Be a Fodor's Correspondent

Your opinion matters. It matters to us. It matters to your fellow Fodor's travelers, too. And we'd like to hear it. In fact, we *need* to hear it.

When you share your experiences and opinions, you become an active member of the Fodor's community. That means we'll not only use your feedback to make our books better, but we'll publish your names and comments whenever possible. Throughout our guides, look for "Word of Mouth," excerpts of your unvarnished feedback.

Here's how you can help improve Fodor's for all of us.

Tell us when we're right. We rely on local writers to give you an insider's perspective. But our writers and staff editors—who are the best in the business—depend on you. Your positive feedback is a vote to renew our recommendations for the next edition.

Tell us when we're wrong. We're proud that we update most of our guides every year. But we're not perfect. Things change. Hotels cut services. Museums change hours. Charming cafés lose charm. If our writer didn't quite capture the essence of a place, tell us how you'd do it differently. If any of our descriptions are inaccurate or inadequate, we'll incorporate your changes in the next edition and will correct factual errors at fodors.com *immediately.*

Tell us what to include. You probably have had fantastic travel experiences that aren't yet in Fodor's. Why not share them with a community of like-minded travelers? Maybe you chanced upon a beach or bistro or B&B that you don't want to keep to yourself. Tell us why we should include it. And share your discoveries and experiences with everyone directly at fodors.com. Your input may lead us to add a new listing or highlight a place we cover with a "Highly Recommended" star or with our highest rating, "Fodor's Choice."

Give us your opinion instantly at our feedback center at www.fodors.com/feedback. You may also e-mail editors@fodors.com with the subject line "China Editor." Or send your nominations, comments, and complaints by mail to China Editor, Fodor's, 1745 Broadway, New York, NY 10019.

You and travelers like you are the heart of the Fodor's community. Make our community richer by sharing your experiences. Be a Fodor's correspondent.

Bon voyage!

D1323280

n Jarrell, Publisher

CONTENTS

CHINA IN FOCUS

CLOSEUPS

MAPS

CONTENTS

ABOUT THIS BOOK

Our Ratings

Sometimes you find terrific travel experiences and sometimes they just find you. But usually the burden is on you to select the right combination of experiences. That's where our ratings come in.

As travelers we've all discovered a place so wonderful that its worthiness is obvious. And sometimes that place is so experiential that superlatives don't do it justice: you just have to be there to know. These sights, properties, and experiences get our highest rating, **Fodor's Choice,** indicated by orange stars throughout this book.

Black stars highlight sights and properties we deem **Highly Recommended,** places that our writers, editors, and readers praise again and again for consistency and excellence.

By default, there's another category: any place we include in this book is by definition worth your time, unless we say otherwise. And we will.

Disagree with any of our choices? Care to nominate a place or suggest that we rate one more highly? Visit our feedback center at www.fodors.com/feedback.

Budget Well

Hotel and restaurant price categories from ¢ to $$$$ are defined in the opening pages of each chapter. For attractions, we always give standard adult admission fees; reductions are usually available for children, students, and senior citizens. Want to pay with plastic? **AE, D, DC, MC, V** following restaurant and hotel listings indicate whether American Express, Discover, Diners Club, MasterCard, and Visa are accepted.

Restaurants

Unless we state otherwise, restaurants are open for lunch and dinner daily. We mention dress only when there's a specific requirement and reservations only when they're essential or not accepted—it's always best to book ahead.

Hotels

Hotels have private bath, phone, TV, and air-conditioning and operate on the European Plan (aka EP, meaning without meals), unless we specify that they use the Continental Plan (CP, with a Continental breakfast), Breakfast Plan (BP, with a full breakfast), or Modified American Plan (MAP, with breakfast and dinner) or are all-inclusive (including all meals and most activities). We always

list facilities but not whether you'll be charged an extra fee to use them, so when pricing accommodations, find out what's included.

Many Listings
★ Fodor's Choice
★ Highly recommended
✉ Physical address
✛ Directions
✉ Mailing address
☎ Telephone
🖷 Fax
⊕ On the Web
✑ E-mail
✑ Admission fee
☺ Open/closed times
▶ Start of walk/itinerary
Ⓜ Metro stations
▭ Credit cards

Hotels & Restaurants
▯ Hotel
↩ Number of rooms
♿ Facilities
🍽 Meal plans
✗ Restaurant
✑ Reservations
👗 Dress code
↘ Smoking
🍷 BYOB
✗▯ Hotel with restaurant that warrants a visit

Outdoors
⛳ Golf
⛺ Camping

Other
☺ Family-friendly
🗗 Contact information
⇨ See also
✉ Branch address
☞ Take note

WHAT'S WHERE

1 Beijing. The capital is in massive flux and the construction never stops. Feel the ancient pulse beneath the current clamor—rock up to Tiananmen Square or get an early start in the Forbidden City.

2 Beijing to Shanghai. Hebei, Shangdong, Anhui, Jiangsu: Discover a cultural and natural treasure trove—Huangshan peaks are islands in a sea of clouds and canal-laced Suzhou is the Venice of the Orient.

3 Shanghai. In the 1920s Shanghai was known as the Whore of the Orient, but we like to think of her as a classy lady who knows how to have a good time. The party stopped for a few decades after the revolution but now Shanghai is back in swing.

4 East Coast. Zhejang, Fujian: Fujian's Xiaman is an undiscovered pearl with all the history, culture and infrastructure of more popular tourist magnets. Zhejang's Hangzhou is the famous southernmost city of the Grand Canal.

5 Hong Kong. A city of contrasts—east and west, old and new, work hard and play harder. Long nights of bar-hopping are offset by tai chi sessions at dawn. Ancient markets and incense-filled temples sit beside modern skyscrapers and luxury malls.

6 **Pearl River Delta.** Guangzhou and Shenzen: The word engine is used metaphorically to describe the Pearl River Delta region, but the vibrations are still palpable here in China's industrial hub.

7 **Southwest.** Guangxi, Guizhou, Yunnan: The mountains are high and the emperor is far away. If you're looking to take a walk on the wild tribal side, then any and all of these three provinces should be high on your to-visit list.

8 **Sichuan, Chongqing.** China's latest industrial revolution is happening in faraway Sichuan and Chongqing, where the Three Gorges Dam, while hotly debated, remains a stunning sight.

9 **The Silk Road.** Shaanxi, Gansu, Qinghai: Distant and mysterious, this was ancient China's lifeline to the outside world. Visit the country's last remaining walled cities—Xian is fascinating for its cultural and its historical importance.

10 **Tibet.** The roof of the world is not the most accessible place, but that's changing thanks to the new train line connecting Lhasa to major cities throughout China. Book ahead because the affect on tourism is already being felt.

QUINTESSENTIAL CHINA

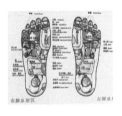

Chinese Chess

Walk through any park in China and chances are good that you'll see people playing China's variant of chess, or xiangqi. Similar in some ways to international chess, there are big differences that are culturally interesting. Western Kings roam the board, but Chinese emperors can't leave the castle (a central box in the rear three rows of the board). Xiangqi has no bishops but instead the shi, who stay inside the palace to protect the king. Naturally, the culture that invented gunpowder has artillery on their chessboards; the cannons can jump across the board for devastating long-range strikes. Similar pieces include horses, which function almost the same as western horses (though they can't jump over blocking pieces). The chariots move like rooks. One of the most interesting differences is that the common soldiers (bing) become more efficient once they hit enemy soil, engaging in lateral guerrilla warfare tactics that western pawns can only dream of.

Reflexology

Foot massage spas are all becoming the rage in China, but if you thought this was a new trend brought on by an upwardly mobile (and naturally more footsore) Chinese populace, think again. While Western medicine sees the foot as mere locomotion, practitioners of traditional Chinese reflexology think that bodily health is reflected in the sole. Each organ is connected to a specific reflex point on the foot. With precise and skillful manipulation of these points, vital functions can be stimulated, toxins eliminated, blood circulation improved, and nerves soothed. Hop up in a chair at one of these foot massage parlors (they're all over the place now), and if your masseuse is skilled, they'll be able to give you a fairly accurate health diagnosis after just a few minutes of looking at the bottoms of your feet. Are you a smoker? Do you suffer from indigestion? Have you been sleeping poorly? Your feet tell all.

Chinese culture is rich, diverse, and will hit you like a ton of bricks. Keep an open mind while you're traveling because this will be an experience of a lifetime.

China Beyond the Han

If America is a melting pot, then China is a massive huo guo, a bubbling hot pot of diverse meats, spices, and vegetables, held together, if you will, by the unifying broth that are the Han Chinese. Officially there are 56 ethnic minorities that make up the great Chinese nation. Though small in number relative to the Han, these minorities have historically been a force to be reckoned with. Rulers of the last dynasty (the Qing) were Manchus. Though Chinese history is rife with examples of inter-tribal war and Han incursion into non-Han territory (Tibet being the latest and most famous example), the revolution, in theory, leveled the playing field. Traveling through areas less dominated by the Han Chinese offers views of the country far different from the usual Beijing-Shanghai-Three Gorges tour. Guangxi, Yunnan, Guizhou, and Sichuan are ethnically diverse, as are the remote provinces along the Silk Road.

All the Tea in China

For a vast majority of the Chinese people the day begins and ends with tea. Whether its being savored in a delicate ceremonial porcelain cup or slurped out of a glass mason jar, you can bet that the imbiber takes tea consumption seriously. Ask a Chinese person about the best tea and the answer will very likely depend on where they're from. The highly prized Pu'er tea has a dark color and heavy, almost earthy flavor. It gets its name from the region of southern Yunnan province where it's grown. Fujian produces the best Wulong teas, thanks to the high mountains and favorable climate. Wulong is usually served with much ceremony. Perhaps the most expensive tea in China is a variant of green tea from the Longjing ("Dragon Well") region of Hangzhuo. Longjing tea is served in clear glasses, so one can watch the delicate dance of the long, thin leaves as they float to the top.

IF YOU LIKE

Strolling Around Pedestrian Malls

In a China increasingly filled with cars, pedestrian malls are becoming all the rage, and for good reason—not only is the air and noise pollution less oppressive when there are no cars around, but also dodging taxis tends to detract from one's shopping enjoyment.

- **Wangfujing, Beijing.** This is considered to be the gold standard of urban Chinese pedestrian malls. This shopping Mecca of restaurants, department stores, and some of the most upscale clothing shops in Asia is just a stone's throw away from the plaza in which Chairman Mao announced communist China's birth. Be aware, Wangfujing is crawling with "art touts," whose job is to lure visitors into local painting shops for an exhibition that usually turns into a sales pitch.

- **Nanjing Dong Lu, Shanghai.** This is the "in" place to spend and be seen. However, avoid the stretch midday in summer, as the bright white street heats up like the inside of a solar panel.

- **Shangxiajiu, Guangzhou.** For sensory stimulation, visit this massive warren of buildings and shops in the heart of old Guangzhou, where the overall decibel level hovers around deafening. Small storefronts sell delicious dried fruit samples and there are a few quiet back alleys to explore.

- **Causeway Bay, Hong Kong.** If you want to understand why the Chinese use ren shan ren hai (people mountain people sea) to describe a crowd scene, visit Causeway Bay any night of the week. Fashion galore and restaurants of all description make this neighborhood a people magnet.

Contemporary Art

China in the 21st century has one of the most vibrant, eclectic, and often downright avant-garde art scenes this side of Paris. Beijing is arguably the center of China's contemporary art scene, and it's in China's capital that well-known artists like sculptor Wang Guangyi (who blends propaganda and icons from the cultural revolution for what some consider cynical effect) and painter Feng Mengbo (whose hallmarks include mixing oil painting and computer graphics) ply their trades.

- **Dashanzi 798 Art District, Beijing.** This former military electronics complex in Beijing's Chaoyang district houses dozens of galleries and the workshops of many of the city's up-and-coming artists.

- **Shanghart Gallery, Shanghai.** Opened in 1996, the Shanghart Gallery is among the most "in" places for contemporary art in the city. As always, competition between Shanghai and Beijing is fierce, and while nobody in China seriously considers Shanghai a contender for the art crown of China, that doesn't stop the Pearl of the Orient from trying.

- **Guangdong Museum of Art, Guangzhou.** Denizens of the Pearl River Delta, though normally thought of as caring more about making money than art, have a number of museums and galleries worth visiting. This museum is well respected throughout China.

- **He Xiangning Museum, Shenzhen.** This beautiful new museum in the Overseas Chinese Town district hosts an annual exhibit each autumn featuring the best works of art students from all over China.

Bicycling

In the not too distant past, China was known as "The Bicycle Kingdom," but as cars become more popular, the iconic sea of bicycles that once filled the avenues of Beijing and Shanghai has dried to a trickle. But this doesn't mean that bicycling enthusiasts should lose heart. While the two-wheeled herd has thinned out considerably, you'll hardly be riding alone. Most hotels will be able to help you out with bicycle rentals, or a brand new flying pigeon (the bike of China) should only set you back a few hundred Yuan.

- **Beijing.** Though notorious for its bad air and automobile gridlock, the capital is still our favorite urban bicycling ground. Its wide avenues and impossible-to-maneuver-by-car back alleyways make it an ideal city to tour by bicycle.

- **Xian.** The city center is small enough to make it perfect for exploring by bike. For a unique experience, take a tour on top of the city wall, the only one left fully intact in all of China.

- **Shanghai.** The Pearl of the Orient is also two-wheel friendly, though you'll be asked to dismount and walk along the Nanjing pedestrian area.

- **Chengdu.** The greenest city in China is also as flat as a Ping-Pong table, which makes it one of our favorites for exploring by bike.

Sculptures and Tombs

The ancient Egyptians may be best at burying their dead kings in gaudy opulence, but the Chinese give them a run for their money when it comes to craftsmanship for the post-mortem care of royalty.

- **Terracotta Warriors, Xian.** The Terracotta warriors are perhaps the best known example of sculptures-as-tomb-guardians in the world. These meticulously crafted soldiers were created as part of the elaborate funeral ritual of the first Qing emperor, buried in the ground outside of what would later become the Silk Road city of Xian, and only discovered millennia later by a modern-day farmer tilling soil.

- **Ming Tomb, Nanjing.** The Ming emperors were particularly interested in making sure that their resting places were both remembered and protected. The Nanjing Ming Tomb was Built as a burial site for the emperor Hong Wu, the warrior monk who established the Ming Dynasty, and is guarded by a grand procession of stone animals–real and mythical—all kneeling in tribute to the emperor as they guard his remains for all eternity.

- **Tomb of the Southern Yue Kings, Guangzhou.** Construction workers breaking ground to build Guangzhou's China hotel were in for quite a shock when they came across an intact underground tomb belonging to the ancient emperor Wen Di. The discovery was interesting in that it led historians to reevaluate the area's place in Chinese dynastical history. Though the discovery barely hindered the construction of the hotel, the tomb itself was not merely faithfully restored, but its treasures form the nucleus of exhibits in the Nan Yue museum next door.

IF YOU LIKE

Antique Villages Come to Life

China is filled with ancient towns and villages, and a fairly recent trend has been the gentrification (sometimes closer to Disneyfication) of historically or culturally significant towns in the name of preservation. Other places, however, look closer to the way they did hundreds of years ago.

- **Lijiang, Yunnan Province.** Though a fun place to visit, with its tribal themed café, guesthouses, and CD stores, Lijiang is pretty much a for-tourists-only kind of place, but the architecture is still pretty cool.

- **Fuli, Guangxi Province.** Just a quick skip up the river from Yangshuo (itself in the midst of a radical "Disneyfication"), Fuli doesn't seem to have changed much since Sun Yat-sen visited nearly a century ago. This Ming-era town gives visitors a good idea of how local people lived hundreds of years ago.

- **Gulangyu island, Xiamen.** Though the area by the ferry pier has been renovated, most of this car-free island off the coast of Xiamen feels not so much "faux run-down" as genuinely feral, with colonial-era buildings in varied states of glorious disrepair. The beaches on the north side of the island are also quite good for swimming.

- **Dapeng Ancient City, Shenzhen.** Located just a few miles outside of China's newest and most modern metropolis, the walled ancient city of Dapeng—which housed military personnel and their families charged with defending China's southern coast during the Ming and Qing dynasties—is an unpolished gem well worth a visit.

Taking It to the Extreme

An increasing number of Middle Kingdom visitors are coming not merely to see the Great Wall but to engage in more adrenaline-intensive activities (jumping over the Great Wall on a skateboard, for example). This new breed of China traveler will be happy to hear that adventure sports are alive and well in the People's Republic.

- **The Great Wall, Huang Hua.** This crumbling section of the wall, just a few hours outside of Beijing, is far more rugged than the more tourist-popular Badaling section, and offers amazing views and seriously challenging climbs.

- **Rock Climbing, Yangshuo.** Yangshuo has become a major "in" spot for aficionados of rock climbing, and the area has hundreds of routes for climbers of all levels. Possibly one of the most challenging routes is the inside track of Moon Hill, which draws some of the world's best climbers each year.

- **Long Distance Bicycling.** Rural touring is exploding in China, and an increasing number of western visitors are choosing to see the country not by train or tour bus, but by bicycle. Bike Asia runs tours for all levels of experience and endurance, from the rolling hills of Guangxi and Guizhou, to the serious-riders-only mountains of Tibet.

- **Wind Surfing, Qingdao.** It's no accident that this seaside city in Northeast China was chosen to host the Olympic sailing events of 2008. The shape of the beaches combined with average wind speeds makes Qingdao an ideal place for those who get their kicks sailing.

Visiting Specters

There are some places in China where you get the distinct feeling that you're not alone, places where the eyes of those long gone seem to be watching you, probing you with a certain . . . curiosity. Its only natural that a country that measures its age in millennia would have many such places.

- **Summer Palace, Beijing.** Visitors to the residence of Cixi, located in the Summer Palace outside Beijing, have noted that they feel a certain sense of disquiet, as if the "Old Buddha" (as the last empress of China was called) herself were still hanging around. Well known for her canny political sense, it is entirely likely that the Old Buddha still returns to keep an eye on the comings and goings of foreign barbarians in China—a big issue during her reign. Though today she's merely a specter of her former glorious self, we advise visitors to be reverent in her home nonetheless.

- **Hakka Enclosures, Shenzhen.** Eerie presences have been reported roaming around inside the Longgang Hakka Enclosures on the outskirts of Shenzhen. Though the former stronghold and dwelling of the proud Hakka people has been converted into a museum, its been done so in a way so unobtrusive that visitors almost get the sense that the homes within are still occupied, and that their former residents might return at any moment. And they just might at that, so consider yourselves a guest of China's guest people (as the Hakka are known), and tread lightly through their domain.

Adventurous Dining

Much has been written about the cuisine of China, and for a very good reason—it's some of the best (and most laden with variety) to be found on the planet. Most visitors will be happy to stick with well-known dishes, such as Peking duck or kung pao chicken, but for those who want a culinary walk on the wild side, might we suggest a few less known regional favorites?

- **Stinky Tofu, Fujian.** Though it's hotly contested whether this highly odiferous dish originated first in Fujian or later in Taiwan, the overpowering snack is readily available on both sides of the Taiwan straits. Cubes of tofu fermented and deep fried to a crispy brown, the dish smells like extremely ripe cheese. Best enjoyed by those who prefer their food on the pungent side.

- **Yak Butter Tea, Yunnan, Tibet.** This beverage is ubiquitous throughout both Tibet and the higher mountain regions of Yunnan province. Thick and tangy, the main ingredients of yak butter tea are, as the name suggests, yak butter. Though its adherents drink it by the gallon, considering it delicious and healthy, unsuspecting imbibers have likened its flavor to melted blue cheese, or even wood polish.

- **Stewed Chicken Feet, Guangzhou.** To a Cantonese chef, nothing should ever go to waste, and the claws of the humble chicken, stewed until the fat and skin are nearly dripping from its tiny bones is considered a crucial part of any dim sum feast.

GREAT ITINERARIES

BEIJING & THE SILK ROAD

Day 1: Welcome to Beijing

Beijing is the cultural heart of China and the nation's top travel destination. Try to catch the daily flag-raising ceremony in Tiananmen Square. Most first-time visitors to China are drawn here as soon as they recover from the jet lag. As you watch goose-stepping People's Liberation Army soldiers march from the Forbidden City into the world's largest public square under the watchful eye of Mao Zedong, you'll know you're not in Kansas anymore. After the flag-raising, take a stroll around the square and soak in the atmosphere. And of course, a tour of the Forbidden City is an essential Beijing experience.

Logistics: Avoid unlicensed taxi touts who approach you in Beijing's airport. Proceed to the taxi stand outside, where a ride to your hotel should cost in the range of Y100. Tiananmen Square is best approached on foot or by subway, as taxis aren't allowed to let you off anywhere nearby.

Day 2: The Great Wall

If you're really pressed for time, you could visit the Badaling section of the Great Wall in an afternoon, but we recommend a day-trip out to the more impressive sections at Mutianyu, Simatai, or Jinshanling.

Logistics: The most economical way to reach any section of the Great Wall is by group tour bus. If you don't want to be rushed, however, you're better off hiring private transportation for the day.

Day 3: Jewels of the Empire

Beijing is dotted with numerous imperial palaces and pleasure gardens. The lovely Summer Palace in the city's northwest has come to symbolize the decadence that brought about the fall of the Qing dynasty. The Temple of Heaven is considered to be the most perfect example of Ming dynasty architecture and is a great place to take a break from the frenetic pace of the capital.

Logistics: These imperial sites will each take about three or four hours to tour properly, and are best reached by taxi. There's no need to ask the driver to wait, though, as plenty of taxis are constantly coming and going.

Day 4: Capital Entertainment

Beijing is teeming with cultural performances, fabulous restaurants, and sprawling outdoor markets. If you're looking to do some souvenir shopping, plan on spending a few hours at Beijing Curio City or the Silk Alley Market in the Chaoyang District. In the evening, music enthusiasts will want to take in a glass-shattering performance of Beijing Opera. If that's not your thing, experience the city's more modern nightlife around Qianhai Lake, where fashionable bars and shops stay open late.

Logistics: Unless you're willing to try your luck on one of Beijing's public buses, these destinations are best reached by taxi.

Days 5-8: Xian, China's Ancient Capital

For most of China's history, Xian was the nation's capital. As the starting point for the Silk Road, the area is packed with historically significant destinations, most of which can be covered in just a few days. One entire day should be devoted to visiting the Terracotta Warriors Museum and surrounding sites located east of the city.

The famous warriors, built to protect China's first emperor in the afterlife, are only part of a huge tomb complex that stretches for miles. If you've got the time, we also recommend a day-trip to the spectacular peaks of Hua Shan.

Logistics: Flights from Beijing to Xian take about 2 hours with very frequent departures. Trains depart from Beijing's West Rail Station and take 12 hours. Most sites within Xian can be reached by foot. The Terracotta Warriors and Hua Shan are located east of Xian, so you'll want to book a tour or catch one of the cheap public buses.

Travel Note:

If you're not interested in continuing farther west along the Silk Road, Xian is the perfect transportation hub from which to catch a flight or train to Lhasa, Chengdu, Shanghai or any other destination of your choice.

Days 9-10: Dunhuang

Once the border between China and the unknown barbarian lands to the west, Dunhuang was also a major stop for merchants and religious pilgrims traveling the Silk Road. Filled with more than 1,000 years of Buddhist carvings, the Mogao Grottoes are widely considered to be the best surviving example of early religious art in China.

Logistics: Flights from Xian to Dunhuang take 3 hours and depart regularly during the busy summer months, less often in the off-season.

Days 11-14: Urumqi & Turpan

Xinjiang is China's vast western frontier, where the pagodas and temples of the East melt into the bazaars and minarets of Central Asia. The capital of Urumqi is certainly interesting as far as large cities go in China, but for a real taste of the region you'll want to head out to the countryside. Heavenly Lake is perhaps the most beautiful body of water in the whole country. The small city of Turpan provides a fascinating look into the Silk Road history that once defined the area and the Uyghur minority way of life that dominates today. If you've got an extra couple of days, head even farther west to Kashgar, closer to Baghdad than Beijing in both distance and culture.

Logistics: During the busy summer season, flights regularly connect Dunhuang with Urumqi. Other times of the year you'll need to make the long journey by train or make a connecting flight in Lanzhou or Xian. There are multiple daily flights between Urumqi and Kasghar, as well as between Urumqi and Beijing.

GREAT ITINERARIES

SHANGHAI & THE CHINESE HEARTLAND

Day 1: Welcome to Shanghai

Shanghai is all about the country's future, not its past. Once you've settled in, your first stop should be the Bund, Shanghai's unofficial tourist center. This waterfront boulevard is the city's best spot for people-watching and culinary exploration. For a bird's-eye view of China's sprawling economic capital, head across the Huangpu River toward Pudong, where you can mount either the Oriental Pearl Tower or the Jinmao Tower. There's also the Yu Garden, where you can relax among carefully designed landscaping and traditional architecture evoking the China of yore.

Logistics: Unless you fear cutting-edge technology, you'll want to take the ultrafast maglev train from the airport into the city center. Shanghai is suprisingly easy to navigate on foot, although taxis are ubiquitous if your feet get tired. To get between the Bund and Pudong, the Y2 ferry across the Huangpu River departs every 10 minutes.

Day 2: Paris of the East

Shanghai's colonial history adds immeasurably to the city's charm. Be sure to visit the French Concession. Whether you're a fan of colonial architecture or enjoy sipping cappuccino in quiet cafés, this is a pleasant area to spend time. Walk through Xintiandi, where restored traditional houses mix with bars, boutiques, and small museums. Spend some time searching for the perfect souvenir on the Nanjing Lu. Alternatively, you could brush up on your Chinese history at the Shanghai Museum, one of the finest in the country.

Logistics: All of these destinations are clustered together in a square mile located west of the Bund, easily accessible on foot or by taxi.

Day 3-4: Suzhou & Zhouzhuang

Regarded by the Chinese in ancient times as heaven on earth, Suzhou manages to retain many of its charms despite the encroaching forces of modernization. Enjoy strolling through perfectly designed gardens and temples along the gently flowing branches of the Grand Canal. Luckily, Suzhou is close enough to work well as a day-trip. Riding on a gondola past the Zhouzhuang's signature tile-roof wooden houses, you'll understand why it was called the "Venice of the East." If you've only got one day to get out of Shanghai, the area's water villages should be your destination.

Logistics: Transportation between Shanghai and Suzhou is most conveniently available by bus, of either the intercity or tourist variety; seats on a tourist coach to Zhouzhuang are also easily booked. If you're planning to visit both destinations, you'll probably want to spend the night at a hotel in Suzhou.

Day 5-8: Huang Shan

China's top natural scenic attraction, Huang Shan (Yellow Mountain) is an impossibly beautiful collection of 72 jagged peaks famous for grotesquely twisted pine trees and unusual rock formations. This area has provided the inspiration for generations of Chinese poets and artists, which is why its vistas and valleys may seem so familiar to you. There are numerous paths to the top, either by foot or by cable car. To take part

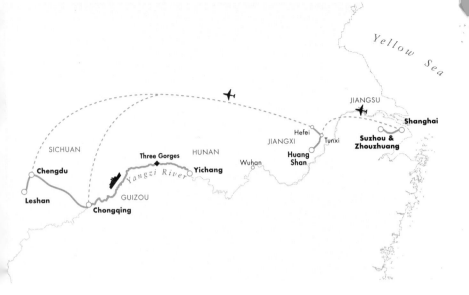

in Huang Shan's essential experience, spend a night at one of the mountaintop guesthouses before waking at dawn to watch the sun rise over an eerie sea of fog.

Logistics: Unless you're willing to spend 10 or more hours on a bus from Shanghai, your best bet is to fly into Huang Shan's airport located nearby in the town of Tunxi. There's no need to book a tour of the mountain, as paths and scenic viewpoints are all well marked in English.

Day 9-10: Chengdu

As the capital of Sichuan Province, Chengdu has long been one of China's great cultural centers. Famous for its fiery local cuisine, the city has also managed to partially maintain a pleasant atmosphere of yesteryear. Essential sites include the Buddhist Wenshu Monastery and for animal lovers, the Giant Panda Breeding Research Base. No matter how little time you have available to spend here, make the day-trip south to Leshan to see the world's largest stone-carved Buddha. With toes the size of a small bus, the seated Grand Buddha is impressive to say the least.

Logistics: Like most tourist hubs, the airport near Huang Shan offers fairly frequent flights to major cities such as Chengdu only during the busy warmer months. You

may find it easier to connect through Hefei or Shanghai. All hotels and travel agencies in Chengdu can book tours to Leshan, or you can travel on your own by public bus.

Travel note: If you're pressed for time and are set on cruising the Yangzi River, skip Chengdu and fly directly to Chongqing.

Day 11-14: The Three Gorges

Despite rising water levels caused by construction of the Three Gorges Dam, a cruise along the Yangzi River through the Three Gorges is impressive. Along the way, you'll pass soon-to-be-submerged abandoned metropolises that were humming with life only a few years ago as well as their modern counterparts built on higher ground. Be sure to book yourself on a luxury boat catering to foreigners, or you'll end up spending three days on a damp, rat-infested ship. Don't miss a visit to the Little Three Gorges, where monkeys play near the water's edge.

Logistics: Boats depart from Chongqing, a three- or four-hour drive east of Chengdu. If you book your tour in Chengdu, transportation to Chongqing is almost always included. Most cruises disembark at Yichang in Hubei Province, where you can get a flight back to most travel hubs.

GREAT ITINERARIES

SOUTHERN CHINA & TIBET

Day 1: Welcome to Hong Kong

Despite the city's return to Chinese rule in 1999, Hong Kong is still a world away from the mainland. To get a feel for the city, take a ride on the Star Ferry, connecting Hong Kong Island with Kowloon. The ferry offers the best possible views of the business district's skyline. Don't miss the smoke-filled Man Mo Temple and Hong Kong's famous assortment of antiques shops and art galleries. Ride the very steep tram to the summit of Victoria Peak, with views of the entire harbor.

Logistics: The new airport is connected to Kowloon and Hong Kong island by express train, taking about 30 minutes. Taxis are available everywhere, although much of the city can be explored by foot. The tram to Victoria Peak is open until midnight.

Day 2: Getting out of the City

While the business districts clustered around the harbor feature some of the world's densest urban jungle, Hong Kong also has a relaxed natural side. The express ferry to Lantau can whisk you away from the city in about 40 minutes. Arriving at the town of Mui Wo, you can catch a bus to the island's top two attractions: Po Lin Monastery, featuring the world's tallest outdoor bronze statue of Buddha, and Tai O, an old fishing village dotted with terrific seafood restaurants. For even greater solitude, take the ferry to one of the smaller Outer Islands.

Logistics: Ferries for Lantau leave from either the Star Ferry Terminal or the Outlying Districts Services Pier just to the west.

On the island, private buses travel between all of the main attractions.

Day 3: Macau

Even with a recent push to become Asia's Las Vegas, Macau is still decidedly quieter and more traditional than Hong Kong. The slower pace of development has left much of the city's colonial charm intact. Start with a visit to Largo do Senado (Senate Square), paved with Portuguese-style tiles and surrounded by brightly colored colonial buildings. The city is home to two beautiful churches, São Domingos and São Paulo, the latter featuring exhibits on the early history of Asian Christianity.

Logistics: TurboJets from Hong Kong to Macau depart frequently and at all times of the day, making the trip in about an hour. If you're not comfortable traveling around the city by taxi, book a tour before you leave Hong Kong.

Day 4-8: Yangshou & Longshen

The scenery in northern Guangxi Province is some of the most beautiful in all of China. Dotted with dramatic groupings of sheer limestone karst mountains, visitors often find themselves loath to leave. You'll see more of the countryside by taking the four-hour Li River Cruise down to Yangshuo as soon as possible. Yangshuo is a laid-back town popular with backpackers, and an excellent base from which to explore natural sites like Green Lotus Peak and Moon Hill. If you've got more time, head back through Guilin to the town of Longsheng, home to the famously photogenic Dragon's Backbone Rice Terraces.

Logistics: For a flight to Guilin you'll need to get to the airport in Shenzhen, just over the border. This can be done by taking a train followed by an airport bus, or by catching the direct TurboJet ferry from Kowloon.

Day 9-14: Northwest Yunnan

Sandwiched between the Tibetan Plateau and Myanmar, foreigners have long been attracted to this area for its mix of minority cultures and stunning natural beauty. Dali, beside the waters of Erhai Lake, is home to the Bai people who settled here 4,000 years ago; the elegant Three Pagodas north of town are one of China's most iconic images. Farther north lies Lijiang, capital of the Naxi people and the only place in the country where traditional Chinese music is said to survive in its original form. The highlight of the region is Tiger Leaping Gorge, one of the deepest river gorges in the world and a popular two- or three-day hike.

Logistics: Most flights from Guilin to either Dali or Lijiang connect through the regional capital. Travel between these destinations is by public bus or tour coach.

Day 15-18: Lhasa

Lhasa is the capital of a nation within a nation, with only tenuous ties to the rest of China. These ties have increased considerably with the opening of the train line to Tibet, yet the city is still unique. Start your tour of the city with a walk around the Barkhor followed by a visit to Jokhang Temple, respectively Tibetan Buddhism's holiest pilgrimage circuit and holiest religious site. Don't miss the Sera Monastery, where monks hold animated theological debates every afternoon. Climb the long steps to the Potala Palace, followed by a visit to what was once the world's largest monastic complex, Drepung Monastery. If you only spend one day outside of Lhasa, make the 2-hour trip to the mountaintop Ganden Monastery, with awe-inspiring views of the surrounding Lhasa River Valley. The 5-day round-trip between Lhasa and Everest Base Camp with a number of stops along the way is the essential Tibet experience.

Logistics: Multiple daily flights connect Kunming with Lhasa. Sites within Lhasa are accessible on foot or by taxi. Travel to sites outside Lhasa, like Everest Base Camp, must be arranged through an official tour operator.

Travel Note: Those wishing to visit Tibet can easily book flight or train tickets from most major transportation hubs.

WHEN TO GO

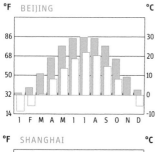

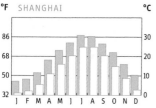

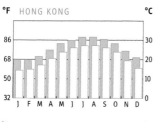

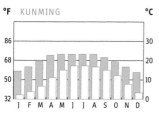

Although temperatures can be scorching, summer is the peak tourist season, and hotels and transportation can be very crowded. If you're traveling during peak season, try to book several months in advance.

The weather is better and the crowds not quite as dense in late spring and early fall, although you need to be prepared for rain. It's easy enough to buy a poncho or an umbrella when you're on the road.

Winter is bitterly cold and not conducive to travel in much of the country, especially North. However, the southern most reaches remain moderate throughout the winter. Try to avoid traveling around Chinese New Year and other national holidays if possible. Many businesses in China shut down and it will seem like the entire population is traveling with you—hotels will be booked solid and major sights will feel like Times Square on New Year's Eve.

Regardless of the weather, avoid traveling during the National Week holiday in October and International Labor Day in May. The entire country goes on vacation and most major destinations resemble mosh pits.

Climate

🔁 Forecasts **Weather Channel Connection** (🌐 www.weather.com).

This is a good source for current weather conditions throughout China

THE AGE OF EMPIRES

When asked his opinion on the historical impact of the French Revolution, Chairman Mao quipped, "It's too early to tell." Though a bit tongue in cheek, China does measure its history in millennia, and in its grand timeline, interactions with the West have been mere blips.

According to historical records, Chinese civilization stretches back to the 15th century BC—markings found on turtle shells carbon dated to around 1500 BC bear some similarity to modern Chinese script. China then resembled city-states rather than a unified nation. Iconic figures such as Lao Tzu (the father of Taoism), Sun Tzu (author of the *Art of War*), and Confucius lived during this period. Generally, 221 BC is accepted as the beginning of Imperial China, when the city-states united under various banners.

Over the next 2,200 years (give or take a few), China alternated between periods of harmony and political upheaval. Its armies conquered new territory and were in turn conquered by external invaders (most of whom wound up themselves being assimilated).

By the early 18th century, the long, slow decline of the Qing—the last of China's Imperial dynasties—was already in progress, making the ancient nation ripe for exploitation by rising European powers. The Imperial era ended with the forced abdication of child Emperor Puyi (whose life is chronicled in Bernardo Bertolucci's *The Last Emperor*), and it's here that the history of modern China, first with the founding of the republic under Sun Yat-sen and then with the establishment of the People's Republic under Mao Zedong, truly begins.

(left) Oracle shell with early Chinese characters. (top, right) The Great Wall stretches 4,163 miles from east to west. (bottom, right) Confucius was born in Qufu, Shandong.

circa 1500 BC

Writing Appears

The earliest accounts of Chinese history are still shrouded in myth and legend, and it wasn't until 1959 that stories were verified by archaeological findings. For millennia, people formed communities in the fertile lands of what is now central China. The first recorded Chinese characters are said to have been developed 3,500 years ago. Though sometimes referred to as the Shang Dynasty, this period was more of a precursor to modern Chinese dynasties than a truly unified kingdom.

722–475 BC

The Warring States Period

China was so far from unified that these centuries are collectively remembered as the Warring States Period. As befitting such a contentious time, military science progressed, iron replaced bronze, and weapons material improved. Some of China's greatest luminaries lived during this period, including the father of Taoism, Lao-tzu, Confucius, and Sun-Tzu, one of the greatest military tacticians and the author of the infamous *Art of War*, which is still studied in military academies around the world.

221–207 BC

The First Dynasty

The Qin Dynasty eventually defeated all of the other warring factions thanks to their cutting-edge military technology, namely the cavalry. The Qin were also called Ch'in, which may be where the word China first originated. The first Emperor, Qin Shi-huang, unified much of the lands and established a legal code and vast bureaucracy to hold it together. The Qin dynasty also standardized the written and spoken language and introduced a common currency.

THE AGE OF EMPIRES

(left) Terracotta warriors in Xian, on the Silk Road. (top right) Buddha statue, Maijishan Cave in Tianshui, Gansa. (bottom left) Sun Tzu, author of The *Art of War*.

In order to protect his newly unified country, Qin Shihuang ordered the creation of the massive Great Wall of China, which was built and rebuilt over the next 1,000 years. He was also a sculpture enthusiast and commissioned a massive army of stone soldiers to follow him into the afterlife. Buried with him, these terra-cotta warriors would remain hidden from the eyes of the world for two thousand years, until they were found by a farmer digging in a field just outside of Xian. These warriors are among the most important archaeological finds of the 20th century.

220–265 BC

Buddhism Arrives

Emperor Qin's dreams of a unified China fell apart, and eventually the kingdom split into three warring factions. But what was bad for stability turned out to be good for literature. The Three Kingdoms Period is still remembered in song and story. *The Romance of the Three Kingdoms* is as popular among Asian bookworms as the *Legend of King Arthur* is among Western readers. It's still widely read and has been translated into almost every language. Variations of the story have been adapted for manga, television series, and video games.

The Three Kingdoms period was filled with court intrigue, murder, and massive battles that, while exciting to read about centuries later, weren't much fun at the time. Armies ravaged the countryside, and most people lived and died in misery. Perhaps it was the carnage and disunity of the time that turned the country into a magnet for forces of harmony; it was during this period that Buddhism was first introduced into China, traveling over the Himalayas from India, via the Silk Road.

(left) Genghis Khan conquered much of China. (top, right) Islamic lecture at madrassa classroom inside Dongguan mosque, Xinning. (bottom, right) Kublai Khan was the first Mongol Emperor of China.

618–845 Religion Diversifies

Chinese spiritual life continued to diversify. Nestorian Monks from Asia Minor arrived bearing news of Christianity, and Saad ibn Abi Waqqas (a companion of the Prophet Muhammad) supposedly visited the Middle Kingdom to spread the word of Islam. During this era, Wu Zetian, onetime concubine, seized power from the Tang Dynasty and became the first (and only) woman to assume the title of emperor. She ruled for 25 years through puppet emperors and finally, for 15 years as Emperor Shengshen.

1271–1368 Ghengis Invades

In Xanadu did Kublai Khan a stately pleasure dome decree . . .

Or so goes the famed Coleridge poem. But Kublai's grandfather Temujin (better known as Ghengis Khan) had bigger things in mind. One of the greatest war tacticians in history, he united the restive nomads of Mongolia's grassy plains and eventually sacked, looted, and pillaged much of the known west and most of the Chinese landmass. By the time Ghengis died in 1227, his grandson was well-tutored and ready to take on the rest of China.

By 1271, Kublai had established a capital in a land-locked city that would only much later become known as Beijing. This marks the beginning of the first (but not last) non-Han dynasty. Kublai Khan kept fighting southward and by 1279, Guangzhou fell to the Mongols, and Khan became the ultimate monarch of China. Though barbarians at heart, the Mongols must be credited for encouraging the arts and a number of early public works projects, including extending the highways and grand canals.

THE AGE OF EMPIRES

(left) Statue of admiral Zheng He. (top right) Forbidden City in Beijing (bottom right) Child emperor Puyi.

Ming Dynasty

1368–1644

Many scholars believe that the Mongols' inability to relate with the Han is what ultimately pushed the Han to rise up and overthrow them. The reign of the Ming Dynasty was the last ethnically Han Dynasty to rule over a unified China. At its apex, the Bright Empire encompassed a landmass easily recognized as China, even by today's mapmakers. The Ming Emperors built a huge army and navy, refurbished the agricultural system, and printed many books using movable type long before Gutenberg. In the 13th century, Emperor Yongle began construction of the famous Forbidden City in Beijing, a veritable icon of China.

Also during the Ming Dynasty, China's best known explorer, Zheng He, plied the seven seas in massive treasure fleets that dwarfed in size and range the ships of Christopher Columbus. A giant both in stature and persona, Admiral Zheng (who was also a eunuch) spent two decades expanding China's knowledge of the world outside of its already impressive borders. He traveled as far as India, Africa, and (some say) even the coast of the New World.

Qing Dynasty

1644–1911

The final dynasty represented a serious case of minority rule. They were Manchus from the northeast. The early Qing dynasty was a brutal period as forces loyal to the new emperor crushed those loyal to the old. The Qing Dynasty peaked in the mid-to-late 18th century but soon after, its military powers began to wane. In the 19th century, Qing control weakened and prosperity diminished. By 1910 China was fractured, a baby sat on the Imperial throne, and the Qing Dynasty was on its deathbed.

(left) Portrait of Marshal Chiang Kai-shek with his wife. (top, right) Mao Zedong on December 6, 1944. (bottom, right) Sun Yat-sen.

The Opium Wars

1834–1860

European powers were hungry to open new territories up for trade, but the Qing weren't buying. The British East India Company, strapped for cash, realized they could sell opium in China at huge profits. The Chinese government quickly banned the nefarious trade and in response, a technologically superior Britain declared war. After a humiliating defeat in the first Opium War, China was forced to cede Hong Kong. Other foreign powers followed with territorial demands of their own.

Republican Era

1912–1949

China's Republican period was chaotic and unstable. The revolutionary Dr. Sun Yat-sen —revered by most Chinese as the father of modern China— was unable to build a cohesive government without the aid of regional warlords and urban gangsters. When he died of cancer in 1925, power passed to Chiang Kai-shek, who set about unifying China under the Kuomintang. What began as a unified group of both left- and right-wingers quickly deteriorated, and by the mid-1920s, civil war between the Communists and Nationalists was brewing.

The '30s and '40s were bleak decades for the Chinese people, caught between a vicious war with Japan and periodic clashes between Kuomintang and Communist forces. After Japan's defeat in 1945, China's civil war kicked into high gear. Though the Kuomintang were armed with superior weapons and backed by American money, the majority of Chinese people rallied behind the Communists. Within four years, the Kuomintang were driven off the mainland to Taiwan, where the Republic of China exists to the present day.

THE AGE OF EMPIRES

(top left) Illiterate soldiers are taught about Mao's *Little Red Book* in Beijing December 1966. (top right) Central Shenzhen, Guangdong (bottom left) Poster of Mao's slogans.

1949 – Present

The People's Republic

On October 1, 1949, Mao Zedong declared from atop Beijing's Gate of Heavenly Peace that "The Chinese People have stood up." And so the People's Republic of China was born. The Communist party set out to overhaul China's ancient feudal system, emphasizing class struggle, redistribution of wealth, and elimination of foreign dominance. The next three decades would see a massive, often painful transformation of Chinese society from feudalism into the modern age.

The Great Leap Forward was a disaster—Chinese peasants were encouraged to cram 100 years of industrial development into as many weeks. Untenable decisions led to industrial and agricultural ruin, widespread famine, and an estimated 30 million deaths. The trauma of this period, however, pales in comparison to The Great Proletarian Cultural Revolution. From 1966–1976, fear and zealotry gripped the nation as young revolutionaries heeded Chairman Mao's call to root out class enemies. During this decade, millions died, millions were imprisoned, and much of China's accumulated religious, historical, and cultural heritage literally went up in smoke.

Like a phoenix rising from its own ashes, China rose from its own self-inflicted destruction. In the early 1980s, Deng Xiao-ping took the first steps in reforming China's stagnant economy. With the maxim "To Get Rich is Glorious," Deng loosened central control on the economy and declared Special Economic Zones, where the seeds of capitalism could be incubated. Two decades later, the nation is one of the world's most vibrant economic engines. Though China's history is measured in millennia, her brightest years may well have only just begun.

Beijing
THE HEART OF THE DRAGON

Watching traditional Beijing opera is a colorful and memorable way to spend an evening.

WORD OF MOUTH

"Have fun! China is great and the people make it that way."

–Michael Thompson

"Beijing is easy to walk around (bring a map), cabs are cheap and plentiful (and, if you have your destinations written in Chinese, it's pretty hard to get lost). We found the great majority of Beijingers (and Chinese everywhere) open, friendly and good-humoured— even more so if you try out a few words in Mandarin."

–Neil_Oz

WELCOME TO BEIJING

TOP REASONS TO GO

★ **The Forbidden City.** This immense palace is the best preserved and most complete collection of imperial architecture in China.

★ **Tiananmen Square.** Walking beneath the red flags of Tiananmen Square is quintessential Beijing: it's likely one of the first spots you'll visit.

★ **Temple of Heaven.** One of the best examples of religious architecture in China, the Temple of Heaven is a pleasant place for wandering and exploring.

★ **Magnificent Markets.** Beijing's markets offer a wide variety of goods, from "Maomorabilia" to silk slippers. Be sure to visit Panjiayuan (aka Dirt Market).

★ **Summer Palace.** Notable sights at this garden complex are the Long Corridor, the Hall of Benevolent Longevity, and the Marble Boat, which Cixi built with money intended for the Chinese navy.

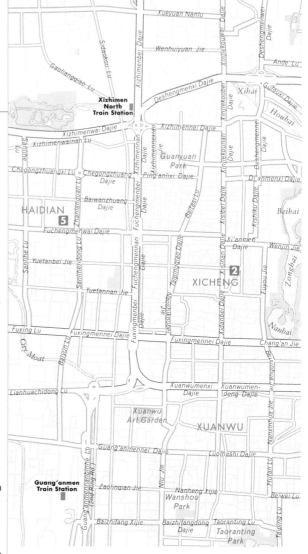

1 Dongcheng District. Dongcheng ("east district") encompasses the Forbidden City, Tiananmen Square, Wangfujing (a major shopping street), the Lama Temple, and many other historical sights dating back to imperial times.

2 Xicheng District. Xicheng ("west district"), directly west of Dongcheng, is a lovely lake district that includes Beihai Park, former playground of the imperial family, and a series of connected lakes bordered by willow trees and courtyard-lined hutongs.

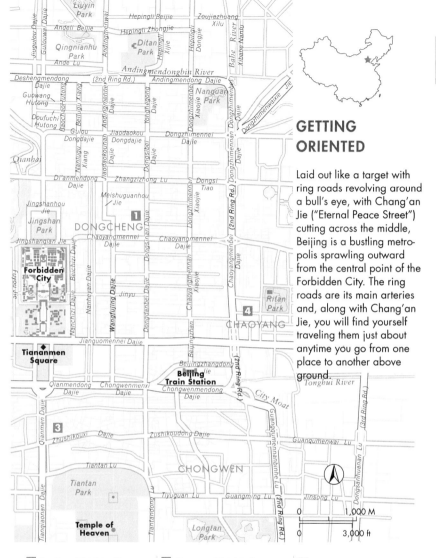

GETTING ORIENTED

Laid out like a target with ring roads revolving around a bull's eye, with Chang'an Jie ("Eternal Peace Street") cutting across the middle, Beijing is a bustling metropolis sprawling outward from the central point of the Forbidden City. The ring roads are its main arteries and, along with Chang'an Jie, you will find yourself traveling them just about anytime you go from one place to another above ground.

3 Southern Districts: Chongwen & Xuanwu. The southern districts include Chongwen in the southeast and Xuanwu in the southwest. These areas have some of the oldest neighborhoods in the city. The magnificent Temple of Heaven is here.

4 Chaoyang District. Chaoyang is the biggest and busiest district, occupying the areas north, east, and south of the eastern Second Ring Road. It's home to foreign embassies, multinational companies, fabulous nightlife, and the newly rising Central Business District, with its gleaming skyscrapers.

5 Haidian District. Haidian is the technology and university district. Northwest of the Third Ring Road, it is home to the Summer Palace, the Beijing Zoo, the Botanical Gardens, and plenty of shops selling electronics.

BEIJING PLANNER

5 Fantastic Days

Day 1: Visit Tiananmen Square in the morning, eat dim sum at Huang Ting, then explore glorious Beihai Park. End the day with evening drinks and goodies in the booming Houhai district.

Day 2: Explore the wonders of the Forbidden City all morning long. Eat lunch or have a drink overlooking the waters of Qianhai. Next head north into Jingshan Park and climb the hill to get a panoramic view of the city. Treat yourself to traditional Peking duck for dinner at Li Qun restaurant.

Day 3: Hire a car and driver to take you to the Great Wall. On the way back, consider a stop at either the Thirteen Ming Tombs or the Summer Palace. Head to Chaoyang or Sanlitun Bar Street in the evening to unwind over a cocktail or two.

Day 4: Time to shop! Our favorite markets are the Panjiayuan, Silk Alley, Hongqiao (Pearl), and Yaxiu (Yashow). Also check out the best shopping streets in town: Liulichang, Wangfujing, and Dazhalan. The Malls at Oriental Plaza are also worth a visit—head to the Food Court for some yummy eats.

Day 5: Reserve half the day for a visit to the Temple of Heaven. Afterward, spring for a pedicab tour through Beijing's amazing ancient hutong neighborhoods, where you can find traditional Chinese food galore.

Visitor Centers

China International Travel Service (CITS), an official government agency, maintains offices in many hotels and at some tourist venues. The Beijing Tourism Administration maintains a 24-hour hotline for tourist inquiries and complaints, with operators fluent in English.

Beijing Tourism Administration Hotline (☎ 010/6513–0828)

China International Travel Service (✉ 28 Jianguomenwai Dajie, Chaoyang District ☎ 010/6515–8565 🖷 010/6515–8603)

Street Vocabulary

Dong is east, **xi** is west, **nan** is south, **bei** is north, and **zhong** means middle. **Jie** and **lu** mean street and road respectively, and **da** means big.

Gongyuan means park. Jingshan Park is Jingshan Gongyuan.

Men, meaning door or gate, indicates a street that once passed through an entrance in the old wall that surrounded the city until it was torn down in the 1960s.

Nei means inside and **wai** means outside.

Qiao, or bridge, is part of the place name at just about every entrance and exit on the ring roads.

Getting Around

On Foot
Though traffic and modernization has put a bit of a cramp in Beijing's walking style, meandering remains one of the best ways of experiencing the capital.

By Bike
The proliferation of cars has made biking a bit less pleasant here. Fortunately, most streets have wide, well-defined bike lanes often separated from other traffic by an island of hedges. If a flat tire or sudden brake failure strikes, seek out the nearest street-side mechanic.

By Subway
The subway is a good way to avoid Beijing's frequent traffic jams. And, with the opening of new lines, Beijing's subway service is becoming increasingly convenient. Beijing has four lines (with more in the works for the Olympics), including a light rail that runs out to the Haidian district. One line circles Beijing beneath the Second Ring Road and the other runs east–west from the city center to the western and eastern suburbs. The subway runs from 5 AM to midnight daily. Fares are Y3 per ride for any distance, and an additional Y2 for transfers to the light rail.

By Taxi
The taxi experience in Beijing has improved significantly. Flag fall for taxis is Y10 for the first 4 km (2½ mi) and Y2 per kilometer thereafter. For all taxis, a 20% nighttime surcharge kicks in at 11 PM and lasts until 5 AM. Taxis are easy to hail during the day, but can be difficult during evening rush hour, especially when it's raining. If you're having difficulty, go to the closest hotel and wait in line there. Few taxi drivers speak English, so ask your hotel concierge to write down your destination in Chinese, or use the end-of-chapter translations in this book. Be sure to take a hotel card with you for the return trip. ■ TIP→ **Be sure to check that the meter has been engaged to avoid fare negotiations at your destination.**

When to Go

The best time to visit Beijing is spring or early fall, when the weather is pleasant and crowds are a bit smaller. Book at least one month in advance for travel during these two times of year. In winter, Beijing's Forbidden City and Summer Palace can look majestic when the traditional tiled roofs are covered with snow and the venues are devoid of tourists. Avoid the three long national holidays: Chinese New Year, which ranges from mid-January to mid-February; Labor Day holiday, the first week of May; and National Day, the first week of October. Millions of Chinese travel during these weeks.

Beijing Temperatures

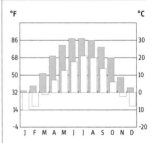

EXPLORING BEIJING

By Paul Mooney, Alex Miller & Dinah Gardner

BEIJING IS A VIBRANT jumble of neighborhoods and districts. It's a city in transition: construction is rampant in preparation for the 2008 Olympics, often leveling lively *hutongs* (ancient alleyway neighborhoods) to make way for the glittering towers that are fast dwarfing their surroundings. Still, day-to-day life seems to pulse the lifeblood of a Beijing that once was.

As you explore Beijing, you'll find that taxis are often the best way to get around. However, if the subway goes where you're headed, it's often a faster option than dealing with traffic, which has become increasingly congested in recent years with the rise of private automobiles. The city is divided into 18 municipal and suburban districts (*qu*). Only six of these districts are central stomping grounds for most visitors: **Dongcheng, Xicheng, Chongwen, Xuanwu, Chaoyang,** and **Haidian.**

Dongcheng District

Dongcheng District, with its idyllic hutongs and plethora of historical sights, is one of Beijing's most pleasant areas. It's also one of the smaller districts in the city, which makes it easy to get around. A day exploring Dongcheng will leave you feeling like you've been introduced to the character of the capital. From the old men playing chess in the hutongs and the sleek, chauffeured Mercedes driving down Chang'an Jie, to the colorful shopping on Wangfujing, Dongcheng offers visitors a thousand little tastes of what makes Beijing a fascinating city.

HIGHLIGHTS From **Wangfujing's** glitzy mall at **Oriental Plaza** to the incense-laden **Lama Temple** and immense **Ditan Park,** Dongcheng has plenty to offer visitors looking for closely packed Beijing thrills. The district is situated north and east of the **Forbidden City,** which is fronted by **Tiananmen Square.** Aside from its historic sites and the massive hotels and office buildings that line major thoroughfares, Dongcheng is a mostly residential district increasingly made up of shiny high-rises. Much of the district is accessible by subway, as it is hemmed in by parts of Lines 1 and 2.

GETTING AROUND Dongcheng is easily accessible by subway, with stops along most of its perimeter: Tiananmen to Jianguomen on Line 1 forms the south side of this district; Jianguomen to Andingmen on Line 2 forms the district's north and east sides. Line 2 stops at the Lama Temple, the Ancient Observatory, Wangfujing, and Tiananmen Square. Taxi travel during peak hours (7 to 9 AM and 4 to 7 PM) is difficult. At other times, traveling by taxi is affordable, convenient, and the fastest option (especially at noon, when much of the city is at lunch, and after 10 PM).

Sights

❷ **Confucius Temple (with the Imperial Academy).** This tranquil temple to China's great sage has endured close to eight centuries of additions and restorations. In 2006 it was once again under scaffolding and is now combined with the Imperial Academy (next door), once the highest educational institution in the country. The highlights here include the

Fodor'sChoice ★

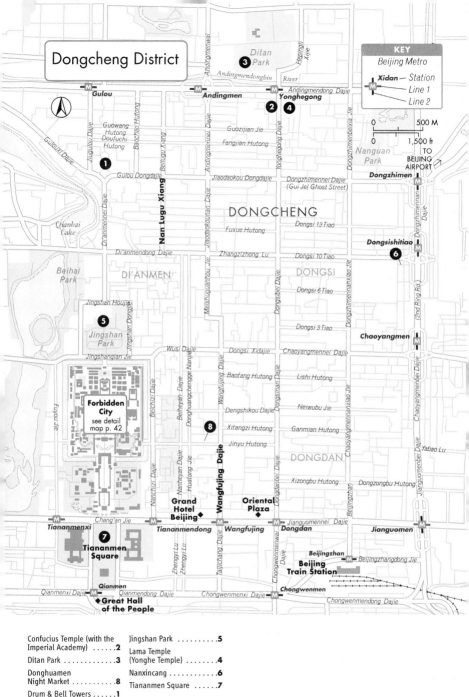

Dongcheng District

see detail map p. 42

cemetery of stone tablets, or stelae, which stand in the main courtyards of the temple. On some stelae you can barely make out the names of thousands of scholars who passed imperial exams.

After you inspect the stelae, wander the Riyong Emperors Lecture Hall. Surrounded by a circular moat (although the building is rectangular in shape), this hall is where emperors would once lecture on the classics.

The Imperial Academy, just next door, was established in 1306 as a rigorous training ground for high-level government officials. This ancient campus would be a glorious place to study today with its washed red walls, gold-tiled roofs, and towering cypresses (some as old as 700 years). The academy was notorious, especially during the early Ming Dynasty era, for the harsh discipline imposed on scholars perfecting their knowledge of the Confucian classics. ✉ *Guozijian Lu off Yunghegong Lu near Lama Temple, Dongcheng District* ☎ *010/8401–1977* 🎫 *Y20 (tickets are reduced if renovations cause restricted access)* 🕙 *Daily 9–5* Ⓜ *Yonghegong.*

❸ Ditan Park (Temple of Earth Park). In this 16th-century park are the Hall of Deities and the square altar where emperors once made sacrifices to the earth god. This is a lovely place for an afternoon stroll. ✉ *Yonghegong Jie, just north of Second Ring Rd., Dongcheng District* ☎ *010/6421–4657* 🎫 *Y2* 🕙 *Daily 6–9.*

★ ❶ Drum Tower. Until the late 1920s, the 24 drums once housed in this tower were Beijing's timepiece. Sadly, all but one of these huge drums have been destroyed, and the survivor is in serious need of renovation. Kublai Khan built the first drum tower on this site in 1272. You can climb to the top of the present tower, which dates from the Ming Dynasty. The nearby **Bell Tower,** renovated after a fire in 1747, offers fabulous views from the top of a long, narrow staircase. The huge 63-ton bronze bell, supported by lacquered wood stanchions, is also worth seeing. ✉ *North end of Dianmen Dajie, Dongcheng District* ☎ *010/6404–1710* 🎫 *Y20 for Drum Tower, Y15 for Bell Tower* 🕙 *Daily 9–4:30* Ⓜ *Gulou.*

❺ Jingshan Park. Climb a winding stone staircase past peach and apple trees to Wanchun Pavilion on Coal Hill, the park's highest point, for views of the Forbidden City and the Bell and Drum towers. Chongzhen, the last Ming emperor, is said to have hanged himself at the foot of this hill as his dynasty collapsed in 1644. ✉ *Jingshanqian Dajie, opposite the north gate of the Forbidden City, Dongcheng District* ☎ *010/6404–4071 or 010/6403–2244* 🎫 *Y5* 🕙 *Daily 6 AM–10 PM.*

❹ Lama Temple (Yonghe Temple). Beijing's most visited religious site and one of the most important functioning Buddhist temples in Beijing, this Tibetan Buddhist masterpiece has five main halls and numerous galleries hung with finely detailed *thangkhas* (painted cloth scrolls). The entire temple is decorated with carved or cast Buddha images—all guarded by somber lamas (monks) dressed in brown robes. Originally a palace for Prince Yongzheng, it was transformed into a temple after a few decades once he became the Qing's third emperor in 1723. The temple flourished under Yongzheng's successor, Emperor Qianlong, housing some 500 resident monks.

FodorśChoice
★

Be sure to visit the Hall of Heavenly Kings, with its statues of Maitreya, the future Buddha, and Weitou, China's guardian of Buddhism. The Pavilion of Ten Thousand Fortunes houses a breathtaking 26-meter (85-foot) Maitreya Buddha carved from a single sandalwood block. While the souvenir shops here add some kitsch, the monks temper this with their own brand of serenity. And although indoor photography is prohibited, the exterior of the temple is quite photogenic. ☒ *12 Yonghegong Dajie, Beixingqiao, Dongcheng District* ☎ *010/6404–3769 or 010/6404–4499* ☒ *Y25* ☉ *Daily 9–5* Ⓜ *Yonghegong.*

> ## WANGFUJING SHOPPING
>
> Beijing's premier shopping street simply glistens with new malls and department stores (namely those at the Oriental Plaza). This pedestrian-only lane overflows with spending opportunities for locals and visitors alike, spanning the shopping spectrum from Adidas to Tiffany's to snack shops and souvenir stalls.

❼ **Tiananmen Square.** The world's largest public square, Tiananmen Square

Fodor'sChoice   owes little to the grand imperial designs of the Yuan, Ming, and Qing—

★   and everything to the successor "dynasty" of Mao Zedong. And looking south, across the proletarian panorama, is the Great Helmsman's tomb. Indeed, it was from the Gate of Heavenly Peace that, on October 1, 1949, Mao Zedong announced the establishment of the People's Republic of China. The young protesters who assembled here in the 1919 May Fourth Movement established an honorable tradition of patriotic dissent, which was repeated in June 1989. But today the square is packed with sightseers, families flying kites, undercover policemen, and earnest tour groups. Wide-eyed visitors converge on Tiananmen Square each day at dawn to watch an honor guard raise the Chinese flag.

Tiananmen is sandwiched between two ancient, grand gates: the Gate of Heavenly Peace to the north, where a portrait of Chairman Mao gazes paternally across the square, and Qianmen ("front gate") in the south. The stern Communist-style block along the western edge is the Great Hall of the People. At the square's center stands the tallest monument in China, the Monument to the People's Heroes, a 125-foot granite obelisk commemorating those who died for the revolutionary cause of the Chinese people. ☒ *Bounded by Changan Jie to the north and Xuanwumen Jie to the south, Dongcheng District* ☒ *Free* ☉ *24 hours year-round* Ⓜ *Tiananmen East.*

Experiences

GETTING TO KNOW MAO

Tiananmen Square is likely one of the first places you'll visit when you arrive in Beijing. For good reason, too: this square is the ultimate symbol of modern China. At the height of the Cultural Revolution, hundreds of thousands of Red Guards crowded the square, chanting Mao's name and waving his Little Red Book. In June 1989 the square was the scene of tragedy when hundreds of student demonstrators were killed by troops breaking up a pro-democracy protest. While exploring the

Continued on page 46

THE FORBIDDEN CITY

Undeniably sumptuous, the Forbidden City, once home to a long line of emperors, is Beijing's most enduring emblem. Magnificent halls, winding lanes, and stately courtyards await you—welcome to the world's largest palace complex.

As you gaze up at roofs of glazed-yellow tiles—a symbol of royalty—try to imagine a time when only the emperor ("the son of God") was permitted to enter this palace, accompanied by select family members, concubines, and eunuch-servants. Now, with its doors flung open, the Forbidden City's mysteries beckon.

The sheer grandeur of the site—with 800 buildings and more than 8,000 rooms—conveys the pomp and circumstance of Imperial China. The shady palaces, musty with age, recall life at court, where corrupt eunuchs and palace officials schemed and bored concubines gossiped.

Building to Glory

Under the third Ming emperor, Yongle, 200,000 laborers built this complex over the course of 14 years, finishing in 1420. Yongle relocated the Ming capital to Beijing (from Nanjing in the south) to strengthen China's northern frontier. After Yongle, the palace was home to 23 Ming and Qing emperors, until the dynastic system crumbled in 1911.

In imperial times, no buildings were allowed to exceed the height of the palace. Moats and massive timber doors

protected the emperor. Gleaming yellow roof tiles marked the vast complex as the royal court's exclusive dominion. Ornate interiors displayed China's most exquisite artisanship, including ceilings covered with turquoise-and-blue dragons, walls draped with priceless scrolls, intricate cloisonné screens, sandalwood thrones padded in delicate silks, and floors of golden-hued bricks. Miraculously, the palace survived fire, war, and imperial China's collapse.

More Than Feng Shui

The Forbidden City embodies Feng Shui, architectural principles used for thousands of years throughout China. Each main hall faces south, opening to a courtyard flanked by lesser buildings. This symmetry repeats itself along a north–south axis that bisects the imperial palace, with a broad walkway paved in marble. This path was reserved exclusively for the emperor's sedan chair. Even court ministers, the empress, and favored concubines were required to trod on pathways and pass through doors set to either side of the Imperial Way.

Take a close look at gates, doors, and woodwork here: most structures have nails in a 9 x 9 formation. Nine is the largest odd number less than the number 10, so it's considered both lucky and important.

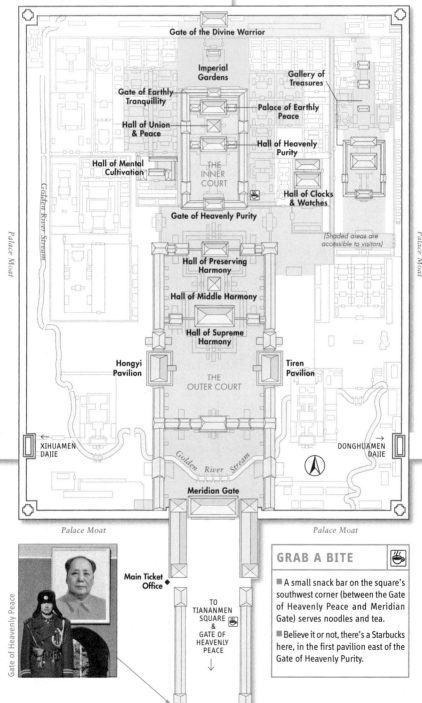

Palace Moat

Palace Moat

Gate of the Divine Warrior

Imperial Gardens

Gallery of Treasures

Gate of Earthly Tranquillity

Palace of Earthly Peace

Hall of Union & Peace

Hall of Heavenly Purity

Hall of Mental Cultivation

THE INNER COURT

Hall of Clocks & Watches

(Shaded areas are accessible to visitors)

Gate of Heavenly Purity

Hall of Preserving Harmony

Hall of Middle Harmony

Hall of Supreme Harmony

Hongyi Pavilion

THE OUTER COURT

Tiren Pavilion

← XIHUAMEN DAJIE

DONGHUAMEN DAJIE →

Golden River Stream

Golden River Stream

Palace Moat

Palace Moat

Meridian Gate

Palace Moat

Palace Moat

Main Ticket Office ◆

TO TIANANMEN SQUARE & GATE OF HEAVENLY PEACE ↓

Gate of Heavenly Peace

GRAB A BITE

■ A small snack bar on the square's southwest corner (between the Gate of Heavenly Peace and Meridian Gate) serves noodles and tea.

■ Believe it or not, there's a Starbucks here, in the first pavilion east of the Gate of Heavenly Purity.

WHAT TO SEE

The most impressive way to reach the Forbidden City is through the **Gate of Heavenly Peace** (Tiananmen), connected to Tiananmen Square. The Great Helmsman himself stood here to establish the People's Republic of China on October 1, 1949.

The **Meridian Gate** (Wumen), sometimes called Five Phoenix Tower, is the main southern entrance to the palace. Here, the emperor announced yearly planting schedules according to the lunar calendar; it's also where errant officials were flogged. The main ticket office and audio-guide rentals are just west of this gate.

The central entrance of the Meridian was reserved for the emperor. The one day the empress was allowed to walk through it was her wedding day.

THE OUTER COURT

The **Hall of Supreme Harmony** (Taihedian) was used for coronations, royal birthdays, and weddings. Bronze vats, once kept brimming with water to fight fires, ring this vast expanse. The hall sits atop three stone tiers with an elaborate drainage system with 1,000 carved dragons. On the top tier, bronze cranes symbolize longevity. Inside, cloisonné cranes flank the imperial throne, above which hangs a heavy bronze ball—placed there to crush any pretender to the throne.

Emperors greeted audiences in the **Hall of Middle Harmony** (Zhonghedian). It also housed the royal plow, with which the emperor would turn a furrow to commence spring planting.

Take a close look at the bronze vats and you'll see the telltale scratch marks of greedy foreign soldiers who scraped the gold with their bayonets.

The highest civil service examinations, which were personally conducted by the emperor, were once administered in the **Hall of Preserving Harmony** (Baohedian). Behind the hall, a 200-ton marble relief of dragons, the palace's most treasured stone carving, adorns the staircase.

A short jaunt to the right is **Hall of Clocks and Watches** (Zhongbiaoguan), where you'll find a collection of early timepieces. It's pure opulence: there's a plethora of jeweled, enameled, and lacquered timepieces (some astride elephants, others implanted in ceramic trees). Our favorites? Those crafted from red sandalwood. *(Admission: Y10)*

The Hall of Supreme Harmony was the site of many imperial weddings.

You'll see that lions in the palace live in pairs. A female lion playing with a cub symbolizes imperial fertility. A male lion, sitting majestically with a sphere beneath his paw, represents power.

Marble dragons will greet you behind the Hall of Preserving Harmony.

■ 24 emperors and two dynasties ruled from within these labyrinthine halls.

■ The emperor was the only non-castrated male allowed in the eastern and western palaces. This served as proof that any pregnant concubine was carrying the royal one's baby.

■ If you prepared for your trip by watching Bertolucci's *The Last Emperor*, you may recognize the passage outside the Hall of Mental Cultivation: this is where young Puyi rode his bike in the film.

■ Women can enter the Forbidden City for half price on March 8, International Women's Day.

■ When it was first built in the 15th century, the palace was called the Purple Forbidden City; today, its official name is the Ancient Palace Museum (Gugong Bowuguan); often it's shortened simply to Gugong.

The Hall of Heavenly Purity

THE INNER COURT

Now you're approaching the very core of the palace. Several emperors chose to live in the Inner Palace with their families. The **Hall of Heavenly Purity** (Qianqinggong) holds another imperial throne; the **Hall of Union and Peace** (Jiaotaidian) was the venue for the empress's annual birthday party; and the **Palace of Earthly Peace** (Kunninggong) was where royal couples consummated their marriages. The banner above the throne bizarrely reads DOING NOTHING.

On either side of the Inner Palace are six western and six eastern palaces—the former living quarters of concubines, eunuchs, and servants. The last building on the western side, the **Hall of Mental Cultivation** (Yangxindian), is the most important of these; starting with Emperor Yongzheng, all Qing Dynasty emperors attended to daily state business in this hall.

AN EMPEROR CHEAT SHEET

JIAJING (1507–1567)

Ming Emperor Jiajing was obsessed with Taoism, which he hoped would give him longevity, but which also led him to ignore state affairs for 25 years. His other fixation was the pursuit of girls: his 18 concubines conspired to strangle him in his sleep, but their plot was uncovered. Nearly all of the girls, and their families, were killed.

YONGZHENG (1678–1735)

The third emperor of the Qing Dynasty, Yongzheng was tyrannical but efficient. He became emperor amid rumors that he had forged his father's will. He appeased his brothers by promoting them, but then proceeded to murder and imprison anyone who posed a challenge, including his own brothers, two of whom died in prison.

1

Animal ornaments decorate the corners of many roofs—the more animals, the more important the building.

FAST FACTS

Address: The main entrance is just north of the Gate of Heavenly Peace, which faces Tiananmen Square on Chang'an Jie.

Web site: www.dpm.org.cn

Admission: Y30

Hours: Oct. 16–Apr. 15, daily 8:30–4:30; Apr. 16–Oct. 15, daily 8:30–5

UNESCO Status: Declared a World Heritage Site in 1987.

■ You must check your bags prior to entry and also pass through a metal detector.

■ Note that the Forbidden City is undergoing major renovations through 2008.

■ The palace is always packed with visitors, but it's impossibly crowded on national holidays.

■ Allow 2–4 hours to explore the palace. There are souvenir shops and restaurants inside.

■ You can hire automated audio guides at the Meridian Gate for Y40 and a Y100 returnable deposit.

The Gallery of Treasures (Zhenbaoguan), actually a series of halls, has breathtaking examples of imperial ornamentation. The first room displays candleholders, wine vessels, tea sets, and a golden pagoda commissioned by Qing emperor Qian Long in honor of his mother. A cabinet on one wall contains the 25 imperial seals. Jade bracelets, golden hair pins, and coral fill the second hall; carved jade landscapes a third. *(Admission: Y10)*

HEAD FOR THE GREEN

North of the Forbidden City's private palaces, beyond the **Gate of Earthly Tranquillity**, lie the most pleasant parts of the Forbidden City: the **Imperial Gardens** (Yuhuayuan), composed of ancient cypress trees and stone mosaic pathways. During festivals, palace inhabitants climbed the Hill of Accumulated Elegance. You can exit the palace at the back of the gardens through the park's **Gate of the Divine Warrior** (Shenwumen).

CIXI (1835–1908)

The Empress Dowager served as de facto ruler of China from 1861 until 1908. She entered the court as a concubine at 16 and soon became Emperor Xianfeng's favorite. She gave birth to his only son to survive: the heir apparent. Ruthless and ambitious, she learned the workings of the imperial court and used every means to gain power.

PUYI (1906–1967)

Puyi, whose life was depicted in Bertolucci's classic *The Last Emperor*, took the throne at age two. The Qing dynasty's last emperor, he was forced to abdicate after the dynasty fell. During an attempted restoration in 1917, he held the throne for 12 days. Puyi was forced out of the Imperial City in 1924 by a warlord.

square, you'll have a chance to gaze up at a portrait of Chairman Mao, a man who inspired both intense love and hate during his lifetime.

Some three decades after his passing, Mao Zedong continues to evoke radically different feelings among the Chinese. Was he the romantic poet-hero who helped the Chinese stand up? Or was he a monster whose wrenching policies caused the deaths of millions of people? Born into a relatively affluent farming family in Hunan in 1893, Mao became active in politics at a young age; he was one of the founding members of the Chinese Communist Party in 1921. When the People's Republic of China was established in 1949, Mao served as chairman of the party and of the state. After getting off to an initially good start in improving the economy, he launched radical economic, political, and agricultural programs in the mid-1950s—often against the advice of his closest comrades—causing serious damage to the nation. The party's official assessment is that Mao was 70% correct and 30% incorrect. His critics, however, reverse this ratio.

AN ANCIENT GRANARY

6 If you have a few hours, visit **Nanxincang,** China's oldest existing granary dating back to the Yongle period (1403–24). It's located on Dongsi Shitiao, just one block west of the Second Ring Road. This valuable historical site is now Beijing's latest entertainment venue, with three art galleries, a teahouse, and several bars and restaurants.

The structures at Nanxincang—just 10 years younger than those of the Forbidden City—were among the more than 300 granaries that existed in this area during imperial days. Have a glass of wine in the second floor of **Yuefu,** an audio and book shop, where you can admire the old interior, then have dinner at one of the excellent restaurants in the compound.

Sifang Jie (☎ 010/6409–6403) specializes in dishes from southwest China.

Fanqian Fanhou (☎ 010/6409–6510) has wonderful Taiwanese cuisine.

Rain Club (☎ 010/6409–6922) offers East-meets-West fusion cuisine.

EVENING MUNCHIES

8 The **Donghuamen Night Market** lies at the northern end of Wangfujing's wide walking boulevard. We'll admit: this is more of a place to look at and perhaps photograph food rather than devour it. In addition to standard street foods, hawkers here also serve up deep-fried scorpions and starfish, plus a variety of insects and other hard-to-identify food items. Most street-market food is usually safe to eat as long as it's hot. The row of interesting outdoor evening stalls here makes for an intriguing walk with great photo ops.

Xicheng District

Xicheng district is home to an eclectic mix of a few of Beijing's favorite things: delicious food, ancient hutongs and courtyard houses, charming lakes, and engaging nightlife. The lakes at Shichahai are fun for all ages, both day and night. Take a boat ride on the lake in the warmer months, or ice skate here in the cold winter months when the lakes are crowded with parents taking their children out for a day of fun. Our top experience? Taking a walk or bicycle tour of the surrounding hutongs: there is no better way to scratch the surface of this sprawling city.

HIGHLIGHTS **Shichahai,** a collection of lakes, comprises Xicheng's foremost attractions. Shichahai's southernmost lake, **Nanhai** ("south lake") is just west of Tiananmen Square; **Zhonghai** ("middle lake") is north of Nanhai and due west of the Forbidden City; and **Beihai** ("north lake") is located in Beihai Park, north of Zhonghai. To the north of Beihai is **Qianhai** ("front lake"). **Houhai** ("rear lake") is a commercialized yet wonderful lake surrounded by chic and cheap bars, good restaurants, and tempting shops. **Soong Qing-ling's former residence** (a lovely spot once inhabited by the wife of the father of modern China, Sun Yat-sen) is on the northeastern side of Houhai.

Xicheng's other main attraction is **Xidan,** an area full of shopping malls and boutiques selling clothing and accessories. There is also *Tushu Dasha* (aka Beijing Book Building), said to be the biggest bookstore in China, which has a small selection of English books in the basement.

GETTING AROUND The Line 1 subway stops include Tiananmen, Xidan, and Fuxingmen while Line 2 makes stops from Fuxingmen to the Drum Tower (Gulou), following Xicheng's perimeter. Xizhimen is a major terminus with access to the northwest via subway. ■ TIP➡ **Shichahai and Beihai Park are more conveniently reached by taxi.** Once you're in the area, definitely spring for a pedicab tour of the fascinating hutong neighborhoods in the area.

Sights

★ ❹ **Beihai Park.** The park is easily recognized by the white Tibetan dagoba perched on a hill just north of the south gate. Also at the south entrance is the **Round City,** which contains a white-jade Buddha, said to have been sent from Burma to Qing emperor Qian Long, and an enormous jade bowl given to Kublai Khan. Nearby, the well-restored **Temple of Eternal Peace** houses a variety of Buddhas and other sacred images. Climb to the dagoba from Yongan Temple. Once there, you can pay an extra Y1 to ascend the Buddha-bedecked **Shanyin Hall** for a view into forbidden Zhongnanhai, where senior Communist Party officials continue to have their offices.

The lake is Beijing's largest and most beautiful public waterway. Amusement-park rides line its east edge, and kiosks stock assorted snacks. On summer weekends the lake teems with paddle boats. The **Five Dragon Pavilion,** on Beihai's northwest shore, was built in 1602 by a Ming Dynasty emperor who liked to fish and view the moon. The halls north of it were added later. Among the restaurants in the park is **Fangshan,** a longstanding and elegant establishment that serves the imperial cuisine of the Manchus. ✉ *South Gate, Weijin Lu, Xicheng District* ☎ *010/ 6404–0610* ✍ *Y10; extra fees for some sights* ☉ *Daily 6* AM*–10* PM.

Qianhai and Houhai. Most people come here to stroll casually around the lakes and enjoy the bars and restaurants that perch on their shores. In summer you can boat, swim, fish, and even, on occasion, windsurf

Xicheng District

Xizhimen
Train Station

XINJIEKOU

XISI

XICHENG

XIDAN

Guanyuan
Park

Beihai

Jingshan
Park

Forbidden
City

Xihai

Houhai

Silver Ingot
Bridge

Qianhai

Han Cang

Fangshan
Restaurant

Shichahai

Zhonghai

Nanhai

Tiananmen

Andingmenxibin River

Ande Lu

Ande Lu

Deshengmendong Dajie
(2nd Ring Rd.)

Deshengmenxi Dajie

Guowang
Hutong
Doufuchi
Hutong

Di'anmenxi Dajie

Di'anmendong Dajie

Jingshan Houjie

Jingshan Qianjie

Jingshanqian Jie

Xichangan Jie

Fuxingmennei Dajie

Xinwenhua Jie

Xirongxian Hutong

Dongrongxian Hutong

500 M

1,500 ft

0

0

on the lakes. In winter sections of the frozen surfaces are fenced off for skating. ⊠ *North side of Dianmen Xi Lu, north of Beihai Lake, Xicheng District.*

SILVER INGOT BRIDGE

Known as **Yin Ding Qiao** in Chinese, this Ming Dynasty Bridge is named for its shape, which resembles a silver ingot turned upside down. It divides Qianhai and Houhai at the lakes' most narrow point. ⊠ *Xicheng District.*

🅞 **Museum of Antique Currency.** This museum in a tiny courtyard house showcases a small but impressive selection of rare Chinese coins. Explanations are in Chinese only. Also in the courtyard are coin and curio dealers. ⊠ *Deshengmen Tower south bldgs., Bei'erhuan Jie, Xicheng District* ☎ *010/6201–8073* 💲 *Y10* ⊗ *Tues.–Sun. 9–4.*

🅢 **Prince Gong's Mansion.** Built during the Ming Dynasty, this grand compound fell to Prince Gong, brother of Qing emperor Xianfeng and later an adviser to Empress Dowager Cixi. With nine courtyards joined by covered walkways, it was once one of Beijing's most lavish residences. The largest hall, now a banquet room, offers summertime Beijing opera and afternoon tea to guests on guided hutong tours. Some literary scholars believe this was the setting of the *Dream of the Red Chamber,* China's best-known classic novel. ⊠ *17 Qianhai Xijie, Xicheng District* ☎ *010/6618–0573* 💲 *Y20* ⊗ *Daily 8–4.*

🅢 **Soong Qing-ling's Former Residence.** Soong Qing-ling (1893–1981) was the youngest daughter of the wealthy, American-educated bible publisher, Charles Soong. At the age of 18, disregarding her family's strong opposition, she eloped to marry the much older Sun Yat-sen. When her husband founded the Republic of China in 1911, Soong Qing-ling became a nationally significant political figure. In 1924 she headed the Women's Department of the Nationalist Party. Then in 1949 she became the vice president of the People's Republic of China as well as honorary president of the All-China Women's Federation. Throughout her career she campaigned tirelessly for the emancipation of women. This former palace was her residence and workplace and now houses a small museum, which documents her life and work. ⊠ *46 Houhai Beiyan, Xicheng District* ☎ *010/6403–5997* 💲 *Y20* ⊗ *Daily 9–5.*

Experiences

SHOPPING ON THE CHEAP

Less than 2 km (1 mi) west of the Forbidden City, the massive shopping area of Xidan swarms with local shoppers and bargain-hunters. Socks, trousers, hats, dresses, and T-shirts galore!

A SNAPSHOT OF OLD BEIJING

Time seems to be standing still in Xicheng's ancient neighborhoods. A street stand sells steamed meat buns beside a parked cart piled high with watermelons. Peddlers shout out while, at the corner, boys crowd around a hawker with dozens of small woven baskets, the size of plums. Inside are crickets. A gaggle of grandmothers sits on short stools nearby, some holding grandchildren, others snoozing in the sun. Pedicabs glide by, on

CLOSE UP

Best Beijing Tours

- **Beijing Hikers.** ☎ 139/1002-5516 or 010/6779-9365 ⊕ www.beijinghikers.com ☎ Y200, including round-trip transportation, park-entrance fees, and end-of-hike refreshments ☉ Weekends 8:30 or 9-4:30 or 5.

- **Beijing Hutong Tourist Agency.** ✉ 26 Di'anmen Xidajie, Dongcheng District ☎ 010/6615-9097 🖷 010/6400-2787.

- **Beijing Panda Tour.** ✉ Grand Rock Plaza, 5th Fl., 13 Xinzhong Xili, Dongcheng District ☎ 010/6417-0468.

- **China International Travel Service.** ✉ 28 Jianguomenwai Dajie, Chaoyang District ☎ 010/6515-8565 🖷 010/6515-8603 ⊕ www.citsusa.com.

- **CycleChina.** ☎ 139/1188-6524 ⊕ www.cyclechina.com.

- **Dragon Bus.** ✉ 28 Jianguomenwai Dajie (behind the Gloria Plaza Hotel), Chaoyang District ☎ 010/6515-8565 ⊕ www.dragontour.com.cn.

- **WildChina.** ✉ Room 801, Oriental Place, 9 East Dongfang Lu, North Dongsanhuan Lu, Chaoyang District ☎ 010/6465-6602 ⊕ www.wildchina.com.

constant prowl for passengers. Along the lake, elderly men are absorbed in the same pastimes that their ancestors enjoyed a century ago. One group is playing Chinese chess, another mah-jongg—the sound of clicking tiles can be heard long before you reach the spot. Elsewhere, a group of men admire birds perched in cages hanging from trees.

WELCOME TO THE HUTONG

For longtime residents of Beijing, there is probably nothing more emblematic of the city than its idyllic—but quickly disappearing—courtyard houses and hutongs. Strolls into a hutong frequently reveal ancient neighborhoods; brick and timber homes; courtyards full of children, *laobaixing* (ordinary folk), and, in winter, mountains of cabbage and coal—not to mention walkways so narrow pedestrians can't pass two abreast. Despite the radical changes that are going on around the city, time seems to stand still in these tiny alleyways. Hutongs have been around for more than 700 years. During imperial days, there were no signs marking the hutongs, whose names were only passed on orally. Some are named after national heroes, some for their geographical location, and others for the businesses that were once conducted there.

One of the best places to explore Beijing's hutongs is the Houhai area, which was home to nobles during the Qing dynasty, and where you can still find some of their homes and gardens. Walk around the lake and plunge into any small lane and just keep wandering around this maze of alleyways. ■ TIP➔ **The Silver Ingot Bridge, which separates the front and rear lakes, is a good place to start.** An easy way to visit the hutongs is with the **Beijing Hutong Tourist Agency** (✉ 26 Di'anmen Xidajie ☎ 010/6615-9097). To experience the inside of one of the beautiful *siheyuan*, or courtyard houses of the Qing dynasty, have dinner at the Red Capital Club, The Source, Baijia Dazhaimen, or Gui Gongfu.

Southern Districts: Chongwen & Xuanwu

Life in the southern part of Beijing has a different rhythm. The major attraction here is the Temple of Heaven, which is heavenly indeed—be sure to set aside part of a day to explore its grounds. Many of the sights in this part of town are ancient reminders of the Beijing that once was. A lazy stroll through Source of Law Temple on a quiet afternoon is sure to remind you of the city's past. Meanwhile, jaunts down the packed shopping streets Qianmen Dajie, Dazhalan, and Liulichang are sure to please the shopper—and gawker—in you.

HIGHLIGHTS **Qianmen Dajie** (a walking street) runs north–south from Qianmen at Tiananmen Square, separating Chongwen and Xuanwu. The ancient, breathtaking **Temple of Heaven,** which has wonderful examples of traditional imperial architecture, is a must-visit. The **Source of Law Temple** is a peaceful old Zen temple that's still operational. **Ox Street** and the **Niujie Mosque** are just about all that remains of Beijing's old Muslim neighborhoods. **Liulichang** is Beijing's historical art street, where the Ming- and Qing-dynasty literati used to swap stories and books. Now a bustling antiques market, Liulichang has great shopping if you're looking for Chinese art or art supplies (though it's rather crammed with tourists).

GETTING AROUND The southern portion of the Line 2 subway runs across the northern fringe of these districts, making stops at Chongwenmen, Qianmen, Hepingmen, Xuanwumen, Changchun Jie, and Xidan. For destinations in the south of Chongwen and Xuanwu, it's advisable to take a taxi, as attractions are a bit more spread out and it may be hard to find your way on foot.

Sights

⑤ Ming Dynasty City Wall Ruins Park. This ancient bit of city wall, following Chongwenmen Dong Dajie, was reconstructed with the original bricks returned by Beijing residents who had taken them to build their own structures when the wall was torn down in the 1960s. It's a well-lighted, nicely landscaped area, flanked by a wide strip of grass with paths full of city residents walking dogs, flying kites, practicing tai chi, and playing with their children. The eastern terminus is the imposing **Dongbianmen Watch Tower,** which has a contemporary Chinese art gallery on the first floor, the Red Gate Gallery, and a historical museum on the upper floors. ☒ *Chongwenmen Dong Dajie, just east of the Chongwenmen subway stop, Chongwen District* Ⓜ *Chongwenmen.*

❶ Niujie (Ox Street) Mosque. More than 1,000 years old, Beijing's oldest
Fodor'sChoice and largest mosque sits at the center of the Muslim quarter. Arches and
★ posts are inscribed with Koranic verse, and a special moon tower helps determine the lunar calendar. The main prayer hall is open only to Muslims and can fit up to 1,000 worshippers. The Spirit Wall stands opposite the main entrance; it serves to prevent ghosts from entering the mosque. From the Tower for Viewing the Moon *imams* (the prayer leaders of a mosque) measure the beginning and end of Ramadan, Islam's

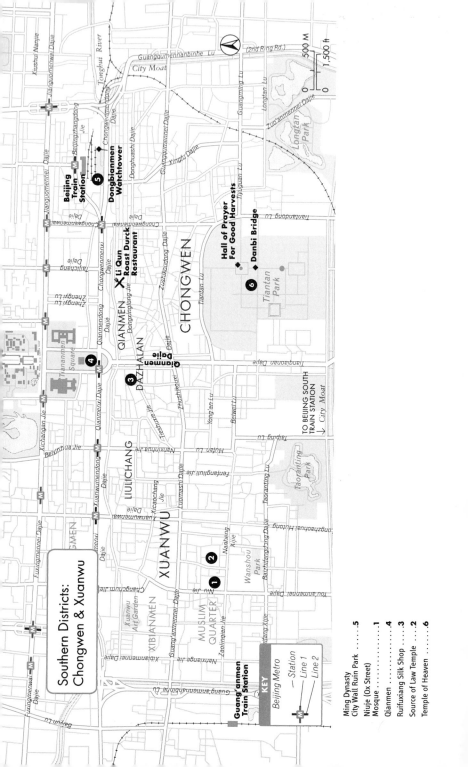

Southern Districts: Chongwen & Xuanwu

KEY

Beijing Metro

— Station
—— Line 1
—— Line 2

Ming Dynasty
City Wall Ruin Park **5**
Niujie (Ox Street)
Mosque **1**
Qianmen **4**
Ruifuxiang Silk Shop **3**
Source of Law Temple **2**
Temple of Heaven **6**

month of fasting and prayer. ⊠ *88 Niu Jie, Xuanwu District* 🎫 *Y10* ⊙ *Daily 8–sunset.*

❹ **Qianmen** (Front Gate). From its top looking south, you can see that Front Gate is actually two gates: Sun-Facing Gate (Zhengyangmen) and Arrow Tower (Jian Lou), which was, until 1915, connected to Zhengyangmen by a defensive half-moon wall. The central gates of both structures opened only for the emperor's biannual ceremonial trips to the Temple of Heaven to the south. ⊠ *Xuanwumen Jie, Xuanwu District* Ⓜ *Qianmen.*

❷ **Source of Law Temple.** This temple is also a school for monks—the Chinese Buddhist Theoretical Institute houses and trains them here. Of course, the temple functions within the boundaries of current regime policy. You can observe both elderly practitioners chanting mantras in the main prayer halls, as well as robed students kicking soccer balls in a side courtyard. Dating from the 7th century but last rebuilt in 1442, the temple holds a fine collection of Ming and Qing statues, including a sleeping Buddha and an unusual grouping of copper-cast Buddhas seated on a 1,000-petal lotus. ⊠ *7 Fayuan Si Qianjie, Xuanwu District* ☎ *010/6353–4171* 🎫 *Y5* ⊙ *Daily 8:30–3:30.*

❻ **Temple of Heaven.** The Temple of Heaven was built in 1420 as a site for imperial sacrifices, meant to please the gods so they would generate bumper harvests. Set in a huge, mushroom-shaped park, it's surrounded by splendid examples of Ming Dynasty architecture, including curved cobalt-blue roofs layered with yellow and green tiles.

Fodor'sChoice ★

Shaped like a semicircle on the northern rim to represent heaven and a square on the south for the earth, the grounds were once believed to be the meeting point of the two. The area is double the size of the Forbidden City. The hallmark structure here is a magnificent blue-roofed wooden tower, originally built in 1420. It burned to the ground in 1889 and was immediately rebuilt using Ming architectural methods (and timber imported from Oregon). The building's design is based on the calendar: 4 center pillars represent the seasons, the next 12 pillars represent months, and 12 outer pillars signify the parts of a day. Together these 28 poles, which correspond to the 28 constellations of heaven, support the structure without nails. A carved dragon swirling down from the ceiling represents the emperor, or "son of heaven."

TEMPLE OF HEAVEN'S MYSTERIES

An almost-magical wall encircling the Imperial Vault of Heaven, the Echo Wall allows anyone to eavesdrop. Extreme quiet is needed to hear the effect. Also, on the courtyard's step are three echo stones, which play with hand claps. The number nine was regarded as a symbol of the power of the emperor, as it is the biggest single-digit odd number, and odd numbers are masculine and were therefore considered more powerful. Nine or multiples of nine are used in the designs of palaces and temples. If you count studs on palace gates, for example, there are usually nine rows of nine.

BEIJING'S SUBWAY

The subway in Beijing can be faster and cheaper than a taxi, but it's also limited. There are only four subway lines—though five more are in the works and should be operational in time for the 2008 Olympics. Line 1 follows Jianguo Lu, starting at Sihui Dong, and passing the China World Trade Center, Jianguomen (one of the embassy districts), the Wangfujing shopping area, Tiananmen Square, the Forbidden City, and Xidan (another major shopping location), all the way to Pingguoyuan ("Apple Orchard") in the far western suburbs. Line 2 (the loop line) runs along a sort of circular route around the center of the city. Line 13 is a commuter rail that runs from Dongzhimen into the northern suburbs and back down to Xizhimen in a crooked upside-down U; the Batong Line (also a light rail) runs from Sihui, just west of the China World Trade Center, to the eastern suburbs.

If both you and your final destination are near the Second Ring Road, or on Chang'an Jie, the best way to get there is probably by subway. It stops just about every mile, and you'll easily spot the entrances (with blue subway logos) dotting the streets. Transferring between Lines 1 and 2 is easy and free, with the standard Y3 ticket including travel between any two destinations. Tickets for Line 13 and the Batong Line are Y5, with transfer to the subway included in this price.

Subway tickets can be purchased at a window either at street-entrance level, or above the steps leading down to the tracks. People unfamiliar with travel in Beijing may find buying a ticket exasperating. There is no line; instead, people crowd around the ticket window and shove their money in.

Trains can be very crowded, especially during rush hour, and it's not uncommon for people to push onto the train before exiting passengers can get off. The crowds also make the subway system an ideal place for pickpockets to work, so be sure to keep your money and wallet in a safe place.

⚠ **Unfortunately, the subway system is not convenient for handicapped people. In some stations, there are no escalators, and sometimes the only entrance or exit is via steep steps.**

Cross the divine pathway on the Danbi Bridge: this will take you to the Hall of Prayer for Good Harvests. The middle section was reserved for the Emperor of Heaven, who was the only one allowed to step foot on the eastern side, while aristocrats and high-ranking officials walked on the western strip. ■ TIP→ Automatic audio guides (Y40) are available for rental at stalls inside all four entrances.

✉ *Yongdingmen Dajie (South Gate), Chongwen District* ☎ *010/6702–8866* 🎫 *all inclusive ticket Apr.—Oct. Y35, Oct.–Apr. Y30; entrance to park only Y15* ⊙ *Daily 8–4:30.*

Experiences

THE MUSLIM QUARTER

Recent urban renewal has wiped out much of Beijing's old Muslim Quarter, an area that dates back to the 900s. The main survivor is the **Niujie Mosque;** it is often crowded with members of Beijing's Muslim community. A few Muslim shops—mainly halal restaurants and butchers—remain in the neighborhood, which is now dominated by high-rise apartment buildings.

DAZHALAN'S DELIGHTS

Dazhalan, a street and neighborhood in Xuanwu, immediately southwest of the Forbidden City, is always packed with people, cars, and bicycles—each competing for the limited space on its narrow streets, already crowded with hawkers' stands and overflowing restaurants. Dive into the hutong and you are immediately rubbing elbows with the masses. Many *laozihao,* or old brand-name shops, continue to do a booming business here. The **Ruifuxiang Silk Shop** (✉ 5 Dazhalan Dajie ☎ 010/6303–5313), established in 1893, has thick bolts of silk, cotton, cashmere, and wool piled high, in more colors than you'll find in a box of crayons. Clerks deftly cut yards of cloth while tailors take measurements for colorful *qipaos* (traditional gowns). In this corner of Beijing, life seems to continue much as it did a century ago.

Chaoyang District

Chaoyang is where you'll find a lot of the action in Beijing: the nightlife in this district is positively sizzling. The bars and clubs are vibrant and full of Chinese office workers and university students as well as foreigners including expats, English teachers, and embassy staff. During the day, all these people work in this area, as it's home to the CBD (Central Business District), as well as the embassies and the residences of the people who run Beijing's portion of the global economy.

HIGHLIGHTS From shopping at **Guomao** (the World Trade Center) to partying in **Sanlitun,** Chaoyang has a little of everything. **Jianguomen** is the embassy area, with some good foreign restaurants, but mostly quiet blocks of gated embassy compounds; in the center there is lovely **Ritan Park,** with its winding paths and lotus-flower ponds.

The fast-rising **Central Business District** (CBD) encompasses the China World Trade Center and a slew of new and impressive skyscrapers, some designed by internationally known architects. Opposite the China World Trade Center is Jian-

RITAN PARK EATS

If you're near Ritan Park and need a pick-me-up, check out **The Stone Boat,** located on the west side of the park alongside the lake. In a beautiful location overlooking the lake, it offers coffee, tea, juices, and mixed drinks along with simple snacks. On the weekends during the warmer months, it also features local music talent. If that's not your cup of tea, try **Vics** (☎ 010/6593–6215) or **Mix** (☎ 010/6530–02889), both just inside the north gate of the Workers' Stadium.

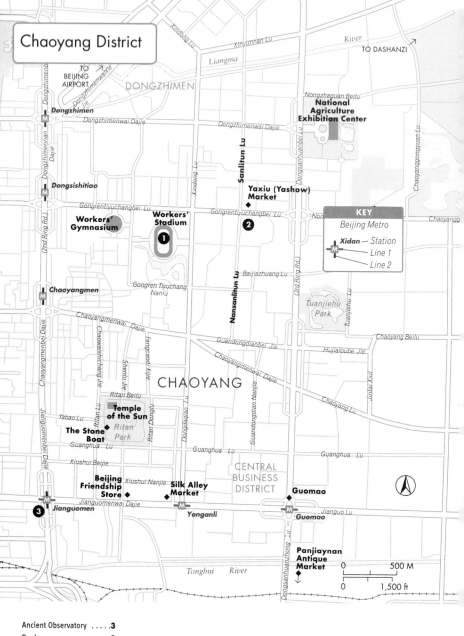

Chaoyang District

TO BEIJING AIRPORT

DONGZHIMEN

Xindong Lu
Xinyunnan Lu
River
TO DASHANZI

Liangma

Dongzhimenbei
Dongzhimenwai
Dongzhimenwai Jie

Dongzhimen

Dongzhimennan Dajie

Dongzhimenwai Dajie

Dongzhimenwai Dajie

Nongzhaguan Beilu

National Agriculture Exhibition Center

Dongsanhuanbei Lu

Chaoyanggongyuan Lu

Dongsishitiao

Gongrentiyuchangbei Lu

Sanlitun Lu

Yaxiu (Yashow) Market

Gongrentiyuchangbei Lu

Workers' Gymnasium

Workers' Stadium

Xindong Lu

1

2

Nong

Chaoyangg

(2nd Ring Rd.)

KEY

Beijing Metro

Xidan— *Station*
— *Line 1*
— *Line 2*

Chaoyangmen

Gongren Tiyuchang Nanlu

Nansanlitun Lu

Baijiazhuang Lu

(3rd Ring Rd.)

Tuanjiehu Park

Chaoyangmenbei Dajie

Chaoyangmenwai Dajie

Chaowaishichang Jie

Shenlu Jie

Fangcaodi Xijie

Guandongdianbei Jie

Chaoyang Beilu

Guandongdian Nanjie

Chaoyangmenwai Dajie

Hujialoube Jie

Tuanjiehu Lu

Tuanjiehu Xilu

CHAOYANG

Dongdaqiao Lu

Chaoyang Lu

Ritan Beilu

Temple of the Sun

Ritan Park

Ritan Donglu

Yabao Lu

The Stone Boat

Guanghua Lu

Guanghua Lu

Guanghua Lu

Xiushui Beijie

Beijing Friendship Store

Xiushui Nanjie

Silk Alley Market

CENTRAL BUSINESS DISTRICT

Guomao

Jianguomenbei Dajie

Jianguomenwai Dajie

Jianguomen

3

Jianguomenwai Dajie

Yonganli

Guomao

Jianguo Lu

Dongsanhuanzhong Lu

Panjiaynan Antique Market

Tonghui River

0   500 M

0   1,500 ft

wai Soho, a collection of gleaming white high-rises in a nicely laid-out complex with dozens of restaurants and shops.

Directly to the north of Ritan Park is the **Workers' Stadium** complex, where many of the biggest visiting acts perform. The famous Sanlitun Bar Street is several blocks east of there and runs north–south; this is the area that's known for great bars catering to foreigners, expats, and young Chinese.

If it's shopping you're looking for, check out **Yaxiu Market** (also called Yashow Market) a former department store that's been turned into five floors of small shops. Or head to the so-called **Silk Alley Market** which is no longer an alley; a mall has been erected near the Yonganli subway station. There's a street of restaurants and bars growing up next to the flower market at **Nurenjie** (aka Ladies' Street). At nearby Lucky Street, there's a string of Asian, Western, and Chinese restaurants and coffee shops. Be sure to check out our favorite, the **Panjiayuan Antique Market,** which is known for more than just antiques—it's a great place to shop for knickknacks, old books, art, and posters.

GETTING AROUND   The heart of Chaoyang district is accessible via Lines 1 and 2, but the district is huge and the sites are broadly distributed. Taking taxis between sites is usually the easiest way to get around. Dashanzi, an art district, is especially far away from central Beijing, and so a taxi is the best bet (about Y25 from the center of town). Buses go everywhere, but as with the rest of the city, they are slow and amazingly crowded, stops are only indicated in Chinese, and, if you don't find a seat, very tiring.

Sights

❸ **Ancient Observatory.** This squat tower of primitive stargazing equipment dates to the time of Genghis Khan, who believed that his fortunes could be read in the stars. Many of the bronze devices on display were gifts from Jesuit missionaries who arrived in Beijing in 1601 and shortly thereafter ensconced themselves as the Ming court's resident stargazers. They offered this technology in a bid to persuade the Chinese of the superiority of the Christian tradition that had produced it. The main astronomical devices are arranged on the roof, whereas, inside, the dusty exhibition rooms shelter ancient star maps with information dating back to the Tang Dynasty.

To China's imperial rulers, interpreting the heavens was key holding on to power; a ruler knew when, say, an eclipse would occur, or could predict the best time to plant crops. Celestial phenomena like eclipses and comets were believed to portend change; if left unheeded they might cost an emperor his legitimacy—or Mandate of Heaven. ✉ *2 Dongbiaobei Hutong, Jianguomenwai Dajie, Chaoyang District* ☎ *010/6524–2202* 🎫 *Y10* ⊙ *Daily 9–4* Ⓜ *Jianguomen.*

Experiences

NIGHTLIFE

❶ A steady stream of Beijing's beautiful people passes through the north gate of the **Workers' Stadium,** drawn toward the hip-hop music that throbs from several of the bars that have displaced spaces once devoted to basketball and Ping-Pong. The crowd runs the gamut from Chinese college

The 2008 Olympic Games

Beijing is undergoing a major makeover as it prepares to host the 2008 Summer Olympics: just about everywhere you look, you'll find feverish activity. Whole city blocks have been razed to make way for state-of-the-art Olympic venues, new hotels, and modern buildings. Subway lines are being expanded, including a welcome new line that will link downtown Beijing with the airport. Furthermore, the Capital International Airport is working on a major expansion.

The Chinese are determined to put on the best games ever. The projects, many designed by top international architects, are impressive to say the least. Twelve brand-new Olympic venues are being built from scratch, with another 11 existing structures being renovated. All will be ready in time for the Olympic trial runs. Check out en.beijing2008.com for more details.

Some say that since Beijing won its bid to host the 2008 Olympics, "the world's largest construction site" has quickly become a rowdy playground for international architects who have shown little regard for traditional Chinese design. Others predict that Beijing will be the scene of a brash, breathtaking architecture that will further open the country—and the world's eyes.

BEIJING CAPITAL AIRPORT, TERMINAL 3
Address: Beijing Capital Airport
Architects: Norman Foster, the preeminent British architect responsible for Hong Kong's widely respected airport

BEIJING LINKED HYBRID
Address: Adjacent to the northeast corner of the Second Ring Road
Architects: New York-based Steven Holl, who won awards for his Museum of Contemporary Art in Helsinki, Finland, and Li Hu, who helped design China's first contemporary museum in Nanjing

CCTV (CENTRAL CHINESE TELEVISION) TOWER & CULTURAL CENTER
Address: 32 Dong San Huan Zhong Lu (32 East Third Ring Middle Road)
Architects: Rem Koolhaas (a Dutch mastermind known for his outlandish ideas and successful Seattle Public Library) and Ole Scheeren (Koolhaas's 30-something German protégé)

NATIONAL STADIUM ("BIRD'S NEST")
Address: Beijing Olympic Park at Bei Si Huan Lu (North Fourth Ring Road).
Architects: Herzog and de Meuron of Switzerland, who won the prestigious Pritzker Prize for work at London's Tate Modern and the Ricola Marketing Building in Laufen, Switzerland

NATIONAL SWIMMING CENTER (THE "WATERCUBE")
Address: Beijing Olympic Park
Architects: PTW, the Australian firm that cut its teeth on venues for the 2000 Games in Sydney

GRAND NATIONAL THEATER
Address: Xi Chang'an Jie (just west of Tiananmen Square)
Architect: French-born Paul Andreu, who designed the groundbreaking Terminal 1 of Paris's Charles de Gaulle airport in 1974.

kids to well-heeled Beijing tycoons to Mongolian prostitutes, plus expats and foreign diplomats. Downstairs in Vics it's wall-to-wall people: drinking, dancing, or lost in conversation. A young woman, French beret pulled down over her eyes, leans against her boyfriend; an older woman straight from the society pages of Hong Kong's newspapers sips wine. There's even a Chinese Elvis, his hair defying physics to remain aloft inches into the air. Welcome to the new China.

SANLITUN BAR STREET

This is one of the hottest streets in the city. Plenty of bars, pubs, and dance spots amp the energy up here, with more refined venues filling out the southern section of the street. Enjoy a drink or meal, along with ❷ some great books, at **The Bookworm**, in the first alley on Sanlitun South Street. Readings and musical events take place throughout the week here, usually in the evenings.

Haidian District

In the last decade or so, with the Chinese Internet and tech booms, the rise of the middle class, and, with it, university education, Haidian, in the northwest corner of the city, has become an educational and tech mecca. The major IT players are all located here (including offices of Microsoft, Siemens, NEC, and Sun). If you want to escape modern life, never fear: Haidian is a huge district, and the outer areas house many interesting cultural sites—in fact, it's the juxtaposition of the Summer Palace, and, say, nearby Zhongguancun (the technology hub) that really makes Haidian the exemplification of the new China.

HIGHLIGHTS **Zhongguancun** is the technology neighborhood, with dozens of big-name corporate headquarters next to malls such as **Hailong Shopping Mall** offering cheap shopping and quality computer components and electronics. The many universities in Haidian have lent a huge, energetic student presence to the entire district, and to the **Wudaokou** area in particular, which has a vibrant nightlife and dining scene dominated by students. You'll also find lots of fascinating and ancient sites in Haidian. The **Summer Palace**, the **Old Summer Palace**, the **Fragrant Hills**, and the **Beijing Botanical Garden** all call this district home. The **Beijing Zoo** is here, too.

GETTING AROUND The Beijing Zoo and Botanical Garden are located near Xizhimen, which you can reach by the Line 2 subway. The Summer Palace, the Old Summer Palace, and the Fragrant Hills are all rather far away in the northwest of the city and are best reached by taxi. To save money, take the train to the Xizhimen subway station and take a taxi from there.

Sights

❶ **Fragrant Hills Park** (Xiangshan Park). This hillside park west of Beijing was once an imperial retreat and hunting ground. From the eastern gate you can hike to the summit on a trail dotted with pavilions and small temples. If you're short on time, ride a cable car to the top. Go during the week to avoid the weekend crowds. ⊠ *Haidian District, northwestern Beijing suburbs near Sanjiadian* ☎ *010/6259–1155* 🚏 *Y10; cable car, Y50* ⊗ *Daily 6–6.*

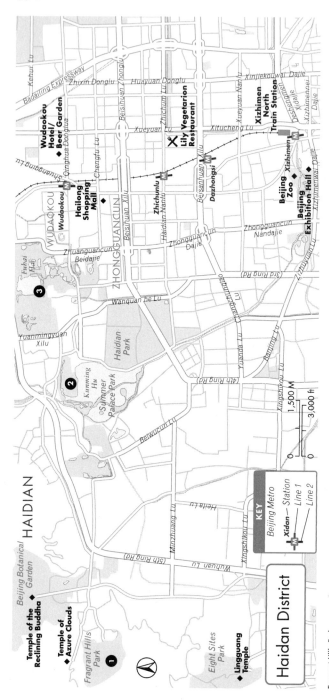

Temple of the Reclining Buddha ◆

Beijing Botanical Garden ◆

HAIDIAN

Temple of Azure Clouds ◆

Fragrant Hills Park

Lingguang Temple ◆

Eight Sites Park

Wuhan Lu

Minzhuang Lu

Heita Lu

Xingshikou Lu

Beiwucun Lu

5th Ring Rd

Yuanmingyuan Xilu

Haidian Park

Summer Palace Park

Kunming Hu

Houhai (Hai)

Wanquan he Lu

Zhuangguancun Lu

WUDAOKOU

Wudaokou

Hailong Shopping Mall ◆

ZHONGGUANCUN

Zhuanguancun Beidajie

Beishuan Xilu

Chengfu Lu

Qinghua Dongtua

Beishuan Zhonglu

Zhixin Donglu

Huayuan Dongtu

Badaling Expressway

Kehui Lu

Wudaokou Hotel/ Beer Garden ◆

Xueyuan Lu

Xinjiekouwai Dajie

Xizhimen North Train Station

Zhichunlu

Haidian Nanlu

Lily Vegetarian Restaurant

Beisihuan Xilu

Dazhongsi

Zhongguancun Dajie

Zhongguancun Nandajie

Beijing Zoo

Xizhimen

Beijing Exhibition Hall ◆

Xizhimen Nanlu

Xueyuan Nanlu

Xitucheng Lu

Xizhimennei Dajie

Xizhimenwai Dajie

Dashengmen Xidalie

3rd Ring Rd

Changchunqiao Lu

Yuanda Lu

Baining Lu

4th Ring Rd

Xingshikou Lu

1,500 M

3,000 ft

KEY

Beijing Metro

Xidan — Station

—— Line 1
---- Line 2

Haidian District

★ ❸ **Old Summer Palace.** Once a grand collection of palaces, this complex was the emperor's summer retreat from the 15th century to 1860, when it was looted and blown up by British and French soldiers. The Western-style buildings—patterned after Versailles in France—were added during the Qing Dynasty and designed by Jesuits. Beijing has chosen to preserve the vast ruin as a "monument to China's national humiliation," though the patriotic slogans that were once scrawled on the rubble have now been cleaned off. The palace is now made up of three idyllic parks: Yuanmingyuan (Garden of Perfection and Light) in the west, Wanchunyuan (Garden of 10,000 Springs) in the south, and Changchunyuan (Garden of Everlasting Spring), where the European ruins of marble palaces can be found, in the east.

> ## OLD SUMMER PALACE
>
> ■ The Old Summer Palace is about the same size as New York City's Central Park.
>
> ■ The park and ruins take on a ghostly beauty after a fresh snowfall.
>
> ■ There's skating on the lake when it's frozen over.
>
> ■ It's a long trek to the European ruins from the main gate.
>
> ■ Electric carts buzz around the park; hop on one heading to Changchunyuan if you feel tired. Tickets are Y5.

An engraved concrete-wall maze known as Huanghuazhen (Yellow Flower), twists and turns around a European-style pavilion. Recently restored and located just to the left of the west gate of Changchunyuan, it was once the site of lantern parties during mid-autumn festivals. The stones of Changchunyuan, which are like a surreal graveyard to European architecture, are perfect from scrambling and exploring. The ruins of ornately carved columns, squat lion statues, and crumbling stone blocks bearing frescoes lie like fallen dominoes. The park costs an extra Y15 to enter, but it's well worth it.

You can even take a boat out on Fuhai Lake: paddle your way around the pink lilies, the occasional sunken fountain, island pavilions, and stone-arched bridges. Stop off and try wild vegetable *baozi* (Chinese steamed buns) at one of the lakeside snack stores. ⊠ *Qinghuan Xi Lu, Haidian District* ☎ *010/6255–1488 or 010/6254–3673* 🎫 *Park Y10; extra Y15 fee for sites* ⊙ *Daily 7–7.*

❷ **Summer Palace.** Emperor Qianlong commissioned this giant royal retreat for his mother's 60th birthday in 1750. Anglo–French forces plundered, then burned, many of the palaces in 1860 and funds were diverted from China's naval budget for the renovations. Empress Dowager Cixi retired here in 1889. Nine years later, she imprisoned her nephew, Emperor Guangxu, after his reform movement failed. In 1903, she moved the seat of government from the Forbidden City to Yiheyuan from which she controlled China until her death in 1908.

 FodorśChoice ★

Nowadays, the place is undoubtedly romantic. Pagodas and temples perch on hillsides; row boats dip under arched stone bridges; and willow branches brush the water. The greenery provides a welcome relief from the bustling city. It's also a fabulous history lesson. You can see first-hand the results of corruption: the opulence here was bought with siphoned money. The entire gardens—complete with boats, theater, palaces and pavilions—were for the dowager's exclusive use. UNESCO placed the Summer Palace on its World Heritage list in 1998.

Peer inside the Hall of Benevolent Longevity—This is where Cixi held court and received foreign dignitaries. It is said that the first electric lights in China shone here. Longevity Hill is strung with pagodas and temples, including the impressive Tower of the Fragrance of

Buddha, Glazed Tile Pagoda, and the Hall that Dispels Clouds. This is the place where you can escape the hordes of visitors. Below is the lovely Kunming Lake, which extends southward for 3 km (2 mi); it's ringed by tree-lined dikes, arched stone bridges, and numerous gazebos. In winter, you can skate on the ice. Although the palace area along Kunming Lake's north shore is usually crowded, the less-traveled southern shore near Humpbacked Bridge is an ideal picnic spot. Be sure to visit the Long Corridor, whose ceiling and wooden rafters are richly painted with thousands of scenes from legends and nature. The wooden walkway skirts the northern shoreline of Kunming Lake for about half a mile until it reaches the marble boat, an elaborate two-deck pavilion built of finely carved stone and stained glass. The boat, in which Cixi often used to take her lunch and dinner, is often used as an example of her shameless extravagance. ☒ *Yiheyuan Lu and Kunminghu Lu, Haidian District, 12 km (7½ mi) northwest of downtown Beijing* ☎ *010/6288–1144* ⊕ *www.summerpalace-china.com (Chinese only)* ☒ *Apr.–Oct. Y50 and Nov.–Mar. Y40 for all exhibits, Apr.–Oct. Y30 and Nov.–Mar. Y20 for everything except the Garden of Virtue & Harmony, Suzhou Street Hall of Serenity, and Wenchang Gallery* ☉ *Daily 6:30—8 (ticket office closes at 6 PM).*

Experiences

SHOPPING FOR THE GOODS

When you're done sightseeing at the Summer palaces, hop a cab to **Hailong Shopping Mall,** a five-story shopping mecca with every kind of computer or electronic device you could possibly want, often at deep discounts. ■ TIP→ Be careful when buying software, though, as most of it is pirated and is illegal to bring back to the United States.

QUICK EATS IN WUDAOKOU

There are plenty of restaurants on campus and around Zhongguancun, but the coolest places to eat in Haidian are in Wudaokou. Try excellent and innovative Korean BBQ at **Hanguokeli** (✉ 35 Chengfu Lu ☎010/6256–3749 Ⓜ Wudaokou). Another hopping eatery is **Youle** (✉ On Shuangqing Lu, just off Chengfu Lu ☎ 010/5872–2028), a Japanese noodle house on the first floor of Weixin Guoji Dasha, or the Weixin International Mansion. Not to be missed is the beer garden at the **Wudaokou Hotel** on Chengfu Lu, one block east of the subway station. The beer garden is a wonderful place to sit around and chat. The **Lily Vegetarian Restaurant** (☎ 010/6202–5284), behind the Jimen Hotel at Jimenqiao, serves up awesome "faux-meat" dishes.

CIXI'S SUMMER PALACE

Her home, in the Hall of Joyful Longevity, is near the beginning of the Long Corridor. The residence is furnished and decorated as Cixi left it. Her private theater, called the Grand Theater Building, just east of the hall, was constructed for her 60th birthday and cost 700,000 taels of silver. At the west end of the beautiful lake you'll find the Marble Boat, which Cixi built with money meant for the Chinese navy.

WHERE TO EAT

By Eileen Wen Mooney

China's economic boom has revolutionized dining culture in Beijing, with the city today boasting a wide variety of regional cuisines, including unusual, tasty specialties from Yunnan, earthy Hakka cooking from southern China, Tibetan yak and *tsampa* (barley flour), Sichuan's spicy flavors, and chewy noodles from Shaanxi. The capital also offers plenty of international cuisine, including French, German, Thai, Japanese, Brazilian, Malaysian, and Italian, among others. You can spend as little as $2 per person for a decent meal to $100-and-up on a lavish banquet. The venues are part of the fun, ranging from swanky restaurants to holes-in-the-wall and refurbished courtyard houses. Beer is available everywhere in Beijing, and although wine was once only available in Western-style restaurants, many Chinese restaurants now have wine menus.

Logistics
People tend to eat around 6 PM, and, although the last order is usually taken around 9 PM, some places remain open until the wee morning hours. Reservations are always a good idea. Book as far ahead as you can, and reconfirm as soon as you arrive. Tipping is not required, although some of the larger hotels will add a 15% service charge to the bill. Small and medium venues only take cash payment, but more established restaurants usually accept credit cards.

Prices
Dining out is still one of the great bargains in Beijing, where it's still possible to have a three-course meal with drinks for less than $10. As in other cities, drinks can push up the price of a meal, so study the drink options and costs carefully.

	WHAT IT COSTS In Yuan				
	$$$$	**$$$**	**$$**	**$**	**¢**
AT DINNER	over Y180	Y121–Y180	Y81–Y120	Y40–Y80	under Y40

Prices are per person for a main course at dinner and do not include the customary 10% service charge.

Dongcheng District

Chinese

$$$$ ✕ **Huang Ting.** Beijing's traditional courtyard houses, which are fast
Fodor'sChoice facing extinction as entire neighborhoods are demolished to make way
★ for new high-rises, provide the theme here. This is arguably Beijing's
best Cantonese restaurant, serving southern favorites such as braised shark
fin with crabmeat, seared abalone with seafood, and steamed scallop
and bean curd in black-bean sauce. The dim sum is delicately refined,
and the deep-fried taro spring rolls and steamed pork buns are not to
be missed. The walls are constructed from original *hutong* bricks taken
from centuries-old courtyard houses that have been destroyed. ⊠ *The
Peninsula, 8 Jinyu Hutong, Wangfujing, Dongcheng District* ☎ *010/
6512–8899 Ext. 6707* 🖃 *AE, MC, V* Ⓜ *Dongdan.*

$$$–$$$$ ✕ **Red Capital Club.** Occupying a meticulously restored courtyard home
Fodor'sChoice in one of Beijing's few remaining traditional Chinese neighborhoods,
★ the Red Capital Club oozes nostalgia. Cultural Revolution memorabilia
and books dating from the Great Leap Forward era (1958–60) adorn
every nook of the small bar, while the theme of the dining room is imperial. The fancifully written menu reads like a fairy tale, with dreamily named dishes. "South of Clouds" is a Yunnan dish of fish baked over
bamboo—it's said to be a favorite of a former Communist marshal.
"Dream of the Red Chamber" is a fantastic eggplant dish cooked according to a recipe in the classic novel by the same name. ⊠ *66 Dongsi
Jiutiao, Dongcheng District* ☎ *010/6402–7150* 🥢 *Reservations essential* 🖃 *AE, DC, MC, V* ☾ *No lunch.*

$$$–$$$$ ✕ **The Source.** The Source serves a set menu of Sichuan specialties,
Fodor'sChoice changing it every two weeks. The menu includes several appetizers, both
★ hot and mild dishes, and a few surprise concoctions from the chef. On
request, the kitchen will tone down the spiciness of your food. The Source's
location was once the backyard of a Qing Dynasty general regarded by
the Qing court as "The Great Wall of China" for his military exploits.
The grounds have been painstakingly renovated; an upper level overlooks a small garden filled with pomegranate and date trees. The central yard's dining is serene and acoustically protected from the hustle
and bustle outside. ⊠ *14 Banchang Hutong, Kuanjie, Dongcheng District* ☎ *010/6400–3736* 🥢 *Reservations essential* 🖃 *AE, DC, MC, V.*

$$–$$$$ ✕ **Din Tai Fung.** The arrival of Din Tai Fung—one of Taipei's most fa-
Fodor'sChoice mous restaurants—was warmly welcomed by Beijing's food fanatics. The
★ restaurant's specialty is *xiaolong bao* (juicy buns wrapped in a light unleavened-dough skin and cooked in a bamboo steamer), which are
served with slivers of tender ginger in a light black vinegar. *Xiaolong
bao* have three different fillings: ground pork, seafood, or crabmeat. If

you can, leave some room for the scrumptious tiny dumplings packed with red-bean paste. This restaurant is frequented by both Beijing's up-and-coming middle class and old Taiwan hands, who are fervently loyal to its delicate morsels. ⊠ *22 Hujiayuan, Yibei Building, Dongcheng District* ☎ *010/6462–4502* ▭ *AE, MC, V.*

$$–$$$ ✕ **Lai Jin Yu Xuan.** A gem tucked inside Zhongshan Park on the west side of the Forbidden City, Lai Jin is known for its Red Mansion banquet, based on dishes from Cao Xueqin's classic novel, *The Dream of the Red Mansion,* written circa 1760. The two-story restaurant sits beside a small pond amid willow and peach trees. The two daily dishes are *qie xiang* (eggplant with nuts) and *jisi haozigan* (shredded chicken with crown-daisy chrysanthemum). To sample more than 40 dishes made famous in this novel, you must order a banquet meal (from Y300–Y440) three days in advance. After your meal, take a lazy stroll across the park to the nearby teahouse with the same name, where you can enjoy a cup of tea in the courtyard surrounded by ancient cypresses and scholar trees. ⊠ *Inside Zhongshan Park, on the west side of the Forbidden City, Dongcheng District* ☎ *010/6605–6676* ▭ *No credit cards.*

$$ ✕ **Gui Gongfu.** Known as the "Lair of Queens" because two former Qing empresses once lived here, this space was also home to the infamous Empress Dowager Cixi and her niece Logyu. A large courtyard house with wisteria and crab-apple trees in the garden make this ideal for dining alfresco in the summer. Some of the dishes are flavored with tea leaves, and are accordingly named. *Lu Yu zhucha,* or "Lu Yu cooking tea," is the restaurant's signature dish: Lu Yu is the author of the ancient *Book of Tea* and the dish is stir-fried beef with chilies and tea leaves. Green-tea flavored noodles and oolong spareribs are also excellent choices. This quiet restaurant attracts people keen to experience a bit of Old Beijing. ⊠ *11 Fang Jia Yuan Hutong, Dongcheng District* ☎ *010/6512–7667* ▭ *AE, V.*

★ $ ✕ **Jingsi Su Shifang.** Soft Buddhist chants hum in this clean, cheerful restaurant, which serves no meat dishes. Carnivores may still be happy here, though, as much of the food is prepared to look and taste like meat. Try the crispy Peking "duck," or a "fish" (made of tofu skin) that even has scales carved into it. *Zaisu jinshen,* another favorite, has a filling that looks and tastes like pork. It is wrapped in tofu skin, deep-fried, and coated with a light sauce. ⊠ *18A Dafosi Dongjie, Dongcheng District* ☎ *010/6400–8941* ▭ *No credit cards.*

¢–$ ✕ **Paomo Guan.** The bright red and blue bamboo shading the front porch of this adorable spot will immediately catch your eye. Paomo Guan focuses on *paomo*—a Shaanxi trademark dish. Guests break a large piece of unleavened flat bread into little pieces and then put them in their bowl. After adding condiments, the waiter takes your bowl to the kitchen where broth—simmered with spices, including star anise, cloves, cardamom, cinnamon sticks, and bay leaves—is poured over the bread bits. ⊠ *59 Chaoyangmennei Nanxiaojie, Dongcheng District* ☎ *010/6559–8135* ▭ *No credit cards.*

Contemporary

★ $$$–$$$$ ✕ **Jing.** Rated "One of the 75 Hottest Tables in the World" by *Condé Nast Traveler* in 2003, Jing serves up East–West fusion cuisine in an ultramodern setting replete with polished red wooden floors, cream-colored chairs, and gauzy curtain dividers. Signature appetizers include outstanding duck rolls, tiger prawns, and fragrant coconut soup. The fillet of barramundi and risotto with seared langoustines are stand-out main courses. For dessert, don't miss the warm chocolate cake with almond ice cream. There's also an excellent selection of international wines. ⊠ *The Peninsula Beijing, 8 Jinyu Hutong, Wangfujing, Dongcheng District* ☎ *010/6523–0175 Ext. 6714* ▭ *AE, DC, MC, V* Ⓜ *Dongdan.*

French

$$ ✕ **Café de la Poste.** In almost every French village, town, or city there is a Café de la Poste, where people go for a cup of coffee, a beer, or a simple family meal. This haunt lives up to its name: It's a steak-lover's paradise, with such favorites as finely sliced marinated beefsteak served with lemon-herb vinaigrette and steak tartare. If the next table orders Banana Flambé, we promise the warm scent of its rum will soon have you smitten enough to order it yourself. ⊠ *58 Yonghegong Dajie, Dongcheng District* ☎ *010/6402–7047* ▭ *No credit cards* Ⓜ *Yonghegong.*

Xicheng District

Chinese

$$$$ ✕ **Mei Fu.** In a plush, restored courtyard on Houhai's south bank, Mei
Fodor'sChoice Fu oozes intimate elegance. The interior is filled with antique furniture
★ and velvet curtains punctuated by pebbled hallways and waterfalls. Black-and-white photos of Mei Lanfang, China's most famous opera star, who performed female roles, hang on the walls. Diners choose from set menus, starting from Y300 per person, which feature typical Jiangsu and Zhejiang cuisine, such as fried shrimp, pineapple salad, and tender leafy vegetables. A Y200 (per person) lunch is also available. ⊠ *24 Daxiangfeng Hutong, south bank of Houhai Lake, Xicheng District* ☎ *010/ 6612–6845* ⌖ *Reservations essential* ▭ *MC, V.*

$$$$ ✕ **Zhang Qun Jia.** You may never guess that behind the old fading wooden door with the number 5 written on it, set on "Bending Pipe Street," lies a gourmet restaurant. "Zhang Qun's Home" was opened in 2003 by a Beijing artist as a place where she and her creative friends could relax. Soon it turned into a small restaurant, serving the home-style specialties of her native Suzhou. The set meal costs Y200 to Y500 a person, and includes a large number of appetizers, hot dishes and a dessert, all selected by Ms. Zhang. ⊠ *5 Yandai Xiejie, Houhai, Xicheng District* ☎ *010/8404–6662* ⌖ *Reservations not accepted* ▭ *No credit cards.*

★ $$$–$$$$ ✕ **Fangshan.** In a traditional courtyard villa on the shore of Beihai, you can get a taste of China's imperial cuisine. Established in 1925 by three royal chefs, Fangshan serves dishes once prepared for the imperial family, based on recipes gathered across China. Fangshan is best known for its filled pastries and steamed breads—traditional snack foods developed to satisfy Empress Dowager Cixi's sweet tooth. To experience Fangshan's exquisite imperial fare, order one of the banquet-style set meals at Y500 per person. Be sure to make reservations two or three days in advance. ⊠ *Beihai Park, northwest of the Forbidden City, Xicheng District, enter through east gate, cross stone bridge, and bear right* ☎ *010/*

6401–1879 🖉 *Reservations essential* 🖃 *AE, DC, MC, V* Ⓜ *Tiananmen West.*

$$ ✗**Xi Xiangzi.** "Spring from Hunan" is a small venue specializing in Hunan
Fodor'sChoice cuisine with a French touch—Aymeric, the owner, is French. The seven-
★ table restaurant has an extensive menu; smoked bean curd (*xianggan*),
and cured meat (*larou*) are prepared splendidly here. In addition to clas-
sic Hunan dishes, you can also sample fondue Bouguignone and banana
flambé. ✉ *36 Ding Fu Jie, Xicheng District* 🕿 *137/0108–0959* 🖉 *Reser-
vations accepted* 🖃 *No credit cards.*

$ ✗**Han Cang.** In the mood for something other than the ubiquitous
Fodor'sChoice home-style Beijing or Sichuan fare? Try Hakka cuisine. Specialties like
★ *sanbei ya* (three-cup duck), *yanju* (salt-baked) shrimp, and *zhi bao luyu*
fish (baked in aluminum foil), are served at this casual restaurant,
flanked by the many watering holes around Houhai. If you're in a
group, be sure to book one of the tables on the second floor so you enjoy
views of the lake. ✉ *Shichahai Dongan, Houhai, Xicheng District,
across the street from the north gate of Beihai Park* 🕿 *010/6404–2259*
🖉 *Reservations recommended* 🖃 *No credit cards.*

¢–$ ✗**Kong Yi Ji.** Named for the down-and-out protagonist of a short story
by Lu Xun (China's most famous contemporary writer), this restaurant
is set behind a small bamboo forest. Upon entering, the first thing you'll
see is a bust of Lu Xun. The old-fashioned menu, which is traditionally
bound with thread, features some of the dishes made famous in the story,
such as *huixiang dou*, or aniseed-flavored broad beans. A wide selec-
tion of *huangjiu*, sweet rice wine, is served in heated silver pots; it's sipped
from a special ceramic cup. ✉ *South shore of Shichahai, Deshengmen-
nei Dajie, Xicheng District* 🕿 *010/6618–4915* 🖉 *Reservations not ac-
cepted* 🖃 *No credit cards.*

¢–$ ✗**Shaguo Ju.** Established in 1741, Shaguo Ju serves a simple Manchu
favorite—*bairou*, or white meat (pork), which first became popular 300
years ago. The first menu pages list all the dishes cooked in the *shaguo*
(the Chinese term for a casserole pot). The classic *shaguo bairou* con-
sists of strips of pork neatly lined-up, concealing bok choy and glass
noodles below. Shaguo Ju emerged as a result of ceremonies held by
imperial officials and wealthy Manchus in the Qing Dynasty, which in-
cluded sacrificial offerings of whole pigs. The meat offerings were later
given away to the nightwatch guards, who shared the "gifts" with friends
and relatives. Such gatherings gradually turned into a small business,
and white meat became very popular. ✉ *60 Xisi Nan Dajie, Xicheng
District* 🕿 *010/6602–1126* 🖃 *No credit cards* Ⓜ *Xidan.*

Southern Districts: Chongwen & Xuanwu

Chinese

★ **$$** ✗**Li Qun Roast Duck Restaurant.** Juicy, whole ducks roasting in a traditional
oven greet you upon entering this simple courtyard house. It's a small,
casual, family-run restaurant far from the crowds and commercialism of
Quanjude, Beijing's most famous Peking duck eatery. Li Qun is a choice
option for those who enjoy a good treasure hunt: the restaurant is hidden deep in a hutong neighborhood. It should take about 10 minutes to

walk there from Chongwenmen Xi Dajie, though you may have to stop several times and ask for directions. It's so well known by locals, however, that when they see foreigners coming down the street, they automatically point in the restaurant's direction. Sure, the restrooms and dining room are a bit shabby, but the restaurant is charming. Ask for an English menu and feast to your heart's content! ⊠ *11 Beixiangfeng, Zhengyi Lu, Chongwen District, northeast of Qianmen* ☎ *010/ 6705–5578* ⚇ *Reservations essential* ▤ *No credit cards* Ⓜ *Chongwen.*

¢ ✕ **Old Beijing Noodle King.** Close to the Temple of Heaven and Hongqiao market, this noodle house serves hand-pulled noodles and traditional Beijing dishes in a lively old-time atmosphere. Waiters shout across the room to announce customers arriving. Try the tasty *zhajiang* noodle accompanied by meat sauce and celery, bean sprout, green beans, soy beans, sliver of cucumber, and red radish. ⊠ *29 Chongwenmen Dajie, Hongqiao Market, Chongwen District* ☎ *010/ 6705–6705* ⚇ *Reservations not accepted* ▤ *No credit cards.*

> ### WORD OF MOUTH
>
> "We liked the Li Qun Roast Duck Restaurant, which is in a hutong area south of Tiananmen Square. It's busy, so get your hotel to book you a table—it's a well-known place. Beijing Duck is roasted, but the crispy skin is served separately, along with pancakes, sliced green onions, and a dipping sauce. By the way, I found that rice wasn't always provided as a matter of course, so you may have to ask for it—the word is mifan, pronounced mee-FAHN."   –Neil_Oz

Chaoyang District

Brazilian

$–$$$$ ✕ **Alameda.** Voted "Restaurant of the Year" in 2005 by *That's Beijing*
Fodor'sChoice   magazine, Alameda has a simple but reliably delicious menu. The week-
★   day Y60 lunch specials are one of the best deals in town. On Saturday, try the *feijoada*—Brazil's national dish—a hearty black-bean stew with pork and vegetables, served with rice. The glass walls and ceiling make it a bright, pleasant place to dine. ⊠ *Sanlitun Beijie, by the Nali shopping complex, Chaoyang District* ☎ *010/6417–8084* ▤ *AE, MC, V.*

Café

★ **$–$$$** ✕ **The Bookworm.** We love this Beijing hotspot when we're craving a double-dose of intellectual stimulation and good food. Thousands of English-language books fill the shelves and may be borrowed for a fee or read inside. New books and magazines are also for sale. This is a popular venue for guest speakers, poetry readings, and live-music performances. The French chef offers a three-course set lunch and dinner. For a nibble, rather than a full meal, sandwiches, salads, and a cheese platter are also available. ⊠ *Building 4, Nan Sanlitun Lu, Chaoyang District* ☎ *010/6586–9507* ▤ *No credit cards.*

Chinese

$–$$$ ✕ **Shin Yeh.** The long line that persists since the restaurant opened proves
Fodor'sChoice   that Shin Yeh diners are hooked. The focus here is on Taiwanese fla-
★   vors and freshness. *Caipudan* is a scrumptious turnip omelet. *Fotiao-*

qiang ("Buddha jumping over the wall") is a delicate soup with medic-inal herbs and seafood. Last but definitely not least, try the *mashu*, a glutinous rice cake rolled in ground peanut. Service is friendly and very attentive. ⊠ *6 Gongti Xilu, Chaoyang District* ☎ *010/6552–5066* ▤ *AE, MC, V.*

¢–$$$ ✕ **La Galerie.** Choose between two outdoor dining areas: one a wooden platform on the park facing the bustling Guanghua Road; the other well hidden in the back, overlooking the greenery of Ritan Park. Inspired Can-tonese food and dim sum fill the menu: *Changfen* (steamed rice noo-dles) are rolled and cut into small pieces then stir-fried with crunchy shrimp, strips of lotus root, and baby bok choy, accompanied by sweet soybean, peanut, and sesame pastes. The *xiajiao* (steamed shrimp dumplings) envelop juicy shrimp and water chestnuts. ⊠ *South gate of Ritan Park, Guanghua Rd., Chaoyang District* ☎ *010/8563–8698* ▤ *AE, MC, V* Ⓜ *Jianguomen.*

$–$$ ✕ **Anping Gujie.** The two-story Anping, with a bar on the first floor and dining upstairs, is located in the sprawling Jianwai Soho complex. Dine amid dark wood, marble tables, velour armchairs, gauzy burgundy drapes, and traditional lamps hung from the ceiling. Hakka and Tai-wanese dishes dominate the menu; our top picks are *caipudan*, a Hakka turnip omelet, and *o a jian*, a popular Taiwanese oyster omelet. *Zha xia juan,* or deep-fried shrimp, and *suzha kezai,* deep-fried oysters, are other toothsome specialties. Conclude your meal with a refreshing dessert of shaved ice with red bean, pineapple, or taro drizzled with sweet condensed milk. ⊠ *Tower A, 106 Jianwai Soho, 39 Dong San-huan Zhonglu, Chaoyang District* ☎ *010/5869–2083* ▤ *AE, MC, V* Ⓜ *Guomao.*

$–$$ ✕ **Jun Wangfu.** Tucked inside Chaoyang Park, Jun Wangfu excels in clas-sical Cantonese fare; it's frequented by Hong Kong expats. The com-prehensive menu includes steamed tofu with scallops, spinach with taro and egg, crispy goose, roast chicken, and steamed fish with ginger and scallion. The fresh baked pastry filled with *durian* (a spiny tropical fruit with a smell so notoriously strong it is often banned from being brought on airplanes) is actually a mouthwatering rarity—don't be scared off by its overpowering odor. ⊠ *19 Chaoyang Gongyuan Nanlu, east of Chaoyang Park south gate, Chaoyang District* ☎ *010/6507–7888.*

$–$$ ✕ **Noodle Loft.** A first-floor noodle bar is surrounded by stools, where several dough masters are working in a flurry, snipping, shaving, and pulling dough into noodles. The stainless-steel stairway leads to a sec-ond dining space, this one spacious, with high ceilings. The black-and-white color scheme plays backdrop to a trendy, pre-clubbing crowd. Do as they do and order yummy fried "cat ears," which are actually small nips of dough, boiled and then topped with meat, scrambled eggs, and shredded cabbage. ⊠ *18 Baiziwan, Chaoyang District* ☎ *010/6774–9950* ▤ *AE, MC, V.*

$–$$ ✕ **South Silk Road.** Serving the specialties of southwest China's Yunnan province in a minimalist setting, South Silk Road is a joy. Waitresses in the colorful outfits of the Bai minority guide you to a sprawling dining room resembling a factory loft. The paintings of Fang Lijun, its artist-owner, are displayed on the walls. Treebark salad, sliced sausages with

Sichuan peppercorn, and *qiguoji* (a clay-pot soup with tonic herbs) are all tasty. One of the house specialties is *guoqiao mixian* ("crossing the bridge" noodles): a scorching bowl of broth, kept boiling by a thin layer of hot oil on top. The fun lies in adding small slivers of raw fish, chicken, ham, and rice noodles, which cook instantly in the pot. Female diners take note: the floor of the restaurant's upper level is made of glass, so don't wear a skirt when you dine here! ⊠ *Building D, Soho New Town, 88 Jianguo Lu, Chaoyang District* ☎ *010/8580–4286* ⊟ *AE, MC, V* Ⓜ *Dawang Lu.*

$–$$ ✕**Three Guizhou Men.** The popularity of this ethnic cuisine prompted three Guizhou friends to set up shop in Beijing. There are many dishes here to recommend, but among the best are "beef on fire" (pieces of beef placed on a bed of chives over burning charcoal) accompanied by ground chilies, spicy lamb with mint leaves, and *mi doufu,* a rice-flour cake in spicy sauce. ⊠ *Jianwai SOHO, Bldg. 7, 39 Dong Sanhuan Zhonglu, Chaoyang District* ☎ *010/5869–0598* ⊟ *AE, MC, V* Ⓜ *Guomao.*

$–$$
Fodor's Choice
★
✕**Yuxiang Renjia.** There are many Sichuan restaurants in Beijing, but if you ask native Sichuanese, Yuxiang Renjia is their top choice. Huge earthen vats filled with pickled vegetables, hanging bunches of dried peppers and garlic, and simply dressed waitresses evoke the Sichuan countryside. The restaurant does an excellent job of preparing provincial classics such as *gongbao jiding* (diced chicken stir-fried with peanuts and dried peppers) and *ganbian sijidou* (green beans stir-fried with olive leaves and minced pork). Thirty different Sichuanese snacks are served for lunch on weekends, all at very reasonable prices. ⊠ *5/F, Lianhe Daxia, 101 Chaowai Dajie, Chaoyang District* ☎ *010/6588–3841* ⊟ *AE, MC, V* Ⓜ *Chaoyangmen.*

★ ¢–$ ✕**Bellagio.** Chic Bellagio is a bright, trendy-but-comfortable restaurant serving up typical Sichuan dishes with a Taiwanese twist. A delicious choice is their *migao* (glutinous rice with dried mushrooms and dried shrimp, stir-fried rice noodles, and meatball soup). You can finish your meal with a Taiwan-style crushed ice and toppings of red bean, green bean, mango, strawberry, or peanut. Bellagio is open until 4 AM, making it a favorite with Beijing's chic clubbing set. The smartly dressed all-female staff—clad in black and white—have identical short haircuts. ⊠ *6 Gongti Xilu, Chaoyang District* ☎ *010/6551–3533* ⊘ *Reservations essential* ⊟ *AE, MC, V.*

¢ ✕**Hai Wan Ju.** Haiwan means "a bowl as deep as the sea," fitting for this eatery that specializes in large bowls of hand-pulled noodles. The interior is simple, with traditional wooden tables and benches. A *xiao er* (a "young brother" in a white mandarin-collar shirt and black pants) greets you with a shout, which is then echoed in a thundering chorus by the rest of the staff. There are two types of noodles here: *guoshui,* noodles that have been rinsed and cooled; and *guotiao,* meaning "straight out of the pot," which is ideal for winter days. Vegetables, including diced celery, radish, green beans, bean sprouts, cucumber, and scallion, are placed on individual small dishes. Unless you specify otherwise, everything will be flipped into your bowl of noodles in one deft motion. ⊠ *36 Songyu Dongli, Chaoyang District* ☎ *010/8731–3518* ⊟ *AE, MC, V.*

1

Continental

★ **$-$$$$** ✕ **Aria.** Aria's outdoor dining is secluded within neatly manicured bushes and roses, providing a perfectly quiet lunch spot amid Beijing's frenetic downtown. Sample the fish fillet topped with crispy pork skin. The best deal at this elegant restaurant is the weekday business lunch: for just Y128 you can enjoy a soup or salad, main course, dessert, and coffee or tea. Renaissance-style paintings decorate the walls. There is a posh dining area and bar on the first floor, and more intimate dining at the top of the spiral staircase. Live jazz plays in the evenings. ⊠ 2/F *China World Hotel, 1 Jianguomenwai Dajie, Chaoyang District* ☎ 010/6505–2266 Ext. 38 ▭ AE, MC, V Ⓜ *Guomao.*

French

$ ✕ **Comptoirs de France Bakery.** This contemporary French-managed café serves a variety of sandwiches, excellent desserts, coffees, and hot chocolates. Besides the standard Americano, cappuccino, and latte, Comptoirs has a choice of unusual hot-chocolate flavors, including banana and Rhum Vieux and orange Cointreau. In the Sichuan peppercorn–infused hot chocolate, the peppercorns float in the brew, giving it a pleasant peppery aroma. ⊠ *China Central Place, Building 15, N 102, 89 Jianguo Rd. (just northeast of Xiandai Soho), Chaoyang District* ☎ 010/6530–5480 ▭ No credit cards.

German

$-$$$ ✕ **Café Constance.** The opening of Café Constance, a German bakery, has brought excellent rye, pumpernickel, and whole-wheat breads to Beijing. The hearty "small" breakfast begins with coffee, fresh fruit, muesli, unsweetened yogurt, eggs and bacon; the big breakfast adds several cold cuts and breads and rolls. This is a true winner if you're looking for a good breakfast, simple meal, or a good cup of java and dessert. ⊠ *Lucky St. B5&C5, 29 Zaoying Lu, Chaoyang District* ☎ 010/5867–0201 ▭ No credit cards.

$$ ✕ **Paulaner Brauhaus.** Traditional German food is dished up in heaping portions at this spacious, bright restaurant in the Kempinski Hotel. Wash it all down with delicious Bavarian beer made right in the restaurant: try the Maibock served in genuine German steins. In summer, you can enjoy your meal outdoors in the beer garden. ⊠ *Kempinski Hotel, 50 Liangmaqiao Lu, Chaoyang District* ☎ 010/6465–3388 ▭ AE, MC, V.

Italian

★ **$-$$$$** ✕ **La Dolce Vita.** The food lives up to the name here: a basket of warm bread is served immediately, a nice treat in a city where good bread is hard to come by. The tough decision is between ravioli, tortellini, and oven-fired pizza. The rice-ball appetizer, with cheese and bits of ham inside, is fantastic. ⊠ *8 Xindong Lu North, Chaoyang District* ☎ 010/6468–2894 ▭ AE, MC, V.

Indian

$-$$$ ✕ **Taj Pavilion.** Beijing's best Indian restaurant, Taj Pavilion serves up all the classics, including chicken tikka masala, *palak panir* (creamy spinach with cheese), and *rogan josht* (tender lamb in curry sauce). Consistently good service and an informal atmosphere make this a well-loved neighborhood haunt. ⊠ *China World Trade Center, L-1 28 West Wing, 1 Jian-guomenwai Dajie, Chaoyang District* ☎ *010/6505–5866* ☐ *AE, MC, V* Ⓜ *Guomao.*

Japanese

$$–$$$$ ✕ **Yotsuba.** This tiny, unassuming restaurant is arguably the best Japan-
Fodor$Choice ese restaurant in town. It consists of a sushi counter—manned by a Japan-
★ ese master working continuously and silently—and two small tatami-style dining areas, evóking an old-time Tokyo restaurant. The seafood is flown in daily from Tokyo's Tsukiji fish market. Reservations are a must for this dinner-only Chaoyang gem. ⊠ *2 Xinyuan Xili Zhongjie, Chaoyang District* ☎ *010/6467–1837* ⌂ *Reservations essential* ☐ *AE, MC, V* ☾ *No lunch.*

Korean

$–$$$ ✕ **Gaon.** A quirky mixture of classic and contemporary decor backdrop traditional Korean food with a modern twist. Korean savory "pan-cakes" are normally too heavy to have with a big meal, but at Gaon they are small and served as appetizers. The *bulgogi* (beef mixed with mushrooms and scallion and served on a hot plate) is subtle yet tasty. We promise you won't leave the restaurant hungry. ⊠ *5/F, East Tower, Twin Towers, B-12 Jianguomenwai Dajie, Chaoyang District* ☎ *010/ 5120–8899* ☐ *No credit cards* Ⓜ *Yonganli.*

Tibetan

$ ✕ **Makye Ame.** Prayer flags lead you to the second floor entrance of this Tibetan restaurant, where a pile of mani stones and a large prayer wheel greet you. Long Tibetan Buddhist trumpets, lanterns, and Tibetan hand-icrafts decorate the walls, and the kitchen serves a range of hearty dishes that run well beyond the Tibetan staples of yak-butter tea and *tsampa* (roasted barley flour). Try the vegetable *pakoda* (a deep-fried dough pocket filled with vegetables), curry potatoes, or roasted lamb spareribs. Heavy wooden tables with brass corners, soft lighting, and Tibetan textiles make this an especially soothing choice. ⊠ *11 Xiushui Nan Jie, 2nd floor, Chaoyang District* ☎ *010/6506–9616* ☐ *No credit cards* Ⓜ *Jianguomen.*

Vietnamese

$–$$ ✕ **Nam Nam.** A sweeping staircase to the second floor, a tiny indoor fish pond, wooden floors, and posters from old Vietnam set the scene in this atmospheric restaurant. The light, delicious cuisine is paired with speedy service. Try the chicken salad, beef noodle soup, or the raw or deep-fried vegetable or meat spring rolls. The portions are on the small side, though, so order plenty. Finish off your meal with a real Vietnamese cof-fee prepared with a slow-dripping filter and accompanied by condensed milk. ⊠ *7 Sanlitun Jie, Sanlitun, Chaoyang District* ☎ *010/6468–6053* ☐ *AE, MC, V.*

Haidian District

Chinese

$–$$$$ ✕ **Baijia Dazhaimen.** Staff dressed in rich-hued, traditional outfits wel-come you at this grand courtyard house. Bowing slightly, they'll say *"Nin* *jixiang"* ("May you have good fortune"). The mansion's spectacular setting was once the garden of Prince Li, son of the first Qing emperor. Cao Xueqin, the author of the Chinese classic *Dream of the Red Chamber,* is said to have lived here as a boy. Featured delicacies include birds' nest soup, braised sea cucumber, abalone, and authentic imperial snacks. On weekends, diners are treated to short, live performances of Beijing opera. ⊠ *15 Suzhou St., Haidian District* ☏ *010/6265–4186* ⊜ *Reservations essential* ⊟ *No credit cards.*

WHERE TO STAY

By Eileen Wen Mooney

China's 1949 Communist victory closed the doors on the opulent accommodations once available to visiting foreigners in Beijing and elsewhere. Functional concrete boxes served the needs of the few "fellow travelers" admitted into the People's Republic of China in the 1950s and '60s. By the late 1970s, China's lack of high-quality hotels had become a distinct embarrassment; the only answer seemed to be opening the market to foreign investment. Many new hotels, built to handle the 2008 Olympic crowds, are emerging; they are bound to change the landscape further in the coming years.

A multitude of polished palaces await you, with attentive service, improved amenities—such as conference centers, health clubs, spas, and nightclubs—and, of course, rising prices. Courtyard hotels usually have a more distinct Chinese character, but those in older buildings may be lacking in facilities. Because of the smaller number of rooms in courtyard hotels, reservations are important for these select accommodations. If you're looking to stay in a more traditional Chinese-style accommodation, consider the LüSongyuan, Haoyuan, Bamboo Garden, and the Red Capital Residence guesthouses.

Reservations & Rates

Booking hotel rooms in advance is always recommended, but the current glut of accommodations here means room availability is rarely a problem, whatever the season. Rates are generally quoted for the room alone; breakfast, whether continental or full, usually is extra. We've noted at the end of each review if breakfast is included in the rate ("CP" for continental breakfast daily and "BP" for full breakfast daily). All hotel prices listed here are based on high-season rates. There may be significant discounts on weekends and in the off-season. All hotels add a 15% service charge to the bill.

	WHAT IT COSTS In Yuan				
	$$$$	$$$	$$	$	¢
FOR 2 PEOPLE	over 1,800	1,401–1,800	1,101–1,400	700–1,100	Under 700

Prices are for two people in a standard double room in high season, excluding 15% service charge.

Dongcheng District

★ **$$$$** 🏨 **Grand Hotel Beijing.** This lovely hotel on the north side of Chang'an Avenue blends the traditions of China's past with modern comforts and technology. It's worth it to book the room with the Forbidden City view. The Red Wall Café, Ming Yuan dining room, Rong Yuan Restaurant, and Old Peking Grill provide a range of cuisines, from Chinese to European. The Grand is convenient to the Forbidden City, Tiananmen Square, and the Imperial Wall Ruins Park, but its service and Western food aren't as up-to-snuff as some other uber-fancy foreign-managed hotels. Even if you don't stay here, visit the rooftop terrace and toast the yellow roofs of the Forbidden City with your sunset drink. The terrace is open only from May through October, from 5 PM to 9:30 PM. ✉ *35 Dongchang'an Jie, Dongcheng District, 100006* ☎ *010/6513–7788* 🖷 *010/6513–0048* ⊕ *www.grandhotelbeijing.com* 🛏 *217 rooms, 50 suites* ⚴ *6 restaurants, bar, in-room fax, in-room safes, cable TV, in-room data ports, pool, health club, sauna, spa, bicycles, shops, Internet, business services, meeting rooms, car rental* ⊟ *AE, DC, MC, V* Ⓜ *Wangfujing.*

$$$$ 🏨 **Grand Hyatt Beijing.** The impressive Grand Hyatt Beijing, with its
Fodor'sChoice bustling lobby, is the centerpiece of Oriental Plaza, a mammoth com-
★ plex that includes a fancy mall, a cinema screening films in English, and a wide range of inexpensive eateries. Rooms and suites, many with floor-to-ceiling windows, are decorated with beige carpets and curtains, cherry-color wood furnishings, and black-and-white photos. The hotel's Olympic-size swimming pool is surrounded by lush vegetation, waterfalls, statues, and comfortable teak chairs and tables. Over the pool, a "virtual sky" ceiling imitates different weather patterns. The gym is equipped with state-of-the-art exercise equipment. The Red Moon on the lobby level is one of the city's chicest bars, with live music every night. The lobby bakery has excellent pastries and coffee, with seating away from the busy main lobby. Shanghai Tang, in the lower level, offers well-crafted and innovative Chinese clothing, accessories, and home items. ■ TIP→ **The hotel is within walking distance to Tiananmen Square and the Forbidden City.** ✉ *1 Dongchang'an Jie, Dongcheng District, 100738, corner of Wangfujing* ☎ *010/8518–1234* 🖷 *010/8518–0000* ⊕ *www.beijing.grand.hyatt.com* 🛏 *825 rooms, 155 suites* ⚴ *5 restaurants, cable TV, in-room data ports, indoor pool, health club, sauna, spa, steam room, bar, shops, Internet, business services, meeting rooms, airport shuttle, no-smoking floors* ⊟ *AE, DC, MC, V* Ⓜ *Wangfujing.*

$$$$ 🏨 **Raffles Beijing Hotel.** Singaporean designer Grace Soh and her team have transformed this hotel into a vivid, charming space, while retaining its history, as highlighted by the black-and-white photographs of dignitaries in the lounge. Think fancy: crystal chandeliers illuminate the lobby, and the grand white staircase is enveloped in a royal-blue carpet. The atrium is adorned with 13 large cloth lanterns in olive green, plum, purple, and yellow—a welcome change to the ubiquitous red. The Presidential Suite is one of the largest, most luxurious suites in Beijing. For dining, choose between French or Italian. The Writer's Bar is replete with large leather armchairs and dark, polished floors. This is a great location for visitors who plan to do some sightseeing: Tiananmen Square, the Forbidden City, and Wangfujing are all nearby. ⊠ *33 Dongchang'an Jie, off Wangfujing Dajie, Dongcheng District, 100004* ☎*010/6526–3388* 🖶 *010/6527–3838* ⊕ *www.beijing.raffles.com* ➴ *171 rooms, 24 suites* ♨ *2 restaurants, lounge, 2 bars, room service, minibars, cable TV, in-room data ports, indoor pool, bar, Internet, business services* ▤ *AE, DC, MC, V* Ⓜ *Wangfujing.*

$$$–$$$$
Fodor's Choice
★

🏨 **Peninsula Beijing.** Guests at the Peninsula Beijing enjoy an impressive combination of ultramodern facilities and traditional luxury. A waterfall cascades through the spacious lobby, which is decorated with Chinese antiques. Rooms have teak-and-rosewood flooring, area rugs, high-quality wood and upholstered furnishings, and flat-screen TVs. A custom bedside control panel lets you adjust lights, temperature, television, and radio. Food fanatics, take note: one on-site restaurant, Jing, serves yummy East-meets-West fusion food. Huang Ting, a second restaurant, provides a rustic setting

for some of Beijing's tastiest dim sum. Work off the meals in the fully equipped gym or swimming pool—or take the 10-minute walk to the Forbidden City. If you're less ambitious, relax in the hotel's steam rooms and saunas. The Peninsula's arcade has designer stores, including Chanel, Jean Paul Gaultier, and Tiffany & Co. ⊠ *8 Jinyu Hutong (Goldfish La.), Wangfujing, Dongcheng District, 100006* ☎ *010/8516–2888* 🖶 *010/6510–6311* ⊕ *www.peninsula.com* ➴ *525 rooms, 59 suites* ♨ *2 restaurants, snack bar, room service, some in-room faxes, in-room safes, minibars, cable TV, in-room data ports, tennis court, indoor pool, health club, hair salon, massage, sauna, steam room, bar, lobby lounge, shops, laundry service, business services, meeting rooms, travel services* ▤ *AE, DC, MC, V* ⦿| *EP* Ⓜ *Dongdan.*

$$–$$$$
🏨 **Beijing Hotel.** One of the capital's oldest hotels, this property was born in 1900 as the Hotel de Pekin. Within sight of Tiananmen Square, it has housed countless foreign delegations, missions, and friends of China, such as Field Marshal Montgomery from Britain and the American writer Edgar Snow. China's longtime premier Zhou Enlai stayed and worked in room #1735. The rooms retain an old-fashioned splendor with French-classic touches. The west wing—now the Grand Hotel—was added in 1955 and the east wing debuted in 1974. This is the place for people in search of some history or proximity to nearby tourist sites, such as Tiananmen Square and the Forbidden City. ⊠ *33 Dongchang'an Jie, off Wangfujing Dajie, Dongcheng District, 100004* ☎*010/6513–7766* 🖶 *010/6523-2395* ⊕ *www.chinabeijinghotel.com.cn* ➴ *800 rooms, 51 suites* ♨ *5 restaurants, room service, minibars, cable TV, in-room data ports, indoor pool, gym, bowling, billiards, tennis court, squash*

court, chess and card rooms, café, Internet, business services, meeting rooms ⊟ *AE, DC, MC, V* Ⓜ *Wangfujing.*

★ ¢–$$$ 🏨 **Zhuyuan Hotel** (Bamboo Garden Hotel). The Bamboo Garden is a charming hotel that was once the residence of Sheng Xuanhuai, a high-ranking Qing official, and, later, of Mao's henchman Kang Sheng. A powerful and sinister character, responsible for "public security" during the Cultural Revolution, Kang nevertheless had fine taste in art and antiques. The Bamboo Garden cannot compete with the high-rise crowd when it comes to comfort and facilities, but its lovely bamboo-filled courtyards and gardens make it a genuine treasure for those looking for a true Chinese experience. It's within walking distance to the colorful Houhai, or Rear Lakes, area, and the Drum and Bell Towers; the neighborhood is perfect if you want to experience the lifestyles of ordinary Beijingers. ⊠ *24 Xiaoshiqiao Hutong, Jiugulou Dajie, Dongcheng District, 100009* ☎ *010/5852–0088* 🖶 *010/5852–0066* 💭 *40 rooms, 4 suites* ⌂ *Restaurant, hair salon, sauna, bicycles, bar* ⊟ *AE, DC, MC, V* Ⓜ *Gulou.*

$$ 🏨 **Red Capital Residence.** Beijing's first boutique courtyard hotel is located
Fodor'sChoice in a carefully restored, traditional Chinese courtyard house in historically
★ preserved Dongsi Hutong. Each of the five rooms is decorated with antiques and according to a different theme, including the "Chairman's Suite," the two "Concubines' Private Courtyards," and the two "Author's Suites" (one inspired by Edgar Snow, an American journalist who lived in Beijing in the 1930s and 1940s, and the other by Han Suyin, a famous novelist). The bathrooms are modern, and all rooms have satellite television. There is also a cigar lounge where you can sit on original furnishings used by China's early revolutionary leaders, as well as a wine bar in a Cultural Revolution–era bomb shelter. Special arrangements can also be made for guests to tour Beijing at night in Madame Mao's Red Flag limousine. The Red Capital Residence offers a continental breakfast; for other meals take the hotel pedicab to the nearby Red Capital Club, a sister establishment also set in a restored courtyard home. ⊠ *9 Dongsi Liutiao, Dongcheng District, 100007* ☎ *010/6402–7150* 🖶 *010/6402–7153* ⊕ *www.redcapitalclub.com.cn* 💭 *5 rooms* ⌂ *Cable TV, bar, laundry service* ⊟ *AE, DC, MC, V* ⦿ *CP.*

$–$$ 🏨 **Crowne Plaza Beijing.** The Crowne Plaza is located on Wangfujing, in the center of Beijing's tourist, shopping, and business districts, and is a great place for walking and window shopping. The hotel underwent a major renovation in 2005, and now has a more modern ambiance. The lobby's champagne bar serves light Japanese and Vietnamese food. Huang Yue, a stylish Cantonese restaurant, is on the second floor. The standard rooms are small, but have top-rate amenities, such as flat-screen TVs and comfortable bathrooms. Craving more space? Try the executive floor, where rooms have extra work space and sprawling bathrooms with showers and separate baths. Take a look at the black-and-white photographs of Beijing covering many of the hotel's warm-hued walls. This is one of the better deals in town, providing a great location and luxury for your dollar. ⊠ *48 Wangfujing Dajie, Dongcheng District, 100006* ☎ *010/6513–3388* 🖷 *010/6513–2513* ⊕ *www.ichotelsgroup.com* ☙ *360 rooms, 27 suites* ♿ *2 restaurants, room service, minibars, cable TV, in-room data ports, indoor pool, gym, hair salon, sauna, bicycles, bar, shops, babysitting, laundry service, business services, travel services, free parking, no-smoking rooms* ⊟ *AE, DC, MC, V* Ⓜ *Wangfujing.*

¢–$$ 🏨 **LüSongyuan.** In 1980, the China Youth Travel Service set up this delightful courtyard hotel on the site of an old Qing Mandarin's residence. The traditional wooden entrance is guarded by two *menshi* (stone lions). Inside are five courtyards, decorated with pavilions, rockeries, and greenery. Rooms are basic, with large windows. Though it calls itself an International Youth Hostel, the hotel has no self-service cooking facilities, but it has a reasonable Chinese restaurant. It's all about location here: you're in the middle of an ancient neighborhood, within walking distance of Houhai, and just a block away from many restaurants and delightful coffee shops on Nan Luogu Xiang. ⊠ *22 Banchang Hutong, Kuanjie, Dongcheng District, 100009* ☎ *010/6401–1116* 🖷 *010/6403–0418* ☙ *55 rooms* ♿ *Restaurant, bar, Internet room* ⊟ *AE, DC, MC, V.*

Fodor's Choice ★

¢–$ 🏨 **Novotel Peace Hotel.** Twenty-two stories of tinted-glass windows play home to a bevy of rooms with floor-to-ceiling windows and accompanying stellar city views. The hotel is a stroll away from plenty of shops and restaurants, as well as Tiananmen Square. Although service is fairly basic, and the ambiance low-key, the hotel offers good value for the location. For dinner, you might try one of the three Chinese restaurants, or Le Cabernet, a French-style brasserie. Our vote? Head out onto the street and try one of the many restaurants in the bustling neighborhood. ⊠ *3 Jinyu Hutong, Wangfujing Dajie, Dongcheng District, 100004* ☎ *010/6512–8833* 🖷 *010/6512–6863* ⊕ *www.accorhotels-asia.com* ☙ *337 rooms, 33 suites* ♿ *4 restaurants, room service, minibars, cable TV, indoor pool, gym, hair salon, sauna, bicycles, 2 bars, dance club, laundry service, concierge, Internet, business services, car rental, parking (fee), no-smoking rooms* ⊟ *AE, DC, MC, V* Ⓜ *Wangfujing.*

Xicheng District

$$$$ 🏨 **Ritz-Carlton Beijing.** A 253-room hotel designed with ample amounts of glass and chrome, the Ritz fits in with many of the city's sleek financial buildings. The interior is stylish and contemporary. There are two restaurants and a café; a lobby lounge also serves afternoon tea and evening cocktails. The enormous health club has an indoor swimming pool and a spa with six treatment rooms. The Ritz-Carlton is located in the western part of the city on the up-and-coming Financial Street, which is being touted as Beijing's Wall Street; it's a smart choice for business visitors with offices or clients on that side of the city. ⊠ *18 Beijing Financial*

St., Xicheng District, 100032 ☎ *010/6601–6666* 🖷 *010/6601–6029* ⊕ *www.ritzcarlton.com* ⤴ *253 rooms, 33 suites* ⚭ *3 restaurants, bar, spa, indoor pool, whirlpool, room service, business services, meeting rooms* ⊟ *AE, DC, MC, V* Ⓜ *Fuchengmen.*

Southern District: Chongwen

★ **$–$$** 🏨 **Courtyard Beijing.** Merging Eastern and Western culture and style, the Courtyard is situated at the heart of the nation's capital. Guests have easy access to many of Beijing's historical sites, and it's connected to the huge New World Shopping Center, one of the busiest in the city, selling a wide variety of international and domestic name-brand products. One problem is that this is a super-congested part of the city. However, there's a subway station just one block away, making quick escapes to quieter areas quite easy. ⊠ *3C Chongwenmenwai Dajie, Chongwen District, 100062* ☎ *010/6708–1188* 🖷 *010/6708–1808* ⊕ *www.courtyard. com/bjscy* ⤴ *283 rooms, 16 suites* ⚭ *Restaurant, babysitting, satellite TV, children's pool, sauna, fitness room, laundry service, Internet* ⊟ *AE, DC, MC, V* Ⓜ *Chongwenmen.*

Chaoyang District

$$$$ 🏨 **China World Hotel.** One of the finest hotels in Beijing, the China
Fodor'sChoice World is part of the prestigious China World Trade Center, which is home
★ to offices, luxury apartments, and premium retail outlets. The lobby, conference center, ballroom, and all guest rooms were given a $30-million renovation in 2003. Marble floors and gold accents in the lobby lead to comfortable, contemporary rooms with marble baths. The dining choices are diverse and enticing: Scene a Café is a casual eatery featuring eight different cuisines, Aria serves a wonderful and inexpensive business lunch, Summer Palace serves dim sum, and Nadaman has superb seafood teppanyaki. The subway station is a one-minute walk away. The hotel is quite popular with business travelers, who crowd here during conferences and exhibitions. ⊠ *1 Jianguomenwai Dajie, Chaoyang District, 100004* ☎ *010/6505–2266* 🖷 *010/6505–3167 or 010/ 6505–0828* ⊕ *www.shangri-la.com* ⤴ *716 rooms, 26 suites* ⚭ *4 restaurants, snack bar, in-room safes, minibars, cable TV, in-room data ports, health club, hair salon, massage, 2 bars, dance club, shops, laundry service, Internet, business services, meeting rooms, airport shuttle, car rental, travel services, parking (fee), no-smoking rooms* ⊟ *AE, DC, MC, V* Ⓜ *Guomao.*

$$$$ 🏨 **St. Regis.** Considered by many to be the best hotel in Beijing, the St.
Fodor'sChoice Regis is a favorite of foreign businesspeople and visiting dignitaries. This
★ is where President Bush stayed during his visit to China, and where Uma Thurman and Quentin Tarantino stayed during the filming of *Kill Bill*. You won't be disappointed: the luxurious interiors combine classical Chinese elegance and fine, modern furnishings. The Press Club Bar, with its grand piano, dark wood, and stocked bookcases, feels like a private club. And the on-site Japanese restaurant has good, moderately priced lunch specials. The Astor Grill is known for its steak and seafood dishes, and Danielli's serves authentic Italian food. We went back for seconds

of waffles with fresh blueberries at the Coffee Garden's incredible breakfast buffet. The St. Regis health club is arguably the most unique in Beijing: the equipment is state-of-the-art; the Jacuzzi is supplied with natural hot spring water pumped up from deep beneath the hotel; and the glass-atrium swimming pool, with plenty of natural light, is a lovely place for a relaxing swim. An added plus is that it's just a 10-minute taxi ride to the Forbidden City. If you can afford it, this is the place to stay. ✉ *21 Jianguomenwai Dajie, Chaoyang District, 100020* ☎ *010/6460–6688* 🖨 *010/6460–3299* ⊕ *www.stregis.com* ⇗ *273 rooms; executive suites* ⏃ *5 restaurants, in-room safes, some kitchenettes, cable TV, in-room data ports, golf privileges, tennis court, 2 indoor pools, health club, hair salon, hot tub, massage, sauna, spa, steam room, bicycles, badminton, billiards, racquetball, squash, 4 bars, 3 lounges, recreation room, shops, babysitting, playground, laundry service, Internet, business services, convention center, airport shuttle, car rental, travel services, parking (fee), no-smoking rooms* ▭ *AE, DC, MC, V* Ⓜ *Jianguomen.*

★ **$$$–$$$$** 🏨 **Kerry Centre Hotel.** The Shangri-La hotel chain opened this palatial, upscale hotel to much fanfare in 1999. Its ultramodern interiors and convenient location close to Beijing's embassy and business district make it an excellent choice for business travelers and anyone who wants to be near shopping. The Forbidden City is a 10- to 15-minute drive away. What really distinguishes it from other glitzy hotels in Beijing is the amazing health club. With a full-service fitness center and spa, a jogging track, squash and tennis courts, and, of course, a pool, it's *the* health club of choice for expats living in Beijing. Centro, the lobby bar, is arguably the most popular hotel bar in the city. The free wireless Internet throughout the lobby, including in the bar and restaurants, is an added plus. ✉ *1 Guang Hua Lu, Chaoyang District, 100020* ☎ *010/6561–8833* 🖨 *010/6561–2626* ⊕ *www.shangri-la.com* ⇗ *487 rooms, 23 suites* ⏃ *2 restaurants, in-room safes, minibars, cable TV, in-room data ports, 2 tennis courts, pool, health club, hot tub, massage, sauna, spa, steam room, basketball, billiards, Ping-Pong, squash, bar, shops, playground, Wi-Fi* ▭ *AE, DC, MC, V* Ⓜ *Guomao.*

$$$–$$$$ 🏨 **Kunlun Hotel.** Kunlun's 2006 renovations unveiled a fresh, new gold-accented look, albeit somewhat overdone. Topped by a revolving restaurant, this 28-story property's impressive presentation and a full range of facilities make up for occasional service lapses. The hotel was named for the Kunlun Mountains, a range between northwestern China and northern Tibet that features prominently in Chinese mythology. The lovely rooms are spacious, with armchairs, entertainment cabinets, slippers, and robes. The business and superior suites, with hardwood floors, marble baths, and new furnishings, are the most attractive. The hotel restaurant serves great Shanghai-style food as well as reliable Thai and Japanese fare in very nicely designed venues. The Kunlun, close to Beijing's rising new diplomatic area, is popular with Chinese business travelers. This shouldn't be your top choice if sightseeing is your priority. ✉ *2 Xinyuan Nan Lu, Sanlitun, Chaoyang District, 100004* ☎ *010/6590–3388* 🖨 *010/6590–3214* ⊕ *www.hotelkunlun.com* ⇗ *701 rooms, 50 suites* ⏃ *6 restaurants, teashop, some kitchens, cable TV, indoor pool, health club, hair salon, hot tub, massage, sauna, steam room, bicycles, billiards,* *bar, lounge, Internet, business services, meeting rooms* ▭ *AE, DC, MC, V* ⦿ *EP.*

$$–$$$$ ⊡ **Swissôtel.** In the large, impressive marble lobby you can enjoy jazz every Friday and Saturday evening. Rooms have high-quality, European-style furnishings in cream and light gray, plus temperature controls and coffeemakers. The hotel health club has an atrium-style swimming pool and an outdoor tennis court. The Western coffee shop has one of the best hotel buffets in Beijing. It's a short walk to the bustling Sanlitun bar area and the Nanxincang complex of restaurants, which are housed in a former Ming Dynasty granary. A subway entrance is just outside the hotel's front door. ⊠ *2 Chaoyang Mennei Dajie, Dongsishiqiao Fly-over Junction (Second Ring Rd.), Chaoyang District, 100027* ☎ *010/6553–2288* 🖷 *010/6501–2501* ⊕ *www.swissotel-beijing.com* ⟿ *362 rooms, 50 suites* ♧ *2 restaurants, room service, some in-room faxes, in-room safes, minibars, cable TV, in-room data ports, indoor pool, gym, hair salon, sauna, bar, shops, babysitting, laundry service, concierge, Internet, business services, meeting rooms, car rental, travel services, no-smoking rooms* ▭ *AE, DC, MC, V* Ⓜ *Dongsi Shitiao.*

$$ ⊡ **Hilton Beijing.** Considered to be one of the city's oldest and most comfortable hotels, the Hilton lies at Beijing's northeast corner; it's a good choice for those wanting easy access to Beijing's airport, which is about a 20-minute drive away. Rooms are simply furnished, and most have two large picture windows and balconies. The hotel underwent a major renovation in 2006, giving the lobby and restaurants a posh new look. One East on Third is designed like a Louisiana mansion, with dark wood and louvered windows, and offers light American cuisine with an extensive wine list. The very cool Zeta Bar has a retro-Beijing ambiance with Bauhaus chairs and Chinese-inspired birdcages hanging above the crescent-shaped bar. A resident DJ spins here every night. ⊠ *1 Dongfang Lu, Dongsanhuan Bei Lu, Chaoyang District, 100027* ☎ *010/5865–5000* 🖷 *010/5865–5800* ⊕ *www.beijing.hilton.com* ⟿ *375 rooms, 12 suites* ♧ *2 restaurants, in-room safes, minibars, refrigerators, cable TV, indoor pool, hot tub, sauna, bicycles, bar, babysitting, business services, meeting rooms, car rental, no-smoking rooms* ▭ *AE, DC, MC, V.*

$–$$$ ⊡ **Traders Hotel.** Inside the China World Trade Center complex, this hotel is connected to its sister property, the China World Hotel, and a shopping mall. The hotel is a favorite of international business travelers, who appreciate its central location, good service, top-notch amenities, and excellent value. Rooms are done up in muted colors, such as beige and light green, with queen- or king-size beds. Guests have access to the excellent health club at the China World Hotel. ⊠ *1 Jianguomenwai Dajie, Chaoyang District, 100004* ☎ *010/6505–2277* 🖷 *010/6505–0828* ⊕ *www.shangri-la.com* ⟿ *570 rooms, 27 suites* ♧ *2 restaurants, in-room safes, minibars, cable TV, in-room data ports, massage, bar, shop, babysitting, business services, meeting rooms, airport shuttle, car rental, travel services, no-smoking rooms* ▭ *AE, DC, MC, V* Ⓜ *Guomao.*

$–$$ ⊡ **Gloria Plaza Hotel.** Built in the late 1990s, this hotel is situated in the Jianguomenwai commercial area of Beijing, not far from the embassy district. From the hotel, it's just a 10-minute walk to the Ancient Observatory, Silk Alley Market, Friendship Store, and to the Red Gate Gallery, which exhibits contemporary Chinese art in one of the few remaining towers of the old city wall. ■ TIP→ **A restored section of the city wall begins at the Red Gate Gallery, making for a pleasant stroll.** The simple rooms have good city views. ⊠ *2 Jiangguomen Nan Dajie, Chaoyang District, 100022* ☎ *010/6515–8855* 🖷 *010/6515–8533* ⊕ *www.gphbeijing.com* ↬ *432 rooms, 50 suites* ⚲ *2 restaurants, room service, cable TV, in-room data ports, indoor pool, health club, hot tub, massage, sauna, bar, lobby lounge, laundry service, business services, meeting rooms, airport shuttle, travel services, parking (fee)* ⊟ *AE, DC, MC, V* Ⓜ *Jianguomen.*

$–$$ 🏨 **Jianguo Hotel.** Despite its 1950s-style name ("build the country"), Jianguo Hotel was the very first U.S.–China joint venture hotel in the city. Wonderfully central, it is close to the diplomatic compounds, southern embassy area, and the Silk Alley Market. It's also a reasonable alternative for people taking part in conferences at the more expensive China World Hotel, just one block away. Nearly half the rooms have balconies overlooking busy Jianguomenwai Dajie. The Jianguo has maintained its friendly and cozy feel and continues to attract many diplomats, journalists, and business people. ⊠ *5 Jianguomenwai Dajie, Chaoyang District, 100020* ☎ *010/6500–2233* 🖷 *010/6501–0539* ⊕ *www.hoteljianguo. com* ↬ *462 rooms, 68 suites* ⚲ *4 restaurants, in-room safes, cable TV, indoor pool, hair salon, massage, bar, shop, laundry service, concierge, Internet, business services, meeting rooms, no-smoking rooms* ⊟ *AE, DC, MC, V* Ⓜ *Yonganli.*

$–$$ 🏨 **Jinglun Hotel.** The rooms of the elegantly refurbished Jinglun Hotel are decorated in a minimalist style. Just a 10-minute drive to Tiananmen Square, and a few minutes from the China World Trade Center, the Jinglun is a well-appointed business and leisure hotel with competitive prices. The tiny, crowded lobby gives way to simple rooms with white-linen beds accented by dark purple, olive-green, and yellow cushions. ⊠ *3 Jianguomenwai Dajie, Chaoyang District, 100020* ☎ *010/6500–2266* 🖷 *010/6500–2022* ⊕ *www.jinglunhotel.com* ↬ *642 rooms, 126 suites* ⚲ *Restaurant, in-room safes, minibars, refrigerators, cable TV, indoor pool, gym, hair salon, hot tub, massage, sauna, bicycles, bar, shops, babysitting, Internet, business services, car rental, travel services* ⊟ *AE, DC, MC, V* Ⓜ *Yonganli.*

★ **$–$$** 🏨 **Kempinski Hotel.** This fashionable hotel forms part of the Lufthansa Center, together with a department store, offices, and apartments. It's within walking distance of the Sanlitun bar area, with its dozens of bars and restaurants, popular Ladies' Street, and Lucky Street, home to more than a dozen moderately priced Western and Asian restaurants. ■ TIP→ **There is an excellent German restaurant here, the Paulaner Brauhaus, which has its own microbrewery.** A deli, with an outstanding bakery frequented by expats, is also on-site. We love the newly designed Kranzler's Coffee Shop, which has an excellent Sunday brunch. A gym and swimming pool are on the 18th floor ⊠ *50 Liangmaqiao Lu, Chaoyang District, 100016* ☎ *010/6465–3388* ⊕ *www.kempinski-beijing.com* 🖷 *010/ 6465–3366* ↬ *526 rooms, 114 suites* ⚲ *6 restaurants, room service, in-room safes, some minibars, cable TV, in-room data ports, indoor pool, gym, bicycles, 2 bars, shops, laundry service, concierge, business services, meeting rooms, car rental, travel services* ⊟ *AE, DC, MC, V.*

¢–$ ▦ **Scitech Hotel.** This is part of the Scitech complex, comprised of an office tower, hotel, and shopping center. The hotel enjoys a good location on busy Jianguomenwai Dajie, opposite the Friendship Store. You are greeted by a small fountain in the lobby, which also has a small teahouse off to one side. The rooms are nondescript and the service is nothing to write home about, but the room rates are quite reasonable for this area. ⊠ *22 Jianguomenwai Dajie, Chaoyang District, 100004* ☎ *010/6512–3388* 🖷 *010/6512–3542* ⊕ *www.scitechgroup.com* ⇌ *294 rooms, 32 suites* ♨ *3 restaurants, room service, in-room safes, minibars, cable TV, tennis court, indoor pool, gym, hair salon, hot tub, sauna, bar, dance club, shops, babysitting, laundry service, business services, meeting rooms, car rental, parking (fee), no-smoking rooms* ⊟ *AE, DC, MC, V* ⵘ❙ *EP* Ⓜ *Yonganli.*

¢ ▦ **Zhaolong International Youth Hostel.** If partaking in Beijing's lively nightlife scene is on your itinerary, consider this clean and comfortable youth hostel in Sanlitun for your stay. The hostel offers clean rooms with two to six beds each, a reading room, a kitchen, and bicycle rentals. ⊠ *2 Gongti Bei Lu, Sanlitun, Chaoyang District, 100027* ☎ *010/6597–2299 Ext. 6111* 🖷 *010/6597–2288* ⊕ *www.zhaolonghotel.com.cn* ⇌ *30 rooms* ♨ *Bar, laundry facilities; no room phones, no room TVs* ⊟ *AE, MC, V* ⵘ❙ *CP.*

Haidian District

$$$ ▦ **Shangri-La Hotel.** Set in delightful landscaped gardens in the western part of the city, 30 minutes from downtown, this Shangri-La is a wonderful retreat for business travelers and those visitors who don't mind being far from the city center. The lobby and restaurants underwent a major renovation in early 2004, and a new wing, the Horizon Tower, was completed in 2006. ⊠ *29 Zizhuyuan Lu, Haidian District, 100084* ☎ *010/6841–2211* 🖷 *010/6841–8002* ⊕ *www.shangri-la.com* ⇌ *616 rooms, 19 suites, 15 1- to 3-bedroom apartments* ♨ *3 restaurants, room service, in-room safes, some kitchenettes, minibars, cable TV, in-room data ports, indoor pool, gym, health club, hair salon, massage, sauna, bar, lobby lounge, shops, babysitting, laundry service, Internet, business services, meeting rooms, car rental, travel services, parking (fee)* ⊟ *AE, DC, MC, V.*

$–$$ ▦ **Friendship Hotel.** The Friendship's name is telling: it was built in 1954 to house foreigners, mostly Soviet, who had come to help build New China. Beijing Friendship Hotel is one of the largest "garden-style" hotels in Asia. The architecture is Chinese traditional and the public spaces are classic and elegant. Rooms are large with modern, if somewhat outdated, furnishings. With 14 restaurants, an Olympic-size pool, and a driving range, the hotel aims to be a one-stop destination. Its location far from the main tourist stops means that it's better situated for people who need to be close to the university area or to Zhongguancun, in the northwest of Beijing. ⊠ *3 Baishiqiao Lu, Haidian District, 100873* ☎ *010/6849–8888* 🖷 *010/6849–8866* ⊕ *www.cbw.com/hotel/friendship* ⇌ *1,700 rooms, 200 suites* ♨ *14 restaurants, minibars, cable TV, driving range, tennis courts, 2 pools (1 indoor), gym, massage, sauna,*

1

billiards, bowling, bar, dance club, theater, business services, meeting rooms, car rental ⊟ AE, DC, MC, V.

Beijing Airport Area

★ $$ ▣ **Sino-Swiss Hotel.** This nine-story contemporary hotel near the airport overlooks a gorgeous outdoor pool surrounded by trees, shrubs, and colorful umbrellas. All the rooms and public areas are completely up-to-date. You'll find large standard rooms with deep-blue carpeting and white bedcovers. The restaurant Mongolian Gher offers barbecue and live entertainment inside a traditional-style felt yurt (a tentlike structure), whereas Swiss Chalet serves familiar continental food to tables on the outdoor terrace. The hotel caters to business travelers with a full-service conference center and duplex business suites. Just five minutes from the airport, the Sino-Swiss Hotel is convenient if you have an early morning flight or get stuck at the airport. ⊠ *9 Xiao Tianzhu Nan Lu (Box 6913), Beijing Capital Airport, Shunyi County, 100621* ☎ *010/ 6456–5588* 🖷 *010/6456–1588* ⊕ *www.sino-swisshotel.com* ↩ *408 rooms, 35 suites* ⏦ *4 restaurants, in-room safes, minibars, cable TV, 2 tennis courts, 2 pools (1 indoor), gym, hot tub, massage, sauna, bicycles, billiards, Ping-Pong, squash, 2 bars, shop, laundry service, business services, meeting rooms ⊟ AE, DC, MC, V* ⧂ *BP.*

ARTS & NIGHTLIFE

By Dinah Gardner

No longer Shanghai's staid sister, Beijing is reinventing herself as a party town, but without the pretensions of her southern sibling. A frenzy of building and refurbishing in recent years means there's now a venue for every breed of boozer, from sports pub to fancy cocktail lounge. There are also more dance clubs than you can count. Bars aside, Beijing has an active, if not international-standard, stage scene. Besides musicals, though, there's not much to see in English. For a fun night on the town that you can enjoy no other place in the world, Beijing Opera, acrobatics, and kung-fu performances remain the best bets.

The Arts

All of the free-listings magazines will have reviews of plays as well as concerts and dance performances; *Time Out Beijing* and *That's Beijing* carry the most critical and comprehensive coverage. The cheapest seats start at around Y50 and can go up to over Y1,000 for world-class international ballets and musicals. Most visitors to Beijing hunt out the big visual spectacles, such as Beijing Opera or kung-fu displays. These long-running shows are tailored for travelers: your hotel will be able to recommend performances and venues, and will likely be able to help you book tickets.

Acrobatics & Kung Fu

Fodor'sChoice **Chaoyang Theater.** This is the queen bee of acrobatics venues, especially ★ designed to cultivate tourist awe. Spectacular individual and team acrobatic displays involving bicycles, seesaws, catapults, swings, and

Continued on page 94

BEIJING OPERA

"OPULENT" MAY BE AN UNDERSTATEMENT

For hundreds of years, Beijing opera troupes have delighted audiences—from members of the royal court to marketplace crowds at makeshift stages—with rich costumes, elaborate makeup, jaw-dropping acrobatics, and tales of betrayal and intrigue.

Nowadays, the weird and wonderful operas staged in Beijing's customized theaters are more than likely of the Jing Ju style, which emerged during the Qing Dynasty. There are more than 350 other kinds of Chinese opera, each distinguished by different dialects, music, costumes, and stories.

Why go? For the same amount of time as a movie (and about $20 per person), a night at the opera guarantees you a glimpse at China's past—not to mention a fascinating mix of drama, color, movement, and sound.

INTRODUCING BEIJING OPERA

A RICH & CURIOUS HISTORY

To master the art of Beijing opera's leaping acrobatics, stylized movements, sword dances, and dramatic makeup techniques, actors begin their grueling training as young children. The work pays off: nowhere else in the world can you see a performer in heavy, opulent costume, so artfully singing, miming, turning flips, and brandishing swords.

Opera instrumentation consists of the percussive Wuchang, that is, the gongs, drums, cymbals, and wooden clappers that accompany exaggerated body movements and acrobatics, and the melodic Wenchang, including the Chinese fiddle (*erhu*), the lutelike *pipa*, horns, and flutes.

Neophytes may find two hours of the staccato clanging and nasal singing of Beijing opera hard to take (and most young Chinese fed on a diet of western-style pop agree). But this dramatic, colorful experience might be one of the most memorable of your trip.

FALSETTOS & BACK FLIPS & GONGS, OH MY!

Beijing opera was born out of a wedding between two provincial opera styles from Anhui and Hubei in the 19th century—during China's last dynasty, the Qing Dynasty. It also borrowed from other regional operas and Kunqu, a 500-year-old Chinese musical-theater style. Even though Beijing opera is relatively young, many of its stories are extracted from epics written as far back as the 12th century.

After Mao Zedong took the helm in 1949, opera was molded to reflect the ideals of Chinese communism. The biggest changes occurred under Mao's wife,

Jiang Qing, during the Cultural Revolution (1966–1976). Traditional operas were banned; only the so-called eight model plays could be staged. These starred people in plain work clothes singing about the glories of Communism. Traditional opera was reinstated gradually following Mao's death in 1976.

■TIP→ **If you're especially keen to follow the opera closely, choose a theater that displays English subtitles above the stage. Don't mind if things get lost in translation? Sit back and enjoy—the stage antics will be entertainment enough.**

MEI LANFANG: GAY ICON & OPERA HERO(INE)

Born in Beijing into a family of performers, Mei Lanfang (1894–1961) perfected the art of female impersonation during his five decades on stage. He is credited with popularizing Beijing opera overseas and was so hip in his day that there was a brand of cigarettes named after him. *The Worlds of Mei Lanfang* (2000) is an American-made documentary about the star, with footage of his performances. You can visit his house at 9 Huguosi, Xicheng District. 🚇 Y10 🕐 Tues.–Sun. 9–4 ☎ 010/6618-0351 🌐 www.meilanfang.com.cn.

Mei Lanfang's gender-bending chops earned him a special place in the hearts of gay activists.

ALL GUSSIED UP

All smiles: elaborate swirls and designs make for quite a done-up countenance.

Towering headdresses and flowing, cotton-candy-soft beards are all part of Beijing opera culture.

The richly embroidered silks in Beijing opera—called *xing tou*—are largely based on Ming Dynasty fashions. These nearly fetishistic costumes are key to identifying each character. The emperor is draped in a yellow robe with a colorful dragon on the back; scholars usually dress in blue and wear a cap with wings; generals don padded armor with bold embroidery; and bandits are often adorned in black capes and trousers.

Painstakingly detailed costumes and towering, bejeweled headdresses enhance the movements of the actors. For example, soldiers wear helmets with pheasant plumes that are waggled and brushed through the air. Cascading sleeves—called water sleeves—are waved and swept to express sorrow or respect.

PAINTED FACES

There are more than 1,000 different kinds of makeup patterns used in Beijing opera. Colors symbolize character traits. For example, red conveys bravery or loyalty, white signifies treachery, yellow suggests brutality, black stands for integrity or fierceness, and purple expresses wisdom. Bandits often have blue faces; gods and spirits are marked with gold and silver.

FACE CHANGING (*BIAN LIAN*)

A specialty of Sichuan opera (Chuan Ju) is the art of face changing, where actors swap masks with lightning speed. One method is to blow into a tiny box of colored powder to camouflage the switch. More spectacular is the mask-pulling routine, in which several masks are painted on thin fabric and attached to the face. Flicking a cloak or sleeve allows the performer to pull the masks off as needed. Masters whisk through as many as 10 masks in 20 seconds.

NOW YOU KNOW

The two most famous Beijing operas are *Peony Pavilion* and *Farewell My Concubine*.

In contrast to the ostentatious costumes, Beijing opera sets are quite sparse: the traditional stage is a simple platform with a silk backdrop.

THE FOUR MAJOR PLAYERS

There are four archetypal characters in Beijing opera: Sheng, Dan, Jing, and Chou. Each one can have variations. The Dan roles, for example, include Qingyi, a shy maiden, and the more promiscuous Huadan. A performer typically devotes a lifetime to perfecting one role.

During the Qing Dynasty, women were banned from performing, so men played the Dan role. These female impersonators were often the most popular actors. Women began performing again in the 1930s; nowadays most female roles are played by women.

SHENG Male characters: Scholars, statesmen

CHOU Clowns: Not always good-natured, wears white patches around eyes/nose

JING Warriors: The roles with the most elaborately painted faces

DAN Female characters: Coquettes, old ladies, warriors, maidens

WHERE TO WATCH

Embellished eyebrows, perfect tendrils of hair, and striking lips–a performer prepares for the show.

Shorter shows put on at venues such as Liyuan Theater are full of acrobatics and fantastic costumes. You can catch an opera performance any night of the week in Beijing, but there will be more options on weekends. Shows usually start around 7 PM and cost between 50 and 200 Yuan. All the free-listing magazines have information, and staff at your hotel can recommend performances and help book tickets. You can also buy tickets online through ⊕ www.piao.com.cn; register online and pay by credit card or phone ☎ 010/6417-7845. Piao.com will send the tickets to your hotel. ■**TIP**→ **You can also get a taste of Chinese opera for free before you spring for tickets if you have access to a television: nonstop opera is broadcast on CCTV channel 11.**

★ **CHANG'AN GRAND THEATER** At this contemporary theater, like at a cabaret, you sit at tables and can eat and drink while watching lively, colorful performances of Beijing opera. ■**TIP**→ **A great perk? English subtitles appear above the stage.** ✉ 7 Jianguomennei Dajie, Dongcheng District ☎ 010/6510-1310

HUGUANG GUILDHALL The city's oldest Beijing opera theater, the Guildhall has staged performances since 1807. The hall has been restored to display its original architecture. Although it's the most atmospheric place to take in an opera, it's not the liveliest. The last we heard, the Huguang monkey king was looking washed out. ✉ 3 Hufangqiao, Xuanwu District ☎ 010/6351-8284 ⊕ www.beijinghuguang.com

LAO SHE TEAHOUSE Performances vary, but usually include Beijing opera and such arts as acrobatics, magic, or comedy. The teahouse is named after Lao She, a playwright and novelist who died in 1966. ✉ 3 Qianmenxi Dajie, 3rd floor, Xuanwu District ☎ 010/6303-6830 ⊕ www.laosheteahouse.com

★ **Fodor's Choice** | **LIYUAN THEATER** Though it's unashamedly touristy, it's our top pick. You can watch performers put on makeup before the show (come early) and then graze on snacks and sip tea while watching English-subtitled shows. Glossy brochures complement the crooning. ✉ Qianmen Hotel, 175 Yongan Lu, Xuanwu District ☎ 010/6301-6688 Ext. 8860 or 010/6303-2301

TIANQIAO HAPPY TEAHOUSE In an old, traditional theater, the teahouse hosts Beijing operas as well as acrobatics, jugglers, and contortionists. ✉ 113 Tianqiao Shichang, Xuanwu District ☎ 010/6303-9013

RENT IT: *FAREWELL MY CONCUBINE*

Before your trip, rent Chen Kaige's *Farewell My Concubine*, a 1993 film that follows the life, loves, and careers of two male opera performers against a background of political turmoil. It also depicts the brutality of opera schools, where children were forced to practice grueling routines (think splits, balancing water jugs, and head stands).

barrels are performed here nightly. ⊠ *36 Dongsanhuan Bei Lu, Chaoyang District* ☎ *010/6507–2421* ⊕ *www.acrobatics.com.cn.*

★ **The Red Theatre.** If it's Vegas-style stage antics you're after, the Legend of Kung Fu show is what you want. Extravagant martial arts are complemented by neon, fog, and heavy-handed sound effects. Shows are garish but also sometimes glorious. ⊠ *44 Xingfu Da Jie, Chongwen District* ☎ *101/6710–3671.*

Universal Theater (Heaven & Earth). The China Acrobatic Troupe—made up of extremely bendy pre-teens—puts on a nightly repertoire of breathtaking, and usually flawless, stunts here. Stunning! ⊠ *10 Dongzhimen Nan Da Jie, Chaoyang District* ☎ *010/6416–9893.*

Wan Sheng Theater (Tianqiao Acrobatic Theater). The Beijing Acrobatics Troupe of China are famous for their weird, fun shows. Content includes a flashy show of offbeat contortions and tricks, with a lot of high-wire action. ⊠ *95 Tianqiao Market, Xuanwu District* ☎ *010/6303–7449.*

Music

Beijing Concert Hall. Beijing's main venue for Chinese and Western classical-music concerts also hosts folk dancing and singing, and many celebratory events throughout the year. The venue is the home of the China National Symphony Orchestra. ⊠ *1 Bei Xinhua Jie, Xicheng District* ☎ *010/6605–5812.*

Fodor'sChoice **Forbidden City Concert Hall.** With a seating capacity of 1,400, this is one
★ of Beijing's largest concert halls. It is also one of the most well-appointed, with plush seating and top-notch acoustics. Despite the modern building, you'll walk through ancient courtyards to get to the hall—highly romantic. ⊠ *In Zhongshan Park, Xichangan Jie, Xicheng District, on the west side of Tiananmen Square* ☎ *010/6559–8285* Ⓜ *Tiananmen West.*

Poly Plaza International Theater. This is a modern shopping-center–like complex on top of Dongsi Shitiao subway station. One of Beijing's better-known theaters, the Poly hosts Chinese and international concerts, ballets, and musicals. ■ TIP➔ **If you're seeking a performance in English, this is your best bet.** ⊠ *1/F Poly Plaza, 14 Dongzhimen Nandajie, Dongcheng District* ☎ *010/6506–5343* Ⓜ *Dongsi Shitiao.*

Workers' Stadium. The Workers' Stadium is a Beijing landmark for expatriates—it's surrounded by a network of bar streets. It's usually host to soccer matches, but pop concerts are also sometimes held here (Britney Spears, anyone?). ⊠ *Gongti Bei Lu, Chaoyang District* ☎ *010/6501–6655.*

Theater

Beijing Exhibition Theater. Chinese plays, Western and Chinese operas, and ballet performances are staged in this Soviet-style building that's part of the Exhibition Center complex. Talk about a wide range of shows: in 2006, the musical *West Side Story* was staged and the Black Eyed Peas played, as well. ⊠ *135 Xizhimenwai Dajie, Xicheng District* ☎ *010/6835–4455.*

Capital Theater. This is a busy, modern theater near the Wangfujing shopping street. It often has performances by the respected Beijing Peo-

1

ple's Art Theatre and various international acts. ✉ *22 Wangfujing Dajie, Dongcheng District* ☎ *010/6524–9847* Ⓜ *Wangfujing.*

Ⓒ **China National Puppet Theater.** Shadow and hand-puppet shows convey traditional stories—it's lively entertainment for children and adults alike. This venue also attracts overseas performers, including the Moscow Puppet Theater. ✉ *1 Anhuaxili, Chaoyang District* ☎ *010/6425–4849.*

Nightlife

Sanlitun—the heart of Beijing's nightlife—offers mainly live-music pubs; it's quite popular with locals. Snuck away in the alleyway behind the giant 3.3 shopping center on Bar Street is an eclectic bunch of bars that range from grungy dance club to rooftop lounge bars serving swanky cocktails and Belgian beer. South Sanlitun Street plays to a more refined crowd of drinkers. Houhai, once a quiet lakeside neighborhood home to Beijing's *laobaixing* (ordinary folk), has exploded into a bumping bar scene. This is a great place to come for a drink at dusk: park yourself on an outdoor seat and enjoy.

Bars & Dance Clubs

DONGCHENG & XICHENG DISTRICTS

Candy Floss Café. Beijing's funky young set are falling over themselves to get to this little courtyard bar. Although the drinks are pricey and pretty average, the place is adorable. The central courtyard has been planted with a fairy-tale garden, complete with ponds, stepping stones, gnomes, thick foliage, and a romantic weeping willow. The interior is like stepping into a friend's living room. It's hard to find, though: walk behind the Central Academy of Drama on Nanluogu Xiang, and take your first left. ✉ *35 Dongmianhua Hutong, Dongcheng District* ☎ *010/6405–5775.*

★ **Drum & Bell.** This bar has a perfect location—right between the Drum and Bell towers. The terrace is a comfy perch for a summer afternoon drink, where you scan the surrounding hutong rooftops. Don't get too plastered, though, because the staircase down is very steep. On the ground floor there are jumbles of sofas tossed with Cultural Revolution memorabilia. ✉ *41 Zhonglouwan Hutong, Dongcheng District* ☎ *010/8403–3600* Ⓜ *Gulou.*

★ **East Shore Live Jazz Café.** The closest thing Beijing has to New Orleans is this bar. Expect cigar smoke, velvet, sepia photographs of jazz greats, and plenty of vintage instruments on display. Owner, local jazz legend Liu Yuan, says he wants to use the bar to promote homegrown jazz talents. On top of the live swing and jazz, the bar boasts the best views of Houhai, either through the floor-to-ceiling windows (complete with telescope) in the bar or from the small, sparsely furnished rooftop. ■ TIP→ There are no guardrails on the roof, so drink and step with extreme care. ✉ *Qianhai Nanyan Lu, 2nd fl., next to the Post Office, Xicheng District* ☎ *010/8403–2131.*

Fodor'sChoice
★

No Name Bar. The first bar to open in Houhai is still around—even though rumors abound that it's on the demolition list. It's also the best by far: many expats still list No Name as their favorite bar in the city. The ser-

CLOSE UP

Fringe Art: The Dashanzi 798 Art District

IF YOU ARE KEEN to see what the city's art scene has to offer beyond calligraphy, the Dashanzi 798 Art District boasts a thriving contemporary art community. Just as the city comes of age in the international, political, and economic arena, so too are local Chinese artists. Exploration of social taboos, use of digital media, and clever installations are juxtaposed among more orthodox forms of canvas paintings and photography. Some efforts may seem like trite knockoffs of American pop art, and Mao references run rampant, but keep in mind this level of expression is still new and evolving for the public arena. Complete freedom of expression is not tolerated and governmental closings are not unheard of (though they're increasingly rare). Chinese artists have also learned the benefits of subversive subtlety.

Built in the 1950s, the factory was a major industrial project designed by East German architects backed by Soviet aid. The factory's decline started in the 1980s, just as Beijing's contemporary art scene began to emerge. The massive relocation of pollutant factories outside the city in preparation for the 2008 Summer Olympic Games has further accelerated the decline of the area's manufacturing roots and allowed for the incubation of modern art as students and artists take over deserted factories to establish their own galleries and studios. The recent government declaration of Dashanzi as a protected arts district has paved the way for a resurgence of new, inventive local galleries, as well as design studios, restaurants, cafés, and bars. The annual Dashanzi

International Arts Festival—held each May—continues to draw international attention to the 798 area.

The Dashanzi compound is immensely walkable; keep in mind this is solely a pedestrian affair unless you arrive by private car. Cabs are not allowed to enter the compound and you will be required to disembark at any of the entrance gates. Though it's open on weekdays (except Monday), most people visit on weekends, when throngs of locals and foreigners congregate to see what's on display.

Directions to Dashanzi: Traveling from the city by car, take the Dashanzi (# 2) exit off the Airport Expressway. Just as you come to the end of the exit ramp, ask the driver to stop at the intersection. Cross the road and walk against oncoming traffic until you see 797 Microphone. Enter through the main gate, onto Jiuxianqiao Road. ■ TIP→ **It may be helpful to ask your hotel staff to instruct the taxi driver before you set off.**

✉ *4 Jiuxianqiao Rd., Dashanzi, Chaoyang District* ☏ *010/6438–4862 or 010/6437–6248* ⊕ *www.798space. com.*

To get a feel for what sells abroad, drop by internationally owned galleries such as White Space Beijing or Art Seasons. These established galleries house perennially hot artists such as Liu Fei, Zhao Bo, and Chen Ke. Time-Zone 8 Book Shop is an avant-garde bookshop in the heart of Dashanzi; it stashes an international range of art, design, and architecture books and magazines, including books on and by Chinese artists.

–by Katharine Mitchell

(top) The Juyongguan section of the Great Wall of China is considered one of the three greatest passes. The others are Jiayuguan Pass and Shanhai Pass. (bottom) The Bailin Buddhist Temple in Shijiazhuang, Hebei.

(top) Take a sunrise camel trip on the Silk Road in Dunhuang, Gansu. (bottom) Pudong, literally "the east side of the river," is Shanghai's financial, economic, and commercial center.

(top) Located in the remote town of Xiahe, the Labrang Monastery is a little piece of Tibet along the Gansu-Qinghai border. (bottom) A colorful Chinese New Year celebration.

(top) In the Longsheng Longji Rice Terraces in Guangxi, patterns have been cut into the hills up to a height of 2,625 feet. (bottom left) Native son Chow Yun-Fat in *Crouching Tiger, Hidden Dragon*. (bottom right) Cormorant fishermen on the Li River near Guilin train their birds to do all the work.

(top left) The Chinese introduced tea to the world; learn all about it at the Flagstaff House Museum of Tea Ware, Hong Kong. (top right) *Manpower* sculpture by Rosanna Li, Grotto Fine Art gallery, Hong Kong. (bottom) The new China is crackling with energy, and crossing the street can sometimes be a dangerous sport.

(top) In the heyday of colonial encroachment, the Bund was Shanghai's main drag, with 52 architectural styles including Gothic, Baroque, and Romanesque. (bottom) In Cantonese opera, makeup and hair give clues to the characters' personality.

(top) The Great Buddha in Leshan, Sichuan, is a UNESCO World Heritage Site and the largest buddha in the world. Each of its big toes are 28 feet long. (bottom left) Architects and designers strive for auspicious feng shui in Hong Kong. (bottom right) In the countryside, the traditional blue Mao uniforms are still fairly common.

Nine-Dragon Wall at Beihai Park in Beijing is one of three walls of its kind in China. Built in 1756 during the Qing Dynasty, the famous wall has nine dragons playing in the clouds.

vice is refreshingly low key—a nice change from the sycophantic staff at neighboring venues—and it's all tumbledown elegance with rattan and potted plants. Locals refer to it by the owner's name: Bai Feng. Anyone from tourists to the old-China hands can be found here. ✉ *3 Qianhai East Bank, Xicheng District* ☎ *010/6401–8541.*

Tango. A huge warehouse-style top-floor club makes this the odd one out in the China Clubland, and that's a good thing. Without the usual gaudiness, Tango is a solid club, roomy enough to take the crowds, and often playing some good tunes. ✉ *79 Hepingli Xijie, South Gate of Ditan Park, Dongcheng District* ☎ *010/6428–2288.*

CHAOYANG DISTRICT **Babyface East.** Now a nationwide brand of clubs spread across China, Babyface East is often full of young-money types rattling dice and drinking Chivas-and-green-tea cocktails. It attracts some good dance DJs, including the occasional international name. The interior is best described as quintessential Chinese club, with bling-bling gaudiness and scantily clad dancers. Prepare to be crushed while you shake your groove thing on the weekend. ✉ *6 Gongti Xi Lu, Chaoyang District* ☎ *010/6551–9091* ⊕ *www.faceclub.com.cn/.*

Brown's. Set inside a massive, multilevel space, Brown's could be called a wannabe Hard Rock Café. Still, it's a fun party pub where you can dance on the bar and dodge pyrotechnic cocktails. It's heavy on the big-screen sports, drink choices (including 500 different shooters), and cheesy 1980s music. Weekend nights are wild, but for the rest of the time you'll be drinking with a well-behaved crowd of relaxed locals and expats. ✉ *Sanlitun Nan Lu, above the Loft, Chaoyang District* ☎ *010/6591–2717.*

Fodor'sChoice ★ **Centro.** We don't always vote for hotel bars, but this one is decidedly different. It's huge and luxurious, with cavernous wine cellars—and it also has Bruce Lee, the city's favorite cocktail master. Drinks are expensive. Come for the early-evening happy hour, when the prices are more polite. Feast your eyes on the nouveau riche showing off their labels. ✉ *1/F Kerry Center Hotel, 1 Guanghua Lu, Chaoyang District* ☎ *010/6561–8833 Ext. 42* Ⓜ *Guomao.*

The Den. Sour staff and crumbling elegance are indeed this bar's attraction. The owner runs the city's amateur rugby club, and you'll find players and their supporters drinking rowdily here. Open 24 hours a day, it's guaranteed to be buzzing every night. There's a disco upstairs. ✉ *4 Gongti Donglu, next to the City Hotel, Chaoyang District* ☎ *010/6592–6290.*

★ **Press Club Bar.** This haunt offers soft leather chairs, tinkling piano ser-enades, brass rails, and a whiff of history. Stuffy and pompous say some; tip-top cocktails worth the trip say others. Rumor has it you can taste Beijing's best Bloody Mary here. ⊠ *1/F St Regis Hotel, 21 Jiang-guomenwai Da Jie, Chaoyang District* ☎ *010/6460–6688 Ext. 2360* Ⓜ *Jianguomen.*

★ **Stone Boat.** This watering hole is a pavilion-style hut on the edge of a pretty lake in Ritan Park. There are ducks, feisty fisherman, and park joggers to observe while you sip chilled white wine. This is one of Beijing's nicest outdoor bars, as long as you don't mind having to use the public toilets opposite the building. The delicious peace is shattered by often amateur-ish DJs on weekend nights. ⊠ *Lakeside, southwest corner of Ritan Park, Chaoyang District* ☎ *010/6501–9986* Ⓜ *Jianguomen.*

Top Club & Lounge. This top-floor club, decked out in deep red, looks like a Ming Dynasty disco. Sofas are squishy, the bar staff quirky, and the rooftop gives wide-open views of the crane-pocked construction val-leys in the area. There are DJs every night, and Thursday is especially gay friendly. Top Club attracts a more mellow crowd than its neighbor, zippy Bar Blu. ⊠ *Tongli Studios, 4th fl., Sanlitun Beilu, Chaoyang Dis-trict* ☎ *010/6413–1019.*

Fodor'sChoice **Q Bar.** George and Echo's cocktails—strong, authentic, and not super
★ expensive—are a small legend here in Beijing. This tucked-away orange lounge bar adds an unpretentious note to an evening out. Don't be put off by the fact it's in a bland motel stuck in the 1980s: the drinks are worth it (especially the whiskey sours!). ⊠ *Top floor of Eastern Inn Hotel, Sanlitun Nan Lu, Chaoyang District* ☎ *010/6595–9239.*

★ **Yugong Yishan.** This Beijing institution is a chilled-out live-music club at the back of the parking lot opposite the Workers' Stadium. It plays host to a range of live bands from blues to jazz to Afro-Caribbean beats and attracts an equally diverse crowd. It occasionally charges an entrance fee, depending on the band. ⊠ *1 Gongti Beilu, Chaoyang District* ☎ *010/6415–0687.*

CHAOYANG **The World of Suzie Wong.** It's no coincidence this bar is named after a
WEST GATE 1957 novel about a Hong Kong prostitute. Come here late at night and you'll find a healthy supply of modern Suzie Wongs and a crowd of expat clients. The sleaze factor is enhanced by its 1930s opium-den design, with China-chic beds overrun with cushions. Suzie Wong's, however, has a good reputation for mixing a more-than-decent cocktail. ⊠ *1A South Nongzhanguan Lu, Chaoyang West Gate, Chaoyang District* ☎ *010/6593–6049 or 010/6500–3377* ⊕ *www.suziewong.com.cn.*

SHOPPING

By Katharine Mitchell

Large markets and malls in Beijing are generally open from 9 AM to 9 PM, though some shops close at 7 PM. It's always best to call ahead if you hope to shop in the early morning or late evenings. Weekdays are always less crowded, and shops tend to be quieter just after lunch, when many Chinese people (including some merchants) take a rest.

Major credit cards are accepted in select venues. Cash is the driving currency and ATMs abound. Before accepting those pink, Mao-faced Y100 notes, most vendors will hold them up to the light, tug at the corners, and feel the surface. Counterfeiting is becoming increasingly more difficult, but no one, including you, wants to be cheated. In some department stores, you must settle your bill at a central payment counter.

Malls & Department Stores

Beijing Department Store. Wangfujing's grand dame continues to attract large crowds with stores selling everything from jewelry to clothing to sports equipment. ⊠ *255 Wangfujing Dajie, Dongcheng District* ☏ *010/ 6512–6677* Ⓜ *Wangfujing.*

Beijing Friendship Store. Years ago, this was the only place sanctioned to sell foreign goods, but with so many cheaper and more glamorous options now, this old mainstay has lost its allure. However, if the thought of bargaining in a loud, crowded market makes your head hurt, or if you're on a single-sweep shopping spree for goods of guaranteed quality, then the Friendship Store will be your haven. There's plenty of traditional Chinese goods and handicrafts, including tablecloths, silk and cashmere, porcelain, watercolor paintings, traditional Chinese medicine, teas, jade and gold jewelry, rugs (both silk and wool), and foreign groceries. ⊠ *17 Jianguomenwai Dajie, Chaoyang District* ☏ *010/6500–3311* Ⓜ *Jianguomen.*

★ **China World Shopping Mall.** Rising up alongside the China World Trade Center, the two towers of Guomao rule the roost with tiers of top-flight designers, such as **Prada, Marc Jacobs, Hermès,** and **Dior.** For quality souvenirs, check out **Tian Fu,** a branch of the famous Chinese tea sellers, or **Emperor,** which sells silk bedding and table linens. ⊠ *1 Jianguomenwai Dajie, Chaoyang District* ☏ *010/6505–2288* Ⓜ *Guomao.*

The Kerry Centre Mall. Located inside a Shangri-La–owned hotel and business center, the Kerry Centre Mall comprises a group of small but top-notch clothing shops, in addition to two golf stores, a post office, and an international food court. Lush piles of silk and wool carpets from Xinjiang & Henan provinces line the walls of **Aladdin Jia Ju Carpets (# B28).** On the mall's entrance level, **Dave's Custom Tailoring** (☏ 010/ 8529–9433) turns out quality men's suits in about 10 days. A few doors down, **Mystery Garments** embellishes linens and silks with Chinese embroidery from Guizhou. Additional branches are in the Holiday Inn Lido and the Oriental Plaza. The designers at Hong Kong–owned **Blanc de Chine** cite Ming and Qing dynasty furniture as inspiration, but their sleek black and gray designs also suggest more contemporary influence. ⊠ *1 Guanghua Rd., Chaoyang District* ☏ *010/8529–9450* Ⓜ *Guomao.*

Lufthansa Youyi Shopping Center. A high-end shopping mall attached to the ritzy Kempinski Hotel, this center is well visited by expat parents, who rave about the selection of children's clothing and baby goods on the sixth floor. International dealers in crystal and glass applaud the jewels and vases sold at **Liuligongfang** on the first floor. ⊠ *52 Liangmao-*

qiao Lu, Chaoyang District ☎ *010/ 6465–1188* ⊕ *www.kempinski-beijing.com.*

★ **Malls at Oriental Plaza.** This enormous shopping complex originates at the southern end of Wangfujing, where it meets Chang'an Jie, and stretches a city block east to Dongan Dajie. A true city within a city, it's conveniently organized by "street" names, such as Gourmet Street (aka the Food Court) and Sky Avenue. Upscale shops include **Max Mara** and **Sisley.** ✉ *1 Dongchang'an Jie, Dongcheng District* ☎ *010/ 8518–6363* Ⓜ *Wangfujing.*

Sun Dongan Plaza. A massive shopping center with dozens of designer shops also makes a concession to Old Peking with a traditional-style shopping street on the second floor. On the third floor, the **Mu Zhen Liao Chinese Fashion Boutique** sells high-quality, ready-made *qipaos* (Chinese-style dresses) as well as tailor-made ones. The store is especially popular with brides-to-be. ✉ *138 Wangfujing Dajie, Dongcheng District* ☎ *010/6528–1788* Ⓜ *Wangfujing.*

3D3, the Fashion Center at Sanlitun. Across the street from Tong Li, the Fashion Center at Sanlitun is a tidy, five-story mall stocked with princess punk fashions, from halter-tops to spaghetti-strap gowns. Men head to the fourth floor for shops with names such as **Manly. Mughal's Beijing,** a rooftop Pakistani/Xinjiang restaurant, offers a yummy alternative to the Western bars crowding Sanlitun below. Look for a red "3D3" sign as you approach. ✉ *33 Sanlitun Jie, Chaoyang District* ☎ *001/6417–3333* ⊕ *www.3d3.cn.*

Markets

Alien Street. Big-footed women rejoice: you'll find size 9+ shoes on Alien Street. A more apt name for this short-but-crammed market strip is Russian Street. All shop signs are in Chinese and Cyrillic; swarms of Russian shoppers and traders trawl the aisles and alleyways; and advertisements picture blond models wearing bikinis and minks. Several Russian restaurants and more shoe stores are located behind Yabao Lu on Ritan Bei Lu, and a giant new shopping center is in construction directly across from the Beijing Auterlima Shoes Market. ✉ *Yabao Lu, Chaoyang District* Ⓜ *Chaoyangmen.*

Beijing Curio City. This complex has four stories of kitsch and curio shops and a few furniture vendors, some selling authentic antiques. Prices are high (driven by tour groups), so don't be afraid to low-ball. If you

---

GREAT SOUVENIRS

- A pearl necklace with matching earrings
- A hand-embroidered silk qipao, tailored to the perfect fit
- Knockoff designer handbags
- Canisters of tea
- Beijing 2008 Olympic memorabilia
- Traditional Chinese scrolls
- Calligraphy brushes
- Reproduction Communist propaganda posters
- A jade pendant representing your Chinese zodiac
- Decorative name chop carved with your Chinese or English name

are looking for antique furniture, try **Dong Fa** ⟨floor⟩ (# 111). ⊠ *Dongsanhuan Nan Lu, Chaoya⟨ng⟩ Ring Rd. at Panjiayuan Bridge* ☎ *010/6774–77⟨ ⟩Ext. 63.*

★ ☺ **Hongqiao Market.** Hongqiao is full of tourist goods⟨ ⟩and cheap watches, but it's best known for its th⟨ ⟩hence its nickname: the Pearl Market. Freshwater, s⟨ ⟩white: the quantity is overwhelming and quality v⟨ary⟩ ᵦy stall. Prices range wildly. Fanghua Pearls (No. 4318), on the fourth floor, displays quality necklaces and earrings, with photos of Barbara Bush and Margaret Thatcher shopping there to prove it. Fanghua has a second store devoted to fine jade and precious stones. As a bonus to your pearl excursion, hold your nose and dive into the fish and meat market in the basement: a veritable aquarium of sea cucumbers, crab, dragon shrimp, squid, eel, and umpteen varieties of fish. Also, promise the kiddos a shopping spree of their own in the toy market directly behind the Hongqiao building. ⊠ *Tiantan Lu, between Chongemenwai Lu and Tiyuguan Dajie, Chongwen District, east of the northern entrance to Temple of Heaven* ☎ *010/6711–7630.*

Fodor'sChoice ★ **Panjiayuan Antique Market.** Every weekend, the sun rises over thousands of pilgrims rummaging through Panjiayuan in search of antiques and the most curious of curios. With over 3,000 vendors crowding an area of 48,500 square meters (159,118 square feet), not every jade bracelet, oracle bone, porcelain vase, and ancient silk screen is authentic, but most people are here for the reproductions anyway. Behold the bounty: watercolors, scrolls, calligraphy, Buddhist statues, opera costumes, old Russian SLR cameras, curio cabinets, Tibetan jewelry, tiny satin lotus-flower shoes, rotary telephones, jade dragons, antique mirrors, infinite displays of "Maomorabilia." If you're buying jade, first observe the Chinese customers, how they hold a flashlight to the milky-green stone to test its authenticity. As with all Chinese markets, *bargain, bargain, bargain,* as many vendors inflate their prices astronomically for *waiguoren* ("outside country people"). A strip of enclosed stores form a perimeter around the surprisingly orderly rows of open-air stalls. The friendly owner of the eponymous **Li Shu Lan** decorates her shop (# 24-D) with antiques from her *laojia,* or countryside hometown. Stop by the **Bei Zhong Bao Pearl Shop** (# 7-A) for medium-quality freshwater pearls cultivated by the Hu family. Also here are a sculpture zoo, book bazaar, reproduction-furniture shops, and a two-story minimarket stashing propaganda posters and Communist literature, as well as comic books, canceled stamps, and old coins. ■ TIP→ **A weekend-only market, it opens at sunrise and empties by 4 PM.** Show the taxi driver the Chinese characters for Panjiayuan Shichang. ⊠ *Third Ring Rd. at Panjiayuan Bridge, Chaoyang District.*

Ritan Office Building Market. Don't let the gray-brick and red-trim exterior fool you: the offices inside the Ritan Building are strung with racks of brand-name dresses and funky-fab accessories. Unlike the tacky variations made on knockoff labels sold in less-expensive markets, the collections here, for the most part, retain their integrity—perhaps because many of these dresses are actually designer labels. ■ TIP→ **They're also more expensive, and bargaining is discouraged.** Of note, the owner Liu Xingxing tailors and sells Hunan silk qipaos (# 1019). The **Ruby Cashmere Shop** (# 1009) sells genuine cashmere sweaters and scarves at reduced prices. Upstairs, the burning incense and bright red walls of You Gi (# 2006) provide a welcome atmosphere for perusing an over-

EARLY-BIRD CATCHES

A common superstition in Chinese markets is that if you don't make a sale with your very first customer of the day, the rest of the day will go badly. So set out early, and if you know you're the first customer of the day, bargain relentlessly.

priced but eccentric collection of Nepalese and Indian clothing and jewelry. ☒ *15A Guanghua Lu, just east of the south entrance to Ritan Park, opposite the Vietnam Embassy, Chaoyang District* ☎ *010/8561–9556.*

Fodor's Choice **Silk Alley Market.** Once a delightfully chaotic sprawl of hundreds of out-
★ door stalls, the Silk Alley Market is now corralled inside a 35,052-square-meter (115,000-square-foot) shopping center. The government has cracked down on certain copycat items, so if you don't see that certain knockoff Louis Vuitton purse or Chanel jacket, just ask; it might magically appear from a stack of plastic storage bins. You will face no dearth, however, of knockoff Pumas and Nikes or North Face jackets. Also ubiquitous are fake Pashmina scarves wrapped in cellophane. Chinese handicrafts and children's clothes are on the top floors. Bargain relentlessly, and guard your wallet against pickpockets. Seek the second-floor cashmere shop (# B2-0088) for quality sweaters and scarves. ☒ *8 Xiushui Dong Jie, Chaoyang District* ☎ *139/0113-6086 or 010/ 5169–9003* ⊕ *www.xiushui.com.cn* Ⓜ *Yonganli.*

★ **Yaxiu Market.** Especially popular among younger Western shoppers, Yaxiu is yet another indoor arena stuffed to the gills with knockoff brand-name clothing and shoes. Prices are slightly cheaper than Silk Alley, but the haggling no less cruel. Don't be alarmed if you see women sniffing sneakers or suede jackets: they're simply testing if the leather is real. The giant sign outside this bustling clothes market near Sanlitun reads Yashow, but it's written YAXIU in pinyin. ☒ *58 Gongti Bei Lu, Chaoyang District* ☎ *010/6416–8699.*

Zhaojia Chaowai Market. Beijing's best-known venue for affordable antique and reproduction furniture houses scores of independent vendors who sell everything from authentic Qing Dynasty–era chests to traditional baskets, ceramics, carpets, and curios. Be sure to bargain; vendors routinely sell items for less than half their starting price. ☒*43 Huawei Bei Li, Chaoyang District, directly across from Pianjiayuan Market* ☎ *010/6770–6402.*

Specialty Shops

Books

Beijing Book Building. This is a multilevel fortress stocked with hundreds of thousands of books, magazines, maps, and learning materials. The

AVOID SCAMS

Fakes abound—everything from jade, cashmere, Pashminas, silk, and leather to handbags, antiques, and Calvin Klein underwear. Fake is great, if that's what you're after, but do reserve your big purchases for accredited shops or merchants who can prove the quality of their product. Some countries limit the number of knockoffs you can bring back into the country, so don't go overboard on the handbags. If you're buying authentic antiques, you'll need to show customs agents your receipts, embossed with an official red seal.

Chinese medicine is wonderful, but not when practiced by lab-coated "doctors" sitting behind a card table on the street corner. If you're seeking Chinese medical treatment, visit a local hospital, Tongrentang medicine shop, or ask your hotel concierge for a legitimate recommendation.

Deception is the only real "art" practiced by the charming "art students" who will invite you to their college's art show. The art works are, in fact, usually painted by hand, but they are mass-produced copies. If you want to support Beijing's burgeoning art scene, explore the galleries of Dashanzi, visit an artists' village, or drop by one of the galleries listed in Chapter 5.

Bargaining is acceptable, and expected, in markets and mom-and-pop shops, though not in malls. The bottom line of bargaining is to pay what you think is fair. No matter how much you haggle, foreigners will almost always be charged more than the local price.

English-language selection is slim, yet travelers still love browsing here. ✉ *17 Changan Jie, Xicheng District* ☎ *010/6607–8498* Ⓜ *Xidan.***The Bookworm.** Book lovers, hipsters, and aspiring poets take note: this lending library and bookstore offers a spacious second-story reading room with a full café and bar. All are welcome to browse: the magazine and new-books section are a stupendous sight for English-starved travelers. The store frequently hosts poetry readings and lectures; check their Web site for schedule. ✉ *4 Sanlitun Nan Lu, set back slightly in a parking lot, Chaoyang District* ☎ *010/6586–9507* ⊕ *www.beijingbookworm.com.*

Foreign Languages Bookstore. Head directly to the third floor, which is reserved for imported publications. Classics perpetually roost on the shelves of this state-owned shop, but bestsellers, biographies, and decent books about China also make the cut (though don't expect to read anything on the Tiananmen Square incidents). Find maps, Chinese-language learning materials, and children's books here, too, as well as a Starbucks on the ground floor. ✉ *235 Wangfujing Dajie, Dongcheng District* ☎ *010/6512–6903* Ⓜ *Wangfujing.*

Chinese Medicine

★ **Tongrentang.** A first-time consultation with a Chinese doctor can feel a bit like a reading with a fortune-teller. With one test of the pulse, many traditional Chinese doctors can describe the patient's medical history and diagnose current maladies. China's most famous traditional Chinese medicine shop, Tongrentang, is the jewel of Dazhalan, the charming pedestrian street just south of Qianmen. Palatial, hushed, and dimly lighted, this 300-year-old old shop even smells healthy. Browse the glassed displays of deer antlers and pickled snakes, dried seahorse and frog, and delicate tangles of roots with precious price tags of Y48,000. ■ TIP➜ If you don't speak Chinese and wish to have a consultation with a doctor, bring along a translator. ⊠ *24 Dazhalan, Qianmen, Exit C, Chongwen District* Ⓜ *Qianmen.*

Computers & Electronics

Bainaohui Computer Shopping Mall. Next door to the Wonderful Electronic Shopping Mall is Bainao, literally "one hundred computers." Home to hundreds of laptops and PCs, this retail mall is crammed with individual vendors. The Chinese word for computer translates literally as "electric brain." ⊠ *10 Chaoyangmenwai Da Jie, Chaoyang District* ☎ *010/6599–5912* Ⓜ *Chaoyangmen.*

Wonderful Electronic Shopping Mall. Cameras, tripods, flash disks, MP3s (called an MP-San in Chinese) abound. If you forgot the USB cable for your digital recorder or need extra camera batteries, this is the place to shop. There's an even larger electronics market in the Haidian District, but unless you're a real computer geek, the journey is too far. ⊠ *12 Chaoyangmenwai Da Jie, Chaoyang District* ☎ *010/8561–4335* Ⓜ *Chaoyangmen.*

Fashion Designers & Boutiques

Heyan'er. He Yan's design philosophy is stated in her label: BU YAN BU YU, or NO TALKING. Her linen and cotton tunics and collarless jackets speak for themselves. From earth tones to aubergine hues and peacock patterns, He Yan's designs echo traditional Tibetan styles. ⊠ *15-2 Gongti Bei Lu* ☎ *010/6415–9442* ⊠ *Holiday Inn Lido, 6 Fangyuan Xi Lu* ☎ *010/6437–6854.*

The Red Phoenix. In this cramped-but-charming Sanlitun studio/showroom, fashion diva Gu Lin designs embroidered satin qipaos, cropped jackets, and men's clothing for stylish foreigners and China's *xin xin ren lei* (literally the "new, new human being," referring to the country's latest flock of successful young professionals). ⊠ *30 Sanlitun Bei Jie, close to the intersection at Dongzhimen Lu at the north entrance of Bar St.* ☎ *010/6416–4423.*

Tongli Studio. Though Tongli Studio is overhyped, this cluster of internationally owned boutiques, cafés, and rooftop bars are worth a gander if you're already cruising Sanlitun. **Feng Ling Fashion** displays sexy thigh-high embroidered silk boots and punky qipaos emblazoned with red stars. At **Things of the Jing,** Londoner Gabrielle Harris alchemizes silver with images of feudal-era Chinese women to create funky-elegant earrings and pendants. **Radiance** carries pagoda-shaped ceramic birdfeeders. ⊠ *43 Sanlitun Hou Jie, Chaoyang District* ☎ *010/6417–7715* ⊕ *www.tonglistudio.com.*

EXPLORING TEA STREET

Tea Street. Maliandao hosts the ultimate tea party every day of the week. Literally hundreds of tea shops perfume the air of this prime tea-shopping district, west of the city center. Midway down this near-mile-long strip looms the **Teajoy Market,** the Silk Alley of teas. Unless you're an absolute fanatic, it's best to visit a handful of individual shops, crashing tea parties wherever you go. Vendors will invite you to sit down in heavy wooden chairs to nibble on pumpkin seeds and sample their large selections of black, white, oolong, jasmine, and chrysanthemum teas. Prices range from a few kuai for a decorative container of loose green tea to thousands of yuan for an elaborate gift set. Tea Street is also the place to stock up on clay and porcelain teapots and service sets. Green and flower teas are sold loose; black teas are sold pressed into disks and wrapped in natural-colored paper. Despite the huge selection of drinking vessels available, you'll find that most locals prefer to drink their tea from a recycled glass jar. ⊠ *Located near Guanganmen Wai Dajie, Xuanwu District.*

Jewelry

Shard Box Store. The signature collection here includes small to mid-size jewelry boxes fashioned from the broken shards of antique porcelain. Supposedly the shards were collected during the Cultural Revolution, when scores of antique porcelain were smashed in accordance with the law. Birds, trees, pining lovers, and dragons decorate these affordable ceramic-and-metal containers, which range from Y20 to Y200. ⊠ *1 Ritan Bei Lu, near the Fangcaodi Primary School, Chaoyang District* ☎ *010/8561–3712* ⊠ *2 Jiangtai Lu, near the Holiday Inn Lido* ☎ *010/ 5135-7638.*

Treasure House. Embedded in the Embassy District, a few stores down from foreign-goods meccas April Gourmand and Jenny Lou's, Treasure House has a modest but slick collection, including silver cuff links and charms inscribed with the Chinese symbols for happiness and longevity. ⊠ *5 Sanlitun Xiwujie* ☎ *001/8451–6096.*

Silk & Fabrics

Beijing Silk Shop. Since 1830, the Beijing Silk Shop has been supplying the city with quality silks and fabrics. This formerly musty store is being renovated; expect a supreme shopping experience in the new space by the 2008 Olympic games. Until then, focus on the silk, not the decor. To reach the shop, walk all the way down Dazhalan, then head directly onto Dazhalan West Street. ⚠ **Two other, much larger stores on Dazhalan major in silk. Ruifuxiang, at No. 5, is housed in a beautiful two-story building, as is Century Silk Store at No. 33.** ⊠ *50 Dazhalan Xi Jie, Xuanwu District* ☎ *010/6301–6658* Ⓜ *Qianmen.*

Beijing Yuanlong Silk Corporation. Jars of silkworm pupa and baskets of cocoons greet you on the second floor of Yuanlong. A tour guide will walk you through the silk quilt-making process while women in white lab coats demonstrate how to clean, soak, and stretch the silk of cocoons. It's touristy but fun if you've never seen the process. Silk quilts and duvets are for sale, as well as an on-site tailor for making qipaos. Quilts are craftily compacted into tiny rectangles—especially handy for international travelers. ■ TIP→ **You should avoid this spot entirely if tour buses are lined up in the parking lot.** ✉ *55 Tiantan Lu, Chongwen District, between the north gate of Temple of Heaven Park and Hongqiao* ☎ *010/ 6701–2859.*

China Star Silk Store. In the Wangfujing area, this is a great place to consider buying a qipao, the traditional Chinese silk dress. ✉ *133 Wangfujing Dajie, Dongcheng District* ☎ *010/6525–7945* Ⓜ *Wangfujing.*

SIDE TRIPS FROM BEIJING

By Alex Miller   Not only is Beijing a fascinating city to visit, but its outskirts are packed with history- and culture-laden sites for the admirer of early empires and their antiquities. First and foremost, a trip to the Great Wall is a must—you simply can't miss it! After the Great Wall, there are a variety of wonderful things to do and see: you can go horseback riding at Yesanpo, take a dip at the beach and gorge yourself with fresh seafood in Beidaihe, or travel to Laolongtou (the Old Dragon's Head), and see another section of the Great Wall in all its majesty as it collides with the ocean. Buddhist temples and ancient tombs, as well as historical bridges and anthropological digs, are all located within a few hours of Beijing. For all these sites, getting there is half the fun—traveling through rural China, even for a day trip, is always something of an adventure.

Thirteen Ming Tombs

48 km (30 mi) north of Beijing.

A narrow valley just north of Changping is the final resting place for 13 of the Ming Dynasty's 16 emperors (the first Ming emperor was buried in Nanjing; the burial site of the second one is unknown; and the seventh Ming emperor was dethroned and buried in an ordinary tomb in western Beijing). Ming monarchs once journeyed here each year to kowtow before their clan forefathers and make offerings to their memory. The area's vast scale and imperial grandeur convey the importance attached to ancestral worship in ancient China.

The road to the Thirteen Ming Tombs begins beneath an imposing stone portico that stands at the valley entrance. Beyond the entrance, the **Shenlu** (💲 Y16 ☉ Daily 9–5:30), or Spirit Way, once reserved for imperial travel, passes through an outer pavilion and between rows of stone sculptures— imperial advisers and huge, serene elephants, lions, horses, and other creatures—on its 7-km (4½-mi) journey to the burial sites.

The spirit way leads to **Changling** (☎ 010/6076–1886 💲 Y30), the head tomb built for Emperor Yongle in 1427. The designs of Yongle's great masterpiece, the Forbidden City, are echoed in this structure. The tomb is open daily from 8:30 to 4:30.

Changling and a second tomb, **Dingling** (☎ 010/6076–1424 ✉ Y60 Mar.–June and Sept.–Nov.; Y40 July and Aug. and Dec.–Feb.), were rebuilt in the 1980s and opened to the public. Both complexes suffer from over-restoration and over-crowding, but they're worth visiting if only for the tomb relics on display in the small museums at each site. Dingling is particularly worth seeing because this tomb of Emperor Wanli is the only Ming Dynasty tomb that has been excavated. Unfortunately, this was done in 1956 when China's archaeological skills were sadly lacking, resulting in irrecoverable losses. Nonetheless, it is interesting to compare this underground vault with the tomb of Emperor Qianlong at Qingdongling. Dingling is open daily from 8:30 to 5:30. Allow ample time for a hike or drive northwest from Changling to the six fenced-off **unrestored tombs,** a short distance farther up the valley. Here, crumbling walls conceal vast courtyards shaded by pine trees. At each tomb, a stone altar rests beneath a stela tower and burial mound. In some cases the wall that circles the burial chamber is accessible on steep stone stairways that ascend from either side of the altar. At the valley's terminus (about 5 km [3 mi] northwest of Changling), the **Zhaoling tomb** (✉ Y30) rests beside a traditional walled village. This thriving hamlet is well worth exploring.

Picnics amid the Ming ruins have been a favorite weekend activity among Beijing-based diplomats for nearly a century. The signs prohibiting this activity are largely ignored; if you do choose to picnic here, though, be sure to carry out all trash. ✉ *Near Changping, Changping County.*

> **WORD OF MOUTH**
>
> "In several visits to Beijing I have used Jane Yeo as a private guide. She has a masterful knowledge of Beijing, its history, and sights. Her English is excellent. She can accommodate single travelers as well as groups and will customize a tour to exactly what you would like to see. She also knows wonderful restaurants and places to shop. Her fees are reasonable. My expectations are always exceeded, and my traveling companions have also been pleased with her services. Her website is www. janeyeotours.com." —eastwest

Fahai Temple

20 km (12 mi) west of Beijing.

The stunning works of Buddhist mural art at Fahai Temple are among the most underappreciated sights in Beijing. Li Tong, a favored eunuch in the court of Emperor Zhengtong (1436–49), donated funds to construct Fahai Temple in 1443. The project was highly ambitious: Li Tong invited only celebrated imperial and court painters to decorate the temple. As a result, the murals in the only surviving chamber of that period, Daxiongbaodian (the Mahavira Hall), are considered the finest examples of Buddhist mural art from the Ming Dynasty. Sadly, statues of various Buddhas and one of Li Tong himself were destroyed during China's Cultural Revolution.

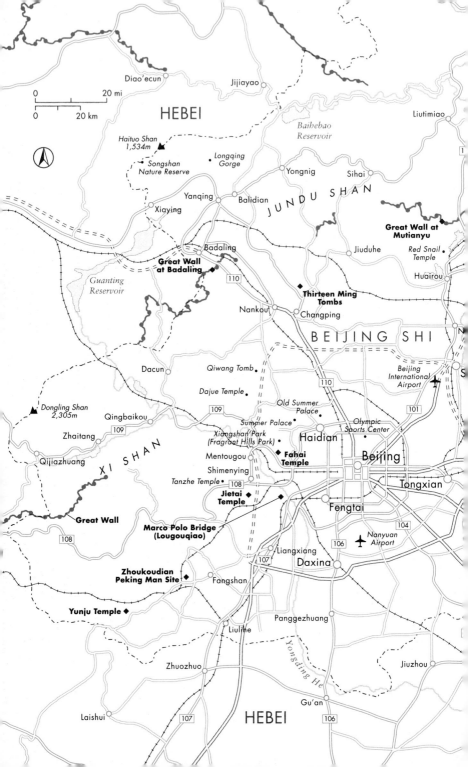

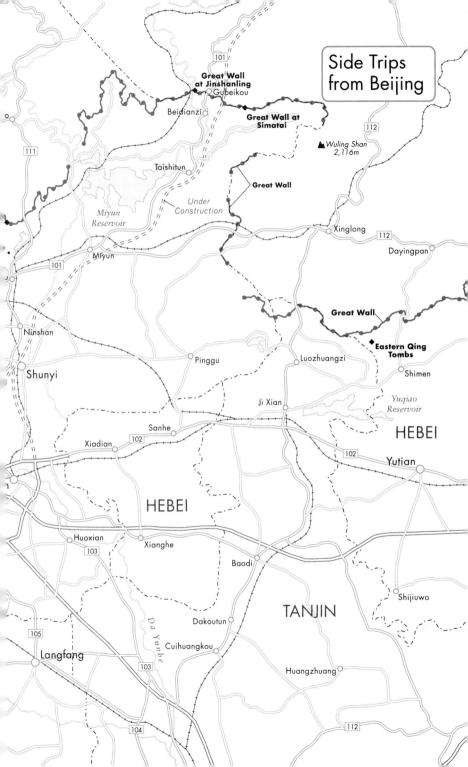

Side Trips
from Beijing

YESANPO & BEIDAIHE

Yesanpo is a sleepy village between Beijing and neighboring Hebei province. Go here if you're craving a slower-paced scene and some outdoor fun. The accommodations aren't first class, but there are lots of great things to do. Leave Beijing from Beijing West Station for the 2-hour ride. Traditionally, locals have houses with extra rooms for guests, and owners will strive to make your stay as comfortable as possible. A clean room with two beds and an air conditioner should run you no more than Y150. There are also a few hotels on the main street by the train station with rooms running approximately Y200. This scenic town is nestled in a valley. The area is best toured on horseback, and horses are available for rent at Y300 per day (with a guide), or Y100 for an hour or so. Yesanpo is also known for its whole barbecued lamb. At the time of this writing, trains leave Beijing West station at 6:38 AM and 2:40 PM. They come back twice daily.

Chairman Mao and the party's favorite spot for sand, sun, and seafood, **Beidaihe** is one of China's premier beach resorts (though it's definitely no Bali). This crowded spot is just a 2½-hour train ride from Beijing Station. Nearly every building in town has been converted to a hotel, and every restaurant has tanks of pick-your-own seafood lining the street.

The most famous of the nine murals in Mahavira Hall is a large-scale triptych featuring Guanyin (the Bodhisattva of Compassion) and Wenshu (the Bodhisattva of Marvelous Virtue and Gentle Majesty) in the center, and Poxian (the Buddha of Universal Virtue) on either side. The depiction of Guanyin follows the theme of "moon in water," which compares the Buddhist belief in the illusoriness of the material world to the reflection of the moon in the water. Typically painted with Guanyin are her legendary mount Jin Sun and her assistant Shancai Tongzi. Wenshu is often presented with a lion, symbolic of the bodhisattva's wisdom and strength of will, while Poxian is shown near a six-tusked elephant, each tusk representing one of the qualities that leads to enlightenment. On the opposite wall is the *Sovereign Sakra and Brahma* mural, with a panoply of characters from the Buddhist canon.

The murals were painted during the time of the European Renaissance, and though the subject matter is traditional, there are comparable experiments in perspective taking place in the depiction of the figures, as compared with examples from earlier dynasties. Also of note is a highly unusual decorative technique; many contours in the hall's murals, particularly on jewelry, armor, and weapons, have been set in bold relief by the application of fine gold threads.

The temple grounds are also beautiful, but of overriding interest are the murals themselves. Plans are in the works to limit access to the poorly lit original murals by one day creating a visitor center with well-illuminated

Continued on page 120

THE GREAT WALL

- One misconception is that the Great Wall is the only man-made structure visible from space. We say there's no better way to see it than up close.

- Sections of this magnificent, ancient wall were built from the 5th century BC until the 17th century AD.

- The Great Wall is the longest man-made structure on earth. It was designated a UNESCO World Heritage Site in 1987.

For some people, the Great Wall is the main reason for a trip to China; for any visitor to Beijing, it's a must-see. Originally intended to keep foreigners out, the world's most famous wall has become the icon of an increasingly open nation. One of the country's most accessible attractions, the Great Wall promises both breathtaking scenery and cultural illumination. As you explore this snaking structure, often compared to a dragon, try to imagine the monumental task of building such a behemoth, and how imposing it must have appeared from horseback, to a nomadic invader trying to penetrate its near-perfect strategic location. Even for those who have conquered it, the Great Wall still has a way of defying imagination.

Built by successive dynasties over two millennia, the Great Wall isn't one structure built at one time, but a series of defensive installations that shrank and grew. Especially vulnerable spots were more heavily fortified, while some mountainous regions were left un-walled altogether. The actual length of the wall remains a topic of considerable debate: at its longest, some estimates say the protective cordon spans 6,437 km (4,000 mi)—a distance wider than the United States. Although attacks, age, and pillaging (not to mention today's tourist invasion) have caused the crumbling of up to two-thirds of its length, new sections are being uncovered even today.

As kingdoms scrambled to protect themselves from marauding nomads, portions of wall cropped up, leading to a motley collection of northern borders. It was the first emperor of a unified China, Qin Shi-huang (circa 259–210 BC), founder of the Qin Dynasty, who linked these fortifications into a single network. By some accounts, Qin mustered nearly a million people, or one-fifth of China's workforce, to build this massive barricade, a mobilization that claimed countless lives and gave rise to many tragic folktales.

The Ming Dynasty fortified the wall like never before: for an estimated 5,000 km (3,107 mi), it stood 26 feet tall and 30 feet wide at its base. However, the wall failed to prevent the Manchu invasion that toppled the Ming in 1644. That historical failure hasn't tarnished the Great Wall's image, however. Although China once viewed it as a model of feudal oppression, the Great Wall is now touted as the national symbol. "Love China, Restore the Great Wall," declared Deng Xiaoping in 1984. Since then large sections have been repaired and opened to visitors, turning it also into a symbol of the tension between preservation and restoration in China.

AN ETERNAL WAIT

One legend concerns Lady Meng, whose husband was kidnapped on their wedding night and forced to work on the Great Wall. She traveled to the work site to await his return, believing her determination would bring him back. She waited so long that, in the end, she turned into a rock, which to this day stands at the head of the Great Wall in the beautiful seaside town of Qinhuangdao.

MATERIALS & TECHNIQUES

During the 2nd century BC, the wall was largely composed of packed earth and piled stone.

Some sections, like those in the Taklimakan Desert, were fortified with twigs, sand, and even rice (the jury's still out on whether workers' remains were used, as well).

The more substantial brick-and-mortar ruins that wind across the mountains north of Beijing date from the Ming Dynasty (14th–17th centuries). Some Ming mortar kilns still exist in valleys around Beijing.

YOUR GUIDE TO THE GREAT WALL

As a visitor to Beijing, you simply must set aside a day to visit one of the glorious Great Wall sites just outside the capital. The closest, Badaling, is just an hour from the city's center—in general, the farther you go, the more rugged the terrain. So choose your adventure wisely!

BADALING, the most accessible section of the Great Wall, is where most tours go. This location is rife with Disneylike commercialism, though: from the cable car you'll see both the heavily reconstructed portions of wall and crowds of souvenir stalls.

If you seek the wall less traveled, book a trip to fantastic **MUTIANYU**, which is about the same distance as Badaling from Beijing. You can enjoy much more solitude here, as well as amazing views from the towers and walls.

Mutianyu

Badaling

70 km; 1 hour by car

90 km; 1.25 hours by car

★ BEIJING

TRANSPORTATION

CARS: The easiest and most comfortable way to visit the wall is by private car. Though taxis are occasionally willing to make the trip to more accessible sections like Badaling and Mutianyu, most hotels can arrange a four-passenger car and an English-speaking driver for Y400–Y600 (about 8 hours). Settle details in advance, and remember that it's polite to invite your driver to eat meals with you. To ensure your driver doesn't return to Beijing without you, pay after the trip is over.

TOURS: In addition to the tour buses that gather around Tiananmen Square, most hotels and tour companies offer trips (in comfortable, air-conditioned buses or vans) to Badaling, Mutianyu, Simatai, and Jinshanling.
■ **TIP**→ **Smaller, private tours are generally more rewarding than large bus trips.** Trips will run between Y100 and Y500 per person, but costs vary depending on the group size, and can sometimes be negotiated. Wherever you're headed, book in advance.

TOUR OPERATORS

OUR TOP PICKS

■ **CITS (China International Tour Service)** runs bus tours to the Great Wall at Badaling (with Ming Tombs), and private tours to Badaling, Mutianyu, and Simatai. (Y370–Y640 per person) ✉ 28 Jianguomen Wai Dajie, Chaoyang District ☎ 010/6522-2991 ⊕ www.cits.net

■ **Beijing Service** leads private guided tours by car to Badaling, Mutianyu, and Simatai (Y260–Y680). ☎ 010/5166-7026 ✐ travel@beijingservice.com ⊕ www.beijingservice.com

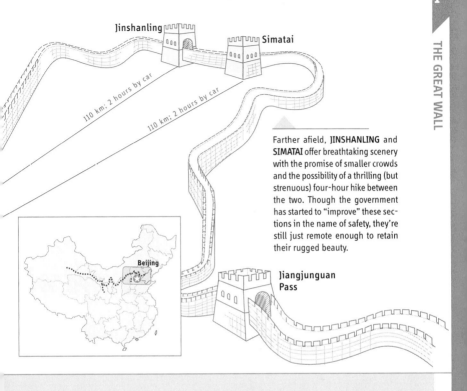

Jinshanling

Simatai

110 km; 2 hours by car

110 km; 2 hours by car

Beijing

Farther afield, **JINSHANLING** and **SIMATAI** offer breathtaking scenery with the promise of smaller crowds and the possibility of a thrilling (but strenuous) four-hour hike between the two. Though the government has started to "improve" these sections in the name of safety, they're still just remote enough to retain their rugged beauty.

Jiangjunguan Pass

■ **Great Wall Adventure Tour** organizes private bus and car trips to Jinshanling–Simatai (Y380–Y650) and Mutianyu (Y160–Y350). ☎ 138/1108-9985 ✍ greatwall@greatwalladventure.com ⊕ www.greatwalladventure.com

ADDITIONAL TOURS

■ **Abercrombie & Kent** also offers pricey personalized group tours to the wall. Call for prices. ☎ 010/6507-7125 ⊕ www.abercrombiekent.com

■ **Cycle China** runs good guided hiking tours of the unrestored Wall at Jiankou,

as well as personalized tours to Simatai and Mutianyu. (Y300–Y600). ☎ 010/6402-5653, ⊕ www.cyclechina.com

■ **David Spindler**, a Great Wall expert, runs private tours to various sites. Contact him for prices, schedules, and details through Wild China ☎ 010/6465-6602 Ext. 314 ✍ info@wildchina.com ⊕ www.wildchina.com

■ **Dragon Bus Tours**, which picks up at major hotels, has tours to Badaling (with Ming Tombs), Mutianyu, and a bus

to Simatai—with an occasional stop at a souvenir factory. (Y280-350; Y140 for Simatai) ☎ 010/6515-8565 ✍ service@beijinghighlights.com

■ **Gray Line/Panda Tours**, with branches in a dozen high-end hotels in Beijing, runs bus tours to Badaling (and Ming Tombs), Mutianyu, and Simatai—but beware of stops at souvenir factories. (Y280-Y590 per person) ✉ 5/F, Grand Rock Plaza, No. 13 Xinzhongxili ☎ 010/6525-8372 ⊕ www.pandatourchina.cn

GREAT WALL AT BADALING

GETTING THERE

Distance: 70 km (43 mi) northwest of Beijing, in Yanqing County

Tours: Beijing Service, CITS, Dragon Bus Tours, Gray Line/Panda Tours

By Car: A car for four people to Badaling should run no more than Y600 for eight hours, sometimes including a stop at the Thirteen Ming Tombs.

By Bus: It's hard to wander south of Tiananmen Square without encountering the many buses going to Badaling. Choose wisely: look for the 1 or 5 bus at Qianmen, across from the southeastern corner of Tiananmen Square (departs 6:30 AM–11:30 AM for Y12–Y18 per person).

FAST FACTS

Phone: 010/6912–1383

Hours: Daily 6:30 AM– 7 PM

Admission: Y40 Nov.–Mar.; Y45 Apr.–Nov.; cable car is an additional Y40 one-way, Y60 round-trip

Web Site: www.badaling. gov.cn

Only one hour by car from downtown Beijing, the Great Wall at Badaling is where visiting dignitaries go for a quick photo-op. Postcard views abound here, with large sections of the restored Ming Dynasty brick wall rising majestically to either side of the fort. In the distance, portions of the early-16th-century Great Wall disintegrate into more romantic but inaccessible ruins.

Badaling is convenient to the Thirteen Ming Tombs and outfitted with tourist-friendly facilities, so it's popular with tour groups and is thus often crowded, especially on weekends. ■ TIP→ **People with disabilities find access to the wall at Badaling better than elsewhere in the Beijing area.** You can either take the cable car to the top, or you can walk up the gently sloping steps, relying on handrails if necessary. On a clear day you can see for miles across leafy, undulating terrain from atop the battlements. The admission price also includes access to the China Great Wall Museum and the Great Wall Circle Vision Theater.

■ TIP→ **Most tours to Badaling will take you to the Thirteen Ming Tombs, as well. If you don't want a stop at the tombs—or at a tourist-trapping jade factory or herbal medicine center along the way—be sure to confirm the itinerary before booking.**

1

GREAT WALL AT MUTIANYU

GETTING THERE

Distance: 90 km (56 mi) northeast of Beijing, in Huairou County

Tours: CITS, Gray Line/ Panda Tours, Great Wall Adventure Tour

By Car: A car to Mutianyu should cost no more than Y500 for the day—it takes about an hour to get there.

By Bus: Take Bus 916/ 936 from Dongzhimen to Huairou (Y5). From there take a minibus to Mutianyu (Y25–Y30) or hire a taxi to take you there and back to the bus station (about Y50 each way, Y100–Y150 round-trip after bargaining). On weekends and national holidays, the tourist Bus 6 from outside the South Cathedral at Xuanwumen goes directly to Mutianyu (Y50, leaves 6:30–8:30 AM).

FAST FACTS

Phone: 010/6162–6873 or 010/6162–6022

Hours: Daily 7 AM– 6:30 PM

Admission: Y35 (students half-price); chairlift, Y35; cable car, Y50 one-way, Y55 with toboggan descent

★ **Fodor's Choice** Slightly farther from downtown Beijing than Badaling, the Great Wall at Mutianyu is more spectacular and, despite the occasional annoyances of souvenir stands, significantly less crowded. This long section of wall, first built during the Northern Qi Dynasty (6th century) and restored and rebuilt throughout history, can offer a solitary Great Wall experience, with unforgettable views of towers winding across mountains and woodlands. On a clear day, you'll swear you can see the deserts of Mongolia in the distance.

The lowest point on the wall is a strenuous one-hour climb above the parking lot. As an alternative, you can take a cable car on a breathtaking ride to the highest restored section (this is how President Bill Clinton ascended in 1998), from which several hiking trails descend. Take a gorgeous 1½-hour walk east to reach another cable car that returns to the same parking lot. Mutianyu is also known for its toboggan run.

■ TIP➔ **For those taking a car, the road from Huairou, a suburb of Beijing, to Mutianyu follows a river upstream and is lined with restaurants selling fresh trout. In addition, Hongluo Temple is a short drive from the bottom of the mountain.**

GREAT WALL AT SIMATAI

GETTING THERE

Distance: At around 110 km (68 mi) northeast of Beijing, Simatai is farther than Badaling and Mutianyu, but is well worth the trip—the road runs through lovely farmland, and few visitors make the trek.

Tours: Most hotels offer tours here, as do CITS, Gray Line/Panda Tours, and Great Wall Adventure Tour.

By Car: A car to Simatai should be no more than Y700 for the day. If you plan to hike from Jinshanling to Simatai, or vice versa, have your car drop you off at one and pick you up at the other.

By Bus: Take the early-morning Bus 916 from the bus station at Dongzhimen (Y20), starting at 6 AM. On weekends and holidays, a luxury bus leaves Qianmen at 8:30 AM (Y85 round-trip) and leaves Simatai at 3 PM.

FAST FACTS

Phone: 010/6903–5025 or 010/6903–1051

Hours: Daily 8 AM–5 PM

Admission: Y20; cable car, Y40 one-way, Y60 round-trip. If you hike to Jinshanling, you will have to buy another Y5 ticket at the border.

★ Remote and largely unrestored, the Great Wall at Simatai is ideal if you're seeking adventure. Near the frontier garrison at Gubeikou, the wall traverses towering peaks and hangs precariously above cliffs. Be prepared for no-handrails hiking, tough climbs, and unparalleled vistas. Several trails lead to the wall from the parking lot.

In summer, a cable car takes you two-thirds of the way up; from there it's a steep 40-minute climb to the summit. Heading east from the Miyun reservoir at a moderate pace will take you to Wangjing Ta, the 12th watchtower, after about 3 hours. For a longer hike, head west over the bridge toward the restored Jinshanling section.

The hike to Jinshanling is a strenuous 9 km (5.6 mi), usually taking around 4 hours up and down sublime sections of the wall. Be aware that crossing to Jinshanling costs Y5. People who wish to hike from one to the other often ask their driver to wait for them at their destination. (Note that hikers usually go from Jinshanling to Simatai, where buses back to Beijing are easier to find.)

GREAT WALL AT JINSHANLING

GETTING THERE

Distance: 110 km (68 mi) northeast from Beijing

Tours: CITS, Cycle China, Gray Line/Panda Tours, Great Wall Adventure Tour

By Car: A car should be no more than Y700; the ride is about two hours. If you plan to hike from Jinshanling to Simatai, as many do, it makes sense to be dropped off at Jinshanling and have your car pick you up at Simatai.

By Train: Take train L671, which departs at 7:25 AM from Beijing North Railway Station, to Gubeikou; there switch to a local minibus or taxi to Jinshanling.

By Bus: Take a minibus from Dongzhimen long-distance bus station to Miyun (Y8) and then change to a local bus or taxi. Or take a Chengde-bound bus from Dongzhimen and get off at Jinshanling; a cab can bring you to the entrance for Y10.

★ Though it lacks the rugged adventure of Simatai, Jinshanling is perhaps the least restored of the major Great Wall sections near Beijing, as well as the least visited. Besides being the starting point for a fantastic four-hour hike to Simatai, Jinshanling also serves as one of the few sections of the Great Wall on which you can camp overnight.

A starry night here is gorgeous and unforgettable—go with a tour group such as Cycle China. Don't forget to pack a piece of charcoal and paper to make rubbings of bricks that still bear the stamp of the date they were made.

FAST FACTS

Phone: 031/4883–0222 or 0138/3144–8986

Hours: Daily 8 AM–5 PM

Admission: Y30; Y50 for overnight stays. If you hike to Simatai, you will have to buy another Y5 ticket at the border.

GREAT WALL MARATHON

Not for the faint of heart, the Great Wall Marathon (and half marathon) takes place each May. The marathon covers approximately 6.5 km (4 mi) of the Great Wall, with the rest of the course running through lovely valleys in rural Tianjin.
⊕ www.great-wall-marathon.com

reproductions. For now, visitors stumble through the dark temple with rented flashlights (free with your ticket). Viewing the murals in this way, it's easy to imagine oneself as a sort of modern-day Indiana Jones unraveling a story of the Buddha as depicted in ancient murals of unrivaled beauty. Fahai Temple is only a short taxi ride from Beijing's Pingguoyuan subway station. ⊠ *Moshikou Lu, Shijingshan District, Beijing, take an approximate Y10-taxi ride from Pinguoyuan subway station directly to the temple* ☎ *010/8871–5776* 🎫 *Y20* ☉ *Daily 9–4:30.*

Eunuchs have played an important role throughout Chinese history, often holding great influence over affairs of state, yet surprisingly little is known about them. The **Beijing Eunuch Culture Exhibition Hall,** near the magnificent **Tian Yi Mu,** begins to redress this lack of information. Tian Yi (1534–1605) was only nine when he was castrated and sent into the service of the Ming emperor Jiajing. He spent the next 63 years of his life serving three emperors and rose to one of the highest ranks in the land, the Director of Ceremonies. His tomb, though not as magnificent as the Thirteen Ming Tombs, nonetheless befits a man of such high social status. Particularly noteworthy in the tomb complex are the stone carvings around the base of the central mound depicting ancient anecdotes. The four smaller tombs on either side belong to other eunuchs who wished to pay tribute to Tian Yi by being buried in the same compound with him.

The small exhibition hall at the front of the tomb complex contains limited background information, most of it in Chinese, about famous eunuchs. Keep an eye out for the ancient Chinese character meaning "to castrate," which resembles two knives, one inverted, side by side. Also here is a list of all the temples in Beijing that were founded by eunuchs. The hall and tomb are a five-minute walk from Fahai Temple; just ask people the way to Tian Yi Mu. ⊠ *80 Moshikou Lu, Shijingshan District, Beijing* ☎ *010/8872–4148* 🎫 *Y8* ☉ *Daily 9–5.*

Jietai Temple

★ *35 km (22 mi) west of Beijing.*

On a wooded hill west of Beijing, Jietai Temple is one of China's most famous ancient Buddhist sites. Its four main halls occupy terraces on a gentle slope up to Ma'an Shan (Saddle Hill). Originally built in AD 622, the temple complex expanded over the centuries and grew to its current scale in a major renovation conducted by devotees during the Qing Dynasty (1644–1912). The temple buildings, plus three magnificent bronze Buddhas in the Mahavira Hall, date from this period. There is also a huge, potbellied Maitreya Buddha carved from the roots of what must have been a truly enormous tree. To the right of this hall, just above twin pagodas, is the Ordination Terrace, a platform built of white marble and topped with a massive bronze Sakyamuni (Buddha) seated on a lotus flower. Tranquil courtyards, where ornate stelae and well-kept gardens bask beneath the Scholar Tree and other ancient pines, add to the temple's beauty. Many modern devotees from Beijing visit the temple on weekends. ⊠ *Mentougou County* ☎ *010/6980–6611* ✉ *Y35* ⊙ *Daily 8–5.*

EN ROUTE Farther along the road past Jietai Temple, **Tanzhe Temple** is a Buddhist complex nestled in a grove of *zhe* (cudrania) trees. Established around AD 400 and once home to more than 500 monks, Tanzhe was heavily damaged during the Cultural Revolution; it has since been restored, but if you look closely at some of the huge stone tablets, or *bei*, littered around the site you'll see that many of the inscriptions have been destroyed. The complex makes an ideal side trip from Jietai Temple or Marco Polo Bridge. ⊠ *Mentougou County* ☎ *010/6086–2500* ✛ *10 km (6 mi) northeast of Jietai Temple, 45 km (28 mi) west of Beijing* ✉ *Y35* ⊙ *Daily 8–5.*

Marco Polo Bridge

16 km (10 mi) southwest of Beijing's Guanganmen Gate.

Built in 1192 and reconstructed after severe flooding during the Qing Dynasty, this impressive span—known as Marco Polo Bridge because it was praised by the Italian wayfarer—is Beijing's oldest bridge. Its 11 segmented stone arches cross the Yongding River on what was once the imperial highway that linked Beijing with central China. The bridge's marble balustrades support nearly 485 carved stone lions that decorate elaborate handrails. Note the giant stone slabs that comprise the bridge's original roadbed. Carved imperial stelae at either end of the span commemorate the bridge and surrounding scenery.

The Marco Polo Bridge is best remembered in modern times as the spot where invading Japanese armies clashed with Chinese soldiers on June 7, 1937. The assault began Japan's brutal eight-year occupation of eastern China, which ended with Tokyo's surrender at the end of World War II. The bridge has become a popular field-trip destination for Beijing students. On the Beijing side of the span is the **Memorial Hall of the War of Resistance Against Japan.** Below the bridge on the opposite shore, local entrepreneurs rent horses (the asking price is Y120 per hour, but you should bargain) and lead tours of the often-dry grassy riverbed. ⊠ *Near Xidaokou, Fengtai District, Beijing* ☎ *010/8389–3919* ✉ *Y10* ⊙ *Daily 8:30–6.*

Zhoukoudian Peking Man Site

48 km (30 mi) southwest of Beijing.

This area of lime mines and craggy foothills ranks among the world's great paleontological sites (and served as the setting for Amy Tan's *The Bonesetter's Daughter*). In 1929 anthropologists, drawn to Zhoukoudian by apparently human "dragon bones" found in a Beijing apothecary, unearthed a complete cranium and other fossils dubbed homo erectus pekinensis, or Peking Man. These early remains, believed to be nearly 700,000 years old, suggest (as do similar homo-erectus discoveries in Indonesia) that humankind's most recent ancestor originated in Asia, not Europe (though today some scientists posit that humans evolved in Africa first and migrated to Asia). A large-scale excavation in the early 1930s further unearthed six skullcaps and other hominid remains, stone tools, evidence of fire, plus a multitude of animal bones, many at the bottom of a large sinkhole believed to be a trap for woolly rhinos and other large game. Sadly, the Peking Man fossils disappeared under mysterious circumstances during World War II, leaving researchers only plaster casts to contemplate. Subsequent digs at Zhoukoudian have yielded nothing equivalent to Peking Man, although archaeologists haven't yet abandoned the search. Trails lead to several hillside excavation sites. A small museum showcases a few (dusty) Peking Man statues, a collection of Paleolithic artifacts, two mummies, and some fine animal fossils, including a bear skeleton and a saber-toothed tiger skull. Because of the importance of Peking Man and the potential for other finds in the area, Zhoukoudian is a UNESCO World Heritage Site, but it may not be of much interest to those without a particular inclination for the subject. If you should find yourself here with little to do after your museum visit and the few dig locations, consider a little hike into the surrounding hills, which are named the Dragon Bone Mountains. ✉ *Zhoukoudian* ☎ *010/6930–1272* 💴 *Y30* ⊙ *Daily 9:30–5.*

Yunju Temple

75 km (47 mi) southwest of Beijing.

Yunju Temple is best known for its mind-boggling collection of 14,278 minutely carved Buddhist tablets. To protect the Buddhist canon from destruction by Taoist emperors, the devout Tang-era monk Jing Wan carved Buddhist scriptures into stone slabs that he hid in sealed caves in the cliffs of a mountain. Jing Wan spent 30 years creating these tablets until his death in AD 637; his disciples continued his work for the next millennium into the 17th century, thereby compiling one of the most extensive Buddhist libraries in the world. A small pagoda at the center of the temple complex commemorates the remarkable monk. Although the tablets were originally stored inside Shijing Mountain behind the temple, they are now housed in rooms built along the temple's southern perimeter.

Four central prayer halls, arranged along the hillside above the main gate, contain impressive Ming-era bronze Buddhas. The last in this row, the Dabei Hall, displays the spectacular *Thousand-Arm Avalokiteshvara*. This 13-foot-tall bronze sculpture—which actually has 24 arms and 5 heads and stands in a giant lotus flower—is believed to embody boundless compassion. A group of pagodas, led by the 98-foot-tall Northern Pagoda, is all that remains of the original Tang complex. These pagodas are remarkable for their Buddhist reliefs and ornamental patterns. Heavily damaged during the Japanese occupation and again by Maoist radicals in the 1960s, the temple complex remains under renovation. ✉ *Off Fangshan Lu, Nanshangle Xiang, Fangshan County* ☎ *010/6138–9612* 💴 *Y40* ⊙ *Daily 8:30–5:30.*

Eastern Qing Tombs

Fodor'sChoice *125 km (78 mi) east of Beijing.*
★

Modeled on the Thirteen Ming Tombs, the Eastern Qing Tombs replicate the Ming spirit ways, walled tomb complexes, and subterranean burial chambers. But they're even more extravagant in their scale and grandeur, and far less touristy. The ruins contain the remains of 5 emperors, 14 empresses, and 136 imperial concubines, all laid to rest in a broad valley chosen by Emperor Shunzhi (1638–61) while on a hunting expedition. By the Qing's collapse in 1911, the tomb complex covered some 18 square mi (46 sq km) of farmland and forested hillside, making it the most expansive burial ground in all China.

The Eastern Qing Tombs are in much better repair than their older Ming counterparts. Although several of the tomb complexes have undergone extensive renovation, none is overdone. Peeling paint, grassy courtyards, and numerous stone bridges and pathways convey a sense of the area's original grandeur. Often, visitors are so few that you may feel as if you've stumbled upon an ancient ruin unknown beyond the valley's farming villages.

Of the nine tombs open to the public, two are not to be missed. The first is **Yuling,** the resting place of the Qing Dynasty's most powerful sovereign, Emperor Qianlong (1711–99), who ruled China for 59 years. Beyond the outer courtyards, Qianlong's burial chamber is accessible from inside Stela Hall, where an entry tunnel descends some 65 feet (20 m) into the ground and ends at the first of three elaborately carved marble gates. Beyond, exquisite carvings of Buddhist images and sutras rendered in Tibetan adorn the tomb's walls and ceiling. Qianlong was laid to rest, along with his empress and two concubines, in the third and final marble vault, amid priceless offerings looted by warlords early in the 20th century.

Dingdongling was built for the infamous Empress Dowager Cixi (1835–1911). Known for her failure to halt Western-imperialist encroachment, Cixi once spent funds allotted to strengthen China's navy on a traditional stone boat for the lake at the Summer Palace. Her burial compound, reputed to have cost 72 tons of silver, is the most elaborate (if not the largest) at the Eastern Qing Tombs. Many of its stone carvings are considered significant because the phoenix, which symbolized the female, is level with, or even above, the imperial (male) dragon—a feature, ordered, no doubt, by the empress herself. A peripheral hall paneled in gold leaf displays some of the luxuries amassed by Cixi and her entourage, including embroidered gowns, jewelry, imported cigarettes, and even a coat for one of her dogs. In a bow to tourist kitsch, the compound's main hall contains a wax statue of Cixi sitting Buddha-like on a lotus petal flanked by a chambermaid and a eunuch.

The Eastern Qing Tombs are a two- to three-hour drive from the capital. The rural scenery is dramatic, and the trip is one of the best full-day excursions outside Beijing. Consider bringing a bed sheet, a bottle

TIANJIN

Tianjin is a huge port city of 10 million people, just 96 km (60 mi) from Beijing, which is known to Beijingers for its *baozi* (steamed buns), wonderful antiques market, and international architecture, including British, French, American, German, Japanese, Russian, Italian, Austrian-Hungarian, and Belgian examples. For the best antique shopping in China, head to Tianjin on a Wednesday evening train, check into your hotel, have dinner, and go to bed so you can wake up early for the **Shenyangdao Antiques Market,** which opens at 4 AM every Thursday and is well picked over by mid-morning. When buying at Shenyangdao, be wary of items dubbed genuine antiques. They do exist, but are very rare; even the prettiest, oldest-looking pieces can be fake. Some are made with antique wood that has been recently recycled into "antiques" by skilled artisans. The casual collector should remember: Buy things because you like them, not because you think they are inherently valuable. Feel free to haggle relentlessly. Trains (Y30) to Tianjin leave Beijing Station every hour from 6 AM until 5:30 PM, and buses (Y25) leave around the clock.

of wine, and boxed lunches, as the grounds are ideal for a picnic. ⊠ *Near Malanguan, Hebei province, Zunhua County* ☎ *0315/694–5348* ⚏ *Y80* ☺ *Daily 8:30–5.*

BEIJING ESSENTIALS

Transportation

By Victoria
Patience

BY AIR

Beijing is one of China's three major international hubs, along with Shanghai and Hong Kong. You can catch a nonstop flight here from New York (13¾ hours), Chicago (13½ hours), Sydney (11½ hours), Los Angeles (13 hours), and London (11 hours). Note that Air China is the only operator that runs nonstop Los Angeles and London flights. Otherwise flights from Los Angeles generally stop in Tokyo, Seoul, Hong Kong, or Vancouver, taking between 17 and 25 hours.

The efficient Beijing Capital International Airport (PEK) is 27 km (17 mi) northeast of the city center. There are two terminals, connected by a walkway. China Southern's domestic flights operate out of Terminal 1; all other airlines out of Terminal 2. If you can't find your flight on the departure board when you arrive, check that you're in the correct terminal. Beijing's airport tax (enigmatically known as the "airport construction fee") is Y90 for international flights and Y50 for domestic. You pay before check-in by purchasing a coupon from the booths inside the terminal, which is then collected at the entrance to the main departure hall. Clearing customs and immigration can take a while, especially in the morning, so make sure you arrive at least two hours before your scheduled flight time.

Airline Contacts Air Canada ☎ 010/6468-2001 ⊕ www.aircanada.com. **Air China** ☎ 010/6601-7755 ⊕ www.airchina.com. **Air France** ☎ 010/6588-1388 ⊕ www.airfrance.com. **All Nippon** ☎ 010/6590-9191 ⊕ www.fly-ana.com. **Asiana** ☎ 010/6468-4000 ⊕ www.us.flyasiana.com. **Austrian Airlines** ☎ 010/6462-2161 ⊕ www.austrianair.com. **British Airways** ☎ 010/6512-4070 ⊕ www.ba.com. **Cathay Pacific** ☎ 010/8486-8532 ⊕ www.cathaypacific.com. **China Eastern** ☎ 010/6468-1166 ⊕ www.ce-air.com. **China Southern** ☎ 010/6459-0539 or 010/6459-6490 ⊕ www.cs-air.com/en. **Continental Airlines** ☎ 800/523-3273 for U.S. and Mexico reservations, 800/231-0856 for international reservations ⊕ www.continental.com. **Delta Airlines** ☎ 800/221-1212 for U.S. reservations, 800/241-4141 for international reservations ⊕ www.delta.com. **Emirates** ☎ Shanghai: 021/3222-9999 ⊕ www.emirates.com. **Japan Airlines** ☎ 010/6513-0888 ⊕ www.jal.com. **KLM** ☎ 010/6505-3505 ⊕ www.klm.com. **Lufthansa** ☎ 010/6468-8838 ⊕ www.lufthansa.com. **Korean Air** ☎ 010/6505-0088 ⊕ www.koreanair.com. **Northwest** ☎ 010/6505-3505 ⊕ www.nwa.com. **Northwest Airlines** ☎ 800/225-2525 ⊕ www.nwa.com. **Singapore Airlines** ☎ 010/6505-2233 ⊕ www.singaporeair.com. **Thai Airways** ☎ 010/8515-0088 ⊕ www.thaiair.com. **United** ☎ 010/6463-1111, 800/810-8282 in China ⊕ www.ual.com. **United Airlines** ☎ 800/864-8331 for U.S. reservations, 800/538-2929 for international reservations ⊕ www.united.com.

Airport Information Beijing Capital International Airport (PEK) ☎ 010/6456-3604 ⊕ www.bcia.com.cn.

GROUND TRANSPORT The easiest way to get from the airport to Beijing is by taxi. In addition, most major hotels have representatives at the airport able to arrange a car or minivan. When departing from Beijing by plane, prebook airport transport through your hotel.

When you arrive, head for the clearly labeled taxi line just outside the terminal, beyond a small covered parking area. The (usually long) line moves quickly. Ignore offers from touts trying to coax you away from the line—they're privateers looking to rip you off. At the head of the line, a dispatcher will give you your taxi's number, useful in case of complaints or forgotten luggage. Prices per kilometer are displayed on the side of the cab. Insist that drivers use their meters, and do not negotiate a fare. If the driver is unwilling to comply, feel free to change taxis.

Most of the taxis serving the airport are large-model cars, with a flag-fall of Y12 (good for 3½ km) plus Y2 per additional kilometer. The trip to the center of Beijing costs around Y100, including the Y10 toll for the airport expressway. If you're caught in rush-hour traffic, expect standing surcharges. In light traffic it takes about 40 minutes to reach the city center, during rush-hour expect a 1-hour cab ride. After 11 PM, taxis impose a 20% late-night surcharge.

Air-conditioned airport shuttle buses are a cheaper way of getting into town. There are six numbered routes, all of which leave from outside the arrivals area. Tickets cost Y16—buy them from the ticket booth just inside the arrivals hall. Most services run every 15 to 30 minutes. There's a detailed route map on the airport Web site.

BY BUS

China has fabulous luxury long-distance buses with air-conditioning and movies. However, buying tickets on them can be complicated if you don't speak Chinese and you may end up on a cramped school bus. Taking a train or an internal flight is often much easier. Buses depart from the city's several long-distance bus stations. The main ones are: Dongzhimen (Northeast); Muxiyuan (at Haihutun in the South); Beijiao, also called Deshengmen (North); and Majuan or Guangqumen (East).

Unless you know Beijing well, public buses aren't the best choice for getting around. There are hundreds of routes, which are hot and crowded in summer and cold and crowded in winter. Just getting on and off can be, quite literally, a fight. Pickpocketing is rife so watch your belongings very carefully.

The Beijing Public Transportation Corporation is the city's largest bus service provider. Routes 1 to 199 are regular city buses, and cost a flat fare of Y1. Routes 201 through 212 only run at night, costing Y2. Routes numbered 300 or higher are suburban, and fares depend on how far you're going—have your destination written in Chinese, as you have to tell the conductor so they can calculate your fare. Newer, air-conditioned buses have an 800 route number; prices vary, but start at Y3. They also run more expensive tourist buses going to sights in and around the city— to the Summer Palace and Great Wall, for example. Prices start at Y40.

🚌 Bus Information **Beijiao** ✉ Deshengmenwai Dajie, Xicheng District ☎ 010/ 6204-7096. **Dongzhimen** ✉ Dongzhimenwaixie Jie, Chaoyang District ☎ 010/6467-4995 or 010/6460-8131. **Muxiyuan** ✉ Yongwai Chezan Lu, Fengtai District ☎ 010/6726-7149 or 010/6722-4641. **Majuan** ✉ Guangqumenwai Dajie, Chaoyang District ☎ 010/ 6771-7620 or 010/6771-7622. **Xizhimen** ✉ 2 Haidian Tou Duicun ☎ 010/6217-6075.
🚌 **Beijing Public Transportation Corporation** ⊕ www.bjbus.com.

BY SUBWAY

With street-level traffic getting more crazed by the minute, Beijing's quick and efficient subway system is an excellent way to get about town. After operating for years with only two lines, the network is growing exponentially—seven new lines are under construction, and a couple more are being planned.

At this writing, there are four lines open. Line 1 (red) runs east–west under Chang'an Jie, crossing through the heart of the city. The circle line, or Line 2 (blue), runs roughly under the Second Ring Road. There are interchange stations between lines 1 and 2 at Fuxingmen and Jianguomen. The two remaining lines are mainly used by commuters and are less useful for sightseeing. The Batong Line extends Line 1 eastward, whereas Line 13 loops north off Line 2. The first north–south line, Line 5, is due to open in mid-2007, and two other lines are scheduled to open in time for the 2008 Olympics.

Subway stations are marked by blue signs with a "D" (for *di tie,* or subway) in a circle. Signs are not always obvious, so be prepared to hunt around for entrances or ask directions; *Di tie zhan zai nar?* (Where's the subway station?) is a useful phrase to remember.

Stations are usually clean and safe, as are trains. Navigating the subway is very straightforward: station names are clearly displayed in Chinese and pinyin, and there are maps in each station. Once on board, each stop is clearly announced on a loudspeaker.

TICKET/PASS PRICE	
Single fare anywhere on lines 1 and 2	Y3
Single fare on Line 13	Y3
Single fare on Batong Line	Y2
Single transfer ticket lines 1, 2, and 13	Y5
Single transfer ticket lines 1, 2, and Batong	Y4

BY TAXI

Taxis are plentiful, easy to spot, and by far the most comfortable way to get around Beijing, though increasing traffic means they're not always the fastest. There's a flagfall of Y10 for the first 4 km (2½ mi), then Y2 per kilometer thereafter. After 11 PM flagfall goes up to Y11, and there's a 20% surcharge per kilometer. Drivers usually know the terrain well, but most don't speak English; having your destination written in Chinese is a good idea. (Keep a card with the name of your hotel on it for the return trip.) Hotel doormen can also help you tell the driver where you're going. It's a good idea to study a map and have some idea where you are, as some drivers will take you for a ride—a much longer one—if they think they can get away with it.

🚩 Complaints **Transport Complaints Unit** ☎ 2889-9999.

BY TRAIN

China's enormous rail network is one of the world's busiest. Trains are usually safe and run strictly to schedule. Although there are certain intricacies to buying tickets, once you've got one, trips are generally hassle-free. Beijing is a major rail hub. Services to all over China leave from its four huge stations. The Trans-Siberian Railway and services to Shanghai, among others, leave from Beijing Zhan, the main station. Trains to Hong Kong and to areas in the west and south of China leave from Beijing Xi Zhan (West). Most of the Z-series trains (nonstop luxury services) come into these two stations. Lesser lines to the north and east of the country leave from Beijing Bei Zhan (North) and Beijing Dong Zhan (East).

You can buy most tickets 10 days in advance; 2 to 3 days ahead is usually enough time, except during the three national holidays—Chinese New Year (2 days in mid-January to February), Labor Day (May 1), and National Day (October 1). If you can, avoid traveling then—-tickets sell out weeks in advance.

The cheapest rates are at the train station itself; there are special ticket offices for foreigners at both the Beijing Zhan (1st floor) and Beijing Xi Zhan (2nd floor). You can only pay using cash. Most travel agents, including CITS, can book tickets for a small surcharge (Y20 to Y50), saving you the hassle of going to the station. You can also buy tickets through online retailers like China Train Ticket. They'll deliver the tickets to your hotel (keep in mind you often end up paying double the station rate).

Overpriced dining cars serve meals that are often inedible, so you'd do better to make use of the massive thermoses of boiled water in each compartment and take along your own noodles or instant soup, as the locals do.

Trains are always crowded, but you are guaranteed your designated seat, though not always the overhead luggage rack. Note that theft on trains is increasing; on overnight trains, sleep with your valuables or else keep them on the inside of the bunk.

You can find out just about everything about Chinese train travel at Seat 61's fabulous Web site. China Highlights has a searchable online timetable for major train routes. The tour operator Travel China Guide has an English-language Web site that can help you figure out train schedules and fares.

⚠ **Note that the information numbers at train stations are usually only in Chinese.**

🚩 **Beijing Bei Zhan** ✉ North Station, 1 Xizhimenwai Beibinhelu, Xicheng District ☎ 010/6223-1003. **Beijing Nan Zhan** ✉ South Station, Yongdingmen, Chongwen District ☎ 010/6303-0031. **Beijing Xi Zhan** ✉ West Station, Lianhuachi Dong Lu, Haidian District ☎ 010/5182-6253. **Beijing Zhan** ✉ Main Station, Beijing Zhan Jie, Dongcheng District ☎ 010/6563-3262. **China Highlights** ⊕ www.chinahighlights.com/china-trains/index.htm. **Seat 61** ⊕ www.seat61.com/China.htm. **Travel China Guide** ⊕ www.travelchinaguide.com/china-trains/index.htm.

Contacts & Resources

BANKS & CURRENCY EXCHANGE

Out of the Chinese banks, your best bet for ATMs is the Bank of China, which accepts most foreign cards. That said, machines frequently refuse to give cash for mysterious reasons. Move on and try another. Citibank and HSBC have lots of branches in Beijing, and accept all major cards. On-screen instructions appear automatically in English.

The Chinese currency is officially called the yuan (Y), and is also known as *renminbi* (RMB), or "People's Money." You may also hear it called *kuai,* an informal expression like "buck." It's pegged to the dollar at around Y8.

Both old and new styles of bills circulate simultaneously in China, and many denominations have both coins and bills. The Bank of China issues bills in denominations of 1 (burgundy), 2 (green), 5 (brown or purple), 10 (turquoise), 20 (brown), 50 (blue or occasionally yellow), and 100 (red). There are Y1 coins, too. The Yuan subdivides into 10-cent units called *jiao* or *mao*; these come in bills and coins of 1, 2, and 5. The smallest denomination is the *fen,* which comes in coins (and occasionally tiny notes) of 1, 2, and 5. Counterfeiting is rife in China, and even small stores inspect notes with ultraviolet lamps. Change can be a problem—don't expect much success paying for a Y13 purchase with a Y100 note, for example.

Exchange rates in China are fixed by the government daily, so it's equally good at branches of the Bank of China, at big department stores, or at your hotel's exchange desk, which has the added advantage of often being open 24 hours a day. Any lower rates are illegal, so you're exposing yourself to scams. A passport is required. Hold on to your exchange receipt, which you need to convert your extra yuan back into dollars.

COMMUNICATIONS

INTERNET Beijing is a very Internet-friendly place for travelers with laptop computers. Most mid- to high-end hotels have in-room Internet access—if the hotel doesn't have a server you can usually access a government-provided ISP, which only charges you for the phone call. Wi-Fi is growing exponentially. Café chains like Starbucks are good places to try.

⚠ **Remember that there is strict government control of the Internet in China. There's usually no problem with Web-based mail, but you may be unable to access news and even blogging sites.**

Most hotels usually have a computer with Internet access that you can use. Internet cafés are ubiquitous; it's an unstable business and new ones open and close all the time—ask your hotel for a recommendation. Prices vary considerably. Near the northern university districts you could pay as little as Y2 to Y3 per hour; slicker downtown places could cost 10 times that.

🔲 Cybercafes ⊕ www.cybercafes.com lists over 4,000 Internet cafés worldwide.

PHONES The country code for China is 86; the city code for Beijing is 10, and the city code for Shanghai is 21. To call China from the United States or Canada, dial the international access code (011), followed by the country code (86), the area or city code, and the eight-digit phone number.

Numbers beginning with 800 within China are toll-free. Note that a call from China to a toll-free number in the United States or Hong Kong is a full-tariff international call.

CALLING WITHIN CHINA The Chinese phone system is cheap and efficient. You can make local and long-distance calls from your hotel or any public phone on the street. Some pay phones accept coins, but it's easier to buy an IC calling card, available at convenience stores and newsstands (*see* ⇨ Calling Cards, *below*). Local calls are generally free from landlines, though your hotel might charge a nominal rate. Long-distance rates in China are very low. Calling from your hotel room is a viable option, as hotels can only add a 15% service charge.

Beijing's city code is 010, and Beijing phone numbers have eight digits. When calling within the city, you don't need to use "010." In general, city codes appear written with a 0 in front of them; if not, you need to add this when calling another city within China.

For directory assistance, dial 114, or 2689–0114 for help in English (though you may not get through). If you want information for other cities, dial the city code followed by 114 (note that this is considered a long-distance call). For example, if you're in Beijing and need directory assistance for a Shanghai number, dial 021–114. The operators do not speak English, so if you don't speak Chinese you're best off asking your hotel for help.

To make long-distance calls from a public phone you need an IC card (⇨ Calling Cards, *below*). To place a long-distance call, dial 0, the city code, and the eight-digit phone number.

CALLING OUTSIDE CHINA To make an international call from within China, dial 00 (the international access code within China) and then the country code, area code, and phone number. The country code for the United States is 1.

IDD (international direct dialing) service is available at all hotels, post offices, major shopping centers, and airports. By international standards prices aren't unreasonable, but it's vastly cheaper to use a long-distance calling card, known as an IP card (⇨ Calling Cards, *below*), whose rates also beat AT&T, MCI, and Sprint hands-down.

CALLING CARDS Calling cards are a key part of the Chinese phone system. There are two kinds: the IC card (integrated circuit; *àicei ka*), for local and domestic long-distance calls on pay phones; and the IP card (Internet protocol; *aipi ka*) for international calls from any phone. You can buy both at post offices, convenience stores, and street vendors.

IC cards come in values of Y20, Y50, and Y100 and can be used in any pay phone with a card slot—most Beijing pay phones have them. Local calls using them cost around Y0.30 a minute, and less on weekends and after 6 PM.

To use IP cards, you first dial a local access number. This is often free from hotels, however at public phones you need an IC card to dial the access number. You then enter a card number and PIN, and finally the phone number complete with international dial codes. When calling from a pay phone both cards' minutes are deducted at the same time, one for local access (IC card) and one for the long-distance call you placed (IP card). There are countless different card brands; China Unicom is one that's usually reliable. IP cards come with values of Y20, Y30, Y50, and Y100. However, the going rate for them is up to half that, so bargain vendors down.

MOBILE PHONES If you have a GSM phone, pick up a local SIM card (*sim ka*) from any branch of China Mobile or China Unicom. You'll be presented with a list of possible phone numbers, with varying prices—an "unlucky" phone number (one with lots of 4s) could be as cheap as Y50, whereas an auspicious one (full of 8s) could fetch Y300 or more. You then buy prepaid cards to charge minutes onto your SIM—do this straight away as you need credit to receive calls. Local calls to landlines cost Y0.25 a minute, and to cell phones Y0.60. International calls from cell phones are very expensive. Remember to bring an adapter for your phone charger. You can also buy cheap handsets from China Mobile. If you're planning to stay even a couple of days this is probably cheaper than renting a phone.

Beijing Limo rents cell phones, which they can deliver to your hotel or at the airport. Renting a handset starts at $5 a day, and you buy a prepaid package with a certain amount of call time; prices start at $50. Beijing Impression travel agency rents handsets at similar rates, and you buy a regular prepaid card for calls.

Beijing Impression ☏ 010/8446-7137 ⊕ www.beijingimpression.com. **Beijing Limo** ☏ 010/6546-1588 ⊕ www.beijinglimo.com. **Cellular Abroad** ☏ 800/287-5072 ⊕ www.cellularabroad.com rents and sells GMS phones and sells SIM cards that work in many countries. **China Mobile** ☏ English-language assistance 1860 ⊕ www.chinamobile.com is China's main mobile-service provider. **China Unicom** ☏ English-language assistance 1001 is China's second-largest main mobile-phone company. **Mobal** ☏ 888/888-9162 ⊕ www.mobalrental.com rents mobiles and sells GSM phones (starting at $49) that will operate in 140 countries. Per-call rates vary throughout the world. **Planet Fone** ☏ 888/988-4777 ⊕ www.planetfone.com rents cell phones, but the per-minute rates are expensive.

EMERGENCIES

The best place to head in a medical emergency is the Beijing United Family Health Center, which has 24-hour emergency services. Asia Emergency Assistance Center (AEA) has 24-hour emergency and pharmacy assistance. SOS is another international clinic with a good reputation; they also arrange Medivac.

Beijing has different numbers for each emergency service, though staff often don't speak English. If in doubt, call the U.S. embassy first: staff members are available 24 hours a day to help handle emergencies and facilitate communication with local agencies.

Doctors & Dentists Asia Emergency Assistance Center ✉ 2-1-1 Tayuan Diplomatic Office Bldg., 14 Liangmahe Nan Lu, Chaoyang District ☏ 010/6462-9112 during office hrs, 010/6462-9100 after hrs. **Beijing United Family Health Center** ✉ 2 Jiangtai Lu, near Lido Hotel, Chaoyang District ☏ 010/6433-3960, 010/6433-2345 for emergencies ⊕ www.unitedfamilyhospitals.com. **SOS International** ✉ Building C, BITIC Leasing Center, 1 North Road, Xing Fu San Cun, Chaoyang District ☏ 010/6462-9112 ⊕ www.internationalsos.com.

U.S. Embassy ✉ 3 Xiushui Bei Jie, Chaoyang District ☏ 010/6532-3431 Ext. 229 or 010/6532-3831 Ext. 264 🖷 010/6532-2483 ⊕ beijing.usembassy-china.org.cn.

General Emergency Contacts Fire ☏ 119. **Police** ☏ 110. **Medical Emergency** ☏ 120. **Traffic Accident** ☏ 122.

Hospitals & Clinics Asia Emergency Assistance Center (private) ✉ 2-1-1 Tayuan Diplomatic Office Bldg., 14 Liangmahe Nan Lu, Chaoyang District ☏ 010/6462-9112 during office hrs, 010/6462-9100 after hrs. **Beijing United Family Health Center** (private) ✉ 2 Jiangtai Lu, near Lido Hotel, Chaoyang District ☏ 010/6433-3960, 010/6433-2345 for emergencies ⊕ www.unitedfamilyhospitals.com. **China Academy of Medical Science (Peking Union Hospital)** (public) ✉ 1 Shui Fu Yuan, Dongcheng District ☏ 010/6529-5120. **Hong Kong International Medical Clinic** (private) ✉ Office Tower, 9th fl., Hong Kong Macau Center-Swissotel, 2 Chaoyangmen Bei Da Jie, Chaoyang District ☏ 010/6553-2288 ⊕ www.hkclinic.com. **Sino-Japanese Friendship Hospital** (public) ✉ Ying Hua Dong Lu, He Ping Li ☏ 010/6422-2965. **SOS International** (private) ✉ Building

C, BITIC Leasing Center, 1 North Road, Xing Fu San Cun, Chaoyang District ☎010/6462-9112 ⊕ www.internationalsos.com.

🔳 Pharmacies The most reliable places to buy prescription medication and over-the-counter remedies are the 24-hour pharmacies at the Beijing United Family Health Center and the International Medical Center. During the day, the Watsons chain is good for over-the-counter medication.

Beijing United Family Health Center (private) ⊠ 2 Jiangtai Lu, near Lido Hotel, Chaoyang District ☎ 010/6433-3960, 010/6433-2345 for emergencies ⊕ www.unitedfamilyhospitals.com. **International Medical Center (IMC)** (private) ⊠ Beijing Lufthansa Center, Room 106, 50 Liangmaqiao Lu, Chaoyang District ☎ 010/6465-1561. **Watsons** ⊠ Holiday Inn Lido Hotel, Jichang Lu, Chaoyang District ⊠ Full Link Plaza, 18 Chaoyangmenwai Dajie, Chaoyang District.

MAIL

Sending international mail from China is reliable. Airmail letters to any place in the world should take 5 to 14 days. Express Mail Service (EMS) is available to many international destinations. Letters within Beijing arrive the next day, and mail to the rest of China takes a day or two longer. Domestic mail can be subject to search so don't send sensitive materials, such as religious or political literature, as you might cause the recipient trouble.

Service is more reliable if you mail letters from post offices rather than mailboxes. Buy envelopes here, too, as there are standardized sizes in China. You need to glue stamps onto envelopes as they're not self-adhesive. Most post offices are open daily between 8 and 7. Your hotel can usually send letters for you, too.

You can use the Roman alphabet to write an address. Do not use red ink, which has a negative connotation. You must also include a six-digit zip code for mail within China. The Beijing municipality is assigned the zip code 100000, and each neighboring county starts with 10. For example, the code for Fangshan, to the immediate southwest of Beijing proper, is 102400.

Sending airmail postcards costs Y4.20 and letters Y5.40 to Y6.50.

🔳 Main Branches **International Post and Telecommunications Office** ⊠ Jianguomen Bei Dajie, Chaoyang District ☎ 010/6512-8114.

🔳 Express Services **DHL** ☎ 010/6466-5566 ⊕ www.cn.dhl.com. **FedEx** ☎ 010/6462-3183 ⊕ www.fedex.com. **UPS** ☎ 010/6505-5005 ⊕ www.ups.com.

At a Glance

ENGLISH	PINYIN	CHINESE CHARACTERS
EXPLORING		
Ancient Observatory	Gǔguānxiàngtái	古观象台
Beihai Park	Běihǎi gōngyuán	北海公园
Bell Tower	Zhōnglóu	钟楼
Chang'an Jie	Cháng'ān jiē	长安街
Chaoyang District	cháoyáng qū	朝阳区
Chongwen District	chóng wén qū	崇文区
Confucius Temple	Kǒngzǐ Miào	孔子庙
Ditan Park	Dìtán gōngyuán	地坛公园
Dongcheng District	dōngchéngqū	东城区
Donghuamen Night Market	Dōnghuámén yèshì	东华门夜市
Drum Tower	Gǔlóu	鼓楼
Forbidden City	zǐ jìn chéng	紫禁城
Great Hall of the People	Rénmín Dàhuìtáng	人民大会堂
Haidian District	hǎi diàn qū	海淀区
Houhai	hòu hǎi	后海
Houhai (rear lake)	hòu hǎi	后海
Imperial Academy	Guózǐjiàn	国子监
Jingshan Park	jǐng shān gōngyuán	景山公园
Lama Temple	Yōnghé Gōng	雍和宫
Liulichang	Liúlichǎng	琉璃厂
Mao Zedong Memorial Hall	Máo zhǔ xí jì niàn táng	毛主席纪念堂
Ming Dynasty City Wall Ruins Park	Míng chéng qiáng yí zhǐ gōng yuán	明城墙遗址公园
Monument to the People's Heroes	Rénmín Yīngxióng Jìniànbēi	人民英雄纪念碑
Museum of Antique Currency	gǔdài qiánbì zhǎnlǎnguǎn	古代钱币展览馆
Nanhai ("south lake")	Nánhǎi	南海
Niujie (Ox Street) Mosque	Niújiē Qīngzhēnsì	牛街清真寺
Old Summer Palace	Yuánmíngyuán	圆明园
Oriental Plaza	dōngfāng guǎngchǎng	东方广场
Prince Gong's Palace	Gōng Wángfǔ	恭王府
Qianmen ("front gate")	Qiánmén	前门
Sanlitun	sān lǐ tún	三里屯

Silver Ingot Bridge	yíndìng qiáo	银锭桥
Soong Ching-ling's Former Residence	Sòng Qìng Líng Gùjū	宋庆铃故居
Source of Law Temple	Fǎyuán Sì	法源寺
Subway	dìtiě	地铁
Summer Palace	Yíhéyuán	颐和园
Temple of Heaven	Tiāntán	天坛
Tiananmen Square	Tiān'ānmén Guǎngchǎng	天安门广场
Wangfujing	Wángfǔjǐng	王府井
Workers' Stadium	gōngrén tǐyùchǎng	工人体育场
Xicheng District	xīchéngqū	西城区
Xidan	Xīdān	西单
Xuanwu District	xuān wǔ qū	宣武区
WHERE TO STAY		
Beijing Hotel	Běijīng fàndiàn	北京饭店
China World Hotel	zhōngguó dàfàndiàn	中国大饭店
Courtyard Beijing	Běijīng wàn yí jiǔdiàn	北京万怡酒店
Crowne Plaza Beijing	Běijīng guójì yìyuàn huángguān jiàrì jiǔdiàn	北京国际艺苑皇冠假日酒店
Friendship Hotel	yǒuyì Bīnguǎn	友谊宾馆
Gloria Plaza Hotel	Běijīng kǎi lái dà jiǔdiàn	北京凯莱大酒店
Grand Hotel Beijing	Běijīng guìbīn lóu fàndiàn	北京贵宾楼饭店
Grand Hyatt Beijing	Běijīng dōngfāng jūn yuè jiǔdiàn	北京东方君悦酒店
Hilton Beijing	Běijīng xī ěr dùn jiǔdiàn	北京稀尔顿酒店
Jianguo Hotel	jiànguó fàndiàn	建国饭店
Jinglun Hotel	jīng lún fàndiàn	京伦饭店
Kempinski Hotel	kǎi bīn sī jī fàndiàn	凯宾斯基饭店
Kerry Centre Hotel	Běijīng jiā lǐ zhōngxīn fàndiàn	北京嘉里中心饭店
Kunlun Hotel	Běijīng Kūnlún fàndiàn	北京昆仑饭店
LüSongyuan	lǚ sōng yuán bīnguǎn	侣松园宾馆
Novotel Peace Hotel	hépíng bīnguǎn	和平宾馆
Peninsula Beijing	wángfǔ bàndǎo jiǔdiàn	王府半岛酒店
Raffles Beijing Hotel	Běijīng fàndiàn lái fó shì	北京饭店莱佛士

Red Capital Residence	xīn hóng zī kèzhàn	新红资客栈
Ritz-Carlton Beijing	Běijīng jīnróng jiē lǐ sī kǎ'ěrdùn jiǔdiàn	北京金融街丽思卡尔顿酒店
St. Regis	Běijīng guójì jùlèbù fàndiàn	北京国际俱乐部饭店
Scitech Hotel	Sài tè fàn diàn	塞特饭店
Shangri-La Hotel	Běijīng xiānggélǐlā fàndiàn	北京香格里拉饭店
Sino-Swiss Hotel	Běijīng guódū dàfàndiàn	北京国都大饭店
Swissôtel	gǎng Ào zhōngxīn ruìshì jiǔdiàn	港澳中心瑞士酒店
Traders Hotel	guó mào fàndiàn	国贸饭店
Zhaolong International Youth Hostel	Zhào lóng qīng nián lǚshè	兆龙青年旅舍
Zhaolong Hotel	zhào lóng fàndiàn	兆龙饭店
Zhuyuan Hotel	zhú yuán bīnguǎn	竹园宾馆

WHERE TO EAT

Anping Gujie	Ānpíng gǔ jiē	安平古街
Aria	ā lì yǎ	阿郦雅
Baijia Dazhaimen	bái jiā dà zháimén	白家大宅门
Bellagio	lùgǎng xiǎo zhèn	鹿港小镇
Café de la Poste	yúnyóu yì	云游驿
Comptoirs de France Bakery	fǎ pài	法派
Din Tai Fung	dǐng tài fēng	鼎泰丰
La Dolce Vita	tiánmì shēnghuó	甜蜜生活
Fangshan	fǎng shàn	仿膳
La Galerie	Zhōngguó yìyuàn	中国艺苑
Gaon	gāo ēn	高恩
Gui Gongfu	guì gōngfǔ	桂公府
Hai Wan Ju	hǎiwǎn jū	海碗居
Han Cang	hàn cāng	汉仓
Huang Ting	huáng tíng	凰庭
Jing	jīng	京
Jingsi Su Shifang	jìngsī sùshí fāng	静思素食坊
Jun Wangfu	jūnwáng fǔ	君王府
Kong Yi Ji	kǒng yǐ jǐ	孔乙己
Lai Jin Yu Xuan	láijīn yǔ xuān	来今雨轩

Li Qun Roast Duck Restaurant	lì qún kǎoyādiàn	利群烤鸭店
Makye Ame	mǎ jí ā mǐ	玛吉阿米
Mei Fu	méi fǔ	梅府
Noodle Loft	miàn kù	面酷
Old Beijing Noodle King	lǎo Běijīng zhájiàngmiàn dàwáng	老北京炸酱面大王
Paulaner Brauhaus	pǔ lā nà píjiǔ fāng cāntīng	普拉那啤酒坊餐厅
RBL	kù bīng	库冰
Red Capital Club	xīn hóng zī jùlèbù	新红资俱乐部
Shaguo Ju	shāguō jū	沙锅居
Shin Yeh	xīn yè	欣叶
The Source	dū jiāng yuán	都江源
South Silk Road	chá mǎ gǔdào	茶马古道
Taj Pavilion	tài jī lóu	泰姬楼
Three Guizhou Men	sān gè guìzhōu rén	三个贵州人
Xi Xiangzi	Xī xiāng zi	西厢子
Yotsuba	sì yè	四叶
Yuxiang Renjia	yú xiāngrén jiā	渝乡人家

ARTS & NIGHTLIFE

Beijing Concert Hall	Běijīng Yīnyuètīng	北京音乐厅
Beijing Exhibition Theater	Běijīng Zhǎnlǎnguǎn Jùchǎng	北京展览馆剧场
Candy Floss Café	Miánhuātáng Kāfēiguǎn	棉花糖咖啡馆
Capital Theater	Shǒudū Jùchǎng	首都剧场
Centro	Xuàn Kù	炫酷
Chaoyang Theater	Cháoyáng Jùchǎng	朝阳剧场
China National Puppet Theater	Zhōngguó Guójiā Mù'ǒujù Yuàn	中国国家木偶剧院
The Den	Dūnhuáng	敦煌
Drum & Bell	Gǔzhōng Kāfēiguǎn	鼓钟咖啡馆
East Shore Live Jazz Café	Dōng'àn Kāfēi	东岸咖啡
Forbidden City Concert Hall	Zhōngshān Gōngyuán Yīnyuè Táng	中山公园音乐堂
Liyuan Theater	Lí yuán jù chǎng	梨园剧场
No Name Bar (Bai Feng's)	Wúmíng Jiǔbā	无名酒吧

Poly Plaza International Theater	Bǎolì Jùyuàn	保利剧院
Press Club Bar	Jìzhě Bā	记者吧
The Red Theatre	Hóng Jùchǎng	红剧场
Stone Boat	Shífǎng	石舫
Tango	Tàn gē	探戈
Universal Theater	Tiāndì Jùchǎng	天地剧场
Wan Sheng Theater (Tianqiao Acrobatic Theater)	Tiānqiáo Zájì Jùchǎng	天桥杂技剧场
Workers' Stadium	Gōngréntǐ Yùchǎng	工人体育场
The World of Suzie Wong	Sūxīhuáng Jùlèbù	苏西黄俱乐部
Yugong Yishan	Yúgōng Yíshān	愚公移山

SHOPPING		
Alien Street	Yǎ Bǎo Lù	雅宝路
Bainaohui Computer Shopping Mall	Bǎi Nǎo Huì Diàn Nǎo Guǎng Chǎng	百脑汇电脑广场
Beijing Curio City	Beǐ Jīng Gǔ Wán Chéng	北京古玩城
Beijing Department Store	Běi jīng shì bǎi huò dà lóu	北京市百货大楼
Beijing Friendship Store	Běi jīng yǒu yì shāng diàn	北京友谊商店
Beijing Silk Shop	Běi jīng sī chóu diàn	北京丝绸店
Beijing Yuanlong Silk Corporation	Yuán lóng sī chóu	元隆丝绸
The Bookworm	Shū Chóng	书虫
China Star Silk Store	Míng xīng zhōng shì fú zhuāng diàn	明星中式服装店
China World Shopping Mall	guó mào shāng chéng	国贸商城
Dazhalan	Dà zhà lán	大栅栏
Fashion Center at San Li Tun	Sān lǐ tún sān diǎn sān fú shì dà shà	三里屯3.3服饰大厦
Foreign Languages Bookstore	Wài wén shū diàn	外文书店
Heyan'er	Hé Yàn Fú Zhuāng Diàn	何燕服装店
Hongqiao Market	Hóng qiáo shì chǎng	红桥市场
The Kerry Centre Mall	Jiā lǐ zhōng xīn	嘉里中心
Liulichang Jie	Liú Lì Chǎng Jiē	琉璃厂街
Lufthansa Youyi Shopping Center	Yàn shā yǒu yì shāng chéng	燕莎友谊商城

Malls at Oriental Plaza	Dōng fāng guǎng chǎng gòu wù zhōng xīn	东方广场购物中心
Panjiayuan Antique Market	Pān Jiā Yuán Shì Chǎng	潘家园市场
The Red Phoenix	Hóng Fèng Huáng Fú Zhuāng	红凤凰服装工作室
Ritan Office Building Market	Rì tán shāng wù lóu	日坛商务楼
Sanlitun	Sān lǐ tún	三里屯
Shard Box Store	Shèn Dé Gé	慎德阁
Silk Alley Market	Xiù Shuǐ Shì Chǎng	秀水市场
Sun Dongan Plaza	Xīn Dōng ān Shì Chǎng	新东安市场
Tea Street	Mǎ Lián Dào Chá Yè Chéng	马连道茶叶批发市场
Tongli Studio	Tóng Lǐ	同里
Tongrentang	Tóng rén táng	同仁堂
Treasure House	Bǎo yuè zhāi	宝月斋
Wonderful Electronic Shopping Mall	Lán dǎo dà shà	蓝岛大厦
Yaxiu Market	Yǎ Xiù shì chǎng	雅秀市场
SIDE TRIPS		
Beidaihe	Běidàihé	北戴河
Eastern Qing Tombs	qīng dōnglíng	清东陵
Fahai Temple	fǎhǎi sì	法海寺
The Great Wall	Cháng chéng	长城
Jietai Temple	jiè tái sì	界台寺
Marco Polo Bridge	lú gōu qiáo	卢沟桥
Tanzhe Temple	tán zhè sì	潭柘寺
Thirteen Ming Tombs	míng Shísānlíng	明十三陵
Tianjin	Tiānjīn	天津
Yesanpo	yě sān pō	野三坡
Yunju Temple	yún jū sì	云居寺
Zhaoling tomb	zhāo líng	昭陵
Zhoukoudian Peking Man Site	Zhōu kǒu diàn běi jīng rén yí zhǐ	周口店北京人遗址

Beijing to Shanghai

HEBEI, SHANDONG, JIANGSU & ANHUI

Working the land in the Jiangxi province.

WORD OF MOUTH

"From Beijing you can take a train to Shanhaiguan, which is where the great wall meets the ocean (spectacular)."

—Steve

WELCOME TO
BEIJING TO SHANGHAI

TOP REASONS TO GO

★ **Qingdao:** Life's a beach in China's premier seaside city. Enjoy some of the country's best seafood washed down with Tsingdao beer, the local brew. Stroll around the interesting and well-preserved architecture from the days when the Germans were in charge.

★ **Huangshan:** Yellow Mountain's towering granite peaks overlooking rice paddies and green fields have been a place of pilgrimage for centuries.

★ **Chengde:** Originally a summer retreat for an emperor, this city's magnificent temples, parks, and palaces now attract weekenders from the capital.

★ **Suzhou:** Classical gardens and a network of crisscrossing canals that run throughout the moated city are the pride of the province.

★ **Tongli:** A fine example of a town built on water, Tongli is a wonderful place to wander around quaint side streets and alleyways that open onto canals and bridges.

Delicately carved ornaments on the roof of the Bailin Zen Buddhist Temple in Shijiazhuang, Hebei.

INNER MONGOL

Chengde

LIAONING

Changping   BEIJING   GREAT WALL

BEIJING   Panshan

Shanhaiguan

Beidaihe

Tangshan

SHANXI

Tianjin

Baoding

TIANJIN   *Bohai Bay*

HEBEI   Hejian

Cangzhou

Shijiazhuang

Weihai

Laizhou Bay   Yantai

Dezhou   Laiyang

Handan   Ji'nan   Weifang

Zibo   SHANDONG   Laoshan

Mt. Tai   Ti'an   **Qingdao**

Qufu

Jining   Linyi   *Haizhou Bay*

Heze   Lianyungang

Xuzhou

HENAN   *Yellow River*

Qingjiang

JIANGSU

Bengbu   Yangzhou   Nantong

Nanjing   Zhenjiang

Hefei   Wuxi   **Shanghai**

Dabie Mountain   ANHUI   Suzhou   Tongli

Zhouzhuang

HUBEI   *Yangtze River*   *Wangpan Bay*

ZHEJIANG

Huangshan

0 ─────── 100 mi

JIANGXI   0 ─────── 100 km

Yellow Sea

1 Hebei: Wrapped around the nation's capital, Hebei's attractions are definitely worth a side trip or two. Chengde's size belies the amount of imperial architecture on display, and in warm weather, the seaside resorts of Beidaihe and Shanghaiguan are good destinations to see the Chinese at play.

2 Shandong: Destinations in this province range from the religious to the bacchanal. Take a pilgrimage to Taishan, the most revered of all China's sacred mountains and Qufu, the birthplace of Confucius. For the more earthly pleasures of sun, beer, and Bavarian architecture don't miss the beach town of Qingdao, China's windsurfing capital.

3 Jiangsu: Here, history is omnipresent. Attractions range from stately monuments, memorials to horrific events, ancient peaks, and elegant gardens. The provincial capital Nanjing has been important for centuries and was the country's capital for six dynastic periods. Nearby Suzhou is justly renowned for its gardens.

The winding paths up Huangshan are sometime treacherous but always spectacular.

4 Anhui: It may be one of China's poorest provinces, but it is rich in sublime mountain scenery at Huangshan. The peaks are a sacred site in China, and once you have ascended its photogenic summit, you will understand why.

GETTING ORIENTED

Stretching from Hebei, which is very much culturally and geographically Northern China, to the more refined province of Jiangsu, Eastern China is easily accessible thanks to a well-developed tourist infrastructure. All four provinces have air and train links to both of the mainland's major transport hubs—Beijing and Shanghai. The port cities of Qinghuangdao in Hebei and Qingdao in Shandong provide another option for the adventurous traveler. No matter what month you're traveling, it's great weather in some part of the region. In spring and summer, head to the coast at Qingdao and farther north, Beidaihe and Shanghaiguan. Save the sometimes arduous ascents up Huangshan and Taishan for autumn or the beginning of winter, when the crowds and temperatures have died down.

Altar inside imperial mausoleum, Nanjing Jiangsu.

BEIJING TO SHANGHAI PLANNER

Contrasts and Comparisons

Traveling through Eastern China is a lesson in extremes. Here, you'll find Jiangsu and Shandong, two of China's richest provinces next door to Anhui, one of its poorest.

Winters can be bone-chillingly cold, especially in Hebei Province, whereas the summers can leave visitors wilting—Nanjing is known as one of the furnaces of China.

An interesting contrast can be made between the region's present and past glories. Traditional Chinese culture is generally regarded to have started with the birth of Confucius in 551 BC in Qufu. His quintessentially Chinese philosophical tradition became the official state philosophy but would ebb and flow in importance.

Few regions in China have seen the rise and fall of more dynasties than here, with Nanjing as the country's capital for several of them.

When Not to Go

The only thing that makes traveling the country of 1.3 billion more difficult is when the 1.3 billion are also on vacation. The eastern region of China is heavily populated, and during the three weeklong public holiday periods, it seems like everyone takes to the road (or train, or plane).

Hotels in major destinations are booked solid and even the quietest of destinations become packed with fellow travelers. Try to avoid traveling during the Chinese New Year, which is based on the lunar calendar and changes date every year. The National Week holiday in October, and the International Labor Day holiday in May can be easily avoided with a bit of planning.

Another bit of advice: buy a good map. Cities change quickly so it's worth making sure you have an up-to-date map to help you navigate.

What to Buy

For centuries, buyers from around the world lusted after the luxury fabrics produced in Suzhou. Silk-spinning worms were in such high demand that to take one abroad was punishable by death. The Suzhou Arts and Crafts Museum contains some of the most accomplished silk embroideries you'll find in China. Another place to try is the Suzhou Silk Museum Shop.

The superlative mountain vistas at Huangshan and Taishan have inspired artists for centuries. Painters flock to this area, and the most serious of them will camp out for weeks at a time. Most of the best artwork goes straight to Shanghai or Beijing, but good pieces are available in the towns nearest to the mountains such as Tunxi near Huangshan or Tai'an, the gateway to Taishan.

Nanjing is a major commercial center and a convenient place to pick up the traditional crafts that come from Jiangsu. Interesting souvenirs include teapots, carvings, flowing silks, folk paper cuttings, and copies of the lavish embroidered robes once worn by emperors.

World Heritage Sites

It's not surprising that a country that counts its history in millennia would also have 33 UNESCO World Heritage sites—and seven of them in this region alone.

The newest additions to China's world heritage list are the two traditional villages of Xidi and Hongcun in Anhui. UNESCO states that they "preserve to a remarkable extent the appearance of nonurban settlements of a type that largely disappeared or was transformed during the last century."

In Jiangsu, UNESCO has acknowledged Suzhou for its nine classical gardens. Farther north, another site that blends harmoniously into nature is Chengde's Mountain Resort's vast complex of palaces, temples, and imperial gardens.

In addition to Taishan, Shandong Province has the temple, cemetery, and family mansion of Confucius in Qufu on the UNESCO list. The Qufu complex of monuments has managed to retain its outstanding artistic and historic character.

WHAT IT COSTS In Yuan

$$$$	$$$	$$	$	¢
RESTAURANTS				
over 165	100–165	50–99	25–49	under 25
HOTELS				
over 1,800	1,400–1,800	1,100–1,399	700–1,099	under 700

Restaurant prices are for a main course, excluding tax and tips. Hotel prices are for a standard double room, including taxes.

Food Facts

Since the weather can be extreme—freezing winters and boiling summers—regional cuisine ranges from freshly caught seafood to dishes memorable for their liberal use of peppers and salted ingredients that liven up a winter diet of noodles and dumplings.

Every locality has their own specialties—wild game such as deer and hare in Chengdu, or Qufu's very own Confucius-family-style cuisine, a drawn-out banquet featuring dishes that have been refined over the past 2,000 years.

Dishes in and around Shanghai place emphasis on fresh ingredients, aroma, and tenderness. Shallots and garlic are frequently used so don't expect subtlety. In the coastal haven of Qingdao, seafood is of course the catch of the day.

Jiangsu cuisine, also called Huaiyang cuisine, is popular in the lower reaches of the Yangtze River. Using fish and crustaceans as the main ingredients, food is light, fresh, and slightly sweet. Its presentation is delicately elegant, befitting the province that borders Shanghai.

Inland in Anhui, food is famously salty and relies heavily on ham and soy sauce to enhance flavors. Try *Bagongshan doufu jiao*, a dish of minced pork wrapped in tofu or *qingceng bing*, which means thousand-layer pancakes. They're made of ham, eggs, and spring onions.

If you're not a meat eater, don't miss the vegetarian options available in or near any Buddhist temple. Chefs manipulate tofu, wheat gluten, and vegetables to create interpretations of meat that even the most voracious carnivore will appreciate.

By Helena
Iveson & Will
Thomson

WITH DIZZYING SPEED, China is transforming itself. A visit today is completely unlike one five years ago, or five years from now. With modern transportation, reliable communication, and comfortable lodgings, the eastern provinces of China are not difficult to travel through. However, modernization has brought problems. In cities like Nanjing, the air quality is often so bad that a haze hangs over the city and with car traffic increasing, crossing streets has become a game of chance. But this entire region is the epicenter of the New China, the epitome of the Old China, and is as exciting as anywhere in the country.

But at the same time, the area's history persists in solemn tombs, stately monuments, and elegant gardens. This is where Confucius was born, and where the Great Wall meets the sea. Described by Marco Polo as the finest and noblest city in the world, Hangzhou is famous for West Lake, which has long inspired poets, painters, and other artists. The largest artificial waterway in the world, the Grand Canal, extends from Beijing to Hangzhou. Nearby Suzhou is famous for its many well-preserved gardens. Classic scenery can also be found at Huangshan, one of China's traditional Five Famous Mountains, in Anhui province. The mountain's peaks rising from the mist have inspired whole schools of Chinese painting.

HEBEI

Many visitors travel through Hebei without a backward glance on the way to and from the capital, but the province has several sites worth a detour. Chengde is a must for history buffs and fans of the outdoors. The town's glory days were during the 18th century when the Emperor Kangxi made the town his summer retreat and hunting ground, filling the place with a palace and temples. The emperors may be long gone, but the town still serves as a holiday destination—today it is busloads of Beijing residents enjoying the scenery. Farther south, the seaside resorts of Beidaihe and Shanhaiguan, where the Great Wall meets the sea, are also remote places where foreign visitors get the rare opportunity to mingle with Chinese vacationers.

Chengde

 An increasingly common stop on the China tour circuit, some visitors regard Chengde as one of the highlights of their trip. With the Wulie River running through the town and the Yanshan Mountains serving as an impressive backdrop, Chengde is filled with magnificent examples of imperial architecture that make it well worth the journey.

Chengde was just another village until the Qing Dynasty emperor Kangxi stumbled upon it during a hunting trip. Now it is a UNESCO World Heritage site, home to one of the largest intact imperial gardens in China, the magnificent Mountain Resort, and the Eight Outer Monasteries. Be aware that although children might enjoy the imperial gardens, there's little else to entertain younger visitors. It's best to visit in summer or early autumn, as some tourist facilities close in the off-season.

Exploring

It isn't worth spending much time wandering around the city itself, but the massive size of the Mountain Resort, twice as large as Beijing's Summer Palace, means you will be doing plenty of walking. The other monasteries are all close to the city.

Fodor'sChoice

★ At the **Mountain Resort** (Bishu Shanzhuang), Emperor Kangxi ordered construction of the first palaces in 1703. Within a decade, dozens of ornate temples, pagodas, and spectacular gardens were spread over 1,500 acres. By the end of the 18th century, when Chengde reached its heyday, nearly 100 imperial structures filled the town.

Besides luxurious quarters for the emperor and his court, great palaces and temples were completed both to house visiting dignitaries and to impress them with the grandeur of the Chinese empire. Its interconnected palaces, in different styles of architecture, reflect China's diversity. Replicas of famous temples representing China's different religions stand on hillsides surrounding the palace as though paying homage to the court.

Today numerous buildings remain; some have been restored but many have grass coming up through the cracks. Only eight of the temples are open for visitors (two of the originals were demolished, and another two are dilapidated). Some rooms have been lovingly restored and contain period furniture, ornaments, and costumed mannequins frozen in time. The surrounding landscape of lakes, grassy meadows, and cool forests is lovely for a stroll. Mountains in the northern half of the park and a giant pagoda in the center afford panoramas of the city of Chengde to the south and the temples to the north and east. The Mountain Resort and the temples are so big that even with a massive influx of summer tourists they don't feel crowded. ⊠ *Center of town* 🎫 *Y90* ☉ *Daily 5:30 AM–6:30 PM.*

Viewing Chengde's **Eight Outer Monasteries** from above, it looks as though Emperor Kangxi built a Disneyland for China's religions. Originally there were a dozen temples, and each was built to reflect the architectural styles of a different minority group. The Eight Outer Monasteries are grouped on the eastern and northern slopes of the Mountain Resort in two different sections close to the Wulie River. The eastern temples of Anyuan, Pule, and Puren can be reached by bus number 10 from the Mountain Resort, and the northern temples of Putuozongcheng, Ximifushou, Puning Si, Puyou, and Shuxiang can be reached by taking bus number 6 from the same place. Only Puning Si is still in active use by monks. ⊠ *North of the Imperial Summer Villa* 🎫 *Y20–Y50* ☉ *Daily 8:30–6.*

❷ On the western bank of the Wulie River, the **Temple of Universal Peace** (Puning Si; ⊠ Puning Si Lu 🎫 Y50 ☉ Daily 8–5), is an interesting blend

of traditional Chinese temple and Buddhist monastery. The fascinating compound is well worth a visit, particularly to see the awe-inspiring 72-foot tall statue of Guanyin, a Buddhist deity, the tallest wooden statue in the world. The temple was built in 1755 during the reign of Emperor Qianlong and modeled on the Samye Temple, the earliest Buddhist monastery in Tibet.

> **WORD OF MOUTH**
>
> "The outer temples, especially Xumifushou and the Potola (which are within walking distance of each other) are really excellent. There are several casual eating places under an awning in front of the Potola that are good for lunch." —someotherguy

❶ The **Temple of the Potaraka Doctrine** (Putuozongcheng Miao; ✉ Shizhigou Lu 🎫 Y40 🕙 Daily 8–6) is modeled on the Potala Monastery in Lhasa, which is why it is known as the Little Potala. The temple, started in 1767, is the largest of the eight surviving temples in Chengde. Inside the imposing gate is a pavilion housing three stelae, the largest one inscribed with THE RECORD OF THE TEMPLE OF THE POTARAKA DOCTRINE in Han, Manchu, Mongolian, and Tibetan languages.

❹ The **Temple of Universal Happiness** (Pule Si; ✉ East of Mountain Resort 🎫 Y30 🕙 Daily 8–5:30) was built in 1766 when the imagery of Tibetan and Mongol Buddhism played an important role in the political and cultural arenas, especially in court circles. The architecture of the main building, the Pavilion of the Brilliance of the Rising Sun (Xuguangge) is similar to Beijing's Temple of Heaven. Look for the high, square, boxlike ceilings with a wooden Tibetan-style mandala motif. On top of the building's outer walls were eight brilliantly painted pagodas supported by lotus flower stands, only one of which remains. The lotus traditionally represents purity and is a common motif in Buddhist temples.

❸ A cable car and a hiking trail lead up to **Club Rock** (Bangchui Feng), a somewhat phallic protrusion which has spawned a local legend: if the rock should fall, so will the virility of local men. 🎫 *Y25* 🕙 *Daily 8–6.*

Tours

All hotels in Chengde run tours covering the city's main sites. The cheapest tours are in Chinese only and around Y30, not including admission to the various sites. An English-speaking guide costs around Y100.

Where to Stay & Eat

Given Chengde's role as a royal hunting ground, it's no surprise that the local specialty is wild game. Venison, rabbit, and pheasant are available at many restaurants. The town is also well-known for its medicinal beverages. Try almond juice if you suffer from asthma or if you have stomach problems, date juice is supposed to help relieve discomfort.

¢–$ ✕ **Da Qinghua.** Overlooking Lizheng Gate, this cheerful place with a rustic wooden exterior is a good choice if you want to sample local dishes. Be sure to try the specialty: homemade dumplings filled with pheasant and local mushrooms. The picture menu is useful—the staff does not speak English. To find the place, look out for the dragons on the build-

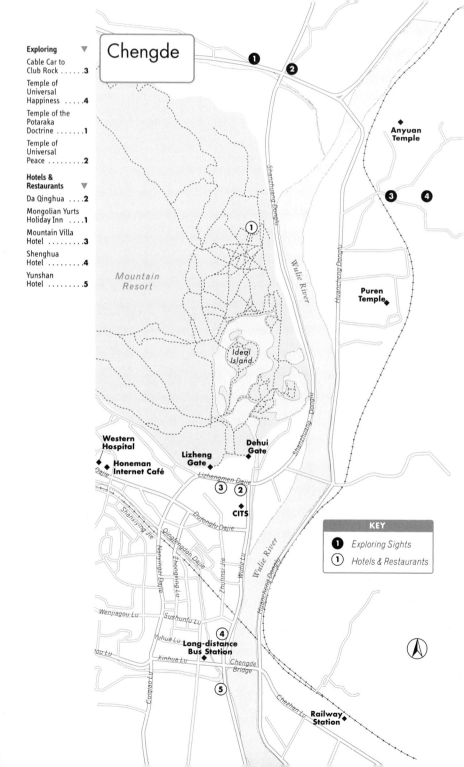

Chengde

Anyuan
Temple

Mountain
Resort

Puren
Temple

Ideal
Island

Western
Hospital

Honeman
Internet Café

Lizheng
Gate

Dehui
Gate

Shanzhuang Donglu

Wulie River

Huancheng Donglu

Shanzhuang Donglu

Lizhengmen Dajie

Dutongfu Dajie

CITS

Shanxiying Jie

Qingfengdun Dajie

Nanyingzi Dajie

Zhongxing Lu

Zhulinsi Jie

Wulie Lu

Huancheng Dongxlu

Wulie River

Wenjiagou Lu

Sushunfu Lu

Yuhua Lu

...ou Lu

Xinhua Lu

Long-distance
Bus Station

Chengde
Bridge

Chezhan Lu

Railway
Station

KEY

❶ *Exploring Sights*

① *Hotels & Restaurants*

2

ing's exterior. ⊠ *19 Lizhengmen Da Jie* ☎ *0314/202–3611* ▭ *No credit cards.*

$–$$ ✕⊡ **Shenghua Hotel.** A modern tower of glass and steel, the city's newest luxury hotel soars to 14 stories. Although the reception areas are quite dark, the rooms have plenty of windows to make them feel light and airy. An excellent restaurant serves local specialties such as stir-fried venison. The bilingual tour operator on staff can help you plan tours of the region. ⊠ *22 Wulie Lu, 067000* ☎ *0314/227–1000* ⊕ *www. shenghuahotel.com* ⤶ *111 rooms* ⌂ *3 restaurants, in-room safes, refrigerators, cable TV, fitness room, sauna, bar, concierge, in-room data ports, hair salon, laundry service* ▭ *AE, DC, MC, V.*

$ ✕⊡ **Yunshan Hotel.** Despite a facade that resembles a waffle, the Yunshan Hotel has a pleasing interior design. An octagonal lobby capped with a massive skylight leads to nicely furnished guest rooms. Two restaurants—one serving Chinese food, the other Western food—make this a reliable choice. A few English speakers at the tour desk can help arrange tours. ⊠ *2 Banbishan Lu, 067000* ☎ *0314/205–5588* ⤶ *230 rooms* ⌂ *2 restaurants, in-room safes, cable TV, hair salon, gym, spa, bar, business services* ▭ *AE, DC, MC, V.*

¢–$ ✕⊡ **Mountain Villa Hotel.** This hotel has perhaps the best location in town: opposite the main gate of the Mountain Resort. The reception area is impressive, if a little gaudy, with a massive chandelier hanging above. Some of the guest rooms are beginning to look a little tired, so ask to see a few before you decide. The cheerful staff and a full array of services make this an excellent choice if you are visiting for a night or so. ⊠ *11 Lizhengmen, 067000* ☎ *0314/209–1188* ⊕ *www.hemvhotel. com* ⤶ *390 rooms, 10 suites* ⌂ *6 restaurants, in-room safes, hair salon, gym, sauna, bicycles, bar, business services* ▭ *AE, DC, MC, V.*

¢ ✕⊡ **Mongolian Yurts Holiday Inn.** This hotel, no relation to the international chain, is made up of 30 yurts. They may not be the type used by Genghis Khan—for one thing, they are made of concrete—but they can sleep two or three people and have modern touches like television sets. Located inside the Mountain Resort, with its quiet and clean air, this makes for a peaceful and unusual stay. The restaurant continues the Mongolian theme so expect plenty of mutton on the menu. ⊠ *Inside the Mountain Resort* ☎ *0314/216–3094* ⤶ *30 yurts* ⌂ *Restaurant; no a/c* ▭ *No credit cards* ⊗ *Closed Nov.–Mar.*

Nightlife & the Arts

Puning Song and Dance (⊠ Temple of Universal Peace, Puning Si Lu ☎ 0314/216–2007) has an hour-long show that is a little touristy, but it's a great way to see the beautiful Temple of Universal Peace lighted at night. The Y150 admission includes transport to and from your hotel.

Shopping

The streets opposite the Temple of Universal Peace are full of stalls that sell a gaudy selection of souvenirs from beads to bronze figurines. Bargain hard!

To & from Chengde

4 hrs (255 km [158 mi]) by train northeast of Beijing; 7 hrs (470 km [291 mi]) by train southwest of Shenyang.

Most tourists arrive via Beijing on one of the two daily direct trains. About an hour outside of Beijing, look out the window for a glimpse of the Great Wall.

There are also buses every 20 minutes from Beijing's Dongzhimen bus station. In 2008, a new expressway will open that will cut the four-hour journey down to just over 2 hours.

Beidaihe

❷ English railway engineers came across this small fishing village in the 1890s, and it was not long after that wealthy Chinese and foreign diplomats were visiting in droves. After Mao Zedong came to power, the new rulers developed a taste for sea air. Today the seaside retreat has an interesting mix of beachy kitsch and political posturing (watch out for the rousing propaganda posters along the beachfront). Beidaihe is terrifyingly crowded during the summer and practically empty the rest of the time.

Exploring
The best way to get around on a sunny day is to rent a bicycle and cruise up and down the seafront. The relaxed pace of life and the rare opportunity to witness the Chinese relaxing makes Beidaihe worth visiting.

North of the middle beach is **Lianfeng Hill Park** (Lianfengshan Gongyuan), where quiet paths through pine forest lead to the quiet **Guanyin Temple** (Guanyin Si). Look out for the aviary, known as the Birds Singing Forest. There are also good views of the sea from the top of Lianfeng Hill. ⊠ *West side of town* ☞ *Y25* ☉ *Daily 8–5.*

Emperor Qin Shi Huang's Palace (Qinhuang Gong) is a 20th-century replica built in homage to the first Qin Dynasty emperor's visit to Beidaihe. Rooms here contain mannequins in period costumes, impressive weapons, and embroideries. ⊠ *Near Shan Zhuang* ☞ *Y30* ☉ *Daily 8–5.*

Where to Stay & Eat
In summer, seafood restaurants line the beach, and you only need to point at the most appetizing thing squirming in red buckets for the waiter to serve up a delicious fresh meal. A plateful of fresh mussels should cost about Y12, fresh crabs a little more. More good seafood restaurants are clustered on Haining Lu near the beach.

¢–$$ ✕ **Kiesslings.** Opened by Austrians six decades ago, this is the town's only foreign-owned restaurant. It serves both Chinese and Western dishes, but is best known for its tasty baked goods at breakfast. Its decor is a little old-fashioned, but that is part of its charm. The restaurant is usually open from May through September, but call ahead to make sure. ⊠ *Dongjing Lu, behind Beidaihe Guesthouse for Diplomatic Missions* ☎ *0335/404–1043* ☰ *No credit cards.*

> **BIKING**
>
> Bikes are available for hire from the **Beidaihe Guesthouse for Diplomatic Missions** ⊠ *1 Baosan Lu* ☎ *0335/428–0000.* It costs about Y30 for half a day and you will need to leave either a deposit of around Y200 or your passport.

2

$ ⊞ **Beidaihe Guesthouse for Diplomatic Missions** (Beidaihe Waijiao Renyuan Binguan). Specifically catering to foreign visitors, the guesthouse has several staff members who speak English remarkably well. Reflecting its past as a lodging for Russian diplomats, it has a building reserved for "distinguished guests." The attractive complex, made up of low-slung buildings from the 1960s, is set among cypress and pines in a peaceful spot overlooking its own private beach. Rates for more expensive rooms include breakfast. ⊠ *1 Baosan Lu, 066100* ☎ *0335/428–0000* ⇨ *153 rooms, 12 suites* ◊ *Restaurant, cable TV, gym, bar, dry cleaning, tennis court, beach* ▭ *AE, DC, MC, V* ⊙ *Closed Nov.–Mar.*

¢ ⊞ **Jinshan Hotel.** On a quiet stretch of sand, this hotel is made up of five two-story buildings linked by tree-lined paths. The rooms are clean and comfortable, although they are beginning to show their age. One of the town's branches of the China International Travel Service (CITS) is on the premises. Stay here in summer, as fewer of the facilities are open low season. ⊠ *4 Dongsan Lu, 066100* ☎ *0335/404–1338* ⇨ *267 rooms* ◊ *2 restaurants, gym, bar, business services, travel services* ▭ *AE, DC, MC, V.*

To & from Beidaihe

4 hrs (260 km [160 mi]) by express train east of Beijing; 5 hrs (395 km [245 mi]) by train southwest of Shenyang; 1 hr (35 km [22 mi]) by minibus southwest of Shanhaiguan.

Most visitors come directly from Beijing, and the train is the most convenient option, being quicker and more comfortable than buses. There are nine double-decker tourist trains each day, and the journey takes about three hours. Bear in mind that the train station in Beidaihe is not in the center of town. If you arrive late at night, taxi drivers may try to charge exorbitant rates.

The nearest airport is 5 km (3 mi) away at Qinhuangdao, and has flights to Dalian, Nanjing, Shanghai, Taiyuan, and Yantai.

Shanhaiguan

❸ On the northern tip of the Bohai Coast, Shanhaiguan is the end of the road for the Great Wall. This is where the eastern end of the massive structure meets the sea. During the Ming Dynasty, Shanhaiguan was fortified to prevent hoards of mounted invaders from Manchuria from invading the city. Now local tourists swarm the town during the summer. But despite the town's noteworthy history, Shanhaiguan doesn't seem to have captured the imagination of foreign visitors. An impressive wall still surrounds the old town, though the warriors on the battlements are now mannequins.

Exploring

The **First Gate Under Heaven** (Tianxiadiyiguan) is the city's eastern portal. Walking along the top (you have to pay an extra Y2, but it's worth it), you can gaze down at the fortifications and imagine how intimidating they must have been to potential invaders. Not that it worked forever: the Manchus overran the city in 1644. Through binoculars, you can see the Great Wall snaking up nearby mountains. ⊠ *East side of the city* 🖃 *Y40, includes admission to Great Wall Museum* ⊙ *Daily 6:30–4.*

The **Great Wall Museum** (Changcheng Bowuguan), housed in a Qing Dynasty–style building past the First Gate Under Heaven, has a diverting collection of historic photographs and cases full of military artifacts, including the fierce-looking weaponry used by attackers and defenders. There are some English captions, but they are not everywhere. At the time of writing, some artifacts were part of a traveling exhibition. ⊠ *South of First Gate Under Heaven* 🖃 *Y40, includes admission to First Gate Under Heaven* ⊙ *Daily 7–4.*

Legend has it that the Great Wall once extended into the Bohai Sea, ending with a giant carved dragon head. The structure that today is called **Old Dragon Head** (Lao Long Tou) has been totally rebuilt, so don't expect to walk on the original structure. It is still a dramatic sight, with the Great Wall jutting out into the sea with waves smashing at its base. On the beach there are motorboats that will take you out to snap a few photos. Some Ming Dynasty naval barracks have also been re-created, and you can dress up in imperial costumes and pretend you are a naval officer. 🖃 *Y50* ⊙ *Daily 8–5.*

One way to leave behind the crowds at Old Dragon Head behind is to climb the wall as it climbs **Jiao Mountain** (Jiao Shan), about 4 km (2½ mi) from the city. The beginning of the section has been retrofitted with handrails and ladders up the sides of watchtowers, but you can keep climbing until you reach the "real" wall. On a clear day the view makes it definitely worth the effort. There is no public transportation, but Jiao Shan is only a 10-minute taxi ride from Shanhaiguan. 🖃 *Y15, Y20 for cable car* ⊙ *Daily 8–5.*

About 8 km (5 mi) down the coast from Old Dragon Head is **Mengjiangnu Miao,** a shrine commemorating a local legend. As the story goes, a woman's husband died while building the Great Wall. She wept as she searched for his body, and in sympathy the Wall split open before her, revealing the bones of her husband and others buried within. Overcome with grief, she threw herself into the sea. The temple has statues of the woman, a symbol of wifely dedication. The shrine is a 10-minute taxi ride northeast of town. 🖃 *Y30* ⊙ *Daily 7–4.*

Where to Stay & Eat

¢–$ ✕ **Wang Yan Lou.** Probably the most upmarket option in town, Wang Yan Lou serves excellent local seafood. Don't be put off by the bland exterior or the plastic tablecloths—the food is better than appearances would suggest. The menu is only in Chinese. ⊠ *Guancheng Xi Lu* 🕾 *No phone* ▭ *No credit cards.*

¢ 🖾 **First Pass Hotel.** Built to resemble a mansion from the time of the Qing Dynasty, this hotel is one of the best in Shanhaiguan. The owners have put a great deal of effort into the common areas, with ornate woodwork on the balconies and colorful lanterns lighting the corridors at night, but the guest rooms are basic. The restaurant, in one of the many court-

Extreme Climbs on the Great Wall

IF YOU WANT TO WALK AROUND THE GREAT WALL, BUT AVOID THE HORDES OF TOURISTS, persistent postcard sellers, and Kentucky Fried Chicken outlets that blight the other sections, then Huanghua is your best bet. This is the place to go for a challenging hike in a remote and beautiful mountainous setting.

Huanghua is a rugged, unrestored part of the Wall about 37 mi (60 km) from Beijing. It's the best place around if you like challenging types of hikes. Here the wall lies in two sections, almost 7 mi (11 km) long. A reservoir divides the two parts and local fishermen are always at work among the parapets and beacon towers.

In summer, the whole area is buried in swathes of yellow flowers (*huang hua* in Chinese) making it a great time to visit. In winter, the sections can be icy and too dangerous to climb.

A SENSE OF HISTORY
According to legend, the Ming Dynasty general who oversaw construction spared no expense and built the Wall to the highest possible standard. He ended up being beheaded for going over budget. But thanks to his thoroughness, you really feel as if you're walking through the past as you huff up those steep inclines. There is almost no rebuilt brickwork here (aside from an initial walkway that allows you to safely ascend onto the wall). Be aware that the natural weathering of the bricks makes the climb a little precarious.

This reason alone keeps the tour buses away, so it's a worthwhile trade-off.

THE COST
Not long ago, the main danger at Huanghua wasn't the crumbling bricks or sheer drops, but the locals keen to extort an entrance fee of a few yuan from visitors. They sometimes carried pitchforks and other sharp implements for added incentive. The government stamped that practice out, and now everyone must pay a flat rate of Y25 before entering the area.

GETTING THERE
Despite being only 37 mi (60 km) from Beijing, there are no direct public transportation options—but this helps limit the crowds. However, it does not take much effort to reach Huanghua. From Beijing's Dongzhimen long-distance bus station, catch Bus 916 to Huairou, which leaves every 20 minutes from 5:30 AM to 6:30 PM. If the traffic is awful, this part of the journey can take up to 3 hours, but at the minimum it will take about 70 minutes. When you arrive at the transit station, taxi drivers will find you before you find them, all keen to take you on the remaining 30-minute journey to the wall itself. If you are an avid bargainer, you can hire a taxi for Y30 per car—don't do a per person deal.

Another option is to hire a car for the day to take you to Huanghua from Beijing: expect to pay about Y400. You can approach any taxi driver or ask your hotel to help arrange this.

yards, serves standard northern Chinese cuisine, so expect dumplings for breakfast and noodles for lunch. The patient staff, although there isn't an English speaker in the bunch, will arrange air and train tickets. ⊠ *1 Dong Da Jie, 066200* ☎ *0335/513–2188* 🔊 *120 rooms* ⚭ *Restaurant, laundry service, travel services; no room TVs* ▭ *No credit cards.*

¢ 🏠 **North Street Hotel.** Inside the city wall, this family-run lodging is a great deal as long as you don't expect too many comforts. Basic but clean rooms are clustered around a pretty courtyard. The place may be a little noisy if the hotel is full. Still, the hotel has a lot more atmosphere than many nearby establishments. ⊠ *2 Mujia Hutong, 066200* ☎ *0335/505–1680* 🔊 *64 rooms* ⚭ *No phones, no room TVs* ▭ *No credit cards.*

To & from Shanhaiguan

1 hr (35 km [22 mi]) by minibus northeast of Beidaihe; 5 hrs (280 km [174 mi]) by minibus east of Beijing; 5 hrs (360 km [223 mi]) southwest of Shenyang.

Some trains from Beijing to Beidaihe continue on to Shanhaiguan, but they tend to be the slower trains and take around 5 hours. To save time you should catch a train to the nearby town of Qinghuangdao, about 3 hours from Beijing. Once in Qinghuangdao, catch a bus or a taxi to Shanghaiguan.

HEBEI ESSENTIALS

Transportation

BY AIR

The nearest airport is in the industrial city of Qinhuangdao. It is being revamped in time for the 2008 Beijing Olympics as the city is hosting most of the soccer matches. Currently, there are frequent flights to Dalian and infrequent flights to other Chinese cities.

🛈 Airport Information **Qinhuangdao Airport** ⊠ 169 Yingbin Lu, Qinhuangdao ☎ 0335/306-2579.

BY BOAT & FERRY

Qinhuangdao is one of the biggest harbors in China, and one of the few ice-free ports in northern China. Destinations include Dalian (14 hours), Shanghai (28 hours), Qingdao (12 hours), and Tianjin (18 hours). Contact CITS in Qinghuangdao for prices and schedules.

🛈 Boat & Ferry Information **Qinhuangdao CITS** ⊠ 100 Heping Dajie ☎ 0335/323-1117.

Qinhuangdao Tourism Bureau ⊠ 11 Gangcheng Dajie ☎ 0335/366-1001.

BY BUS

Long-distance buses are uncomfortable and slow, but they're the only transport linking Chengde with Beidaihe and Shanhaiguan. Several daily buses make this trip, all departing in the early morning from Chengde's long-distance bus station near the Shenghua Hotel. In 2008, two new highways to Chengde and Qinghuangdao should reduce the journey from Beijing to just over two hours to both destinations, making buses a more attractive option.

An excellent minibus service runs between Beidaihe, Qinhuangdao, and Shanhaiguan. Buses leave every 30 minutes and cost Y6 for the somewhat circuitous ride, with frequent stops between Beidaihe and Shanhaiguan. The bus station in Beidaihe is at the intersection of Heishi Lu and Haining Lu, and in Shanhaiguan it is in front of the train station. Buy tickets on the bus.

🚍 Bus Information **Beidaihe Station** ✉ Beining Lu and Haining Lu. **Shanhaiguan Station** ✉ Xinkai Xi Lu. **Chengde Station** ✉ Wulie Lu at Xinhua Lu.

BY TAXI

The half-hour taxi ride between Beidaihe and Shanhaiguan costs about Y80. Within all the towns in the region, taxis are an inexpensive way to get around.

BY TRAIN

Trains from Beijing all pass through Beidaihe, Shanhaiguan, and Qinghuangdao. Shanhaiguan has the least number of trains, so it might be worth booking a ticket to Qinghuangdao and then catching a bus to Shanhaiguan.

Chengde is on a northern rail line between Beijing and Shenyang. The journey takes 4½ hours from the capital. No trains run between Chengde and Beidaihe or Shanhaiguan.

🚍 Train Information **Chengde Train Station** ✉ Chezhan Lu, Chengde. **Beidaihe Train Station** ✉ Chezhan Lu, Beidaihe. **Shanhaiguan Train Station** ✉ Off Nanguan Da Jie, Shanhaiguan.

Contacts & Resources

EMERGENCIES

In Chengde, Chengde Chinese-Western Hospital is your best option. If you are ill in Beidaihe or Shanhaiguan, you are better off going to Qinghuangdao—it has superior medical facilities.

🚍 **Chengde Chinese-Western Hospital** ✉ 12 Xi Da Jie, Chengde ☎ 0314/202-2222. **Qinghuangdao Hospital** ✉ 281 Hebei Lu, Qinghuangdao ☎ 0335/404-1695.

TRAVEL AGENCIES

Chengde's branch of the China International Travel Service (CITS) has a helpful English-speaking staff that will be able to answer any questions about the region. It charges about Y100 per person for a full-day tour with an English-speaking guide.

🚍 Local Agent Referrals **Chengde CITS** ✉ 11 Zhonghua Lu ☎ 0314/202-7483.

VISITOR INFORMATION

If you're in Beidaihe and Shanhaiguan, contact CITS in Qinhuangdao. In Chengde, contact CITS.

🚍 Tourist Information **Chende CITS** ✉ 11 Zhonghua Lu, Chengde ☎ 0314/202-7483. **Qinhuangdao CITS** ✉ 100 Heping Dajie, Qinhuangdao ☎ 0335/323-1117. **Qinhuangdao Tourism Bureau** ✉ 11 Gangcheng Dajie, Qinhuangdao ☎ 0335/366-1001.

SHANDONG

More than 92 million people call Shandong home, but an annual influx of domestic tourists considerably add to that number. Most flock to this region for Qingdao, China's most attractive coastal city and best known for its beer and Bavarian architecture, the well-preserved town of Qufu, home of the philosopher Confucius, and Mount Tai, the most revered of all China's sacred mountains. Business is booming in Shandong, so expect even more visitors in the future.

Ji'nan

❹ It may be Shandong's provincial capital, but Ji'nan is overshadowed in almost every way by its coastal rival Qingdao. However, this modern and easygoing place is an enjoyable transit point to other destinations. It's a good place to stay if you are going to visit the nearby destinations of Qufu, Taishan, or Qingdao.

In 1901, Ji'nan was hauled into the 20th century by the construction of a railway line linking it to Qingdao. German, English, and Japanese companies found Ji'nan to be a convenient place to do business, and a few buildings they constructed can still be seen in the downtown (although they are increasingly overshadowed by new shopping centers and hotels).

Ji'nan's three main sites are Thousand Buddha Mountain, Big Bright Lake, and Gushing from the Ground Spring. These and a handful of other attractions easily occupy visitors for a day or so.

Exploring

Ji'nan's downtown area is relatively compact, with the Hueheng River looping through its center. Thousand Buddha Mountain overlooks the city from the southeast. The grid of streets south of the main railway station, which bear the most European influence, are worth walking by foot. The rest of the sites are best reached via taxi.

Legends about **Big Bright Lake** (Daming Hu) have been around for nearly 1,500 years. Water from springs fill the lake, which in turn empties into the Gulf of Bohai. Small temples surround the large lake, making it a great place for a stroll. ☒ *Daming Hu Lu* 🎫 *Y15* ⊙ *Daily 6–5:30.*

Gushing from the Ground Spring (Baotu Quan). Ji'nan's nickname is the City of Springs because of the more than 100 natural springs that once dotted the landscape. Many have since dried up, but Baotu Quan is still flowing, making the adjacent park attractive and lush. ☒ *Quancheng Lu* 🎫 *Y15* ⊙ *Daily 6–9.*

One interesting architectural legacy of the foreign occupation is an imposing redbrick **Protestant Church**, with its landmark twin towers. Built in 1927, it is still in use. ☒ *425 Jing Si Lu.*

NEED A BREAK?

Shandong Elite Teahouse (☒ 9 Qianfoshan Lu 🕾 No phone) makes for a lovely break any time of the day. The teahouse serves many varieties of tea at polished wooden tables. The exquisite traditional Chinese teahouse setting is decorated with lattice wooden paneling, vases, and musical instruments.

On the southern outskirts of the city is **Thousand Buddha Mountain** (Qianfoshan), one of the country's most sacred religious sites. It was called Mt. Li in ancient times. In the early days of Sui Dynasty many statues were chiseled into the rock, and it became known as Thousand Buddha Mountain. It is still the focus of religious festivals, although most of the statues have been lost to the ravages of time and the Cultural Revolution. If visiting in March or September, look out for the park's temple fairs. Getting to the top of the mountain requires a 30-minute climb or a ride on the cable car (Y25 round-trip). Either way you'll be rewarded with a good view of Ji'nan—air quality permitting. For your child (or the child in you), there's an excellent slide to whiz you back to the bottom. ☒ 18 *Jing Shiyi Lu, off Qianfoshan Lu* ☒ *Y15* ☉ *Daily 5* AM*–9* PM.

Tours

The town's attractions are all within a short taxi ride from the city center, so there is no need to arrange a tour to see them.

Where to Stay & Eat

¢–$$ ✕ **Kiwi Corner.** Opened by a woman from New Zealand, this restaurant is a good place to meet local expats. The kitchen serves up Western favorites when you need a change from Chinese food. The lasagna and salad are especially tasty. The location, among office buildings, is the main drawback. ☒ *22 Minziqian Lu* ☎ *No phone* ▭ *No credit cards.*

¢–$ ✕ **Foshan Yuan.** Near Thousand Buddha Mountain is this excellent restaurant specializing in vegetarian re-creations of traditional dishes. Try the crispy duck or the three-cup chicken and you'll be amazed at how perfectly the kitchen captures the flavors of the original dishes. Whatever you order, make sure to sample the very tasty spicy carrot dumplings. There is—unusual for these parts—an English menu. The restaurant closes at 9 PM, when the staff prepares food for homeless people. ☒ *Foshan Yuan Jie* ☎ *0531/8602–7566* ▭ *No credit cards.*

¢–$ ✕ **Jiu Wan Ban.** On a street filled with 24-hour joints, this cheerful place is the one locals rate as the best. You choose from pre-plated platters of fresh local fish, which are then cooked as you watch. Try the seafood version *xiaolongbao*, the little dumplings that are a specialty of Shanghai. ☒ *12 Chaoshan Jie* ☎ *0531/8612–7228* ▭ *No credit cards.*

¢–$ ✕ **Yuan Jiudian.** On the bustling street in the center of the city is this homey place. The kitchen serves up reliably good local favorites like *di san xian,* a mix of potatoes, peppers, and eggplant fried in a soy-flavored sauce.

The roast duck is also tasty. The staff does not speak English, but is patient with foreigners. ⊠ *Eastern end of Foshan Jie* ☎ *0531/8252–8577* ▤ *No credit cards.*

★ **$$–$$$$** ✕▥ **Crowne Plaza Ji'nan.** The city's newest hotel is already ranked among the best in China. The armload of awards it has collected is understandable, as this hotel in the heart of the shopping district is a great choice for business or leisure travelers. The English-speaking staff provides remarkably good service. The guest rooms are spacious and decorated in relaxing shades of oatmeal and cream; the bathrooms are excellent, with deep tubs and separate showers. With three bars, the hotel serves as a lively hub for the city's expat community. ⊠ *3 Tianditan Jie, 250011* ☎ *0531/8602–9999* ⊕ *www.ichotelsgroup.com* ➳ *227 rooms, 79 suites* ⚒ *6 restaurants, room service, refrigerators, cable TV, pool, health club, 3 bars, babysitting, laundry service, in-room broadband, business center, no-smoking rooms* ▤ *AE, DC, MC, V.*

$$–$$$$ ✕▥ **Sofitel Silver Plaza Ji'nan.** In the center of town, this 49-story cylinder looks vaguely like a tube of lipstick. Inside you find a lobby that incorporates classical design elements like massive marble columns and chandeliers. If that wasn't classy enough, there's a violinist who serenades guests as they arrive. The elegant guest rooms are spacious, but the marble bathrooms, which come with separate tub and shower, are on the small side. Among its six restaurants, be sure to try the rooftop Silver Sky Revolving Restaurant. In addition to a panoramic view of the city, you'll be treated to a hearty buffet dinner and live music. There is regular shuttle service to the airport. ⊠ *66 Luoyuan Dajie, 250063* ☎ *0531/8606–8888* ⊕ *www.sofitel.com/asia* ➳ *220 rooms, 106 suites* ⚒ *6 restaurants, room service, refrigerators, cable TV, pool, gym, bar, laundry service, concierge, in-room broadband, business services, airport shuttle* ▤ *AE, DC, MC, V.*

¢ ▥ **Silver Plaza Quancheng Hotel.** Located in the center of the city, this business hotel is a great place to stay even if you're not in town to close a deal. The common areas are bright and welcoming, and the rooms are spacious and relaxing. Try to avoid those overlooking the street, as these can be noisy. The restaurant serves up good renditions of local specialties and has an English menu. The service can be a bit brusque, mainly because of the huge number of people coming through the door. ⊠ *2 Nanmen Jie St., 250011* ☎ *0531/8692–4815* ➳ *350 rooms* ⚒ *Restaurant, room service, cable TV, gym, bar, business services* ▤ *AE, DC, MC, V.*

Nightlife

Although not in the same ballpark as Beijing, Shanghai, or even Qingdao, there is a burgeoning bar scene in Ji'nan centered around Foshan Jie.

The newest arrival is **Banjo** (⊠ 54 Foshan Jie), a pleasant bar that jostles for a place among a row of Chinese, Japanese, and Korean restaurants that are very lively at night. For a touch of the Irish, head to the **Downtown Café** (⊠ 11 Foshan Jie), which has a menu of pub grub and a wide selection of beers.

Shopping

Shandong Curio's City (✉ 283 Quancheng Lu ☎ No phone) is a cluster of small antiques shops huddled around an attractive courtyard. Jade, jewelry, and local antiques are beautifully displayed.

Shen's Embroidery Arts (✉ 66 Luoyuan Dajie ☎ 0531/8981–6158) is in the lobby of the Sofitel Silver Plaza, but don't write it off as another lackluster hotel gift shop. The embroidered paintings found here are extremely labor intensive, making them unusual, though expensive, souvenirs.

Side Trip to Mount Tai

Reaching 5,067 feet above sea level, **Mount Tai** (Taishan) is the most venerated of the five sacred mountains of China. A destination for pilgrims for 3,000 years, the mountain was named a UNESCO World Heritage Site in 1987. Confucius is said to have climbed the mountain and said as he scanned the horizon: "The world is very small." Much later, the Marxist Mao Zedong reached the top and even more famously said: "The East is red." If you are keen to reach a ripe old age, legend has it that climbing Mount Tai means you'll live to 100. It is possible to climb the cut-stone steps to the summit in a day, but many people prefer to stay overnight on the mountain. The classic photo—sunrise over the cloud-hugged mountainside—is actually a rare sight because of the mist. Human sacrifices were made on the summit, but today you will only encounter large crowds throughout the year.

WHERE TO STAY 🏨 **Shengqi Hotel.** This is the only real hotel on the summit but it's overpriced considering the barely adequate rooms. Still, there are unusual
¢–$ extras such as a bell that rings when it's time to get up for sunrise. ✉ *Summit of Mount Tai* ☎ *0538/822–3866* 🛏 *66 rooms* 🍴 *Restaurant, cable TV, laundry facilities, business services* ▭ *AE, DC, MC, V.*

TO & FROM **Mount Tai** is near the town of Tai'an, a major stop on the Shanghai-Beijing railway. Dozens of trains travel through Tai'an daily. Buses from
MOUNT TAI Ji'nan to Tai'an leave the bus terminal opposite the main train station every 25 minutes between 5 AM and 6 PM. From any spot in Tai'an, a taxi to Taishan takes less than 15 minutes and costs about Y10. ✉ *About 50 km (30 mi) south of Ji'nan* 🎫 *Y100.*

Side Trip to Qufu

Qufu is the birthplace of the country's most famous philosopher, Confucius, and so it's of massive significance to the Chinese people. Confucius's impact was immense in China, and his code of conduct was to dominate daily life until it fell out of favor during the Cultural Revolution. His teachings—that son must respect father, wife must respect husband, ordinary citizens must respect officials—were swept away by Mao Zedong because of their associations with the past. Qufu suffered greatly during the Cultural Revolution, with the Red Guards smashing statues and burning buildings. But the pendulum has swung

> **WORD OF MOUTH**
>
> "Qufu isn't often included in tours, but I think you'll be very glad it is included in yours for the Confucius Temple, Mansion, and Cemetery."
> –PeterN_H

back, and Confucius's teachings are back in favor. That's why you'll see the large crowds in Qufu. It's a lovely place, with timbered houses surrounded by the town walls.

EXPLORING Within the city walls, the **Confucius Temple** (⊠ Banbi Jie 🖾 Y30 ⊙ Daily 8–5) is actually a cluster of temples that occupy about a fifth of the city center. The 466 buildings cover more than 50 acres, making this one of the largest architectural complexes left from ancient China, comparable to Beijing's Forbidden City or Chengde's Summer Resort. The Hall of Great Achievements is one of the most ornate of the temples; don't miss its 28 stone pillars carved with dragons. The courtyards are full of gnarled trees and the many memorial halls are interesting because of the fine calligraphy, stone columns, and old furnishings on display. The complex is at the top of the list of places to visit, so you're likely to find a crowd.

Adjacent to the Confucius Temple is the **Confucius Family Mansion** (⊠ Banbi Jie 🖾 Y20 ⊙ Daily 8–5). Although not as big as the Confucius Temple, the private home consists of around 450 rooms. It dates from the 16th century and well illustrates the power and glory enjoyed by Confucius's descendants.

Confucius and his descendants have been buried in this tree-shaded cemetery for the past 2,000 years. Surrounded by a 10-km (6-mi) wall, **Confucian Forest** (⊠ Lindao Lu 🖾 Y20 ⊙ Daily 7:30–6) has over 100,000 pine and cypress trees. This is one of the only places in the city where you can escape the crowds.

WHERE TO STAY 🏨 **Queli Hotel.** This hotel is a good choice if you're staying overnight in
¢ Qufu, being just a short walk to the Confucius Temple and Confucius Family Mansion. The traditional Chinese architecture is attractive, though the rooms are spartan and have small bathrooms. The local specialty is a somewhat shortened version of a 196-course banquet traditionally served only to emperors. The restaurant here puts out a good spread. ⊠ 1 Queli Lu, 273100 🖷 0537/441–2022 ⇗ 150 rooms ⚒ Restaurant, gym, bar, laundry service, business services ▭ AE, DC, MC, V.

TO & FROM QUFU Regular buses run trips from Ji'- nan to Qufu. The Qufu Bus Station is located south of the town center at the intersection of Shen Dao and Jingxuan Lu.

To & from Ji'nan

4½ hrs (500 km [220 mi]) by train south of Beijing; 4 hrs (305 km [189 mi]) by train west of Qingdao.

> ## CONFUSING CONFUCIUS
>
> Many locals claim to be direct descendants of Confucius, and they take great pride in their heritage. Although the philosopher would have raised an eyebrow, the townspeople sell Confucius-brand cookies, wine, and many other items.

Your best option if traveling from Beijing is to catch the daily T35 express train, which leaves the capital at 1:30 PM and arrives at Ji'nan's main train station 4½ hours later. A hard seat is Y73, a soft seat Y110. The return train, the T36, leaves Ji'nan at 9:55 PM. There are also buses, but the journey can take more than 7 hours.

Jinan Yao Qiang International Airport is 25 mi (40 km) away from the city center. The journey takes 45 minutes in a taxi and costs around Y100.

Qingdao

❺ Qingdao has had a turbulent century, but it's emerged as one of China's most charming cities. It was a sleepy fishing village until the end of the 19th century, when Germany, using the killing of two German missionaries as a pretext, set up another European concession to take advantage of Qingdao's coastal position. The German presence lasted only until 1914, but locals continued to build German-style houses, and large parts of the old town make visitors feel as if they have stumbled into a town in the Black Forest. Unlike many cities that had foreign concessions, Qingdao has recognized the historical value of these buildings and is now enthusiastic about preserving them. With its seafront promenades, winding colonial streets, and pretty parks, Qingdao is probably China's best city for strolling.

Nationally and internationally known for being home to the country's best-known beer, Tsingtao, Qingdao is very accommodating when it comes to alcohol consumption. (Look for beer being sold on the streets in plastic bags.) But wine drinkers should take heart, as the region is also developing a much-talked-about wine industry.

The city is already a destination for golfers, having many of the country's best courses. Qingdao is also host of the sailing events of the 2008 Olympics. Though some sailing fans worry about the lack of wind, money is being pumped in from the capital, including $370 million for an International Sailing Center. Expect plenty of changes, including a striking new skyscraper overlooking the beach, called—what else?—the Sail.

In Qingdao, taxis are a cheap way to get around. Getting anywhere in town will cost less than Y25.

Exploring

❺ A landmark in Qingdao is the **Catholic Church** (Tianzhu Jiaotang), with its towering 200-foot twin steeples and red-tile roof. It was built by the Germans in 1934 and was badly damaged during the Cultural Revolution. Now though, it's a relaxing and peaceful place. ⊠ *15 Zhejiang Lu* 🔳 *Y6* ☉ *Mon.–Sat. 8–5, Sun. 10–5.*

❽ The striking former **German Governor's Residence** (Qingdao Ying Binguan) was transformed into a museum in 1996. Built in 1903 as the official residence of the governor-general of the then-German concession, it is set on a hill overlooking the old city. The interior is warm and welcoming, with wood paneling and a wide staircase leading from the foyer up to the bedrooms. Among the famous leaders who stayed here is a Who's Who of names from recent Chinese history: Mao Zedong, Zhou Enlai, and Deng Xiaoping ⊠ *26 Longshan Lu, below Xinhao Hill Park* 🔳 *Y10* ☉ *Daily 8:30–4:30.*

❻ **Guanhaishan Park** (Guanhaishan gongyuan) is tiny but charming. This was where the German high officials would practice their golf swing while

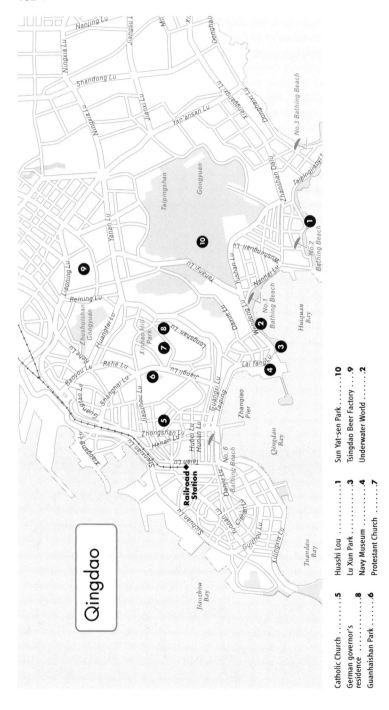

Qingdao

looking down over the rest of the city. ⊠ *15 Guanhai Er Lu* 🔁 *Free* ⊙ *Daily 7–5.*

❶ After the German Governor's Residence, the castle-like **Huashi Lou** is Qingdao's second most famous example of traditional German architecture. It was built as a villa for a Russian aristocrat but soon became a retreat for the governor. Look out for wedding parties using the grounds as a backdrop for their photos. ⊠ *18 Huanghai Lu* 🔁 *Y5* ⊙ *Daily 8–5:30.*

❸ Built in 1929, **Lu Xun Park** (Lu Xun Gongyuan), faces the rocky coastline of Huiquan Bay. It was named in 1950 for the distinguished Chinese writer and commentator Lu Xun. ⊠ *West end of No. 1 Bathing Beach* 🔁 *Y5* ⊙ *Daily 8–5.*

❹ In the upper yard of the **Navy Museum** (Haijun Bowuguan) you'll find an indoor exhibition documenting the history of the Chinese navy. Outside are the big guns, including Russian-made fighter planes, fixed-turret and antiaircraft naval guns, rockets, tanks, ground artillery, naval vessels (including three moored in the adjacent harbor), and even an old biplane. The displays are looking a bit dusty, so this museum is for hardcore naval fans only. ⊠ *8 Lai Yang Lu* ☎ *0532/286–6784* 🔁 *Y30* ⊙ *Daily 8:30–5.*

❼ Qingdao's **Protestant Church** (Jidu Jiaotang) is easy to spot: look out for the large green spire resembling those topping medieval castles. It was built in 1910 at the southwest entrance of Xinhao Hill Park. If you climb up to the bell tower, you are rewarded with an excellent view. ⊠ *15 Jiangsu Lu* 🔁 *Y7* ⊙ *Daily 8:30–4:30.*

NEED A BREAK? | It may bear more than a passing resemblance to a certain Seattle-based chain, but **SPR** (⊠ 29 Taiping Lu ☎ 0532/8299–6699 ▭ No credit cards) is a homegrown chain. It's a great place to relax with a cappuccino or fill up on a slice of pizza.

❿ The largest of the city's parks, **Sun Yat-sen Park** (Zhongshan Gongyuan), named for Dr. Sun Yat-sen, has plenty of exotic plants. It's pretty throughout the year, but is at its best in spring. ⊠ *28 Wendeng Lu* 🔁 *Y10* ⊙ *Daily 5 AM–9 PM.*

❾ Beer fans should make a pilgrimage to the **Tsingdao Beer Factory** (Tsingdao Pijiu Chang). A guide walks you through the facility, then gives you a multitude of freshly made beer samples. There is also an excellent museum on the history of the brewery, built in 1903 by—who else?—the

Germans. ⊠ *56 Dengzhou Lu* ☎ *0532/383–3437* 📧 *Y50* 🕙 *Daily 8:30–4:30.*

🧒 ❷ If you have children in tow, they will be enthralled by one of the city' newest attractions, **Underwater World** (Qingdao Haidi Shijie). The facility claims to have the world's largest aquarium, and it is kept filled with exotic creatures from the deep. Especially popular is an underwater tunnel where you can see sharks swim over your head. ⊠ *1 Laiyang Lu* ☎ *0532/8287–8218* ⊕ *www.qdunderwaterworld.com* 📧 *Y100* 🕙 *Daily 8:30–5.*

Where to Stay & Eat

It is no surprise to learn that Qingdao's specialty is seafood. Locals flock to Minjiang Jie, where the time between choosing a fish from tanks and having it arrive steaming on your plate is about three minutes. Many places don't have menus, but displays of popular dishes help you know exactly what you're getting.

> **IN THE NEWS**
>
> Qingdao also has a lively foreign-restaurant scene, but places tend to open and close very quickly. Get a copy of the local expat magazine *Redstar* from your hotel for the latest information.

$–$$ ✕ **La Villa** (La Wei La Faguo Canting). It may have an Italian name, but this French restaurant serves up reliable renditions of classic dishes such as coq au vin. The French-trained chef also serves up steaks and other hearty fare. The cozy wooden interior makes this popular with local expats. ⊠ *5 Xianggang Zhong Lu* ☎ *0532/8388–6833* ▭ *DC, MC, V.*

$–$$ ✕ **Qingdao Restaurant** (Qingdao Caiguan). At this popular restaurant there isn't an English menu—in fact, there's no menu of any kind. Instead, you wander around displays of uncooked dishes laid out on ice and tanks filled with mussels and crabs, all ready to be whisked away to the kitchen and cooked to order. The decor isn't exciting, but the food is excellent and the service is doting. ⊠ *17 Aomen Lu* ☎ *0532/8386–0098* ▭ *DC, MC, V.*

¢–$ ✕ **Chui Zhu Yuan.** Don't be offended when you're brought a bib and plastic gloves when you walk into this brightly lighted restaurant. You'll need them for the signature dish: tiny lobsters served in a rich, spicy sauce. There might be some work getting to the fleshy bits, but that's half the fun. Other Qingdao specialties, like spicy clams, are excellent. ⊠ *129 Minjiang Lu* ☎ *0532/8576–5286* ▭ *No credit cards.*

¢–$ ✕ **Guo Fu Cheng.** On a street lined with lively eateries, this inexpensive hot-pot restaurant stands head and shoulders above the rest. You and your dining companions will all have a private hot pot, so you can choose what meat and seafood to add to the steaming liquid. If you don't want to do all the work yourself, the kitchen is happy to take care of things. Be warned: the spicy hot pot is *seriously* spicy. ⊠ *72 Yunxiao Lu, off Minjiang Lu* ☎ *0532/8578–7018* ▭ *No credit cards.*

¢–$ ✕ **Zhong Shan Restaurant.** In the same neighborhood as the Catholic Church, this spartan but spotless place is where locals come for seafood. The restaurant is in an attractive building from the 1930s, and its price list seems to be from the same era. A bowl of seafood wontons is Y3, and a large plate of fresh oysters with a garlic-and-vinegar dip is yours for an astounding Y15. ☒*46 Hunan Road, at Zhong Shan Lu* ☎ *0532/ 8287–9073* ▭ *No credit cards.*

$$–$$$ 🏨 **Crowne Plaza.** The tallest building in the eastern end of the city, the Crowne Plaza towers over the competition. The service is attentive, especially considering the massive number of guests that constantly stream through the doors. The rooms in the cylindrical tower are spacious, and some have views of the ocean and the new Olympic Sailing Center. The hotel is adjacent to a ritzy shopping center filled with outposts of Prada and Louis Vuitton. ☒ *76 Xianggang Zhong Rd., 266071* ☎ *0532/8571–8888* ⊕ *www. crowneplaza.com* ⟟ *388 rooms* ♨ *5 restaurants, room service, cable TV, pool, health club, bar, in-room broadband, business services, airport shuttle* ▭ *AE, DC, MC, V.*

$$–$$$ 🏨 **Shangri-La.** Only a block from the scenic coastline, the Shangri-La is also close to some of the best shopping and eating in town. Legions of bellboys wait to take you and your luggage up to your well-appointed room. Q Bar, popular with local expats, is a stylish place for a pre-dinner drink. ☒ *9 Xiang Gang Zhong Lu, 266071* ☎ *0532/388– 3838* ⊕ *www.shangri-la.com* ⟟ *402 rooms* ♨ *2 restaurants, room service, in-room fax, refrigerators, cable TV, tennis court, pool, gym, bar, broadband, business services* ▭ *AE, DC, MC, V.*

$–$$ 🏨 **Huiquan Dynasty Hotel.** Opposite the city's most popular beach, this well-established hotel revels in its enviable location. Diners at the 25th-floor revolving restaurant enjoy great views of the ocean. It is worth paying for a room overlooking the ocean even if you don't plan on spending a lot of time admiring the view, as the rooms in the rear overlook a busy road. There is a branch of the CITS travel agency on the premises. ☒ *6 Nanhai Lu, 266003* ☎ *0532/829–9988* 🖷 *0532/8287–1122* ⊕ *www. hqdynastyhotel.com* ⟟ *405 rooms* ♨ *Restaurant, room service, gym, swimming pool, bar, laundry service, in-room broadband, business services, travel services* ▭ *AE, DC, MC, V.*

¢ 🏨 **Badaguan Hotel.** If your priority is peace and quiet, this hotel in the scenic Badaguan neighborhood is a good choice. Set in established gardens, it feels miles away from the hustle and bustle of the city. The guest rooms look a little dusty, but are otherwise more than adequate. The location near Number 2 Beach makes up for any deficiencies. ☒ *19 Shanhaiguan Lu, 266071* ☎ *0532/387–2168* ⟟ *300 rooms* ♨ *Restaurant, tennis court, gym, business services* ▭ *AE, DC, MC, V.*

Nightlife & the Arts

In a German-style building dating from the 1930s, **Café Roland** (☒ 9 Taiping Jiao Er Lu ☎ 0532/8387–5734) has a lovely wooden interior and a view of Number 3 Beach. The **Sailing Club and Bar** (☒6 Nanhai Lu ☎0532/ 8286–4645) lets you enjoy a quiet drink as you gaze at the sailboats float-

---

RAISE A GLASS

The **International Beer Festival,** in August, is Qingdao's biggest event of the year, with gallons of beer for tasting. You may not see any lederhosen, but it's still great fun. The **Cherry Festival** takes place in April and May. In early September the **Mt. Daze Grape Festival** celebrates the fruit of the vine.

---

ing past. It's easy to imagine yourself transported to somewhere in Europe. But for the best beer in town, head to the source: **Tsingdao Brewery Bar** (⌗ 56 DengZhou Lu ☎ 0532/8383–3437). Things can get rowdy because the prices are intentionally kept low, but if cost is more of a consideration than ambiance, this can be an excellent night out.

Sports & the Outdoors

Chinese visitors come to Qingdao in the tens of thousands for the beaches. Each of the seven sandy beaches that run along the coast for more than 6 mi (10 km) have a variety of facilities ranging from changing rooms to kiosks renting inflatable toys. Sometimes the water quality isn't the greatest, so it's worth inquiring at your hotel.

BEACHES **Number 1 Beach** is the busiest, and in summer it can be difficult to find a place for your towel. If your goal is peace and quiet, head to **Number 2 Beach,** as fewer Chinese tourists venture out that way. In the summer, watch out for the armies of brides and bridegrooms using the beaches as backdrops for their wedding photos.

GOLF The 18-hole **Qingdao International Golf Club** (⌗ Song Ling Lu ☎ 0532/899–0001) is 20 minutes from downtown. It has driving ranges, a pro, and a fine-dining restaurant.

WATER SPORTS With the sailing center for the 2008 Olympics, the Qingdao waterfront is completely transformed. Besides the athletic facilities, there is a conference center, a luxury hotel, a cruise-ship terminal, a yacht club, and a marina. There are also several other places that will help you get on or in the water.

Located near Number 1 Beach, **Qingdao Qin Hai Diving Club** (⌗ 5 Huiquan Lu ☎ 0532/8387–7977) is the only government-certified diving club in northern China. All equipment is provided, and you can get your diving certificate in 12 classes.

The Sailing Club and Bar (⌗ 6 Nanhai Lu ☎ 0532/8286–4645) has sailing and windsurfing equipment for rent in the summer. The prices are very reasonable, ranging from Y60 to Y180 an hour for a boat. If the water is too cold for you, there are wet suits available.

One of the country's largest yacht clubs, **Yinhai International Yacht Club** (⌗ 30 Donghai Zhong Lu ☎ 0532/8588–6666 ⊕ www.yinhai.com.cn) has more than 30 yachts for rent, and offers lessons to beginners and more experienced sailors. The club is in the east of town, near the Olympic Sailing Center.

Shopping

The north end of Zhongshan Lu has a cluster of antiques and cultural artifacts shops. The **Ju Bao Zhai Art Shop** (⌗ 169 Zhongshan Lu ☎ 0532/8282–4184) offers a selection of porcelain, metal, and stoneware. The largest antiques shop on the street is the **Qingdao Art and Craft Store** (⌗ 212 Zhongshan Lu ☎ 0532/8281–7948), with 4 floors of porcelain, scroll paintings, silk, gold, jade, and other stones.

Very near the Catholic Church is **Michael's** (⌗ 15 Zhejiang Lu ☎ 0532/8286–6790), a gallery specializing in calligraphy. Aside from the lovely writing on display, the building itself, which dates from the 1930s, makes a visit worthwhile.

Side Trips from Qingdao

Rising to a height of more than 3,280 feet, **Mount Lao** (Laoshan) is nearly as famous as the province's other famous mountain, Mount Tai. A place of pilgrimage for centuries, Laoshan once had 9 palaces, 8 temples, and 72 convents. Many of these places have been lost over the years, but a number of the temples remaining are worth a look for their elegant architecture and their excellent views out to sea. With sheer cliffs and cascading waterfalls, the beautiful mountain is widely recognized in China as a source of the country's best-known mineral water (a vital ingredient in the local brew, Tsingtao). It is possible to see the mountain's sights in less than a day. Tourist buses to Laoshan leave from the main pier in Qingdao. ✉ *40 km (25 mi) east of Qingdao* 🖃 *Y50* 🕙 *Daily 7–5.*

Near Laoshan is **Huadong Winery,** Shandong's best winery. Although not as famous as the province's brewery, it has nevertheless already won a string of prizes. Some judge the chardonnay, grown from vines imported from France in the 1980s, to be on par with those from California. (This is perhaps because the wine-growing area of Shandong is on the same latitude as the Napa Valley.) The beautiful scenery alone makes this a worthwhile side trip from Qingdao. Visit the winery's **Qingdao Office** (✉ 15 Donghai Xi Lu ☎ 0532/8387–4778) to book a tour. ✉ *Jiulong Po* ☎ *0532/8387–4889.*

To & from Qingdao

12 hrs (540 km [335 mi]) by train or 2 hrs by plane southeast of Beijing; 6 hrs by train (310 km [192 mi]) east of Ji'nan.

Three express trains link Qingdao to Beijing (8 hours), and there are also direct trains to Shanghai (18 hours) and Guangzhou (28 hours). It's best to buy tickets from travel agents or through your hotel, as there are few English speakers at the station.

The long-distance bus terminal is opposite the train station. Here you can catch buses to Ji'nan (3½ hours), Shanghai (11 hours), and Beijing (16 hours).

The international airport is 30 km (19 mi) north of the city. In a taxi, the journey takes 40 minutes and costs around Y80. Some hotels have airport shuttles, so inquire when you make your reservations.

SHANDONG ESSENTIALS

Transportation

BY AIR

Regular flights link Ji'nan Yiao Qiang Airport with Beijing, Shanghai, Hong Kong, and other major Chinese cities. The airport is 40 km (25 mi) northeast of downtown Ji'nan.

Qingdao Liu Ting Airport is 30 km (19 mi) from the city center. Direct flights link Qingdao with Osaka and Seoul, as well as Hong Kong and other major Chinese cities.

🚹 Airport Information **Ji'nan Yao Qiang Airport** ⊠ Near Yiao Qiang Village ☎ 0531/694-9400. **Qingdao Liuting Airport** ⊠ Near Liu Ting Village ☎ 0532/8471-5177 ⊕ www.qdairport.com.

BY BOAT & FERRY

Some routes have been canceled because most travelers prefer to fly, but if time is not a consideration, going to Incheon in South Korea (four boats a week) or Shimonoseki in Japan (once every two weeks) is possible. For up-to-date information, consult a travel agent or the schedule at the passenger ferry terminal.

🚹 Boat & Ferry Information **Qingdao Ferry Terminal** ⊠ 6 Xinjiang Lu, 1 mi (2 km) north of the train station, Qingdao ☎ 0532/8282-5001.

BY BUS

Regular buses link Ji'nan with Tai'an (1 hour) and Qufu (3 hours). Buses ply the route between Ji'nan and Qingdao every 20 minutes, taking four to five hours. The bus terminals in Qingdao and Tai'an are opposite their respective train stations.

🚹 Bus Depot **Ji'nan Long-Distance Bus Station** ⊠ 23 Jiluo Lu ☎ 0531/96369. **Tai'an Bus Station** ⊠ 235 Dongyue Jie ☎ No phone. **Qufu Bus Station** ⊠ Shen Dao Lu and Jingxuan Lu ☎ 0543/7441-2554. **Qingdao Long-Distance Bus Station** ⊠ 2 Wenzhou Lu ☎ 0532/8267-6842.

BY TRAIN

Ji'nan is on the Beijing–Shanghai line and the Beijing–Qingdao line, so there is no shortage of trains. On an express train, the journey from the capital takes 4½ hours. Tai'an is also on the Beijing–Shanghai rail line.

Direct trains link Qingdao with Beijing (8 hrs), Shanghai (19 hrs), Shenyang (24 hrs), Yantai (4 hours), Xi'an (22 hours), and Guangzhou (28 hours).

🚹 Train Information **Ji'nan Station** ⊠ Jingyi Jie ☎ 0531/242-8862. **Qingdao Station** ⊠ Yingzhe Dajie ☎ 0538/8296-2777. **Tai'an Station** ⊠ Yingzhe Dajie ☎ 0538/824-6222.

Contacts & Resources

EMERGENCIES

Shandong uses the same emergency numbers as the rest of China. **Police** (☎ 110), the **fire department** (☎ 119), and the **first-aid hotline** (☎ 120).

The best hospital in Ji'nan is Shengli Hospital. In Qingdao, the International Clinic at Qingdao Municipal Hospital has doctors from Korea and America who can speak English.

🚹 **Shengli Hospital** ⊠ 324 Jingwu Lu, Ji'nan ☎ 0531/793-8911. **Qingdao Municipal Hospital** ⊠ 5 DongHai Zhong Lu, Qingdao ☎ 0532/8593-7690.

INTERNET SERVICES

Most major hotels provide free in-room broadband service for their guests. If you need an Internet café, there are a few choices. In Ji'nan, there are several smoky places near the train station: look out for the WANG BA signs.

TRAVEL AGENCIES
China International Travel Service (CITS) is the country's national travel service, intended mostly for foreign visitors. This does not guarantee that attendants speak good English, but they can usually summon someone who can. The staff can book train tickets, plane tickets, arrange tours, and reserve rooms at hotels.

🖪 Ji'nan CITS ✉ 6th fl., Building 30, 1 Jiefeng Lu ☎ 0531/8292-7250. **Qingdao CITS** ✉ Yuyuan Dasha Office Building, 73 Xianggang Zhong Lu ☎ 0532/8389-3062.

VISITOR INFORMATION
Qingdao is more prepared for foreign travelers than Ji'nan, and this is reflected in the quality of tourist information available. The staff at Qingdao's tourist office speaks excellent English and can advise you on worthwhile destinations in the region.

🖪 Tourist Information **Qingdao Tourist Administration** ✉ 7 Minjiang Lu, Qingdao ☎ 0532/8591-2027. **Ji'nan Tourist Service** ✉ 86 Jingshi Lu, Ji'nan ☎ 0531/260-0660.

JIANGSU

Jiangsu is defined by water. The region is crossed by one of the world's great rivers, the mystical Yangtze. Here you'll find an ancient feat of engineering, the Grand Canal. This massive waterway allowed merchants to ship the province's plentiful rice, vegetables, and tea to the north. Within the cities, daily life was historically tied to the water. Many old neighborhoods are still crisscrossed by countless small canals.

As a result of its trading position, Jiansu has long been an economic and political center of China. The founder of the Ming Dynasty brought the capital to Nanjing before his son moved it back north to Beijing, but Nanjing and Jiangsu retained their nationwide importance. After the 1911 revolution, the province once again hosted the nation's capital, in Nanjing.

Planning a trip in the province is remarkably easy. The cities are quite close together, and connected by many buses and trains. Autumn tends to be warm and dry, with ideal walking temperatures. Spring can be rainy and windy, but the hills burst with blooms. Summers are infamously oppressive, hot, and humid. The winter is mild, but January and February are often rainy.

Top Tours
Jiangsu Huate International Travel Service has a number of guides who speak English. Jinling Business International Travel Service offers a range of options for travelers. The company has its own fleet of comfortable cars with knowledgeable drivers. It can arrange trips throughout the region.

🖪 Tour-Operator Recommendations **Jiangsu Huate International Travel Service** ✉ 33 Jingxiang He Lu, Nanjing ☎ 025/8337-8598 ⊕ www.hitravels.com. **Jinling Business International Travel Service** ✉ Jinling Hotel, 2 Hanzhong Lu, Nanjing ☎ 025/8473-0501 ⊕ www.travelspace.cn.

Nanjing

6 The name Nanjing means Southern Capital, and for six dynastic periods the city was the administrative capital of China. Never as successful a capital as Beijing, the locals chalk up the failures of several dynasties here to bad timing, but it could be that the laid-back atmosphere of the Yangtze Delta just isn't as suited to political intrigue as the north.

Nanjing offers travelers significantly more sites of historical importance than the economic powerhouse of nearby Shanghai. One of the most impressive is the massive Ming Dynasty sections of the city wall, built to surround and protect the city in the 14th century. There are also a number of traditional monuments, tombs, and gates that reflect the glory of Nanjing's capital days.

> ### IN THE NEWS
>
> Currently under construction, Nanjing Public Library will be one of the largest in Asia. It's a massive public project, one that speaks to China's desire to recover its historical place in the world. When completed, it will be one of China's most advanced places of learning, with a technology center and multimedia auditorium.

The city lies on the Yangtze, and the colossal Second Bridge or the more subdued park at Sparrow Rock are great places for viewing the river. The sheer amount of activity is testimony to its continued importance as a corridor for shipping and trade. Downtown, the streets are choked with traffic, but the chaotic scene is easily avoided with a visit to any of the large parks. You can also take a short ride to ZiJin Mountain. Quiet trails lead between Ming Tombs and the grand mausoleum of Sun Yat-sen.

Exploring Nanjing

5 **Confucian Temple** (Fuzimiao). The traditional-style temple overlooks the Qinhuai, a tributary of the Yangtze. The surrounding area is the city's busiest shopping and entertainment district and lit with neon at night. The back alleys behind the temple, once home to China's most famous district of courtesans, now house a toy market and excellent curio shops. This area has the best bazaars for souvenirs and crafts. Evening tours of the Qinghuai River leave from in front of the temple. The cost is Y40 per person ⊠ *Zhongshan Lu and Jiankang Lu, on the Qinhuai River* 🖆 *Y15* ⊕ *www.njfzm.com* ☉ *Daily 8:30–5:30.*

11 **Drum Tower** (Gulou). The traditional center of ancient Chinese cities, the 1382 Drum Tower housed the drums used to signal important events, from the changing of the guard to an enemy attack or a fire. Today it holds only one drum. If you're in the area, you can duck inside to see the 1st-floor art exhibition. ⊠ *1 Dafang Xiang, beside Gulou People's Square* 🕾 *025/8663–1059* 🖆 *Y5* ☉ *Daily 8:30–5:30.*

9 **Ming Tomb** (Ming Xiaoling). The ancient tomb of the founder of the Ming Dynasty, called Tomb of Filial Piety, is one of the largest burial mounds in China. The emperor Hong Wu was born a peasant and orphaned early

Fodor'sChoice
★

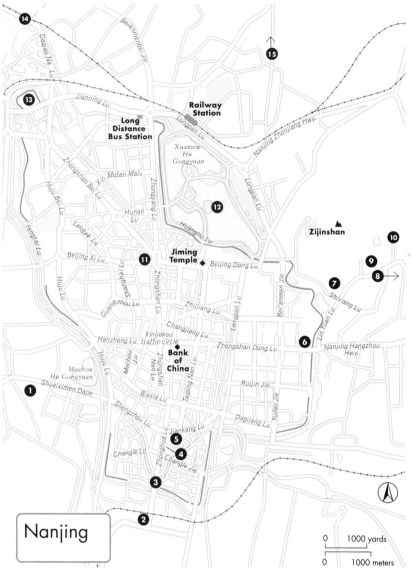

Nanjing

on. He became a monk and eventually led the army that overthrew the Yuan Dynasty. He chose Nanjing for the capital of the Ming Dynasty, but his son returned the capital to Beijing. Visitors approach the tomb through a grand entrance of stone animals. The lions, elephants, camels, and mythical creatures kneel in tribute to the emperor and stand as guardians to the tomb. Winding paths behind them make

> ## GETTING AROUND
>
> Once you're on Purple Mountain, the best way to get around is Bus Y3, a tourist bus that runs from the train station to Ming Tomb, Sun Yat-sen Botanical Gardens, Sun Yat-sen Mausoleum, and Spirit Valley Pagoda.

the Ming Tomb area a rewarding place to explore, but as in all Chinese tombs the entrance is hidden to foil looters. For detailed history, buy a book at the entrance shop; English signage is sparse. ⊠ *Mingling Lu, on Purple Mountain* 🔁 *Y50* ⊙ *Daily 8:30–5.*

❶ Nanjing Massacre Memorial (Datusha Jinianguan). In the winter of 1937, Japanese forces occupied Nanjing. In the space of a few days, thousands of Chinese were killed in the chaos, which became commonly known as the "Rape of Nanjing." This monument commemorates the victims, many of whom were buried in a mass grave. Be advised, however: this is not for the squeamish. Skeletons have been exhumed from the "Grave of Ten Thousand" and are displayed with gruesomely detailed explanations as to how each lost his or her life. The memorial also displays artifacts from the Sino-Japanese reconciliation after World War II, which ended the conflict between the two countries on a less strident, more hopeful note. To get here, take Bus 7 and 37 from Xinjiekou. ⊠ *418 Shui Ximen Da Jie, west of Mouchou Lake Park* ☎ *025/8650–1033* ⊕ *www.nj1937.org* 🔁 *Free* ⊙ *Tues.–Sun. 8:30–4:30.*

❻ Nanjing Museum (Nanjing Bowuyuan). With one of the largest and most impressive collections in China, the Nanjing Museum has excellent displays that set objects in historical context. For instance, beside the shelves of ancient pottery there is a re-created kiln to illustrate how traditional objects were formed. The permanent collection includes excellent works in jade, silk, and bronzes. There's also a treasure room with some eye-popping displays. In a modern hall the museum's curators have pushed the envelope—and pushed some buttons—with some controversial temporary exhibits. ⊠ *Zhongshan Dong Lu, inside Zhongshan Gate, east of the city center* ☎ *025/8480–2119* ⊕ *www.njmuseum. com/english* 🔁 *Y20* ⊙ *Daily 9–4:30.*

❼ Plum Blossom Hill and Sun Yat-sen Botanical Gardens (Meihuashan and Zhongshan Zhiwuyuan). This hillside explodes with plum blossoms in early spring. The garden is a nice place for a picnic, but is only worth a special trip when the flowers are in bloom. The exhibits at the botanical gardens, on the other hand, are a rewarding experience for anyone interested in the flora of China. ⊠ *1 Shixiang Lu, northeast of Nanjing Museum* 🔁 *Y50* ⊙ *Daily 6:30 AM–6:30 PM.*

❷ Rain Flower Terrace and Martyrs Memorial (Yuhua Tai Lieshi Lingyuan). The terrace gets its name from the legend of Yunzhang, a 15th-century Buddhist monk who supposedly pleased the gods so much with his recitation of a sutra that they showered flowers on this spot. The site was used for a more grim purpose in the 1930s, when the Nationalists used it to execute their left-wing political enemies. The site was transformed into a memorial park with massive statues of heroic martyrs, soaring obelisks, flower arrangements of the hammer and sickle, and a moving museum that uses personal objects to convey the lives of some of those executed here. ⊠ *215 Yuhua Lu, outside Zhonghua Gate* 🎫 *Y35* ⊙ *Park daily 7 AM–10 PM, memorial daily 8–5:30.*

🕑 ❸ **South Gate of City Wall** (Zhonghua Men). Built as the linchpin of the city's defenses, this is less of a gate than a complete fortress, with multiple courtyards and tunnels where several thousand soldiers could withstand a siege. It was even attacked; armies wisely avoided it in favor of the less heavily fortified areas to the north. Today bonsai enthusiasts have displays in several of the courtyards. ⊠ *Southern end of Zhonghua Lu, south side of city wall* 🎫 *Y15* ⊙ *Daily 8–6.*

❶❺ **Sparrow's Rock** (Yanzi Ji). North of the city, this small park overlooking the Yangtze is worth the trip. Paths wind up the hill to several lookout points for what may be Nanjing's best view of this great river. The park's name comes from the massive boulder over the water that supposedly resembles a bird. To get here, take Bus 8 to the last stop. ⊠ *Northeast of Mount Mufu, on the Yangtze* 🎫 *Y6* ⊙ *Daily 7:30–6.*

❽ **Spirit Valley Temple and Pagoda** (Linggu Si and Linggu Ta). The temple commemorates Xuan Zang, the monk who brought Buddhist scriptures back from India. Farther up the hill is a 9-story granite pagoda with a staircase that spirals up the central pillar. The top is dizzyingly high. This pagoda was built as a solemn memorial to those killed by the Nationalists in 1929; today, vendors sell plastic balloons to throw off the top balcony. On the grounds is the brick Beamless Hall. The magnificent 14th-century architecture is now given over to propagandistic "historical" reenactments. Although the temple and pagoda may not be worth a special trip, they are close to Ming Tomb and other attractions around Purple Mountain. ⊠ *Ta Lu, southeast of Sun Yat-sen Memorial* ☎ *025/ 8444–6111* 🎫 *Pagoda Y15, temple Y2* ⊙ *Sept.–May daily 8:30–5, June–Aug. daily 6:30 AM–6:30 PM.*

❶⓿ **Sun Yat-sen Memorial** (Zhongshan Ling). Acknowledged by the Nationalist and Communist governments alike, the father of modern China lies

---

CAUTION

Be careful when crossing the street—look both ways, and again, and keep looking as you cross. This is where the implications of China's immense population are most apparent. Nanjing has seen an explosion of private auto ownership in the past decade, and no comparable program of driver education. Pedestrians may have the green walk light, but they are not necessarily given the right of way when cars make right turns. Motorbikes and bicycles ignore all lights and signage as a rule, and even take over the sidewalks. The good news is that Nanjing has several quiet pedestrian areas, where you truly let down your guard.

PEDESTRIAN STREETS

You can escape city traffic and do a little shopping in any of the following areas.

■ The **Confucius Temple Area** (Fuzimiao) are souvenir and shopping streets around the Qinghuai River. ✛ *By the intersection of Zhongshan Lu and Jiankang Lu.*

■ **Hunan Road** is a section of streets filled with snack shops and restaurants, and is one of the best places to fill up before venturing back out into traffic. ✛ *Hunan Lu, west of Zhongshan North Rd. and east of Zhongyang Lu.*

■ In the **Xinjiekou City Center**, around the big malls and shopping centers are several bustling walking streets. ✛ *Xinjiekou between Huaihai Lu and Zhongshan Lu.*

buried in a delicately carved marble sarcophagus. His resting place is the quiet center of a solemn and imposing monument to the ideas that overthrew the imperial system. On the mountain are steep trails up the pine-covered slopes that feel worlds away from the bustle of Nanjing. A popular destination for Chinese tourists, the mausoleum can get crowded on weekends; try to visit on a weekday. ⊠ *Lingyuan Lu, east of the Ming Tomb* ✇ *Y40* ⊙ *Sept.–May daily 8:30–5, June–Aug. daily 6:30 AM–6:30 PM.*

❹ **Taiping Heavenly Kingdom Museum** (Taiping Tianguo Lishi Bowuguan). Commemorating a particularly fascinating period of Chinese history, this museum follows the life of Hong Xiuquan, a Christian who led a peasant revolt in 1859. He ultimately captured Nanjing and ruled for 11 years. Hong, who set himself up as emperor, claimed to be the younger brother of Jesus. On display are artifacts from the period. After browsing the museum, you can walk around the grounds of the Ming Dynasty garden compound that houses the museum. During the day, it is the calmest spot in Nanjing. In the evening from 6 to 11 there are performances of opera and storytelling. Reasonably priced English-speaking guides make up for the lack of English signage. ⊠ *128 Zhanyuan Lu, beside the Confucian Temple* ☎ *025/5223–8687* ✇ *Y50* ⊙ *Daily 8–4:30.*

⓬ **Xuanwu Lake Park** (Xuanwu Hu Gongyuan). More lake than park, this pleasant garden is bounded by one of the longer sections of the monumental city wall, which you can climb for a good view of the water. Purple Mountain rises in the east, and the glittering skyscrapers of modern Nanjing are reflected on the calm water. Causeways lined with trees and benches connect several large islands in the lake. ⊠ *Off Hunan Lu, in the northeast corner of the city, outside the city wall* ✇ *Y20* ⊙ *Daily 8–8.*

⓮ **Yangtze River Bridge** (Changjiang Daqiao). Completed in 1968 at the height of the Cultural Revolution, the bridge is decorated in stirring Socialist-realist style. Huge stylized flags made of red glass rise from the bridge's piers, and groups of giant-size peasants, workers, and soldiers stride forward heroically. Look closely and you'll even see one African—a reminder of Mao's support for revolutionaries around the world. The Great Bridge Park lies on the south side. From here you can take an elevator from the park up to a small museum. ⊠ *End of Daqiao Nan, northwest section of the city* 🏛 *Free* ☉ *Daily 9–5.*

⑬ Yuejiang Lou Tower. This massive tower complex, built in the new millennium in Ming Dynasty style, looks out over a broad sweep of the Yangtze River. The founding emperor of the Ming Dynasty wrote a poem describing his plans to have a tower built here where he could view the river. Other imperial business got in the way, and for several centuries the building remained on paper. The grand tower and its surrounding buildings were built in 2001 in a historically accurate style, but it somehow seems too sterile. ⊠ *202 Jianning Lu, northwest corner of the city* 🏛 *025/5880–3977* 🌐 *www.yuejiangtower.com* 🏷 *Y30* ☉ *Daily 8–6.*

Tours

Major hotels will often arrange a tour guide for a group. Nanjing China Travel Service can arrange almost any type of tour of the city.

🗂 Tour Guides **Nanjing China Travel Service** ⊠ 12 Baizi Ting, south of the Drum Tower 🏛 025/8336–6227 🌐 www.njcts.com.

Where to Stay & Eat

For more information on bars and restaurants in Nanjing, pick up a copy of the local bilingual *Map Magazine* at your hotel. It has listings and reviews of many popular spots in the city, as well as upcoming cultural events.

$$–$$$ ✕ **Blue Marlin.** Palladian windows and a broad arched ceiling distinguish this dining room. The owner attended culinary school in Germany, which is why the place serves European-influenced cuisine. Specials include fish, steak, pasta—even foie gras. ⊠ *8 Changjiang Hou Jie, across from the Nanjing Library* 🏛 *025/8453–7376* 🖃 *No credit cards.*

★ $$–$$$ ✕ **Dingshan Meishi Cheng.** One of Nanjing's finest restaurants, Dingshan Meishi Cheng serves local cuisine in a traditional setting. The food here is not as hot as that from Sichuan, nor as sweet as that from Shanghai. There's a set-price menu that includes 4 cold dishes, 4 hot dishes, and a whopping 18 small dessert dishes, all for Y60. ⊠ *5 Zhanyuan Lu, near Confucian Temple* 🏛 *025/5220–9217* 🖃 *AE, MC, V.*

$–$$ ✕ **Baguo Buyi.** Nanjing cuisine is generally mild, but if you are craving

Fodor'sChoice something spicy, Baguo Buyi is one of the best places to try authentic

★ Sichuan cuisine. The food is searingly hot, in sharp contrast to the sweeter flavors of eastern Chinese cuisine. The stew of beef and yellow tofu is delicious, as is the steamed river fish served in a caldron of peppercorns. The dining room is decorated with traditional wood carvings and antique furniture. ☒ *211 Longpan Zhong Lu, at Yixian Qiao* ☏ *025/8460–8801* ▭ *No credit cards.*

$–$$ ✕ **Hong Ni Restaurant.** It's hard to miss the Hong Ni—its facade lights up the neighborhood with a three-story neon extravaganza. Although the exterior is pure Las Vegas, the cuisine is excellent Yangzi Delta food from neighboring Zhejiang province. Prices are reasonable and everything is served in a sleek dining room. It's conveniently located downtown, near the Xinjiekou traffic circle, and many members of the staff speak English. ☒ *23 Hongwu Lu* ☏ *025/8689–9777* ▭ *No credit cards.*

$–$$ ✕ **Jimingsi Vegetarian Restaurant.** Inside the Jiming Temple, this establishment cooks up excellent Chinese fare with absolutely no meat. Although the menu lists pork, fish, chicken, and goose dishes, the food is in fact all vegetarian. The chefs ingeniously use tofu, wheat gluten, and vegetables to create interpretations of meat, often more savory than the real thing. An English menu features a limited selection of the best dishes. Tofu threads and the Sichuan "fish" are among the best. The restaurant has a lovely view of the temple grounds as well as access to the city wall. ☒ *Jiming Temple, off Beijing Dong Lu, south of Xuanwu Lake Park* ☏ *025/8771–3690* ▭ *No credit cards* ☉ *No dinner.*

★ $–$$ ✕ **Shizi Lou.** Anchoring the strip of restaurants of Shizi Qiao, near the Shanzi Road Market, Shizi Lou is a great introduction to Huaiyang fare. Resembling an indoor market, you can walk between stands and point to the dishes you want to sample. The "stinky tofu" is very good and not as malodorous as it's billed. The place is famous for local meatballs, with a dozen types from which to choose. ☒ *29 Hunan Lu, near Shizi Bridge* ☏ *025/8360–7888* ▭ *No credit cards.*

$$$–$$$$ ⌂ **Jinling Hotel.** Nanjing's best-known hotel has a great location in the center of the city. It's a huge modern building connected to a shopping center. The travel agency on the 1st floor provides friendly and efficient service. On the 2nd floor is the most authentic Japanese food in town. The guest rooms have every comfort. ☒ *2 Xinjiekou, 210005* ☏ *025/ 8471–1888 or 025/8471–1999* ⇆ *570 rooms, 30 suites* ⌂ *7 restaurants, 2 cafés, gym, hair salon, bar, business services, meeting room* ▭ *AE, MC, V.*

$$$ ⌂ **Sheraton Nanjing Kingsley Hotel and Towers.** Top-rate facilities make this attractive hotel a favorite among business travelers; if you're not on an expense account, the prices may seem a bit steep. The rooms are as comfortable as any at this chain. It's also home to Nanjing's only Irish pub, Danny's, with Guinness on tap and a group of expat regulars. ☒ *169 Hanzhong Lu, 210029* ☏ *025/8666–8888* ⊕ *www.sheraton.com* ⇆ *350 rooms* ⌂ *2 restaurants, tennis court, pool, gym, 3 bars, business services, meeting rooms, no-smoking floor* ▭ *AE, DC, MC, V.*

$–$$ ⌂ **Celebrity City Hotel.** Unlike many of the city's lodgings, you won't forget you're in China when you step through the door at this modern hotel. The hotel combines the best of the East (elegant bamboo and silk brocade) and the West (sleek glass and steel). Two good restaurants are here, one serving spicy Hunan food, and one re-creating the feasts of the imperial past (for imperial prices). Half of one floor is dedicated to mah-

FodorsChoice
★

jongg rooms. Rooms aren't palatial, but they are intelligently designed, with sleek furnishings, privacy, and high ceilings. ⊠ *30 Zhongshan Bei Lu, 210008* ☎ *025/8312–3333* 🛏 *288 rooms, 77 suites* ♨ *2 restaurants, pool, gym, sauna, bar, no-smoking floors* ⊟ *AE, MC, V.*

$–$$ 🏨 **Mandarin Garden Hotel.** While many hotels of its caliber seem impersonal, this well-appointed establishment is warm and friendly. Its setting on the north side of the Confucian Temple keeps you far from the noise of the city. The excellent rooftop bar affords a good view of the skyline. The Galaxy Restaurant on the 2nd floor serves Cantonese food. Guests are treated to an excellent breakfast buffet. ⊠ *9 Zhuang Yuan Jing, 210001* ☎ *0255/220–2555 or 0255/220–2988* ⊕ *www.njzyl-hotel.com* 🛏 *500 rooms, 24 suites* ♨ *12 restaurants, pool, gym, hair salon, sauna, squash, bar, business services, meeting room, no-smoking floor* ⊟ *AE, MC, V.*

$ 🏨 **Central Hotel.** This lodging caters to travelers by arranging day tours in and around Nanjing. The 24-hour travel desk also sets up tours to more distant destinations. The modern rooms are stylish and reasonably priced. The sleek sauna and beautiful star-shape courtyard pool are inviting after a long day of sightseeing. ⊠ *75 Zhongshan Lu, 210005* ☎ *025/8473–3888* 🛏 *354 rooms, 22 suites* ♨ *2 restaurants, coffee shop, pool, gym, sauna, bar, dance club, shops, business services, meeting room* ⊟ *AE, MC, V.*

¢–$$$ 🏨 **Grand Hotel.** This elliptical building in the center of town is a good base for seeing the sights. It overlooks the busy shopping centers and office buildings in the commercial center of the city. Along with standard amenities, it has a good Western restaurant. ⊠ *208 Guangzhou Lu, 210024* ☎ *025/8331–1999* ⊕ *www.njgrandhotel.com* 🛏 *294 rooms, 11 suites* ♨ *Restaurant, tennis court, pool, gym, hair salon, sauna, bar, meeting room* ⊟ *AE, DC, MC, V.*

¢–$ 🏨 **Lakeview Xuanwu Hotel.** This modern hotel's guest rooms have excellent views of Xuanwu Lake. If you don't feel like venturing far from your room for dinner, the 20th-floor revolving restaurant serves an all-you-can-eat buffet with Western and Chinese cuisine. The hotel can also help you arrange day trips around the city. ⊠ *193 Zhongyang Lu, 210009* ☎ *025/8335–8888* 🛏 *270 rooms, 30 suites* ♨ *6 restaurants, gym, massage, sauna, bar, business services, meeting room* ⊟ *AE, DC, MC, V.*

¢ 🏨 **Nanjing Hotel.** Built in 1936, the old-fashioned hotel surrounded by lawns and trees seems pleasantly out of place in such a busy area of town. The staff is well trained and friendly. A separate section has simpler rooms that are less attractive, but are also half the standard rate. Rooms have different amenities, so ask to see a few before you decide. ⊠ *259 Zhong-shan Bei Lu, 210003* ☎ *025/8682–6666* 🛏 *307 rooms, 14 suites* ♨ *3 restaurants, gym, hair salon, massage, sauna, business services, meeting room* ⊟ *AE, MC, V.*

Nightlife

Nanjing's nightlife centers around the newly constructed 1912 neighborhood, named for the year the Republic of China was founded. A few dozen restaurants, bars, and clubs are packed into several blocks at the intersection of Taiping Lu and Changjiang Lu, a 15-minute walk northeast of the city center. Locals start with dinner, relax over drinks, charge up with coffee, hit the dance floor at a trendy club, stagger out to a late-night tea shop, and catch a cab back home—all without ever having to cross a lane of traffic. All the bars get going by about 10 PM, and close at 2 AM.

A highlight of the club scene, **Red Club** (⊠ Off Taiping Lu ☎ 025/8452–2568) has a bar and dance floor downstairs. **Scarlet Bar** (⊠ Off Taiping Lu ☎ 025/8335–1916) is a longstanding favorite popular with expats for its excellent music. At **Swank** (⊠ Off Taiping Lu ☎ No phone), the dance floor is packed with a trendy crowd.

★ **Base 77** (⊠ 129 Hanzhong Lu ☎ 025/8470–2006) has the best live music in town. The house band is remarkably versatile, even incorporating instruments like the mandolin and fiddle. **Behind the Wall** (⊠ 150 Shanghai Lu ☎ 025/8391–5630) is a great escape from the smoke and noise of most Chinese bars. It doubles as a Mexican restaurant during the day, which is why the staff can mix up a mean margarita. On weekends the music ranges from a solo guitar to a string quartet.

Shopping

The best place to buy traditional crafts, art, and souvenirs is the warren of small shops in the center of the city. The lavish embroidered robes once worn by the emperors were traditionally produced in Nanjing, and the **Brocade Research Institute** (⊠ 240 Chating Dong Jie, behind Nanjing Massacre Memorial ☎ 025/8651–8580) has a fascinating museum and workshop where the brocades are still produced using massive traditional looms. Their gift shop sells beautiful examples of traditional brocade.

Nanjing is a convenient place to pick up many of the traditional crafts of Jiangsu—purple sand teapots, flowing silks, interesting carvings, and folk paper cuttings. The **Nanjing Arts & Crafts Company** (⊠ 31 Beijing Dong Lu ☎ 025/5771–1189) has a range of items, from jade and lacquerware to tapestries.

In the courtyard of the Confucian Temple, the **Chaotian Gong Antique Market** (⊠ Zhongshan Lu and Jiankang Lu ☎ No phone) has an array of curios, ranging from genuine antiques to fakes of varying quality. Vendors' opening prices can border on the ludicrous side, especially with foreign customers, but some good-natured bargaining can yield good buys. The market is open every day, but is liveliest on weekend mornings.

The **Shanxi Lu Night Market** (⊠ Hunan Lu and Matai Jie ☎ No phone) has all sorts of odd items and some good finds waiting to be unearthed by savvy shoppers.

Northwest of the Drum Tower, the **Fabric Market** (⊠ 215 Zhongshan Bei Lu ☎ No phone) sells silks, linen, and traditional cotton fabrics. Bargaining is necessary, but the prices are reasonable. Prices range, but a good basic ballpark to pay is Y40 to Y60 per meter of silk. The vendors can also arrange tailoring.

To & from Nanjing

2½ hrs (309 km [192 mi]) by fast train west of Shanghai; 4½ hrs by normal train.

Bus travel in this area of China is considerably more comfortable than elsewhere, thanks to a highway linking the cities, and a fleet of new luxury buses. Buses for Shanghai leave from the Zhong Shan Nan Road Bus Station. The trip takes between three and four hours. Buses bound for Suzhou depart from the Zhongshan Nan Road Station, and can be as quick as two hours. Buses bound for Yangzhou leave frequently from the Long Distance Bust Station and take one hour.

Trains to Shanghai leave every half hour or so. There are several different kinds of trains, depending on the number of stops. For a speedier journey, request a K- or T-coded ticket. Fast trains take about 3 hours, whereas the slower ones can be as long as 4½ hours. One train each day makes the trip in 2½ hours. Trains to Suzhou are on the Shanghai line, and all stop there with the exception of the direct train. Travel time is two to three hours.

Yangzhou

❼ Yangzhou has quietly transformed itself into one of the most pleasant cities in Eastern China. With a population of half a million—miniscule by Chinese standards—the town has a laid-back feel. Yangzhou is small enough to be seen in one day, but is charming enough to make you want to linger for a few days.

Because of its location on the Grand Canal, Yangzhou flourished in the Tang Dynasty. Drawing on thousands of years as a trade center for salt and silk, Yangzhou maintains a cosmopolitan feel. Indeed, some of the most interesting sites in Yangzhou demonstrate a blending of cultures: Japanese relations are evidenced in the monument to Jianzhen, a monk who helped spread Buddhist teachings to Japan. European influence is seen in the Sino-Victorian gardens of He Yuan, and Persian contact is preserved in the tomb of Puddahidin, a 13th-century trader and descendant of Mohammed.

Exploring Yangzhou

The **Da Ming Temple** (Daming Si) is one of the more interesting Buddhist shrines in Eastern China. Maybe the most arresting detail is the mural behind the main laughing Buddha image, where an image of the gender-bending god Guanyin stands on a turtle's head. Another highlight on the temple grounds is the Fifth Spring Under Heaven. Most of the ancient Tang Dynasty springs are no longer usable, but this one still flows. The high mineral content of the water makes it especially suited for tea, which you can sip in a small teahouse overlooking the temple gardens. Also on the grounds is a Tang-style monument to a Chinese missionary who traveled to Japan, Jian Zhen. ⊠ *8 Pingshan Tang Lu, next to Slender West Lake* ☎ *0514/734–0720* ✉ *Mar.–June and Sept.–Nov. Y45; Jan.–Feb., July, Aug., and Dec. Y30* ☉ *Daily 8–5:30.*

The **Garden Tomb of Puhaddin** (Puhading Mu) faces the Grand Canal, from where you climb a stairway to a graveyard of marble slab headstones. In the back is a garden with a charming pavilion that blends Chinese and Muslim design, with Arabic inscriptions. Largely ignored by local tourists, a visit to the garden tomb is an eye-opening look at Chinese history. ⊠ *Laopai Lu at Quanfu Lu, near Jiefang Bridge* ⛳ *Y10* ⏲ *Daily 7:30–4:30.*

Rather than flowers, **Ge Garden** (Ge Yuan) is planted with over 60 varieties of bamboo and is a virtual rainbow of greens. There are yellow stalks, striped stalks, huge treelike stands, and dwarf bamboo with delicate leaves. The emerald stalks stand out against whitewashed walls and black undulating rooflines. Note the loose bricks in the path, arranged to clack as you walk. Catch your breath with a cup of tea in the tea hall. ⊠ *10 Yangfu Dong Lu, east of Yangzhou Hotel* ☎ *0514/736–5553* ⛳ *Y40* ⏲ *Daily 7:15–6.*

Dating from the 1880s, the Victorian-influenced **He Garden** (He Yuan) is notable for its melding of European and Chinese architecture. While Ge Garden flows in traditional style, He Garden has a more rigid design. However, the attention to detail and perspective subtly brings together design values of East and West, making the garden more than a mere imitation of European design. ⊠ *66 Xuning Men Dalu, southeast corner of the city* ☎ *0514/723–2360* ⛳ *Y40* ⏲ *Daily 7:30–5:30.*

Originally part of a river, **Slender West Lake** (Shou xi hu) was created during the Qing Dynasty by rich salt merchants hoping to impress the emperor on his visit to Yangzhou. The park is planted in willows, bamboo, and flowers, and can be enjoyed briskly in 45 minutes or savored for a full afternoon. The grounds are scattered with pavilions, tearooms, and bowed bridges. The **fishing terrace** marks the spot where the emperor decided he'd try his hand at angling. The merchants reportedly had their servants wade into the lake and hook a fish on each line he cast. Another mark left by the emperor is in the form of the **White Pagoda,** actually a *dagoba,* a Buddhist monument shaped like a bottle. The emperor casually remarked that Slender West Lake only lacked a dagoba like the one in Beijing. By the time the sun shone through the morning mist, there was the emperor's dagoba—more or less. The permanent structure was completed much later. Apparently all the flattery had the desired effect, because Yangzhou prospered up until the 20th century as a center of trade in China. ⊠ *28 Da Hongqiao Lu, in the northern part of the city* ☎ *0514/733–0189* ⛳ *Y80* ⏲ *Daily 6:30–6.*

Fodor'sChoice Unremarkable when it was built, **Wang's Residence** (Wangshi Xiaoyuan) ★ is now one of Yangzhou's highlights. This courtyard house was one of many large private homes owned by Yangzhou's prosperous merchant class. It alone was spared the wrath of the Cultural Revolution because it had been converted into a factory during the turbulent 20th century. The highlight is the detailed carvings, chief among them the crisscrossing bamboo design carved in layers out of *nanmu,* a glimmering wood now extinct in this area of China. There's even a bomb shelter in the small inner garden that serves as a reminder of the Japanese invasion. English translations are few, but there are a few guides who can lead in English—however the house speaks for itself. ⊠ *14 Di Gong Di, between Taizhou Lu and Guoqing Lu* ☎ *0514/732–8869* ⛳ *Y15* ⏲ *Daily 8–5:30.*

CLOSE UP

Adopting in China

FOR SOME, THE GARDENS, THE ARCHITECTURE, HISTORY, AND SCENERY are all secondary reasons to visit Yangzhou. Theirs is a more personal and momentous trip. On the outskirts of town there is a white-tiled compound called the Yangzhou Social Welfare Institute. This is where American parents and Chinese children come together to form families. Since Chinese law began promoting foreign adoption in 1991, there has been a huge surge in the number of families adopting from China, surpassing all other nations in the number of orphans placed in America. More than 50,000 children have been brought to the United States from China in the past 15 years.

Over 95% of children in orphanages are female. There persists a strong preference for boys, especially in rural areas. This is largely due to a combination of bias and traditional social structures whereby girls marry out and males help provide for the family. An unintended consequence of the One Child Policy exacerbates prejudices against women. Some Chinese parents, so desperate to have a male child, have taken drastic measures like gender-selective

abortion and even abandoning their girls on the steps of orphanages.

In the next years, the first wave of American-adopted Chinese girls will be growing into their teens. As they come of age, their trans-racial families face unique challenges as they grapple with questions of racial and cultural identity. Focused support groups, social organizations, and even specialized heritage tour groups address these questions and assist children in learning more about their places of birth.

For more information on adoption in China:

Families with Children from China runs listservs and provides a wealth of resources on adoption (⊕ www.fwcc. org). Tour information is available from the nonprofit group **Our Chinese Daughters Foundation** (⊕ www.ocdf. org). **The China Centre of Adoption Affairs** (CCAA; ⊕ www.china-ccaa. org) is the Chinese government's official source for procedural and legal information. *Adoptive Families* (⊕ www.adoptivefamilies.com) is a national magazine on general adoption issues.

Tours

Not only for the young, China Youth Travel can put together any kind of trip, from morning boat rides around Slender West Lake to evening cruises down the Great Canal. The staff speaks English, and has the most experience working with foreign travelers.

🎟 Tour-Operator Recommendations **Yangzhou China Youth Travel Agency** ✉ 6 Si-wangting Lu ☎ 0514/793-0606.

Where to Stay & Eat

$-$$ ✕ **Fu Chun Teahouse.** With history going back more than a century, Fu Chun serves traditional local food. It's best known for its desserts; try the sweet rice buns, layer cakes, or any of their other bite-size snacks. Wash it all down with flavorful green tea. ✉ *59 Tai Zhou Lu* ☎ *0514/723–3326* 🗐 *No credit cards.*

¢–$$ ✕ **De Yue Restaurant.** Started 20 years ago with just six tables, this sprawling restaurant is a testament to the quality of the food. Specialties include salted goose, flaky white fish, and shrimp in rice wine. ✉ *139 Wen Chang Lu* ☎ *0514/511–1908* 🗐 *No credit cards.*

$–$$ 🏨 **Metropark Hotel.** This modern hotel is conveniently located in the city center. Past the grand lobby are guest rooms with Asian-inspired decor. The helpful staff can arrange a car and driver if you want to explore the area. ✉ *559 Wenchang Quanfu Lu* ☎ *0514/732–2888* ⊕ *www.metroparkhotels.com* ⇥ *220 rooms, 25 suites* ♨ *4 restaurants, in-room safe, cable TV, in-room broadband, gym, babysitting, bar, business services, meeting rooms* 🗐 *AE, MC, V.*

$–$$ 🏨 **XiYuan Hotel.** These rooms border on drab, but the location is good and the hotel is quiet. ✉ *1 Feng Le Shang Jie, 215325* ☎ *0514/780–7888* ⊕ *www.xiyuan-hotel.com* ⇥ *258 rooms, 12 suites* ♨ *4 restaurants, travel services, babysitting, business services, meeting rooms; no-smoking floor* 🗐 *AE, MC, V.*

¢–$ 🏨 **Yangzhou Hotel.** Although this hotel looks a little worn around the edges, it does have a prime location overlooking the canals. Frequent discounts make it a real bargain. If you like going to bed early though, ask for a room facing away from the street. One of the city's biggest nightclubs is next door, and the noise can continue past midnight. ✉ *5 Feng Le Shang Jie, 225002* ☎ *0514/780–5888* ⇥ *141 rooms, 6 suites* ♨ *Restaurant, pool, massage, bar, nightclub, business services* 🗐 *AE, MC, V.*

Nightlife

The two best nightlife options are near the Yangzhou Hotel. At **Banana Club** (✉ 15 Fengle Shangjie ☎ 0514/780–5888) a DJ spins tunes for a mostly local crowd. The laid-back **Cellar Bar** (✉ 8 Fengle Shangjie ☎ 0514/216–6866) has a good mix of locals and expats. The beer is cheap, and the service is friendly.

To & from Yangzhou

1 hr (106 km [66 mi]) Northeast of Nanjing, 3½ hrs (300 km [185 mi]) from Shanghai.

The best way to get to or from Yangzhou is by bus. It lies on the Beijing–Shanghai and Nanjing–Nantong highways. Huaihai Road Bus Station has departures from 6:30 in the morning until 6:30 in the evening. Suzhou is 230 km (143 mi) south, about 2 hours away. Shanghai, about 300 km (186 mi) away, takes 3½ hours. Trains to Yangzhou are not as convenient as the bus. It takes 5 hours to reach Shanghai,

---

REPLANTING GARDENS

The sad story is that many of the country's historic gardens have been recently pieced back together. Most were ravaged during the Cultural Revolution, when for years Red Guard troops were encouraged to smash China's heritage to pieces. To this day, China is still replanting gardens, repairing temples, and restoring historic architecture.

and there are limited connections each day. It takes about 1½ hours to reach Nanjing.

Suzhou

8 Suzhou has long been renowned as a place of culture, beauty, and sophistication. It produced scores of artists, writers, and politicians over the centuries, and it developed a local culture based on refinement and taste. Famous around the world for its carefully designed classical gardens, Suzhou's elegance extends even to its local dialect—Chinese often say that two people arguing in the Suzhou dialect sound more pleasant than lovers talking in standard Chinese.

Unlike in other cities in Eastern China, glass-and-steel office parks have been barred from old city center, and this preservation makes Suzhou a pleasant place to explore. There is excellent English signage on the roads, and the local tourism board has even set up a convenient information center to get you on the right track.

Only an hour outside of Shanghai, the tourist trail here is well-worn, and during the high season you will find yourself sharing these gardens with packs of foreign and domestic tour groups. It is worth strategizing and getting up early to hit the most popular places before the crowds descend.

Exploring Suzhou

Suzhou is threaded by a network of narrow waterways. The canals that now seem quaint were once choked with countless small boats ferrying goods between the city's merchants. All of these small channels lead eventually to imperial China's main conduit of trade and travel, the **Grand Canal** (Da Yunhe), which passes through the outskirts of town. The **Precious Belt Bridge** (Baodai Qiao), is an ancient bridge of 53 arches that bound over Tantai Lake where it meets the Grand Canal. ⊠ *Beyond Pingmen Gate, north on Renmin Lu.*

2 **Blue Wave Pavilion** (Canglang Ting). The Blue Wave Pavilion is the oldest existing garden in Suzhou, dating back more than 900 years to the Song Dynasty. With a simple design, the garden grounds feel a little wilder than the relative newcomers. The central pond is an expansive stretch of water that reflects the upturned eaves of the surrounding buildings. Over 100 different lattice designs shading the windows provide visual variety as you saunter the long corridor over the water. A rocky hill rises in the center of the pond, atop which stands the square Blue Wave Pavilion. The **Pure Fragrance Pavilion** showcases Qing Dynasty furniture at its most extreme; the entire suite is created from gnarled banyan root. ⊠ *East of Renmin Lu, between Shiquan Jie and Xinshi Lu* 🎟 Y30 ⏱ *Daily 7:30–5:30.*

13 **Hanshan Temple** (Hanshan Si). Best known as a subject of one of the

> ## WATER WHEELS
>
> The old city is circled by a moat, and you can take an "aquatic bus" that leaves from the bus station. The cost is Y15 per person.

Suzhou

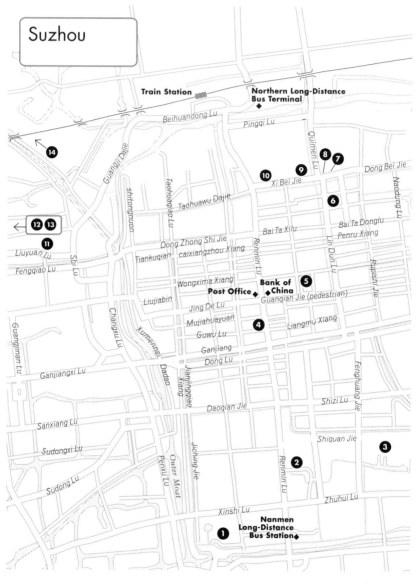

Train Station

**Northern Long-Distance
Bus Terminal** ◆

Beihuandong Lu

Pingqi Lu

Guangji Dajie

Qumen Lu

⑧ ⑦

Dong Bei Jie

⑩ ⑨ ⑥

Xi Bei Jie

Naodong Lu

shitongnuon

Taohuaqiao Lu

Taohuawu Dajie

Bai Ta Xilu

Bai Ta Donglu

Penru Xiang

Dong Zhong Shi Jie

Lin Dun Lu

Rupshi Jie

⑭

Tiankuqian· caixiangzhou Xiang

Renmin Lu

⑫ ⑬

Liuyuan Lu

Sai Lu

Wongxima Xiang

Post Office ◆

**Bank of
China** ⑤

⑪

Fengqiao Lu

Liujiabin

Jing De Lu

Guanqian Jie (pedestrian)

Guangjinan Lu

Changxu Lu

Mujiahuayuan

④

Liangmu Xiang

Guwu Lu

Ganjiang

Ganjiangxi Lu

Xumennei Dadao

Dong Lu

Jianjingqiao Xiang

Daoqian Jie

Shizi Lu

Fenghuang Jie

Sanxiang Lu

Shiquan Jie

Sudongxi Lu

Jiching Jie

③

Sudong Lu

Penxi Lu

Outer Moat

Renmin Lu

②

Zhuhui Lu

Xinshi Lu

**Nanmen
Long-Distance
Bus Station** ◆

①

Tang Dynasty's most famous poems, which described the sound of its massive bell at midnight, this large, pristinely painted temple may leave those unfamiliar with the ancient poetry feeling a little underwhelmed. The place has the frenetic feel of a tourist attraction, rather than the serenity of a temple. Literary pilgrims can line up to ring the temple bell themselves for an extra charge. ⊠ *24 Hanshan Si Nong* ☎ *0512/6533–6634* ⊕ *www. hanshansi.org* ✉ *Y15* ☉ *Daily 8–5.*

❼ Humble Administrator's Garden (Zhuo Zheng Yuan). More than half of *FodorsChoice* Suzhou's largest garden is taken up by ponds and lakes. The garden was built in 1509 by Wang Xianjun, an official dismissed from the imperial court. He chose the garden's name from a Tang Dynasty line of poetry reading "humble people govern," perhaps a bit of sarcasm considering the grand scale of his private residence. ⊠ *178 Dongbei Jie, 1 block east of Lindun Lu* ☎ *0512/6751–0286* ⊕ *www.szzzy.cn* ✉ *Y70* ☉ *Daily 7:30–5:30.*

❹ Joyous Garden (Yi Yuan). The youngest garden in Suzhou, Joyous Garden was built in 1874. It borrows elements from Suzhou's other famous garden: rooms from the Humble Administrator's, a pond from the Master of the Nets. The most unusual original feature in the garden is an oversize mirror, inspired by a tale of the founder of Zen Buddhism, who stared at a wall for years to find enlightenment. The garden's designer hung the mirror opposite a pavilion, to let the building contemplate its own reflection. From April to October, the garden doubles as a popular teahouse in the evening. ⊠ *343 Renmin Lu, 1 block south of the Temple of Mystery* ☎ *0512/6524–9317* ✉ *Y15* ☉ *Daily 7:30 AM–midnight.*

⓫ Lingering Garden (Liu Yuan). Windows frame other windows, undulating rooflines recall waves, and a closed corridor transforms into a room open to the pond at this interesting garden. The compound provides an endless array of architectural surprises: in a corner an unexpected skylight illuminates a planted nook; windows are placed to frame bamboo as perfectly as if they were painted. The **Mandarin Duck Hall** is particularly impressive, with a lovely moon gate engraved with vines and flowers. In the back of the garden stands a 70-foot-tall rock moved here from Lake Taihu. Ongoing solo musical performances on erhu and zither enliven the halls. ⊠ *79 Liuyuan Lu, west of the moat* ☎ *0512/6533–7903* ⊕ *www.gardenly.com* ✉ *Y40* ☉ *Daily 7:30–5:30 (last ticket sold at 5).*

★ ❻ Lion's Grove Garden (Shizi Lin). This garden uses countless gnarled formations from nearby Lake Taihu to create a surreal moonscape. A labyrinth of man-made caves surrounds a small lake. There's a popular local saying that if you talk to rocks, you won't need a psychologist, making this garden a good place to spend a 50-minute hour. A tearoom on the 2nd floor of the main pavilion overlooks the lake. ☒ *23 Yuanlin Lu, 3 blocks south of the Humble Administrator's Garden* ☏ *0512/ 6727–8316* ⊕ *www.szszl.com* ☒ *Y30* ☉ *Daily 7:30–5:30.*

★ ❸ **Master of the Nets Garden** (Wangshi Yuan). All elements of Suzhou style are here in precise balance: rock hills, layered planting, and charming pavilions overlooking a central pond. The garden is a favorite spot on tour group itineraries. To avoid the crowds, visit in the evening, when you can saunter from room to room enjoying traditional opera, flute, and dulcimer performances—as the master himself might have done. Performances are held from mid-March to mid-November. ☒ *11 Kuo Jia Tou Gang, west of Shiquan Lu* ☏ *0512/6529–3190* ⊕ *www.szwsy. com* ☒ *Y30* ☉ *Daily 7:30–5 (last ticket sold at 4:30).*

❿ **North Temple Pagoda** (Beisi Ta). One of the symbols of ancient Suzhou, this temple towers over the old city. This complex has a 1,700-year history, dating to the Three Kingdoms Period. The wooden pagoda has nine levels; you can climb as high as the eighth level for what might be the best view of Suzhou. Within the grounds are the Copper Buddha Hall and Plum Garden, which, built in 1985, lacks the history and the complexity of Suzhou's other gardens. ☒ *Xibei Jie and Renmin Lu, 2 blocks west of Humble Administrator's Garden* ☏ *0512/6753–1197* ☒ *Y15; Y10 more to climb pagoda* ☉ *Mar.–Oct., daily 7:45–6.*

❶ **Pan Gate** (Pan Men). Traffic into old Suzhou came both by road and canals, so the city's gates were designed to control access by both land and water. This gate—more of a small fortress—is the only one that remains. In addition to the imposing wooden gates on land, a double sluice gate can be used to seal off the canal and prevent boats from entering. A park is filled with colorful flowers, in contrast to the subdued traditional gardens elsewhere in the city. A small platform extends over a pond where voracious carp turn the water into a thrashing sheet of orange and yellow as they compete for food that tourists throw down. You can climb the **Ruiguang Pagoda,** a tall, slender spire originally built more than 1,000 years ago. ☒ *1 Dong Dajie, southwest corner of the old city* ☏ *0512/6530–0827* ⊕ *www. szpmjq.com* ☒ *Y25* ☉ *Daily 8–4:45.*

❾ **Suzhou Arts and Crafts Museum.** The highlight here is watching artists in action. They carve jade, cut latticework fans from thin sheets of sandalwood, and fashion traditional calligraphy brushes. Perhaps most amazing is the careful attention to detail of the women embroidering silk. The attached shop is a good place to pick up quality crafts. ⊠ *58 Xibei Lu, between Humble Administrator's Garden and the North Pagoda* ☎ *0512/6753–4874* ☑ *Y15* ⊙ *Daily 9–5.*

❽ **Suzhou Museum.** This is the most modern building to emerge amid a neighborhood of traditional architecture. The museum is the valedictory work for 90-year-old modernist master I. M. Pei. A controversy erupted over whether to allow Pei to construct the glass-and-steel structure in historical Suzhou. Like his crystal pyramid in the courtyard of the Louvre, this building thrives on juxtapositions of old and new. The museum, not yet open as of this writing, will house historical objects from Suzhou's ancient past. ⊠ *Dongbei Jie, next to Humble Administrator's Garden* ☎ *0512/6754–1534.*

WORD OF MOUTH

"Once you get inside the old town (of Tongli), there are no motorized vehicles, just bikes and pedestrian traffic. Nothing really seems to be rebuilt here, so you can get a feel for the old ways of living, people still doing their laundry & washing vegetables in the canal. Stopped and had tea at a cute tea shop. Good local art here in Tongli, as well as inexpensive embroidered wall art."   –quimbymoy

❺ **Temple of Mystery** (Xuanmiao Guan). One of the best-preserved Taoist compounds, the Temple of Mystery backs a large square that is now a lively market. Founded in the 3rd century, the temple is a rare example of a wooden structure that has lasted centuries, still retaining parts from the 12th century. Fortunately, it suffered very little damage in the Cultural Revolution and retains a splendid ceiling of carefully arranged beams and braces painted in their original colors. Taoist music is performed throughout the day. ⊠ *Guanqian Jie* ☎ *0512/6727–6616* ⊕ *www.szxmg.com* ☑ *Y10* ⊙ *Daily 8:30–5.*

❿❹ **Tiger Hill** (Huqiu). This hill is the burial place of the King of the State of Wu, who founded the city in 514 BC. At the top of the approach is a huge sheet of stone called **Thousand Man Rock,** where legend has it that the workers who built the tomb were thanked for their work with an elaborate banquet. The wine, alas, was drugged, so they died to keep the secret of the tomb's entrance. Modern archaeologists think they have discovered it hidden under the artificial lake. The secret may be out, but the king's wish to rest in peace is ensured by the fact that excavating the tomb would bring down the fragile Song Dynasty pagoda that stands above. The **Leaning Pagoda** is one of the most impressive monuments in Suzhou, with Persian influence evident in the arches and other architectural elements. A helpful audio guide explains many of the park's legends. ⊠ *Huqiu Lu, northwest of the city* ☎ *0512/6532–3488* ☑ *Y60* ⊙ *Daily 7:30–5.*

❶❷ **West Garden Temple** (Xi Yuan Si). This temple is most notable for the **Hall of 500 Arhats** (Wubai Luohan Tang), which houses 500 gold-painted statues of these Buddhist guides. They are humorous carvings: one struggling with dragons, another cradling a cat. ⊠ *8 Xiwan Lu, across from Lingering Garden* ☑ *Y6* ⊙ *Daily 7–5.*

Exploring the Water Villages

CENTURIES-OLD VILLAGES, preserved almost in their original state, are scattered around Suzhou. Bowed bridges span narrow canals, as traditional oared boats paddle by, creating an almost perfect picture of a way of life long past. A trip to one of these villages will probably be a highlight of your trip to Eastern China.

Be careful which village you choose, though. The tourist dollars that flow in may have saved these villages from the wrecking ball, but they have also changed their character to differing degrees. Those closest to the larger cities can be the most swamped by tour groups. Trekking to an out-of-the-way destination can pay off by letting you find a village that you will have all to yourself.

The most famous of the water villages is undoubtedly **Zhouzhuang.** Its fame is partly due to its proximity, just 45 minutes from Suzhou and an hour away from Shanghai. As a result, more than 2.5 million visitors head here each year to catch a glimpse of old China. Its charm is reduced by the sheer number of tourists who elbow their way through the streets. Next to the "ancient memorial archway," which isn't ancient at all, is a ticket window. The steep entrance fee of Y100 gets you into the water village-turned-gift shop.

Crowds aside, Zhouzhuang is fun for families. Several residences, some 500 years old, let you see what life was like in the Ming and Qing dynasties. There are several storefronts where you can see brick making, bamboo carving, and basket weaving—traditional crafts that up until recently were in widespread use throughout the countryside. The food is typical country fare, making it a nice break from the fancier cuisine of Suzhou and Shanghai. The most famous dish, a fatty cut of pork leg, is a bit oily for most Western palates. But there are also pickled vegetables and wild greens to sample. For crafts, skip the snuff bottles and teapots, which are of low quality. Opt for something you

probably won't find elsewhere: homemade rice wine, rough-hewn ox-horn combs, and bamboo rice baskets.

Buses to Zhouzhuang leave from Suzhou's North Bus station every half hour between 7 AM and 5 PM. The 1½-hour trip is Y15 to Y25.

The pick of the water villages is **Tongli**, 30 minutes from Zhouzhuang and 1½ hours from Suzhou. There's a more reasonable entrance fee of Y60. A number of locals still live and work here, making this village seem more authentic than Zhouzhuang. The streets are cobbled, and the complete absence of cars make Tongli feel like it's from a different era. You can still find yourself wandering on quaint side streets or creeping down impossibly narrow alleyways that open onto canals and bridges. Tongli is the largest of the water villages, imminently photographable, and a pleasure to explore. Near the entrance gate are several private homes offering beds, and throughout the village are tea shops and small tables set out in front of the canals. Hiring a boat (Y60 for up to 6 people) to float down the canals gives you a different perspective on the town.

A favorite spot in Tongli is Tuisi Garden, a slightly smaller version of the private courtyard parks found in Suzhou. Tongli is also home to the **Ancient Chinese Sexual Culture Museum** (✉ Entrance to town

☎ 0512/6332-2973), housed in a former girl's school. The controversial exhibition of ancient erotic toys and art is the project of a retired university professor.

Buses to Tongli leave from the square in front of Suzhou Tran Station every 20 to 30 minutes between 7 AM and 5 PM. The journey is Y6 to Y10.

Even farther off the beaten path is **Luzhi**, about a half hour from Suzhou and Zhouzhuang. It has been described as a "museum of bridges." There are over 40 here, in all different shapes and sizes. Many of the older women in the village preserve traditional customs, wearing traditional headdresses and skirts. Luzhi is also notable for the spectacular **Baosheng Temple** (✉ Luzhi ☎ 0512/6501-0067), a yellow-walled compound that is famous for its breathtaking collection of Buddhist arhats. Arranged on a wall of stone, these clay sculptures are the work of Yang Huizhi, a famous Tang Dynasty sculptor. They depict Buddhist disciples who have gained enlightenment; these works, made over 1,000 years ago, impart the character and artistry of their creator. The temple also features a well-preserved bell from the end of the Ming Dynasty.

Luzhi-bound buses leave from the square in front of Suzhou Train Station every 30 minutes between 6:30 AM and 6:30 PM. The 40-minute drive is Y10.

Where to Stay & Eat

In addition to the restaurants below, Shiquan Jie is quickly becoming one of the city's restaurant hubs, with both Suzhou-style restaurants and Chinese regional cuisine from Xinjiang to Yunnan. Many offer English menus, and are popular with both locals and guests at nearby hotels.

★ **$-$$$** ✕ **Deyuelou.** This restaurant has served Suzhou-style food for more than 400 years. The menu boasts a wide array of fish dishes as well as a particularly tasty *deyue tongji* (braised chicken). It also specializes in an attractive type of food presentation, the ancient art of "garden foods"—an assortment of small dishes arranged to resemble various sorts of gardens, with foods portraying flowers, trees, and rocks. You can also try the local-style dim sum. ✉ *27 Taijian Nong, south of the Temple of Mystery* ☎ *0512/6523–8940* ▭ *AE, MC, V.*

★ **$-$$** ✕ **Pine and Crane** (Songhelou). The food here is the type once served on riverboats during banquet cruises—hence the popular designation "boat food." A particularly good dish here is the *songshu guiyu*, or "squirrel-shape Mandarin fish." (Don't let the English translation turn you off: it's a sweet-and-sour boneless fried river fish.) The other fish dishes here are just as delicious. The venerable restaurant has a sleek, tasteful decor. ✉ *18 Taijian Nong, south of the Temple of Mystery* ☎ *0512/6523–3270* ▭ *AE, MC, V.*

¢ ✕ **Huangtianyuan.** Here the specialty is the local favorite of *gaotuan* (rice gluten), made by pounding rice to a fine paste. In business since 1821, the eatery's menu changes with the seasons. A year-round house specialty is *babao fan* (syrupy rice with various sweets, nuts, and fruit bits). The sweets here come in all sizes and colors, including green rice balls and red bean-filled dumplings. All the desserts are subtly sweet, not the sugary concoctions that Westerners are used to. ✉ *86 Guanqian Jie* ☎ *0512/6727–7033* ▭ *No credit cards.*

$$$-$$$$
Fodor's Choice
★
🏨 **Sheraton Suzhou Hotel & Towers.** Suzhou's most luxurious hotel has a two-story stone entrance topped by a pagoda lobby that is modeled after the Pan Gate. (If you want to compare, it sits behind the hotel.) The garden views from the courtyard-facing rooms are stunning. Guests have access to a fitness center and a striking Roman-style pool. But for a nightly rate that is twice the average Chinese monthly salary, the accommodations are not huge, Internet access is only available in the most expensive rooms, and the location is less than central. The Garden Brasserie presents an Asian-style buffet, and high tea is served on weekends. ✉ *259 Xinshi Lu, 215007* ☎ *0512/6510–3388* ⊕ *www.sheraton-suzhou.com* ⤳ *370 rooms, 30 suites* ⚁ *3 restaurants, room service, cable TV, some in-room data ports, pool, gym, hot tub, massage, sauna, steam room, bar, shop, babysitting, dry cleaning, laundry service, concierge, concierge floor, Internet room, business services, no-smoking rooms, no-smoking floors* ▭ *AE, DC, MC, V.*

★ **$-$$$** 🏨 **Gloria Plaza Hotel Suzhou.** From the watercolor paintings lining the halls to the cascading waterfall windows of its Sampan Restaurant, the Gloria Plaza Hotel stands out as an inviting property. The large standard rooms dwarf the furniture inside; rooms on the executive floor fill the space better by adding a pullout couch. The hotel is a five-minute walk from Guanqian Jie's restaurants and nightclubs. The business facilities are useful not just for those on a business trip, but for anyone who wants to stay connected. ✉ *535 Ganjiang Dong Lu, 215006* ☎ *0512/6521–8855* ⊕ *www.gphsuzhou.com* ⇗ *281 rooms, 13 suites* ⚏ *2 restaurants, room service, in-room safes, minibars, cable TV, in-room data ports, gym, massage, sauna, steam room, bar, babysitting, laundry service, concierge, Internet room, business services, no-smoking rooms* ▭ *AE, DC, MC, V.*

$–$$ ☷ **Bamboo Grove Hotel.** A modern hotel that caters to international travelers, the Bamboo Grove offers more amenities than you might expect. The three-story open lobby, stylish garden courtyard, and vast restaurant are attractive places to relax. The guest rooms are bland but comfortable. The hotel's bamboo logo pops up everywhere, from the backs of chairs to the cute cotton robes hanging in the closets. ✉ *168 Zhuhui Lu, 215006* ☎ *0512/6520–5601* ⊕ *www.bg-hotel.com* ⇗ *319 rooms, 37 suites* ⚏ *2 restaurants, room service, in-room safes, minibars, cable TV, in-room data ports, 2 tennis courts, pool, gym, hair salon, massage, sauna, steam room, bar, shops, babysitting, dry cleaning, laundry service, concierge, Internet room, business services, meeting rooms, no-smoking rooms* ▭ *AE, DC, MC, V.*

$–$$ ☷ **Lidu (Jasper) Hotel Suzhou.** "Jasper" refers to this hotel's decor: bright-green headboards and chairs add a splash of color to the comfortably sized rooms. The hotel's lengthy list of recreation facilities from pool to bowling makes it a good place to return to after a day of exploring. ✉ *168 Ganjiang Xi Lu, 215002* ☎ *0512/6511–9358* ⇗ *124 rooms, 5 suites* ⚏ *2 restaurants, room service, in-room safes, minibars, cable TV, in-room data ports, gym, hair salon, massage, sauna, bar, shops, babysitting, dry cleaning, laundry service, Internet room, business services, meeting rooms, travel services, no-smoking rooms* ▭ *AE, DC, MC, V.*

$ ☷ **Nanyuan Guest House.** After a day of exploring Suzhou's gardens, return to a garden of your own. The 10 acres surrounding the Nanyuan Guest House are pleasantly planted with bamboo, and rocks and ponds are sprinkled throughout its courtyards. The selling point, however, is the location two blocks from the Master of the Nets Garden. The apricot-and-mauve rooms are spread among six buildings. ✉ *249 Shiquan Jie, 215006* ☎ *0512/6519–7661* 🖷 *0512/6519–8806* ⇗ *93 rooms, 7 suites* ⚏ *2 restaurants, room service, minibars, cable TV, hair salon, massage, sauna, bar, laundry service, Internet room, business services, meeting rooms* ▭ *AE, DC, MC, V.*

¢–$ ☷ **Lexiang Hotel.** Catering mainly to Chinese guests, this hotel is filled with furnishings in a classical Chinese style. It has a fine location, just down the street from the Joyous Garden and a block from the beautiful Temple of Mystery. ✉ *18 Dajingxiang, 215006* ☎ *0512/6524–4164* ⇗ *197 rooms, 15 suites* ⚏ *3 restaurants, gym, hair salon, bar, business services, meeting room* ▭ *AE, MC, V.*

¢–$ ☷ **Suzhou Hotel.** On Perfect 10 Street, this hotel has a location to match. It is a short walk from the Master of the Nets Garden and a stretch of restaurants, bars, and clubs. In the Chinese-style suites, lovely moon gates separate the bedrooms from the sitting areas. The guest rooms are tastefully appointed. The inner-facing rooms overlook a garden. Even with the window open, the only noise is the croaking of frogs in a pond. The

Fodor's Choice
★

hotel is popular with tour groups. ⊠ *115 Shiquan Jie, 215006* ☎ *0512/ 6520–4646* ⊕ *www.suzhou-hotel.com* ⌑ *283 rooms, 23 suites* ⚅ *2 restaurants, room service, minibars, cable TV, gym, hair salon, massage, sauna, bar, dry cleaning, laundry service, business services, no-smoking floors* ⊟ *AE, MC, V.*

Nightlife & the Arts

NIGHTLIFE At night, Perfect Ten Street, the stretch of Shiquan Jie between Renmin Lu and Hengfeng Lu is home to a thriving cluster of bars and clubs. You won't find huge dance floors, but you will find perfect places for a glass of wine or a conversation.

Despite the suggestive name, **Action Bar** (⊠ 699 Shiquan Jie ☎ 0512/ 6219–8066) is a nothing-fancy place with a drop-in feel. The crowd ranges from locals to tourists to traveling business executives. **Pulp Fiction** (⊠ Shiquan Jie, east of Hengfeng Lu ☎ No phone) is Suzhou's main expat bar, so you can be sure there are dart boards and pool tables—and it organizes quirky events. At the top of a flight of stairs is **Whiskey Jack's** (⊠ 150 Shiquan Jie ☎ 0512/6526–7626) where bands play regularly.

THE ARTS Mid-March to mid-November, there are traditional opera and music performances at the **Master of the Nets Garden** (⊠ Shiquan Jie ☎ 0512/ 6826–7737). The nightly concerts begin at 7:30 and cost is Y80. The show presents a taste of various scenes from opera, as well as an opportunity to hear classical Chinese instruments. It can be a bit crowded during the peak tourist season.

Shopping

Districts around the gardens and temples teem with silk shops and outdoor markets. The city's long history of wealth and culture have encouraged a tradition of elegant and finely worked craft objects. One of the best-known crafts is double-sided embroidery, where two separate designs are carefully stitched on both sides of a sheet of silk. The city is also famous for its finely latticed sandalwood fans. Both are available at the Suzhou Arts and Crafts Museum. The area outside the gate of the Master of the Nets Garden has dozens of small stalls selling curios and inexpensive but interesting souvenirs.

The **Friendship Store** (⊠ 504 Renmin Lu ☎ 0512/6523–6165) has a selection of local products in silk, wood, and jade. Since 1956 the **Suzhou Antiques Store** (⊠ 328 Renmin Lu ☎ 0512/6522–8368) has been selling antiques, calligraphy, jades, and other items. You can get jewelry and carvings at the **Suzhou Jade Carving Factory** (⊠ 33 Baita Xi Lu ☎ 0512/6727–1224).

Near the North Pagoda, the **Suzhou Silk Museum Shop** (⊠ 661 Renmin Lu ☎ 0512/6753–4941) is really the reason to come to the Silk Museum. For local artworks and calligraphy, visit the **Wumen Artstore** (⊠ 105 Liuyuan Lu ☎ 0512/6533–4808).

To & from Suzhou

Approximately 3½ hrs (225 km [140 mi]) by train on Nanjing–Shanghai rail line southeast of Nanjing, or 1 hr (84 km [52 mi]) by train west of Shanghai.

Buses bound for Nanjing (2 hours) and Yanzhou (3 hours) depart from the North Bus Station. Frequent trains to Nanjing take two to three hours. It's a popular route, so be sure to buy tickets in advance. Trains to Yangzhou take 3½ hours.

Buses to Shanghai take about an hour. Train, which depart about every 20 minutes, take anywhere from 40 minutes to 1½ hours.

2

JIANGSU ESSENTIALS

Transportation

BY AIR

Most flights from Europe or North America go through Shanghai or Beijing before continuing on to Nanjing's Lukou Airport, but there are direct flights from Asian hubs like Seoul, Nagoya, and Bangkok. From Nanjing, several flights leave daily for Shanghai, Beijing, Guangzhou, Xiamen, Wuhan, and Hong Kong; flights leave daily for Xi'an and Chengdu; and several flights leave weekly for Zhengzhou and Hangzhou. You can buy tickets at any travel agency, at major hotels, or at the CITS office.

Taxis from Nanjing Lukou Airport, 36 km (22 mi) southwest of the city, should take about 20 minutes. The fare should be Y120.

🚹 Airport Information **Nanjing Lukou Airport** ✉Jiangning Qu ☎025/248-0063 🖷025/248-0025.

🚹 Airlines & Contacts **CAAC (Air China)** ✉ 50 Ruijin Lu, Nanjing ☎ 025/8449-9378. **China Eastern Airlines** ✉658 Renmin Lu, Suzhou ☎0512/6522-2788. **Dragonair** ✉208 Guangzhou Lu, Room 810, Nanjing ☎ 025/8331-1999 Ext. 810.

BY BUS

Frequent bus service runs between Nanjing, Yangzhou, and Suzhou, as well as from these cities to Shanghai. Most routes have buses with air-conditioning and other amenities. Nanjing's bus station lies west of the railway station at Zhongyang Men. The Suzhou Bus Station is just outside the Ping Gate. About 6 km (4 mi) west of the city is the Yangzhou Bus Station.

🚹 Bus Information **Nanjing Bus Station** ✉Jianing Lu and Zhongyang Lu ☎025/8550-4973. **Suzhou Bus Station** ✉ 29 Xihui Lu ☎0512/6753-0686. **Yangzhou Bus Station** ✉Jiangyang Zhong Lu ☎0514/786-1812.

BY TRAIN

Nanjing and Suzhou are on the same rail line, which continues on to Shanghai. Yangzhou is reached through Nanjing, but one of the frequent buses from Nanjing is a better option. Tickets can be purchased either through your hotel or at the stations, although the lines are long and vendors can be curt with non-Chinese speakers.

🚹 Bus Information **Nanjing Train Station** ✉Long Pan Lu ☎025/8582-2222. **Suzhou Train Station** ✉Beihuan Xi Lu ☎0512/6753-2831. **Yangzhou Train Station** ✉Wenhe Xi Lu ☎0514/268-6282.

Contacts & Resources

EMERGENCIES

All of the establishments below are open 24 hours.

First Aid Station ⊠ 231 Zhongshan Lu, Nanjing ☎ 025/8663-3858. **Yangzhou No. 1 People's Hospital** ⊠ 45 Taizhou Lu, Yangzhou ☎ 0514/790-7353. **People's Hospital No. 2** ⊠ 26 Daoqian Jie, Suzhou ☎ 0512/6522-3691.

VISITOR INFORMATION

Hotels are the chief source of tourist information in Yangzhou. It's best to do any planning you need in Nanjing or Suzhou, where both the staffs at hotels and travel agencies tend to be much better informed. You can also try China International Travel Service (CITS).

Tourist Information CITS ⊠ 202/1 Zhongshan Bei Lu, Nanjing ☎ 025/8342-8999 ⊠ 18 Da Jing Xiang, Suzhou ☎ 0512/6522-3783 ⊕ www.citssz.com.

ANHUI

Eastern China's most rural province, Anhui has a rugged terrain that forces families to fight their hardscrabble farmland for every acre of harvest. Today it remains significantly poorer than its neighbors, with an average income half of that in neighboring Zhejiang. But what Anhui lacks in material wealth, it makes up for in splendid natural landscape. Travelers here enjoy countryside largely untouched by the last century. Near Huangshan (Yellow Mountain), towering granite peaks loom over green fields, and round-shouldered water buffalo plow the flooded rice paddies.

The foothills of Huangshan have a remarkable wealth of historical architecture. Tiny communities dot the landscape in Shexian and Yixian counties. Many of these villages were far enough out of the way that even the zealous Red Guards of the Cultural Revolution left them alone. Today there are whole villages that remain exactly as they have been for 200 years.

Anhui boasts significant contributions to Chinese civilization. Of the treasures of classical Chinese education, Anhui produces the most famous paper and ink. Hui opera, an ancient musical form developed in the province, was a major influence in Beijing Opera. Hui cuisine is considered one of the country's finest culinary traditions, making use of mountain vegetables and simple, bold flavors.

Most of the province's attractions for tourists lie in the south, accessible from Shanghai, Hangzhou, and Nanjing.

Huangshan (Yellow Mountain)

❾
Fodor'sChoice
★

Eastern China's most impressive natural landscape, Huangshan has peaks that rise like islands through roiling seas of clouds. A favorite retreat of emperors and poets of old, its peaks have inspired some of China's most outstanding artworks and literary endeavors. They were so beguiling, in fact, that years of labor went into their paths, which are actual stone steps rising up—sometimes gradually into the forest, sometimes sharply through a stone tunnel and into the mist above. Since 1990, the area has been listed as a UNESCO World Heritage Site.

The common English translation—Yellow Mountain—is misleading. Huangshan is not a single mountain, but rather a series of peaks that stretches across four counties. To complicate matters, the name is not a reference to color. The region was originally called the "Black Mountains," but a Tang Dynasty emperor renamed it to honor Huangdi, the Yellow Emperor. And according to legend, it was from these slopes that he rode off to heaven on the back of a dragon.

The mountain is renowned for its gnarled stone formations, crooked pines, and seas of mists. Most of these trees and rocks have names; some are obvious, whereas others require dedicated squinting and a leap of the imagination. Generations of Chinese poets and travelers have humanized these peaks and forests through this practice, and left their indelible mark on the area.

Be forewarned, though: Huangshan has its own weather. More than 200 days a year, precipitation obscures the famous views. It can be sunny below, but up in the mountains it's raining. But even on the foggiest of days the wind is likely to part the mist long enough to make out mysterious peaks. 🎟 Y200.

Exploring

There are two primary hiking routes up the mountain. The Eastern Steps, a straightforward path through forests, is both the shortest and the easiest. The Southern Steps (some guidebooks call these the Western Steps, which causes confusion with another set of steps used primarily by porters) require more effort, but they pay off with remarkable scenery. The steep, winding path reveals sheer peaks and precipitous lookouts over mist-enshrouded valleys.

Climbing up is physically taxing, but climbing down is mentally exhausting, requiring far more concentration. If you have the time and the leg muscles, it's nice to ascend the South Steps, where the scenery stretches before you. The breathtaking views are a good excuse to stop and, well, catch your breath.

EASTERN STEPS The Eastern Steps begin at the **Cloud Valley Temple Cable Car Station** (🎟 Y65 ☉ weekdays 6:30 AM–4:30 PM, weekends 6:30 AM–5 PM). The cable car takes eight minutes to traverse what takes hikers three or more hours. Large windows provide an aerial view of the mountain and bamboo forests below. This area was once home to several monasteries, nunneries, and

TO HIKE OR NOT

Huangshan can be seen in a day or over the course of several days, depending on your schedule and stamina. The least strenuous way to take in the famous mountain is to ride a cable car up in the morning, hike around the summit, and catch another cable car down. Far more rewarding is an overnight stay on the summit, allowing you to experience the ascent on foot.

temples. By the beginning of the 20th century they had been abandoned, but the name Cloud Valley Temple Area remains.

If you opt to hike, the Eastern Steps are quicker than the Southern Steps, but the scenery isn't as rewarding and there are fewer scenic side routes. Along the way is a **Fascinating Pavilion,** most notable as a rest stop along the way. There's a short half-hour side hike to **Pipeng,** with a good view out over a number of the smaller eastern peaks. By the time you reach **Cloud Valley,** the landscape that makes Huangshan famous begins to come into view. **Beginning to Believe Peak** is the start of the awe-inspiring landscape, and the first true majestic vista on this path.

SOUTHERN STEPS The steep Southern Steps are by far the tougher path. However, the climb pays off with great views. There are also some beautiful optional side trails. Although the Eastern Steps feel like a walk through the woods, the Southern Steps truly feel the ascent into the clouds. The steps begin around the Hot Springs, at the **Mercy Light Temple** area. **Midway Mountain Temple** has facilities to rest, eat, and even stay overnight, but no temple. It's here that the splendor of Huangshan comes into full view. At the **Three Islands at Penglai,** a trio of peaks poke out from a sea of mist. If you're feeling energetic, a side tour of **Heavenly Capital Peak** affords spectacular views out over the rest of the range. This may not be the highest peak in the range, but it is one of the steepest.

The **Jade Screen Cable Car** (📧 Y65 ⊙ weekdays 6:30 AM–4:30 PM, weekends 6:30 AM–5 PM) runs parallel to the Southern Steps, leaving riders close to the Welcoming Guests Pine. It can close unexpectedly in inclement weather.

THE SUMMIT The entrance to the summit area is announced by the **Welcoming Guest Pine,** a lone pine clinging to the edge of a cliff, one branch outstretched. Behind it, a sheer stone slope rises out of the clouds. Continuing up, you can climb **Lotus Peak,** the tallest in the province. A walk through **Turtle Cave,** an arched pathway straight through the hillside, brings the weary traveler to **Bright Top Peak,** just slightly lower than Lotus, and an easier climb.

The newly opened **Xihai Grand Canyon** loop starts at the Cloud Dispelling Pavilion and ends at the Haixin Ting Pavilion. Rock formations called "Upside Down Boot" and "Lady Playing Piano" may be clumsily named, but they are stunning. The farther along you walk, the fewer travelers you'll come across. At the southern end of the loop, near Haixin, the trail reaches the **Immortal's Walk Bridge,** a dizzying arch over the misty abyss that leads to a terrace on one of the mountain's spires. A huge landscape spreads out beneath, without a single tour group in sight.

WHAT TO BRING

Stock up on water and snacks at the bottom of the Southern Steps. By midway up the mountain everything is sold at double the price or even quadruple the normal rate. Consider bringing a plastic poncho. It's handier than an umbrella because it won't catch the wind, and will leave you with both hands free to climb on wet steps.

A highlight of any trip is sunrise, visible from several places on the mountain. Most hikers arrive well after dawn, but you'll be rewarded with the spectacle of Huangshan materializing from the shadows if you arrive just before first light. A popular spot near the Beihai Hotel is the **Dawn Pavilion.** There are several less crowded peaks with equally good views a little farther from the hotels. **Refreshing Terrace, Lion Peak,** and **Red Cloud Peak** all provide unobstructed views of the rising sun.

> ### HIKING GEAR
>
> Huangshan still has sheer drop-offs and steep, uneven, rain-slicked steps. A walking stick (sturdy wooden dragon-head staffs are on sale around the mountain) will help steady your ascent. It can get very cold on the peaks and rain can come unexpectedly. Dress in layers, and consider bringing a hooded sweatshirt to stay warm.

Compared to the ascent, the summit area is relatively level, but there is still a good amount of stair-climbing. It takes about three to four hours to walk the full summit circle, and considerably more if you take side trails.

Tours

Tours up the mountain are unnecessary. Waiting around for slower members of your entourage or having to huff and puff to catch up to the power-climbers can be frustrating. A better bet is to buy a good map from one of the local vendors and chart the path you want to take.

Where to Stay & Eat

Five areas of Huangshan offer lodging. Tangkou, a village that has sprung up to serve mountain climbers, has the most for travelers, including hotels, restaurants, grocery stores, and shops to gear up for the long climb ahead. Tangkou sits near the front gate of the park, and buses run regularly to the trailheads for both the Southern and Eastern steps. If you want to take the shorter route up the Eastern Steps, the Cloud Valley Temple Area is a convenient option. At this writing, the Hot Springs were undergoing a major renovation. The formerly dingy mineral springs should be operating again in 2008. In the meantime, the area still makes convenient a base to hike up the scenic Southern Steps.

There are several small, basic huts along the Southern Steps, but it would be better to push to the end of the path to the hotels in the Summit Area. Although these lodgings tend to be more expensive than those below, they are your only option if you want to catch the sunrise. As a bonus, you'll have the dew-drenched forests to yourself for a few hours before the latecomers arrive. Reservations are strongly recommended, especially for weekends, as this is a popular destination for Chinese travelers, as well as those from Japan and Korea.

$$–$$$ ✕**Celebrity's Banquet.** The best restaurant on the summit, Celebrity's Banquet celebrates local culture with a range of traditional Hui dishes. There are soups of dried vegetables, jellied tofu, braised pork, and a delicately flavored pumpkin soup that shouldn't be missed. ⊠ *Xihai Hotel, Grand Canyon Loop, Summit Area* ☎ *0559/558–8888* ⊟ *AE, MC, V.*

$–$$$ ✕ **Tangzhen Hotel Restaurant.** This budget hotel is nothing to write home about, but the food is especially good. Locals come from all around the area to dine here. Specialties include cured mandarin fish, pork with bamboo, and mountain stone frogs. ⊠ *At the main entrance to Huangshan, Tangkou* ☎ *0559/556–2665* ▭ *No credit cards.*

$$–$$$$ ⊞ **Jade Screen Tower.** The views from this hotel are unmatched, though like most of the hotels on the summit, the rooms are on the small side. Nonetheless the location is good, at the top of the Southern Steps near the cable car station; it's the first proper hotel you'll reach after a long climb. ⊠ *Past Welcoming Guest Pine, Summit Area, 242709* ☎ *0559/ 558–2288* ⤵ *29 rooms, 1 suite* ⚒ *2 restaurants, massage, sauna, business services* ▭ *AE, MC, V.*

$$–$$$ ⊞ **Baiyun Hotel.** This hotel offers comfortable rooms and a good location on the summit—a short walk away from Bright Top Peak. An excellent restaurant downstairs serves great river fish, as well as mountain vegetables and mushroom dishes. ⊠ *Tianhai Area, Summit Area, 242709* ☎ *0559/558–2708* ⊕ *www.hsbyhotel.com* ⤵ *80 rooms, 1 suite* ⚒ *Restaurant, massage, sauna, bar* ▭ *AE, MC, V.*

$$ ⊞ **Beihai Hotel.** This is one of the nicest places to stay on the mountain. A few extras like the sauna are a welcome end to a day of hiking. The rooms are set among rhododendrons and azaleas on the hillside. Ask for the front-facing rooms, which have been recently renovated and have better views—and rent for the same price as the rooms in the back. ⊠ *Huangshan Scenic Area, Summit Area, 242709* ☎ *0559/556–2555* ⤵ *137 rooms, 2 suites* ⚒ *Restaurant, massage, sauna, bar* ▭ *AE, MC, V.*

¢–$$ ⊞ **Huangshan Xingang Hotel.** Because practically every guest is coming up or down the mountain, the staff here is a great repository of knowledge of what to see, how to climb, and the best routes to take. Like most hotels in the area, this place has rooms that are somewhat small, but are clean and get lots of sun. They are good places to rest up for the climb ahead. ⊠ *At the main entrance to Huangshan, Tangkou, 242709* ☎ *0559/556–1048* ⊕ *www.hsxghotel.com* ⤵ *115 rooms, 2 suites* ⚒ *Restaurant, massage, sauna* ▭ *AE, MC, V.*

¢ ⊞ **Peach Blossom Hotel.** A winding road takes you over a bridge and past a double waterfall to this resort between the main gate of the mountain park and the beginning of the Southern Steps. The no-frills rooms are clean and comfortable. The Peach Blossom also has great Chinese and Western food, with specialties like bamboo chicken. ⊠ *Huangshan Scenic Area, Hot Springs, 242709* ☎ *0559/558–5666* ⤵ *141 rooms, 4 suites* ⚒ *Restaurant, café, bar* ▭ *AE, MC, V.*

¢ ⊞ **Yungu Hotel.** Tucked in among the trees, these traditional-style buildings blend well in the forest landscape. Cheaper than staying on the summit, the guest rooms here are also larger and better outfitted. ⊠ *Next to the cable-car station, Cloud Valley Temple Area, 242709* ☎ *0559/ 558–6444* ⤵ *100 rooms* ⚒ *2 restaurants, café, massage, bar* ▭ *AE, DC, MC, V.*

To & from Huangshan

5½ hrs (250 km [155 mi]) by train west of Nanjing; 3½ hrs by long-distance bus.

Most long-distance transportation, including trains and airplanes, arrives in Tunxi, the largest city near Yellow Mountain. Be aware, however, that Tunxi is still 1 to 1½ hours away from Yellow Mountain. Minibuses to Tangkou and other destinations around the base of the mountain leave from the plaza in front of Tunxi's train station. The cost should be Y15 to Y30. There are also plenty of taxi drivers who are happy to offer their services, usually for around Y70 per carload.

Some buses from Nanjing, Hangzhou, and Shanghai go directly to Tangkou, the entrance at the base of the mountain. The airport is close toTunxi, about a Y15 to Y20 cab ride from the mountain.

Tunxi

⑩ Tunxi, also called Huangshan City, is the gateway to the Yellow Mountain area. Apart from being a transportation hub, Tunxi also has a charming strip of shops and restaurants and is a convenient place from which to take trips to Shexian and Yixian counties, famous for their historical architecture.

Exploring
In Tunxi, the best place to pick up souvenirs is along **Old Street** (Lao Jie). The street is quiet in the daytime, but comes alive in the early evening. Shops stay open until about 10 or 11. As in any tourist-oriented area, there's a lot of trash, but you will find some treasures.

Tours
Believe it or not, tours from Tunxi to Yellow Mountain can sometimes be more economical than going it alone. Some Tunxi companies offer trips that include accommodations for little more than the cost of the admission price to the park. And there's no need to spend the day with strangers—you can hike on your own, joining the rest of the group in time to catch the bus back.

Guides are a good idea if you are exploring the countryside around Huangshan. CTS has private village tours in Yixian county and architecture tours in Shexian counties.

🚩 **Tour-Operator Recommendations CTS** ✉ 12 Qianyuan Bei Lu, Tunxi ☎ 0559/211–5832 ✉ 1Binjiang Xi Lu, Tunxi ☎ 0559/254–2391.

Where to Stay & Eat

$–$$ ✕ **Diyilou.** All sorts of small dishes are sold at this lively shop. Diners
Fodor'sChoice order by pointing to sample dishes, so the lack of an English menu is
★ no problem. With hundreds of dishes on rotation, there's something for everyone. Local specialties include tender bamboo shoots, four-mushroom soup, red-braised tofu, and a white mushroom-wrapped meatball that is not to be missed. ✉ *247 Tunxi Lao Jie, at Lao Jie* ☎ *0559/253–9797* 🍴 *AE, MC, V.*

¢–$$ 🏨 **Huashan Hotel.** This large hotel sits at a perfect location in Tunxi, just a block away from the shopping district of Old Street. The lobby is enormous, as are the guest rooms. Some are a bit musty; ask to see a few before you decide. The service is thorough, if a little confused at times. ✉ *3 Yanan Lu, 1 block north of Old St., 245000* ☎ *0559/254–2811*

⌨ *186 rooms, 14 suites* ♨ *2 restaurants, pool, tennis court, gym, sauna* 🖃 *AE, MC, V.*

Shopping

When shopping along Lao Jie, the best offerings are traditional calligraphy ink and paper. The best inkstones are sold at **Sanbai Yanzhai** (✉ 173 Lao Jie ☎ 0559/253–5538).

Another traditional craft is bamboo carving. The **Stone and Bamboo Shop** (✉ 122 Lao Jie ☎ 0559/751–5042) sells exquisite examples of traditional carving.

Side Trips from Tunxi

SHEXIAN COUNTY Shexian County has several sites of interest. **Huizhou Old Town** (✉ Shexian County Center ☎ 0559/653–1586 🎟 Y15 ⊙ Daily 7:30–6:30) boasts a centuries-old city wall and a magnificent four-sided memorial gate guarded by sculptures of frolicking lions.

The most famous series of **Memorial Arches** (✉ 3 mi (5 km) west of Huizhou Old Town ☎ No phone 🎟 Y50 ⊙ Daily 8–5:30) are in Tangyue village. Dating from the Ming and Qing dynasties, these archways represent traditional values like morality, piety, and *female* chastity.

The **Huashan Mysterious Grottoes** (✉ Between Xiongcun and Tunxi ☎ 0559/253–9888 🎟 Y70 ⊙ Daily 7:30–6:30) are a combination of natural caves and rooms carved into the rock. No one is quite certain when or why they were built, but they are impressive, and newly illuminated with colored lights.

Near Huizhou Old Town, **Yuliang Village** (✉ ☎ No phone 🎟 Y20 ⊙ Daily 7:30–6:30) overlooks a Tang Dynasty dam with water gurgling over its sloped sides. Fishermen in wooden skiffs still make their living here. A narrow street parallel to the river is a nice place for a stroll. Most families leave their doors open, allowing a peak into homes where pages from magazines are used as wallpaper and aluminum foil is a common decoration.

If you're traveling by bus from Tunxi, head to Shexian Bus Station in Huizhou Old City, where you can connect with minibuses or taxis to outlying scenic spots. However, if you are traveling with several people, it will be well worth hiring a car and driver for the day. Many of these places are remote, and you may find the bulk of your day wasted waiting on minibuses or trying to find a taxi.

YIXIAN COUNTY Yixian County is the site of some beautiful villages filled with ancient architecture. A UNESCO World Heritage site, **Xidi Village** (✉ Yixian Xidi Village ☎ 0559/515–4030 🎟 Y80 ⊙ Daily 6:30–6:30) is known for its exquisite memorial gate. There were once a dozen gates, but they were destroyed during the Cultural Revolution. The existing gate was left standing as a "bad example" to be criticized. There are several houses with excellent examples of brick carving and an impressive Clan Temple with massive ginkgo columns and beams.

An arched bridge leads to **Hongcun Village** (✉ Eastern Yixian County ☎ 0559/251–7464 🎟 Y90 ⊙ Daily 6:30–6:30). From above, the village is said to resemble a buffalo. Two 600-year-old trees mark its horns, a lake its belly, and even irrigation streams are its intestines. In recent years, a number of films have been partially shot here, including Ang Lee's *Crouching Tiger, Hidden Dragon*. Several large halls and old houses are open to tour. The Salt Merchants House is especially well preserved, with intricate decorations and carvings that were unharmed during the Cultural Revolution.

To get to destinations in Yixian County, take the buses that leave from in front of Tunxi's train station. They cost about Y9, and depart every 20 minutes. Because of a nearby military base, a police-issued travel permit costing Y50 is required for travel in Yixian County. However, the ticket offices at the gates of Xidi Village and Hongcun Village can take care of this for you. A passport is necessary to register for the permits.

To & from Tunxi

5½ hrs (250 km [155 mi]) by train west of Nanjing; 3½ hrs by long-distance bus.

Unless you arrive on a long-distance bus that is bound for Tangkou, or have joined a chartered excursion to Yellow Mountain, your bus or train is probably bound for Tunxi, around 40 mi (65 km) from the mountain.

ANHUI ESSENTIALS

Transportation

BY AIR

If you plan on flying to Yellow Mountain, you'll land at the Huangshan City Airport near Tunxi, about 1 to 1½ hours away. There are daily flights to Beijing and Guangzhou, Shanghai twice daily, and Hong Kong twice a week.

Taxis to the airport from Tunxi cost about Y15 to Y20.

🚹 Airport Information **Huangshan City Airport** ✉ West of Tunxi on Yingbin Dadao ☎ 0559/293-4111.
🚹 Airlines & Contacts **CAAC** ✉ 23 Huashan Lu, Tunxi ☎ 0559/953-4111 ✉ 49Huang-shan Donglu, Tuxni ☎ 0559/254-1222.

BY BUS

Buses are a convenient way of getting to Tunxi from Zhejiang, Jiangsu, and even Shanghai. Buses that run hourly from Hangzhou take 3½ hours and cost Y65. The route takes you through some gorgeous scenery. Buses from Nanjing take around 5 hours and cost Y80. From Shanghai, buses take eight to nine hours and cost Y120.

🚹 **Tunxi Bus Station** ✉ 95 Huangshan Dong Lu, Tunxi ☎ 0559/235-3952.

BY TAXI

In Tunxi, minibuses and taxis that congregate around the train station will take you to Yellow Mountain. For about Y20 they will drop you at the main gate at the bottom of the mountain or at the beginning of the climbing section.

BY TRAIN
Trains travel to Tunxi, where you can catch a minivan or taxi to Yellow Mountain. The ride takes about an hour. It's best to arrive early in the day, as many drivers are not eager to traverse the winding road in the dark.

Trains leave three times a day to Nanjing and Shanghai (7 hours, Y60). The most popular way to travel is a sleeper train that arrives in Shanghai and Nanjing in the early morning. The cost is Y160.

🚆 **Huangshan Train Station** ✉ Northern end of Qianyuan Beilu, Tunxi ☎ 0559/211-6222.

Contacts & Resources

EMERGENCIES
In case of an emergency, contact your hotel manager for assistance. If you speak Chinese (or are traveling with someone who does), the following numbers may prove useful: **Police** (☎ 110), the **fire department** (☎ 119), and the **first-aid hotline** (☎ 120).

🚑 **People's Hospital of Huangshan City** ✉ 4 Liyuan Lu, Huangshan ☎ 0559/253-1528. **Beihai Medical Center** ✉ Across from Beihai Hotel, Huangshan ☎ 0559/558-2555. **Jade Screen Tower First-Aid Station** ✉ Jade Screen Tower Hotel ☎ 0559/558-2288.

TRAVEL AGENCIES
The Tunxi branches of China Travel Service—better known as CTS—can arrange transportation and book a place to stay on the mountain. It also has info on getting out and exploring the surrounding countryside. You can also get info from China International Travel Service, or CITS.

🏢 **CITS** ✉ 2 Binjiang Xi Lu, Tunxi ☎ 0559/251-5303. **CTS** ✉ 12 Qianyuan Bei Lu, Tunxi ☎ 0559/211-5832 📠 1Binjiang Xi Lu, Tunxi ☎ 0559/254-2391.

VISITOR INFORMATION
The best place for current information about the region is the English-language Hangshan Travel Net, run in conjunction with the local CTS. The site is the brainchild of CTS's Victor Zhang, one of the area's most knowledgeable guides. He has arranged tea tours, bike tours, and architecture tours. Once you're in the area, you can also drop by CTS's offices for travel tips.

🏢 Tourist Information **CTS** ✉ 12 Qianyuan Bei Lu, Tunxi ☎ 0559/211-5832 📠 1Binjiang Xi Lu, Tunxi ☎ 0559/254-2391 ⊕ www.uhuangshan.com.

At a Glance

ENGLISH	PINYIN	CHINESE CHARACTERS
HEBEI	Héběi	河北
CHENGDE	Chéngdé	承德
EXPLORING		
CITS	Zhōng Guó Guó Jì Lǚxíng Shè	中国国际旅行社
Club Rock	Bàngchuí Fēng	棒槌峰
Eight Outer Monasteries	Wài Bā Miào	外八庙
Huanghua Great Wall	Huánghuā Chángchéng	黄花长城
Mountain Resort	Bìshǔ Shānzhuāng	避暑山庄
Temple of Universal Peace	Pǔníng Sì	普宁寺
Temple of the Potaraka Doctrine	Pùtuó Zōngchéng Sì	普陀宗乘寺
Temple of Universal Happiness	Pùlè Sì	普乐寺
WHERE TO STAY, EAT & DRINK		
Mongolian Yurts Holiday Inn	Ménggù Bāodù Jiàcūn	蒙古包度假村
Da Qinghua Jiao Zi	Dà Qīnghuā Jiǎo Zǐ	大清花饺子
Hong Men Internet Bar	Hóngmén Wǎng Bā	鸿门网吧
Mountain Villa Hotel	Shānzhuāng Bīnguǎn	山庄宾馆
Shenghua Hotel	Shènghuá Dà Jiǔdiàn	盛华大酒店
Yunshan Hotel	Chéngdé Yúnshān Fàndiàn	承德云山饭店
BEIDAIHE	Běidàihé	北戴河
EXPLORING		
Guanyin Temple	Guānyīn Sì	观音寺
Lianfeng Hill Park	Líanfēngshān Gōng yuán	联峰山公园
Emperor Qin Shi Huang's Palace	Qínhuáng Gōng	秦皇宫
WHERE TO STAY, EAT & DRINK		
Kiesslings	Qǐshìlín Cāntīng	起士林餐厅
Beidaihe Guesthouse for Diplomatic Missions	Běidàihé WàiJiāo RénYuán Bīnguǎn	北戴河外交人员宾馆
Jinshan Hotel	Jīnshān Dà JiǔDiàn	金山大酒店
SHANHAIGUAN	Shān Hǎi Guān	山海关
EXPLORING		
First Gate Under Heaven	Tiānxià Dìyīguān	天下第一关
Great Wall Museum	Chángchéng Bówùguǎn	长城博物馆

Jiao Mountain	Jiǎo Shān	角山
Mengjiangnu Miao	Mèng Jiāng Nǚ Miào	孟姜女庙
Old Dragon Head	Lǎo Lóng Tóu	老龙头
WHERE TO STAY, EAT & DRINK		
First Pass Hotel	Jīngshān Bīnguǎn	京山宾馆
North Street Hotel	Běi Jiē Zhāo dài suǒ	北街招待所
Wang Yan Lou	Wàng Yān lóu	王严楼
SHANDONG	Shāndōng	山东
JI'NAN	Jìnán	济南
EXPLORING		
Big Bright Lake	Dàmíng Hú	大明湖
Confucius Family Mansion	Kǒng fǔ	孔府
Confucius Forest	Kǒng lín	孔林
Confucius Temple	Kǒng miào	孔庙
Gushing from the Ground Spring	Bàotǔquán	暴土泉
Mt. Tai	Tàishān	泰山
Protestant church	Jīdū Jiàotáng	基督教堂
Thousand Buddha Mountain	Qiān FóShān	千佛山
QUFU	Qūfù	曲阜
WHERE TO STAY & EAT		
Crowne Plaza Ji'nan	Jǐnán guìhé huángguānjiàrì jiǔdiàn	济南贵和皇冠假日酒店
Foshan Yuan		
Jiu Wan Ban	Jiǔwǎnbān	九晚班
Kiwi Corner	Qíyìguǒ Jiǎo	奇异果角
Queli Hotel	Quèlǐ bīnshě	阙里宾舍
Shandong Elite Teahouse	Shāndōng gāorényīděng cháguǎn	山东高人一等茶馆
Silver Plaza Quancheng Hotel	Yínzuò quánchéng dàjiǔdiàn	银座泉城大酒店
Sofitel Silver Plaza	Jǐnán suǒfēitè yínzuò dàfàndiàn	济南索菲特银座大饭店
Shengqi Hotel	Shēngqǐ fàndiàn	升起酒店
Tai'an	Tài ān	泰安

2

Yuan Jiudian	Yuán Jiǔdiàn	园酒店
QINGDAO	Qīngdǎo	青岛
EXPLORING		
Catholic church	Tiānzhǔ Jiàotáng	教堂
German governor's residence	Qīngdǎo yíng bīnguǎn	青岛迎宾馆
Guanhaishan Park	Guānhǎishān gōngyuán	观海山公园
Huashi Lou	Huā shí lóu	花石楼
Lu Xun Park	Lǔxùn gōngyuán	鲁迅公园
Mount Lao	Láo shān	崂山
Navy Museum	Hǎijūn bówùguǎn	海军博物馆
Protestant church	Jīdū Jiàotáng	基督教堂
Qingdao Tourism Administration	Qīngdǎo lǚyóu guǎlǐjú	青岛旅游管理局
Sun Yat-sen Park	Zhōngshān gōngyuán	中山公园
Tsingdao Beer Factory	Qīngdǎo píjīchǎng	青岛啤酒厂
Underwater World	Shuǐxià (ǎidǐ) shìjiè	水下（海底）世界
WHERE TO STAY & EAT		
Badaguan Hotel	Bādàguān bīnguǎn	八大关宾馆
Café Roland	Lǎngyuán jiǔbā	朗园酒吧
Chui Zhu Yuan	Chuī zhǔ yuán	炊主园
Crowne Plaza	Huángguān jiǔdiàn	皇冠酒店
Guo Fu Cheng	Guō fù chéng	郭富城
Huadong Winery CO.,LTD	Huádōng pútáo niàngjiǔ yǒuxiàn gōngsī	华东葡萄酿酒有限公司
Huiquan Dynasty Hotel	Huìquán wángcháo dàfàndiàn	汇泉王朝大饭店
La Villa	Lāwéilā fǎguó cāntīng	拉维拉法国餐厅
Sailing Club and Bar	Hánghǎi jùlèbù jiǔbā	航海俱乐部酒吧
Shangri-La	Xiāng gé lǐ lā	香格里拉
SPR coffee	SPR kāfēi	SPR 咖啡
Tsingtao Brewery Bar	Qīngdǎo píjiǔbā	青岛啤酒吧
Zhongshan restaurant	Zhōngshān fàndiàn	中山饭店
JIANGSU	Jiāngsū	江苏
NANJING	Nán jīng	南京

EXPLORING

CITS	zhōng guó guó jì lǚ xíng shè	中国国际旅行社
1912	Yī jiǔ yī èr	一九一二
Baguo Buyi	Bāguó bùyī	巴国布衣
Behind the Wall	Dá àn bā	答案
Bellagio	Lùgǎng xiǎozhèn	鹿港小镇
Blue Marlin	Lánqiāngyú xīcán jiǔbā	蓝枪鱼西餐酒吧
Brocade Research Institute	Nánjīng yúnjǐn yánjiūsuǒ	南京云锦研究所
Central Hotel	Zhōngxīn dàjiǔdiàn	中心大酒店
Chaotian Gong Antique Market	Cháotiāngōng gǔwàn shìchǎng	朝天宫古玩市场
City Garden Coffee Shop	Chéngshì huāyuán kāfēidiàn	城市花园咖啡店
Confucian Temple	FūzǐMiào	夫子庙
Danfengyulu Coffee Shop	Dānfèng yǔ lù kāfēidiàn	丹凤雨露咖啡店
Dingshan Meishi Cheng	Dīngshān měishíchéng	丁山美食城
Drum Tower	Gǔ lóu	鼓楼
Golden Eagle department store	Jīnyīng guójì gòuwùzhōngxīn	金鹰国际购物中心
Grand Hotel	Gǔ nán dū fàn diàn	古南都饭店
Hong Ni Restaurant	Hóngní dàjiǔdiàn	红泥大酒店
Jimingsi Vegetarian Restaurant	Jīmíngsìsùzhāi	鸡鸣寺素斋
Jinling Hotel	Jīnlíng fàndiàn	金陵饭店
Lukou Airport	Lùkǒu jīchǎng	禄口机场
Magazine Café	Zázhì kāfēI	杂志咖啡
Mandarin Garden Hotel	Zhuàngyuánlóu jiǔdiàn	状元楼酒店
Meiling Palace	Měilíng gōng	美龄宫
Ming Tomb	Míng Xiào líng	明孝陵
Nanjing Arts & Crafts Company	Nánjīng gōngyì měishù pǐn gōngsī	南京工艺美术品公司
Nanjing Bus Station	Nánjīng qìchēzhàn	南京汽车站
Nanjing City's Zhongshan Matou (Ferry Terminal)	Nánjīng zhōngshān mǎtóu	南京中山码头
Nanjing Hilton	Nánjīng xī ěr dùn	南京希尔顿
Nanjing Hotel	Nánjīng fàndiàn	南京饭店

2

Nanjing Massacre Memorial	Nánjīng dàtúshā jìniànguǎn	南京大屠杀纪念馆
Nanjing Museum	Nánjīng bówùyuàn	南京博物院
Oriental Plaza	Dōngfáng shāngshà	东方商厦
Plum Blossom Hill and Middle Mountain (Sun Yat-sen) Botanical Gardens	Méihuāshān hé zhōngshān zhíwùyuán	梅花山和中山（孙中山）植物园
Rain Flower Terrace and Martyrs Memorial	Yǔhuātái hé lièshìjìniànguǎn	雨花台和烈士纪念馆
Ramada	Huáměidá	华美达
Red Club	Hóng bā	红吧
Scarlet	Luànshì jiārén	乱世佳人
Shaanxi Lu night market	Shānxī lù yèshì	山西路夜市
Sheraton Nanjing Kingsley Hotel and Towers	Nánjīng xīláidēng dàjiǔdiàn	南京喜来登大酒店
SoHo Silk Market	Sūháo sīchóu chéng	苏豪丝绸城
South Gate of City Wall	Zhōnghuá mén	中华门
Sparrow's Rock	Yànzǐjī	燕子矶
Spirit Valley Temple and Pagoda	Línggǔsì hé línggǔtǎ	灵谷寺和灵谷塔
Sun Yat-sen Memorial	Sūnzhōngshān jìniànguǎn	孙中山纪念馆
Swank	Wánkè bā	玩客吧
T'Oberay New Zealand Coffee	Dùbóruì xīnxīlán kāfēi	杜伯瑞新西兰咖啡
Tea Station	Chákè lǎozhàn	茶客老站
The Coffee Beanery	Bīnlè kāfēi	滨乐咖啡
Tiandi Restaurant	Yíjiāqīn měishi tiāndi	一家亲美食天地
WHERE TO STAY & EAT		
Xinjiekou department store	Xīnjiēkǒu bǎihuò gōngsī	新街口百货公司
Xuanwu Hotel	Xuánwǔ fàndiàn	玄武饭店
Xuanwu Lake Park	Xuánwǔhú gōngyuán	玄武湖公园
Yangzi River Bridge	Nánjīng chángjiāng dàqiáo	南京长江大桥
Yuejiang Lou Tower	Yuèjiāng lóu	阅江楼
YANGZHOU	Yáng zhōu	扬州
EXPLORING		
DaMing Temple	Dà míng sì	大明寺

Fifth Spring Under Heaven	Tiānxià dìwǔ quán	天下第五泉
fishing terrace	Diàoyú tái	钓鱼台
Five Pavilion Bridge	Wǔ tíng qiáo	五亭桥
Garden Tomb of Puhaddin	Pǔhādīng mù yuán	普哈丁墓园
Ge Garden	Gè yuán	个园
He Garden	Hé yuán	何园
Slender West Lake	Shòu xīhú	瘦西湖
Wang's Residence	Wāngshì xiǎoyuàn	汪氏小苑
White Pagoda	Bái tǎ	白塔
Yangzhou Bus Station	Yángzhōu qìchēzhàn	扬州汽车站
Yangzhou China Youth Travel Agency	Yángzhōu zhōngguó qīngnián lǚxíngshè	扬州中国青年旅行社

WHERE TO STAY & EAT

DeYue Restaurant	Déyuè jiǔjiā	得月酒家
Fu Chun Teahouse	Fùchūn cháshè	富春茶社
Grand Metropole Hotel	Jīnghuá guójì dájiǔdiàn	京华国际大酒店
XiYuan Hotel	Xīyuán dàjiǔdiàn	西园大酒店
Yangzhou Hotel	Yángzhōu bīnguǎn	扬州宾馆

EXPLORING THE WATER VILLAGES

Ancient Chinese Sexual Culture Museum	Zhōngguó gǔdài xìngwénhuà bówùguǎn	中国古代性文化博物馆
Baosheng Temple	Bǎoshèng sì	保圣寺
Luzhi	Lù zhí	甪直
Tong Li	Tóng lǐ	同里
Zhouzhuang	Zhōu zhuāng	周庄
SUZHOU	Sū zhōu	苏州

EXPLORING

Blue Wave Pavilion	Cānglàng tíng	沧浪亭
Grand Canal	Dà yùnhé	大运河
Hall of 500 Arhats	WǔbǎI luóhàn táng	五百罗汉堂
Hanshan Temple	Hánshān sì	寒山寺
Humble Administrator's Garden	Zhuózhèng yuán	拙政园
Joyous Garden	Yí yuán	怡园
Leaning Pagoda	Xié tǎ	斜塔

Lingering Garden	Liú yuán	留园
Lion's Grove Garden	Shīzī lín	狮子林
Mandarin Duck Hall	Yuānyàng tīng	鸳鸯厅
Master of the Nets Garden	Wǎngshī yuán	网师园
North Temple Pagoda	Běisì tǎ	北寺塔
Overnight Boat	Géyè chuán	隔夜船
Pan Gate	Pán mén	盘门
Precious Belt Bridge	Bǎodài qiáo	宝带桥
Pure Fragrance Pavilion	Qīngxiāng guǎn	清香馆
Ruiguang Pagoda	Ruìguāng tǎ	瑞光塔
Suzhou Arts and Crafts Museum	Sūzhōu gōngyìměishù bówùguǎn	苏州工艺美术博物馆
Suzhou Bus Station	Sūzhōu qìchē zhàn	苏州汽车站
Suzhou Ferry Terminal	Sūzhōu mǎtóu	苏州码头
Suzhou International Travel Service	Sūzhōu guójì lǚxíngshè	苏州国际旅行社
Suzhou Taihu International Travel Service	Sūzhōu tàihú guójì lǚxíngshè	苏州太湖国际旅行社
Temple of Mystery	Xuánmiào guàn	玄妙观
Tiger Hill	Hǔ qiū	虎丘
West Garden Temple	Xīyuán sì	西园寺
WHERE TO STAY & EAT		
Bamboo Grove Hotel	Sūzhōu zhúhuī fàndiàn	苏州竹辉饭店
Deyuelou	Déyuè lóu	得月楼
Friendship Store	Yǒuyí shāngdiàn	友谊商店
Gloria Plaza Hotel Suzhou	Sūzhōu kǎilái dàjiǔdiàn	苏州凯莱大酒店
Huangtianyuan	Huángtiān yuán	黄天园
Lexiang Hotel	Lèxiāng fàndiàn	乐乡饭店
Lidu (Jasper) Hotel Suzhou	Sūzhōu lìdū dàjiǔdiàn	苏州丽都大酒店
Master of the Nets Garden	Wǎngshī yuán	网师园
Nanlin Hotel	Nánlín dàjiǔdiàn	南林大酒店
Nanyuan Guest House	Sūzhōu nányuán bīnguǎn	苏州南园宾馆
Pine and Crane	Sōnghè lóu	松鹤楼
Sheraton Suzhou Hotel & Towers	Xīláidēng dàjiǔdiàn	喜来登大酒店

Suzhou Antiques Store	Sūzhōu wénwù shāngdiàn	苏州文物商店
Suzhou Arts and Crafts Museum	Sūzhōu gōngyìměishù bówùguǎn	苏州工艺美术博物馆
Suzhou Hotel	Sūzhōu fàndiàn	苏州饭店
Suzhou Silk Museum Shop	Sūzhōu sīchóu bówùguǎn shāngdiàn	苏州丝绸博物馆商店
Wumen Artstore	Wúmén yìyuàn	吴门艺苑
Wuyuegong Restaurant Theater	Wúyuè gōng	吴越宫

Shanghai

HEAD OF THE DRAGON

The hyper-modern skyline of the Pudong district.

WORD OF MOUTH

"Shanghai is not about shopping as it is about experiencing a cosmopolitan China. Shanghai is like a woman or a man, whichever you prefer, a city that is alive and is waiting for you to get to know her." —sbobao

"Shanghai grabbed me, and I'd go back any time. You have a great chance to see a great country at a pivotal point in its history, and nowhere illustrates this more dramatically than Shanghai." —Neil_Oz

WELCOME TO SHANGHAI

TOP REASONS TO GO

★ **Futuristic Views.** Shanghai is the country's future, and the city's skyline is its banner. If you head to the top of either the Pearl Tower or the pagoda-inspired Jin Mao you'll be in for a bird's-eye view of the city and its surroundings.

★ **Shopping Overload.** Shanghai has possibly the best shopping on the mainland, from designer boutiques to market stalls. The Bund and the glamorous Plaza 66 are the up-and-coming designer areas for the ultrachic. If you want something more "Chinese," the boutiques in and around Xintiandi offer very stylish fusion pieces.

★ **Shanghai Museum.** China's best museum houses an incomparable collection that includes paintings, sculpture, ceramics, calligraphy, furniture, and fantastic bronzes.

★ **Yu Garden.** The Garden offers an atmosphere of peace and beauty amid the clamor of the city, with rocks, trees, and walls curved to resemble dragons, bridges, and pavilions.

1 The Bund. Famous waterfront boulevard is lined with art-deco buildings and souvenir stands. It's great for people-watching, being watched yourself, shopping for increasingly chic clothes, and sampling some of Shanghai's most famous restaurants. It's also where you'll get that postcard view of the futuristic skyline in Pudong.

2 Xintiandi. Shopping, bars, restaurants, and museums mix together in restored traditional shikumen (stone gate) houses. Xintiandi is a popular location for hanging out and people-watching, and there are a few great boutiques. The small museums have interesting exhibits related to Shanghai's and the Communist Party's history.

GETTING ORIENTED

Few places in the world are undergoing as much change as high-powered Shanghai. The city's landscape changes every day, as old neighborhoods are swept away to make room for the new face of China. Art Deco rubs shoulders with French Colonial remnants and futuristic design. Shanghai is also where you'll see China at its most sophisticated. Get here quickly, though, before the future is all that's left.

Lujiazui Financial Distirct, Pudong

3 Former French Concession. Whether you're an architecture fanatic, a photographer, a romantic, or just plain curious, a wander through these streets is always a wonderful way to pass an afternoon. Take your time and allow for breaks at cafés or in small boutiques in Pudong.

4 Nanjing Lu. People come from all over China to shop on what was once China's premier shopping street. Pedestrian-only Nanjing Lu is undergoing a massive face-lift, and trendy designer boutiques are beginning to emerge alongside pre-1960s department stores and old-fashioned silk shops.

SHANGHAI PLANNER

City of the Future

As the most Westernized city in China after Hong Kong, Shanghai is on the cutting edge of China's race for modernization. It isn't an ancient Chinese city with loads of historic temples and ruins to visit. It's a young new city more akin to Hong Kong than Beijing. The street scene and on-the-go vibe reflect China's future more than its past. Almost a quarter of the world's construction cranes stand in this city of 15 million. On the other hand, architectural remnants of a strong colonial past survive along the charming, winding, bustling streets that make this city undeniably and intimately Chinese.

When to Go

The best time to visit Shanghai is early fall, when the weather is good and crowds diminish. Although temperatures are scorching and the humidity can be unbearable, summer is the peak tourist season, and hotels and transportation can get very crowded. If possible, book several months in advance for summer travel.

Avoid the three national holidays: Chinese New Year, which ranges from mid-January to mid-February; the Labor Day holiday during the first week of May; and the National Day holiday during the first week of October. Imagine 1.2 billion people on the move, and you'll understand why it isn't a good time to travel.

Navigating

Shanghai is divided into east and west sides by the Huangpu River. The metro area is huge, but the city center is a relatively small district in Puxi (west of the river). On the east side lies the district that many think is Shanghai's future—Pudong (east of the river). The city is loosely laid out on a grid and most neighborhoods are easily explored on foot. Massive construction makes pavements uneven and the air dusty, but if you can put up with this, walking is the best way to really get a feel for the city and its people. Taxis are readily available and good for traveling longer distances.

Major east–west roads are named for Chinese cities and divide the city into *bei* (north), *zhong* (middle), and *nan* (south) sections. North–south roads divide the city into *dong* (east), *zhong* (middle), and *xi* (west) segments. The heart of the city is found on its chief east–west streets— Nanjing Lu, Huaihai Lu, and Yanan Lu.

■ TIP→ Transport cards costing Y10 are available from the metro stations and can be charged with however much money you like. These can be used in taxis, on metros, and on some buses. They aren't discounted, but they'll save you time you would have spent joining queues and fumbling for cash.

Navigating Vocabulary

Below are some terms you'll see over and over again. These words will appear on maps and street signs, and they are part of the name of just about every place you go:

Dong is east, **xi** is west, **nan** is south, **bei** is north, and **zhong** means middle. **Jie** and **lu** mean street and road respectively, and **da** means big.

Qiao, or bridge, is part of the place name at just about every entrance and exit on the ring roads.

Men, meaning door or gate, indicates a street that once passed through an entrance in the fortification wall that surrounded the city hundreds of years ago. The entrances to parks and some other places are also referred to as *men.*

Getting Around

By Taxi: Taxis are plentiful, cheap, and easy to spot. Your hotel concierge can call for one by phone or you can hail one on the street. Taxi stands are cropping up all over the city, but during peak hours or in rainy weather it's still every man for himself and fights for the free taxis can get physical. The available ones have a small lit-up sign on the passenger side. If you're choosing a cab from a line, peek at the driver's license on the dashboard. The lower the license number, the more experienced the driver. Drivers with a number below 200,000 can usually get you where you're going.

Most cab drivers don't speak English, so it's best to give them a piece of paper with your destination written in Chinese. (Keep a card with the name of your hotel on it handy for the return trip.) Hotel doormen can help you tell the driver where you're going. It's a good idea to study a map and have some idea of where you are, as some drivers will take you for a ride—a much longer one—if they think they can get away with it.

By Subway: The subway is great way to get someplace fast without getting stuck in Shanghai's traffic-choked streets. As the subway is improved and extended, more English maps and exit signs are being included. The new electronic ticket machines have an English option that gives maps in English so you can pick your destination.

Stations are clean and glass walls are being installed to protect passenger safety. If you aren't sure which exit to take, take any and negotiate your way when above ground. In-car announcements for each station are given in both Chinese and English. Pick up a subway or city map at your hotel because at many stations you may not find an English-language route map until after you've bought your ticket and cleared the turnstile. Keep your ticket handy; you'll need to insert it into a second turnstile as you exit at your destination. Transport cards are swiped at entry and exit.

By Ferry: Ferries run around the clock every 10 minutes between the Bund and Pudong's terminal just south of the Riverside Promenade. The per-person fare is Y2 per person each way.

By Bus: Taking the bus is not recommended as they are often crowded, slow, and nearly impossible to negotiate without speaking Chinese.

Opening Hours

Almost all businesses close for Chinese New Year (sometime in mid-January to mid-February) and other major holidays.

Shops: Stores are generally open daily 9 to 7; some stores stay open as late as 10 PM especially in summer.

Temples & Museums: Most temples and parks are open daily 8 to 5. Museums and most other sights are generally open 9 to 5, six days a week, with Monday being the most common closed day.

Banks & Offices: Most banks and government offices are open weekdays 9 to 5, although some close for lunch (sometime between noon and 2). Bank branches and CITS tour desks in hotels often keep longer hours and are usually open Saturday morning. Many hotel currency-exchange desks stay open 24 hours.

Visitor Centers

China International Travel Service (CITS), an official government agency, maintains offices in many hotels and at some tourist venues. The Shanghai Tourism Administration maintains a 24-hour hotline for tourist inquiries and complaints, with operators fluent in English.

China International Travel Service (CITS) (⊠ 1277 Beijing Xi Lu, Jing'an ☎021/6289–4510). **Shanghai Tourist Information Services** (⊠ Yu Garden, 159 Jiujiaochang Lu, Huangpu ☎ 021/5355–5032 ⊠ Hongqiao International Airport ☎ 021/6268-8899). **Tourist Hotline** (☎021/6439–0630 or 021/6439-8947).

EXPLORING SHANGHAI

By Elyse
Singleton

Central Shanghai is cut in two by the Huangpu River. To the east is the city's new financial district, glitzy modern Pudong, where the iconic Pearl TV Tower sits. On the west lies Puxi, the old city, home to most of Shanghai's tourist attractions. Pudong and Puxi are linked by three bridges, two tunnels, three subway crossings, and various ferries.

The focus of Puxi is Huangpu District, Shanghai's downtown. It contains the linchpin of Shanghai's tourist scene, the Bund, a good place to get your bearings. Nanjing Lu (Shanghai's answer to Fifth Avenue) connects the Bund to Renmin (People's) Square. Also in Puxi are traditional Nanshi, the Former (sometimes called Old French Concession) French Concession, ultratrendy Xintiandi, and Xuhui and Jing'an.

A rough grid system governs the streets of central Shanghai. East–west streets take their names from Chinese cities (Beijing Lu or Yan'an Lu, for example); provinces or regions give their names to north–south streets (such as Heinan Lu or Sichuan Lu). As in many U.S. cities, Shanghai's street names change slightly along their length with the addition of a compass point. Thus Beijing Xi Lu and Beijing Dong Lu are Beijing Road East and Beijing Road West, respectively.

Old City

Tucked away in the east of Puxi are the remnants of Shanghai's Old City. Once encircled by a thick wall, a fragment of which still remains, the Old City has a sense of history among its fast disappearing old *shikumen* (stone gatehouses), temples, and markets. Delve into narrow alleyways where residents still hang their washing out on bamboo poles and chamber pots are still in use. Burn incense with the locals in small temples, sip tea in a teahouse, or get a taste of Chinese snacks and street food. This is the place to get a feeling for Shanghai's past, but you'd better get there soon, as the wrecker's ball knows no mercy.

GETTING
AROUND

At press time, Shanghai's ever expanding metro system had not yet reached Old City. However, it's a short walk east from Henan Zhong Lu station on Line 2, and a slightly longer, but interesting walk south from Huangpi Nan Lu on Line 1. ■ TIP→ Be warned that taxis are nearly impossible to find in this area when you want to leave.

Sights

❶ **Old City Wall.** The Old City used to be completely surrounded by a wall, built in 1553 as a defense against Japanese pirates. Most of it was torn down in 1912, except for one

> **NAVIGATING**
>
> Shanghai is a large, sprawling city, and the size of its districts reflects that. We have simplified your experience by creating a series of smaller neighborhoods, centered around the attractions. However, because you may still need to know the official districts, we have listed them at the end of each entry. They'll be useful in dealing with the local tourist resources, hotels, and taxi drivers.

SHANGHAI THEN & NOW

A port city, lying at the mouth of Asia's longest and most important river, Shanghai is famous as a place where internationalism has thrived. Opened to the world as a treaty port in 1842, Shanghai for decades was not one city but a divided territory. The British, French, and Americans each claimed their own concessions, neighborhoods where their laws and culture—rather than China's—were the rule.

By the 1920s and '30s, Shanghai was a place of sepia-lighted nightclubs, French villas, and opium dens. Here rich taipans walked the same streets as gamblers, prostitutes, and beggars, and Jews fleeing persecution in Russia lived alongside Chinese intellectuals and revolutionaries.

But now Shanghai draws more parallels to New York City than Paris. Pudong New Area, China's 21st-century financial, economic, and commercial center is home to

the tallest hotel in the world, and the world's first commercial "Maglev" (magnetic levitation) train. As Shanghai prepares to host the 2010 World Expo, Pudong is again immersed in a decade-long round of construction. Puxi, the west side of the river and the city center, has also gone through staggering change. Charming old houses are making way for shiny high-rises. The population is moving from alley housing in the city center to spanking-new apartments in the suburbs.

Shanghai's open policy has also made the city a magnet for foreign investors. As millions of dollars pour in, especially to Pudong, Shanghai has again become home to tens of thousands of expatriates. Higher salaries and higher buildings, more business and more entertainment—they all define the fast-paced lives of China's most cosmopolitan and open people.

40-meter-long (50-yard-long) piece that still stands at Dajing Lu and Renmin Lu. You can walk through the remnants and check out the rather simple museum nearby, which is dedicated to the history of Old City (the captions are in Chinese). Stroll through the tiny neighboring alley of Dajing Lu for a lively panorama of crowded market life in the Old City. ☒ *269 Dajing Lu, at Renmin Lu, Huangpu* ☎ *021/6385–2443* 🖾 *Y5* ☉ *Daily 9–4.*

Experiences

SHANGHAI'S BEST GARDEN

Yu Garden. Since the 18th century, this complex, with its traditional red walls and upturned tile roofs, has been a marketplace and social center where local residents gather, shop, and practice *qi gong* in the evenings. Although a bit overrun by tourists and not as impressive as the ancient palace gardens of Beijing, Yu Garden is a piece of Shanghai's past, and one of the few old sights left in the city.

To get to the garden itself, you must wind your way through the bazaar. The garden was commissioned by the Ming Dynasty official Pan Yund-

uan in 1559 and built by the renowned architect, Zhang Nanyang, over 19 years. When it was finally finished it won international praise as "the best garden in southeastern China," an accolade that would be hard to defend today, especially when compared with the beautiful gardens of Suzhou. In the mid-1800s the Society of Small Swords used the garden as a gathering place for meetings. It was here that they planned their uprising with the Taiping rebels against the French colonists. The French destroyed the garden during the first Opium War, but the area was later rebuilt and renovated.

Winding walkways and corridors bring you over stone bridges and carp-filled ponds and through bamboo stands and rock gardens. Within the park are an **old opera stage**, a **museum** dedicated to the Society of Small Swords rebellion, and an **exhibition hall**, opened in 2003, of Chinese calligraphy and paintings. One caveat: the park is almost always thronged with Chinese tour groups, especially on weekends. As with most sights in Shanghai, don't expect a tranquil time alone. ⊠ *218 Anren Lu, bordered by Fuyou Lu, Jiujiaochang Lu, Fangbang Lu, and Anren Lu, Huangpu* 🕾 *021/6326–0830 or 021/6328–3251* 🎟 *Y30* ☉ *Gardens, daily 8:30–5.*

FEEL THE SPIRIT

❸ **Temple of the City God** (Chenghuang Miao) lies at the southeast end of the bazaar. This Taoist Temple of the City God was built during the early part of the Ming Dynasty and later destroyed. The main hall was re-built in 1926 and has been renovated many times over the years. Inside are gleaming gold figures, and atop the roof you'll see statues of crusading warriors—flags raised, arrows drawn. ✉ *Xi Dajie Lu, Huangpu* ☎ *021/6386–8649* 🚇 *Y5* ☉ *Daily 8:30–5 (doors close at 4:30).*

❹ **Chen Xiangge Temple.** If you find yourself passing by this tiny temple on your exploration of the Old City, you can make an offering to Buddha with the free incense sticks that accompany your admission. Built in 1600 by the same man who built Yu Garden, it was destroyed during the Cultural Revolution and rebuilt in the 1990s. The temple is now a nunnery, and you can often hear the women's chants rising from the halls beyond the main courtyard. ✉ *29 Chenxiangge Lu, Huangpu* ☎ *021/6320–0400* 🚇 *Y5* ☉ *Daily 7–4.*

> **GRAB A BITE**
>
> The **Huxinting Teahouse** (✉ 257 Yuyuan Lu, Huangpu District ☎ 021/6373–6950 downstairs, 021/6355–8270 upstairs), Shanghai's oldest, opened in 1856 and stands on a man-made lake in the middle of the Yu Garden, at the center of the Bridge of the Nine Turnings. Although tea is cheaper on the 1st floor, be sure to sit on the top floor by a window overlooking the lake. Upstairs, a bottomless cup of tea comes with Chinese snacks. A traditional tea ceremony is performed every night from 8:30 PM to 10 PM. An ensemble with erhu (a two-stringed instrument), pipa (a type of flute), and other traditional instruments performs Monday from 1:30 to 5 PM and Friday through Sunday from 6:30 to 9 PM.

Xintiandi & City Center

Xintiandi is Shanghai's showpiece restoration project. Reproduction shikumen houses contain expensive bars, restaurants, and chic boutiques. It's at its most magical on a warm night when locals, expats, and visitors alike pull up a chair at one of the outside seating areas and watch the world go by. Nearby, the area around People's Square has some magnificent examples of modern and historical architecture and a smattering of some of Shanghai's best museums. The adjoining People's Park is a pleasant green space where it's possible to escape the clamor of the city for a while.

GETTING AROUND People's Square metro station is at present the main point of convergence for Shanghai's metro lines. The underground passageways can be confusing, so it's best to take the first exit and then find your way above ground. Xintiandi is a block or two south of Line 1's Huangpi Nan Lu metro station.

Sights

⓬ **Site of the First National Congress of the Communist Party.** The secret meeting on July 31, 1921 that marked the first National Congress was held at the Bo Wen Girls' School, where 13 delegates from Marxist, Commu-

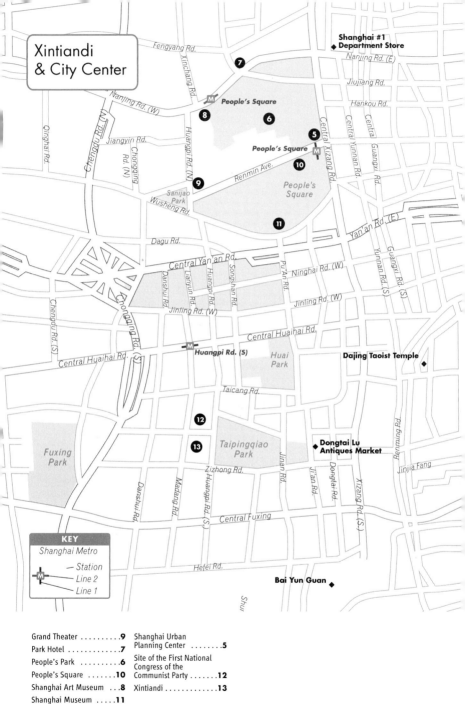

Xintiandi & City Center

nist, and Socialist groups gathered from around the country. Today, ironically, the site is surrounded by Xintiandi, Shanghai's center of conspicuous consumption. The upstairs of this restored shikumen is a well-curated museum explaining the rise of communism in China. Downstairs lies the very room where the first delegates worked. It remains frozen in time— the table set with matches and teacups. ⊠ *374 Huangpi Nan Lu, Luwan* ☎ *021/5383–2171* ⌺ *Y3* ⊙ *Daily 9–5, last ticket sold at 4.*

❾ Grand Theater. The spectacular front wall of glass shines as brightly as the star power in this magnificent theater. Its three stages host the best domestic and international performances, including the debut of *Les Misérables* in China in 2002 and *Cats* in 2003. The dramatic curved roof atop a square base is meant to invoke the Chinese traditional saying, "the earth is square and the sky is round." ■ TIP→ **See it at night.** ⊠ *300 Renmin Dadao, Huangpu* ☎ *021/6386–8686* ⌺ *Tour, Y40* ⊙ *Tours Mon. 9–11.*

❼ Park Hotel. This art-deco structure overlooking People's Park was originally the tallest hotel in Shanghai. Completed in 1934, it had luxury rooms, a nightclub, and chic restaurants. Today it's more subdued, and the lobby is the most vivid reminder of its glorious past. It was also apparently an early inspiration for famous architect I. M. Pei (of the glass pyramids at the Louvre). ⊠ *170 Nanjing Xi Lu, Huangpu* ☎ *021/6327–5225.*

❻ People's Park. In colonial days, this park was the northern half of the city's racetrack. Today the 30 acres of flower beds, lotus ponds, and trees are crisscrossed by a large number of paved paths. There's also an art gallery, the **Museum of Contemporary Art,** and a bar and restaurant, **Barbarossa** inside. ⊠ *231 Nanjing Xi Lu, Huangpu* ☎ *021/6327–1333* ⌺ *Free* ⊙ *Daily 6–6 in winter and 5–7 in summer.*

Fodor'sChoice **People's Square.** Once the southern half of the city's racetrack, Shang-
★ hai's main square has become a social and cultural center. The Shang-
❿ hai Museum, Municipal Offices, Grand Theater, and Shanghai Urban Planning Center surround it. During the day, visitors and residents stroll, fly kites, and take their children to feed the pigeons. In the evening, kids roller-skate, ballroom dancers hold group lessons, and families relax together. Weekends here are especially busy. ⊠ *Bordered by Weihai Lu on south, Xizang Lu on east, Huangpi Bei Lu on west, and Fuzhou Lu on north, Huangpu.*

❺ Shanghai Urban Planning Center. To understand the true scale of Shanghai and its ongoing building boom, visit the Master Plan Hall of this museum. Sprawled out on the 3rd floor is a 6,400-square-foot planning model of Shanghai—the largest model of its kind in the world— showing the metropolis as city planners expect it to look in 2020. You'll find familiar existing landmarks like the Pearl Tower and Shanghai Center as well as future sites like the so-called Flower Bridge, an esplanade over the Huangpu River to be built for Expo 2010. ⊠ *100 Renmin Dadao, Huangpu* ☎ *021/6372–2077* ⌺ *Y30 unless there is a special exhibition* ⊙ *Mon.–Thurs. 9–5, Fri.–Sun. 9–6, last ticket sold 1 hr before closing.*

Experiences

FALL IN LOVE WITH XINTIANDI

⑬ Xintiandi. By WWII, around 70% of Shanghai's residents lived in shikumen or "stone gatehouses." Over the last two decades, most have been razed in the name of progress, but this 8-acre collection of stone gatehouses was renovated into an upscale shopping and dining complex and renamed Xintiandi, or "New Heaven on Earth." The restaurants are busy from lunchtime until past midnight, especially those with patios for watching the passing parade of shoppers. Just off the main thoroughfare is the visitor's center and the **Shikumen Museum** (✉ House 25, North Block, 123 Xingye Lu, Luwan District ☎ 021/3307–0337), a shikumen restored to 1920s style and filled with furniture and artifacts collected from nearby houses. Exhibits explain the European influence on shikumen design, the history of the Xintiandi renovation, as well as future plans for the entire 128-acre project. ✉ *181 Taicang Lu, Luwan, bordered by Taicang Lu, Madang Lu, Zizhong Lu, and Huangpi Nan Lu* ☎ *021/6311–2288* ⊕ *www.xintiandi.com* ✉ *Museum Y20* ⊙ *Museum, daily 10–10.*

DISCOVER THE ART SCENE

⑧ Shanghai Art Museum. At the northwest corner of People's Park, the former site of the Shanghai Library was once a clubhouse for Shanghai's sports groups, including the Shanghai Race Club. The building is now the home of the state-run Shanghai Art Museum. Its permanent collection includes paintings, calligraphy, and sculpture, but its rotating exhibitions have favored modern artwork. There's a museum store, a café, and a rooftop restaurant. ✉ *325 Nanjing Xi Lu, at Huangpi Bei Lu, Huangpu* ☎ *021/6327–2829* 🖷 *021/6327–2425* ✉ *Varies, depending on exhibition. Generally Y20* ⊙ *Daily 9–5.*

Fodor'sChoice
★
⑪ Shanghai Museum. Truly one of Shanghai's treasures, this museum has the country's premier collection of relics and artifacts. Eleven galleries exhibit Chinese artistry in all its forms: paintings, bronzes, sculpture, ceramics, calligraphy, jade, Ming and Qing dynasty furniture, coins, seals, and art by indigenous populations. Its bronze collection is one of the best in the world, and its dress and costume gallery showcases intricate handiwork from several of China's 52 minority groups. If you opt not to rent the excellent acoustic guide, information is well presented in English. You can relax in the museum's pleasant tearoom or buy postcards, crafts, and reproductions of the artwork in the stellar bookshop. ✉ *201 Renmin*

> ### WORD OF MOUTH
>
> "The Art Museum is THE must-do in Shanghai. It's by far the best museum in Asia. Be sure to rent the headphones. You can wander the galleries in any order and dial up the commentary for wherever you happen to be. You will not be able to do the whole museum unless you plan to spend an entire day there. Take a few moments at the beginning to decide which areas interest you the most and target those. The exhibits are arranged by medium: ceramics, jade, bronze, etc."
>
> —Lindsey

Da Dao, Huangpu ☎ *021/6372–3500* ⊕ *www.shanghaimuseum.net* ☞ *Y20, Y60 with acoustic guide* ◔ *Daily 9–4.*

The Bund & Nanjing Dong Lu

The city's most recognizable sightseeing spot, the Bund, on the bank of Shanghai's Huangpu River, is lined with pre-1949 buildings. Some of them have been developed into hip "lifestyle" complexes with spas, restaurants, bars, galleries, and designer boutiques. The Bund is also an ideal spot for that photo of Pudong's famous skyline. Leading away from the Bund, Nanjing Dong Lu is a shadow of the stylish street it once was, but it's still a popular shopping spot for the locals. Some of the adjacent streets still have a faded glamour. The best time to visit is at night to stroll the neon-lighted pedestrian road.

GETTING AROUND
The simplest way to get here is to take metro Line 2 to Henan Zhong Lu station and then head east for the Bund, or west for the main shopping area of Nanjing Dong Lu. Alternatively, you can get off at People's Square station and walk east.

Sights

⑭ The Bund. Shanghai's waterfront boulevard best shows both the city's
Fodor'sChoice
★
pre-1949 past and its focus on the future. Today the municipal government has renovated the old buildings of this most foreign face of the city, highlighting them as tourist attractions, and even tried for a while to sell them back to the very owners it forced out after 1949.

On the riverfront side of the Bund, Shanghai's street life is in full force. The city rebuilt the promenade, making it an ideal gathering place for both tourists and residents. In the morning, just after dawn, the Bund is full of people ballroom dancing, doing aerobics, and practicing kung fu, qi gong, and tai chi. The rest of the day people walk the embankment, snapping photos of the Oriental Pearl Tower, the Huangpu River, and each other. Be prepared for the aggressive souvenir hawkers; while you can't completely avoid them, try ignoring them or telling them *"bu yao,"* which means "Don't want." In the evenings lovers come out for romantic walks amid the floodlit buildings and tower. ⊠ *5 blocks of Zhongshan Dong Yi Lu between Jinling Lu and Suzhou Creek, Huangpu.*

Experiences

FIND ART DECO ON THE BUND

⑮ Bank of China. Here, old Shanghai's Western architecture (British art deco in this case) mixes with Chinese elements. In 1937 it was designed to be the highest building in the city and surpassed the neighboring Cathay Hotel (now the Peace Hotel) by a hair, except for the green tower on the Cathay's roof. ⊠ *23 The Bund, Zhongshan Dong Yi Lu, Huangpu* ☎ *021/6329–1979.*

⑰ Former Hong Kong and Shanghai Bank Building (HSBC). One of the Bund's most impressive buildings—some say it's the area's pièce de résistance—the domed structure was built by the British in 1921–23, when it was the second-largest bank building in the world. After 1949 the building

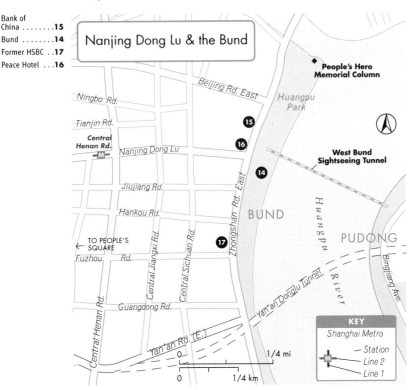

Nanjing Dong Lu & the Bund

was turned into Communist Party offices and City Hall; now it is used by the Pudong Development Bank. In 1997 the bank made the news when it uncovered a beautiful 1920s Italian-tile mosaic in the building's dome. In the 1950s the mosaic was deemed too extravagant for a Communist government office, so it was covered by white paint, which protected it from being found by the Red Guards during the Cultural Revolution. It was then forgotten until the Pudong Development Bank renovated the building. If you walk in and look up, you'll see the circular mosaic in the dome—an outer circle painted with scenes of the cities where the HSBC had branches at the time: London, Paris, New York, Bangkok, Tokyo, Calcutta, Hong Kong, and Shanghai; a middle circle made up of the 12 signs of the zodiac; and the center painted with a large sun and Ceres, the Roman goddess of abundance. ☒ *12 The Bund, Zhongshan Dong Yi Lu, Huangpu* ☏ *021/6161–6188* ☒ *Free* ☉ *Daily 9–6.*

★ ❶ **Peace Hotel** (Heping Fandian). This hotel at the corner of the Bund and Nanjing Lu is among Shanghai's most treasured old buildings. If any establishment will give you a sense of Shanghai's past, it's this one. Its high ceilings, ornate woodwork, and art-deco fixtures are still intact, and the ballroom evokes old Shanghai cabarets and gala parties.

The south building was formerly the Palace Hotel. Built in 1906, it is the oldest building on the Bund. The north building, formerly the Cathay Hotel, built in 1929, is more famous historically. It was known as the private playroom of its owner, Victor Sassoon, a wealthy landowner who invested in the opium trade. The Cathay was actually part of a complete office and hotel structure collectively called Sassoon House. Victor Sassoon himself lived and entertained his guests in the green penthouse. The hotel was rated on a par with the likes of Raffles in Singapore and the Peninsula in Hong Kong. It was *the* place to stay in old Shanghai; Noel Coward wrote *Private Lives* here. In the evenings, the famous Peace Hotel Old Jazz Band plays in the German-style pub on the 1st floor. ✉ *20 Nanjing Dong Lu, Huangpu* ☎ *021/ 6321–6888* ⊕ *www.shanghaipeacehotel.com.*

Former French Concession

With its tree-lined streets and crumbling old villas, the Former French Concession is possibly Shanghai's most atmospheric area. It's a wonderful place to go wandering and make serendipitous discoveries of stately architecture, groovy boutiques and galleries, or cozy cafés. Here, much of Shanghai's past beauty remains, although many of the old buildings are in desperate states of disrepair. One of the major roads through this area, Huaihai Lu, is a popular shopping location with shops selling international and local brands. It's also where many of Shanghai's restaurants, bars, and clubs are located, so if you are looking for an evening out, this is a good area to head for.

GETTING HERE Any of the four Line 1 metro stops (Huangpi Nan Lu, Shaanxi Nan Lu, Changshu Lu, or Hengshan Lu) will land you somewhere in the French Concession area. There are usually plenty of taxis except on rainy days or at peak hours.

Sights

⓱ **Fuxing Park.** The grounds of this European-style park—known as French Park before 1949—provide a bit of greenery in crowded Shanghai. Here you'll find people practicing tai chi and lovers strolling hand in hand. ✉ *105 Fuxing Zhong Lu, Luwan* ☎ *021/5386–1069* ✈ *Free* ⊙ *Daily 6 AM–6 PM.*

Experiences

SEE HOW THEY LIVED

㉒ **Soong Qingling's Former Residence.** Although she first came to national attention as the wife of Dr. Sun Yat-sen, Soong Ching-ling became revered in her own right for her dedication to the Communist Party. Indeed, many mainland Chinese regard her as the "Mother of China." (On the other hand, Soong's sister, Meiling, married Chiang Kai-shek, who was the head of the Nationalist government from 1927 to 1949, at which point the couple fled to Taiwan.) This three-story house, built in 1920 by a German ship owner, was Soong's primary residence from 1948 to 1963. It has been preserved as it was during her lifetime and includes her 4,000 books in the study and furniture in the bedroom that her parents gave as her dowry. The small museum next door has some nice dis-

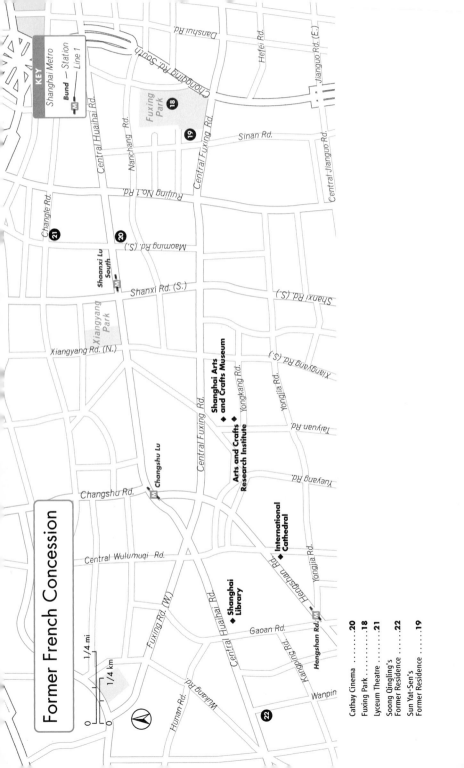

Former French Concession

KEY

Shanghai Metro
Bund — Station
— Line 1

Fuxing Park

Sinan Rd.

Danshu Rd.

Hefei Rd.

Jianguo Rd. (E.)

Central Huaihai Rd.

Nanchang Rd.

Ruijing No.1 Rd.

Central Fuxing Rd.

Changle Rd.

Maoming Rd. (S.)

Shaanxi Lu
South

Shanxi Rd. (S.)

Xiangyang
Park

Xiangyang Rd. (N.)

Shanxi Rd. (S.)

Xiangyang Rd. (S.)

Central Fuxing Rd.

Shanghai Arts
and Crafts Museum

Arts and Crafts
Research Institute

Yongkang Rd.

Yongjia Rd.

Taiyuan Rd.

Central Jianguo Rd.

Chongming Rd. South

Chandong Rd.

Changshu Lu

Changshu Rd.

International
Cathedral

Hengshan Rd.

Yongjia Rd.

Yueyang Rd.

Central Wulumuqi Rd.

Fuxing Rd. (W.)

Shanghai
Library

Central Huaihai Rd.

Gaoan Rd.

Kangping Rd.

Hengshan Rd.

Hunan Rd.

Wukang Rd.

Wanpin

1/4 mi

1/4 km

Cathay Cinema	**20**
Fuxing Park	**18**
Lyceum Theatre	**21**
Soong Qingling's Former Residence	**22**
Sun Yat-Sen's Former Residence	**19**

plays from Soong Qingling and Sun Yat-sen's life, including wedding pictures from their 1915 wedding in Tokyo. ☒ *1843 Huaihai Zhonglu, Xuhui* ☏ *021/6431–4965* ✉ *Y8* ☺ *Daily 9–4:30.*

⑲ Sun Yat-sen's Former Residence. Dr. Sun Yat-sen, the father of the Chinese republic, lived in this two-story house for six years, from 1919 to 1924. His wife, Soong Qingling, continued to live here after his death until 1937. Today it's been turned into a museum, and tours are conducted in Chinese and English. ☒ *7 Xiangshan Lu, Luwan* ☏ *021/6437–2954* ✉ *Y8* ☺ *Daily 9–4:30.*

SEEK OUT ART DECO

⑳ Cathay Cinema. Once part of millionaire Victor Sassoon's holdings, the art-deco Cathay Cinema was one of the first movie theaters in Shanghai. The building still serves as a theater, showing a mix of Chinese and Western films. ☒ *870 Huaihai Zhonglu, at Maoming Nan Lu, Luwan* ☏ *021/5404–1122.*

㉑ Lyceum Theatre. In the days of old Shanghai, the Lyceum was the home of the British Amateur Drama Club. The old stage got a face-lift in 2003 and is still in use as a concert hall. ☒ *57 Maoming Nan Lu, Luwan* ☏ *021/6217–8530.*

Nanjing Xi Lu & Jing'an

Shanghai's glitziest malls and some five-star hotels are along the main street in this area, Nanjing Xi Lu. So, if you're into designer threads, luxury spas, or expensive brunches, you can satisfy your spending urges and max out your credit here. For those of a more spiritual bent, Jingan Temple, although still being reconstructed, is one of Shanghai's largest temples. The small Jingan Park across the street is popular with couples. Behind the temple is an interesting network of back streets.

GETTING HERE Metro Line 2 takes you to Jingan Si station. If you want to take a taxi afterward, joining the queue at the Shanghai Centre/Portman Ritz-Carlton is a good idea, especially when it's raining.

Sights

㉔ Jingan Temple. Originally built about AD 300, the Jingan Temple has been rebuilt and renovated numerous times. The sound of power tools often drowns out the monks' chanting. The temple's Southern-style halls, which face a central courtyard, gleam with new wood carvings of elephants and lotus flowers, but the hall interiors have stark, new concrete walls, and feel generally antiseptic. The temple's main draw is its copper Hongwu bell, cast in 1183 and weighing in at 3.5 tons. ☒ *1686 Nanjing Xi Lu, next to the Jingan Si subway entrance, Jingan* ☏ *021/6256–6366* ✉ *Y10* ☺ *Daily 7:30–5.*

㉕ Paramount. Built in 1933, socialites referred to the Paramount as the finest dance hall in Asia. Now, at night, the domed roof of this art-deco dance hall glow blue and inside people dance the afternoon and the night away. ☒ *218 Yuyuan Lu, Jingan* ☏ *021/6249–8866* ✉ *Varies depending on the dance session time* ☺ *Daily.*

BEST CITY TOURS

Getting around Shanghai independently is the best way to see the city, and an increasing number of travelers are doing just that. Organized tours are often rushed and on-again and off-again in style, which is a shame as Shanghai really is a great city to walk around. English is increasingly spoken especially in tourist-frequented areas and restaurants. If you get lost, there's often a friendly local nearby to help you out. All the same, here are some day-tour options that might help you get your bearings on that stressful first afternoon.

BOAT TOURS

A boat tour on the Huangpu River affords a great view of the Pudong skyline and the Bund, but after that it's mostly ports and cranes.

Huangpu River Cruises launches several small boats for one-hour daytime cruises as well as its unmistakable dragon boat for two-night cruises. The company also runs a 3½-hour trip up and down the Huangpu River between the Bund and Wusong, the point where the Huangpu meets the Yangzi River. You'll see barges, bridges, and factories, but not much scenery. All tours depart from the Bund at 239 Zhongshan Dong Lu. You can purchase all tickets at the

dock or through **CITS** (⇨ see Visitor Information, below); prices range from Y35 to Y90. ✉ 239 Zhongshan Dong Er Lu (the Bund), Huangpu District ☎ 021/6374-4461.

Shanghai Oriental Leisure Company runs 40-minute boat tours along the Bund from the Pearl Tower's cruise dock in Pudong. Daytime cruises cost Y40, nighttime Y50. Follow the brown signs from the Pearl Tower to the dock. ✉ Oriental Pearl Cruise Dock, 1 Shiji Dadao, Pudong ☎ 021/5879-1888 Ext. 80435.

BUS TOURS

The Shanghai Sightseeing Bus Center has more than 50 routes, including 10 tour routes that make a circuit of Shanghai's main tourist attractions. There are also one-stop itineraries and weekend overnight trips to sights in Zhejiang and Jiangsu provinces. One-day trips range from Y30 to Y200; overnight trips cost as much as Y400. You can buy tickets up to a week in advance. The main ticket office and station, beneath Staircase No. 5 at Shanghai Stadium, has plenty of English signage to help you through the ticketing process. ✉ No. 5 Staircase, Gate 12, Shanghai Stadium, 666 Tianyaoqiao Lu, Xuhui District ☎ 021/6426-5555.

㉓ Shanghai Exhibition Center. This mammoth piece of Russian architecture was built as a sign of Sino-Soviet friendship after 1949. Today, it hosts conventions and special touring exhibitions. The complex has a restaurant that caters largely to tour groups. ✉ *1000 Yanan Zhonglu, Jingan* ☎ *021/6279-0279* ☉ *Daily 9–4.*

Experiences

GET YOUR HANDS DIRTY

Enjoy Mandarin offers a range of cultural encounters ranging from language to seal cutting, so you can even make your own souvenirs. Pri-

Nanjing Xi Lu & Jing'an

vate classes cost Y120 per hour and classes lasting a few hours can be booked a day in advance. ⊠ *Room 411, Qing Gong Building, 1576 Nan Jing Xi Rd., Jing'an* ☎ *021/6258–6885* ⊕ *www.enjoymandarin.com.*

Pudong

Shanghai residents used to say that it was better to have a bed in Puxi than an apartment in Pudong, but the neighborhood has come a long way in recent years from a rural area to one that represents a futuristic city of wide boulevards and towering skyscrapers topped (although soon to be out-floored) by the pagodalike elegance of the Jinmao Tower. Apartments here are some of the most expensive in Shanghai. Although a little on the bland side, it is home to expat compounds designed in a medley of bizarre architectural styles, international schools, and malls. However, there are quite a few sites here worth visiting, particularly if you have children.

GETTING HERE The Bund Tourist Tunnel is a strange and rather garish way of making the journey under the Huangpu River to Pudong. You might get a few laughs from the light displays. Otherwise you can take the metro on Line 2 to Lujiazui, or catch the ferry from the Bund.

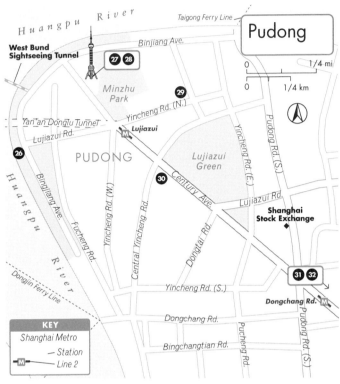

Experiences

CHECK OUT CHINA'S FUTURE

★ **30** **Jinmao Tower** (Jinmao Dasha). This gorgeous 88-floor (8 being the Chinese number implying wealth and prosperity) industrial art-deco pagoda is among the five tallest buildings in the world and the tallest in China—at least for the time being, as a massive skyscraper being built next door will soon eclipse it. In it is also the highest hotel in the world—the Grand Hyatt Shanghai takes up the 53rd to 87th floors. The 88th-floor observation deck, reached in 45 seconds by two high-speed elevators, offers a 360-degree view of the city. The Jinmao combines the classic 13-tier Buddhist pagoda design with postmodern steel and glass. Check out the Hyatt's dramatic 33-story atrium or the Cloud Nine bar on the 87th floor. ✉ *88 Shiji Dadao, Pudong* ☎ *021/5047–0088* 🎫 *Observation deck Y50* 🕐 *Daily 8:30 AM–9 PM.*

★ **27** **Oriental Pearl Tower.** The tallest tower in Asia (1,535 feet or 468 meters) has become the pride and joy of the city, a symbol of the brashness and glitz of today's Shanghai. This UFO-like structure is especially kitschy at night, when it flashes with colored lights against the classic beauty of the Bund. Its three spheres are supposed to represent pearls (as in "Shanghai, Pearl of the Orient"). An elevator takes you to observation decks in the tower's three spheres. Go to the top sphere for a 360-degree bird's-eye view of the city or grab a bite in the Tower's revolving restaurant. On the bottom floor is the Shanghai History Museum. ⇨ *see* below ⊠ *1 Shiji Dadao, Pudong* ☎ *021/5879–1888* ✉ *Y135, all three spheres plus museum; Y70 and Y85 for the lower spheres* ☉ *Daily 8* AM*–9:30* PM.

USE YOUR LEGS

㉜ Century Park. This giant swathe of green in Pudong is a great place to take children as it has a variety of vehicles for hire, good flat paths for rollerblading, and pleasure boats. On a fine day, pack a picnic as there are also designated picnic areas as well as woods and grass to play on. ⊠ *1001 Jinxiu Lu, Pudong* ☎ *021/3876–0588* ✉ *Y10.* ☉ *Daily 7* AM*–6* PM.

㉖ Riverside Promenade. Although the park that runs 2,750 yards (2514 meters) along the Huangpu River is sugary-sterile in its experimental suburbia, it still offers the most beautiful views of the Bund. You can stroll on the grass and concrete and view a perspective of Puxi unavailable from the west side. If you're here in the summer, you can ENJOY WADING, as a sign indicates, in the chocolate-color Huangpu River from the park's wave platform. ⊠ *Bingjiang Dadao, Pudong* ✉ *Free.*

FOR THE KIDS

★ **㉘ Shanghai History Museum.** This impressive museum in the base of the Pearl Tower recalls Shanghai's pre-1949 history. Inside you can stroll down a re-created Shanghai street circa 1900 or check out a streetcar that used to operate in the concessions. Dioramas depict battle scenes from the Opium Wars, shops found in a typical turn-of-the-20th-century Shanghai neighborhood, and grand Former French Concession buildings of yesteryear. ⊠ *1 Shiji Dadao, Pudong* ☎ *021/5879–1888* ✉ *Y35* ☉ *Daily 8* AM*–9:30* PM.

㉙ Shanghai Ocean Aquarium. As you stroll through the aquarium's 12,000-foot-long, (3658 meters) clear, sightseeing tunnel, you may feel like you're walking your way through the seven seas—or at least five of them. The aquarium's 10,000 fish span 300 species, 5 oceans, and 4 continents. You'll also find penguins and species representing all 12 of the Chinese zodiac animals, such as the tiger barb, sea dragon, and seahorse. ⊠ *158 Yincheng Bei Lu, Pudong* ☎ *021/5877–9988* ⊕ *www.aquarium. sh.cn* ✉ *Y110 adults, Y70 children* ☉ *Daily 9* AM*–9* PM*; last tickets sold at 8:30.*

㉛ Shanghai Science and Technology Museum. This museum, a favorite attraction for kids in Shanghai, has more than 100 hands-on exhibits in its 6 main galleries. Earth Exploration takes you through fossil layers to the earth's core for a lesson in plate tectonics. Spectrum of Life introduces you to the animal and plant kingdoms within its simulated rain forest. Light of Wisdom explains basic principles of light and sound through interactive exhibits, and simulators in AV Paradise put you in a plane cockpit and on television. Children's Technoland has a voice-activated fountain and miniature construction site. In Cradle of Designers, you can record a CD or assemble a souvenir. Two IMAX theaters and an IWERKS 4D theater show larger-than-life movies, but mostly in Chinese. All signs are in English; the best times to visit are weekday afternoons. ⊠ *1388 Lujiazui Huan Lu, Pudong* ☎ *021/6854–2000* 🖅 *Y60; there are separate prices for the IMAX and IWERKS* ⊙ *Tues.–Sun. 9 AM–4:30 PM.*

North Shanghai

Although often neglected in favor of their more glamorous neighboring areas, the northern Shanghai districts of Putuo, Hongkou, and Zhabei still offer some interesting sights. Hongkou District, particularly, is still relatively undeveloped and unchanged, and buildings from the past are still visible behind cheap clothing stores. An area with an interesting history, it has the most sights worth seeing as well as the lush green sweep of Lu Xun Park. The old buildings and warehouses around Suzhou Creek, which feeds into the Huangpu, are slowly being turned into a hip and happening arty area, particularly the M50 development. Also in Putuo District is another one of Shanghai's main temples, the Jade Buddha Temple.

GETTING HERE For the Jade Buddha Temple and M50, you can hop off the metro Line 1 at Shanghai Railway Station, but you still have to get across Suzhou Creek. You can take the Pearl Line to East Baoxing Lu and Hongkou Stadium for Lu Xun Park and Duolun Lu. The best way to get around these areas is by taxi.

Sights

❸❸ **Duolun Lu.** Designated Shanghai's "Cultural Street," Duolun Road takes you back in time to the 1930s, when the 1-km- (½-mi-) long lane was a favorite haunt of writer Lu Xun and fellow social activists. Bronze statues of those literary luminaries dot the lawns between the well-preserved villas and row houses, whose 1st floors are now home to antiques shops, cafés, and art galleries. As the street takes a 90-degree turn, its architecture shifts 180 degrees with the seven-story stark gray **Shanghai Doland Museum of Art.** ⊠ *Off Sichuan Bei Lu, Hongkou.*

★ ❸❻ **Jade Buddha Temple.** Completed in 1918, this temple is fairly new by Chinese standards. During the Cultural Revolution, in order to save the temple when the Red Guards came to destroy it, the monks pasted portraits of Mao Zedong on the outside walls so the Guards couldn't tear them down without destroying Mao's face as well. The temple is built in the style of the Song Dynasty, with symmetrical halls and courtyards, upturned eaves, and bright yellow walls. The temple's great treasure is its 6½-foot-high, (2 meter)-pound seated Buddha made of white jade with a robe of precious gems, originally brought to Shanghai from Burma. Other Buddhas, statues, and frightening guardian gods of the temple populate the halls, as well as a collection of Buddhist scriptures and paintings. The 100 monks who live and work here can sometimes be seen worshipping. It's madness at festival times. ⊠ *170 Anyuan Lu, Putuo* ☎ *021/6266–3668* 🖅 *Y10 plus an extra Y10 for the Jade Buddha* ⊙ *Daily 8–4:30.*

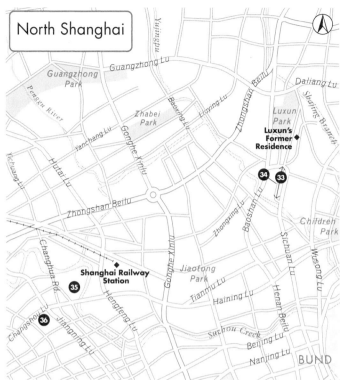

North Shanghai

3

Experiences

MODERN ART FIX

35 **M50** is a cluster of art galleries and artists studios by Suzhou Creek. This is home to some of Shanghai's hottest galleries and where you will see works from China's best artists as well as new and not so well-known ones. There are also a couple of shops selling music and art supplies and a branch of Shirtflag. Don't be shy about nosing around—there are galleries in many floors of these old factories and warehouses and sometimes artists will be around for a chat. ✉ *50 Moganshan Lu, Putuo* 🔄 *Free* ☉ *Daily, although most galleries are closed on Mon. Opening times vary depending on the gallery.*

34 **Shanghai Doland Museum of Modern Art.** Opened in December 2003, this is Shanghai's first official venue for modern art. The six-story museum's 14,400 square feet of exhibition space include a tiny shop selling art books and a metal spiral staircase that's a work of art in itself. The exhibitions, which change frequently, are cutting edge for Shanghai. They've showcased electronic art from American artists, examined gender issues among Chinese, and featured musical performances ranging from Chinese electronica to the *dombra,* a traditional Kazak stringed instrument.

TEE OFF

With its own international tournament—the Volvo China Open—and several courses designed by prestigious names, Shanghai is making its mark on the golf scene. Approximately 20 clubs dot the countryside within a two-hour arc of downtown. All clubs and driving ranges run on a membership basis, but most allow nonmembers to play when accompanied by a member. A few even welcome the public. Most clubs are outside the city, in the suburbs and outlying counties of Shanghai.

Shanghai International Golf and Country Club. This 18-hole course designed by Robert Trent Jones Jr. is the most difficult course to get into in Shanghai. There are water hazards at almost every hole. ⊠ 961 Yin Zhu Lu, Zhu Jia Jiao, Qingpu District ☎ 021/5972-8111.

Shanghai Silport Golf Club. This club hosts the Volvo China Open. Its 27-hole course on Dianshan Lake was designed by Bobby J. Martin; a new 9 holes designed by Roger Packard opened in 2004. ⊠ 1 Xubao Lu, Dianshan Lake Town, Kunshan City, Jiangsu Province ☎ 0512/5748-1111.

Tianma Country Club. Tianma is the most accessible course to the public. Its 18 holes have lovely views of Sheshan Mountain. ⊠ 3958 Zhaokun Lu, Tianma Town, Songjiang District ☎ 021/5766-1666.

Tomson Shanghai Pudong Golf Club. The closest course to the city center, Tomson has 18 holes and a driving range designed by Shunsuke Kato. Robert Trent Jones Jr. has inked a deal to develop the club's second course. ⊠ 1 Longdong Dadao, Pudong ☎ 021/5833-8888.

⊠ *27 Duolun Lu, Hongkou* ☎ *021/6587–2530* ⊕ *www.duolunart. com* ☷ *Varies according to the exhibition* ☉ *Daily 10–5:30.*

Xujiahui, Hongqiao & Gubei

Buyers throng into the large malls in the shopping precinct at Xujiahui, which shines with neon and giant billboard advertisements. Farther down the road are the districts of Hongqiao and Gubei where wealthy expats live in high-walled compounds and drive huge SUVs. You're likely to find a larger concentration of Western-style restaurants and supermarkets here if you are feeling homesick.

GETTING HERE Metro Line 1 takes you right into the depths of the Grand Gateway Mall at Xujiahui. For the other sights, they are fairly far-flung, so it might be a good idea to jump into a taxi. If you are going to places like the Shanghai Botanical Gardens from the center of town, be prepared for a large taxi bill. Otherwise, you can get off at Shanghai South Railway Station.

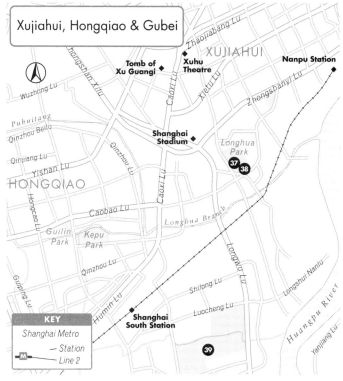

Xujiahui, Hongqiao & Gubei

KEY

Shanghai Metro

— *Station*

-Ⓜ- *Line 2*

Sights

㊲ Longhua Martyrs Cemetery may seem a tranquil place now, but it is a site that has had a bloody history. It was used as an execution ground from the 19th century and was the site of the executions of many Communists, particularly during the Guomingdang crackdown in 1927. Nowadays, the site is full of large Soviet-style sculpture and immaculate lawns. The most chilling is the small unkempt grassy execution area accessed by a tunnel where the remains of murdered Communists were found with leg irons still on in the 1950s. ⊠ *180 Longhua Lu, Xuhui* ☎ *021/ 6468–5995* 🚇 *Y1 with an extra Y4 to enter the museum* ☉ *Daily 6–5, Museum 9–4.*

★ **㊳ Longhua Temple** (Longhua Si). Shanghai's largest and most active temple has as its centerpiece a seven-story, eight-sided pagoda. While the temple is thought to have been built in the 3rd century, the pagoda dates from the 10th century; it's not open to visitors. Near the front entrance of the temple stands a three-story bell tower, where a 3.3-ton bronze bell is rung at midnight every New Year's Eve. Along the side corridors of the temple you'll find the Longhua Hotel, a vegetarian restaurant, and a room filled seven rows deep with small golden statues. The third hall is the most impressive. Its three giant Buddhas sit beneath a swirled red and gold dome. ⊠ *2853 Longhua Lu, Xuhui* ☎ *021/6456–6085 or 021/6457–6327* 💷 *Y10 with free incense and an extra Y50 to strike the bell* ☉ *Daily 7–4:30.*

㊴ Shanghai Botanical Garden. Spread over 200 acres, the Shanghai Botanical Garden has separate areas for peonies and roses, azaleas and osmanthus, bamboo and orchids, and medicinal plants. Its Penjing Garden is among the world's best. *Penjing* translates as "pot scenery," and describes the Chinese art of creating a miniature landscape in a container. More than 2,000 bonsai trees line the Penjing Garden's courtyards and corridors, whose cut-out windows perfectly frame these miniature masterpieces. The world-class Chinese Cymbidium Garden has more than 300 varieties. Within the glass canopy of the Grand Conservatory are towering palms and more than 3,500 varieties of tropical plants. Opened in 1978, the garden's buildings are showing their age, but the natural beauty of the gardens blooms anew each year. Admission to the garden is free on the 10th of each month. ⊠ *1111 Longwu Lu, Xuhui* ☎ *021/5436–3369* 💷 *Y15 for entrance through main gate only* ☉ *Daily 7–5.*

WHERE TO EAT

By David
Taylor

When eating out, you'll notice most Chinese restaurants in Shanghai have large, round tables. The reason will become clear the first time you eat a late dinner at a local restaurant and are surrounded by jovial, laughing groups of people toasting and topping off from communal bottles of beer, sharing cigarettes, and spinning the lazy Susan loaded with food.

Dining out with friends and family isn't just a favorite social activity; it's a ritual. Whether feting guests or demonstrating their growing wealth, hosts will order massive, showy spreads. Although take-away boxes for leftovers are starting to become popular, proud hosts wouldn't deign to use them. Shanghai's standing as China's most international city is reflected in its dining scene. You can enjoy *jiaozi* (dumplings) for breakfast, foie gras for lunch, and Kobe beef teppanyaki for dinner.

It's traditional to order several dishes, plus rice, to share among your party. Tipping is not expected, but sophistication comes at a price. Although you can easily eat as the locals do at Chinese restaurants for less than Y40, even simple Western meals will cost you a more Western price.

Most restaurants in Shanghai offer set lunches—multicourse feasts—at a fraction of the usual price. It's the best dining deal going, allowing you to eat at local Chinese restaurants for Y25 or less and at such places at M on the Bund without completely blowing your budget. Also, check out the "Restaurant Events" section of *That's Shanghai,* or *SH Magazine,* which list dining discounts and promotions around town.

Meal Times

Dining in Shanghai can be a protracted affair. Dinner hours in restaurants begin at around 5 PM, but often carry on late into the night. Many of the classic, local restaurants popular with the Shanghainese only close after the last diners have left, which sometimes keeps them open until the wee hours of the morning. Generally, though, dinner is eaten between 6 and 11 PM, with fine dining generally happening later than casual meals.

Prices

From an American or European point of view, fine dining in Shanghai can be very economical. Even in the fanciest restaurants, main courses are unlikely to cost more than US$35. However, in Shanghai, like everywhere else, fame is on par with price. The famous restaurants charge as much as the international market will bear—prices that often don't reflect the quality of the dining experience.

For the adventuresome, great local food can be found everywhere for laughably cheap prices, even in fairly nice restaurants. The food is good and inexpensive ($1 to $5 per dish), and the experience of eating at a small, unknown restaurant is pure China. We recommend you try it at least once.

WHAT IT COSTS In Yuan				
$$$$	**$$$**	**$$**	**$**	**¢**
AT DINNER	over Y300	Y151–Y300	Y81–Y150	Y40–Y80	under Y40

Prices are for a main course at dinner.

Old City

Mediterranean

¢–$ ✕ **Mediterranean Café.** Buried in the east end of town, the Med is a hidden gem. Small and unpretentious, it is one of the few places in town serving authentic Mediterranean food. With highlights of genuine bagels (one of the only places to find them in town), kosher-deli foods, feta and falafels, this is a perfect lunch destination. We recommend the pita falafel—hot, green, and crunchy, served with an Israeli salad—and the latkes, which are perfectly fried potato pancakes served with sour cream. ⊠ *415 Dagu Lu Rd., Huangpu* ☎ *021/6327–0897 or 021/6295–9511* ⊟ *No credit cards.*

Shanghainese

$–$$$ ✕ **Lu Bo Lang.** A popular stop for visiting dignitaries, Lu Bo Lang is a perfect photo op of a restaurant. The traditional three-story Chinese pavilion with upturned eaves sits next to the Bridge of Nine Turnings in the Yu Garden complex. The food is good but not great, with many expensive fish choices on the menu. Among the best dishes are the crabmeat with bean curd, the braised eggplant with chili sauce, and the sweet *osmanthus* cake, made with the sweetly fragrant flower of the same name. ⊠ *115 Yuyuan Lu, Huangpu* ☎ *021/6328–0602* ✍ *Reservations essential* ⊟ *AE, DC, MC, V.*

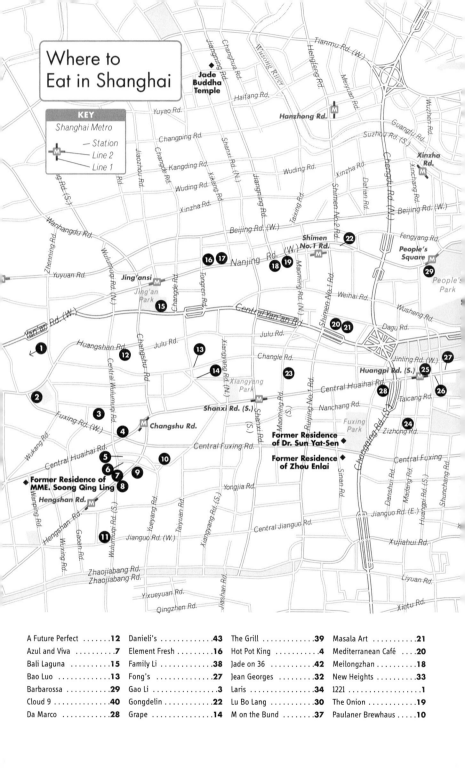

Where to Eat in Shanghai

KEY

Shanghai Metro

— Station
Line 2
Line 1

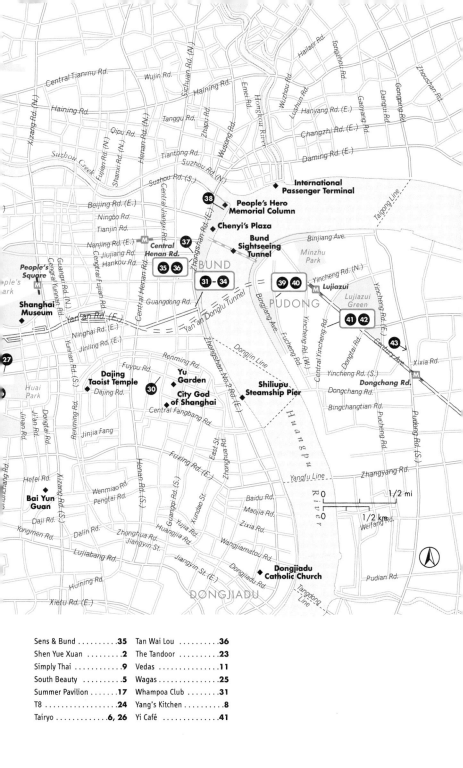

Xintiandi & City Center

Café

¢–$ ✕ **Wagas.** Serving sandwiches, salads, and coffees, Wagas is a popular lunch stop. The food is decent, and the service adequate, but there is little distinctive about this easily accessible chain café. It's popular with locals for its reasonable prices, English menus, and speedy service and is good for a quick refill when shopping. ⊠ *Hong Kong New World Plaza, 300 Huaihai Zhong Lu, Luwan* ☎ *021/6335–3739* ▭ *No credit cards.*

Contemporary

$$–$$$ ✕ **T8.** A favorite haunt for celebrities, T8 has garnered its share of head-
Fodor's Choice lines for its stunning interior and inspired contemporary cuisine. The
★ restaurant occupies a traditional shikumen house within Xintiandi and has modernized the space with raw stone floors, carved-wood screens, and imaginative lighting that transforms shelves full of glasses into a modern-art sculpture. The show kitchen turns out such Thai- and Chinese-inspired dishes as a slow-cooked, Sichuan-flavored lamb pie, and nori-wrapped sashimi-grade tuna. Like the clientele, the wine list is exclusive, with many labels unavailable elsewhere in Shanghai. ⊠ *House 8, North Block, Xintiandi, 181 Taicang Lu, Luwan* ☎ *021/6355–8999* ⌕ *Reservations essential* ▭ *AE, DC, MC, V* ⊘ *No lunch Tues.*

Japanese

$–$$ ✕ **Tairyo.** Teppanyaki has invaded Shanghai. More down to earth than a sophisticated sushi bar, teppanyaki (Japanese barbecue) is a gastronomic experience serving sushi, sashimi, barbecued meats, and a wide variety of Western and Eastern dishes. It does have à la carte, but at Y150 for all you can eat and drink, Tairyo's main attraction is obvious. Just walk in, take a seat at the grill, and indulge while the chef prepares your dinner as you watch. We recommend the Mongolian King Steak, but the menu has English and pictures, so pick and choose. This is a perfect, no-effort dinner destination. Private rooms are available for groups larger than seven (reservations essential). ⊠ *Hong Kong New World Plaza, South Building, 283 Huaihai Rd., 3rd fl., Luwan* ☎ *021/6390–7244* ▭ *AE, DC, MC, V.*

Middle Eastern

$–$$ ✕ **Barbarossa.** Modern Middle Eastern food in a setting taken from the *Arabian Nights,* Barbarossa is rapidly becoming a destination of choice. The decoration is amazing, albeit possibly flammable, with billowing draperies swathing the space, and the food is good and reasonably priced. At around 10 PM, Barbarossa becomes a club, so don't aim for a late dinner unless you like mingling with the party people. ⊠ *People's Square, 231 Nanjing Xi Rd., next to the Shanghai Art Museum, Luwan* ☎ *021/6318–0220* ▭ *AE, DC, MC, V.*

Vietnamese

$–$$ ✕ **Fong's.** Don't be deterred by Fong's location in an office plaza. Inside, chirping birds, gauze curtains, bamboo furniture, and hostesses wearing *ao dai* (a long Vietnamese dress with side slits worn over pants) set a romanticized scene for Fong's excellent French-style Vietnamese cuisine. The English menu (with photos) focuses on traditional dishes like spring rolls and a wonderfully smoky fried vermicelli with seafood, but it also includes bouillabaisse and other French specialties. Service is adequate but may seem distant in this busy and justifiably popular restaurant. ⊠ *Lippo Plaza, 222 Huaihai Zhonglu, 2nd fl., Luwan* ☎ *021/6387–7228* ▭ *AE, DC, MC, V.*

Nanjing Dong Lu & the Bund

American

★ **$–$$$** ✕ **New Heights.** Perched atop prestigious Three on the Bund, New Heights is a surprisingly unpretentious restaurant. With a gorgeous terrace overlooking the river and a solid menu of generally North American standard fare, this is an excellent destination for the weary Bund tourist. We recommend it for a late lunch basking in the afternoon sun on the terrace. Try the hamburger with a cold beer. ⊠ *Three on the Bund, 7th fl., 3 Zhong Shan Dong Yi Rd., Huangpu* ☎ *021/6321–0909* ▭ *AE, DC, MC, V.*

Cantonese

$$$$ ✕ **Family Li Imperial Cuisine.** This spectacular restaurant, a newer branch of the famous Beijing Imperial restaurant, deserves a visit despite high prices (set menus begin at Y1,000). Using family recipes smuggled from the Forbidden City a century ago, Family Li gives the closest thing to a taste of imperial food. There are only nine rooms, and only set menus are served. Reservations more than 24 hours in advance are a must. ⊠ *Huangpu Park, 500 East Zhongshan Yi Rd., Huangpu* ☎ *021/5308–1919* ⌕ *Reservations essential* ▭ *AE, DC, MC, V.*

$$–$$$$ ✕ **Whampoa Club.** A new addition to the Bund scene, Whampoa Club is nouveau Chinese at its best. With a focus on fresh seafood and interesting interpretations of Shanghai classics, this is a destination worth checking out. As befits a celebrity venue, prices are steep, but generally worth the expense. ⊠ *Three on the Bund, 4th fl., 3 Zhongshan Dong Yi Lu, Huangpu* ☎ *021/6323–3355* ⌕ *Reservations essential* ▭ *AE, DC, MC, V.*

$$–$$$$ ✕ **Tan Wai Lou.** Bund 18's signature Chinese restaurant, Tan Wai Lou serves up nouveau-Cantonese cuisine in a refined setting. The food is good and well presented, though the non-Chinese service (dishes are presented in courses and not shared) can be a little jarring for a diner expecting a classic Chinese meal. Still, the seafood is very fresh and the view of the Huangpu spectacular. ⊠ *Bund18, 5th fl., 18 Zhongshan Dong Yi Rd., Huangpu* ☎ *021/6339–1188* ⌕ *Reservations essential* ▭ *AE, DC, MC, V.*

Contemporary

$$–$$$$ ✕ **Laris.** The signature restaurant of star Australian chef David Laris, this is one of the few Bund restaurants with the owner/chef in residence. The innovative continental-inspired cuisine is good and well presented, though service can often be problematic and sloppy, with complaints about the haughty staff being all too common. In our opinion, Laris survives more on hype than on substance. ⊠ *Three on the Bund, 6th fl., 3 Zhongshan Dong Yi Lu, Huangpu* ☎ *021/6321–9922* ⌕ *Reservations essential* ▭ *AE, DC, MC, V.*

THE SCENE

OLD CITY

The Old City can be a good location to find some traditional-style food in an authentic environment. We recommend that the adventurous go out into the side streets around Fangbang Lu in search of authentic Chinese snacks. When dining in small local restaurants, always ask the price first—with no English menu, many sellers in this area aren't above raising the price.

XINTIANDI & CITY CENTER

Xintiandi and the City Center contain some of the finest restaurants of the city, for any type of cuisine. Xintiandi's beautifully restored traditional shikumen (stone gatehouse) dwellings house world-class restaurants like T8, and in the area surrounding People's Square are popular spots such as the JW Marriott's restaurants and the trendy Middle Eastern food of Barbarossa.

NANJING DONG LU & THE BUND

The stellar view of the river and Pudong has attracted some of the finest restaurant development in town, including the showcase restaurants at Bund 18, Sens & Bund, and Three on the Bund. However, many visitors complain that the Bund restaurants are more style than substance, and rely too heavily on their fame and location. We find that although service and quality can occasionally lapse, it's well worth your effort to experience what this area has to offer.

FORMER FRENCH CONCESSION

Brimming with fine-dining options, the Old French Concession is the place to go for diverse dining, from traditional French to local Shanghainese. With its maze of tree-lined streets and small bistros, the Concession is an excellent area to explore the cuisine and the city.

PUDONG

The skyscraper-rich financial district is home to a surprising number of high-class eateries. The many five-star hotels boast some of Shanghai's most popular restaurants, including the Shangri-la's Yi Café and the Hyatt's towering Cloud 9.

NANJING XI LU & JING'AN

A business hub that is home to some of the finest hotels in the city, the Jing'an area is understandably heavy on Western-dining options. Familiar American franchises rub shoulders with Buddhist restaurants and popular expat destinations like Element Fresh, making this a vibrant dining destination.

NORTH SHANGHAI

Often neglected, North Shanghai is a historic neighborhood, with several fine options for eating. This is not a place to go in search of Western dining, but it has a selection of good Chinese restaurants.

HONGQIAO & GUBEI

The neighborhoods of Hongqiao, with its conference centers and hotels, and Gubei, with its high-end residential properties, have a few great options. The most noteworthy is Giovanni's in the Sheraton, a solidly traditional Italian bistro that is often overlooked.

$$–$$$$ ✕ **M on the Bund.** The original international restaurant on the Bund, M has long had a reputation of being a place to see and be seen. However, it's been fading somewhat of late, in the face of the new competitors nearby. Still, the brunch is a landmark affair, business lunches are good, and the food can occasionally reach dizzying heights. ✉ *20 Guangdong Lu, 7th fl., Huangpu* ☎ *021/6350–9988* ⌕ *Reservations essential* ⊟ *AE, DC, MC, V* ⊘ *No lunch Mon.*

French

$$–$$$$ ✕ **Jean Georges.** One of the fine-dining warhorses of the Bund, Jean Georges is the Shanghai project of celebrity Chef Jean Georges Vongerichten. The dark and intimate dining room in the historic Three on the Bund brings the right note of class to the experience, though the service can occasionally be lacking. The contemporary French cuisine is generally well executed, although very expensive. This is a showcase restaurant and at its best, Jean Georges is on the top of the scene; however, it's too often that it falls just a little short of perfection. ✉ *Three on the Bund, 4th fl., 3 Zhong Shan Dong Yi Rd., Huangpu* ☎ *021/ 6321–7733* ⊟ *AE, DC, MC, V.*

$$–$$$$ ✕ **Sens & Bund.** The Shanghai branch of the France-based Jardin du Sens Group, Sens & Bund serves contemporary Mediterranean cuisine that is a study in elegant contrasts. The food is good, the service well-trained, and the ambiance relaxing. The prices are quite high, but the overall quality and consistency makes this a better choice than many of its neighbors. ✉ *Bund 18, 1 Zhongshan Dong Yi Rd., 6th fl., Huangpu* ☎ *021/ 6323–9898* ⊟ *AE, DC, MC, V.*

Former French Concession

Cantonese

¢ ✕ **Shen Yue Xuan.** Dim sum is the big draw at Shen Yue Xuan. It's the featured fare at breakfast and lunch and has its own separate menu. The restaurant's Cantonese–Shanghainese dinner menu has a healthy slant, though the amount of grease often counteracts these efforts. The two-story restaurant is nestled in Dingxiang Garden, a verdant 35-acre playground the late Qing Dynasty–mandarin Li Hongzhang gave to his concubine Ding Xiang. There's outdoor seating on a large terrace, and the 2nd floor overlooks the garden. Book early if you want a table by the window. ✉ *849 Huashan Lu, Xuhui* ☎ *021/6251–1166* ⌕ *Reservations essential* ⊟ *AE, DC, MC, V.*

★ ¢–$ ✕ **Grape.** Entry-level Chinese food at inexpensive prices has been the Grape's calling card since the mid-1980s. This cheerful two-story restaurant remains a favorite among expatriates and travelers wandering the Former French Concession. The English menu, with photos, includes such recognizable fare as sweet-and-sour pork and lemon chicken as well as delicious dishes like garlic shrimp and *jiachang doufu* (home-style bean curd), all of which are served with a smile. ✉ *55 Xinle Lu, Luwan* ☎ *021/ 5404–0486* ⊟ *No credit cards.*

¢–$ ✕ **Hot Pot King.** *Huo guo*, or hotpot, is a popular Chinese ritual of at-the-table cooking, in which you simmer fresh ingredients in a broth. Hot Pot King reigns over the hotpot scene in Shanghai because of its extensive menu as well as its refined setting. The most popular of the 17 broths is the yin-yang, half spicy red, half basic white pork-bone broth. Add in a mixture of veggies, seafood, meat, and dumplings for a well-rounded pot, then dip each morsel in the sauces mixed tableside by your waiter. The minimalist white and gray interior has glass-enclosed booths and well-spaced tables, a nice change from the usual crowded, noisy, hotpot joints. ⊠ *1416 Huaihai Rd., 2nd fl., Xuhui* ☎ *021/6473–6380* ⊟ *AE, DC, MC, V.*

Contemporary

★ **$–$$** ✕ **Azul and Viva.** In creating his continent-hopping New World cuisine, owner Eduardo Vargas drew upon his globe-trotting childhood and seven years as a restaurant consultant in Asia. As a result, the menus in Azul, the tapas bar downstairs, and Viva, the restaurant upstairs, feature a delicious, delicate balance of flavors that should please any palate. Classics like beef carpaccio contrast cutting-edge dishes like coffee-glazed pork. Lunch and weekend brunch specials are lower priced. The relaxed, romantic interior—dim lighting, plush pillows, and splashes of color against muted backdrops—invites you to take your time on your culinary world tour. ⊠ *18 Dongping Lu, Xuhui* ☎ *021/6433–1172* ⊟ *AE, DC, MC, V.*

> **WORD OF MOUTH**
>
> "Azul was one of the highlights of the trip: funky dj-in', great tapas (especially the calamari and as Paddies we really appreciated the magnificent mashed spuds!), cool cocktails, and laid back vibe."
> –Jenny, Ireland

$–$$ ✕ **A Future Perfect.** Hidden away down a little lane off Huashan Road, Fodor'sChoice AFP has the kind of terrace space that most Shanghai-restaurant own-★ ers can only dream of: spacious, tranquil, yet intimate. It is a must for those hot afternoons and evenings in Shanghai when you need a break from shopping and sightseeing, and deserve some good food and good drinks. We recommend being adventurous; try the caviar blinis and Tunaba-lulla (a large portion of excellently prepared tuna) if you like seafood, or the 300 T (300 grams of tenderloin) for a carnivorous treat. The menu is fresh and there is plenty to satisfy any tastes. AFP has an on-site bakery, and serves breakfast every morning. ⊠ *16, La. 351 Huashan Lu, Xuhui* ☎ *021/6248–8020* ⊟ *AE, DC, MC, V.*

German

$$–$$$$ ✕ **Paulaner Brauhaus.** There's a shortage of good German food in Shanghai. Paulaner Brauhaus does its best to fill the void with a menu of classic German dishes; Wiener schnitzel, bratwurst, and apple strudel, accompanied by the house-brewed lager. The food isn't inspiring, and seems pricy, but the beer is excellent. The Fenyang Lu location is more laid-back, with a courtyard beer garden in the summer. The Xintiandi branch, open for lunch, is great for people-watching. ⊠ *150 Fenyang Lu, Xuhui* ☎ *021/6474–5700* ☉ *No lunch* ⊠ *House 19-20, North Block Xintiandi, 181 Taicang Lu, Luwan* ☎ *021/6320–3935* ⊟ *AE, DC, MC, V.*

Indian

$–$$$ ✕ **The Tandoor.** Don't miss the unbelievable *murgh malei kebab* (tandoori chicken marinated in cheese and yogurt mixture) or try some vegetable curries—*palak aloo* (spinach with peas) or *dal makhani* (lentil). Decorated with mirrors, Indian artwork, and Chinese characters dangling from the ceiling, the restaurant is ingeniously designed to show the route of Buddhism from India to China. The management and staff, all from India, remain close at hand throughout the meal to answer questions and attend to your needs. ✉ *Jinjiang Hotel, South Building, 59 Maoming Nan Lu, Luwan* ☎ *021/6472–5494* ✍ *Reservations essential* ▭ *AE, DC, MC, V.*

★ $ ✕ **Vedas.** In the heart of the Old French Concession, Vedas is a popular destination for quality Indian food at affordable prices. Decor is dark and comfortable. The menu focuses on northern Indian cuisine, and the hand-pulled naan bread, thick and succulent curries, fiery vindaloos, and house-made chutneys are excellent. Vedas is extremely popular, and always bustling. Don't expect an intimate, tranquil dining experience, but do expect spectacular food and great service in a pleasant if busy environment. ✉ *550 Jianguo Xi Lu, Xuhui* ☎ *021/6445–8100* ✍ *Reservations essential* ▭ *AE, DC, MC, V.*

Italian

$–$$$ ✕ **Da Marco.** Its reasonably priced authentic Italian fare makes Da Marco a universal favorite in Shanghai. The original location, on Dong Zhu An Bang Lu, is a magnet for Italian expats in search of a late dinner, whereas the Yandang Lu location attracts a mix of locals, expats, and tourists. Lasagna, ravioli, Caprese salad, and pizza (11 types) are among the classic dishes on the menu. The wine list includes many selections under Y200. Three-course set lunches are a popular option. You can choose alfresco dining under the bright orange awning or a comfy seat on the banquette in the sunshine-yellow dining room. ✉ *62 Yandang Lu, Luwan* ☎ *021/6385–5998* ✍ *Reservations essential* ▭ *AE, DC, MC, V.*

Japanese

$–$$ ✕ **Tairyo.** After indulging in the Y150 all-you-can-eat teppanyaki special at Tairyo, you might feel as big as the three sumo wrestlers in the restaurant's wall-sized mural. Although locals seem to prefer the cheaper à la carte menu, Westerners come here for the endless delicious servings of sashimi, scallops, lemon prawns, and some of the best beef in town. Beer, sake, wine, and plum wine are included in the price, too. ✉ *139 Ruijin Yi Lu, Luwan* ☎ *021/5382–8818* ✉ *15 Dongping Rd., Xuhui* ☎ *021/6445–4734* ✍ *Reservations essential* ▭ *AE, DC, MC, V.*

Korean

¢ ✕ **Gao Li Korean Restaurant.** Hidden on a small lane, Gao Li is a bit of a hole in the wall, but its eight tables are packed with patrons until 2 AM. It serves great, cheap food and specializes in tender and delicious grilled meats. You do the cooking, placing thin cuts of meat on a small gas grill and then wrapping them in a lettuce leaf and adding chili sauce. The noodle dishes are some of the best in town: try the cold Korean noo-

dles for dessert. ⊠ *No. 1, 181 Wuyuan Lu, Xuhui* ☎ *021/6431–5236*
☐ *AE, DC, MC, V.*

Shanghainese

¢–$$ ✕ **Yang's Kitchen.** Traditional Shang-
hainese food without the usual
renao (hot and noisy atmosphere)
draws customers down the narrow
laneway to the restored villa that's
now home to Yang's Kitchen. The
19-page menu includes familiar
dishes like mandarin fish, the oblig-
atory *xiaolongbao*, as well as 22
soups. An apricot-and-white side
dining room with small tables
spaced widely for privacy is popu-
lar among couples and solo diners
seeking a quiet and inexpensive
meal. ⊠ *No. 3, 9 Hengshan Lu,*
Xuhui ☎ *021/6445–8418* ☐ *AE,*
DC, MC, V.

WORD OF MOUTH
"One place where you won't have to worry about being surrounded by the Americans you saw on the Bund. A true local hangout. Enormous, noisy and authentic. Go with a group, the bigger the better. But study the gigantic menu carefully. "Shredded chicken" is a pigeon in seven pieces, including the head. With anything you order, you'll be tasting the 'real thing.' " –John Mihalec, Connecticut

¢–$ ✕ **Bao Luo.** Although its English menu caters to tourists, Bao Luo is Chi-
nese dining as the Chinese enjoy it, a fact confirmed by the usual long
wait for a table. The freshness of the ingredients comes through in every
dish, from perfectly steamed broccoli to tender stewed crab and pork
meatballs. Tables are packed tightly in this small two-story restaurant,
and the light-wood interior merely serves as backdrop to the can't-miss
cuisine. However, look closely for the red-scroll neon sign with a tiny
BL, or you may miss the restaurant altogether. ⊠ *271 Fumin Lu, by*
Changle Lu, Jing'an ☎ *021/5403–7239* ⌕ *Reservations essential* ☐ *No*
credit cards.

Sichuan

★ $–$$ ✕ **South Beauty.** The elegant interior and spicy fare are both worth be-
holding at South Beauty. As the sliding-glass front door opens—reveal-
ing a walkway between two cascading walls of water—it splits the
restaurant's trademark red Chinese-opera mask in two. Likewise, the
menu is split down the middle between cooler Cantonese cuisine and
sizzling hot Sichuan fare. Don't be fooled: even dishes with a one-pepper rating, like sautéed baby lobster, will singe your sinuses. ⊠ *28 Tao-*
jiang Lu, Xuhui ☎ *021/6445–2581* ⌕ *Reservations essential* ☐ *AE,*
DC, MC, V.

Thai

¢–$$ ✕ **Simply Thai.** Unpretentious Thai fare at moderate prices has earned
Fodor'sChoice this restaurant a loyal expat clientele. Customers flock to the tree-
★ shaded patio to savor such favorites as green and red curries (on the spicy
side) and stir-fried rice noodles with chicken (on the tame side). The ap-
petizers are all first-rate, especially the crispy spring rolls and samosas.
The wine list includes a half-dozen bottles under Y200 ($25), a rarity
in Shanghai. The branch in Xintiandi is a bit noisier but features the

same great food and prices. ✉ *5C Dongping Rd., Xuhui* ☎ *021/ 6445–9551* ⌖ *Reservations essential* ▭ *AE, DC, MC, V.*

Pudong

Contemporary

$–$$$ ✗ **Cloud 9.** Pudong can be an intimidating concrete jungle, with little respite in sight. If you're looking for refreshment on your Pudong safari, try Cloud 9 on the 87th floor of the Hyatt. Be aware, this is not a cheap lounge—there is a Y120 minimum and dress code, but the view is spectacular. Kick back and drink in the city laid out beneath you, while nibbling at their tasty Asian-inspired tapas and snacks. ✉ *Grand Hyatt, 87th fl., 88 Shiji Dadao, Pudong* ☎ *021/5049–1234* ⌖ *Reservations essential* ▭ *AE, DC, MC, V.*

$$–$$$$ ✗ **The Grill.** Part of the Hyatt's three-in-one, open-kitchen restaurant concept, the Grill shares the 56th floor with two other restaurants (serving Japanese and Italian cuisine). At the Grill you can feast on a great seafood platter or unbelievably tender steak. ✉ *Grand Hyatt, 88 Shiji Dadao, Pudong* ☎*021/5049–1234* ⌖*Reservations essential* ▭*AE, DC, MC, V.*

> ### WORD OF MOUTH
>
> "I was looking for a good steak, and The Grill delivered! There is not a more magnificent view anywhere than the Grand Hyatt Hotel, and you want a good rib-eye steak, this is a can't miss in Shanghai."
>
> –Dan Hooker, New Jersey

International

$$$$
Fodor's Choice
★
✗ **Jade on 36.** This is a restaurant that must be experienced to be believed. Perched on the 36th floor of the Shangri-La tower, the Jade lounge/restaurant is simply beautiful. There is no à la carte menu; instead, diners choose from a selection of set menus named simply for colors and sizes. The cuisine is innovative and extremely fresh, the service impeccable, and the view pleasant. Menus vary from five to eight courses, with an emphasis on fresh seafood and tender meats. The jumbo shrimp in a jar is especially enjoyable, as is the signature lemon tart. It's an expensive indulgence, but worth every penny. ✉ *Pudong Shangri-La, 36th fl., 33 Fu Cheng Lu, Pudong* ☎ *021/6882–8888* ▭ *AE, DC, MC, V.*

$$$ ✗ **Yi Café.** Popular and busy, the Yi Café at the Shangri-La is open-kitchen dining at its finest, serving a world of cuisines. The Yi Café is very popular with the Lujiazui business set, as well as with local diners for the quality and variety of the food. It's a great place to people-watch over a selection of the finest dishes Asia has to offer. This experience doesn't come cheap, at Y268 per person, but it's worth it. The restaurant is slightly underrepresented in Western cuisine, focusing more on Asian dishes. ✉ *Pudong Shangri-La, 2nd fl., 33 Fu Cheng Lu, Pudong* ☎ *021/ 6882–8888* ▭ *AE, DC, MC, V.*

Italian

★ **$$–$$$** ✗ **Danieli's.** This is one of the finest Italian restaurants in the city, and worth the commute to Pudong. The intimate dining area is spacious without being overwhelming, and the staff is very well trained. Their business lunch is famed for its speed and quality, but it is at dinner that Danieli's really shines. The menu is well balanced with seasonal dishes, and boasts an excellent five-course set menu. Prices can be expensive, especially for wine, but it is worth the money. We recommend the set menu with a bottle of the superb Green Point by Chandon sparkling wine. ⊠ *St. Regis, 889 Dongfang Lu, Pudong* ☎ *021/5050–4567* ♧ *Reservations essential* ▭ *AE, DC, MC, V.*

Sichuan

$–$$ ✕ **South Beauty.** From its perch atop the top floor of the Super Brand Mall, the Pudong branch of South Beauty has a sweeping view of the beauty of the Bund. Although half of its menu is Cantonese, the restaurant is known for its sizzling hot Sichuan fare. Even dishes with a one-pepper rating will scorch your mouth. ⊠ *Super Brand Mall, 10th fl., 168 Lujiazui Lu, Pudong* ☎ *021/5047–1817* ▭ *AE, DC, MC, V.*

Nanjing Xi Lu & Jing'an

American

★ $–$$ ✕ **Element Fresh.** Freshly made and generously portioned salads and sandwiches draw crowds of people to this bright lunch spot in the Shanghai Center. The creative menu of innovative sandwiches, light pasta dishes and excellent salads has made Element Fresh one of the most popular lunch destinations in the city. For the health-conscious, an equally creative drink menu has long lists of fresh fruit juices and smoothies. ⊠ *Shanghai Center, 1376 Nanjing Xi Lu, Jing'an* ☎ *021/6279–8682* ▭ *AE, DC, MC, V.*

Cantonese

$$–$$$$ ✕ **Summer Pavilion.** Helmed by Ho Wing, the former chef of Hong Kong's famed Jockey Club, Summer Pavilion serves delicious Cantonese specialties ranging from simple dim sum to delicacies such as shark fin, bird's nest soup, and abalone. As befits the Portman Ritz-Carlton, the restaurant's dining room is elegant, with black and gold accents and a raised platform that makes you feel as though you're center stage—a sense heightened by the attentive servers, who stand close, but not too close, at hand, anticipating your needs. ⊠ *Portman Ritz-Carlton, 2nd fl., 1376 Nanjing Xi Lu, Jing'an* ☎ *021/6279–8888* ♧ *Reservations essential* ▭ *AE, DC, MC, V.*

$–$$ ✕ **The Onion.** On the high-traffic sector of Nanjing Xi Lu, Onion is a simple concept Cantonese restaurant, serving quality Cantonese dishes at reasonable prices. The decor is light and airy, with well-spaced tables and efficient service. The menu is extensive and bilingual, with lunch specials and dim sum. This is a very low stress restaurant, and a great destination for a simple and satisfying meal. ⊠ *881 Nanjing Xi Lu, 3rd fl., Jing'an* ☎ *021/6267–5477* ▭ *No credit cards.*

Indonesian

$–$$ ✕ **Bali Laguna.** Overlooking the lily pond in Jing'an Park and with interior and alfresco dining, Bali Laguna is a popular choice for couples. Balinese music piped along the statue- and palm-lined walkway sets the mood even before the sarong-clad hostess welcomes you inside the traditional, three-story, Indonesian-style house or to a pond-side table. The menu is

WHERE TO REFUEL AROUND TOWN

When all you want is a quick, inexpensive bite, look for these local chains. They all have English menus and branches in Shanghai's tourist areas.

Ajisen Noodles: This Japanese-style noodle joint has an English menu with photos, and fast service.

Bi Feng Tang: Dim sum is the sum of the menu, from chickens' feet to less exotic items such as shrimp wontons and barbecue pork pastries.

Sumo Sushi: Sit along the carousel and watch the chefs slice and dice

fresh made-to-order sushi. You can order set lunches, à la carte, or all you can eat.

Gino Café: The inexpensive Italian fare at this café chain includes pizza, pasta, sandwiches, and good desserts.

Manabe: This Japanese coffeehouse chain serves Western fast food, such as club sandwiches and breakfast fare, as well as Japanese snacks and a long list of teas.

heavy on seafood, such as grilled fish cakes and chili crab, which captures the fire of Indonesian cuisine. Quench it with a Nusa Dua Sunset or other Bali-inspired cocktail. ⊠ *Jing'an Park, 189 Huashan Lu, Jing'an* ☎ *021/6248–6970* ⬧ *Reservations essential* ▭ *AE, DC, MC, V.*

Shanghainese

★ **$–$$** ✕ **1221.** This stylish but casual eatery is a favorite of hip Chinese and expatriate regulars. The dining room is streamlined chic, its crisp white tablecloths contrasting the warm golden walls. Shanghainese food is the mainstay, with a few Sichuan dishes. From the extensive 26-page menu (in English, pinyin, and Chinese), you can order dishes like sliced *you tiao* (fried bread sticks) with shredded beef, a whole chicken in a green-onion soy sauce, and *shaguo shizi tou* (pork meatballs). ⊠ *1221 Yanan Xi Lu, Changning* ☎ *021/6213–6585 or 021/6213–2441* ⬧ *Reservations essential* ▭ *AE, DC, MC, V.*

$–$$$
Fodor'sChoice
★ ✕ **Meilongzhen.** Probably Shanghai's most famous restaurant, Meilongzhen is one of the oldest dining establishments in town, dating from 1938. The building served as the Communist Party headquarters in the 1930s, and the traditional Chinese dining rooms still have their intricate woodwork, and mahogany and marble furniture. The exhaustive menu has more than 80 seafood options, including such traditional Shanghainese fare as mandarin fish, and dishes with a more Sichuan flair, like shredded spicy eel and prawns in chili sauce. Since this is a stop for most tour buses, expect a wait if you haven't booked ahead. ⊠ *No. 22, 1081 Nanjing Xi Lu, Jing'an* ☎ *021/6253–5353* ⬧ *Reservations essential* ▭ *AE, DC, MC, V.*

Vegetarian

¢–$ ✕ **Gongdelin.** A two-story gold engraving of Buddha pays tribute to the origins of the inventive vegetarian dishes this restaurant has served for 80 years. Chefs transform tofu into such surprising and tasty creations as mock duck, eel, and pork. The interior is just as inspired, with Ming-style, wood-and-marble tables; metal latticework; and a soothing fountain. Tables fill up quickly after 6 PM, so either arrive early or buy some goodies to go at the take-out counter. ⊠ *445 Nanjing Xi Lu, Huangpu* ☎ *021/6327–0218* ▤ *AE, DC, MC, V.*

> **WORD OF MOUTH**
>
> "I would go back to Shanghai just to eat at this place—the vegetarian cuisine is amazing!!!"
> —Rebecca Schmal, Canada

Hongqiao & Gubei

Café

¢–$ ✕ **Wagas.** Serving sandwiches, salads, and coffees, Wagas is a popular lunch stop and good for a quick refill when shopping. The food is decent and the service speedy, but there is little else that is distinctive about this easily accessible chain café. ⊠ *Maxdo Building, 86 Xia Xia Lu, Luwan* ☎ *021/5208–1978* ▤ *No credit cards.*

Cantonese

$–$$ ✕ **The Dynasty.** Although its cuisine is mostly Cantonese, Dynasty does serve some other regional fare, such as first-rate Peking duck and Sichuan-influenced hot-and-sour soup. The Cantonese seafood dishes, especially the prawns and lobster, are particularly good, and the shrimp *jiaozi* (dumplings) are delicious. Keyhole cutouts in the subdued pewter walls showcase Chinese vases and artifacts. Thick carpets mute any hotel noise, but the prices quickly remind you this is indeed a hotel restaurant. ⊠ *Renaissance Yangtze, 2099 Yanan Xi Lu, Changning* ☎ *021/ 6275–0000* ⌖ *Reservations essential* ▤ *AE, DC, MC, V.*

Italian

★ $$–$$$ ✕ **Giovanni's.** Its Italian courtyard with a penthouse view provides a wonderful backdrop for Giovanni's traditional Italian fare. The antipasta and calamari are delicious, and the pastas are served perfectly al dente. Once dark and gloomy, Giovanni's has recently been renovated into a bright and colorful bistro. Seasonal promotions add a taste of Tuscany and other regions to the menu. ⊠ *Sheraton Grand Tai Ping Yang, 27th fl., 5 Zunyi Nan Lu, Changning* ☎ *021/6275–8888* ⌖ *Reservations essential* ▤ *AE, DC, MC, V.*

Taiwanese

¢–$ ✕ **Bellagio.** Taiwanese expatriates pack the bright, sunlit dining room of Bellagio for an authentic taste of home. Red fabric–covered chairs and black streamlined tables contrast the white walls and decorative moldings. Waiters, chic in black sweaters, move efficiently between the closely spaced tables. The menu includes such traditional entrées as three-cup chicken as well as 25 noodle dishes spanning all of Southeast Asia. Save room for dessert: shaved-ice snacks are obligatory Taiwanese treats and come in 14 varieties. ✉ *778 Huangjin Cheng Dao, by Gubei Lu, Changning* ☎ *021/6278–0722* ⌨ *Reservations not accepted* ▭ *AE, DC, MC, V.*

WHERE TO STAY

By Rachel King Berlin

Although China has become a hot destination for leisure travelers, Shanghai's stature as China's business capital means that its hotels still cater primarily to business clientele and can be divided into two categories: modern Western-style hotels that are elegant and nicely appointed; or hotels built during the city's glory days, which became state-run after 1949. The latter may lack great service, modern fixings, and convenient facilities, but they often make up for it in charm, tradition, history, and value.

Judging by the number of five-star and Western chain hotels now in Shanghai, the city has proven just how grandly it has opened to the outside world. The Grand Hyatt, JW Marriott, Westin, Portman Ritz-Carlton, and St. Regis aren't merely hotels; they're landmarks on the Shanghai skyline and standard-bearers for all lodgings in town. Even the historic properties that make up the other half of Shanghai's hotel market feel the pressure to update their rooms and facilities. And as Shanghai speeds up its preparations for the World Expo in 2010, newcomers, like the Regent, are setting the bar even higher with their ultramodern settings and top-notch service.

Reservations & Rates

Increasing competition on the hotel scene means there are bargains to be had, especially during the low season from November through March.

Avoid traveling during the three national holidays—Chinese New Year (mid-January to mid-February), Labor Day (May 1), and National Day (October 1)—when rooms and prices will be at a premium.

WHAT IT COSTS In Yuan				
$$$$	**$$$**	**$$**	**$**	**¢**
FOR 2 PEOPLE over 1,800	1,401–1,800	1,101–1,400	700–1,100	Under 700

Prices are for two people in a standard double room in high season, excluding 10% to 15% service charge.

Old City

★ **$$$$**   **The Westin Shanghai.** With its distinctive room layouts, glittering glass staircase, and 90-plus works of art on display, the Westin Shanghai is a masterpiece, fittingly located near the majestic Bund. Crowne Deluxe rooms are miniature suites; sliding doors divide the sitting area, bathroom, and bedroom (the only problem is that all these divisions make the rooms feel on the small side). Luxurious amenities include rain-forest showers, extra deep tubs, and Westin's trademark Heavenly Bed. Pampering continues at the Banyan Tree spa—China's first—and stellar EEST restaurant, a sunny three-in-one venue with full Thai, Japanese, and Cantonese menus. Sunday champagne brunch at the Stage restaurant is considered the best in town by Shanghai's glitterati. Service is so attentive that extra staff stand in front of the check-in counter to assist. ⊠ *Bund Center, 88 Henan Zhonglu, Huangpu 200002* ☎ *021/6335–1888 or 888/ 625–5144* 🖷 *021/6335–2888* ⊕ *www.westin.com/shanghai* �’276 *rooms, 25 suites* △ *3 restaurants, grocery, patisserie, room service, in-room faxes, in-room safes, minibars, cable TV, in-room data ports, indoor pool, health club, hair salon, hot tub, sauna, spa, steam room, bar, lobby lounge, piano, shops, babysitting, dry cleaning, laundry service, concierge, concierge floor, Internet, business services, convention center, travel services, some free parking, no-smoking floors* ⊟ *AE, DC, MC, V.*

> **MONEY-SAVING TIPS**
>
> ■ Since Shanghai's hotels target business travelers, there are often excellent deals available on weekends at many of the upmarket establishments. Reductions on room rates are also widely available from November to March, except over Chinese New Year when an influx of domestic tourists causes prices to spike.
>
> ■ Don't be shy to practice your bargaining skills when making reservations—the Chinese are used to the first price always being up for negotiation. If you're staying for several nights, some three- or four-star hotels will throw in breakfast or give you a discounted rate, so always be sure to ask.

Xintiandi & City Center

$$$$ ▦ **88 Xintiandi.** Although it targets business travelers, 88 Xintiandi is a shopper's and gourmand's delight. The boutique hotel is in the heart of Xintiandi, its balconies overlooking the top-dollar shops and restaurants below. The rooms, all mini- or full-size suites with kitchens, are likewise upscale. Beds are elevated on a central, gauze-curtained platform; sitting areas have large TVs and DVD players. Stylish wood screens accent the rooms and common areas. Deluxe rooms and the executive lounge overlook man-made Lake Taipingqiao, and guests have access to the comprehensive Alexander City Club gym next door. Renovations will be complete by the end of 2007 and will add such amenities as plasma TVs, DVD players, foot massage machines, printers, scanners, and juicers to all rooms. ⊠ *380 Huangpi Nan Lu, Luwan 200021* ☎ *021/5383–8833* 🖷 *021/5353–8877* ⊕ *www.88xintiandi.com* �’ *12 suites, 41 rooms* △ *Restaurant, room service, in-room faxes, in-room safes, kitchens, minibars, microwaves, refrigerators, cable TV, in-room VCRs, in-room data ports, indoor pool, gym, bar, babysitting, laundry service, concierge, business services, parking (fee), no-smoking floors* ⊟ *AE, DC, MC, V.*

$$$$ ▦ **JW Marriott.** For the best views in Puxi, look no farther. The JW Marriott's futuristic 60-story tower on the edge of People's Square turns heads with its 90-degree twist, which divides the executive apartments below from the 22-story hotel above. The interior follows classic lines with subtle Chinese accents. Celadon vases, wedding boxes, and ornamental jades complement the soft green-and-yellow palette and warm fiddle-back wood in the spacious rooms, but the real eye-catcher is the amazing cityscape vista from every room. The largely business clientele appreciates the one-touch "At Your Service" call button, and the Mandara Spa, indoor and outdoor pools, excellent restaurants, JW Lounge (with 60-plus martinis), and proximity to many of the major tourist attractions are big draws for leisure travelers. ⊠ *399 Nanjing Xi Lu, Huangpu 200003* ☎ *021/*

> ## STREET SNACKS
>
> Shanghai's street snacks are the city's main culinary claim to fame. You'll see countless sidewalk stands selling the famed xiaolongbao (Shanghai's signature steamed dumplings, filled with pork or crab and soup broth), as well as various types of bing (Chinese pancakes), and baozi (filled or unfilled steamed buns).

5359–4969 or 888/236–2427 🖷 *021/6375–5988* ⊕ *www.marriotthotels. com/shajw* ⟿ *305 rooms, 37 suites* ⟁ *3 restaurants, coffee shop, room service, some in-room faxes, in-room safes, minibars, cable TV, in-room data ports, 2 pools (1 indoor), health club, hot tub, sauna, spa, steam room, lobby lounge, lounge, library, piano, shops, babysitting, dry cleaning, laundry service, concierge, concierge floor, Internet, business services, convention center, travel services, parking (fee), no-smoking rooms, no-smoking floor* ▭ *AE, DC, MC, V.*

$$$$ 🖬 **Radisson Hotel Shanghai New World.** A prominent figure not only on People's Square, but also on the Shanghai skyline, the dome-topped Radisson New World is best known for its revolving restaurant, Epicure on 45. Rooms are divided between the lower Park Tower and the higher City Tower. Park Tower rooms are more expensive, but have the best views, facing People's Square. Though the hotel caters primarily to business travelers, suites—each with a huge living room, kitchen/dining room, and spacious bath—are convenient for families. In addition, most rooms have flat-screen TVs, and DVD players are available by request. Many travelers still prefer the tranquil garden setting of the Radisson's Xingguo hotel in the French Concession, but it cannot compete with the New World's central location and city views. ■ TIP➔ **Be sure to ask about special weekend packages.** ⊠ *88 Nanjing Dong Lu, Huangpu 200003* ☎ *021/6359–9999* 🖷 *021/6358–9705* ⊕ *www. radisson.com* ⟿ *429 rooms, 91 suites* ⟁ *3 restaurants, patisserie, room service, in-room data ports, in-room safes, minibar, cable TV, indoor pool, gym, health club, hair salon, spa, virtual golf, squash, billiards, bar, lobby lounge, shops, babysitting, laundry service, concierge, Internet, business services, convention center, travel services, parking (fee), no-smoking floors* ▭ *AE, DC, MC, V.*

$$ 🖬 **Park Hotel** (Guoji Fandian). Once Shanghai's tallest building, the 20-story Park Hotel is now dwarfed on the Puxi skyline and eclipsed by other hotels whose glory days are present instead of past. Recently named a China Cultural Heritage Site, this 1934 art-deco structure overlooking People's Park still has great views and a musty charm, particularly in its restored marble lobby. Rooms are clean and bright, with prints of historic buildings from around the world. But bathrooms are tiny, and the

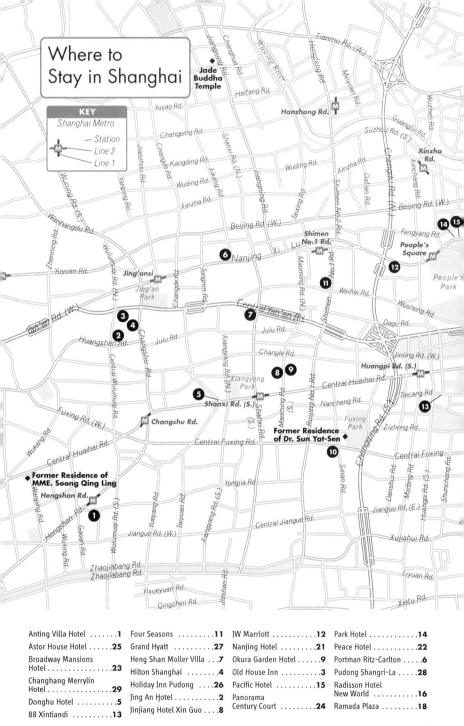

Where to Stay in Shanghai

KEY

Shanghai Metro

— Station
Ⓜ Line 2
  Line 1

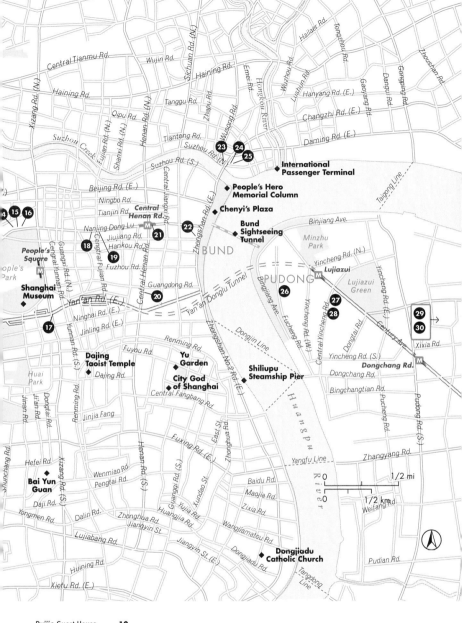

hotel's limited English service and facilities have definitely slipped to second-rate. ⊠ *170 Nanjing Xi Lu, Huangpu 200003* ☏ *021/6327–5225* 📠 *021/6327–6958* 🗗 *225 rooms, 25 suites* ⚅ *3 restaurants, in-room safes, minibars, cable TV, some in-room data ports, gym, hair salon, sauna, billiards, 2 bars, lobby lounge, piano, shop, dry cleaning, laundry service, concierge, Internet, business services, meeting rooms, travel services, some free parking, no-smoking rooms* 🖃 *AE, DC, MC, V.*

$ 🖫 **Pacific Hotel.** This 1926 property has done an admirable job of preserving its charm. The marble lobby and the downstairs bar, decorated with art-deco leather chairs and archived photos of 1920s Shanghai, sweep you back to the city's glory days. In the original Italian-style front building, 6th- and 7th-floor rooms have wood floors, ornate molded ceilings, and great views of People's Park. (Bathrooms, though, are rather institutional.) The smaller rooms in the rear building lack the fine detail and views but are still comfortable and are a bit quieter. Amenities fall short, and soundproofing could be better, but the hotel's proud history, prime location, and prices make it an appealing choice. ⊠ *108 Nanjing Xi Lu, Huangpu 200003* ☏ *021/6327–6226* 📠 *021/6372–3634* ⊕ *www.pacifichotelsh.com* 🗗 *177 rooms, 5 suites* ⚅ *Restaurant, 2 bars, room service, minibars, cable TV, in-room data ports, Wi-Fi, some in-room safes, lobby lounge, shop, hair salon, spa, laundry service, dry cleaning, Internet, business services, meeting rooms, travel services, parking (fee)* 🖃 *AE, DC, MC, V.*

¢–$ 🖫 **YMCA Hotel.** Its central location within a 15-minute walk of People's Square, Xintiandi, and the Bund makes the YMCA Hotel a top destination for budget travelers. Built in 1929 as an actual YMCA, the 11-story brick building retains some of its original features: a templelike exterior and painted ceiling beams on the 2nd floor. The four dormitory rooms have single beds, rather than bunks. This is also a good chance for you to practice your bargaining skills, as discounts are almost always available. ⊠ *123 Xizang Nan Lu, Huangpu 200021* ☏ *021/6326–1040* 📠 *021/6320–1957* ⊕ *www.ymcahotel.com* 🗗 *140 rooms, 6 suites, 4 rooms with shared bath* ⚅ *2 restaurants, bar, coffee shop, grocery, room service, some in-room safes, in-room data ports, minibars, cable TV, gym (fee), hair salon, massage, billiards, Ping-Pong, recreation room, shops, laundry service, Internet, business services, meeting rooms, airport shuttle, travel services* 🖃 *AE, DC, MC, V.*

Nanjing Dong Lu & the Bund

$$$–$$$$
Fodor'sChoice
★
🖫 **Ramada Plaza.** With its ornate lobby resembling a European opera house, the Ramada Plaza Shanghai brings a touch of grandeur to the Nanjing Road pedestrian walkway. Statues of Greek gods reign from atop intricate inlaid tables. Soaring marble columns direct the eye skyward toward a stained-glass skylight. Although the fair-size rooms lack any great views, they do face in toward a dramatic atrium, topped by yet another courtyard and the executive lounge. In 2005, an indoor swimming pool, one of the largest in Shanghai, was added, housed inside an addition reminiscent of an ancient Chinese palace. Given the lush setting and ace location, the Ramada Plaza is a good value for the money, and you can usually get a room for less than the rack rate. ⊠ *719 Nan-*

*jing Dong Lu, Huangpu 200001 ☎ 021/6350–0000 or 800/854–7854
🖷 021/6350–6666 ⊕ www.ramadainternational.com ⇨ 376 rooms, 36
suites ♨ 4 restaurants, patisserie, room service, in-room safes, minibars,
cable TV, in-room data ports, some in-room hot tubs, indoor pool, gym,
hair salon, massage, sauna, spa, steam room, billiards, lobby lounge,
nightclub, shops, babysitting, dry cleaning, laundry service, concierge,
concierge floor, Internet, business services, convention center, travel
services, free parking, no-smoking floors ▭ AE, DC, MC, V.*

$$–$$$$ 🖥 **Peace Hotel.** The allure of the Peace Hotel is as one of Shanghai's most
treasured historic buildings. That said, as a place to stay, it's an unfor-
tunate disappointment. Though the art-deco lobby and international suites
still retain some of the hotel's past glamour, the rooms tend toward small
and stuffy, with nondescript worn furnishings. The south building,
opened in 1906 as the Palace Hotel, is the oldest structure on the Bund,
but its rooms are the hotel's most modern (and least expensive), with
larger bathrooms and nicer furniture. There are rumors of renovations
in 2007, but even that won't fix the staff's curt service. ⊠ *20 Nanjing
Dong Lu, Huangpu 200002 ☎ 021/6321–6888 🖷 021/6329–0300
⊕ www.shanghaipeacehotel.com ⇨ 411 rooms, 9 suites ♨ 2 restau-
rants, room service, Wi-Fi, in-room safes, minibars, gym, hair salon, mas-
sage, sauna, spa, steam room, billiards, Ping-Pong, 2 bars, lobby lounge,
piano, shops, babysitting, playground, dry cleaning, laundry service,
concierge, concierge floor, convention center, travel services, free park-
ing, no-smoking rooms ▭ AE, DC, MC, V.*

$$$ 🖥 **Sofitel Hyland.** Directly on the Nanjing Road pedestrian mall, the Sof-
itel Hyland is a convenient base for shopping and exploring the city cen-
ter and the Bund. The rooms in this 30-story French-managed hotel are
somewhat small, but were spruced up in 2006 with prints of Chinese
emperors and small replicas of terra-cotta warrior statues. The top-floor
Sky Lounge serves Sunday brunch amid views of the Bund and downtown, and Le Pub 505 brews up its own beer. ⊠ *505 Nanjing Dong
Lu, Huangpu 200001 ☎ 021/6351–5888 🖷 021/6351–4088 ⊕ www.
accorhotels-asia.com ⇨ 299 rooms, 73 suites ♨ 3 restaurants, room
service, in-room safes, minibars, cable TV, in-room data ports, pool, gym,
health club, hair salon, massage, sauna, spa, steam room, 2 bars, lobby
lounge, pub, piano, shops, dry cleaning, laundry service, concierge floor,
Internet, business services, convention center, airport shuttle, travel
services, parking (fee), no-smoking floors ▭ AE, DC, MC, V.*

¢ 🖥 **Nanjing Hotel.** A frequent choice for budget tour groups, the Nanjing Hotel is only half a block yet a world away from the modern bustle of the Nanjing Dong Lu pedestrian walkway. Step out the front door
and you'll see China as the locals do: fruit vendors balancing their
loads, trash men ringing their hand bells. The hotel's proximity to the
metro line and the Bund compensate for the street noise and lack of views.
Built in 1931, the eight-story building is dated, yet rooms are fair-sized
with Internet access and a few satellite channels. ■ TIP➜ **Though 5th-floor
rooms were refurbished in 2006, opt for a room on the 6th floor, which is quieter.** ⊠ *200 Shanxi Lu, Huangpu 200001 ☎ 021/6322–2888 🖷 021/
6351–6520 ⊕ www.nj-hotel.com ♨ Restaurant, room service, in-room
safes, in-room data ports, minibars, cable TV, shops, laundry service,*

WHICH NEIGHBORHOOD?

Shanghai may have an excellent subway system and cheap, plentiful taxis, but if you want to take full advantage of Shanghai's popular tourist sights, restaurants, and nightlife opt to stay in downtown **Puxi**, incorporating the quiet, leafy green Former French Concession, the historical promenade of the Bund, and the bustling shopping street of Nanjing Road. From these neighborhoods you'll have easy access to all of Shanghai's dynamic neighborhoods.

NANJING LU & THE BUND
Breathtaking views of the Pudong skyline, skyscrapers juxtaposed with Victorian architecture, and easy access to great shopping and some of the city's best restaurants are just a few reasons to stay here. Best of all, most major sites, from the Bund to the Shanghai Museum, are all within comfortable walking distance. If you want to see modern Shanghai, this is the place to be.

FORMER FRENCH CONCESSION
Sneak away from the city's frenetic energy in one of the historical hotels tucked down the Former French Concession's tree-lined streets. Excellent restaurants and shopping abound, the neighborhood's relaxing atmosphere can be a nice break after a hectic day of sightseeing. A short cab or metro ride takes you straight to any of the city's sights on Nanjing Lu and the Bund.

HONGQIAO DEVELOPMENT ZONE
Hongqiao is not a destination for leisure travelers. A combination of residential complexes and business offices, Hongqiao lacks many sights or restaurants. Unless business brings you here or you have an early flight from the Hongqiao airport, there aren't many reasons to stay so far from the action.

PUDONG
Although Pudong—with its shiny new skyscrapers and wide boulevards—can feel impersonal, and it's too far from downtown Puxi for some, it has some of the city's best hotels, all close to Pudong International Airport. Phenomenal views of the Bund are a major bonus. But if you stay here, be prepared to spend at least 30 minutes shuttling back and forth to Puxi (and it could take even longer during rush hour as millions of locals compete to flag down taxis or squeeze into subway cars almost overflowing with commuters).

Internet, business services, meeting rooms, travel services ▤ *AE, DC, MC, V.*

Former French Concession

$$$$ ▦ **Jinjiang Hotel.** The former Cathay Mansions, Grosvenor Gardens, and Grosvenor House, now known collectively as the Jinjiang Hotel, are among the few art-deco buildings left standing in the city. It's here that President Nixon and Premier Zhou Enlai signed the Shanghai Communique in 1972 and all lobbies display photographs of the heads of state who have graced the hotel's grounds, giving the establishment a wonderful air of history. The fabulous luxury suites in the Grosvenor House start at $800 nightly. Rooms in the 1929 Cathay Building are plain but fair-sized with separate showers and tubs. Deluxe rooms are more stylish. The 5-floor Cathay Garden, which reopened in 2005 after extensive renovations, now houses the hotels best non-suite room, with guests praising the spacious modern deco furnishings and deep soak bathtubs. For the best view, snag a room on the 4th or 5th floor. ✉ *59 Maoming Nan Lu, Luwan 200020* ☎ *021/6258–2582* 🖷 *021/6472–5588* 🛏 *328 rooms, 33 suites* ⚫ *5 restaurants, room service, in-room safes, minibars, cable TV, in-room data ports, indoor pool, health club, hair salon, sauna, bowling, 2 bars, lobby lounge, shops, babysitting, Internet, business services, convention center, airport shuttle, travel services, free parking, no-smoking rooms, no-smoking floors* ☰ *AE, DC, MC, V.*

$$$$ 🏨 **Okura Garden Hotel.** Its parklike setting in the heart of the French Concession makes this 33-story Garden Hotel a favorite Shanghai retreat, especially for Japanese travelers familiar with the Okura Group name. The first three floors, which were once old Shanghai's French Club, have been restored, with cascading chandeliers, frescoes, and art-deco details at every turn. Average-size standard rooms are simply furnished with silk wallpaper and European-style furniture and, unlike deluxe rooms and suites, lack flat-screen TVs. The romantic 3rd-floor terrace bar overlooks the 2-acre garden, and the Japanese and French restaurants serve excellent but high-priced food. For those who want to stay connected, cell phones are available for rent at the concierge desk. ✉ *58 Maoming Nan Lu, Luwan 200020* ☎ *021/6415–1111* 🖷 *021/6415–8866* ⊕ *www.gardenhotelshanghai.com* 🛏 *478 rooms, 22 suites* ⚫ *5 restaurants, room service, some in-room faxes, in-room safes, minibars, cable TV, in-room data ports, 2 tennis courts, indoor-outdoor pool, health club, hair salon, hot tub, massage, sauna, 3 bars, lobby lounge, shops, dry cleaning, laundry service, concierge, concierge floor, Internet, business services, convention center, airport shuttle, travel services, some free parking, no-smoking floors* ☰ *AE, DC, MC, V.*

$$$–$$$$ 🏨 **Hilton Shanghai.** Opened in 1988 as Shanghai's first five-star hotel, the Hilton remains a local favorite among businessmen and airline crews. Rooms are comfortable with an understated sand-tone color scheme, but not as cutting-edge as the hotel's younger competitors. But what the Hilton lacks in modern decor it makes up for with its prime location near the restaurants and nightlife of Jing'an Temple and the Former French Concession and its low-key friendly service. The delectable Gourmet Corner now occupies a large storefront in the front lobby, whereas in the rear lies the much-lauded Italian restaurant Leonardo's and the sunlit 24-hour Atrium Café, which resembles a quiet Chinese garden. On the top floors, the conference center, Penthouse Bar, and stellar Sichuan Court restaurant all have stunning views of the ever-expanding Puxi skyline. ✉ *250 Huashan Lu, Xuhui 200040* ☎ *021/6248–0000 or 800/445–8667* 🖷 *021/6248–3848* ⊕ *www.shanghai.hilton.com* 🛏 *692 rooms, 28 suites* ⚫ *6 restaurants, café, coffee shop, room service, some in-room faxes, minibars, cable TV, in-room data ports, tennis court, indoor pool, health club, hair salon, hot tub, Japanese baths,* *sauna, spa, steam room, squash, 3 bars, lobby lounge, shops, babysitting, dry cleaning, laundry service, concierge, concierge floor, Internet, business services, convention center, airport shuttle, travel services, parking (fee), no-smoking floors* ⊟ *AE, DC, MC, V.*

$$$–$$$$ ▢ **Jing An Hotel.** The weekly chamber-music concert in its lobby is just one example of how the Jing An Hotel has retained its elegance and charm after 70 years. In a 1½-acre garden, the Spanish-style main building's lobby has beautiful stained-glass windows. The ornate upstairs dining rooms often host prominent city officials. Although facilities are lacking compared to the newer hotels in town and the rooms in the Jing An New Building should be avoided at all costs (bathrooms are barely the size of a closet), the hotel's proximity to the subway line and its lush Former French Concession setting make this oft-overlooked property a winner. ⊠ *370 Huashan Lu, Xuhui 200040* ☏ *021/6248–0088* ⊟ *021/ 6249–6100* ⊕ *www.jinganhotel.net* ⇗ *210 rooms, 17 suites* ⌂ *2 restaurants, coffee shop, room service, in-room safes, minibars, cable TV, in-room data ports, gym, hair salon, massage, sauna, lobby lounge, piano bar, shops, babysitting, dry cleaning, laundry service, concierge, Internet, business services, meeting rooms, airport shuttle, travel services, parking (fee), no-smoking rooms* ⊟ *AE, DC, MC, V.*

$$–$$$$ ▢ **Donghu Hotel.** Just off the frenzied shopping street of Huaihai Road, the Donghu Hotel remains one of Shanghai's best preserved hotels from the city's 1920s heyday. The hotel's seven buildings have a surprising array of restaurants—Korean barbecue and Japanese, in addition to the standard Chinese and Western fare—an indoor pool, and a wide variety of room options. "Superior" rooms in Building 7 don't quite live up to their title and are simply furnished with twin beds and rather mismatched yellow wallpaper and red carpet. We suggest the Donghu deluxe rooms across the street at Building 1—with their traditional Chinese furniture and dark-wood paneling, these spacious rooms make you feel as if you've stepped back in time. ⊠ *70 Donghu Lu, Xuhui 200031* ☏ *021/6415–8158* ⊟ *021/6415–7759* ⊕ *www.donghuhotel. com* ⇗ *240 rooms, 30 suites* ⌂ *6 restaurants, room service, some in-room safes, minibars, cable TV, in-room data ports, indoor pool, gym, hair salon, billiards, piano, dry cleaning, laundry service, concierge, Internet, business services, convention center, travel services, parking (fee)* ⊟ *AE, DC, MC, V.*

★ $$–$$$$ ▢ **Ruijin Guest House.** Formerly the Morriss Estate, the Ruijin Hotel showcases how opulently *taipans* (expatriate millionaire businessmen) lived in Shanghai's heyday of the 1930s. Rooms within the two preserved villas—No. 1 and Old No. 3—are rich with detail: high ceilings, ornate plaster molding, bamboo-etched glass. The two other buildings are significantly shorter on charm but still overlook the verdant grounds, which are shared with several top-notch restaurants (including the hip Face Bar) and provide direct access to the bars on Maoming Road. New No. 3 may lack the historic cachet of the other buildings, but its standard rooms, which come with a king-size bed and Jacuzzi, are definitely a steal. ⊠ *118 Ruijin Er Lu, Luwan 200020* ☏ *021/6472–5222* ⊟ *021/ 6473–2277* ⊕ *www.shedi.net.cn/outedi/ruijin* ⇗ *62 rooms, 20 suites* ⌂ *Restaurant, coffee shop, room service, in-room safes, minibars, cable*

TV, hair salon, 2 bars, lobby lounge, shops, laundry service, Internet, business services, convention center, free parking, no-smoking rooms ⊟ *AE, DC, MC, V.*

$$ ⊞ **Anting Villa Hotel.** Two blocks from the metro and the Hengshan Road–nightlife district, the Anting Villa Hotel is a convenient and surprisingly quiet retreat tucked away down a small side street. Superior rooms in the 10-story hotel tower have been refurbished in a "Spanish style" with garishly bright red pillowcases and leather-covered furniture; some rooms now come with flat-screen TVs. It's worth it to pay a little extra for a garden-view room with vistas of the cedar-shaded grounds and namesake 1932 Spanish-style villa. Although English service is limited, the hotel's staff is eager and friendly. Full gym facilities, including a tennis court and pool, are planned for 2007. ⊠ *46 Anting Lu, Xuhui 200031* ☎ *021/6433–1188* 🖷 *021/6433–9726* ⊕ *www.sinohotel.com* 📖 *135 rooms, 11 suites* ⚭ *Restaurant, café, room service, in-room safes, in-room data ports, minibars, cable TV, hair salon, massage, piano, shops, babysitting, laundry service, Internet, business services, meeting rooms, travel services, free parking, no-smoking rooms* ⊟ *AE, DC, MC, V.*

$ ⊞ **Old House Inn.** Hidden down a small lane, Old House Inn is one of
Fodor'sChoice Shanghai's only boutique hotels and a must if you're looking for a per-
★ sonalized experience that the larger hotels just can't offer. What this tiny gem lacks in amenities (there's no elevator, gym, concierge, or business facilities), it makes up for with its authentic Chinese style and charm. All rooms are decorated with antique dark-wood furniture and traditional porcelains and the friendly staff is so eager to please that they'll even run down to the end of the lane and find you a taxi. Adjacent to the hotel is the swanky A Future Perfect restaurant, popular with both expats and trendy locals for its outdoor café. ■ TIP→ **Book well in advance to snag one of the moderately priced king-size rooms.** ⊠ *No. 16, Lane 351 Huashan Lu, Xuhui 200040* ☎ *021/6248–6118* 🖷 *021/6249–6869* ⊕ *www.oldhouse.cn* 📖 *12 rooms* ⚭ *Restaurant, bar, in-room data ports, in-room safes, minibars, cable TV, dry cleaning, laundry service, free parking* ⊟ *AE, DC, MC, V.*

Pudong

★ **$$$$** ⊞ **Grand Hyatt.** Views, views, views are what the world's highest hotel is all about—occupying floors 53 through 87 of the spectacular Jinmao Tower, the Grand Hyatt's interior is defined by art-deco lines juxtaposed with space-age grillwork and sleek furnishings and textures. The 33-story central atrium is a marvel in itself—a seemingly endless cylinder with an outer-space aura. Room amenities are space-age as well: CAT 5 optical lines for laptop use; Internet connections on the flat-screen TV through a cordless keyboard; and three high-pressure shower heads in the bathroom. Views from the rooms are spectacular; corner rooms have two walls of pure glass for endless panoramas of the Oriental Pearl Tower, majesty of the Bund, and expanse of the city below. ■ TIP→ **But watch out—being that high up puts you literally in the clouds, and at the mercy of Shanghai's foggy weather.** ⊠ *Jinmao Dasha, 88 Shiji Dadao, Pudong 200121* ☎ *021/ 5049–1234 or 800/233–1234* 🖷 *021/5049–1111* ⊕ *www.shanghai. grand.hyatt.com* 📖 *510 rooms, 45 suites* ⚭ *5 restaurants, café, coffee* *shop, food court, room service, in-room safes, minibars, cable TV, in-room data ports, indoor pool, health club, hair salon, sauna, spa, steam room, 3 bars, lobby lounge, piano bar, nightclub, shops, dry cleaning, laundry service, concierge, concierge floor, Internet, business services, convention center, parking (fee), some free parking* ⊟ *AE, DC, MC, V.*

$$$$ 🏨 **Pudong Shangri-La.** The Shangri-La occupies one of the most prized
Fodor'sChoice locations in Shanghai: overlooking the Huangpu River, opposite the Bund,
★ near the Pearl Tower in Lujiazui. The hotel's breathtaking water's-edge views, white-glove service, and spacious rooms attract a mix of business and leisure travelers. The addition of a second tower in 2005 made the Shangri-La the largest luxury hotel in Shanghai, with almost 1,000 guest rooms and 10 dining choices. Although rooms in Tower 2, behind the original hotel, come with 32-inch plasma TVs, DVD players, and fax machines, many return guests still prefer the rooms in Tower 1 for their gloriously unobstructed views of the Bund. ⊠ *33 Fucheng Lu, Pudong 200120* ☎ *021/6882–8888 or 800/942–5050* 🖷 *021/6882–6688* ⊕ *www.shangri-la.com* ⇆ *916 rooms, 65 suites* ♠ *8 restaurants, patisserie, room service, in-room safes, minibars, cable TV, in-room data ports, some in-room faxes, tennis court, 2 indoor pools, 2 gyms, hair salon, hot tub, massage, sauna, steam room, spa, 2 bars, 2 lobby lounges, nightclub, shops, babysitting, dry cleaning, laundry service, concierge, concierge floor, Internet, business services, convention center, travel services, parking (fee), no-smoking floors* ⊟ *AE, DC, MC, V.*

$$$$ 🏨 **The St. Regis.** Every guest is a VIP at the St. Regis. The amphitheater-
Fodor'sChoice like lobby sets the stage for the most indulgent hotel experience in
★ Shanghai. The 318 rooms in this 40-story red-granite tower—its design lauded by *Architectural Digest*—spare no expense, with Bose wave radios, Herman Miller Aeron chairs, and rain-forest showers that give you the feeling of being under a waterfall. At 500 square feet (152 sq. m), standard rooms compare to other hotels' suites. The two women's-only floors are unique in Shanghai. Butlers address all your needs 24/7 (you can even contact them by e-mail) from in-room check-in to room service, and as part of a new program, they can arrange to escort guests personally to visit local artist studios. The hotel's location—15 minutes from the riverfront—is a drawback, but the fitness center and 24-hour gym, along with the remarkable Danieli's Italian restaurant add to this pampering property's appeal. ⊠ *889 Dongfang Lu, Pudong 200122* ☎ *021/5050–4567 or 800/325–3589* 🖷 *021/6875–6789* ⊕ *www.stregis.com/shanghai* ⇆ *274 rooms, 44 suites* ♠ *3 restaurants, room service, some in-room faxes, in-room safes, minibars, cable TV, in-room data ports, Wi-Fi, tennis court, indoor pool, health club, hair salon, hot tub, sauna, spa, steam room, 2 bars, lounge, shops, babysitting, dry cleaning, laundry service, concierge, Internet, business services, convention center, travel services, parking (fee), no-smoking floors* ⊟ *AE, DC, MC, V.*

$$$–$$$$ 🏨 **Holiday Inn Pudong.** In the commercial district of Pudong, this Holiday Inn is well-situated for travelers with business in the area and just a four-block walk to metro Line 2 into Puxi. Rooms are simply decorated—beige walls, bird's-eye maple furniture—but provide plenty of room to spread out your suitcases. The gym and indoor pool are quite large. For entertainment, there's a KTV (karaoke) club, a lobby piano

KID-FRIENDLY HOTELS

The **Somerset Grand,** in the Former French Concession, is the best option for families, with fully equipped kitchens in large apartmentlike suites. The hotel has a playroom and a pool, and it's within walking distance of the shops and movie theater at Xintiandi. The **City Hotel,** also in the Former French Concession, has smallish, somewhat tired rooms but there's an indoor playroom for kids. Rooms on the executive floors are larger and more up-to-date. The **Radisson Hotel Shanghai New World,** directly on Nanjing Lu by People's Square, has large (though pricey) family suites that come with spacious living room and dining area. Suites with kitchens at competitive rates are the main draw at the **Somerset Xuhui,** between the Former French Concession and Xujiahui. It's a bit far from the action on Nanjing Lu, but there's an indoor playroom and a sizeable pool.

bar, and an Irish pub with Guinness and Kilkenny on tap. ⊠ *899 Dong-fang Lu, Pudong 200122* ☎ *021/5830–6666 or 800/465–4329* 📠 *021/ 5830–5555* ⊕ *www.holiday-inn.com* 🛏 *285 rooms, 30 suites* ⚴ *3 restaurants, coffee shop, patisserie, in-room safes, minibars, cable TV, indoor pool, gym, hair salon, massage, sauna, steam room, billiards, 2 bars, piano bar, pub, babysitting, dry cleaning, laundry service, concierge, concierge floor, Internet, business services, convention center, travel services, parking (fee), no-smoking floors* ⊟ *AE, DC, MC, V.*

¢–$ 🏨 **Changhang Merrylin Hotel.** The Merrylin Corporation is better known throughout China for its restaurants than its hotels, and Changhang Mer-rylin Hotel's exceptional Chinese restaurant overshadows its fair-size inexpensive rooms. Decor aspires to European grandeur but comes off as amusingly tacky. Reliefs and golden statues of frolicking nymphs dom-inate the lobby, and rooms are decked out in gold-flecked wallpaper and crackled white-painted fixtures. Service can be brusque, but the loca-tion is convenient, within 3 blocks of the 10-story Next Age Depart-ment Store and metro Line 2 to Puxi. ⊠ *818 Zhangyang Lu, Pudong 200122* ☎ *021/5835–5555* 📠 *021/5835–7799* 🛏 *192 rooms, 32 suites* ⚴ *3 restaurants, room service, minibars, cable TV, hair salon, lobby lounge, shops, dry cleaning, laundry service, concierge, Internet, busi-ness services, meeting rooms, airport shuttle, parking (fee)* ⊟ *AE, DC, MC, V.*

Nanjing Xi Lu & Jing'an

$$$$ 🏨 **The Four Seasons.** With palm trees, fountains, and golden-hued mar-ble as warm as sunshine, the lobby of the Four Seasons establishes the hotel's theme as an elegant oasis in bustling downtown Puxi. Opened in 2002, this 37-story luxury hotel caters to its largely business clien-tele. It has impeccable service, a 24-hour business center, a gym, and butler service. The spacious rooms—just 12 to 15 per floor—include safes big enough for a laptop, DVD/CD players, and marble showers and tubs (one of each). Nanjing Road and the Shanghai Museum are

within a 10-minute walk, but there are convincing reasons to stay in: the Jazz 37 club; the exceptional Si Ji Xuan Cantonese restaurant; and ■ TIP→ you don't want to miss one of the spa's indulgent Balinese treatments. ⊠ *500 Weihai Lu, Jing'an 200041* ☏ *021/6256–8888 or 800/819–5053* 🖷 *021/6256–5678* ⊕ *www.fourseasons.com* ↰ *360 rooms, 79 suites* ♨ *4 restaurants, room service, some in-room faxes, in-room safes, minibars, cable TV, in-room VCRs, in-room data ports, Wi-Fi, pool, gym, hair salon, hot tub, spa, steam room, bar, lounge, shop, babysitting, dry cleaning, laundry service, concierge, concierge floor, Internet, business services, convention center, travel services, parking (fee), no-smoking floors* ⊟ *AE, DC, MC, V.*

$$$$ ⊡ **The Portman Ritz-Carlton.** Outstanding facilities and a high-profile location in the Shanghai Center have made the Portman Ritz-Carlton one of the city's top attractions since its opening in 1998. The 50-story hotel devotes three floors solely to its fitness center and another four to its executive club rooms. The two-story lobby—a popular networking spot and the location of the best afternoon tea in town—exudes cool refinement with its ebony, marble, and chrome touches. Renovations to be completed in 2007 will spruce up all guest rooms with plasma TVs and DVD players. In addition to the Shanghai Center's surrounding shops, banks, airline offices, and restaurants, the hotel has its own deli and four top-notch restaurants. Though the hotel touts its consistent rankings as one of the best employers and hotels in Asia, there have been complaints that service has slipped and there are often long lines for the concierge and taxi stand. ⊠ *1376 Nanjing Xi Lu, Jing'an 200040* ☏ *021/6279–8888 or 800/241–3333* 🖷 *021/6279–8887* ⊕ *www.ritzcarlton.com* ↰ *510 rooms, 68 suites* ♨ *4 restaurants, snack bar, room service, in-room safes, minibars, cable TV, in-room data ports, tennis court, indoor-outdoor pool, health club, hair salon, hot tub, massage, sauna, steam room, racquetball, squash, 2 bars, shops, babysitting, dry cleaning, laundry service, concierge, concierge floor, Internet, business services, convention center, helipad, parking (fee), no-smoking rooms* ⊟ *AE, DC, MC, V.*

$–$$$$ ⊡ **Heng Shan Moller Villa.** Part gingerbread dollhouse, part castle, the Heng Shan Moller Villa was built by British businessman Eric Moller to resemble a castle his daughter envisioned in a dream. The family fled Shanghai in 1941, and after 1949 the house was the Communist Youth League's headquarters. Opened as a boutique hotel in 2002, the original villa has 11 deluxe rooms and has been ostentatiously restored with parquet floors, chintzy crystal chandeliers, and too much gold paint. Standard rooms in the new Building No. 2 are disappointingly plain and service is merely perfunctory. Guests have access to the neighboring Shanghai Grand Club's excellent fitness center. ⊠ *30 Shaanxi Nan Lu, Luwan 200040* ☏ *021/6247–8881 Ext. 607* 🖷 *021/6289–1020* ⊕ *www.mollervilla.com* ↰ *40 rooms, 5 suites* ♨ *6 restaurants, coffee shop, some in-room safes, minibars, cable TV, in-room data ports, hair salon, shop, laundry service, Internet, business services, meeting rooms, free parking* ⊟ *AE, DC, MC, V.*

North Shanghai

$–$$$$ **Astor House Hotel.** The oldest hotel in China, the Astor House Hotel does an admirable job of capturing the feeling of Victorian Shanghai. The lobby's dark-wood columns and vaulted ceilings are accented by potted orchids and photos of famous visitors from the hotel's illustrious past (including Charlie Chaplin, Ulysses Grant, and Albert Einstein). The hotel has maintained its popularity with both budget and business travelers with its spacious, high-ceilinged rooms, often decorated with historical memorabilia, which more than compensate for the hotel's lack of views. We especially like Executive Room A, with its hardwood floors, oriental carpet, and rain shower. ■ TIP→ **Skip the renovated modern penthouse rooms—they lack the historical charm of the lower floors.** ✉ *15 Huangpu Lu, Hongkou 200080* ☎ *021/6324–6388* 🖷 *021/6324–3179* ⊕ *www.astorhotel.com* ✈ *127 rooms, 3 suites* ⅋ *2 restaurants, café, room service, in-room data ports, some in-room faxes, some in-room safes, some minibars, cable TV, some in-room VCRs, gym, hair salon, bar, piano, shops, baby-sitting, dry cleaning, laundry service, concierge, Internet, business services, convention center, free parking, no-smoking rooms* ▭ *AE, DC, MC, V.*

$ 🏠 **Broadway Mansions Hotel.** One of Shanghai's revered old buildings, the Broadway Mansions Hotel has anchored the north end of the Bund since 1934. Although the good-size rooms were last updated in 2001, the worn wood furniture, industrial bathrooms, and steam radiators betray their age. In contrast, business rooms are strikingly modern, with cool gray-and-tan interiors, glass-topped desks and nightstands, and separate marble showers and tubs. River-view rooms cost Y100 extra; request a higher floor to reduce the street noise. ✉ *20 Suzhou Bei Lu, Hongkou 200080* ☎ *021/6324–6260 Ext. 2326* 🖷 *021/6306–5147* ⊕ *www.broadwaymansions.com* ✈ *161 rooms, 72 suites* ⅋ *2 restaurants, café, patisserie, room service, some in-room faxes, some in-room safes, minibars, cable TV, in-room data ports, gym, hair salon, massage, sauna, 2 bars, piano, babysitting, laundry service, concierge floor, Internet, business services, meeting rooms, airport shuttle, some free parking* ▭ *AE, DC, MC, V.*

$ 🏠 **Panorama Century Court.** In a part of town dominated by historic properties, Panorama Century Court stands out for its modern facilities, competitive prices, and great Bund views from across the Waibaidu Bridge. The 32-story Accor-owned hotel attracts European tourists familiar with the brand as well as business travelers. One- to three-bedroom suites all include living rooms and tiny kitchens, but you'll have to request utensils. Standard rooms have thoughtfully designed bathrooms with handy shelves for toiletries. If you want to take full advantage of the view, ■ TIP→ **ask for a room above the 18th floor—otherwise your river view will be blocked by a billboard.** ✉ *53 Huangpu Lu, Hongkou 200080* ☎ *021/5393–0008* 🖷 *021/5393–0009* ✈ *62 rooms, 92 suites* ⅋ *Restaurant, room service, in-room safes, some kitchens, minibars, microwaves, refrigerators, cable TV, in-room data ports, gym, sauna, steam room, lobby lounge, library, piano, laundry facilities, laundry service, concierge, Internet, business services, meeting rooms, free parking* ▭ *AE, DC, MC, V.*

Hongqiao & Gubei

$$$$ 🗔 **The Regent.** This newcomer to town is already giving Shanghai's other five-star hotels a run for their money. All rooms come with 42" flat-screen TVs, luxurious rain showers, and dazzling city views. The Regent's location outside the city center, on the edge of the Former French Concession, is more than compensated by the hotel's choice of eight restaurants, L'Institute de Guerlain Spa, and stunning infinity edge lap pool, where guests can feel as if they are swimming off into Puxi's cityscape. Guests also rave about the studio and corner suite's exceptional showers, which look out through a wall of glass to sweeping views of downtown Shanghai. An extensive gym and outdoor tennis courts add to the hotel's cachet. ⊠ *1116 Yan'an Xi Lu, Hongqiao 200052* ☎ *021/ 6115–9988* 🖷 *021/6115–9977* ⊕ *www.regenthotels.com* 🛏 *511 rooms, 83 suites* ♨ *8 restaurants, patisserie, in-room data ports, in-room safes, minibars, some in-room hot tubs, in-room VCRs by request, 2 tennis courts, indoor pool, gym, health club, hair salon, spa, bar, lobby lounge, babysitting, dry cleaning, laundry service, concierge, concierge floor, Internet, business services, convention center, travel services, free parking, no-smoking rooms, no-smoking floors* 🖃 *AE, DC, MC, V.*

$$$$ 🗔 **Sheraton Grand Tai Ping Yang.** Even after 16 years, the Sheraton Grand
Fodor'sChoice is still the go-to hotel for savvy business travelers staying in Hongqiao.
★ Formerly the Westin, this Japanese-managed property has four club floors, one-touch service by phone, and golf privileges at Shanghai International Golf Club. Oriental rugs, antique pottery, folding Chinese screens, and wooden masks and statues, all chosen by the hotel's General Manager on his travels, add personal touches that cannot be found at any other hotel in town. Spacious standard rooms include large desks and ergonomic chairs, and the plush grand rooms have oriental carpets and overstuffed chairs in the separate bed and sitting rooms. A grand staircase sweeps you from the formal lobby up to the 2nd floor and the exceptional Bauernstube deli. Giovanni's serves Italian food as impressive as its views from atop the 27th floor. ⊠ *5 Zunyi Nan Lu, Hongqiao 200336* ☎ *021/ 6275–8888 or 888/625–5144* 🖷 *021/6275–5420* ⊕ *www.sheratongrandshanghai.com* 🛏 *474 rooms, 22 suites* ♨ *5 restaurants, café, coffee shop, room service, in-room safes, minibars, cable TV, some in-room faxes, some in-room hot tubs, in-room data ports, Wi-Fi, in-room VCRs by request, golf privileges, pool, tennis court, gym, health club, jogging track, hair salon, massage, sauna, steam room, 2 bars, lobby lounge, piano, library, shops, babysitting, dry cleaning, laundry service, concierge, concierge floor, Internet, business services, convention center, travel services, parking (fee), no-smoking floors* 🖃 *AE, DC, MC, V.*

ARTS & NIGHTLIFE

By Lisa Movius   Fueled equally by expatriates and an increasingly adventurous population of locals, Shanghai boasts an active and diverse nightlife. It is hardly the *buyecheng* (city that never sleeps) of the 1930s pop song "Ye Lai Xiang"—most places peter out after 1 or 2 AM—but until then there's a bit of something for everyone. Offerings range from world-class swank to dark and dingy dens or from young Shanghainese kids screaming experimental punk to Filipino cover bands singing "Hotel California" in a hotel basement. Prices, scenes, crowds, and ambiance can range just as wildly.

Shanghai lacks the sort of performing-arts scene one would expect from a city its size, but it's getting there. The city has two world-class, state-of-the-art spaces in the Shanghai Grand Theater and the Oriental Art Center, but stodgy government management means their offerings are spotty at best. Things like acrobatics are solely of interest to tourists, and unrelated to this modern city's cultural life, however traditional forms of Chinese opera remain popular with older citizens and are even enjoying resurgences with the younger generation. The city also has several competent symphonies. The Shanghai Ballet and the Shanghai Folk Dance Troupe are excellent, although forced by official directive to restrain their creativity; both perform at the various theaters around town.

The Arts

Acrobatics

Shanghai Acrobatics Troupe. The Shanghai Acrobatics Troupe performs remarkable gravity-defying stunts at both the Shanghai Center Theater and Shanghai Circus World, a glittering gold and green dome located in the center of Jing'anthat that seats more than 1,600 people. ⊠ *Shanghai Center Theater, 1376 Nanjing Xi Lu, Jing'an* ☎ *021/6279–8945* ✉ *Shanghai Circus World 2266 Gong He Xin Lu, Zhabei* ☎ *021/6652–7750* ☉ *Shows daily at 7:30 PM* 🎟 *Y50–Y150.*

Chinese Opera

Kunju Opera Troupe. Kun opera, or Kunju, originated in Jiangsu Province more than 400 years ago. Because of the profound influence it exerted on other Chinese opera styles, it's often called the mother of Chinese opera. It's located in the lower part of the Former French Concession. ⊠ *9 Shaoxing Lu, Luwan* ☎ *021/6437–1012* 🎟 *Y20–Y50* ☉ *Performances Sat. at 1:30.*

Yifu Theatre. Not only Beijing Opera, but also China's other regional operas, such as Huju, Kunju, and Yueju, are performed regularly at this theater in the heart of the city center. Considered the marquee theater for opera in Shanghai, it's just a block off People's Square. Call the box office for schedule and ticket information. ⊠ *701 Fuzhou Lu, Huangpu* ☎ *021/6351–4668.*

Dance & Classical Music

Jing An Hotel. Every Sunday, the Shanghai Symphony Orchestra performs chamber music in the lobby of the Jing An Hotel. Past concerts have included pieces by Bach, Ravel, and Chinese composer Huang Yongxi. ⊠ *San Diego Hall, Jing An Hotel, 370 Huashan Lu, Jing'an* ☎ *021/6248–1888 Ext. 687* 🎟 *Y20.*

Shanghai Concert Hall. City officials spent $6 million in 2003 to move this 73-year-old hall two blocks to avoid the rumble from the nearby highway. Only then did they discover that they had moved it to sit over

BEST SPAS

The **Banyan Tree Spa** (✉ Westin Shanghai, 88 Henan Zhong Lu, 3rd fl., Huangpu District ☎ 021/6335–1888), the first China outpost of this ultraluxurious spa chain, occupies the 3rd floor of the Westin Shanghai. The spa's 13 chambers as well as its treatments are designed to reflect wu sing, the five elemental energies of Chinese philosophy: earth, gold, water, wood, and fire. Relax and enjoy one of five different massages (Y780 plus service charge), facials, body scrubs, or indulgent packages that combine all three.

Dragonfly (✉ 20 Donghu Lu, Xuhui District ☎ 021/5405–0008) is a therapeutic retreat center that has claimed the middle ground between expensive hotel spas and workmanlike blind-man massage parlors. Don the suede-soft treatment robes for traditional Chinese massage (Y120), or take them off for an aromatic oil massage (Y200).

The Three on the Bund complex includes the first **Evian Spa** (✉ Three on the Bund, Zhongshan Dong Yi Lu, Huangpu District ☎ 021/6321–6622) outside of France. Its 14 theme rooms offer treatments from head to toe and 9 different massages, including an Indian head massage (Y600) or a hot-stone aromatherapy massage (Y900).

With its exposed wood beams, unpolished bricks, and soothing fountains, the **Mandara Spa** (✉ 399 Nanjing Xi Lu, Huangpu District ☎ 021/5359–4969) in the JW Marriott resembles a traditional Chinese water town. Face, beauty, and body treatments include the spa's signature Mandara massage (Y960), a 90-minute treatment in which two therapists administer a blend of five massage styles: Shiatsu, Thai, Lomi Lomi, Swedish, and Balinese.

an even more rumbly subway line. Oops. It's the home of the Shanghai Symphony Orchestra and also hosts top-level classical musicians from around China and the world. ✉ *523 Yanan Dong Lu, Jing'an* ☎ *021/6386–9153.*

Shanghai Oriental Art Center. Designed to resemble a white magnolia in full bloom, the glass-shrouded Shanghai Oriental Art Center is an attempt to kick-start Pudong's performing-art scene, although thus far it has featured mostly unimpressive acts. This $94-million center hopes eventually to rival the Shanghai Grand Theater and includes a 2,000-seat symphony hall, 1,100-seat theater, and 300-seat auditorium. ✉ *425 Dingxiang Lu, Pudong* ☎ *021/3842–4800.*

★ **Xiahemi Warehouse.** Experimental-dance troupe Niao and other avant-garde performers use this small, underground space for rehearsals and occasional performances. ✉ *Longcao Lu, La. 200, No. 100, 3rd fl, Xujiahui* ☎ *021/5448–3368.*

Theater

Lyceum Theatre. Although the recent renovation of Shanghai's oldest theater sadly replaced the sumptuous dark wood with glaring marble and glass, the design of the space makes for an intimate theater experience. The Lyceum regularly hosts drama and music from around China as well as smaller local plays and Chinese opera performances.
✉ *57 Maoming Nan Lu, Luwan* ☎ *021/6217–8539.*

★ **Majestic Theatre.** Once Asia's largest movie theater, this elegantly restored, beautiful 1930s art-deco gem regularly presents top-ticket theater from China's major troupes, as well as novelty acts and some Western performances. The venue does not have an affiliated drama troupe, so the space is open to all sundry comers. ✉ *66 Jiangning Lu, Jing'an* ☎ *021/6217–4409.*

Fodor'sChoice **Shanghai Dramatic Arts Center.** Shanghai's premier theater venue and
★ troupe, with several busy stages, the Dramatic Arts Center presents an award-winning lineup of its own original pieces, plus those of other cutting-edge groups around China. It also stages Chinese-language adaptations, sometimes very inventive, of Western works, such as a festival of Samuel Beckett works reinterpreted through Chinese opera. It also invites a steady lineup of renowned international performers, such as the Royal Shakespeare Company. Despite being a state-owned institution, the Shanghai Dramatic Arts Center manages to offset sumptuous historical epics with small, provocative plays that examine burning social issues like infidelity, divorce, finances, and AIDS. ✉ *288 Anfu Lu, Xuhui* ☎ *021/6473–4567.*

Shanghai Grand Theater. As the premier stage in town, the Shanghai Grand Theater hosts top national and international performances. When Broadway shows come to Shanghai—such as *The Lion King* in 2006—they play here. ✉ *300 Renmin Dadao, Huangpu* ☎ *021/6372–8701, 021/ 6372–8702, or 021/6372–3833.*

Nightlife

Bars

XINTIANDI & CITY **Barbarossa.** Above the lily pond in People's Park and next to the MoCA,
CENTER this beautiful Moroccan restaurant switches into a bar at night. Usually quiet and classy, it becomes crowded and crazy on Thursday, when women drink free. ✉ *231 Nanjing Xi Lu, Huangpu* ☎ *021/6318–0220.*

TMSK. Short for Tou Ming Si Kao, this exquisitely designed little bar is an aesthete's dream. Glisteningly modern, TMSK is stunning—as are the prices of its drinks. ✉ *Xintiandi North Block, Unit 2, House 11, 181 Taicang Lu, Luwan* ☎ *021/6326–2227.*

NANJING DONG
LU & THE BUND

Bar Rouge. The gem in the crown of the trendy, upscale Bund 18 complex, Bar Rouge is the destination du jour of Shanghai's beautiful people. It has retained that distinction for a surprisingly long time, considering the fickle nature of Shanghai's denizens of the dark. Pouting models and visiting celebrities are among the regular clientele. ☒ *Bund 18 7F, 18 Zhongshan Dong Lu, Huangpu* ☏ *021/6339–1199.*

Glamour Bar. The lounge of the perennial favorite **M on the Bund,** Glamour Bar offers beautiful decor in a classy, low-key setting. However, ■ TIP➔ bar patrons are forbidden from visiting the restaurant's balcony and enjoying the view that made the place famous, so visitors not planning to eat should head to other Bund locations instead. ☒ *7F, 20 Guangdong Lu, Huangpu* ☏ *021/6350–9988.*

★ **Three on the Bund.** The sophisticated Three complex, suitably enough, encloses three different bars: the swanky, dark-wood paneled **Bar JG** on the 4th floor; the sleek white **Laris** on the 6th floor; and topped off by the more casual **New Heights/Third Degree** on the 7th floor. ☒ *3 Zhongshan Dong Lu, Huangpu* ☏ *021/6321–0909.*

FORMER FRENCH
CONCESSION

★ **Arch Bar and Café.** For an artsy expatriate circle, head to Arch. Its location in Shanghai's copy of the Flatiron building and in a popular residential district attracts architects and design professionals. ☒ *439 Wukang Lu, Xuhui* ☏ *021/6466–0807.*

Fodor'sChoice
★ **Cotton's.** This friendly, laid-back favorite moved many times before settling into the current old garden house. Busy without being loud, Cotton's is a rare place where you can have a conversation with friends—or make some new ones. ☒ *132 Anting Lu, Xuhui* ☏ *021/6433–7995.*

Face. Once the see-and-be-seen place in Shanghai, Face's hipster clientele have mostly moved to Manifesto with former owner Charlie, leaving it mostly a tourist destination. But it's still beautiful: candlelit tables outside and a four-poster bed inside are the most vied-for spots in this colonial villa with Indonesian furnishings. ☒ *Bldg. 4, Ruijin Hotel, 118 Ruijin Er Lu, Luwan* ☏ *021/6466–4328.*

★ **Time Passage.** Shanghai has always been a place more inclined toward slick nightclubs and posh wine bars than mellow, conversation dives, but Time Passage has always been the exception. Cheap beers, friendly service, and a cool, if grungy, atmosphere makes it the best way to start—

WHAT'S ON

Nightlife is a difficult business in Shanghai, and, aside from a few stalwarts, venues can open and close faster than the speed of apartment block construction, and even places that retain the same name and location can rapidly change owners, concepts, and clientele. For up-to-date information, check out *That's Shanghai* and *City Weekend,* monthly and bi-weekly expatriate magazines available at Western bars, restaurants, and hotels throughout town; or *Shanghai Daily,* the English-language newspaper.

or end—a night on the town. ⊠ *Huashan Lu, La. 1038, No. 183, by Fuxing Lu, Xuhui* ☎ *021/6240–2588.*

Windows. Shanghai's budget-drinking chain, Windows lures patrons with Y10 drinks. Packed solid on weekends, chill on weekdays, it's the place to meet foreign students and hard-core booze hounds. ⊠ *Windows Roadside: 186 Maoming Nan Lu, Luwan* ☎*021/6445–7863* ⊠ *Windows Scorecard: 681 Huaihai Zhong Lu 3F, Xuhui* ☎ *021/5382–7757* ⊠ *Windows Tembo: 66 Shaanxi Bei Lu, Jing'an* ☎ *021/5116–8857* ⊠ *Windows Too: J104, Jingan Si Plaza J104, 1669 Nanjing Xi Lu, Jing'an* ☎*021/3214–0351.*

PUDONG **Dublin Exchange.** Dublin Exchange is a great place for a Pudong pint. Its upmarket Irish banker's-club ambiance caters to the growing wannabe Wall Street that is Lujiazui. ⊠ *HSBC Bldg., 2nd fl., 101 Yincheng Dong Lu, Pudong* ☎ *021/6841–2052.*

NANJING XI LU & **Manifesto.** The mastermind behind Face opened this coolly minimalist
JING'AN yet warmly welcoming space and took most of his clientele with him.
★ Popular with foreigners and local white-collars alike, it serves up standard cocktails plus excellent tapas from its sister restaurant Mesa. ⊠ *748 Julu Lu, Jing'an* ☎ *021/6289–9108.*

HONGQIAO **The Door.** The stunningly extravagant interior of the Door distracts from
Fodor'sChoice the bar's overpriced drinks. Take in the soaring wood-beam ceilings, slid-
★ ing doors, and the museum's worth of antiques as you listen to the eclectic house band, which plays modern, funky riffs on Chinese music on the *erhu, pipa,* and other traditional instruments. ⊠ *4F, 1468 Hongqiao Lu, Changning* ☎ *021/6295–3737.*

Dance Clubs

XINTIANDI & CITY **Pegasus.** It began life as just another
CENTER dance club, but Pegasus took wing after restyling itself into the top place for aspiring hip-hop DJs to battle it out. Regular mix-off competitions really pull in the crowds. ⊠ *Golden Bell Plaza 2F, 98 Huaihai Zhong Lu, Luwan* ☎ *021/5385–8187.*

FORMER FRENCH **California Club.** Celebrity guest DJs
CONCESSION play everything from tribal to disco for the bold and beautiful crowd at this hip establishment. The club is part of the Lan Kwai Fong complex at Park 97, which also includes Baci and Tokio Joe's restaurants. ⊠ *Park 97, 2A Gaolan Lu, Luwan* ☎ *021/5383–2328.*

Judy's Too. A veteran on the club scene, Judy's Too is infamous for its hard-partying, meat-market crowd.

GETTING AROUND

Although downtown Shanghai is fairly compact, suburban sprawl is creeping in nefariously. Most nightlife destinations are downtown, but pockets of activity are creeping up in farther-flung areas. Go by taxi: it's fairly safe and fairly affordable. Prices are rising, and some drivers will take advantage of drunk or ignorant passengers and go the "scenic" route, so be sure to keep your wits about you and your eyes on the route. Also, many taxi drivers are new and from out of town, so some simply do not know where they are going.

TOP NIGHTLIFE NEIGHBORHOODS

Once exclusive province of downtown, bars and clubs now dot all parts of Shanghai. There are, however, a few concentrations for those hoping to hop conveniently.

Maoming Nan Lu, has long been Shanghai's nightlife hub, with the slightly seedy offerings of the main drag contrasting with the classy, upscale venues—most notably, **Face**—in the adjacent Ruijin Guest House, a hotel complex that takes up an entire city block. Threats to shut it down have yet to materialize, but much of the action has migrated elsewhere, to the new **Tongren Lu** bar street. Tongren Lu does have some good clubs for those who like their nightlife on the wild side. The infamous **Julu Lu** bar street is still

going strong. All three of these are crowded with "fishing girls," who ask gents to give them money to buy drinks in exchange for their company (or something more)—and then they either pocket the money or take a cut from the bar.

Those looking for less-blatant sexual commerce should head to the popular bar, restaurant, and shopping complex of **Xintiandi,** an old Shanghai pastiche with an array of clean and pleasant but pricey bars. **The Bund** is gradually emerging as a center for upscale dining and drinking, and several new spaces slated to open in the upcoming years will serve to cement its position. **Hengshan Lu** and **Fuxing Park** also offer concentrations of bars and clubs.

The den of iniquity was memorialized in Wei Hui's racy novel *Shanghai Baby,* among others. ✉ *176 Maoming Nan Lu, by Yongjia Lu, Luwan* ☎ *021/6473–1417.*

Real Love. Still going strong despite the fickleness of Shanghai's nightlife patrons, Real Love remains the most popular place for young Shanghainese to bop to pop tunes. It is worth going just to watch the sincere, eager young crowd—quite a contrast from the jaded clientele at most of the city's clubs. Such is the popularity that it creates traffic jams on Hengshan Lu most nights. ✉ *10 Hengshan Lu, Xuhui* ☎ *021/6474–6830.*

NANJING XI LU & JING'AN

Fodor'sChoice ★

Mint. One of Shanghai's most popular clubs, as much for its location in a gorgeous old Bauhaus mansion as for its dance music, Mint has special guest DJs most weekends. ✉ *333 Tongren Lu, 2F, Jing'an* ☎ *021/6247–9666.*

NORTH SHANHAI ★

Pier One. Looking to single-handedly transform the Suzhou Creek district from an artists' colony into a clubbing destination, Pier One occupies a cavernous historic warehouse. The space includes a dance club, **Minx,** with schedules online at www.minx.com.cn, an **Art Deco** lounge bar, **Jacuzzi Monsoon,** and the **Mimosa Supperclub** restaurant. ✉ *82 Yi Chang Lu, next to Suzhou Creek at Shaanxi Bei Lu, Zhabei* ☎ *021/5155–8310.*

Karaoke

Karaoke is ubiquitous in Shanghai. Many KTV bars employ "KTV girls" who sing along with (male) guests and serve cognac and expensive snacks. (At most establishments, KTV girls are also prostitutes.) That said, karaoke is a popular—and sometimes legitimate—pastime among locals. Many bars also have KTV rooms, but these places are dedicated karaoke establishments.

Haoledi. Crowded at all hours with locals of all ages crooning pop favorites, the popular Haoledi chain has branches virtually everywhere. These listed are just a few of the outlets downtown. ⊠ *1111 Zhaojiabang Lu, Xuhui* ☎ *021/6311–5858* ⊠ *180 Xizang Zhong Lu, Luwan* ☎ *021/6311–5858* ⊠ *438 Huaihai Zhong Lu, Luwan* ☎ *021/ 6311–5858.*

Party World. This giant establishment is one of Shanghai's most popular KTV bars, and among the few that's dedicated to the KTV instead of the KTV girls. Its warren of rooms is packed nightly. ⊠ *459 Wulumuqi Bei Lu, Jing'an* ☎ *021/6374–1111* ⊠ *109 Yandan Lu, inside Fuxing Park, Luwan* ☎ *021/5306–3888* ⊠ *68 Zhejiang Lu Huangpu* ☎ *021/6374–1111.*

Live Music

XINTIANDI & CITY CENTER **CJW.** The acronym says it all: cigars, jazz, and wine are what this swank lounge is all about. Its second location atop the Bund Center throws in a breathtaking view of the river. ⊠ *Xintiandi, House 2, 123 Xingye Lu, Luwan* ☎ *021/6385–6677* ⊠ *Bund Center 50F, 222 Yanan Dong Lu, Huangpu* ☎ *021/6329–9932.*

FORMER FRENCH CONCESSION **Club JZ.** Reincarnated in a new venue, JZ continues its role as the king of Shanghai's jazz offerings. Most nights the solid house band grooves, ★ but occasionally guest performers from around the world take the stage. ⊠ *46 Fuxing Xi Lu, Xuhui* ☎ *021/6431–0269.*

Cotton Club. A dark and smoky jazz and blues club, the Cotton Club is an institution in Shanghai and still one of the best places to catch live jazz. The house band is a mix of Chinese and foreign musicians with a sound akin to Blues Traveler. ⊠ *8 Fuxing Xi Lu, Xuhui* ☎ *021/ 6437–7110.*

★ **House of Blues and Jazz.** Decked out in memorabilia from Shanghai's jazz era of the 1930s, Blues and Jazz would be a great bar even without the music. But the several nightly sets make it a must visit. Owner Lin Dongfu, a local television personality, ensures a steady stream of minor celebrities, if the band isn't entertainment enough. ⊠ *158 Maoming Nan Lu, Luwan* ☎ *021/6437–5280.*

★ **Tanghui.** Weekends at Tanghui see some of Shanghai rock's perennial favorites rocking out downstairs.

WHAT TO WEAR
The Shanghai dress code is fairly laid-back, and even nicer establishments are unlikely to turn away the casually dressed. Women in Shanghai like to doll it up, and are very brand-conscious, but one need not feel obliged to follow suit; men usually head out in jeans and a tee or polo shirt. Smoking is universal in China's bars and clubs, so wear clothing that washes well or that you don't mind carrying a souvenir fragrance of smoke and stale beer.

BEST HOTEL BARS

Cloud 9. Perched on the 87th floor of the Grand Hyatt, Cloud 9 is the highest bar in the world. It has unparalleled views of Shanghai from among—and often above—the clouds. The sky-high views come with sky-high prices: ■ TIP→ there's a two-drink minimum in the evening, so go in the late afternoon to avoid this. The class is offset with kitsch, as Chinese fortune-tellers and various artisans ply their skills to customers. ⊠ Grand Hyatt, 88 Shiji Dadao, Pudong ☎ 021/5049–1234.

Jade on 36. This gorgeous, swanky new spot in the new tower of the Pudong Shangri-La has swish drinks in a swish setting. Exquisite design and corresponding views (when Shanghai's pollution levels cooperate) have made Jade popular with the "in" set. ⊠ Pudong Shangri-La, Tower 2, 36F 33 Fucheng, Pudong ☎ 021/6882–3636.

Jazz Bar. Within the historic and romantic Peace Hotel, this German-style pub has earned its fame due to the nightly performances (tickets, Y80) of the Peace Hotel Old Jazz Band. The musicians, whose average age is above 70, played jazz in dance halls in pre-1949

Shanghai. However, they're not quite as swingin' as in their prime, and a sense of tradition, rather than the quality of the music, has sustained these performances. ⊠ Peace Hotel, 20 Nanjing Dong Lu, Huangpu ☎ 021/6321–6888.

Jazz 37. The Four Seasons' jazz bar matches its penthouse view with a stylish interior. Grab a canary-yellow leather chair by the white grand piano for some top-quality live jazz. ⊠ The Four Seasons, 37F, 500 Weihai Lu, Jing'an ☎ 021/6256–8888.

JW Lounge. At the top of the JW Marriott, this lounge has a panoramic view of downtown Shanghai. ⊠ JW Marriott, 40F, 399 Nanjing Xi Lu, Huangpu ☎ 021/5359–4969.

Ye Lai Xiang (The Garden Hotel Bar). Few people know the real name of the Garden Hotel's terrace bar. Considered one of the most romantic spots in town for a drink when the weather is nice, this 3rd-floor terrace overlooks the fountain and hotel's namesake 2-acre garden. ⊠ Okura Garden Hotel, 58 Maoming Nan Lu, Luwan ☎ 021/6415–1111.

The rest of the week brings a more eclectic line up. Lounges on the 2nd and 3rd floors facilitate DJ parties or just hanging out. ⊠ *85 Huating Lu, Xuhui* ☎ *021/6281–5646.*

Yuyintang Warehouse. No one or thing has done as much to bring Shanghai rock out from the underground and into the open than the Yuyintang collective. Headed by sound engineer and former musician Zhang Haisheng, the group started organizing regular concerts around town and eventually opened their own space. Regular concerts, usually on Friday and Saturday nights or Sunday afternoons, spotlight the best and latest in Chinese music. Visit www.yuyintang.com for a schedule. ⊠ *Longcao Lu, La. 200, No. 100, 1F, Xuhui* ☎ *021/6436–0072.*

SHOPPING

By Elyse
Singleton

When in Shanghai, do as the locals do and hit the shops hard. Ask some-one in the street their favorite hobby, and if they don't say basketball or PC games, they will probably say shopping. New stores open each day—from glittering luxury behemoths to tiny boutiques with barely any breathing room. Shopping here is a voyage of discovery that is best done on foot so as to discover the little surprises, especially in areas like the former French Concession.

Shanghai gets up late and opening hours really vary. Malls don't usu-ally open until 10 and boutiques at 11 AM. The upside is stores tend to stay open later, with many closing at 10 PM. Markets generally start ear-lier, at around 8:30 or 9:30 AM, and close at around 6 PM. Most stores are open seven days a week.

Malls & Department Stores

NANJING DONG
LU & THE BUND

Shanghai No. 1 Department Store. Shanghai's largest state-owned store attracts masses of Chinese shoppers, especially on weekends. It sells every-thing from porcelain dinnerware to badminton racquets and is popu-lar with much of Shanghai's male population who want no-nonsense, one-stop shopping. ⊠ *830 Nanjing Dong Lu, Huangpu* ☎ *021/6322–3344.*

Brilliance Shimao International Plaza. This mall near People's Square (it was finished in 2006) stocks some high-end designers such as Givenchy mixed in with midrange ones such as Lacoste and Esprit. ⊠ *829 Nan-jing Dong Lu, Huangpu* ☎ *021/3313–4718.*

Raffles City. Near People's Square, Raffles City has midrange foreign and local designer stores including funky streetwear such as Miss Sixty, Roxy, and FCUK. It also has a movie theater showing both Chinese and some foreign films, and a food court in the basement with snacks and drinks. ⊠ *268 Xizang Zhong Lu, Huangpu* ☎ *021/6340–3600.*

PUDONG

Next Age. This veritable behemoth of a department store–meets-mall has loads of foreign brands, especially in the beauty department. ⊠ *501 Zhangyang Lu, Pudong* ☎ *021/5830–1111.*

Super Brand Mall. At 10 stories, this is one of Asia's largest malls. It has a massive Lotus supermarket along with a mind-boggling array of shops and food stops, and a movie complex. It can be overwhelming if you don't love to shop. ⊠ *168 Lujiazui Lu, Pudong* ☎ *021/6887–7888.*

Xinmei Union Square. Smaller, newer, and funkier than Pudong's other malls, Xinmei has a focus on hip foreign brands such as Miss Sixty, G-Star Raw, Fornarina, and Swatch. ⊠ *999 Pudong Nan Lu, Pudong* ☎ *021/5134–1888.*

XUJIAHUI &
SOUTH
SHANGHAI

Grand Gateway. Look for the dome; beneath you'll find more than 1.4-million-square feet of shopping and entertainment, including a movie complex, restaurants, and floor after floor of clothing stores, plus a large number of Shanghai's shoppers. ✉ *1 Hongqiao Lu, Xuhui* ☎ *021/6407–0115.*

Specialty Shops

Antiques

XINTIANDI & CITY CENTER   **Shanghai Art Deco.** It looks like an old junk shop but Shanghai Art Deco has a wonderful selection of radios, old tin advertising signs, furniture, and retro household items like Revolution-era teapots and double happiness trays. ✉ *107 Dongtai Lu, Luwan* ☎ *021/6387–6048.*

★ **Zhen Zhen.** Friendly owner Mr. Liu sells a range of lamps, gramophones, fans, and other electrical equipment salvaged from Shanghai's glorious past. Some of his stock has been bought by chic restaurants like M on the Bund, and most are in some kind of working order. A small glass lamp base will set you back about Y100. ✉ *11 Dongtai Lu, Luwan* ☎ *021/6385–8793.*

NANJING DONG LU & THE BUND   **Shanghai Antique and Curio Store.** A pleasant departure from the touristy shops in area, this government-owned store is an excellent place to gauge whether you are being taken for a ride elsewhere. Goods start as low as Y20 for small pieces of embroidery, and items range from ceramics to wedding baskets (traditionally used to hold part of the brides' dowry). Be aware that some of the pieces may not be taken out of the country, as a sign in the ceramics store warns. ✉ *192–246 Guangdong Lu, Huangpu* ☎ *021/6321–5868.*

★ **Madame Mao's Dowry.** A covetable collection of mostly revolutionary-propaganda items from the '50s, '60s, and '70s sourced from the countryside and areas in Sichuan province and around Beijing and Tianjin mixed in with hip designs from local and international designers. Although this could be your one-stop shopping experience, remember this is communism at capitalist prices: Y800 for a small Revolution-era teapot and around Y1,800 for a Revolution-era mirror. ✉ *70 Fuxing Xi Lu, Xuhui* ☎ *021/6437–1255* ✉ *Gallery: 50 Moganshan Lu, Building 6, 5th fl., Putuo* ☎ *021/6276–9932.*

NORTH SHANGHAI   **Henry Antique Warehouse.** Named the number-one shop in Shanghai by *Shanghai 8 Days,* an expat magazine, this company is the antique Chinese–furniture research, teaching, and training institute for Tongji University. Part of the showroom sometimes serves as an exhibition hall for the modern designs created jointly by students and the warehouse's 50 craftsmen. Wandering through the pieces on display is a trek through Chinese history; from intricately carved traditional altar tables to 1920s deco furniture. ✉ *796 Suining Lu, Changning* ☎ *021/5219–4871* ⊕ *www.antique-designer.com.*

XUJIAHUI & SOUTH SHANGHAI   **Hu & Hu Antiques.** Co-owner Marybelle Hu worked at Taipei's National Palace Museum as well as Sotheby's in Los Angeles before opening this shop with sister-in-law Lin in 1998. Their bright, airy showroom ★ contains Tibetan chests and other rich furniture as well as a large selection of accessories, from lanterns to mooncake molds. Their prices

Continued on page 284

MARKETS
A GUIDE TO BUYING SILK, PEARLS & POTTERY

Chinese markets are hectic and crowded, but great fun for the savvy shopper. The intensity of the bargaining and the sheer number of goods available are pretty much unsurpassed anywhere else in the world.

Nowadays wealthier Chinese may prefer to flash their cash in department stores and designer boutiques, but generally, markets are still the best places to shop. Teens spend their pocket money at cheap clothing markets. Grandparents, often toting their grandchildren, go to their local neighborhood food market almost daily to pick up fresh items such as tofu, fish, meat, fruit, and vegetables. Markets are also great places to mix with the locals, see the drama of bargaining take place, and watch as the Chinese banter, play with their children, challenge each other to cards, debate, or just lounge.

Some markets have a mishmash of items, whereas others are more specialized, dealing in one particular ware. Markets play an essential part in the everyday life of the Chinese and prices paid are always a great topic of conversation. A compliment on a choice article will often elicit the price paid in reply and a discussion may ensue on where to get the same thing at an even lower cost.

GREAT FINDS

The prices we list below are meant to give you an idea of what you can pay for certain items. Actual post-bargaining prices will of course depend on how well you haggle, while pre-bargaining prices are often based on how much the vendor thinks he or she can get out of you.

PEARLS

Many freshwater pearls are grown in Taihu; seawater pearls come from Japan or the South Seas. Some have been dyed and others mixed with semiprecious stones. Designs can be pretty wild and the clasps are not of very high quality, but necklaces and bracelets are cheap. Post-bargaining, a plain, short strand of pearls should cost around Y40.

ETHNIC-MINORITY HANDICRAFTS

Brightly colored skirts from the Miao minority and embroidered jackets from the Yunnan area are great boho souvenirs. The heavy, elaborate jewelry could decorate a side table or hang on a wall. Colorful children's shoes are embellished with animal faces and bells. After bargaining, a skirt in the markets should go for between Y220 to Y300, and a pair of children's shoes for Y40 to Y60.

RETRO

Odd items from the hedonistic '20s to the revolutionary '60s and '70s include treasures like old light fixtures and tin advertising signs. A rare sign such as one banning foreigners from entry may cost as much as Y10,000, but small items such as teapots can be bought for around Y250. Retro items are harder to bargain down for than mass-produced items.

"MAOMORABILIA"

The Chairman's image is readily available on badges, bags, lighters, watches, ad infinitum. Pop-art-like figurines of Mao and his Red Guards clutching red books are kitschy but iconic. For soundbites and quotes from the Great Helmsman, buy the Little Red Book itself. Pre-bargaining, a badge costs Y25, a bag Y50, and a ceramic figurine Y380. Just keep in mind that many posters are fakes.

CERAMICS

Most ceramics you'll find in markets are factory-made, so you probably won't stumble upon a bargain Ming Dynasty vase, but ceramics in a variety of colors can be picked up at reasonable prices. Opt for pretty pieces decorated with butterflies, or for the more risqué, copulating couples. A bowl-and-plate set goes for around Y25, a larger serving plate Y50.

BIRDCAGES

Wooden birdcages with domed roofs make charming decorations, with or without occupants. They are often seen being carried by old men as they promenade their feathered friends. A pre-bargaining price for a medium-size wooden cage is around Y180.

JADE

A symbol of purity and beauty for the Chinese, jade comes in a range of colors. Subtle and simple bangles vie for attention with large sculptures on market stalls. A lavender jade Guanyin (Goddess of Mercy) pendant runs at Y260 and a green jade bangle about Y280 before bargaining.

PROPAGANDA AND COMIC BOOKS

Follow the actions of Chinese revolutionary hero, Lei Feng, or look for scenes from Chinese history and lots of *gongfu* (Chinese martial arts) stories. Most titles are in Chinese and often in black and white, but look out for titles like *Tintin and the Blue Lotus*, set in Shanghai and translated into Chinese. You can bargain down to around Y15 for less popular titles.

SILK

Bolts and bolts of silk brocade with blossoms, butterflies, bamboo, and other patterns dazzle the eye. An enormous range of items made from silk, from purses to slippers to traditional dresses, are available at most markets. Silk brocade costs around Y35 per meter, a price that is generally only negotiable if you buy large quantities.

MAH-JONGG SETS

The clack-clack of mah-jongg tiles can be heard late into the night on the streets of most cities in summer. Cheap plastic sets go for about Y50. Far more aesthetically pleasing are ceramic sets in slender drawers of painted cases. These run about Y250 after bargaining, from a starting price of Y450. Some sets come with instructions, but if not, instructions for the "game of four winds" can be downloaded in English at www.mahjongg.com.

SHOPPING KNOW-HOW

When to Go

Avoid weekends if you can and try to go early in the morning, from 8 AM to 10 AM, or at the end of the day just before 6 PM. Rainy days are also good bets for avoiding the crowds and getting better prices.

Bringin' Home the Goods

Although that faux-Gucci handbag is tempting, remember that some countries have heavy penalties for the import of counterfeit goods. Likewise, that animal fur may be cheap, but you may get fined a lot more at your home airport than what you paid for it. Counterfeit goods are generally prohibited in the United States, but there's some gray area regarding goods with a "confusingly similar" trademark. Each person is allowed to bring in one such item, as long as it's for personal use and not for resale. For more details, go to the travel section of www.cbp.gov. The HM and Revenue Customs Web site, www.hmrc.gov.uk, has a list of banned and prohibited goods for the United Kingdom.

⚠The Chinese government has regular and very public crackdowns on fake goods, so that store you went to today may have different items tomorrow. In Shanghai, for example, pressure from the Chinese government and other countries to protect intellectual property rights led to the demise of one of the city's largest and most popular markets, Xiangyang.

BEFORE YOU GO

■ Be prepared to be grabbed, pushed, followed, stared at, and even to have people whispering offers of items to buy in your ear. In China, personal space and privacy are not valued in the same way as in the West, so the invasion of it is common. Move away but remain calm and polite. No one will understand if you get upset anyway.

■ Many Chinese love to touch foreign children, so if you have kids, make sure they're aware of and prepared for this.

■ Keep money and valuables in a safe place. Pickpockets and bag-slashers are becoming common.

■ Pick up a cheap infrared laser pointer to detect counterfeit bills. The light illuminates the hidden anti-counterfeit ultraviolet mark in the real notes.

■ Check for fake items, e.g. silk and pearls.

■ Learn some basic greetings and numbers in Chinese. The local people will really appreciate it.

HOW TO BARGAIN

Successful bargaining requires the dramatic skills of a Hollywood actor. Here's a step-by-step guide to getting the price you want and having fun at the same time.

DO'S	DONT'S

Browsing in a silk shop

Chinese slippers at a ladies' market

- Start by deciding what you're willing to pay for an item.

- Look at the vendor and point to the item to indicate your interest.

- The vendor will quote you a price, usually by punching numbers into a calculator and showing it to you.

- Here, expressions of shock are required from you, which will never be as great as those of the vendor, who will put in an Oscar-worthy performance at your prices.

- Next it's up to you to punch in a number that's around 75% of the original price—or lower if you feel daring.

- Pass the calculator back and forth until you meet somewhere in the middle, probably at up to (and sometimes less than) 50% of the original quote.

- Don't enter into negotiations if you aren't seriously considering the purchase.

- Don't haggle over small sums of money.

- If the vendor isn't budging, walk away; he'll likely call you back.

- It's better to bargain if the vendor is alone. He's unlikely to come down on the price if there's an audience.

- Saving face is everything in China. Don't belittle or make the vendor angry, and don't get angry yourself.

- Remain pleasant and smile often.

- Buying more than one of something gets you a better deal.

- Dress down and leave your jewelry and watches in the hotel safe on the day you go marketing. You'll get a lower starting price if you don't flash your wealth.

SHANGHAI MARKETS

Antiques Market of Shanghai Old Town God Temple. (Huabao Building). Prices are high due to the prime location of this basement market in the main Yu Garden shopping complex. Shop No. 22 has revolution-era materials, including an original Little Red Book for Y180. No. 200 has textiles and embroidery starting at Y50 for a 5-cm-square patch. ☒ *Yu Garden, 265 Fangbang Zhonglu, Huangpu* ✛ *On the corner of Fangbang Lu* ☎ *021/6355-9999* ☼ *Daily 10 AM–6 PM.*

Cang Bao Antiques Building (Cang Bao Lou). During the week, you can browse four floors of booths that sell everything from Mao paraphernalia to real and fake antique porcelain. There are pearls in a wide range of colors and styles, starting from Y10 for a simple bracelet. Curios and other jewelry are on the ground floor, and check out the third floor for old photos, clothing, books, and obscure household kitsch. On Sunday the action starts long before sunrise, when, according to a local saying, only ghosts should be awake, hence the market's nickname: *guishi* or "ghost market." Hawkers from the provinces arrive early to lay out their goods on the sidewalk

or inside on the fourth floor. Ivory, jade, and wood carvings are among the many goods sold here, all at negotiable prices. ☒ *457 Fangbang Zhonglu, Huangpu* ✛ *End of Fangbang Lu near the gate to Henan Zhong Lu* ☼ *Weekdays 9–5:30, weekends 6 AM–5:30 PM.*

★ **Fodor's Choice** **Dongtai Lu Market.** Mao statues, tiny shoes for women with bound feet (though foot-binding is rarely practiced in China anymore), ethnic minority-crafted clothing and embroidery, ceramic bracelets, gramophones —it's all here. This is one of the best places in town to buy gifts and souvenirs, and it's within walking distance of the shops at Xintiandi. Most of the stalls sell similar items, so your bargaining power is high as you can just walk to another store if you don't like the price. Real antiques are rare. Squeeze behind the stalls to check out the shops in the back. ☒ *1266 Nanjing Xi Lu, Jing'an* ☎ *021/5306-8888* ✛ *Just west of Xizang Lu* ☼ *Daily 9 AM–6 PM.*

Fuyou Gate Market. This department-store-meets-market with a wild variety of items spreads over three floors. On the ground floor, shop No. 156 sells Nepali and Indian clothing and jewelry; No. 186 sells brightly colored Chinese folk textiles, including children's shoes; and on the second floor, shop No. 1 sells Korean stationery. ☒ *427 Fuyou Lu, Huangpu* ✛ *Take bus No. 66 from Xizang Nan Lu* ☼ *Daily 7 AM–5:30 PM.*

Fuyuan Market. The first floor of this market, also in the Yu Garden area, specializes in Chinese medicine. You can get jujube seeds for insomnia and kudzu vine flower for hangovers, or just wander around and marvel at the weird-looking ginseng. ☒ *338 Fuyou Lu, Huangpu* ✛ *Across the street and just east of Fuyou Gate Market* ☼ *Daily 8 AM–5:30 PM.*

Pu'an Lu Children's Market. A mecca for parents, children, and doting relatives, this underground market sells toys, accessories, shoes, and clothing for kids. Hunt out French and Swedish clothing brands, and big-name toy manufacturers such as Lego and Barbie, as well as some beautiful Japanese wooden toys. You might find a pretty dress for Y29 or a small wooden Noah's ark for Y35. ⊠ *10 Pu'an Lu Lu, Luwan* ⊹ *Take metro Line 1 to Huangpi Nan Lu and walk east down Huaihai Lu a few blocks, then turn left* ☉ *Daily 9:30 AM–6:30 PM.*

Qi Pu Clothing Wholesale Market. Three large buildings (and counting) are stuffed to the rafters with cheap clothing here. It's good for children's clothes, but women's clothing tends to be very petite, and shoe lovers with big feet will be heartbroken. You're most likely to come away with fake designer sneakers and a T-shirt printed with misspelled or vaguely obscene English. ⊠ *168 and 183 Qipu Lu, by Henan Bei Lu, Zhabei* ⊹ *Take bus No. 66 from Xizang Nan Lu to Qipu Lu, or take the long walk north from the Henan Zhong Lu metro stop* ☎ *021/ 5102–0001* ☉ *Daily 6 AM–6 PM.*

★ **Fodor's Choice** **South Bund Soft-Spinning Material Market.** The unusual name alludes to the veritable treasure chest of fabrics, from lurid synthetics to silk brocades, spread over three floors. Shop No. 313 can produce embroidery based on a digital image for Y40, while Nos. 231, 399, 353, and 161 are Aladdin's caves of buttons and braids. No. 189 has masses of silk brocade from a negotiable Y35 per meter. Most stores have a tailoring service with prices starting at Y40 for a shirt and Y50 for a pair of pants. Be warned: the tailoring is very hit or miss. Opt for a tailor whose display clothes are similar to those you want to have made. ⊠ *399 Lujiabang Lu, Huangpu* ⊹ *Near the Zhongshan Er Lu end of Lujiabang Lu* ☉ *Daily 8:30 AM–6:30 PM.*

Taikang Antiques Market. Here on lovely Sinan Lu, owners lounge around and smoke as you wander under the low ceilings. It makes a nice change from the tourist scramble of Yuyuan and Dongtai Lu. There are a lot of ceramics, some furniture, and plenty of junk. Shop C28 is crammed with revolutionary propaganda, B113 has old pictures and photos, and C6 has old *qipao* and silks. ⊠ *113 Sinan Lu, Luwan* ⊹ *About 6 blocks south of Huaihai Lu* ☉ *Daily 9:30 AM–6 PM.*

Wenmiao Book Market. The Sunday book market at Shanghai's only Confucian temple is worth a look for old propaganda material, comic books, and other cheap paperbacks mainly in Chinese. Look about under the tables for the cheapest items or flip through someone else's photo album. You can pick up a propaganda magazine for Y15 and then head out to the street to eat or have sticker photos made. ⊠ *Wenmiao Lu, off Huaihai Lu, Huangpu* ☉ *Sun. 10 AM– 4 PM* ⊠ *Y1.*

WHERE TO EAT

Street vendors selling snacks and meals surround most markets. Wenmiao market has a particularly good selection of street food, including cold noodles served from carts, fried meat on sticks, and in summer, fresh coconut milk. At the South Bund Soft-Spinning Market, on Nancang Jie, you'll find similar offerings. Rumor has it that you can even eat snake there; look for the baskets outside the small food vendors' stores. Dongtai Lu is close to Xintiandi, where you can choose from a wide selection of cafés, bars, and restaurants.

■ TIP→→ **Avoid tap water, ice, and uncooked food. Cooked food from street vendors is generally safe unless it looks like it has been sitting around for a while.**

are a bit higher than their competitors, but so is their standard of service. ⊠ *Alley 1885, 8 Caobao Lu, Minhang* ☎ *021/3431–1212* ⊕ *www. hu-hu.com.*

Art

NANJING DONG
LU & THE BUND
★

Studio Rouge. A small but well-chosen collection of mainly photography and paintings by emerging and established artists crowd this simple shop. Look for Studio Rouge Black Box opening up at M50 in Moganshan Lu; it will house the works of more international artists. Prices start at US$600 for a limited-edition silk screen. ⊠ *17 Fuzhou Lu, Huangpu* ☎ *021/6323–0833.*

FORMER FRENCH
CONCESSION

Art Scene. A 1930s French Concession villa serves as a beautiful, albeit contrasting, backdrop for this gallery's contemporary Chinese artwork. Like the established and emerging artists it represents, the gallery is making a name for itself internationally, having participated in Art Chicago and the San Francisco International Art Exposition. ⊠ *No. 8, La. 37, Fuxing Xi Lu, Xuhui* ☎ *021/6437–0631.*

NORTH
SHANGHAI

M50. This complex on Moganshan Lu is soon going to be one of the hippest places in Shanghai. Get down to these old warehouses before the crowds do. It's a great place to spend time wandering around the smaller galleries, chatting to the artists, and seeing China's more established artists' work as well. ⊠ *50 Moganshan Lu, Putuo* ☎ *No phone.*

ShanghART. The city's first modern-art gallery, ShanghART is *the* place to check out the work of art-world movers and shakers such as Ding Yi, Xue Song, and Shen Fan. Here you can familiarize yourself with Shanghai's young contemporary avant-garde artists, who are garnering increasing international attention. The gallery represents 30 local artists as well as putting on great shows and openings in its adjacent H Space. They sell some catalogs of artists they represent and of past shows. ⊠ *50 Moganshan Lu, Putuo* ☎ *021/6359–3923* ⊕ *www.shanghartgallery.com.*

Books

NANJING DONG
LU & THE BUND

Foreign Languages Bookstore. On the 1st floor, find a selection of English-language books about China and Chinese language. Head to the 4th floor for English-language classic novels and children's books. Prices start at Y10 for paper-cut cards. ⊠ *390 Fuzhou Lu, Huangpu* ☎ *021/ 6322–3200, 021/6322–3271, or 021/6322–3219.*

XINTIANDI & CITY
CENTER

Chaterhouse Books. An oasis for the starved reader, this bookstore stocks a good range of magazines in English and other languages and English books, including children's books and a comprehensive selection of travel guides. ⊠ *Shop B1-E Shanghai Times Square, 99 Huaihai Zhong Lu, Luwan* ☎ *021/6391–8237.*

Chinese Medicine

NANJING DONG
LU & THE BUND

Shanghai No. 1 Dispensary. If you've got an illness, this place has something to cure it. The flagship store on Nanjing Dong Lu carries Eastern and Western medicines from ginseng to hairy antler, and aspirin to acupuncture needles. ⊠ *616 Nanjing Dong Lu, Huangpu* ☎ *021/6322–4567.*

Clothing & Shoes

NANJING DONG LU & THE BUND

Bund 18. The glamorous collection of shops here sell high-end designer clothing and accessories such as Marni, Ermenegildo Zegna, Cartier, and Giorgio Armani. The boutique **Younik** stands out by specializing in Shanghai-based designers, including Lu Kun. ⊠ *18 Zhongshan Dong Yi Lu, Huangpu* ☏ *021/6323–7066.*

★ **Suzhou Cobblers.** Beautifully embroidered handmade shoes and slippers with quirky designs such as cabbages are sold alongside funky bags made from rice sacks. Women's shoes start at Y480 and can be made to order for an extra Y50. Children's shoes are also available. Also sold here are sweet knitted toys and children's sweaters. ⊠ *17 Fuzhou Lu, Room 101, Huangpu* ☏ *139–181–877–60 (mobile)* ⊕ *www.suzhou-cobblers.com.*

Three on the Bund. Like Bund 18 (*above*), Three on the Bund is a luxury complex that stocks mainly European-designer brands. ⊠ *3 Zhongshan Dong Yi Lu, Huangpu* ☏ *021/6323–0101.*

FORMER FRENCH CONCESSION

Boutique Cashmere Lover. The small collection of wickedly soft cashmere and blends is contemporary in design; some have Chinese details. Made to order is available. A man's pure-cashmere sweater is around Y1,580. ⊠ *200 Taikang Lu, Room 409, Luwan* ☏ *021/6473–7829.*

Feel. The qipao may be a traditional Chinese dress, but Feel makes it a style for modern times as well. Pop across the lane to Feel Handicrafts, which has great lamps. ⊠ *La. 210, No. 3, Room 110, Taikang Lu, Luwan* ☏ *021/5465–4519/6466–8065.*

Rouge Baiser Elise. Yet another French designer in Shanghai, Rouge Baiser Elise has beautiful linen and cotton homeware and clothing, including children's clothes. Items can be made to order in your choice of color, and children's names can be sewn onto clothing for no extra cost. Handmade pieces have subtle embroidery, and everything looks distinctly French. Go just to check out the beautiful building. Prices start at Y150 for socks. ⊠ *299-2 Fuxing Xi Lu, Xuhui* ☏ *021/6431–8019* ⊕ *www.rougebaiser-elise.com.*

★ **Shanghai Tang.** This is perhaps one of China's leading fashion brands with distinctive acid-bright silks, soft as a baby's bottom cashmere, and funky homeware. Sigh at the beautiful fabrics and designs and gasp at the prices, which start at Y50 for a greeting card. ⊠ *Xintiandi 15, North Block 181, Taicang Lu, Luwan* ☏ *021/6384–1601* ⊠ *JinJiang Hotel, Shop E, 59 Maoming Nan Lu, Luwan* ☏ *021/5466–3006* ⊠ *Shangri-La Hotel, Lobby Level, 33 Fucheng Lu, Pudong* ☏ *021/ 5877–6632* ⊕ *www.shanghaitang.com.*

BUDDHIST PARAPHERNALIA

Around the **Jade Buddha Temple** (⊠ Yufo Si, corner of Anyuan Lu and Jiangning Lu, Putuo) are a cluster of stores selling Buddhist items including monks' clothing, prayer beads, lotus lamps, and candles and incense for the temple. Get an embroidered monk's bag for Y15.

3

AVOIDING SCAMS

■ Fake antiques are often hidden among real treasures and vice versa. Some stores may tell you whether a piece is old or new, you only have their word to prove it. Also be aware of age; the majority of pieces date from the late Qing Dynasty (1644–1911). Technically, only items dated after 1795 can be legally exported. In some stores, only domestic customers may purchase these items to prevent illegal exportation.

■ China is famous for its silk, but some unscrupulous vendors will try to pass off synthetics at silk prices. Ask the shopkeeper to burn a small scrap from the bolt you're considering. If the burned threads bead up and smell like plastic, the fabric is synthetic. If the threads turn into ash and smell like burned hair, the fabric is real silk. (The same goes for wool.) For brocade silk, fair-market prices range from Y30 to Y40 a meter; for synthetics, Y10 to Y28. You'll pay more in retail shops.

■ On tourist stretches such as the Yu Gardens and Nanjing Dong Lu, you may be approached by young people claiming to be students who invite you to an "art exhibition." Unless you are in the market for imitation artwork at high prices, decline and keep moving.

■ Check for fake pearls before purchasing. Real pearls will feel gritty when you bite them, and they also feel cool to the touch. Taking a knife to the surface to see if it scrapes off or burning the pearl are common tactics used by vendors to show that it is real.

■ Real jade makes a distinctive chiming sound when struck and will stick slightly to your hand when underwater.

★ **Shanghai Trio.** Chinese fabrics mixed with French flair, irresistible children's clothes in bright colors and sweet little kimonos, great utilitarian satchels that scream urban chic, and crafty necklaces are the stars of this range. The most luxurious item is a Y3,000 cashmere qipao-style coat. ⊠ *Xintiandi 181, Taicang Lu, Luwan* ☎ *021/6355–2974.*

★ **Shirtflag.** A hipper-than-thou collection of witty and slickly designed T-shirts, accessories, and notebooks at this fun shop takes on propaganda art with a humorous and funky edge. Get Mao's head on a pair of Converse-style canvas sneakers for Y150. ⊠ *Room 8, No.7, La. 210 Taikang Lu, Luwan* ☎ *021/6466–7009* ⊠ *330 Nanchang Lu, Luwan* ☎ *021/5465–3011* ⊠ *Room 505, 168 Lujiazui Lu, Pudong* ☎ *021/ 5047–1650* ⊠ *336 Changle Lu, 1st fl., Xuhui* ☎ *021/6255–7699* ⊕ *www.shirtflag.com.*

Gifts & Souvenirs

FORMER FRENCH CONCESSION **Arts and Crafts Research Institute.** Shanghai artisans create pieces of traditional Chinese arts and crafts such as embroidery and paper-cutting right before your eyes at this institute. You can purchase everything from paper-cuts to snuff bottles, although at prices higher than you'll pay at the stalls around Yu Garden. ⊠ *79 Fenyang Lu, Xuhui* ☎ *021/6437–2509* ✉ *Y8.*

Harvest Studio. Drop in for an embroidery class or just to watch the Miao women with their distinctive hair knots embroidering, and sometimes singing. This studio sells Miao-embroidered pillows, purses, and clothing as well as the silver jewelry that traditionally adorns the Miao ceremonial costume. ⊠ *3 La. 210, Room 118, Taikang Lu, Luwan* ☎ *021/ 6473–4566.*

XINTIANDI & CITY
CENTER
Fodor'sChoice
★
Shanghai Museum Shop. The selection of books on China and Chinese culture at the main store is impressive, and there are some children's books. Very expensive reproduction ceramics are available as well as smaller gift items such as magnets, scarves, and notebooks. Cool purchases like a Chinese architecture–ink stamp (Y90) make great gifts. A delicate bracelet with Chinese charms costs Y150. ⊠ *Shanghai Museum, 201 Renmin Dadao, Huangpu* ☎ *021/6372–3500* ✉ *123 Taicang Lu, Luwan* ☎ *021/6384–7900.*

Pearls & Jewelry

NANJING DONG
LU & THE BUND
Ling Ling Pearls & Jewelry. Traditional pearl necklaces and inexpensive fashion jewelry stand out for being hipper than the competition. Contemporary looking pearl and stone combinations are priced high, but large discounts are often given sans haggling. It's one of many stalls in the Pearl City complex. ⊠ *2F, Pearl City, 558 Nanjing Dong Lu, 2nd fl., Huangpu* ☎ *021/6322–9299* ⊕ *www.linglingspearl.com.*

FORMER FRENCH
CONCESSION
★
Amy Lin's Pearls and Jewelry. Friendly owner Amy Lin has sold pearls to European first ladies and American presidents but treats all her customers like royalty. Her shop just near the old Xiangyang Market has inexpensive trinket bracelets, strings of seed pearls, and stunning Australian seawater pearl necklaces. ⊠ *77 Xiangyang Nan Lu, Xuhui* ☎ *021/ 5403–9673 or 021/6275–3954* ⊕ *www.amy-pearl.com.*

Silk

FORMER FRENCH
CONCESSION
Silk King (Shanghai Silk Commercial Company). With so many branches, it seems that there is a Silk King on every corner, and for good reason. The shop is respected for its quality silk and wool, and the average price of silk is Y138 per meter. But though the quality may be guaranteed, the patterns are a little dowdy. ⊠ *139 Tianping Lu, Xuhui* ☎ *021/6282–5013* ✉ *590 Huaihai Zhonglu, Luwan* ☎ *021/6372–0561* ✉ *1226 Huaihai Zhonglu, Xuhui* ☎ *021/6437–3370.*

Tea

FORMER FRENCH
CONCESSION
Shanghai Huangshan Tea Company. The nine Shanghai locations of this teashop sell traditional Yixing teapots as well as a huge selection of China's best teas by weight. The higher the price the better the tea. ⊠ *605 Huaihai Zhonglu, Luwan* ☎ *021/5306–2974.*

> **WORD OF MOUTH**
>
> "The tea [at Huangshan Tea Company] is packaged nicely for gifts and they had very pretty flowering jasmine. Next door is a little bakery called Lily's. They had excellent egg custard tarts with really flaky pastry! What a nice treat."–quimbymoy

Tianshan Tea City. This place stocks all the tea in China and then some. More than 300 vendors occupy the three floors. You can buy such famous teas as West Lake dragon well tea and Wuyi red-robe tea, and the tea set to serve it in. ✉ *520 Zhongshan Xi Lu, Changning* ☎ *021/ 6228–6688* ⊕ *www.dabutong.com.*

SHANGHAI ESSENTIALS

Transportation

BY AIR

Shanghai is one of China's three major international hubs, along with Beijing and Hong Kong. Shanghai has two major airports: most international flights go through ultramodern Pudong International Airport (PVG), 45 km (30 mi) east of the city, wheras domestic routes operate out of the older Hongqiao International Airport (SHA), 15 km (9 mi) west of the city center.

Both Pudong and Hongqiao have a departure tax of Y90 for international flights and Y50 for domestic. You pay before check-in by purchasing a coupon from booths (near the check-in counters at Pudong, or just inside the terminal at Hongqiao); this coupon is collected at the entrance to the main departure hall.

If you're feeling sci-fi, consider taking the flashy MagLev (magnetic levitation) train, which floats above its tracks at 430 kph (267 mph), whipping you to the Longyang Lu subway station in just eight minutes. Though exciting, the trip isn't very practical. Unless you're staying in eastern Pudong, you'll need to transfer to the subway to get downtown. The MagLev runs between 7 AM and 9 PM and costs Y50 one-way, so if there's more than two of you it makes economic sense to take a cab and save the ride for another day.

■ TIP➔ **Many hotels offer free airport transfers to their guests—ask when you book.** Otherwise, shuttle buses link Pudong Airport with a number of hotels (routes starting with a letter) and transport hubs (routes starting with a number) in the city center.

MagLev Train (☎ 021/2890-7777 ⊕ www.smtdc.com). **Pudong Airport Shuttle Buses** (☎ 021/6834-6612).

Taking a taxi is the most comfortable way into town from Pudong International Airport. Expect to pay around Y150 to Y160 for the hour-long trip to Puxi; getting to the closer Pudong area takes 40 minutes and costs Y120. Note that at rush hour, journey times can easily double.

From Hongqiao, a taxi to Puxi starts at Y60 and takes 30 to 40 minutes; expect an hour for the costlier trip to Pudong hotels. A taxi from one airport to the other takes about an hour and costs Y200 to Y240.

🛄 Airport Information **Hongqiao International Airport** ☎ 021/6268-8918 ⊕ www. shanghaiairport.com. **Pudong International Airport** ☎ 021/9608-1388 ⊕ www. shanghaiairport.com.

BY BIKE

Cycling is still the primary form of transportation for many Shanghai residents, despite the government's best efforts to discourage it by banning bikes on main roads. Shanghai's frenzied traffic is not for the faint of heart, though fortunately most secondary streets have wide, well-defined bike lanes. The pancake-flat city landscape means that gears just aren't necessary.

BY BUS

TO SHANGHAI China has some fabulous luxury long-distance buses with air-conditioning and movies. Many intercity services depart more regularly than trains. However, buying tickets for them can be complicated if you don't speak Chinese—you may end up on one of the cramped old-style affairs, much like an old-fashioned school bus. Drivers don't usually speak English, either. Taking a train or an internal flight is often much easier.

Most of Shanghai's long-distance services leave from the monstrous Shanghai Long Distance bus station, across the square from the Shanghai Railway Station in Zhabei. You buy tickets in the massive circular ticket lobby; allow time for the walk to the departure gate.

WITHIN SHANGHAI Shanghai claims to have more bus lines than any other city on earth—around 1,000—though so much choice probably hinders rather than helps. In fact, unless you know Shanghai well, public buses aren't the best choice for getting around. Although there are more and more air-conditioned services, most buses are hot and crowded in summer and cold and crowded in winter. Just getting on and off can be, quite literally, a fight. Pickpocketing is rife so watch your belongings very carefully. Fares on regular services cost Y1; air-conditioned routes cost Y2; longer routes can cost up to Y4. To buy a ticket you drop the right change into the box next to the driver as you get on, or swipe your Jiatong card. If you do decide to take city buses, Micah Sittig's encyclopedic Web site has English translations of all of Shanghai's routes.

There are some exceptions to the no-bus rule. Bus route 911 runs down Huaihai Lu through the Old French Concession, with great views over the compound walls of the beautiful old Shanghai buildings that line the thoroughfare. Route 936 runs between Pudong and Puxi, passing the Shanghai Zoo, and number 20 passes by the Bund, Jing'an Temple, Nanjing Road, and Renmin Square.

🚹 Bus Information **Shanghai Long-distance Bus Station** ✉ North Square, Shanghai Railway Station, 1662 Zhongxing Lu, Zhabei District ☎ 021/6605-0000.
🚹 Local Bus Information **Micah Sittig's Shanghai Bus Route Translations** ⊕ http://msittig.wubi.org/bus/talk/. **Passenger Hotline** Chinese only ☎ 021/1608-8160.

BY CAR

Highways connect Shanghai to neighboring cities such as Suzhou and Nanjing in the west, and Hangzhou in the south. However, due to government restrictions, it's virtually impossible for nonresidents of China to drive. You can, however, hire a car and driver through your hotel's transportation service or through Hertz or Avis, both of which have several locations throughout the city.

BY FERRY

More than 20 ferry lines cross the Huangpu River between Pudong and Puxi. The most convenient ferry for tourists runs daily between the Bund in Puxi and Pudong's terminal just south of the Riverside Promenade. There are no seats, merely an empty lower deck that welcomes the masses with their bikes and scooters. The per-person fare is Y2 each way. The ferries leave the dock every 10 minutes, 24 hours a day.

Boats leave from Shanghai's Wusong Passenger Terminal for destinations along the Yangzi River such as Wuhan and Chongqing; coastal cities such as Nantong, Dalian, and Ningbo; and the outlying island of Putuoshan. First-class cabins have comfortable beds and their own washbasin.

The Shanghai Ferry Company and the China-Japan International Ferry Company both operate services to Osaka, Japan, from the International Passenger Terminal at Waihongqiao. Boats leave at midday on Tuesday and Saturday, respectively; the trip takes around two days. There are restaurants, a game room, and even karaoke on board.

You can purchase tickets for both international and domestic services (in Chinese) at each terminal, or through China International Travel Service (CITS) for a small surcharge.

🛈 **China-Japan International Ferry Company** ✉ 908 Dongdaming Lu, Hongkou District ☎ 021/6595-7988. **China International Travel Service (CITS)** ☎ 021/6289-8899 ⊕ www.cits.com.cn. **Pudong-Puxi ferry** ✉ Puxi dock, the Bund at Jinling Lu, Huangpu District ✉ Pudong dock, 1 Dongchang Lu, south of Binjiang Da Dao, Pudong. **Shanghai Ferry Company** ☎ 021/6537-5111 ⊕ www.shanghai-ferry.co.jp.

BY SUBWAY

Shanghai's quick and efficient subway system—called the Shanghai Metro—is an excellent way to get around town. The network is growing exponentially—at this writing, there are five lines open; four more are under construction, as are line extensions.

Line 1 runs north–south, crossing the Old French Concession, with a stop at the Shanghai Railway Station. It intersects with Line 2 at People's Square, a labyrinth of a station with 2 levels, 20 exits, and *lots* of people. Line 2, which will eventually link Hongqiao International Airport with Pudong International Airport, is an east–west line that runs under Nanjing Lu along part of its length, and crosses to Pudong close to the Bund. You can transfer from it to the MagLev at Longyang Station in Pudong. Line 3 (formerly known as the Pearl Line) starts in north Shanghai and loops around the west of the city center; useful stops include Shanghai South Railway Station. Line 4 is a circle line that goes around Puxi and through Pudong, crossing the Huangpu River at two places—at this writing, its southwest segment was yet to open. Line 5 is a commuter spur line connecting southwest Shanghai to Line 1.

Subway stations are marked by signs with a jagged red "M" for Metro. Signs are not always obvious, so be prepared to hunt around for entrances or ask directions. Fares depend on how far you travel: most trips within the city center cost Y3 to Y5, with the maximum fare at Y8. Trains run regularly, with three to six minutes between trains on average. Generally speaking, you can change lines without having to buy a new ticket; changes marked TRANSFER are the exception.

🚹 **Shanghai Metro Passenger Information** ☎ 021/6318-9000 ⊕ www.shmetro.com.

BY TAXI

Taxis are plentiful, easy to spot, and by far the most comfortable way to get around Shanghai, though increasing traffic means they're not always the fastest. Almost all are Volkswagen Santanas or Passats, and they come in a rainbow of colors, which reflect the company they work for. These include teal (Dazhong; most locals' first choice), green (Bashi), yellow (Qiangsheng), red (Premium cab), dark blue (Blue Union), and white (Jinjiang). All are metered.

There's a base fee of Y11 for the first 3 km (2 mi), then Y2 per km for the first 10 km (6 mi), then Y3 per kilometer thereafter. After 10 PM the base fee goes up to Y14, and there's a 20% surcharge per kilometer. You also pay for waiting time in traffic. Tipping is unheard of—indeed most taxi drivers return even the smallest change. In compact central Shanghai, outrageous traffic drags out otherwise short cab rides.

🚹 Taxi Companies **Centralized Taxi Reservations** Chinese only ☎ 021/96965. **Dazhong Taxi Company** ☎ 021/96222. **Jinjiang Taxi** Chinese only ☎ 021/96961. **Qiangsheng Taxi** Chinese only ☎ 021/6258-0000. **Shanghai Taxi Authority** ☎ 021/6323-2150.

BY TRAIN

Shanghai is connected to many destinations in China by direct train. Trains to southern China, including Hong Kong, will eventually leave from the gleaming Shanghai South Railway Station in Xuihui. Trains to northern and western China leave from the older Shanghai Railway Station. Both stations have easy transfers to the subway. The best train to catch to Beijing is the overnight express that leaves around 6 PM and arrives in Beijing the next morning. The express train for Hong Kong departs around noon and arrives at the Kowloon station 24 hours later.

🚹 **Shanghai Railway Station** ✉303 Moling Lu, Zhabei District ☎021/6317-9090. **Shanghai South Railway Station** ✉ Between Liuzhou Lu and Humin Lu, Xuhui District ☎ 021/6317-6060.

Contacts & Resources

BANKS & CURRENCY EXCHANGE

In Shanghai, American Express, MasterCard, and Visa are accepted at most major hotels and a growing number of upmarket stores and restaurants. Diners Club is accepted at many hotels and some restaurants.

INTERNET

Shanghai is a very Internet-friendly place for those bearing laptops. Most mid- to high-end hotels have in-room Internet access; if the hotel doesn't have a server but you have a room phone you can usually access a government-provided ISP, which only charges you for the phone call. Wi-Fi is growing exponentially—many hotels and even cafés provide it free.

PHONES

Shanghai's city code is 021, and Shanghai phone numbers have eight digits—you only need to dial these when calling within the city.

EMERGENCIES

Shanghai has different numbers for each emergency service, but staff often don't speak English. If in doubt, call the U.S. embassy first: staff members are available 24 hours a day to help handle emergencies and facilitate communication with local agencies.

In a medical emergency don't call for an ambulance. The Shanghai Ambulance Service is merely a transport system that takes you to the closest hospital, not the hospital of your choice. If possible, take a taxi to the hospital; you'll get there faster. The best place to head in a medical emergency is the Shanghai United Family Hospital or the World Link Medical Center, which have 24-hour emergency services (including dental) and pharmacy assistance. The Shanghai East International Medical Center has similar services but no dentistry. SOS is an international medical service that arranges Medivac. Huashan and Huadong hospitals are both local hospitals with foreigners' clinics. Although cheaper than the international clinics, their hygiene standards aren't as high.

The most reliable places to buy prescription medication is at the 24-hour pharmacy at the World Link Medical Center and the Shanghai United Family Health Center (⇨ Medical Services *above*). During the day, the Watson's chain is good for over-the-counter medication; there are several branches all over town.

🚩 Medical Services **Huadong Hospital** ⊠ Foreigners' Clinic, 2F, 221 Yanan Xi Lu, Jing'an District ☎ 021/6248–3180 Ext. 30106. **Huashan Hospital** ⊠ Foreigners' Clinic, 15F, 12 Wulumuqi Zhong Lu, Jing'an District ☎ 021/6248–3986, 021/6248–9999 Ext. 2531 for 24-hour hotline. **Shanghai East International Medical Center** ⊠ 551 Pudong Nan Lu., Pudong District ☎ 021/5879–9999 ⊕ www.seimc.com.cn.

Shanghai United Family Health Center private ⊠ 1139 Xian Zia Lu, Changning District ☎ 021/5133–1900, 021/5133–1999 emergencies ⊕ www.unitedfamilyhospitals.com. **SOS International Shanghai Office** ⊠ Sun Tong Infoport Plaza, 22nd fl., Unit D–G, 55 Huaihai Xi Lu, Xuhui District ☎ 021/5298–9538 general inquiries, 021/6295–0099 emergencies ⊕ www.internationalsos.com.

World Link Medical Center ⊠ Room 203, West Tower, Shanghai Center, 1376 Nanjing Xi Lu, Jing'an District ⊠ Hongqiao Clinic ⊠ Mandarin City, 1F, Unit 30, 788 Hongxu Lu, Minhang District ⊠ Jian Qiao Clinic ⊠ 51 Hongfeng Lu, Jian Qao, Pudong ☎ 021/6445–5999 ⊕ www.worldlink-shanghai.com.

🚩 Foreign Consulates **United States Consulate** ⊠ 1469 Huaihai Zhong Lu, Xuhui District ☎ 021/6433–6880, 021/6433–3936 after-hours emergencies ⊠ Citizen Services Section, Westgate Mall, 8th fl., 1038 Nanjing Xi Lu, Jing'an District ☎ 021/3217–4650 ⊕ http://shanghai.usconsulate.gov.

🚩 General Emergency Contacts **Fire** ☎ 119. **International SOS Medical Services 24-hour Alarm Center** ☎ 021/6295–0099. **Police** ☎ 110, 021/6357–6666 (English). **Shanghai Ambulance Service** ☎ 120.

🚩 Pharmacies **Watson's Pharmacy** ⊠ Westgate Mall, 1038 Nanjing Xi Lu, Jiang'an District.

MAIL

The Shanghai municipality's postal code is 200000, and each of the city's districts differs in the fifth and sixth digits; for example, Xuhui district is 200030. Forest green signs identify the many branches of China Post in Shanghai. The main post office is at 276 Suzhou Bei Lu, and there are also English-speaking staff at the Shanghai Center and Xuhui branches.

🏠 Main Branches **Post Office** ✉ 276 Suzhou Bei Lu, Hongkou District ✉ Shanghai Center, 1376 Nanjing Xi Lu, Jing'an District ✉ 133 Huaihai Lu, Xuhui District ☎ 021/ 6393-6666 Ext. 00.

At a Glance

ENGLISH	PINYIN	CHINESE CHARACTERS
EXPLORING		
Old City Wall	dàjìng gé	大境阁
Bank of China	zhōngguó yínháng	中国银行
Bund	wàitān	外滩
Cathay Cinema	guótài diànyǐngyuàn	国泰电影院
Century Park	shìjì gōngyuán	世纪公园
Chen Xiangge Temple	chén xiāng gé	沉香阁
Duolun Lu	duōlún lù	多伦路
Former Hong Kong and Shanghai Bank Building	pǔdōng fāzhǎn yínháng	浦东发展银行
Fuxing Park	fùxīng góngyuán	复兴公园
Grand Theatre	shànghǎi dà jùyuàn	上海大剧院
Jade Buddha Temple	yùfó sì	玉佛寺
Jingan Temple	jìng'ān sì	静安寺
Jinmao Tower	jīnmào dàshà	金茂大厦
Longhua Martyrs Cemetery	lónghuá lièshì língyuán	龙华烈士陵园
Longhua Temple	lónghuá sì	龙华寺
Lu Xun Park	lǔxùn gōngyuán	鲁迅公园
Lyceum Theatre	lánxīndàjùyuàn	兰心大剧院
M50	chūnmíng yìshù chānyèyuán	春明艺术产业园
Oriental Pearl Tower	dōngfāng míngzhū diànshìtǎ	东方明珠电视塔
Paramount	bǎilèmén	百乐门
Park Hotel	guójì fàndiàn	国际饭店
Peace Hotel	hépíng fàndiàn	和平饭店
People's Park	rénmín góngyuán	人民公园
People's Square	rénmín guǎngchǎng	人民广场
Shanghai Botanical Garden	shànghǎi zhíwùyuán	上海植物园
Shanghai Doland Museum of Modern Art	duōlún xiàndài meishù guǎn	多伦现代美术馆
Shanghai Exhibition Centre	shànghǎi zhǎnlǎn Zhōngxīn	上海展览中心
Shanghai History Museum	shànghǎi lìshǐ bówùguǎn	上海历史博物馆
Shanghai Museum	shànghǎi bówùguǎn	上海博物馆

Shanghai Ocean Aquarium	shànghǎi hǎiyáng shuǐzúguǎn	上海海洋水族馆
Shanghai Science and Technology Museum	shànghǎi kējìguǎn	上海科技馆
Shanghai Urban Planning Centre	shànghǎi chéngshì guīhuà zhǎnlǎnguǎn	上海城市规划展览馆
Site of the First National Congress of the Chinese Communist Party	zhōnggòng yīdà huìzhǐ	中共一大会址
Soong Qingling's Mausoleum	sòng qìnglíng língmù	宋庆龄陵墓
Sun Yat-sen's Former Residence	sūn zhōng shān gùjū	孙中山故居
Xintiandi	xīntiāndì	新天地
Yu Garden	yù yuán	豫园

WHERE TO EAT

1221	Yī èr èr Yī Cāntīng	1221餐厅
Bali Laguna	Dōushì Táohuā Yuán	都市桃花源
Bao Luo	Bǎo Luó	保罗
Barbarossa	Bā Bā Lù Shā	芭芭露莎
Bellagio	Bǎi Lè Gōng	百乐宫
Cloud 9	Jǐ Zhòng Tiān	九重天
Da Marco	Dà Mǎ Ke	大马可
Element Fresh	Xīn Yuánsù	新元素
Family Li Imperial Cuisine	Lǐ Jiā Cài	历家菜
Gao Li Korean Restaurant	Gāolì Cāntīng	高丽餐厅
Giovanni's	Jí Fàn Ní Sī	吉范尼斯
Gongdelin	Gōngdé Lín	功德林
Grape	Pútáo Yuán	葡萄园
Hot Pot King	Lái Fú Lóu	来福楼
Jade on 36	Fěicuì Sān Shí Liù	翡翠36
Laris	Lù Wéi Xuān	陆唯轩
Lu Bo Lang	Lǜbō Láng Jiǔlóu	绿波廊酒楼
M on the Bund	Mǐ Shì Xīcān Tīng	米氏西餐厅
Mediterranean Café	Dìzhōnghǎi Xīcān Tīng	地中海西餐厅
Meilongzhen	Méi Lóng Zhèn	梅龙镇
New Heights	Xīnshìjiǎo Cāntīng Jiǔláng	新视角餐厅酒廊

Paulaner Brauhaus	Bǎoláinà Cāntīng	宝莱纳餐厅
Sens & Bund	Yǎ Dé	雅德
Shen Yue Xuan	Shēn Yuè Xuān	申粤轩
Simply Thai	Tiān tài Cāntīng	天泰餐厅
South Beauty	Qiào Jiāng Nán	俏江南
Summer Pavilion	Xià Yuàn	夏苑
T8	T Bā	T8
Tairyo	Tai Láng	太郎
Tan Wai Lou	Tān Wai Lóu	滩外楼
The Dynasty	Mǎn Fú Lóu	满福楼
The Grill	Meishì Shāokǎo	美式烧烤
The Onion	Yáng cōng Cāntīng	洋葱餐厅
The Tandoor	Tiāndōulǐ Yìndù Cāntīng	天都里印度餐厅
Wagas	Huá Jiā Sī	华佳思
Whampoa Club	Huáng Pǔ Huì	黄埔会
Yang's Kitchen	Yángjiā Chúfáng	杨家厨房
Yi Café	Yí Kāfēi	怡咖啡
WHERE TO STAY		
88 Xintiandi	88 Xīntiāndì Jiǔdiàn	88新天地酒店
Anting Villa Hotel	Āntíng Biéshù Huāyuán Jiǔdiàn	安亭别墅花园酒店
Astor House Hotel	Pǔjiāng Fàndiàn	浦江饭店
Broadway Mansions Hotel	Shànghǎi Dàshà	上海大厦
Changhang Merrylin Hotel	Chánghàng Měilín'gé Dàjiǔdiàn	长航美林阁大酒店
Donghu Hotel	Dōnghú Bīnguǎn	东湖宾馆
Grand Hyatt	Shànghǎi Jīnmào Jūnyuè Dàjiǔdiàn	上海金茂君悦大酒店
Heng Shan Moller Villa	Héngshān Mǎlè Biéshù Fàndiàn	衡山马勒别墅饭店
Hilton Shanghai	Shànghǎi Jìng'ān Xī'ěrdùn Jiǔdiàn	上海静安希尔顿酒店
Holiday Inn Pudong	Shànghǎi Pǔdōng Jiàrì Jiǔdiàn	上海浦东假日酒店
Jin Jiang Hotel	Jǐnjiāng Fàndiàn	锦江饭店
Jing An Hotel	Jìng'ān Bīnguǎn	静安宾馆

JW Marriott	J.W. Wànháo Jiǔdiàn	JW万豪酒店
Nanjing Hotel	Nánjīng Fàndiàn	南京饭店
Okura Garden Hotel	Huāyuán Fàndiàn	花园饭店
Old House Inn	Lǎoshíguāng Jiǔdiàn	老时光酒店
Pacific Hotel	Jīnmén Dàjiǔdiàn	金门大酒店
Panorama Century Court	Hǎiwān Dàshà	海湾大厦
Park Hotel	Guójì Fàndiàn	国际饭店
Peace Hotel	Hépíng Fàndiàn	和平饭店
Pudong Shangri-la	Pǔdōng Xiānggélǐlā Jiǔdiàn	浦东香格里拉酒店
Radisson Hotel Shanghai New World	Xīnshìjiè Lìshēng Dàjiǔdiàn	新世界丽笙大酒店
Ramada Plaza	Nánxīn Yǎhuá Měidá Dàjiǔdiàn	南新雅华美达大酒店
Ruijin Guest House	Ruìjīn Bīnguǎn	瑞金宾馆
Sheraton Grand Tai Ping Yang	Shànghǎi Tàipíngyáng Dàfàndiàn	上海太平洋大饭店
Sofitel Hyland Hotel	Suǒfēitè Hǎilún Bīnguǎn	索菲特海仑宾馆
The Four Seasons	Sìjì Jiǔdiàn	四季酒店
The Portman Ritz-Carlton	Bōtèmàn Lìjiā Jiǔdiàn	波特曼丽嘉酒店
The Regent	Shànghǎi Lóngzhīmèng Lìjīng Dàjiǔdiàn	上海龙之梦丽晶大酒店
The St. Regis	Shànghǎi Ruìjí Hóngtǎ Dàjiǔdiàn	上海瑞吉红塔大酒店
Westin	Wēisītīng Dàfàndiàn	威斯汀大饭店
YMCA	Qīngniánhuì Jiǔdiàn	青年会酒店

ARTS & NIGHTLIFE

Shanghai Acrobatics Troupe	Shànghǎi Zájìtuán	上海杂技团
Kunju Opera Troupe	Shànghǎi Kūnjùtuán	上海昆剧团
Yifu Theatre	Yìfū Wǔtái	逸夫舞台
Jing An Hotel	Jìng'ān Bīnguǎn	静安宾馆
Shanghai Concert Hall	Shànghǎi Yīnyuètīng	上海音乐厅
Shanghai Grand Theatre	Shànghǎi Dàjùyuàn	上海大剧院
Shanghai Oriental Art Center	Shànghǎi Dōngfāng Yìshù Zhōngxīn	上海东方艺术中心
Xiahemi Warehouse	Xiàhé Mǐcāng	下河米仓

Lyceum Theatre	Lánxīn Dàxìyuàn	兰馨大戏院
Majestic Theatre	Měiqí Dàxìyuàn	美琪大戏院
Shanghai Dramatic Arts Center	Shànghǎi Huàjù Yìshù Zhōngxīn	上海话剧艺术中心
Barbarossa	Bābālùshā Jiǔbā	巴巴路莎酒吧
TMSK	Tòumíng Sīkǎo Jiǔbā	透明思考酒吧
Glamour Bar	Mèilì Jiǔbā	魅力酒吧
Three on the Bund	Wàitān Sānhào	外滩三号
Arch Bar and Café	Jiǔjiān Jiǔbā	玖间酒吧
Cotton's	Miánhuā Jiǔbā	棉花酒吧
Time Passage	Shíguāng Tōngdào Jiǔbā	时光通道酒吧
Dublin Exchange	Dūbólín Kāfēiguǎn	都柏林咖啡馆
The Door	Qiánmén Jiǔbā	乾门酒吧
Real Love	Zhēn'ài Jiǔbā	真爱酒吧
Pier One	Yīhào Mǎtóu	一号码头
Jade on 36	Fēicuì Sān Shí Liù Jiǔ Bā	翡翠36酒吧
Jazz Bar	Juéshì Bā	爵士吧
Jazz 37	Juésh Sān Shí Qī Jiǔ Bā	爵士37酒吧
Ye Lai Xiang	Yèláixiāng Jiǔbā	夜来香酒吧
Haoledi	Hǎolèdī KTV	好乐迪KTV
Party World	Qiánguì KTV	钱柜KTV
CJW	CJW Juéshìyuè Jiǔbā	CJW爵士乐酒吧
Club JZ	Chúncuì Juéshìyuè Jiǔbā	纯粹爵士乐酒吧
Cotton Club	Miánhuā Jùlèbù	棉花俱乐部
House of Blues and Jazz	Bùlǔsī Yǔ Juéshì Zhīwū	布鲁斯与爵士之屋
Tanghui	Tánghuì Jiǔbā	堂会酒吧
Yuyintang Warehouse	Yù Yīn Táng	育音堂
SHOPPING		
Amy Lin's Pearls and Jewelry	aìmǐnlínshì zhūbǎo	艾敏林氏珠宝
Art Scene	yìshù jǐng	艺术景
Arts and Crafts Research Institute	shànghǎi gōngyì meishù yánjiū suǒ	上海工艺美术研究所
Brilliance Shimao International Plaza	bǎilián shìmào guójì guǎngchǎng	百联世茂国际广场
Bund 18	wàitān shíbā hào	外滩十八号

3

Chaterhouse Books	sānlián shūdiàn	三联书店
Feel	jīnfěn shìjiā	金粉世家
Foreign Languages Bookstore	wàiwén shūdiàn	外文书店
Grand Gateway	gǎnghuì guǎngchǎng	港汇广场
Harvest Studio	shànghǎi yíngjiāfǎng gōngzuòshǐ	上海盈稼坊工作室
Henry Antique Warehouse	hànruì gǔdiǎn jiājù	汉瑞古典家俱
Hu & Hu Antiques	gǔyuè jiājù	古悦家俱
Ling Ling Pearls & Jewelry	línglíng zhūbǎo	玲玲珠宝
M50	Chūnmíng yìshù chǎnyèyuán	春明艺术产业园
Madame Mao's Dowry	máotài shèjì	毛太设计
Next Age	dìyī bābǎibàn	第一八佰伴
Raffles City	láifùshì guǎngchǎng	来福士广场
Shanghai Antique and Curio Store	shànghǎi wénwù shāngdiàn	上海文物商店
Shanghai Art Deco	shànghǎi huáijiù	上海怀旧
Shanghai Museum Shop	shànghǎi bówùguǎn shāngdiàn	上海博物馆商店
Shanghai No. 1 Department Store	dìyī bǎihuò	第一百货
Shanghai No. 1 Dispensary	yīyào yī diàn	医药一店
Shanghai Tang	shànghǎi tān	上海滩
Shanghai Trio	shànghǎi zǔhé	上海组合
ShanghArt	xiáng gé nà huàláng	香格纳画廊
Shirtflag	zédóng shíshàng	泽东时尚
Silk King	zhēnsī dàwáng	真丝大王
Studio Rouge	hóngzhài dāngdài yìshù huàláng	红寨当代艺术画廊
Super Brand Mall	zhèngdà guǎngchǎng	正大广场
Three on the Bund	wàitān sān hào	外滩三号
Tianshan Tea City	dàbùtóng tiānshān cháchéng	大不同天山茶城
Xinmei Union Square	xīnméi liánhé guǎngchǎng	新梅联合广场
Zhen Zhen	zhēn zhēn gǔwán diàn	珍珍古玩店

Eastern China

ZHEJIANG & FUJIAN

The main canal in the Zhejiang province.

WORD OF MOUTH

"Xiamen deserves its title of 'Garden on the Sea.' The perpetual spring with its luxuriant flowers and trees gives it another name, 'Green Island.' The legend that it was once a habitat of egrets brings about another beautiful name 'Egret Island.' "

—chinajack

WELCOME TO EASTERN CHINA

Chinese tour boat in West Lake.

TOP REASONS TO GO

★ **Teatime in Hangzhou.** Sip sublime Longjing tea and buy silk in the footsteps of Marco Polo at Hangzhou's romantic West Lake.

★ **Qiantian Tidal Bore.** Marvel at one of nature's most enthralling spectacles: the mighty tidal-bore at the mouth of Zhejiang's Qiantian River.

★ **Shaoxing Wine.** Dramatized by one of China's most famous writers Lu Xun, Shaoxing wine is celebrated throughout the region. Potent for sure, Shaoxing wine is de-rigeur for local dining.

★ **Hakka Roundhouses.** The founder of modern China, Dr. Sun Yat-sen, came from China's proud Hakka minority peoples, whose ancient tradition of rounded-home architecture is now treasured for its graceful lines and organic construction material. As these people succumb to China's fast-paced economic changes, this legacy of living is quickly disappearing.

1 Hangzhou. Described by Marco Polo as the finest and noblest city in the world, Hangzhou is famous for the inspiringly beautiful West Lake. In recent years, Hangzhou has also emerged as one of China's most vibrant cities. A little way outside the city, visit the planta-tions that produce the area's famous Longjing tea, or stroll in forested hills to take in the views of the surrounding area.

2 Shaoxing. Shaoxing is famed for its historic homes and many traditional bridges. This small, well-preserved town is perhaps the best place to experience the historic atmos-phere of a traditional Yangzi Delta town. Visit the stunning Figure 8 Bridge, which was erected over 800 years ago. Bearded moss hangs from its arches like the characters in local author Lu Xun's sagas. Don't miss the Catholic church with Italian–Chinese inspired decor.

Elderly Hakka woman.

3 Xiamen. With a bird's-eye view of the Taiwan Straight, Xiamen is well poised to profit from the windfall of increased economic activity between Taiwan and the mainland. Loaded with expats, its trendy clubs and upscale restaurants are now becoming as common-place as Xiamen's famous beaches and botanical gardens. Still, Xiamen moves to its own, early-20th-century tempo.

GETTING ORIENTED

4

With thousands of miles of coastline, the provinces of Zhejiang and Fujian are considered the rounded belly section of China's east coast. Indeed, their shores know where the East China Sea ends and the South China Sea begins. Zhejiang Province's primary ports of call are the cities of Ningbo and Hangzhou, both of which are within two hours of Shanghai by bus. Hangzhou is also famous as the southernmost city of the Grand Canal. Directly south of Zhejiang is the lush and mountainous province of Fu-jian. Famed for its proximity with the Taiwan Straight, the wealthy coastal cities of Fujian are convenient to each other, but the province's mountainous inte-rior make them a long train trip away from the rest of the region.

Local women picking some of China's most famous tea—Longjing was a favorite of Mao's and one of the most expensive brews in Hangzhou.

EASTERN CHINA PLANNER

Follow the Coast

Few tour routes these days have exclusive planners just for China's central coast, which is a pity. After all, the provinces of Zhejiang and Fujian have much on offer for bicyclists, hikers, ocean swimmers, and windsurfers. And as one of China's first Special Economic Zones, Xiamen is currently awash with cash but still hasn't lost its old-world charm. Fall and spring are the ideal times to visit the region. Spring, especially April and May, have very comfortable temperatures and the trees and flowers are in full bloom. Hot and muggy summer is not the best time to visit—many of the cities are uncomfortable from mid-June though August. The region has a long and very pleasant fall season—moderate weather and clear skies lasting into early December. Chinese tourists flood in during the two "Golden Week" holidays at the start of May and October, so try to avoid those two weeks. Most of the region's sights are open daily.

With the Kids

One of our favorite child-friendly places is the garden behind the Pagoda of Six Harmonies in Hangzhou. Start by climbing the stairs of the seven-story Pagoda itself. The views from the top overlooking the river are excellent and worth the hike. Visit the garden and play among the miniature re-creations of China's most famous pagodas and temples—it's as educational as it is fun. With the tall trees and cozy benches, this park is an ideal place to picnic. The best time to visit is about 4 PM, before the sun dips and the tower closes. There are also several gift shops next to the tower that sell everything from shell necklaces to kiddie *qi-paos*. If you want to avoid crowds, remember, on the 18th day of the 8th lunar month, the pagoda is packed with people, all wanting the best seat for "Qiantang River Bore," when the river reverses itself and large waves form.

The pagoda is 2½ km (1½ mi) south of West Lake. ⊠ *Fuxing Jie, on the Qiantang River* 🎫 *Y15* ⊗ *Daily 6–6:30.*

Wired on the Beach

Xiamen is a city that's doing a lot of catch-up, and it's doing it in style! It now has at least a dozen laid-back cafés with wireless networks—even a local McDonald's has Wi-Fi. Recently, China's largest wine importer, ASC Wines, began pouring a steady stream of fine vino into the island of old Amoy. In sum: this once sleepy little coastal city is now becoming very special to big money—even more so than when it first became a Special Economic Zone in 1980. Yet Xiamen's main attraction is still its subdued beach scene. One of the best places for an endless Xiamen summer is Siming, just east of downtown. Framed by mountains and defined by clean beaches, its sunsets are timeless. The beaches of Gulangyu island are another favorite, particularly because cars have been banned from the isle altogether. Cobblestone streets, colonial buildings, towering tree canopies, and its rich milieu of pianists and other musicians make this one of China's most popular seaside destinations.

Wonders of West Lake

A famous poem that says, "Of all the lakes, north, south, east and west, the one at West Lake is the best." Why? Because this ancient man-made lake casts the mold for scores of manicured lakes across China. Start exploring where Pinghai Road meets Harbin Road in the northeastern part of the lake. There's a fabulous boardwalk with weeping willows, restaurants, and a lakeside teahouse.

Wending north, you can cross the street to ascend a small hill capped with the Baochu Pagoda. Here, the views of West Lake are some of the best in the city. Once you climb down, you can venture to the Baidi and Sudi Causeways, through the middle of the lake. Don't miss the classical Lingyin Temple, nestled in the nearby hills.

Take a guided boat from the southern shore by night, when the Three Pools Mirroring the Moon pagoda is alight. This stone pagoda has six incised circles. When candles are set inside them, the light appears as romantic moons.

WHAT IT COSTS In Yuan

RESTAURANTS				
$$$$	$$$	$$	$	¢
over 165	100–165	50–99	25–49	under 25
HOTELS				
$$$$	$$$	$$	$	¢
over 1,800	1,400–1,800	1,100–1,399	700–1,099	under 700

Restaurant prices are for a main course, excluding tax and tips. Hotel prices are for a standard double room, including taxes.

On the Menu

Zhejiang cuisine is often steamed or roasted and has a more subtle, salty flavor; specialties include yellow croaker with Chinese cabbage, sea eel, drunken chicken, and stewed chicken. In Shaoxing locals traditionally start the day by downing a bowl or two of *huang jiu* (rice wine), the true breakfast of champions. Shaoxing's most famous dish is its deep-fried *chou dofu*, or stinky tofu. Try it with a touch of the local chili sauce.

The cuisine of Fujian is considered by some to have its own characteristics. Spareribs are a specialty, as are soups and stews using a soy and rice-wine stock. The coastal cities of Fujian offer a wonderful range of seafood, including river eel with leeks, fried jumbo prawns, and steamed crab.

What To Wear

Dress is usually casual, but is a little formal in the hotel restaurants, especially the western sections. Reservations are not necessary; in fact, many restaurants are loath to give out their phone numbers.

Be Sure to Avoid

Shark's fin soup is a great delicacy here, and in other places like Hong Kong. We, however, do not recommend ordering it. The harvesting of shark fins is exceptionally cruel and the zeal with which they are being hunted has led to a shocking decline in global shark populations. And if this isn't enough to turn you off, shark fins are known to contain high levels of toxic mercury.

4

By Will
Thomson and
Joshua Samuel
Brown

A MICROCOSM OF THE FORCES at play in contemporary China is presented in the provinces here on the eastern coast of the country. The rich legacy of the past and the challenges and aspirations for China's future combine in a present that is dizzying in its variety and speed of transformation. Zhejiang and Fujian have long been some of the most affluent provinces in China and today they're once again enjoying prosperity.

Zhejiang has always been a hub of culture, learning, and commerce. The cities, with their elegant gardens, elaborate temples, and fine crafts, evoke the sophisticated and refined world of classical China's literati. Since the Southern Song Dynasty (1127–79), large numbers of Fujianese have emigrated around Southeast Asia. As a result, Fujian province has strong ties with overseas Chinese. In 1979 Fujian was allowed to form the first Special Economic Zone (SEZ)—a testing ground for capitalist market economy—at Xiamen. Today Xiamen is a pleasant city with a vibrant economy.

ZHEJIANG

The province of Zhejiang showcases the region's agricultural prowess and dedication to nature, even as it is one of the most populous urban regions of China. The capital city of Hangzhou is famous for West Lake, a huge green park embodying this devotion and relationship with natural beauty. A center of culture and trade, Zhejiang is also one of China's wealthiest provinces. Hangzhou served as one of the eight ancient capital cities of the country, after the Song Dynasty rulers fled Jurchen invaders. Throughout history, the city also benefited from its position as the last stop on the Grand Canal, the conduit for supplying grains and goods to the imperial north.

Shaoxing showcases another aspect of Zhejiang life. The small-town flavor of this city on canals remains, despite a growing population and overall economic boom in the province. Several high-profile figures helped put Shaoxing on the map, including former Premier Zhou Enlai, and novelist Lu Xun.

In addition to its cities, Zhejiang's farms are also among the most prosperous, and rural incomes are some three to four times higher than in many other areas of the country. Geographically, the river-basin plains in the north near Shanghai give way to mountains in the south of the province. Besides grain, the province also is recognized in China for its tea, crafts, silk production, and long tradition of sculpture and carving.

Hangzhou

❶ Residents of Hangzhou are immensely proud of their city, and will often point to a classical saying that identifies it as an "earthly paradise." Indeed, Hangzhou is one of the country's most enjoyable cities. The green spaces and hilly landscape that surround the city make Hangzhou unique in Eastern China. Add to the experience a thriving arts scene, sophisticated restaurants, and vibrant nightlife, and Hangzhou vies with nearby Shanghai as the hippest city in the East.

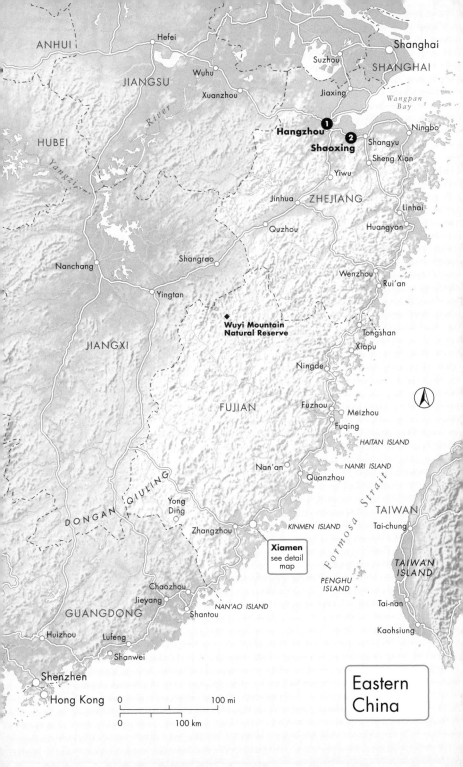

Exploring

West Lake (Xihu). With arched bridges stretching over the water, West Lake is the heart of leisure in Hangzhou. Originally a bay, the whole area was built up gradually throughout the years, a combination of natural changes and human shaping of the land. The shores are idyllic and imminently photographable, enhanced by meandering paths, artificial islands, and countless pavilions with upturned roofs.

Two pedestrian causeways cross the lake: **Baidi** in the north and **Sudi** in the west. They are both named for two poet–governors from different eras who invested in landscaping and developing the lake. Ideal for strolling or biking, both walkways are lined with willow and peach trees, crossed by bridges, and dotted with benches where you can pause to admire the views. ⊠ *East of the city, along Nanshan Lu.*

The Bai Causeway ends at the largest island on West Lake, **Solitary Hill Island** (Gushan). A palace for the exclusive use of the emperor during his visits to Hangzhou once stood here. On its southern side is a small, carefully composed park around several pavilions and a pond. A path leads up the hill to the **Seal Engraver's Society** (Xileng Yinshe) (☎ 0571/8781–5910 ☒ Y5 ☉ Daily 9–5). Professional carvers here will design and execute seals. The trip up the hill to the society is worth it, even for those who aren't particularly interested in this unusual art form. The society's garden has one of the best views of the lake. Solitary Hill Island is home to the **Zhejiang Provincial Museum** (Zhejiang Bowuguan) (☎ 0571/8797–1177 ⊕ www.zhejiangmuseum.com ☒ Free ☉ Weekdays 8:30–4:30). The museum has a good collection of archaeological finds, as well as bronzes and paintings. ⊠ *West Lake ☒ Free ☉ Daily 8–dusk.*

NEED A BREAK?

On the crest of the hill inside the Seal Engraver's Society is a small **teahouse** where you can drink local teas. Order a cup and have a seat on the hilltop veranda. The view will make clear why locals have loved this place for centuries.

On the southern side of the lake is the man-made island of **Three Pools Reflecting the Moon** (Santan Yinyue). Here you'll find walkways surrounding several large ponds, all connected by zigzagging bridges. Off the island's southern shore are three stone Ming Dynasty pagodas. During the Mid-Autumn Moon Festival, held in the middle of September, lanterns are lit in the pagodas, creating the three golden disks that give the island its name. Boats costing between Y35 and Y45 run between here and Solitary Hill Island. ⊠ *West Lake ☒ Y20 ☉ Daily 7–5:30.*

Along the eastern bank of the lake is **Orioles Singing in the Willow Waves** (Liulang Wenying), a nice place to watch boats on the lake. This park comes alive during the Lantern Festival, held in the winter. Paper lanterns are set to float on the river, under the willow bows. ⊠ *Near the intersection of Hefang Jie and Nanshan Lu.*

FodorśChoice ★ On the southeastern shore of West Lake is the **Evening Sunlight at Thunder Peak Pagoda** (Leifeng Xizhao). Local legend says that the original Thunder Peak Pagoda was constructed to imprison a snake-turned-human who lost her mortal love on West Lake. The pagoda collapsed in 1924, perhaps finally freeing the White Snake. A new tower, completed in 2002, sits beside the remains of its predecessor. There's a sculpture on each level, including a carving that depicts the tragic story of the White Snake. The foundation dates to AD 976 and is an active archaeological site, where scientists uncovered a miniature silver pagoda containing what is said to be a lock of the Buddha's hair; on display in a separate hall. The view of the lake is breathtaking, particularly at sunset. ⊠ *15 Nanshan Lu* ☎ *0571/8796–4515* ⊕ *www.leifengta.com.cn* 🎫 *Y40* ۞ *Apr.–Nov., daily 8 AM–9 PM; Dec.–Mar., daily 7:30 AM–8:30 PM; last admission 30 mins before closing.*

> ## RENT A BIKE
>
> Shaded by willow trees, West Lake is one of the country's most pleasant places for bicycling. This path, away from car traffic, is also a quick way to move between the area's major sights. There are numerous bike-rental shops around Orioles Singing in the Willow Waves Park. The rental rate is about Y10 per hour. A deposit and some form of identification are usually required.

☺ The well-designed **Hangzhou Aquarium** (Hangzhou Haidi Shijie), on West Lake's eastern shore, centers around a walk-through glass tunnel. The main tank brings you to the bottom of the ocean, with sharks and other denizens of the deep swimming above you. There's also a seal pool and several hands-on exhibits. ⊠ *49 Nanshan Lu* ☎ *0571/8706–9500* 🎫 *Y60* ۞ *Daily 8:30–5.*

The slender spire of Protecting Chu Pagoda rises atop **Precious Stone Hill** (Baoshi Shan). The brick and stone pagoda is visible from just about anywhere on the lake. From the hilltop, you can see around West Lake and across to Hangzhou City. Numerous paths from the lakeside lead up the hill, which is dotted with Buddhist and Taoist shrines. Several caves provide shade and relief from the hot summer sun. ⊠ *North of West Lake.*

At the foot of Qixia Hill is **Yellow Dragon Cave** (Huanglong Dong), famous for a never-ending stream of water spurting from the head of a yellow dragon. Nearby is a garden and a stage for traditional Yue opera performances that are given daily. In a nearby groove you'll see examples of rare "square bamboo." ⊠ *Shuguang Lu* ☎ *0571/8798–5860* 🎫 *Y15* ۞ *Daily 7:30–6.*

Near Solitary Hill Island stands the **Yue Fei Mausoleum** (Yue Fei Mu), a shrine to honor General Yue Fei (1103–42), who led Song armies against foreign invaders. As a young man, his mother tattooed his back with the commandment to "Repay the nation with loyalty." This made Yue Fei a hero of both patriotic loyalty and filial piety. At the height of his success, a jealous rival convinced the emperor to have Yue Fei executed.

A subsequent leader pardoned the warrior and enshrined him as a national hero. Statues of Yue Fei's accusers kneel in shame nearby. Traditionally, visitors would spit on statues of the traitors, but a recent sign near the statue asks them to glare instead. ✉ *Beishan Lu, west of Solitary Hill Island* 🎫 *Y25* ⊘ *Daily 7:30–6.*

Equally celebrated as West Lake and a short ride southwest of the lake is **Dragon Well Tea Park** (Longjing Wencha), set amid rolling tea plantations. This park is named for an ancient well whose water is considered ideal for brewing the famous local Longjing tea. Distinguishing between varieties and grades of tea can be confusing for novices, especially under the high pressure of the eager hawkers. It is worth a preliminary trip to the nearby tea museum to bone up first. The highest quality varieties are very expensive, but once you take a sip you will taste the difference. Opening prices are intentionally high, so be sure to bargain. ✉ *Longjing Lu, next to Dragon Well Temple.*

★ The fascinating **China Tea Museum** (Zhongguo Chaye Bowuguan) explores all the facets of China's tea culture, such as the utensils used in the traditional ceremony. Galleries contain fascinating information about the varieties and quality of leaves, brewing techniques, and gathering methods, all with good English explanations. A shop also offers a range of tea for sale, without the bargaining you'll encounter at Dragon Well Tea Park. ✉ *Off Longjing Lu, north of Dragon Well Tea Park* ⊕ *www.teamuseum.cn* 🎫 *Free* ⊘ *Daily 8:30 AM–4:30 PM.*

In the hills southwest of the lake is **Running Tiger Spring** (Hupao Quan). According to legend, a traveling monk decided this setting would be a perfect location for a temple, but was disappointed to discover that there was no source of water. That night he dreamed of two tigers that ripped up the earth around him. When he awoke he was lying next to a spring. On the grounds is an intriguing "dripping wall," cut out of the mountain. Locals line up with jugs to collect the water that pours from its surface, believing the water has special qualities—and it does. Ask someone in the temple's souvenir shop to float a coin on the surface of the water to prove it. ✉ *Hupao Lu, near the Pagoda of Six Harmonies* 🎫 *Y15* ⊘ *Daily 6 AM–6 PM.*

Fodor'sChoice One of the major Zen Buddhist shrines in China, the **Temple of the Soul's**
★ **Retreat** (Lingyin Si) was founded in AD 326 by Hui Li, a Buddhist monk from India. He looked at the surrounding mountains and exclaimed, "This is the place where the souls of immortals retreat," hence the name. This site is especially notable for religious carvings on the nearby **Peak That Flew from Afar** (Feilai Feng). From the 10th to the 14th century, monks and artists sculpted more than 300 iconographical images on the mountain's face and inside caves. Unfortunately, the destruction wrought by the Red Guards during the Cultural Revolution is nowhere more evident than here. The temple and carvings are among the most popular spots in Hangzhou. To avoid the crowds, try to visit during the week. The temple is about 3 km (2 mi) southwest of West Lake. ✉ *End of Lingyin Si Lu* ☎ *0571/8796–9691* 🎫 *Park Y25, temple Y20* ⊘ *Park daily 6:30 AM–6 PM, temple daily 7–5.*

The Qiantang Tidal Bore

DURING THE AUTUMNAL EQUINOX, when the moon's gravitational pull is at its peak, huge waves crash up the Qiantang River. Every year at this time, crowds gather at a safe distance to watch what begins as a distant line of white waves approaching. As it nears, it becomes a towering, thundering wall of water.

The phenomenon, known as a tidal bore, occurs when strong tides surge against the current of the river. The Qiantang Tidal Bore is the largest in the world, with speeds recorded up to 25 mi an hour, and heights of 30 feet. The Qiantang has the best conditions in the world to produce these tidal waves. Incoming tides are funneled into the shallow riverbed from the Gulf of Hangzhou. The bell shape narrows and concentrates the wave. People have been swept away in the past, so police now enforce a strict viewing distance.

From worm to weave, the **China National Silk Museum** (Zhongguo Sichou Bowuguan) explores traditional silk production, illustrating every step of the way. By the end, you'll comprehend the cost of this fine fiber made from cocoons of mulberry-munching larvae. On display are looms, brocades, and a rotating exhibit of historical robes from different Chinese dynasties. The 1st-floor shop has the city's largest selection of silk, and sells it by the meter. The museum is south of West Lake, on the road to Jade Emperor Hill. ⊠ *73-1 Yuhuangshan Lu* ☎ *0571/8706–2129* ⊕ *www.chinasilkmuseum.com* 🖾 *Free* ☉ *Daily 8–6.*

Atop **Moon Mountain** (Yuelin Shan) stands the impressive **Pagoda of Six Harmonies** (Liuhe Ta). Those who climb to the top of the seven-story pagoda are rewarded with great views across the Qiantang River. Originally lanterns were lit in its windows, and the pagoda served as a lighthouse for ships navigating the river. On the 18th day of the 8th lunar month, the pagoda is packed with people wanting the best seat for Qiantang Reversal. On this day the flow of the river reverses itself, creating large waves that for centuries have delighted observers. Behind the pagoda in an extensive park is an exhibit of 100 or so miniature pagodas, representing every Chinese style. The pagoda is 2½ km (1½ mi) south of West Lake. ⊠ *Fuxing Jie, on the Qiantang River* 🖾 *Y15* ☉ *Daily 6 AM–6:30 PM.*

TOURS

Hotels can set up tours of the city's sights. You can also hire a car, driver, and translator through CITS, which has an office east of West Lake in the building of the Zhejiang Tourism Board. It's relatively inexpensive, and you'll be privy to discounts you wouldn't be able to negotiate for yourself. Smaller travel services tend to be less reliable and less experienced with the needs of foreign travelers.

Taxi drivers at the train station or in front of hotels will often offer tours. Although these can be as good as official ones, your driver's knowledge of English is often minimal.

🗂 CITS ⊠ 1 Shihan Lu, Hangzhou ☎ 0571/8515-2888.

Where to Stay & Eat

$$–$$$$ ✕ **Louwailou Restaurant.** Back in 1848, this place opened as a fish shack

Fodor's Choice on West Lake. Business boomed and it became the most famous restau-

★ rant in the province. Specializing in Zhejiang cuisine, Louwailou makes special use of lake perch, which is steamed and served with vinegar sauce. Another highlight is the classic *su dongpo* pork, slow cooked in yellow-rice wine and tender enough to cut with chopsticks. Hangzhou's most famous dish, Beggar's Chicken, is wrapped in lotus leaves and baked in a clay shell. It's as good as it sounds. ⊠ *30 Gushan Lu, southern tip of Solitary Hill Island* ☎ *0571/8796-9682* ▤ *AE, MC, V.*

$$ ✕ **Haveli.** A sign of the city's cosmopolitan atmosphere, Nanshan Lu is home to several good international restaurants. The best of these is this authentic Indian restaurant, with a solid menu of dishes ranging from lamb vindaloo to chicken tandoor cooked in a traditional oven. End your meal with a fantastic mango-flavored yogurt drink. Choose between the dining room with a high peaked ceiling and exposed wood beams or the large patio. A belly dancer performs nightly. ⊠ *77 Nanshan Lu, south of Orioles Singing in the Willow Waves* ☎ *0571/8707-9177* ⚐ *Reservations essential* ▤ *AE, DC, MC, V.*

¢–$ ✕ **Zhiweiguan Restaurant.** In business for nearly a century, this restaurant's bustling 1st floor is a pay-as-you-go dim-sum counter. No menu necessary: you point to order a bamboo steamer filled with their famous dumplings or a bowl of wonton soup. The 2nd floor is for proper dinner, where the menu is full of well-prepared fish dishes. ⊠ *83 Renhe Lu, east side of West Lake* ☎ *0571/8701-8638* ▤ *No credit cards.*

$–$$ ✕ **Lingyin Si Vegetarian Restaurant.** Inside the Temple of the Soul's Retreat, this restaurant has turned the Buddhist restriction against eating meat into an opportunity to invent a range of delicious vegetarian dishes. Soy replaces chicken and beef, meaning your meal is as benevolent to your health as to the animal world. ⊠ *End of Lingyin Si Lu western shore of West Lake* ☎ *0571/8796-9691* ▤ *No credit cards* ⊘ *No dinner.*

★ $$$$ 🏨 **Sofitel Westlake Hangzhou.** A stone's throw from West Lake, this high-end hotel is situated in a lively neighborhood of restaurants, bars, and shops. Gauzy curtains and etched-glass and -wood columns divide the distinctive lobby, distinguished by a gold-and-black mural of the city's landmarks. The

WORD OF MOUTH
"If just relaxing is the aim, then Hangzhou is a better choice than Shanghai, I'd say, but three nights would almost certainly be enough."   –PeterN_H

rooms—most of which have lake views—are thoughtfully designed, with sleek oval desks, fabric-covered headboards, and a glass privacy screen in the bathroom. A Roman-style pool overcomes its drab basement location. The hotel is a block north of Orioles Singing in the Willow Waves. ⊠ *333 Xihu Dadao, 310002* ☎ *0571/8707–5858* ⊕ *www. accor.com* ⌂ *186 rooms, 15 suites* ♨ *4 restaurants, room service, in-room safes, minibars, cable TV with movies, in-room data ports, Wi-Fi, indoor pool, gym, hair salon, massage, sauna, spa, bar, lobby lounge, piano, shops, dry cleaning, laundry service, concierge, concierge floor, business services, convention center, airport shuttle, no-smoking rooms* ▭ *AE, DC, MC, V.*

$$$–$$$$ 🏨 **Hyatt Regency Hangzhou.** Hangzhou's newest luxury hotel, the Hyatt **Fodor's**Choice Regency combines careful service, comfortable rooms, and a great lo-★ cation. A large pool with a fountain water show overlooks West Lake. Inside there's a day spa, as well as excellent Chinese and Western restaurants. About two blocks north is Hubing Yi Park Boat Dock, where you can catch boats that ply the lake. The rooms are sleekly furnished, and unlike many hotels in China, the beds here are truly soft. Ask for a room on an upper floor for an unobstructed view. ⊠ *28 Hu Bin Lu, 310006* ☎ *0571/8779–1234* ⊕ *www.hyatt.com* ⌂ *390 rooms, 23 suites* ♨ *3 restaurants, room service, in-room safes, minibars, in-room broadband, golf privileges, tennis court, indoor pool, gym, sauna, spa, squash, steam room, 2 bars, shops, children's programs (ages 1–12), dry cleaning, laundry service, concierge, business services, convention center, no-smoking rooms* ▭ *AE, DC, MC, V.*

$$$–$$$$ 🏨 **Lakeview Wanghu Hotel.** True to its name, this hotel has good views of the water from its position near the northeastern shore of West Lake. It's oriented toward business travelers, which is why it emphasizes its meeting facilities and 24-hour business center. An on-site travel agency employs several guides who specialize in working with English-speaking travelers. ⊠ *2 Huancheng Xi Lu, 310006* ☎ *0571/8707–8888* 🖷 *0571/8707–1350* ⊕ *www.wanghuhotel.com* ⌂ *348 rooms, 9 suites* ♨ *2 restaurants, pool, gym, hair salon, sauna, bar, business services, meeting room* ▭ *AE, MC, V.*

$$–$$$$ 🏨 **Shangri-La Hotel Hangzhou.** Set on the site of an ancient temple, the **Fodor's**Choice Shangri-La is itself a scenic and historic landmark. The hotel's 40 hill-★ side acres of camphor and bamboo trees merge seamlessly into the nearby gardens and walkways surrounding West Lake. Spread through two wings, the large rooms have a formal feel, with high ceilings and heavy damask fabrics. Request a room overlooking the lake. The gym and restaurants are all top caliber. A 1st floor garden bar is an elegant spot to relax with a drink. ⊠ *78 Beishan Lu, 310007* ☎ *0571/8797–7951* ⊕ *www.shangri-la.com* ⌂ *355 rooms, 37 suites* ♨ *3 restaurants, room service, in-room safes, minibars, in-room data ports, tennis court, indoor pool, gym, hair salon, hot tub, massage, sauna, steam room, bicycles, billiards, bar, lobby lounge, shops, babysitting, dry cleaning, laundry service, concierge, bike rentals, concierge floor, Internet, business services, convention center, airport shuttle, travel services, no-smoking rooms* ▭ *AE, DC, MC, V.*

¢–$$$ 🖼 **Dragon Hotel.** Within walking distance of Precious Stone Hill and the Yellow Dragon Cave, this hotel stands in relatively peaceful and attractive surroundings. It's a massive place, but feels much smaller because its buildings are spread around peaceful courtyards with ponds, a waterfall, and a gazebo. Two towers house the medium-size guest rooms, which are decorated in pale greens and blues. Although it has plenty of facilities, the hotel lacks the polish of its Western competitors. The hotel is currently undergoing renovations; ask for one of the newly redecorated rooms. ✉ *120 Shuguang Lu, at Hangda Lu, 310007* ☎ *0571/ 8799–8833* ⊕ *www.dragon-hotel.com* 🛏 *499 rooms, 29 suites* ♨ *4 restaurants, room service, in-room safes, minibars, in-room data ports, tennis court, pool, gym, hair salon, hot tub, massage, sauna, bicycles, lobby lounge, shops, babysitting, dry cleaning, laundry service, concierge, Internet, business services, convention center, travel services, no-smoking rooms, no-smoking floors* ▭ *AE, DC, MC, V.*

¢ 🖼 **Dong Po Hotel.** This budget business hotel is clean and comfortable. The smaller rooms are rather utilitarian, but the location in the center of town—two blocks from the lake and two blocks from the night market—makes this a good choice. ✉ *52 Renhe Lu, 310000* ☎ *0571/ 8706–9769* 🛏 *99 rooms, 3 suites* ♨ *Restaurant, business services* ▭ *MC, V.*

¢ 🖼 **Hangzhou Overseas Chinese Hotel.** A budget hotel with a five-star location, the Overseas Chinese Hotel is steps from West Lake. The chipped woodwork and beige color scheme makes it less flashy than its competitors, but the low price makes this hotel a good pick. Rooms on the 5th floor have the best views over the water. You can hire a car and driver through the hotel to tour the outlying area. ✉ *39 Hubin Lu, 310006* ☎ *0571/8768–5555* 🛏 *218 rooms, 4 suites* ♨ *5 restaurants, in-room safes, minibars, hair salon, massage, sauna, 2 bars, shops, babysitting, laundry service, business services, meeting rooms, travel services, car rental* ▭ *AE, DC, MC, V.*

Nightlife & the Arts

The city's most exciting bar is the **Travelers Pub** (✉ 176 Shuguang Lu ☎ 0571/8796–8846), the only venue for live jazz and folk music. A bohemian crowd gathers here during the week, and on weekends hipsters fill the place to capacity. Subtle political murals decorate the wall, and there's even a bulletin board for those looking to meet fellow travelers and artists looking for collaborators.

The laid-back **Kana Pub** (✉ 152 Nanshan Lu ☎ 0571/8706–3228) is an expat favorite for its well-mixed cocktails, live music, and friendly proprietor. The personable staff at the **Shamrock** (✉ 70 Zhongshan Zhong Lu ☎ 0571/8702–8760), the city's first Irish pub, serves Guinness and Kilkenny pints, bottled-beer specials, along with great food.

Yue opera performances take place daily from 8:45 AM to 11:30 AM and 1:45 PM to 4:30 PM at the **Yuanyuan Minsu Theater** (✉ 69 Shuguang Lu ☎ 0571/8797–2468), at the Yellow Dragon Cave. The performances are free with the Y15 park admission.

Art for Art's Sake

THE CONTEMPORARY ARTS SCENE in Hangzhou grows by the year, with a mix of national and international artists calling Hangzhou home. For current art exhibits, grab a copy of *In Touch* (⊕ www.intouchzj.com), an English-language magazine available in many hotels and coffee shops.

Some of the country's hottest artists show their work at **Contrasts** (✉ No. 20-2b Hubin Lu ☎ 0571/8717–2519 ⊕ www.contrastsgallery.com).

At **Loft 49** (✉ 49 Hangyin Lu ☎ 0571/8823–8782 ⊕ www.loft49.cn), industrial spaces have been transformed into studios for the cutting-edge artists, sculptors, and architects. This former printing factory has free galleries and a café.

Frequent exhibits of painting and sculpture are on display at **Red Star** (✉ 280 Jianguo Nan Lu ☎ 0571/8770–3888 ⊕ www.redstarhotel.com).

Shopping

The best souvenirs to buy in Hangzhou are green tea and silk, but all sorts of wooden crafts, silk fans and umbrellas, and antiques are available in small shops sprinkled around town. For the best Longjing tea, head to Dragon Well Tea Park or the China Tea Museum. Around town, especially along Yanan Lu, you can spot the small tea shops by the woklike tea roasters at the entrances.

China Silk City (Zhongguo Sichou Cheng; ✉ 253 Xinhua Lu, between Fengqi Lu and Tiyuchang Lu ☎ 0571/8510–0192) sells silk ties, pajamas, and shirts, plus silk straight off the bolt. A combination health-food store and apothecary, **Fulintang** (✉ 147 Nanshan Lu ☎ 0571/8702–6639) sells herbs and other health-enhancing products. About three blocks north of the China Tea Museum, the **Xihu Longjing Tea Company** (✉ 15 Longjing Lu ☎ 0571/8796–2219) has a nice selection of Longjing tea.

Hangzhou's **Night Market** (✉ Renhe Lu, east of Huansha Lu) is thriving. In addition to Hangzhou's best selection of late-night snacks, you'll find accessories of every kind—ties, scarves, pillow covers—as well as knockoff designer goods and fake antiques. You'll find the same merchandise at many stalls, so don't hesitate to walk away if the price isn't right. It's open nightly 6 PM–10:30 PM.

To & from Hangzhou

2 hrs (180 km [112 mi]) by train or express bus southwest of Shanghai.

Hangzhou is most accessible by train. Already a popular weekend trip from Shanghai, it will become even more so if the government builds a new line that would cut the 1½- to 2½-hour trip down to 30 minutes. Trains to Suzhou take 3 to 4 hours.

WORD OF MOUTH

"Local dishes made with the famous Shaoxing 'yellow wine' are worth trying, and you can get all the same Huaiyang dishes you can get in Hangzhou, too." –PeterN_H

There are buses that will get you to Shanghai in 2 hours or Suzhou in 2½ hours. Hangzhou has several stations spread around the city serving different destinations—buses to Shanghai use the East Bus Station, whereas those to Suzhou use the North Bus Station. Be careful to check that you are headed to the correct terminal.

Shaoxing

★ ❷ Shaoxing is alive in the Chinese imagination thanks to the famous writer Lu Xun, who set many of his classic works in this sleepy southern town. A literary revolutionary, Lu Xun broke tradition by writing in the vernacular of everyday Chinese, instead of the stiff, scholarly prose previously held as the only appropriate language for literature.

Today, much of the city's charm is in exploring its narrow cobbled streets. The older sections of the city are made of low stone houses, connected by canals and crisscrossed by arched bridges. East Lake is no match for the grandeur of Hangzhou's West Lake, but its bizarre rock formations and caves make for interesting tours. Shaoxing is also famous for its celebrated yellow-rice wine, used by cooks everywhere.

Exploring

The **Lu Xun Family Home** (Lu Xun Gu Ju) was once the stomping grounds of literary giant and social critic Lu Xun. The extended Lu family lived around a series of courtyards. Nearby is the local school where Lu honed his writing skills. This is a great place to explore a traditional Shaoxing home and see some beautiful antique furniture. ⊠ *398 Lu Xun Zhong Lu, 1 block east of Xianhen Hotel* ☎ *0575/513–2080* ⊠ *Y60* ☉ *Daily 8:30–4:30.*

> **WORD OF MOUTH**
>
> "I asked a Shaoxing taxi driver about "stinky tofu" and got a dissertation in response. Stinky tofu is either a religion or an all-consuming passion in Shaoxing, I haven't quite figured it out yet!"
> –easytraveler

In a city of bridges, **Figure 8 Bridge** (Bazi Qiao Bridge) is the city's finest and best known. Its long, sloping sides rise to a flat crest that looks like the character for eight, an auspicious number. The current bridge is over 800 years old, and is draped with a thick beard of ivy and vines. It sits in a quiet area of old stone houses with canal-side terraces where people wash clothes and chat with neighbors. ⊠ *Bazi Qiao Zhi Jie, off Renmin Zhong Lu.*

Near the Figure 8 Bridge is the bright pink **Catholic Church of St. Joseph,** dating from the turn of the 20th century. A hybrid of styles, the Italian-inspired interior is decorated with passages from the Bible in Chinese calligraphy. ⊠ *Bazi Qiao Zhi Jie, off Renmin Zhong Lu.*

The city's quiet northern neighborhoods are especially amenable to wandering, with several historic homes and temples that are now preserved as museums. The largest is the **Cai Yuanpei's House** (⊠ On alley north of Xiaoshan Lu, which runs east from Jiefang Lu ☎ 0575/511–0652 ⊠ Y8 ☉ Daily 8–5). The owner was a famous educator during

What's Cooking

SHAOXING SECURED ITS PLACE in the Chinese culinary pantheon with Shaoxing wine, the best yellow-rice wine in the country. Although cooks around the world know the nutty-flavored wine as a marinade and seasoning, in Shaoxing the fermented brew of glutinous rice is put to a variety of uses, from drinking straight up (as early as breakfast) to sipping as a medicine (infused with traditional herbs and remedies). Like grape wines, Shaoxing mellows and improves with age, as its color deepens to a reddish brown. It is local custom to bury a cask when a daughter is born and serve it when she marries.

The wine is excellent accompaniment to Shaoxing snacks such as pickled greens, and the city's most popular street food *chou doufu*, which means "stinking tofu." The golden-fried squares of tender tofu taste great, if you can get past the pungent odor. Also, look for dishes made with another Shaoxing product, fermented bean curd. With a flavor not unlike an aged cheese, it's rarely eaten by itself, but complements fish and sharpens the flavor of meat dishes.

the republic, and his family's large compound is decorated with period furniture.

The **Zhou Enlai Family Home** (✉ 369 Laodong Lu ☎ 0575/513–3368 💴 Y18 ⊙ Daily 8–5) belonged to the first premier of Communist China, who came from a family of prosperous Shaoxing merchants. Zhou is credited with saving some of China's most important historical monuments from destruction at the hands of the Red Guards during the Cultural Revolution. The compound, a showcase of traditional architecture, has been preserved and houses exhibits on Zhou's life, ranging from his high-school essays to vacation snapshots with his wife.

The narrow **East Lake** (Dong Hu) runs along the base of a rocky bluff rising up from the rice paddies of Zhejiang. The crazily shaped cliffs were used as a rock quarry over the centuries, and today their sheer gray faces jut out in sheets of rock. You can hire a local boatman to take you along the base of the cliffs in a traditional black awning boat for Y40. ✉ *Yundong Lu, 3 km (2 mi) east of the city center* 💴 *Y25* ⊙ *Daily 7:30–5:30.*

Where to Stay & Eat

¢–$ ✕**Sanwei Jiulou.** This restaurant serves up local specialties, including warm rice wine served in Shaoxing's distinctive tin kettles. Relaxed and distinctive, it's located in a restored old building and appointed with traditional wood furniture. The second story looks out over the street below. ✉ *2 Lu Xun Lu* ☎ *0575/893–5578* ▭ *No credit cards.*

¢ ✕**Xianheng Winehouse** (Xianheng Jiudian). Shaoxing's most famous fictional character, the small-town scholar Kong Yiji, would sit on a bench here, dining on wine and boiled beans. Forgo the beans, but the fermented bean curd is good, especially with a bowl of local wine. ✉ *179 Lu Xun*

Zhong Lu, 1 block east of the San-
wei Jiulou ☏ *0575/511–6666*
🖃 *No credit cards.*

$–$$ 🏨 **Shaoxing International Hotel**
(Shaoxing Guoji Dajiudian). Surrounded by pleasant gardens, this
hotel offers bright, well-appointed
rooms and a range of facilities. It's
located near the West Bus Station.
🖂 *100 Fushan Xi Lu, 312000*
☏ *0575/516–6788* ⤴ *302 rooms* ⚬ *2 restaurants, minibars, pool, ten-*
nis court, gym, sauna, business services 🖃 *AE, DC, MC, V.*

$–$$ 🏨 **Shaoxing Xianheng Hotel.** Conveniently located near many of the
city's restaurants, the Shaoxing Xianheng offers modern, comfortable
rooms and good service. 🖂 *680 Jiefang Nan Lu, 312000* ☏ *0575/806–*
8688 ⤴ *221 rooms, 8 suites* ⚬ *2 restaurants, pool, tennis court, gym,*
sauna, bar, business services 🖃 *AE, MC, V.*

Shopping

Shaoxing has some interesting local crafts, mainly related to calligraphy and rice wine. The most convenient place to buy souvenirs is the
shopping street called **Lu Xun Zhong Lu.** In addition to calligraphy brushes,
and fans, scrolls, and other items decorated with calligraphy, look for
shops selling the local tin wine pots. The traditional way of serving yellow-rice wine, the pots are placed on the stove to heat up wine for a
cold winter night. Also popular are traditional boatmen's hats, made
of thick waterproof black felt.

To & from Shaoxing

1 hr (68 km [42 mi]) by bus or train east from Hangzhou.

Regular train and luxury bus service runs to Shaoxing from Hangzhou
and Shanghai a few times a day.

ZHEJIANG ESSENTIALS

Transportation

BY AIR

Hangzhou Xiaoshan International Airport, about 27 km (17 mi) southeast of the city, has frequent flights to Hong Kong, Guangzhou, and Beijing, which are all about 2 hours away. There are also flights to other
major cities around the region.

Major hotels offer limousine service to the airport. Taxis to the airport
cost around Y120. A bus leaves from the CAAC office on Tiyuchang Lu
every 30 minutes between 5:30 AM and 8:30 PM. It costs Y15 per person.

🛈 Airport Information **Hangzhou Xiaoshan International Airport** 🖂 Hangzhou Xiaoshan District ☏ 0571/8666-1234.

🛈 Airlines & Contacts **CAAC** 🖂 390 Tiyuchang Lu, Hangzhou ☏ 0571/8515-4259. **Drag-**
onair 🖂 Radisson Plaza Hotel Hangzhou, 333 Ti Yu Chang Lu, Hangzhou ☏ 0571/
8506-8388.

BY BOAT & FERRY

You can travel overnight by ferry between Hangzhou and Suzhou on the Grand Canal. Tickets are available through CITS or at the dock. It's a slow trip compared to buses and trains, and it's at night, so there's little to see.

One of the best ways to experience the charm of West Lake is on one of the many boats that ply the waters. Ferries charge Y35 for trips to the main islands. They depart when there are enough passengers, usually about every 20 minutes. Small private boats charge Y80 for up to four people, but you can choose your own route. You can head out on your own boat for Y20, but you can't dock at the islands.

🚩 Boat & Ferry Information **CITS** ✉ Huancheng Bei Lu, Hangzhou ☎ 0571/8515-3360.

BY BUS TO & FROM ZHEJIANG

The bus hub for the province is Hangzhou, where you'll find four stations. The West Bus Station (Xi Zhan) has several buses daily to the Yellow Mountain, as well as to Nanjing. The East Bus Station (Dong Zhan) is the town's biggest, with several hundred departures per day to destinations like Shaoxing (1 hr), Suzhou (2 ½ hrs), and Shanghai (3 hrs). About 9 km (5 mi) north of the city is the North Bus Station (Bei Zhan), where there are buses to Nanjing (4 to 4½ hours).

Make sure you check with your hotel or travel agent which bus station you need to use.

🚩 Bus Information **East Bus Station** ✉ 215 Liangshan Xi Lu, Hangzhou ☎ 0571/8694-8252. **North Bus Station** ✉ Moganshan Lu-Huayuan Gang, Hangzhou ☎ 0571/8604-6666. **West Bus Station** ✉ 60 Tianmushan Lu, Hangzhou ☎ 0571/8522-2237.

BY BUS WITHIN ZHEJIANG

In addition to regular city buses, Hangzhou has a series of modern, air-conditioned buses that connect most major tourist sights. They are an easy way to get to more isolated sights. Bus Y1 connects Baidi Causeway, Solitary Hill Island, Yue Fei Mausoleum, the Temple of the Soul's Retreat, and Orioles Singing in the Willow Waves. Bus Y3 runs to Precious Stone Hill, the China National Silk Museum, and the China Tea Museum.

Hangzhou's East Bus Station has dozens of buses each day to Shaoxing. In Shaoxing, buses to Hangzhou leave from the main bus station in the north of town, at the intersection of Jiefang Bei Lu and Huan Cheng Bei Lu.

BY TAXI

Hangzhou's taxi fleet is among the most modern and comfortable in China, and makes it easy to get from West Lake to far-flung sights like the Temple of the Soul's Retreat and the China Tea Museum (Y30 to Y45).

Although Shaoxing is small enough that walking is the best way to get between many sights, the city's small red taxis are relatively inexpensive. Most trips are Y15.

Continued on page 326

SPIRITUALITY IN CHINA

Even though it's officially an atheist nation, China has a vibrant religious life. But what are the differences between China's big three faiths of Buddhism, Taoism, and Confucianism? Like much else in the Middle Kingdom, the lines are often blurred.

Walking around the streets of any city in China in the early 21st century, it's hard to believe that only three decades ago the bulk of the Middle Kingdom's centuries-old religious culture was destroyed by revolutionary zealots, and that the few temples, mosques, monasteries, and churches that escaped outright destruction were desecrated and turned into warehouses and factories, or put to other ignoble uses. Those days are long over, and religious life in China has sprung back to life. Even though the official line of the Chinese Communist Party is that the nation is atheist, China is rife with religious diversity.

Perhaps the faith most commonly associated with China is Confucianism, an ethical and philosophical system developed from the teachings of the sage Confucius. Confucianism stresses the importance of relationships in society and of maintaining proper etiquette. These aspects of Confucian thought are associated not merely with China (where its modern-day influence is dubious at best, especially in a crowded subway car), but also with East Asian culture as a whole. Confucianism also places great emphasis on filial piety, the respect that a child should show an elder (or subjects to their ruler). This may account for

(left) Offering up joss sticks.
(below) The Yong he Gong
Lama temple in Beijing.

4

Confucianism's status as the most officially tolerated of modern China's faiths.

Taoism is based on the teachings of the *Tao Te Ching,* a treatise written in the 6th century BC, and blends an emphasis on spiritual harmony with that of the individual's duty to society. Taoism and Confucianism are complementary, though to the outsider, the former might seem more steeped in ritual and mysticism. Think of it this way: Taoism is to Confucianism as Catholicism is to Protestantism. Taoism's mystic quality may be why so many westerners come to China to study "the way," as Taoism is sometimes called.

Buddhism came to China from India in the first century AD and quickly became a major force in the Middle Kingdom. The faith is so ingrained here that many Chinese openly scoff at the idea that the Buddha wasn't Chinese. In a nutshell, Buddhism teaches that attachment leads to suffering, and that the best way to alleviate the world's suffering is to purify one's mind, to abstain from evil, and to

Tian Tan, The Temple of Heaven in Beijing.

cultivate good. In China, there are three major schools: the Chinese school, embraced mainly by Han Chinese; the Tibetan school (or Lamaism) as practiced by Tibetans and Mongolians; and Theravada, practiced by the Dai and other ethnic minority groups in the southwest of the country.

TEMPLE FAUX PAS

Chinese worshippers are easygoing. Even at the smallest temple or shrine, they understand that some people will be visitors and not devotees. Temples in China have relaxed dress codes, but you should follow certain rules of decorum.

■ You're welcome to burn incense, but it's not required. If you do decide to burn a few joss sticks, take them from the communal pile and be sure to make a small donation. This usually goes to temple upkeep or local charities.

The Buddha

■ When burning incense, two sticks signify marriage, and four signify death.

■ Respect signs reading NO PHOTO in front of altars and statues. Taoist temples seem particularly sensitive about photo taking. When in doubt, ask.

■ Avoid stepping in front of a worshipper at an altar or censer (where incense is burned).

■ Speak quietly and silence mobile phones inside of temple grounds.

■ Don't touch Buddhist monks of the opposite sex.

■ Avoid entering a temple during a ceremony.

TEMPLE OBJECTS

For many, temple visits are among the most culturally edifying parts of a China trip. Large or small, Chinese temples incorporate a variety of objects significant to religious practice.

INCENSE

Incense is the most common item in any Chinese temple. In antiquity, Chinese people burned sacrifices both as an offering and as a way of communicating with spirits through the smoke. This later evolved into a way of showing respect for one's ancestors by burning fragrances that the dearly departed might find particularly pleasing.

BAGUA

Taoist temples will have a bagua: an octagonal diagram pointing toward the eight cardinal directions, each representing different points on the compass, elements in nature, family members, and more esoteric meanings. The bagua is often used in conjunction with a compass to make placement decisions in architectural design and in fortune-telling.

"GHOST MONEY"

Sometimes the spirits need more than sweet-smelling smoke, and this is why many Taoists burn "ghost money" (also known as "hell money"), a scented paper resembling cash. Though once more popular in Taiwan and Hong Kong (and looked upon as a particularly capitalist superstition on the mainland), the burning of ghost money is now gaining ground throughout the country.

CENSER

Every Chinese temple will have a censer in which to place joss sticks, either inside the hall or out front. Larger temples often have a number of them. These large stone or bronze bowls are filled with incense ash from hundreds of joss sticks placed by worshippers. Some incense censers are ornate, with sculpted bronze rising above the bowls.

STATUES

Chinese temples are known for being flexible, and statues of various deities, mythical figures, and multiple interpretations of the Buddha abound. Confucius is usually rendered as a wizened man with a long beard, and Taoist temples have an array of demons and deities.

PRAYER WHEEL

Used primarily by Tibetan Buddhists, the prayer wheel is a beautifully embossed hollow metal cylinder mounted on a wooden handle. Inside the cylinder is a tightly wound scroll printed with a mantra. Devotees believe that the spinning of a prayer wheel is a form of prayer that's just as effective as reciting the sacred texts aloud.

CHINESE ASTROLOGY

According to legend, the King of Jade invited 12 animals to visit him in heaven. As the animals rushed to be the first to arrive, the rat snuck a ride on the ox's back. Just as the ox was about to cross the threshold, the rat jumped past him and arrived first. This is why the rat was given first place in the astrological chart. Find the year you were born to determine what your astrological animal is.

RAT

1924 • 1936 • 1948 • 1960 • 1972 • 1984 • 1996 • 2008

Charming and hardworking, Rats are goal setters and perfectionists. Rats are quick to anger, ambitious, and lovers of gossip.

OX

1925 • 1937 • 1949 • 1961 • 1973 • 1985 • 1997 • 2009

Patient and soft-spoken, Oxen inspire confidence in others. Generally easygoing, they can be remarkably stubborn, and they hate to fail or be opposed.

TIGER

1926 • 1938 • 1950 • 1962 • 1974 • 1986 • 1998 • 2010

Sensitive, and thoughtful, Tigers are capable of great sympathy. Tigers can be short-tempered, and are prone to conflict and indecisiveness.

RABBIT

1927 • 1939 • 1951 • 1963 • 1975 • 1987 • 1999 • 2011

Talented and articulate, Rabbits are virtuous, reserved, and have excellent taste. Though fond of gossip, Rabbits tend to be generally kind and even-tempered.

DRAGON

1928 • 1940 • 1952 • 1964 • 1976 • 1988 • 2000 • 2012

Energetic and excitable, short-tempered and stubborn, Dragons are known for their honesty, bravery, and ability to inspire confidence and trust.

SNAKE

1929 • **1941** • **1953** • **1965** • **1977** • **1989** • **2001** • **2013**

Snakes are deep, possessing great wisdom and saying little. Snakes can often be vain and selfish while retaining sympathy for those less fortunate.

HORSE

1930 • **1942** • **1954** • **1966** • **1978** • **1990** • **2002** • **2014**

Horses are thought to be cheerful and perceptive, impatient and hot-blooded. Horses are independent and rarely listen to advice.

GOAT

1931 • **1943** • **1955** • **1967** • **1979** • **1991** • **2003** • **2015**

Wise, gentle, and compassionate, Goats are elegant and highly accomplished in the arts. Goats can also be shy and pessimistic, and often tend toward timidity.

MONKEY

1932 • **1944** • **1956** • **1968** • **1980** • **1992** • **2004** • **2016**

Clever, skillful, and flexible, Monkeys are thought to be erratic geniuses, able to solve problems with ease. Monkeys are also thought of as impatient and easily discouraged.

ROOSTER

1933 • **1945** • **1957** • **1969** • **1981** • **1993** • **2005** • **2017**

Roosters are capable and talented, and tend to like to keep busy. Roosters are known as overachievers, and are frequently loners.

DOG

1934 • **1946** • **1958** • **1970** • **1982** • **1994** • **2006** • **2018**

Dogs are loyal and honest and know how to keep secrets. They can also be selfish and stubborn.

PIG

1935 • **1947** • **1959** • **1971** • **1983** • **1995** • **2007** • **2019**

Gallant and energetic, Pigs have a tendency to be single-minded and determined. Pigs have great fortitude and honesty, and tend to make friends for life.

4

SPIRITUALITY IN CHINA

BY TRAIN

Travel between Shanghai and Hangzhou is quick and convenient: regular trains take about three hours; newer express trains take only two. The train station is crowded and difficult to manage, but hotel travel desks can often book advance tickets for a small fee. Trains also run to Suzhou (3 hours), Nanjing (5½ hours), and most cities in Fujian.

Trains between Hangzhou and Shaoxing take about 1 hour, but do not leave as frequently as buses. The Shaoxing Train Station is 2½ km (1½ mi) north of the city, near the main bus station.

🚆 Train Information **Hangzhou Train Station** ⊠ 1 Huan Cheng Dong Lu, near intersection of Jiang Cheng Lu and Xihu Da Dao ☎ 0571/8782-9418. **Shaoxing Train Station** ⊠ Shaoxing Chezhan Lu ☎ 0575/802-2584.

Contacts & Resources

EMERGENCIES

As one of China's wealthier cities, the standard of medical care in Hangzhou is reasonably high.

🚑 **Hangzhou Red Cross Hospital** ⊠ 38 Huancheng Dong Lu ☎ 0571/8518-6042 or 0571/8518-3137. **Zhejiang Medical University Affiliated Hospital No. 1** ⊠ 261 Qingchun Lu, Hangzhou ☎ 0571/8707-2524. **Shaoxing People's Hospital** ⊠ 61 Shaoxing Dongjie ☎ 0575/522-8888.

MONEY MATTERS

ATMs are ubiquitous, but stick with Bank of China machines, as they are the most reliable. The only time you might need to enter an actual bank branch is to exchange currency or to cash traveler's checks. Make sure to save your receipt, as the local currency cannot be converted into dollars without proof that it was exchanged for dollars.

🏦 **Bank of China** ⊠ 140 Yan An Lu, Hangzhou ☎ 0571/8501-8888 ⊠ 268 Zhongxing Zhong Lu, Shaoxing ☎ 0575/514-3571.

TRAVEL AGENCIES

Most hotels offer visitor information, and there is always CITS.

🏢 Local Agent Referrals **Zhejiang Comfort Travel** ⊠ Shangri-La Hotel Hangzhou, 78 Beishan Lu, Hangzhou ☎ 0571/8796-5005. **Zhejiang Women's International Travel Service** ⊠ 1 508 Wensan Lu, Hangzhou ☎ 0571/8822-5166.

VISITOR INFORMATION

🛈 Tourist Information **Hangzhou Travel and Tourism Bureau** ⊠ 484 Yanan Lu ☎ 0571/8515-2645. **Zhejiang CITS** ⊠ 1 Shihan Lu, Hangzhou, next to the Hangzhou Tourism Bureau ☎ 0571/8516-0877.

FUJIAN

One of China's most beautiful provinces, Fujian has escaped the notice of most visitors. This is because the region, though not too far off the beaten path, is usually passed over in favor of more glamorous destinations like Hong Kong or Shanghai. The city of Xiamen is clean and beautiful, and the surrounding area has some of the best beaches north of Hainan. And Gulangyu is a rarity in modern China: a tree-filled island with undisturbed colonial architecture and absolutely no cars.

Xiamen

By Chinese standards, Xiamen is a new city: its history only dates to the late 12th century. Xiamen was a stronghold for Ming loyalist Zheng Chenggong (better known as Koxinga), who later fled to Taiwan after China was overrun by the Qing. Xiamen's place as a dynasty-straddling city continues to this day due to its proximity to Taiwan. Some see Xiamen as a natural meeting point between the two sides in the decades-long separation. Only a few miles out to sea are islands that still technically belong to "The Republic of China," as Taiwan is still officially known.

A prosperous city due to its importance as a trading port, Xiamen suffered because of China's anxieties over Taiwan. But as one of the first cities opened to foreign trade, Xiamen saw the money come rolling in again. It is today one of the most prosperous cities in China, with beautiful parks, amazing temples, and waterfront promenades that neatly complement the port city's historic architecture. Xiamen has a number of wonderful parks and temples well worth visiting.

Exploring Xiamen

❷ Nanputuo Temple (Nanputuo Si) dates from the Tang Dynasty. It has been restored many times, most recently in the 1980s, following the Cultural Revolution. Built in the exuberant style that visitors to Taiwan will find familiar, it has roofs that are decorated with brightly painted flourishes of clustered flowers, sinewy serpents, and mythical beasts. Pavilions on either side of the main hall contain tablets commemorating the suppression of secret societies by the Qing emperors. As the most important of Xiamen's temples, it is nearly always the center of a great deal of activity as monks and worshippers mix with tour groups. Attached to the temple complex is an excellent vegetarian restaurant. To get here, take Bus 1 or 2 from the port. ⊠ *Siming Nan Lu, next to Xiamen University* ⊡ *Y3* ☉ *Daily 7:30 AM–6:30 PM.*

❶ Housed in a fascinating mix of traditional and colonial buildings close to Nanputuo Temple is **Xiamen University** (Xiamen Daxue). It was founded in the 1920s with the help of Chinese people living abroad. The **Museum of Anthropology** (Renlei Bowuguan), dedicated to the study of the Neolithic era, is one of the most popular destinations. It has a very good collection of fossils, ceramics, paintings, and ornaments. It's open daily 8:30 to 11 and 3 to 5. ⊠ *End of Siming Nan Lu.*

❸ In the southern part of the city, the **Overseas Chinese Museum** (Huaqiao Bowuguan) was founded by the wealthy industrialist Tan Kah-kee. Three halls illustrate, with the help of pictures and documents, personal items, and relics associated with the great waves of emigration from southeastern China during the 19th century. ⊠ *Off Siming Nan Lu, at foot of Fengzhao Shan* ☏ *0592/208–5345* ⊡ *Y10* ☉ *Tues.–Sun. 8:30–11:30 and 2–5:30.*

❹ Surrounding a pretty lake, the **10,000 Rock Botanical Garden** (Wanshi Zhiwuyuan) has a fine collection of more than 4,000 species of tropical and

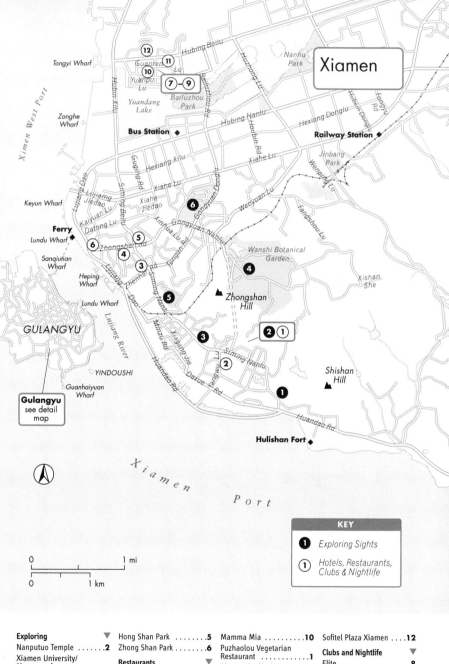

Xiamen

subtropical flora, ranging from eucalyptus and bamboo trees to orchids and ferns. There are several pavilions, of which the most interesting are those forming the **Temple of the Kingdom of Heaven** (Tianjie Si). ✉ *Huyuan Lu, off Wenyuan Lu* 🎫 *Y10* 🕙 *Daily 8–6.*

⑤ The rather hilly **Hong Shan Park** (Hong Shan Gong Yuan) has a small Buddhist temple, a lovely waterfall, and beautiful views of the city and the harbor. There's also a lovely tea shop serving Iron Buddha tea, a Fujian specialty. ✉ *Siming Nan Lu, near Nanputuo Temple* 🎫 *Free.*

⑥ Commemorating Dr. Sun Yat-sen, **Zhong Shan Park** (Zhong Shan Gong Yuan) is centered around a statue to the great man. There is a small zoo, lakes, and canals you can explore by paddleboat. The annual Lantern Festival is held here. ✉ *Zhong Shan Lu and Zhenhai Lu* 🎫 *Free.*

OFF THE BEATEN PATH

JINMEN – History buffs will be fascinated by a trip around this lingering remnant of China's bitter civil war. Though barely a stone's throw from mainland China, this island is still controlled by Taiwan. As of this writing only Xiamen residents are allowed to visit Jinmen, so tour boats only come close enough to let you see Taiwanese guards patrolling the shores or call out to the Taiwanese fishermen netting the waters. However, talks are continually underway between the two sides, and it's entirely possible that rules might be relaxed, allowing casual tourists to visit this cold-war outpost. Tours cost about Y80 per person.

HAKKA ROUNDHOUSES – (Yong Ding Tu Lou). Legend has it that when these four-story-tall structures were first spotted by the American military, fear spread that they were silos for some unknown gigantic missile. They were created centuries before by the Hakka, or "Guest People," an offshoot of the Han Chinese who settled all over southeastern China. These earthen homes are made of raw earth, glutinous rice, and brown sugar, reinforced with bamboo and wood. They are the most beautiful example of Hakka architecture. The roundhouses are in Yong Ding, 210 km (130 mi) northwest of Xiamen. To get here, take a bus from Xiamen to Longyan, then transfer to a minibus headed to Yong Ding. ✉ *Yong Ding* 🎫 *Y20.*

Tours

Xiamen is a great city to explore on your own, but if you'd like to hire a guide, all the major hotels have English-speaking guides. Tours can also be arranged through any China Travel Service office.

Where to Stay & Eat

Although Xiamen is known for its excellent seafood (this is a port city, after all), the city's Buddhist population means it has excellent vegetarian cuisine. Xiamen is probably the best place outside of Taiwan to experience Taiwanese cuisine, and many restaurants advertise their *Taiwan Wei Kou* and *Taiwan Xiao Chi,* meaning "Taiwanese flavor" and "Taiwanese snacks."

★ $$–$$$$ ✕ **Shuyou Seafood Restaurant.** Shuyou means "close friend," and that's how you're treated at this upscale establishment. Considered one of the best seafood restaurants in China (and certainly in Xiamen), Shuyou serves fresh seafood in an opulent setting. Downstairs, the tanks are filled with lobster, prawns, and crabs, and upstairs diners feast on seafood dishes cooked in Cantonese and Fujian styles. If you're in the mood for other fare, the restaurant is also known for its excellent Peking duck and goose liver. ⊠ *Hubin Bei Lu, between Marco Polo and Sofitel hotels* ☎ *0592/509–8888* ☒ *AE, MC, V.*

$–$$ ✕ **Guan Hai Canting.** On the rooftop of the waterfront Lujiang Hotel, this terrace restaurant has beautiful views over the bay. The Cantonese chef prepares delicious seafood dishes and dim-sum specialties like sweet pork buns and shrimp dumplings. ⊠ *54 Lujiang Lu, across from ferry terminal* ☎ *0592/202–2922* ☒ *AE, MC, V.*

$–$$ ✕ **Mamma Mia.** Across from the Marco Polo Xiamen hotel, Mamma Mia serves authentic Italian specialties like risotto, gnocchi, and several different types of pasta. There's also a beautiful bar on the 3rd floor where you can sink into plush chairs. ⊠ *Jianye Lu and Hubin Bei Lu* ☎ *0592/536–2662* ☒ *AE, MC, V.*

$–$$ ✕ **Puzhaolou Vegetarian Restaurant.** The comings and goings of monks add to the atmosphere at this restaurant next to the Nanputuo Temple. Popular dishes include black-fungus soup with tofu and stewed yams with seaweed. You won't find any English menus, so ask for one of the picture menus. ⊠ *Nanputuo Temple, Siming Nan Lu* ☎ *0592/208–5908* ☒ *No credit cards.*

¢–$ ✕ **Dafang Vegetarian Restaurant.** Across from Nanputuo Temple, this reasonably priced restaurant is popular with students. But don't just come for the low prices—it also has excellent food. Try the sweet and sour soup or the mock duck. English menus are available. ⊠ *412-9 Siming Nan Lu* ☎ *0592/209–3236* ☒ *No credit cards.*

¢ ✕ **Huangzehe Peanut Soup Shop.** Peanuts get the star treatment at this popular restaurant near the waterfront. Peanut soups, peanut sweets, and even peanut dumplings show off the culinary potential of the humble goober. ⊠ *24 Zhongshan Lu* ☎ *0592/212–5825* ☒ *No credit cards.*

$$$–$$$$ ⊞ **Sofitel Plaza Xiamen.** The newest (and costliest) luxury hotel in Xiamen, the Sofitel Plaza has a beautiful art-deco lobby. Though not on the beach, many of the nicely appointed guest rooms have a beautiful view of nearby Lake Yuandang. The location is convenient to the city's financial district. The Oasis Bar is a popular spot with Xiamen's trendy set. The guest rooms, with dark-wood furnishings, are beautiful and modern. ⊠ *19 Hubin Bei Lu, 361012* ☎ *0592/507–8888* ⊕ *www.sofitel.com* ↪ *383 rooms, 48 suites* ⬭ *Restaurant, in-room safes, in-room broadband, pool, gym, sauna, bar, business services, airport shuttle, no-smoking floors* ☒ *AE, MC, V.*

★ $$–$$$$ ⊞ **Holiday Inn Crowne Plaza Harbourview.** With an excellent location overlooking the harbor, this hotel is among the best in the city. Rooms are spacious and comfortable, as you'd expect from the chain, and the staff is friendly and attentive. The hotel's restaurants are particularly good, and the 1st-floor coffee shop is the only place in Xiamen to get a good New York–style deli sandwich. Golfers will want to have a drink at the 1st-floor bar, which has a small putting green. ⊠ *12 Zhenhai Lu, 361001* ☎ *0592/202–3333* ⊕ *www.holiday-inn.com* ⤵ *334 rooms, 7 suites* ⚒ *4 restaurants, in-room safes, in-room broadband, pool, fitness room, sauna, bar, business services, no-smoking floors* ⊟ *AE, MC, V.*

$$$ ▦ **Marco Polo Xiamen.** Situated between the historic sights and the commercial district, the Marco Polo has an excellent location. The hotel's glass-roof atrium makes the lobby bar a particularly nice place to relax after a day's sightseeing. Nightly entertainment includes a dance band from the Philippines. The guest rooms are comfortable and well appointed. ⊠ *8 Jianye Lu, 361004* ☎ *0592/509–1888* ⊕ *www.marcopolohotels. com* ⤵ *246 rooms, 38 suites* ⚒ *3 restaurants, in-room safes, in-room broadband, pool, gym, sauna, bar, business services, no-smoking rooms* ⊟ *AE, MC, V.*

$–$$ ▦ **Lujiang Hotel.** In a refurbished colonial building, this hotel has an ideal location opposite the ferry pier and the waterfront boulevard. A rooftop-terrace restaurant looks over the straits. Many of the rooms have ocean views. ⊠ *54 Lujiang Lu, 361001* ☎ *0592/202–2922* ⤵ *153 rooms, 18 suites* ⚒ *4 restaurants, in-room safes, in-room broadband, bar, business services* ⊟ *AE, MC, V.*

Nightlife & the Arts

Although it has nothing to rival Beijing or Shanghai, Xiamen has a few options for night owls. The stretch of Zhongshan Lu near the ferry pier is charming in the evening when the colonial-style buildings are lighted with gentle neon. This waterfront promenade is a particularly popular spot for young couples walking arm in arm. There are a few small pubs where people stop for drinks.

The dimly lit **La Bomba** (⊠ Jianye Lu.1 block north of Marco Polo Xiamen hotel ☎ 0592/531–0707) is popular with locals and expats alike. It has live rock bands on the weekends.

The upscale **Elite** (⊠ Jianye Lu. 1 block north of Marco Polo Xiamen hotel ☎ 0592/533–0707) has a dance floor and a lounge where you can check out the crowd.

Sports & the Outdoors

Xiamen offers some excellent hiking opportunities. Most notable of these are the hills behind the Nanputuo Temple, where winding paths and stone steps carved into the sheer rock face make for a fairly strenuous climb. For a real challenge, hike from Nanputuo Temple to 10,000 Rock Garden. If you're still in the mood for a climb after spending a few hours enjoying the garden's beautiful landscape, another more serpentine trail (a relic of the Japanese occupation) leads to Xiamen University. The hike takes the better part of an afternoon, and is well worth it.

The area around Xiamen is filled with fine public beaches. On nice days, sunbathers abound nearly anywhere along Huandao Lu, the road that circles the island.

To & from Xiamen

3 hrs (200 km [124 mi]) by bus southwest of Fuzhou; (500 km [310 mi]) by bus northeast of Hong Kong.

Xiamen Airport, one of the largest and busiest in China, lies about 12 km (7 mi) northeast of the city. A taxi from downtown should cost no more than Y60.

Dragonair connects Xiamen with many cities in China, as well as international destinations like Jakarta, Manila, Penang, and Singapore. Xiamen Airlines has flights to Bangkok, Hong Kong, and Macau, as well as cities all over China. Philippine Airlines has daily direct flights to Manila.

Xiamen has service to all the main cities along the coast as far as Guangzhou and Shanghai. The long-distance bus station is on Hubin Nan Lu, just south of Yuandang Lake.

Gulangyu

The best way to experience Gulangyu's charm is to explore its meandering streets, stumbling across a particularly distinctive old mansion or the weathered graves of missionaries and merchants. These quiet back alleys are fascinating to wander, with the atmosphere of a quiet Mediterranean city, punctuated by touches of calligraphy or the click of mahjongg tiles to remind you where you really are. And unlike most Chinese communities, you won't take your life in your hands when crossing the street because cars are banned on Gulangyu. This island is easy to reach by ferry from Xiamen.

Gulangyu holds a special place in the country's musical history, thanks to the large number of Christian missionaries who called the island home in the late 19th and early 20th centuries. Gulangyu has more pianos per capita than anyplace else in China, with one home in five having one. "Chopsticks" to Chopin—and everything in between—can be heard being ❷ played by the next generation's prodigies. The **Piano Museum** (Island of Drumming Waves) is a must for any music lover. ⊠ *45 Huangyan Lu* ☎ *0592/206–0238* 🎫 *Y30* ⏱ *Daily 8:15–5:15.*

From the ferry terminal, turn left and follow oceanfront Tianwei Lu until ❶ you come to **Bright Moon Garden** (Haoyue Yuan). The garden is a fitting seaside memorial to Koxinga, and a massive stone statue of the Ming general stares eastward from a perch hanging over the sea. ⊠ *Tianwei Lu* ☎ *No phone* 🎫 *Y15* ⏱ *Daily 8–7.*

❸ Continuing along Tianwei Lu, you'll come to **Shuzhuang Garden** (Shuzhuang Huayuan). The garden is immaculately kept and dotted with pavilions and bridges, some extending out to rocks just offshore. ⊠ *Tianwei Lu* ☎ *No phone* 🎫 *Y40* ⏱ *Daily 8–7.*

❹ Skillfully mixing history and oddities, **Zhen Qi Shi Jie** is one of the country's odder museums. Part of the museum displays the usual historical information about Fujian and Taiwan. The other part is a veritable museum of oddities, offering pickled genetic mutations like two-headed snakes, conjoined twin sheep, and a few live exhibits like gigantic tor-

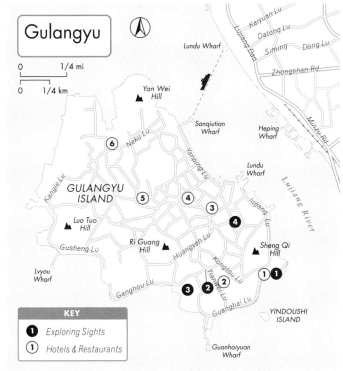

4

toises. The room of ancient Chinese sex toys will please some and mystify others. ⊠ *Long Tou Lu, 2 blocks from ferry terminal* ☏ *0592/206–9933* 🎫 *Y35* ⊙ *Daily 8–6:30.*

Tours

The best—and really, the only—way to see Gulangyu is on foot. Take a morning or afternoon to climb up the narrow, winding streets to see the hundreds of colonial-era mansions (ranging from restored to ramshackle) that are the heart of this fabulous treasure trove of late-19th- and early-20th-century architecture. A good guide is Vivian Wang, a native of the area.

🛈 **Tour-Operator Recommendations Vivian Wang** ☏ 0592/13959-228225.

Where to Stay & Eat in Gulangyu

\$ ✕ **Gang Zai Hou Yu Chang Can Ting.** The name of this restaurant means "Behind Gang Zai Beach," which gives you a clue as to the short distance seafood travels from the ocean to the plate. Gang Zai Hou serves excellent oyster soup, steamed crabs, and just about anything else that swims. ⊠ *14 Gang Hou Lu* ☏ *0592/206–3719* 🚫 *No credit cards.*

\$ ✕ **Long Wen Can Ting.** Serving fresh seafood dishes, this large restaurant near the ferry terminal is popular with tourists from Taiwan. The chef unabashedly admits to being an enthusiastic consumer of his own cuisine—never a bad sign. Specialties include whole steamed fish, oyster soup, and a wide variety of seafood dishes. The decor is traditional Chinese. ⊠ *21 Long Tou Lu* ☎ *0592/206–6369* ▤ *No credit cards.*

$ ✕ **Bright Moon Leisure and Holiday Club.** Located in Bright Moon Garden, this lovely little hotel consists of nine wooden houses perched on seaside cliffs. What the place lacks for in amenities it more than makes up with amazing views. ⊠ *9 Zhangzhou Lu, 361002* ☎ *0592/206–9730* ☞ *15 rooms* ⊘ *Beach, laundry service* ▤ *AE, MC, V.*

¢–$ ✕ **Fu Lin Chun Can Ting.** Serving home-style seafood cooked to order, this closet-size restaurant is almost always packed with locals during peak hours. If it comes from the sea, you'll find it here, with steamed crab, deep-fried shrimp, and whole fish served in a variety of tantalizing styles. ⊠ *109 Long Tou Lu* ☎ *0592/206–2847* ▤ *No credit cards.*

¢ ▥ **Gulangyu International Youth Hostel.** If you're strapped for cash, you'd be hard-pressed to find cheaper accommodations. In the former German Embassy, this place retains a bit of its Bavarian feel. High-ceiling rooms have beds, desks, and antique-lighting fixtures. ⊠ *18 Lu Jiao Lu, 361002* ☎ *0592/206–6066* ☞ *6 rooms* ⊘ *Fans, laundry facilities, Internet room; no a/c in some rooms* ▤ *No credit cards.*

¢ ▥ **Gulangyu Villa Hotel.** On the west side of the island, this hotel has a playful feel. The rooms are clean but simple and the staff is friendly enough. There is a decent Chinese restaurant on the premises. ⊠ *14 Gusheng Lu, 361002* ☎ *0592/206–0160 or 0592/206–3280* ☞ *75 rooms* ⊘ *Restaurant, business services, laundry service* ▤ *No credit cards.*

To & from Gulangyu
5 minutes by boat from Xiamen.

Boats to the island run from early in the morning until midnight from the ferry terminal across from the Lujiang.

FUJIAN ESSENTIALS

Transportation

BY AIR
▮ Airlines & Contacts **Dragonair** ⊠ Seaside Bldg., Jiang Dao Lu, Xiamen ☎ 0592/202-5433. **Philippine Airlines** ⊠ Xiamen Airport ☎ 0592/239-4729 ⊕ www.philippineairlines.com. **Xiamen Airlines** ⊠ 22 Dailiao Lu, Xiamen ☎ 0592/602-2961 ⊕ www.xiamenair. com.cn.
▮ Airport Information **Xiamen Airport** ☎ 0592/602-0017.

BY BUS
▮ Bus Information **Long-Distance Bus Station** ⊠ 56 Hubin Nan Lu, Xiamen ☎ 0592/203-1246.

BY TAXI
In Xiamen, taxis can also be found around hotels or on the streets; they're a convenient way to visit the sights on the edge of town. As most taxi drivers do not speak English, make sure that all your addresses are written in Chinese. Any hotel representative will be happy to do this for you.

BY TRAIN

Rail travel to and from Xiamen isn't as convenient as in many other cities. Many journeys involve changing trains at least once. There is, however, direct service to Shanghai, which takes 27 hours. Service between Xiamen and Beijing takes 34 hours, and service between Xiamen and Kunming takes a whopping 41 hours. For this reason, most visitors to Xiamen prefer to fly.

The railway station is about 3 km (2 mi) northeast of the port; bus service between the station and port is frequent.

🚄 Train Information **Xiamen Train Station** ✉ Xiahe Lu ☎ 0592/505-4340.

Contacts & Resources

EMERGENCIES

Lifeline Medical System, a clinic set up for expatriates, offers English-speaking doctors that are on call 24 hours a day.

🚑 **Lifeline Medical System** ✉ Hubin Bei Lu Xiamen ☎ 0592/203-2834.

INTERNET SERVICES

Because of the number of young people spending days on end playing video games, many Internet cafés ask customers for identification. Some seem hesitant to accept foreign passports. One place where you won't run into any hassle is Javaromas, across from the Marco Polo Xiamen hotel.

🖥 **Javaromas** ✉ 31-13 Jianye Lu, Xiamen ☎ 0592/514-5677.

MONEY MATTERS

In Xiamen, the Bank of China, one block north of the Marco Polo Xiamen hotel, has a 24-hour ATM, as does the HSBC branch on Xiahe Lu.

🏦 **Bank of China** ✉ 10 Zhongshan Lu, Xiamen ☎ 0592/506-6466. **HSBC** ✉ 189 Xiahe Lu, Xiamen ☎ 0592/239-7799.

TRAVEL AGENCIES

China Travel Service, known as CTS, is the best place to make travel bookings and general tourist information. There are two offices in Xiamen that are open weekdays 9 to 7, Saturday 9 to 5, and Sunday 9:30 to 12:30 and 2 to 5.

🧳 **CTS** ✉ 2 Zhongshan Lu, Xiamen ☎ 0592/212-6917 ✉ Hubin Bei Lu, Xiamen ☎ 0592/505-1822.

At a Glance

ENGLISH	PINYIN	CHINESE CHARACTERS
EXPLORING		
ZHEJIANG	Zhèjiāng	浙江
HANGZHOU	Hángzhōu	杭州
Baidi	Báidī	白堤
CAAC	Zhōngguómínháng	中国民航
China Tea Museum	Zhōngguócháyèbówùguǎn	中国茶叶博物馆
Dragon Well Tea Park	Lóngjǐngwénchá	龙井闻茶
East Bus Station	Hángzhōuqìchēdōngzhàn	杭州汽车东站
Evening Sunlight at Thunder Peak Pagoda	Léifēngxīzhào	雷锋夕照
Hangzhou Aquarium	Hángzhōuhǎidǐshìjiè	杭州海底世界
Hangzhou Xiaoshan International Airport	Hángzhōu xiāoshān guójì jīchǎng	杭州萧山国际机场
Hangzhou Travel and Tourism Bureau	Hángzhōushìlǚyóujún	杭州市旅游局
Moon Mountain	Yùelúnshān	月轮山
North Bus Station	Hángzhōuqìchēběizhàn	杭州汽车北站
Orioles Singing in the Willow Waves	Liǔlàng wényīng	柳浪闻莺
Pagoda of Six Harmonies	Liùhétǎ	六和塔
Peak That Flew from Afar	Fēiláifēng	飞来峰
Precious Stone Hill	Bǎoshíshān	宝石山
Protecting Chu Pagoda	Bǎo chù tǎ	宝俶塔
Running Tiger Dream Spring	Hǔpǎomèngquán	虎跑梦泉
Seal Engraver's Society	Xīlíng yìnshè	西泠印社
Solitary Hill Island	Gū shān dǎo	孤山岛
Sudi	Sūdī	苏堤
Temple of the Soul's Retreat	Língyǐnsì	灵隐寺
Three Pools Reflecting the Moon	Sāntányìnyuè	三潭印月
West Bus Station	Hángzhōuqìchēxīzhàn	杭州汽车西站
West Lake	Xīhú	西湖
Yellow Dragon Cave	Huánglóngdòng	黄龙洞
Yue Fei Mausoleum	Yuèfēimù	岳飞墓
Zhejiang Provincial Museum	Zhéjiāngshěng bówùguǎn	浙江省博物馆

Zhejiang CITS	Zhèjiāngzhōngguóguójìlǚxíngshè	浙江中国国际旅行社
Zhejiang Women's International Travel Service	Zhèjiāngfùnǚguójìlǚxíngshè	浙江妇女国际旅行社

China Silk City	Zhōngguósīchóuchéng	中国丝绸城
Dong Po Hotel	Dōngpōbīnguǎn	东坡宾馆
Dragon Hotel	Huánglóngfàndiàn	黄龙饭店
Fulintang	Fúlíntáng	福林堂
Hangzhou Overseas Chinese Hotel	Hángzhōuhuáqiáofàndiàn	杭州华侨饭店
Haveli		
Huanglong Dong Yuanyuan Mingsu Yuan Theater	Huánglóngdòngyuányuányuánbínsúyuán	黄龙洞圆缘民俗园
Hyatt Regency Hangzhou	Hángzhōukǎiyuèjiǔdiàn	杭州凯悦酒店
Kana Pub	Kǎnà jiǔbā	卡那酒吧
Lakeview Wanghu Hotel		
Lingyin Si Vegetarian Restaurant	Língyǐn sì sùzhāi	灵隐寺素斋
Louwailou Restaurant	Lóu wài lóu	楼外楼
Shamrock	Ài ěr lán píjiǔbā	爱尔兰啤酒吧
Shangri-La Hotel Hangzhou	Hángzhōuxiānggélǐlāfàndiàn	杭州香格里拉饭店
Sofitel Westlake Hangzhou	Hángzhōusuǒfēitèxīhúdàjiǔdiàn	杭州索菲特西湖大酒店
Wanghu Hotel	Wànghúbīngua_n	望湖宾馆
Xihu Longjing Tea Company	Xīhúlóngjǐngcháyègōngsī	西湖龙井茶叶公司
Zhiweiguan Restaurant	Zhīwèiguān	知味观

SHAOXING	Shàoxīng	绍兴
Bazi Qiao Bridge	Bāzìqiáo	八字桥
Cai Yuanpei's House	Càiyuánpéi gùjū	蔡元培故居
Catholic Church of St. Joseph	Tiānzhǔjiàotáng	天主教堂
East Lake	Dōnghú	东湖
Lu Xun Family Home	Lǔxùn gùjū	鲁迅故居
Zhou Enlai Family Home	Zhōu ēnlái gùjū	周恩来故居

Sanwei Jiulou	Sānwèijiǔlóu	三味酒楼
Shaoxing International Hotel	Shàoxìngguójìdàjiǔdiàn	绍兴国际大酒店

Shaoxing Xianheng Hotel	Shàoxīng xiánhēng dàjiǔdiàn	绍兴咸亨大酒店
Xianheng Winehouse	Xiánhēng jiǔdiàn	咸亨酒店
FUJIAN	fú jiàn	福建
XIAMEN CITY	xià mén shì	厦门市
EXPLORING		
10,000 Rock Botanical Garden	wàn shí zhí wù yuán	万石植物园
American Express	měi guó yùn tōng	美国运通
Bank of China	zhōng guó yín háng	中国银行
China Travel Service	zhōng guó lǚ xíng shè	中国旅行社
CITS	zhōng guó guó jì lǚ xíng shè	中国国际旅行社
Hakka Roundhouses	kè jiā tǔ lóu	客家土楼
Hong Shan Park	huáng shān gōng yuán	黄山公园
Jinmen	jīn mén	金门
Long-distance Bus Station	cháng tú qì chē zhàn	长途汽车站
Museum of Anthropology	rén lèi bó wù guǎn	人类博物馆
Nanputuo Temple	nán pǔ tuó sì	南普陀寺
Overseas Chinese Museum	huá qiáo bó wù guǎn	华侨博物馆
Temple of the Kingdom of Heaven	tiān jiè sì	天届寺
Xiamen Airport	xià mén jī chǎng	厦门机场
Xiamen Train Station	xià mén huǒ chē zhàn	厦门火车站
Xiamen University	xià mén dà xué	厦门大学
Zhong Shan Park	zhōng shān gōng yuán	中山公园
WHERE TO STAY & EAT		
Dafang Vegetarian	dà fāng sù shí guǎn	大方素食馆
Elite	míng shì xiàn chǎng yīn yuè jiǔ bā	名仕现场音乐酒吧
Guan Hai Canting	guān hǎi cān tīng	观海餐厅
Holiday Inn Crowne Plaza Harbourview	hǎi jǐng huáng guān jià rì jiǔ diàn	海景皇冠假日酒店
Huangzehe Peanut Soup Shop	huáng zé hé huā shēng tāng diàn	黄则和花生汤店
La Bomba	là bèng bā	辣蹦吧
Lujiang Hotel	lù jiāng bīn guǎn	鹭江宾馆
Marco Polo Xiamen	mǎ kě bō luó dà jiǔ diàn	马可波罗大酒店

Puzhaolou Vegetarian Restaurant	pǔ zhào lóu sù cài guǎn	普照楼素菜馆
Shuyou Seafood Restaurant	shū yǒu hǎi xiān dà jiǔ lóu	舒友海鲜大酒楼
Sofitel Plaza Xiamen	suǒ fēi tè dà jiǔ diàn	索菲特大酒店
GULANGYU	gǔ làng yǔ	鼓浪屿

EXPLORING

Bright Moon Garden	hào yuè yuán	皓月园
Piano Museum	gāng qín bó wù guǎn	钢琴博物馆
Shuzhuang Garden	shū zhuāng huā yuán	菽庄花园
Zhen Qi Shi Jie	zhēn qí shì jiè	珍奇世界

WHERE TO STAY & EAT

Bright Moon Leisure and Holiday Club	hàoyuè xiuxian dujià jūlèbù	皓月休闲度假俱乐部
Fu Lin Chun Can Ting	fú lín chūn cān tīng	福林春餐厅
Gang Zai Hou Yu Chang Can Ting	gǎng zǎi hòu yùchǎng cāntīng	港仔后浴场餐厅
Gulangyu International Youth Hostel	gǔ làng yǔ guó jì qīng nián lǚ shè	鼓浪屿国际青年旅社
Gulangyu Villa Hotel	gǔ làng bié shù fàn diàn	鼓浪别墅饭店
Long Wen Can Ting	lóng wén cān tīng	龙文餐厅

Hong Kong

CULTURE, COMMERCE, HIGH STYLE

Retail temples in Kowloon; truly spiritual sights aren't far away, though.

WORD OF MOUTH

" We have visited Hong Kong three times, staying a week or two each time. So, all in all, we have spent a good month there. Just know that Hong Kong is a very engaging city. It's so easy to get around and enjoy yourself unassisted."   —marya

" Hong Kong Harbour, whether seen from the Star Ferry or the Peak or on a walk along the Kowloon Esplanade (and preferably from all three) is one of the best sights in the world. At sunset and twilight it's magical."   —Cicerone

WELCOME TO HONG KONG

TOP REASONS TO GO

★ **Harbor Views.** The skyline that launched a thousand postcards. . . . See it from the Tsim Sha Tsui waterfront, from a Star Ferry in the harbor, or from Victoria Peak.

★ **Cultural Immersion.** Start at the Hong Kong Heritage Museum, which chronicles the city's history, from village life to booming new towns. A Chinese art collection and an interactive Cantonese opera exhibit are two more reasons to come here before experiencing the many other cultural sights.

★ **Horsing Around.** Hong Kongers gamble over US$10 billion annually, and the Happy Valley Racetrack is one of their favorite places to do it. The thousands of screaming punters are as much of a spectacle as the races.

★ **Shopping Immersion.** In Kowloon's street markets, clothes and gadgets compete for space with food carts. Antiques fill shops along Hollywood Road, from Central to Sheung Wan, where herbalists peddle remedies. Designers monopolize Central's malls.

1 Hong Kong Island. It's only 78 square km (30 square mi), but it's where the action is, from high finance to nightlife to luxury shopping. The commercial districts—Western, Central, and Wan Chai among them—are on the north coast. Southside is home to small towns, quiet coves, and reserve areas. Indeed, a 20-minute taxi ride from Central can have you breathing fresh air and seeing only greenery.

2 Kowloon. This peninsula —a mecca for great hotels and shopping—on the Chinese mainland is just across from Central and bounded in the north by the string of mountains that give it its poetic name: *gau lung*, "nine dragons."

3 New Territories. The expanse between Kowloon and the Chinese border feels far removed from urban congestion and rigor. Nature reserves (many with great trails), temples, and traditional Hakka villages fill its 200 square mi. Conversely public housing projects have led to the creation of new towns like Sha Tin and Tsuen Mun.

4 Outer Islands. Off the west coast of Hong Kong Island lie Lamma, Cheung Chau, and Lantau islands. Lantau, which is home to the Tian Tan Buddha, is connected by ferries to Hong Kong Island and by a suspension bridge to west Kowloon. More than 200 other islands also belong to Hong Kong.

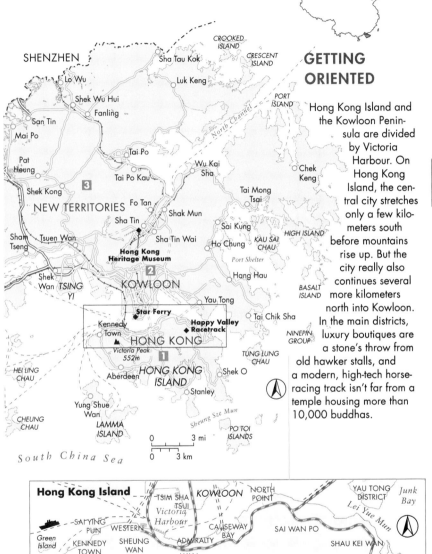

SHENZHEN

Sha Tau Kok

CROOKED ISLAND

CRESCENT ISLAND

Lo Wu

Luk Keng

PORT ISLAND

GETTING ORIENTED

Shek Wu Hui

Fanling

North Channel

San Tin

Mai Po

Tai Po

Wu Kai Sha

Chek Keng

Pat Heung

Tai Po Kau

Tai Mong Tsai

Shek Kong

3

Fo Tan

NEW TERRITORIES

Sha Tin

Shak Mun

Sai Kung

HIGH ISLAND

Sham Tseng

Tsuen Wan

Sha Tin Wai

Ho Chung

KAU SAI CHAU

Hong Kong Heritage Museum

Port Shelter

Shek Wan

TSING YI

2

KOWLOON

Hang Hau

BASALT ISLAND

Yau Tong

Star Ferry

Tai Chik Sha

Kennedy Town

Happy Valley Racetrack

NINEPIN GROUP

HONG KONG

TUNG LUNG CHAU

HEI LING CHAU

Victoria Peak 552m

1

HONG KONG ISLAND

Shek O

Aberdeen

Stanley

Yung Shue Wan

CHEUNG CHAU

LAMMA ISLAND

Sheung Sze Mun

PO TOI ISLANDS

0   3 mi

0   3 km

South China Sea

Hong Kong Island and the Kowloon Peninsula are divided by Victoria Harbour. On Hong Kong Island, the central city stretches only a few kilometers south before mountains rise up. But the city really also continues several more kilometers north into Kowloon. In the main districts, luxury boutiques are a stone's throw from old hawker stalls, and a modern, high-tech horse-racing track isn't far from a temple housing more than 10,000 buddhas.

5

Hong Kong Island

TSIM SHA TSUI

KOWLOON

NORTH POINT

YAU TONG DISTRICT

Junk Bay

Victoria Harbour

Lei Yue Mun

SAI YING PUN

WESTERN

Green Island

KENNEDY TOWN

SHEUNG WAN

ADMIRALTY

CAUSEWAY BAY

SAI WAN PO

SHAU KEI WAN

WESTERN

CENTRAL

WAN CHAI

HAPPY VALLEY

JARDINE'S LOOKOUT

CHAI WAN

PEAK DISTRICT

POK FU LAM

HONG KONG ISLAND

0   1 mile

0   1 kilometer

HONG KONG PLANNER

Looks Deceive

Hong Kong is complex. On the surface it seems every building is a high-rise sculpture of glass and steel and every pedestrian is hurrying to a meeting. But look past the shiny surfaces to the ancient culture that gives the city its exotic flavor and its citizens their unique outlook.

Wording It Right

The official languages are English and Cantonese. Mandarin—the language of China, known in Hong Kong as Putonghua—is gaining in popularity both here and in Macau, where the languages are Portuguese and Cantonese. It can't hurt to learn a few basic Cantonese expressions like "*lei-ho?*" ("hi, how are you?") and "*mm-goi sai*" ("thanks very much").

Staff in hotels, major restaurants, and large stores speak English. Taxi and bus drivers and clerks in small shops, cafés, and market stalls do not. The best people to ask for directions are MTR (transit system) employees or English-speaking policemen, identifiable by the red strips on their epaulettes. Get your concierge to write down your destination in Chinese if you're headed off the trail.

Peruse the Web site of the **New Asia Yale in China Chinese Language Centre** (⊕ www.cuhk.edu. hk/clc) at the Chinese University of Hong Kong for information on language study courses.

Navigating

■ Hong Kong's streets seem utterly chaotic, but getting lost in Central is an achievement. If you manage it, get your bearings by looking up: orient yourself using the waterfront skyscraper TwoIFC. In Kowloon, remember where you are in relation to Nathan Road, where the MTR (underground railway) stations are.

■ The MTR, which links most of the areas you'll want to visit, is quick, safe, clean, and very user-friendly. The KCR transit system links Kowloon with areas in the New Territories.

■ Pay with a rechargeable Octopus card. You can use it on the MTR, KCR, buses, trams, the Star Ferry, the Peak Tram—even at the racetrack.

■ It's often not worth taking the MTR for one stop, as stations are close. Walk or take a bus or tram.

■ Most MTR stations have many exits, so consult the detailed station maps to determine which exit lets you out closest to your destination.

■ If you're crossing Central, use the covered walkways that link its main buildings, thus avoiding stoplights, exhaust fumes, and weather conditions.

■ On Hong Kong Island, Queen's Road changes its suffix every so often, so you get Queen's Road East, Queen's Road Central, and Queen's Road West. These suffixes, however, don't exactly correspond with the districts, so part of Queen's Road Central is actually in Western. As street numbers start again with each new section, be sure you know which part you're headed for, or better still, the intersecting street. The same goes for Des Voeux Road.

Good for Kids

Put the Star Ferry, the Symphony of Lights, the Peak Tram, and a skyscraper climb atop your list. The Hong Kong Heritage Museum has a gallery where 4- to 10-year-olds can dress up in Hakka clothes and reconstruct pottery. Colorful, very hands-on main galleries have plenty for teens.

Ocean Park has a balance of toned-down thrills and high-octane rides, so you could take 3- or 4-year-olds right through to teenagers. A massive aquarium and a giant-panda enclosure round out the offerings. Older kids might enjoy seeing candy-pink dolphins in their natural habitat on DolphinWatch half-day trips. If you want even more beasties, a black jaguar is one of the zoo's most famous residents.

Mallrats can make plenty of like-minded local friends at Times Square, Pacific Place, and Kowloon Tong's Festival Walk, all of which are safe places to let them wander. And, of course, there's always Hong Kong Disney.

Visitor Information

Swing by the Hong Kong Tourist Board (HKTB) visitor center before even leaving the airport. They publish stacks of helpful free exploring booklets, run a plethora of tours all over the territory (and beyond), and operate a multilingual helpline. Their detailed website is a fabulous resource. If you're planning on visiting several museums in a week, pick up an HKTB Museum Tour pass, which gets you into several museums and costs HK$30.

Contacts **Hong Kong Tourist Board** (HKTB; ✉ Hong Kong International Airport, Arrivals Level, Lantau ☾ Daily 7 AM–11 PM ✉ Causeway Bay MTR Station, near Exit F, Causeway Bay ☾ Daily 8–8 ✉ Star Ferry Concourse, Tsim Sha Tsui, Kowloon ☾ Daily 8–8 ☎ 2508–1234 hotline ⊕ www.discoverhongkong.com).

When to Go

Hong Kong's high season, October through late December, sees sunny days and cool, comfortable nights. January, February, and sometimes early March are cool and dank, with long periods of overcast skies and rain. March and April can be either chilly and miserable or sunny and beautiful. By May the temperature is consistently warm and comfortable.

June through September are the cheapest months for one reason: they coincide with the hot, sticky, and very rainy typhoon (hurricane) season. Hong Kong is prepared for blustery assaults; if a big storm approaches, the airwaves crackle with information, and your hotel will post the appropriate signals (a No. 8 signal indicates the worst of winds, and a black warning is the equivalent for rain). This is serious business—bamboo scaffolding can come hurtling through the streets like spears, ships can sink in the harbor, and large areas of the territory can flood. Museums, shops, and transport shut down, too.

HONG KONG TEMPERATURES

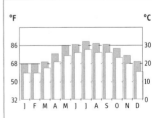

EXPLORING HONG KONG

By Victoria
Patience & Eva
Chui Loiterton

If you're on Hong Kong Island and feeling a little disoriented, remember that the water is always north; in Kowloon it's always south. Central, Admiralty, and Wan Chai, the island's main business districts, are opposite Tsim Sha Tsui on the Kowloon Peninsula. West of Central are Sheung Wan and the other (mainly residential) neighborhoods that make up Western. Central backs onto the slopes of Victoria Peak, so the districts south of it—the Midlevels and the Peak—look down on it. Causeway Bay, Shau Kei Wan, Quarry Bay, North Point, and Chai Wan East run east along the shore after Wan Chai. Developments on the south side of Hong Kong Island are scattered: the beach towns of Shek O and Stanley sit on two peninsulas on the southeast; industrial Aberdeen and Ap Lei Chau are to the west.

Kowloon's southern tip is the Tsim Sha Tsui district, which gives way to Jordan, Yau Ma Tei, Mong Kok, and Prince Edward. Northeast are the New Kowloon districts of Kowloon Tong, Kowloon City, and Wong Tai Sin, beyond which lie the eastern New Territories—mostly made up of mountainous country parks and fishing villages. The Sai Kung Peninsula juts out on the east, and massive Sha Tin New Town is north of New Kowloon, over Lion Rock Mountain. The Kowloon–Canton Railway and a highway run north of this to the Chinese border at Lo Wu.

Western

Western has been called Hong Kong Island's Chinatown, and though it's a strange-sounding epithet, there's a point to it. The area is light-years from the dazzle and bustle of Central, despite being just down the road. And although developers are making short work of the traditional architecture, Western's colonial buildings, rattling trams, old-world medicine shops, and lively markets still recall bygone times.

THE TERRITORY The Midlevels Escalator forms a handy boundary between Western and Central. Several main thoroughfares run parallel to the shore, each farther up the slope: Des Voeux Road (where the trams run), Queen's Road, Hollywood Road (where SoHo starts), and Caine Road (where the Midlevels begin). As to how far west Western goes, it technically reaches all the way to Kennedy Town, where the tramlines end, but there isn't much worth noting beyond Sheung Wan.

GETTING AROUND The most atmospheric way to Sheung Wan is on a tram along Des Voeux Road. From Central or Admiralty, this is probably the quickest mode, too: no traffic, no subway lines, or endless underground walks. There are stops every two or three blocks. In addition, the Sheung Wan MTR station brings you within spitting distance of Western Market.

The Midlevels Escalator is fun up as far as SoHo. If you're going farther, take a bus or a cab; the thrill wares off and it can take 20 minutes to reach the top. Buses 3, 40, and 40M run between the university and the IFC in Central, as does green Minibus 8. Both pass the top of Ladder Street. A taxi from Central to the Midlevels runs HK$20.

Sights

★ ❶ **Hong Kong University Museum & Art Gallery.** Chinese harp music and a faint smell of incense float through its peaceful rooms. The small but excellent collection of Chinese antiquities includes ceramics and bronzes, some dating from 3000 BC; fine paintings; lacquerware; and carvings in jade, stone, and wood. There are some superb ancient pieces: ritual vessels, decorative mirrors, and painted pottery. There are usually two or three well-curated temporary exhibitions on: contemporary artists who work with traditional media often feature. ■ TIP→ **Don't miss part of the museum: the collection is spread between the T. T. Tsui Building and the Fung Ping Shan Building, which you access via a first-floor footbridge.** The museum is out of the way—20 minutes from Central via Buses 3A or 40 M, or a 15-minute uphill walk from Sheung Wan MTR—but it's a must for the true Chinese-art lover. ✉ *94 Bonham Rd., Midlevels, Western* ☎ *2241–5500* ⊕ *www.hku.hk/hkumag* ✉ *Free* ☉ *Mon.–Sat. 9:30–6, Sun. 1:30–5:30.*

❸ **Man Mo Temple.** It's believed to be Hong Kong Island's oldest temple, though no one knows exactly when it was built. The consensus is sometime around the arrival of the British in 1841. It's dedicated to the Taoist gods of literature and of war: Man, who wears green, and Mo, dressed in red. A haze of incense fills the small building—you first catch the fragrance a block away. Huge spirals of the stuff coil down from the ceiling, scattering ash on the worshipping old ladies. The temple bell, cast in Canton in 1847, and the drum next to it are sounded to attract the gods' attention when a prayer is being offered—give it a ring to make sure yours are heard. ■ TIP→ **To check your fortune, stand in front of the altar, select a small bamboo cylinder, and shake it until a stick falls out. The number on the stick corresponds to a written fortune, the English translation of which is in a book that the temple will happily sell you.** ✉ *Hollywood Rd. at Ladder St., Western* ☉ *Daily 8–6* Ⓜ *Sheung Wan, Exit A2.*

Experiences

UPWARD MOBILITY

The unimaginatively named Midlevels is midway up the hill between Victoria Peak and the Western and Central districts. A 1-km-long (½-mi-long) combination of escalators and walkways, known collectively
❺ as the **Midlevels Escalator,** provide free, glass-covered transport up or down the steep incline between Central and Midlevels. The effortless trip provides a view of small Chinese shops, a wet market, the Jamia Mosque at Shelley Street, and gleaming residential high-rises. In fact, you're often so close to the apartments that it's impossible to avoid peering in, perhaps on a family having dinner or watching TV. Starting at Staunton Street, the escalator cuts through SoHo, the fasionable area south of (i.e., above) Hollywood Road that's filled with cafés, bars, and boutiques.

Plan to ride the escalators up between 10:20 AM and 11:30 PM. From 6 to 10 AM they move downhill only, so commuters from Midlevels can get to work. After 11:30 PM the escalators shut down, and that equates to a long walk on steep steps. You can get off at any point and explore side streets where vendors sell porcelain, clothes, and antiques (not necessarily authentic). Most buildings have tiny makeshift altars to ancestors, usually made of colorful red paper with gold Chinese characters, with offerings of fruit and incense. But blink and you'll miss them. ⊠ *Enter across from Central Market, at Queen's Rd. Central and Jubilee St., Central* ⊙ *Daily 6 AM–11:30 PM.*

HEALTHY WAYS

❹ If you don't know your chi from your chin, and you're not sure if you need a dried seahorse or a live snake, **Eu Yan Sang Medical Hall** is the place to educate your vital energies. Glass cases at this reputable store display reindeer antlers, dried fungi, ginseng, and other standard medicinal items; English-language cards explain some of the items' uses. Grave but helpful shop assistants behind hefty wooden counters will sell you purported cures for anything from the common cold to impotence (the cure for the latter is usually slices of reindeer antler boiled into tea). ■ TIP→ **The Hong Kong Tourism Board runs free introductory classes on Chinese medicine here Wednesday at 2:30 PM.** There are other smaller branches all over Hong Kong. From Sheung Wan MTR walk left along Wing Lok Street, right into Wing Wo Street, then left onto Queen's Road Central. ⊠ *152–156 Queen's Rd. Central, Western* ☎ *2544–3870* ⊕ *www. euyansang.com.sg* ⊙ *Daily 9–7:30* Ⓜ *Sheung Wan MTR, Exit E2.*

❷ Brush up on traditional treatments at the **Hong Kong Museum of Medical Sciences.** The least morbid and most enlightening exhibits compare Chinese and western medical practices and show Chinese medicines of both animal and plant origin. Elsewhere dusty displays of old medical equipment send macabre thrills up your spine. The accounts of Hong Kong's various epidemics are sobering. Indeed, the museum was purpose-built in 1906 to hold the Bacteriological Institute, which aimed to curb the chronic bubonic plague outbreaks that had ravaged the city since 1894. Reaching this museum is a healthy experience in itself: you pant up several blocks' worth of stairs to reach the Edwardian building it's in. ■ TIP→ **The cheat's way of getting here is on the Midlevels Escalator: alight at Caine Road and walk west four or five blocks to Ladder Street. The museum is just down the first flight of stairs, on the left.** Alternatively, walk up Ladder Street from Man Mo Temple on Hollywood Road. ⊠ *2 Caine La., Western* ☎ *2549–5123* ⊕ *www.hkmms.org.hk* ▣ *HK$10* ⊙ *Tues.–Sat. 10–5, Sun. 1–5.*

★ In colonial times **Bonham Strand,** a curving thoroughfare in the Sheung Wan district, was a major commercial hub. Sadly, its wooden shop fronts are fast falling victim to real estate development. The few that remain are medicinal mother lodes: wood-clad walls are lined with shelves of jars filled with pungent ingredients such as fungi, barks, and insects. These are consumed dried and ground up—infused in hot water or tea or taken as powder or pills. West of the intersection with Wing Lok Street, the original facades give way to those with big plate-glass windows displaying bundles of hairy-looking forked yellow roots— this is the heart of the ginseng wholesale trade. Ginseng is a broad-spectrum remedy that's a mainstay of Chinese medicine. Don't be surprised, though, to see Wisconsin-grown ginseng, a cheaper alternative to pricey Chinese and Korean varieties, which are said to have more kick (or more kudos).

★ A sharp but musty smell fills the air when you turn down **Wing Lok Street or Des Voeux Road West,** Sheung Wan streets renowned for their dried-seafood stores. Out of shop fronts spill sacks filled to bursting with dried and salted fish, seahorses, shrimp, and abalone—a shellfish that is to China what oysters are to the west. The cucumber look-alikes are sea slugs. Foot-wide fungi, gleaming beans, wrinkly red prunes, nuts, and even rosebuds make up the rest of the stock. A grimmer offering lurks behind a few shop windows: highly prized shark's fins, purported to be an aphrodisiac and used to make the famous soup. ⚠ The fin is the only part of the shark that's used; the rest is usually thrown back into the sea, a practice that's seriously affecting shark populations.

At Possession Street, where Queen's Road Central becomes **Queen's Road West,** shop windows display what looks like clumps of fine vermicelli noodles, ranging in color from pale gold to rich chestnut. It's not pasta, though; these are birds' nests, another of Sheung Wan's intriguing specialties. They're used to make a highly prized (and correspondingly expensive) soup that tastes rather disappointingly like egg white.

In herb shops on Queen's Road West beyond the intersection with Hollywood Road, it's a tough call as to who's more wizened: the clerks or the dried goods they sell. Either way, these stores convey the longevity benefits of Chinese medicine. Forget the gleaming teak counters of Central's tony TCM boutiques, here the herbs, dried mushrooms, and other more mysterious ingredients are displayed in plastic jars and burlap sacks.

NO GIN, JUST TONIC

Downing a glass of herbal health tonic is a normal part of many a Hong Konger's day. The pen-fronted stores that sell them are everywhere: look for small throngs of people surrounding counters full of ornate metal drums with taps on them. There are blends for flu, headaches, colds, and coughs as well as more serious complaints. Many stores have English labels, otherwise tell the server your troubles, and he or she will run you off a glass of whatever works best. Most cost HK$6–HK$20 a dose. Remember, though, that Chinese medicines aren't regulated by the Hong Kong government. Anything that sounds dubious or dangerous might be just that.

Central

Shopping, eating, drinking—Central lives up to its name when it comes to all of these. But it's also Hong Kong's historical heart, packed with architectural reminders of colonial days. They're in stark contrast to the soaring masterpieces of modern architecture. Somehow the mishmash works. With the harbor on one side and Victoria Peak on the other, Central's views—once you get high enough to see them—are unrivaled. It's the liveliest district, packed with people, sights, and life.

■ TIP→ In Hong Kong, the word "nightlife" is synonymous with Lan Kwai Fong, a few narrow lanes in Central filled with bars and clubs just up the hill from the intersection of Queen's Road Central and Pedder Street.

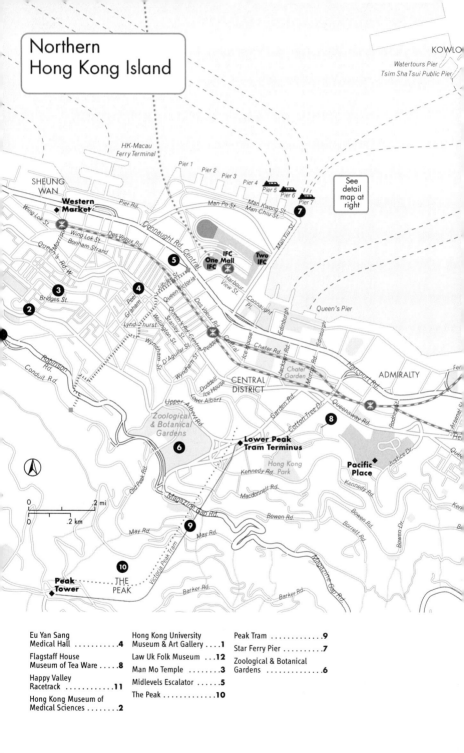

Northern Hong Kong Island

KOWLO
Watertours Pier
Tsim Sha Tsui Public Pier

SHEUNG WAN

HK-Macau Ferry Terminal

Pier 1
Pier 2
Pier 3
Pier 4
Pier 5
Pier 6
Pier 7 **7**

See detail map at right

Western Market

Wing Lok St.
Wing Lok St.
Morrison St.
Queen's Rd. W.
Bonham Strand
Des Voeux Rd.
Pier Rd.
Man Po St.
Man Kwang St.
Man Chiu St.
Man Yiu St.

Connaught Rd. Central

5

IFC
One Mall
IFC

Two IFC

Harbour View St.

Connaught Pl.

3
Bridges St.

2

4

Queen Victoria St.
Pedder St.
Queen's Rd. Central
Graham St.
Lyndhurst
Stanley St.
Wellington St.
D'Aguilar St.
Wyndham St.
Peel St.

Des Voeux Rd.

Ice House St.
Chater Rd.

Queen's Pier

Edinburgh

Robinson Rd.
Conduit Rd.

Dudell
Ice House
Lower Albert
Upper Albert Rd.

Peacock

Central

CENTRAL DISTRICT

Chater Garden

Garden Rd.

Jackson Rd.
Murray Rd.
Edinburgh

Harcourt Rd.

ADMIRALTY

Fer

Zoological & Botanical Gardens

6

Lower Peak Tram Terminus

Hong Kong Park
Kennedy Rd.

Cotton Tree Dr.

Queensway Rd.

Queensway Rd.
Garden Rd.

8

Justice Dr.

Que

He

Old Peak Rd.
Magazine Gap Rd.

Kennedy Rd.
Macdonnell Rd.

Pacific Place
Kennedy Rd.

0   .2 mi
0   .2 km

May Rd.
May Rd.

9

Bowen Rd.

Bowen Rd.
Borrett Rd.
Bowen Dr.
Magazine Gap Rd.

Ken

Be

Victoria Peak Tram

10

Peak Tower
THE PEAK

Barker Rd.

Barker Rd.

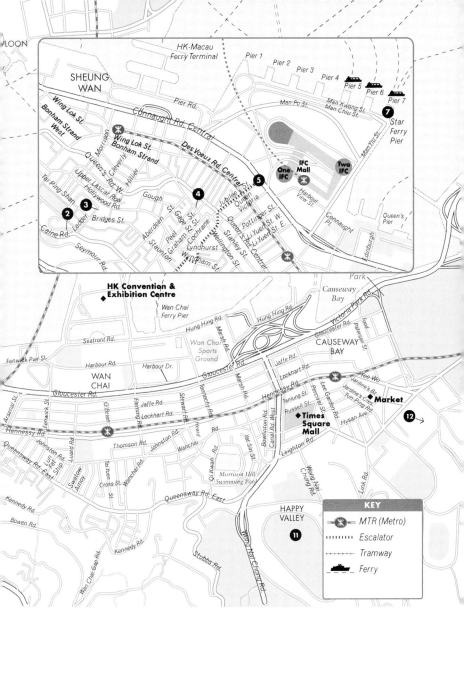

THE TERRITORY The Midlevels Escalator and Cotton Tree Drive form the boundaries of Central with Western and Admiralty districts, respectively. The area between Queen's Road Central and the harbor is all reclaimed land, and streets are laid out more or less geometrically. On the south side of Queen's Road, however, is a rabbit-warren of steep lanes. Overhead walkways connect Central's major buildings.

GETTING AROUND Central MTR station is a mammoth underground warren with a host of far-flung exits. A series of travelators join it with Hong Kong Station, under the IFC Mall, where Tung Chung line and Airport Express trains arrive and depart. Rattling old trams along Des Voeux Road have you at Sheung Wan, Admiralty, and Wan Chai in minutes. They continue to Causeway Bay, Happy Valley, and beyond. Bus routes to and from all over pass through Central's Exchange Square and under the Admiralty Centre in Admiralty.

Star Ferry vessels leave Pier 7 every 6–10 minutes 6:30 AM–11:30 PM; the 7-minute trip costs HK$2.20 (upper deck). Regular and high-speed ferries run from the Outlying Islands Ferry Pier, in front of the IFC, every half hour 6 AM–midnight.

Sights

★ ❽ **Flagstaff House Museum of Tea Ware.** All that's good about British colonial architecture is exemplified in the simple white facade, wooden monsoon shutters, and colonnaded verandas of Flagstaff House. Over 600 pieces of delicate antique teaware from the Tang (618–907) through the Qing (1644–1911) dynasties fill rooms that once housed the commander of the British forces. ■ TIP→ Skip the lengthy, confusing tea-ceremony descriptions; concentrate on the porcelain itself. Look out for the unadorned brownish purple clay of the Yixing pots: unglazed, their beauty hinges on perfect form. The best place to put your Chinese tea theory into practice is the **Lock Cha Tea Shop** (☎ 2801–7177 ⊕ www.lockcha.com), in the K.S. Lo Gallery annex of Flagstaff House. It's half shop, half teahouse, so you can sample brews before you buy. Friendly, knowledgeable staffers prepare the tea *gong-fu* style at carved rosewood tables. Try the Tie Guan Yin, a highly aromatic green tea. ■ TIP→ The Hong Kong Tourist Board runs tea appreciation classes at Lock Cha Tea Shop—phone the shop to book a place. ⊠ *Hong Kong Park, 10 Cotton Tree Dr., Admiralty* ☎ *2869-0690* ⊕ *www.lcsd.gov.hk* ▣ *Free* ☺ *Wed.–Mon. 10–5* Ⓜ *Admiralty MTR, Exit C1.*

☾ ❻ **Hong Kong Zoological & Botanical Gardens.** The city has grown around the gardens, which opened in 1864, and though they're watched over by skyscrapers, a visit to them is still an escape. Paths lined with semi-tropical trees, shrubs, and flowers wind through cramped zoo enclosures. Sloths, orangutans, pink flamingoes, and a depressed-looking black jaguar are among the 30 represented species. Albany Road slices the park in half: jaguars, birds, and the greenhouse are on the eastern side, the other animals are to the west. A pedestrian underpass connects the two sides. In the very early morning the elderly people practicing tai chi chuan here are inspiring. ⊠ *Upper Albert Rd. opposite Government House;*

Leaves of the City

Get up early in Hong Kong, and you'll see old men shuffling along Hong Kong's streets with their pet birds in tow. The destination? A teahouse for some warm brew and a chat with pals, birds chirping away from cages hung nearby.

But tea isn't just for old-timers. Hot black tea comes free—usually in glass beakers that are constantly refilled—with all meals in Chinese restaurants. Pu-erh tea, which is known here as Bo Lei, is the beverage of choice at dim sum places. In fact, another way to say dim sum is *yum cha,* meaning "drink tea."

Afternoon tea is another local fixation. Forget cucumber sandwiches and petit fours. Here we're talking neighborhood joints with Formica tables, grumpy waiters, and menus only in Chinese. Most people go for *nai cha* made with evaporated milk. A really good cup is smooth, sweet, and hung with drops of fat. An even richer version, *cha chow,* is made with condensed milk. If *yuen yeung* (yin yang; half milk tea and half instant coffee) sounds a bit much, *ling-mun cha* (lemon tea) is also on hand. Don't forget to order butter toast or daan-ta (custard tarts).

The bubble (or *boba*) tea craze is strong. These cold brews contain pearly balls of tapioca or coconut jelly. There's also been a return to traditional teas. Chains such as Chinese Urban Healing Tea serve healthy blends in MTR stations all over town—giving Starbucks a run for its money.

enter on Garden Rd., Central ☎ *2530–0154* ⊕ *www.lcsd.gov.hk* ✉ *Free* ☉ *Zoo: daily 6 AM–7 PM. Gardens: daily 6 AM–10 PM.*

Experiences

HARBOR RIDE

❼

Fodor'sChoice

★

Since 1898 the ferry pier has been the gateway to the island for people from Kowloon. If it's your first time in the city, you're all but required to cross the harbor and back on the **Star Ferry** at least once. It's a beautiful, relaxing trip on antiquated, characterful vessels. An evening ride is even better, when the city's neon and skyscrapers light up the sky. The distinctive green-and-white vessels are beloved harbor fixtures; many people prefer the gentle, smooth sailing trip to one on the busy MTR. The ferry's home is Pier 7 of the Outlying Islands Ferry Piers.

There are two classes: a first-class ticket (HK$2.20) gives you a seat on the upper deck, with its air-conditioned compartments. Second-class seats (HK$1.70) are on the lower deck and tend to be noisy because they're near the engine room. For very different experiences, try the upper deck one way and the lower deck on the other. ■ TIP→ **For trips from Central to Tsim Sha Tsui, seats on the eastern side have the best views—the ferries don't turn around, though, so remember to swing the seats so that you face forward.**

Across the way, the pier makes a convenient starting point for any tour of Kowloon. (It also has a bus terminal, which sends buses to all parts of Kowloon and to the New Territories.) As you face the bus station, Ocean Terminal, where luxury cruise ships berth, is on your left; inside and in adjacent Harbour City, are miles of air-conditioned shops. To the right of the ferry pier is Victoria Clock Tower, which dates from 1915 and is all that remains of the old Kowloon–Canton Railway Station. The train station for travel within China is now 2 km [1 mi] to the east in Hung Hom. ⊠ *Central* ⊙ *Daily 6 AM–midnight.*

THE PEAK

9 Hong Kong is very proud of the fact that the **Peak Tram**, its funicular railway, is the world's steepest. Before it opened in 1880 the only way to get up Victoria Peak, the highest hill overlooking Hong Kong Harbour, was to walk or take a bumpy ride in a sedan chair on steep steps. You really can't afford to miss the thrilling tram journey. On the way up, grab a seat on the right-hand side for the best views of the harbor and mountains. The trams, which look like old-fashioned trolley cars, are hauled the whole way in seven minutes by cables attached to electric motors. En route to the upper terminal, 1,805 feet above sea level, the cars pass five intermediate stations. At times they seem to travel at an impossibly vertical angle, but don't fret; it's all perfectly safe.

As you step off the tram, the feeling that you left your stomach somewhere down in Central disappears. The cure? A sharp intake of breath and bout of sighing over the view. Whatever the time, whatever the weather, be it your first visit or your 50th, this is Hong Kong's one unmissable sight. ■ TIP➔ Before buying a return ticket down on the tram, consider taking one of the beautiful low-impact trails back to Central. There are also buses down. Bus 15C, an antique double-decker with an open top, shuttles you to the Peak Tram Terminal from Edinburgh Place, next to City Hall. ⊠ *Between Garden Rd. and Cotton Tree Dr., Central* ☎ *2522–0922* ⊕ *www.thepeak.com.hk* ✉ *HK$20 one-way, HK$30 round-trip* ⊙ *Daily every 15 mins, 7 AM–midnight.*

10 **Victoria Peak**'s Chinese name, Tai Ping Shan, means Mountain of Great Peace, and it certainly seems to inspire momentary hushed awe in visitors at the viewing point, a few yards left along the road from the tram terminal. Spread below you is a glittering forest of skyscrapers; beyond them the harbor and—on a clear day—Kowloon's eight mountains. On a rainy day wisps of cloud catch on the buildings' pointy tops; at night both sides of the harbor burst into color. Consider having dinner at one of the restaurants near the upper terminus. ■ TIP➔ Forsake all else up here and start your visit with the lookout point: there are a hundred other shopping ops in the world, but few views like this.

There are spectacular views in all directions on the **Peak Circle Walk**, an easy going 2.2-mi (3.5-km) paved trail that starts at the Upper Tram Terminus. Start by heading north along fern-encroached Lugard Road. There's another stunning view of Central from the lookout, 20 minutes along, after which the road snakes west to an intersection with Hatton and Harlech roads. From here Lantau, Lamma, and—on incredibly clear days—Macau come into view. The longer option from here is to wind your way down Hatton to the University of Hong Kong campus in the Western district. Alternatively, following Harlech takes you back east to the Peak Tower, with deep green vistas of Pok Fu Lam country park and reservoir to your right. If you fancy getting closer to the view, turn right down Pok Fu Lam Reservoir Road, just before the Peak Tower, which takes you alongside the reservoir. After 1½ mi you hit Pok Fu Lam Road where Bus 7 can carry you back to Central.

You'd think the tram and the view would be enough to tempt people up here, but developers felt differently. The result? The tacky **Peak Tower** (⊠ 128 Peak Rd., Victoria Peak, Central ☎ 2849–7654 ⊙ 7 AM–midnight) is packed with largely forgettable shops, restaurants, and amusement rides. There's also a branch of Ripley's Believe It or Not! Odditorium—by the looks on most of the Mainlanders' faces, they've gone with the "not" option.

Local heroes Jackie Chan and Michelle Yeoh are some of the famous faces resisting meltdown at Asia's first branch of London's famous wax works, **Madame Tussaud's** (⊠ Peak Tower, Level 2, 128 Peak Rd., Victoria Peak, Central ☎ 2849–6966 ⊕ www.madame-tussauds.com ☞ HK$115 ⊙ 10 AM–10 PM). The usual celebrity suspects—from Beckham to Marilyn—are also here in candle form, as is Chinese President Jiang Zemin, not to be upstaged. It may be 1,225 feet above sea level, but the **Peak Galleria** mall scores high on nothing else but the cheese scale. ■ TIP➔ Bypass the overpriced tourist traps inside and head straight up the escalators to the third-floor viewing gallery, which looks down over the Pok Fu Lam country park and reservoir, and, on a clear day, Aberdeen.

Lantau Island

A decade of manic development has seen Lantau become much more than just "the place where the Buddha is." There's a mini-theme park at Ngong Ping to keep the Buddha company. Not to be outdone, Disney has opened a park and resort on the northeast coast. And, of course, there's the airport, built on a massive north coast reclamation. At 55 square mi, Lantau is almost twice the size of Hong Kong Island, so there's room for all this development and the laid-back attractions—beaches, fishing villages, and hiking trails—that make the island a great getaway.

THE TERRITORY Most Lantau roads lead to Tung Chung, the north shore new town, close to Hong Kong International Airport. It's connected to Kowloon by the lengthy Tsing Ma Bridge, which starts near Hong Kong Disneyland, on Lantau's northeast tip. The Tung Chung Road winds through mountains and connects north Lantau with the southern coast. Here, the South Lantau Road stretches from the town of Mui Wo in the east to Tai O in the west, passing Cheung Sha Beach and Ngong Ping.

GETTING AROUND The speediest way to Lantau from Central is the Airport Express, which stops at Tung Chung and the airport—but it'll cost ya (HK$100). Vastly cheaper (HK$26), the MTR's Tung Chung Line runs the same route but takes a bit longer. Plan one leg of your trip by ferry—it's a half-hour trip from Central, with great views. New World First Ferry vessels to Mui Wo leave every 15 minutes from Central's Pier 6.

Lantau is mountainous so bus routes are winding, and rides can be heart-stopping. There's service every half hour from Tung Chung and Mui Wo to Ngong Ping, more frequently to Tai O. The most direct way to Ngong Ping is the 20-minute trip over the mountains on the **Ngong Ping 360 Skyrail** (☎ 2109–9898 ⊕ www.np360.com.hk). The cable car runs weekdays 10–6 and weekends 10–6:30; fares are HK$58–$68 one-way and HK$88–98 round-trip.

You can reach Tung Chung by a red taxi from Kowloon or Central, but the long, toll-ridden trip will cost HK$340 from Central. Blue taxis travel Lantau (but can't leave it)—but hairpin bends make costs add up. If you have the time and the inclination, consider exploring via the well-maintained Lantau Trail.

Sights

☺ ⓭ **Hong Kong Disneyland.** If you're expecting an Asian take on the Magic Kingdom, think again—this park on Lantau Island is aimed at Mainland Chinese hungry for apple-pie Americana. Still, it's as gleaming and polished as all the other Disneys, and it has one big advantage: few visitors, which means short lines. You can go on every ride at least once and see all the attractions in a day. If your kids are theme park–savvy, the incredibly tame rides here won't win their respect. That said, there are loads for little kids. Space Mountain is the only attraction with a height restriction, so there's no ride-exclusion angst for them. ■ TIP→ **Hong Kong Disneyland operates a Fastpass system, which lets you jump the lines at the most popular attractions. Stick your entry ticket into the Fastpass machines at each ride, and you'll be given a time to come back (usually within an hour). You can only have one ride "Fastpass activated" at a time.**

You enter right into **Main St., USA,** an area paying tribute to early-20th-century small-town America. Shops—cute though they are—outnumber attractions here, so save lingering for the 3:30 PM parade, which winds up in the Town Square. Sleeping Beauty's castle, with its trademark turrets, is the gateway to faux-medieval **Fantasyland.** Choose from two spin cycles—the Mad Hatter's Teacups or Cinderella's Carousel—while you wait for your Winnie-the-Pooh Fastpass time.

Throbbing drums let you know you've hit **Adventureland,** on the park's south side. Landscapers have really run amok at attractions like Tarzan's Treehouse, on an island only accessible by rafts, and the Jungle River Cruise. In **Tomorrowland** attractions look more like the *Jetsons* than the future. It's home to rollercoaster-in-the-dark Space Mountain, a humbled version of

> ### FLY THE FRIENDLY SKIES
>
> You might be too dazed to notice when you arrive, but Sir Norman Foster's Y-shape design for the Hong Kong International Airport (aka Chek Lap Kok Airport) is an architectural marvel. With 1.8 mi (2.9 km) of moving walkways, 14 acres of glass, and around 30 acres of carpeting, the international terminal is the world's largest. At $20 billion to build, it's also the world's most expensive. An express train runs between the city and this modern marvel in 23 minutes.

the original. While you're waiting for your Fastpass time, help Buzz Lightyear blast the daylights out of the evil Zurg, or spin out the wait on the Orbitron's flying saucers. ■ TIP➡ Shade is limited so take the lead from locals and make an umbrella your No. 1 accessory—use it as a parasol if the sun blazes down or the traditional way if it pours.

The MTR is the quickest way here: take the Tung Chung Line to Sunny Bay Station, then change to the Disneyland Resort Line, whose special trains have royal-blue plush seating and Mickey-shape windows. ✉ *Lantau Island* ☎ *1–830—830* ⊕ *www.hongkongdisneyland.com* ✉ *HK$350 weekends, holidays and July and Aug.; HK$295 other days.* ☉ *Weekdays 10–8, weekends 10–9* Ⓜ *Disneyland Resort Station.*

⑭ **Tian Tan Buddha.** Hong Kongers love superlatives, even if making them true requires strings of qualifiers. So the Tian Tan Buddha is the world's largest Buddha—that's seated, located outdoors, and made of bronze. It doesn't need the epithets: its vast silhouette against the sky is impressive. Steep stairs lead to the lower podium, essentially forcing you to stare up at all 242½ tons of Buddha as you ascend. (Note: the only way to the upper level, right under the Buddha, is through an underwhelming museum inside the podium. You only get a couple of feet higher up, so it's not worth the effort.)

Fodor'sChoice
★

It's hard to believe today, but from its foundation in 1927 through the early '90s, the **Po Lin Monastery** was a true retreat, virtually inaccessible by road. These days, it's at the heart of Lantau's biggest attraction. The monastery proper has a gaudy and exuberantly commercial orange temple complex with a vegetarian restaurant—a clattering canteen with greasy, uninspiring fare (pick up sandwiches at the Citygate Mall, Tung Chung). It's the Buddha people come for.

The peaceful **Wisdom Path** runs beside 38 halved, towering tree trunks arranged in an infinity shape on a gentle hillside. Each is carved with Chinese characters that make up the Heart Sutra, a 5th-century Buddhist prayer that expresses the doctrine of emptiness. The idea is to walk around the path—which takes 5 minutes—and reflect. To reach it, follow the signposted trail to the left of the Buddha.

People were kicking up a fuss over this attraction before its first stone was laid. **Ngong Ping Village** is a money-making add-on to the Tian Tan Buddha. Indeed, if a trip here is a journey of enlightenment, then Nirvana is much easier to reach than previously thought. If you're hungry there's a Cantonese restaurant, an Asian-fusion place, and a branch of the local *gelatteria* Da Dolce. At the Ngong Ping Teahouse you can watch a tea ceremony and pastry making before partaking of both. ✉ *Ngong Ping, Lantau Island* ☎ *2109—9898 to Ngong Ping Village* ✉ *Buddha: lower podium free, upper podium and museum HK$23 or free with meal ticket. Monastery and path free. Village HK$65. Village and return Skyrail HK$145* ☉ *Buddha daily 10–5:30. Monastery and path daily dawn–dusk. Village weekdays 10–6, weekends 10–6:30.*

5

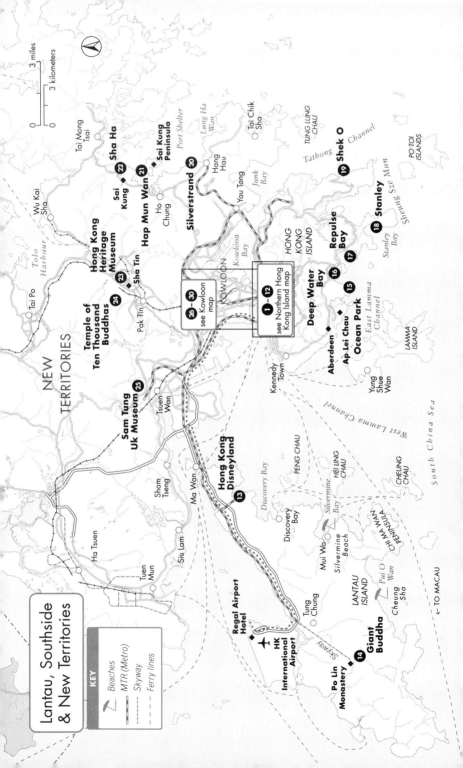

Lantau, Southside & New Territories

KEY

- Beaches
- MTR (Metro)
- Skyway
- Ferry lines

N

0   3 miles
0   3 kilometers

NEW TERRITORIES

Tai Mong Tsai

Sha Ha **22**

Sai Kung **22**

Sai Kung Peninsula **21**

Hap Mun Wan **21**

Hong Kong Heritage Museum

Sha Tin **23**

Silverstrand **20**

Hang Hau

Temple of Ten Thousand Buddhas **24**

Pak Tin

Port Shelter

Lung Ha Wan

Tai Chik Sha

TUNG LUNG CHAU

Shek O **19**

Tathong Channel

PO TOI ISLANDS

Stanley **18**

Repulse Bay **17**

Deep Water Bay **16**

15

Stanley Bay

Sheung Sze Mun

HONG KONG ISLAND

Kowloon Bay

KOWLOON

26–30 see Kowloon map

1–12 see Northern Hong Kong Island map

Ocean Park

Ap Lei Chau

Aberdeen

Kennedy Town

Junk Bay

Yau Tong

Ho Chung

Wu Kai Sha

Tolo Harbour

Tai Po

Sam Tung Uk Museum **25**

Tsuen Wan

Sham Tseng

Ma Wan

Hong Kong Disneyland **13**

Siu Lam

Tuen Mun

Ha Tsuen

Discovery Bay

PENG CHAU

HEI LING CHAU

CHEUNG CHAU

Mui Wo

Silvermine Beach

Silvermine Bay

CHI MA WAN PENINSULA

Pui O Wan

LANTAU ISLAND

Cheung Sha

Tung Chung

HK International Airport

Regal Airport Hotel

Skyway

Giant Buddha **14**

Po Lin Monastery

← TO MACAU

West Lamma Channel

East Lamma Channel

Yung Shue Wan

LAMMA ISLAND

South China Sea

Experience

DOLPHIN-SPOTTING

The Chinese white dolphin (actually from pink to dark gray) is on its way to extinction in the South China Sea. **Hong Kong DolphinWatch** (☎ 2984–1414 ⊕ www.hkdolphinwatch.com ✉ HK$320 ⊙ Wed., Fri., and Sun.) offers half-day dolphin-spotting cruises for HK$320 (which goes toward building a sanctuary); if you don't see one, you get to go again for free. Boats leave from Tung Chung New Pier on North Lantau; buses to Lantau depart from City Hall in Central (8:30 AM) and the Kowloon Hotel in Tsim Sha Tsui (9 AM). Reserve at least two weeks in advance, and plan to pay in advance (credit cards accepted).

Wan Chai, Causeway Bay & Beyond

A few blocks back from the convention center and various office blocks in Wan Chai are crowded alleys where you might stumble across a wet market, a tiny furniture-maker's shop, or an age-old temple. Farther east, Causeway Bay pulses with Hong Kong's best shopping streets. At night, the whole area comes alive with bars, restaurants, and discos, as well as establishments offering some of Wan Chai's more traditional services (think red lights and photos of semi-naked women outside). The island's far eastern districts—Shau Kei Wan, North Point, Quarry Bay, and Chai Wan—are all undeniable parts of the "real" Hong Kong, which means they're full of offices, apartment blocks, and factories.

THE TERRITORY Wan Chai's trams run mostly along Hennessy Road, with a detour along Johnston Road at the neighborhood's western end. Queen's Road East runs parallel to these two streets to the south, and a maze of lanes connect it with Hennessy. The thoroughfares north of Hennessy—Lockhart, Jaffe, and Gloucester, which is a freeway—are laid out in a grid. Causeway Bay's diagonal roads make it hard to navigate, but it's small.

GETTING Both Wan Chai and Causeway Bay have their own MTR stops, but a
AROUND pleasant way to arrive from Central is on the tram along Hennessy Road. All the lines go through Wan Chai, but check the sign at the front if you're going beyond. Some continue to Quarry Bay and North Point, via Causeway Bay, while others go south to Happy Valley. The underground stations are small labyrinths, so read the signs carefully to find the best exit. Traffic begins to take its toll on journey times farther east—the MTR is a better option for Shau Kei Wan and Chai Wan. There are Star Ferries between Tsim Sha Tsui and Wan Chai every 10–12 minutes. They leave from the ferry pier just east of the convention center.

Sight

⓬ Law Uk Folk Museum. This Hakka house was once the home of the Law family, who arrived from Guangdong in the mid-18th-century. It's the perfect example of a triple-*jian,* double-*lang* residence. Jian are enclosed rooms—here, the bedroom, living room, and workroom are at the back. The front storeroom and kitchen are the *lang,* where the walls don't reach up to the roof, and thus allow air in. Although the museum is small, informative texts outside and displays of rural furniture and farm implements inside give a powerful idea of what rural Hong Kong was like.

It's definitely worth a trip to industrial Chai Wan, at the eastern end of the MTR, to see it. Photos show what the area looked like in the 1930s—these days a leafy square is the only reminder of the woodlands and fields that once surrounded this buttermilk-color dwelling. ⊠ *14 Kut Shing St., Chai Wan, Eastern* ☎ *2896–7006* ⊕ *www.lcsd.gov.hk* ⊡ *Free* ⊘ *Mon.–Wed., Fri., and Sat. 10—6, Sun. 1–6* Ⓜ *Chai Wan, Exit B.*

Experience

OFF TO THE RACES

The "sport of kings" is run under a monopoly by the Hong Kong Jockey Club, one of the territory's most powerful entities. It's a multimillion-dollar-a-year business, employing thousands of people and drawing crowds that approach insanity in their eagerness to rid themselves of their hard-earned money. Profits go to charity. The season runs from September through June. Some 65 races are held at one or the other of the two courses—on Saturday or Sunday afternoon at Sha Tin (New Territories) and Wednesday night at Happy Valley—which must rank among the world's great horse-racing experiences.

In the public stands the vibe is electric and loud thanks to feverish gamblers shouting and waving their newspapers madly. Both courses have huge video screens at the finish line so you can see what's happening every foot of the way. ■ TIP➡ The HKTB offers track tours that cost HK$550–HK$1,080 and can include transfers, lunch, and tips on picking a winner.

⑪ **Happy Valley Racetrack.** Hong Kong punters are the world's most avid
FodorsChoice horse-racing fans, and the beloved track in Happy Valley—opened soon
★ after the British first arrived in the territory—is one of their headquarters. The roar of the crowd as the jockeys in bright silk colors race by is a must-see. The joy of the Happy Valley track, even for those who aren't into horses, is that it's smack in the middle of the city and surrounded by towering apartment blocks—indeed, people whose balconies hang over the backstretch often have parties on racing days. The track is a five-minute walk from the Causeway Bay MTR. ⊠ *Hong Kong Jockey Club, 1 Sports Rd., Happy Valley* ☎ *2966–8111* ⊕ *www.hkjc. com* ⊡ *HK$10.*

Sha Tin Racecourse. Whether you enter Sha Tin by road or rail, you'll be amazed to find this metropolis in the middle of the New Territories (⇨ *below*). One of the so-called "new towns," Sha Tin underwent a population explosion starting in the mid-1980s that transformed it from a town of 30,000 to a city of more than a half million. The biggest attraction is the racecourse, which is newer and larger than the one in Happy Valley. In fact it's one of the world's most modern courses and, as such, is the venue for all championship events. The easiest way to get here is by taxi, or you can catch the MTR to Kowloon Tong and transfer to the KCR train, which stops at the Racecourse Station on race days. A walkway from it takes you directly to the track. ⊠ *Tai Po Rd., next to Racecourse KCR station, Sha Tin* ☎ *2966–6520* ⊡ *HK$10.*

Southside

For all the unrelenting urbanity of Hong Kong Island's north coast, its south side consists largely of green hills and a few residential areas around picturesque bays. With sea views, real estate is at a premium; some of Hong Kong's wealthiest residents live in beautiful houses and luxurious apartments here. Southside is a breath of fresh air—literally and figuratively. The people are more relaxed, the pace is slower, and there are lots of breezes.

TRANSPORTATION
FROM CENTRAL
TO . . .

Aberdeen: 30 minutes via Bus 70 or 91. (Ap Lei Chau is 15 minutes from Aberdeen on Bus 90B or 91; 10 minutes by sampan.)

Deep Water Bay: 20 minutes via Bus 6, 64, 260, or 6A.

Ocean Park: 30 minutes via Star Ferry Pier and Bus 629.

Repulse Bay: 30 minutes via Bus 6, 6A, 6X, 66, 64, or 260.

Shek O: 50 minutes via MTR to Shau Ki Wan and then Bus 9 to the last stop.

Stanley: 40 minutes via Bus 6, 6A, 6X, 66, 64, or 260.

Note that express buses skip Aberdeen and Deep Water Bay, heading directly to Repulse Bay and Stanley. Buses run less frequently in the evening, so it's more convenient to grab a taxi (they're everywhere).

Sights

 Ocean Park. When it comes to amusement parks, there's no question where Hong Kongers' loyalties lie. This marine-theme park embraces both high- and low-octane buzzes and spectacular zoological attractions; they even breed endangered species here. And there's an educational twist to many of the attractions. The park stretches out over 170 hilly acres, and you can gaze down at much of it from spookily silent cabins of the mile-long cable car that connects the tamer Lowlands area to the action-packed Headland. ■ TIP→ If all you fancy is roller coasting, enter the park at the Tai Shue Wan Middle Kingdom entrance, and head straight up the escalator to Adventureland. If you're planning to do everything, start at the main entrance.

The highlights of the **Lowland Gardens** are the giant pandas, An An and Jia Jia, who lumber fetchingly around their bamboo-filled enclosure. Paths wind to other enclosures, including a cantilevered butterfly house where rare species are bred, and the traditional Chinese architecture of the Goldfish Pagoda. Cross a rickety bridge to the lush undergrowth of the Amazing Amazon: its inhabitants are richly colored birds like toucans and flamingos. The Dino display focuses on such modern "dragons" as the Chinese alligator.

Hong Kong's biggest roller coaster, the Dragon, is at the **Headland,** where the cable car stops. It might not quite be up to international standards, but it still loops the loops. There's also a Ferris wheel and swinging pirate ship here. If your kids want a ticket to ride but are too small to get past Headland height restrictions, make for **Kids World.** There's a carousel as well as kid-size fairground stalls. You can also sneak in some learning at Dolphin University. (The first-ever dolphins conceived from artificial insemination were born in Ocean Park.)

More than 2,000 fish find their way around the Atoll Reef in **Marine Land.** The 70 inhabitants of the Shark Aquarium look a bit listless, though they may still raise a few hairs on the back of your neck. If you're comfortable with performing animals, head for the Ocean Theatre, where dolphins, orcas, and sea lions clown around with surprising grace. In **Adventureland,** the Wild West–theme Mine Train was designed to feel rickety and screw-loose, which is probably why it rates highest on the scream-o-meter. Expect a light spraying or a heavy drenching at the Raging River: it all depends on your seat (and your luck). Rounding up the adrenaline boosts is the Abyss Turbo Drop, consisting, simply, of a 200-foot vertical plunge. It will definitely give you that sinking feeling.

Ocean Park is 30 minutes from the Admiralty MTR by Bus 620. Buses 70, 75, 90, 97, 260, 6A, 6X, and 29R also run from Central. ⊠ *Tai Shue Wan Rd., Aberdeen, Southside* ☎ *2552–0291* ⊕ *www.oceanpark. hk* 🎟 *HK$185* ⊙ *Tues.–Sun. 10–6.*

Experiences

SUNBATHING

🔟 **Deep Water Bay.** On Island Road, just to the east of Ocean Park and all its amusements, this bay was the setting for the William Holden film *Love Is a Many Splendored Thing* (1955), and its deep coves are still lovely. Near Deep Water Bay are the greens of the Deep Water Bay Golf Course, which is owned by the Hong Kong Golf Club. Not surprisingly, the area has become a multimillionaires' enclave and is home to Hong Kong's richest man, Li Ka-shing, a very private real-estate tycoon.

■ TIP→ For a scenic route to Deep Water Bay, take Bus 70 from Central's Exchange Square to Aberdeen and change to Bus 73, which passes the beach en route to Stanley.

🔟 **Repulse Bay.** It's named after the British warship HMS *Repulse* and not, as some local wags say, after its slightly murky waters. It was home of the now demolished Repulse Bay Hotel, which gained notoriety in December 1941 when Japanese clambered over the hills behind it, entered its gardens, and overtook the British, who were using the hotel as headquarters. Repulse Bay Verandah Restaurant & Bamboo Bar—a great place for British high tea—is a replica of the eating and drinking establishment that once graced the hotel. High tea costs HK$128 and is served weekdays from 3 to 5:30 and weekends from 3:30 to 5:30. You can also grab a bite at one of several Chinese restaurants and snack kiosks that dot the beach. The Lifesaving Club at the beach's east end resembles a Chinese temple, with large statues of Tin Hau, goddess of the sea, and Kwun Yum, goddess of mercy. ⚠ If you opt for a meal in a seafood restaurant here or at any beach, note that physicians caution against eating raw shellfish because of hepatitis outbreaks.

🔟 **Shek O.** This wide beach is almost Mediterranean in appearance with its low-rise houses and shops set on a headland. In Shek O village you can find old mansions, small shops selling inflatable toys and other beach gear, and a few popular Chinese and Thai restaurants. Follow the curving path from the town square across a footbridge to the "island" of Tai Tau Chau, really a large rock with a lookout over the South China Sea. Little more than a century ago, this open water was ruled by pirates. Also near town is the Shek O Golf and Country Club and the superb Shek O Country Park, with great trails and bird-watching: look for Kentish plovers, reef egrets, and black-headed gulls, as well as the colorful rufus-backed shrike and the ubiquitous chatty bulbul.

⑱ Stanley. Notorious during World War II as the home of Japan's largest POW camps in Hong Kong, Stanley is now known primarily for its market, a great place for deals on knickknacks, ceramics, paintings, casual clothing, and sporting goods—including, ironically enough, snow-skiing gear. The old police station, built in 1859, now houses a restaurant. Past the market, on Stanley Main Street, a strip of restaurants and pubs faces the bay. On the other side of the bay a temple honoring Tin Hau, goddess of the sea, is wedged between giant modern housing estates. Stanley's wide main beach is the site of the dragon boat races, usually held in June, in which teams paddle out into the sea, turn around, and, at the sound of the gun, race ferociously back to shore. The beach is popular with the windsurfing, waterskiing, and wake-boarding crowd.

SAIL AWAY: SAMPANS & JUNKS

Named after an English lord, not the Scottish city, the Southside town of Aberdeen (30 minutes from Central via Bus 70 or 91) was once a pirate refuge. After World War II it became commercial as the *tanka* (boat people) attracted visitors to their floating restaurants. In the harbor are some 3,000 junks and sampans, still interspersed with floating restaurants, among them the famous Jumbo Kingdom, its faux-Chinese decorations covered in lights. The tanka still live on houseboats, and though the vessels look picturesque, conditions are depressing.

Elderly women with sea- and sun-weathered skin and croaking voices may invite you aboard a sampan for a harbor ride. It's better to go with one of the licensed operators that depart on 20-minute tours daily from 8 to 6 from the seawall opposite Aberdeen Centre. Tickets are HK$40. A tour lets you see how the fishing community lives and works and how sampans are also homes, sometimes with three generations on one small vessel. Ironically, about 110 yards away are the yachts of the Marina Club and the slightly less exclusive Aberdeen Boat Club.

You can also hire a junk to take you to outer islands: Cheung Chau, Lamma, Lantau, Po Toi, or the islands in Port Shelter, Sai Kung. Sailing on a large (up to 80-feet-long), well-varnished, plushly appointed, air-conditioned junk—which can serve as a platform for swimmers and water-skiers—is a unique Hong Kong experience. Ap Lei Chau Island (Duck's Tongue Island), accessible via sampan or Bus 90B or 91 along the bridge that connects it with Aberdeen, has a yard where junks, yachts, and sampans are built, almost all without formal plans. ■ TIP➔ **Look to your right when crossing the bridge for a superb view of the harbor and its countless junks.** With 80,000 people living on 1 square km (½ square mi), Ap Lei Chau is the world's most densely populated island.

The ritzy restaurant-bar **aqua luna** (☎ 2116—8821 ⊕ www.aqua.com. hk) is on the *Cheung Po Tsai,* a 28-meter junk named for a pirate and created by an 80-year-old local craftsman. It's slow but impressive, with magnificent red sails. A 45-minute cruise through Victoria Harbour costs HK$150 by day and HK$180 at night. Departures are every hour on the half hour 1:30 PM to 10:30 PM from Tsim Sha Tsui Pier, near the Cultural Centre, and 15 minutes later from Queen's Pier, Central.

The **Duk Ling** is a fully restored 25-year-old fishing junk whose large sails are a sight to behold. But the best thing about the *Duk Ling* is that a ride won't cost you a dime. The HKTB offers visitors free one-hour sails from Kowloon Pier (Thursday at 2 PM and 4 PM, Saturday at 10 AM and noon) and from Central's Queen's Pier (Thursday at 3 PM and 5 PM, Saturday at 11 AM and 1 PM). Register first at the HKTB offices at the Star Ferry Pier in Tsim Sha Tsui; when you do, bring your passport to prove you're from out of town.

HIKING

Fodor'sChoice **Dragon's Back.** One of the most popular trails crosses the "rooftop" of
★ Hong Kong Island. Take the Peak Tram from Central up Victoria Peak, and tackle as much or as little of the range as you feel like—there are numerous exits "downhill" to public-transport networks. Surprisingly wild country feels a world away from the urban bustle below, and the panoramas—of Victoria Harbour on one side, and South Island and outlying islands on the other—are spectacular. You can follow the trail all the way to the delightful seaside village of Shek O, where you can relax over an evening dinner before returning to the city by minibus or taxi. The most popular route, and shorter if you're not up for a huge hike, is from Shek O Country Park. Take the MTR from Central to Shaukeiwan, then Bus 9, and alight after the first roundabout, near the crematorium. The entire trip takes the better part of an unforgettable day.

Wilson Trail. The 78-km- (48-mi) long trail runs from Stanley Gap on the south end of Hong Kong Island, through rugged peaks that have a panoramic view of Repulse Bay and the nearby Round and Middle islands, and to Nam Chung in the northeastern New Territories. You have to cross the harbor by MTR at Quarry Bay to complete the entire walk. The trail is smoothed by steps paved with stone, and footbridges aid with steep sections and streams. Clearly marked with signs and information boards, this popular walk is divided into 10 sections, and you can easily take just one or two (figure on three to four hours a section); traversing the whole trail takes about 31 hours.

Kowloon

Just across the harbor from Central, there's street upon street of hardcore consumerism in every imaginable guise. But there's much more to the Kowloon Peninsula than rock-bottom prices and goods of dubious provenance. Island residents rarely venture here—their loss, because Kowloon's dense, gritty urban fabric is the backdrop for Hong Kong's best museums and most interesting spiritual sights.

THE TERRITORY Kowloon's southernmost district is Tsim Sha Tsui (TST), home to the Star Ferry Pier and the Peninsula Hotel. The building-lined waterfront extends a few miles to TST East. Shops and hotels line Nathan Road, which stretches north from the waterfront through the market districts of Jordan, Yau Ma Tei, and Mong Kok.

New Kowloon is the unofficial name for the industrial sprawl beyond Boundary Street. The district immediately north is Kowloon Tong. Two interesting spiritual sights—Wong Tai Sin and Lok Fu—are a little farther east. The tongue sticking out into the sea to the south was the runway of the old Kai Tak Airport. Kowloon City is a stone's throw west.

GETTING AROUND The most romantic way from Hong Kong Island to southern TST is by Star Ferry. There are crossings from Central every 7–10 minutes and a little less often from Wan Chai.

TST is also accessible by MTR. Underground walkways connect the station with Kowloon-Canton Railway's Tsim Sha Tsui East terminus, where KCR East Rail trains depart every 10–15 minutes for the eastern New Territories. The Kowloon Airport Express station is amid a construction wasteland west of TST. One day it will connect with KCR West Rail; for now hotel shuttles link it to the rest of Kowloon.

The MTR is your best bet for Jordan, Yau Ma Tei, Mong Kok, Kowloon Tong, Lok Fu, and Wong Tai Sin. But you'll need a bus or cab to reach Kowloon Tong from Wong Tai Sin or TST East.

Sights

★ ☺ ❷❽ **Bird Garden.** The air fills with warbling and tweeting about a block from this narrow public garden. Around 70 stalls stretch down one side of it, selling all the birds, cages, and accessories a bird owner could need. More gruesome are the heaving bags of creepy-crawlies—old men tending the stalls lift larvae with chopsticks and pop them into the open mouths of baby birds. Birds are a favorite pet in Hong Kong, especially among the elderly, who often take them out for a "walk" in bamboo cages.

Plenty of free birds also swoop in to gorge on spilled food and commiserate with imprisoned brethren. The garden was built to replace the old, mazelike Bird Market, which was closed down during the worst Bird Flu outbreaks. (Government sanitation programs mean the flu is no longer a threat, though all the vendors here ignore signs warning against contact with birds.) From the MTR station walk east along Prince Edward Road for three short blocks, then turn left onto Sai Yee Street, then right onto Flower Market Road, for an aromatic approach. The bird garden is at the end of this flower-market street. ✉ *Yuen Po St., Prince Edward, Kowloon* 🎟 *Free* ☉ *Daily 7 AM–8 PM* Ⓜ *Prince Edward, Exit B1.*

❷❾ **Chi Lin Nunnery.** Not a single nail was used to build this nunnery, which
dates from 1934. Instead, traditional Tang Dynasty architectural techniques involving wooden dowels and bracket-work hold its 228,000 pieces of timber together. Most of the 15 cedar halls house altars to *bodhisattvas* (someone who has reached enlightenment)—bronze plaques explain each one. Feng Shui principles governed construction. The buildings face south toward the sea, to bring abundance; their back is

to the mountain, provider of strength and good energy. Polished wood and gleaming Buddha statues are the only adornments.

The Main Hall is the most imposing—and inspiring—part of the monastery. Overlooking the smaller second courtyard, it honors the first Buddha, known as Sakyamuni. The soaring ceilings are held up by 28 cedar columns, measuring 18 feet each. They also support the roof—no mean feat, given that its traditionally made clay tiles make it weigh 176 tons. Be sure to keep looking up—the lattice work ceilings and complicated beam systems are among the most beautiful parts of the building. Left of the Main Hall is a don't-miss hall dedicated to Avalokitesvra, better known in Hong Kong as Kwun Yum, goddess of mercy and child-bearing, among other things. She's one of the few exceptions to the rule that bodhisattvas are represented as asexual beings.

Courtyards and gardens, where frangipani flowers scent the air, run beside the nunnery. The gardens are filled with bonsai trees and artful rockeries. Nature is also present inside: the various halls and galleries all look onto two courtyards filled with geometric lotus ponds and manicured bushes. ■ TIP→ Consider combining Chi Lin Nunnery with a visit to Sik Sik Yuen Wong Tai Sin Temple, only one MTR stop or a short taxi ride away. ⊠ *5 Chi Lin Dr., Diamond Hill, Kowloon* ☎ *2354–1789* ⊡ *Free* ☉ *Nunnery daily 9–4:30, lotus-pond garden daily 7–7* Ⓜ *Diamond Hill, Exit C2.*

㉖ Hong Kong Museum of Art. An extensive collection of Chinese art is
Fodor'sChoice   packed inside this boxy tiled building on the Tsim Sha Tsui waterfront
★   in Kowloon. It's a heady mix of things that make Hong Kong what it is: Ming ceramics, 2,000-year-old calligraphic scrolls, 1,100 works chronicling colonization, kooky contemporary canvases. Thankfully it's organized into thematic galleries with clear, if uninspiring, explanations. Hong Kong's biggest visiting exhibitions are held here, too.

The Chinese Antiquities Gallery is the place to head if Ming's your thing. A series of low-lit rooms on the third floor houses ceramics from Neolithic times through the Qing dynasty. Unusually, they're displayed by motif rather than by period: dragons, phoenixes, lotus flowers, and bats are some of the auspicious designs. Bronzes, jade, lacquerware, textiles, enamel, and glassware complete this collection of decorative art.

In the Chinese Fine Art Gallery you get a great introduction to Chinese brush painting, often difficult for the Western eye to appreciate. Landscape paintings from the 20th-century Guangdong and Lingnan schools form the bulk of the collection, and modern calligraphy also gets a nod. ■ TIP→ Traditional Chinese landscape paintings are visual records of real or imagined journeys—a kind of travelogue. Pick a starting point and try to travel through the picture, imagining the journey the artist is trying to convey.

The Contemporary Hong Kong Art Gallery showcases a mix of traditional Chinese and Western techniques—often in the same work. Paintings account for most of the pieces from the first half of the 20th century, when local artists used the traditional mediums of brush and ink in innovative ways. Western techniques dominate later work.

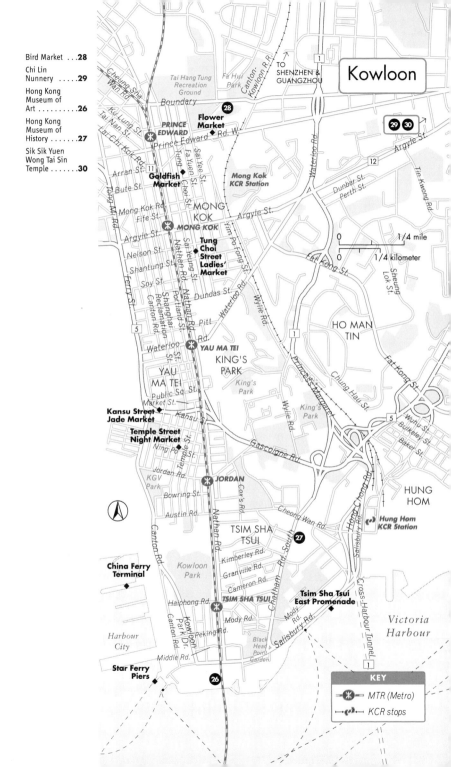

Kowloon

TO
SHENZHEN &
GUANGZHOU

Tai Hang Tung
Recreation
Ground

Fa Hui
Park

Boundary

28

29 **30**

Argyle St.

**PRINCE
EDWARD**

Flower
Market

Prince Edward Rd. W.

Cheung Sha Wan Rd.

Ku Lung St.

Tai Nan St.

Lai Chi Kok Rd.

Sai Yee St.

Fa Yuen St.

Tung Choi St.

12

Waterloo Rd.

Canton-Kowloon R.R.

Dunbar St.

Perth St.

Tin Kwong Rd.

Arran St.

11

**Goldfish
Market**

**Mong Kok
KCR Station**

Tong Mi Rd.

Bute St.

Mong Kok Rd.

Fife St.

**MONG
KOK**

MONG KOK

Argyle St.

Nathan Rd.

Yim Po Fong St.

Argyle St.

Nelson St.

Sai Yeung Choi St.

**Tung
Choi
Street
Ladies'
Market**

Fat Kong St.

Sheung Lok St.

Shantung St.

Soy St.

Ferry St.

5

Shanghai St.

Reclamation St.

Portland St.

Canton Rd.

Dundas St.

Waterloo Rd.

Wylie Rd.

0 ___ 1/4 mile

0 ___ 1/4 kilometer

Pitt St.

YAU MA TEI

**HO MAN
TIN**

Waterloo St.

**YAU
MA TEI**

**KING'S
PARK**

King's
Park

Princess Margaret Rd.

Chung Hau St.

Fat Kong St.

Public Sq. St.

Market St.

King's
Park

5

Wuhu St.

Bulkeley St.

**Kansu Street
Jade Market**

Kansu St.

Gascoigne Rd.

Baker St.

**Temple Street
Night Market**

Ning Po St.

Temple St.

**KGV
Park**

Jordan Rd.

Wylie Rd.

JORDAN

Cox's Rd.

Bowring St.

Cheong Wan Rd.

**HUNG
HOM**

Austin Rd.

Nathan Rd.

Hong Chong Rd.

Salisbury Rd.

**Hung Hom
KCR Station**

**TSIM SHA
TSUI**

27

**China Ferry
Terminal**

Canton Rd.

Kowloon
Park

Kimberley Rd.

Granville Rd.

Chatham Rd. South

Cross-Harbour Tunnel

Cameron Rd.

Victoria
Harbour

Haiphong Rd.

TSIM SHA TSUI

**Tsim Sha Tsui
East Promenade**

Mody Rd.

Mody Rd.

Kowloon Park Dr.

Peking Rd.

**Harbour
City**

Black
Head
Point
Garden

Salisbury Rd.

Middle Rd.

**Star Ferry
Piers**

26

There are educational rooms tucked away on the eastern side of every floor. Kids can emboss traditional motifs on paper or do brass rubbings; there are also free gallery worksheets in English. Guided tours can help you to understand art forms you're not familiar with. There are general museum tours in English Monday through Saturday at 11 AM and 4 PM. If you prefer to tour alone, consider an English-language audioguide: it's informative, if a little dry, and it costs only HK$10.

The museum is a few minutes' walk from either the Star Ferry or Tsim Sha Tsui MTR stop. ✉ *10 Salisbury Rd., Tsim Sha Tsui, Kowloon* ☎ *2721–0116* ⊕ *www.lcsd.gov.hk* ✆ *HK$10; free Wed.* ☉ *Fri. and Sun.–Wed. 10–6, Sat. 10–8* Ⓜ *Tsim Sha Tsui MTR, Exit E.*

★ ㉗ **Hong Kong Museum of History.** A whopping HK$156 million went into making this museum engaging and educational. The permanent Hong Kong Story re-creates life as it was rather than simply displaying relics of it: indeed, actual artifacts are few. The museum's forte is clear explanations of spectacular life-size dioramas, which include village houses and a Central shopping street in colonial times. The ground-floor Folk Culture section is a Technicolor introduction to the history and customs of Hong Kong's main ethnic groups: the Punti, Hakka, and Hoklo. Upstairs, gracious stonewalled galleries whirl you through the Opium Wars and the beginnings of colonial Hong Kong. ■ TIP→ **Unless you're with kids who dig models of cavemen and bears, skip the prehistory and dynastic galleries. Reserve energy for the last two galleries: a chilling account of life under Japanese occupation and a colorful look at Hong Kong life in the '60s.**

Budget at least two hours to stroll through—more if you linger in each gallery. Pick your way through the gift shop's clutter to find local designer Alan Chan's T-shirts, shot glasses, and notebooks. His retro-kitsch aesthetic is based on 1940s cigarette-girl images. To get here from the Tsim Sha Tsui MTR walk along Cameron Road, then left for a block along Chatham Road South. A signposted overpass takes you to the museum. ✉ *100 Chatham Rd. S, Tsim Sha Tsui, Kowloon* ☎ *2724–9042* ⊕ *http://hk.history.museum* ✆ *HK$10; free Wed.* ☉ *Mon. and Wed.–Sat. 10–6, Sun. 10–7* Ⓜ *Tsim Sha Tsui MTR, Exit B2.*

★ ㉚ **Sik Sik Yuen Wong Tai Sin Temple.** There's a very practical approach to prayer at one of Hong Kong's most exuberant places of worship. Here the territory's three major religions—Taoism, Confucianism, and Buddhism—are all celebrated under the same roof. You'd think that highly ornamental religious buildings would look strange with highly visible vending machines and LCD displays in front of them, but Wong Tai Sin pulls it off in cacophonic style. The temple was established in the early 20th century, on a different site, when two Taoist masters arrived from Guangzhou with the portrait of Wong Tai Sin—a shepherd boy said to have healing powers—that still graces the main altar. In the '30s the temple was moved here; continuous renovations make it impossible to distinguish old from new.

Start at the incense-wreathed main courtyard, where the noise of many people shaking out *chim* (sticks with fortunes written on them) forms a constant rhythmic background. After wandering the halls, take time out in the Good Wish Garden—a peaceful riot of rockery—at the back of the complex. At the base of the complex is a small arcade where sooth-sayers and palm readers are happy to interpret Wong Tai Sin's predic-tions for a small fee. At the base of the ramp to the Confucian Hall, look up behind the temple for a view of Lion Rock, a mountain in the shape of a sleeping lion. ■ TIP➔ **If you feel like acquiring a household altar of your own, head for Shanghai Street in Yau Ma Tei, the Kowloon district north of Tsim Sha Tsui, where religious shops abound.** ⊠ *Wong Tai Sin Rd., Wong Tai Sin, Kowloon* ☎ *2327–8141* 📨 *Donations expected. Good Wish Garden: HK$2* ⊗ *Daily 7–5:30* Ⓜ *Wong Tai Sin, Exit B2 or B3.*

New Territories

Rustic villages, incense-filled temples, green hiking trails, pristine beaches—the New Territories have a lot to offer. Until a generation ago, the region was mostly farmland with the occasional walled village. Today, thanks to a government housing program that created "new towns" like Sha Tin and Tuen Mun with up to 500,000 residents, parts of the region are more like the rest of Hong Kong. Within its expansive 518 square km (200 square mi), however, you'll still feel far removed from urban congestion and rigor. It's here where you can visit the area's lush-est parks and sneak glimpses into traditional rural life in the restored walled villages and ancestral clan halls.

THE TERRITORY The New Territories borders mainland China to the north and Sai Kung Peninsula to the east. Places worth visiting are a fair distance from each other, so day trips here take planning and patience. You're definitely on "the other side," where few people speak English. Choose two or three sights to visit in a day, allowing 15–30 minutes of travel time between each, depending on whether you're going by bus or taxi.

GETTING Between the bus, MTR, and the Kowloon–Canton Railway (KCR), you
AROUND can get close to many sights. Set off on the MTR from Central to Tsuen Wan; taxis, buses, and minibuses can transport you from there. For Sha Tin and other spots in the east, take the MTR to Kowloon Tong; trans-fer to the KCR to Sha Tin station. To reach the Sai Kung Peninsula, take the MTR from Central to Choi Hung, then the green Minibus 1A to Sai Kung Town.

To tour at your own pace consider hiring a car and driver. **Ace Hire Car** (☎ 2893–0541) charges HK$160 per hour (three-hour minimum). **DCH Transport** (☎ 2768–2977) is HK$280 an hour (three-hour minimum). You can hire a green **New Territories taxi** (☎ 2527–6324 or 2574–7311) for around HK$100. Ask that the driver meet you at a train station.

Sights

㉓ **Hong Kong Heritage Museum.** This fabulous museum is Hong Kong's
Fodor'sChoice largest, yet it still seems a well-kept secret: chances are you'll have most
★ of its 10 massive galleries to yourself. They ring an inner courtyard, which pours light into the lofty entrance hall. There's lots of ground to cover: prioritize the New Territories Heritage, the T. T. Tsui Gallery, and the Cantonese Opera Halls, all permanent displays, and do the temporary history and art exhibitions if energy levels permit. ■ TIP➔ **Try to time your**

arrival to coincide with one of the hourly (on the hour) English-language presentations in the ground-floor Orientation Theater.

The New Territories Heritage Hall is packed with local history—6,000 years of it. See life as it was in beautiful dioramas of traditional villages—one on land, the other on water (with houses-on-stilts). There's also lots of info and artifacts related to religion and festivals. The last gallery documents the rise of massive urban New Towns. There's even a computer game where you can design your own.

In the T. T. Tsui Gallery of Chinese Art exquisite antique Chinese glass, ceramics, and bronzes fill nine hushed second-floor rooms. The curators have gone for quality over quantity. Look for the 4-foot-tall terracotta Horse and Rider, a beautiful example of the figures enclosed in tombs in the Han Dynasty (206 BC–AD 220). The Tibetan religious statues and *thankga* paintings are unique in Hong Kong.

The Cantonese Opera Hall is all singing, all dancing, and utterly hands-on. The symbolic costumes, tradition-bound stories, and stylized acting of Cantonese opera can be impenetrable: the museum provides simple explanations and stacks of artifacts, including century-old sequined costumes that put anything Vegas dreams up to shame. ■ TIP→ **Don't miss the opera hall's virtual makeup display, where you get your on-screen face painted like an opera character.**

Kids love the Children's Discovery Gallery, where hands-on activities for 4- to 10-year-olds include dressing up in traditional Hakka gear and putting a broken "archaeological find" back together. The Hong Kong Toy Story, charting more than a century of local toys, brings a whole new dimension to that Made in Hong Kong tag in the toy box.

The museum is a five-minute signposted walk from Che Kung Temple KCR Station. If the weather's good, walk back along the leafy riverside path that links the museum with the Sha Tin KCR Station, in New Town Plaza mall, 15 minutes away. ⊠ *1 Man Lam Rd.,, New Territories, Sha Tin* ☎ *2180–8188* ⊕ *hk.heritage.museum* ✑*HK$10* ⊘ *Mon., Wed.–Sat. 10–6, Sun. 10–7* Ⓜ *Che Kung or Sha Tin KCR.*

㉕ Sam Tung Uk Museum. A walled Hakka village from 1786 was saved from demolition to create this museum. It's in the middle of industrial Tsuen Wan, in the western New Territories, so its quiet whitewashed courtyards and small interlocking chambers contrast greatly with the nearby residential towers. Hakka villages were built with security in mind, and this one looks more like a single large house than a village. Indeed, most Hakka village names end in *uk,* which literally means "house"—Sam Tung Uk translates as "Three Beam House." Rigid symmetry dictated the village's construction: the ancestral hall and two common chambers form the central axis, which is flanked by the more private areas. The front door is angled to face west–southwest, in keeping with feng shui principles of alignment between mountain and water. Traditional furniture and farm tools are displayed in each room. ■ TIP→ **Head through the courtyards and start your visit in the exhibition hall at the back, where a display gives helpful background on Hakka culture and preindustrial Tsuen Wan—**

explanations are sparse elsewhere. You can also try on a Hakka hat. ✉ 2 *Kwu Uk La., Tsuen Wan, New Territories* ☎ *2411–2001* ☜ *Free* ⊗ *Mon. and Wed.–Sun. 9–5* Ⓜ *Tsuen Wan, Exit B3.*

★ ㉔ **Temple of Ten Thousand Buddhas.** You climb some 400 steps to reach this temple: but look on the bright side, for each step you get about 32 Buddhas. The uphill path through dense vegetation is lined with life-size golden Buddhas in all kinds of positions. If you're dragging bored kids along, get them to play "Spot the Celebrity Lookalike" on the way. ■ TIP➡ **In summer bring water and insect repellent.** Prepare to be dazzled inside the main temple: its walls are stacked with gilded ceramic statuettes. There are actually nearly 13,000 Buddhas here, a few more than the name suggests. They were made by Shanghai craftsmen and have been donated by worship-

> ### THE HAKKA
>
> The Hakka or "guest" people from northeast China first arrived in Hong Kong during a late-17th-century government effort to populate the coast. They fiercely held onto their language and traditions, were dealt the worst lands, and were scorned by the local Punti community. Their farming lifestyle was notoriously tough; women worked the fields as hard as men (leading to a happy side effect of unbound feet). Even today the Hakka have a reputation for being hardworking and conscientious; education and solidarity are also cultural mainstays. In the New Territories you still might see traditionally dressed women in open-crown, broad-brimmed hats, circled by a curtain of black cloth.

pers since the temple was built in the 1950s. Kwun Yum, goddess of mercy, is one of several deities honored in the courtyard.

The temple is in the foothills of Sha Tin, in the central New Territories. Take Exit B out of the Sha Tin KCR station, walk down the ramp, and take the first left onto Pai Tau Street. Keep to the righthand side of the road and follow it around to the gate where the signposted path starts. ■ TIP➡ **Don't be confused by the big white buildings on the left of Pai Tau Road. They are ancestral halls, not the temple.** ✉ *Off Pai Tau St., Sha Tin, New Territories* ☜ *Free* ⊗ *Daily 9–5:30* Ⓜ *KCR East Rail: Sha Tin.*

Experiences

SUNBATHING

㉑ **Hap Mun Wan.** Half Moon Bay is a brilliant, golden sand beach on a grassy island near Sai Kung Town. It's one of the many small beaches among dozens of small islands near Sai Kung that are popular and easy to reach. Sampans to Half Moon depart from the Sai Kung waterfront, beside the bus station. If you're sharing a sampan with other passengers, remember the color of the flag on the roof: that's the color you need for your return ferry. Shared sampans cost HK$40. ■ TIP➡ **To cruise around the harbor, rent a *kaido* (pronounced "guy-doe," one of the small boats run by private operators for about HK$130 round-trip), and stop at tiny Yim Tin Tsai Island, which has a rustic Catholic mission church built in 1890.** *From Central, take MTR to Choi Hung, then green Minibus 1A to Sai Kung Town.*

㉒ Sha Ha. The sand isn't fine and golden, but the main reason people visit this beach is for the windsurfing. Sha Ha's waters are shallow, even far from shore, and ideal for beginning windsurfers. Feeling exhausted after a day out on the water? Grab something to eat at the restaurants and bars that dot the beach. You can take lessons or rent a board at the **Kent Windsurfing Centre** (✉ Sha Ha, Sai Kung. ☏ 9733—1228). Ask for Eddy. *From Central take MTR to Choi Hung, then green Minibus 1A to Sai Kung Town. It's a 10-min walk along shore to Sha Ha.*

⓴ Silverstrand. Though a little rocky in spots, it has soft sand and is always crowded on summer weekends. Walk down a steep set of steps to reach the small stretch of beach where families enjoy all manner of floating beds and tubes in the sea. Despite the heat, barbecuing is a popular activity here and elsewhere. The local style is to hold special long forks laden with sausages, chicken, or other meats over the coals. *From Central, take MTR to Diamond Hill, then Bus 91. Alight at big roundabout.*

HIKING

Fodor'sChoice ★ Named after a former Hong Kong governor, the 97-km (60-mi) **MacLehose Trail** is the grueling course for the annual charity event, the MacLehose Trailwalker. Top teams finish the hike in an astonishing 15 hours. Mere mortals should allow three to four days from beginning to end or simply tackle one section or another on a day hike or two.

This splendidly isolated trail through the New Territories starts at Tsak Yue Wu, beyond Sai Kung, and circles High Island Reservoir before breaking north. A portion of the MacLehose takes you through the Sai Kung Country Park, Hong Kong's most beloved nature preserve, and up a mountain called Ma On Shan. Turn south for a high-ridge view, and walk through Ma On Shan Country Park. From here you walk west along the ridges of the mountains known as the Eight Dragons, which gave Kowloon its name.

After crossing Tai Po Road, the path follows a ridge to the summit of Tai Mo Shan (Big Hat Mountain), which, at 3,140 feet above sea level, is Hong Kong's tallest mountain. On a clear day you can even see the spire of the Bank of China building in Central from here. Continuing west, the trail drops to Tai Lam Reservoir and Tuen Mun, where you can catch public transport back to the city. To reach Tsak Yue Wu, take the MTR to Choi Hung and then Bus 92 or 96R, or Minibus 1 to Sai Kung Town. From Sai Kung Town, take Bus 94 to the country park.

To the east of Sha Tin, **Sai Kung Peninsula** has a few small towns and Hong Kong's most beloved nature preserve. The hikes through the hills surrounding High Island Reservoir are spectacular, and the beaches are among the territory's cleanest. Seafood restaurants dot the waterfront at Sai Kung town as well as the tiny fishing village of Po Toi O in Clear Water Bay. Take the MTR to Choi Hung and then Bus 92 or 96R, or Minibus 1 to Sai Kung Town. Instead of taking the bus, you can also catch a taxi along Clearwater Bay Road, which will take you into forested areas and land that's only partially developed with Spanish-style villas overlooking the sea. At Sai Kung town, you can rent a sampan that will take you to one of the many islands in the area for a day at the beach. Sai Kung Country Park has several hiking trails that wind through majestic hills overlooking the water. This excursion will take a full day, and you should only go if it's sunny.

WHERE TO EAT

By Robin
Goldstein

Besides losing your culinary inhibitions, what's the best way to have a memorable meal in Hong Kong? First, choose a restaurant that's full rather than empty. Then check out what's on everyone else's plate. Don't be shy about pointing to an interesting dish at your neighbor's table. This is often the best way to order, as many local specialties don't appear on the English version of the menu.

Whether Cantonese, traditional Italian or French, or celebrity-chef chic, most of the pricier restaurants lie within five-star hotels. While you shouldn't let these places monopolize your culinary exposure to Hong Kong, some are really world-class. That said, while you're here you must have at least one dim sum breakfast or lunch in a traditional teahouse. Those steaming bamboo baskets you see conceal delicious dumplings, buns, and pastries—all as comforting as they are exotic.

Meal Times
Locals eat lunch between noon and 1:30 PM; dinner is around 8. Dim sum begins as early as 10 AM. Reservations aren't usually necessary except during Chinese holidays or at of-the-moment or high-end hotel restaurants like Alain Ducasse's SPOON or the Caprice. Certain classic dishes (e.g., beggar's chicken, whose preparation in a clay pot takes hours) require advance notice of at least 24 hours. You'll also need reservations for a meal at one of the so-called private kitchens—unlicensed culinary speakeasies, which are often the city's hottest tickets. Book several days ahead, and if possible, join forces with other people. Some private kitchens only take reservations for parties of four or more.

Prices
The ranges in our chart reflect actual prices of main courses on dinner menus (unless dinner isn't served). That said, the custom of sharing dishes affects the ultimate cost of your dinner. Further, we exclude outrageously expensive dishes—abalone, bird's nest soup, shark's fin soup— and seafood at market prices when we assign ranges to properties.

Don't be shocked when you see that you've been charged for everything: tea, rice, and those side dishes placed automatically on your table. Tips are expected (10% average gratuity), even if the bill includes a service charge, which *won't* go to the waitstaff.

WHAT IT COSTS In HK$					
	$$$$	$$$	$$	$	¢
AT DINNER	over $300	$201–$300	$101–$200	$50–$100	under $50

Prices are per person for a main course at dinner and do not include the customary 10% service charge.

Western, Central & the Admiralty

American

$–$$$ × **Dan Ryan's.** If, after a few days of goose web and thousand-year egg, you have a sudden burger craving, this is the place. You'll find good approximations of the kind expats dream about when they think of the States. The popular bar and grill is often standing room only, so call ahead. Apart from burgers and beer, the menu offers a smattering of international dishes—pasta and the like—but we recommend avoiding anything complicated (and certainly anything with fish). Stick to the simple, rib-sticking fare, served up without fuss. ⊠ *114 Pacific Pl., 88 Queensway, Admiralty* ☎ *2845–4600* ⊕ *www.danryans.com* ⌔ *Reservations essential* ⊟ *AE, DC, MC, V* Ⓜ *Admiralty.*

Cantonese

$$$$ × **Lung King Heen.** It's made a serious case for being the best Cantonese restaurant in Hong Kong—and consequently, the world. Where other contenders tend to get too caught up in prestige dishes, and hotel restaurants in name-brand chefs, here there's a complete focus on taste. When you try a little lobster-and-scallop dumpling, or a dish of house-made XO sauce that is this divine, you will be forced to reevaluate your entire conception of Chinese cuisine. ⊠ *Four Seasons Hotel, 8 Finance St. Central* ☎ *3196–8888* ⊕ *www.fourseasons.com* ⌔ *Reservations essential* ⊟ *AE, DC, MC, V* Ⓜ *Central.*

Fodor'sChoice ★

¢–$$ × **Yung Kee.** Since 1950 this massive eatery has served Cantonese food amid riotous decor and writhing gold dragons. Convenient to both hotels and businesses, Yung Kee specializes in roast goose with beautifully crisp skin, but the place is equally well known for dim sum. More adventurous palates may wish to check out the meltingly tender thousand-year-old eggs with ginger. Among the good seafood offerings are sautéed fillet of pomfret with chili and black-bean sauce, or braised garoupa. ⊠ *32–40 Wellington St., Central* ☎ *2522–1624* ⊕ *www.yungkee. com.hk* ⊟ *AE, DC, MC, V* Ⓜ *Central.*

¢ × **Mak's Noodles Limited.** Mak's looks like any other Hong Kong noodle shop, but it's one of the best known in town, with a reputation that belies its humble decor. The staff is attentive, and the menu includes some particularly inventive dishes, such as tasty pork-chutney noodles. The real test of a good noodle shop, however, is its wontons, and here they're fresh, delicate, and filled with whole shrimp. And don't miss the *sui kau,* filled with minced chicken and shrimp. ⊠ *77 Wellington St., Central* ☎ *2854–3810* ⊟ *No credit cards* Ⓜ *Central.*

ANCIENT CHINESE SECRET

If you keep an open mind about food, you can lose yourself in the magic of a cuisine whose traditions have been braising for millennia. It, like many of Hong Kong's residents, has its roots in Guangdong (Canton) Province. Cantonese cooks believe that the secret to bringing out the natural flavors of food is to cook it quickly at very high temperatures. The resulting dishes are then served and eaten immediately.

Contemporary

★ **$$$$** ✕ **Amber.** When the Landmark Mandarin Oriental hotel opened in 2005 its aim was to be seen as the preeminent hotel on Hong Kong Island. It only made sense, therefore, that it would contain a flagship power-lunch restaurant that aspires to a similar level of impeccable, modern style. At his best, chef Richard Ekkebus shows shades of true genius, as when he serves a gentle bisque of New Zealand scampi daringly paired with chicken-liver custard, unexpected but passionate bedfellows. Amber also excels with desserts, for instance a crisp hazelnut and Caraibe chocolate bar served with a "moccachino." Prices are high, but so is the ambition—and the wavelike amber sculpture that soars like a grandiose pipe organ above the room. ⊠ *Landmark Mandarin Oriental Hotel, 15 Queen's Rd., Central* ☎ *2132–0066* ▤ *AE, DC, MC, V* Ⓜ *Central.*

$$$$ ✕ **Bo Innovation.** One of the most deservedly renowned of Hong Kong's "private kitchens," Bo Innovation is a little gem that serves a kind of Japanese-Chinese-French fusion. It feels more upscale than most speakeasies, with sleek lines, dim lighting, and an open kitchen. The food, likewise, is unusually original. Chef-renaissance man Alvin Leung has a particular way with foie gras, which seems to make its way into most dishes in some way or another. Don't be shocked if it winds up paired with toro sashimi—two rich softnesses blending into one. And if you engage in a conversation with Alvin, you might end up learning something about musical acoustics—or wines from Burgundy. ⊠ *UG/F, 32— 38 Ice House, Central* ☎ *2850–8371* ⊕ *www.boinnovation.com* ⌂ *Reservations essential* ▤ *AE, MC, V* ☾ *Closed Sun. No lunch Sat.* Ⓜ *Central.*

☾ **$$–$$$$** ✕ **café TOO.** It'll amuse the buffet-loving kids, at least: the innovative café TOO introduces all-day dining and drama with seven separate cooking "theaters" and a brigade of 30 chefs. The liveliness and bustle make it a good place to stop for breakfast or lunch. Take your pick from seafood, sushi, and sashimi; Peking duck and dim sum; a carving station for roasts, poultry, and game; noodles and pastas; and pizzas, curries, tandooris, antipasto, cured meats, salads, or sandwiches. You can even have a late-night snack here from 10:30 PM to midnight. ⊠ *7/F, Island Shangri-La, Pacific Place, Supreme Court Rd., Admiralty* ☎ *2820–8571* ⊕ *www. shangri-la.com* ▤ *AE, DC, MC, V* Ⓜ *Admiralty.*

Eclectic

☾ **$$–$$$$** ✕ **Café Deco Bar & Grill.** As at most restaurants that cater to captive audiences, dining up at the Peak is a crapshoot. This huge eatery in the Peak Galleria mall—at this writing, the only one with real views—is no exception: you come for the views, not the food. The best strategy might be to come here in time for sunset, hit Café Deco just for drinks and appetizers, and enjoy the vistas; then head down to the city for dinner. The overambitious menu, which haphazardly traverses five or six continents, is dramatically prepared by chefs in open kitchens (which will, at least, amuse the

5

kids). Oysters are good and the pizza is okay, but you should avoid the insipid Southeast Asian fare and overpriced steaks. When you book (and you must), be sure to request a table with a view, as many tables in the place have none, which defeats the purpose of coming. ⊠ *1st level, Peak Galleria, 118 Peak Rd., The Peak, Central* ☏ *2849–5111* ⊕ *www. cafedecogroup.com* ⌕ *Reservations essential* ▤ *AE, DC, MC, V.*

$$–$$$$ ✕ **Jimmy's Kitchen.** One of the oldest restaurants in Hong Kong, Jimmy's opened in 1928 and has been catering to a loyal clientele of mostly Old China Hands ever since. The setting is shamelessly colonial, with dark-wood booths and brass fittings. The menu features comfort food as charmingly old-fashioned as the place itself: everything from corned beef and cabbage to a traditional mixed grill. Other specialties include borscht, goulash, and bangers and mash, plus Asian selections ranging from curry to fried rice. Homey desserts include bread-and-butter pudding. ⊠ *South China Bldg., 1–3 Wyndham St., basement, Central* ☏ *2526–5293* ▤ *AE, DC, MC, V* Ⓜ *Central.*

French

★ $$$$ ✕ **Restaurant Pétrus.** Commanding breathtaking views atop the Island Shangri-La, Restaurant Pétrus scales the upper Hong Kong heights of prestige, formality, and price. This is one of the city's few flagship hotel restaurants that have not attempted to reinvent themselves as fusion; sometimes traditional French haute cuisine is what you want. Likewise, the design of the place is in the old-school restaurant-as-ballroom mode. The kitchen has a particularly good way with (surprise!) foie gras, and the wine list is memorable, with verticals of Chateau Pétrus among the roughly 1,000 celebrated vintages. ⊠ *56/F, Island Shangri-La, Pacific Place, Supreme Court Rd., Admiralty* ☏ *2820–8590* ⊕ *www. shangri-la.com* ⌕ *Reservations essential* 🏛 *Jacket required* ▤ *AE, DC, MC, V* Ⓜ *Admiralty.*

Italian

$$$$ ✕ **Toscana.** One of the best Italian restaurants in Asia, Toscana is not content to serve just the classics, as many Hong Kong Italian joints, however fancy, are wont to do. Rather, Umberto Bombana's cuisine is something more exciting, more artistic. He begins by flying just about every ingredient in from Italy, right down to the eggs. Then, the master chef embarks upon inspired flights of fancy. Delicately seared foie gras might meet up with Sicilian lemon, or a dish of pasta that distills the sweetest essence from scampi (a sweet Adriatic shellfish) yet seamlessly marries it to tomato. All this is served up in a room that is sumptuous and elegant without being stuffy—equally suited for a business lunch or a romantic dinner. ⊠ *Ritz-Carlton, 3 Connaught Rd., Central* ☏ *2532–2062* ⊕ *www. ritzcarlton.com* ▤ *AE, DC, MC, V* ☻ *Closed Sun.* Ⓜ *Central.*

FodorsChoice ★

$$–$$$ ✕ **DiVino.** This ultracool wine bar feels like something straight out of Milan, bringing with it small plates

> ### WORD OF MOUTH
>
> "Quite popular with the after-work crowd, DiVino makes for an energizing start to a big night out in Hong Kong." —Nicole

for casual snacking and mixed platters ideal for sharing. Not surprisingly, it's popular with the drinks-after-work crowd—and you get complimentary savory treats with your wine from 6 to 8 PM. But don't underestimate the cuisine: the tailor-made cold-cut platters, for starters, are superb. The cheese board is served with warm, crusty bread. Heavier pasta main courses include gnocchi with lamb and mushroom sauce. The place also stays open for revelry late into the evening. ⊠ *Shop 1, 73 Wyndham St., Central* ☎ *2167–8883* ⊕ *www.divino.com.hk* ⊟ *AE, DC, MC, V* ☻ *Closed Sun. No lunch Sat.* Ⓜ *Central.*

Japanese

$$$–$$$$ ✕ **Dragon-I.** If you can stomach the scene at this top of the scenesters, an evening at Dragon-I can be a memorable experience. The hip, "orientalist" interior is a window into the world of Hong Kong's Beautiful People. A velvet rope shows up at some point each evening, and the models all put in an appearance on Wednesday nights (and along follows everyone else). Happily, the Japanese fusion food and sushi generally keeps up—just don't come with lofty expectations, and be prepared to spend a lot for small portions. Dim sum lunch on the terrace (an exception to the general Japanese culinary theme) is a lower-impact way to go. ⊠ *UG/F, The Centrium, 60 Wyndham St., Central* ☎ *3110–1222* ⊕ *www.dragon-i.com.hk* ⌔ *Reservations essential* ⊟ *AE, DC, MC, V* ☻ *Closed Sun.* Ⓜ *Central.*

Sichuan

$$–$$$ ✕ **Lumiere.** Modern, sexy Lumiere, in the IFC Mall, bills itself as a "Szechuan Bistro and Bar," and its menu blends Sichuan and South American cuisines. Although main courses are Sichuan in inspiration, like spicy jumbo crab claws, the starters include ceviche. Mongolian mutton slices also get high marks, as does the unique cocktail list at the long bar, which overlooks the harbor. Drinks are classified into "fruity," "creamy," and "sweet-and-sour," and also categorized by strength. Here, too, there's South America to thank, as in a "Caipiritini"—or, if you prefer, there's always the 1970 Pétrus. ⊠ *3101–3107, Podium Level 3, International Finance Center Mall, Central* ☎ *2393–3393* ⊕ *www.cuisinecuisine.hk* ⊟ *AE, DC, MC, V* Ⓜ *Central.*

$–$$ ✕ **Yellow Door Kitchen.** A sunny, casual Sichuan private kitchen (unlicensed
Fodor$Choice restaurant), the Yellow Door is still one of the most talked-about places
★ to eat in SoHo, even though it's been open since 2002. The space is down-home and personal, with good food and good feelings. Many of the spices and ingredients are shipped in from Sichuan province to create such wonders as bean curd and meat cooked in spicy Sichuan sauce and a memorable stuffed Hangzhou-style "8-treasure duck," which is stuffed with sticky rice and braised. The HK$250 set dinner, including eight starters, six mains, and dessert, is a great value. ⊠ *6/F, 37 Cochrane St., SoHo, Western* ☎ *2858–6555* ⊕ *www.yellowdoorkitchen.com.hk* ⊟ *AE, DC, MC, V* ☻ *Closed Sun. No lunch Sat.* Ⓜ *Central.*

5

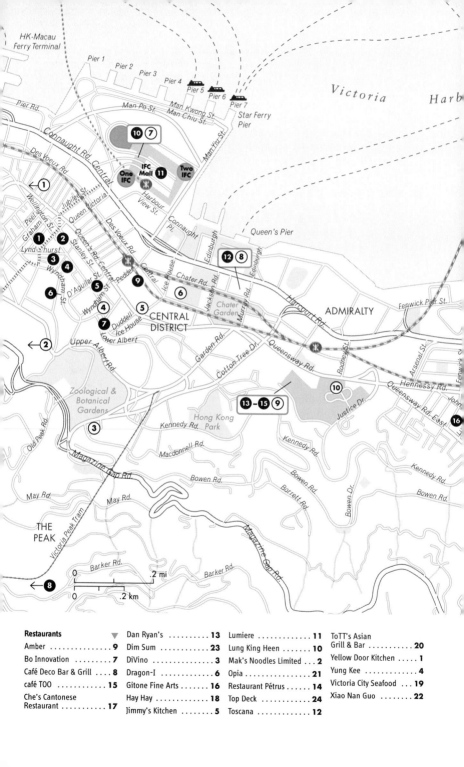

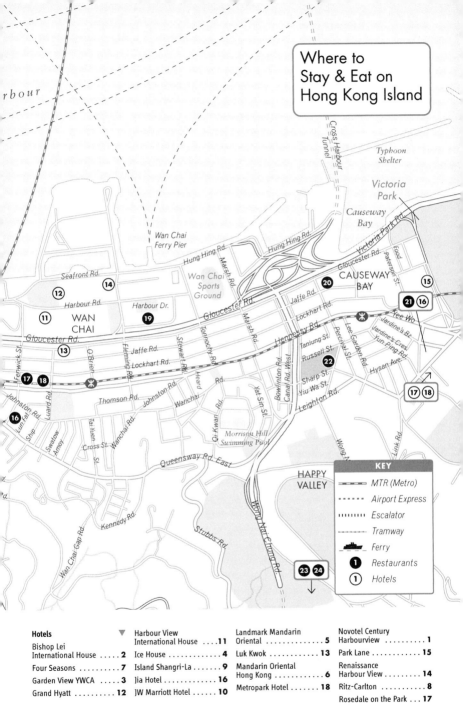

Where to Stay & Eat on Hong Kong Island

Typhoon Shelter

Victoria Park

Causeway Bay

CAUSEWAY BAY

Cross Harbour Tunnel

Wan Chai Ferry Pier

Wan Chai Sports Ground

WAN CHAI

Hung Hing Rd.
Hung Hing Rd.
Marsh Rd.
Gloucester Rd.
Gloucester Rd.
Jaffe Rd.
Lockhart Rd.
Hennessy Rd.
Tanlung St.
Russell St.
Jardine's Bz.
Yun Ping Rd.
Lee Garden Rd.
Percival St.
Hysan Ave.
Yat Sin St.
Tonnochy Rd.
Canal Rd. West
Bowrington Rd.
Leighton Rd.
Sharp St.
Yiu Wa St.
Link Rd.

Seafront Rd.
Harbour Rd.
Harbour Dr.
Gloucester Rd.
Jaffe Rd.
Lockhart Rd.
Fleming Rd.
Stewart Rd.
O'Brien
Thomson Rd.
Johnston Rd.
Wanchai
Tai Yuen Rd.
Wanchai Rd.
Cross St.
Swatow
Amoy
Ship
Lun Fat
Luard Rd.
Fenwick St.
Gloucester Rd.
Johnston Rd.
Heard Rd.
Qi Kwan Rd.

Victoria Park Rd.
Gloucester Rd.
Paterson St.
Yee Wo
Jardine's Bz.
Food

Morrison Hill Swimming Pool

Queensway Rd. East

HAPPY VALLEY

Kennedy Rd.
Stubbs Rd.
Wan Chai Gap Rd.
Wong Nai Chung Rd.

KEY

▬▬▬	MTR (Metro)
- - - - -	Airport Express
‖‖‖‖‖	Escalator
··············	Tramway
🚢	Ferry
❶	Restaurants
①	Hotels

Wan Chai & Causeway Bay

Cantonese

$–$$ ✕ **Che's Cantonese Restaurant.** Smartly dressed locals-in-the-know head
Fodor'sChoice for this casually elegant dim sum specialist, which is in the middle of
★ the downtown bustle yet well concealed on the fourth floor of an office building. From the elevator, you'll step into a classy Cantonese
world. It's hard to find a single better dim sum dish than Che's crispy
pork buns, whose sugary baked pastry conceals the brilliant saltiness
of stewed pork within. Other dim sum to try include pan-fried turnip
cake; rich, tender braised duck web (foot) in abalone sauce; and a refreshing dessert of cold pomelo and sago with mango juice for a calm-
ing end to an exciting meal. ⊠ *4/F, The Broadway, 54–62 Lockhart Rd.,
Wan Chai* ☎ *2528–1123* ▤ *AE, DC, MC, V* Ⓜ *Wan Chai.*

$–$$ ✕ **Dim Sum.** This elegant jewel breaks with tradition and serves dim sum
Fodor'sChoice all day and night. The original menu goes beyond common Cantonese
★ morsels like *har gau* (steamed shrimp dumplings), embracing dishes more
popular in the north, including chili prawn dumplings, Beijing onion
cakes, and steamed buns. Lobster bisque and abalone dumplings are also
popular. Lunch reservations are not taken on weekends, so there's always a long line. Arrive early, or admire the antique telephones and old
Chinese posters while you wait. Even if it feels somewhat contrived, it's
worth it. ⊠ *63 Sing Woo Rd., Happy Valley, Causeway Bay* ☎ *2834–8893*
▤ *AE, DC, MC, V* Ⓜ *Causeway Bay.*

¢ ✕ **Hay Hay.** The best food in Hong Kong can hide out in the dingiest
storefronts, and nowhere is this more true than at Hay Hay, a restaurant whose business card contains not a word of English. Surprisingly,
though, there's an English menu lurking somewhere in the back office,
but you shouldn't bother with it. Instead, just point to what looks good
on other tables—it's likely to be a delicious plate of rice, sweet, tender
roast goose or pork, and greens; or an exemplary noodle soup with slices
of roast meat resting on top. Apply the hot sauce liberally, and don't
expect the staff to speak a word of English. ⊠ *72–86 Lockhart Rd., corner of Ward St., Wan Chai* ☎ *2143–6183* ▤ *No credit cards* Ⓜ *Wan
Chai.*

Contemporary

★ **$$$$** ✕ **Opia.** The Philippe Starck–designed Jia Hotel is one of Hong Kong's
hottest, hippest spots, whether to eat, drink, or stay. Opia is its restaurant. Sip a smooth cocktail in the bar-lounge before being seated for dinner at one of the minimalist tables, and keep in mind that the place doesn't
really get going until 9 PM or so. The culinary theme is Australian, but
that won't help you predict what's on the menu: it might be better dubbed
Euro-Japanese-Thai, with dishes like yellowfin tuna sashimi with bonito
panna cotta and Wagyu red beef curry with pumpkin. DJs spin on
Wednesday and weekends. ⊠ *UG/F, 32—38 Ice House, Causeway Bay*
☎ *2850–8371* ⊕ *www.jiahongkong.com* ✍ *Reservations essential*
▤ *AE, MC, V* Ⓜ *Causeway Bay.*

$$–$$$$ ✕ **ToTT's Asian Grill & Bar.** The funky interior—zebra-stripe chairs, a
central oval bar, and designer tableware—is matched by the East-meets-
West cuisine at this restaurant on top of the Excelsior hotel, which

looks down on Causeway Bay and the marina. It's one of the very best dinner views in town, with a fun, lively vibe to boot. Best on the menu are steaks, with excellent imported meat cooked properly to order; there's also an extensive wine list. Live music kicks in late during the evening, offering a chance to burn a few calories on the dance floor.

✉ *Excelsior Hotel, 281 Gloucester Rd., Causeway Bay* ☎ *2837–6786* ▱ *AE, DC, MC, V* Ⓜ *Causeway Bay.*

Shanghainese

$$ ✕ **Gitone Fine Arts.** This pottery-studio-cum-restaurant-speakeasy has acquired quite a following since its 1995 opening. An artistic couple runs the studio and gallery, and turn it into a cozy, unlicensed "private dining" restaurant at night. The menu varies completely from day to day, but there are generally both Shanghainese and Cantonese options. Go for the Shanghai-style meal, as this is the specialty—it will include up to 16 small courses making up a long night of adventurous tasting. The pork leg braised in sweet soy, when available, is outstanding; it's a Shanghainese classic. Booking is absolutely essential, and unless you get lucky on a particular night, you must have at least a group of four. ✉ *1/F, 100 Queen's Road E, Wan Chai* ☎ *9025–7777* ⌖ *Reservations essential* ▱ *AE, DC, MC, V* Ⓜ *Wan Chai.*

¢–$ ✕ **Xiao Nan Guo.** First, a disclosure: this is a chain restaurant. But in this case it's not a bad thing, since it's part of a Shanghai chain, and you want your Shanghainese food to be authentic. In the years since it came to Hong Kong, Xiao Nan Guo has developed a serious following, particularly for dim sum. The feeling is casual and unpretentious, with a bright, expansive, bustling dining room lined with round tables. The focus is really on the food: soup dumplings are excellent, as you'd expect, but don't forget about the fatty "Lion's Head" meatballs, or the pork belly. ✉ *Shop 1201, 12/F Times Sq., 1 Matheson Rd., Causeway Bay* ☎ *2506–0009* ✉ *Shop 1201, 12/F Times Sq., 1 Matheson Rd., Causeway Bay* ☎ *2874–8899* ⊕ *www.aqua.com.hk* ▱ *AE, DC, MC, V* Ⓜ *Causeway Bay* ☉ *No lunch.*

Seafood

★ **$–$$$$** ✕ **Victoria City Seafood.** This perennially popular restaurant excels at Cantonese dim sum, Shanghainese, and seafood. It's a big, bright, banquet-style space, generally packed with large groups. Not to be missed are the spectacular soup dumplings with hairy crab roe; steamed blood with leek and egg tarts; and stir-fried rice rolls with XO sauce. Seafood, which you select live from the tank, might include whitebait in chili sauce, steamed prawns in vinegar sauce, whole local garoupa with ginger, or crab cooked with fried garlic. There's an Admiralty branch, too. ✉ *Sun Hung Kai Center, 3 Harbour Rd., Wan Chai* ☎ *2827–9938* ✉ *5/F Citic Tower, 1 Tim Mei Ave., Admiralty* ☎ *2877–2211* ▱ *AE, DC, MC, V* Ⓜ *Wan Chai.*

Southside

Eclectic

★ ✕ **Top Deck.** For a long time, the Jumbo Floating Restaurant and Dragon
☽ **$$-$$$$** Court were the only places to eat at Aberdeen's famed Jumbo Kingdom.
But times change, and now there's Top Deck, a classier, less kitschy, if
equally pricey alfresco option on the roof deck of the big boat, beneath
a three-story pagoda. It has a vastly better view (and breeze) than the
indoor restaurants beneath. If the weather permits, you should sit out-
doors rather than at one of the few indoor tables. The menu is some-
what haphazard (Thai, Japanese, Indian, Italian, steak) but generally good.
The raw bar is the best option, if you like seafood. There's a jazz band
playing on Wednesday, and a Sunday brunch every week. ⊠ *Shum Wan
Pier Path, Wong Chuk Hang, Aberdeen, Southside* ☎ *2552–3331*
⊕ *www.cafedecogroup.com* ⊟ *AE, MC, V* ⊗ *Closed Mon.*

Kowloon

Beijingese

$-$$ ✕ **Spring Deer.** With shades of pastel blue and green in a somber interior, and waiters in bland uniforms, this Peking duck specialist looks
like something out of 1950s communist Beijing. The crowd, too, is hi-
lariously old-school, which only adds to your duck experience. You'll
see locals with noodle dishes, stir-fried wok meat dishes, and so forth,
and they're good, but the Peking duck is the showstopper—it might be
the best in town. Even the peanuts for snacking, which are boiled to a
delectable softness, go above and beyond. ⊠ *1/F, 42 Mody Rd., Tsim
Sha Tsui, Kowloon* ☎ *2366–4012* ⊟ *AE, DC, MC, V* Ⓜ *Tsim Tsa Shui.*

Cantonese

$ ✕ **Happy Garden Noodle & Congee Kitchen.** For a taste of down-to-earth
Hong Kong fare without the fear of feeling like an interloper in Chi-
nese-only local joints, this is the place to go. With helpful waitresses and
an English menu, this small place is great for a typical local breakfast,
an easy lunch, and even a big dinner. A popular morning combination
is congee and a glutinous rice dumpling wrapped in a lotus leaf. A bowl
of wonton soup or a plate of fried rice or noodles makes a simple but
satisfying lunch. For dinner, the diced chicken with cashews and sweet-
and-sour pork are delicious. ⊠ *G/F, 72 Canton Rd., Tsim Sha Tsui,
Kowloon* ☎ *2377–2603* ⊟ *No credit cards* Ⓜ *Tsim Sha Tsui.*

¢ ✕ **Hing Fat Restaurant.** There are so many simple roast meat and noodle soup shops in the area around lower Nathan Road that it can be
hard to choose from among them. The popular Hing Fat is a reliable
choice both for soup dumplings and for Cantonese-style roast meats—
and the place is open all night, which is a definite plus. If you've made
a long night of it, plop down here among the locals for late-night refu-
eling within easy reach of the big Tsim Sha Tsui hotels. ⊠ *G/F, 8–10
Ashley Rd., Tsim Sha Tsui, Kowloon* ☎ *2736–7788* ⊟ *No credit cards*
Ⓜ *Tsim Sha Tsui.*

Contemporary

★ **$$$$**   ✕ **SPOON by Alain Ducasse.** Even if culinary legend Alain Ducasse is not exactly presiding over this kitchen, his inspiration is felt at this sleek restaurant, especially in preparations such as steamed foie gras, which balances the richness of seared foie gras with the resilience

of a cold terrine de foie gras. Despite the odd Asian flavor (seaweed pesto and shiitake mushrooms), the menu is contemporary French, liberally employing lobster, truffle, and other luxury ingredients with a keen sense of balance. The best, if priciest, way to go is the multicourse tasting menu. The tables overlooking the harbor provide a romantic setting—or reserve the kitchenside chef's table for a completely different experience. ⊠ *Hotel InterContinental Hong Kong, 18 Salisbury Rd., lobby level, Tsim Sha Tsui, Kowloon* ☎ *2313–2256* ⊕ *www.ichotelsgroup.com* ⌂ *Reservations essential* ▭ *AE, DC, MC, V* Ⓜ *Tsim Sha Tsui.*

Steak House

★ **$$$–$$$$**   ✕ **Steak House.** This restaurant with its lively, informal din, salad buffet, and gleaming harbor views, serves the best steak in the city. After being seated, you are made to choose from among 10 steak knives, 12 mustards, and eight kinds of rock salt—gimmicky, but fun. But the main event is of course the meat: wagyu steaks come from Australia, are aged for more than a year, and the results are shockingly tender, buttery, and flavorful. Other delicious cuts are flown in from the United States; and all of it is lovingly seared on Hong Kong's only charcoal grill. There isn't a jacket-and-tie policy but note that shorts are not allowed. ⊠ *Hotel InterContinental Hong Kong, 18 Salisbury Rd., Tsim Sha Tsui, Kowloon* ☎ *2721–1211* ⊕ *www.ichotelsgroup.com* ⌂ *Reservations essential* ▭ *AE, DC, MC, V* Ⓜ *Tsim Sha Tsui.*

WHERE TO STAY

By Robin Goldstein

Hong Kong has a truly postmodern skyline, and you might say that it has the hotels to match. Space is at a premium, so rooms are often cramped and expensive. But they're also tricked out with cutting-edge conveniences and luxurious amenities. Digs with rainfall-style showers, 42-inch plasma TVs, and iPod docks are more the rule than the exception. And it's hard to find a hotel without wireless Internet or a spa these days. Then there's that Hong Kong trademark—unparalleled harbor and skyline views.

Reserve well in advance, and plan to pay dearly. Hong Kong is now overrun as much by the new breed of vacationing upper-middle-class Mainlanders as by the international business set. Room shortages mean that the age of the under-US$100 hotel room is vanishing; top spots run US$500–$600.

Book well in advance. Never is this more true than for stays in March or in September through early December, high seasons for conventions. Most hotels operate on the European plan, with no meals included. All rooms have private baths unless indicated otherwise. We always list the facilities available, but we don't specify whether they cost extra; so when pricing accommodations, always ask what's included and what's not.

WHAT IT COSTS In HK$				
$$$$	**$$$**	**$$**	**$**	**¢**
FOR 2 PEOPLE over $3,000	$2,101–3,000	$1,101–2,100	$700–1,100	under $700

Prices are for two people in a standard double room in high season, excluding 10% service charge and a 3% government tax.

Western, Central & the Admiralty

$$$$
Fodor'sChoice
★
Four Seasons. When the Four Seasons opened, in the shadow of the world's sixth-tallest building, there was a collective intake of breath: with the elegantly colorful Chinese-theme rooms and their more muted Western counterparts, the place displays equal levels of effortless modern style, yet they're not about trendy minimalism; the *smallest* of them is a roomy 500 square feet. World-class linens, feng shui elevator banks, heated infinity pools, tropical rain showers, 42-inch plasma TVs, skyline-view hot-rock massages in the city's most cutting-edge spa, clairvoyant service, fantastic restaurants . . . and this list doesn't even include the holistic effect of staying in a place that's redefining the world's very notion of an urban luxury hotel. ⊠ *International Finance Center, 8 Finance Rd., Central* ☎ *3196–8888* ⊕ *www.fourseasons.com* ✆ *345 rooms, 54 suites* ⚹ *5 restaurants, room service, minibars, cable TV with movies, in-room DVDs, Wi-Fi, in-room stereos, 2 pools, gym, spa, room service, health club, hair salon, shops, hot tub, massage, sauna, 3 bars, lounge, dry cleaning, laundry service, concierge, business services, meeting rooms* ⊟ *AE, DC, MC, V* Ⓜ *Sheung Wan.*

$$$$
Fodor'sChoice
★
Island Shangri-La. This trademark elliptical building has become an icon of Hong Kong, as has *The Great Motherland of China*, the world's largest Chinese landscape painting, housed in a 16-story glass-top atrium with elevators soaring up and down. The lobby of the deluxe hotel, affectionately known to locals as the "Island Shang,"

> **WORD OF MOUTH**
>
> "Everything, without exception, was absolutely perfect at the Island Shangri-La. I cannot imagine a hotel doing better!"   –Yves

sparkles with more than 780 dazzling Austrian crystal chandeliers hanging from high ceilings and huge, sunlighted windows. Take the elevator up from the 39th floor and see the mainland's misty mountains drift by. Rooms are some of the largest on Hong Kong Island and have magnificent views; all have large desks and all-in-one bedside control panels. ⊠ *Supreme Court Rd., 2 Pacific Pl., Admiralty* ☎ *2877–3838,*

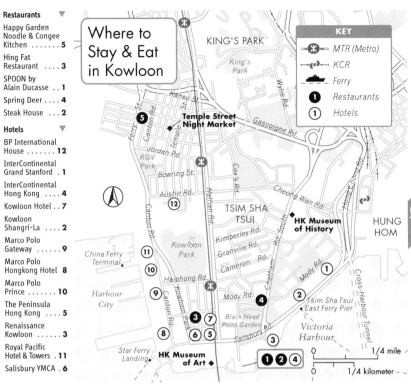

Restaurants ▼

Happy Garden
Noodle & Congee
Kitchen **5**

Hing Fat
Restaurant **3**

SPOON by
Alain Ducasse . . **1**

Spring Deer **4**

Steak House . . **2**

Hotels ▼

BP International
House **12**

InterContinental
Grand Stanford . **1**

InterContinental
Hong Kong **4**

Kowloon Hotel . . **7**

Kowloon
Shangri-La **2**

Marco Polo
Gateway **9**

Marco Polo
Hongkong Hotel **8**

Marco Polo
Prince **10**

The Peninsula
Hong Kong **5**

Renaissance
Kowloon **3**

Royal Pacific
Hotel & Towers . **11**

Salisbury YMCA . **6**

800/942–5050 *in U.S.* ⊕ *www.shangri-la.com* ↩ *531 rooms, 34 suites*
⑁ *4 restaurants, room service, in-room safes, minibars, cable TV with*
movies, DVD players, Wi-Fi, pool, gym, health club, hair salon, hot tub,
massage, sauna, spa, steam room, 3 lounges, shops, babysitting, dry clean-
ing, laundry service, concierge, business services, meeting rooms, no-smok-
ing floors ▭ *AE, DC, MC, V* Ⓜ *Admiralty.*

★ ⑁ **$$$$** ▦ **JW Marriott Hotel.** With its spacious, sunlight-filled lobby with floor-
to-ceiling windows revealing fantastic views of the harbor, you might
be tempted to spend hours drinking tea or cocktails at this high-end Marriott. Rooms have harbor or mountain views, ample work space, and
thoughtful amenities such as irons and ironing boards, complimentary
coffee, tea, and mineral water, and high-speed Internet access. Suites have
stereos and CD alarm clocks. There's a 24-hour gym and an outdoor
pool, and even tai chi lessons every Saturday. ⊠ *Pacific Place, 88*
Queensway, Admiralty ☎ *2810–8366, 800/228–9290 in U.S.* ⊕ *www.*
marriott.com ↩ *577 rooms, 25 suites* ⑁ *4 restaurants, room service,*
in-room safes, minibars, cable TV with movies, Wi-Fi, pool, health
club, spa, 3 bars, shop, babysitting, dry cleaning, laundry service,
concierge, business services, meeting rooms, no-smoking floors ▭ *AE,*
DC, MC, V Ⓜ *Admiralty.*

$$$$ 🏨 **Landmark Mandarin Oriental.** Hong Kong hotels are like computers:
FodorśChoice every year, the new technology outdoes the old by such a staggering mar-
★ gin that you're left wondering why anyone would stick by their old models. The design of this boutique-size hotel is dazzling, and a complete
departure from the Mandarin's standard MO. The three room types are
named for their square footage; the midrange L600 is the most interesting, with a round bathroom fascinatingly placed at the center of the
space. Everything from iPod docks to surround-sound speakers are controlled through your TV remote, and the 21,000-square-foot spa has
Turkish baths and tropical-rain saunas. And all of this is implausibly
concealed within the financial mitochondrion of the city. ⊠ *15 Queen's
Rd., Central* ☎ *2132–0188* ⊕ *www.mandarinoriental.com/landmark
⤸ 113 rooms ⚱ 3 restaurants, room service, minibars, cable TV with
movies, in-room DVDs, Wi-Fi, in-room stereos, pool, gym, health club,
hot tub, massage, shop, spa, sauna, bar, lounge, dry cleaning, laundry
service, concierge, business services* ⊟ *AE, DC, MC, V* Ⓜ *Central.*

$$$$ 🏨 **Mandarin Oriental Hong Kong.** The legendary Mandarin has served
FodorśChoice the international elite since 1963, has completed a top-to-bottom ren-
★ ovation that included the installation of one of the city's most elaborate spas. Five new categories of rooms, from "study" to "harbour,"
span a wider price range than ever before. All have been updated to a
space-age standard: flat panel LCDs, iPod docks, Hermès toiletries.
⊠ *5 Connaught Rd., Central* ☎ *2522–0111* ⊕ *www.mandarin-oriental.
com ⤸ 434 rooms, 68 suites ⚱ 6 restaurants, room service, in-room
safes, minibars, cable TV with movies, in-room data ports, indoor pool,
gym, health club, hair salon, hot tub, sauna, spa, 4 bars, dry cleaning,
laundry service, concierge, business services, meeting rooms, no-smoking floors* ⊟ *AE, DC, MC, V* Ⓜ *Central.*

★ **$$$–$$$$** 🏨 **Ritz-Carlton.** Refined elegance and superb hospitality are signatures
of the Ritz-Carlton. Although gilt-frame mirrors and crystal chandeliers
evoke old-world Europe, the design does give the occasional nod to Asia.
Service is in the stratosphere, as you'd expect from a Ritz-Carlton, and
every room has either a harbor view or a Peak-and-skyscraper view. The
upper club floors have a private concierge, and a lounge with free food
and drinks all day long, where you'll likely see elite business deals being
transacted in hushed tones. The small lobby is less impressive than
those of its peers, but on the flip side, its location, right aside Central's
main plaza, is unbeatable. ⊠ *3 Connaught Rd., Central* ☎ *2877–6666,
800/241–3333 in U.S.* ⊕ *www.ritzcarlton.com/hotels/hong_kong ⤸ 187
rooms, 29 suites ⚱ 6 restaurants, room service, in-room safes, minibars,
cable TV with movies, in-room DVDs, Wi-Fi, pool, gym, health club,
hot tub, massage, sauna, bar, lounge, shop, babysitting, dry cleaning,
laundry service, concierge, business services, meeting rooms, no-smok-
ing floors* ⊟ *AE, DC, MC, V* Ⓜ *Central.*

↻ **$$** 🏨 **Garden View YWCA.** Don't be put off by the name: this attractive cylin-
FodorśChoice drical guesthouse on a hill overlooks the botanical gardens and harbor,
★ and its well-designed rooms make excellent use of small irregular shapes
and emphasize each room's picture windows. If you want to do your
own cooking, ask for one with a kitchenette (which will include a mi-
crowave oven); if not, the coffee shop serves European and Asian food.

You can also use the swimming pool and gymnasium in the adjacent YWCA. Garden View is a five-minute drive (Bus 12A or Minibus 1A) from Central and a few minutes from the Peak tram station. ✉ *1 MacDonnell Rd., Midlevels, Western* ☎ *2877–3737* 🌐 *www.ywca.org.hk* *133 rooms* *Coffee shop, some kitchenettes, minibars, cable TV, in-room data ports, pool, gym, laundry service, in-room broadband, business services, no-smoking floors* 💳 *AE, DC, MC, V* Ⓜ *Central.*

★ $–$$ **Ice House.** Consider yourself lucky to be alive at the right time: the apart-hotel accommodation concept has finally hit Hong Kong, and at the Ice House, it's done right. These chic, modern studio apartments are available to rent by the day or week, not just by the month (which, by the way, is quite reasonable at around HK$14,000). Sunlight is plentiful, and the glass cube showers are an amusing touch. The location is excellent, next to the Foreign Correspondents' Club and Lan Kwai Fong, and there's free unlimited broadband, a dedicated phone line, and other business amenities. There's housekeeping service every day but Sunday. ✉ *38 Ice House St., Central* ☎ *2836–7333* 🌐 *www.icehouse.com.hk* *30 rooms* *Kitchenettes, minibars, cable TV, in-room broadband, laundry service, business services* 💳 *AE, DC, MC, V.*

★ $–$$ **Novotel Century Harbourview.** This modern hotel is surrounded by traditional Chinese streets full of stores selling antiques, herbal medicines, and bric-a-brac, seemingly unchanged with the passage of time. Rooms are small but have city or harbor views. A free shuttle bus takes you to the Airport Express Hong Kong Station and the HK Convention & Exhibition Centre. Biz Café in the lobby has Internet facilities and is open from early morning for breakfast to late night for supper and drinks. The rooftop pool and gym have panoramic views. ✉ *508 Queen's Rd. W, Western* ☎ *2974–1234* 🌐 *www.accorhotels.com/asia* *262 rooms, 12 suites* *Restaurant, coffee shop, room service, in-room safes, minibars, cable TV with movies, in-room broadband, pool, gym, massage, 2 bars, babysitting, laundry service, business services, meeting rooms, no-smoking floors* 💳 *AE, DC, MC, V* Ⓜ *Sheung Wan.*

$ **Bishop Lei International House.** Owned and operated by the Catholic diocese of Hong Kong, this guesthouse is up the Midlevels Escalator at the top of SoHo. Rooms are quite small but functional, and half have harbor views. Although it's economically priced, there is a fully equipped business center, a workout room, a pool, and a restaurant serving Chinese and Western meals. ✉ *4 Robinson Rd., Midlevels, Western* ☎ *2868–0828* 🌐 *www.bishopleihtl.com.hk* *104 rooms, 101 suites* *Restaurant, in-room safes, minibars, cable TV, in-room broadband, pool, gym, babysitting, laundry service, business services, meeting rooms, no-smoking floors* 💳 *AE, DC, MC, V* Ⓜ *Central.*

Fodor'sChoice ★

WORD OF MOUTH

"Bishop Lei is a fantastic value for Hong Kong. The location is great (about a 2-minute walk from the moving sidewalk), the bus is outside the door, the front desk staff are helpful, and it's about a 40-minute walk to the top of the Peak." –Anna

Lantau Island

★ ⚑ **Hong Kong Disneyland Hotel.** Modeled in Victorian style after the
⚑ **$$$–$$$$** Grand Floridian in Florida's Walt Disney World Resort, this top-flight
hotel is beautifully executed on every level, from the spacious rooms with
balconies overlooking the sea to the Hidden-Mickey topiary gardens and
grand, imposing ballrooms that wouldn't be out of place in a fairy-tale
secret castle. There's a full daily schedule of activities, many aimed at
children; and downstairs, Disney characters meet and greet guests dur-
ing the enormous buffet breakfast—a good way to get your kids to for-
give you for the three days you spent sampling the geese hanging from
their necks in Mong Kok. Don't overlook Disneyland as a place to stay
before or after your early-morning or late-night flight—it's minutes
from the airport. ⊠ *Hong Kong Disneyland Resort, Lantau Island*
☎ *1–830–830* ⊕ *www.hongkongdisneyland.com* ⮒ *400 rooms* ⚐ *3
restaurants, room service, in-room safes, children's programs, mini-
bars, cable TV with movies, in-room broadband, pool, gym, spa, health
club, massage, 2 bars, lounge,*
shops, dry cleaning, laundry serv-
ice, business services, meeting rooms
⊟ *AE, DC, MC, V.*

$$$ ⚑ **Regal Airport Hotel.** Ideal for pas-
sengers in transit, this is one of the
world's largest airport hotels. It's
some distance from the city, but
the high-speed rail system can have
you on Hong Kong Island in 25

> **WORD OF MOUTH**
>
> "I found the Regal to be a very
> stylish, opulent, and relaxing
> haven after a very long day of
> flying."   –Brian

minutes. It's also connected to the passenger terminal by an air-conditioned, moving walkway. Some rooms have terrific views of planes
landing from afar; those with balconies overlook two swimming pools
and feel like you're staying in a resort. ⊠ *9 Cheong Ted Rd., Lantau
Island* ☎ *2286–8888* ⊕ *www.regalhotel.com* ⮒ *1,103 rooms, 27 suites*
⚐ *7 restaurants, coffee shop, room service, in-room safes, minibars, cable
TV with movies, Wi-Fi, indoor-outdoor pool, exercise equipment, gym,
bar, 2 lounges, shop, dry cleaning, laundry service, business services, meeting rooms, no-smoking floors* ⊟ *AE, DC, MC, V.*

★ ⚑ **$$** ⚑ **Disney's Hollywood Hotel.** Like its pricier sister, the Disneyland Hotel,
Disney's Hollywood Hotel could theoretically be viewed simply as one
of Asia's best airport hotels. But that would hardly do justice to the cre-
ativity and attention to detail that so brightly color every aspect of your
stay here. The theme is the golden age of Hollywood, and if you're from
the United States you'll smile at the loving display of Americana here,
from the New York–theme restaurant to the art-deco frontage of the
cocktail lounge. Of course, this is Disneyland, and there are the Chef
Mickey restaurants, too. Rooms are on the smaller side, and a bit more
"Goofy" than they are at the Disneyland Hotel. ⊠ *Hong Kong Disney-
land Resort, Lantau Island* ☎ *1–830–830* ⊕ *www.hongkongdisneyland.
com* ⮒ *600 rooms* ⚐ *3 restaurants, room service, in-room safes, chil-
dren's programs, minibars, cable TV with movies, in-room broadband,
pool, gym, spa, health club, massage, 2 bars, shops, dry cleaning, laun-
dry service, business services, meeting rooms* ⊟ *AE, DC, MC, V.*

Wan Chai & Causeway Bay

★ ☾ $$$$ 🏨 **Grand Hyatt.** A ceiling painted by Italian artist Paola Dindo tops the Hyatt's art-deco–style lobby, and black-and-white photographs of classic Chinese scenes hang on the walls. The elegant guest rooms have sweeping harbor views, many with interesting zigzag window frames; amenities include large interactive TVs with cordless keyboards. The

One Harbour Road Cantonese restaurant is notable—as is JJ's nightclub and Thai restaurant—and the ground-floor breakfast buffet is a decadent feast. The Plateau spa has a Zen-like calm and there are extensive outdoor facilities. The hotel is especially convenient if you're spending time at the Hong Kong Convention & Exhibition Centre, which is connected to the building. ⊠ *1 Harbour Rd., Wan Chai* ☎ *2588–1234* ⊕ *www.hongkong.grand.hyatt.com* 🛏 *519 rooms, 51 suites* ♿ *7 restaurants, room service, in-room safes, minibars, cable TV with movies, Wi-Fi, driving range, 2 tennis courts, pool, exercise equipment, gym, health club, hair salon, spa, 3 bars, lounge, nightclub, babysitting, dry cleaning, laundry service, concierge, business services, meeting rooms, no-smoking floors* ⊟ *AE, DC, MC, V* Ⓜ *Wan Chai.*

★ $$$–$$$$ 🏨 **Park Lane.** With an imposing facade that wouldn't look out of place in London, this elegant hotel overlooks Victoria Park and backs onto one of Hong Kong Island's busiest shopping, entertainment, and business areas, Causeway Bay. There's a grand lobby, and rooms have marble bathrooms, elegant handcrafted furniture, and marvelous views of the harbor, Victoria Park, or the city. The rooftop restaurant has a panoramic view and serves international cuisine with a touch of Asian flavor. ⊠ *310 Gloucester Rd., Causeway Bay* ☎ *2293–8888* ⊕ *www.parklane.com.hk* 🛏 *759 rooms, 33 suites* ♿ *2 restaurants, room service, in-room safes, minibars, cable TV with movies, in-room broadband, gym, health club, hair salon, massage, sauna, spa, bar, shop, babysitting, dry cleaning, laundry service, concierge, business services, meeting rooms, no-smoking floor* ⊟ *AE, DC, MC, V* Ⓜ *Causeway Bay.*

$$–$$$ 🏨 **Jia.** The first boutique hotel designed by Philippe Starck in Asia is a
Fodor's Choice wonder to behold, beginning with the (see-and-be-) scene in the lobby,
★ bar, and restaurant, making it one of the hippest places to drink or dine in town. Although the sculptural furniture and accompanying trendiness won't be everyone's cup of tea, this is still a groundbreaking concept that is helping to redefine the modern Hong Kong hotel landscape. For instance, it doesn't have rooms; rather, it has "apartments," with mini-kitchens, dining tables, and cookware. You can choose between smaller "studios" or the larger one-bedroom "suites," which have separate bedrooms. Will the design of this hotel feel "so 2006" 10 years hence? Perhaps. But for the moment, Jia is the place. ⊠ *1–5 Irving St., Causeway Bay* ☎ *3196–9000* ⊕ *www.jiahongkong.com* 🛏 *54 rooms* ♿ *Restaurant, room service, minibars, Wi-Fi, in-room stereos, in-room*

DVDs, kitchenettes, bar, lounge, dry cleaning, laundry service, meeting room, no-smoking rooms ⊟ *AE, DC, MC, V* Ⓜ *Causeway Bay.*

$$–$$$ 🏨 **Luk Kwok.** This contemporary hotel and office tower designed by Hong Kong's leading architect, Remo Riva, replaced the Wan Chai landmark of the same name immortalized in Richard Mason's novel *The World of Suzie Wong.* The Luk Kwok's appeal, aside from its slightly kitschy classic Asian feel, is its proximity to the Hong Kong Convention & Exhibition Centre, the Academy for Performing Arts, and the Arts Centre. Guest rooms in the building's 19th to 29th floors are simply furnished, and the higher floors have mountain or city views. There's also a good Chinese restaurant. ⊠ *72 Gloucester Rd., Wan Chai* ☎ *2866–2166* ⊕ *www.lukkwokhotel.com* ↘ *195 rooms, 2 suites* ⌂ *Restaurant, room service, in-room safes, minibars, cable TV with movies, in-room broadband, health club, lounge, dry cleaning, laundry service, concierge, business services, meeting rooms, babysitting, no-smoking floors* ⊟ *AE, DC, MC, V* Ⓜ *Wan Chai.*

★ $$–$$$ 🏨 **Metropark Hotel.** At this contemporary hotel with Euro-boutique flair you'll get a prime location and unobstructed views for a lower cost than many other hotels. Most rooms look out at Victoria Park or the harbor through the floor-to-ceiling windows, and all rooms are equipped with high-speed Internet access. The tiny lobby leads into Vic's, a tapas bar; the trendy Café du Parc has French and Japanese fusion food. Free shuttle buses to and from the Hong Kong Convention & Exhibition Centre run regularly. ⊠ *148 Tung Lo Wan Rd., Causeway Bay* ☎ *2600–1000* ⊕ *www.metroparkhotel.com* ↘ *266 rooms, 56 suites* ⌂ *Restaurant, room service, in-room safes, minibars, cable TV, in-room broadband, pool, gym, sauna, spa, bar, babysitting, dry cleaning, laundry service, business services, meeting rooms, no-smoking floor* ⊟ *AE, DC, MC, V* Ⓜ *Causeway Bay.*

☾ $$–$$$ 🏨 **Renaissance Harbour View.** Sharing the Hong Kong Convention & Ex-
Fodor'sChoice hibition Centre complex with the Grand Hyatt is this more modest but
★ attractive hotel. Guest rooms are medium size with plenty of beveled-glass mirrors that reflect the modern decor. Many rooms have good harbor views and all have high-speed Internet access. Grounds are extensive and include a large outdoor pool, plus gardens, a playground, and jogging trails, which makes this a good place to stay if you are with children. The wonderfully scenic, soaring lobby lounge has a live jazz band in the evening. ⊠ *1 Harbour Rd., Wan Chai* ☎ *2802–8888* ⊕ *www.renaissancehotels.com* ↘ *809 rooms, 53 suites* ⌂ *4 restaurants, room service, in-room fax, in-room safes, minibars, cable TV with movies, Wi-Fi, driving range, 2 tennis courts, pool, gym, health club, hair salon, sauna, 2 bars, shops, babysitting, playground, dry cleaning, laundry service, concierge, business services, meeting rooms, no-smoking floors* ⊟ *AE, DC, MC, V* Ⓜ *Wan Chai.*

$$ 🏨 **Harbour View International House.** This waterfront YMCA property has small but relatively inexpensive—rooms near the Wan Chai Star Ferry Pier. Rooms are not luxurious but have the basic amenities; the best ones face the harbor. The hotel is well placed for attending cultural events: both the Arts Centre and the Academy for Performing Arts are next door. It's also just opposite the Hong Kong Convention & Exhibition Cen-

tre. The 16-story hostel provides free shuttle service to Causeway Bay and the Central Star Ferry. You can use the superb YMCA Kowloon facilities, just a short ferry ride away, for a small fee. ✉ *4 Harbour Rd., Wan Chai* ☎ *2802–0111* ⊕ *www.harbour.ymca.org.hk* 🛏 *320 rooms* ♨ *Restaurant, room service, minibars, cable TV, in-room broadband, babysitting, laundry service, concierge, business services, meeting rooms, no-smoking floor* ▤ *AE, DC, MC, V* Ⓜ *Wan Chai.*

★ **$$** 🖳 **Rosedale on the Park.** This "cyber boutique hotel," the first of its kind in Hong Kong, has lots of high-tech extras. All public areas have computers, and you can rent a printer, computer, or fax for use in your room, where you also have broadband Internet access and a cordless telephone that can be used anywhere on the property. Mobile phones are also available for rent during your stay. Although only the top few floors have park or stadium views, all rooms are bright and comfortable. Next to Victoria Park and only a five-minute walk to the MTR subway, it's a great location for shopping—and the price is one of the best values in the category. You're in Hong Kong, after all, so why not take advantage of all that technology? ✉ *8 Shelter St., Causeway Bay* ☎ *2127–8888* ⊕ *www.rosedale.com.hk* 🛏 *229 rooms, 45 suites* ♨ *2 restaurants, room service, in-room safes, minibars, cable TV with movies, Wi-Fi, lounge, babysitting, dry cleaning, laundry service, business services, meeting rooms, no-smoking floors* ▤ *AE, DC, MC, V* Ⓜ *Causeway Bay.*

Kowloon

$$$$ 🖳 **InterContinental Hong Kong.** Perhaps one of the most attractive hotels in Asia, the InterContinental Hong Kong is opulent inside while it offers some of the finest views of the Hong Kong skyline outside. Simply coming here for a spectacularly conceived cocktail at 8 PM to take in the skyline light show is a memorable Hong Kong experience, perhaps equivalent to tea at the Peninsula. The lobby has a delicious airy quality, and the impeccably modern rooms are just as exciting, with luxuriously large beds, desks with ergonomically designed chairs, and superlative showers in the bathrooms. Corner suites have 180-degree harbour views, Dom Perignon is the house champagne in the executive lounge, and the spa is worth e-mailing home about. The incredible restaurant lineup, meanwhile, is soon to include Nobu—to give Alain Ducasse a bit of company, perhaps. ✉ *18 Salisbury Rd., Tsim Sha Tsui, Kowloon* ☎ *2721–1211, 800/327–0200 in U.S.* ⊕ *www.ichotelsgroup. com* 🛏 *495 rooms, 92 suites* ♨ *5 restaurants, minibars, room service, cable TV with movies, Wi-Fi, pool, gym, health club, hot tub, sauna, spa, steam room, shop, babysitting, dry cleaning, laundry service, concierge, business services, meeting rooms, no-smoking floors* ▤ *AE, DC, MC, V* Ⓜ *Tsim Sha Tsui.*

Fodor's Choice ★

$$$$ 🖳 **The Peninsula Hong Kong.** Established in 1928, the Peninsula has long been synonymous with impeccable taste and colonial glamour. And many people adore this hotel. But time may well have left this hotel behind. These days, the Pen's rooms just feel gaudy and overpriced, with stodgy, uncomfortable sofas, awkward desks, chandeliers, and outdated TV systems. The spa is decked out with faux-Roman statues that are all show without a sense of style. Even the hotel's famous Rolls-Royces

5

feel dingy these days. And at about US$600 for the cheapest harbor-view room, it seems the only thing keeping up with the times is the price. If you must see the place, there is still the famous high tea in the lobby bar. ⊠ *Salisbury Rd., Tsim Sha Tsui, Kowloon* ☎ *2366–6251* ⊕ *www.peninsula. com* ⇝ *246 rooms, 54 suites* ⚘ *7 restaurants, room service, in-room fax, in-room safes, minibars, cable TV with movies, in-room VCRs, in-room broadband, pool, gym, health club, hair salon, hot tub, spa, bar, shops, babysitting, dry cleaning, laundry service, concierge, business services, meeting rooms, helipad, no-smoking floors* ⊟ *AE, DC, MC, V* Ⓜ *Tsim Sha Tsui.*

★ **$$$–$$$$** ⊡ **Kowloon Shangri-La.** Catering mainly to business travelers, this upscale hotel has a 24-hour business center with teleconferencing facilities as well as some strange features, such as the elevator carpets that are changed at midnight to indicate the day of the week. You'll feel like a tycoon in the posh lobby; the guest rooms all have magnificent harbor or city views, and although it doesn't have quite the glamour or services of the Island Shangri-La (or the accompanying sky-high prices) it's still a wonderful place to stay. Complimentary newspapers are delivered daily to your room; club rooms have combination fax/printer/copier/scanners, as well as DVD players and even TVs in the bathroom. A wireless telephone system allows guests to receive calls throughout the hotel. Attention to detail and outstanding service, in a city where service is already tops, set this hotel apart. ⊠ *64 Mody Rd., Tsim Sha Tsui East, Kowloon* ☎ *2721–2111, 800/942–5050 in U.S.* ⊕ *www.shangri-la.com* ⇝ *700 rooms, 25 suites* ⚘ *5 restaurants, room service, in-room safes, minibars, cable TV with movies, Wi-Fi, indoor pool, gym, health club, hair salon, sauna, spa, bar, lounge, shops, babysitting, dry cleaning, laundry service, concierge, business services, meeting rooms, no-smoking floor* ⊟ *AE, DC, MC, V* Ⓜ *Tsim Sha Tsui.*

☾ **$$$–$$$$** ⊡ **Marco Polo Hongkong Hotel.** Next to the Star Ferry and Cultural Centre and part of the wharf-side Harbour City complex, this is the largest and best of three Marco Polo hotels along the same street. Spacious rooms have special touches such as a choice of 11 types of pillows and, for children, miniature bathrobes, mild shampoos, and rubber ducks. The Continental Club floors include 24-hour butler service. All three hotels share the pool, gym, and spa that are at this location. ⊠ *Harbour City, Canton Rd., Tsim Sha Tsui, Kowloon* ☎ *2113–0088* ⊕ *www. marcopolohotels.com* ⇝ *621 rooms, 44 suites* ⚘ *7 restaurants, room*

TEA FOR TWO?

The British haven't been in the tea business as long as the Chinese, but they know a thing or two. Afternoon tea in the soaring grand lobby of this icon is all very Noel Coward. A string quartet plays as liveried waiters pour from silver pots. Three tiers' worth of salmon sandwiches, petit fours, and Valrhona truffles keep you munching. There's clotted Devonshire cream for the airy scones—so popular the Pen makes 1,000 a day. All this comes to a snip of what a suite here costs: HK$340 for two. You can't make reservations, though; to avoid lines come at 2 on the dot or after 5:30.

service, in-room safes, minibars, cable TV with movies, in-room broad-band, pool, gym, hair salon, spa, lounge, shops, babysitting, dry clean-ing, laundry service, concierge, business services, meeting rooms, no-smoking floors ⊟ *AE, DC, MC, V* Ⓜ *Tsim Sha Tsui.*

$$$ 🏨 **Marco Polo Prince.** Like its neighboring Marco Polo namesakes in the Harbour City complex (the Hongkong and Gateway), the Prince is con-venient to upscale shops, cinemas, and the restaurants and shops of Tsim Sha Tsui. It's also near the China Hong Kong Terminal, where ferries, boats, and buses depart for mainland China. Most of the small but com-fortable rooms overlook expansive Kowloon Park, and some suites have views of Victoria Harbour. You can use the pool, gym, and spa at the Marco Polo Hongkong, a five-minute walk away. ⊠ *Harbour City, Canton Rd., Tsim Sha Tsui, Kowloon* ☎ *2113–1888* ⊕ *www. marcopolohotels.com* 🛏 *343 rooms, 51 suites* 🍴 *4 restaurants, snack bar, room service, in-room safes, minibars, cable TV with movies, in-room broadband, hair salon, bar, shop, babysitting, dry cleaning, laun-dry service, business services, meeting rooms, no-smoking floors* ⊟ *AE, DC, MC, V* Ⓜ *Tsim Sha Tsui.*

$$–$$$ 🏨 **InterContinental Grand Stanford Hong Kong.** More than half the rooms in this luxury hotel, the lesser sibling of the larger InterContinental Hong Kong in downtown Tsim Sha Tsui, have an unobstructed harbor view. The elegant lobby is spacious, the staff is helpful and friendly, and the modern comfortable rooms are decorated in warm earth tones with fine wood fittings and large desks. Executive rooms have a direct-line fax machine and amenities include trouser presses. The restaurants are well known locally, including Mistral (Italian), Belvedere (regional French), and Tiffany's New York Bar, which celebrates the Roaring 1920s with antique furniture, Tiffany-style glass ceilings, and a live band. ⊠ *70 Mody Rd., Tsim Sha Tsui East, Kowloon* ☎ *2721–5161* ⊕ *www.grandstanford. com* 🛏 *554 rooms, 25 suites* 🍴 *4 restaurants, room service, in-room safes, minibars, cable TV with movies, in-room data ports, pool, gym, health club, sauna, spa, bar, shop, babysitting, dry cleaning, laundry serv-ice, business services, meeting rooms, no-smoking floors* ⊟ *AE, DC, MC, V* Ⓜ *Tsim Sha Tsui.*

$$–$$$ 🏨 **Marco Polo Gateway.** This 16-story hotel, popular with Japanese tour groups, is in the shopping and commercial area along Canton Road and close to the Tsim Sha Tsui MTR station. The tastefully decorated rooms and suites have large windows and comfortable beds. The most notable restaurant is La Brasserie, serving French provincial cuisine in a typical brasserie style (long bar, dark wood, leather seats, red-checkered table-cloths). The business center is well supplied, and the staff is helpful. You can use the pool, gym, and spa at the nearby Marco Polo Hongkong Hotel. ⊠ *Harbour City, Canton Rd., Tsim Sha Tsui, Kowloon* ☎ *2113–0888* ⊕ *www.marcopolohotels.com* 🛏 *377 rooms, 56 suites* 🍴 *3 restaurants, room service, in-room safes, minibars, cable TV with movies, in-room broadband, hair salon, bar, shops, babysitting, dry clean-ing, laundry service, business services, meeting rooms, no-smoking floors* ⊟ *AE, DC, MC, V* Ⓜ *Tsim Sha Tsui.*

$$ 🏨 **BP International House.** Built by the Boy Scouts Association, this hotel next to Kowloon Park offers an excellent value for the money. A portrait of association founder Baron Robert Baden-Powell, hangs in the spacious modern lobby. The hostel-like rooms are small and spartan but have regular hotel amenities and panoramic views of Victoria Harbour and clear views of the busiest part of Kowloon. Ask to see your room before settling in, as some rooms are better than others. A multipurpose hall hosts exhibitions, conventions, and concerts, and the health club is one of the biggest in town. There are Internet terminals available for use. ✉ *8 Austin Rd., Jordan, Kowloon* ☎ *2376–1111* ⊕ *www.bpih. com.hk* 🖾 *529 rooms, 4 suites ⌂ 2 restaurants, cable TV with movies, health club, spa, dry cleaning, laundry facilities, laundry service* ▭ *AE, DC, MC, V* Ⓜ *Jordan.*

\$\$ 🏨 **Kowloon Hotel.** The mirrored exterior and the chrome, glass, and marble lobby reflect the hotel's high-tech orientation. Kowloon means "nine dragons" in Cantonese, and is the theme here. Triangular windows and a pointed lobby ceiling, made from hundreds of hand-blown Venetian-glass pyramids, represent dragons' teeth. The Kowloon is the lesser sibling to the adjacent Peninsula hotel, so you can sign up for services at the Pen and charge them to your room account here; similarly, all the facilities at the Peninsula are open to you. Rooms are small, but each has a computer with free Internet service and fax. ✉ *19–21 Nathan Rd., Tsim Sha Tsui, Kowloon* ☎ *2929–2888* ⊕ *www.harbour-plaza.com* 🖾 *730 rooms, 12 suites ⌂ 3 restaurants, room service, in-room fax, minibars, cable TV with movies, in-room broadband, babysitting, dry cleaning, laundry service, business services, meeting room, no-smoking floors* ▭ *AE, DC, MC, V* Ⓜ *Tsim Sha Tsui.*

\$\$ 🏨 **Renaissance Kowloon.** Part of a large shopping complex, and now a member of the Marriott chain, this popular hotel on the Tsim Sha Tsui waterfront has perfect views of Hong Kong Island from its upper club floors, rivaled only by the adjacent hotel InterContinental Hong Kong, part of the same complex. Long escalators lead from the shopping area to the hotel's large second-floor lobby. The comfortable, modern guest rooms are homey and have plenty of space for working and relaxing. Greenery surrounds the outdoor pool, which stays open throughout the year. The Panorama restaurant, one of three in the hotel, has one of the best harbor views in town. ✉ *22 Salisbury Rd., Tsim Sha Tsui, Kowloon* ☎ *2369–4111* ⊕ *www.marriott.com* 🖾 *492 rooms, 53 suites ⌂ 3 restaurants, room service, in-room safes, minibars, cable TV with movies, Wi-Fi, pool, gym, health club, hair salon, sauna, spa, lounge, babysitting, dry cleaning, laundry service, business services, meeting rooms, no-smoking floors* ▭ *AE, DC, MC, V* Ⓜ *Tsim Sha Tsui.*

\$–\$\$ 🏨 **Royal Pacific Hotel & Towers.** On the Tsim Sha Tsui waterfront, the Royal Pacific is part of the Hong Kong China City complex, which includes the terminal for ferries to mainland China. Guest rooms are arranged in two blocks, the hotel and tower wings. Tower-wing rooms have harbor views and are luxuriously furnished, while more inexpensive hotel-wing rooms have Kowloon street and park views and are smaller but just as attractive. The hotel connects to Kowloon Park by a footbridge and is close to shops and cinemas. ✉ *33 Canton Rd., Tsim Sha Tsui, Kowloon* ☎ *2736–1188* ⊕ *www.royalpacific.com.hk* 🖾 *641 rooms, 32 suites ⌂ 3 restaurants, room service, in-room safes, minibars,* *cable TV with movies, in-room broadband, gym, health club, sauna, spa, steam room, squash, bar, babysitting, dry cleaning, laundry service, business services, meeting rooms* ☰ *AE, DC, MC, V* Ⓜ *Tsim Sha Tsui.*

☾ **$–$$** ⊞ **Salisbury YMCA.** This upscale
Fodor's Choice YMCA is Hong Kong's most pop-
★ ular and is great value for your money. Next to the Peninsula and opposite the Cultural Centre, Space Museum, and Art Museum, it's in an excellent location for theater, art, and concert crawls. The pastel-color rooms have harbor views and broadband Internet access. The Y

WORD OF MOUTH

"Not a YMCA as such, but an excellent hotel. It offers good value for money, especially the (partial) harbor view rooms. The Peninsula right next door charges much more for similar views. There's friendly service, modern rooms, and lots of facilities, including a pool. The location is also perfect—on the Kowloon side, close to the Star Ferry terminal and MTR."
–F. Schubert

5

also has a chapel, a garden, a conference room with a built-in stage, a children's library, and excellent health and fitness facilities, which include a dance studio and even a climbing wall. Restaurants in the area are cheap and good, and the shopping is great. ⊠ *41 Salisbury Rd., Tsim Sha Tsui, Kowloon* ☎ *2369–2211* ⊕ *www.ymcahk.org.hk* ⇌ *303 rooms, 62 suites* ⌂ *2 restaurants, room service, in-room safes, minibars, cable TV, in-room broadband, indoor pool, gym, health club, hair salon, spa, squash, lounge, shops, babysitting, laundry facilities, business services, meeting room, no-smoking floors* ☰ *AE, DC, MC, V* Ⓜ *Tsim Sha Tsui.*

AFTER DARK

By Eva Chui
Loiterton

A riot of neon, heralding frenetic after-hours action, announces Hong Kong's nightlife districts. Hectic workdays make way for busy nighttime scenes. Clubs and bars fill to capacity, evening markets pack in bargain hunters, restaurants welcome diners, cinemas pop corn as fast as they can, and theaters and concert halls prepare for full houses.

Partying in Hong Kong is a way of life; it starts at the beginning of the week with a drink or two after work, progressing to serious barhopping, and clubbing if it's the weekend. Work hard, play harder is the motto here, and people follow it seriously. It's perfectly normal to pop into two or three bars before heading to a nightclub . . . or two. You simply cannot go home without a Hong Kong nightlife story to tell!

Central

Hong Kong is proud of its own *très* chic SoHo—SOuth of HOllywood Road—a small warren of streets between Central and Midlevels. This area is filled with cosmopolitan restaurants as well as a handful of bars. Below SoHo is the infamous Lan Kwai Fong, a hillside section around Central's D'Aguilar Street that has many good bistros and a large selection of bars. Along with the drink-swinging hordes, busloads of

Asian tourists offload here—not to enjoy a beverage, but only to have their picture taken beneath the LAN KWAI FONG street sign.

Bars

Barco. Had enough of the crowds and looking for a quiet drink and conversation that you can actually hear? Barco is the place. One of many small drinking holes popping up in SoHo, it's cozy, with a small lounge area and a courtyard in the back. ⊠ *42 Staunton St., SoHo, Central* ☎ *2857–4478* ☞ *Closes 1 AM.*

Boca Tapas and Wine Bar. What better combination than delicious tapas and some lovely wine? The 80-bottle list has top Australian, Argentinean, Italian, and French wines and more. Boca—"mouth" in Spanish—has a diverse tapas menu, too, ranging from traditional chorizo and stuffed olives to Asian bites such as spicy spring rolls and satay sticks. ⊠ *64 Peel St., SoHo, Central* ☎ *2548–1717* ☞ *Closes 2 AM.*

★ **California.** Set in a semi-basement, but with large open windows at the top so the crowds in Lan Kwai Fong can easily peer down, California is a slice of the West Coast for homesick expats or Western visitors looking for a more familiar environment. It's a mini-institution, having survived the notoriously high turnover rate in the area, and remains one of the busiest bars in Lan Kwai Fong. ⊠ *32–34 D'Aguilar St., Lan Kwai Fong, Central* ☎ *2521–1345* ☞ *Closes 3 AM.*

D'Apartment. Visit the library, lounge, or even the bedroom in this hip basement "apartment." The tiny library is dimly lighted and stacked with real books, but there's no chance of dozing off with the music blaring in the next room. The bedroom has a lush bedlike sofa to laze on, and, don't worry, there are no neighbors to complain about the racket. ⊠ *California Entertainment Bldg., 34–36 D'Aguilar St., basement, Lan Kwai Fong, Central* ☎ *2523–2002* ☞ *Closes 3 AM.*

F.I.N.D.S. The name of this red-hot bar comes from the first letters of Finland, Iceland, Norway, Denmark, and Sweden. In keeping with the theme, the light-blue-and-white interior is also kept quite cold at this Scandinavian ice bar, but the crowds that frequent it are anything but icy. There's a large terrace to escape the smoke-filled haze indoors, and from here you can check out the crowds below in Lan Kwai Fong. About 30 premium vodkas are served, and if that doesn't tickle your fancy, try one of the many house cocktails with corny names such as the Edvard Munch, made with lime aquavit and ginger wine. The party continues after hours at the Drop nightclub. ⊠ *2/F, LKF Tower, 33 Wyndham St., entrance of D'Aguilar St., Central* ☎ *2522–9318* ☞ *Closes 3 AM.*

NIGHTLIFE SAVVY

Hong Kong is a safe place, but as in every tourist destination the art of the tourist rip-off has been perfected. If you're unsure, visit places signposted as members of the Hong Kong Tourist Board (HKTB). For listings and quirky reviews of all that's on, pick up *Hong Kong Magazine,* distributed free in Central's bars each Thursday. The nightlife coverage in *BC Magazine* is almost as extensive. Another good source of nightlife and cultural information is the daily newspaper, the *South China Morning Post.* The free monthly newspaper *City News* lists City Hall performances and events.

Globe. Between Lan Kwai Fong and SoHo, the Globe is one of the few laid-back places in the area to knock back a beer or two with down-to-earth folks. It's the local pub for homesick expats who live in the area. ✉ *39 Hollywood Rd., Central* ☎ *2543–1941* ⏰ *Closes 2* AM.

Goccia. The beautiful people flock to this cool bar (with a restaurant upstairs) and it's packed wall to wall most nights. *Goccia*—a drop in Italian—occupies a long room on the ground floor, and if it had a VIP table, it would have to be one by the window facing the street where you can see and be seen. ✉ *73 Wyndham St., Central* ☎ *2167–8181* ⏰ *Closes 3* AM.

Insomnia. It's *almost* open 24/7 (closing for only three hours 6–9 AM), hence the name. Live music is what really draws people here; there's a small stage and a dance floor at the back, but you'll have to fight your way there on weekends through the perfumed women and suited men. You might have more breathing room if you stay near the front bar, by the arched windows. ✉ *38–44 D'Aguilar St., Lan Kwai Fong, Central* ☎ *2525–0957.*

The Keg. As its name implies, beer and more beer is the beverage of choice at this small pub. Large wooden barrels serve as tables and the floors are covered with discarded peanut shells. All manner of sports coverage reigns on the TV screens. ✉ *52 D'Aguilar St., Lan Kwai Fong, Central* ☎ *2810–0369* ⏰ *Closes 3* AM.

La Dolce Vita. This tiny bar, beneath its sister restaurant **Post 97** and next to its other sibling **Club 97**, often spills onto the pavement. One of the first modern bars to pop up when the area gained popularity, La Dolce Vita has a sleek interior and a crowd to match. It's a popular stomping ground for the name-dropping masses. ✉ *9 Lan Kwai Fong, Lan Kwai Fong, Central* ☎ *2810–9333* ⏰ *Closes 3* AM.

Le Jardin. For a gregarious, cosmopolitan vibe, check out this casual bar with its lovely outdoor terrace overlooking a not-so-lovely alley. It's atop a flight of steps above Indian, Malaysian, and Vietnamese restaurants below, but the leafy garden setting is worth it. ✉ *1/F, 10 Wing Wah La., Central* ☎ *2526–2717* ⏰ *Closes 3* AM.

Lux. The well-heeled drink martinis and designer beers at this swanky corner spot. It has a prime location in Lan Kwai Fong and is another great bar to people-watch; they also serve excellent food in booths at the back. ✉ *U/F, California Tower, 30–32 D'Aguilar St., Lan Kwai Fong, Central* ☎ *2868–9538* ⏰ *Closes 4* AM.

MO Bar. This plush bar in the Landmark Mandarin Oriental is where the banking set goes to relax. You'll

THE FONG

A curious, L-shape cobblestone lane in Central is a pulsating center of nightlife and dining. Lan Kwai Fong, or just "the Fong," is a spot that really shines after the sun sets. There are more than 20 bars, restaurants, and clubs within just a few blocks. You can start with a predinner drink at any number of bars, then enjoy some of the territory's finest dining, before stopping at a nightclub to boogie the night away. Since most of the ground-floor establishments spill out onto the pavement, there's an audible buzz about the place, lending it a festive air that's unmatched elsewhere in town.

pay top dollar for the martinis, but the striking interior makes it worthwhile. A huge red light circle dominates an entire wall, the "O" being a Chinese symbol of shared experience. There's also a drawbridge and an elevated lily pond. ⊠ *The Landmark Mandarin Oriental Hotel, 15 Queen's Road Central, The Landmark, Central* ☏ *2132–0077* ⌇ *Closes 2 AM.*

RED Bar. Although its mall location may not seem appealing, once you arrive at RED, you'll throw all your preconceived notions into the harbor. On the roof of IFC Mall, RED has breathtaking views of Victoria Habour as well as skyscrapers. There's also a restaurant here and it's part of the Pure Fitness group of gyms. That's right, so after a session at the gym, grab some dinner, and then relax with a cocktail while watching the breathtaking sunset. You've earned it. ⊠ *Level 4, Two IFC, 8 Finance St., Central* ☏ *8129–8882* ⌇ *Closes 2 AM.*

Staunton's Wine Bar & Cafe. Adjacent to Hong Kong's famous outdoor escalator is this hip bistro-style café and bar. Partly alfresco, it's the perfect place to people-watch. You can come for a drink at night, or for coffee or a meal during the day. It's also a Sunday-morning favorite for nursing hangovers over brunch. ⊠ *10–12 Staunton St., SoHo, Central* ☏ *2973–6611* ⌇ *Closes 3 AM.*

Discos & Nightclubs

★ **C Club.** The upwardly mobile and occasionally some minor Hong Kong celebrities party here. There's a large dance floor, a flashy bar, and plenty of nooks to lounge in. But be warned: no sneakers, no shorts, no jeans. Weekends command a HK$200 door charge that includes one standard drink. ⊠ *32–34 D'Aguilar St., basement, Lan Kwai Fong, Central* ☏ *2526–1139* ⌇ *Closes 4 AM.*

Club 97. A glamorous and glitzy nightspot, Club 97 draws mobs of beautiful people. It started off life as a members-only club, but that rule has since been disregarded. The space is dominated by a circular bar in the center of the room, and has a small dance floor surrounded by cozy nooks. ⊠ *9–11 Lan Kwai Fong, Central* ☏ *2186–1897* ⌇ *Closes 4 AM.*

★ **dragon-i.** A place to prance, pose, and preen, dragon-i is owned by local party boy and social celebrity Gilbert Yeung. The entrance is marked by an enormous birdcage (filled with real budgies and canaries) made entirely of bamboo poles. Have a drink on the wonderful alfresco deck by the doorway or step inside the rich, red playroom, which doubles as a restaurant in the early evening. Take a trip to the bathroom to see arguably the biggest cubicles in Hong Kong, with floor-to-ceiling silver tiles and double-height mirrored ceilings. ⊠ *Upper G/F, The Centrium, 60 Wyndham St., Central* ☏ *3110–1222* ⌇ *Closes 5 AM.*

★ **Drop.** Although it has been around for a number of years, this A-list club is still a favorite. Drop is where international celebrities party when they're in town—usually until the sun rises. It may take some effort to find, but that only adds an air of exclusivity to the speakeasylike location. The excellent martinis are their forte. Things don't get going until late. ⊠ *On Lok Mansion, 39–43 Hollywood Rd., basement, entrance off Cochrine St., Central* ☏ *2543–8856* ⌇ *Closes 6 AM.*

The Edge. A young crowd flocks to this nightclub, situated directly beneath dragon i. A rotating lineup of DJs keep the hip-hop throng coming back for more, especially on Saturday nights when people line up for hours to get in—it's arguably the biggest hip-hop night in town. ✉ *G/F, The Centrium, 60 Wyndham St., Central* ☎ *2523–6690.*

Hei Hei Club. Two Jacuzzis and a 2-foot pool aren't often found at nightclubs, but Hei Hei—"Double Happiness" in Chinese—encourages clubbers to bring their swimwear. But the Playboy Mansion it's not. The aquatic features are on two outdoor terraces; the rest of Hei Hei's 7,000 square feet is a bar and dance floor blasting hip-hop and R&B. ✉ *3/F, On Hing Terr., Central* ☎ *2899–2068.*

AFTER THE PARTY

The ever-reliable MTR shuts down at 1 AM, and taxis are your only way home after that. They can easily be flagged down; when the light on the car roof is on, it's available for hire. If the cab has an "out of service" sign over its round "for hire" neon sign on the dashboard, it means it's a cross-harbor taxi.

Volar. Barking dogs and beefy bouncers front the entrance to Volar, a hugely popular nightclub. In a cavernous basement, different rooms feature the latest hip-hop, house, and tech-funk spun by a roster of international DJs. On weekends, the lines to enter are long. ✉ *B/F, 39–44 D'Aguilar St., Lan Kwai Fong, Central* ☎ *2810–1272.*

Gay & Lesbian Spots

Meilanfang Bar. Named after the most accomplished Peking Opera artist of the last century (on whom the film *Farewell My Concubine* was loosely based) Meilanfang is the newest gay bar in Central. How better to pay tribute to a man whose livelihood was made by impersonating females on stage (men commonly played female roles), paving the way for present-day drag queens? The busy bar is appropriately decked out in a riot of traditional bright Chinese opera colors. Locals called it "M Bar." ✉ *14 On Wo La., Sheung Wan* ☎ *2152–2121.*

Propaganda. Off a quaint but steep cobblestone street, this is *the* most popular gay club in Hong Kong, with a near-monopoly on the scene (it's known as P P to the locals, Props to the expatriate lot). The art-deco bar area has elegant booths and tables and soft lighting; on the other hand, the dance floor has lap poles on either side for go-go boys to flaunt their wares. It's pretty empty during the week; the crowds arrive well after midnight on weekends. The entrance fee of HK$180 on Friday and Saturday nights includes one standard drink. ✉ *Lower G/F, 1 Hollywood Rd., Central* ☎ *2868–1316* ☞ *Closes 5:30 AM.*

Rice Bar. This friendly bar is no-smoking—an impressive move, and they still manage to keep the business coming in. Weekends are very crowded from midnight, and if you're willing to go topless, you'll be rewarded with free drinks. The owner also owns a gay café around the corner called Billy Boy. ✉ *33 Jervois St., Sheung Wan* ☎ *2851–4800* ☞ *Closes 3 AM.*

Music Clubs

The Cavern. Cover bands dressed up as Abba, the Monkees, and even Bruce Springsteen keep the crowds on their feet and singing at this bar.

Pop music rules—the cheesier, the better. The place is impossible to miss, not only for its loud music, but for its bright, lollypop-color mural on the exterior wall, and tables on the pavement, straddling Lan Kwai Fong. ⊠ *Shop 1, G/F, LKF Tower, 33 Wyndham St, entrance on D'Aguliar St., Central* ☎ *2121–8969* ☞ *Closes 4* AM.

★ **Fringe Club.** The arts-minded mingle in this historic redbrick building that also houses the members-only Foreign Correspondents' Club. The Fringe is the headquarters for Hong Kong's alternative arts scene and normally stages live music twice a week. ⊠ *2 Lower Albert Rd., Central* ☎ *2521–7251* ☞ *Closes 3* AM.

Wan Chai

Wan Chai nightlife has cleaned up its act and is no longer the seedy area that inspired *The World of Suzie Wong*. The hostess bars are still here though, and "freelance" girls stalk the street corners. Tattoo parlors do a heavy trade in the early mornings when the inebriated, convinced it's a good idea at the time, get inked. But these establishments now share the streets with hip bars and pubs. Still, the busiest nights are still when there's a navy ship in the harbor, on an R&R stopover.

Bars

★ **Brown.** Much like a New York neighborhood restaurant, Brown is comfy and homey for those who need to wind down from a hectic day (either working or shopping). Spacious high ceilings give the space an airy feel, and there are sink-down-and-chill sofas at the back. The small courtyard is a favorite for weekend brunches. ⊠ *18A Sing Woo Rd., Happy Valley,* ☎ *2891–8558* ☞ *Closes 1:30* AM.

Carnegies. Named after the Scotsman Andrew Carnegie, whose family sailed to America in the late 1800s (he was a famous patron of the arts and the founder of Carnegie Hall in New York City), this rock-and-roll bar lives up to its name. Although Carnegie himself probably didn't imagine bar-top dancing to classic rock tunes at an establishment bearing his name, the Scottish owners feel that the spirit of his love of music lives on regardless. ⊠ *53–55 Lockhart Rd., Wan Chai* ☎ *2866–6289* ☞ *Closes 4* AM.

Old China Hand Hand. Once full of gritty booths and stark lighting, this pub now has a facade that opens onto the street, absorbing all the hustle and bustle of Lockhart Road. It's open 24/7, and has been here from time immemorial. The kitchen serves typical pub fare and is something of an institution for those wishing to sober up with greasy grub after a long night out. ⊠ *104 Lockhart Rd., Wan Chai* ☎ *2865–4378.*

★ **1/5.** Walk upstairs through the narrow corridor with a mirrored ceiling to enter a large, dimly lighted bar with triple-height ceilings and brown velour lounge areas. In the hip Star Street area, this is the bar of choice for those who want an alternative to Lan Kwai Fong and SoHo. There are often international DJs spinning vinyl, and popular manicure and martini nights are held each Wednesday for HK$120. ⊠ *1/F, Starcrest Bldg., 9 Star St., Wan Chai* ☎ *2520–2515* ☞ *Closes 3* AM.

Mes Amis. In the heart of Wan Chai, on the corner of Lockhart and Luard roads, Mes Amis is a friendly bar that also serves good food. Its corner setting and open bi-fold doors means that none of the action outside is missed, and vice versa. ✉ *83 Lockhart Rd., Wan Chai* ☏ *2527–6680* ☞ *Closes 6* AM.

Klong Bar & Grill. Named after the many canals that intersect the Thai capital of Bangkok, Klong's ground-floor bar opens onto the street serving up tasty grilled snacks to go with Singha beers. Head upstairs to knock back more Singhas at the U-shape bar, or you can sit in booths or crossed-legged on the raised floor, Thai-style—shoes off, please. ✉ *54–62 Lockhart Rd., Wan Chai* ☏ *2217–8330* ☞ *Closes 3* AM.

Discos & Nightclubs

Boracay. This disco is a Hong Kong institution—its basement space isn't very large, but that doesn't stop the crowds from heading down there. The dance floor gets going in the wee hours, and keeps going. There's a bit of a sleaze factor here, but when it's late, who cares? ✉ *Basement, 20 Luard Rd., Wan Chai* ☏ *2529–3461* ☞ *Closes 5* AM.

Joe Bananas. With the ever-changing face of bars in Wan Chai, Joe Bananas has been the one constant in the area's nightlife. Its reputation for all-night partying and general good times remains unchallenged. This disco and bar strictly excludes the military and people dressed too casually: no shorts, sneakers, or T-shirts (the only exception is the Rugby Sevens weekend when even Joe can't turn away the thirsty swarm). The wet T-shirt contest nights are obviously popular. Arrive before 11 PM to avoid the line. ✉ *23 Luard Rd., Wan Chai* ☏ *2529–1811* ☞ *Closes 6* AM.

Tribeca. A "New York-style nightclub," Tribeca occupies the space that formerly housed Manhattan (is there a trend in names here?) and more recently Club Ing. Unlike many other nightclubs in Hong Kong, it has a huge space—one of the largest in the city—full of dance floors, bars, lounges, and the requisite VIP areas. The plush interior attempts to emulate a swanky nightclub in the Big Apple, and judging by the crowds who flock here, it's doing it well. ✉ *4/F, Convention Plaza, 1 Harbour Rd., Wan Chai* ☏ *2836–3690* ☞ *Closes 4* AM.

Kowloon

Central and Wan Chai are undoubtedly the king and queen of nightlife in Hong Kong. If you're staying in a hotel, however, or having dinner on *the other side,* that is, Kowloon, a fun place in Tsim Sha Tsui for nightlife is an out-of-the-way strip called Knutsford Terrace.

Bars

Aqua. Felix at the Peninsula Hotel has had a stronghold in the sophisticated bar-with-a-view competition for years, but now its crown has been handed over to Aqua. Inside One Peking, a curvaceous skyscraper dominating the Kowloon skyline, this very cool bar is on the mezzanine level of the top floor. The high ceilings and raking glass walls offer up unrivaled views of Hong Kong Island and the magical lights of the harbor filled with ferries and ships. ✉ *29th and 30th floors, One Peking, 1 Peking Rd., Tsim Sha Tsui, Kowloon* ☏ *3427–2288* ☞ *Closes 2* AM.

Bahama Mama's. You'll find tropical rhythms at the Caribbean-inspired bar, where world music plays and the kitsch props include a surfboard

Hostess Clubs

The many hostess clubs found in Hong Kong are clubs in name only. Some of these are multimillion-dollar operations with plush interiors with hundreds of hostess-companions. Computerized clocks on each table tabulate companionship charges in timed units; the costs are clearly detailed on table cards, as are standard drink tabs. The clubs also have dozens of luxuriously furnished private rooms, with partitioned lounges and the ubiquitous karaoke setup. Local and visiting businessmen adore these rooms—and the multilingual hostesses. Business is so good that the clubs are willing to allow visitors *not* asking for companionship.

The better clubs are on a par with music lounges in deluxe hotels, though they cost a little more. Their happy hours start in the afternoon, when many have a sort of tea-dance ambiance, and continue through to mid-evening. Peak hours are 10 PM to 4 AM. Think twice before succumbing to the city's raunchier hideaways. If you stumble into one, check out cover and hostess charges *before* you get too comfortable. Many so-called hostess clubs are in fact fronts for prostitution. In Wan Chai, for instance, hostess clubs are dotted among regular bars, too many to mention by name. But most, if not all of them are sad little places full of leering men watching girls with vacant expressions performing halfhearted pole dances dressed in leotards.

The reputable **Club BBoss** (⌧ Mandarin Plaza, Tsim Sha Tsui East, Kowloon ☎ 2369–2883 ☞ Closes 4 AM) is Hong Kong's grandest and most boisterous hostess club, tended by a staff of more than 1,000, and frequented by local company executives. If your VIP room is too far from the entrance, you can hire an electrified vintage Rolls-Royce and purr around an indoor roadway. Be warned that this is tycoon territory—a bottle of brandy can cost HK$18,000.

---

over the bar and the silhouette of a curvaceous woman showering behind a screen over the restroom entrance. ⌧ *4–5 Knutsford Terr., Tsim Sha Tsui, Kowloon* ☎ *2368–2121* ☞ *Closes 4 AM.*

Balalaika. Vodka is served in a -20°C (-36°F) room at this Russian-theme bar, but don't be alarmed at the freezing temperature—they provide you with fur coats and traditional Russian fur hats. Take your pick from the 15 varieties of vodka from five different countries. ⌧ *2/F, 10 Knutsford Terr., Tsim Sha Tsui, Kowloon* ☎ *2312–6222* ☞ *Closes 1 AM.*

★ **Delaney's.** Both branches of the pioneer of Hong Kong Irish pubs have interiors that were made in Ireland and shipped to Hong Kong, and the mood is as authentic as the furnishings. There is Guinness and Delaney's ale (a specialty microbrew) on tap, corner snugs (small private rooms), and a menu of Irish food, plus a happy hour that runs from 5 to 9 PM daily. ⌧ *71–77 Peking Rd., basement, Tsim Sha Tsui, Kowloon* ☎ *2301–3980* ⌧ *G/F, 1 Capital Pl., 18 Luard Rd., Wan Chai* ☎ *2804–2880* ☞ *Closes 3 AM.*

Fodor'sChoice
★ **Felix.** High up in the Peninsula Hotel, this bar is immensely popular with visitors; it not only has a brilliant view of the island, but the interior was designed by the visionary Philippe Starck. Don't forget to check out the padded mini-disco room. ⊠ *28/F, the Peninsula Hong Kong, Salisbury Rd., Tsim Sha Tsui, Kowloon* ☎ *2920–2888* ♺ *Closes 2* AM.

SHOPPING

By Victoria
Patience &
Sofia Suárez

They say the only way to get to know a place is to do what the locals do. When in Rome, scoot around on a Vespa and drink espresso. When in Hong Kong, shop. For most people in this city, shopping is a leisure activity in itself, whether that means picking out a four-figure party dress, rifling through bins at an outlet, upgrading a cell phone, or selecting the freshest fish for dinner. Shopping is so sacred that sales periods are calendar events, and most stores close on just three days a year—Christmas Day and the first two days of Chinese New Year. Imagine that: 362 days of unbridled purchasing ops. Opening hours are equally conducive to whiling your life away browsing the racks: all shops are open until 7 or 8 PM; many don't close their doors until midnight.

It's true that the days when everything in Hong Kong was mind-bogglingly cheap are over. It *is* still a tax-free port, though, so you can get some good deals. But it isn't just about the savings. Sharp contrasts and the sheer variety of experiences available make shopping here very different from back home. You might find a bargain or two elbowing your way through a chaotic open-air market filled with haggling vendors selling designer knockoffs, the air reeking of the *chou tofu* ("stinky" tofu) bubbling at a nearby food stand. But then you could find a designer number going for half the usual price in a hushed marble-floor mall, Vivaldi piping through the loudspeaker, or the air reeking of designer fragrances worn by fellow shoppers. What's more, in Hong Kong, the two extremes are often within spitting distance of each other.

Malls

If you are short on time, visit one of Hong Kong's many malls. On Hong Kong Island, the main ones are Cityplaza (Eastern); IFC (Central); Island Beverley (Causeway Bay); The Landmark (Central); Pacific Place, which contains the three lesser arcades of Admiralty Centre, United Centre, and Queensway Plaza (Admiralty); and Times Square (Causeway Bay). In Kowloon, next to the Star Ferry, is Harbour City, encompassing the Ocean Terminal, Marco Polo Hong Kong Hotel Arcade, Ocean Centre, and Gateway Arcade. Farther flung malls include Festival Walk in Kowloon Tong and Langham Place in Mong Kok.

Chinese Department Stores

★ **Chinese Arts & Crafts.** Head to this long-established mainland company to blitz through that list of presents in one fell swoop. It stocks a variety of well-priced brocades, silk clothing, carpets, and cheap porcelain. Incongruously scattered throughout are specialty items like large globes with lapis oceans and landmasses inlaid with semiprecious stones for a mere HK$70,000. Other more accessible gifts include appliqué table-

---

TRICKS OF THE TRADE

Be wary of absurd discounts, which are designed purely to get you in the door. Product switches are also common—after you've paid, they pack a cheaper model. The consensus is to avoid electronics shops in Tsim Sha Tsui, whose fearsome reputation is well-earned. Check purchases carefully, ensuring clothes are the size you wanted, jewelry is what you picked, and electronics come with the plug and accessories you paid for.

Always get an itemized receipt. Without one, forget about getting refunds. Shops displaying the Hong Kong Tourism Board's (HKTB) QUALITY TOURISM SERVICE sticker (an easily recognizable junk boat) are good bets. You can complain about prices or treatment at them to the HKTB (☎ 2508–1234). For complaints about all other shops, call the Hong Kong Consumer Council (☎ 2929–2222).

---

cloths and cushion covers or silk dressing gowns. ✉ *Pacific Place, Admiralty* ☎ *2827–6667 for information* ⊕ *www.chineseartsandcrafts.com.hk* Ⓜ *Admiralty, Exit F* ✉ *Asia Standard Tower, 59 Queen's Rd. Central, Central* Ⓜ *Central, Exit D2* ✉ *Star House, 3 Salisbury Rd., Tsim Sha Tsui, Kowloon* Ⓜ *Tsim Sha Tsui, Exit F.*

Sincere. Hong Kong's most eclectic department store stocks everything from frying pans to jelly beans. Run by the same family for more than a century, Sincere has several local claims to fame: it was the first store in Hong Kong to give paid days off to employees, the first to hire women in sales positions—beginning with the founder's wife and sister-in-law—and the first to establish a fixed-price policy backed up by the regionally novel idea of issuing receipts. Although you probably won't have heard of its clothes or cosmetic brands, mostly imported from China, you might come across a bargain. ✉ *173 Des Voeux Rd., Central* ☎ *2544–2688* ⊕ *www.sincere.com.hk* Ⓜ *Sheung Wan, Exit E3.*

Fodor'sChoice ★ **Yue Hwa Chinese Products Emporium.** Its five floors contain Chinese goods, ranging from clothing and housewares through tea and traditional medicine. The logic behind the store's layout is hard to fathom, so go with time to rifle around. As well as the predictable tablecloths, silk pajamas, and chopstick sets, there are cheap 'n' colorful porcelain sets and offbeat local favorites like mini-massage chairs. The top floor is entirely given over to tea—you can pick up a HK$50 packet of leaves or an antique Yixing teapot stretching into the thousands. ✉ *55 Des Voeux Rd., Central* Ⓜ *Central, Exit B* ✉ *1 Kowloon Park Dr., Tsim Sha Tsui, Kowloon* Ⓜ *Tsim Sha Tsui, Exit E.*

Wing On. Great values on household appliances, kitchenware, and crockery have made Wing On a favorite with locals on a budget since it opened in 1907. It also stocks clothes, cosmetics, and sportswear, but don't expect to find big brands (or even brands you know). You *can* count on rock-bottom prices and an-off-the-tourist-trail experience, though. ✉ *211 Des Voeux Rd. Central, Sheung Wan, Western* ☎ *2852–1888* ⊕ *www.wingonet.com* Ⓜ *Sheung Wan, Exit E3.*

Markets

Flower Market. Huge bucketfuls of roses and gerbera spill out onto the sidewalk along Flower Market Road. Delicate orchids and vivid birds of paradise are some of the more exotic blooms. During Chinese New Year there's a roaring trade in narcissi, poinsettias, and bright yellow chrysanthemums, all auspicious flowers. ⊠ *Flower Market Rd., off Prince Edward Rd. W, Mong Kok, Kowloon* ☉ *Daily 7 AM–7:30 PM* Ⓜ *Prince Edward, Exit B1.*

☺ **Goldfish Market.** Goldfish are considered auspicious in Hong Kong (though aquariums have to be positioned correctly to bring good luck), and this small collection of shops is a favorite local source. Shop fronts are decorated with bag upon bag of glistening, pop-eyed creatures, waiting for someone to take them home. Some of the fishes inside shops are serious rarities and fetch unbelievable prices. ⊠ *Tung Choi St., Mong Kok, Kowloon* ☉ *Daily 10–6* Ⓜ *Mong Kok, Exit B2.*

Jardine's Bazaar and Jardine's Crescent. These two small parallel streets are so crammed with clothing stalls it's difficult to make your way through. Most offer bargains on the usual clothes, children's gear, bags and chopstick sets. Surrounding boutiques are also worth a look for local and Japanese fashions, though sizes are small. ⊠ *Jardine's Bazaar, Causeway Bay* ☉ *Daily noon–10 PM* Ⓜ *Causeway Bay, Exit F.*

Kansu Street Jade Market. Jade in every imaginable shade of green, from the milkiest apple-tone to the richest emerald, fills the stalls of this Kowloon market. If you know your stuff and haggle insistently, you can get fabulous bargains. Otherwise stick to cheap trinkets. Some of the so-called "jade" sold here is actually aventurine, bowenite, soapstone, serpentine, and Australian jade—all inferior to the real thing. Strings of freshwater pearls also go for a song, although you may have to have them restrung. ⊠ *Kansu St. off Nathan Rd., Yau Ma Tei, Kowloon* ☉ *Daily 10–4* Ⓜ *Yau Ma Tei, Exit C.*

★ **Ladies' Market.** Block upon block of tightly packed stalls overflow with clothes, bags, and knickknacks along Tung Choi Street in Mong Kok. Despite the name there are clothes for women, men, and children here. Most offerings are imitations or no-name brands; rifle around enough and you can often pick up some cheap 'n' cheerful basics. Haggling is the rule here. ⊠ *Tung Choi St., Mong Kok, Kowloon* ☉ *Daily noon–11 PM* Ⓜ *Mong Kok, Exit B2.*

★ **Stanley Village Market.** This was once Hong Kong's most famed bargain trove, but its ever-growing popularity means that Stanley Village Market no longer has the best prices around. Still, you can pick up some good buys in sportswear and casual clothing if you comb through

BARGAINING POWER

Prices are always negotiable at markets, and you can expect discounts in small shops, too, especially for electronics or if you buy several things at once. The norm ranges from 10% to 50% off. Be firm and decisive—walking away from a stall can often produce a radical price drop. Don't let anyone guilt-trip you; rest assured that no Hong Kong salesperson will sell you anything that doesn't cut them a profit.

the stalls. Good value linens—especially appliqué tablecloths—also abound. Dozens and dozens of shops line a main street so narrow that awnings from each side meet in the middle, and on weekends your elbows will come in handy. ⊠ *Stanley Village, Southside* ⊗ *Daily 11–6.*

★ **Temple Street Night Market.** Each night, as it gets dark, the lamps strung between the stalls of this Yau Ma Tei street market slowly light up, and the air fills with the smells wafting from myriad food carts. Hawkers try to catch your eye by flinging clothes up from their stalls. Cantonese opera competes with pop music, and vendors' cries and shoppers' haggling. Fortune-tellers and the odd magician or acrobat set up shop in the street. Granted, neither the clothes nor cheap gadgets on sale here are much to get excited about, but it's the atmosphere people come for—any purchases are a bonus. ⊠ *Temple St., Mong Kok, Kowloon* Ⓜ *Jordan, Exit A* ⊗ *Daily 5 PM–midnight; best after 8 PM.*

> **FAKING IT**
>
> The government has cracked down on designer fakes. Depending on how strict the police are being when you visit, you may not find the choice of knockoffs you were hoping for. Bear in mind that designer fakes are illegal, and as such you could get into trouble if you get caught with them going through customs.

Specialty Shops

Art & Antiques

Alisan Fine Arts. In a quiet corner of the sleek Prince's Building shopping arcade is this established authority on contemporary Chinese artists. Styles range from traditional to modern abstract, and media include oil, acrylic, and Chinese ink. Founded in 1981 by Alice King, this was one of the first galleries in Hong Kong to promote the genre. ⊠ *Prince's Bldg., 10 Chater Rd., Central* ☎ *2526–1091* ⊕ *www.alisan. com.hk* Ⓜ *Central.*

Altfield Gallery. If only your entire home could be outfitted by Altfield. Established in 1980, the elegant gallery carries exquisite antique Chinese furniture; Asia-related maps and topographical prints; Southeast Asian sculpture and decorative arts from around Asia, including silver artifacts and rugs. ⊠ *Prince's Bldg., 10 Chater Rd., Central* ☎ *2537–6370* ⊕ *www.altfield.com.hk* Ⓜ *Central.*

China Art. The Chiang family runs this retail and wholesale operation that specializes in craftsman-restored Chinese antiques, especially furniture. Their honest approach is apparent in its exhibitions and has inspired a coffee table book, *Antiques in the Raw.* ⊠ *G/F, 15 Hollywood Rd., Central* ☎ *2234–9924* ⊕ *www.chinaart.com.hk* Ⓜ *Central.*

Grotto Fine Art. Director and chief curator Henry Au-yeung writes, curates, and gives lectures on 20th-century Chinese art. His hidden gallery (hence the "grotto" in the name) focuses exclusively on local Chinese artists, with an interest in the newest and most avant-garde works. Look for paintings, sculptures, prints, photography, mixed-media pieces, and conceptual installations. ⊠ *2/F, 31C–D Wyndham St., Central* ☎ *2121–2270* ⊕ *www.grottofineart.com* Ⓜ *Central.*

Hanart TZ Gallery. This is a rare opportunity to compare and contrast cutting-edge and experimental art from mainland China, Taiwan, and Hong Kong selected by one of the field's most respected authorities. Unassuming curatorial director, Johnson Chang Tsong-zung, also cofounded the Asia Art Archive, and has curated exhibitions at the

São Paulo and Venice biennials. ⊠ *2/F, Henley Bldg., 5 Queen's Rd., Central* ☎ *2526–9019* ⊕ *www.hanart.com* Ⓜ *Central.*

Schoeni Art Gallery. Known for vigorously promoting Chinese art on a global scale, this gallery, founded by Manfred Schoeni in 1992, has represented and supported various artists from mainland China with styles ranging from neorealism to postmodernism. Manfred's daughter Nicole now pinpoints exciting new artists for her prominent clientele. Informative past exhibition catalogs are placed atop Chinese antiques, which are also presented in this huge space. You're likely to pass the Hollywood Road branch first, but Old Baily Street gallery is the better of the two. ⊠ *Upper G/F, 21–31 Old Bailey St., Central* ☎ *2525–5225* ⊕ *www.schoeni.com.hk* Ⓜ *Central.*

Teresa Coleman Fine Arts Ltd. You can't miss the spectacular textiles hanging in the window of this busy corner shop. Specialist Teresa Coleman sells embroidered costumes from the Imperial Court, antique textiles, painted and carved fans, jewelry, lacquered boxes, and engravings and prints. ⊠ *79 Wyndham St., Central* ☎ *2526–2450* ⊕ *www. teresacoleman.com* Ⓜ *Central.*

Yue Po Chai Antique Co. One of Hollywood Road's oldest shops is at the Cat Street end, next to Man Mo Temple. Its vast and varied stock includes porcelain, stone carvings, and ceramics. ⊠ *G/F, 132–136 Hollywood Rd., Central* ☎ *2540–4374* Ⓜ *Central.*

Clothing: HK Couture

Barney Cheng. One of the best-known, local designers, Barney Cheng creates haute-couture prêt-à-porter collections, infusing his glam, often sequined, pieces with wit. When the Kennedy Center in Washington, D.C., hosted an exhibition titled "The New China Chic," Cheng was invited to display his works alongside those by Vera Wang and Anna Sui. ⊠ *12/F, World Wide Commercial Bldg., 34 Wyndham St., Central* ☎ *2530–2829* ⊕ *www.barneycheng.com* Ⓜ *Central.*

Lu Lu Cheung. A fixture on the Hong Kong fashion scene for more than a decade, Lu Lu Cheung's designs ooze comfort and warmth. In both daytime and evening wear, natural fabrics and forms are represented in practical yet imaginative ways. ⊠ *The Landmark, Central* ☎ *2537–7515* ⊕ *www.lulucheung.com.hk* Ⓜ *Central* ⊠ *New Town Plaza, Shatin Centre St., New Territories Shatin* Ⓜ *KCR Shatin.*

Olivia Couture. The surroundings are functional, but the gowns, wedding dresses, and *cheongsams* by local designer Olivia Yip are lavish. With a growing clientele, including socialites looking to stand out, Yip is quietly making a name for herself and her Parisian-influenced pieces.

⊠ *G/F, Bartlock Centre, 3 Yiu Wah St., Causeway Bay* ☎ *2838–6636* ⊕ *www.oliviacouture.com* Ⓜ *Causeway Bay.*

Ranee K. Designer Ranee Kok Chui-Wah's showrooms are scarlet dens cluttered with her one-off dresses and eclectic women's wear that bring new meanings to "when East meets West." Known for her quirky *cheongsams* and dresses, she has also collaborated with brands such as Furla and Shanghai Tang. ⊠ *G/F, 47K Staunton St., SoHo, Central* ☎ *2108–4068* ⊕ *www.raneek.com* Ⓜ *Central* ⊠ *G/F, 62K Leighton Rd., Causeway Bay* Ⓜ *Causeway Bay.*

Fodor'sChoice **Shanghai Tang.** In addition to the brilliantly hued—and expensive—displays of silk and cashmere clothing, you'll find custom-made suits starting at around HK$5,000, including fabric from a large selection of Chinese silks. You can also have a *cheongsam* (a sexy slit-skirt silk dress with a Mandarin collar) made for HK$2,500–HK$3,500, including fabric (⇨ *also,* Clothing–Tailor Made, *below*). Ready-to-wear Mandarin suits and unisex kimonos are all in the HK$1,500–HK$2,000 range. Among the Chinese souvenirs are novelty watches with mah-jongg tiles or dim sum instead of numbers. There's a second location inside the Peninsula Hong Kong. ⊠ *12 Pedder St., Central* ☎ *2525–7333* ⊕ *www.shanghaitang.com* Ⓜ *Central* ⊠ *Peninsula Hong Kong, Salisbury Rd., Tsim Sha Tsui, Kowloon* Ⓜ *Tsim Sha Tsui.*

★ **Sin Sin Atelier.** Sin Sin's conceptual, minimalist clothes, jewelry, and accessories retain a Hong Kong character, while drawing from other influences—especially Japan. Yet the pieces are ultimately a unique expression of her ebullient spirit. A regular performer in Hong Kong community theater, Sin Sin prefers to introduce her collections via unusual presentations such as modern dance performances rather than catwalk shows. She also has an art space directly across the road and a fine art gallery up the hill in SoHo. ⊠ *G/F, 52 Sai St., off Hollywood Rd. at Cat St. end, Western* ☎ *2521–0308* ⊕ *www.sinsin.com.hk.*

Spy Henry Lau. Local bad boy Henry Lau brings an edgy attitude to his fashion for men and women. Bold and often dark, his clothing and accessories lines are not for the fainthearted. ⊠ *1/F, Cleveland Mansion, 5 Cleveland St., Causeway Bay* ☎ *2317–6928 customer service* ⊕ *www.spyhenrylau.com* Ⓜ *Causeway Bay* ⊠ *Shop C, G/F, 11 Sharp St., Causeway Bay* Ⓜ *Causeway Bay.*

Vivienne Tam. You know when you walk into a Vivienne Tam boutique—the strong Chinese motif prints and modern updates of traditional women's clothing are truly distinct. Don't let the bold ready-to-wear collections distract you from the very pretty accessories, which include footwear with Asian embellishments such as jade. Tam is one of the best-known Hong Kong designers and, even though she's now based outside the SAR, the city still claims her as their own. ⊠ *Pacific Place, 88 Queensway, Admiralty* ☎ *2918–0238* ⊕ *www.viviennetam.com* Ⓜ *Admiralty* ⊠ *Harbour City, Canton Rd., Tsim Sha Tsui, Kowloon* Ⓜ *Tsim Sha Tsui* ⊠ *IFC Mall, 8 Finance St., Central* Ⓜ *Central.*

Clothing: HK Casual

Blue Star. The cheap basics in this shop—part of the Giordano family of stores—deliver on the motto: "Variety, Efficiency, Economy." Pick

The Choice Is Joyce

LOCAL SOCIALITES and couture addicts still thank Joyce Ma, the fairy godmother of luxury retail in Hong Kong, for bringing must-have labels to the city. Others may be catching up, but her Joyce boutiques are still ultrachic havens outfitted with a *Vogue*-worthy wish list of designers and beauty brands.

Joyce Beauty. Love finding unique beauty products from around the world? Then this is the place for you, with cult perfumes, luxurious skin solutions, and new discoveries to be made. Bring your credit card—"bargain" isn't in the vocabulary here. ⊠ *Times Square, 1 Matheson St., Causeway Bay* ☎ *2970–2319* Ⓜ *Causeway Bay* ✉ *G/F, New World Tower, 16–18 Queen's Rd. Central, Central* Ⓜ *Central* ✉ *Lane Crawford, IFC Mall, 8 Finance St., Central* Ⓜ *Central* ✉ *The Gateway, 3–27 Canton Rd., Tsim Sha Tsui, Kowloon* Ⓜ *Tsim Sha Tsui.*

Joyce Boutique. Not so much a shop as a fashion institution, Joyce Boutique's hushed interior houses the worship-worthy creations of fashion's greatest gods and goddesses. McCartney, Galliano, Dolce &

Gabbana, Prada, Miyake: the stock list is practically a mantra. Joyce sells unique household items, too, so your home can live up to your wardrobe. ⊠ *New World Tower, 16 Queen's Rd., Central* ☎ *2810–1120* ⊕ *www.joyce. com* Ⓜ *Central, Exit G* ✉ *Pacific Place, 88 Queensway, Admiralty* Ⓜ *Admiralty, Exit F* ✉ *Harbour City, Tsim Sha Tsui, Kowloon* Ⓜ *Tsim Sha Tsui, Exit F.*

Joyce Warehouse. Fashionistas who've fallen on hard times can breathe a sigh of relief. Joyce's outlet on Ap Lei Chau, the island offshore from Aberdeen in Southside, stocks last season's duds from the likes of Jil Sander, Armani, Ann Demeulemeester, Costume National, and Missoni. Prices for each garment are reduced by about 10% each month, so the longer the piece stays on the rack, the less it costs. Bus 90B gets you from Exchange Square to Ap Lei Chau in 25 minutes; then hop a taxi for the four-minute taxi ride to Horizon Plaza. ⊠ *21/F, Horizon Plaza, 2 Lee Wing St., Southside* ☎ *2814–8313* ⊙ *Tues.–Sat. 10–6, Sun. noon–6.*

5

up plain, unbranded T-shirts, shorts, and other casual wear. Fashionistas may turn their noses up at the straightforward designs, but Blue Star jeans fit very well for as little as HK$116. ⊠ *G/F, Li Dong Bldg., 7–11 Li Yuen St. E, Central* ☎ *2921–2481, 2786–8295 customer service and branch information* Ⓜ *Central* ✉ *G/F, Circle Apartment, 13–15 Tai Yuen St., Wan Chai* Ⓜ *Wan Chai* ✉ *G/F, Golden Crown Court, 66 Nathan Rd., Tsim Sha Tsui, Kowloon* Ⓜ *Tsim Sha Tsui.*

Giordano. Hong Kong's version of the Gap is the most established and ubiquitous local source of basic T-shirts, jeans, and casual wear. A few of its hundreds of stores are listed here, but you'll have no problem finding one on almost every major street. Customer service is good, even if the young, energetic staff screeches "hello" then "bye-bye" at every customer in a particularly jarring way. Through the Web site, you can even order custom-made jeans. Diffusion lines include the more sophisticated Giordano Ladies and the even cheaper Blue Star. ⊠ *G/F, Capitol Centre, 5–19 Jardine's Crescent, Causeway Bay* ☎ *2923–7111* ⊕ *www.giordano.com.hk* Ⓜ *Causeway Bay* ⊠ *G/F and M/F, On Lok Yuen Bldg., 27 Des Voeux Rd., Central* Ⓜ *Central* ⊠ *G/F and 1/F., 65–69 Peking Rd., Tsim Sha Tsui, Kowloon* Ⓜ *Tsim Sha Tsui.*

Giordano Ladies. If Giordano is the Gap, Giordano Ladies is the Banana Republic, albeit with a more Zen approach. It's clean-line modern classics in neutral black, gray, white, and beige; each collection is brightened by a highlight color: red one season, blue the next. Everything is elegant enough for the office and comfortable enough for the plane. ⊠ *1/F, Capitol Centre, 5–19 Jardine's Cresecent Causeway Bay* ☎ *2923–7118* ⊕ *www.giordanoladies.com* Ⓜ *Causeway Bay* ⊠ *Man Yee Bldg., 60–68 Des Voeux Rd., Central* Ⓜ *Central* ⊠ *1/F, Manson House, 74–78 Nathan Rd., Tsim Sha Tsui, Kowloon* Ⓜ *Tsim Sha Tsui.*

Clothing: Tailor Made

A-Man Hing Cheong Co., Ltd. People often gasp at the very mention of A-Man Hing Cheong in the Mandarin Oriental Hotel. For some it symbolizes the ultimate in fine tailoring with a reputation that extends back to its founding in 1898. For others it's the lofty prices that elicit a reaction. Regardless, this is a trustworthy source of European-cut suits, custom shirts, and excellent service. ⊠ *Mezzanine, Mandarin Oriental, 5 Connaught Rd., Central* ☎ *2522–3336* Ⓜ *Central.*

Ascot Chang. This self-titled "gentleman's shirtmaker" makes it easy to find the perfect shirt, even if you could get a better deal in a less prominent shop. Ascot Chang has upheld exacting Shanghainese tailoring traditions in Hong Kong since 1955, and now has stores in New York, Beverly Hills, Manila, and Shanghai, in addition to offering online ordering and regular American tours. The focus is on the fit and details, from 22 stitches per inch to collar linings crafted to maintain their shape. Among the countless fabrics, Swiss 200s two-ply Egyptian cotton by Alumo is one of the most coveted and expensive. Ascot Chang does pajamas, robes, boxer shorts, and women's blouses, too. It also has developed ready-made lines of shirts, T-shirts, and neckties. ⊠ *Prince's Bldg., 10 Chater Rd., Central* ☎ *2523–3663* ⊕ *www.ascotchang.com* Ⓜ *Central* ⊠ *IFC Mall, 8 Finance St., Central* Ⓜ *Central* ⊠ *Peninsula Hong Kong, Salisbury Rd., Tsim Sha Tsui, Kowloon* Ⓜ *Tsim Sha Tsui* ⊠ *New World Centre (InterContinental Hong Kong), 18–24 Salisbury Rd., Tsim Sha Tsui, Kowloon* Ⓜ *Tsim Sha Tsui.*

Blanc de Chine. Blanc de Chine has catered to high society and celebrities, such as actor Jackie Chan, for years. That's easy when you're housed on the second floor of an old colonial building (just upstairs from Shanghai Tang) and you rely on word of mouth. The small, refined tailoring shop neatly displays exquisite fabrics. Next door is the Blanc de Chine boutique filled with lovely ready-made womenswear, menswear, and home accessories. With newer stores in New York and Beijing, it appears the word is getting out. Items here are extravagances, but they're worth every penny. ⊠ *Pedder Bldg., 12 Pedder St., Central* ☎ *2104–7934* ⊕ *www.blancdechine.com* Ⓜ *Central.*

Continued on page 416

IT SUITS YOU

No trip to Hong Kong would be complete without a visit to one of its world-famous tailors, as many celebrities and dignitaries can attest. In often humble, fabric-cluttered settings, customer records contain the measurements of notables such as Jude Law, Kate Moss, David Bowie, Luciano Pavarotti, and Queen Elizabeth II.

Prince Charles, who has his pick of Savile Row craftsmen, placed a few orders while in the territory for the 1997 handover. When Bill Clinton passed through, word has it that tailors were up until 4 AM to accommodate him.

Like some of their international clientele, who often make up a third of their total business, a handful of tailors are famous themselves. They even go on world tours for their fans. Picking the right tailor can be daunting in a city where the phone book lists about 500 of them. A good suit will last for 20 years if cared for correctly. A bad one will probably leave your closet only for its trip to the thrift store. All the more reason to make thoughtful, educated choices.

TIP

The special economic zone of Shenzhen on the mainland, just a train ride away, is known for competitively priced and speedy tailoring. Quality doesn't always measure up, though, so buyer beware.

5 STEPS TO SIZING THINGS UP

If you've ever owned a custom-made garment, you understand the joy of clothes crafted to fit your every measurement. In Hong Kong, prices rival exclusive ready-to-wear brands.

Hong Kong is best known for men's tailoring, but whether you're looking for a classic men's business suit or an evening gown, these steps will help you size things up.

1. SET YOUR STYLE

Be clear about what you want. Bring samples—a favorite piece of clothing or magazine photos. Also, Hong Kong tailors are trained in classic, structured garments. Straying from these could lead to disappointment. There are three basic suit styles. Experienced tailors can advise on the best one for your shape.

The **American cut** is considered traditional by some, shapeless by others. Its jacket has notched lapels, a center vent, and two or three buttons. The trousers are lean, with flat fronts. The **British cut** also has notched lapels and two- or three-button jackets, but it features side vents and pleated trousers. The double-breasted **Italian cut** has wide lapels and pleated trousers—a look in remission these days.

2. CHOOSE YOUR FABRIC

You're getting a deal on workmanship, so consider splurging on, say, a luxurious blend of cashmere, mink, and wool. When having something copied, though, choose a fabric similar to the original. And buy for the climate you live in, not the climate of your tailor. (How often will you wear seersucker in Alaska?) Take your time selecting: fabric is the main factor affecting cost.

Examine fabric on a large scale. Small swatches are deceiving. Those strong pinstripes might be elegant on a tiny card, but a full suit of them could make you look like an extra from *The Godfather*.

3. MEASURE UP

Meticulous measuring is the mark of a superior craftsman, so be patient. And for accuracy, stand as you normally would (you can't suck in that gut forever). Tailors often record your information so you can have more garments sent to you without returning to Hong Kong. Still, double check measurements at home before each order.

4. PLACE YOUR ORDER

Consider ordering two pairs of trousers per suit. They wear faster than jackets, and alternating between two will help them last longer.

Most tailors require a deposit of 30%–50% of the total cost. Request a receipt detailing price, fabric, style, measurements, fittings, and production schedule. Also ask for a swatch to compare with the final product.

5. GET FIT

There should be at least two fittings. The first is usually for major alterations. Subsequent fittings are supposed to be for minor adjustments, but don't settle for less than perfect: keep sending it back until they get it right.

Bring the right clothes, such as a dress shirt and appropriate shoes, to try on a suit. Having someone you trust at the final fitting helps ensure you haven't overlooked anything.

Try jackets buttoned and unbuttoned. Examine every detail. Are shoulder seams puckered or smooth? Do patterns meet? Is the collar too loose or tight? (About two fingers' space is right.)

FINDING A TAILOR

- As soon as you arrive, visit established tailors to compare workmanship and cost.

- Ask if the work is bespoke (made from scratch) or made-to-measure (based on existing patterns but handmade according to your measurements).

- You get what you pay for. Assume the workmanship and fabric will match the price.

- A fine suit requires six or more days to create. That said, be wary but not dismissive of "24-hour tailors." Hong Kong's most famous craftsmen have turned out suits in a day.

5

IT SUITS YOU

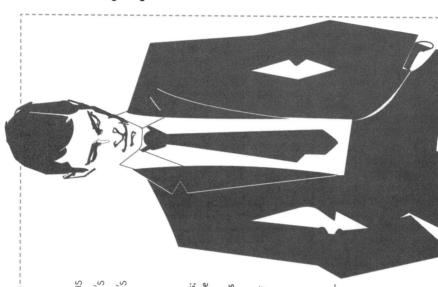

MEN'S TAILORING

Although most tailors can accommodate women—and a few even focus on womenswear (see listings)—Hong Kong tailors are best known for men's suits and shirts. Many shirtmakers also do pajamas, boxer shorts, and women's shirts. To help you with all the options, here are some basics.

JACKETS

Buttons: Plastic buttons can make exquisite tailoring look cheap. Select natural materials like horn. (No two natural buttons will be exactly alike.) Ask for extras, too.

Cuffs: The rule is the number of buttons on each cuff should match the total number on the front of the jacket.

Double- or Single-Breasted: Single-breasted jackets are more versatile: you can dress them up or down and wear them open or buttoned. Two buttons are most popular, but single-breasted jackets can have from one to four.

Lining: The interior (sleeves and pockets, too) should be lined with a beautifully stitched, high-quality fabric like silk. The lining affects both how the jacket falls and how readily it glides on and off.

Pockets: Standard jackets have straight pockets; modern designs have slanted ones. Both can be a slot style or have flaps, which may add girth. A small ticket pocket above a standard pocket is a nice touch.

Stitching: Handstitched lapels subtly show off fine tailoring; the discerning request handstitched buttonholes as well. At the first fitting, stitches should be snug and free of any fraying.

Vent: The vent was created to allow cavalry officers to sit in their saddles comfortably. Although you probably won't go riding in your suit, don't skip the vent. Unvented jackets simply aren't flattering.

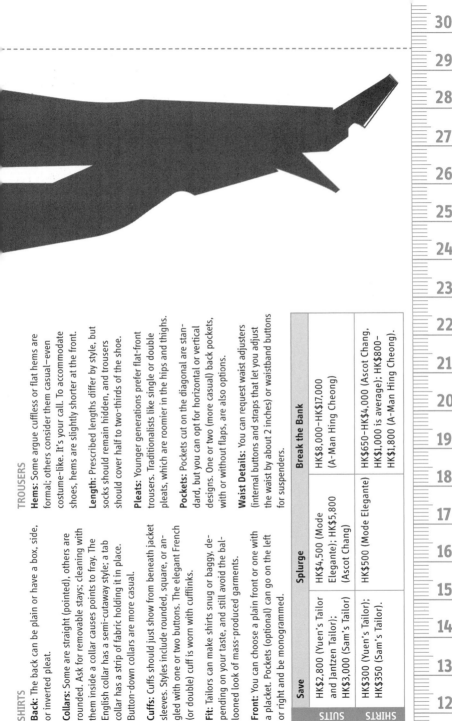

SHIRTS

Back: The back can be plain or have a box, side, or inverted pleat.

Collars: Some are straight (pointed), others are rounded. Ask for removable stays; cleaning with them inside a collar causes points to fray. The English collar has a semi-cutaway style; a tab collar has a strip of fabric holding it in place. Button-down collars are more casual.

Cuffs: Cuffs should just show from beneath jacket sleeves. Styles include rounded, square, or angled with one or two buttons. The elegant French (or double) cuff is worn with cufflinks.

Fit: Tailors can make shirts snug or baggy, depending on your taste, and still avoid the ballooned look of mass-produced garments.

Front: You can choose a plain front or one with a placket. Pockets (optional) can go on the left or right and be monogrammed.

TROUSERS

Hems: Some argue cuffless or flat hems are formal; others consider them casual—even costume-like. It's your call. To accommodate shoes, hems are slightly shorter at the front.

Length: Prescribed lengths differ by style, but socks should remain hidden, and trousers should cover half to two-thirds of the shoe.

Pleats: Younger generations prefer flat-front trousers. Traditionalists like single or double pleats, which are roomier in the hips and thighs.

Pockets: Pockets cut on the diagonal are standard, but you can opt for horizontal or vertical designs. One or two (more casual) back pockets, with or without flaps, are also options.

Waist Details: You can request waist adjusters (internal buttons and straps that let you adjust the waist by about 2 inches) or waistband buttons for suspenders.

	Save	Splurge	Break the Bank
SUITS	HK$2,800 (Yuen's Tailor and Jantzen Tailor); HK$3,000 (Sam's Tailor)	HK$4,500 (Mode Elegante); HK$5,800 (Ascot Chang)	HK$8,000–HK$17,000 (A-Man Hing Cheong)
SHIRTS	HK$300 (Yuen's Tailor); HK$350 (Sam's Tailor).	HK$500 (Mode Elegante)	HK$650–HK$4,000 (Ascot Chang, HK$1,000 is average); HK$800–HK$1,800 (A-Man Hing Cheong).

David's Shirts Ltd. Like so many of its competitors, the popular David's Shirts has global reach and even a branch in New York City. But customers still enjoy the personalized service of a smaller business supervised by David Chu himself since 1961. All the work is done in-house by Shanghainese tailors with at least 20 years' experience each. There are more than 6,000 imported European fabrics to choose from, each prewashed. Examples of shirts, suits, and accessories—including 30 collar, 12 cuff, and 10 pocket styles—help you choose. Single-needle tailoring, French seams, 22 stitches per inch, handpicked, double-stitched shell buttons, German interlining—it's all here. Your details, down to which side you wear your wristwatch, are kept on file. ⊠ *G/F, Wing Lee Bldg., 33 Kimberley Rd.,, Tsim Sha Tsui, Kowloon* ☎ *2367–9556* ⊕ *www.davidsshirts.com* ⊠ *Mezzanine, Mandarin Oriental, 5 Connaught Rd., Central* Ⓜ *Central.*

Jantzen Tailor. You'll have to push past a lively crowd and eclectic shops in a mall preferred by Filipina domestic helpers to get to Jantzen. Catering to expatriate bankers since 1972, this reputable yet reasonable tailor specializes in classic shirts; it also makes suits and women's garments. The comprehensive Web site displays their commitment to quality, such as hand-sewn button shanks, Gygil interlining, and Coats brand thread. ⊠ *2/F World Wide House, 19 Des Voeux Rd., Central* ☎ *2570–5901* ⊕ *www.jantzentailor.com* Ⓜ *Central.*

Linva Tailors. It's one of the best of the old-fashioned *cheongsam* tailors, in operation since the 1960s. Master tailor, Mr. Leung, takes clients through the entire process and reveals a surprising number of variations in style. Prices are affordable, but vary according to fabric, which ranges from basics to special brocades and beautifully embroidered silks. ⊠ *38 Cochrane St., Central* ☎ *2544–2456* Ⓜ *Central.*

Maxwell's Clothiers Ltd. After you've found a handful of reputable, high-quality tailors, one way to choose between them is price. Maxwell's is known for its competitive rates. It's also a wonderful place to have favorite shirts and suits copied and for straightforward, structured women's shirts and suits. It was founded by third-generation tailor Ken Maxwell in 1961, and follows Shanghai tailoring traditions while also providing the fabled 24-hour suit upon request. The showroom and workshop are in Kowloon, but son, Andy, and his team take appointments in the United States, Canada, and Europe twice annually. The motto of this family business is, "Simply let the garment do the talking." ⊠ *7/F, Han Hing Mansion, 38–40 Hankow Rd., Tsim Sha Tsui, Kowloon* ☎ *2366–6705* ⊕ *www.maxwellsclothiers.com* Ⓜ *Tsim Sha Tsui.*

Mode Elegante. Don't be deterred by the somewhat dated mannequins in the windows. Mode Elegante is a favorite source for custom-made suits among women and men in the know. Tailors here specialize in European cuts. You'll have your choice of fabrics from the United Kingdom, Italy, and elsewhere. Your records are put on file so you can place orders from abroad. They'll even ship the completed garment to you almost anywhere on the planet. Alternatively, you can make an appointment with director Gary Zee, one of Hong Kong's traveling tailors who makes regular visits to North America, Europe, and Japan. ⊠ *Peninsula Hong Kong, Salisbury Rd., Tsim Sha Tsui, Kowloon* ☎ *2366–8153* ⊕ *www.modeelegante.com* Ⓜ *Tsim Sha Tsui.*

Raj Mirpuri. This establishment is best known for its Seven-Fold Tie. Most ties are made of several pieces of fabric and lined to give the illusion of weight. The Seven-Fold Tie is handmade from a single piece of silk that's folded seven times for a luxurious finish inspired by Renaissance craftsmanship. Raj Mirpuri further differentiates itself with bespoke (truly tailored to your measurements) rather than made-to-measure (based on an existing pattern) tailoring, with prices to match. They make suits, shirts, and accessories for men and women, and have stores in London, Geneva, and Zurich. ⊠ *8/F Star House, 3 Salisbury Rd., Tsim Sha Tsui, Kowloon* ☎ *2317–0804* ⊕ *www.mirpuri.com* Ⓜ *Tsim Sha Tsui.*

Fodor'sChoice **Sam's Tailor.** You won't find the legendary Sam's in a chic hotel or sleek
★ mall. But don't be fooled. These digs in humble Burlington House, a tailoring hub, have hosted everyone from U.S. presidents to performers such as the Black Eyed Peas, Kylie Minogue, and Blondie. This former uniform tailor to the British troops once even made a suit for Prince Charles in a record hour and 52 minutes. The men's and women's tailor does accept 24-hour suit or shirt orders, but will take about two days if you're not in a hurry. Founded by Naraindas Melwani in the 1950s, "Sam" is now his son, Manu Melwani, who runs the show with the help of his own son, Roshan, and about 55 tailors behind the scenes. In 2004 Sam's introduced a computerized bodysuit that takes measurements without subjecting you to the tape measure. (Actually, they now use a combination of both.) These tailors also make annual trips to Europe and North America. (Schedule updates are listed on the Web site.) ⊠ *Burlington House, 90–94 Nathan Rd., Tsim Sha Tsui, Kowloon* ☎ *2367–9423* ⊕ *www.samstailor.com* Ⓜ *Tsim Sha Tsui.*

★ **Shanghai Tang—Imperial Tailors.** Upscale Chinese lifestyle brand, Shanghai Tang, has the Imperial Tailors service in select stores. A fabulous interior evokes the charm of 1930s Shanghai, and gives an indication of what to expect in terms of craftsmanship and price. From silk to velvet, brocade to voile, fabrics are displayed on the side walls, along with examples of fine tailoring. The expert tailors here can make conservative or contemporary versions of the *cheongsam*. Men can also have a Chinese *tang* suit made to order. ⊠ *G/F, 12 Pedder St., Central* ☎ *2525–7333* ⊕ *www.shanghaitang.com* Ⓜ *Central.*

W. W. Chan & Sons Tailors Ltd. Chan is known for excellent quality suits and shirts, classic cuts, and has an array of fine European fabrics. It's comforting to know that you'll be measured and fitted by the same master tailor from start to finish. The Kowloon headquarters features a mirrored, hexagonal changing room so you can check every angle. Tailors from here travel to the United States several times a year to fill orders for their customers. ⊠ *2/F Burlington House, 92–94 Nathan Rd., Tsim Sha Tsui, Kowloon* ☎ *2366–9738* ⊕ *www.wwchan.com* Ⓜ *Tsim Sha Tsui.*

Yuen's Tailor. Need a kilt? This is where the Hong Kong Highlanders Reel Club comes for custom-made kilts. The Yuen repertoire, however, extends to well-made suits and shirts. The tiny shop is on an unimpressive gray walkway and is filled from floor to ceiling with sumptuous European fabrics. It's a good place to have clothes copied; prices are competitive. ⊠ *2/F, Escalator Link Alley, 80 Des Voeux Rd., Central* ☎ *2854–9649* Ⓜ *Central.*

Electronics

Variety and novelty—not prices—are the reasons to buy electronic goods and accessories in Hong Kong these days. Products are often launched in this keen, active electronics market before they are in the United States and Europe. The street sweepers may wear old-fashioned rattan Hakka hats, but even they carry cutting-edge, almost impossibly tiny phones. Indeed, cell phones are status symbols—often they're changed seasonally, like fashion accessories.

Broadway. Like its more famous competitor, Fortress, Broadway is a large electronic goods chain. It caters primarily to the local market, so some staff members speak better English than others. Look for familar name-brand cameras, computers, sound systems, home appliances, and mobile phones. Just a few of the many shops are listed here. ⊠ *Times Square, 1 Matheson St., Causeway Bay* ☎ *2506–0228* ⊕ *www.ibroadway.com. hk* Ⓜ *Causeway Bay* ⊠ *Ocean Centre, Harbour City, Canton Rd., Tsim Sha Tsui, Kowloon* Ⓜ *Tsim Sha Tsui* ⊠ *G/F, 48–50 Sai Yeung Choi St. S, Mong Kok, Kowloon* Ⓜ *Mong Kok.*

DG Lifestyle Store. An appointed Apple Center, DG carries Macintosh and iPod products. High-design gadgets, accessories, and software by other brands are add-ons that meld with the sleek Apple design philosophy. ⊠ *In Square, Windsor House, 311 Gloucester Rd., Causeway Bay* ☎ *2504–4122* ⊕ *www.dg-lifestyle.com* Ⓜ *Causeway Bay* ⊠ *IFC Mall, 8 Finance St., Central* Ⓜ *Central* ⊠ *New Town Plaza, Shatin Centre St., New Territories Shatin* Ⓜ *KCR Shatin.*

★ **Fortress.** Part of billionaire Li Ka-shing's empire, the extensive chain of shops sells electronics with warranties—a safety precaution that draws the crowds. It also has good deals on printers and accessories, although selection varies by shop. You can spot a Fortress by looking for the big orange sign. For the full list of shops, visit the Web site. ⊠ *Times Square, 1 Matheson St., Causeway Bay* ☎ *2506–0031* ⊕ *www.fortress. com.hk* Ⓜ *Causeway Bay* ⊠ *Ocean Centre, Harbour City, Canton Rd., Tsim Sha Tsui, Kowloon* Ⓜ *Tsim Sha Tsui* ⊠ *Lower G/F, Melbourne Plaza, 33 Queen's Rd. Central, Central* Ⓜ *Central.*

★ **Windsor House Computer Plaza.** Clean, wide corridors distinguish this less frantic computer arcade from the others. It has three floors of computer products with a wide selection of Mac and PC computer games, video games, laptops, desktops, and accessories. This is a reputable center with competitive prices. ⊠ *10/F–12/F, Windsor House, 311 Gloucester Rd., Causeway Bay* ☎ *2895–6796* Ⓜ *Causeway Bay.*

Jewelry

Artland Watch Co Ltd. Elegant but uncomplicated, the interior of this established watch retailer is like its service. The informed staff will guide you through the countless luxury brands on show and in the catalogs from which you can also order. Prices here aren't the best in Hong Kong, but they're still lower than at home. ⊠ *G/F, Mirador Mansion, 54–64B Nathan Rd., Tsim Sha Tsui, Kowloon* ☎ *2366–1074* Ⓜ *Tsim Sha Tsui* ⊠ *G/F, New Henry House, 10 Ice House St., Central* Ⓜ *Central.*

Chocolate Rain. The collections—dreamed up by a Hong Kong fine arts graduate—consist of pieces handcrafted of recycled materials, jade, crystals, precious stones, and mother of pearl. The showroom also doubles as a classroom for jewelry-making courses. ⊠ G/F, 63 Peel St., SoHo, Central ☎ 2975–8318 ⊕ www.chocolaterain.com Ⓜ Central.

Edward Chiu. Everything about Edward Chiu is *fabulous*, from the way he dresses to his high-end jade jewelry. The minimalist, geometric pieces use the entire jade spectrum, from deep greens to lavenders. He's also famous for contrasting black-and-white jade, setting it in precious metals and adding diamond or pearl touches. ⊠ IFC Mall, 8 Finance St., Central ☎ 2525–2618 ⊕ www.edwardchiu.com Ⓜ Central.

Eldorado Watch Co Ltd. At this deep emporium of watch brands, seek the advice of one of the older staffers who look like they've been there since the British landed. Brands include: Rolex, Patek Philippe, Girard-Perregaux, etc. ⊠ G/F, Peter Bldg., 58–62 Queen's Rd., Central ☎ 2522–7155 Ⓜ Central.

Qeelin. With ancient Chinese culture for inspiration and *In The Mood for Love* actress Maggie Cheung as the muse, something extraordinary was bound to come from Qeelin. Its name was cleverly derived from the Chinese characters for male ("qi") and female ("lin"), and symbolizes harmony, balance, and peace. The restrained beauty and meaningful creations of designer Dennis Chan are exemplified in two main collections: Wulu, a minimalist form representing the mythical gourd as well as the lucky Number 8; and Tien Di, literally "Heaven and Earth," symbolizing everlasting love. Classic gold, platinum, and diamonds mix with colored jades, black diamonds, and unusual materials for a truly unique effect. ⊠ IFC Mall, 8 Finance St., Central ☎ 2389–8863 ⊕ www. qeelin.com Ⓜ Central ⊠ Peninsula Shopping Arcade, Salisbury Rd., Tsim Sha Tsui, Kowloon Ⓜ Tsim Sha Tsui.

Ronald Abram Jewellers. Large white and rare-color diamonds sourced from all over the world are a specialty here, but the shop also deals in emeralds, sapphires, and rubies. With years of expertise, Abram dispenses advice on both the aesthetic merits and the investment potential of each stone or piece of jewelry. ⊠ Mezzanine, Mandarin Oriental, 5 Connaught Rd., Central ☎ 2810–7677 ⊕ www.ronaldabram.com Ⓜ Central.

Sandra Pearls. Without a recommendation like this, you might be wary of the lustrous pearls hanging at this little Jade Market stall. The charming owner, Sandra, does, in fact, sell genuine and reasonable cultured and freshwater pearl necklaces and earrings. Some pieces are made from shell, which Sandra is always quick to point out, and could pass muster among the snobbiest collectors. ⊠ Stall 381 and Stall 447, Jade Market, Kansu St., Yau Ma Tei, Kowloon ☎ 9485–2895 Ⓜ Yau Ma Tei.

Scorva Ltd. After years of experience in the watch industry, Hong Kong–based Satyajeet Sethi has applied his passion for design to a line of bold luxury timepieces. Made from steel and various precious metals, the watches come in various colors with special details such as chronograph features and diamonds. ⊠ Hollywood Plaza, 610 Nathan Rd., Mong Kok, Kowloon ☎ 3690–2760 ⊕ www.scorva.com.

Super Star Jewellery. Discreetly tucked in a corner of Central, Super Star looks like any other small Hong Kong jewelry shop—with walls lined by display cases filled with the usual classic designs (old-fashioned to some) in predominantly gold and precious stones. What makes them stand out are the good prices and personalized service. Their cultured pearls and mixed strands of colored freshwater pearls are not all shown, so ask Lily or one of her colleagues to bring them out. ✉ *The Galleria, 9 Queen's Rd. Central, Central* ☎ *2521–0507* Ⓜ *Central.*

TSL Jewellery. One of the big Hong Kong chains, TSL (Tse Sui Luen) specializes in diamond jewelry and manufactures, retails, and exports its designs. Its range of 100-facet stones includes the Estrella cut, which reflects nine symmetrical hearts and comes with international certification. Although its contemporary designs use platinum settings, TSL also sells pure, bright yellow gold items targeted at Chinese customers. ✉ *G9–10, Park Lane Shopper's Blvd., Nathan Rd., Tsim Sha Tsui, Kowloon* ☎ *2332–4618* ⊕ *www.tsljewellery.com* Ⓜ *Tsim Sha Tsui* ✉ *G/F, 35 Queen's Rd. Central, Central* Ⓜ *Central.*

Tayma Fine Jewellery. Unusual colored "connoisseur" gemstones are set by hand in custom designs by Hong Kong–based jeweler Tayma Page Allies. The collection is designed to bring out the personality of the individual wearer, and includes oversize cocktail rings, distinctive bracelets, pretty earrings, and more. ✉ *Prince's Bldg., 10 Chater Rd., Central* ☎ *2525–5280* ⊕ *www.taymajewellery.com* Ⓜ *Central.*

SIDE TRIP TO MACAU

By Hiram Chu   Macau—on the western bank of the Pearl River Delta, less than an hour from Hong Kong by hydrofoil—can legitimately lay claim to being a hybrid of east and west. In 1999, after 450 years of Portuguese rule, the Macau Peninsula and the islands of Taipa and Coloane became a Special Administrative Region (SAR) of the People's Republic of China.

The many contrasts in this tiny enclave of 450,000 people serve as reminders of how very different cultures have embraced one another's traditions for hundreds of years. Though Macau's population is 95% ethnic Chinese there are still vibrant pockets of Portuguese and Filipino expats. And some of the thousands of Eurasians—who consider themselves neither Portuguese nor Chinese, but something in between—can trace the intermarriage of their ancestors back a century or two. Most people visit Macau to gamble, eat cheap seafood, and shop without crowds. But don't overlook its timeless charms and unique culture, born from centuries of both Portuguese and Chinese influence.

Exploring Macau

Chances are you'll arrive at the Macau Ferry Terminal after sailing from Hong Kong. There's not much to see within walking distance of the terminal, so hop into one of the waiting taxis, buses, or pedicabs and head directly to the historic center, less than 10 minutes away. The short stretch of road named Avenida Almeida Ribeiro, more commonly known as San Ma Lo, is Macau's commercial and cultural heart. The region's biggest and best casinos are minutes away in the Downtown peninsula area and next to the ferry terminal in the Outer Harbour area.

THE BASICS

■ **Passports & Visas:** To enter Macau, Americans, Canadians, European Union citizens, and others only need a valid passport for stays of up to 20 days. Check the government's Web site (www.fsm. gov.mo) for more information.

■ **Currency:** The official currency is the pataca (abbreviated as MOP) with a fixed exchange rate of MOP$1.032 to HKD$1, which is roughly MOP$8 to US$1. Patacas come in 10, 20, 50, 100, 500, and 1000 MOP banknotes plus 1, 5, and 10 MOP coins. 1 pataca is divided into 100 avos and come in 10, 20, and 50 avos coins. That said, Hong Kong dollars are accepted on a 1:1 basis throughout Macau.

■ **Language:** Chinese and Portuguese are Macau's official languages. Both Cantonese and Mandarin are widely spoken. English is often used in commerce, but relying on it will be frustrating outside of tourist areas and with most taxi drivers.

Downtown Macau

Fodor's Choice
★
Fortaleza da Guia. The Guia Fortress, built between 1622 and 1638 on Macau's highest hill, was key to protecting the Portuguese from invaders. You can walk the steep, winding road up to the fortress or take a five-minute cable-car ride from the entrance of Flora Garden on Avenida Sidonio Pais. Once inside the fort, notice the Guia Lighthouse (you can't go inside, but you can get a good look at the exterior) that's lighted every night. Next to it is the Guia Chapel, built by Clarist nuns to provide soldiers with religious services.

Largo do Senado. The charming Senado Square, Macau's hub for centuries, is lined with neoclassical-style colonial buildings painted bright pastels. Only pedestrians are allowed on its shiny black-and-white azulejos, and the alleys off it are packed with great restaurants and shops. Take your time wandering. There are plenty of benches on which to rest after all your shopping and sightseeing. Come back at night, when locals of all ages gather to chat, and the square is beautifully lighted.

The magnificent yellow **Igreja de São Domingo** (St. Dominick's Church) beckons you to take a closer look. You can do so for free each day from 10 to 6. The cream-and-white interior takes on a heavenly golden glow when lighted up for services.

The imposing white facade of **Santa Casa da Misericordia** is hard to ignore. Founded in 1569 by Dom Belchior, Macau's first bishop, the Holy House of Mercy is the China coast's oldest Christian charity, and it continues to take care of the poor with soup kitchens and health clinics as well as to provide housing for the elderly. The exterior is neoclassical but the interior is done in a contrasting opulent modern style. It's open daily 10–1 and 2–5:30; admission is MOP$8.

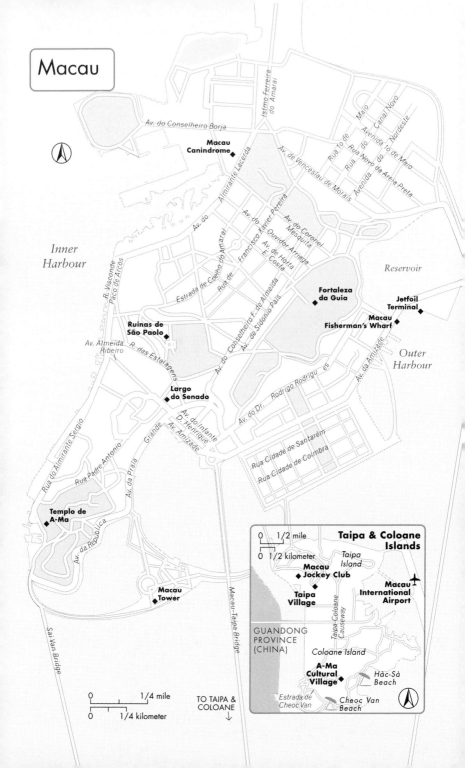

Macau

Inner
Harbour

Av. do Conselheiro Borja

Istmo Ferreira do Amaral

Av. de Venceslau de Morais

Macau Canindrome

Almirante Lacerda

Av. do

Estrada de Coelho do Amaral

Av. do Coronel Mesquita

Av. do Xavier Pereira

Rua de Francisco Xavier Pereira

Av. do Ouvidor Arriaga

Av. de Horta E. Costa

Av. do Conselheiro f. de Almeida

Av. de Sidónio Pais

R. Visconde Paço de Arcos

Ruínas de São Paolo

Av. Almeida Ribeiro

R. das Estalagens

Largo do Senado

Av. do Infante D. Henrique

Av. da Amizade

Rua do Almirante Sérgio

Rua Padre Antonio

Av. da Praia Grande

Av. do Dr. Rodrigo Rodrigues

Rua Cidade de Santarém

Rua Cidade de Coimbra

Fortaleza da Guia

Reservoir

Jetfoil Terminal

Macau Fisherman's Wharf

Av. da Amizade

Outer
Harbour

Templo de A-Ma

Av. da República

Macau Tower

Sai Van Bridge

Macau-Taipa Bridge

TO TAIPA &
COLOANE
↓

0   1/4 mile
0   1/4 kilometer

Taipa & Coloane Islands

0   1/2 mile
0   1/2 kilometer

Taipa Island

Macau Jockey Club

Taipa Village

Macau International Airport

Taipa-Coloane Causeway

GUANDONG
PROVINCE
(CHINA)

Coloane Island

A-Ma Cultural Village

Hác-Sá Beach

Estrada de Cheoc Van

Cheoc Van Beach

The neoclassical **Edificio do Leal Senado** (Senate Building) was built in 1784 as a municipal chamber and is still used by the government. A beautiful foyer and garden, open Tuesday through Sunday from 9 to 9, frequently host art and historical exhibitions. Admission is free.

Macau Canidrome. Asia's only greyhound track looks rundown compared to the pristine jockey club and the glitzy casinos, but it offers a true taste of Macau. It opened in 1932 and attracts a steady crowd of older gamblers several times a week for the slower-pace, lower-stakes gambling rush of betting on fast dogs chasing an electronic rabbit. Check out the parade of race dogs before each race. ☎ 853/333–399 ⊕ *www.macauyydog.com* ✉ *Public stands: MOP$2. Private boxes: MOP$80.* ☉ *Tues., Thurs., and weekends 6 PM–11 PM; first race at 7:30.*

Ⓒ **Macau Fisherman's Wharf.** This complex of amusements, shops, restaurants, and convention facilities is split into themed areas, including China's Tang Dynasty, a Middle East Bazaar, Tibet's Lhasa, African deserts, and ancient Rome. Each has unique dining and shopping options along with amusement rides for younger children. Crowds are thin, so the rides usually have no line. Come if you have kids in tow. Otherwise skip it. ✉ *Av. da Amizade at Av. Dr. Sun Yat-Sen, Downtown* ☎ *853/299–3300* ⊕ *www.fishermanswharf.com.mo* ✉ *Rides and shows MOP$10–MOP$100* ☉ *Amusement rides daily 10–9. Restaurants daily 10–10.*

Macau Tower & Convention & Entertainment Centre. Rising above everything else in the city, the world's 10th largest freestanding tower (1,100 feet) recalls a similar structure in Auckland. And it should as both were designed by New Zealand architect Gordon Moller. A. J. Hackett, the extreme sports company, is another bit of Kiwi flavor at the tower. The company offers a variety of thrills, including the Mast Climb, which challenges the daring and strong of heart and body to make a two-hour climb 300 feet up the tower's mast for incomparable views of Macau and China. On the Ironwalk, you clamber up the tower's legs and shafts as if you were rock climbing. What's that? You prefer walking to climbing? Well then perhaps you could take the Skywalk, an open-air stroll around the tower's exterior—without any gates or handrails. Even more intense is the Skyjump, which is listed in the *Guinness Book of World Records* as the world's highest decelerator descent. You essentially bungee jump—free-falling for 765 feet—while control wires prevent you from swinging into the tower. Prices range from MOP$233 for the Skywalk to MOP$688 for the Mast Climb. There are discounts for groups and multiple experiences. Yikes! ✉ *Largo da Torre de Macau, Downtown* ☎ *853/988–8656* ⊕ *www.macautower.com.mo.*

> ### WORLD HERITAGE
>
> In 2005 the "Historic Centre of Macao" was listed as China's 31st UNESCO World Heritage Site. The term "center" is misleading as the site is really a collection of churches, buildings, and neighborhoods that colorfully illustrate Macau's 400-year history. Included in it are China's oldest examples of western architecture and the region's most extensive concentration of missionary churches.

Ruínas de São Paulo (Ruins of St. Paul's Church). Only the magnificent, towering facade, with its intricate carvings and bronze statues, remains from the original church. This widely adopted symbol of Macau was built between 1602 and 1640 by Jesuit priests and Japanese Christians. The church, an adjacent college, and Mount Fortress once formed East Asia's first Western-style university and was collectively regarded as the Acropolis of Asia. Most of the structures were destroyed by fire in 1835, but the ruins remain popular with visitors, and there are snack bars and antiques and other shops at the foot of the site.

Behind the facade of São Paulo is the **Museum of Sacred Art,** which holds statues, crucifixes, and the bones of Japanese and Indo-Chinese Christian martyrs. There are also some intriguing Asian interpretations of Christian images, including samurai angels and a Chinese Virgin and child. The museum is free and open Sunday through Monday 9–6.

The **Templo de Na Tcha** is a small Chinese temple that was built in 1888, during the Macauan plague. The hope was that Na Tcha Temple would appeal to a mythical Chinese character who granted wishes and could save lives. The **Troco das Antigas Muralhas de Defesa** (Section of the Old City Walls) is all that remains of Macau's original defensive barrier and borders the left side of the Na Tcha Temple. These crumbling yellow walls were built in the mid-16th century and illustrate the durability of *chunambo:* compacted layers of clay, soil, sand, straw, crushed rocks, and oyster shells. ⊠ *Downtown* ☎ *Free* ☉ *Daily 8–5.*

Templo de A-Ma (A-Ma Temple). Properly called Ma Kok Temple but known to locals as simply A-Ma, it's thought to be Macau's oldest building. The structure has its origins in the Ming Dynasty (1368–1644), and was influenced by Confucianism, Taoism, and Buddhism. Vivid-red calligraphy on large boulders tells the story of the goddess A-Ma (also known as Tin Hau), the patron of fishermen. The entrance is obscured by overhanging trees; a small gate opens onto prayer halls, pavilions, and caves carved directly into the hillside. A small museum has temple artifacts. ⊠ *Rua de São Tiago da Barra, Largo da Barra, Downtown* ☉ *Daily 7–6* ☎ *Free.*

Taipa

Taipa village's narrow, winding streets are packed with restaurants, bakeries, shop houses, temples, and other buildings with South Chinese and Portuguese design elements. The aptly named Rua do Cunha (Food Street) has many great Chinese, Macanese, Portuguese, and Thai restaurants. Several shops sell homemade Macanese snacks, including steamed milk pudding, almond cakes, beef jerky, and coconut candy.

Macau Jockey Club. The MJC operates year-round. A five-story, open-air grandstand accommodates as many as 15,000 spectators, and, of course, hundreds of private suites and VIP boxes for high rollers and celebrity visitors. All the facilities are top quality, and you can even get a great meal here. Horses have a comfortable lifestyle, too, with more than 1,250 air-conditioned stalls, an equine hospital, and an equine swimming pool. There's also a riding school for aspiring jockeys. Sand-track races are held weeknights at 7, and grass track races take place weekends at 2, except in summer when the heat and humidity forces all races to be held in the evenings. You can place bets at more than 80 stations throughout Macau and Hong Kong as well as through the Internet. Stop by the northeast exit to visit the large Four Face Buddha statue where you can say a short prayer for luck. ⊠ *Estrada Governador Albano de Oliveira, Taipa* ☎ *853/821–188* ⊕ *www.macauhorse.com* ⊠ *General admission is free, grandstand seating is MOP$20.*

Coloane

Quiet, relaxed Coloane Village is home to traditional Mediterranean-style houses painted in pastels as well as the baroque-style Chapel of St. Francis Xavier and the Taoist Tam Kung Temple. The surrounding small narrow alleys have surprises at every turn; among many things you may encounter are fishermen repairing their junks or a local baptism at the chapel. The village's heart is a small square with a fountain with a bronze Cupid. The surrounding Macanese and Chinese open-air restaurants are among the region's best; some are the unheralded favorites of chefs visiting from Hong Kong and elsewhere in Asia.

A-Ma Cultural Village. A path just south of Seac Pai Van Park leads to A-Ma Cultural Village, a huge complex built in a traditional Qing Dynasty style. It pays homage to Macau's namesake, the goddess of the sea. The vibrancy and color of the details in the bell and drum towers, the tiled roofs, and the carved marble altars are truly awe-inspiring. It's as if you've been transported back to the height of the Qing Empire. Other remarkable details include the striking rows of stairs leading to Tian Hou Palace at the entrance. Each row features painstaking detailed marble and stone carvings of auspicious Chinese symbols: a roaring tiger, double lions, five cranes, the double phoenix, and a splendid imperial dragon. The grounds here also have an arboretum with more than 100 species of local and exotic flora. ⊠ *Off Estrada de Seac Pai Van, Coloane* ⊠ *Free* ☉ *Tues.–Sun. 8–6.*

Cheoc Van Beach is perfect for romantic walks. It's in a sheltered cove with a seafood restaurant to one side, the Marine Club, with kayak rentals on the other side, and a charming pousada overlooking the ocean. Note: there are lots of stray, though generally friendly, dogs on this beach.

Hàc-Sà translated from the Chinese means "black sand," though the sands of the area's biggest beach are actually a deep gray. Playgrounds, picnic areas, and restaurants are all within walking distance. A sports complex has an Olympic-size swimming pool, tennis courts, and other sports facilities. Also nearby is the Hàc-Sà Reservoir BBQ park with picnic and barbecue facilities, boat rentals, and water sports outfitters.

Where to Eat

	WHAT IT COSTS In patacas				
	$$$$	**$$$**	**$$**	**$**	**¢**
AT DINNER	over $300	$201–$300	$151–$200	$80–$150	under $80

Prices are for two main courses, a small side dish, and two beverages at dinner and do not include the customary 10% service charge.

$$$$ ✕ **Restaurante Perola.** With its brilliant turquoise tiles, ironwork chandeliers, and dark wood, the sophisticated Perola evokes the seafaring heritage of Portugal and Macau. The emphasis is on the freshest seafood, and there are numerous imported Portuguese ingredients in the dishes. Here you can try an excellent *cataplana,* a savory stew of fish, shellfish, and pork served in a gleaming copper pot, as well as a tangy, juicy African chicken. Rich coffees and wines complement the sublime desserts. ⊠ *203 Largo de Monte Carlo, 3rd fl. Sands Casino, Outer Harbour, Macau* ☎ *853/883–377* ▭ *AE, DC, MC, V* ☉ *Closed Mon.*

$$$ ✕ **Os Gatos.** The Portuguese name "Os Gatos" means "cats" and sitting on the sunny outdoor terrace of the Pousada de São Tiago, a 17th-century fortress overlooking the South China Sea, you do feel like a feline basking in the afternoon sun. The large brick terrace is shaded by several leafy trees while the air-conditioned interior has hand-carved furniture and painted tiles from Portugal. The mixed Mediterranean, Italian, and Macanese dishes on the menu are straightforward and enjoyable, though somewhat disappointing when compared with the beautiful setting. There are good versions of seafood paella, baked crab with saffron and sage, and chicken piri-piri, but the best deal is the afternoon tea beginning at 3 PM. A popular buffet lunch and dinner is served daily. ⊠ *Pousada de São Tiago, Av. da República, Inner Harbour, Macau* ☎ *853/ 968–686* ▭ *AE, DC, MC, V.*

$$ ✕ **Litoral.** Litoral serves authentic Macanese dishes that are simple, straightforward, and deliciously satisfying. Tastefully decorated with white-washed walls and dark-wood beams, must-try dishes include the tamarind pork with shrimp paste as well as codfish baked with potato and garlic and a creamy Portuguese green soup. For dessert, try the *bebinca de leite,* a coconut-milk custard, or the traditional egg pudding, *pudim abade de priscos.* You should make reservations if you're planning a weekend meal. ⊠ *261 Rua do Almirante Sergio, Inner Harbour Macau* ☎ *853/ 967–878* ▭ *AE, DC, MC, V.*

$$ ✕ **Pizzeria Toscana.** The owners have roots in Pisa and have created a warm, rustic interior to match the menu of refined comfort food on the menu. The *bresaola involtini* (air-cured beef with shredded Parmesan) and fresh salmon carpaccio antipasti are a tasty way to begin your meal; then try the grilled king prawns, homemade tortellini, and, of course, the perfect wood-fired pizzas. And you can finish your meal with the best cappuccinos in town. ⊠ *Av. da Amizade, opposite Macau Ferry Terminal, Outer Harbour, Macau* ☎ *853/726–637* ⌕ *Reservations essential* ▭ *AE, DC, MC, V.*

$ ✕ **Fat Siu Lau.** Fat Siu Lau has kept its customers coming back for more
Fodor's Choice than 100 years with delicious Macanese favorites and modern cre-
★ ations. For best results, try ordering whatever you see the chatty Cantonese stuffing themselves with on the surrounding tables, and you won't be disappointed! It will probably be whole curry crab, grilled prawns in a butter garlic sauce, and the famous roasted pigeon marinated in a secret marinade. A newly opened Fat Siu Lau 2 is on Macau Lan Kwai Fong Street and offers the same great food. Reservations are strongly recommended. ⊠ *Rua da Felicidade, Downtown, Macau* ☎ *853/573– 580* ▭ *AE, DC, MC, V.*

¢ ✕ **Pastelaria Koi Kei.** When walking along the street toward the Ruins
Fodor'sChoice of St. Paul's Church, you will no doubt be accosted by dozens of ag-
★ gressive salespeople trying to force samples of Macanese snacks into your
hands. Don't be shy and have a taste or two because competition is fierce
for the tourist dollar and they expect you to shop around. Along the
street are several *pastelarias* (pastry shops) where you can buy almond
cakes, ginger candy, beef jerky, and egg rolls, but one of the oldest and
best is Pastelaria Koi Kei. The Portuguese custards are excellent. You'll
see lots of Hong Kong visitors hauling the bakery's distinctive tan bags,
heavy with snacks, back home for friends and relatives. Koi Kei has
branches throughout Macau. ✉ *70–72 Rua Felcidade, base of Ruins
of St. Paul's, Downtown, Macau* ☎ *853/938–102* ⊟ *AE, DC, MC, V.*

Where to Stay

	WHAT IT COSTS In Patacas				
	$$$$	**$$$**	**$$**	**$**	**¢**
FOR 2 PEOPLE	Over $1,500	$1,001–1,500	$801–1,000	$300–800	Under $300

Prices are for two people in a standard double room on a typical Saturday night,
not including 10% service charge and 5% tax.

Macau

★ **$$$$** ☷ **Mandarin Oriental.** The Mandarin Oriental is synonymous with elegance and understated opulence, and its Macau location doesn't disappoint. This hotel is also widely known for deluxe treatments in the
enormous spa complex next to the gorgeous, tropical swimming pool
on the landscaped grounds. You'll feel like you're in a lush rain forest
as you look out from the traditional Mediterranean architecture of the
hotel. ✉ *956–1110 Av. da Amizade, Outer Harbour* ☎ *853/567–888,
2881–1988 in Hong Kong, 800/526–6566 in U.S.* ⊕ *www.
mandarinoriental.com* ↜ *407 rooms, 28 suites* ♨ *4 restaurants, café,
room service, in-room safes, minibars, refrigerators, cable TV with
movies, in-room data ports, 2 tennis courts, 2 pools, gym, hot tubs (indoor and outdoor), massage, sauna, spa, squash, bar, casino, children's
programs (ages 3–12), dry cleaning, laundry service, business services,
meeting rooms* ⊟ *AE, DC, MC, V.*

★ **$$$$** ☷ **Pousada de São Tiago.** The spirit of the structure's past life as a 17th-
century fortress permeates every part of this romantic and charming lodging, making it an ideal location for a honeymoon or two. Your first sight
is the front entrance, an ascending stone tunnel carved into the mountainside with water seeping through in quiet trickles, just as it has done
for centuries. The location's namesake comes from a small chapel dedicated to São Tiago, the patron saint of the Portuguese army. Each
room has imported Portuguese furniture and a careful balance between
modern luxury and Portuguese charm. Note, though, that the service
can be slow. Sip an unforgettable cocktail on Cafe da Barra's terrace as
the sun sets, painting the ocean waters a warm orange. ✉ *Av. da
República, Inner Harbour* ☎ *853/378–111, 2739–1216 in Hong Kong*
⊕ *www.saotiago.com.mo* ↜ *20 rooms, 4 suites* ♨ *Restaurant, room*

5

service, minibars, cable TV, pool, bar, dry cleaning, laundry service ⊟ *AE, DC, MC, V.*

★ $$$$ ☷ **Sands Macau.** Casino tycoon Sheldon Anderson's first venture in Macau, the Sands, is nothing if not luxurious. Spacious rooms have deep, soft carpets, comfortable, large beds, and huge marble bathrooms, and you get efficient, professional service from the smartly dressed staff, all of whom speak excellent English. You can opt for one of the 51 luxury suites, ranging in size from 1,000 to 8,000 square feet, with in-room hot tubs, a massage table for in-room service, karaoke rooms, plasma TVs, remote-control drapes and lighting, plus personal butler service to keep it all running smoothly. ⊠ *Largo de Monte Carlo 203, Outer Harbour* ☎ *853/883–388* ⊕ *www.sands.com.mo* ⇴ *407 rooms, 28 suites* ♿ *7 restaurants, room service, in-room safes, minibars, cable TV with movies, in-room broadband, tennis courts, 2 public pools plus private plunge pools, gyms, spa, sauna, squash, bar, casino, dry cleaning, laundry service, business services, meeting rooms* ⊟ *AE, DC, MC, V.*

$$$ ☷ **Hotel Lisboa.** Macau's infamous landmark, with its distinctive, slightly bizarre architecture, rumored connections to organized crime, open prostitution, and no-limit VIP rooms, is in the heart of downtown Macau. No expense is spared, with plush custom-made carpets, luxurious beds, beautifully tiled bathrooms with Hermès toiletries, and hot tubs in every room. The lobby is a bit gaudy and ostentatious but always interesting because of the art on display from owner Dr. Stanley Ho's private collection. The multifloor casino remains one of the biggest in Macau, and the VIP rooms are legendary. But the Lisboa has more than just gambling, with high-end shopping arcades, extensive dining options, deluxe spa facilities, and a huge outdoor heated pool. ⊠ *Av. da Amizade, Downtown Peninsula* ☎ *853/577–666, 2559–1028, 800/ 969–130 in Hong Kong* ⊕ *www.hotelisboa.com* ⇴ *1,000 rooms, 100 suites* ♿ *18 restaurants, room service, in-room safes, minibars, cable TV with movies, in-room broadband, tennis courts, gym, central pool, spa, sauna, squash, bar, casino, dry cleaning, laundry service, business services, meeting room* ⊟ *AE, DC, MC, V.*

★ $$ ☷ **Hotel Sintra.** Minutes from the Lisboa and Senado Square, the Hotel Sintra has carpeted rooms with soothing brown-and-cream color schemes and comfortable beds. The staff is smartly dressed and helpful, though their English inconsistent. Breakfast is a buffet spread that includes steamed breads, noodles, and rice. There's a shopping arcade and free shuttle buses from the Macau Ferry Terminal. ⊠ *Av. De D. Joao IV, Downtown Peninsula* ☎ *853/710–111* ⊕ *www.hotelsintra.com* ⇴ *112 rooms, 2 suites* ♿ *4 restaurants, bar, room service, in-room safes, minibars, cable TV, sauna, shopping arcade, laundry service, banquet and conference facilities, shuttle bus* ⊟ *AE, DC, MC, V.*

★ $ ☷ **Metropole Hotel.** The Metropole offers no-frills accommodations in one of the best locations in the city. Minutes away from all of Macau's major casinos, shopping, and sightseeing, the Metropole provides friendly staff to compensate for minimalist guest rooms, a meager breakfast, and not many guest amenities apart from the free shuttle bus from the Macau Ferry Terminal. ⊠ *Av. de Praia Grande 493–501, Downtown* ☎ *853/388–166* ⊕ *www.mctshmi.com* ⇴ *112 rooms, 2 suites* ♿ *2* *restaurants, room service, in-room safes, minibars, cable TV, laundry service, shuttle bus* ⊟ *AE, DC, MC, V.*

Coloane

$$$$
Fodor'sChoice
★ 🏨 **Westin Resort.** Built into the side of a cliff, the Westin is surrounded by the black sands of Hàc-Sà Beach and lapping waves of the South China Sea; this is where you truly get away from it all. Every room faces the ocean; the place glows as much because of the sunny tropical color scheme as because of the sunshine. The vast private terraces are ideal for alfresco dining and naps in the afternoon sun. Guests also receive access to the PGA-standard, 18-hole Macau Golf and Country, which is on rocky plateaus above the hotel. ⊠ *Hàc-Sà Beach, Coloane Island South* ☎ *853/871–111 or 2803–2002, 800/228–3000 in Hong Kong* ⊕ *www. westin-macau.com* ⇆ *200 rooms, 8 suites* ⟺ *4 restaurants, room service, in-room safes, minibars, cable TV with movies, in-room data ports, driving range, 18-hole golf course, miniature golf, 8 tennis courts, 2 pools (1 indoor), health club, hot tubs (indoor and outdoor), massage, bicycles, badminton, squash, 2 bars, shops, babysitting, business services, meeting rooms, car rental, no-smoking rooms* ⊟ *AE, DC, MC, V.*

★ **$$$$** 🏨 **Pousada de Coloane.** At Cheoc-Van Beach at the most southern tip of Coloane Island, Pousada de Coloane offers a quiet, natural setting, nestled within the lush hills and mountains of Macau's south. There are ample opportunities for kayaking, hiking, and swimming. A long winding path paved with Portuguese azulejo tiles leads you to the spacious terrace overlooking the beach and is ideal for outdoor wedding receptions and other celebrations. Facilities include a small pool, a comfortable fireplace, and a small bar in the restaurant. The Terrace restaurant offers traditional Portuguese, Macanese, and Chinese favorites cooked in a heavy, homestyle tradition served in generous portions to ensure you are full, but flavors can be bland. There are seafood restaurants down on the beach that you might consider trying instead. All 30 rooms have private double hot tubs and balconies overlooking the beach and mountains. ⊠ *Cheoc Van Beach, Coloane Island South* ☎ *853/882–143* ⊕ *www.hotelpcoloane.com.mo* ⇆ *30 rooms, 10 suites* ⟺ *Restaurant, room service, minibars, cable TV, pool, bar, dry cleaning, laundry service, Internet room* ⊟ *AE, DC, MC, V.*

Nightlife

Macau's nightlife is more civilized than in its wild past and, outside of the casinos and a few restaurants, the city shuts down after 11 PM. You can slip into any of dark, elegant lounge bars inside the city's larger hotels, and enjoy live music and expensive cocktails, but don't expect much energy or big crowds.

Macau's Lan Kwai Fong has a collection of bars along a small stretch of street in the New Reclaimation Area, within sight of Macau's harbor. Although it takes its name from the legendary bar area in Hong Kong, in reality, it's a bunch of nice, quiet spots to meet with friends or watch sports on a big-screen TV. A large number of expats come to this area to relax and drink in the evenings; don't expect the thumping music you might find in the original LKF in Hong Kong. Go the way locals do and just hop into a cab and tell him "Lan Kwai Fong" and you'll be there in 10 minutes or less, no matter where you are.

Casinos

The average gaming table in Macau grosses almost nine times the average one in Las Vegas, and the world's highest grossing casino, the legendary Lisboa, brings in more than 7 million dollars *per day*. Small wonder that international casino groups have swarmed the region, driving Macau's explosive double-digit growth.

From the late 1960s until 2001, Macau native Dr. Stanley Ho owned all the casinos, helping him to become one of the world's wealthiest people. One of the first steps the Chinese government took after the 1999 handover was to break up Dr. Ho's monopoly and award casino licenses to several consortiums from Las Vegas. The grand plan to transform Macau from a quiet town that offered gambling into one of the world's top gaming destinations is well underway.

THE SCENE Gambling is lightly regulated, so there are only a few things to remember. No one under age 18 is allowed into casinos. Most casinos use Hong Kong dollars in their gaming and not Macau patacas, but you can easily exchange currencies at cashiers. High- and no-limit VIP rooms are available on request. Minimum bets range from HK$50,000 to HK$100,000 per hand. You can get cash from credit cards and ATMs 24 hours a day. Most casinos don't have strict dress codes outside of their VIP rooms, but you're better off not wearing shorts or sleeveless shirts. Minimum bets for most tables are higher than those in Las Vegas, but there are lower limits for slots and video gambling.

The players here may not look sophisticated, but don't be fooled. Chinese men and women have long embraced gambling, so many of Macau's gamblers are truly hard-core. Average bets are high, and many people gamble until they're exhausted or broke, usually the latter. Macau is also famous for gambling's sister industries of pawn shops, loan sharks, seedy saunas, and prostitution. This underbelly is hidden, though. You won't encounter such things unless you seek them out.

THE CREAM OF
THE CROP **Sands Macao Casino Hotel** (⊠ Largo de Monte Carlo 203, Downtown Macau ☎ 853/883–388 ⊕ www.sands.com.mo). **Mandarin Oriental Casino Hotel** (⊠ 956-1110 Av. da Amizade, Downtown Macau ☎ 853/567–888 ⊕ www.mandarinoriental.com). **Wynn Macau** (⊠ 6-8 Av. da Amizade, Downtown Macau ☎ 853/889–966 ⊕ www.wynnmacau.com). **Venetian Macao Resort Hotel** (⊠ Cotai Strip, Macau ☎ 853/883–311 ⊕ www.venetianmacao.com).

THE LANDMARKS **Hotel Casino Lisboa** (⊠ 2-4 Av. de Lisboa, Downtown Macau ☎ 853/377–666 ⊕ www.hotelisboa.com). **Hyatt Regency Hotel Casino** (⊠ 2 Estrata Almirante, Marques Esparteiro Taipa ☎ 853/831–537 ⊕ www.macau.hyatt.com). **Jai Alai Casino** (⊠ Jai Alai Building, Av. de Amizade, Downtown Macau ☎ 853/726–086). **Macau Jockey Club Casino** (⊠ Grandview Hotel, Estrada Governador Albano de Oliveira 142, Taipa ☎ 853/837–788). **Golden Dragon Casino** (⊠ Hotel Golden Dragon Rua de Malaca, Downtown Macau ☎ 853/727–979).

Macau Essentials

Transportation

BY AIR

The Macau International Airport is a busy regional hub with capacity for more than 6 million passengers per year and regular daily service to all major cities in China and the rest of Asia. Downtown Macau is a 15-minute taxi ride away and the China Border Gate is 20 minutes. The graceful arched Friendship Bridge connects the airport's reclaimed island to Taipa Island.

International flights do come into Macau, but there are no flights from Hong Kong, which is only 10 minutes away by plane. There are, however, 16-minute flights between Hong Kong's Shun Tak Centre and the Macau Ferry Terminal that leave every 30 minutes from 9:30 AM to 10:30 PM daily. Prices are HK$1,268 Monday to Thursday and HK$1,477 Friday to Sunday and holidays. Reservations are essential.

📷 **East Asia Airlines** ☎ 2108–9898 Shun Tak Centre, 853/727–288 Macau Terminal ⊕ www.helihongkong.com. **Macau International Airport** ☎ 853/861–111 ⊕ www.macau-airport.gov.mo.

BY BUS

Public buses are clean and affordable; trips to anywhere in the main peninsula cost MOP$2.50, service to Taipa Island is MOP$3.30, and service to Coloane and the airport is MOP$5. Buses require exact change upon boarding and detailed bus schedules are posted at all stops, though they are in Chinese and Portuguese only. Also available are replicas of 1920s London buses known as Tour Machines. They can be found at the Macau Ferry Terminal and the cost of one chartered bus for a party of up to nine people goes for MOP$300–MOP$380 per hour.

BY CAR

In contrast to Hong Kong's British system of driving on the left-hand side of the road, Macau has a system similar to the United States of driving on the right-hand side of the road. Road signs are in Chinese and Portuguese only, though. Common sense and careful driving will help you get around most problems. International drivers' licenses are accepted in Macau.

Avis Car Rental is the only choice in town for traditional car rentals. Cars go for MOP$450 to MOP$600 on weekdays and MOP$500 to MOP$650 on weekends. Book in advance for a discount, but as always, you must ask for it.

If you have a taste for the nontraditional, you can also rent *mokes*, motor vehicles that look like a jeep crossed with a British taxi. They're a slice of Macanese life, fun to drive, and ideal for touring. Rental rates are MOP$350 for 24 hours, plus a whopping MOP$3,000 deposit but thankfully credit cards are accepted. The price includes third-party insurance, and the helpful staff will often give a discount if asked. Hotel packages also include special moke-rental deals and you can contact Happy Mokes for additional details.

🚗 **Avis Rent A Car** ☎ 853/336-789 in Macau, 2576-6831 in Hong Kong ⊕ www.avis.com. **Happy Mokes** ☎ 2523-5690 in Hong Kong, 853/831-212, 853/439-393 in Macau.

BY FERRY

Ferries run every 15 minutes 24 hours a day with a reduced schedule from 1:30 AM to 7 AM. Spring's typhoon season sees regular disruptions in service. Call the ferry office for information when the weather is bad.

Prices for the three classes of tickets—economy, first, and super—run HK$142–HK$260. VIP cabins cost HK$1,650 and up. Weekday traffic is light, so you can buy tickets a few minutes before departure. Weekend tickets, on the other hand, often sell out, so make reservations. You can do so up to 28 days in advance with travel agents and at most Hong Kong hotels and large MTR stations. You can also book by phone and pay with American Express, Diners Club, and Visa cards, but you must pick tickets up at least a half hour before departure.

Most ferries leave from Hong Kong's Shun Tak Centre (Sheung Wan MTR Station) in Central, though limited service is also available from Kowloon's Tsim Sha Tsui Ferry Terminal. In Macau all service is handled by the Macau Ferry Terminal. The trip takes 55 minutes one-way. Buses and cabs await you on the Macau side.

🚢 **Ferry Reservations & Turbojet Tickets** ☎ 2859-3333 for schedules, 2921-6688 for bookings ⊕ www.turbojet.com.hk. **First Ferry** ✉ Shun Tak Centre, 200 Connaught Rd., Sheung Wan, Hong Kong ☎ 2131-8181 ⊕ www.nwff.com.hk.

BY TAXI

Taxis are inexpensive and plentiful in Macau and the small geographic size of the region makes taxi rides an affordable luxury. The black cabs with cream-color roofs can be flagged on the street and the yellow cabs are radio taxis, which can be arranged through your hotel's concierge. All are metered, air-conditioned, and reasonably comfortable. Drivers often don't speak or read much English, so you should carry a bilingual map or name card for your destination in Chinese. The base charge is MOP$10 for the first 1¾ km (about 1¼ mi) and MOP$1 per additional 800 feet. Drivers don't expect a tip but will gladly accept one if offered. Expect to pay about MOP$15 for a trip from the ferry terminal to downtown Macau and MOP$20 from the airport.

Resources

VISITOR INFORMATION

The Macau Government Tourist Office (MGTO) is well managed and generously funded. It has an excellent and helpful staff and a comprehensive Web site with information on everything from the latest exhibitions and festivals to the top sights, restaurants, and hotels.

🏛 **MGTO** ✉ Macau Ferry Terminal, Macau ☎ 853/726-416 ⊕ www.macautourism.gov.mo ✉ Macau International Airport, Arrival Hall ☎ 853/861-436 ✉ Shun Tak Centre, 200 Connaught Rd., Sheung Wan, Hong Kong ☎ 2857-2287 ✉ Hong Kong International Airport, Hong Kong ☎ 2769-7970 or 2382-7110.

TOURS

Two basic tours of Macau are available. One covers mainland Macau and the most famous sites, with stops at the Chinese border, Kun Iam

Temple, the ruins of St. Paul's, and Penha Hill. This type of tour lasts about 3½ hours. The other typical tour consists of a two-hour trip across the bridge to the islands of Taipa and Coloane to see old Chinese villages, lesser-known temples, the main beaches, and the Macau Jockey Club. Tours travel by liner bus or minibus.

The most comfortable way to tour is by chauffeur-driven minivan. A car with a maximum of four passengers costs HK$200 an hour with Avis and you can also charter a regular taxi for touring, though few drivers speak English. Depending on your bargaining prowess, the cost will be HK$50–HK$70 per hour.

Most travelers going to Macau on a day-trip can book a tour with travel agents in Hong Kong, but it's not essential. If you do prearrange your trip, you'll have the convenience of transportation from Hong Kong to Macau all set, with your guide waiting in the arrival hall, which can be a real time-saver. There are several licensed tour operators in Macau and the ones listed below cater to English-speaking visitors.

🔳 Tour Operators **Able Tours** Also operates Grayline tours ✉ Room 1015, Avenida da Amizade, Ferry Terminal, Macau ☎ 853/725-813. **Estoril Tours** ✉ Shop 333, Shun Tak Centre, 200 Connaught Rd., 3/F, Central, Hong Kong ☎ 2559-1028 ⊕ www.estoril.com. **Sintra Tours** ✉ Hotel Sintra, 58-62 Av. Dom João IV, Macau ☎ 853/710-361.

HONG KONG ESSENTIALS

Transportation

By Victoria
Patience

BY AIR

Cathay Pacific is Hong Kong's flagship carrier. It maintains high standards, with friendly service, good in-flight food, and an excellent track record for safety—all of which drive its prices higher than some of the other regional carriers. Cathay has nonstop flights from both Los Angeles and San Francisco on the west coast and from New York–JFK on the east. Singapore Airlines is usually slightly less expensive and offers direct flights to San Francisco on the west coast and Newark on the east coast. Considerably less comfortable, Continental also frequently offers good price deals, and has a nonstop flight to Hong Kong from Newark.

The sleek, sophisticated Hong Kong International Airport (HKG) is never called by its official name; it's universally referred to as Chek Lap Kok, which is where it's located. At almost a mile long, its Y-shape passenger terminal is the world's biggest. Walkways connect the check-in and arrival halls with nearby gates. An electric train glides to gates at the end of the terminal. There's Wi-Fi access all over the terminal after check-in, but you have to pay for it. The Internet is free at the PCs in the Cyber Lounges near Gates 20 and 60. You can also surf the Net or make calls from the high-tech PowerPhones throughout the terminal.

Check in at least two hours before departing from Chek Lap Kok. If you're flying to anyplace but the United States and plan on taking the train to the airport, most major airlines let you use the In-Town check-in service at the Hong Kong or Kowloon Airport Express stations. You can check your bags up to 24 hours before your flight. The service closes 1½ hours before your flight time. After September 11, 2001, carriers flying to the United States discontinued In-Town check-in indefinitely.

🛪 **Airline Contacts Cathay Pacific Airways** ☎ 800/233-2742 in U.S., 800/268-6868 in Canada, 2747-1888 in Hong Kong ⊕ www.cathay-usa.com. **Continental Airlines** ☎ 800/523-3273 for U.S. and Mexico reservations, 800/231-0856 for international reservations, 852/3198-5777 in Hong Kong. ⊕ www.continental.com. **Singapore Airlines** ☎ 800/742-3333 in U.S., 852/2520-2233 in Hong Kong ⊕ www.singaporeair.com. 🛪 **Airport Information Hong Kong International Airport** ☎ 852/2181-0000 ⊕ www.hkairport.com.

GROUND TRANSPORT The Airport Express train service is the quickest and most convenient way to and from the airport. Gleaming, high-speed trains whisk you to Kowloon in 19 minutes and Central in 24 minutes. Trains run every 12 minutes between 5:50 AM and 1:15 AM daily. There's plenty of luggage space, legroom, and comfortable seating with TV screens on the backs of the passenger seats showing tourist information and the latest news.

The Airport Express station is connected to the MTR's Tung Chung, Kowloon, and Central stations—the latter is via a long, underground walkway with no luggage carts, however. One-way or same-day return fare to or from Central is HK$100; from Kowloon, HK$90. Round-trip tickets valid for one month cost HK$180 for Central and HK$160 for Kowloon. The Airport Express also runs free shuttle buses every 12 minutes between major hotels and its Hong Kong and Kowloon stations—there are seven routes. To board, you must show your ticket, boarding pass, or Airport Express ticket.

Citybus runs five buses ("A" precedes the bus number) from Chek Lap Kok to popular destinations. They have fewer stops than regular buses, which have an "E" before their number, so are more expensive. Two useful routes are the A11, serving Central, Admiralty, Wan Chai, and Causeway Bay; and the A21, going to Tsim Sha Tsui, Jordan, and Mong Kok. There's plenty of space and onboard announcements in English, so you won't miss your stop. Several small shuttle buses with an "S" before their number run to nearby Tung Chung MTR station, where you can get the MTR to Central and Kowloon. The trains follow the airport express route, but are a little slower and ¼ of the cost.

Taxis from the airport are reliable and plentiful and cost around HK$340 for Hong Kong Island destinations and HK$270 for Kowloon destinations, plus HK$5 per piece of luggage. Two limo services in the arrivals hall, Parklane and Intercontinental, will run you into town in style. Depending on the zone and the type of car, limo rides from the airport range from HK$500 to HK$600.

🛪 **Airport Express** ☎ 2881-8888 for MTR hotline ⊕ www.mtr.com.hk. **Citybus** ☎ 2873-0818 ⊕ www.citybus.com.hk. **Intercontinental Hire Car** ☎ 2261-2155 ⊕ www.trans-island.com.hk. **Parklane Limousine Service** ☎ 2261-0303 ⊕ www.hongkonglimo.com.

BY BOAT & FERRY

The landmark double-bowed, green-and-white Star Ferry vessels connect Central and Wan Chai with Kowloon in seven minutes daily from

6:30 AM to 11:30 PM; the ride costs HK$2.20 on the upper deck, making it the cheapest scenic tour in town.

New World First Ferry (NWFF) Services Ltd. runs nine routes from Central to the outlying islands of Lantau and Cheung Chau. Discovery Bay Transportation Service has high-speed boats (they even have Wi-Fi) leaving for Lantau every 10–30 minutes from Pier 3. Trips take 25–30 minutes and cost HK$27.

Pick up printed schedules at the Hong Kong Tourist Board (HKTB) info centers at the Tsim Sha Tsui Star Ferry Concourse and in Causeway Bay MTR station; as well as through the HKTB Visitor Hot Line. Or, you can simply pick one up at the ferry ticket counters. For information about ferry service to Macau, *see* Macau Essentials.

🚢 **Discovery Bay Transportation Service** ☎ 2987-7351 ⊕ www.hkri.com.hk. **HKTB Visitor Hot Line** ☎ 2508-1234. **New World First Ferry** ☎ 2131-8181 ⊕ www.nwff.com.hk. **Star Ferry** ☎ 2367-7065 ⊕ www.starferry.com.hk.

BY BUS

An efficient network of double-decker buses covers most of Hong Kong. Using them is a tricky business, though, as drivers don't usually speak English, and the route maps on bus shelters and company Web sites are so complex as to be off-putting. To compound this, there are several companies and no central Web site or pocket bus maps.

When determining bus direction, buses ending with the letter "L" will eventually connect to the Kowloon–Canton Railway; buses ending with the letter "M" connect to an MTR station; "As" go to the airport; and buses ending with the letter "X" are express.

Rattling along Hong Kong's roads at breakneck speed are numerous minibuses, which seat 16 people. They're cream with green or red roofs and display their route number and a fixed price prominently. They stop at designated spots, and you pay as you board. If you want to get off, shout *"Bah-see jam yau lok"* ("Next stop, please") to the driver and hold on tight as he screeches to a halt. Though slightly more expensive than buses, minibuses are quicker and more comfortable.

FARES Double-decker bus fares range from HK$1.20 to HK$45; minibus fares from HK$2 to HK$20. For both you must pay exact change upon entering the bus. You can also use an Octopus card on both.

🚌 **Bus Information Citybus** ☎ 2873-0818 ⊕ www.citybus.com.hk; Hong Kong Island, cross-harbor and airport routes. **Kowloon Motor Bus** (KMB) ☎ 2745-4466 ⊕ www.kmb.com.hk; mainly serves Kowloon and New Territories. **Long Win Bus Company** ☎ 2261-2791 ⊕ www.kmb.com.hk; serves north Lantau, including Tung Chung. **New World First Bus** ☎ 2136-8888 ⊕ www.nwfb.com.hk; runs services on Hong Kong Island and in New Kowloon. **Octopus Cards** ☎ 2266-2222 ⊕ www.octopuscards.com.

BY CAR

The best advice we can give is don't drive in Hong Kong. Gasoline costs up to twice what it does in the United States, and parking is scarce *and* prohibitively expensive. What's more, local bus and truck drivers seem to think slamming on their breaks (and sending their passengers flying forward) is the only way to stop.

🚗 Local Agency **Hawk Rent-a-Car** ☎ 2516-9822 ⊕ www.hawkrentacar.com.hk
🚗 Major Agencies **Alamo** ☎ 800/522-9696 ⊕ www.alamo.com. **Avis**
☎ 800/331-1084 ⊕ www.avis.com. **Budget** ☎ 800/472-3325 ⊕ www.
budget.com. **Hertz** ☎ 800/654-3001 ⊕ www.hertz.com. **National Car
Rental** ☎ 800/227-7368 ⊕ www.nationalcar.com.
🚗 Road Rules **Hong Kong Government Transport Department Road Safety Code**
⊕ http://www.td.gov.hk/road_safety/index.htm.

BY SUBWAY

By far the best way to get around is on the Mass Transit Railway or
MTR. There are five main lines: the Island Line runs along the north
coast of Hong Kong Island; the Tsuen Wan Line goes from Central under
the harbor to Tsim Sha Tsui then up to the western New Territories. Tsim
Sha Tsui links to eastern New Kowloon via the Kwun Tong Line; also
serving this area is the Tseung Kwan O Line, which crosses back over
the harbor at Quarry Bay. Finally, the Tung Chung Line connects Central and west Kowloon with Tung Chung on Lantau, near the airport.

The MTR's highly modern trains are fast, clean, and very safe, as are
the stations. Platforms and exits are clearly signposted, and all MTR
areas are air-conditioned. Most stations have wheelchair access, and all
have convenience stores and services. Trains run every 2–5 minutes between 6 AM and 1 AM daily. Station entrances are marked with a simple line symbol resembling a man with arms and legs outstretched.

FARES &
SCHEDULES
You buy tickets from ticket machines (using coins or notes) or from English-speaking workers at the counters by the turnstile entrances. Fares
are not zoned, but depend on which stations you're traveling between.
There are no monthly or weekly tickets. If you're going to do more than
one or two trips on the MTR (or any other form of transport), get yourself a rechargeable Octopus card. It saves you time lining up for tickets, and you get a discount on your fares, too.

Fares range from HK$4 to HK$26. The special Tourist MTR One-Day
Pass (HK$50) allows you unlimited rides in a day. The three-day Air-
port Express Tourist Octopus (HK$220–HK$300) includes single journeys from–to the airport, unlimited MTR travel, and HK$20 worth of
trips on other transport.
🚇 **HKTB Visitor Hot Line** ☎ 2508-1234. **MTR** ☎ 2881-8888 ⊕ www.mtr.com.hk. **Octopus Cards** ☎ 2266-2222 ⊕ www.octopuscards.com.

BY TAXI

During the day, heavy traffic means that taxis around Central and Tsim
Sha Tsui aren't the way to go. Outside these areas, or after dark, they're
much more useful. Drivers usually know the terrain well, but as many
don't speak English, having your destination written in Chinese is a good
idea. You can hail cabs on the street, provided it's a stopping area (i.e.,
not on double yellow lines). Note that it's sometimes hard to find a taxi
around 4 PM when the drivers switch shifts.

Fares for the red taxis operating in urban areas start at HK$15 for the
first 2 km (1½ mi), then HK$1.40 for each ⅕ km (⅒ mi) or minute of

waiting time (so fares add up fast in traffic). There's a surcharge of HK$5 for each piece of luggage you put in the trunk, and surcharges of HK$20 for the Cross-Harbour Tunnel, HK$40 for the Eastern Harbour Tunnel, and HK$50 for the Western Harbour Tunnel. The Tsing Ma Bridge surcharge is HK$30. The Aberdeen, Lion Rock, and Junk Bay tunnels also carry surcharges (HK$5 to HK$10).

In the New Territories taxis are green; on Lantau they're blue. Fares are slightly lower than in urban areas, but although urban taxis may travel into rural zones, rural taxis can't cross into urban zones.

Backseat passengers must wear a seat belt or face a HK$5,000 fine. Most locals don't tip; however, if you do by rounding off the fare by a few Hong Kong dollars—you're sure to earn yourself a winning smile from your underpaid and overworked driver. Taxis are usually reliable, but if you have a problem, note the taxi's license number, which is usually on the dashboard, and call the Transport Complaints Unit.

In urban areas, it's as easy and safe to hail a cab on the street as to call one. There are hundreds of companies and no central booking number, so it's best to get your hotel or restaurant to call a company they work with. Note that there's a HK$5 surcharge for phone bookings.

🚹 Complaints **Transport Complaints Unit** ☎ 2889-9999.

BY TRAIN

The ultraefficient Kowloon–Canton Railway (KCR) connects Kowloon to the eastern and western New Territories. Trains run every 5–8 minutes, and connections to the MTR are usually quick. It's a commuter service and, like the MTR, has sparkling clean trains and stations—smoking and eating are forbidden in both. At this writing the KCR has three main lines, but there are all kinds of ambitious projects underway to extend its service network. Fares range from HK$4.50 to HK$36.50; you can pay by Octopus card or buy tickets from sales counters or ticket machines.

🚹 Train Information **Kowloon-Canton Railway Corporation** ☎ 2939-3399 ⊕ www. kcrc.com. **HKTB Visitor Hotline** ☎ 2508-1234. **Octopus Cards** ☎ 2266-2222 ⊕ www. octopuscards.com.

BY TRAM

Hong Kong Tramways runs old-fashioned double-decker trams along the north shore of Hong Kong Island. Routes start in Kennedy Town (in the west), and go through Central, Wan Chai, Causeway Bay, North Point, and Quarry Bay to Shau Kei Wan. A branch line turns off in Wan Chai toward Happy Valley. Destinations are marked on the front of each tram; you board at the back and get off at the front, paying HK$2 (by Octopus or with exact change) as you leave. Avoid trams at rush hours, which are generally weekdays from 7:30 to 9 AM and 5 to 7 PM. Although trams move slowly, for short hops between Central and Western or Admiralty they can be quicker than the MTR. A leisurely top-deck ride from Western to Causeway Bay is a great city tour.

🚹 Tram Information **Hong Kong Tramways** ☎ 2548-7102 ⊕ www.hktramways.com. **Octopus Cards** ☎ 2266-2222 ⊕ www.octopuscards.com.

Contacts & Resources

BANKS & CURRENCY EXCHANGE

Cash and plastic are the way to go in Hong Kong. Banks and some hotels accept traveler's checks, but local restaurateurs and shop assistants won't be interested. Major credit cards are widely accepted though they may not be accepted at small shops, and in some shops you get better rates paying in cash. When adding tips to restaurant bills, be sure to write "HK$" and not just "$."

Reliable, safe ATMs are widely available throughout Hong Kong—some may carry the sign ETC instead of ATM. MTR stations are a good place to look if you're having trouble locating one. If your card was issued from a bank in an English-speaking country, the instructions on the ATM machine will appear in English. You can withdraw cash in multiples of HK$100.

The Hong Kong dollar is divided into 100 cents. There are bronze-color coins for 10, 20, and 50 cents; silver-color ones for 1, 2, and 5 dollars; and chunky bimetallic 10-dollar pieces. There's also a green 10-dollar bill, as well as bills for HK$20 (blue-green), HK$50 (purple), HK$100 (red), HK$500 (brown), and HK$1,000 (yellow). Don't be surprised if two bills of the same value look different: three local banks (HSBC, Standard Chartered, and Bank of China) all issue bills and each has its own design. Although the image of Queen Elizabeth II doesn't appear on new coins, old ones bearing her image are still valid.

At this writing, there were approximately 7.8 Hong Kong dollars to 1 U.S. dollar. There are no currency restrictions in Hong Kong. You can exchange currency at the airport, in hotels, in banks, and through private money changers scattered through the tourist areas. Banks usually have the best rates, but as they charge a flat HK$50 fee for nonaccount holders, it's better to change large sums infrequently. Currency exchange offices have no fees, but they offset that with poor rates. Stick to ATMs wherever you can.

BUSINESS & TRADE SERVICES

BUSINESS CENTERS Hong Kong has many business centers outside hotels, and some are considerably cheaper than hotel facilities. Others cost about the same but offer private desks (from HK$250 per hour for desk space to upward of HK$8,000 a month for an office). Amenities include a private address and phone-answering and forwarding services. Many centers are affiliated with accountants and lawyers who can expedite company registration. Some will even process visas and wrap gifts for you.

The American Chamber of Commerce can arrange a Breakfast Briefing Program at your hotel for a fee based on group size. The chamber hosts luncheons and seminars, and its Young Professionals Committee holds cocktail parties at least once a month. Facilities include a library and China trade services.

American Chamber of Commerce ✉ Bank of America Tower, 12 Harcourt Rd., Room 1904, Central ☎ 2526-0165 ⊕ www.amcham.org.hk. **The Executive Centre**

☎ 2297-0222 ⊕ www. executivecentre.com. **Harbour International Business Centre**
☎ 2529-0356 ⊕ www.hibc.com. **Regus** ☎ 2166-8000 ⊕ www.regus.hk.

CONVENTION
CENTER

The Hong Kong Convention & Exhibition Centre is a state-of-the-art, 693,000-square-foot complex on the Wan Chai waterfront, capable of handling 140,000 visitors a day. There are five exhibition halls and two main convention halls. One of Asia's largest complexes, the center houses two hotels, the 570-room Grand Hyatt and the 860-room Renaissance Harbour View; an apartment block; and a 54-story trade center.

🚩 **Hong Kong Convention & Exhibition Centre** ✉ 1 Expo Dr., Wan Chai ☎ 2582-8888 ⊕ www.hkcec.com.hk.

TRADE
INFORMATION

🚩 **Hong Kong General Chamber of Commerce** ☎ 2529-9229 ⊕ www.chamber.org. hk. **Hong Kong Trade Development Council** ☎ 2584-4333 ⊕ www.tdctrade.com. **Hong Kong Trade & Industry Department** ☎ 2392-2922 ⊕ www.tid.gov.hk. **Innovation & Technology Commission** ☎ 2737-2573 ⊕ www.itc.gov.hk.

COMMUNICATIONS

INTERNET

Hong Kong is an Internet-friendly place for those bearing laptops. All mid- to high-end hotels have in-room Internet access; Wi-Fi is common both in hotels and in public places, including many cafés, bars, and restaurants. All business centers have high-speed access. Laptops and Blackberries are so ubiquitous in Hong Kong that things get tough if you haven't got one. Internet cafés are practically nonexistent; the only place to check e-mail on the go is at one of the many branches of the Pacific Coffee Company—you can log on to one of their free terminals if you buy a coffee (HK$20–HK$30).

🚩 **Pacific Coffee Company** ⊕ www.pacificcoffee.com.

PHONES

Hong Kong was the first city in the world with a fully digitized local phone network, and the service is efficient and cheap. Even international calls are inexpensive relative to those in the United States. You can expect clear connections and helpful directory assistance. Don't hang up if you hear Cantonese when calling automated and prerecorded hotlines; English is usually the second or third language option. The country code for Hong Kong is 852; there are no local area codes. Hong Kong phone numbers have eight digits: landline numbers usually start with a 2 (mobiles with a 9).

If you're old enough to talk in Hong Kong, you're old enough for a cell phone, which means public phones are dwindling. MTR stations still always have one or two: local calls to both land and cell lines cost HK$1 per 5 minutes. If you're planning to call abroad from a pay phone, buy a phone card. Convenience stores like 7-Eleven sell stored-value Hello cards (only for use at pay phones) and SmartCards (a PIN-activated card you can use from any phone). Some pay phones accept credit cards.

Restaurants and shopkeepers will usually let you use their phone for free, as the phone company doesn't charge for individual local calls. Many small stores keep their phone on the counter facing the street. Hotels may charge as much as HK$5 for a local call, though.

Dial 1081 for directory assistance from English-speaking operators. If a number is constantly busy and you think it might be out of order, call 109 and the operator will check the line. The operators are very helpful, if you talk slowly and clearly.

International rates from Hong Kong are reasonable, even more so between 9 PM and 8 AM. The international dial code is 001, then the country code. The country code is 1 for the United States. So to call the United States you dial 0011. Dial 10013 for international inquiries and for assistance with direct dialing. Dial 10010 for collect and operator-assisted calls to most countries, including the United States. Dial 10011 for credit-card, collect, and international conference calls.

MOBILE PHONES Most GSM-compatible mobile handsets work in Hong Kong. If you can unlock your phone, buying a SIM card locally is the cheapest and easiest way to make calls. Local phone company PCCW sells them for around HK$200 from their "i-shops" all over town. Local calls cost around HK$0.50 a minute. Otherwise, you can rent handsets from CSL (HK$35 a day) with prepaid SIM cards (HK$48–HK$180). There's a stand at the airport and shops all over town. If you're only in town for a day or two, this is a good-value option.

🚩 **CSL** ☎ 2512-3123 on Hong Kong Island, 2393-5597 in Kowloon ⊕ www.one2free. com. **PCCW** ☎ 2888-8888 ⊕ www.pccw.com.

EMERGENCIES

Hong Kong is an incredibly safe place—day and night. The police do a good job maintaining law and order, but there are still a few pickpockets about, especially in Tsim Sha Tsui. So exercise the same caution you would in any large city: be aware and avoid carrying large amounts of cash or valuables with you, and you should have no problems.

Locals and police are helpful in emergencies. Most officers speak some English or will contact someone who does. For police, fire, and ambulance emergencies, dial 999. The Queen Mary hospital has a 24-hour pharmacy; otherwise local chain Watson's has a pharmacy department at their numerous shops; they're usually open until 9 PM.

🚩 Consulate **U.S. Consulate General** ✉ 26 Garden Rd., Central ☎ 2523-9011 ⊕ www. usconsulate.org.hk.

🚩 General Emergency Contacts **Police, fire & ambulance** ☎ 999. **Hong Kong Police & Taxi Complaint Hotline** ☎ 2527-7177.

🚩 Hospitals & Clinics **Hong Kong Central Hospital** ✉ (private) 1 Lower Albert Rd., Central ☎ 2522-3141 ⊕ www.hkch.org. **Hong Kong Baptist Hospital** ✉ (private) 223 Waterloo Rd., Kowloon ☎ 2229-8888 ⊕ www.hkbh.org.hk. **Queen Mary Hospital** ✉ (public) 102 Pok Fu Lam Rd., Pok Fu Lam, Western ☎ 2855-3838 ⊕ www.ha.org. hk/qmh.

🚩 Pharmacies **Watson's** ☎ 2868-4388.

MAIL

Hong Kong's postal system has an excellent reputation. Airmail letters to any place in the world should take three to eight days. The Kowloon Central Post Office and the General Post Office in Central are open 8 AM to 6 PM Monday through Saturday.

Letters sent from Hong Kong are thought of as going to one of two zones. Zone 1 includes China, Japan, Taiwan, South Korea, Southeast Asia, Indonesia, and Asia. Zone 2 is everywhere else. International airmail costs HK$2.40 or HK$3 for a letter or postcard weighing less than 20 grams mailed to a Zone 1 or 2 address, respectively. To send a letter within Hong Kong, the cost is HK$1.40. Packages sent airmail to the United States often take two weeks. The post office also has an overnight express service called Speedpost.

🛈 Express Services **DHL** ☎ 2400-3388 ⊕ www.dhl.com.hk. **Federal Express** ☎ 2730-3333 ⊕ www.fedex.com/hk_english. **UPS** ☎ 2735-3535 ⊕ www.ups.com.

🛈 Main Postal Branches **General Post Office** ✉ 2 Connaught Rd., Central ☎ 2921-2222 ⊕ www.hongkongpost.com. **Kowloon Central Post Office** ✉ 10 Middle Rd., Tsim Tsa Shui.

5

Pearl River Delta

GUANGZHOU & SHENZEN

Pizhou Exhibition Hall in Guangzhou, Guangdong province.

WORD OF MOUTH

"My favorite 'local' activities are good inexpensive foot massages and adventurous eating."

—CJbryant

PEARL RIVER DELTA: GUANGZHOU & SHENZEN

TOP REASONS TO GO

★ **Feel the Buzz!** This region is the undisputed engine driving China's current economic boom, and whether you're in Guangzhou or Shenzhen, you're sure to feel the buzz of this formerly Socialist nation on a serious capitalist joyride.

★ **Explore the Ancient.** Though thoroughly modern, the Pearl River Delta has by no means lost touch with its ancient roots. From the temples of Guangzhou to the Ming Dynasty–walled city of Dapeng in Shenzhen, a journey through the PRD is a journey through the centuries.

★ **Soak Up Some Colonial Splendor.** Guangzhou is rife with well-preserved examples of architecture dating back to the 19th century, when European merchants amassed fortunes in the opium trade, and the buildings from which they once plied their trade still stand.

★ **Shopping! Shopping! Shopping!** Need We Say More?

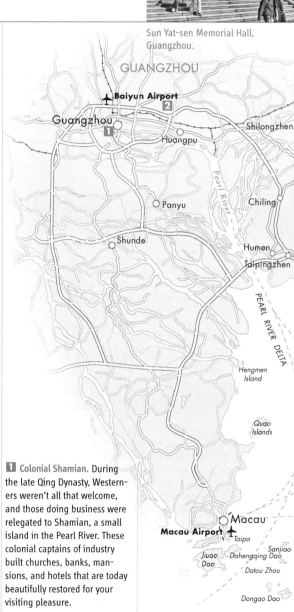

Sun Yat-sen Memorial Hall, Guangzhou.

GUANGZHOU

Baiyun Airport ✈ **2**

Guangzhou **1**

Shilongzhen

Huangpu

Pearl River

Panyu

Chiling

Shunde

Humen
Taipingzhen

PEARL RIVER DELTA

Hengmen Island

Quao Islands

Macau

Macau Airport ✈ Taipa

Jiuao Dao   Dahengqing Dao   Sanjiao

Datou Zhou

Dongao Dao

1 Colonial Shamian. During the late Qing Dynasty, Westerners weren't all that welcome, and those doing business were relegated to Shamian, a small island in the Pearl River. These colonial captains of industry built churches, banks, mansions, and hotels that are today beautifully restored for your visiting pleasure.

2 White Cloud Mountain. Take a trip away from the madding crowd at White Cloud Mountain. Climb to the top of Santailing Park, listen to the birds in Bird Spring Valley Park, and check out Jinye Pond, whose waters are said to be so clear that it acts as a mirror, clearly reflecting the surrounding mountains.

3 Overseas Chinese Town. Culture's the name of the game in Shenzhen's Overseas Chinese Town (OCT District) area, and scattered around the neighborhood are an array of sculptures commissioned by the city fathers to "class up the joint." If you don't like your art alfresco, check out the rotating exhibits at the He Xiangning Art Museum.

4 Mission Hills. The Chinese have gone mad for golfing and nowhere else in the country is the passion for golf as well-catered to as in the Pearl River Delta. If you've come to the middle kingdom to hit the links, the world-class Mission Hills Golf Club will blow your mind.

GETTING ORIENTED

The Pearl River Delta is a massive triangle. Guangzhou is at the top, Shenzhen on the east corner, and Zhuhai on the west. The area as a whole is just a bit too spread out for any one corner to make a good base of operations from which to explore the others, so we recommend beginning at one corner and making your way around. Guangzhou is fairly dense, so leave yourself three days in which to soak it all in before heading down to Shenzhen. From Shenzhen's Shekou Harbor it's a one-hour ferry ride to Zhuhai, which takes less than a day to explore before returning either back to Guangzhou or into nearby Macau or Hong Kong.

6

Dongguan

KCR Rail Link

Shenzhen Airport ✈

Baoan

Shekou

ZHONGSHAN

Dongjiaozui

0 ——— 10 mi

4

0 ——— 10 km

3 Shenzhen

HONG KONG

Tsing Yi

Chek Lap Kok
Hong Kong Airport ✈

Hong Kong

Kowloon

Lantau Island

Victoria

Lamma Island

Putai Islands

Wailingding Dao

Sanmen
Liedao

Dangan Dao

Chu Chou

Citic Plaza.

PEARL RIVER DELTA PLANNER

Whither the Weather?

When to go is a major question every traveler needs to ask themselves, and certainly in a place like the Pearl River Delta, where summer temperatures and humidity can make the area feel like the inside of a clothes dryer halfway through the dry cycle and winter brings an all-pervading chill and dampness that sucks the joy from any endeavor no matter how well planned.

The answer, naturally, is spring and autumn, but this is complicated by a few factors. Unless you have friends in the hotel industry, don't even think about visiting Guangzhou during the annual spring trade fair, when prices of hotels skyrocket.

Don't travel anywhere in China during the Golden Week holiday, which takes place annually from October 1 through 7. So what do we recommend? September, October (excluding Golden Week), and early to mid-November.

A Little Medicinal Shopping?

Guangzhou's Qingping Market has undergone a radical rebirth over the past few years. Once notorious as a filthy wet market from which weak-stomached travelers were advised to steer clear, this sprawling maze of shops and stalls has been transformed into a traditional Chinese–medicine market. On the grounds where caged cats, chickens, and turtles once awaited doom, a new mall has risen, one with wide aisles and escalators, and 100 or so stalls of varying sizes filled with merchants dealing in everything from acupuncture needles to zebra testicles.

Whether you chose to shop in the new mall or in the surrounding alleyways (still filled with shops of a less gentrified nature, offering both Chinese medicine and livestock), you're in for a serious *only in China* experience. How much are a pair of dried lizards on sticks really worth? How many ounces of dried sea horse are needed to make broth for a family of four? And how will you explain that sack full of dried geckos to the customs officer at home?

Cabaret, Chinese-style

If you only go to one multimedia cabaret dinner–theater in Guangzhou, it has to be *The Magic Phantom* at Guangzhou's Mo Li Fang Theater. We mean this both as a recommendation and a literal statement, as this original, quirky, and very well-executed production is the only example of multimedia cabaret dinner–theater we've yet to come across in Guangzhou (or anywhere else in China).

The performance is in Chinese, but the combination of elements from traditional Beijing Opera, Hong Kong Cinema, puppetry, karaoke, acrobatics, dancing, and computer animation makes it a feast for the senses regardless of linguistic skill. And then there's the meal fit for a king, featuring eight separate courses served in crystal dishes. As the audience eats each dish, their ingredients, health benefits, and historical significance are explained by a Beijing-trained opera singer (who happens to speak a little English as well). Tickets can be booked at the front desk of better hotels, and performances are held nightly, with matinees on Saturday and Sunday.

Getting Around

Guangzhou is a chaotic city, famed for noise, crowds, and endless traffic jams—many a vacation hour has been wasted inside of taxicabs. Although taxis in Guangzhou are cheap and plentiful, traffic in the city is reaching nightmare proportions.

Many casual visitors are reluctant to take the Guangzhou metro, perhaps feeling that without the proper linguistic skills such a journey might be fraught with confusion. We think that this is a shame. The Guangzhou metro is quick, convenient, and a boon to day-trippers.

For walking-tour-friendly neighborhoods, we recommend Dongshankou station. This is a lovely little area with plenty of shopping opportunities. Tree-lined streets just off the avenue are filled with enclosed gardens and old houses with traditional architecture. The area surrounding the Linhex station is the most modern part of the city. This is a good neighborhood to walk around with your head tilted skyward.

Of course, if you really want to continue on an anti-car trip, get off at Gongyuanqian station (where Lines 1 and 2 intersect) and walk to the Beijing Road Pedestrian Mall: the hip, trendy, and carfree heart of young consumerism in Guangzhou.

WHAT IT COSTS In Yuan

RESTAURANTS				
$$$$	$$$	$$	$	¢
over 165	100–165	50–99	25–49	under 25
HOTELS				
$$$$	$$$	$$	$	¢
over 1,800	1,400–1,800	1,100–1,399	700–1,099	under 700

Restaurant prices are for a main course, excluding tax and tips. Hotel prices are for a standard double room, including taxes.

Ancient Days

Don't let the *Blade Runner*–like skyline fool you. China's newest city isn't all glass and steel. Areas outside the city are resplendent with examples of ancient Chinese culture.

Like the rapidly disappearing hutong neighborhoods of Beijing, **Dapeng Fortress**–an ancient city– is a living museum. The old town contains homes, temples, shops, and courtyards that look pretty much the way they did when they were built over the course of the Ming (AD 1368–1644) and Qing (1644–1911) dynasties. For the most part, the residences are occupied, the shops are doing business, and the temples are active houses of worship. Dapeng's ancient city is surrounded by an old stone wall, and entered through a series of gates built at the cardinal points.

Likewise, the **Hakka Folk Customs Museum and Enclosures** are an amazingly well-preserved example of a walled community. Now more a museum than anything else–persecution of Hakkas went out of vogue after the collapse of the Qing Dynasty, led by Sun Yat-sen, himself a member of the clan–the enclosures still stand as an excellent example of an ancient community built with defense in mind. The Hakkas built their homes inside of an exterior wall, complete with vertical-arrow slits for discouraging unwanted visitors. Many of the homes inside the fort are still furnished, and visitors may get the feeling that the original inhabitants have just popped out for a bit of hunting and might come back any minute, crossbows cocked.

6

By Joshua
Samuel Brown

THE PEARL RIVER DELTA is China's workshop, its fastest-growing, ever-changing, and most affluent region. It is the industrial engine powering China's meteoric economic rise—and it shows. Earth-at-night satellite photos give a telling view of Asia. Tokyo, Seoul, and Taiwan glow brightly, but it's the boomtown cities along the Pearl River Delta that burn brightest. You will find some of the greatest shopping, a flourishing nightlife, and a culinary scene, which less-prosperous regions can only dream of.

The Pear River Delta is also among China's most polluted regions, and this is saying a lot. From the southern suburbs of Guangzhou city to the northern edge of Shenzhen, industry stretches in all directions. As far as the eye can see, tens of thousands of factories churn out the lion's share of the world's consumer products. This hyper-industry has polluted the entire area's soil, water, and air so badly that in Hong Kong (on the region's southern tip) pollution is an overriding public concern. On a bad day, the air quality in Guangzhou can actually be described as *abusive*. On top of all of this, much of the region is noisy and chaotic.

So with all this in mind, why would the pleasure traveler even visit Pearl River Delta? The answers are myriad. History enthusiasts head to Guangzhou, Guangdong province's ancient capital, and the historic center of both Cantonese culture and the revolution that overthrew the last dynasty. Gourmands flock to both Guangzhou and Shenzhen to indulge in some of the best examples of Chinese cuisine—and increasingly, the world—at all price ranges. Culture vultures don't mind putting up with the pollution and chaos for a chance to visit the many temples, shrines, and museums scattered throughout the region. And shop-a-holics? A visit to the Pearl River Delta will quickly dismiss any lingering notions that China is still a nation bound by the tenets of Marx and Mao.

GUANGZHOU

❶ Guangzhou (also known as Canton), the capital of Guangdong province, is both a modern boomtown and an ancient port city. This metropolis of over 7 million people has all the expected accoutrements of a competitive, modern Chinese city: Skyscrapers, heavy traffic, efficient metro, and serious crowds. Guangzhou is an old city with a long history. Exploring its riverfront, parks, temples, and markets, one is constantly reminded the impact its irrepressible culture, language, and cuisine has made on the world.

The city has long been considered China's gateway to the West, and the Cantonese have a reputation for being China's most savvy entertainers. From the late 18th century, Western merchants set up trading houses in Guangzhou where they negotiated the purchase of tea.

In the early 20th century, Guangzhou was a hotbed of revolutionary zeal, first as the birthplace of the movement to overthrow the last dynasty (culminating in the 1911 Revolution), and then as a battleground between Nationalists and Communists in the years leading to the 1949 Communist revolution. Following the open-door policy of Deng Xiaop-

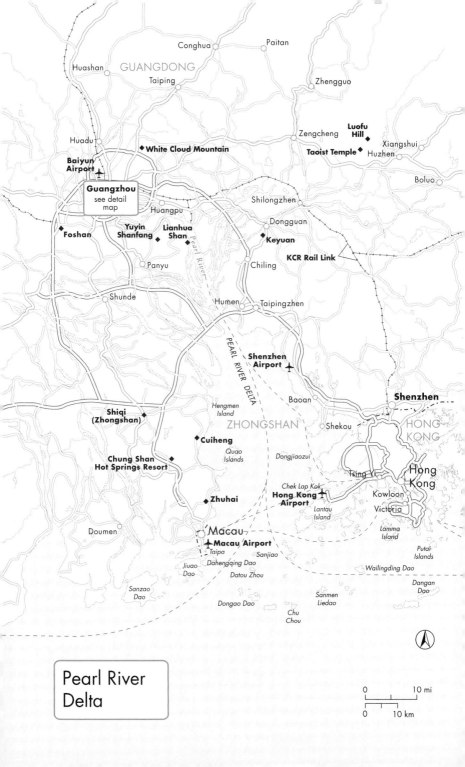

Pearl River Delta

ing in 1979, the port city was able to resume its role as a commercial gateway to China.

Rapid modernization during the 1980s and '90s has taken its toll not just on the environment but also on the pace of city life. On bad days the clouds of building-site dust, aggressive driving, shop touts, and persistent beggars can be overwhelming. But in Guangzhou's parks, temples, winding old-quarter backstreets, restaurants, river islets, and museums, the old city and a more refined way of life is never far away.

Exploring

Guangzhou is a massive, sprawling metropolis divided into several districts and many more neighborhoods. Roughly speaking, the city is divided in half by the Pearl River, which runs from east to west and separates the Haizhu District (a large island) from the districts in the north. Most of the explorations we're recommending will keep you north of the Pearl River, since this is where the majority of the more culturally edifying parts of Guangzhou lie.

Cultural Attractions

❷ The Qingping Market has undergone a few changes over the past few years; the sprawling cluster of stalls was once infamous for its wet market, a hotbed of animal slaughter. Though it always had a good selection of general knickknacks, as well as a large section of goods of various apothicarial value (ginseng, fungi, and herbs, as well as more cruelly obtained items like bear bile and essence of tiger prostate), the wet market scared all but the heartiest visitors away. Following SARS, the government decided to do away with the bloodier, less hygienic stalls. A large section of the old market was been cleared away to make room for a shiny new mall-like structure with stalls dedicated to sales of traditional medicines. The funkier and older outdoor section of the market still exists off to one side, but for the most part items on sale are of the flora and not the fauna variety. Merchants of tiger claws and bear bile are still engaged in their cruel trade on the base of the bridge leading to Shamian Island. Even though most of these merchants are dressed Tibetan style (perhaps to engender the sympathy of foreigners?) the majority of them are Han Chinese engaged in a despicable trade.

❶ Shamian Island. More than a century ago the mandarins of Guangzhou designated a 44-acre sandbank outside the city walls in the Pearl River as an enclave for foreign merchants. The foreigners had previously lived and done business in a row of houses known as the Thirteen Factories, near the present Shamian, but local resentment after the Opium Wars—sometimes leading to murderous attacks—made it prudent to confine them to a protected area, which was linked to the city by two bridges that were closed at 10 every night.

The island soon became a bustling township, as trading companies from

CAUTION	

Like any other urban area, Guangzhou has its fair share of pickpockets, so keep your wallet in a front pocket and your bags in front of you.

Britain, the United States, France, Holland, Italy, Germany, Portugal, and Japan built stone mansions along the waterfront. With spacious gardens and private wharves, these served as homes, offices, and warehouses. There were churches for Catholics and Protestants, banks, a yacht club, football grounds, a cricket field, and the Victory hotel.

Shamian was attacked in the 1920s but survived until the 1949 Revolution when its mansions became government offices or apartment houses and the churches were turned into factories. In recent years, however, the island has resumed much of its old character. Many colonial buildings have been restored, and both

> **WORD OF MOUTH**
>
> "Shamian Island has a few interesting craft-type shops and colonial buildings."
>
> —cjbryant

churches have been beautifully renovated and reopened to worshippers. Worth visiting is **Our Lady of Lourdes Catholic Church** (⊠ Shamian Dajie at Yijie), with its cream-and-white neo-Gothic tower. A park with shady walks and benches has been created in the center of the island, where local residents come to chat with friends, walk around with their caged birds, or practice tai chi.

NEED A BREAK?

Have an espresso in Chinese colonial splendor at the **Shamian Island Blenz** (⊠ 46 Shamian Ave.), across from **Customs Hotel** in a building dating back to the late Qing Dynasty. Comfy couches, strong coffee, and free Internet access are available in this old building that once housed Guangzhou's U.S. Bank in the pre-revolutionary days. Right on the park, Blenz is a great place to watch people practice tai chi and traditional Chinese fan dancing.

⑦ Bright Filial Piety Temple (Guangxiao Si). This is the oldest Buddhist temple in Guangzhou and by far the most charming. The gilded wooden laughing Buddha sitting at the entrance adds to the temple's warm, welcoming atmosphere. A huge bronze incense burner, wreathed in joss-stick smoke, stands in the main courtyard. Beyond the main hall, noted for its ceiling of red-lacquer timbers, is another courtyard that contains several treasures, among them a small brick pagoda said to contain the tonsure hair of Hui-neng (the sixth patriarch of Chan Buddhism), and a couple of iron pagodas, which are the oldest of their kind in China. Above them spread the leafy branches of a myrobalan plum tree and a banyan, called Buddha's Tree because it is said Hui-neng became enlightened in its shade. ⊠ *Corner of Renmin Bei and Guangxiao Lu, 2 blocks north of metro station Ximenkou* Ⓜ *Ximenkou* 🚇 *Y5* ⊙ *Daily 6:30–5.*

❸ Chen Family Temple (Chen Jia Ci). The Chen family is one of the Pearl River Delta's oldest and biggest clans. In the late 19th century local members, who had become rich as merchants, decided to build a memorial temple. They invited contributions from the Chens—and kindred Chans—who had emigrated overseas. Money flowed in from 72 countries, and no expense was spared. One of the temple's highlights is a huge and skillfully carved ridgepole frieze. It stretches 90 feet along the main roof and depicts scenes from the epic *Romance of Three Kingdoms*, with

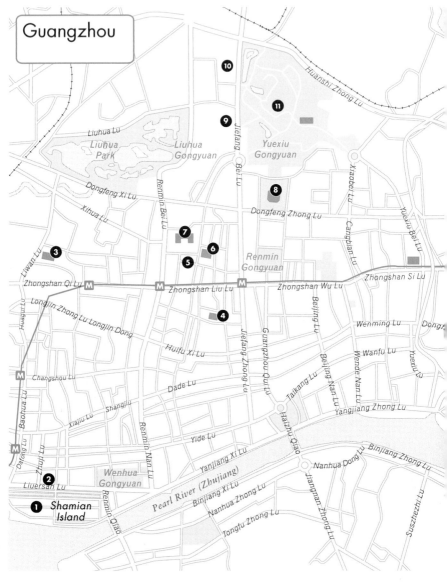

Guangzhou

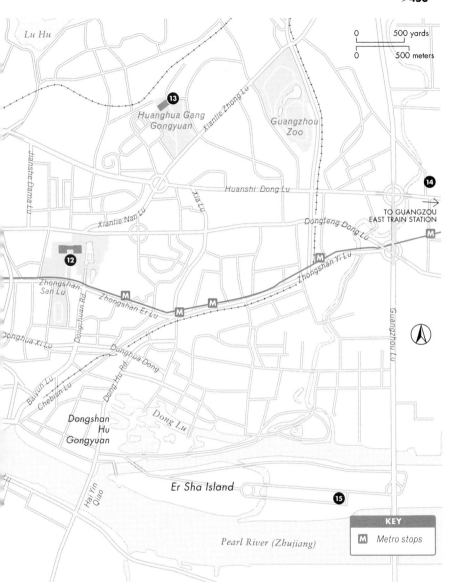

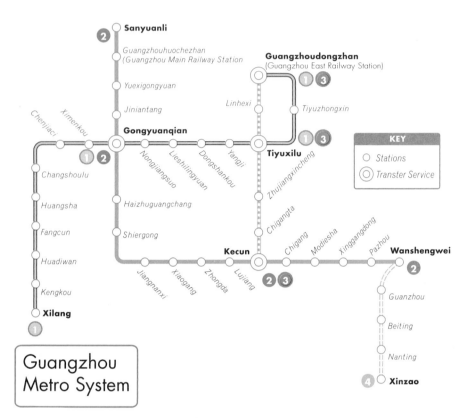

Guangzhou Metro System

thousands of figures against a backdrop of ornate houses, monumental gates, and lush scenery. Elsewhere in the huge compound of pavilions and courtyards are friezes of delicately carved stone and wood, as well as fine iron castings and a dazzling altar covered with gold leaf. The temple also houses a folk-arts museum and shop. ⊠ *7 Zhongshan Qi Lu* ☜ *Y5* ☉ *Daily 8:30–5* Ⓜ *Chengjia Ci metro station.*

❹ **Huaisheng Mosque** (Huaisheng Si Guang). In the cosmopolitan era of the Tang Dynasty (618–907) a Muslim missionary named Abu Wangus, said to be an uncle of the prophet Mohammed, came to southern China. He converted many Chinese to Islam and built this mosque in Guangzhou as their house of worship. His tomb in the northern part of the city has been a place of pilgrimage for visiting Muslims, but the mosque is his best-known memorial. A high wall encloses the mosque, which is dominated by the smooth, white minaret. Rising to 33 meters (108 feet), it can be climbed using an interior spiral staircase, and the views from the top—where a muezzin calls the faithful to prayer—are spectacular. ⊠ *Guangta Lu, 3 blocks southwest of the Gongyuanqian metro station* ☜*Free* ☉*Sat.–Thurs. 8–5, except Muslim holy days* Ⓜ *Gongyuanqian.*

❺ **Guangxiao Temple** (Guangxiao si). This impressively restored temple and city-gate complex, also known as the Five Celestials Shrine, was once the front gate for the wall that surrounded the city. The shrine and remaining sections of the wall in Yuexiu Park are the only pieces of old Guangzhou's fortifications still standing. The complex also has an impressive 3D model of how the city looked when the air was clean, the roads were filled with horse-drawn carts, and foreigners were confined on pain of death to one small section

of the city. ⊠ *Renmin Bei Lu, 3 blocks north of the Ximenkou metro* Ⓜ *Ximenkou* 🚇 *10* ⊗ *Daily 8–5.*

❻ **Six Banyan Temple** (Liu Rong Si Hua Ta). Look at any ancient scroll painting or lithograph by early Western travelers, and you'll see two landmarks rising above old Guangzhou. One is the minaret of the mosque; the other is the 56-meter (184-foot) pagoda of the Six Banyan Temple. Still providing an excellent lookout, the pagoda appears to have nine stories, each with doorways and encircling balconies. Inside, however, there are 17 levels. Thanks to its arrangement of colored, carved roofs, it is popularly known as the Flowery Pagoda.

The temple was founded in the 5th century, but because of a series of fires, most of the existing buildings date from the 11th century. It was built by the Zen master Tanyu and is still a very active place of worship, with a community of monks and regular attendance by Zen Buddhists. It was originally called Purificatory Wisdom Temple but changed its name after a visit by the Song Dynasty poet Su Dongpo, who was so delighted by six banyan trees growing in the courtyard that he left an inscription with the characters for six banyans. ⊠ *Haizhu Bei Lu, south of Yuexiu Park* 🚇 *Y10* ⊗ *Daily 8–5.*

Parks & Museums

⓯ **Guangdong Museum of Art** is a major cultural establishment of the "new Canton," and regularly hosts the works of painters, sculptors, and other artists from around China and the world. An excellent sculpture garden surrounds the large complex with exhibitions both large and small. Located on Ersha Island, the Web site offers a map to help you find your way—so print it out before you go. ⊠ *38 Yanyu Lu, Er Sha Island* ☎ *020/8735–1468* ⊕ *www.GDMoA.org* ⊗ *Tues.–Sun. 9–5.*

★ ⓾ **Orchid Garden** (Lanpu). This garden offers a wonderfully convenient retreat from the noise and crowds of the city. It's spread over 20 acres, with paths that wind through groves of bamboo and tropical trees to a series of classic teahouses. Here you can sit and enjoy a wide variety of Chinese teas, brewed the traditional way. There are tables inside and on terraces that overlook the ponds. As for the orchids, there are 10,000 pots with more than 2,000 species of the flower, which present a magical sight when they bloom (peak time is May and June). ⊠ *Jiefang Bei Lu* 🚇 *Y5* ⊗ *Daily 8:30 AM–11 PM.*

CLOSE UP

Underground in Guangzhou

LIVING UP TO ITS MOTTO "gets you there on time," Guangzhou's subway system is cheap, clean, and (unlike Beijing's) reasonably efficient. Divided into four lines that span both sides of the Pearl River, most of the areas of interest to casual visitors are found on lines 1 or 2 (the red and yellow lines on the maps).

The terminus of Line 1 is Guangzhoudongzhan, or Guangzhou East Train Station, which is where trains leave for Hong Kong. This area is also the heart of the Tienhe, Guangzhou's newest financial district. Gongyuanqian is the interchange for Lines 1 and 2. The most interesting temples and shrines are within walking distance of stations along Line 1, with signs in English pointing the way.

★ ➒ **Tomb of the Southern Yue Kings.** Until recently only specialist historians realized that Guangzhou had once been a royal capital. In 1983 bulldozers clearing ground to build the China Hotel uncovered the intact tomb of Emperor Wen Di, who ruled Nan Yue (southern China) from 137 BC to 122 BC. The tomb was faithfully restored and its treasures placed in the adjoining **Nan Yue Museum.**

The tomb contained the skeletons of the king and 15 courtiers—guards, cooks, concubines, and a musician—who were buried alive to attend him in death. Also buried were several thousand funerary objects, clearly designed to show off the extraordinary accomplishments of the southern empire. The tomb itself—built entirely of stone slabs—is behind the museum and is remarkable for its compact size. ⊠ 867 Jiefang Bei Lu, around the corner from the China Hotel ☎ Y15 ⊙ Daily 9:30–5:30.

★ ☾ ⓫ **Yuexiu Park** (Yuexiu Gongyuan). To get away from the bustle, retreat into Yuexiu Park in the heart of town. The park covers 247 rolling acres and includes landscaped gardens, man-made lakes, recreational areas, and playgrounds. Children and adults get a kick out of the fish-feeding ponds.

Be sure to visit the famous **Five Rams Statue** (Wuyang Suxiang), which celebrates the legend of the five celestials who came to Guangzhou riding on goats to bring grains to the people. Guangzhou families like to take each other's photo in front of the statue before setting off to enjoy the park. ⊠ Jiefang Bei Lu, across from China Hotel ☎ Y5 ⊙ Daily 6 AM–9 PM.

Revolutionary Memorials

In the center of the city are memorials to people who changed Chinese history in the 20th century,

> **WORD OF MOUTH**
>
> "There is a teahouse on a small island in the lake and they had the most extensive assortment of high-end Xixing teapots I've seen anywhere. They also had quite an assortment of teas."
> —Kathie

using Guangzhou as a base of operations. The most famous were local boy Dr. Sun Yat-sen, who led the overthrow of the Qing Dynasty, and Communist Party–founders Mao Zedong and Zhou Enlai. There were many others, thousands of whom died in the struggles. All are recalled in different ways.

⑬ Mausoleum of the 72 Martyrs (Huanghua Gang Qishi'er Lieshi Mu). In a prelude to the successful revolution of 1911 a group of 88 revolutionaries staged the Guangzhou armed uprising, only to be defeated and executed by the authorities. Of those killed, 72 were buried here. Their memorial, built in 1918, incorporates a mixture of international symbols of freedom and democracy, including replicas of the Statue of Liberty. ⊠ *Xianlie Zhong Lu* 🖂 *Y10* 🕙 *Daily 6 AM–8:30 PM.*

⑫ Memorial Garden for the Martyrs (Lieshi Lingyuan). Built in 1957, this garden has been planted around a tumulus that contains the remains of 5,000 revolutionaries killed in the 1927 destruction of the Guangzhou Commune by the Nationalists. This was the execution site of many victims. On the grounds is the **Revolutionary Museum,** which displays pictures and memorabilia of Guangdong's 20th-century rebellions. ⊠ *Zhongshan San Lu* 🖂 *Y5* 🕙 *Daily 6 AM–9 PM.*

⑧ Sun Yat-sen Memorial Hall (Zhongshan Jinian Tang.) Dr. Sun's Memorial Hall is a handsome pavilion that stands in a garden behind a bronze statue of the leader. Built in 1929–31 with funds mostly from overseas Chinese, the building is a classic octagon, with sweeping roofs of blue tiles over carved wooden eaves and verandas of red-lacquer columns. Inside is an auditorium with seating for 5,000 and a stage for plays, concerts, and ceremonial occasions. ⊠ *Dongfeng Zhong Lu* 🖂 *Y10* 🕙 *Daily 8–5:30.*

Tianhe-District Sights

The Tianhe District is Guangzhou's newly designated business and upmarket residential area. It is the site of the new Guangzhou East Railway Station, the terminus for Hong Kong trains, a world-class sports stadium, and a growing number of office/apartment skyscrapers. Among the buildings is the 80-story **GITIC Plaza** which soars 396 meters (1,300 feet) and is China's second-tallest building. The **Guangzhou East Railway Station** (⊠ Linhe Lu), with its vast entrance hall is worth a peak, even if you don't have a train to catch.

⑭ A hub for most of Guangzhou's sporting events, the **Tianhe Stadium Complex** (⊠ Huanshi Dong Lu, East Guangzhou) has two indoor and two outdoor arenas that are equipped for international soccer matches, track-and-field competitions, as well as pop concerts and large-scale ceremonies. The complex is surrounded by a pleasantly landscaped park, with outdoor cafés and tree-shaded benches. The park includes a bowling center with 38 lanes and lots of video games.

Tours

The aptly named China Travel Service (CTS) (*see* Visitor Information *in* Pearl River Delta Essentials, *below*) is still the most trusted name in arranging tours throughout China. Their Web site ⊕ www.ctshk.com/english/index.htm has links to their many offices worldwide; they have 40 offices in Hong Kong, Kowloon, and the New Territories and can arrange just about any type of travel experience that might interest you in Guangzhou or the Pearl River Delta. CTS can also assist with visas and booking discount hotel rooms.

Where to Eat

For centuries Guangzhou has been known as a city of gourmands, and in the last decade, it has undergone a gastronomic renaissance the likes of which few cities will ever know. At the heart of this is commerce, as business travelers bring the ingredients, spices, and culinary traditions from their homes with them. Popping up alongside venerable Cantonese restaurants are eateries specializing in flavors from around the world. Guangzhou has more excellent Indian, Italian, Thai, and Vietnamese restaurants than you can shake a joss stick at, and owing to the recent influx of Middle Eastern traders, there are some parts of town where it's easier to find a falafel than a shrimp dumpling. Of course this isn't to say that Guangzhou's traditional delicacies have been usurped. Amazing seafood dishes and braised and barbecued meats are still available in delicious variety, and succulent dim sum still rules the roost as the city's hometown favorite.

$$$$ ✕ **Chiu Chou City.** The Landmark Canton hotel's Chiu Chou City has the reputation as one of Canton's more well-known culinary experiences and is often fairly crowded with locals looking for good regional cuisine. The decor is old-school Chinese-restaurant style, with large round tables and cloth-covered chairs, but if you like, or want to explore, Chiu Chou regional dishes, such as goose cooked in its own blood and dipped in white vinegar and chopped-garlic sauce, or the ever popular *yin-yang* soup (green vegetable soup and white congee soup served together to form a yin-and-yang symbol), this place might be for you. ⊠ *Landmark Canton hotel, 8 Qiao Guang Lu, Colonial Canton* ☎ *020/8335–5988* ▭ *AE, DC, MC, V.*

$$$$ ✕ **Connoisseur.** This premier restaurant feels like regency France with its arched columns and gilded capitals, gold-framed mirrors, lustrous drapes, and immaculate table settings. The resident French chef specializes in lamb and steak dishes. ⊠ *Garden Hotel, 368 Huanshi Dong Lu, 3rd fl., Huanshi Road* ☎ *020/3964–3962* ▭ *AE, DC, MC, V* ✆ *No lunch.*

$$$$ ✕ **The Roof.** With panoramic 18th-floor views, this restaurant oozes understated splendor. The menu offers seasonal specialties and classic staples, such as saddle of lamb marinated in mint and yogurt, fettuccine, scallops in saffron sauce, and prime cuts of U.S. beef. ⊠ *China Hotel, Liuhua Lu, Station District* ☎ *020/8666–6888 Ext. 71892* ▭ *AE, DC, MC, V* ✆ *Closed Sun. No lunch.*

$$$$ ✕ **Silk Road Grill Room.** This grill room in the White Swan Hotel is the place to see and be seen. The service is impeccable. You can choose between the set menu, which includes an appetizer, cold dish, soup, entrée, dessert, and drink (excluding wine), or à la carte. Highlight entrées include prime rib and sea-bass fillet. ⊠ *White Swan Hotel, Yi Shamian Lu, Shamian Island* ☎ *020/8188–6968* ▭ *AE, DC, MC, V* ✆ *Reservations essential* ✆ *No lunch.*

$$$–$$$$
Fodor'sChoice
★

✕ **La Seine.** This upscale restaurant on Er Sha Island offers a daily lunch buffet. Dinner highlights include classic French fare, such as beef tenderloin, escargot, and foie gras. An ideal place to eat before or after a show. ⊠ *Xinghai Concert Hall, 33 Qing Bo Lu, Er Sha Island, close to Xinghai Concert Hall and Guangzhou Museum* ☎ *020/8735–2531* ⌂ *Reservations essential* ☰ *AE, DC, MC, V.*

$$$ ✕ **Lai Wan Market.** A re-creation of the old Canton waterfront, this theme restaurant has booths shaped like flower boats and small wooden stools at low counters. The Market is known for its dim sum and two kinds of rice, one made with pork, beef, fish, and seafood, the other with fish, beef, and pork liver. ⊠ *Garden Hotel, 368 Huanshi Dong Lu, 2nd fl., Huanshi Road* ☎ *020/8333–8989 Ext. 3922* ☰ *AE, DC, MC, V.*

$$–$$$ ✕ **Banxi Restaurant.** On the edge of Liwan Lake, this restaurant has a series of teahouse rooms and landscaped gardens interconnected by zigzag paths and bridges that give the feel of a Taoist temple. One room is built on a floating houseboat. The food is as tasty as it looks with dishes such as scallop and crab soup and quail eggs cooked with shrimp roe on a bed of green vegetables. ⊠ *151 Longjin Xi Lu, Liwan Park* ☎ *020/8181–5718* ☰ *AE, MC, V.*

$$–$$$ ✕ **Tang Yuan.** The location alone beats out most other restaurants in Guangzhou. It is in a faux colonial-style mansion on an island in Liuhuahu Park. Cuisine is pure old-school Cantonese, with expensive dishes like abalone and shark's fin soup being served alongside more rational staples like crispy fried pigeon, carbon-roasted mackerel, and stuffed garlic prawns. Naturally, there's plenty of dim sum, and the "Cantonese combo plate" features a variety of roasted meats sure to please carnivores. Although the food at Tang Yuan is excellent, most people come here for the opulence as well. Admission fee for the park is waived for guests of the restaurant, and a golf cart waits at the park's entrance on Liuhua Road to whisk diners to the restaurant's palatial front door. ⊠ *Lihuahu Park, Dongfeng Xi Lu and Renmin Bei Lu, 2 blocks west of Yuexiu Gongyuan metro station* ☎ *020/8668–8863* ☰ *AE, DC, MC, V.*

$–$$$ ✕ **Datong Restaurant.** Occupying all eight stories of an old riverfront building, with an open terrace on the top floor, this is one of the city's veteran dining establishments. The restaurant is popular with locals all hours of the day, so arrive early to be guaranteed a seat. The atmosphere is chaotic and noisy, but the morning and afternoon dim sum and huge menu are well worth it. Famous dishes include stewed-chicken claws (delicious, by the way), crispy-skin chicken, and roasted *Xishi* duck. Probably not the best place for vegetarians. ⊠ *Nanfang Dasha, 63 Yanjiang Xi Lu, Colonial Canton* ☎ *020/8188–8988* ☰ *AE, DC, MC, V.*

$–$$$ ✕ **Dongjiang Seafood Restaurant.** There are two Dongjiang Seafood restaurants in Guangzhou. Both are renowned for their culinary excellence and authentic Canton decor, but we recommend the Pearl River location (on Qiao Guang and Yan Jiang roads). It features a seafood market where you can wander around and choose your own meal. The staff will try to steer you toward the most expensive items first, so make sure you check prices beforehand. Some of our favorites include the braised duck stuffed with eight delicacies and glutinous rice, stuffed

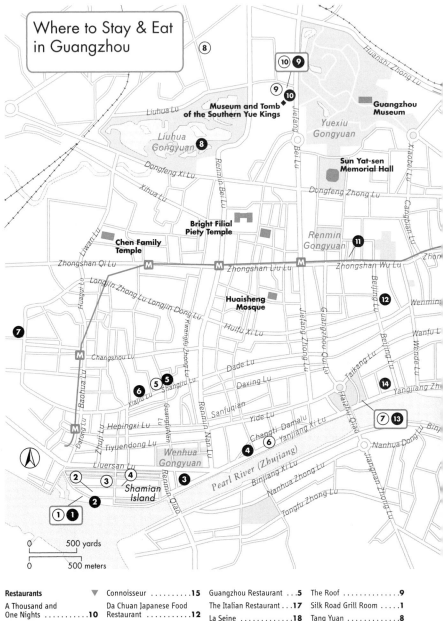

Where to Stay & Eat in Guangzhou

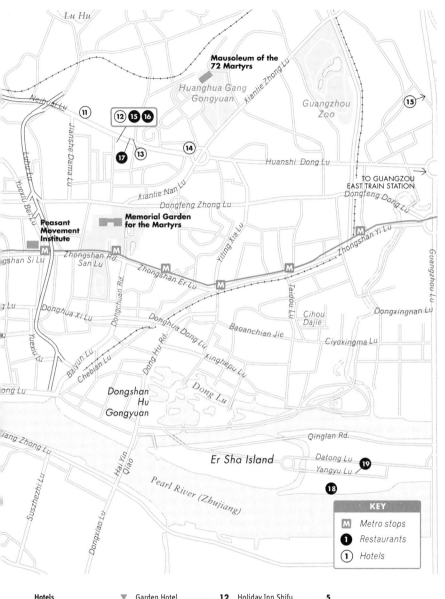

giant prawns, crab in black-bean sauce, and salt-roast chicken. ✉ *No. 2 Qiao Guang Rd., Pearl River, 2 blocks SE of Haizhu Shichang metro* ☎ *020/8318–4901* ▤ *AE, DC, MC, V.*

$–$$$ ✗ **Guangzhou Restaurant.** One of the oldest eateries in the city, Guangzhou Restaurant was opened in 1936 and has a string of culinary awards. The setting is classic Canton, with courtyards of flowery bushes surrounded by dining rooms of various sizes. The food is reputed to be among the best in the city, with house specialties like "Eight Treasures," a mix of fowl, pork, and mushrooms served in a bowl made of winter melon. Other Cantonese dishes include duck feet stuffed with shrimp, roasted goose, and of course, dim sum. Meals here can be cheap or very expensive, depending on how exotic you're looking to get. ✉ *2 Wenchang Nan Lu, Ancestral Guangzhou* ☎ *020/8138–8801* ▤ *AE, DC, MC, V.*

$–$$$ ✗ **Tao Tao Ju.** Prepare yourself for the garish decor, shouted conversations of fellow diners, and a menu comprised of enough weird animal parts to send vegetarians running. Tao Tao Ju (which, roughly translated, means "house of happiness") is one of the most revered traditional Cantonese restaurants in the city. Soups are a big thing here, and the menu (available in English) has many that you're unlikely to find elsewhere. The kudzu and snakehead soup is delicious, and they have over 200 varieties of dim sum. They're also open from 6:30 AM to midnight, so it's a good place to stop for a late-night meal. ✉ *20 Dishipu Lu, Shangxiajiu* ☎ *020/8139–6111* ▤ *AE, DC, MC, V.*

$$ ✗ **Back Street Jazz Bar & Restaurant.** Tall bamboo groves masks a space-age interior of glass walls, sliding-metal doors, and Plexiglas walkways in this cantina attached to the Guangdong Art Museum. Food is pure world fusion, with dishes like deep-fried salmon and lotus root, Thai chicken salad, and honey apple–foie gras. The softly lit red-neon bar serves mojitos, fruit martinis, and a wide selection of wines. Back Street has an in-house jazz band playing nightly from 10 until midnight, and often hosts international bands. ✉ *38 Yanyu Lu, East Gate of the Guangdong Museum of Art, Ersha Island* ☎ *020/3839–9090* ▤ *AE, DC, MC, V.*

$–$$ ✗ **Lucy's.** With cuisines from so many cultures represented on its menu (Asian curries, mixed grills, Tex-Mex dishes, fish-and-chips, noodles, burgers, sandwiches, and much more), a UN–think tank could happily share a table. A favorite among foreigners, the outdoor dining area is lovely, and even the indoor dining area has a few trees growing through the roof. Take-out service is available. ✉ *3 Shamian Nan Jie, 1 block from White Swan Hotel* ☎ *020/8121–5106* ▤ *No credit cards.*

$–$$ ✗ **A Thousand and One Nights.** Possibly due to its being part of a chain operating throughout China, this cavernous Middle Eastern restaurant gets written up a lot, and is crowded with Westerners on most nights. But despite the authentic Arabic decor, belly dancers, and menu filled with kebabs and babaghanoush, A Thousand and One Nights seems to be coasting on reputation, and Guangzhou has better Arab fare by far. But if you're at the China Hotel and don't feel like hopping in a taxi to the Nile, you could do worse than a meal here. ✉ *899 Jie Fang Bei Rd., next to the China Hotel, Yuexiu Gongyuan metro* ☎ *020/3618–2280* ▤ *AE, DC, MC, V* Ⓜ *Yuexiu Gongyuan.*

$ ✕ **Da Chuan Japanese Food Restaurant.** This local eatery is located in a busy shopping area on Beijing Road. The best value is a sushi set meal, or you can dive into à la carte dishes plucked straight off the rotating sushi bar. ✉ *294 Beijing Rd., 4th fl., Beijing Road Pedestrian Mall* ☎ *020/8319–0283* ▭ *No credit cards.*

$ ✕ **The Italian Restaurant.** This aptly named restaurant is a popular hangout for Western expats who work in the neighborhood. It offers a cheerful home-away-from-home feel, complete with flags from various countries hanging from the ceiling and beers from around the world. The food is inexpensive and good, with pizzas, pastas, and excellent brochette prepared by an Italian chef. The owner is an entrepreneur with a number of other restaurants and bars in the neighborhood. His reputation for catering to Western tastes is hardly undeserved. ✉ *East Tower, Pearl Building, 3rd fl., 360 Huanshi Zhong Lu, 1 block west of Garden Hotel* ☎ *020/8586–6783* ▭ *AE, DC, MC, V* ☉ *Daily.*

$ ✕ **Nile Restaurant.** This lovely little three-story restaurant on the banks of the Pearl River serves excellent Middle Eastern food, including falafel, shwarma, and a variety of Middle Eastern salads. The Nile is worth noting for two reasons: the decor, including the uniforms worn by the waitstaff, is straight out of the movie *Cleopatra*; and the menu has a large number of vegetarian dishes, not always the easiest thing to find in Guangzhou. For our vegetarian friends, we recommend the lentil soup, babaghanoush, and the falafel salad. Nile also serves excellent breakfasts. ✉ *31 Yanjian W. Rd., 2 blocks east of Shamian Island* ☎ *020/8101–2986* ▭ *No credit cards* ☉ *Daily.*

Where to Stay

The purpose of your visit to Guangzhou is likely to determine where you stay. Business people increasingly choose the upcoming Tianhe District, close to Guangzhou East Railway Station and the city's growing thicket of office skyscrapers. Visitors are more likely to choose a hotel on the oasislike Shamian Island, in the heart of the city. Though traffic is still hellish, getting around is easier now than it has been in years past. Recently completed expressways and a growing underground-train system have vastly reduced cross-city travel time.

$$–$$$$ ▦ **China Hotel.** Managed by Marriott, this hotel is part of a multicomplex that includes office and apartment blocks, a shopping mall big enough to get lost in, and a wide enough range of restaurants to satisfy any appetite. The hotel is favored by business travelers because it's connected to the metro and close to the Trade Fair Exhibition Hall. The 66-room executive floor has big private lounges, and the piano bar in the lobby offers champagne brunches. There's a walk-in humidor on the premises and the 4th-floor gym is open around the clock. ✉ *Liuhua Lu, 510015* ☎ *020/8666–6888* ⤸ *1,013 rooms, 74 suites* ♨ *4 restaurants, tennis court, pool, gym, nightclub, shops, piano bar, business services, in-room broadband, meeting room* ▭ *AE, DC, MC, V* Ⓜ *Yuexu Gongyuan metro.*

$$–$$$$ ▦ **Holiday Inn City Centre.** This centrally located hotel is bound to offer stiff competition to the Garden Hotel just down the road. The large taste-

ful rooms are arranged according to Chinese feng-shui principles. The top three executive floors have suites and a lounge–restaurant area with stellar views of smog-shrouded Guangzhou. In addition to all of its lovely facilities, the hotel also has enough meeting rooms to host a small Tony Robbins seminar. ✉ *28 Guangming Lu, Overseas Chinese Village, Huanshi Dong Road, 510095* ☎ *020/6128–6868* ⊕ *www.guangzhou.holiday-inn.com* ➷ *430 rooms, 38 suites* ♨ *4 restaurants, pool, gym, lounge, business services, in-room broadband, meeting rooms, car rental, travel services* ▭ *AE, DC, MC, V.*

TIGHTWAD TIP	

All hotels in Guangzhou have in-room Internet access for those traveling with laptops. Although it's almost always free at the cheaper hotels, more expensive properties charge anywhere from Y100 to Y120 to "buy" a block of 24 hours of surfing time.

$$–$$$$ ▦ **Holiday Inn Shifu.** The newest hotel in Guangzhou, and the only four-star hotel in popular tourist area Shangxiajiu, Holiday Inn Shifu is 14 stories, with rooms ranging in price from Y1,080 to Y2,680. There's a lovely rooftop pool and an adjacent bar with views of old Guangzhou. The Shifu is also a stone's throw from the newly renovated Qingping Market, which is a must-see for first-time visitors. ✉ *No.188 Di Shi Fu Rd., Xiangxiajiu, 510140, signs from Changshou metro exit point the way* ☎ *020/8138–0088* ➷ *280 rooms, 6 suites* ♨ *2 restaurants, pool, gym, sauna, business services, in-room broadband, bar, meeting room* ▭ *AE, DC, MC, V* Ⓜ *Changshuo.*

$$–$$$$ ▦ **White Swan Hotel.** Occupying a marvelous site on Shamian Island, beside the Pearl River, this huge luxury complex has landscaped gardens, two pools, a jogging track, and a separate gym and spa. Its presidential suite is just that: reserved for heads of state, it has been occupied by such luminaries as Richard Nixon and Kim Jong-il. Its restaurants are second to none; the windows of the elegant lobby bar and coffee shop frame the panorama of river traffic. ✉ *Yi Shamian Lu, Shamian Island, Colonial Canton, 510133* ☎ *020/8188–6968, 852/2524–0192 in Hong Kong* ⊕ *www.whiteswanhotel.com* ➷ *843 rooms, 92 suites* ♨ *9 restaurants, 2 pools, gym, bar, shops, business services, in-room broadband, meeting rooms, travel services* ▭ *AE, DC, MC, V.*

$–$$$$ ▦ **Guangdong Victory Hotel.** Over the past few years, this Shamian Island hotel has undergone upgrades that have bumped it up from budget class. The two wings, both originally colonial guesthouses, have been beautifully renovated. The main building has a pink-and-white facade, an imposing portico, and twin domes on the roof, where you'll find a pool and an excellent sauna facility. Standard rooms are more than adequate, and the hotel still retains a fairly inexpensive dining room on the 1st floor. ✉ *53 Yi Shamian Lu, Shamian Island, 510130* ☎ *020/8121–6688* ⊕ *www.gd-victory-hotel.com* ➷ *328 rooms* ♨ *4 restaurants, dining room, pool, gym, sauna, business services, in-room broadband, meeting rooms* ▭ *AE, DC, MC, V.*

FodorśChoice ★

$$–$$$ ▦ **Garden Hotel.** In the northern business suburbs, this huge, aging hotel is famous for its spectacular garden that includes an artificial hill, a waterfall, and pavilions. The cavernous lobby, decorated with enormous murals, has a bar–lounge set around an ornamental pool. Though long considered the standard of luxury in Guangzhou, other hotels are now giving the Garden a run for its money. ⊠ *368 Huanshi Dong Lu, Huanshi Road, 510064* ☎ *020/8333–8989* ⊕ *www.thegardenhotel.com.cn* ⌑ *1,028 rooms, 63 suites* ⌂ *7 restaurants, 2 tennis courts, pool, gym, squash, bar, lounge, pub, shops, business services, in-room broadband, convention center* ▭ *AE, DC, MC, V.*

$$–$$$ ▣ **Tian Lun International Hotel.** A new, upscale boutique hotel located next to Guangzhou East Railway Station, offers large luxury rooms with a sleek edge. The colors are kept to soft blacks, grays, and beige. The buffet in the 2nd-floor café is beautifully arranged around a centerpiece of coral, and the high ceilings lend an air of sophistication. ⊠ *172 Linhe Lu Central, Tianhe District, 510610, next to Guangzhou East Railway Station* ☎ *020/8393–6388* ⊕ *www.tianlun-hotel.com* ⌑ *382 rooms, 23 suites* ⌂ *2 restaurants, business services, in-room broadband, pool, gym, sauna* ▭ *AE, DC, MC, V.*

$–$$$ ▣ **Dong Fang.** Across from Liuhua Park and the trade-fair headquarters, this complex is built around a 22½-acre garden with pavilions, carp-filled pools, and rock gardens. The lobby is done up in a Renaissance motif, complete with Romanesque pillars and gold-and-white floor tiling. The shopping concourse has Chinese antiques and carpets. The hotel has recently added an 86,000-square-foot convention center. Discounts of up to 30% for rooms in the off-season are not unheard of. ⊠ *120 Liuhua Lu, 510016* ☎ *020/8666–9900, 852/2528–0555 in Hong Kong* ⌑ *772 rooms, 114 suites* ⌂ *6 restaurants, gym, hair salon, spa, business services, in-room broadband, meeting room* ▭ *AE, DC, MC, V.*

$–$$$ ▣ **Guangdong International Hotel.** This 15-year-old towering hotel in the finance district is somewhat of an institution in Guangzhou, but it has a tired feel, as if the leap from state to private ownership hasn't been made in full. The hotel does have extensive recreation facilities and an indoor gym, as well as a large rooftop pool with an excellent view. For the money though, the nearby City Centre Holiday Inn is a better buy. ⊠ *339 Huanshi Dong Lu, Huanshi Road, 510098* ☎ *020/8331–1888* ⌑ *603 rooms, 200 suites* ⌂ *3 restaurants, tennis court, pool, gym, bar, shops, business services, in-room broadband* ▭ *AE, DC, MC, V.*

$–$$$ ▣ **Landmark Canton.** Towering above Haizhu Square and the main bridge across the river, this hotel is in the heart of central Guangzhou. It's managed by China Travel Service of Hong Kong, so a lot of its guests tend to be Hong Kongers on holiday, but the hotel has its fair share of foreign guests as well. There's a great chocolate shop in the lobby, and a small but very pretty Chinese garden and carp pond in the courtyard. The Landmark's location allows it to boast that most guest rooms have great views of the river and city. ⊠ *8 Qiao Guang Lu, 510115* ☎ *020/ 8335–5988* ⌑ *688 rooms, 103 suites* ⌂ *3 restaurants, pool, gym, bar, dance club, shops, business services, meeting room* ▭ *AE, DC, MC, V* Ⓜ *Haizhu Guangchang.*

¢–$ ▣ **Élan Hotel.** If you like cheap, funky, and hip little hotels, this is the spot for you. Guangzhou's first attempt at a boutique hotel has compact, Ikea-inspired rooms with bold color palettes and clean lines. Celine Dion muzak wafting through the hallways can be an annoyance, but the warm, cozy beds guarantee a restful sleep. The small 1st-floor restaurant serves cheap northeast Chinese food that is as authentic and tasty. ⊠ *32 Zhan Qian Heng Rd., 510010, 2 blocks south of Guangzhou main railway station* ☎ *020/8622–1788* ⊕ *www.hotel-elan.com* ↘ *76 rooms, 8 suites* △ *Restaurant, business services, in-room broadband* ⊟ *AE, DC, MC, V.*

¢ 🏨 **The Customs Hotel.** This clean and inexpensive hotel has both character and an excellent location. The newly opened four-story establishment has an attractive colonial facade that blends well with the surrounding area. The bright interior surrounds an inner courtyard. Standard rooms are tastefully decorated with Republican-era furniture made of dark wood, though the suites seem more cluttered. If possible, get a room facing Shamian Avenue, the quiet, tree-lined street, which runs the length of the island. There is a karaoke bar and a lovely backyard garden. ⊠ *No.35 Shamian Ave., Shamian Island, Colonial Guangzhou, 510130* ☎ *20/8110–2388* ↘ *49 rooms, 7 suites* △ *2 restaurants, gym, bar, business services, in-room broadband* ⊟ *AE, DC, MC, V.*

¢ 🏨 **HallBell De Fond.** This inexplicably named budget hotel is not a bad place for the price. However, a few of the rooms are a bit funky, the beds hard, and some of the wooden furniture seems rickety. We got the feeling that the hotel's clientele was primarily comprised of businesspeople on a strict budget, and patrons of the bar street below using the place for trysts. There are two common rooms with televisions, free Internet access, and the definite prospect of meeting interesting people. ⊠ *16F Zhujiang Building, 358 Huanshi Dong Lu, Huanshi Road* ☎ *20/6122–4388* ⊕ *www.hallbell.com* ↘ *50 rooms* △ *Business services, in-room broadband* ⊟ *MC, V.*

¢ 🏨 **Shamian.** This is a great hotel for visitors on a budget. Its rooms are a little spartan and the lobby cramped, but it is clean and friendly and the location—right in the middle of Shamian Island—is second to none. ⊠ *52 Shamian Nan Jie, Shamian Island, 510130* ☎ *020/8121–8288* ⊕ *www.gdshamianhotel.com* ↘ *58 rooms, 20 suites* △ *Restaurant, business services* ⊟ *AE, DC, MC, V.*

¢–$ 🏨 **Aiqun Hotel.** When it was built in the 1930s, this 16-story hotel was the tallest building in Pearl River Delta. Though it once hosted dignitaries of great importance during China's Republican era, these days this elegant art-deco hotel hosts visitors from around China and international travelers on a budget. Rooms are clean, comfortable, and tastefully furnished with rich mahogany, faux colonial-era furniture. The revolving restaurant on the 16th floor of the new wing offers great views of the surrounding area. ⊠ *No.113 Yanjiang Rd., Pearl River District, 510120* ☎ *020/8186–6668* ↘ *220 rooms, 20 suites* △ *4 restaurants, business services, meeting room, in-room broadband* ⊟ *AE, DC, MC, V.*

Nightlife & the Arts

Though not as happening as Shanghai or Beijing, the Guangzhou nightlife scene is anything but boring. Western-style clubs vie for increasingly hip and knowledgeable crowds and invest serious money on international DJs and design. A wide variety of pubs, sports bars, coffee shops, and cafés have also sprung up. Bars tend to stay open until 2 AM; clubs continue to 5 AM.

Pubs & Bars

Bingjiang xilu (✉ South of Shamian Island, across the Pearl River) is *the* street for barhopping. Very popular with a younger crowd, it has great views, and if you get bored with looking north across the river you can always cross the bridge to **Yanjiang Xilu** and drink at some of the bars on that side.

Huanshi Dong Lu and the area behind the Garden Hotel is popular with locals and expats (short- and long-term). Two favorites are **Gypsy** and **Cave,** both located on opposite ends of the Zhujiang Building. Cave has a distinct meat-market vibe and features nightly performances by a scantily clad woman whose specialty is dancing with snakes. Gypsy reeks of hashish and is much mellower.

The Paddy Field (✉38 Huale Lu , behind Garden Hotel ☎020/8360–1379) makes you long for Ireland. There are darts, pints of Guinness and Kilkenny, and football matches on a massive screen.

Popular with foreigners and locals alike, **1920 Restaurant** (✉ 183 Yan-jiang Zhong Lu ☎ 020/8333–6156) serves up Bavarian food and imported wheat beers on a lovely outdoor patio. Meals start from Y30, beers from Y28.

The popular **Café Lounge** (✉ China Hotel, lobby ☎ 020/8666–6888) has a mellow vibe, big comfortable bar stools, quiet tables for two, live music on weekends, and a fine selection of cigars.

The big attraction of the **Hare & Moon** (✉ White Swan Hotel, Yi Shamian Lu, Shamian Island ☎ 020/8188–6968) is the panorama of the Pearl River as it flows past the picture windows.

Dance Clubs

Though normally thought of as inauspicious in Chinese culture, the number 4 is anything but at Guangzhou's newly renovated **Yes Club** (✉ 132 Dongfeng Xi Lu, across from Liuhua Lake Park ☎ 020 8136–8688 🖳 Free), which actually has four separate clubs under one roof for four distinctly different clubbing experiences. **Super Yes** has techno and electronica, whereas **Mini Yes** offers house and break beat. **Funky Yes** offers a more eclectic mixture of R&B and hip-hop, and **Club Yes** is a total chill-out zone, with softer music and lighting, and a fine selection of wine and cigars. Taken as a whole, the more than 6,000-square-foot megaclub is definitely the biggest in Guangzhou.

Baby Face (✉83 Changdi Da Ma Lu ☎020/8335–5771 🖳Y20) is where the stylish go to strike a pose. It fills up quickly on weekends with most tables reserved. Arrive early and be prepared to spend.

Deep Anger Music Power House (✉ 183 Yanjiang Lu ☎ 020/8317–7158 🖳 Free ☉ Daily 8 PM–2 AM) is a cool dance club located in a building that was a theater back in the days of Sun Yat-sen. Lounge lizards and history buffs will enjoy sipping a beer here.

Art & Culture in Guangzhou

If you think Guangzhou's high culture begins and ends with Cantonese opera, think again, pilgrim—the art and performance scene here is vibrant, and getting more so every day. Even cynics who believe that Guangzhou's mainstream masses care more for dim sum than for dance are waking up to the fact that the city is undergoing a cultural broadening, as evidenced by the opening of small art spaces, more eclectic forms of theater, and more national attention being focused on the city's major museums. Of course, purists need not panic; the Cantonese opera has hardly disappeared.

> **IN THE NEWS**
>
> Some good publications to check out for regularly updated info on ongoing cultural happenings are *City Weekends, City Guide, South China City Talk,* and *That's PRD.*

Xinghai Concert Hall (⊠ 33 Qing Bo Lu, Er Sha Island ☏ 020/8735–2222 Ext. 312 for English ⊕ www.concerthall.com.cn) is the home of the Guangzhou Symphony Orchestra, and puts on an amazing array of concerts featuring national and international performers. Their Web site, unfortunately, is only in Chinese, but your hotel should be able to call to find out what's going on. The concert hall is surrounded by a fantastic sculpture garden, and is next door to the Guangzhou Museum of Art, making the two an excellent mid-afternoon to evening trip.

Mo Li Fang Theater (⊠ 292 Changdida Ma Lu ☏ 020/8132–2600 ☏ Y 290 includes dinner) presents nightly performances of their original multimedia dinner–theater cabaret *The Magic Phantom,* combining elements of traditional Beijing Opera, Hong Kong Cinema, puppetry, karaoke, acrobatics, dancing, and computer animation. The play is in Putonghua, but the story is fairly simple: A young prince of the kingdom of Nanyue finds a magic ring that allows him to travel through time and space. His travels take him and his consort to prohibition-era Chicago, Republican-era Shanghai, and outer space. As if this weren't enough to justify the price of admission, each member of the audience is served a pre-performance meal literally fit for a king, with eight separate and sumptuous dishes served in crystal bowls by waiters in full ancient costume. An evening well spent for all senses—see our front section for more about this terrific show, which begins at 7 PM nightly with matinees Saturdays and Sundays. Tickets are available at the box office, or through the front desk of most hotels.

Guang Ming Theatre (⊠ 293 Nan Hua Zhong Lu ☏ 020/3415–4721) is a well-known place to catch Cantonese opera as well as other performances.

Guangdong Puppet Art Center (⊠ 21 Fenyuan St. ☏ 020/8431–0227) hosts live puppet shows every Saturday and Sunday at 10:30 AM and 3 PM.

Guangdong Modern Dance Company (⊠ 13 Shuiyinhenglu, Shaheding ☏ 020/8704–9512 ⊕ www.gdmdc.com) is mainland China's first professional modern-dance company, and the troupe is regularly praised by publications as diverse and respected as the *New York Times* and the *Toronto Sun.* This theater is their home base, so if you're a fan of dance, check out their English-language Web site for a full performance schedule.

Galleries & Performance Spaces

Park 19 (✉ 19 Xiaogang Hauyuan, Jingnan Donglu ☎ 020/8425–2689 ⊕ www.park19.com ☷ Call for hours) is Guangzhou's newest and hippest art spot, which offers several floors of studio and performance space, and is definitely worth checking out. Call or check their Web site for current happenings and hours.

If eclectic art is your thing, then **Vitamin Creative Space** (✉ 29 Hengyi Jie, inside of Xinggang Cheng, Haizhu District ☎ 020/8429–6760) might be worth the trip. But be warned, it's located in the back of a semi-enclosed vegetable market and not easy to find even if you speak Chinese. Call first (the curator speaks English) and someone will escort you from in front of the market. Hours are somewhat erratic, but the art can be as wonderfully weird as anything you're likely to find in China.

Shopping

It's no surprise that the world's busiest manufacturing city offers an amazing array of shopping options. Whatever the item may be, if it's being sold chances are good that somebody's selling it in Guangzhou.

Malls & Markets

Shangxiajiu (✉ Follow signs from Changshoulu metro) is a massive warren of old buildings and shops and considered the user-friendly heart of old Guangzhou. The half-mile main street is a pedestrian mall boasting nearly 250 shops and department stores. The buildings in Shangxiajiu are old, but the stores are the same ones as in "modern Guangzhou." Even though the overall decibel level hovers around deafening, the area isn't without its charms. Our favorite shops are the small storefronts offering dried-fruit samples, which are very addictive. The area draws a big, younger crowd, but there are a few quiet back alleys that keep it from feeling too overwhelming. There's also a wide variety of street stalls selling a large selection of delicious edibles.

Beijing Road Pedestrian Mall (✉ Follow signs from Gongyuanqian metro) offers an interesting contrast to Shangxiajiu. Shangxiajiu offers new stores in old buildings, whereas Beijing Road makes no pretense at being anything other than a fully modern, neon-draped pedestrian mall, similar to Beijing's Wangfujing Street or Shanghai's Nanjing Street. Pedestrianized and open from around 10 AM until 10 PM, this is where city teenagers buy sensible, midrange Hong Kong–style clothes and increasingly garish local brands. Noisy and fun, the street is lined with cheap food stalls, cafés, and the ubiquitous fast-food chains like KFC and McDonald's.

Haizhu Plaza (✉ Haizhu Sq., north of Haizhu Bridge, Haizhu Ⓜ Guangchang metro ☷ Daily 10–6) is a massive, two-story flea and souvenir market where casual shoppers and wholesale buyers alike bargain for kitsch—think toys, faux antiques, and cultural revolution–themed knickknacks. Merchants keep calculators at hand for entering figures in the heat of negotiation, and vendors sell a variety of snacks from carts located by the exits.

The **Friendship Store** (✉ 369 Huanshi Dong Lu, across from the Garden Hotel) is an old stalwart, dating back from days of postrevolutionary

Continued on page 476

21ST ★
CENTURY
CHINA

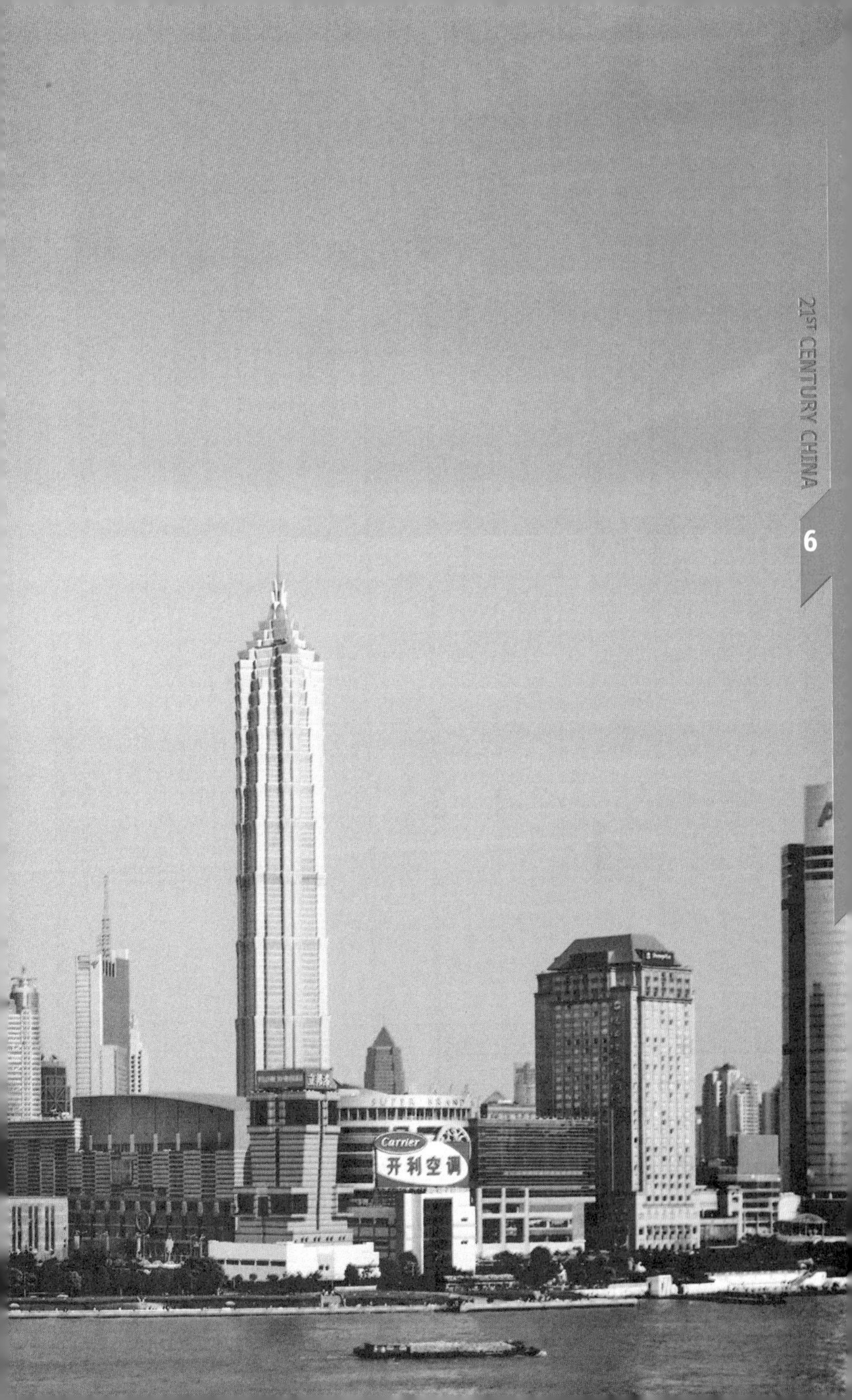
Carrier
开利空调

BEIJING

A Chinese Century?

The SARS hiccup aside, China's economy has been red hot since joining the World Trade Organization in 2001. One of the engines driving the global economy, it helped revive Japan's sagging economy and the slumping international shipping industry. Worldwide commodities markets have also been boosted by China's increasing hunger for everything from copper to coffee.

The country that was long written off as just a cheap exporter is now a net importer. It's the fourth-largest economy in the world after the United States, Japan, and Germany, whose economies are growing at less than half the rate.

Such development is nothing short of remarkable, but national problems such as energy, the environment, and wealth inequality are threatening the country.

Internationally, it's how China and the United States cooperate on global issues, and how they manage their own complex relationship, that may have the greatest impact on the rest of the century. Since Nixon first opened the door in 1972, the two countries have managed to forge a working relationship. But Yuan revaluation, trade issues, energy supply (especially oil), and both countries' military role in the Asia-Pacific region are all issues that could sour this budding friendship.

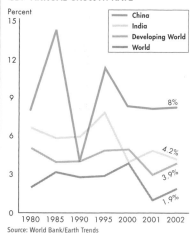

GDP-ANNUAL GROWTH RATE

Percent

Legend:
- China
- India
- Developing World
- World

8%
4.2%
3.9%
1.9%

1980 1985 1990 1995 2000 2001 2002

Source: World Bank/Earth Trends

(top) Architectural stars (or starchitects) like Rem Koolhaas, Li Hu, Paul Andreu, and Jacques Herzog and Pierre de Meuron (Olympic Stadium, above) are descending on Beijing for construction of state-of-the-art Olympic venues. (right) Hong Kong skyline.

HONG KONG

Fueling the Chinese Dream

China is now the number two energy consumer in the world, after the United States. Its consumption has exploded by an average of 5% yearly since 1998. This thirst for fuel is evident on roads all over the country. The land of the bicycle is now car-crazy. Three million vehicles were recently sold, and higher sales are predicted in the coming years.

Back in 2005, the country consumed 320 million tons of crude oil, roughly one-third of which was imported. It's expecting to import 500 million tons by 2020, two-thirds of its projected total imports.

Where will China get this oil? Much comes from countries with troubled relations with the West such as Iran and Sudan, but it is also working on importing more from traditional U.S. suppliers such as Saudi Arabia.

There's also a growing demand for electricity, 75% of which comes from coal. In the coming 25 years, the greenhouse gases produced by China's coal burning will probably exceed that of all industrial nations combined. And the country will continue to rely on coal for electricity in the years to come, despite large hydropower projects and a plan to increase the number of nuclear power plants.

Aside from developing clean, renewable energy sources, China needs to improve its poor energy efficiency—it uses nine times the energy Japan does to produce one GDP unit. But plans are being made to improve energy efficiency by 20% from 2006 to 2010.

WORLD OIL CONSUMPTION

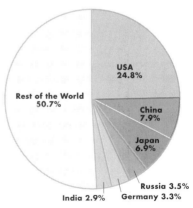

USA 24.8%

Rest of the World 50.7%

China 7.9%

Japan 6.9%

Russia 3.5%

Germany 3.3%

India 2.9%

Source: http://www.nationmaster.com/

Can China Go Green?

A devastated environment is a major result of China's economic transformation. For example, because of deforestation around the capital, Beijing is threatened by the encroaching Gobi Desert, which dumped 300,000 tons of sand on the city in one week in 2006. Industrial carelessness and lack of regulation result in accidents such as the 50-mile benzene spill in a river near Harbin in late 2005.

Cities have been smoggy for decades because of pollution from factories, vehicles, and especially coal. But air quality is now becoming obscured by water issues. In mid-2006, the Water Resources Ministry reported that 320 million urban residents—more than the population of the United States—did not have access to clean drinking water.

Much of this is the result of a development-at-any-cost mentality, particularly in the wake of economic reform. Companies and factories, many of which are foreign-owned, have only recently had to deal with environmental laws— "scoff laws"—that are often circumvented by

bribing local officials. And average citizens don't have freedom of speech or access to political tools to fight environmentally damaging projects.

Is the central government waking up? In 2006, the vice-chairman of China's increasingly outspoken State Environmental Protection Agency put it bluntly: "We will face tremendous problems if we do not change our development patterns."

Mind the Gap

China has come a long way from the days when everyone had an "iron rice bowl," or a state-appointed job that was basically guaranteed regardless of one's abilities or work performance.

Since 1980, the country has quadrupled per capita income and raised more than 220 million of its citizens out of poverty. A belt of prosperity is emerging along the coast, but hundreds of millions still live on less than $1 per day.

(left) Owning a car is the new Chinese dream. (top right) The Three Gorges Dam will be the largest in the world, supplying the hydroelectric power of 18 nuclear plants. (bottom right) China's cities are some of the most polluted in the world.

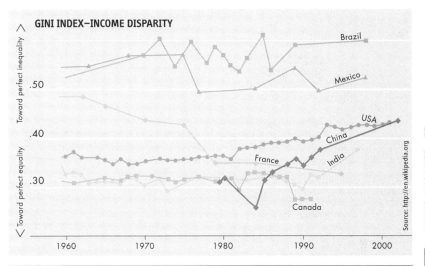

GINI INDEX—INCOME DISPARITY

Toward perfect inequality ⟩

Toward perfect equality ⟨

Brazil

Mexico

USA

China

France

India

Canada

.50

.40

.30

1960   1970   1980   1990   2000

Source: http://en.wikipedia.org

21ST CENTURY CHINA

6

Economists use a statistical yardstick known as the Gini coefficient to measure wealth inequality in a society, with zero being perfect equality and one being perfect inequality. The World Bank estimates that China's national Gini coefficient rose from 0.30 to 0.45 from 1982, a 50% jump in two decades. In 2006, some academics estimated China's current Gini coefficient to be closer to, or even higher than, Latin America's 0.52.

As economic inequality has grown, so has discontent, particularly in rural areas. The country recorded 87,000 public protests in 2005, an increase of 11,000 over the year before.

Many of these protests are incited by the acts of local, particularly rural, officials whose corruption policies are sometimes beyond Beijing's sphere of influence.

Most protests are focused on specific incidents or officials rather than general dissent against the government, but the growing frequency of such events is not going unnoticed by the central government. In 2005, 8,400 officials were arrested on corruption-related charges.

CHINA IN NUMBERS

	CHINA	U.S.
Area in sq km:	9,560,960	9,631,420
Population	1.3 bil	300 mil
Men (15–64 yrs)	482 mil	100 mil
Women (15–64 yrs)	456 mil	101 mil
Population growth	0.59%	0.91%
Life expectancy: men	70.8	75
Life expectancy: women	74.6	80.8
GDP per head	$1,090	$37,240
Health spending, % GDP	5.8	14.6
Doctors per 1000 pop.	1.6	2.8
Hospital beds per 1000 pop.	1.6	3.0
Infant mortality rate per 1000 births	23.12	6.43
Education spending, % GDP	2.1	5.7
Adult literacy: men	95.1%	99%
Adult literacy: women	86.5%	99%
Internet users	111 mil	204 mil

China's earliest flirtation with capitalism. The Guangzhou Friendship Store occupies a five-story building with departments selling a wide range of designer wear, children's wear, luggage, and household appliances.

La Perle (⊠ 367 Huanshi Dong Lu, across from the Garden Hotel ⊗ Daily 10–10) is next to the Friendship Store, and a bit more upscale. They have genuine designer clothes at expensive rates, with shops such as Versace, Louis Vuitton, Polo, and Prada.

Antiques & Traditional Crafts
On Shamian Island, the area between the White Swan and Victory hotels has a number of small family-owned shops that sell paintings, carvings, pottery, knickknacks, and antiques.

Guangzhou Arts Centre (⊠ 698 Renmin Bei Lu ☎ 020/8667–9898) has a fine selection of painted scrolls.

Guangzhou Ji Ya Zhai (⊠ 7 Xinwen Lu, Zhongshan Wulu ☎ 020/8333–0079) is a specialist in Chinese calligraphy and painting.

The **South Jade Carving Factory** (⊠ 15 Xia Jiu Lu, Shangxiajiu ☎ 020/8138–8040) offers a wide variety of jade and jadeite products at reasonable prices. On the 2nd floor visitors can watch jade being carved.

The **White Swan Arcade** (⊠ White Swan Hotel, Yi Shamian Lu, Shamian Island) has some of the city's finest upmarket specialty shops. They sell genuine Chinese antiques, traditional craft items, works of modern and classical art, Japanese kimonos and swords, jewelry, cameras, and books published in and about China.

Bookstores
Guangzhou Books Center (⊠ 123 Tianhe Lu ☎ 020/3886–4208) is a chain with seven floors of books on every subject, including some bargain-priced art books in English.

Xinhua Bookstore (⊠ 276 Beijing Rd. ☎ 020/8333–2636) sells an extensive catalog of books on a wide range of subjects at very affordable prices.

Side Trip to White Cloud Mountain

17 km (10½ mi) north of Guangzhou.

White Cloud Mountain gets its name from the halo of clouds that, in the days before heavy pollution, appeared around the peak following a rainstorm. The mountain is part of a 28-square-km- (17-square-mi-) resort area and consists of 6 parks, 30 peaks, and myriad gullies. **Santailing Park** is home to the enormous Yuntai Garden, of interest to anybody with a thing for botany. **Fei'eling Park** has a nice sculpture garden, and **Luhu Park** is home to Jinye Pond, as pure and azure a body of water as you're likely to find within 100 miles. All in all, a trip to White Cloud Mountain is a good way to get out of the city—maybe for a day of hiking—without traveling too far. Buses 11 and 24 both stop here, though a taxi shouldn't set you back more than Y100. 🚌 20Y. ⊗ *Daily 9–5.*

To & from Guangzhou
120 km (74½ mi; 1½ hrs) north of Hong Kong.

Most travelers enter Guangzhou either by train or plane. Long-distance trains pull in at the Guangzhou East Station. This station is also on the metro line, so getting to your destination right off the train is a fairly simple matter. One-way tickets to or from Hong Kong cost between Y210 and Y250, and between Y130 and Y170 to Shenzhen.

Guangzhou is connected to Shenzhen (approximately 100 km [62 mi] to the south) by the aptly named Guangzhou–Shenzhen expressway. Buses from Guangzhou to Hong Kong leave from both the Guangzhou East Station and from major hotels such as the China and the Garden hotels, and cost about Y180. You can, in a pinch, get a taxi from the station to the Shenzhen–Hong Kong border, but be prepared to pay upward of Y400.

SHENZHEN

Shenzen may be China's youngest city, but this is one metropolis that's definitely come of age. A small farming town until 1980, Shenzhen was chosen by Deng Xiaoping as an incubator in which the seeds of China's economic reform were to be nurtured. The results are the stuff of legend; a quarter century later, Shenzhen is now China's richest, and, according to some, its most vibrant city.

Shenzhen is the wealthiest per capita of any Chinese city (a fact that irks second-place Shanghai to no end). As such, Shenzhen offers a vast variety of ways for the city's middle class and nouveau riche to be parted from their money.

Until recently, few visitors saw Shenzhen as a long-term destination in itself, choosing instead to think of China's youngest city as a place to pass through on the way from Hong Kong to Guangzhou. But over the last several years, this has changed as more expats chose to call Shenzhen home, and more travelers discover that the city is a unique destination in itself.

Exploring Shenzhen

Sprawling Shenzhen is composed of six districts. Luohu and Futian are the "downtown" districts, with most of the major shopping areas, financial districts, and hundreds of hotels. If beautiful beaches and Soviet-era aircraft carriers-cum-theme parks are your thing, you won't want to miss the Yantian district. Shekou District is an area extremely popular with locals and visitors alike for its waterfront dining and plethora of bars and restaurants. Nanshan is Shenzhen's arts and theme-park district. Surrounding these smaller districts like a misshapen croissant are Shenzhen's two largest (and least urban) districts: Bao'an to the east and Longgang to the west.

Luohu & Futian
Though Luohu and Futian are the smallest districts in the city, for many it is this urban jungle of skyscrapers, markets, restaurants, and hotels

Avoid the Luohu Border-Crossing Crush

AT LUOHU (the main border crossing between Hong Kong and mainland China) the masses are funneled through a large three-story building. From the outside this building looks huge, but from the inside–especially when you're surrounded by a quarter million other people waiting to be processed–the crossing can be reminiscent of a scene from *Soylent Green.*

ALTERNATIVE ROUTES
If you're just going through Shenzhen en route to or from Guangzhou, take the through train from Kowloon to Guangzhou. The immigration line at the Guangzhou East station is a comparative piece of cake, even on the worst days. It's possible to buy tickets on the fly on this commuter train, but we advise booking anywhere from a few hours to a day or two in advance.

If you're heading into Shenzhen, why not trade the mad crush of Luohu for an hourlong ferry ride followed by a quick trip through the much less popular border crossing at Shekou Harbor? Although this won't bring you into downtown Shenzhen, you'll be no farther from attractions like the amusement parks and Mission Hills Golf Club.

---

that defines Shenzhen. Luohu (*Lo Wu* in Cantonese) is the area beginning right at the border crossing with Hong Kong. Jienshi Road is the street that ends at the border, and like many border areas, has more than just a bit of a rough feel about it. Single men walking on this road (which parallels the train tracks leading north to Guangzhou and south to Hong Kong) will be harassed by countless women shouting out "massage" and "missy" (ironically, this street also has a number of good, reputable massage parlors as well as a number of excellent restaurants).

Futian, Shenzhen's trading hub, is also where the Shenzhen's gourmands go for a night of gastronomic pleasure. The Zhenhua Road–restaurant district in Futian is where scores of excellent restaurants compete for the patronage of Shenzhen's very discriminating diners.

Nanshan & Shekou

Nanshan is where you'll find Shenzhen's most stylish district, Huaqiao Cheng, or Overseas Chinese Town (often called the OCT District). Here you will find the **OCT park,** an urban expanse of greenery and sculpture (whose highlights include pieces like Fu Zhongwang's "Earth Gate," a Gothic-looking locked

> **UNDERGROUND SHENZEN**
>
> Shenzhen's brand-new metro runs from the terminus at Luohu station to the Windows of the World Station in OCT. What's more, many stations have sculptures, murals, and other objets d'art. The metro is cheap, easy to use, and has announcements in Chinese and English. Stored-value tickets are available at any station for Y100, and can be cashed in for any unused balance at the end of your trip.

iron door buried in the ground, and French sculptor Bernar Vernet's *230.5*, a postmodern monument of forged steel that fits well with Shenzhen's industrious nature). There are two excellent museums, the **Hexiangning Museum of Contemporary Chinese Art**, and the more underground-feeling **OCAT** (Overseas Chinese Art Terminal). The OCT also has three popular theme parks.

> **PLAY TIME**
>
> The theme parks in OCT could all be visited in a single day, but for the sake of sanity, we recommend only visiting two for the day. They are connected by an elevated monorail that costs Y20. Splendid China and Windows on the World have some "cultural" value, and Happy Kingdom is fun for kids.

Shekou was the first Special Economic Zone, marking the earliest baby step of modern China's transformation from state planned to market economy. Nowadays the neighborhood is best known for **Sea World Plaza**, a pedestrian mall featuring restaurants, bars, and a completely landlocked oceangoing vessel (now transformed into a bar, hotel, and nightclub complex), and the Shekou bar street.

Splendid China features China's 74 best-known historical and geographical sights collected and miniaturized to 1:15 scale. Built in 1991 and popularized by Deng Xiaoping (who stopped in for a photo op on his famous 1992 journey south promoting free enterprise), it is still a big draw with the patriotic camera-wielding masses, and not a few Westerners "doing China" in a day. The 74-acre site includes a waist-high Great Wall, a fun-size Forbidden City, and little Potala Palace. ✉ *OCT District, Shenzhen* ☎ *0755/2660–0626* 💰 *Y140* ☉ *Daily 10–10* Ⓜ *Windows of the World metro station.*

Windows of the World gives a similar miniature makeover to 130 of the world's most famous landmarks and is China's biggest and busiest homegrown theme park. Divided into eight geographical areas interconnected by winding paths and a full-size monorail, it includes randomly scaled Taj Mahal, Mount Rushmore, Sydney Harbor Opera House, and a 100-meter- (328-foot-) high Eiffel Tower that can be seen from miles away. There is also a fireworks show at 9 PM on weekends and holidays which, for adults, is best viewed from across the street at the Crowne Plaza's rooftop V-Bar. ✉ *OCT, Nanshan District, Shenzhen* ☎ *0755/ 2660–8000* ⊕ *www.szwwco.com* 💰 *Y140* ☉ *Daily 9 AM–10 PM* Ⓜ *Windows of the World metro station.*

Shenzhen is a great city for art lovers. In addition to its statue-filled Overseas Chinese Town Park, the OCT neighborhood is packed with other museums. The **He Xiangning Art Museum** is free on Friday and features contemporary and classical art from all over China. ✉ *Shenzhen shi Huaqiaocheng Shennan Dadao 9013 hao, OCT, Nanshan District* ☎ *0755/2660–4540* ☉ *Tues.–Sun. 10–6* Ⓜ *Huaqiaocheng metro station.*

The **OCT Contemporary Art Terminal.** Shenzhen shi Huaqiaocheng Enping Lu is where you'll find works from the hippest artists from Beijing and beyond. ✉ *OCT, Nanshan District* ☎ *0755/2691–6199* ☉ *Call for hrs* Ⓜ *Huaqiaocheng metro station.*

Yantian, Longgang & Bao'an

Though these three districts make up the bulk of Shenzhen's land area, most casual visitors to the city never hear of them, let alone visit them. We think this is a pity, as it's these outer regions where you'll find both the prettiest scenery and the most culturally edifying places in the Pearl River Delta, not to mention China's most famous golf course, Mission Hills.

Just east of Luohu, Yantian is Shenzhen's beach district. **Dameisha** and **Xiaomeisha** are two beaches adjacent to one another, which offer sun, surf, and strange statues of colorful winged men doing what appears to be beachfront tai chi. Dameisha is a public beach, whereas Xiaomeisha has a Y20 admission price. Both are about 40 minutes from Luohu by taxi. Yantian is also the home of **Minsk World,** a decommissioned Soviet-era aircraft carrier turned into a tourist attraction.

Minsk World. When a group of Shenzhen businessmen bought a decommissioned Soviet-era aircraft carrier in the late 1990s, Western intelligence agencies wondered if it was a military move by the Chinese. But the truth was revealed when these savvy entrepreneurs turned this massive warship into Minsk World, Shenzhen's most popular—and perhaps strangest—tourist attraction. Parked in perpetuity on the top deck of the ship (which is as long as three football fields placed end to end, and gets wickedly hot in the summer) are several Soviet fighter planes and helicopters. Every hour on the hour comely young ladies in military costumes perform a dance routine combining sensuality with martial flair and twirling rifles. A visit to Minsk World will be of greatest interest to military buffs. Even casual visitors should find it educational enough to warrant spending the afternoon. ⊠ *Shatoujiao, Dapeng Bay, Yantian District, Shenzhen* ☎ *Y110* ☉ *Daily 10–9.*

Longgang, Shenzen's ancient heart, is where you'll find the sights that belie the city's reputation as a place of new money and no history. **Dapeng Fortress** is a Ming Dynasty–era walled city where visitors can wander down narrow cobblestone streets and walk on parapets that were ancient even in the days of the last Qing empress. The **Hakka Folk Customs Museum and Enclosures** is another walled town. This one was built (and formerly occupied) by the Hakka—Han Chinese who are said to have migrated from north to south ages ago, bringing with them their own cuisine and traditions; not to mention peculiar building design. Both of these slices of ancient China are about an hour away from the modern heart of Luohu by taxi.

Finally, the Bao'an District is famous for Mission Hills, the finest golf club in China and the largest in the world (according to the *Guinness Book of World Records*).

Dapeng Fortress was built over 600 years ago, and is an excellent example of a Ming Dynasty–military encampment (1368–1644). The fortress was originally built to resist Japanese pirates who'd been harassing the southern coastal areas of Guangdong. However, the fortress is best known as the site of the British Naval attack of September 4, 1839, in which British forces attacked China in what is widely considered the beginning of the Opium Wars. As local legend goes, Chinese troops in fishing boats, led by General Lai Enjue, defeated the better-equipped enemy. Today, visitors flock to the fortress to admire the inside of the walled town, which is replete with ornately carved beams and columns, with poetic couplets painted over each door. ⊠ *Pengcheng Village, Dapeng Town, Longgang District, Shenzhen* ☎ *No phone* ☜ *Y20* ☉ *Daily 10–9.*

Hakka Folk Customs Museum and Enclosures is actually a large series of concentric circular homes built inside of an exterior wall that basically turns the whole place into a large fort. Inside of the enclosure are a large number of old Hakka residences, some of which are still filled with tools and furniture left over from the Qing Dynasty. The site is somewhat feral; once you pass the ticket booth, you're pretty much on your own and free to stroll around the grounds and explore inside the residences themselves, many of which seem to have been left in a mostly natural state. Although some restoration projects pretty things up to the point of making the site look unreal, the opposite is true here. Parts of the enclosures are so real as to seem downright spooky; visitors might get the feeling that the original inhabitants may return at any moment, crossbows cocked. ⊠ *Luoruihe Village, Longgang Township, Longgang District, Shenzhen* ☎ *0755/2883–5108* ☜ *Y20* ☉ *Daily 10–6.*

If you're interested in watching art in the making, spend an afternoon at the **Dafen Oil Painting Village,** a small town 20 minutes by taxi from Luohu, which employs thousands of artists painting everything from originals to copies of classics. Where do all those oil paintings you find in motels come from? Visit Dafen and you'll know. Be aware, opening hours are sporadic. ⊠ *Shen Hui Rd., Bu Ji St., Longgang District* ☎ *0755/ 8473–2622.*

Where to Eat

Shenzhen is packed with people from other provinces, and its main culinary strength lies in this diversity. From the heavy mutton stews of Xinjiang to the spicy seafood dishes of Fujian, Shenzhen is home to thousands of restaurants existing not to please the fickle palates of visitors, but to alleviate the homesickness of people pining for native provinces left behind. Furthermore, over the past few years, Shenzhen has attracted a slew of restaurateurs from abroad, making the city a veritable culinary mecca, not merely for those with a taste for Chinese cuisine, but for international gourmands as well.

★ **$$$–$$$$** ✕ **Blue Italian Seafood & Grill.** Arguably one of the finest Italian restaurants in China, the decor, as the name suggests, is blue—blue walls, ceilings, and mellow indigo lighting. The food is expensive but worth every penny. If you're really in the mood for decadence, try the dessert tray—chocolates, pastries, and eight different types of mousse surround a caramelized sugar statue of David. ⊠ *Crowne Plaza Hotel, 3rd fl., 9026 Shen Nan Rd., OCT District* ☎ *0755/2693–6888 Ext. 8022, 8023, or 8106* ⊟ *AE, DC, MC, V.*

$$–$$$ ✕ **Greenland Lounge.** This favorite is known for its international-style buffet and truly unique selection of Chinese teas. The glass-domed roof and smart-casual ambiance make this a popular spot for Shenzhen's movers and shakers. ✉ *Lobby, Pavilion Hotel, 4002 Huaqiang Rd. N, Futian District* ☎ *0755/ 8207–8888* 🖃 *AE, DC, MC, V.*

$$–$$$
Fodor'sChoice
★
✕ **360.** The newest (and possibly brightest) star on the Shenzhen haute-cuisine scene, 360 takes up the top two floors of the Shangri-la hotel, and offers sumptuous dishes like homemade pasta with eggplant, zucchini, and pesto sauce and ginger-crusted-salmon fillet with couscous and lemon celery sauce. Ambiance is chic, and the view from any table in the house is breathtaking. For food, decor, and view we can't recommend this place highly enough. ✉ *31st fl., Shangri-la hotel, 1002 Jianshi Rd. Luohu* ☎ *0755/ 8396–1380* 🖃 *AE, DC, MC, V* Ⓜ *Luohu metro.*

> ### ADVENTUROUS EATING
>
> The Futian District's Zhen Hua Road, just two blocks north of the Hua Qiang metro station, is one of the few food streets that has not succumbed to the franchise blight of McDonald's and KFC. There are very few English menus and even less Western food, so be prepared to be adventurous. Two good choices are the North Sea Fishing Village Restaurant, whose waitstaff speak a bit of English, and has live seafood in tanks out front allowing diners to point and choose, and Lao Yuan Zi, a restaurant with a definite *Crouching Tiger Hidden Dragon* vibe.

$–$$ ✕ **Sunday Chiu Chow King.** The dim sum and other Cantonese dishes are good, but what really sets this place apart is the excellent Chaozhou (or Chiu Chow) cuisine. The restaurant is well known on both sides of the border, and usually packed on the weekends with noisy diners from Hong Kong. Try the crispy fried tofu and steamed seafood balls, or the yin-yang soup (it's the soup that looks like a yin-and-yang symbol, made up of rice congee on one side and creamed spinach on the other, just point to the picture on the menu). All of these are Chaozhou specialty dishes. ✉ *Jen Shi Rd. 1076, 9th–10th fls., Luohu, 2 blocks north of Shangri-La Hotel* ☎ *0755/ 8231–0222* 🖃 *V* Ⓜ *Luohu metro station.*

★ **$–$$** ✕ **Yokohama.** Here they offer excellent sushi with amazing views of the fishing boats and ferries of Shekou Harbor to the east, and the hills of Shekou to the north. Sashimi is the freshest around, and other dishes are the real deal. The clientele is mostly Japanese, which is always a good sign. Try a side dish of *oshinko* (traditional Japanese pickles)—unlike many lesser Japanese restaurants in China, Yokohama takes no shortcuts with its oshinko and offers eight different types. ✉ *Shekou Harbor, Nanhai Hotel, 10th fl., Shekou District* ☎ *0755/2669–5557* 🖃 *AE, DC, MC, V.*

$ ✕ **Little India.** This is definitely more than your average curry house. The Nepalese chef offers cuisine from both northern India and Nepal. The restaurant is especially known for its tandoori dishes, and for its selection of baked *nan* breads. Little India is also the only restaurant in the Sea World Plaza that offers hookahs, though they'll gently ask you to smoke on the outdoor pavilion during peak hours. ✉ *Shop 73-74, Sea World Plaza, Shekou District* ☎ *0755/2685–2688* 🖃 *MC, V.*

$–$$ ✕ **Shenzhen North Sea Restaurant.** This is a popular Shenzen franchise (there are two other locations) where diners can pick their own seafood

CLOSE UP

To Your Health!

GOOD-BYE STARBUCKS, hello Wong Chun Loong! For decades the Loong-beverage franchise has dominated the Guangzhou scene, and for good reason. They serve drinks that are thirst-quenching, healthy, and taste good (sometimes). The most popular drink is *Huomaren*, a beverage made from crushed hemp seeds (it's the brown beverage displayed on the counter) and *yezi*, or coconut milk. A cup of either only costs Y2.

Wong Chun Loong also brews Chinese medicinal teas—some of the bitterest stuff you're ever likely to taste. If you'd like to try some, point to your throat and say *"wo gan mao"*–"I have a cold." If you're nice, they may give you a free piece of candy to cut the aftertaste.

There are about 800 branches in the city, so if you walk a few blocks in any direction, you're bound to stumble on one of them.

from one of the tanks outside and have it cooked to order. The restaurant is known for its quality and freshness, and is busy on any given night. We've chosen the branch on the Zhen Hua Road food street simply because it's easy to find and a few of the waitresses understand a bit of English. ✉ *79 Zhen Hua Rd., Futian District, 2 blocks north of the Huaqiang metro station* ☎ *0755/8322–1852* ⊟ *MC, V.*

$ ✕ **Lao Yuan Zi.** They have Sichuan and Hunan food so spicy that scientists are looking into the connection between Lao Yuan Zi's cuisine and global warming. A favorite dish is the hotpot, made with fiery red chilies and a variety of meat and vegetables. A plethora of cold-vegetable dishes abound, as do meat, seafood, and vegetable dishes of all sorts. If you order the Sichuan hotpot, the best strategy is to keep a bowl of white rice close at hand; beer won't douse this fire fast enough. Be warned; this place can get rather noisy. ✉ *1,2/F, Qi Che Building, at the intersection of Zhen Hua and Yan Nan Rds., Futian District, 2 blocks north of the Hua Qiang metro station* ☎ *020/8332–8400* ⊟ *No credit cards.*

¢–$ ✕ **Foodfeast.** This is the only place in Shekou for genuine Hakka cuisine, including rich soups made with pork and bitter melon, serious Hakka-style dumplings, stewed clay-pot dishes and roasted chicken, duck, and fatty pork. Try the durian pancake, if you're a fan of the enormously smelly "king of fruits." (Durian's odor is so strong that it is sometimes banned from subways.) Foodfeast is unpretentious, the sort of place where Sun Yet-sen might have taken tea while plotting the revolution against the Manchu Dynasty. ✉ *Sea World Hotel, 1st fl., Taizi Rd. #7, Shekou District* ☎ *0755/2540–4730* ⊟ *No credit cards.*

Where to Stay

$$$$ ✕ **Crowne Plaza.** This hotel holds its own among the best hotels in **Fodor'sChoice** Asia. Theme is pure Italian Renaissance, right down to the Venetian-★ gondolier uniforms worn by the staff, and the wide spiral staircases and long hallways gives the place an M. C. Escher feel. The Crowne's swimming pool is the largest in Shenzen, and extends from an indoor pool under a domed roof to a connected outdoor pool with a swim-up bar. One regular patron told us that she comes back "because anywhere you look in this hotel there's something interesting." The Crowne also has a number of excellent restaurants, including Blue, Marcos, and JK. ⊠ *OCT District, 518053, across from Windows of the World metro station* ☎ *0755/2693–6888* ⊕ *www.crowneplaza.com* ↪ *340 rooms, 50 suites* ☖ *5 restaurants, pool, gym, sauna, 2 bars, business services, meeting room* ⊟ *AE, DC, MC, V.*

$$$$ ✕⊡ **The Pavilion.** With a great location in the heart of the Futian business district, and a gorgeous interior (check out the domed-glass roof over a central piano bar–teahouse), the Pavilion is one of the top international-class hotels in Shenzhen. Service is good, especially for a locally managed hotel, and most staff members speak English. In addition to the teahouse, the Pavilion has Western, Chinese, Korean, and Japanese restaurants, all very tastefully done-up. The meeting rooms have everything an international traveler could need. ⊠ *4002 Huaqiang Bei Lu, Futian District, 518028* ☎ *0755/ 8207–8888* ⊕ *www.pavilionhotel. com* ↪ *297 rooms, 19 suites* ☖ *4 restaurants, pool, gym, sauna, business services, meeting room* ⊟ *AE, DC, MC, V.*

$$$–$$$$ ⊡ **Landmark Shenzhen.** Since completing its ambitious renovation program in 2006, The Landmark has become Shenzhen's first *all suite* hotel; every room is a suite, boasting a 42-inch plasma television and extra large bathrooms. In addition, the hotel has five excellent restaurants, including a wine and cigar bar with a walk-in humidor. However, what makes this hotel truly unique is its personalized butler service, managed by Robert Watson, director of the Guild of Professional English Butlers and the former principal tutor at the Lady Apsley School for Butlers in London. As for amenities, this hotel basically has it all. If you're looking to experience the life of China's new elite, this is the place to do it. ⊠ *3018 Nanhu Lu, 3 blocks NE of Shenzhen main station, Shenzhen 518001* ☎ *0755/8217–2288* ⊕ *www.szlandmark.com* ↪ *253 suites* ☖ *5 restaurants, driving range, pool, gym, bar, shops, business services, meeting rooms* ⊟ *AE, DC, MC, V.*

★ **$$$–$$$$** ✕⊡ **Shangri-La Shenzhen.** The location (practically straddling the border with Hong Kong) has made it a popular meeting place, and it's a city landmark. Rooms are first class, hospitality is excellent, and the hotel features in-house wireless Internet and top-notch spa facilities. What really makes Shangri-La worth a visit is the newly renovated 360 Lounge and Restaurant, which takes up the top two floors of the hotel and offers a view of Shenzhen. The Shangri-La also has a number of other excellent restaurants, making it a good choice for first-time visitors who might not want to come into contact with the neighborhood's rougher edges. ⊠ *1002 Jianshe Lu, Luohu District, Shenzhen 518001, Luohu, east side of train station* ☎ *0755/8233–0888* ⊕ *www.shangri-la.com* ↪ *553 rooms, 30 suites* ☖ *6 restaurants, pool, gym, hair salon, bar, shops, business services, meeting rooms* ⊟ *AE, DC, MC, V.*

¢–$ ⊡ **Cruise Inn.** Pearlescent tiled floors and stained-glass ceilings are the first thing you'll notice in the lobby of this newly opened hotel inside of the landlocked and permanently docked good ship *Minghua*, the cen-

Sleeping on the Cheap

SPAS ARE A RECENT and much welcome trend in Shenzhen, and the city offers a number of excellent places to get soaked, sauna'd, and massaged to your heart's content. Although some of these places are thinly disguised houses of ill repute, many more cater to a higher class of clientele looking for a legitimate massage and sauna.

The way a Chinese sauna works is this: you check in, lock up your belongings in a guarded locker room (you keep one key and the attendants keep the other), and have a shower and steam, and then soak as long as you like. Afterward, dressed in the spa's pajamas, you relax in a common area (usually well stocked with food and beverages, a couple of plasma-screen televisions piping in Hong Kong television, and comfortable chaise longues) until you're ready for your massage.

A well-known money-saving tip among Chinese travelers on overnight business is to check in to one of these places in the mid- to late evening and

catch a few hours' sleep in the common area after your massage. Your admission price—usually around Y200—entitles you to stick around until 9 AM the next day, and the common areas are generally pretty quiet after 2 AM (and guests are always provided blankets), making this a good strategy for anyone on a shoestring budget.

One such place in the Futian District that's both clean, cheerful, and co-ed is the **Shanshui Korean Spa** (✉ No.1 Hua Fa Bei Lu,, Futian District, 2 blocks north of Hua Qiang metro station ☎ 0755/6135–8862). Shanshui (which means "mountain water") is a Korean-themed spa. Although the hot tubs in both areas are somewhat small, the spa offers a rather interesting co-ed dry-sauna filled with small, rounded stones, which visitors are meant to sink down into for a full-body experience. Y165 gets you a massage, full sauna privileges, a light snack, and a night's stay should you be so inclined.

6

---

tral feature of Shekou's Sea World Plaza. Rooms are clean, comfortable, and nautically themed. The Romantic Sea View room has a waterbed and a view of the ocean and driving range; the Captain's Suite looks out over the bar street, and has two plasma-screen televisions and a Jacuzzi. If a whimsical maritime *Alice in Wonderland*-style inn is what you're looking for, then look no farther. ✉ *Minghua Ship, Sea World, Shekou 518069* ☎ *0755/2682–5555* ⊕ *www.honlux.com* ⇲ *110 rooms, 1 suite* ♨ *3 restaurants, coffee shop, 2 bars, dance club, driving range, bicycles* ⊟ *AE, DC, MC, V.*

¢–$ ✕🖳 **Nan Hai.** This hotel's retro space-age exterior, featuring rounded balconies that look as if they might detach from the mother ship at any moment, is the first sight greeting visitors on the Hong Kong–Shekou ferry. Although one of Shenzhen's older luxury hotels, the Nan Hai still holds its own in the moderate-luxury class, offering a lobby piano bar, attractive rooms with balconies and sea views, and a number of excellent restaurants, including Yokohama. ⊠ *1 Gongye Yilu, Shekou 18069* ☎ *0755/2669–2888* ⊕ *www.nanhai-hotel.com* ⟿ *358 rooms, 86 suites* ⚒ *5 restaurants, 2 tennis courts, pool, hair salon, piano bar, dance club, meeting rooms* ⊟ *AE, DC, MC, V.*

¢–$$ 🖵 **Shenzhen Sea view.** Staying in the OCT District but can't afford the Crowne Plaza? The nearby Sea view hotel is a good bet, albeit far less luxurious. Though rack prices are steep, discounts of up to 40% are usually available. The Sea view is clean, comfortable, has a water view, and thanks to its location across the street from the He Xiangning Art Museum, it is very popular with visiting artists. The 2nd-floor restaurant serves excellent Western food, and the 3rd-floor Cantonese restaurant is good for dim sum. ⊠ *No. 3-5 Guangqiao St., OCT, Nanshan District, Directly in front of Huaqiao Cheng metro* ☎ *0755/2660–2222* ⟿ *446 rooms, 11 suites* ⚒ *2 restaurants, coffee shop, gym, sauna* ⊟ *AE, DC, MC, V.*

¢–$ 🖵 **Shanshui Trends Hotel.** This budget hotel in the Futian District appeals mostly to business travelers. With a round bed and view of the interior food court, the Romance Suite is a bit musty and distinctly unromantic. However, the Japanese Suite, with its wooden tub and traditional tatami mats was much nicer. Shanshui Trends is a good deal for travelers on a shoestring, located in one of Shenzhen's most happening food districts. Discounts of up to 30% are available. ⊠ *No.1 Hua Fa Bei Lu,, Futian District, 2 blocks north of Hua Qiang metro station* ☎ *0755/6135–8802* ⟿ *197 rooms, 2 suites* ⚒ *Spa, gym* ⊟ *AE, DC, MC, V.*

Nightlife & the Arts

Shenzhen's nightlife is so happening that it's not unusual to run into people—expats and Chinese—who've come in from Hong Kong and Guangzhou just to party. The two major nightlife centers in Shenzhen are the Luohu District and Shekou District (Luohu tends to be flashier and Shekou a bit more laid-back), but there are also a couple of cool spots in the OCT District as well. ■ TIP→ **A great English-language Web site that lists the latest on what's happening in Shenzhen's ever-evolving party scene is** ⊕ **www.shenzhenparty.com.**

Baby Face (⊠ Beside Lushan Hotel, Luohu District ☎ 0755/9234–2565 ⊕ www.babyface.com.cn) is the Shenzhen branch of one of China's most popular nightspots, offering imported DJs, a late-night-party scene, and extremely chic clientele (so don't show up in sandals).

True Colors (⊠ 3F Dongyuan Mansion, 1 Dongyuan Lu, Futian District ☎ 0755/8212–9333) has one of the coolest party scenes in Shenzhen and attracts top-name international DJs. Musical tastes range from trance to house, and the party usually doesn't break up until dawn.

V-Bar (⊠ Crowne Plaza Hotel, rooftop OCT District ☎ 0755/2693–6888) is without a doubt the hottest nightspot in the OCT, featuring a live band, a holographic globe hovering over a circular bar, and a fireworks show on the weekends at 9 PM courtesy of the Windows of the World theme park across the street. The V-Bar is the only bar in town with an attached swimming pool.

Browns Wine Bar & Cigar House (✉ Portofino, OCT District, Shenzhen ☎ 0755/8608–2379) is the perfect, low-key place for quiet conversation over a bottle of wine and a Cuban cigar. Browns has an admirable stock of vintage wines, cognacs, and Armagnacs, and a walk-in humidor to insure that all cigars are kept fresh. This is a good spot for those who appreciate old-money ambiance and fine cigars.

Soho Nightclub (✉ TaiZi Bar St, Shekou District ☎ 0755/ 2669–0148 or 0755/2669–2148) is the place in Shekou to dance, drink, and party. If you need a rest from dancing, be sure to slip out to the outdoor garden for a cocktail.

> **OUT IN SHENZHEN**
>
> One of the byproducts of China's rapid modernization has been the shedding of old taboos. Although it's an overstatement to say being gay is no longer taboo, it is safe to say that the closet door has been opened in a big way. And no place is this more true than in Shenzhen, which has always prided itself as being ahead of the curve.

3 colors Bar (✉ Jing Yuan Building, 2nd fl., SongYuan Rd., Luohu District ☎ 0755/2588–7000) is a lively dance club that's very in with Shenzhen's gay crowd. It's a fun place so there's often a wide mix of people.

Er Ding Mu (✉ Jiang Nan Chun Hotel, 3rd fl., Ai Hua Rd. No.23, Futian District, at Nanyuan and Ai Hua Rds. ☎ 0755/8365–1879 or 131/ 4883–9798) is another popular gay club, offering a more relaxed spot for a mostly younger male crowd to unwind and hook up.

Shopping

The ever-upwardly mobile denizens of the city (not to mention bargain hunters from neighboring Hong Kong) are always looking for places to spend their hard-earned yuan, and from computer parts to fashion, shoes to cell phones, China's first city of capitalism pretty much has it all.

Dongmen Shopping Plaza (✉ Laojie Metro Station, Luohu District, Shenzhen ☎ No phone) is Shenzhen's oldest shopping area. It's a sprawling pedestrian plaza with both large shopping centers for name-brand watches, shoes, bags, cosmetics, and clothes, and plenty of smaller outdoor shops. Foot fetishists won't want to miss the huge **Dongmen Shoes City,** close to the east side of the plaza. If you're into people-watching, grab a glass of bubble-milk tea and soak up the sights—the plaza is like a low-rent version of the fashionista youth culture in Tokyo's Ginza.

CITIC City Plaza (✉ 1095 Shennan Rd., Shenzhen ☎ 0755/2594–1502 ☺ Daily 10:30 AM to 10 PM Ⓜ Kexueguan metro station) offers upscale shopping for the time-conscious business traveler. Shops include Japanese department stores **Seibu and Jusco, Louis Vuitton, Polo,** and **Tommy Hilfiger.** There's also a food court on the lower level that's not a bad place to take a break over some coffee or a bowl of noodle soup.

Louhu Lo Wu (Commercial City) (✉ Adjacent to the Hong Kong Border Crossing/Luohu metro station, Shenzhen ☎ No phone ☺ Daily 10

AM–10 PM) is a venerable stalwart of Shenzhen mixed-bag shopping. On one hand, its location (straddling the Hong Kong–Shenzhen border) makes it a good place to do last-minute shopping for pirate DVDs, shoddy electronics, and phony versions of just about any name brand you can think of, and stalls selling semiprecious stones and feng-shui knickknacks on the 2nd floor is pretty cool. On the other hand, Luohu Commercial City has some of the most aggressive touts you're likely to find in Shenzhen. If having "DVD? Rolex watch?" shouted every 20 seconds doesn't bother you, this place might be worth the trip.

San Dao Plaza (✉ Jen Shi Rd. 1076 Luohu Shenzhen ☎ No phone ⊘ 9 AM–8 PM Ⓜ Luohu metro station). This four-story extravaganza is the area's best market for medicinal herbs, tea, and tea-related products. The top two floors contain a series of stalls where merchants sell a wide range of Chinese teas. Visitors are generally invited to *lai, he cha,* or come drink tea. Don't worry, it isn't considered rude to have a cup without buying anything, but if you're a tea aficionado you'll find it hard to leave empty-handed. Downstairs, there is also a large vegetable market and small shops selling traditional Chinese herbal medicines, incense, and religious items. If you speak a little Chinese, you can have your fortune told.

Golf

Shenzen has an abundance of golf courses, the most famous being the **Mission Hills Golf Club** (✉ Nan Shan, Da Wei, Sha He, Bao'an District, Shenzhen ☎ 0755/2690–9999, 852/2826–0238 in Hong Kong ⊕ www.missionhillsgroup.com). The club has 10 celebrity-designed 18-hole courses (2 of which offer nighttime playing), as well as a spectacular clubhouse, a tennis court, 2 restaurants, and an outdoor pool. There's also a five-star hotel on the premises for golfers serious about trying every course. Mission Hills offers a shuttle bus service from Hong Kong and Shenzhen (call Shenzhen: 0755/2802–0888 or Hong Kong: 852/2973–0303 for schedule). Greens fees: Y600 weekdays and Y1,000 weekends; caddies Y150.

The **Guangzhou Luhu Golf & Country Club** (✉ Lujing Rd. ☎ 020/8350–7777) has 18 holes spread over 180 acres of Luhu Park, 20 minutes from the Guangzhou Railway Station and 30 minutes from Baiyun Airport. The 6,820-yard, par-72 course was designed by world-renowned course-architect Dave Thomas. The club also offers a 75-bay driving range and a clubhouse with restaurants, pro shop, and a gym. Members' guests and those from affiliated clubs pay Y637 in greens fees on weekdays, Y1,274 on weekends. Nonmembers pay Y849 and Y1,486, respectively. These prices include a caddie. Clubs can be rented for Y265. The club is a member of the International Associate Club network.

FORE!

Although manufacturing is undoubtedly the Pearl River Delta's raison d'etre, golfing may well come in as a close second—the area has over 30 golf courses.

White Swan Hotel Golf Practice Center (⊠ White Swan Hotel, Yi Shamian Lu Shamain Island ☎ 020/8188–6968) is a good driving range on Shamian Island if you are pressed for time or don't want to leave the city. Admission is Y70, a rental of one club is Y30, and a box of 20 balls is Y10.

The **Sand River Golf Club** (⊠ 1 Baishi Lu, Nanshan District Shenzhen ☎ 0755/2690–0111 ⊙ Daily 7 AM–9 PM) is another popular club, though not nearly as large as Mission Hills. Sand River offers two courses, one of which is designed by Gary Player and floodlighted for night playing. Other facilities include a large driving range, a lake, and various resort amenities. Greens fees: 9-holes Y330 weekdays and Y550 weekends. Greens fees: Y660 weekdays and Y1,100 weekends; caddies Y160 to Y180.

The **Lakewood Golf Club** (⊠ Da'nan Mountain, Jinding District ☎ 0756/338–3666) is about 20 minutes from the Zhuhai Ferry Terminal, and is the most popular of the city's five golf clubs. Both its Mountain Course and its Lake Course are 18 holes, and are said to be challenging. Visitor packages, including greens fees and a caddy are Y420 for weekdays and Y820 weekends. Golf carts cost Y200.

Side Trips to Zhongshan and Zhuhai

Two other cities worth visiting in the Pearl River Delta are Zhongshan and Zhuhai. Though some casual visitors might choose to spend more than one day in this region, both are small enough to be seen in an afternoon.

Zhongshan is 78 km (48 mi) from Guangzhou and 61 km (38 mi) northwest of Macau. Until recently it was a picturesque port, where a cantilever bridge over the Qi River was raised twice a day to allow small freighters to pass. Today, the old town has been all but obliterated by modern high-rises, and the surrounding farms are now factories. However, there are still a few spots of historical note worth seeing.

Zhongshan is the birthplace of Sun Yat-sen and home to the **Sun Yat-sen Memorial Hall** (⊠ Sunwen Zhong Lu ☎ Y10 ⊙ Daily 8–4:50). Considered the father of the Chinese revolution that overthrew the corrupt Qing Dynasty, he is one of the few political figures respected on both sides of the Taiwan Straits.

The **Xishan Temple** (⊠ Xishan Park ☎ Y5 ⊙ Daily 8–5) is a beautifully restored temple that's also worth a visit.

Probably the most popular spot in town is **Sunwen Xilu,** a pedestrian mall lined with dozens of restored buildings. At the end of the street is the lovely **Zhongshan Park,** where there is the seven-story Fufeng Pagoda (about the only thing in Zhongshan not named after Sun Yat-sen), and also the world's largest statue of . . . you guessed it, Sun Yat-sen.

Buses travel daily to Zhongshan from bus stations throughout the Pearl River Delta.

Bordering Macau, and a little over an hour away by ferry from Hong Kong and Shenzen, most people don't see **Zhuhai** as a major destination in its own right. The city does, however, have a nice long coastline and many small offshore islands. Lover's Road, a 20-km (12½-mi) stretch of road hugging the shoreline, is Zhuhai's signature attraction, as beach-side drives are a rarity in China. The road leads to the **Macau Crossing** and has enough bars and restaurants to draw a steady crowd of Macau partygoers. Near the Macau border, across from the bus station, is **Yingbin Street,** a popular shopping area. Cheap seafood restaurants stay open well after midnight and, thanks to a variety of hawkers, street musicians, and food stalls, it makes for a fascinating, if slightly earthy, evening stroll.

To & from Shenzen

1 hr by express train, 2½ hrs by express bus (112 km [70 mi]) from Guangzhou. Walk across border from Hong Kong's Luohu KCR (Kowloon–Canton Railway) train station.

Tens of thousands of people cross from Hong Kong into Shenzhen (and back) daily, usually over the Luohu border crossing. Over the weekends, numbers can triple. Most visitors take the KCR train (⊕ www.kcrc.com) from Kowloon to the crossing and walk into Shenzhen. A more expensive—but infinitely more pleasant—way to is by taking the ferry from Hong Kong or Kowloon into Shekou Harbor. Here, immigration lines are a fraction of what they can be in Luohu. Shenzhen Party maintains an updated schedule for trains and ferries at ⊕ www.shenzhenparty.com/comingtoshenzhen/index.html.

The **Turbojet Company** (☎ 852/2921–6688 [#3 for English] ⊕ www.ctshk.com) runs regular ferries connecting Hong Kong, Shenzen, Macau, and Zhuhai. Check their Web site for schedules and prices.

PEARL RIVER DELTA ESSENTIALS

Transportation

BY AIR

Guangzhou's Baiyun Airport in Huada city is expected to establish Guangzhou as a regional air hub connecting the city to 40 international destinations by 2007. The airport currently offers 10 flights per day to both Hong Kong (Y670) and Beijing (Y1,240) between 9 AM and 9 PM. It has direct flights to Paris, Los Angeles, Singapore, Bangkok, Sydney, Jakarta, and Phnom Penh and a number of cities in North America. International airport tax is Y90, domestic departure tax is Y50.

Shenzhen Airport is very busy, with flights to 50 cities. There is commuter service by catamaran ferries and buses between the airport and Hong Kong. Bus service links the Shenzhen Railway Station, via Huaren Dasha, direct to Shenzhen Airport for Y25 (one-way). Zhuhai International Airport operates only domestically, to 24 cities.

⚑ Airline & Contacts Civil Aviation Administration of China, CAAC represented by China Southern ⊠ 181 Huanshi Lu, on left as you exit Guangzhou railway station (Guangzhou main station metro) ☎ 020/8668–2000, 24-hr hotline.

📄 Airport Information **Shenzhen Airport** ☎ 0755/2777-7821. **Zhuhai International Airport** ☎ 0756/889-5494.

BY BOAT & FERRY

📄 Boat & Ferry Information The **Turbojet Company** ☎ 852/2921-6688 (press 3 for English) ⊕ www.ctshk.com runs regular ferries connecting Hong Kong, Shenzen, Macau, and Zhuhai. Check their Web site for schedules and prices. **Macau Ferry Terminal** ⊠ Shun Tak Centre, Connaught Rd., Central ☎ 853/2546-3528.

BY BUS

Air-conditioned express buses crisscross most of the Pearl River Delta region several times a day. Ask at your hotel for the closest bus station.
📄 Bus Depots **Guangdong Provincial Bus Station** ⊠ 145 Huanshi Xi Lu ☎ 020/8666-1297. **Guangzhou Bus Station** ⊠ 158 Huanshi Xi Lu ☎ 020/8668-4259. **Tianhe Bus Station** ⊠ Yuangang, Tianhe District ☎ 020/8774-1083. **Shenzhen Luohu Bus Station** ⊠ 1st-2nd fls., East Plaza, Luohu District ☎ 755/8232-1670 **Zhuhai Gongbei Bus Station** ⊠ No.1 Lianhua Rd., Gongbei District ☎ 756/888-8554. **Zhongshan Bus Station** ⊠ Fuhua Rd., Shiqiben West District ☎ 760/863-3825.
📄 Bus Information **Citybus** ☎ 852/2873-0818.

BY SUBWAY

Guangzhou's clean and efficient underground metro currently has two lines connecting 36 stations, including the new East and old Central railway stations. Tickets range from Y2 to Y7. Shenzhen's metro, the newest in China, has two lines, and tickets range between Y2 and Y8.
📄 Metro Information **Metro** ☎ 020/8310-6622 for information in English, 020/8310-6666.

BY TRAIN

Shenzhen can easily be reached from Hong Kong by taking the KCR light railway from Hong Kong's Kowloon Tong KCR station to Luohu Railway Station and then crossing over to Shenzhen on foot. Trains depart from Luohu to Hong Kong every five minutes.

Five express trains (Y234 first-class, Y190 second-class) depart daily for Guangzhou East Railway Station from Hong Kong's Kowloon Station. The trip takes about 1¾ hours. The last train back to Hong Kong leaves at 5:25 PM. Trains between Shenzhen's Luohu Railway Station and Guangzhou East Railway Station run every hour and cost between Y80 and Y100.
📄 Train Stations **Guangzhou East Railway Station** ⊠ Lin Hezhong Rd., Tianhe District ☎ 020/6134-6222. **Guangzhou Railway Station** ⊠ Huanshi Lu ☎ 020/6135-7222. **Shenzhen Railway Station** ⊠ Luohu District ☎ 020/8232-8647.

Contacts & Resources

EMERGENCIES

In case of an emergency, contact your hotel manager for assistance. If you speak Chinese (or are traveling with someone who does), the following numbers may prove useful.
📄 General Contacts **Police** ☎ 110, the **fire department** ☎ 119, and the **first-aid hotline** ☎ 120.

F Hospitals **Shenzhen People's Hospital** ⊠ Dongmen Rd. N, Shenzhen ☎ 0755/2553–3018 Ext. 2553 or 1387 (Outpatient Dept.).

INTERNET SERVICES

Most major hotels in town provide broadband Internet service in the rooms, though increasingly guests are expected to pay between Y50 and Y100 per day. If you still hanker for an Internet café, otherwise known as *wang ba,* they're scattered all over almost any Chinese city.

VISITOR INFORMATION

With more than 30 branches all over Hong Kong, and many offices around the world, China Travel Services is probably the best place to make travel-bookings arrangements in mainland China. They are open weekdays 9 AM to 7 PM, Saturday 9 AM to 5 PM, and Sunday and holidays 9:30 to 12:30 and 2 PM to 5 PM.

F **China Travel Services** ⊠ China Travel Bldg, ground floor, 77 Queen's Rd., Central District, Hong Kong ☎ 852/2851-1700 or 852/2522-0450 ⊕ www.ctshk.com/english/index.htm.

At a Glance

ENGLISH	PINYIN	CHINESE CHARACTERS
EXPLORING		
GUANGZHOU	Guāng Zhōu	广州
Bright Filial Piety Temple	Guāngxiào Sì	光孝寺
Nan Yue Museum	Nán Yuè Bówùguǎn	南越博物馆
Chen Family Temple	Chénjiā Cí	陈家祠
Citybus Hong Kong Office	Xiānggǎng Chéngbā Bàngōngshì	香港城巴办公室
Five Rams Statue	Wǔyáng Sùxiàng	五羊塑像
GITIC Plaza	Zhōngxìn Guǎngchǎng	中信广场
Guangdong Museum of Art	Guǎngdōng Měishù Guǎn	广东美术馆
Guangdong Provincial Bus Station	Guǎngdōng Shěng Chángtú Qìchēzhàn	广东省长途汽车站
Guangxiao Temple	Guāngxiào sì	光孝寺
Guangzhou Bus Station	Guǎngzhōu Qìchēzhàn	广州汽车站
Guangzhou East Railway Station	Guǎngzhōu dōngzhàn	广州东站
Guangzhou Museum	Guǎngzhōu Bówùguǎn	广州博物馆
Huaisheng Mosque	Huáishèng Sì	怀圣寺
Liuhua Park	Liúhuāhú Gōngyuán	流花湖公园
Garden for the Martyrs	Lièshì Língyuán	烈士陵园
Mausoleum of the 72 Martyrs	Huánghuā Gǎng Qīshí'èr Lièshì Líng Yuán	黄花岗七十二烈士陵园
Orchid Garden	Lánpǔ Gōngyuán	兰圃公园
Our Lady of Lourdes	Shāmiàn Táng	沙面堂
Peasant Movement Institute	Nóngmín Yùndòng Jiǎngxí Suǒ	农民运动讲习所
Qingping Market	Qīngpíng Shìchǎng	清平市场
Revolutionary Museum	Qǐyì Bówùguǎn	起义博物馆
Shamian Island	Shāmiàn Dǎo	沙面岛
Six Banyan Temple	Liù Róng Si	六榕寺
Sun Yat-sen Memorial Hall	Sūn Zhōngshān Jìniàn Táng	孙中山纪念堂
Teem Plaza	Tiānhé Chéng	天河城
Tianhe Bus Station	Tiānhé Bāshì Zhàn	天河巴士站

6

Tianhe Stadium Complex	Tiānhé Tǐyù Zhōngxīn	天河体育中心
Tomb of the Southern Yue Kings	Nányuè Wáng Mù	南岳王墓
Tower Controlling the Sea	Zhènhǎi Lóu	镇海楼
White Cloud Mountain	Báiyúnshān	白云山
Yuexiu Park	Yuèxiù Gōngyuán	越秀公园
WHERE TO STAY & EAT		
Aiqun Hotel	Āiqún Jiǔdiàn	爱群酒店
Banxi Restaurant	Bànxī Jiǔjiā	泮溪酒家
Beijing Road Pedestrian Mall	Běijīng Lù Bùxíngjiē	北京路步行街
Café Elles	Mùzǐ Bā	木子吧
China Hotel	Zhōngguó Dàjiǔdiàn	中国大酒店
Chiu Chou City	Cháozhōu Chéng	潮州城
Connoisseur	Míng Shì Gé	名仕阁
Customs Hotel, The	Hǎiguān Bīnguǎn	海关宾馆
Da Chuan Japanese Food Restaurant	Dàchuān Rìběn Liàolǐ	大川日本料理
Datong Restaurant	Dátóng Jiǔdiàn	大同酒店
Dong Fang Hotel	Dōngfāng Bīnguǎn	东方宾馆
Dongjiang Seafood Restaurant	Dōngjiāng Hǎixiān Cāntīng	东江海鲜餐厅
Elan Hotel	Mǐlánhuā Jiǔdiàn	米兰花酒店
Garden Hotel	Huā yuán jiǔdiàn	花园酒店
Guangdong International Hotel	Guǎngdōng Jiāyì Guójì Jiǔdiàn	广东嘉逸国际酒店
Guangzhou Restaurant	Guǎngzhōu Jiǔjiā	广州酒家
Haizhu Plaza	Hǎizhū guǎngchǎng	海珠广场
Hare & Moon	Yuètù Jiǔbā	月兔酒吧
Haveli Restaurant and Bar	Táng Yuè Gōng	唐乐宫
Holiday Inn City Centre	Wénhuà Jiàrì Jiǔdiàn	文化假日酒店
Holiday Inn Shifu	Shífǔ Jiàrì Jiǔdiàn	十甫假日酒店
Huanshi East Road	Huánshì Dōng Lù	环市东路
Italian Restaurant, The	Xiǎojiē Fēngqíng	小街风情
Kathleen's	Kǎisèlín Kāfēi	凯瑟林咖啡
La Seine	Sàinàhé Fǎguó Xīcāntīng	塞纳河法国西餐厅

L'Africain	Fēizhōu Bā	非洲吧
Lai Wan Market	Lìwān Tíng	荔湾亭
Landmark Canton	Huáxià Dà Jiǔdiàn	华夏大酒店
Lucy's	Lùsī Jiǔbā	露丝酒吧
Mo Li Fang Theater	Mólìfāng Jùyuàn	魔立方剧院
Nan Yue Museum	Nányuè Bówùguǎn	南岳博物馆
Nile Restaurant	Níluóhé Cāntīng	尼罗河餐厅
Park 19	Park Yāojiǔ Yìshù Kōngjiān	Park 19 艺术空间
Roof, The	Líng Xiāo Gé	凌宵阁
Shamian Hotel	Shāmiàn Bīnguǎn	沙面宾馆
Silk Road Grill Room	Sīchóu Zhīlù Páfáng	"丝绸之路"扒房
Tang Yuan	Táng Yuàn	唐苑
Tao Tao Ju	Táotáo Jū	陶陶居
Thousand And One Nights	Yī Qiān Líng Yī Yè	一千零一夜
Tian Lun International Hotel	Tiānlún Wànyí Jiǔdiàn	天伦万怡酒店
Victory Hotel	Shènglì Bīnguǎn	胜利宾馆
White Swan Hotel	Báitiāné Jiǔdiàn	白天鹅酒店
White Swan Arcade	Báitiānér Shāngchǎng	白天鹅商场
Yidu Restaurant	Yìdū Jiǔjiā	艺都酒家

SHENZHEN	Shen Zhèn	深圳
EXPLORING		
Huaqiaocheng Station	Huánqiáochéng Zhàn	华侨城站
Bao'an	Bǎoān	保安
Dapeng Fortress	Dà Péng Gǔ Chéng	大鹏古城
Futian	Fú Tián	福田
Happy Kingdom	Huānlè Gǔ	欢乐谷
He Xiangning Art Museum	Héxiāngníng Měishùguǎn	何香凝美术馆
Longgang	Lónggǎng	龙岗
Longgang Hakka Customs Museum	Lónggǎng Kèjiārén Bówùguǎn	龙岗客家人博物馆
Lover's Road	Qíng Rén Lù	情人路
Luohu	LuóHú	罗湖
Macau Ferry Terminal	Àomén Mǎtóu	澳门码头
Minsk World	Míng Sī Kè Hángmǔ Shìjiè	明思克航母世界

6

Nanshan	Nán Shān	南山
OCT Contemporary Art Terminal	OCT Dāngdài Yìshù Zhōngxīn	OCT当代艺术中心
Oil Painting Village	Dàfēn Yóuhuà Shìjiè	大芬油画世界
Overseas Chinese Town	Huáqiáo Chéng	华侨城
Pengcheng Village	Péngchéng Cūn	鹏城村
Shekou	Shékǒu	蛇口
Shenzhen Airport	Shēnzhèn Jīchǎng	深圳机场
Splendid China	Jǐnxiù Zhōnghuá	锦绣中华
Windows of the World	Shìjiè Zhīchuāng	世界之窗
Yantian	Yántián	盐田
Yingbin Street	Yínbīn Dàdào	迎宾大道
Zhuhai	Zhūhǎi	珠海
Zhuhai International Airport	Zhūhǎi Guójì Jīchǎng	珠海国际机场
WHERE TO STAY & EAT		
Blue Italian Seafood & Grill	Yìdàlì Cāntīng	意大利餐厅
CITIC City Plaza	Shēnzhèn Zhōngxìn Dàshà	深圳中信大厦
Crowne Plaza	Wēinísī Huángguān Jiàrì Jiǔdiàn	威尼斯皇冠假日酒店
Cruise Inn	Míng Huá Lún Jiǔ Diàn	明华轮酒店
Foodfeast	Lǎolóng Fēngwèi Shífǔ	老隆风味食府
Fuhua Hotel	Zhōngshān Fùhuá Jiǔdiàn	中山富华酒店
Futian District, Shenzhen	Shēn Zhèn Fú Tián	深圳福田
Grand Bay View	Zhūhǎi Hǎiwān Dà Jiǔdiàn	珠海海湾大酒店
Greenland Lounge	Lǜ Jiàn Láng Dàtángbā	绿涧廊大堂吧
Holiday Inn Zhuhai	Zhūhǎi Yuècái Jiàrì Jiǔdiàn	珠海粤财假日酒店
Huaqiao Cheng Metro	Huáqiáochéng Dìtiězhàn	华侨城地铁站
Jinye Hotel	Jīnyè Jiǔdiàn	金叶酒店
Landmark Shenzhen	Fùyuàn Jiǔdiàn	富苑酒店
Lao Yuan Zi	Láo Yuàn Zī	老院子
Little India	Xiǎo Yìndù Cāntīng	小印度餐厅
Nan Hai	Nánhǎi	南海
OCT	HuáQiáo Chéng	华侨城
Paradise Hill	ShíjǐngShān Lǚyóu Zhōngxīn Dà Jiǔdiàn	石景山旅游中心大酒店

San Dao Plaza	Sān Dǎo Zhōngxīn	三岛中心
Shangri-La Shenzhen	Shēn Zhèn Xiāng Gé Lǐ Lā Jiǔ Diàn	深圳香格里拉酒店
Shanshui Trends Hotel	Shānshuǐ Hánguó Jiǔdiàn	山水韩国酒店
Shenzhen North Sea Restaurant	Shēn Zhèn Běi Hǎi Yú Cūn Jiǔ Jiā	深圳北海渔村酒家
Shenzhen Seaview Hotel	Shēn Zhèn Huá Qiáo Chéng Hǎi Jǐng Jiǔ Diàn	深圳华侨城海景酒店
Sun Yat-sen Memorial Hall	Zhōngshān Jìniàn Táng	中山纪念堂
Sunday Chiu Chow King	Sāndǎo Cháohuáng Yuècài Jiǔlóu	三岛潮皇粤菜酒楼
The Pavilion	Shèngtíngyuàn Jiǔdiàn	圣廷苑酒店
Xishan Temple	Xīshān Miào	西山庙
Yokohama	Héngbīn Rìběn Liàolǐ	横滨日本料理
Zhongshan City	Zhōngshān Shì	中山市

6

The Southwest

GUANGXI, GUIZHOU & YUNNAN

A lazy ride down the Li River at sunset, Guilin.

WORD OF MOUTH

"Guilin is without dispute the most scenic city in China. Hilltops pop up from nowhere like trees in the forest and they are shaped like buns, camels, fish, saw-teeth, horses, etc. It is a city you must visit or you will miss those beautiful landscape there. Rivers flow around like green silk ribbons while the hills reveal themselves as jade hair-pins."

–jadeleo

WELCOME TO
THE SOUTHWEST

TOP REASONS
TO GO

★ **Lose Yourself in Lijiang:** Treasured by the Chinese and now designated as a UNESCO World Heritage Site, the winding cobblestone lanes of Lijiang beckon to all.

★ **Lush Xihuangbanna Rain Forests:** Hugging the borders of Laos and Myanmar, this small city in Yunnan is home to the legendary Dai minority people, who make you feel far from the rest of China.

★ **Trek Tiger Leaping Gorge:** Explore the deepest gorge in the world, and one of the most scenic spots in all of Yunnan, and possibly China.

★ **Guizhou's Eye-Popping Huangguoshu Pubu:** Travel to the Baishuio River in Guizhou, where the largest waterfall in China plummets to 230 feet.

★ **Ballooning Yangshuo:** Float over this strange lunarlike landscape of limestone karsts.

Miao Minority during their New Year Celebration in Kaili, Guizhou province.

1 Guangxi. Home to a number of ethnic minorites, the sublime scenery of Guangxi's rivers, valleys, and stone peaks have drawn travelers here for centuries. The "dragon's spine" terraced rice fields of **Longsheng** and the limestone karst rock formations that surround **Guilin** and **Yangshuo** make this one of the most beautiful provinces in China.

2 Guizhou. Off the beaten tourist track and with little tourism infrastructure, this fascintating region is known for its undulating mountains, terraced fields, traditional villages, frequent festivals, and China's largest waterfall, **Huangguoshu Pubu.** More than a third of the population is made up of Dong, Hui, Yao, Zhuang, and Miao (known in the west as the Hmong) peoples.

City gate of Qingyan ancient city Guizhou.

CHONGQING
Chongqing

Zunyi

GUIZHOU
Guiyang   **2**   Kaili
Anshun   Duyun
Huangguoshu
Pubu

HUNAN

Longsheng

Guilin
1

Yangshou

Bose   GUANGXI   Liuzhou

Nanning

Fangcheng

GUANGDONG

Beihai
Gulf of
Tonkin

7

GETTING ORIENTED

Southwestern China is a tropical land of mythical mountains, shrouded with mist and speckled with tribal minority peoples. Given its historic significance and breathtaking scenery, it's not surprising that this is also one of China's top travel destinations. The Southwest begins on the beaches of the South China Sea in Guangxi province. The rugged and seldom-visited province of Guizhou is over 70% mountains and 20% rivers. Yunnan brushes up against Laos and Myanmar. The capital city of Kunming is about to experience a transportation revolution—the new Kunming to Bangkok highway is slated to open, making this region one of the most dynamic travel destinations on earth.

An old bridge in Lijiang.

3 Yunnan. Nestled in Yunnan, the laid-back atmosphere of **Dali** is a drawcard for those who've loved Yangshuo, and it's the perfect jumping-off point for **Lijiang** and **Tiger Leaping Gorge**. As the former capital of the ancient Nanzhau Kingdom, Dali's storied streets are as varied as its Dali Lake is placid. Popular pastimes here include tai-qi by the lake and lingering late in cafés.

SOUTHWEST PLANNER

On the Menu

One would be remiss not to sample some of Southwestern China's best dishes. From dairy-based Dai dishes with fresh pepper to chicken steamed in clay pots and bitter melon served with eggs, Southwest China's cuisine is unique.

Bordering Sichuan and Hunan provinces to the north and Myanmar, Laos, and Vietnam to the south, the region is sandwiched between some of the spiciest cuisines on earth. Yet meals retain a palatable earthiness, defined by river fish, terraced rice, mountain medicinal herb, and more wild mushrooms than you can shake a digging stick at.

Particularly popular are soup-based dishes served with thin, spaghetti-like rice-noodles that come with fresh mint, oil, slices of pork, carrots, and corn. Other amazing delicacies involve steaming sticky rice inside bamboo. The province sees its fair share of Tibetan delights too, including Yak meat and yoghurt-wine.

Packing for the Weather

Southwest China has subtropical temperatures toward the borders with Sichuan and Hunan, and Tropic of Cancer-like heat and humidity around the borders of Myanmar, Laos, and Vietnam.

Be sure to pack plenty of sunblock, spare pairs of socks, a windbreaker, hat, sunglasses, hiking boots, running shoes, and sandals. Light cotton clothes are a good bet, but bring something warm if you're visiting the mountains.

In summer, the monsoons can be heavy. Keep abreast of weather reports on the Internet at any of the numerous cafés, hostels, and hotels.

The best time of year is spring, in April or early May. Winter months can be surprisingly cold (except on the south coast of Guangxi and Yunnan), and the summertime heat is stifling. Mid-September can also be a comfortable time to travel. The falls at Huangguoshu are at their best in the rainy season from May through October.

Backpacker's Paradise

Be forewarned: Yangshuo is bliss for hipster backpackers. There's an aura about this subtropical destination that's akin to Bangkok's hippie laden Khao-San Road. Yangshuo's 20,000 surrounding karst lime mountains are part and parcel of the tried-and-true Southeast Asia backpacker circuit that was forged in the 1970s and remain well trodden to this day.

The city first blossomed among the more seasoned and adventurous backpackers in the 1980s and came into swing during the late 1990s.

Today, Yangshuo's main strip known as "Xijie" or "West Street" throbs with the commingling cacophony of Hong Kong canto-pop, reggae, hip-hop, and classic rock. Here, too, you can order everything from lasagna to enchiladas to pad-thai noodles. It's also the ideal place to get the lowdown on the best deals from English-speaking wait-staff or expats.

Minority Festivals

This region is known for its colorful, and sometimes wild, minority festivals. If at all possible, try to find one when you're in the area.

At Hidden Lake near Kunming, the Yi and Bai peoples hold their sacred Torch Festivals on June 24. They throw handfuls of pine resin into bonfires, alighting the night with clouds of magical sparks. The mid-April Dai Water Splashing Festival in the rain forests of Xishuangbanna is liquid pandemonium. Its purpose is to wash away the sorrow of the old year and refresh you for the new.

Dali has two festivals of note—the Third Moon Fair (usually April) in honor of Guanyin, the bodhisattva of mercy; and the Three Temples Festival (usually May). The Sister's Meal Festival is dedicated to unmarried women. During the great rice harvest, special brightly colored dishes are made and at nightfall, there's much ado about courtship, dancing, and old-fashioned flirting. It's so sweet that this festival, like all of Southwestern China's heralded holidays, will leave travelers yearning for more.

WHAT IT COSTS In Yuan

RESTAURANTS				
$$$$	$$$	$$	$	¢
over 165	100–165	50–99	25–49	under 25
HOTELS				
$$$$	$$$	$$	$	¢
over 1,800	1,400–1,800	1,100–1,399	700–1,099	under 700

Restaurant prices are for a main course, excluding tax and tips. Hotel prices are for a standard double room, including taxes.

Guangxi's Silver-Toothed Touts

Aggressive touts are a fact of life for Western travelers in hyper-capitalist China, and the more well-trafficked the area, the more numerous said touts. Guangxi province is known for the tenacity of its touts—mostly older, tribal women with silver teeth (as is the local custom). To these wandering merchants, a Western traveler is a coin purse with legs.

It's not uncommon for half a dozen of these women to surround you at any given site, shouting "water" and "postcard." They'll follow you around until you buy something from each of them.

It's hard for travelers to maintain equilibrium when confronted with a gaggle of old women who seem doggedly intent on turning a hiking trip around, say, the Longsheng Rice Terraces into a no-win trinket-buying binge. Polite "no, thank you's" can soon become expletive-laden tirades, inevitably leading to remorse for cursing a poverty-stricken old woman.

What's worse, cursing accomplishes nothing. No sooner will the last bitter word leave your lips than Granny will thrust a pack of commemorative postcards at you and shout "10 yuan!"

Our advice is to consider the purchasing of minor souvenirs or unwanted sodas as part of the experience, keep a few yuan handy for just that, and to deal with it smilingly. Failing that, you can always run. But remember, these old women know all the shortcuts, and you'll tire out and need to buy a beverage anyway. And maybe some postcards as well.

Joshua Samual
Brown and
Christopher
Horton

The southwestern provinces are, without a doubt, the most alluring destinations in the country. This region lays claim to some of the most breathtaking scenery in all of China—the moonscapelike limestone karsts and river scenery of Yangshou, China's mightiest waterfall in Guizhou, to the Yunnan's tropical rain forests and spectacular Tiger Leaping Gorge.

But don't just visit for the pretty scenery. This area is rich in ethnic diversity and culture. Yunnan is home to almost a third of all China's ethnic minorities and in 1958, Guangxi became an autonomous region in an attempt to quell the friction between the Zhuang minority and the ethnic Han majority. Yunnan, Guanxi, and Guizhou represent the complex tapestry of ethnic diversity that has long been China.

GUANGXI

Known throughout China for its fairy-tale scenery, Guangxi's rivers, valleys, and stone peaks have inspired painters and poets for centuries. From the distinctive terraced rice fields of Longsheng, which resemble a dragon's spine, to the karst rock formations that surround Guilin and Yangshuo and rise from the coastal plain in the south, Guangxi is quite possibly the most picturesque of China's provinces.

As in neighboring Guizhou, a significant portion of Guangxi's population is tribal: the Dong, Gelao, Hui, Jing, Maonan, Miao, Shui, Yao, Yi, and, in particular, the Zhuang people, who constitute about a third of the province's population. Guangxi has often been the object of struggle between these indigenous peoples and the Han, who established their authority only in the 19th century. Today it is one of five autonomous regions, which, in theory, have an element of self-government.

The climate is subtropical, affected by seasonal monsoons, with long, hot, humid, and frequently wet summers and mild winters. Guangxi is one of the most popular travel destinations in China among Chinese and Westerners alike.

Guilin

Guilin has the good fortune of being situated in the middle of some of the world's most beautiful landscapes. This landscape of limestone karst hills and mountains, rising almost vertically from the earth, has a dreamy, hypnotic quality. They were formed 200 million years ago, when the area was under the sea. As the land beneath began to push upward, the sea receded, and the effects of the ensuing erosion over thousands of years produced this sublime scenery.

Architecturally, the city lacks charm, having been heavily bombed during the Sino-Japanese War and rebuilt in the utilitarian style popular in the 1950s. Still, the river city is replete with beautiful parks and bridges, and has a number of historical sites that make it worthy of exploration. It's also a good base from which to explore Northern Guangxi province.

Exploring Guilin

② The 492-foot **Peak of Solitary Beauty** (Duxiu Feng), with carved stone stairs leading to the top, offers an unparalleled view of Guangxi. It's

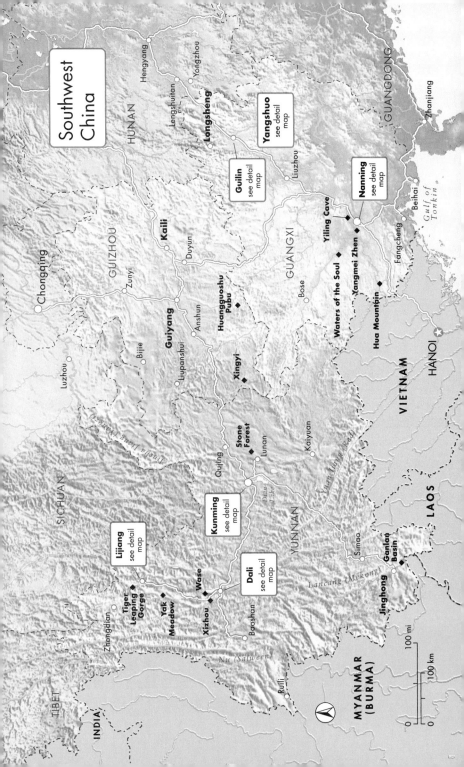

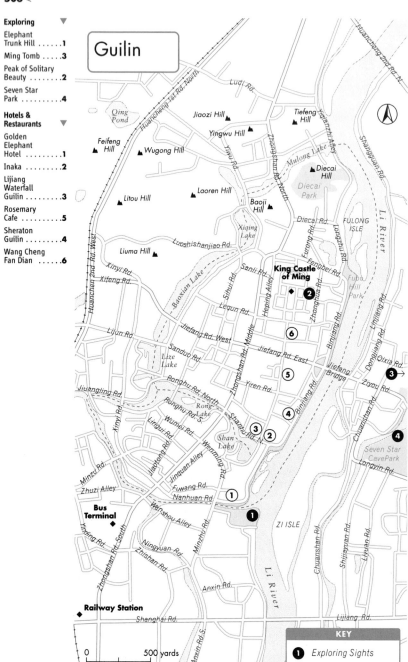

Guilin

Qing Pond

Ludi Rd.

Huancheng 1st Rd. North

Huancheng 2nd Rd. N.

Jiaozi Hill

Tiefeng Hill

Feifeng Hill

Yingwu Hill

Wugong Hill

Hanzhi Alley

Shangguan Rd.

Mulong Lake

Diecai Hill

Yiyu Rd.

Zhongshan Rd. North

Diecai Park

Li River

Litou Hill

Laoren Hill

Baoji Hill

Diecai Rd.

FULONG ISLE

Xiqing Lake

Furong Rd.

Longzhu Rd.

Huanchen 2nd Rd. West

Liuma Hill

Luoshishanjiao Rd.

Baoxian Lake

Fengbei Rd.

Fubo Hill Park

Xinyi Rd.

Sanli Rd.

King Castle of Ming

Xifeng Rd.

Sihui Rd.

Heping Alley

Zhongshan Rd.

Binjiang Rd.

Lijiang Rd.

◆ ❷

Lequn Rd.

Lijun Rd.

Jiefang Rd. West

❻

Sanduo Rd.

Jiefang Rd. East

Dongxia Rd.

Qixia Rd.

Jiuangling Rd.

Lize Lake

Zhongshan Rd. Middle

Yiren Rd.

Jiefang Bridge

Ziyou Rd.

Chuanshan Rd.

❸ ➔

Ronghu Rd. North

❺

Xinyi Rd.

Ronghu Rd. S.

Rong Lake

Binjiang Rd.

❹

Linggui Rd.

Wumei Rd.

Shanhu Rd. N.

Shan Lake

③ ②

❹

Jiaotong Rd.

Wenming Alley

Seven Star CavePark

Longyin Rd.

Minzu Rd.

Jinquan Alley

Zhuzi Alley

Fuwang Rd.

①

Wenshou Alley

Nanhuan Rd.

❶

ZI ISLE

Yinding Rd. South

Bus Terminal ◆

Ningyuan Rd.

Minzhi Rd.

Chuanshan Rd.

Shijiayuan Rd.

Liyan Rd.

Zhongshan Rd. South

Zhishan Rd.

Anxin Rd.

Li River

Railway Station ◆

Anxin Rd. S.

Shanghai Rd.

Lijiang Rd.

KEY
❶ *Exploring Sights*
① *Hotels & Restaurants*

0 ——— 500 yards

0 ——— 500 meters

CLOSE UP

The Zhuang & the Miao

THE ZHUANG PEOPLE ARE China's largest minority population, totaling more than 16 million. Most Zhuang are located in Guangxi Zhuang Autonomous Region (where they constitute more than 85% of the population) as well as Guizhou, Yunnan, and Guangdong provinces. The Zhuang language is part of the Tai-Kadai family, related to Thai and fellow Chinese minority the Dai. Historically, the Zhuang have had almost constant friction with China's Han majority, but that's beginning to improve since the Guangxi Zhuang Autonomous region was established in 1958. In many ways the Zhuang are gradually becoming assimilated into the dominant Han Chinese culture, but to date they have been able to preserve their strong culture and its music and dance traditions. Clothing varies from region to region and mostly consists of collarless, embroidered jackets buttoned to the left, loose wide trousers or pleated skirts, embroidered belts or black square headbands.

The Miao are also a large minority group and spread across much of southern China. Throughout their history, the Miao have had to deal with Han China's southward expansion, which drove them into marginal, chiefly mountainous areas in southern China and northern areas of Myanmar, Thailand, Laos, and Vietnam. Living in such isolated regions, the Miao group developed into several subsets, including Black, Red, Green, and Big Flowery Miao. Most of China's nearly 10 million Miao are located in Guizhou province, where local markets feature the intricate and expert craftsmanship of the Miao, who specialize in jewelry, embroidery, and batik. Their beautiful craftsmanship aside, the Miao are also renowned for their festivals, particularly the Lusheng festival, which takes place from the 11th to the 18th of the first lunar month. Named after a Miao reed instrument, Lusheng is a week of lively music, dancing, horse races, and bullfights. The Guizhou city of Kaili is the center of Miao festivals, hosting more than 120 each year.

7

one of the attractions of the **Princess City Solitary Beauty Park** (Wang Cheng Jing Chu). In the oddly named park, surrounded by an ancient wall outside of which vendors hawk their wares, sits the heart of old Guilin. Inside are the decaying remains of an ancient Ming Dynasty palace built in 1393 and Guilin's Confucius temple. Sun Yat-sen lived here for a few months in the winter of 1921 (a fact duly noted on the wall by the outside gate). Cixi, the last empress of China, inscribed the character for "longevity" on a rock within these walls. ⊠ *Heart of Old Guilin, in center of city, 2 blocks north of Zhengyang Lu pedestrian mall* ☎ *No phone* 🎫 *Y50* ☉ *Daily 8–6.*

❹ Dominating the eastern part of Guilin, **Seven Star Park** (Qixing Gongyuan) gets its name from the arrangement of its hills, said to resemble the Big Dipper. At the center of this huge park on the east side of the Li river is **Putuo Mountain** (Putuoshan), atop of which sits a lovely pavilion housing a number of famous examples of Tang calligraphy. Indeed, calligraphy abounds on the side of this hill, mostly the work of Ming Dynasty Taoist philosopher Pan Changjing. Nearby is **Seven Star Cliff** (Qixing Dong) with several large caves open for exploration. The largest contains rock formations that are thought to resemble a lion with a ball, an elephant, and other figures. An inscription in the cave dates from AD 590. Seven Star Park also contains Guilin City Zoo, which is only worth a stop if you have kids in tow. It costs an additional Y30. ✢ *1 km (½ mi) east of downtown Guilin* ☎ *No phone* 🎫 *Y30* ☉ *Daily 8–5.*

❶ A very popular destination, **Elephant Trunk Hill** (Xiangbi Shan) once appeared on Chinese currency bills. On the banks of the river in the southern part of the city, it takes its name from a rock formation arching into the river like the trunk of an elephant. Nearby is a grotto covered in poetic inscriptions inspired by the beauty of the place, some by the greatest poets of the Song Dynasty. ⊠ *Bing Jiang Lu, across from Golden Elephant Hotel* ☎ *No phone* 🎫 *Y25* ☉ *Daily 7 AM–7 PM.*

❸ East of the town is the **Ming Tomb** (Zhu Shouqian Ling), the tomb of Zhu Shouqian, the nephew of the first Ming emperor, who founded a principality here. It makes a pleasant excursion by bicycle. To get here, take Jiefang Dong Lu east about 9 km (5 mi). ⊠ *Jiefang Dong Lu* ☎ *No phone* 🎫 *Y40* ☉ *Daily 8:30–5:30.*

Where to Stay & Eat

Being on a river, Guilin restaurants serve catfish and other freshwater fish. Horse is a local specialty, so equestrians will want to avoid restaurants on Zhengyang Lu (just south of the Peak of Solitary Beauty), all of which seem to specialize in *ma rou*.

$$–$$$ ✕ **Inaka.** Resembling a Japanese home, this excellent restaurant sits at the southern end of Guilin's Zhengyang Lu pedestrian mall. The interior, calling to mind a temple, has a low-key vibe. The sashimi and sushi—not easy to find in cities away from the coast—are fresh and excellent. The best deals are the four-course lunch specials, which begin with miso soup and end with a dessert made from sweetened bean curd. ⊠ *1 Zhengyang Lu* ☎ *0773/280–2888* ▭ *MC, V.*

¢–$$ ⨉ **Rosemary Café.** Every city has at least one restaurant that serves as a home away from home for expats. In Guilin, Rosemary Café unquestionably fills the bill. The kitchen serves up a wide selection of familiar dishes, including soups like vegetarian vegetable and chicken noodle. There are great hamburgers, and sandwiches of all sorts. You might eat your meal to the sounds of Tom Waits's latest release—not an easy find in China. ⊠ *Yiren Lu, 1 block east of clock tower on Zhenyang Lu pedestrian mall* ☎ *0773/ 281–0063* ⊟ *No credit cards.*

> ### WORD OF MOUTH
>
> I think 4 full days in Yangshuo is probably too much. May want to spend two in and around Guilin.
> –rkkwan

¢–$ ⨉ **Wang Cheng Fan Dian.** This restaurant south of the Peak of Solitary Beauty is extremely popular with students from the nearby college. It serves a wide variety of dishes, including many made with horse, including noodles stir-fried with horse and a spicy hotpot with horse and vegetables. ⊠ *56 Zhengyang Lu, 1 block north of pedestrian mall* ☎ *0773/ 282–2284* ⊟ *No credit cards.*

$$$–$$$$ 🏨 **Lijiang Waterfall Guilin** (Lijiang Da Pubu Jiudian). Overlooking the river, this luxury hotel also has breathtaking views of the Elephant Trunk Hill, Seven Star Park, and the famous peaks surrounding the city. Rooms are clean, spacious, and as the hotel is one of the city's newest, extremely modern. Five excellent restaurants offer Asian and Western cuisine. ⊠ *1 North Shanhu Lu, 541001, South end of Zhengyang Lu pedestrian mall* ☎ *0773/282–2881* ⊕ *www.waterfallguilin.com* 🛏 *430 rooms, 23 suites* ♨ *5 restaurants, in-room safes, minibars, cable TV, in-room broadband, pool, gym, sauna, bar, dry cleaning, concierge, business services, meeting rooms, airport shuttle, no-smoking floors* ⊟ *AE, MC, V.*

★ $$–$$$$ ⨉🏨 **Sheraton Guilin** (Guilin Dayu Dafandian). This modern business hotel has a nice location overlooking the river. The lobby is very chic, with its sunny atrium and glass elevators that whisk you up to your room. Clean and spacious, the rooms are decorated in shades of cream and tan. The formal restaurant serves excellent Chinese cuisine, and a small café attracts homesick expats and stylish locals with its Western-style dishes. ⊠ *15 Binjiang Lu, on west bank of Li River, 541001* ☎ *0773/282–5588* ⊕ *www.sheraton.com/guilin* 🛏 *411 rooms, 19 suites* ♨ *3 restaurants, room service, in-room safes, minibars, cable TV, in-room broadband, bar, nightclub, shops, meeting rooms, travel services* ⊟ *AE, MC, V.*

★ ¢ 🏨 **Golden Elephant Hotel.** If you're on a budget, this clean, comfortable hotel will fit the bill. The guest rooms are on the frumpy side, and the beds a bit hard; however, many have terrific views of Elephant Trunk Hill. The Korean restaurant on the 1st floor is particularly good. ⊠ *8 Bingjiang Lu, 541002* ☎ *0773/289–2821* 🛏 *50 rooms* ♨ *2 restaurants, cable TV, in-room broadband, business services, no-smoking rooms* ⊟ *AE, MC, V.*

Nightlife & the Arts

Zhengyang Lu, the city's pedestrian mall, picks up when the sun goes down. At the center is a three-story-tall clock tower, around which you'll find a number of vendors selling roasted nuts, barbecued meat, pearl milk tea, and—oddly enough—fried chicken on a stick. There is also a number of shops selling a surprisingly hip selection of CDs from jazz and funk to rock and hip-hop.

The largest nightclub on the strip is the two-story **Music Barbie Club** (✉ Zhengyang Lu ☎ 0773/282–6818), where the city's trendy crowd dances the night away to techno.

To & from Guilin

15 hrs (500 km [310 mi]) by train northwest of Hong Kong; 28 hrs (1,675 km [1,039 mi]) by train southwest of Beijing.

About 26 km (16 mi) from the city center, Guilin Airport has flights to cities throughout China as well as throughout Asia. An airport shuttle bus, which operates daily from 6:30 AM to 8 PM, runs between the airport and the Aviation Building located at 18 Shanghai Lu, across the street from the main bus station. The cost is Y20 per person.

Most long-distance trains come to Guilin's South Railway Station. Guilin is linked by daily rail service with most major cities in China; an international train from Beijing to Hanoi passes through Guilin twice a week in both directions.

Short- and long-distance buses connect Guilin to surrounding cities like Yangshuo, Quanzhou, Lipu, and Longsheng. Long-distance sleeper coaches travel to cities throughout the Pearl River Delta.

Yangshuo

Once considered a side trip from Guilin, Yangshuo has taken center stage as the province's top tourist destination. Despite its well-developed tourist infrastructure, Yangshuo retains a small-town feel. At the heart of the city is West Street, a pedestrian mall extending to the Li River. Many visitors are content to spend a few days just wandering up and down the main drag, eating, drinking, and gazing over the low-slung traditional structures facing toward the fang-shaped peaks that surround the town. Yangshuo is fast becoming a destination for adventure travel, and the countryside is filled with opportunities for biking, hiking, rock climbing, caving, and even hot-air ballooning.

Exploring Yangshuo

❶ Probably the most popular destination in Yangshuo, **Moon Hill** (Yue Liang Shan) gets its name from the large hole through the center of this karst peak. There are more than a dozen rock-climbing routes on the northwest side. ✉ *Yangshuo–Gaotian Rd.* ☎ *No phone* 🎫 *Y15* ⊙ *Daily 7 AM–7 PM.*

❷ In the center of town, **Yangshuo Park** (Yangshuo Gong Yuan) is where older people come to play chess while children scamper about in small playgrounds. The park has a number of statues and ponds worth seeing, and Yangshuo Park Peak has a small pagoda offering excellent views of the surrounding town. For a more intense climb with even better views, ascend the television tower, across the street from the park's entrance.

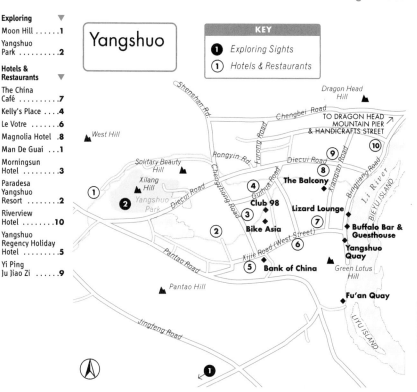

Yangshuo

KEY

❶ *Exploring Sights*

① *Hotels & Restaurants*

Dragon Head
Hill

Shensham Rd.

Chengbei Road

TO DRAGON HEAD
MOUNTAIN PIER
& HANDICRAFTS STREET

West Hill

Rongyin Rd.

Furong Road

Diecui Road

⑨

⑩

Li River

BIEYU ISLAND

Binjiang Road

Xianqian Road

Solitary Beauty
Hill

Xilang
Hill

Yangshuo
Park

Diecui Road

Chengzhong Road

Guihua Road

The Balcony

Club 98

④

⑧

Lizard Lounge

③

Bike Asia

②

⑦

**Buffalo Bar &
Guesthouse**

⑥

**Yangshuo
Quay**

Xijie Road (West Street)

⑤

Bank of China

Green Lotus
Hill

Fu'an Quay

LIYU ISLAND

Pantao Road

Pantao Hill

Jingfeng Road

❶

7

✉ *Die Chui Lu, at Pan Tao Lu, across from Yangshuo Bus Station* ☎ *No
phone* 💲 *Y15* 🕐 *Daily 6 AM–midnight.*

Tours

If getting wet and muddy underground is your idea of a good time, look
no farther than Water Cave, the area's deepest and largest underground
grotto in the area. Accessible only by a flat-bottom boat, Water Cave
has hikes among stalactites, a mud bath, and a number of crystal-clear
pools perfect for washing off all that mud. Tours can be arranged
through Guilin Yangshuo Rainbow Travel.

Other good travel agents include Jamie Mo at Charm Yangshuo Tour.
Independent guide Lucy Chen has a reputation for leading great small
and medium-sized tours through the area.

🎯 Tour-Operator Recommendations **Charm Yangshuo Tour** ✉ Pan Tao Lu ☎ 0773/
881–4355. **Lucy Chen** ✉ 4 Cheng Shong Jie ☎ 1397/7351-1663.

Where to Stay & Eat

$–$$ ✕ **Le Votre.** A restored building dating from the Qing Dynasty is the set-
ting for this French restaurant. The dining room looks more like a museum than a restaurant. The restaurant serves excellent Western-style
specialties like grilled lamb chops and pasta primavera, as well as fine
pizza. ✉ *79 Xi Jie* ☎ *0773/882–8040* 💳 *No credit cards.*

★ ¢–$$ ✕ **Yi Ping Ju Jiao Zi.** Don't let the lack of an English name scare you—this place serves some of the best northern-style dumplings in the area. Don't leave without trying them, either steamed or fried. You'll also find excellent local specialties like *pi jiu yu* (beer fish) and *tien luo niang* (stuffed river snails). English menus are available. ✉ *21 Xian Tian Jie, across from Magnolia Hotel* ☎ *0773/890–2058* ▭ *No credit cards.*

¢ ✕ **China Café.** In all of Yangshuo, there's only one restaurant that requires reservations—and even then, only for one dish. This place serves an addictive rotisserie chicken that is made from a highly guarded local recipe. The kitchen makes between 12 and 18 chicken roasts each night, so diners in the know call the chef's mobile number at least an hour in advance. ✉ *34 Xi Jie* ☎ *1380/783–0498* ▭ *No credit cards.*

¢–$ ✕ **Kelly's Place.** Beloved by expats, this closet-size café is an escape from the hustle and bustle of West Street. On any given night, English teachers can be found drinking beer on the cobblestone pavilion. There are tasty Chinese-style dumpling soups. This is the only place in town to find vegetarian burgers. ✉ *43 Gui Hua Lu, 1 block north of Xi Jie* ☎ *0773/881–3233* ▭ *No credit cards.*

¢–$ ✕ **Man De Guai.** At this family-owned restaurant, popular with locals but almost unknown to travelers, you'll find an amazing array of local dishes. There are no English menus, but the owners will bring you into the kitchen and let you pick out what you want. This place is hard to find: look for it on the small street two blocks north of the bus station, next to the large statue of Kuan Yin, the Buddha of Compassion. ✉ *41 Yang Shuo Xie Bi Nian Dong* ☎ *0773/691–0959* ▭ *No credit cards.*

$–$$$ ▥ **Paradesa Yangshuo Resort** (Yangshuo Bai). Once the premier hotel of Yangshuo, the Paradise now has a lot of competition. The guest rooms are comfortable and some have nice views of the surrounding peaks. This is the only hotel in town with a babysitting service. Ask about seasonal and group discounts. ✉ *116 Xi Jie, 541900* ☎ *0773/882–2109* ⊕ *www.paradiseyangshuo.com* ⬎ *145 rooms* ♨ *2 restaurants, minibars, cable TV, in-room broadband, pool, gym, shops, business services, massage, babysitting, laundry service, dry cleaning, Internet room, no-smoking rooms* ▭ *AE, MC, V.*

¢ ▥ **Magnolia Hotel** (Baiyu Lan Jiu Dian). Built around a traditional courtyard, the Magnolia has a glass-roofed lobby overlooking a lovely carp pond. Rooms have big windows that let in a lot of light, with most having amazing views of the mountains, the river, or both. The family suite is particularly nice: two adjoining rooms that give parents and children a little privacy. ✉ *7 Due Cui Lu, 541900* ☎ *0773/881–9288* ⊕ *www.yangshuoren.com/magnolia.htm* ⬎ *26 rooms, 1 suite* ♨ *Cable TV, Wi-Fi, dry cleaning, laundry service, in-room broadband, business services, no-smoking rooms* ▭ *AE, MC, V.*

¢ ▥ **Morningsun Hotel** (Chen Guang Jiu Dian). With a lovely enclosed courtyard, the Morningsun Hotel has the look and feel of a Ming Dynasty guesthouse. The guest rooms also have a traditional feel (except for the postmodern bathrooms, which are all brass and glass). The staff at this family-run establishment is extremely friendly. Reserve ahead, as the hotel tends to fill up on weekends and holidays. ✉ *4 Chenzhong Jie, 541900* ☎ *0773/881–3899* ⊕ *www.morningsunhotel.com* ⬎ *21 rooms*

FodorsChoice
★

⟁ *Restaurant, laundry services, business services, Internet room, no-smoking rooms* ☰ *AE, MC, V.*

¢ 🖼 **Riverview Hotel** (Wangjiang Lou Kezhan). With its curvaceous tile roof and balconies with stunning views of the Lijiang River, the Riverview is one of the town's nicest budget hotels. The guest rooms are tastefully appointed with dark-wood furniture. The 1st-floor restaurant has a patio facing the water, which is a great place to have your morning coffee. ✉ *11 Bin Jiang Lu, 541900* ☎ *0773/882–2688* ⊕ *www.riverview.com.cn* ↪ *38 rooms* ⟁ *Restaurant, cable TV, bar, laundry service, Internet room* ☰ *AE, MC, V.*

¢ 🖼 **Yangshuo Regency Holiday Hotel.** Located at the entrance to the tourist district, this newcomer has clean rooms with soft beds and nice views of the surrounding mountains. Its location makes it a good base for exploring the area. It faces the main road through town, so some rooms are a bit noisy. ✉ *117 Xi Jie, 541900* ☎ *0773/881–7198* ⊕ *www.ys-holidayhotel.com* ↪ *52 rooms* ⟁ *2 restaurants, minibars, shops, massage, business services, laundry service, dry cleaning, in-room broadband, Internet room, no-smoking rooms* ☰ *AE, MC, V.*

Nightlife

Yangshuo is a great spot for nightlife. West Street hums with activity until well past midnight during the week, and even later on weekends. A number of bars and clubs in the area are worth a visit.

Its Chinese name means "Little Horse's Heaven," but in English this place is known as **The Balcony** (✉ 28 Xian Qian Jie ☎ 773/881–2331). The place has chic decor, a fine selection of imported liquor, and a lovely balcony. While rock and roll is favored at the surrounding bars, owner Xiao Ma is more a fan of trip-hop and acid jazz, so that's what you'll most likely hear.

With a fine selection of Australian beers, **Buffalo Bar** (✉ 50 Xian Qian Jie ☎ 773 881–3644) is especially popular with expats. You can meet a few around the pool table. **Club 98** (✉ 42 Gui Hua Jie ☎ 773 881–4605) serves mixed drinks and imported beers. The bar also has a cool pavilion extending over a small creek that joins the Li River.

The Outdoors

BIKING Cheaply made mountain bikes are available for rent all over Yangshuo at a cost of about Y10 per day. However, if you want a better quality mountain bike, **Bike Asia** (✉ 42 Gui Hua Lu ☎ 0773/882–6521 ⊕ www.bikeasia.com) rents them for Y30 per day. The company leads short trips to the villages along the Li River, as well as longer trips throughout China.

BOATING Starting as a humble spring at the top of Mao Er Mountain, the majestic Li River snakes through

> **WORD OF MOUTH**
>
> Go straight to Yangshuo and hire a small boat to take you along the best part of the Li River, the section between the nearby village of Xingping and Yangdi. It's widely acknowledged that this section of the Li River has the best scenery, and a small boat cruise is much more peaceful than a ride aboard the noisy cruise boats from Guilin.
> –Lil1210

7

Guangxi, connecting Yangshuo to many other towns along the way. One of the country's most scenic—and thus far, unpolluted—rivers, its banks are filled with stone embankments where people practice tai chi. The best spots for swimming can be found north of the city, where the stone walls give way to sand. Several local companies offer rides on bamboo rafts along the Li River and on the Yu Long River, a smaller tributary. You can bargain with them at the stone quay at the end of West Street.

Kayaking is a popular activity in and around Yangshuo. With a small fleet of lightweight fiberglass kayaks, **George Chen** (⊠ 80 West St. ☎ 135/5766–4617) offers half-day trips on the nearby Yulong River. Trips cater to a variety of skill levels, traveling on smooth water or rushing rapids.

HOT-AIR BALLOONING **Guilin Flying Hot Air Balloon** (☎ 0773/881–4919 ⊕ www.chinahotairballoon.com) glides above the winding rivers and stunning peaks of Yangshuo—an unforgettable experience that will be a highlight of your trip. Hourlong trips cost Y800 per person.

ROCK CLIMBING Yangshuo is the undisputed rock-climbing capital of China. The oldest and most trusted climbing club in Yangshuo is **Chinaclimb** (⊠ 45 Xian Qian Jie ☎ 0773/881–1033 ⊕ www.chinaclimb.com). Led by a mostly Australian staff, climbs are perfect for novices and experts alike. Half-day treks cost between Y200 and Y300, including equipment and transportation.

Shopping

West Street is filled with shops selling everything from batik tapestries to T-shirts with cheesy sayings like I SURVIVED SARS. You should also explore Dragon Head Mountain Pier Handicrafts Street (Long Tou Shan Ma Tou Gong Yu Jie), a cobblestone street running along the river. Busts of Mao, painted fans, and marble chess sets can be found here. Merchants are used to dealing with tourists, and will generally ask for high prices. You can bargain them down to half of the original asking price.

Working behind a small table, **Meng Hui** (⊠ Dragon Head Mountain Pier Handicrafts St. ☎ 1363/514–1394) is not your average calligrapher. His work, on scrolls and fans, is the sort that Confucius might have appreciated. After a car accident cost him his right arm, he learned how to paint with a calligrapher's brush strapped to his right shoulder. His work is in demand, and is often bought by tourists from Beijing and Shanghai. Despite all the attention he receives, his fees are very reasonable. The artist can be found most nights on Xi Jie selling scrolls and paintings from his bicycle.

Yangshuo does have a great place to buy books, albeit mostly second-hand books. **Johnny Lu's Café and Books** (⊠ 7 Cheng Zhong Jie ☎ 1323/783–1208) has a full selection of travel books.

Side Trip from Yangshuo

Yangshuo is an exceptional base from which to explore the villages along the Li River, many of which date back hundreds of years. About 8 km (5 mi) southeast of Yangshuo sits **Fuli,** a Ming Dynasty town built on the river's northern banks. Fuli has narrow, winding cobblestone streets and a number of ancient temples worth exploring. This village is where you'll find the **Peng Family Painted Scroll Factory** (⊠ 55 Fuli Ing Bei Jie ☎ 0773/894–2416), a family-run shop that's been producing hand-made scrolls and painted fans for generations. You'll find these for sale in Yangshuo for two or three times the price you can get them for here. From Fuli you can travel up the river to other villages such as Xinzhai, Degongzha, and Puyi, which has a large weekend market. Many of the people living in these villages still dress in traditional clothing.

To & from Yangshuo
1 hr (70 km [43 mi]) by bus south of Guilin.

Express luxury buses travel between Guilin and Yangshuo every half hour between 7 AM and 8 PM. The trip takes just over an hour in these air-conditioned and smoke-free buses that cost Y15. Slightly cheaper are regular minibuses, which are slower and filled with smokers.

To get here from Hong Kong, Guangzhou, or Shenzhen, the cheapest option is an overnight bus. Express buses go directly to Yangshuo without a stop at Guilin. Tickets are available from any travel agent.

Arriving via train or airplane means traveling through Guilin. Taxis from Guilin Airport are Y300, and from Guilin Train Station are Y200.

A prettier option is the boat that traverses the Li River from Guilin to Yangshuo, taking approximately four hours. At Y380 for a round-trip ticket, it's costlier than other modes of travel. Tickets are available from any travel agent.

Longsheng Longji Rice Terraces

A mesmerizing pattern of undulating fields have been cut into the hills up to a height of 2,625 feet at the **Longsheng Longji Rice Terraces.** These terraces, known as the "Dragon's Backbone," are amazing in both their scale and their beauty. The terraces are worked, as they have been for untold generations, by rice farmers from the local Yao, Dong, Zhuang, and Miao communities, who build their houses in villages on the terraced hills.

> **WORD OF MOUTH**
>
> The rice terraces are absolutely stunning. This was definitely the highlight of my month in China. I could easily see myself staying for an entire summer.
>
> –Lil1210

While terrace farming has long been a common practice in the hilly regions of southern China, these are the largest in the country. On a clear day, the view from the top is stunning. ☞ *Y30.*

Where to Stay & Eat

✿ ✕⊞ **Li Qing Guesthouse.** In the nearby village of Ping An, the Li Qing Guesthouse is operated by two sisters, Liao Yan Li and Liao Yan Qing. The guesthouse is made up of two houses; the older one has dorm-style rooms, and the newer one has single and double rooms with private baths. The restaurant is extremely popular with visitors, and in addition to more well-known Chinese dishes serves a number of traditional dishes like bamboo stuffed with sticky rice, and stir-fried mountain vegetables. ⊠ *Ji Lu, Ping An* ☎ *0773/758–3048* ⌨ *12 rooms* ⌂ *Restaurant, Internet room* ⊟ *No credit cards.*

To & from Longsheng

3 hrs (120 km [74 mi]) by bus northwest of Guilin.

Buses heading to Guilin leave every 15 minutes and take about 4 hours (Y15). The express bus to Guilin takes 3 hours and departs Longshen every two hours (Y20).

Nanning

Built along the banks of the Yong River, Nanning is the capital of Guangxi province. The city isn't a major tourist draw, but does have a few interesting sites. Many travelers stop here for a visa before continuing into Vietnam.

Exploring

❶ Surrounding White Dragon Lake, **White Dragon Park** (Bailong Gongyuan) has some 200 species of rare trees and flowers. Here you'll find the remains of fortifications built by a warlord in the early part of the 20th century. ⊠ *Renmin Dong Lu* ⌨ *Y5* ⊙ *Daily 8:30–6.*

❷ The **Guangxi Provincial Museum** (Guangxi Sheng Bowuguan) focuses on the numerous indigenous peoples in the area. In the back is a magnificent life-size reconstruction of houses, pagodas, and drum towers set among attractive pools and bridges. A collection of more than 300 bronze drums made by local people is also on display. ⊠ *Minzu Dadao* ⌨ *Y5* ⊙ *Daily 8:30–11:30 and 2:30–5.*

❸ In the southeastern part of the city, **South Lake** (Nanhu) covers more than 200 acres. There's a bonsai exhibition and an orchid garden in the surrounding park. Close by is a botanical garden specializing in herbs. ⊠ *Gucheng Lu* ⌨ *Y2* ⊙ *Daily 8–5.*

Where to Stay & Eat

$-$$ ✕ **Nanhu Fish Restaurant** (Nan Hu Yu Fandian). In an ugly concrete building near South Lake, this restaurant serves excellent seafood. Can't decide? Try the dried scallops in hot-pepper and garlic sauce. ⊠ *43 Xinhu Lu* ☎ *0771/585–9705* ⊟ *No credit cards.*

★ **$-$$** ☷ **Majestic Hotel** (Mingyuan Xindu Jiudian). This older luxury hotel, close to the main square, has been refurbished reasonably well and is efficiently run. Its low price, excellent location, and fine gym make it a top choice in Nanning. ⊠ *38 Xinmin Lu, 530012* ☎ *0771/283–0808* ⌨ *298 rooms* ⌂ *2 restaurants, in-room safes, minibars, in-room broadband, pool, gym, bar, babysitting, laundry service* ⊟ *AE, DC, MC, V.*

¢ ☷ **Tao Yuan Hotel** (Tao Yuan Fan Dian). The guest rooms at this budget hotel are clean and comfortable. There is a decent gym, a fairly swinging bar, and a pair of restaurants, one serving good Cantonese dim sum, the other spicy Sichuanese cuisine. ⊠ *74 Tao Yuan Lu, 530021* ☎ *0771/ 209–6868* ⌨ *400 rooms* ⌂ *2 restaurants, room service, in-room broadband, gym, bar, dry cleaning, concierge, business services, airport shuttle* ⊟ *AE, DC, MC, V.*

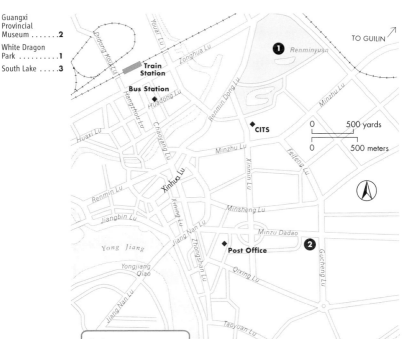

To & from Nanning

5 hrs (350 km [217 mi]) by train southwest of Guilin; 24 hrs (440 km [273 mi]) by train southeast of Guiyang; 16 hrs (600 km [372 mi]) by train west of Hong Kong.

Guangxi's roads have been vastly improved in recent years, making express bus travel a convenient alternative. Frequent bus service is available to Guangzhou and Guilin.

For longer hauls, trains run daily to Beijing, Chengdu, Guangzhou, Kunming, Shanghai, and Xian. Daily flights are available to Shanghai, Shenzhen, Kunming, and Beijing.

GUANGXI ESSENTIALS

Transportation

BY AIR

Guilin and Nanning have flights to China and the rest of the region. Guilin Liangjiang International Airport (KWL), about 26 km (16 mi) from the city, is the gateway to Yangshuo. Nanning Wuxu International Airport is 31 km (19 mi) southwest of Nanning.

🚹 Airport Information **Guilin Liangjiang International Airport** ☎ 0773/284-5359. **Nanning Wuxu International Airport** ☎ 0771/209-5160.

BY BUS

From Guilin's long-distance bus station on Zhongshan Lu, you can catch buses bound for cities throughout Guangxi, Guizhou, Yunnan, and the Pearl River Delta. Buses and minibuses headed to Yangshuo depart regularly from the Guilin Train Station.

There are frequent buses between Nanning and Guilin (6 hours). There is no direct service between Nanning and Yangshuo, meaning there's a change of buses in Guilin.

🚹 Bus Stations **Yangshuo Bus Station** ✉ Pan Tao Lu, across from Yangshuo Park ☎ 0773/882-2188. **Guilin Bus Station** ✉ Off Zhongshan Nan Lu ☎ 0773/382-2153. **Nanning Bus Station** ✉ 65 Huadong Lu ☎ 0771/242-4529.

BY TRAIN

Guilin's train station, located in the southern part of the city, has service to most major cities in China. The fastest direct trains to Beijing or Shanghai take 27 hours, to Kunming 19 hours, and to Guangzhuo 15.

Nanning's station is at the northwestern edge of town, and offers frequent service to Guilin. The fastest of these takes 4 hours. Most trains to other major cities are routed through Guilin; the Kunming train, however, comes to Nanning first, making that trip a breezy 15 hours.

🚹 Train Information **Guilin Railway Station** ✉ Off Zhongshan Nan Lu ☎ 0773/383-3124. **Nanning Station** ✉ North end of Chaoyang Lu ☎ 0771/243-2468.

Contacts & Resources

EMERGENCIES

For emergencies, contact your hotel. The Public Security Bureau, or PSB, is where you must go should your passport be lost or stolen during your travels in Guangxi.

🚹 **PSB Guilin** ✉ 16 Shi Jia Yuan Rd., Guilin ☎ 773/582-9930. **PSB Nanning** ✉ 5 Ke Yuan East Rd, Xi Xiang Tang ☎ 0771/289-1302. **PSB Yangshuo** ✉ Pan Tao Lu ☎ 0773/882-2178.

MONEY MATTERS

Money can be changed in the major hotels or at the Bank of China. Both the Guilin and Nanning airports have branches and ATMs, and all Bank of China ATMs take international cards.

🚹 Banks **Bank of China** ✉ 5 Shan Hu Bei Lu, Guilin ☎ 0773/280-2867 ✉ 39 Gu Cheng Lu, Nanning ☎ 0771/281-1267.

VISITOR INFORMATION

🚹 Tourist Information **China International Travel Service (CITS)** ✉ 41 Bin Jiang Lu, Guilin ☎ 0773/282-3518 ✉ 40 Xinmin Lu, Nanning ☎ 0771/532-0165 ✉ Xi Jie, near Pantao Lu, Yangshuo ☎ 0773/882-7102. **China Travel Service (CTS)** ✉ 14 Bin Jiang Lu, Guilin ☎ 0773/283-3986.

Continued on page 526

FOR ALL THE TEA IN CHINA

Legend has it that the first cup dates from 2737 BC, when Camellia sinensis leaves fell into water being boiled for Emperor Shenong. He loved the result, tea was born, and so were many traditions.

Historically, when a girl accepted a marriage proposal she drank tea, a gesture symbolizing fidelity (tea plants die if uprooted). Betrothal gifts were known as "tea gifts," engagements as "accepting tea," and marriages as "eating tea." Today the bride and groom kneel before their parents, offering cups of tea in thanks.

Serving tea is a sign of respect. Young people proffer it to their parents or grandparents; subordinates do the same for their bosses. Pouring tea also signifies submission, so it's a way to say you're sorry.

When you're served tea, show your thanks by tapping the table with your index and middle fingers.

And forget about adding milk or sugar. Not only is most Chinese tea best without it, but why dilute and sweeten a beverage long known by herbalists to be good for you? Even modern medicine acknowledges that tea's powerful antioxidants reduce the risk of cancer and heart disease. It's also thought to be such a good source of fluoride that Mao Zedong eschewed toothpaste for a green-tea rinse. Smiles, everyone.

HISTORICAL BREW

Tea in the morning; tea in the evening, tea at suppertime...

The Rise and Fall of Empires

Tea has a long and tumultuous history, making and breaking empires in both the East and the West. Bricks of tea were used as currency, and Chinese statesmen kept rebellious northern nomads in check by refusing to sell it to them.

Rumor has it that tea caused the downfall of the Song Empire. Apparently, tea-whisking was Emperor Huizong's favorite pastime: he was so obsessed with court tea culture that he forgot all about trivial little matters like defense. The country became vulnerable to invasion and fell to the Mongols in 1279.

Genghis preferred *airag* (fermented mare's milk), but after the Mongol's defeat, the drink of kings returned with a vengeance to the court of the Ming Dynasty (1368–1644). Tea as we know it today dates to this period: the first Ming emperor, Hongwu, set the trend of using loose-leaf tea by refusing to accept tea tribute gifts in any other form.

Tea Goes International

The first Europeans to encounter the beverage were navigators and missionaries who visited China in the mid-16th century. In 1610, Dutch traders began importing tea from China into Europe, with the Portuguese hot on their heels. It was initially marketed as a health drink and took a while to catch on. By the 1640s, tea had become popular amongst both the Dutch and Portuguese aristocracy, initially the only ones who could afford it.

Although we think of tea as a quintessentially British drink, it actually arrived in America two years before it appeared in Britain. When the British acquired New Amsterdam (later New York) in 1664, the colony consumed more tea than all the British isles put together.

Tea was available in Britain from about 1554 onward, but Brits were wary of the stuff at first. What tipped the scales in tea's favor was nothing less than celebrity product endorsement. King Charles II

as Native Americans peacefully boarded British ships in Boston harbor and emptied 342 chests of tea into the water. The act came to be known as the Boston Tea Party and was a vital catalyst in starting the American Revolution.

The War of Independence wasn't the only war sparked by tea. In Britain, taxes were axed and, as tea was suddenly affordable for everyone, demand grew exponentially. But China remained the world's only supplier so that by the mid-19th century, tea was causing a massive trade deficit. The British started exporting opium into China in exchange for tea, provoking two Opium Wars. In the 1880s, attempts to grow tea in India were finally successful and Indian tea began to overtake Chinese tea on the market.

married the Portuguese princess Catherine of Braganza in 1662. She arrived in England with tea and fine porcelain tea ware in her dowry and a healthy addiction to the stuff. Members of the royalty were the 16th-century's trendsetters: tea became the thing to drink at court; pretty soon the general public was hooked, too.

These days, over 3.2 million tonnes of tea are produced annually worldwide. After water, tea is the world's favorite drink. Though Britain and Ireland now consume far more tea per capita than China, tea is still a regular presence at the Chinese table and is inextricably bound to Chinese culture.

Storms in a Teacup

Tea quickly became a very important—and troublemaking—commodity. Religious leaders thought the drink sinful and doctors declared it a health risk. In Britain, ale-brewers were losing profits and pressure-groups successfully persuaded the government to tax tea at 119%. On top of all this, the immensely powerful British East India Company held the monopoly on tea importation.

Tea's value skyrocketed: by 1706, the retail price of green tea in London was equivalent to $300 for 100 g (3.5 oz), far beyond the reach of normal people. Tea-smuggling quickly became a massive—and often cut-throat—business. To make sought-after tea supplies stretch even further, they were routinely mixed with twigs, leaves, animal dung, and even poisonous chemicals.

Back in the New World, Americans were fed up with paying taxes that went straight back to Britain. Things came to a head when a group of patriots dressed

ANCIENT TRADE ROUTES

The Ancient Tea and Horse Caravan Road, also known as the Southern Silk Road, is a trade corridor dating back to the Tang Dynasty (618–907). The 4,000-km route emerged more than 1,200 years ago and was actually still in use until recently.

Back in the heyday of the Caravan Road, Xishuangbanna, Dali, Lijiang, and many other parts of Yunnan were important outposts on the route. Tea, horses, salt, medicinal herbs, and Indian spices all featured prominently in this massive network.

During World War II, the route was used to smuggle supplies from India into the interior of Japanese-occupied China.

DRINKING IN THE CULTURE

The way tea was prepared historically bears little resemblance to the steep-a-tea-bag method many Westerners employ today. Tea originally came in bricks of compressed leaves bound with sheep's blood or manure. Chunks were broken, ground into a powder, and whisked into hot water. In the first tea manual, *Cha Jing (The Way of Tea)*, Tang Dynasty writer Lu Yu describes preparing powdered tea using 28 pieces of teaware, including big brewing pans and shallow drinking bowls.

The potters of Yixing (near Shanghai) gradually transformed wine vessels into small pots for steeping tea. Yixing pottery is ideal for brewing: its fine unglazed clay is highly porous, and if you always use the same kind of tea, the pot will take on its flavor.

Today the most elaborate Chinese tea service—which requires only two pots and enough cups for all involved—is called *gong fu cha* (skilled tea method). Although you can experience it at many teahouses, most people consider it too involved for every day. They simply brew their leaf tea in three-piece lidded cups, called *gaiwan*, tilting the lid as they drink so that it acts as a strainer.

THE CEREMONY

1 Rinse teapot with hot water.

2 Fill with black or oolong to one third of its height.

3 Half-fill teapot with hot water and empty immediately to rinse leaves.

4 Fill pot with hot water, let leaves steep for a minute; no bubbles should form.

5 Pour tea into small cups, moving the spout continuously over each, so all have the same strength of tea.

6 Pour the excess into a second teapot.

7 Using the same leaves, repeat the process up to five times, extending the steeping time slightly.

Gaiwan

TEA TIMELINE

Yunnan Pu-erh Tea Bricks

350 AD	"Tea" appears in Chinese dictionary.
618–1644	Tea falls into and out of favor at Chinese court.
7th c.	Tea introduced to Japan.
1610–1650	Dutch and Portuguese traders bring tea to Europe.
1662	British King Charles II marries Portugal's Catherine of Braganza, a tea addict. Tea craze sweeps the court.
1689	Tea taxation starts in Britain; peaks at 119%.

HOW TEA IS MADE

Chinese tea is grown on large plantations and nearly always picked by hand. Pluckers remove only the top two leaves. A skilled plucker can collect up to 35 kg (77 lbs) of leaves in a day; that's 9 kg (almost 20 lbs) of tea or 3,500 cups. After a week, new top leaves will have grown, and bushes can be plucked again. Climate and soil play an important role on a tea plantation, much as they do in a vineyard. But what really differentiates black, green, and oolong teas is the way leaves are processed.

Plucked leaves arrive at factory

Leaves left to wilt in warm, humid environment

STEAM
GREEN TEA: Steam leaves to prevent oxidation

OXIDATION
Leaves broken to encourage oxidation.
BLACK TEA: 4 hrs
OOLONG: 1-2 hrs

FIRING
(that is, dried in warm ovens or large woks)

GREEN TEA
Curled, packed flat, or rolled into pellets

OOLONG TEA
Formed/packed like green tea

BLACK TEA

WHITE TEA
Only new buds; processed like green tea

PU-ERH TEA
Green, black, and oolong are fermented and compressed

FLAVORED TEA
Flavorings added to black or oolong

Boston Tea Party

1773	Boston Tea Party: Americans dump 342 chests of tea into Boston Harbor, protesting British taxes.
1784	British tea taxes slashed; consumption soars.
1835	Tea cultivation starts in Assam, India.
1880s	India and Ceylon produce more tea than China.
1904	Englishman Richard Blechynden creates iced tea at St. Louis World's Fair.
1908	New York importer Thomas Sullivan sends clients samples in silk bags—the first tea bags.
2004	Chinese tea exports overtake India's for the first time since the 1880s.

TYPES OF TEA

 Some teas are simply named for the region that produces them (Yunnan or Assam); others are evocatively named to reflect a particular blend. Some are transliterated (like Keemun); others translated (Iron Goddess of Mercy). Confused? Keep two things in mind. First, the universal word for tea comes from *one* Chinese character—pronounced either "te" (Xiamen dialect) or "cha" (Cantonese and Mandarin). Second, all types of tea come from *one* plant.

	BLACK	PU-ERH	GREEN
Overview	It's popular in the West so it makes up the bulk of China's tea exports. It has a fuller, heavier flavor than green tea, though this varies enormously according to type.	Pu-erh tea is green, black, or oolong that's fermented from a few months to 50 years and compressed into balls during aging. Pu-erh is popular in Hong Kong, where it's called Bo Lei.	Most tea grown and consumed in China is green. It's delicate, so allow the boiling water to cool for a minute before brewing to prevent "cooking" the tea.
Flavor	From light and fresh to rich and chocolatey	Rich, earthy	Light, aromatic
Color	Golden brown to dark mahogany	Reddish brown	Light straw-yellow to bright green
Caffeine per Serving	40 mg	20–40 mg	20 mg
Ideal Water Temperature	203°F	203°F	160°F
Steeping Time	3–5 mins.	3–5 mins.	1–2 mins.
Examples	Dian Hong (dark, chocolatey aftertaste; unlike other Chinese teas, can take milk). Keemun (Qi Men; mild, smoky; once used in English breakfast blends). Lapsang Souchong (dried over smoking pine; strong flavor). Yunnan Golden (full bodied, malty).	Buying Pu-erh is like buying wine: there are different producers and different vintages, and prices vary greatly.	Bi Luo Chun (Green Snail Spring; leaves rolled into pellets; rich, fragrant). Chun Mee (Eyebrow; pale yellow; floral). Hou Kui (Monkey Tea; nutty, sweet; flowery aftertaste). Long Ding (Dragon Mountain; sweet, minty). Long Jing (Dragon's Well; bright green; nutty).

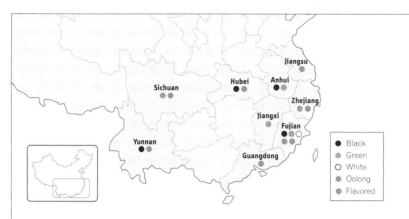

- ● Black
- ● Green
- ○ White
- ◑ Oolong
- ● Flavored

	WHITE	OOLONG	FLAVORED
Overview	The rare white tea is made from the newest buds, picked unopened at daybreak and processed like green tea. Small batches mean high prices. It's a tea for refined palates.	Halfway between green and black tea, this tea is more popular in China than elsewhere. The *gong fu cha* ceremony best reveals its complexities.	Petals, bark, and other natural ingredients are added to black or green tea to create these brews. Earl Grey is black tea scented with Bergamot (a recipe supposedly given to the tea's 18th-century namesake by a Mandarin). Jasmine tea is green tea dried with jasmine petals.
Flavor	Very subtle	Aromatic, lighter than black tea	
Color	Very pale yellow	Pale green to pale brown	Others include lychee congou and rose congou: black tea dried with lychee juice or rose petals. Flavor, color, caffeine content, and ideal preparation depend on the tea component of the blend.
Caffeine per Serving	15 mg	30 mg	
Ideal Water Temperature	185°F	203°F	
Steeping Time	4–15 mins.	1–9 mins.	
Examples	Bai Hao Yin Zhen (Silver Needle; finest white tea; sweet and very delicate, anti-toxin qualities). Bai Mu Dan (White Peony; smooth and refreshing).	Da Hong Pao (Scarlet Robe; the real stuff comes from only 4 bushes; full bodied, strongly floral). Tie Guan Yin (Iron Goddess of Mercy; legend has it a farmer repaired an iron statue of the goddess, who rewarded him with the tea bush shoot; prized; golden yellow; floral).	Don't confuse flavored teas with the caffeine-free herbal teas made from herbs, roots, and blossoms (e.g., chamomile, peppermint, rosehips, licorice, ginger).

GUIZHOU

With its undulating mountains, terraced fields, and traditional villages, Guizhou is among China's most interesting provinces. Although beautiful, it has less tourism infrastructure than neighboring Guangxi or Yunnan. One of the least visited provinces in southern China, Guizhou attracts those intent on heading off the beaten path.

Guizhou is home to many different tribes, including the Dong, Hui, Yao, Zhuang, and Miao (known in the west as the Hmong) peoples. More than a third of Guizhou's population comes from these tribes. The countryside is sprinkled with villages dominated by impressive towers. The province is known for its festivals, and frequent travelers claim that you can't travel through the province without running into at least one or more celebration.

Guiyang

With its large boulevards and metropolitan atmosphere, the capital city of Guiyang is a pleasant place to begin an exploration of the province. Like most cities in China it is fast losing its older quarters, however enough remain to make a short stay here worthwhile. The main streets of the sprawling town are Zhonghua Lu and Yan'an Lu.

Filled with bamboo groves, **Riverbank Park** (Hebin Gongyuan), sits on the banks of the Nanning River. This is a great place to come with children, as there is a Ferris wheel and other rides. In the park you'll find the **Hua Jia Pavilion** (Hua Jia Lou), an attractive Ming Dynasty pagoda painted with dragons and phoenixes. Also within the boundaries of the park is the colorful Ming Dynasty **Wen Chang Pavilion** (Wen Chang Lou), surrounded with buildings that house a collection of ancient coins and tools. ✉ *Huangcheng Dong Lu, off Minsheng Lu* 🎟 *Y2* ⏲ *Daily 9–5.*

Just outside the city, **Qianlingshan Park** (Qianlingshan Gongyuan) covers 740 acres. It has a bit of everything, including thousands of different species of plants and a collection of birds and monkeys (many of whom roam wild through the park). Dominating the park is a 4,265-foot-high mountain that has fine views of the town from its western peak. The **Cave of the Unicorn** (Qiling Dong), discovered in 1531, was used as a prison for the two Nationalist generals Yang Hucheng and Chang Hsueliang, who were accused by the Guomindang of collaborating with the Communists when Chiang Kai-shek was captured at Xian in 1937. ✉ *Zhaoshan Lu, 1½ km (1 mi) northwest of city* 🎟 *Y2* ⏲ *Daily 8 AM–10 PM.*

Filled with ornamental gardens, **Huaxi Park** (Huaxi Gongyuan) sits on the banks of the Huaxi, known as the River of Flowers. The Huaxi Waterfall is nearby. ✉ *18 km (11 mi) south of Guiyang* 🎟 *Y5* ⏲ *Daily 8–6.*

★ **Underground Gardens** (Dixia Gongyuan) is the poetic name for a cave about 25 km (15 mi) south of the city. In the cave, at a depth of 1,925 feet, a path weaves its way through the various rock formations, which are illuminated to emphasize their similarity with animals, fruit, and other living things. ⊠ *25 km (15 mi) south of Guiyang* ☎ *0851/511–4014* 🚍 *Y5* ⊙ *Daily 8:30–11:30 and 2:30–5.*

Tours

For tours of the area, contact the China International Travel Service (CITS) or the Guizhou Overseas Travel Service.

🔲 Tour-Operator Recommendations & Contacts **China International Travel Service (CITS)** ⊠ 20-40 Yan'an Zhong Lu, Guiyang ☎ 0851/581–6348. **Guizhou Overseas Travel Service** ⊠ 20 Yan'an Zhong Lu, Guiyang ☎ 0851/657–3212.

Where to Stay & Eat

Every province has a number of dishes that locals are fiercely proud of. In Guizhou, this is unquestionably *suan tang yu,* or sour fish soup. It combines a mouth-numbing number of herbs, spices, and local vegetables to make a dish that is at once spicy and savory. Another wonderfully named dish is *lian ai dougu guo,* or "the bean curd in love." It's a strip of vegetable- or meat-stuffed tofu that is toasted to a golden brown and sprinkled with sesame oil. It's a popular dish with couples, hence the name.

$$ ✕ **Jinqiao Restaurant** (Jinqiao Fandian). Although the decor is rather plain, the menu at this good restaurant offers regional food from Beijing and Canton. ⊠ *34 Ruijin Zhong Lu* ☎ *0851/582–5310* 🚫 *No credit cards.*

★ **¢–$** ✕ **Hongfu Temple Vegetarian Restaurant** (Hongfu Si Sucaiguan). With a wide range of dishes, this is considered one of the city's finest vegetarian restaurants. But it doesn't stay open late, so show up before 8 PM. ⊠ *Qianlin Park* ☎ *0851/682–5606* 🚫 *No credit cards.*

★ **¢–$** ✕ **Kaili Sour Sour Fish Restaurant** (Kaili Suan Tang Yu Jiudian). This is where you can order the city's signature dish, sour fish soup. It's cooked at your table, so you are able to add just the right amount of seasonings. Should yours be too spicy, remember that a bit of white rice—*not* water—is the best method of dousing culinary flames. ⊠ *55 Shengfu Lu* ☎ *No phone* 🚫 *No credit cards.*

¢–$ 🏨 **Nenghui Jiudian.** This handsome modern hotel delivers accommodations and facilities above its official three-star designation. Guest rooms are large and bright with high ceilings, big firm beds, modern furniture, and sparkling bathrooms. Its central location makes it a good base for exploring the city. ⊠ *38 Ruijin Nan Lu, 550003* ☎ *0851/589–8888* 🛏 *117 rooms* 🍴 *Restaurant, in-room safes, minibars, cable TV, in-room broadband, gym, sauna, bar, lounge, shops, dry cleaning, concierge, business services* 🚫 *AE, DC, MC, V.*

★ **¢** 🏨 **Guizhou Park Hotel** (Guizhou Fandian). The most luxurious hotel in town is this sleek glass tower close to Qianlingshan Park. The rooms are well appointed, but you'd be hard-pressed to find anything in them that lets you know you're in China. The 32-story hotel's roof garden is a great place to look out over the majestic scene that is Guizhuo province. ⊠ *66 Beijing Lu, 550004* ☎ *0851/682–3888* 🛏 *410 rooms* 🍴 *2 restaurants, in-room safes, minibars, cable TV, pool, bar, business services, meeting rooms, travel services* 🚫 *AE, DC, MC, V.*

Festivals of Guizhou

ITS COLORFUL FOLK FESTIVALS are one of the big draws to Guizhou. Since the province is comprised of various ethnic groups—including the Dong, Hui, Yao, Zhuang, and Miao peoples—Guizhuo is a veritable gallery of traditional customs. A wide variety of festivals are held throughout the year, both in Guiyang and elsewhere in the province. Many of these festivals are named after the specific dates on which they're held. Keep in mind that these dates are according to a lunar calendar, so the festival called "Month Four Day Eight" is not on April 8, but on the eighth day of the fourth lunar month (usually sometime in May).

Siyueba, which literally translates as "Month Four Day Eight," is when the Miao, Buyi, Dong, Yao, Zhuang, Yi, and other peoples of the province celebrate spring. Similar to Mardi Gras (but without the drinking or bawdy behavior), the festival is a major holiday in the region. Guiyang is a great place to check out the festival, as the area around the fountain in the city center erupts with music, dancing, and general merrymaking that can go on all night.

An important traditional festival of Guiyang's Buyi population is **Liuyueliu,** or "Six Month Six." Held in midsummer, as the name implies, this festival sees thousands of Buyi people from the region gathering on the banks of the Huaxi River. As the story goes, a beautiful Buyi maiden embroidered an image of mountains and rivers of immense beauty. It was so inspiring that a miscreant devised to steal it, and on the sixth day of the sixth month he sent his minions to take it by force. The maiden cast her embroidery into the air, where it was transformed into the beautiful mountains and rivers seen here today.

Among the Miao people who live in and around Kaili, a bullfight is a contest between the bulls themselves. The **Miao Bullfight Festival** traditionally takes place between the planting of rice seedlings and their harvest a few months later, usually between the sixth and eighth lunar month. Owners of bulls meet beforehand to size up the competition before agreeing to the fight. The atmosphere on the day of the fight is lively, with drinking, music, and exchanging of gifts. Using fireworks, the bulls are enticed into combat until one falls down or runs away.

An important fertility festival among the Miao people is the **Sister's Meal Festival** when unmarried women harvest rice from the terraced fields and prepare a special dish of sticky rice colored blue, pink, and yellow. Men arrive to serenade the women, and the women offer gifts of rice wine and small packets of rice wrapped in cloth. In the evenings, women dressed in all their finery to dance.

Side Trip to Huangguoshu Pubu

Fodor'sChoice ★ The Baishuio River streams over nine sets of rocks, creating nine waterfalls over a course of 2 km (1 mi). At the highest point, Huangguoshu Pubu (literally, Yellow Fruit Trees Falls) drops an eye-popping 230 feet. The largest in China, these falls are set in a lush countryside where you'll find numerous villages. You can enjoy them from afar or by wading across the **Rhinoceros Pool** (Xiniu Jian) to the **Water Curtain Cave** (Shui Lian Dong) hidden behind the main falls. Seven kilometers (4½ mi) downstream is the **Star Bridge Falls** (Xing Qiao Pu). The falls are at their best from May through October. Buses from Guiyang's main bus terminal make the trip here in two to three hours. Any travel agent can help you with the arrangements. ✉ *160 km (99 mi) southwest of Guiyang* ☎ *No phone* 🎟 *Y90* ⊗ *Dawn–dusk.*

To & from Guiyang

17 hrs (350 km [217 mi]) northwest of Guilin; 25 hrs (425 km [264 mi]) northwest of Nanning; (850 km [527 mi]) by train northwest of Hong Kong; 29 hrs (1,650 km [1,023 mi]) by train southwest of Beijing.

Guiyang Airport lies to the southwest of the city. There are direct flights between Guiyang and most of the main cities in China, including Beijing, Chengdu, Guangzhou, Guilin, Hong Kong, Shanghai, Xiamen, and Xian.

From Guiyang's station there is regular bus service to Anshun (2 hrs), Kaili (5 hrs), and Xingyi (approximately 12 hrs over very bad roads). There are also special tour buses to Huangguoshu Pubu from the Guiyang Railway Station that take about two hours.

Direct trains link Guiyang with Chongqing (9 hrs), Guilin (16½ hrs), Kunming (10 hrs), Liuzhou (13 hrs), Nanning (24½ hrs), and Shanghai (30 hrs). The train station is at the southern edge of the city.

Kaili

Capital of the Qian Dongnan Autonomous Region, Kaili serves as the starting point for a journey to the Miao and Dong villages that dominate eastern Guizhou. More than two-thirds of the population here is Miao, and their villages are along the eastern and northeastern outskirts of Kaili. The Dong communities are located to the southeast. To get a real flavor for these peoples, try to catch a glimpse of a local festival; there are more than 100 festivals annually, many in fall or spring.

Kaili is a pleasant place to visit, thanks to its laid-back atmosphere. In Jinquanhu Park, the **Drum Tower** (Gu Lou) is the Dong people's gathering place for celebrations. The **Minorities Museum** (Zhou Minzu Bowuguan; ✉ 5 Guangchang Lu 🎟 Y10 ⊗ Mon.–Sat. 9–5) displays arts, crafts, and relics of the local indigenous peoples.

Outside town the local villages are of great interest. To the north is the Wuyang River, which passes by many mountains, caves, and Miao villages. At **Shibing**, you can take boat rides (contact CITS, *below* in Guizhou Essentials) through spectacular limestone gorges and arrange stops at these towns. South of Kaili are the Dong villages of **Leishan, Rongjiang,** and **Zhaoxing.** The latter village, set in a beautiful landscape, is known for its five drum towers.

Where to Stay & Eat

¢ ✕🏨 **Guotai Dajiudian.** This hotel, in the center of town, is the best in Kaili. (No wonder it attracts well-heeled foreign tour groups.) The guest rooms are extremely comfortable, and the bathrooms are squeaky clean. The staff—mostly made up of members of the Miao minority group—is very friendly. The restaurant serves a variety of traditional Miao dishes, as well as many from the rest of the country. ⊠ *6 Beijing Dong Lu, 556000* ☎*0855/826–9888* ⌂*73 rooms* ⌂ *2 restaurants, room service, cable TV, in-room broadband, hair salon, laundry service, business services* ⊟ *No credit cards.*

To & from Kaili
3 hrs (about 200 km [124 mi]) by train east of Guiyang.

The Kaili long-distance buses leave for Guiyan every three hours (Y40 to Y60). In the morning there are also minivans to Guiyan at the local bus station in the western part of town.

GUIZHOU ESSENTIALS

Transportation

BY AIR
▟ Airport Information **Guiyang Airport** ✈ Southwest of the city ☎ 0851/549-8908.

BY BUS
▟ Bus Information **Guiyang Station** ⊠ Yan'an Xi Lu ☎ 0851/685-5336.

BY TRAIN
▟ Train Information **Guiyang Railway Station** ⊠ Zunyi Lu ☎ 0851/818-1222.

Contacts & Resources

EMERGENCIES
For emergencies, contact your hotel. The Public Security Bureau, or PSB, is where you must go should your passport be lost or stolen during your travels.
▟ **PSB** ⊠ 5 Zhuxin Lu, Guiyang ☎ 0851/676-5230.

MONEY MATTERS
Change money at your hotel or at the Bank of China in Guiyang and Kaili.
▟ Bank **Bank of China** ⊠ 30 Dusi Lu, Guiyang ☎ 0851/581-5261 ⊠ Beijing Donglu near the city's main roundabout, Kaili.

TOURS
Quite possibly the only multilingual identical twin tour guides operating in China, Jennifer and Louisa Wu are members of the Miao minority and speak English, Mandarin, and a number of other Chinese languages fluently. They are both highly familiar with Guizhuo and Yunnan, and divide their time leading short- and long-term tours around these provinces. Rates for a group are negotiable, but generally average around Y250 per day.
▟ **Jennifer and Louisa Wu** ☎ 1370/844-3445.

VISITOR INFORMATION
The China International Travel Service (CITS) is the best place to get information about the region.

▣ Tourist Information **China International Travel Service (CITS)** ✉ 20-40 Yan'an Zhong Lu, Guiyang ☎ 0851/581-6348.

YUNNAN

Hidden deep in southwestern China, Yunnan is one of the country's most fascinating provinces. Its rugged and varied terrain contains some of China's most beautiful natural scenery, as well as the headwaters of three of Asia's most important rivers: the Yangtze, Mekong, and Salween. Stunning mountains, picturesque highland meadows, and steamy tropical jungles are inhabited by Bai, Dai, Naxi, Hani, and dozens of other ethnic groups, many of which can only be found in Yunnan.

Yunnan sits atop the Yunnan-Guizhou Plateau, a prime piece of real estate with the Himalayas to the northwest and Myanmar, Laos, and Vietnam to the south. Yunnan was central to the Ancient Tea and Horse Caravan Route, an important trade route that connected China with the rest of Southeast Asia for thousands of years. Today, Yunnan is one of the top travel destinations in China, with Lijiang, Dali, and Jinghong getting most of the attention. There are also countless lesser-known but equally amazing places sprinkled throughout the province.

Roughly the size of California, Yunnan is only now becoming accessible to the outside world. Increasingly convenient air travel makes it possible to have breakfast by the Mekong in Jinghong and dinner overlooking the old mountain town of Lijiang the same day. Far from being overrun by tourism, Yunnan still has plenty of places that are off the beaten path.

Kunming

Kunming is one of China's most pleasant cities, a product of its year-round mild climate. It's one of the few Chinese cities that regularly has blue skies. Because of this, the Chinese have nicknamed it the "City of Spring."

Not too long ago Kunming was still a sleepy backwater, but in recent years it has grown bigger and wealthier. An unfortunate side effect of this rapid development has been the wholesale demolition of the rustic old city, the most recent victim being the much-loved Jingxing Street Bird and Flower Market. Another drawback is the severe pollution of nearby Dianchi Lake.

BIKING AROUND KUNMING

Kunming is one of the best cities in China for biking. Small brown signs point toward historical and cultural sights. The signs are in Chinese, but you should be able to find the sites if you follow the arrows. Start at Green Lake Park and explore the numerous winding lanes shooting off in every direction from the park. Heading south you'll find the few remaining pockets of old Kunming. Continuing south there are several small parks, temples, pagodas, and other monuments that make nice places to stop.

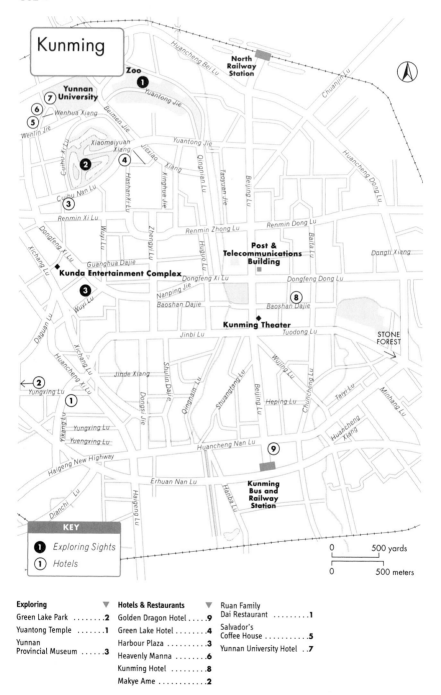

Kunming

Kunming's city center, particularly around Cuihu Park, has a relaxed atmosphere. Although the city has little in the way of must-see attractions, its cool climate and friendly population make it a good place to spend a few days.

WORD OF MOUTH

I like Kunming for 2 days, and Dali for 2 or less (it is noisy and not v. interesting). In Dali you'll see many minorities dressed in their own dress & many natural areas of great beauty. The people appear to be much more Tibetan than Chinese.

                          —merckxxx

Exploring Kunming

❷ In the north-central part of the city, **Green Lake Park** (Cuihu Gongyuan) is filled with willow- and bamboo-covered islands connected by stone bridges. Green Lake itself was once part of Dianchi Lake, but it was severed from that larger body of water in the late 1970s. The park is a favorite gathering place for Kunming's older residents, who begin to congregate in the park for singing and dancing beginning around 2:30 PM and stay until the gates close at 11 PM. In summers, the lake is filled with pink and white lotus blossoms. In winter the park fills with vacationing seagulls from Siberia. ⊠ *Cuihu Nan Lu* ☞ *Free* ☉ *Daily 7–11.*

FodorsChoice ★

★ ❸ **Yuantong Temple** (Yuantong Si), the largest temple in the city, dates back some 1,200 years to the Tang Dynasty. The compound consists of a series of gates leading to the inner temple, which is surrounded by a pond brimming with fish and turtles. The chanting of worshippers in the serene environment makes it hard to believe you're in a big city. In the back of the compound is a temple housing a statue of Sakyamuni, a gift from the king of Thailand. ⊠ *30 Yuantong Jie* ☞ *Y4* ☉ *Daily 8–6.*

❶ The **Yunnan Provincial Museum** (Yunnansheng Bowuguan) is a window into the region's interesting history. The museum focuses primarily on the Dian Kingdom, which ruled much of Yunnan from 1000 BC to 1 BC. Most of what you see here is more than 2,000 years old. Exhibits have good English captions. ⊠ *118 Wuyi Lu* ☎ *0871/362–7718* ☞ *Y10* ☉ *Daily 9–5:30.*

Tours

There are no group tours of Kumming that are worth your time. Beware of local companies that run tours that spend more time in shops than attractions.

Where to Stay & Eat

The local cuisine in Kunming is slightly more sour but just as spicy as Sichuan fare. The cooking styles of Yunnan's ethnic populations, particularly the Dai, are increasingly popular. If you can't handle super-spicy food (most locals are addicted to peppers), tell the staff you don't want any spice; chances are your dish will still come out mildly spicy.

$–$$$$ ✕**Makye Ame.** As much a cultural experience as a gastronomical adventure, Makye Ame is known for its Tibetan and Indian song-and-dance performances. The shows are enjoyable, but rather loud. For a quieter meal, ask for one of the rooms in the back or the cozy teahouse upstairs. Food-wise, Makye Ame serves a large variety of Tibetan dishes guaran-

Ethnic Minorities of the Southwest

YUNNAN IS LIKE NO OTHER PLACE in China with 26 of the counties' 56 ethnic minorities living within its borders. Many of the groups in this region have long resisted Han influence and as a result, the province has a multicultural flavor all its own.

NAXI

Primarily living in the area around Lijiang and neighboring Sichuan, the Naxi culture is extremely unique, even when compared with other minority groups in China. The society is traditionally matriarchal, with women dominating relationships, keeping custody of children, and essentially running the show. Some Naxis practice Buddhism or Taoism, but it is the shamanistic culture of the Dongba and Samba that set their spiritualism apart from other groups. The Dongba (male shamans) and Samba (female shamans) serve their communities as mediators, entering trancelike states and communicating with the spiritual world in order to solve problems on earth. Naxi script, like Chinese script, is made up of ideograms. These pictographs are vivid representations of body parts, animals, and geography used to express concrete and abstract concepts. Despite numbering less than 300,000 the Naxi are one of the better-known ethnic groups in China.

BAI

The Bai, also known as the Minjia, are one of the more prominent minorities in Yunnan, although they are also found in Guizhou and Hunan provinces. Primarily centered around the Dali Bai Autonomous Region, the Bai are known for their agricultural skills and unique architecture style. The Bai also have some of the most colorful costumes, particularly the rainbow-colored hats worn by women. The Bai, along with the Yi people, were part of the Nanzhao Kingdom, which briefly rose to regional dominance in southwest China and Southeast Asia during the Tang Dynasty, before giving way to the Kingdom of Dali. The Dali region and the Bai have essentially been a part of the Chinese sphere of influence since the Yuan Dynasty, during which the Yuan's Mongolian armies conquered the area in the 13th century. The Bai people's highly efficient and productive rice paddies were seen as an asset by the Yuan, who let them operate under relative autonomy. Today the Bai and their festivals, including the Third Moon Festival and Torch Festival, are major attractions for domestic and international tourists.

DAI

Related to Thais and speakers of languages belonging to the Tai-Kadai family, the Dai seem much more Southeast Asian than Chinese. In China, they are primarily located in the Xishuangbanna, Dehong, and Jingpo regions of southern Yunnan, but can also be found in Myanmar, Laos, and Thailand. They practice Theravada Buddhism, the dominant form of Buddhism in Southeast Asia. The linguistic, cultural, and religious connections with Southeast Asia give Dai-inhabited regions a decidedly un-Chinese feel. Within China, they are

most famous for their spicy and flavorful food and their Water Splashing Festival (water is used to wash away demons and sins of the past and bless the future). Many grow rice and produce such crops as pineapples, so villages are concentrated near the Mekong (Lancang) and Red (Honghe) rivers. The Dai population here has ebbed and flowed with China's political tide and many are now returning after the turmoil of the 1960s and 70s.

YI

Descendants of the Qiang people of northwestern China, the Yi (aka Sani) are scattered across southwestern China in Yunnan, Sichuan, and Guizhou provinces as well as Guangxi Zhuang Autonomous Region. The largest concentration of the more than 6½ million Qiang descendants are in Sichuan's Liangshan region. They live in isolated, mountainous regions and are known for being fierce warriors. Notable traits include their syllabic writing system, ancient literature, and traditional medicine—all of which are still being used today. The Yi also sport extravagant costumes that vary according to geographical region. Massive black mortarboard-style hats, blue turbans, ornate red headdresses, and other headwear complement the brilliantly colored vests and pants. Their language is part of the Tibeto-Burman language family and similar to Burmese. Some Yi also live in Vietnam, where they are called the Lolo.

(left) Young unmarried Bai women. Yunnan province. (right) Yi Girl in traditional costume. Puge, Sichuan Province

Yunnan Cuisine

DIAN CUISINE is the term for Han Chinese cuisine found in Yunnan, especially around Kunming. Dian-style dishes are similar to Sichuan dishes and tend to favor spicy and sour flavors. Rice is a staple here, as is a type of rice noodle called *mixian*. A favorite dish is *guoqiao mixian*, a boiling oily broth served with raw pork and vegetables that you cook yourself. *Qiguo ji* (steampot chicken), another trademark Dian-style dish, uses a special earthenware pot to steam chicken and vegetables into a savory soup.

One thing that sets Dian cuisine apart from the rest of China is the dairy products. *Rubing* is made from goat's milk and is typically fried and served with dried chili peppers or sugar. It is a little drier and less pungent than regular goat cheese. *Rushan*, or "milk fan," is a long strip of a cheese that is spread with a salty or sweet sauce. Wrapped around a chopstick, it makes a handy snack.

Street barbecue is a major part of the Yunnan culinary experience. Every kind of meat and vegetable are on offer, as well as quail eggs, *chou doufu* (stinky tofu), and *erkuai* (rice pancakes with sweet or savory fillings). Most restaurants in Yunnan close early, but barbecue stands stay open until the wee hours, making them a good place for a late-night snack.

teed to please, including stone-cooked yak, *malai kafta* (large potato and cashew balls in a curried yogurt sauce), and an incomparable *xianggu* (shiitake-mushroom) platter. A cold Lhasa beer or some homemade yogurt wine rounds out one of the city's more memorable meals. ✉ *Jinhuapu Lu, next to Yimen Hotel* ☎ *0871/833–6300* ▭ *No credit cards.*

¢–$ ✕ **Heavenly Manna.** Truly from heaven, this place serves some of the best food in the city. There are delicious regional specialties such as steampot chicken, bitter melon with egg, and corn in duck egg yolks, as well as local interpretations of traditional Chinese dishes. Manna is a favorite lunch and dinner spot for locals, so it can be difficult to find seating at peak hours. There's an English menu. ✉ *74 Wenhua Xiang* ☎ *0871/536–9399* ▭ *No credit cards.*

¢–$ ✕ **Ruan Family Dai Restaurant** (Ruanjia Daiwei Yuan). Located in the back of Chuangku, a cluster of art galleries on Xiba Lu, this restaurant is one of the best places in town to try the delicious cuisine of the Dai. Here you'll find everything from purple rice in pineapple to fried beef with mint to tapioca in coconut milk. There's no English menu, so you may have to be inspired by what your fellow diners have ordered. Don't forget to take advantage of the unlimited free *shuijiu*, a sakelike rice wine that goes down smooth and takes the edge off the spicy food. Come early, as the restaurant stops taking orders around 8 PM. ✉ *101 Xiba Lu* ☎ *0871/363–3023* ▭ *No credit cards.*

🕐 ¢–$$ ✕ **Salvador's Coffee House.** It has the city's best espresso drinks—made
FodorsChoice from local beans—but Salvador's is more than just a coffeehouse. Eas-
★ ily the best Western restaurant in Kunming, Salvador's makes its own bagels, pesto, hummus, salsa—even the Indian chai is powdered on the

premises. Popular main dishes include burritos, quesadillas, and falafel. Salvador's has free Wi-Fi, comfy sofas for lounging, and outdoor seating ideal for people-watching on bustling Wenhua Xiang. Lots of people come with the kids for ice cream. ⊠ *76 Wenhua Xiang* ☎ *0871/536–3525* ⊟ *No credit cards.*

¢–$ ⌂ **Golden Dragon Hotel** (Jinlong Fandian). Although a bit on the drab side, this locally owned hotel offers moderately priced rooms and a reasonable standard of service. The location is very convenient to the railway and bus stations. ⊠ *575 Beijing Lu, 650011* ☎ *0871/313–3015* ⊅ *150 rooms* ⌂ *2 restaurants, pool, hair salon, bar, shops, TV, business services, in-room broadband* ⊟ *AE, DC, MC, V.*

¢–$ ⌂ **Green Lake Hotel** (Cuihu Binguan). In a pleasant part of town, this former Hilton still holds itself to the same high standards. The grand marble-and-wood lobby is filled with plush chairs and sofas and the coffee shop has excellent coffee drinks and homemade ice cream. The guest rooms are Kunming's cleanest and most comfortable. The restaurant hosts regular performances of traditional music. ⊠ *6 Cuihu Nan Lu, 650031* ☎ *0871/515–8888* ⊕ *www.greenlakehotel.com.cn/e_index.htm* ⊅ *301 rooms, 6 suites* ⌂ *4 restaurants, pool, hot tub, gym, massage, bar, nightclub, shops, in-room safes, business services, in-room broadband* ⊟ *AE, DC, MC, V.*

$$–$ ✕⌂ **Harbour Plaza.** With one of the best locations in town, this hotel sits beside Cuihu Park. With good Cantonese and Japanese restaurants and a revolving lounge up top, Harbour Plaza has plenty of food and drink options. It's also a short stroll from some of the best bars and restaurants in town. ⊠ *20 Honghuaqiao, 650031* ☎ *0871/538–6688* ⊕ *www.harbour-plaza.com/en/home.aspx* ⊅ *315 rooms, 14 suites* ⌂ *2 restaurants, coffee shop, lounge, in-room safes, cable TV, gym, pool, massage, sauna, business services, in-room broadband* ⊟ *AE, DC, MC, V.*

¢ ⌂ **Kunming Hotel.** The oldest of the luxury hotels in town is centrally located and has reasonably comfortable rooms, although they have not been renovated for some years. There is a pool and a practice range for golfers on the premises. ⊠ *52 Dongfeng Dong Lu, 650051* ☎ *0871/316–2063* ⊕ *www.kmhotel.com.cn/enhome.htm* ⊅ *267 rooms, 53 suites* ⌂ *3 restaurants, driving range, pool, gym, 2 bars, business services* ⊟ *AE, DC, MC, V.*

¢ ⌂ **Yunnan University Hotel.** In the heart of the university area, Yunnan University Hotel is one of the city's best bargains. Standard rooms all have clean bathrooms. Located on the west side of Yunnan University, the hotel has backdoor access to one of China's most beautiful college campuses. ⊠ *Yieryi Dajie, 650031* ☎ *0871/503–4195* ⊅ *84 rooms* ⌂ *Restaurant, laundry; no room phones, no room TVs* ⊟ *V* ⏐◯⏐ *BP.*

Kunming's Flying Tigers

DESPITE ITS LOCATION in the hinterland of Southwest China, Kunming played a crucial role in World War II by preventing Japanese forces from taking control of all of China. At the center of this role was the American Volunteer Group, best known by its local nickname *feihu*, or the Flying Tigers, because of the shark faces painted on their fuselages.

The group of around 300 American servicemen was led by the mysterious Claire L. Chennault. A retired captain in the U.S. Air Force, Chennault first came to Kunming in 1938 when Madame Chiang Kai-shek, wife of the country's leader, asked him to organize a Chinese air force to counter the relentless attacks from the Japanese, who were busily bombing much of China with little opposition.

Supply routes to China's capital were being taken out one after another leaving just one road. Chennault argued that a group of American pilots could defend this crucial supply artery, as well as push the Japanese out of the region.

The Flying Tigers were tenacious fighters. They swept through much of China, putting an end to the constant bombing by Japanese forces. Their record was second-to-none in World War II. They had over 50 enemy encounters and were never defeated.

Nightlife & the Arts

NIGHTLIFE   When evening falls, Kunming's growing expat population tends to congregate at the bars, cafés, and restaurants of Wenlin Jie and Wenhua Xiang (literally Culture Forest Street and Culture Alley). **Chapter One** (✉ 146 Wenlin Jie ☎ 0871/536–5635) is one of the favorite bars for expats.

THE ARTS   Kunming's nascent art scene can be taken in at **Chuangku** (✉ 101 Xiba Lu ☎ No phone). A group of warehouses that have been converted into galleries, Chuangku is also home to a smattering of cafés and restaurants.

Chinese dance legend Yang Liping may have retired after breaking her leg during her last tour in 2005, but the Yunnan native's award-winning dance and musical production **Dynamic Yunnan** (✉ Kunming Theater, 427 Beijing Lu ☎ 0871/319 2141) still plays to full-capacity crowds. An impressive fusion of the storytelling, songs, and dances of indigenous groups with modern theatrical techniques, Dynamic Yunnan is a must-see for music and dance aficionados.

Shopping

If you're looking for a good deal on tea, look no farther than the wholesale tea market at the southeast corner of Beijing Lu and Wujing Lu. There are a couple of small entrances to the large market on Wujing Lu. Within the market you'll find an amazing variety of green teas, black teas, flower teas, and herbal teas. It's a wholesale market, but all vendors will sell you small quantities, usually at mind-blowingly low prices.

Qianju Jie is one of the more popular shopping streets in the city, near the intersection of Wenlin Jie and Wenhua Xiang. On Wenhua Xiang is

Mandarin Books (⊠ 52 Wenhua Xiang 9–10 ☎ 0871/551–6579), one of the best foreign-language bookstores in all of China.

Side Trip from Kunming

One of the most interesting sites near Kunming is a geological phenomenon known as the **Stone Forest** (Shilin). This cluster of dark gray-limestone karst formations has been twisted into unusual shapes since being formed beneath the sea 270 million years ago. Many have been given names to describe their resemblances to real or mythological animals (phoenixes, elephants, and turtles). The journey here takes you through the hilly countryside dotted with timber-frame architecture typical of the area.

You can take walks through the park, which is dotted with small lakes and pools. Here you'll find plenty of Sani women eager to act as guides and sell you their handicrafts. The area where most tourists venture has, inevitably, become rather commercialized, but there are plenty of similar formations in other parts of the park if you wander off the main trail.

The Stone Forest is 125 km (78 mi) southeast of Kunming. There are several ways to get here, the best being a car and driver. One can be arranged through your hotel and should cost between Y500 and Y600. Another option is the cheap bus tours (Y20 round-trip) that leave each morning from the area around the train station. This trip takes at least four hours, as the driver makes numerous stops at souvenir stands and junk stores along the way. ⊠ *Lunan* 🚆 *Y80* ⊗ *24 hrs.*

To & from Kunming

11 hrs (400 km [248 mi]) by train southwest of Guiyang; 21 hrs (650 km [403 mi]) by train southwest of Chengdu; 27 hrs (1,200 km [744 mi]) by train west of Hong Kong; 45 hrs (2,000 km [1,240 mi]) by train southwest of Beijing.

Buses are still the main form of transportation in the region. Luxury buses with bathrooms are available at the Xizhan bus station on Xichang Lu, north of Yieryi Dajie. Smaller buses are available outside the train station at the south end of Beijing Lu.

There is train service from Kunming to Dali, and service to Lijiang is slated to be added sometime in 2007. The train station is at the south end of Beijing Lu.

There are also daily flights from Kunming to Dali, Lijiang, and Jinghong. The prices are highest during national holidays. The airport is at the south end of Chuncheng Lu, in the city's southeastern section.

Dali

Dali is one of those rare places that feels completely cut off from the rest of the world, yet has high-speed Internet access. The rustic town is perched at the foot of the towering Cangshan Mountains and overlooks lovely Erhai Lake. Its typically sunny weather, sleepy atmosphere, and gorgeous sunsets have made it one of Yunnan's most popular destinations.

Home to the Bai people, Dali has been inhabited for more than 4,000 years, serving as a major rice-production base for the region. Today, tourism is rejuvenating the town. The upside of this building boom is a greater variety of restaurants and hotels; the downside is that the old town is constantly being demolished and reconstructed, the most recent addition being a massive shopping complex called "Foreigner Street Plaza" that looks like it was copied from a strip mall and comes complete with its own chiming four-sided clock. A major highway has also been built near the old town.

Exploring Dali

Dali's old town, called Dali Gucheng, is surrounded by reconstructed versions of the old city wall and gates. Go to the wall's southwest corner and take the stairs to the top for a great view of the city and the surrounding mountains. Outside of the bustling center of the old town are countless little alleys lined with old Bai-style homes that are interesting for exploring.

> ## THE TORCH FESTIVAL
>
> One of the more exciting festivals in southwest China is the Torch Festival, which is celebrated by both the Yi and Bai minorities in June or July. Dali's old town is one of the best (and worst) places to catch the festival. The chaotic celebration is rivaled only by Chinese New Year. However, many local children like to frighten travelers with the flames, especially on the Foreigner Street. Anyone who wants to see the festival without worrying about getting singed by pyromaniac children might want to go to Xizhou or other places with fewer foreigners.

Dali has two popular pedestrian streets, Huguo Lu and Renmin Lu, both of which run east–west, or uphill–downhill. Huguo Lu, better known as Foreigner Street, is lined with the cafés that made Dali famous in the 1990s, but the street has begun to lose its luster. High rents and cut-throat competition have taken a toll on quality and service.

The most famous landmark in Dali, the **Three Pagodas** (San Ta), appears on just about every calendar of Chinese scenery. The largest, 215 feet high, dates from AD 836 and is decorated on each of its 16 stories with Buddhas carved from local marble. The other two pagodas, also richly decorated, are more elegant in style. When the water is still, you can ponder their reflection in a nearby pool. The pagodas are a 20-minute walk from the old town. ⊠ *1 km (½ mi) north of Dali Gucheng* 🚃 *Y40* ⊙ *Daily 7 AM–8 PM.*

Tours

China Minority Travel lets you explore the villages surrounding Erhai Lake. The first stop on the day-trip is nearby Xizhou, a village that resembles Dali before the tourism boom. Afterward, enjoy lunch on the ferry across Erhai Lake before arriving at Wase to explore the village's market. The trip is $225 for up to five people, including a guide, transportation, and lunch.

🚹 Tour-Operator Recommendations **China Minority Travel** ⊠ 63 Boai Lu ☎ 0872/267-9549 ⊕ www.china-travel.nl.

Dali & the Nanzhao Kingdom

THE IDYLLIC SCENERY belies Dali's importance as the center of power for the Nanzhao Kingdom. The easily defensible area around Erhai Lake was the Kingdom's birthplace, which began as the Bai- and Yi-dominated Damengguo in 649. Almost a century later, Damengguo was expanded to include the six surrounding kingdoms ruled by powerful Bai families. This expansion was supported by the ruling Chinese Tang Dynasty, and the kingdom was renamed Nanzhao.

The primarily Buddhist Nanzhao Kingdom was essentially a vassal state of the Tang Dynasty until AD 750, when it rebelled. Tang armies were sent in 751 and 754 to suppress the insurgents, but they suffered humiliating defeats. Emboldened by their victories, Nanzhao troops helped the kingdom acquire a significant amount of territory. Before reaching its high point with the capture of Chengdu and Sichuan in 829, the Nanzhao Kingdom had expanded to include all of present-day Yunnan, as well as parts of present-day Burma, Laos, and Thailand.

Although the capture of Chengdu was a major victory for Nanzhao, it appears to have led directly to its decline. The Tang Dynasty couldn't stand for such an incursion and sent large numbers of troops to the area. They eventually evicted Nanzhao forces from Sichuan by 873. About 30 years later, the Nanzhao leaders were finally overthrown, ending the story of their meteoric rise and fall.

7

Where to Stay & Eat

For a taste of authentic local Bai dishes like *paojiao zhurou* (pork with pickled peppers) or *chao rubing* (fried goat cheese), try any of the local restaurants on Renmin Lu just east of the intersection with Fuxing Lu. None of these restaurants have English menus or service, but they generally have their ingredients on display. Just point out what you want and chances are you'll get what you're looking for.

$–$$ ✕ **The Dining Room.** Can't decide between Yunnan and Sichuan food? This restaurant, one of the best places to get a home-cooked meal, serves both. The menu is mostly off-the-cuff, so it's best to wander into the kitchen and see what's cooking. Run by a young Chinese couple, the restaurant feels like someone's living room; there are comfy sofas and even a Sony PlayStation 2. ✉ *266 Renmin Lu* ☎ *0872/267–0266* ⊟ *No credit cards.*

¢–$$ ✕ **La Stella's Pizzeria.** Located at the top of Foreigner Street, Stella's has
Fodor'sChoice emerged as one of the best restaurants in town. The pizzas, cooked in
★ a wood-fired oven, feature traditional toppings, as well as Chinese favorites such as corn. Other highlights include lasagna, nachos, and Greek salads. The Chinese food is also worth a try. ✉ *21 Huguo Lu* ☎ *0872/267–9251* ⊟ *No credit cards.*

★ ¢–$$ ✕ **Café de Jack.** In business since 1989, Café de Jack has always managed to change with the times. It still serves some of the best coffee in town, but now it also has an Internet station and a Wi-Fi connection.

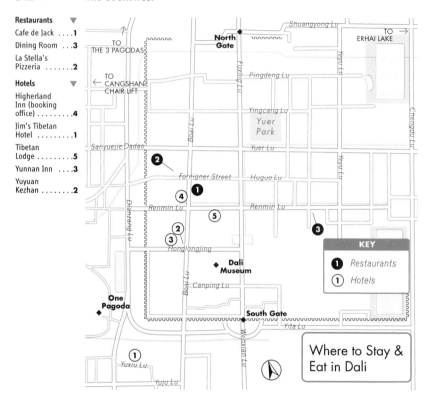

Where to Stay &
Eat in Dali

The 1st floor feels like a bar, whereas the 2nd floor is more like a restaurant. Kick back with a beer on the rooftop on afternoons when the weather's good. ⊠ *82 Boai Lu* ☎ *0872/267–1572* ▭ *No credit cards.*

¢–$$ ⊡ **Higherland Inn.** Up in the verdant mountains behind the old town sits the Higherland Inn. At 8,500 feet, it's the perfect place to start a hike or just enjoy the view. The walls are a little thin, so it's not the best place for light sleepers. Meals are similar to those you'd find in town, and feature both Chinese and Western dishes. There is a booking office in Dali at 67 Bo'ai Lu, near Renmin Lu; reserve ahead to get a discount on the Y30 fee to ascend the mountains. ⊠*Cangshan Daorendong, 671003* ☎*0872/266–1599* ▭*8 rooms* ♢ *Restaurant, library* ▭ *No credit cards.*

☾ ¢ ⊡ **Jim's Tibetan Hotel.** Outside the south gate, this is one of the city's newest lodgings. It's in the quiet Yulu Xiaoqu neighborhood, making it ideal for those wanting to avoid the hubbub of the old town. Decorated in traditional Tibetan and Bai styles, the hotel is run by a Tibetan and Dutch couple that speaks fluent English. This is the only place in Dali with a playground for kids. Ask about booking tours of Dali and beyond. ⊠ *13 Yuxiu Lu, 671003* ☎ *0872/267–7824* ⊕ *www.china-travel.nl* ▭*13 rooms* ♢ *Restaurant, bar, Wi-Fi, travel services* ▭ *No credit cards.*

¢ ⊡ **Tibetan Lodge.** Conveniently located near the top of Renmin Lu, Tibetan Lodge puts you in the middle of a long stretch of bars and restaurants. The guest rooms are clean and well equipped. Tibetan Lodge has bicycles for rent plus a variety of tour options. ⊠ *58 Renmin Lu, 671003* ☎ *0872/266–4177* ⟟ *20 rooms* ⟁ *Restaurant, bar, Internet room, bicycles* ⊟ *No credit cards.*

★ ¢ ⊡ **Yunnan Inn.** Owned by acclaimed Chinese artist Fang Lijun, this guesthouse is in a class by itself. Eschewing traditional architecture for a more modern feel, Fang has created one of the city's most pleasant places to stay. Great rooftop views and the chance to visit Fang's studio set this guesthouse apart. Even better, standard rooms start at just Y80. ⊠ *3 Honglongjing, 671003* ☎ *0872/266–3741* ⟟ *10 rooms* ⟁ *Restaurant, bar, Internet room* ⊟ *No credit cards.*

¢ ⊡ **Yuyuan Kezhan.** There is no restaurant or bar, but this family-run guesthouse offers some of the nicest rooms in its price range. Its location, on a quite street near the center of old town, is great. Despite its minimal amenities, the guesthouse does laundry and has Internet access. ⊠ *8 Honglongjing, 671003* ☎ *0872/267–3267* ⟟ *19 rooms* ⟁ *Laundry service, Internet room* ⊟ *No credit cards.*

Nightlife & the Arts

There's not much in the way of cultural events in Dali, but the heart of the old town can occasionally be happening at night. The **Bird Bar** (⊠ 22 Renmin Lu ☎ 0872/266–1843) has the best pool table in town and often holds impromptu pool tournaments. **Café de Jack** (⊠ 82 Boai Lu ☎ 0872/267–1572) often has live music in the evenings.

Shopping

Foreigner Street is lined with Bai women who have been selling the same jewelry, fabrics, and Communist kitsch for the last 15 years. That said, sometimes there is the occasional find. Don't be afraid to walk away when bargaining; vendors will often drop their prices at the last minute.

Boai Lu and Renmin Lu are peppered with a variety of shops featuring outdoor clothing and equipment; handicrafts from India, Nepal, and Southeast Asia; as well as Chinese antiques. Fuxing Lu, aimed primarily at Chinese tourists, is where you'll find local teas, specialty foods, and most prominently, jade. Much of it is low quality, so buy only if you know something about jade.

Side Trips from Dali

★ With a peak that rises to more than 14,765 feet, **Cangshan** (Green Mountain) can be seen from just about any place in Dali. A 16-km (10-mi) path carved into the side of the mountain halfway between the summit and the old town offers spectacular views of Dali and the surrounding villages. There are also several temples, grottoes, and waterfalls just off the main trail. If you don't want to climb several thousand feet to get to the path,

---

> **CAFÉ SOCIETY**
>
> Dali has some of the best coffee shops in China, particularly on Renmin Lu. Coffee drinks made with Yunnan-grown beans can be found at **Tea Utopia** (⊠ 59 Renmin Lu ☎ 0872/267-3777). For Dali's best coffee and tea, head to **Guiqu Laixi** (⊠ 258 Renmin Lu ☎ 0872/267-6737), whose owner is a well-traveled Chinese antique collector who has decorated the place with a rustic yet refined feel.

7

there is a cable car (more like a ski lift) that will take you up and back for Y60. To get to the cable car, follow Yuer Lu to the foot of the mountain. In 2006 a new Y30 charge was added for ascending the mountains in any way, bringing the cost of taking the cable car up the mountain to Y90 and footing it to Y30.

Almost any street off Fuxing Lu will bring you to the shore of **Erhai Lake** (Erhai Hu). You may catch a glimpse of fishermen with their teams of cormorants tied to their boats.

Cormorants have a collar around their necks that prevents them from swallowing the fish they have caught.

In good weather, ferries are a wonderful way to see the lake and the surrounding mountains. The ferries usually cost between Y30 and Y70 (depending on your ability to bargain). More interesting perhaps—and cheaper—would be to hire one of the local fishermen to paddle wherever you want to go. Boats depart from the village of Zhoucheng.

A number of interesting communities lie fairly close to Dali. Among the prettiest towns in the area is **Xizhou,** about 20 km (12 mi) north of Dali. It has managed to preserve a fair amount of its Bai architecture. The daily morning market and occasional festivals of traditional music attract a fair number of tourists from neighboring Dali. Buses to Xizhou leave from Dali's west gate and cost Y4.

There are a handful of towns with markets known for local crafts, household goods, and antiques (beware of fakes!). **Shaping** has the most popular market, taking place every Monday morning. The town sits on the lake's northern shore, and can be most easily reached by boat or by hiring a car and driver.

Wase is another popular area market, featuring Bai clothing. The town is on the opposite side of the lake from Dali and can be reached by car or boat.

To & from Dali

5 hrs (250 km [155 mi]) by bus northwest of Kunming; 4 hrs (140 km [87 mi]) by bus south of Lijiang.

Bus tickets can be purchased at any local travel agency. Most buses drop you off in the new town, which has little to recommend it. A 25-minute cab ride gets you from the new town to the old town. It should cost Y35 to Y40, depending on your haggling skills.

From Dali, there are frequent flights to Kunming. Taxis between the old town and the airport cost Y90.

Lijiang

Lijiang is probably the most famous travel destination in Yunnan, as its old town was named a UNESCO World Heritage Site. At the base of majestic Jade Dragon Snow Mountain, Lijiang is home to the Naxi people, who are related to Tibetans but have their own language and culture.

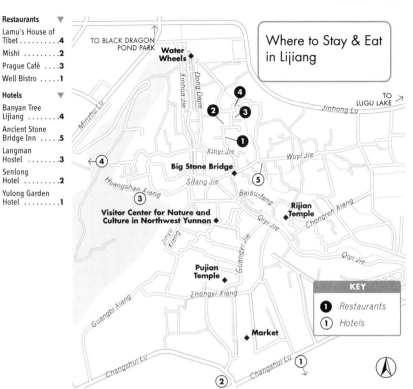

Where to Stay & Eat in Lijiang

TO BLACK DRAGON POND PARK

TO LUGU LAKE

Water Wheels

Xinhua Jie

Dong Dajie

Minzhu Lu

Jinhong Lu

Xinyi Jie

Wuyi Jie

Big Stone Bridge

Sifang Jie

Huangshan Xiang

Baisuifang

Qiyi Jie

Rijian Temple

Chongren Xiang

Visitor Center for Nature and Culture in Northwest Yunnan ◆

Jinyu Xiang

Guangyi Jie

Qiyi Jie

Pujian Temple ◆

Zhongyi Xiang

Guangbi Xiang

Market ◆

Changshui Lu

Changshui Lu

KEY

❶ Restaurants

① Hotels

7

The main attraction for most travelers to Lijiang is the old town, a labyrinth of winding alleys, fish-filled streams, and old Naxi houses with tile rooftops. Traditional Naxi singing and dancing are on display nightly at Sifang Jie, the square in old town's center.

Exploring Lijiang

Because there are so many shops and markets, much of Lijiang's old town feels more like a Special Economic Zone than a UNESCO-protected site. However, it is still possible to get away from the cacophony of the town's center for an interesting stroll. Helpful English maps have been installed around town to help you navigate the maze.

The **Visitor Center for Nature and Culture in Northwest Yunnan** is a small but fascinating museum of the region's cultural and biological diversity. Exhibits include one in which area villagers were given cameras to document their daily lives. One exhibit compares photos taken in the 1920s with those taken

WORD OF MOUTH

The town is very touristy. However, I would say that during our time there, it was probably more than 99% Asian tourists. We saw very few Westerners.

–walkinaround

Naxi Music of Lijiang

THE NAXI CULTURE is rich in artistic elements—the Naxi pictographs, architecture, Dongba shamans, and, not least of all, the music. It is a complex and intricate musical blending of Han and Naxi musical traditions that has commonly served as entertainment, as well as a measuring stick for Confucian social relationships—Naxi musicians and members of social clubs related to the music were considered to be of a higher status than the average Naxi villager.

Today, Naxi music, with its 500 years of history, is a sonic time capsule, giving us the opportunity to hear songs dating as far back as the Tang, Song, and Yuan Dynasties. Most of the Naxi-inhabited counties around Lijiang feature their own orchestras specializing in the two extant versions of Naxi music: Baisha fine music and Dongjing music. A third type, Huangjing music, fell out of practice over the centuries and has since been lost.

THE ROOTS OF RHYTHM

Legend has it Baisha fine music developed as a result of Kublai Khan's gratitude for Naxi assistance during his conquest of Yunnan during the Yuan Dynasty. The Khan is believed to have left a group of his best musicians and their musical canon with the Naxi in Lijiang. Baisha fine music is one of the grander Chinese musical styles, with large orchestras including the Chinese flute, the lute, and the zither.

Dongjing music came to this region from central China during the Ming and Qing dynasties and is based on Taoist classics. It is the better preserved of the two musical styles, most likely because the Naxi incorporated more of their indigenous music into it.

BEAUTY IS IN THE EAR OF THE BEHOLDER

Naxi orchestras have their own standards for what makes for a quality Naxi musical experience, the key factor being age. In the eyes of the Naxi, the older the musicians, the better. Perhaps this is because fewer and fewer are learning the traditional styles. The musicians' instruments are also old, often much older than the septuagenarians playing the music—the craftsmanship 100 years ago was better than today. Naxi orchestras refuse to play any modern music. They only jam to centuries-old tunes.

For many travelers, Naxi music is an aural step back in time. Others find it screechy and grating. But regardless of one's level of appreciation, it is an interesting link to China's and Lijiang's past.

You can catch a show at a number of venues in Lijiang's old town and the new city. The most famous groups are the Baihua and Dayan orchestras. Tickets can typically be purchased starting at Y100 at most hotels and guesthouses.

more recently to document the effect of development upon the area. The museum is funded by the Nature Conservancy. ⊠ *42 Xianwen Xiang, at Guangyi Jie* ☎ *0888/511–5969* ✉ *Free* ☉ *Daily 9–6.*

If you can find it, the **Pujian Temple** (Pujian Si) is a tsranquil place to get away from the crowds. You can refuel with some local snacks from the temple's vegetarian snack restaurant. Try fried Naxi potatoes (they're purple), *jidoufen*, a bean concoction that can be eaten hot as a porridge, or cold and cut up like noodles—the ubiquitous Naxi *baba* bread is also quite good. Wash it all down with a pot of Tibetan yak butter tea and get back to finding your way around town. ⊠ *Qi Yi Jie* 🚅 *Free* ☉ *Daily 8–6.*

Outside the old town, the **Black Dragon Pool Park** (Heilong Tan Gongyuan) has a tranquil pavilion where locals come to play cards and drink tea. The park is home to the **Dongba Research Institute Museum** (Dongba Yanjiu Suo), a museum devoted to Naxi Dongba culture. ⊠ *Xinde Lu* 🚅 *Y20* ☉ *Daily 6:30 AM–8 PM.*

Tours

There are no group tours of Lijiang, so you'll have to explore its twisting streets on your own. It's a confusing place to navigate, so pick up one of the free maps available at restaurants, cafés, and guesthouses throughout the old town. Wooden maps installed throughout the town help you find your way.

Where to Stay & Eat

$$–$$$$
Fodor'sChoice
★
✕ **Mishi.** Easily the best restaurant in the old town, Swedish-owned Mishi serves the perfect balance of local and international cuisine. The relaxing environment combines Scandinavian design with traditional Naxi sensibilities. Standout dishes include sizzling yak meat on a roof tile, pan-fried salmon with lemon butter, and fried spareribs. In a town full of bars, Mishi has one of the best selections of liquor and beer, which go perfectly with the plush seating inside or the relaxing interior courtyard. ⊠ *52 Mishi Xiang, off Xinyi Jie* 🕾 *0888/518–7605* ▭ *No credit cards.*

¢–$
✕ **Lamu's House of Tibet.** The two-story restaurant serves Tibetan, Chinese, and Naxi cuisine, as well as familiar dishes like lasagna and french fries. The pleasant atmosphere, traditional Tibetan decor, and helpful staff make Lamu's one of Lijiang's better dining options. ⊠ *56 Xinyi Jie* 🕾 *139/8704–9750* ▭ *No credit cards.*

¢–$
✕ **Prague Café.** The town's top choice for good coffee, Prague Café also serves good food, especially the American breakfast. Favorite meals include Japanese-style *katsudon*, pork cutlets in a savory sauce. The restaurant also has a nice book collection and free Internet access. ⊠ *80 Mishi Xiang, at Xinyi Jie* 🕾 *0888/512–3753* ▭ *No credit cards.*

¢–$
✕ **Well Bistro.** Near the Old Well, this small eatery serves a nice variety of international food at reasonable prices in a pretty setting away from the town square. Its coffee is very good and it's a top choice for breakfast. This is one of the best places in town to hunker down with a hot drink and a good book on a cold or rainy day. ⊠ *32 Mishi Xiang, at Xinyi Jie* 🕾 *0888/518–6431* ▭ *No credit cards.*

$$$$ 🏨 **Banyan Tree Lijiang.** The only luxury resort near Lijiang, Banyan Tree is made up of villas designed to resemble Naxi courtyard homes. Each self-contained accommodation features its own hot tub or swimming pool. Located in the old Naxi capital of Baisha at the foot of mist-covered Jade Dragon Snow Mountain, the hotel has spectacular unobstructed views. It has all the amenities you would expect in a world-class resort, from Thai massage in the spa to fine dining in the Bai Yun restaurant. ⊠ *Yuerong Rd., 674100* ☎ *0888/533–1111* ⊕ *www. banyantree.com* 📞 *55 villas* 🔥 *2 restaurants, room service, in-room safes, cable TV, gym, spa, bar, dry cleaning, laundry service, in-room broadband, airport shuttle* ⊟ *DC, MC, V.*

¢ 🏨 **Ancient Stone Bridge Inn.** Two of the rooms in this guesthouse look directly out over a brook, a small pedestrian street, and pair of bridges. It's a bit more expensive than the average guesthouse, but the perfect setting may justify the extra few yuan. The front door is locked at midnight. ⊠ *71 Wuyi Jie Xingrenxia, 674100* ☎ *0888/518–4001 or 139/ 8882–5829* 📞 *10 rooms* 🔥 *Cable TV, laundry service* ⊟ *No credit cards.*

¢ 🏨 **Langman Hostel.** The best guesthouse in the old town, Langman Hostel is also the best bargain. This Taiwanese- and Korean-run guesthouse straddles both sides of an alley near the town square. On one side you'll find the guesthouse and its clean standard rooms with private bathrooms. Across the way is a Korean and Chinese restaurant with a stunning balcony and a view of the crowded tile roofs of the old town and the surrounding mountains. This is one of the best vantage points for enjoying a Lijiang sunset. It's at the top of a steep hill, so take a taxi. ⊠ *60 Huangshan Xiang Shangduan, off Xinhua Jie, 674100* ☎ *0888/ 512-7289* 📞 *9 rooms* 🔥 *Restaurant, Internet room* ⊟ *No credit cards.*

¢ 🏨 **Senlong Hotel.** Although slightly overpriced, this is the most modern of the hotels in old town. There is a lovely garden area in the courtyard, and the rooms are large and nicely furnished. The restaurant serves a wide variety of local dishes. ⊠ *Minzu Lu, 674100* ☎ *0888/512–0666* 📞 *243 rooms* 🔥 *Restaurant, sauna, business services* ⊟ *No credit cards.*

¢ 🏨 **Yulong Garden Hotel.** This hotel offers a pleasant combination of traditional architecture and modern convenience. It's a good option for visitors who want the amenities of a hotel, like an on-site restaurant and bar. It may not be special, but is very clean and well maintained, and the water is reliable. ⊠ *Dinghong Lu, 674100* ☎ *0888/518–2888* 📞 *150 rooms* 🔥 *Restaurant, massage, sauna, bar, business services, laundry service* ⊟ *AE, MC, V.*

Nightlife & the Arts

Traditional Naxi music and dancing can be found in the town square at Sifang Jie beginning in the afternoon and lasting into the evening. There is also a variety of cultural performances held daily around Lijiang.

The most impressive cultural event is **Lijiang Impression** (⊠ Ganhai Scenic District ☎ 0888/888–8888), produced by internationally acclaimed mainland director Zhang Yimou (*Red Sorghum, Raise the Red Lantern*). He takes Lijiang's Dongba culture and beautiful surroundings as his muse. Set at the base of Jade Dragon Snow Mountain and using the mountain as an integral part of the scenery, this music and dance performance makes full use of its spectacular location. Tickets for the show, which takes place daily at 1:20, are Y190.

At the Meeting Hall of Lijiang, the **Mountain Spirit Show** (⊠ Minzu Lu ☎ No phone) offers fire eating and other extraordinary feats by the Yi shamen. The performance, daily at 8 PM, costs Y120.

Side Trips from Lijiang

Towering majestically over Lijiang, the 18,360-foot **Jade Dragon Snow Mountain** (Yulong Xue Shan) is one of non-Tibetan China's most spectacular peaks. The mountain's jagged, snow-covered face is one of the defining sights of a trip to Lijiang. The well-maintained road to the scenic area is a nice drive, passing numerous villages and offering fine valley and mountain views. The park entrance is about a 30-minute drive from old town. Taxis should cost Y35 to Y40 one-way, and Y100 or more if you want the driver to wait for you. Most hotels and guesthouses can book trips to the mountain. 🖾 *Y80* 🕙 *Daily 7–5.*

¢ 🏠 **Wenhai Ecolodge.** Only accessible by foot or on horseback, Wenhai Ecolodge is one of the country's first "green" resorts. It's located in the mountain valley that is home to Lake Wenhai, a seasonal lake that appears between July and March. When the basin is filled, the lake is home to black-necked cranes, black storks, and several varieties of duck. There is excellent hiking in the valley, and the chance to come across some of the area's endangered plants and animals such as the giant laughing thrush and the winter wren. The 12-room lodge is designed to minimize environmental impact and has excellent views of nearby Jade Dragon Snow Mountain. It's highly recommended for nature lovers and conservation-minded travelers. Room price includes three meals per day. ⊠ *Lake Wenhai* ☎ *1390/888–1817* ⊕ *www.northwestyunnan.com/wenhai ecolodge.htm* 🛏 *12 rooms* 🍴 *Restaurant* 🚫 *No credit cards* 🍽 *FAP.*

★ A 2½-hour drive from Lijiang, **Tiger Leaping Gorge** (Hutiao Xia) is home to some of China's most breathtaking mountain scenery. See it now, before completion of a dam on the Jinsha River that will partially fill this massive chasm. Measuring about 16 km (10 mi), the gorge can be leisurely hiked in two days. There are two trails, the more popular running between Qiaotou in the west and Daju in the east. The easiest way to tackle the trek from Lijiang is to take the 8:30 AM or 9 AM bus on Xin Da Jie to Qiaotou and hike toward Daju.

There are several guesthouses in the gorge, scattered at distances to accommodate hikers at any stage of their trek. All offer food, hot showers, and beds for Y10 to Y20. These guesthouses have put up signs and arrows to let hikers know how much farther until the next lodging. If you don't mind not hiking the whole gorge, stop in Walnut Garden, where you can take one of the regular buses back to Lijiang. If you continue to Daju, there are only two buses a day to Lijiang, at 8:30 AM and 1 PM.

Nuisances along the trail include fake "toll collectors" who will attempt to take your money and aggressive local dogs. The former requires patience and politeness to deal with, the latter the ability to stand one's ground—and it's useful to have a large stick.

To & from Lijiang

4 hrs (150 km [93 mi]) by bus north of Dali; 8 hrs (320 km [198 mi]) by bus northwest of Kunming; 20 hrs (550 km [341 mi]) by bus southwest of Chengdu.

Lijiang's main bus stations are located on Xin Da Jie and the south side of Xiangelila Da Dao. Train service linking Lijiang to Dali and Kunming is expected to begin by 2008.

There are daily flights between Lijiang and Kunming. The airport is 30 mi west of Lijiang.

Jinghong & the Xishuangbanna Region

Jinghong is the capital of southern Yunnan's Xishuangbanna Dai Autonomous Region, which borders Laos and Myanmar. Xishuangbanna is home to the Dai, a people related to Thais and Laotians who, like their cousins to the south, are known for their love of very spicy food.

Jinghong sits on the banks of the muddy Mekong, although this stretch of the legendary river is known locally as the Lancang. This is where China meets Southeast Asia; it feels more and more like Laos or Thailand the farther you travel from Jinghong. Even inside the city, the architecture, the clothing, and even the barbecue seem much more like what you'd find in Vientiane or Chiang Mai.

Jinghong has experienced a bit of a boom because of tourism; it now has its own airport with flights to Kunming and other cities. But despite the increase in economic activity, Jinghong still moves at about the same speed as the Mekong.

Exploring Jinghong

Even a short walk around Jinghong reveals its colorful mix of Dai, Chinese, Thai, and Burmese influences. It's a small enough town that you can cover most of it on foot in a day. Bordered by the Lancang River to the east, the city quickly begins to thin out as you head west.

The **Lancang River** (Lancang Jiang) is the name of the Mekong River in China, where it originates before flowing into Southeast Asia. It is easiest to access the river from Jinghong at the Xishuangbanna Bridge—

there is a path there that follows alongside the river and is ideal for strolling or biking. A growing number of local operations offer a variety of boat, raft, and dinghy trips along the famed river.

On the southeastern edge of Jinghong is **Manting Park** (Manting Gongyuan), a pleasant park where you can have a closer look at some of the area's indigenous plants. Also worth exploring is the large peacock aviary. The park is especially lively around mid-April when people gather here to celebrate the Water Splashing Festival. ⊠ *Manting Lu* 🖾 *Y15* ⊙ *Daily 7:30 AM–7:30 PM.*

★ **Xishuangbanna Tropical Flower & Plant Garden** (Xishuangbanna Redai Huahuiyuan) is an interesting place to spend several hours walking among fragrant frangipani, massive lily pads, drooping jackfruit, and thousands of other colorful and peculiar plants. This is one of China's finest gardens, featuring a well-designed layout arranged into themed sections including tropical fruits, palms, and rubber trees. Don't walk through too fast or you'll miss out on some of the more unique plants such as *tiaowu cao,* or "dancing grass," which actually stands up if you sing at it. Each plant's placard features English and Latin names. ⊠ *99 Xuanwei Dadao* 🖾 *Y40* ⊙ *Daily 7:30–6.*

> ## THE WATER SPLASHING FESTIVAL
>
> The Dai Water Splashing Festival is held in Dai-inhabited areas of southern Yunnan, including the cities of Jinghong and Ruili. Originally, water was poured gently upon the backs of family members to wash away the sins of the past year and provide blessings for the coming year. Today, it has become a water war, replete with squirt guns, buckets of ice water, and other weapons. It is quite a bit of fun, and a great way to cool off. Just remember to leave any cameras, watches, or cell phones back in your room.

Tours

There are currently no group tours of Jinghong, but most hotels offer travel services to destinations outside of the city.

Where to Stay & Eat

$–$$ ✕ **Foguang Yuan.** Tucked away behind a school and a police station, Foguang Yuan is a hidden gem. The restaurant is actually several dining areas built around a patch of jungle. The Dai architecture and beautiful tropical setting alone merit a visit, but the restaurant also serves an excellent array of Dai and Chinese classics. There are no English menus, so venture into the kitchen and point to what looks good. Brave diners can sample the large selection of *paojiu,* or flavored liquors. ⊠ *Nonglin Nan Lu* ☎ *0691/213–8608* ☲ *No credit cards.*

¢–$$ ✕ **Meimei Café.** This is a good place to compare notes with other travelers, as many people come here to buy tickets or book tours. One of the few places in Jinghong with English-speaking staff, Meimei Café serves Western, Chinese, and Dai food, as well as good coffee and juice drinks. ⊠ *Jingde Lu, at Galan Nan Lu* ☎ *0691/212–7324* ☲ *No credit cards.*

¢–$ ✕ **Forest Café.** Run by the brother-sister team of Sarah and Stone Chen, both of whom are fluent in English, this café serves the best Western-style breakfasts in town. The kitchen makes its own whole-wheat bread and uses only organic mountain rice in its dishes. The friendly and knowledgable staff can arrange transportation as well as trips to a variety of local villages. ⊠ *Galan Nan Lu at Jingde Lu* ☎ *0691/898–5122* ▤ *No credit cards.*

¢–$$ ⌺ **Crown Hotel.** In the heart of Jinghong, this hotel has several low-slung buildings that are set in a parklike setting with a large swimming pool. Standard rooms start at Y480, but if you haggle a bit you can get a much better rate. There is also a good night market outside the hotel. ⊠ *70 Mengle Dadao, 666100* ☎ *0691/219–9888* ⌨ *88 rooms* ⌂ *Restaurant, massage, sauna, nightclub, laundry service* ▤ *No credit cards.*

¢ ⌺ **Jin Banna Hotel.** A good deal for budget travelers, you can get a bed in a dorm-style room for about what you'd pay for dinner. The standard rooms are clean and have private bathrooms. Don't expect much in the way of service or amenities, however. ⊠ *55 Mengle Dadao, 666100* ☎ *0691/212–4901* ⌨ *100 rooms* ⌂ *Restaurant, business services* ▤ *AE, MC, V.*

Nightlife & the Arts

Evening is when Jinghong comes alive, with locals taking advantage of the cooler temperatures to go out for a stroll or a late meal. Manting Park and the city's other smaller green spaces often feature local music and dance performances.

Zhuanghong Lu, in the northern part of town, is filled with Burmese jade and goods from Thailand. There is a massive night market by the Xishuangbanna Bridge in the city's northeast. There is a much smaller night market on Mengla Lu outside the Crown Hotel.

Side Trips from Jinghong

One of China's first serious attempts at ecotourism, the 900-acre **Sanchahe Nature Reserve** is home to wild elephants. Two hours north of Jinghong, the park also features a butterfly farm and a cable car that offers breathtaking views. Lodging is in "tree houses" about 25 feet above ground—a unique place to spend a night. It is best to avoid visiting during the summer, when the weather can be rainy. Arrange transportation through your hotel or a travel agency.

One of the more scenic areas of Xishuangbanna is **Ganlan Basin** (Ganlanba), 37 km (23 mi) from Jinghong. Minority peoples still live in bamboo huts here, amid the beautiful rain forest. The area is famous in Yunnan for its tropical flowers and the millions of butterflies that inhabit this valley. If you want to spend a few days hiking and investigating the basin, you can stay at one of the many village guesthouses, most of which accept foreigners.

To & from Jinghong

12 hrs (400 km [248 mi]) by bus southwest of Kunming; 12 hrs (425 km [264 mi]) by bus south of Dali.

Jinghong has an international airport with service to Kunming and Chengdu, as well as destinations in Thailand, Cambodia, and Laos. It is located about 15 minutes west of the city. Security checks are quick because there are only a few flights each day.

Jinghong's Number Two Bus Station, just north of the intersection of Mengle Dadao and Xuanwei Lu, is where to catch buses bound for Kunming (12 hours) and Dali (18 hours).

YUNNAN ESSENTIALS

Transportation

BY AIR

Kunming is a busy air hub with flight links all over China, as well as to Dali, Lijiang, Jinghong, and Zhongdian. The airport is at the southern end of Chuncheng Lu about 20 minutes by taxi from the center of town and should cost Y20 to Y30.

Jinghong Airport is located about 15 minutes west of the city center. Take the Number 1 bus into town for Y2, or opt for a Y30 taxi.

Dali's Airport is located at the southern tip of Erhai Lake. Other than irregular bus service, taxis are the only way to get to and from the airport. The standard fare to or from the old town is Y90.

Lijiang Airport is located about half an hour west of the city. There is a Y20 bus from the airport that terminates on the edge of the old town. Otherwise, a taxi to the old town will run you Y80.

There are weekly flights from Zhongdian to Lhasa, Tibet. The airport is northwest of the city.

Yunnan is served by China Eastern Air, Shanghai Airlines, and Dragonair, among other airlines.

🛫 Airport Information **Dali Airport** ☎ 0872/242-8909. **Jinghong Airport** ☎ 0691/212-3003. **Kunming Airport** ☎ 0871/711-3232. **Lijiang** ☎ 0888/517-3088. **Zhongdian** ☎ 0887/822-9916.

BY BUS

Kunming's long-distance bus station is in the south of the city. Buses leave for Dali (6 hours), Lijiang (15 hours), Shilin (Stone Forest; 3 hours), Xishuangbanna (26 hours), and Guiyang (13 hours).

🚌 Bus Stations **Kunming Bus Station** ✉ Beijing Lu, Kunming ☎ 0871/534-9414 or 0871/351-1534.

BY CAR

You can't drive your own rental car on mainland China, but cars with drivers can be hired through your hotel. Expect to pay Y200 to Y700 per day, depending on where you begin your trip. (Kunming will be more expensive than other cities.) This is a good option if you are going to places where it is doubtful that there will be taxis or buses.

BY TRAIN

Direct service links Kunming with Guangzhou (25 hrs), Chengdu (24 hrs), Chongqing (21 hrs), Emeishan (21 hrs), Guilin (23 hrs), Guiyang (13 hrs), Beijing (46 hrs), and Shanghai (60 hrs). The newly renovated station is on the southern edge of the city.

🚆 Train Stations **Kunming Train Station** ✉ Beijing Lu, Kunming ☎ 0871/534-9414 or 0871/351-1534.

Contacts & Resources

EMERGENCIES

The Public Security Bureau (PSB) may be of help to foreign visitors in need of assistance. You must contact the PSB in the case of lost passports. The PSB can be reached by calling 110, the Chinese equivalent of 911.

🚓 **PSB** ✉ Beijing Lu, Kunming ✉ Huguo Lu, Dali ☎ 110 ✉ Fuhui Lu, Lijiang ☎ 110 ✉ Xuanwei Dadao, Jinghong ☎ 110.

🏥 Hospitals **Dali First Municipal People's Hospital** ✉ 217 Taian Lu, Dali ☎ 0872/212-4462. **Jinghong People's Hospital** ✉ 41 Galan Zhong Lu, Jinghong ☎ 0691/212-3221. **Lijiang People's Hospital** ✉ Fuhui Lu, Lijiang ☎ 0888/512-2393. **Xiehe Hospital** ✉ 338 Huancheng Nan Lu, Kunming ☎ 0871/357-9999.

MONEY MATTERS

Foreign bank cards on the Cirrus or Plus systems can be used at ATMs displaying their respective logos. Bank of China and ICBC are your best bets. When traveling to remote parts of the region, be sure to have cash on hand, as ATMs accepting foreign cards are much rarer.

🏦 Banks **Bank of China** ✉ Renmin Dong Lu, Kunming ✉ Fuxing Lu, Dali ✉ Dong Dajie, Lijiang ✉ Mengle Dadao, Jinghong. **ICBC** ✉ Huguo Lu, Dali.

VISITOR INFORMATION

ℹ Tourist Information **China International Travel Service (CITS)** ✉ 1–8 Wuyi Lu, 220 Huancheng Nan Lu, Kunming ☎ 0871/313-2332 ✉ Galan Zhong Lu, Jinghong ☎ 0691/213-1165 ✉ Xin Dajie, Lijiang ☎ 0888/512-3508.

At a Glance

ENGLISH	PINYIN	CHINESE CHARACTERS
EXPLORING		
Guangxi	guǎng xī	广西
GUILIN	guì lín	桂林
Elephant Trunk Hill	xiàng bí shān	象鼻山
Guilin Bus Station	guì lín qì chē zhàn	桂林汽车站
Guilin Liangjiang International Airport	guì lín liǎng jiāng guó jì jī chǎng	桂林两江国际机场
Guilin Railway Station	guì lín huǒ chē zhàn	桂林火车站
Ming Tomb	jìng jiāng wáng líng	靖江王陵
Peak of Solitary Beauty	dú xiù fēng	独秀峰
Seven Star Park	qī xīng gōng yuán	七星公园
WHERE TO STAY & EAT		
Golden Elephant Hotel	guì lín jīn xiàng dà jiǔ diàn	桂林金象大酒店
Inaka	tián shè rì běn liào lǐ	田舍日本料理
Lijiang Waterfall Guilin	guì lín lí jiāng dà pù bù fàn diàn	桂林漓江大瀑布饭店
Rosemary Cafe	mí dié xiāng	迷迭香
Sheraton Guilin	guì lín xǐ lái dēng dà yǔ fàn diàn	桂林喜来登大宇大饭店
Wang Cheng Fan Dian	wáng chéng fàn diàn	王城饭店
YANGSHUO	yáng shuò	阳朔
EXPLORING		
Moon Hill	yuè liàng shān	月亮山
Yangshuo Bus Station	yáng shuò qì chē zhàn	阳朔汽车站
Yangshuo Park	yáng shuò gōng yuán	阳朔公园
WHERE TO STAY & EAT		
Le Votre	lè dé	乐得
Magnolia Hotel	bái yù lán jiǔ diàn	白玉兰酒店
Man De Guai	mǎn dé guǎi qīng shuǐ yú diàn	满得拐清水鱼店
Morningsun Hotel	chén guāng jiǔ diàn	晨光酒店
Paradesa Yangshuo Resort	yáng shuò bǎi lè lái dù jià fàn diàn	阳朔百乐来度假饭店
Riverview Hotel	wàng jiāng lóu kè zhàn	望江楼客栈

7

Yangshuo Regency Holiday Hotel	yáng shuò lì jǐng jià rì bīn guǎn	阳塑丽景假日宾馆
Yi Ping Ju Jiao Zi.	yáng shuò yī pǐn jiào zī	阳朔一品居饺子
Longsheng Longji Rice Terraces	lóng shèng lóng jǐ tī tián	龙胜龙脊梯田
Li Qing Guesthouse	lì qíng fàn diàn	丽晴饭店
NANNING	nán níng	南宁
EXPLORING		
Guangxi Provincial Museum	guǎng xī shěng bó wù guǎn	广西省博物馆
Nanning Bus Station	nán níng qì chē zhàn	南宁汽车站
Nanning Railway Station	nán níng huǒ chē zhàn	南宁火车站
Nanning Wuxu International Airport	nán níng wú xū guó jì jī chǎng	南宁吴圩国际机场
South Lake	nán hú	南湖
White Dragon Park	bái lóng gōng yuán	白龙公园
WHERE TO STAY & EAT		
Majestic Hotel	míng yuán xīn dū jiǔ diàn	明园新都酒店
Nanhu Fish Restaurant	nán hú yú cān guǎn	南湖鱼餐馆
Tao Yuan Hotel	táo yuán fàn diàn	桃园饭店
GUIZHOU	guì zhōu	贵州
GUIYANG	guì yáng	贵阳
EXPLORING		
Cave of the Unicorn	qí lín dòng	麒麟洞
China International Travel Service	zhōng guó guó jì lǚ xíng shè	中国国际旅行社
Guizhou Overseas Travel Service	guì zhōu hǎi wài lǚ xíng shè	贵州海外旅行社
Hua Jia Pavilion	huá jiā gé lóu	华家阁楼
Huangguoshu Pubu	huáng guǒ shù pù bù	黄果树瀑布
Huaxi Park	huā xī gōng yuán	花溪公园
Qianlingshan Park	qián líng shān gōng yuán	黔灵山公园
Rhinoceros Pool	xī niú tán	犀牛潭
Riverbank Park	hé bīn gōng yuán	河滨公园
Star Bridge Falls	tiān xīng qiáo pù	天星桥瀑
Underground Gardens	dì xià gōng yuán	地下公园
Water Curtain Cave	shuǐ lián dòng	水帘洞
Wen Chang Pavilion	wén chāng gé	文昌阁

WHERE TO STAY & EAT		
Jinqiao Restaurant	jīn qiáo fàn diàn	金桥饭店
Hongfu Temple Vegetarian Restaurant	hóng fú sì sù cài guǎn	弘福寺素菜馆
Kaili Sour Sour Fish Restaurant	lǎo kǎi lǐ suān tāng yú shěng fǔ diàn	老凯里酸汤鱼省府店
Nenghui Jiudian	néng huī jiǔ diàn	能辉酒店
Guizhou Park Hotel	guì zhōu fàn diàn	贵州饭店
KAILI	kǎi lǐ	凯里

EXPLORING		
Drum Tower	gǔ lóu	鼓楼
Guiyang Railway Station	guì yáng huǒ chē zhàn	贵阳火车站
Guiyang Station	guì yáng shì cháng tú qì chē zǒng zhàn	贵阳市长途汽车总站
Jinquanhu Park	jīn quán hú	金泉湖
Leishan	léi shān	雷山
Minorities Museum	míng zú bó wù guǎn	民族博物馆
Rongjiang	róng jiāng	榕江
Shibing	shī bǐng	施秉
Zhaoxing	zhào xīng	肇兴

WHERE TO STAY & EAT		
Guotai Dajiudian	guó tài dà jiǔ diàn	国泰大酒店
YUNNAN	Yúnnán	云南
KUNMING	Kūnmíng	昆明

EXPLORING		
Green Lake Park	Cuìhú Gōngyuá	翠湖公园
Stone Forest	Shílín	石林
Yuantong Temple	Yuántōng Sì	圆通寺
Yunnan Provincial Museum	Yúnnán Shěng Bówùguǎn	云南省博物馆

WHERE TO STAY & EAT		
Golden Dragon Hotel	Jīnlóng Fàndiàn	金龙饭店
Green Lake Hotel	Cuìhú Bīnguǎn	翠湖宾馆
Harbour Plaza	Hǎiyì Jiǔdiàn	海逸酒店
Heavenly Manna	Mǎnǎ	吗哪
Kunming Hotel	Kūnmíng Fàndiàn	昆明饭店
Makye Ame	Mǎjí Āmǐ	玛吉阿米

7

Ruan Family Dai Restaurant	Ruǎnjiā Dǎiwèi Cāntīng	阮家傣味餐厅
Salvador's Coffee House	Sàěrwǎduō Kāfēi Guǎn	萨尔瓦多咖啡馆
Yunnan University Hotel	Yúndà Bīnguǎn	云大宾馆
DALI	Dàlǐ	大理
EXPLORING		
Cangshan	Cángshān	苍山
Erhai Lake	Ěrhǎi Hú	洱海湖
Three Pagodas	Sāntǎ	三塔
Xizhou	Xǐzhōu	喜洲
WHERE TO STAY & EAT		
Bird Bar	Niǎobā	鸟吧
Café de Jack	Yīnghuā Yuán	樱花园
Higherland Inn	Gāodì	高地
Jim's Tibetan Hotel	Jímǔ Zàngshì Jiǔdiàn	吉姆藏式酒店
La Stella's Pizzeria	Xīnxīng Bǐsà Fáng	新星比萨房
Lazy Lizard	Gǔnlóng	滚龙
The Dining Room	Shítáng	食堂
Yunnan Inn	Fēngyuè Shānshuǐ	风月山水
Yuyuan Kezhan	Yùyuán Kèzhàn	玉园客栈
LIJIANG	Lìjiāng	丽江
EXPLORING		
Black Dragon Pool Park	Hēi Lóng Tán Gōngyuán	黑龙潭公园
Dongba Institute Museum	Dōngbā Yájiūsuò	东巴研究所
Jade Dragon Snow Mountain	Yùlóng Xuěshān	玉龙雪山
Pujian Temple	Pǔjiān Sì	普坚寺
Tiger Leaping Gorge	Hǔtào Xiá	虎跳峡
WHERE TO STAY & EAT		
Ancient Stone Bridge Inn	Dàshíqiáo Kèzhàn	大石桥客栈
Banyan Tree Lijiang	Lìjiāng Yuèróng Zhuāng	丽江悦榕庄
Lamu's House of Tibet	Xīzàngwū Xīcān Guǎn	西藏屋西餐馆
Langman Hostel	Làngmàn Yìshēng	浪漫一生
Mishi	Mǐsīxiāng	米思香
Prague Café	Bùlāgé	布拉格
Senlong Hotel	Sēnlóng Dàjiǔdiàn	森龙大酒店
Well Bistro	Jǐngzhuó Cānguǎn	井卓餐馆

Yulong Garden Hotel	Yùlóng Huāyuán Dàjiǔdiàn	玉龙花园大酒店
JINGHONG/XISHUANGBANNA	Jǐnghóng/Xīshuāngbǎnnà	景洪/西双版纳
EXPLORING		
Manting Park	Màntīng Gōngyuán	曼听公园
Lancang River	Láncáng Jiāng	澜沧江
Sanchahe Nature Reserve	Sānchāhé Sēnlín Gōngyuán	三岔河森林公园
Ganlan Basin	Gǎnlǎnbà	橄榄坝
Xishuangbanna Tropical Flower and Plant Garden	Xīshuāngbǎnnà Rèdài Huāhuì Yuán	西双版纳热带花卉园
WHERE TO STAY & EAT		
Crown Hotel	Huángguān Dàjiǔdiàn	皇冠大酒店
Foguang Yuan	Fóguāng Yuán	佛光园
Forest Café	Sēnlín Kāfēi Guǎn	森林咖啡馆
Jin Banna Hotel	Jīn Bǎnnà Jiǔdiàn	金版纳酒店
Meimei Café	Měiměi Kāfēi	美美咖啡

7

Sichuan & Chongqing

You're not in Kansas anymore! The Litang Horse Festival, Sichuan

WORD OF MOUTH

"Tiny, bustling alleyways are everywhere. People are everywhere. Bikes are everywhere. Best of all, trees and greenery are everywhere. [Chengdu] is a fantastically green city, there are rivers and canals throughout, apartments have rooftop gardens spilling over the sides and streets are lined with huge old plane trees. It's really attractive."

—Neil_Oz

www.fodors.com/forums

WELCOME TO SICHUAN & CHONGQING

TOP REASONS TO GO

★ **Emeishan:** Hike 10,000 feet, to the top of one of China's holy mountains and UNESCO World Heritage Site.

★ **Giant Panda Breeding Research Base:** Stroll through the peaceful bamboo groves, bone up on the latest in genetic biology and ecological preservation, and check out the cute baby pandas.

★ **Horseback riding in Songpan:** Marvel at the raw beauty of Northern Sichuan's pristine mountain forests and emerald-green lakes from the back of these gentle beasts.

★ **Liquid Fire:** Savor some of the spiciest food on the planet in Chongqing's many hotpot places.

★ **An engineering miracle or madness:** Enjoy a lazy riverboat ride through the surreal Three Gorges, and stand in awe of one of China's latest engineering feats, the mighty Three Gorges Dam.

Medieval Buddhist cave art at Dazu

1 Chengdu. Sichuan's capital and culinary hub, it is also one of the last bastions of the art of tea drinking. While bent on modernizing, the capital city still retains its laid-back character. Kick back and enjoy!

Horse race at the Litang Horse Festival, Sichuan Province.

2 Emeishan. One of China's holy mountains, it has almost 50 km (31 mi) of paths leading to the summit. Take time out to enjoy the lush mountains around Emeishan, which also produce some of the best tea in the world.

GANSU

SHAANXI

Wanzhou THREE GORGES
Yangzi River

HUBEI

Jinyun
Mountian CHONGQING
Neijiang Fengdu

Chongqing

Dazu

Luzhou HUNAN

Yibin

GUIZHOU

0   50 mi
0   50 km

Tourist boat at the Three Little Gorges, Yangzi River.

GETTING ORIENTED

If you're after a China experience where the cuisine is fiery and pandas can be found in the forests gnawing on bamboo, Sichuan province in Southwestern China is a good bet. Sichuan's capital of Chengdu is dab smack in the middle of the province and the logical point to begin your sojourn. Chengdu's flat, gridlike layout is ideal for strolls and biking. It's also acclaimed for its many outdoor gear shops that can equip one for any of Sichuan's local and neighboring natural wonders. For those interested in witnessing the mighty Three Gorges Dam, the city of Chongqing, 150 miles southeast of Chengdu, is where the best Yangzi tour boats begin their journey downriver, through the Gorges and to the dam.

8

3 Jiuzhaigou Natural Preserve. Nestled between the snowcapped peaks of the Aba Autonomous Prefecture in northern Sichuan lies the **Jiuzhaigou Natural Preserve,** a wonderland of turquoise pools and interwoven waterfalls that has long been home to the Qiang and Tibetan peoples.

4 Chongqing. Formerly part of Sichuan proper, **Chongqing** is its own exploding municipality with well over 15 million residents. Chongqing's meandering alleys will appeal to those who love getting lost in Venice-like twisting streets. This is also the jumping-off point for the **Three Gorges** river ride.

SICHUAN & CHONGQING PLANNER

The Developing West

China's recent economic campaign to "Develop the West" is taking off in earnest in both Sichuan and Chongqing. Apart from the cascade of cash brought to Western China from the Three Gorges Dam project, local authorities have been priming the pump with tourism and infrastructure improvement. One such plan is the Shanghai to Lhasa Highway that is slated to open sometime in 2008.

The Weather

Chengdu and eastern Sichuan are hot and humid, with temperatures around 35° to 50°F in winter and 75° to 85°F in summer. Chongqing is known for its broiling summer temperatures—sometimes over 100°F. The western plateau is cold but intensely sunny (bring sunscreen and sunglasses). In winter temperatures drop to -15°F. Summers are around 65°F.

Walking Shoes

If you plan on spending time in Sichuan and Chongqing, bring good walking shoes or hiking boots. These two peppery provinces in Western China have everything from hard-core trekking to hilly urban strolls.

When visiting Chongqing, think of San Francisco and you'll have an idea of what to expect of the city's numerous wending, hilly streets. Thankfully, this charming conurbation on the Yangtze River is riddled with steps for ascending steep inclines.

Sichuan's capital of Chengdu couldn't be different. The streets are broad, laid out in grid-fashion and ideal for biking and long urban treks.

If you're traveling between these two cities, be aware of the recent spate of road construction projects. It's not uncommon to wait for a few hours in a long traffic line. If you're stuck, take advantage of the opportunity and explore a little of the local nature.

The Jewel of Jiuzhaigou

The Jiuzhaigou Natural Preserve's cerulean and aqua pools are among the most beautiful in the world. Its raw natural beauty has been compared to Yellowstone National Park. And so have the size of the crowds—throngs of Chinese tourists descend daily on this 800-ki (497-mi) stretch of lush forests, piercing peaks, languid lakes, and clear pools. UNESCO has given it heritage status for its "Man and Biosphere" program. Within the park itself, you can also meet tribes of ethnic Tibetans and Qingnan peoples.

If you want to truly experience Jiuzhaigou as the Chinese do, sign up with any of the numerous package tours found in Chengdu and Chongqing. A word to the wise: be prepared to be herded along with a flag and a bullhorn. That being said, the folks on Chinese tours are boisterous and full of curious energy. Foreigners who join them are in for a full cultural immersion. It'll be an experience you won't soon forget.

Bear Science

Mysterious, endangered, and cuddly are a few of the monikers typically associated with China's most well-known symbol. Dwindling in population would be another—but not if the folks at Sichuan's Panda Breeding Research Base have any say in the matter. Amid their tranquil bamboo groves, crack crews of scientists are committed to making sure that these bears breed safely.

In a controlled environment, they help pandas breed and care for the young. Given China's recent economic reforms, pandas face a mixed future. On the one hand, economic growth and overpopulation are increasingly affecting their habitat. On the other hand, more state and international resources are pouring into these special research institutes.

What will be the ultimate fate of these stoic creatures? It's hard to say. One thing is certain though: those who visit ecological preserves such as this one are part of the solution.

Chongqing & the Yangtze River

Some call the Yangtze China's dragon river, with its tail at Chongqing and mouth at Shanghai. The Yangtze is one of the richest rivers in the world in terms of sites and currently, the Three Gorges Damn is its signature draw.

If you're planning a tour of this legendary river, you'll definitely be spending some time in Chongqing. Some advice—take your time here. There are over 30 million people in Chongqing and the city is ablaze with neon. For those interested in seeing a working river port, visit the Chaotianmen Docks. Historians at heart will relish the U.S. Chiang Kai-shek Criminal Acts Exhibition Hall & SACO Prison.

Chongqing is brimming with history, a thriving food scene, teahouses, bookshops, and clubs. The adjacent villages are nestled in rolling hills, so before parachuting in to seize the Yangtze by the horns, allow a few days of proper Chongqing trekking.

Leaving from Chongqing allows for lots of daytime sightseeing through Yichang, Shashi and Qutang, Wu and Xiling Gorges. However, this trip moves fast and can be frustrating for shutterbugs.

Make sure that the tour goes to the Shennong section of the dam. Its steep, foliage-laden hills are some of the most majestic in China—as one might expect to find along the world's third largest river.

WHAT IT COSTS In Yuan

RESTAURANTS				
$$$$	$$$	$$	$	¢
over 165	100–165	50–99	25–49	under 25

HOTELS				
$$$$	$$$	$$	$	¢
over 1,800	1,400–1,800	1,100–1,399	700–1,099	under 700

Restaurant prices are for a main course, excluding tax and tips.
Hotel prices are for a standard double room, including taxes.

By Sascha Matuszak **TRANSCENDING MODERN BORDERS,** Southwest China harks back thousands of years to the trade routes that extended north from Burma and India through the sunny highlands of Yunnan and Guangxi into the wilds of Sichuan and Guizhou. The peoples that once ruled this wide swath of land can still be found in its valleys, hills, and mountains: the Yi, spanning the entire region with their cultural and political base in southern Sichuan; the Naxi, straddling the salt-, horse-, and tea-trade routes between Tibet, Sichuan, and Yunnan; the Miao, centered in Guizhou with close cousins as far away as the Hmong people of Vietnam; the Mosu, a matriarchal society gathered around Lugu Lake; and, of course, the Tibetans and the Han, arbiters of power in the region for millennia.

This region possesses some of the world's most amazing scenery. Southwest China is dominated by the snowcapped Himalayas marching in from the west. Its lush foothills, green valleys, and spectacular gorges eventually smooth out into the central plains. Extremely diverse flora and fauna make the area a hotbed of scientific research—there are more than 100 panda reserves dotting the mountains of Southwest China. But the people have made their mark, too. There are numerous UNESCO World Heritage Sites sprinkled throughout Southwest China, including dazzling Buddhist and Taoist monuments constructed hundreds of years ago.

SICHUAN

Throughout history, Sichuan has been known as the "Storehouse of Heaven," due not only to its abundance of flora and fauna, but also to its varied cuisine, culture, and customs.

Geographically, it is dominated by the Sichuan Basin, which covers much of the eastern part of the province. The Sichuan Basin—also known as the Red Basin because of the reddish sandstone that predominates in the region—accounts for almost half its area. On all sides the province is surrounded by mountains: the Dabashan in the northeast, the Wushan in the east, the Qinghai Massif in the west, and the Yunnan and Guizhou plateaus in the south.

DID YOU KNOW?

With an area of 567,000 square km (219,000 square mi), Sichuan is larger than France (although it forms only one-seventeenth of China).

Sichuan's relative isolation made communication with the outside world difficult and fostered the development of valley, plains, and mountain cultures with distinct characteristics. The Tibetans living deep in the foothills of the Himalayas share space with Qiang, Hui, and Han settlers. In the mountains to the south toward Yunnan, there are dozens of peoples living side by side, such as the Yi, Naxi, Mosu, Miao, and Bai. These cultures all have their own religions and philosophies, with Buddhism and Taoism being the dominant religions in the area.

The mountain of Emeishan is a pilgrimage site for millions of Buddhists, as is the Great Buddha in nearby Leshan. In Songpan, north of the capital city of Chengdu, Muslims, Buddhists, Christians, and Taoists live alongside each other in harmony. One of China's most famous national

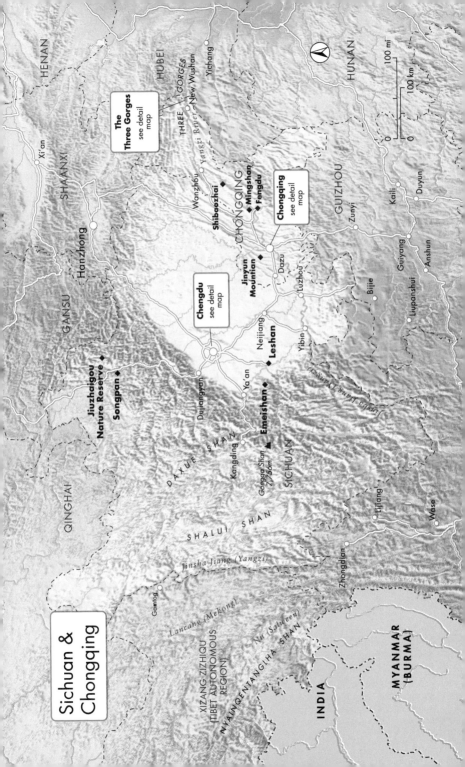

Sichuan & Chongqing

HENAN

SHAANXI

Xi'an

HUBEI

THREE GORGES

Yichang

New Wushan

The Three Gorges
see detail map

Hanzhong

Wanzhou

Yangzi River

HUNAN

100 mi

100 km

Shibaozhai

Mingshan

Fengdu

CHONGQING

Chongqing
see detail map

GUIZHOU

Zunyi

Duyun

Kaili

GANSU

Dujiangyan

Chengdu
see detail map

Jinyun Mountain

Dazu

Luzhou

Guiyang

Anshun

Liupanshui

Bijie

Jiuzhaigou Nature Reserve

Songpan

Neijiang

Leshan

Yibin

Ya'an

Kangding

DAXUE SHAN

Emeishan

Gongga Shan 7,556m

SICHUAN

QINGHAI

SHALUI SHAN

Jinsha Jiang (Yangzi)

Lijiang

Wase

Ganzi

Zhongdian

Lancang (Mekong)

Nu (Salween)

XIZANG ZIZHIQU
(TIBET AUTONOMOUS REGION)

NYAINQENTANGLHA SHAN

INDIA

MYANMAR
(BURMA)

parks is in Jiuzhaigou, far to the north in Aba Prefecture. The natural springs, dense forests, dramatic cliffs, and sprawling waterfalls make Jiuzhaigou Nature Reserve one of the country's most popular tourist destinations. And if you need more urban comforts, Chengdu is an increasingly international city with food from all over the world, topnotch hotels, dizzying nightlife, and what must be more teahouses per square inch than any other city in the world.

Chengdu

Don't go to Chengdu when you're young—is what the Chinese advise the children who might be corrupted by this modern, energetic city. But despite all of the hustle and bustle, Chengdu manages to be one of the most leisurely places in all of China. Most visitors end up joining the locals as they while away the day playing mah-jongg, sipping fragrant green tea, and cracking sunflower seeds.

The city is changing at a dizzying pace. Much of the old city has been razed to make room for modern high-rises. But there is still much to see here in terms of history and culture. Its temples and memorials display the importance Chengdu holds as the cosmopolitan capital of western China. The city is also a great center for Sichuan cooking, which many believe to be the best in China. The Sichuanese cuisine is famous for its spicy peppers and strong flavors and Chengdu does not disappoint. There are too many good restaurants to list and oftentimes the hole in the wall around the corner may serve the most authentic and tasty Sichuan dishes you'll encounter.

All roads into Southwest China lead through Chengdu. As the gateway city to Tibet, the permits and supplies needed for your trip there are best handled. Journeys south to Yunnan or north to Xi'an pass through here as well. Lying in the middle of Sichuan Province, Chengdu is also a good base for excursions to the scenic spots dotting Sichuan.

Exploring Chengdu

Chengdu is easy to negotiate, built as it is along a main north–south artery and surrounded by two ring roads. Bikes are a great way to get around the city. If you are traveling on foot, many of the city's sights are within walking distance of Tian Fu Plaza. You can snag a cab or brave the buses if you are going farther afield.

❶ **Du Fu's Thatched Cottage** (Du Fu Caotang) is named for the famous poet Du Fu (712–770) of the Tang Dynasty, whose poetry continues to be read today. A Manchurian, he came to Chengdu from Xi'an and built a small hut overlooking the bamboo and plum tree–lined Huanhua River. During the four years he spent here he wrote well over 240 poems. After his death the area be-

> **GETTING AROUND**
>
> The Chengdu Tourism Bureau has instituted a shuttle bus between the city's three major sights: Du Fu's Cottage, the Memorial of the Marquis of Wu, and the Tomb of Emperor Wang Jian. With your ticket stub, you can hop aboard the bus free of charge. The bus leaves every 20 minutes.

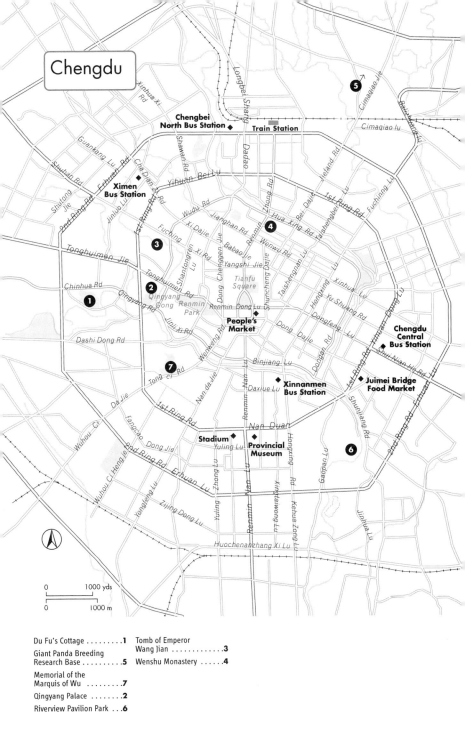

Chengdu

came a garden; a temple was added during the Northern Song Dynasty (960–1126). A replica of his cottage now stands among several other structures, all built during the Qing Dynasty. Some of Du Fu's calligraphy and poems are on display here. English-speaking guides are available, as are English translations of his poems. ✉ *Caotang Lu, off Yihuan Xi Lu* ☎ *028/8734–1220* 🎟 *Y60* ⊙ *Daily 7:30–7.*

❻ The four-story wooden pavilion in **Riverview Pavilion Park** (Wangjiang Lou Gongyuan), dating from the Qing Dynasty, offers splendid views of the Fu River and the surrounding countryside. The poet Xue Tao, who lived in Chengdu during the Tang Dynasty, was said to have spent time near the river, from which she apparently drew water to make paper for her poems. The pavilion stands amid more than 120 species of bamboo, a plant particularly revered by the poet. There are also several other pavilions to enjoy in the park. ✉ *Wangjiang Lu* 🎟 *Y20* ⊙ *Daily 8–5.*

NEED A BREAK? Not many people know that some of the best green tea comes from the mountains of western Sichuan. In Chengdu, *hua cha* (flower tea) is the most popular. Hua cha has such a potent aroma because it has been doctored up with jasmine or chrysanthemum. If you want to sample some good tea, head to People's Park, Wen Shu Temple, or Kuan Xiangzi, the last street of the old city that remains intact.

❼ The **Memorial of the Marquis of Wu** (Wuhou Ci) is a shrine to the heroes that made the Shu Kingdom legendary during the Three Kingdoms Period. The temple here was constructed in 221 to entomb the earthly remains of Shu Emperor Liu Bei. During the Ming Dynasty, Liu Bei's subjects were also housed here, most notably Zhu Ge Liang. Liu Bei's most trusted advisor during the Three Kingdoms Period, Zhu Ge Liang is a legendary figure in Sichuan and, in some respects, more honored than his master. The temple burned during the wars that toppled the Ming Dynasty and was rebuilt in 1671–72 during the Qing Dynasty. The main shrine, Zhaolie Temple, is dedicated to Liu Bei; the rear shrine, Wu Hou Temple, to Zhu Ge Liang. There is also the Sworn Brotherhood Shrine, which commemorates Liu Bei, Zhang Fei, and Guan Yu's "Oath in the Peach Garden." English guides are available for Y80 for groups up to 10 people.

The Sichuan Opera performs here nightly from 8 to 10. The Y180 ticket is expensive, but the face-changing, fire-breathing, lyre-playing ensemble might make you forget that. If that doesn't work, get a free massage from one of the elegantly dressed masseuses touring the audience area. ✉ *231 Wuhou Ci Dajie* ☎ *028/8555–2397* 🎟 *Y60* ⊙ *May–Oct., daily 7:30–9; Nov.–Apr., daily 8–6:30.*

In the northwest section of Chengdu stands the 49-foot-high, 262-feet-
❸ in-diameter **Tomb of Emperor Wang**

> ### WORD OF MOUTH
>
> "We spent a very pleasant afternoon at the Chengdu panda center. They give you a tour on a tourist train through the area. We saw lots of adult and baby pandas—and also red pandas."
>
> –JaneB

Jian (Wang Jian Mu), which honors the ruler of the Kingdom of Shu from AD 847 to 918. Made of red sandstone, it is distinguished by the male figures that support the platform for the coffin and the carvings of musicians, thought to be the best surviving record of a Tang Dynasty musical troupe. There are a lovely park and teahouse on the grounds, both quite popular among locals. ⊠ *Off Fuqin Dong Lu* ⊠ *Y20* ⊙ *Daily 8:30–5:30.*

First built during the Tang Dynasty, **Qingyang Palace** (Qingyang Gong) is the oldest Taoist temple in the city and one of the most famous in the country. Six courtyards open out onto each other before arriving at the sculptures of two goats, which represent one of the earthly incarnations of Lao Tzu (the legendary founder of Taoism). If you arrive midmorning, you will be able to watch the day's first worshippers before the stampede of afternoon pilgrims arrives. The temple grounds are filled with nuns and monks training at the Two Immortals Monastery, the only such facility in Southwest China. There is a small teahouse on the premises. ⊠ *Yihuan Xi Lu at Xi Erduan Lu and Qing Yang Zheng Lu* ☎ *028/8776–6584* ⊠ *Y5* ⊙ *Daily 8–6.*

② In the northern part of town, the large **Wenshu Monastery** (Wenshu Yuan) is a major tourist attraction in Chengdu. It is currently undergoing extensive renovations, both inside and outside the temple walls. Originally constructed during the Sui Dynasty (605 BC–617 BC), the monastery fell in the flames of war during the Ming Dynasty. The temple was rebuilt during the Qing Dynasty. In this complex you can find a fine cup of green tea and the best vegetarian food in the city. ⊠ *Wenshu Yuan Jie off Renmin Zhong Lu* ⊠ *Y5* ⊙ *Daily 10:30–7:30.*

FodorśChoice
★

★ ☾ **⑤** The **Giant Panda Breeding Research Base** (Daxiongmao Bowuguan) is worth the 45-minute drive to walk the peaceful bamboo groves, snap pictures of the lolling pandas, and catch a glimpse of the tiny baby pandas that are born with startling regularity. For those interested in efforts to save these creatures, the research center is excellent. Visit early in the morning, when the pandas are most active. To get here, book a tour through your hotel for about Y70 per person. ⊠ *Jiefang Lu* ☎ *028/8350–5513* ⊠ *Y30* ⊙ *Daily 7–6:30.*

8

Where to Stay & Eat

In Chengdu, hotpot is easy to find. A walk down just about any street will yield at least one restaurant serving this local specialty: a boiling vat of chili oil, red peppers, and mouth-numbing spices into which you dip duck intestines, beef tripe, chicken livers, or (for the less adventurous) bamboo shoots and mushrooms. Hotpot restaurants tend to be open-air affairs, often spilling out onto the sidewalk.

★ $$$–$$$$ ✕ **Huang Cheng Lao Ma.** Built and run by artists, this amazing restaurant on Second Ring Road South is

> ## WORD OF MOUTH
>
> "Chengdu is the capital of Sichuan province, so if you're interested in their type of spicy food, it's the place to go."
>
> –rkkwan

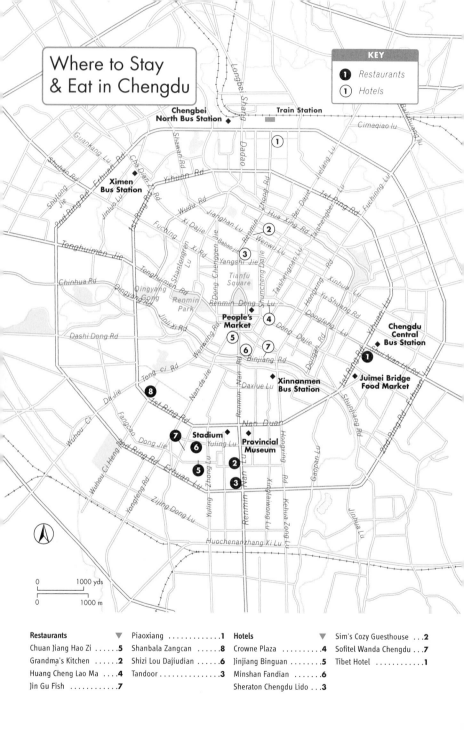

Where to Stay & Eat in Chengdu

KEY
- **1** Restaurants
- **①** Hotels

Chengbei North Bus Station ◆
Train Station
Cimaqiao lu

Ximen Bus Station ◆

Chengdu Central Bus Station ◆

Juimei Bridge Food Market

People's Market

Tianfu Square

Renmin Park

Xinnanmen Bus Station

Stadium ◆

Provincial Museum ◆

0 — 1000 yds
0 — 1000 m

a must for visitors to Chengdu. Huang Cheng Lao Ma is a massive brick-and-stone building with sculpted pillars rising up either side with a stone facade depicting scenes from old Chengdu. The hotpot here comes in traditional spicy varieties and also wild mushroom, seafood, and "soft/clear soup" styles (soft soup—qing tang means no spices!). Not only will you get an idea of the creativity in architecture and cuisine still visible in modern China, but there are often photo exhibitions from local artists. The top floor is a high-class teahouse. ⊠ *Erhuan Lu, Nan San Duan* ☎ *028/8513–9999* ▭ *No credit cards.*

★ **$$–$$$$** ✕ **Chuan Jiang Hao Zi.** The most popular hotpot restaurant in Chengdu, this place is in the restaurant district of Yulin. Always crowded, you can spot this place by the line of people at the front door chewing sunflower seeds as they wait for a table. The hotpot here is classic Sichuan style, with plenty of fresh meat and vegetables from which to choose. Even if you call ahead for a reservation, the policy seems to be first-come, first-served. ⊠ *1 Hua Zi Lu, across from the Yulin Middle School* ☎ *028/8555–5636* ▭ *No credit cards.*

★ **$$–$$$$** ✕ **Piaoxiang.** This restaurant is renowned for its efforts to update Sichuanese dishes, transforming traditional into something wonderful. Simple fare like *dou hua* (soft tofu) and *hue guo rou* (twice-cooked pork) is fresh and tasty, and includes much less oil than your average spot. The menu is mostly ribs, tofu, and chili sauce, but more refined than the typical street stall. ⊠ *60 Yihuan Lu, Dong San Duan* ☎ *028/8437–9999* ▭ *No credit cards.*

¢–**$$$$** ✕ **Jin Gu Fish** (Jin Gu Yu). This great seafood place sits right in the middle of Yulin, the restaurant district of Chengdu. If you are not sure which of the spicy fish dishes to order, ask the manager to put together a meal for you. If it's on the menu, try the spicy *ya yu*, a style of fish from the mountains of western Sichuan. ⊠ *16 Yulin Dong Lu* ☎ *028/8556–8850* ▭ *No credit cards.*

$$–$$$ ✕ **Tandoor.** Just a couple of blocks from the American Consulate, this restaurant serves the city's best northern Indian fare. The decor, a sophisticated combination of wood and mirrors, makes a meal here seem like a special occasion. It's no surprise that the devoted Punjabi chef serves up delicious tandoori chicken, and there's also freshly baked breads. ⊠ *Sunjoy Inn, 34 Renmin Nan Lu, Si Duan* ☎ *028/8554–1958* ▭ *AE, DC, MC, V.*

$–$$ ✕ **Shizi Lou Dajiudian.** The specialty here is Sichuan-style hotpot—very spicy and delicious. It's more expensive than your run-of-the-mill places, but worth it. If you're lucky, your visit might coincide with evening entertainment, most often live local music. ⊠ *2 Mannian Lu, off Er Xi Lu, Dong San Duan* ☎ *028/8433–3975* ▭ *No credit cards.*

¢–**$$$** ✕ **Grandma's Kitchen.** If you're sick of hotpot, this is the place to go. Hamburgers and other solid American foods are served up at decent prices. It's an excellent choice for breakfast, but also a good standby any time of day. The Renmin Nan Lu branch is cozy (some may argue a bit too much so), but most people there are too busy enjoying their food to notice. ⊠ *73/75 Kehua Bei Lu* ☎ *028/8524–2835* ⊠ *22 Renmin Nan Lu* ☎ *028/8555–3856* ▭ *No credit cards.*

8

¢ ✕ **Shanbala Zangcan.** For a taste of Tibet, this is the place. Groups of Tibetan cowboys crowd around tables shooting the breeze as solitary monks eats quietly in the corner. Everything here is traditional—the kitchen makes its own yogurt and uses yak meat from the grasslands, not beef from the corner grocery. The tea, which arrives in a big pot, is delicious. No English menus are available, but the friendly staff does its best to assist you. Some bread, yak noodles, and a few dumplings will satisfy almost anyone. The restaurant sits on a street of Tibetan establishments near Southwest Nationalities University. ✉ *3 Wuhou Ci Dong Jie* ☎ *028/8553-8665* ▤ *No credit cards.*

$–$$$ ⊡ **Sofitel Wanda Chengdu.** One of Chengdu's finest luxury hotels, this concave glass tower sits beside the Fu Nan River. The restaurants are amazing—as might be expected from a European-based hotelier—so expect to be taken on a culinary journey that takes you from China to Japan to France. The reception area is magnificent, with skylight illuminating the marble corridors. The guest rooms are quiet and restful, done up in subdued shades of cream and oatmeal. ✉ *15 Binjiang Zhong Lu, 610041* ☎ *028/6666-9999* 🖷 *028/6666-3333* ⊕ *www.sofitel.com* ⟿ *262 rooms* ⚘ *3 restaurants, in-room safes, cable TV, in-room broadband, fitness center, indoor pool, sauna, 4 bars, business services, travel services* ▤ *AE, DC, MC, V.*

$–$$ ⊡ **Crowne Plaza.** In the heart of Chengdu, this luxury hotel puts you very close to attractions like Du Fu's Thatched Cottage. The guest rooms are among the most spacious that you'll find in the city, although the decor is a little staid. The restaurants are not as snazzy as at the other top-notch hotels, but they serve an interesting array of cuisines. ✉ *31 Zong Fu Jie, 610016* ☎ *028/8678-6666* 🖷 *028/8678-9789* ⊕ *www. crowneplaza.com* ⟿ *434 rooms, 80 suites* ⚘ *4 restaurants, cable TV, in-room broadband, fitness center, 2 bars, laundry service, business services, travel services* ▤ *AE, DC, MC, V.*

$–$$ ⊡ **Sheraton Chengdu Lido.** Located in a quiet section of the central business district, the Sheraton Chengdu Lido was one of the city's first luxury hotels. It's still among the best, as you'll know as soon as you walk into the marble lobby. The rooms are immaculate and very comfortable, and the service is very conscientious. Amenities, such as the glass-roofed swimming pool, are world-class. The location puts you closer to many popular attractions, including the Giant Panda Breeding Research Base. ✉ *15 Renmin Zhong Lu, Yi Duan, 610015* ☎ *028/8676-8999* 🖷 *028/ 8676-8888* ⊕ *www.starwoodhotels.com* ⟿ *421 rooms* ⚘ *4 restaurants, cable TV, Internet, fitness center, pool, sauna, 2 bars, laundry service, business services, travel services* ▤ *AE, DC, MC, V.*

¢–$ ⊡ **Jinjiang Binguan.** For years this was the city's best hotel—foreign dignitaries as well as bigwigs from Beijing could always be found milling around the lobby. Now with five-star hotels all over the city, the Jinjiang has lost a little of its luster. But the hotel has one of the finest Chinese restaurants in the city, as well as a dance club that is surprisingly popular. Although a bit dated, the guest rooms have cable TV, Internet, and spacious bathrooms. ✉ *80 Renmin Lu, Er Duan, 610012* ☎ *028/8550-6666* 🖷 *028/ 8550-7550* ⊕ *www.jjhotel.com* ⟿ *523 rooms* ⚘ *2 restaurants, cable TV,* *in-room broadband, bar, dance club, shops, laundry service, Internet room, business services, meeting rooms* ⊟ *AE, MC, V.*

¢ ⊞ **Minshan Fandian.** In the heart of downtown, this gleaming white tower is one of the city's best hotels. The lobby is covered with gleaming marble, and the guest rooms enlivened by bold floral prints. The Taibai Lou restaurant, which opens out onto a lovely garden, is one of Chengdu's popular places for Sichuan cooking. ⊠ *55 Renmin Nan Lu, Er Duan, 610016* ☎ *028/8558–3333* 🖷 *028/8558–2154* ⤵ *422 rooms* ⚲ *2 restaurants, cable TV, in-room broadband, bar, shops, business services* ⊟ *AE, DC, MC, V.*

¢ ⊞ **Sim's Cozy Guesthouse.** Serving as the German Consulate at the beginning of the 20th century, this traditional building has survived longer than most in this modern-minded city. It is a beautiful, quiet place, with large comfortable rooms and clean common areas. The owners, from Singapore and Japan, having traveled extensively throughout the region are very helpful in planning your excursions. ⊠ *42 Xizhushi Jie, 610017* ☎🖷 *028/8691–4422* ⊕ *www.gogosc.com* ⤵ *22 rooms* ⚲ *Restaurant, laundry service, bar, Internet room; no room TVs* ⊟ *No credit cards.*

¢ ⊞ **Tibet Hotel** (Xizang Fandian). Near the train station, this hotel built by the Tibet Autonomous Region Government is a good option for those planning trips to Tibet. There is a tourist office in the hotel lobby specializing in travel to Tibet. The Tibetan restaurant suffers from a surprising lack of Tibetan food. The guest rooms are clean and comfortable. ⊠ *10 Renmin Bei Lu, 610081* ☎ *028/8318–3388* 🖷 *028/8318–5678* ⤵ *360 rooms* ⚲ *3 restaurants, cable TV, business services, travel services* ⊟ *AE, DC, MC, V.*

Nightlife & the Arts

Chengdu's nightlife is not limited to weekends, so you'll see people packing the bars and clubs all week long.

One of the city's most popular discos is the **Babi Club** (⊠ Er Huan Lu Nan San Duan). This and other clubs on the Second Ring Road South are packed until the wee hours with Chivas-chugging Chinese business executives. A crew of "beer girls" walk around serving Carlsberg, Heineken, and a host of other imported beers for Y100 to Y120 for a six-pack. A huge entertainment complex known simply as **69** (⊠ Ke Hua Lu) sits just south of the Jiu Yuan Bridge. In addition to dancing, you can also enjoy tipsy locals crooning along to the karaoke machine.

■ TIP→ For a listing of the hottest establishments, check out the English-language magazine *Go West,* available at many bars; it usually comes out once a month.

For the classic pub feel, the **Shamrock Irish Bar** (⊠ 15 Ren Min Nan Lu, Si Duan) is an old standby around the corner from the U. S. Consulate. On weekends this pub is filled with expats, students, and a smattering of travelers here to listen to live music or offerings from the DJ. Guinness on tap is Y40, and other beers range from Y10 to Y25. The Western-style food is authentic and hearty. South of the U.S. Consulate is the **Bookworm** (⊠ 28 Ren Min Nan Lu, Si Duan), a relaxed spot with clinking classes, comfy chairs, and a thousand books from which to choose.

8

Shopping

The main shopping street is **Chunxi Lu,** east of Tianfu Square. Most shops here cater to the growing middle class in China, so you'll find lots of shops selling high-end clothing.

The best place to shop for souvenirs is **Song Xian Qiao Antique City** (⊠ 22 Huan Hua Bei Lu), the country's second-largest antiques market. This place is massive, with more than 500 separate stalls selling everything from Mao-era currency to fake Buddha statues to wonderful watercolor paintings. It's near Du Fu's Cottage and Wu Hou Temple.

To & from Chengdu

4 hrs (240 km [149 mi]) by bus northwest of Chongqing; 32 hrs (1,450 km [900 mi]) by train southwest of Beijing; 40 hrs (1,300 km [806 mi]) by train northwest of Hong Kong.

Chengdu is the transportation hub of Western China. Bus, train, and plane connections are as convenient as they get in China. Shuangliu International Airport is about 16 km (10 mi) southwest to the center of Chengdu. From here you can fly to Beijing (2½ hours), Canton (2 hours), Kunming (1 hour), Shanghai (2½ hours), or many other domestic destinations. There are a few international connections, but these may be canceled without notice. The reliable international flights are to Hong Kong (2 hours), Singapore (4 hours), Bangkok (3 hours), and Tokyo (6 hours).

Chengdu sits on the Kunming–Beijing railway line, therefore connections are reliable. The most popular trips are to Kunming (18 hours), Xi'an (18 hours), and Chongqing (5 hours). The Chengdu North Railway Station is located in the northern part of the city. It's a Y20 cab ride from Tian Fu Plaza.

There are several bus stations in Chengdu, so make sure you are headed to the correct one. The Xinnanmen Bus Station, in the city center, has buses to almost every town in Sichuan. The Wuguiqiao Bus Station, east of the city, is used mainly for travelers to Chongqing or Yibin. The Chadianzi Bus Station, in the northwestern part of the city, has buses to destinations in the mountains to the north and west. Less frequently used by tourists are the Northern Bus Station, which has a few lines to Chongqing and other towns in northern and eastern Sichuan and the Shiyangchang Bus Station, which has buses to Leshan and Emeishan.

Emeishan

The 10,000-foot-high Emeishan (literally, Lofty Eyebrow Mountain) sits in the southern part of Sichuan. One of the country's holiest places, the mountain is a pilgrimage site for Buddhists. The temples here survived the Cultural Revolution better than most others in China, due in part to courageous monks. Still, of the hundreds of temples that once were found here, only 20 remain.

■ TIP→ When coming to Emeishan, bring enough cash to last your whole visit. Although there are banks in Emei Town, the ATMs are unreliable when dealing with foreign banks. There is no place to exchange money, except on the black market.

Exploring

You can reach the Golden Summit of Emeishan in just over two days. It's a difficult climb—the stairs up the mountain somehow make it seem more arduous. On the first day, hike until a bit before nightfall and stay in one of the temples along the way for Y15 to Y40 per person. Start out early on the second day, reaching the summit by nightfall. On the third day, rise early in the morning and walk to the Golden Summit, where you may catch a spectacular sunrise. It's a wonderful journey, despite its difficulty. You will find the natural surroundings as enchanting as the temples—most likely more so.

MONKEY BUSINESS

The mountain is known for its wily golden monkeys who have been known to steal items (such as cameras) and hang them in trees. They will try to surround you, screaming, pointing, and jumping in an intimidating manner. A sound strategy is to walk quickly through the band before they can increase in numbers.

The most common route to the top is past Long Life Monastery. This route takes you past the Elephant Bathing Pool, the crossroads for tourists and pilgrims headed up or down the mountain. The pool was once used by Bodhisattva Puxian to wash the grime off of his white elephant. This place is usually crowded, but once you ascend from here you will be mostly free of the madding crowd.

A recommended route down is the long shoulder of the mountain past Magic Peak Monastery, another highlight of the climb. The monks here personify the compassion and simplicity of Buddhism, and the surrounding scenery is beyond compare. After a hard climb down, sharing a simple meal in the courtyard then staying the night in the monastery is magical.

The best times to climb are in the spring or fall. The summer can be uncomfortably hot at the lower altitudes, but once you ascend to the mountain's upper reaches you might want to stay a few extra days to avoid the stifling summer heat below. The true beauty of Emeishan appears after you have cleared the halfway point, leaving behind most of the tourists. Bring a change of clothes for the sweaty part of the journey and a warm jacket for the summit. Water and food are available on the mountain, carried by pipe-puffing porters to the stalls along the way.

DID YOU KNOW?

The mountain is part of a lush and beautiful range that stretches from Ya'an in the north to Xichang in the south. These mountains produce some of the world's best green tea. Although not as famous as Dragonwell or Iron Goddess, these green teas are prized by tea lovers the world over. Emei's local tea is called Zhu Ye Qing (Jade Bamboo Leaf), and there are several types and grades. It is possible to buy organic Zhu Ye Qing around the mountain and in Emei Town. Look for the Long Dong Organic Brand.

For an easier pilgrimage, use the Y30 minibus service from Declare Nation Temple (Baoguo Si) up to **Jieyin Dian,** from where the climb to the top will take about two hours. To avoid climbing altogether, ride the cable car (Y40 up, Y30 down) to the summit from Jieyin Dian (although there are often long lines).

Direct bus (3 hours) service links Chengdu with Baoguo Si, at the foot of the mountain. Trains from Chengdu stop in the town of Emei, about 6 km (4 mi) from the mountain.

Where to Stay & Eat

★ ¢–$ ✕ **Teddy Bear Café.** Arriving at the Emei Bus Station, you will likely be approached by touts offering to take you to the Teddy Bear Café. It's a good idea to go with them. Despite its odd name and spartan decor, the Teddy Bear is a great place to eat. The café has everything from hamburgers to Chinese dishes. The eggplant, crispy but not overcooked, is one of the best dishes. The sign outside says LOCAL PRICES, and it's the truth. The owners are friendly, know the area well, and will help you in any way they can, doing everything from loaning walking sticks to arranging guides. They even have an exceptionally clean and comfortable hotel in back. ⊠ *43 Baoguosi Lu, Emei* ☎ *0833/559–0135* ⊟ *No credit cards.*

¢ ▦ **Baoguo Monastery.** This monastery, at the foot of the mountain, is one of the many accommodations available to those journeying to the Golden Summit. Few people stay here because it sits near the start of the path up the mountain, but if you are arriving late then this quiet, if slightly damp, hotel is a good option. ⊠ *Baoguo Si, 614201* ☎ *No phone* ⇥ *20 rooms* ⌂ *Restaurant* ⊟ *No credit cards.*

¢ ▦ **Emeishan Hotel** (Emeishan Dajiudian). This hotel sits at the foot of the mountain, offering good access for those going on early hikes. The rooms are comfortable, and have clean bathrooms. ⊠ *Baoguo Si, 614201* ☎ *0833/552–6888* ⊟ *0833/559–1061* ⇥ *200 rooms* ⌂ *Restaurant, cable TV, bar, business services, meeting rooms* ⊟ *No credit cards.*

To & from Emeishan

★ *3 hrs (100 km [62 mi]) by train southwest of Chengdu.*

The best way to get here is by bus. There are departures from Chengdu every half hour and from Leshan every hour on the hour between 7 AM and 6 PM. Also from Leshan are buses that go directly to Emeishan's Baoguo Si. They depart every half hour from 9 to 5.

A train from the Chengdu North Railway Station bound for Kunming passes through Emei Town.

Leshan

Leshan is famous for the Great Buddha, carved into the mountainside at the confluence of the Dadu, Qingyi, and Min rivers. The Great Buddha—a UNESCO World Heritage Site—was initiated by the monk Haitong, who never saw its completion. The statue, blissfully reclining, has overlooked the swirling, choppy waters for 1,300 years. The city just spent Y3 billion on a new museum up the Dadu River from the Great Buddha. It should be completed by 2007.

Exploring

At 233 feet, the **Grand Buddha** (Da Fo) is the tallest stone Buddha and among the tallest sculptures in the world. The big toes are each 28 feet in length. The construction of the Grand Buddha was started in AD 713 by a monk who wished to placate the rivers that habitually took local fishermen's lives. Although the project took more than 90 years to complete, it had no noticeable effect on the waters. It is possible to clamber down, by means of a cliff-hewn stairway, from the head to the platform where the feet rest. You can also take a boat ride (about Y30) to see the statue in all its grandeur from the river. ✍ *Y70* ☉ *Oct.–May, daily 7:30 AM–9 PM; Nov.–Apr., daily 9–4:30.*

There are also several temples or pagodas in the vicinity, including **Wu You Temple** (Wuyou Si), a Ming Dynasty temple with a commanding view of the city. You might find yourself staring intently at the lifelike figures and wonder about the person they were modeled after. ✍ *Y35* ☉ *Oct.–May, daily 7:30 AM–9 PM; Nov.–Apr., daily 9 AM to 4:30 PM.*

Tours

Boats at a dock about 1,500 feet up the river from the main gate will take you for a bumpy ride to within camera distance of the Grand Buddha. The 40-minute trip is Y40 per person. From the boat you will be able to see two heavily eroded guardians that flank the main statue.

Where to Stay & Eat

$$–$$$$ ✕ **San Jiang.** This Chinese restaurant run by a husband and wife team serves up some great fish dishes. The buffets here are guaranteed to please; the food is primarily fish from the waters around the feet of the Grand Buddha and local specialties like *dou hua* (soft tofu) and bamboo shoots. The restaurant is one of several facing the water, so there's a nice view. ✉*North of the main gate to the Grand Buddha* ☎*130/0642–2361* ▭*No credit cards.*

¢ ▦ **Jiazhou Bingguan.** Located on the opposite side of the river from the Grand Buddha, this hotel has comfortable accommodations and clean bathrooms. There is a café across the parking lot with passable Western food. ✉ *19 Baitu Lu, 614010* ☎ *0833/213–9888* 🖷 *0833/213–3233* 🛏 *120 rooms* ⚒ *Restaurant, cable TV, business services* ▭ *No credit cards.*

To & from Leshan

★ *3 hrs (165 km [102 mi]) by bus south of Chengdu.*

Buses to Leshan leave from Chengdu's Xinnamen Bus Station every 30 minutes between 7:30 AM and 7:30 PM. From Leshan's Xiao Ba Bus Station, you can take Bus 13 directly to the Grand Buddha's main gate.

Buses from Chongqing to Leshan's Xiao Ba Bus Station leave every hour from 6:30 AM to 6:30 PM.

Jiuzhaigou Nature Reserve

★ *8–10 hrs (350 km [217 mi]) by bus north of Leshan; 4–6 hrs (225 km [140 mi]) by bus northwest of Chengdu.*

High among the snowcapped peaks of the Aba Autonomous Prefecture of northern Sichuan lies the **Jiuzhaigou Nature Reserve** (Jiuzhaigou Ziran Bao Hu Qu), a spectacular national park filled with lush valleys, jagged peaks, a dozen large waterfalls, and most famously, a collection of iridescent lakes and pools. Jiuzhaigou has become one of the country's most popular tourist destinations, with more than 1½ million people visiting every year. Not surprisingly, it has undergone tremendous changes in recent years.

A UNESCO World Heritage Site, Jiuzhaigou Nature Reserve is both a natural reserve and a collection of villages, mostly of Tibetan and Qinang origin. (The name Jiuzhaigou translates as "Nine Villages.") The dramatic increase in tourism has had great impact upon the locals, many of whom have been removed from their homes in order to "protect" the park.

> **WORD OF MOUTH**
>
> "Jiuzhaigou was really something else—there aren't words to describe this place. It's superb scenery, absolutely gorgeous. What makes it even better is there are several beautiful Tibetan villages and temples in the valley where Tibetans go about their everyday lives."
>
> –Neil_Oz

Management of Jiuzhaigou Nature Reserve has been turned over to a private company, so admission is much more expensive than in previous years, but there are also more services available, such as the introduction of an environment-friendly transportation route through the park—plied by so-called green buses that have reduced emissions to protect the environment. For those who want to avoid tour buses and local guides, there are walkways and signs directing travelers along the way. There are now many hotels around the park, including a five-star resort tucked back in the wilderness.

This region is spectacular, with limestone and karst formations, temperate rain forests, and dozens of bright turquoise, orange, and emerald-green pools. The park shelters 76 mammal species, including pandas, black bears, and deer. The climate is wet in the spring and fall, very snowy and cold in the winter, and bright and warm in the summer. ✉ *Y310* 🕙 *Apr.–Nov., daily 6:30 AM–6 PM; Dec.–Mar., daily 7:30 AM–5 PM.*

Exploring

Exploring the park is made easier by frequent ranger stations and signs in English. As you explore the Y-shaped Jiuzhaigou Nature Reserve, your first stop will undoubtedly be the Zaru Valley, on your left. You'll find the Zaru Temple and the Hejiao Stockade farther up the Zaru Valley. Deeper in the valley you'll pass the stunning Shunzheng Terrace Waterfall before you reach Mirror Lake and Nuorilang Falls. On the right side of this path you'll find the fabled Nine Villages, where it is possible to have a meal with the locals. These sights alone are worth the trip, and many tourists head back after marveling at Mirror Lake.

From Mirror Lake you can veer left to the Zechawa Village, an impossibly beautiful small Tibetan community. From the village, the path travels through a temperate rain forest interspersed with dozens of turquoise-colored pools. At the far end of the left branch of the Y is Long Lake, a beautiful and peaceful place that carries barely a trace of the modernization happening all around. Down the right branch of the Y is a series of amazing small lakes, including Five Flower Lake and Arrow Bamboo Lake, crisscrossed by wooden walkways.

Where to Stay & Eat

Did someone say yak? Near the main gate of Jiuzhaigou Nature Reserve you'll find restaurants selling dried yak, cured yak, pickled yak, smoked yak, yak hotpot, fried yak, and—well, you get the point. And we aren't just talking about the main dishes; make sure to sample the *sampas* (barley-and-yak-butter tea cakes).

$$$$ ✕⊡ **Jiuzhai Paradise International Resort.** Tucked away in a valley 15 km (9 mi) from the Jiuzhaigou Nature Reserve, this is the region's most luxurious lodging. The sprawling complex was designed around a Qiang-style village that sits under a glass dome. The foyer is truly one of a kind, covered by a glass-and-metal dome that lets in sunlight during the day and allows glimpses of the moon at night. The rooms are extravagantly decorated, and there's a nightly performance by Tibetan dancers. A daily bus takes you to the national park's main gate. ⊠ *Near Jiuzhaigou Nature Preserve, 623402* ☎ *0837/778–9999* 🖷 *0837/778–9898* ⊕ *www. jiuzhaiparadise.com* ⬐ *405 rooms, 45 suites* ⟁ *4 restaurants, room service, cable TV, pool, gym, sauna, spa, bar, Internet room, business center, meeting rooms* ⊟ *AE, MC, V.*

$–$$$ ✕⊡ **Sheraton Jouzhaigou Resort.** This is the region's first luxury hotel, located about a thousand feet from the mouth of the Jiu Zhai Valley. With dozens of peaked roofs, the resort vaguely resembles an ancient castle. Surrounded by the mountains, the hotel has incredible views from its nicely decorated guest rooms. ⊠ *Jiu Zhai Gou Scenic Spot, Jiuzhaigou, 623402* ☎ *0837/773–9988* 🖷 *0837/779–9900* ⊕ *www.starwoodhotels.com* ⬐ *428 rooms* ⟁ *3 restaurants, room service, cable TV, pool, gym, spa, tour operator, bar, dry cleaning, laundry service, Internet room* ⊟ *AE, MC, V.*

¢ ⊡ **YouU Hostel.** All things considered, this may be the best lodging in the area. The hostel is a 15-minute cab ride south of the Jiu Zhai Valley. The owners are artists and travelers—evident in their tasteful decor and their knowledge of the surrounding area. The rooms, which run the gamut from dorm-style to suites, are spotless, cozy, and comfortable. The café has the finest Western food in the area—not surprising, as the chef once ran the

> ### WORD OF MOUTH
>
> "Some of my relatives just came back from China, and suffered from some mild to moderate altitude sickness at Huanglong National Park in Sichuan province . . . If you're planning a trip to Jiuzhaigou and Huanglong, and flying directly from Chengdu, please give yourself a lot of time to acclimate before going to Huanglong."
> –rkkwan

8

kitchen at Grandma's in Chengdu. The steaks are juicy and tender, the pasta is perfect, and the coffee is some of the best around. The setting is charming and peaceful. ⊠ *Building 4, Khampa Lingka Plaza, 623402* ☎*0837/776–3111* 🖶*0837/776–3966* 🖰*160 rooms, 15 suites* ♿ *Restaurant, Wi-Fi, laundry facilities* ▤ *MC, V.*

To & from Jiuzhaigou

There are several buses each day that shuttle passengers from Chengdu's Xinnanmen Bus Station or Chadianzi Bus Station.

You can also fly to Jiuhuang Airport, located 2½ hours south of Jiuzhaigou in Huanglong. There are numerous shuttle buses that can take you from the airport to Songpan (2 hours) or to the Jiu Zhai Valley (2 hours). If you have booked a hotel, it will be able to arrange a transfer; otherwise a shuttle bus will cost Y60 to Y80.

Songpan

Anyone who visited Songpan more than a few years ago won't recognize the place. The village with a couple of dirt roads and no accommodations has become a small town with several decent hotels and a fine restaurant. The locals, taking advantage of the tourism boom, have spruced up the streets and built nice new wooden signs, often with English translations. The old town is not that old any longer, but the mosque by the river is a beautiful sight in the morning when the sunlight reflects off of the minaret.

Most people visit Songpan for the horses, and they do not leave disappointed. These horseback-riding treks through the surrounding countryside are for as long as you want, but four days seems to be the maximum.

Horse Treks

Once hapless squabblers, **Shun Jiang** (☎ 139/0904–3565) and **Happy Trails Horse Trekking** (☎ 139/0904–3513) have merged, which should make arranging a horseback-riding adventure less of a hassle. (They still operate separate offices, both just south of the bus station.) The treks take you into the mountains and past Tibetan villages that haven't changed for centuries. They're Y150 per person, per day. Prices are somewhat negotiable.

> **WORD OF MOUTH**
>
> "Actually this is anything but a one-horse town—there are ponies everywhere!"
>
> –Neil_Oz

Where to Stay & Eat

You can't leave Songpan without trying goat. There are restaurants up and down the main drag that prepare this local specialty. If you spy an Islamic crescent moon above the restaurant in question, it is a good bet the fare is excellent.

¢–$$ ✕ **Emma's Kitchen.** Not far from the bus station, this place is where most visitors end up at one time or another. The owner speaks English, knows

Continued on page 589

A CULINARY TOUR OF CHINA

For centuries, the collective culinary fragrances of China have drifted far beyond its borders and tantalized the entire world. In the decades following the revolution, most Westerners couldn't get anything close to genuine Chinese cuisine. But with China's arms now open to the world, a vast variety of Chinese flavors are more widely accessible than ever.

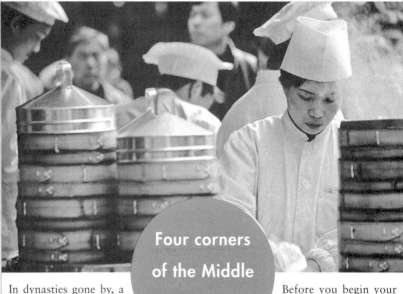

Four corners of the Middle Kingdom

In dynasties gone by, a visitor to China might have to undertake a journey of a thousand li just to feel the burn of an authentic Sichuanese hotpot, and another to savor the crispy skin and juicy flesh of a genuine Beijing roast duck. Luckily for us, the vast majority of regional Chinese cuisines have made successful internal migrations. As a result, Sichuanese cuisine can be found in Guangzhou, Cantonese dim sum in Urumuqi, and the cumin-spiced lamb-on-a-stick, for which the Uigher people of Xinjiang are famous, is now grilled all over China.

Before you begin your journey, remember, a true scholar of Middle Kingdom cuisine should first eliminate the very term "Chinese food" from their vocabulary. It hardly encompasses the variety of provincial cuisines and regional dishes that China has to offer, from succulent Shanghainese dumplings to fiery Sichuanese hotpots.

To guide you on your gastronomic journey, we've divided the country's gourmet map along the points of the compass—North, South, East, and West. Bon voyage and *bon appétit!*

NORTH

THE BASICS

Cuisine from China's Northeast is called *dongbei cai,* and it's more wheat than rice based. Vegetables like kale, cabbage, and potatoes are combined with robust, thick soy sauces, garlic (often raw), and scallions.

Even though many Han Chinese from southern climates find mutton too gamey, up north it's a regular staple. In many northern cities, you can't walk more than a block without coming across a small sidewalk grill with *yang rou chua'r,* or lamb-on-a-stick.

NOT TO BE MISSED

The most famous of all the northern dishes is Peking duck, and if you've ever had it well prepared, you'll know why Beijingers are proud of the dish named for their city.

The fowl is cleaned, stuffed with burning millet stalks and other aromatic combustibles, and then slow-cooked in an oven heated by a fire made of fragrant wood. Properly cooked, Peking duck should have crispy skin, juicy meat, and none of the grease. Peking duck is served with pancakes, scallions, and a delicious soy-based sauce with just a hint of sweetness.

The ultimate window dressing.

LEGEND HAS IT

Looking for the best roast duck in Beijing? You won't find it in a luxury hotel. But if you happen to find yourself wandering through the Qianmendong hutong just south of Tiananmen Square, you may stumble upon a little courtyard home with a sign in English reading LI QUN ROAST DUCK. This small and unassuming restaurant is widely considered as having the best Peking roast duck in the capital. Rumor has it that the late leader Deng Xiaoping used to send his driver out to bring him back Li Qun's amazing ducks.

THE CAPITAL CITY'S NAMESAKE DISH

Soy-based hoisin sauce

A perfectly prepared duck

Pancakes

Scallions

SOUTH

(left) Preparing for the feast. (top right) Dim sum as art. (bottom right) Meat-filled Beijing dumplings.

THE BASICS

The dish most associated with Southern Chinese cuisine is dim sum, which is found in great variety and abundance in Guangdong province, as well as Hong Kong and Macau. Bite-size dim sum is usually eaten early in the day. Any good dim sum place should have dozens of varieties. Some of the most popular dishes are *har gao*, a shrimp dumpling with a rice-flour skin, *siu maai*, a pork dumpling with a wrapping made of wheat flour, and *chaahabao*, a steamed or baked bun filled with sweetened pork and onions. Adventerous eaters should order the chicken claws. Trust us, they taste better than they look.

The Cantonese saying *"fei qin zou shou"* roughly translates to *"if it flies, swims or runs, it's food."*

For our money, the best southern food comes from Chaozhou (Chiuchow), a coastal city only a few hours' drive north of its larger neighbors. Unlike dim sum, Chaozuo cuisine is extremely light and understated. Deep-fried bean curd is also a remarkably fresh Chaozuo dish.

NOT TO BE MISSED

One Chaozuo dish that appeals equally to the eye and the palate is the plain-sounding mashed vegetable with minced chicken soup. The dish is served in a large bowl, and resembles a green-and-white yin-yang. As befitting a dish resembling a Buddhist symbol, a vegetarian version substituting rice gruel for chicken broth is usually offered.

SOUTHWEST AND FAR WEST

Southwest

THE BASICS

When a person from the Southwest asks you if you like spicy food, consider your answer well. Natives of Sichuan and Hunan take the use of chilies, wild pepper, and garlic to blistering new heights. These two areas have been competing for the "spiciest province in China" title for centuries. The penchant for fiery food is likely due to the weather—hot and humid in the summer and harshly cold in the winter. But no matter what the temperature, if you're eating Sichuan or Hunan dishes, be prepared to sweat.

Southwest China shares some culinary traits with both Southeast Asia and India. This is likely due to the influences of travelers from both regions in centuries past. Traditional Chinese medicine also makes itself felt in the regional cuisine. Theory has it that sweating expels toxins and equalizes body temperature.

As Chairman Mao's hometown province, Hunan has a number of dishes with revolutionary names. The most popular are red-cooked Hunan fish *(hongshao wuchangyu)* and red-cooked pork *(hongshao rou)*, which was said to have been a personal favorite of the Great Helmsman.

The hotter the better.

NOT TO BE MISSED

One dish you won't want to miss out on in Sichuan is *mala zigi*, or "peppery and hot chicken." It's one part chicken meat and three parts fried chilies and a Sichuanese wild pepper called *huajiao* that's so spicy it effectively numbs the tongue. At first it feels like eating Tiger Balm, but the hot-cool-numb sensation produced by crunching on the pepper is oddly addictive.

KUNG PAO CHICKEN

One of the most famous Chinese dishes, Kung Pao chicken (or *gongbao jiding*), enjoys a legend of its own.

Though shrouded in myth, its origin exemplifies the improvisational skills found in any good Chinese chef. The story of Kung Pao chicken has to do with a certain Qing Dynasty-era (1644-1911) provincial governor named Ding Baozhen, who arrived home unexpectedly one day with a group of friends in tow. His cook, caught in between

shopping trips, had only the chicken breast and a few vegetables he was planning to cook for his own dinner. The crafty chef diced the chicken into tiny bits and fried it up with everything he could find in the cupboard—some peanuts, sugar, onion, garlic, bits of ginger, and a few handfuls of dried red peppers—and hoped for the best.

(top left) Chowing down at Kashgar's Sunday Market. (center left) Eat, drink, and be merry! (bottom left) Monk stirring tsampa barley. (right) Juggling hot noodles in the Xinjiang province.

Far West

THE BASICS

Religion is the primary shaper of culinary tradition in China's Far West. Being a primarily Muslim province, chefs in Xinjiang don't use pork products of any kind. Instead, meals are likely to be heavy on spiced lamb. Baked flat breads coated in sesame seeds are a specialty. Whole lamb roasted on a spit, fine spicy tomato salads, and lightly spiced mutton and vegetable soups are also favorites.

NOT TO BE MISSED

In Tibet, climate is the major factor dictating cuisine. High and dry, the Tibetan plateau is hardly suited for rice cultivation. Whereas a Han meal might include rice, Tibetan cuisine tends to include tsampa, a ground barley usually cooked into a porridge. Another staple that's definitely an acquired taste is yak butter tea. Dumplings, known as *momo*, are wholesome and filling. Of course, if you want to go all out, order the yak penis with caterpillar fungus.

EAST

(top left) Flash cooking with the wok. (top right) Juicy steamer dumplings. (bottom right) Harvesting China's staple. (bottom left) Shanghai's sublime hairy crab.

THE BASICS

The rice, seafood, and fresh vegetable-based cooking of the southern coastal provinces of Zhejiang and Jiangsu are known collectively as *huiyang cai.* As the area's biggest city, Shanghai has become a major center of the culinary arts. Some popular dishes in Shanghai are stir-fried freshwater eels and finely ground white pepper, and red-stewed fish—a boiled carp in sweet and sour sauce. Another Shanghai favorite are *xiaolong bao,* or little steamer dumplings. Similar to Cantonese dim sum, xiaolong bao tend to be more moist. The perfect steamed dumpling is meant to explode in your mouth in a juicy burst of meat.

NOT TO BE MISSED

Drunken anything! Shanghai chefs are known for their love of cooking with wine. Dishes like drunken chicken, drunken pigeon, and drunken crab are all delectable meals cooked with prodigious amounts of Shaoxing wine. People with an aversion to alcohol should definitely avoid these. Another meal not to be missed is hairy freshwater crabs, which only come into season in October. One enthusiast of the dish was 15th-century poet and essayist Li Yu, who wrote of the dish in near-erotic terms. "Meat as white as jade, golden roe . . . to use seasoning to improve its taste is like holding up a torch to brighten the sunshine."

everything about the area, and lets you log onto the Internet. Oh, she also makes a great pizza. ✣ *South of the bus station* ☎ *0837/880–2958.*

¢ ⊡ **Songzhou Traffic Hotel.** When you want bang for your buck, this is the place. Located on the 2nd floor of the long-distance bus station, this hotel has clean private rooms and dorm-style accommodations. Another perk is the English-speaking manager. ✉ *Long Distance Bus Station* ☎ *0837/ 723–1818* ⇱ *100 rooms* ♨ *Cable TV, travel services* ▭ *No credit cards.*

To & from Songpan
6–8 hrs (350 km [217 mi]) by bus northwest of Chengdu.

Buses from Chengdu's Chadianzi and Xinnanmen bus stations shuttle passengers every day from 6:30 AM to 7 PM.

Although most travelers use the Jiuhuang Airport (located in Songpan Township, but actually almost three hours away in Huanglong) to go to the Jiu Zhai Valley, it is possible to fly into Jiuhuang and take a shuttle or taxi to Songpan. The ride should cost around Y100 per person, depending on the size of your group.

SICHUAN ESSENTIALS

Transportation

BY AIR
Chengdu Shuangliu International Airport is about 16 km (10 mi) southwest of the city. Chengdu has flights to all the major cities of China, including Beijing, Guangzhou, Chongqing, Guilin, Guiyang, Hong Kong, Kunming, Nanking, and Shanghai. Bus service links the airport terminal and downtown Chengdu.

Near Songpan, Jiuzhaigou Huanglong Airport has reopened after an expansion in 2006. Don't be fooled by the name, as the airport is about 88 km (55 mi) from Jiuzhaigou. Shuttle buses make the 1½-hour trip. ❼ Airport Information **Chengdu Shuangliu International Airport** ☎ 028/8570-2649 ⊕ www.cdairport.com. **Jiuzhaigou Huanglong Airport.**

BY BUS
There are four bus stations in Chengdu. The main one is Xinnanmen Bus Station. It is located in the city center and operates routes to Emeishan, Leshan, and other popular tourist destinations.

Chadianzi takes you to points northwest, such as Jiuzhaigou and Songpan.The North Railway/Bus Station has service to to Chingqing and Yibin, as well as northern Sichuan and Wu Gui Qiao. It is located 40 minutes east of the city center by taxi.

Ximen Bus Station is for closer destinations, those within an hour or so of the city. ❼ Bus Information **Chadianzi Bus Station** ⊠ Sanhuan Lu, Chengdu. **Wu Qui Qiao Bus Station** ⊠ Dongguichun Sanzhu, Chengdu. **Ximen Bus Station** ⊠ Yuejingchun Yizhu, Chengdu. **Xinnanmen Bus Station** ⊠ 57 Linjiang Lu, Chengdu.

8

BY TRAIN

There are trains from Chengdu to Dazu (7 hours), Emeishan (3 hours), Kunming (23 hours), and Xi'an (16 hours). It is also possible by train to get to Guangzhou (40 hours), Lanzhou (26 hours), Beijing (25 hours), Shanghai (45 hours), and Ürümqi (42 hours).

🚆 Train Information **Chengdu Train Station** ✉ Erhuan Lu ☎ 028/8370-9580.

Contacts & Resources

CONSULATE

🚆 United States **U.S. Consulate** ✉ 4 Lingshiguan Lu, Chengdu ☎ 028/8558-3992.

EMERGENCIES

🚆 **Public Security Bureau** PSB; Foreigner's Police ✉ Wenwu Lu, part of Xinhua Dong Lu; 40 Wenmiaohou Jie, Chengdu ☎ 110 or 028/8674-4683.

MONEY MATTERS

In Chengdu, money can be exchanged in the major hotels and at the Bank of China.

🚆 **Bank of China** ✉ Renmin Nan Lu, Chengdu.

VISITOR INFORMATION

There's a China International Travel Service (CITS) office in Chengdu.

🚆 Tourist Information **China International Travel Service** CITS ✉ 65 Renmin Nan Lu, Chengdu.

CHONGQING & THE YANGTZE RIVER

After decades of lobbying for special economic status, in 1997 Beijing finally allowed Chongqing to formally separate from Sichuan. This maneuver facilitated Chongqing's rise from a stunted once-capital to the region's industrial powerhouse and allowed for the long-planned Three Gorges Dam Project to move forward.

Called the Mountain City (also the name of the local beer), Chongqing has features unlike any other Chinese city. Instead of the ubiquitous bicycle, Chongqing has the Stickman Army. Stickmen are peasants for hire who wander the streets of Chongqing carrying stuff up and down the hills. The city is also riddled with tunnels, many of which were dug during the sieges of WWII. Built on the side of a mountain, the city has an upper and a lower level, so it's not unusual for buildings to have two or more "ground floors."

DID YOU KNOW? Chongqing is the heart of the BaYu Culture—vibrant, colorful, and proud—with its own version of Sichuan Opera, its own cuisine, and a history of rebelliousness. Chongqingese are known for their directness and fiery tempers.

The city is the major jumping-off point for the Three Gorges Cruise down the Yangtze River. The classic novel, *The Three Kingdoms,* takes place along this stretch of the river, and the cliffs are lined with caves and tombs dating back to the Yellow Emperor. The Three Gorges Dam is now complete and the water level is steadily rising—millions of people have been

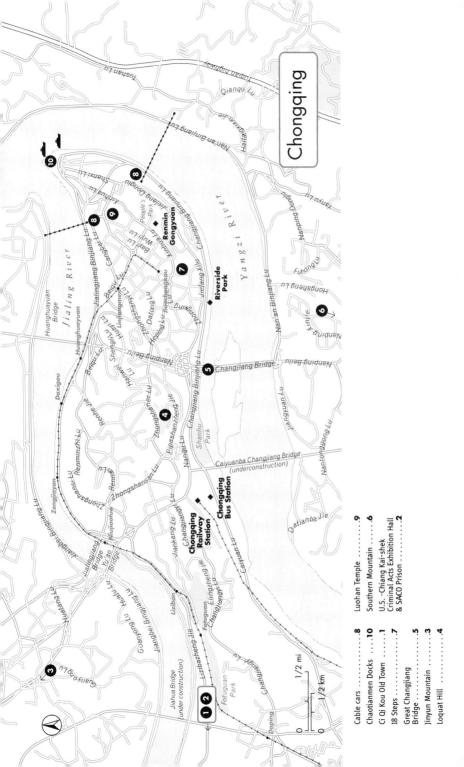

Chongqing

displaced, entire villages swamped, and countless historical artifacts lost forever—but China needs energy to keep its economic miracle running and the western regions need a reliable inland port with deep water capacity, therefore the dam stays.

Chongqing

Contrary to popular opinion, Chongqing is not just a dump that's only visited as a jumping-off spot for the ride down the Yangtze. For starters, because of the summertime heat and humidity, Chongqing comes alive at night. Few places have as many night food markets with such delicious, diverse, and agreeably priced fare. There's a great club scene in all parts of the city, especially in the Jie Fang Bei area. And the hills that distinguish Chongqing don't stop at the city limits—the lush countryside is dotted with villages locked in time and the mountains are riddled with caves. Finally, Chongqing is rich in early-20th-century Chinese historical sites. It will take a determined traveler plenty of time to fully explore all that the Mountain City has to offer. But if time is limited, a night or two in the city and perhaps a day-trip to Dazu before heading down the river is the norm.

Exploring Chongqing

★ ❽ Be sure to ride on both of the **cable cars** that dangle above the city. One links the north and south shores of the Jialing River, from Canbai Lu to the Jinsha Jie station and gives excellent views of the docks, the city, and the confluence of the Jialing and Yangtze rivers. The other crosses the Yangtze itself and starts close to Xinhua Lu. Be sure to take a map and study the city while up in the air. It's a good opportunity to rise above it all and get a grip on the city.

Jianling River Cable Car ✉ *40 Canbai Lu* ☎ *023/6383–4320* 💲 *Y1.50* ⊙ *Daily 9 AM–6 PM.* **Yangtze River Cable Car** ✉ *24 Xinhua Lu* ☎ *023/ 6287–7799* 💲 *Y2* ⊙ *Daily 6:15 AM–10 PM.*

❿ Perhaps not as busy and bustling as once upon a time, **Chaotianmen Docks** (Chaotianmen Matou) still offer an opportunity to get a glimpse of China at work and see the various boats departing for the Three Gorges river cruise. It's also a nice place to witness the unique merging of the muddy-brown Yangtze River and the blue-green Jialing River. ✉ *Shaanxi Lu.*

NEED A BREAK?

If you'd like to sit and relax, the **Unique Coffee House** (✉ 100 Nan Bing Rd., Sunlight Pavilion ☎ 023/6068-9122 ▭ No credit cards) is perched on top of a wall overlooking the Yangtze and sits right across from the evening

18 STEPS

Chongqing has the dubious distinction of being the most-bombarded city ever. During WWII, people would hide in the tunnels throughout the city to escape devastation. One of these tunnels is located in the district known as 18 Steps, in present-day Jie Fang Bei District. The tunnel still exists today but serves a very different purpose. It emits a constant flow of cool air and area residents gather here to cool themselves on sweltering summer days.

cruise-boat launch. The view is splendid, the coffee is good, and the boss is knowledgeable and speaks English. There is also a small selection of cakes and muffins.

★ ❸ In Beibie Town, just north of the city, **Jinyun Mountain** (Jinyun Shan) has some pretty views and a smattering of pavilions from the Ming and Qing dynasties. Three contain imposing statues of the Giant Buddha, the Amitabha Buddha, and the famous general of the Three Kingdoms Period, Guan Yu. The park also has a set of **hot springs,** where it is possible to bathe in the 30°C (86°F) water, either in a swimming pool or in the privacy of cubicles with their own baths. ⊠ *Jinyun Shan, 45 min (50 km [30 mi]) by bus north of city* ☒ *Y15* ☯ *Daily 8:30–6.*

❹ The 804-foot **Loquat Hill** (Pipa Shan) has great views of the bustle on the river below. At night, enjoy the city lights. There's also a small park with no entrance fee. ⊠ *Zhongshan Er Lu* ☯ *Daily 8 AM–7 PM.*

❻ **Southern Mountain** (Nan Shan) is the highest point in the city and at 935 feet, it is the most popular place from which to view Chongqing. For a thousand years Nan Shan has been the route over which travelers and traders of medicine, tea, spices, and silk entered the city and headed on to Sichuan. Besides spectacular views, the following sites are also on the mountaintop: **The Chongqing Anti-Japanese War Ruins Museum** (☒ Y20) is a collection of new houses built where the Nationalist Army had its headquarters during WWII. There are a few pictures and maps here, but we found the price too steep for what was offered. For the highest view of Chongqing City, check out the **Viewing Pavilion** (☒ Y20 ☯ Daily 8 AM–6 PM), a half-moon pavilion facing north across the Yangtze River. The **Luo Jun Cave Taoist Temple** (☒ Y6 ☯ Daily 7:30 AM–4:30 PM) is a 1,700-year-old temple that has been completely renovated but still sees very little traffic. The main temple entrance is accessible from the far side of the mountain, but we recommend slipping through the back door, which is a nice walk up the mountain's main road. The main temple sits on top of five caves that were used by Taoist monks centuries ago for meditation and contemplation. ⊠ *Nanping District, south side of the city, near Nan An Bin Jiang Lu* ☯ *Daily 7 AM–11 PM.*

Originally built about 1,000 years ago (Song Dynasty) and rebuilt in ❾ 1752, and again in 1945, the **Luohan Temple** (Luohan Si) is a popular place of worship and a small community of monks is still active here. One of the main attractions is the 500 lifelike painted clay arhats—Buddhist disciples who have succeeded in freeing themselves from the earthly chains of delusion and material greed. At the

8

GETTING AROUND

Chongqing's light-rail line from the city center to the zoo in the south is worth the Y7 round-trip ticket price. The two stations in the city center (Jiao Chang Kou and Ling Jiang Men) are easily accessible from Liberation Monument. The line curves north to the Jialing River—above ground—and goes through six riverside stations before it heads south to the terminal station at the zoo.

time of this writing, the temple was under construction, so the 1,000-Hand Guanyin couldn't be viewed. At the back of the temple, you can order tea, get a massage, and eat a vegetarian meal every day at 11 AM for Y2. ⊠ *Minzu Lu* ⊡ *Y5* ⊙ *Daily 8* AM–5 PM.

❶ Ci Qi Kou Old Town (Ci Qi Kou Gu Cheng.) Perched in the west of the city overlooking the Jialing River, this refurbished old district dates back to the late Ming Dynasty. There is a main drag with dozens of souvenir and snack shops, including the peaceful Baolun Si temple, which dates back 1,500 years. If you stay until late into the evening, head down the alleys off of the main drag and have a bowl of "Night Owl Noodles." It's spicy, meaty, and filling. ⊠ *Take Bus 462 from Liberation Monument to Chongqing University and connect with one of dozens of minivans and small buses to Ci Qi Kou for Y1–Y2; the ride takes about 40 mins.*

❼ 18 Steps (Shi Ba Ti) is one of the coolest places in the city, literally and figuratively. The neighborhood is just south of Liberation Monument and hasn't changed since the early 20th century. The name refers to the steps leading from the upper level of Jie Fang Bei down to the slums below. The infamous 18 Steps tunnel, the scene of horrible carnage during WWII, serves as a congregation point for the whole neighborhood. Find the tunnel, pull up a mat and sip tea while the locals stare at you incredulously. At the top of the steps is a teahouse with a treasure trove of WWII memorabilia. ⊠ *18 Steps, Jie Fang Bei District, walk in a southerly direction from Liberation Monument and ask about "Shi Ba Ti" as you go.*

NEED A BREAK? There are dozens of hole-in-the-wall restaurants all along the stone steps that serve the cheapest, tastiest food in town.

❷ U.S.-Chiang Kai-shek Criminal Acts Exhibition Hall & SACO Prison (Zhongmei Hezuosuo). SACO stands for the Sino-American Cooperation Organization, a collaboration between Chiang Kai-shek and the U.S. government and dedicated to the training and supervision of agents for the Nationalist Party government that fought the Communists before retreating to Taiwan. It was jointly run by the Chinese and the Americans, who built prisons outside Chongqing where sympathizers of the Communist Party were imprisoned and tortured. The exhibition hall houses a few photographs and examples of the restraining devices used on the prisoners but has nothing in English. The prisons are a considerable walk from the exhibition hall. The SACO museum is actually a complex of four separate sites located in the Sha Ping Ba suburb in northwest Chongqing at the foot of and atop Gele Mountain. Each site is Y10 or you can buy a ticket to the entire complex for Y40. There is also the option to

WORD OF MOUTH

"We like spicy food and have experienced no problems with the spicy hotpots we've encountered before, but they are chicken broth compared to Chongqing hotpots! Your whole mouth goes numb. Your lips tingle."

–Marija

hire a car and a guide with passable English for Y140. The prisons are not worth the price, but Gele Mountain is worth the climb; it is peaceful and often misty, and has several small pavilions, a playground, and a monument to the Martyrs at the summit. ⊠ *Foot of Gele Mountain, Sha Ping Ba District* 🎫 *Y40 or Y10 per site* ☉ *Daily 8:30–5.*

Tours

Chongqing is beautiful at night. High-rises ring the hills in and around the city, each giving off a neon glow that reflects off of the rushing rivers below. A night boat cruise is a romantic way to appreciate the charms of the Mountain City. Tickets can be bought at any hotel, or at the **Chaotianmen Donghai Travel Booking Office.** Cruises can be booked with or without dinner. ⊠ *18 Xingyi St., across from the port* 🕾 *023/6380—3350 or 023/6372–8026* 🎫 *Y100–Y120* ☉ *Daily 9* AM*–6* PM.

Where to Stay & Eat

$$–$$$$ ✕ **Champs Elysee 1902.** This former French Marine ballroom takes up three floors and has spectacular views of the riverboats. Dishes such as baked snail with herb and garlic butter, fried goose liver, escargot with baked goose liver, and baked mussels are enough to make a Frenchman homesick. The coffee (Blue Mountain Brew) is a nice ending to the meal. ⊠ *No. 142 Qiantaixing, Danxishi, Nan An District* 🕾 *023/625–0888* 🖃 *MC, V.*

$–$$$$ ✕ **Yizhishi Fandian.** This multilevel eatery is one of Sichuan's most famous. The food upstairs is more expensive but delicious—indulge in top-notch local dishes such as tea-smoked duck. The pastries and *jiaozi* (dumplings) downstairs are a perfect breakfast nosh. ⊠ *114 Zourong Lu* 🕾 *023/6384–1456* 🖃 *No credit cards.*

$–$$$ ✕ **Lao Sichuan.** The best-known restaurant in Chongqing because it's been in existence for as long as anyone can remember, the Old Sichuan has traditional and exotic food (for example, chili-braised frogs) at reasonable prices. The hot-pepper dishes are as spicy as you'd get in Sichuan. ⊠ *186 Minzu Lu* 🕾 *023/6382–6644* 🖃 *AE, MC, V.*

$ ✕ **Pizza Amalfi.** For weary travelers looking for some culinary familiarity, this pizzeria hits the spot. The food is pricey for what it is, but they speak English and offer take-out and delivery service. ⊠ *Minzu Lu near Liberation Monument* 🕾 *023/6381–7868 or 023/6091–4480* 🖃 *No credit cards.*

★ ¢ ✕🏨 **Chongqing Fandian.** This hotel is located in the center of town in an art-deco–style building. The well-equipped rooms make it an excellent value and the restaurant, Chiao Tiang Gong—one of the city's older, more famous eateries—serves very good local and regional food in pleasant modern surroundings. ⊠ *41–43 Xinhua Lu, 630011* 🕾 *023/*

> ## A SPOT OF TEA
>
> **Qi Xiang Ju** (⊠ Liang Lu Kou Ti Yu Guan, next to the Liang Lu Kou Sports Facility), which translates literally into "Strange Aroma Spot," is a small collection of tables and trees in the heart of the city. Some of the best tea in town is served here and it's a favorite hangout for artists, journalists, and the nouveau rich of Chongqing.

8

6160–9999 🖨 023/6384–3085
🛏197 rooms ⌂2 restaurants, minibars, bar, shops ▤MC, V.

¢–$$$ 🖼 **Hilton Hotel.** The Hilton is lo-
cated in a leafy, quiet neighbor-
hood west of Liberation
Monument. The hotel chain that
gave Paris her fortune literally drips
with class. Plush rooms have the
firmest beds in town and fabulous
bathrooms to boot. The rooftop
pool is the perfect place to unwind.
✉ 139 Zhongshan San Lu, 400015
☎ 023/8903–9999 ⊕ www.hilton.
com 🛏 434 rooms and suites ⌂ 4
restaurants, Wi-Fi, spa, pool, busi-
ness services, ballroom, meeting
rooms ▤ AE, MC, V.

¢–$$$ ✕🖼 **J.W. Marriott.** The Marriott is located just off the main drag of the
city within short walking distance to virtually any site near Liberation
Monument. The service is impeccable, the rooms plush and comfy, and
the amenities are first-class. The shopping arcade on the ground floor is
a nice way to spend an hour or two, and if you're in the mood for steak
and excellent views, visit the restaurant on the top floor. ✉ 77 Qing Nian
Lu, Yu Zhong District, 400010 ☎023/6388–8888 ⊕www.marriotthotels.
com 🛏 484 rooms ⌂ 5 restaurants, pool, gym, sauna, shops, cigar bar,
business center ▤ AE, MC, V.

¢–$ 🖼 **Holiday Inn Yangtze Chongqing** (Yangzijiang Jiari Fandian). This in-
ternational standard hotel is just outside the city center. Try to reserve
a room on the hotel's north side, where you can enjoy full views of the
Yangtze River. It's located right across from the International Conference and Exhibition Center and there are lots of in-house amenities. ✉ 15
Nanping Bei Lu, 400060 ☎ 023/6280–3380 🖨 023/6280–0884 🛏 365
rooms ⌂ 5 restaurants, pool, gym, bar, dance club, business services ▤AE,
MC, V.

¢ 🖼 **Yu Du Da Jiu Dian.** A fine option if the foreign hotels are out of your
price range but you still want to feel like royalty. The hotel's great location makes up for the mediocrity of the Chinese restaurant inside. The
entire street down from the Liberation Monument is filled with food
stands during the afternoon and evening hours, so you won't starve. Next
door, on the 3rd floor is the Newcastle Arms, an English-style pub with
Y20 beers and Y300 bottles of booze. ✉ 168 Bayi Lu, 400015 ☎ 023/
6383–8888 🖨 023/6381–8168 🛏 160 rooms ⌂ Tearoom, restaurant,
massage ▤ AE, MC, V.

Nightlife & the Arts

Hong Ya Cave (Hong Ya Dong) (✉Bin Jiang Lu, south bank of the Yangtze,
Nanping District) is a recently built complex that fuses Ba Yu cultural
performances with traditional Chinese architecture and elements of the
American mall. The complex overlooks the Jialing River and has a
brightly lit waterfall and paved streets built right into the mountainside.

The main attraction is the Ba Yu dance performance, a dancing primer for Chongqing customs and folklore. At times it's a bit racy, and the historical aspects of Ba Yu culture have been dumbed-down for the benefit of travelers, but the costumes, choreography, and the bit on the Devil Town of Fengdu make it an evening well spent. For the **Ba Yu Theatre** (☎ 023/6303–9968 or 023/6303–9969 ticket reservations ✉ Y80–Y280 ⊙ Shows Wed. and Sun. 8 PM).

River Side Road (Nan An Bing Jiang Lu) (✉ Nan An Bin Jiang Lu, south bank of the Yangtze, Nanping District) stretches the length of the Yangtze River's south bank. The road is still under construction (with no definate date set for completion) and has not yet fulfilled its potential as the Champs Elysee of Chongqing, but there are a few good places to eat and a slew of enormous clubs along the road.

De Yi World (De Yi Shi Jie) (✉ Ci Qi Lu, Yu Zhong District, near Jie Fang Bei, around the corner from the Marriott Hotel) is a large complex of bars, karaoke rooms, and dance clubs. If you want to party with the locals, we recommend **Falling** (✉ Basement of De Yi World Complex ☎ No phone ✉ Free ⊙ 6 PM–sunrise), a cramped club with a little dance floor that is packed on weekends. The music is good for Chinese club standards, and foreign DJs sometimes come and spin for a night or two. When you're tired of dancing, go next door and grab a Guinness and some greasy snacks at **The Celtic Man** (✉ Basement of De Yi World ☎ 023/6379–8158 ⊙ 5 PM–5 AM)

Shopping

Carrefour (Jialefu), near Chaotian Men port, is the largest foreign-owned department store in China, with outlets in virtually every major city in the nation. The France-based giant sells everything from congee to caviar plus a decent import section with all the goodies one misses from home. Carrefour is located right next to the largest fish market in the city (✉ Cangbai Lu ⊙ 9 AM–11 PM).

Side Trip to Dazu

★ *3 hrs (160 km [99 mi]) by bus northwest of Chongqing.*

The Buddhist caves outside of this sprawling city were recently named a UNESCO site. They rival those at Datong, Dunhuang, and Luoyang. The sculptures, ranging from teeny-tiny to gigantic, contain unusual domestic detail, as well as purely religious works. There are two major sites at Dazu—Bei Shan and Baoding Shan. Work at the caves began in the 9th century (during the Song and Tang dynasties) and continued for more than 250 years.

Baoding Shan is the more impressive of the two sites and where the carvings were completed according to a plan. Here you will find visions of hell reminiscent of similar scenes from medieval Europe; the Wheel of Life; a magnificent 100-foot reclining Buddha; and a gold, thousand-armed statue of the goddess of mercy.

The best way to reach Dazu is to book a tour through your hotel or a travel agency. Every agency gives the Dazu tour for between Y210 and Y220, which includes transportation, lunch, and the entrance fee. If you would like to go it alone, there are minibuses by Liberation Monument that can take you there for about Y150 to Y200 round-trip. Be sure to leave early as seats sell out. 🎫 *Y85* ⊗ *Daily 8–5.*

¢ 🏨 **Dazu Binguan.** Most foreign guests end up staying in this clean

but unimaginative hotel. The on-site travel agency can help you buy bus or train tickets. ⊠ *47 Gongnong Jie, 402360* ☎ *023/4372–2476* 📠 *023/4372–2967* 🛏 *132 rooms* ⚐ *Restaurant, business services* ▭ *DC, MC, V.*

To & from Chongqing

4 hrs (240 km [149 mi]) by bus southeast of Chengdu; 3 hrs (1,800 km [1,116 mi]) by plane southwest of Beijing; 34 hrs (1,025 km [636 mi]) by train northwest of Hong Kong.

Chongqing is located smack-dab in the middle of China, connected by rail, bus, and plane to every major city in the country. Rail connections from the east coast are frequent and relatively fast—30-plus hours from Shanghai, Beijing, or Canton. Trains also link Chongqing with the far western regions with daily departures to Xi'an, Lanzhou, and Kunming. Buses are great for shorter excursions into neighboring Sichuan, but long-distance bus rides from Chongqing can be harrowing. The Chongqing airport is well connected, with daily flights to all major cities in China. For travel between the east coast and Chongqing, flying is your most comfortable option. For trips to Chengdu, the express train is the best bet, although there are bus and plane connections as well.

The Three Gorges

The third-longest river in the world after the Amazon and the Nile, the Yangtze cuts across 6,380 km (3,956 mi) and seven provinces before flowing out into the East China Sea. After descending from the mountain ranges of Qinghai and Tibet, the Yangtze crosses through Yunnan to Sichuan, winding its way through the lush countryside between Sichuan and Hubei before flowing northward toward Anhui and Jiangsu. Before the 20th century, many lost their lives trying to pass through the fearsome stretch of water running through what is known as the Three Gorges—the complicated system of narrow cliffs between Fengjie, in Sichuan, and Yichang, in Hubei.

The spectacular scenery of the Three Gorges—Qutang, Wu, and Xiling—has survived the rising waters of the newly dammed Yangtze River. A trip through the Three Gorges offers a glimpse of a way of life that is rapidly disappearing: panoramas of hills covered with rice fields; fishermen scooping the waters with large nets from the shores; cliffs and clouds parting to reveal narrow passages of water barely wide enough for two boats—these are the images that have persisted for centuries. If you can pull your mind away from the hype and hyperbole surround-

Damming the Yangtze

THE THREE GORGES dam project has been a dream for the Chinese leadership since Liberation in 1949. Harnessing the power of the mighty Yangtze River as it rushes through the gorges can help satiate China's voracious appetite for energy as well as generate untold millions in income for provincial and central government coffers. At 607 feet high and more than 1-mi wide, the dam will produce enough electricity to supply the factories and cities of both the developed east and the underdeveloped heartland, hopefully putting an end to the rampant blackouts that threaten to choke China's economic revolution. The dam, when completed in 2009, will be the largest ever constructed, the cornerstone for the Communist Party's development program, and an international symbol of China's global power status. The reservoir created by the dam will increase Chongqing's ability to send freight down the Yangtze River—a potential boon for logistics companies now relying on outdated trains and motley fleets of rickety cargo trucks—and provide critical flood control for long-suffering downstream cities like Wuhan.

Since construction began, however, critics have railed against a project they consider a hubristic, expensive, and poorly planned attempt to impress the rest of the planet while destroying land, homes, and the history of a vast swath of China. Costs are difficult to assess in secretive China, but estimates have been put as high as $75 billion, give or take a few billion that may have gone to lining the pockets of countless officials during former Chairman Li Peng's reign over the project. Rampant corruption has led to accusations of "tofu engineering," a serious allegation considering the millions of lives at stake if the dam were to collapse.

The project has been vilified by environmentalists worldwide. The reservoir, though instrumental in jump-starting hinterland exports to the outside world, will also back up the muddy Yangtze, potentially silting up the dam and thereby reducing electricity output. A more sinister possibility is the creation of a 300-mi-long cesspool, as the notoriously filthy and toxic towns of central China pour their wastes into an almost stagnant river.

The dam has also created a swarming diaspora of migrant workers and displaced persons who have swelled the nearby cities of Wuhan, Chongqing, Xi'an, and other cities as far away as Lanzhou and Urumqi. The submergence of entire towns and villages has coincided with the inundation of countless relics and artifacts from the cradle of Chinese civilization. The Three Gorges area is the site of some of the most famous battles of the Three Kingdoms period and has cliff-side tombs dating back to the dawn of civilization as we know it.

Regardless of the pitfalls and dangers, the Chinese are going through with their great project and banking hard that the benefits will outweigh the costs. Hopefully the dam will be a defiant success in the face of a wall of skepticism. The alternative is unimaginable suffering for the inhabitants along this strip of the Yangtze River.

ing the Three Gorges project, you will find yourself dreaming of kung fu warriors, splendidly clad princes and princesses, and clashing armies from a bygone age. Even though the towns along the river—Fengdu, Shibaozhi, and others—have been conquered by the prevailing religion of today's mercantile China, the sites along the river are magical. How you experience your journey will depend on your mindset and on your preparation—this trip can be as amazing as you want it to be.

DID YOU KNOW?

The Three Gorges area is steeped in legends and history. To best appreciate the trip, read the classic book, *The Three Kingdoms,* and augment it with a few history books.

Boat Tour Options

There are a number of riverboat options, depending on how much money you want to spend and how comfortably you want to travel. Riverboat rides essentially come in two forms: luxury and domestic. Domestic cruises are much cheaper and have fewer amenities. No matter which option you choose, be sure to book ahead as berths are limited.

LUXURY CRUISE BOATS

The foreign-owned ships, such as the Victoria Series boats, are big, quadruple-decker liners that are by far the most comfortable option—and they're built with entertainment in mind. In addition to spacious decks from which to soak up the breathtaking views, many boats are equipped with a gym, a ballroom, a business center with Internet connection, and bars and restaurants. There are also a few shops in case you run out of film or other necessities.

WORD OF MOUTH

"Meals on the Victoria Queen are eaten at assigned tables. Breakfast and lunch are buffets. Dinner is served family-style at the tables. We were very pleasantly surprised by the quality of the food. There was good variety, both Chinese and European, and the food was well prepared."

–Marija

The ticket price includes the admission cost for most of the sites along the way, except the Little Three Gorges. A one-way package tour ranges from Y4,583 to Y3,793 and the boats themselves are divided into three-, four-, and five-star service. Prices fluctuate so be sure to check ahead.

Changjiang Cruise Overseas Travel Co. Cruise Marketing Center ✉ Chao Tian Men Plaza, Chongqing 400010 ☎ 0086/27-8566-8414 ⊕ www.ccotc.com.

DOMESTIC BOATS

These are the less expensive, less luxurious option and are divided into four classes. Suites offer almost all of the amenities of Luxury Cruise Boats and are available for Y2,084 one-way. First-class sleeps two people and costs Y1,042 one-way to Yichang. Spartan rooms come with two beds, a private bathroom, TV, and air-conditioning. Second-class sleeps four people and costs Y503 for a one-way ticket. Third-class sleeps six to eight people and costs Y347 one-way. Both second- and third-classes have bunk beds, shared bathrooms that aren't always kept clean, and views from lower decks are sometimes limited. Unlike the Luxury

Cruise lines, these prices do not include the price of entry to sites along the way. The domestic boats serve good Chinese food, depending on the class you choose. Avoid any Western dishes that are on the menu. There are no shops on board, so be sure to stock up beforehand. If you go in winter, bring an extra blanket and dress warmly.

> **WORD OF MOUTH**
>
> "Because of the new dam the river level is rising and the gorges will never look the way they do now again."
>
> —thursdaysd

The tour operators have been consolidated into one company, and most tours get booked through them. Offices can be found throughout the Chaotianmen District.

🛈 **Chongqing Port International Travel Service** ✉ 18 Xingyi St., Chaotianmen, Yu Zhong District, Chongqing ☎ 023/6310-0595 ⊕ www.cqpits.com.cn.

HYDROFOIL This option is used by those returning from Yichang to Chongqing, who don't want to do the whole trip over again, in reverse. Prices may vary, but currently it is Y280 from Yichang to Chongqing and takes about six hours. You have to get off at Wanxian and take a bus back into Chongqing. This costs Y120 and takes another 3½ hours. If you're pressed for time, there is an airport in Yinchang with daily flights to Chongqing at 7 PM for Y700.

Sights en Route

On the banks of the Yangtze, **Fengdu,** also known as Guicheng or the "city of devils," is filled with temples, buildings, and statues depicting demons and devils. During the Tang Dynasty, the names of two local princely families, Yin (meaning "hell") and Wang (meaning "king"), were linked through marriage, making them known as Yinwang, or the "king of hell." Ever since, people have believed that the town is populated by ghosts. You can take a series of staircases or a cable car to the top of the mountain. 🎫 *Y60* 🕑 *Daily* 6 AM–6 PM.

The bamboo-covered **Ming Hill** (Mingshan) has a Buddhist temple, a pavilion, and pagodas with brightly painted dragons and swans emanating from the eaves. The hill has a nice view of the Yangtze River.

Stone Treasure Stronghold (Shibaozhai) is actually a rectangular rock with sheer cliffs, into which is built an impressive 12-story pagoda, constructed by Emperor Qianlong (1736–96) during the Qing Dynasty. Wall carvings and historical inscriptions describing the construction of the building can be seen along the circuitous stairway that leads from the center of the pagoda to the top. 🎫 *Y60* 🕑 *Daily* 6 AM–6 PM.

Three Gorges (San Xia). The Three Gorges lie in the heart of China, along the fault lines of what once were flourishing kingdoms. Those great kingdoms have now vanished into history and become, collectively, China.

❶ The westernmost gorge, **Qutang Gorge** (Qutang Xia) is the shortest, at 8 km (5 mi). The currents here are quite strong due to the natural gate formed by the two mountains, Chijia and Baiyan. Both are craggy monsters rising out of the depths, with shoulders forming weird peaks such as "Rhinoceros views the Moon" and "Elephant Peak." There are cliff inscriptions along the way, so be sure to have your guide point them out and explain their significance. Several are from the Warring States period over 1,000 years ago. Warriors' coffins from that period were discovered in the caves on these mountains, and some still remain.

Next, a short turn leads to Wushan, at the entrance to Wu Gorge. Here you can change to a smaller boat navigated by local boatmen to the ❷ **Little Three Gorges** (Xiao San Xia) (✉ Y150). The Little Three Gorges (Dragon Gate Gorge, Misty Gorge, and Emerald Gorge) are spectacular and not to be missed. They are striking and silent, rising dramat-

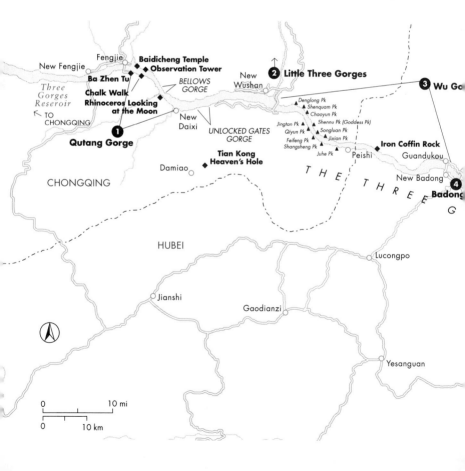

ically out of the river to rival the Three Gorges themselves. If you have time, take a trip to the old town of Dachang near the end of the Little Three.

❸ The impressive **Wu Gorge** (Wu Xia) is 33 km (20 mi) long. Its cliffs are so sheer and narrow that they seem to be closing in upon each other as you approach in the boat. Some of the cliff formations are noted for their resemblances to people and animals. Most notably is the Goddess Peak, a beautiful pillar of white stone among 12 other peaks along the route.

❹ At the city of **Badong** in Hubei, just outside the eastern end of Wu Gorge, boats leave for Shennongjia on the Shennong River, one of the wildest and strangest parts of the country.

❺ **Xiling Gorge** (Xiling Xia), 66 km (41 mi) long, is the longest and deepest of all the gorges, with cliffs that rise up to 4,000 feet. There are no stops along here and it is undoubtedly the most peaceful and contemplative leg of the journey.

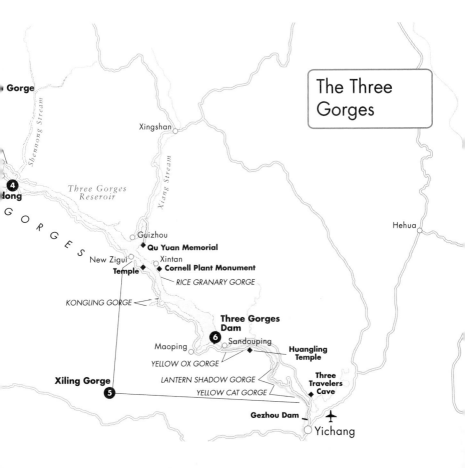

❻ Xiling Gorge ends at the **Three Gorges Dam** (San Xia Da Ba). Nothing that you've seen or read about this project can possibly prepare you for its massive scale. Sit back in awe as the boat approaches this great dam and then slowly slips through the inner workings, into the lower reaches of the river. ➱ *Y190.*

CHONGQING ESSENTIALS

Transportation

BY AIR

Traffic permitting, Chongqing's Jiangbei International Airport is a 1½-hour drive north by taxi from the city center. The airport flies to every major domestic, and some international hubs, mostly within Asia. Book tickets at any hotel or the travel agencies around Liberation Monument. 🛪 Airlines & Contacts **China Southwest Airlines** ✉ Zhongshan San Lu ☏ 023/6366-0444. **CAAC Chongqing** ✉ 161 Zhongshan San Lu, Chongqing ☏ 023/6360-3223.

BY BOAT & FERRY

Boats go on the Yangtze from Chongqing all the way to Shanghai (seven days), but the most popular route is the cruise downstream from Chongqing to Yichang or Wuhan (three to four days) or upstream from Wuhan to Chongqing. Most major sights, including the Three Gorges and Three Little Gorges, lie between Chongqing and Yichang. Tourist boats offer air-conditioned cabins with a television and private bath; the ordinary passenger steamers used by most Chinese offer minimal comforts. Tickets can be arranged through CITS or your travel agent.

BY BUS & TRAIN

The shared train and bus station may be the most inconvenient, crowded, and annoying station in the world. It is eternally under construction, but the station will soon be moved to a spot farther north of the city center. Once your taxi has maneuvered through the corrugated tin walls and piles of baggage, finding buses or trains is not hard. Touts are eager to help just in case. 🛪 **Cai Yuan Ba Train and Bus Station** ✉ Off of Nan Qu Lu.

From Chongqing to Chendu is a well-trodden path. The bus departs every hour, takes five to six hours, and costs Y110. Buses are viable as far as Yibin or within the municipality itself (Dazu and Beibei), but trains are recommended for all other destinations.

There are trains leaving Chongqing every minute for every conceivable city in China. If you're going to Chengdu, we recommend the new express train. It's a comfy, double-decker train with air-conditioning and good food. The trip only takes 4½ hours, basically half of the original time. Trains leave every day from Chongqing at 8 AM, 1 PM (sleeper), and 3:01 PM. Tickets cost Y52 one-way for hard-seat class and Y81 for soft-seat class. Sleeper-seats cost Y98 to Y106.

Trains run daily to the following destinations: Beijing (Y238 to Y658, 25 hours, 2 daily departures at 12:26 AM and 8:17 PM); Guangzhou (Y118 to Y533, 38 hours, 5 departures daily at 1:02 AM, 4:35 PM, 7:35 PM, 9:11 PM, and 10:33 PM); Guiyang (Y62 to Y127, 10+ hours, 3 departures daily at 7:39 AM, 7:55 PM, and 11:07 PM); Kunming (Y143 to Y400, 20+ hours, 2 departures daily at 12:38 PM and 2:42 PM); Shanghai (Y271 to Y754, 30+ hours, 1 departure daily at 8:07 PM); Xi'an (Y53 to Y120, 14 hours, 1 departure daily at 9:27 AM).

Contacts & Resources

EMERGENCIES

🚹 **Public Security Bureau** PSB; Foreigner's Police ⊠ Linjiang Lu, Chongqing ☎ 110 or 023/6375-8200.

INTERNET SERVICES

Most hotels in the city center are wired and there are Internet cafés in the smaller streets that radiate from the Liberation Monument.

🚹 **Gao Shou Internet Bar** ⊠ Ci Qi Lu, Yu Zhong District, basement of De Yi World, around the corner from the Marriott and next to the Falling Club.

MONEY MATTERS

You can change money in Chongqing in the hotels or at the Bank of China. There are plenty of Banks of China scattered throughout the city.

🚹 **Bank of China** ⊠ Minzu Lu, Chongqing.

VISITOR INFORMATION

🚹 Tourist Information **CITS** ⊠ Renmin Binguan hotel, Renmin Lu, Chongqing ☎ 028/8668-7058 or 028/8665-7598.

8

At a Glance

ENGLISH	PINYIN	CHINESE CHARACTERS
EXPLORING		
SICHUAN	Sì Chuān	四川
CHENGDU	Chéng Dū	成都
Du Fu's Thatched Cottage	Dùfǔ Cǎotáng	杜甫草堂
Chengdu Train Station	Chéng Dū Huǒ Chē Zhàn	成都火车站
Giant Panda Breeding Research Base	Dàxióngmāo Bówùguǎn	大熊猫博物馆
Memorial of the Marquis of Wu	Wǔ Hóu Cí	武侯祠
Qingyang Palace	Qīngyáng Gōng	青羊宫
Riverview Pavilion Park	Wàng Jiāng Lóu Gōng Yuán	望江楼公园
Tomb of Emperor Wang Jian	Wáng Jiàn Mù	王建墓
Wenshu Monastery	Wénshū Yuàn	文殊院
WHERE TO STAY & EAT		
Chengdu Grand Hotel	Chéngdū Dàfàndiàn	成都大饭店
Chuan Jiang Hao Zi	Chuān Jiāng Hào Zǐ	川江号子
Crowne Plaza	Zǒng Fǔ Huáng Guān Jià Rì Jiǔ Diàn	总府皇冠假日酒店
Grandma's Kitchen	Zǔ mǔ De Chú Fáng	祖母的厨房
Huang Cheng Lao Ma	Huáng Chéng Lǎo Mǎ	皇城老妈
Jin Gu Fish	Jīn Gǔ Yú	金骨鱼
Jinjiang Binguan	Jǐn Jiāng Bīn Guǎn	锦江宾馆
Minshan Fandian	Mín Shān Fàn Diàn	岷山饭店
Piaoxiang	Piāo Xiāng	飘香
Shanbala Zangcan	Xiāng Bā Lā Zàng Cān	香巴拉藏餐
Shizi Lou Dajiudian	Shī zǐ Lóu Dà Jiǔ Diàn	狮子楼大酒店
Sim's Cozy Guest House	Guān Huá Qīng Nián Lǚ Guǎn	观华青年旅馆
Sofitel Wanda Chengdu	Suò Fēi Tè Wàn Dá Dà Jiǔ Diàn	索菲特万达大饭店
Songzhou Traffic Hotel	Jiāo Tōng Fàn Diàn	交通饭店
Tandoor	Tǎn Dào Yìn Dù Cān Tīng	坦道印度餐厅
Tibet Hotel	Xī Zàng Fàn Diàn	西藏饭店
EMEISHAN	É Méi Shān	峨嵋山
EXPLORING		
Elephant Bathing Pool	Xǐ Xiàng Chí	洗象池
Golden Summit	Jīndǐngsì	金顶寺

Jieyin Dian	Jiē Yǐn Diàn	接引店
Long Life Monastery	Cháng Shòu Sì	长寿寺
Magic Peak Monastery	Xiān Fēng Sì	仙峰寺
WHERE TO STAY & EAT		
Baoguo Monastery	Bào Guó Sì	报国寺
Emeishan Hotel	É Méi Shān Dà Jiǔ Diàn	峨嵋山大酒店
Teddy Bear Café	Xiǎo Xióng Kāfēi	小熊咖啡
LESHAN	Lè Shān	乐山
EXPLORING		
Grand Buddha	Lè Shān Dà Fó	乐山大佛
Wuyou Temple	Wū Yóu Sì	乌尤寺
WHERE TO STAY & EAT		
Jiazhou Garden Hotel	Jiāzhōu Huāyuán Jiǔdià	加州花园酒店
San Jiang	Sān Jiāng	三江
JIUZHAIGOU NATURE RESERVE	Jiǔ Zhài Gōu Zì Rán Bǎo Hù Qū	九寨沟自然保护区
WHERE TO STAY & EAT		
Jiuzhai Paradise International Resort	Jiǔzhài Tiāntáng Guójì Huìyì Dùjià Zhōng Xīn	九寨天堂国际会议度假中心
Sheraton Jouzhaigou Resort	Jiǔzhàigōu Xǐláidēng Guójì Dàjiǔdiàn	九寨沟喜来登国际大酒店
YouU Hostel	Yōuyóu Dùjià Qīngnián Jiǔdiàn	悠游度假青年酒店
SONGPAN	Sōng Pān	松潘
WHERE TO STAY & EAT		
Emma's Kitchen	Ài Mǎ Xiǎo Chú	艾玛小厨
Songzhou Traffic Hotel	Sōngzhōu Jiāotōng Fàndiàn	松洲交通饭店
CHONGQING	Chóng Qìng	重庆
EXPLORING		
Baoding Shan	Bǎo Dìng Shān	保定山
Cable cars	Diàn Lǎn Chē	电缆车
Chaotianmen Docks	Cháo Tiān Mén Mǎ Tóu	朝天门码头
Dazu	Dà Zú	大足
Jinyun Mountain	Jìn Yún Shān	缙云山
Loquat Hill	Pí Pá Shān	琵琶山
Southern Mountain	Nán Shān	南山
Chongqing Train Station	Chóng Qìng Huǒ Chē Zhàn	重庆火车站

8

Ci Qi Kou Old Town	Cí Qì Kǒu Lǎo Jiē	瓷器口老街
18 Steps	Shíbā Tī	十八梯
U.S.-Chiang Kai-Shek Criminal Acts Exhibition Hall & SACO Prison	Zhōngměi Hézuòsuǒ	中美合作所

WHERE TO STAY & EAT		
Champs Elysee 1902	Xiāng Shě Lì Xiè	香舍丽榭
Chongqing Fandian	Chóngqìng Fàndiàn	重庆饭店
Hilton Hotel	Xī Ěr Dùn Jiǔ Diàn	希尔顿酒店
Holiday Inn Yangzi Chongqing	Yāngzǐjiāng Jiàrì Fàndiàn	扬子江假日饭店
J.W. Marriott	Wàn Háo Jiǔ Diàn	JW 万豪酒店
Lao Sichuan	Lǎo Sìchuān	老四川
Qi Xiang Ju (ED: literally strange aroma spot)	Qí Xiāng Jū	奇香居
Yizhishi Restaurant	Yí Zhiī Shí Dà Jiǔ Lóu	颐之时大酒楼
Yu Du Da Jiu Dian	Yúdū Dàjiǔdiàn	渝都大酒店
THE YANGTZE RIVERBOAT RIDE	Chángjiāng Yóulún Yóu	长江游轮旅游

EXPLORING		
Badong	Bādōng	巴东
Dazu Binguan	Dàzú Bīnguǎn	大足宾馆
Fengdu	Fēngdū	丰都
Little Three Gorges	Xiǎo Sān Xiá	小三峡
Luohan Temple	Luóhàn Sì	罗汉寺
Ming Hill	Míngshān	明山
Qutang Gorge	Qú Táng Xiá	瞿塘峡
Shibaozhai	Shíbǎozhài	石堡寨
Three Gorges	Sānxiá	三峡
Three Gorges Dam	Sānxiá Dàbà	三峡大坝
U.S. Consulate	Měiguó Lǐngshìguǎn	美国邻事馆
Wu Gorge	Wūxiá	巫峡
Wushan	Wūshān	巫山
Xiling Gorge	Xīlíng Xiá	西岭峡
Yangzi River	Cháng Jiāng	长江

The Silk Road

SHAANZI, GANSU, QUINGHAI, XINJIANG

A boy taking the reigns in Xiahe, Gansu

WORD OF MOUTH

"Make sure you go to the night market in Dunhuang. People set up folding lawn chairs and sell you tea and fruits. It is one of my most magical memories."

—epi

WELCOME TO THE SILK ROAD

TOP REASONS TO GO

★ **Terracotta Warriors:** Visit one of the nation's most haunting and memorable sites—the vast life-size army of soldiers, built to outlast death.

★ **Discover Dunhuang:** Satisfy your inner archaeologist at the magnificent Mogao Caves and scale the shifting slopes of Singing Sand Mountain.

★ **Seek Solace at Kumbum Monastery:** Visit one of the six great monasteries of the Tibetan Buddhist sect known as Yellow Hat, reputedly the birthplace of the sect's founder, Tsong Khapa.

★ **Tour Turpan:** Discover the ruins of ancient city-states Jiaohe and Gaochang, destroyed by Genghis Khan and his unstoppable Mongol hordes.

★ **Kashgar & the Karakorum Highway:** Explore Central Asia's largest and liveliest bazaar before heading south to the snow-capped Pamir Mountains and crystal-clear Lake Karakul.

Karakoram Highway.

RUSSIA

KAZAKHSTAN

Altay

Karamay

JUNGGAR PENDI

Ürümqi

Qijiaojing

KYRGYZSTAN

Turpan

TIEN SHAN

Aksu

Korla

Sugun

4

Kashgar

XINJIANG UYGUR ZIZHIQU

Lop Nur

TAJIKISTAN

Tashkurgan

TAKLIMAKAN PENDI

ALTUN SHAN

Hotan

Qiemo

PAKISTAN

KARAKORAM

KUNLUN SHAN

INDIA

KASHMIR

(TIBETIAN PLATEAU)

TIBET

Tanggula Mountain Pass

0   200 mi

0   200 km

1 Shaanxi: Visit the tomb of China's first emperor and its army of thousands of lifelike terra-cotta warriors in Xian. Climb the sheer face of sacred Mount Hua Shan. Shaanxi is the starting point of the fabled Silk Road that brought silks, spices, and other precious goods from the Middle Kingdom to Rome more than two millennia ago.

2 Gansu: Arid, mountainous, and home to more than a dozen different ethnicities, Gansu has served as a corridor to the West for thousands of years. Heralded sites include the Mogao Caves, Singing Sand Mountain, and the remote Labrang Monastery.

3 Qinghai: Away from the industrialized cities and under the epic sky and vast open plains, seminomadic herders, clad in brown robes slashed with fluorescent pink sashes, still roam the grasslands, herding yak and goats the way their ancestors did for centuries before them—on horseback.

Terracotta Soldiers.

GETTING ORIENTED

There was no single "Silk Road," but rather hundreds of old routes and scores of trading posts that formed a vibrant overland trade network between China, Central Asia, and Europe. The current "Silk Road" received its moniker from the German scholar Baron Ferdinand von Richtofen in the mid-19th century. The Chinese section he noted stretched from Xian in Shaanxi Province, through Gansu's narrow Hexi Corridor to Dunhuang. After passing through the famed Jade Gate dividing China from the outside world, it webbed out in three directions to several key cities in Xinjiang: Ürümqi in the north, Korla in the center, Hotan in the south, and Kashgar in the west.

MONGOLIA

Anxi
Dunhuang
Mogao Caves Jiayuguan
Zhangye
INNER MONGOL
Har Hu
Jinchang
Yinchuan
QAIDAM PENDI
Qinghai Hu
Xining
NINGXIA
Great Wall
Golmud
Lanzhou
SHAN
QINGHAI
Kumbum Monastary
GANSU
3
Yellow
2 Tianshui
Jinsha Jiang (Yangzi)
Maijishan Grottoes
1 Xi'an
HEN
SHAANXI
SICHUAN
HUBEI

Kashgar bazaar.

4 Xinjiang: Chinese in name only, Xinjiang is a land of vast deserts and ancient Silk Road settlements. The region's remote western city of Kashgar is about equidistant with Baghdad as it is Beijing. Wander too far west and you'll find yourself in Afghanistan. The region is populated by Uyghurs, a Turkic-speaking Muslim people that form China's largest minority group.

THE SILK ROAD PLANNER

Northwestern Fare

The cuisine in Shaanxi revolves around noodles and *jiaozis* (dumplings) rather than rice, and lamb is the meat of choice. A Xian Muslim specialty is *yangroù paomo*, a spicy lamb soup poured over broken pieces of flat bread. Other popular Muslim street foods are *heletiao* (buckwheat noodles marinated in soy sauce and garlic) and *roùjiamo* (pita bread filled with beef or pork and topped with cumin and green peppers).

Gansu and Qinghai don't offer much in the way of culinary surprises, but in Xinjiang, where temperatures can reach scorching levels, you'll find a variety of local ices, ice cream, and *durap* (a refreshing mix of yogurt, honey, and crushed ice). Traditional Uyghur dishes like *bamian* (lamb and vegetables served over noodles) and *kevap* (spicy lamb kebabs) are ubiquitous. Grapes from Turpan and melons from the oasis town of Hami are famous throughout China.

The Jade Road

The residents of Xinjiang are apt to point out that the Silk Road isn't the first road they knew. That honor goes to the "Jade Road," which was established nearly 7,000 years ago. Running from Hotan into today's Qinghai and Gansu provinces, the Jade Road was the artery for Xinjiang's legendary white jade trade. Primarily mined from the Hotan River, Xinjiang jade comes in a number of hues, although small white stones with a reddish-brown exterior are the most highly valued.

Sensous and smooth to the touch, this "lamb's fat jade" is cloudy with translucent qualities. Chinese emperors have craved it for centuries. Good places to hunt around for all manner of jade in Ürümqi include the swirling International Grand Bazaar and the Xinjiang Antique Store.

Visitors who wish to know more about this region's heady history of jade, silk, and more should visit the Xinjiang Autonomous Region Museum. Here's a quick tip: buy fast. The availability of quality jade has dropped in recent years, and scientists fear the precious stone is being mined to exhaustion.

Treasures of Shaanxi

Shaanxi gave birth to 13 major Chinese dynasties. From its bosom came the Zhou, Qin, Han and Tang states. The latter dynasty, the Tang, is considered to be China's Golden Age. In fact, many of the dynasties forged along the banks of the Yellow River in Shaanxi created long-lasting cultural trends that still define China to this day.

For a taste of this central province's rich past, consider first hitting the Shaanxi History Museum. Once you've steeped yourself in its chronology, local "must-see" desinations like Xian's Drum Towers, Muslim Quarter, and Great Goose Pagodas will make much more sense. So, too, will the awe-inspiring army of terra-cotta warriors at the tomb of China's first emperor. True fans of history can even make the trip to China's own "Valley of the Kings" near Xianyang.

Qinghai Surprise

With the opening of the Qinghai-Tibet Railway in 2006, Qinghai is now seeing an increase in activity. One of the railway's most scenic stretches cuts through the Kunlun and Tanggula mountains along the Tibetan border. Visitors can now marvel at the region's stunning scenery from the safety of train cars featuring free oxygen supplies. The infusion of tourists is naturally affecting how one experiences the Silk Road. Now. Travelers in Xining (or Lanzhou or Xian, for that matter) can flip a coin and decide to head farther west to Xinjiang or break south to Lhasa.

Should you be tempted to join the throngs headed for Tibet, make sure to take in a few of Qinghai's must-see sites beforehand. The capital city of Xining itself is worth getting to know. The city is small and friendly by Chinese standards, with a bit of charming Tibetan flair. Take note of the city's nearest ethereal retreats. On the northwest edge of the city is the famed North Monastery, a solemn Daoist destination. The Kumbum Monastery is a testament of Tibetan tranquillity. For a truly heavenly display, crane your neck skyward at Bird Island on Qinghai Lake several hundred miles to the west of Xining. Your soul will be richer for it.

WHAT IT COSTS In Yuan

RESTAURANTS				
$$$$	$$$	$$	$	¢
over 165	100–165	50–99	25–49	under 25

HOTELS				
$$$$	$$$	$$	$	¢
over 1,800	1,400–1,800	1,100–1,399	700–1,099	under 700

Restaurant prices are for a main course, excluding tax and tips. Hotel prices are for a standard double room, including taxes.

How's the Weather?

The best time to visit the region is from early May to late October, when the weather is warm. This is also the high tourist season, when many festivals take place and the land is in bloom with grasses and flowers.

Spring is a double-edged sword. At no other time of the year (and in no other part of China) do wildflowers make such a colorful, riotous appearance on the mountain meadows, rolling grasslands, and lush valleys. That said, much of northwest China is desert and spring is when warm winds whip across the land causing dust devils and sandstorms. By May most of the fury has died down.

Dry, sunny summers provide blue skies and long days, optimal for exploring and photographing the region. Lunchtime, however, can be insufferably hot and most tourists follow the locals' lead in taking a midday break. If you plan to explore mountain areas, summer gives the most access and fluctuates between chilly nights and warm, bright days.

Clear skies last well into fall, usually through October. The changing leaves explode into a symphony of yellow, orange, and red, once again creating ideal opportunities for the shutterbug. Cold weather, however, can come quickly and unannounced. If you visit in fall, bring an extra set of warm clothes.

Winter brings sub-freezing temperatures, and a noticeable dearth of tourists and travelers. Although solitude may have its own charms, many interesting sights close for the off-season, making it the least desirable time to visit.

9

SHAANXI

By Michael
Manning

Shaanxi has more often than not been the axis around which the Chinese universe revolved. It was here more than 6,000 years ago that Neolithic tribes established the earliest permanent settlements in China. In 221 BC, the territories of the Middle Kingdom were unified here under the Qin Dynasty (from which the word "China" is derived). Propitiously located at the eastern terminus of the famed Silk Road, Shaanxi later gave birth to one of the ancient world's greatest capitals, Chang'an, a city enriched financially and culturally by the influence of foreign trade.

But nothing lasts forever: as the Silk Road fell into disuse and China isolated itself from the outside world, Shaanxi's fortunes declined. Flood, drought, and political unrest among the province's large Muslim population made Shaanxi a very difficult place to live for most of the past 1,000 years. It's only since the founding of the People's Republic in 1949 that the area has regained some of its former prominence, both as a center of industry and as a travel destination. It's a telling sign of Shaanxi's long separation from the rest of China that the government policy of "developing the west" has set the province squarely in its sights, despite the fact that the capital city of Xi'an is merely 13 hours by train from Beijing.

Xian

Many first-time visitors to Xian are seeking the massive terra-cotta army standing guard over the tomb of China's first emperor. Whether or not that experience lives up to their expectations, one thing is certain: Xian has so much to offer that it would be a pity not to spend at least a few days exploring the city.

Xian was known in ancient times as Chang'an (meaning Long Peace) and was one of the largest and most cultured cities in the world. During the Tang Dynasty—considered by many Chinese to be the nation's cultural pinnacle—the city became an important center for the arts. Not surprisingly, this creative explosion coincided with the height of trade on the Silk Road, bringing Turkish fashions to court and foreigners from as far away as Persia and Rome. Although the caravan drivers of yesteryear have long since turned to dust, their memory lives on in the variety of faces seen in Xian.

Exploring Xian

❿ Banpo Matriarchal Clan Village (Banpo Bowuguan). About 5 km (3 mi) east of the city are the remains of a 6,000-year-old Yangshao village, including living quarters, a pottery-making center, and a graveyard. The residents of this matriarchal community of 200 to 300 people survived mainly by fishing, hunting, and gathering, although there is ample evidence of attempts at animal domestication and organized agriculture.

Stone farming and hunting implements, domestic objects, and pottery inscribed with ancient Chinese characters are all on display in small galleries near the entrance. There's also enough left in the ground—pottery, building foundations, and a few skeletons—to make things interesting. The archaeological site has been under renovation since 2003, with no end in sight. With any luck, English descriptions will show up sooner rather than later. Unless you're interested in documenting one of China's great tourist oddities, avoid the awful model village that sits in a state of semi-disrepair toward the rear of the property. ✉ *139 Banpo Lu, off Changdong Lu* ☎ *029/8353–2482* 💲 *Y20* ⊙ *Mon.–Sat. 8–6.*

3 **Bell Tower** (Zhonglou). Xian's most recognizable structure, the Bell Tower was built in the late 14th century to mark what was then the center of the city. Remember its location so you can use it as a reference point. The tower marks the point where Xida Jie (West Main Street) becomes Dongda Jie (East Main Street) and Bei Dajie (North Main Street) becomes Nanda Jie (South Main Street). To reach the tower, which stands isolated in the middle of a traffic circle, use any of eight entrances to the underground passageway. Once inside the building, you'll see Ming Dynasty bells on display. Concerts are given six times daily (9, 10:30, 11:30, 2:30, 4, and 5:30). For Y5 you can make your own music by ringing a copy of the large iron bell that gives the tower its name. Don't miss the panoramic views of the city from the 3rd-floor balcony. ✉ *Junction of Dongda Jie, Xida Jie, Bei Dajie, and Nanda Jie* ☎ *No phone* 💲 *Y20, Y30 includes admission to Drum Tower* ⊙ *Apr.–Oct., daily 8:30 AM–9:30 PM; Nov.–Mar., daily 8:30 AM–6 PM.*

9 **Big Wild Goose Pagoda** (Da Yan Ta). This impressively tall pagoda lies 4 km (2½ mi) southeast of South Gate, on the grounds of the still-active Temple of Thanksgiving (Da Ci'en Si). The pagoda was constructed adjacent to the Tang palace in the 7th century AD to house scriptures brought back from India by monk Xuan Zang. It's been rebuilt numerous times since then, most recently during the Qing Dynasty, in Ming style. If you can make it here in the late afternoon, the pagoda and temple look radiant under the setting sun's golden light. A park and huge plaza were constructed around the temple in 2004, and locals gather here after work to fly kites, stroll hand in hand, and practice tai chi. The main entrance gate to the temple is found on the plaza's southern edge. ✉ *Yanta Lu* ☎ *029/8525–5141* 💲 *Y25; additional Y20 to climb the pagoda* ⊙ *Daily 8–6.*

5 **Culture Street** (Wenhua Jie). Located just inside the city wall, this lively pedestrian street is lined with houses that have been rebuilt in traditional Ming style. Shops sell a wide variety of wares, including charming calligraphy and watercolors. If you're coming from South Gate, halfway down the first block you'll find Guanzhong Academy, built in 1609. Take a peek through the gates, as entrance is forbidden. Continue east along the city wall to reach the Forest of Stone Tablets. ⊹ *1 block north of South Gate.*

2 **Drum Tower** (Gulou). Originally built in 1380, this 111-foot-high Ming Dynasty building—which used to hold the alarm drums for the imperial city—marks the southern end of Xian's Muslim Quarter. Various ancient drums are on display inside the building, and concerts are given daily at 9, 10:30, 11:30, 2:30, 4, and 5:30. After passing through the tower's massive base, turn left down a small side street called Hua Jue

Northwestern China and the Silk Road

Lake Balkash

KAZAKHSTAN

Alakol

Altay

Karamay

JUNGGAR PENDI

Bishkek

Almaty

Ysyk-Kol

KYRGYZSTAN

Shihezi

Changji

Ürümqi

Heavenly Lake

Bezeklik Thousand Buddha Caves

Qi

Grape Valley

Turpan

Torugart Pass

TIEN SHAN

Aksu

City of Jiaohe Ruins

Artux

Sugun

Kashgar
see detail map

Mor Ta

Korla

Atsana-Karakhoja Tombs

City of Gaochang Ruins

Tashkurgan

XINJIANG UYGUR ZIZHIQU

TAKLIMAKAN PENDI

Lop Nur

KARAKORAM

Hotan

Qiemo

ALTUN SHAN

Karakorum Shankou Pass

KUNLUN SHAN

KASHMIR

QINGSHAN GAOYUAN
(TIBETIAN PLATEAU)

XIZANG ZIZHIQU
(TIBET AUTONOMOUS REGION)

Tanggula Mountain Pass

TANGGULA SHAN

GANGDISE SHAN

H I M A L A Y A S

INDIA

NEPAL

Lhasa

0   150 mi

0   150 km

Kathmandu

Xiang to find everything from shadow puppets to Mao memorabilia—truly a souvenir heaven. After clearing that gauntlet, you'll find yourself deep inside the Muslim Quarter at the entrance to the Great Mosque. ✉ *Bei Yuan Men, 1 block west of the Bell Tower* ☎ *No phone* 🎟 *Y20, Y30 includes admission to Bell Tower* ☉ *Apr.–Oct., daily 8:30 AM–9:30 PM; Nov.–Mar., daily 8:30 AM–6 PM.*

★ ❹ **Forest of Stone Tablets Museum** (Xian Beilin). As the name suggests, there is no shortage here of historical stone tablets engraved with content ranging from descriptions of administrative projects to artistic renditions of landscape, portraiture, and calligraphy. One of the world's first dictionaries and a number of Tang Dynasty classics are housed here. One tablet, known as the Popular Nestorian Stela, dates from AD 781 and records the interaction between the emperor and a traveling Nestorian priest. After presenting the empire with translated Nestorian Christian texts, the priest was allowed to open a church in Xian. English descriptions are rare. ✉ *15 Sanxue Jie, end of Culture St.* 🎟 *Y30* ☉ *Mar.–Nov., daily 8:15–6:45; Dec.–Feb., daily 8:15–5:15.*

❶ **Great Mosque** (Da Qingzhen Si). This lushly landscaped mosque with four graceful courtyards may have been established as early as AD 742, during the Tang Dynasty, but the remaining buildings date mostly from the 18th century. Amazingly, it was left standing during the Cultural Revolution. Stone tablets mark the various pavilions, often bearing inscriptions in both Chinese and Ara-

> ## WORD OF MOUTH
>
> "We really enjoyed Xi'an. I'm glad we spent the time we did there. But if you only want to see the warriors and the museum, you'll be fine with only one day."
> –cactuslady.

bic. Be sure to look above the doors and gates: there are some remarkable designs, including three-dimensional Arabic script that makes the stone look as malleable as cake frosting. Non-Muslims are not allowed in the prayer hall, as the mosque is still an active place of worship. The place is a bit hard to find. After passing through the Drum Tower, follow a small curving market street called Hua Jue Xiang on the left. (You'll see an English sign posted on a brick wall next to the street's entrance reading GREAT MOSQUE.) When you reach a small intersection, the mosque's entrance is on the left. The bustling **Muslim Quarter** surrounding the mosque is the center of the city's Hui (Chinese Muslim) community. It's a great place to wander, and aside from the wonderful selection of souvenirs found near the mosque's entrance you'll find endless food stalls offering everything from cold sesame noodles to panfried dumplings to spicy mutton kebabs. ✉ *30 Hua Jue Xiang* 🎟 *Y12* ☉ *May–Sept., daily 8–7; Oct.–Apr., daily 8–5.*

❽ **Shaanxi History Museum** (Shaanxi Lishi Bowuguan). Although museums
Fodor's Choice in China are often underwhelming, this is a notable exception. The works
★ in this imposing two-story structure, built in 1991, range from crude Paleolithic stone tools to gorgeously sculpted ceramics from the Tang Dynasty. Several terra-cotta warriors taken from the tombs outside town are on display. The exhibits, which have English descriptions, leave

no doubt that China has long been the world's most advanced culture. ⊠ *91 Xiaozai Dong Lu* ☎ *029/8525–4727* 🖅 *Y35* ⊙ *Daily 8:30–6.*

★ ➐ **Small Goose Pagoda** (Xiao Yan Ta). Once part of the 7th-century AD Jianfu Temple, this 13-tier pagoda was built by Empress Wu Zetian in 707 to honor her predecessor, Emperor Gao Zong. The pagoda housed Buddhist texts brought back from India by the pilgrim Yiqing in the 8th century. A tremendous earthquake in 1555 lopped off the top two stories of what was originally a 15-story structure; climbing to the top lets you examine the damage. The shaded grounds surrounding the pagoda are pleasant, and the pavilions are a good place to relax on a hot day. ⊠ *Youyi Xilu, west of Nanguan Zhengjie* ☎ *029/8525–3455* 🖅 *Y18; additional Y10 to climb the pagoda* ⊙ *Daily 8–8.*

➏ **South Gate** (Nanmen). This is the most impressive of the 13 gates leading through Xian's 39-foot-high city walls. This was the original site of Tang Dynasty fortifications; the walls you see today were built at the beginning of the Ming Dynasty. Recent repairs mean you can travel the entire 14 km (9 mi) around the city on the top of the wall. The trip by bike takes about 2 hours, but the views are worth the effort. Rental bikes are Y15 for 90 minutes. An open-air shuttle bus costs Y50. ⊠ *Nanda Jie* 🖅 *Y40* ⊙ *Daily 8 AM–9 PM.*

Around Xian

Famen Temple (Famen Si), originally built in the 3rd century AD, was the site of an amazing find during renovations in 1981. A sacred crypt housing four of Sakyamani Buddha's finger bones was discovered to hold more than 25,000 coins and 1,000 sacrificial objects of jade, gold, and silver. Many of these objects are now on display in the on-site museum. ⊠ *125 km (80 mi) west of Xian in the town of Famen* 🖅 *Y60* ⊙ *Daily 8–6.*

Huaqing Hot Springs, a pleasure palace during the Tang Dynasty, gets mixed reviews from visitors. For history buffs, the site contains General Chiang Kai-shek's living quarters, where the infamous Xian Incident unfolded. You'll probably be happier spending your time on **Li Shan,** the small mountain directly behind Huaqing Hot Springs. The slopes are home to the spot where Chiang was captured, as well as China's first beacon tower and a number of small temples. Many people prefer to take the cable car to the top and walk down. Tickets (Y25 one-way, Y45 round-trip) can be purchased at the hot springs; look for the blue metal gate just west of the ticket booth. ⊠ *30 km (19 mi) east of Xian in the town of Lintong* 🖅 *Y45 entrance* ⊙ *Daily 8–6.*

Fodor'sChoice **Terracotta Warriors Museum** (Bingmayong Bowuguan). Discovered in ★ 1974 by farmers digging a well, this archaeological site includes more than 7,000 terra-cotta soldiers standing guard over the tomb of Qin Shihuang, the first emperor of a unified China. The warriors, 1,000 of which have been painstakingly pieced together, come in various forms: archers, infantry, charioteers, and cavalry. Incredibly, each of the life-size statues is unique, including different mustaches, beards, and hairstyles. An exhibition hall displays artifacts unearthed from distant sections of the tomb, including two magnificently crafted miniature bronze chariots. ⊠ *30 km (19 mi) east of Xian in the town of Lintong* 🖅 *Mar.–Nov.,*

9

Y90; Dec.–Feb., Y65 ⊙ Daily 8:30–5:30.

The **Tomb of the First Qin Emperor**—consisting mainly of a large burial mound—is a fairly disappointing visit these days, but must have been impressive in its heyday. According to ancient records, the underground palace took more than 40 years to build. You can climb to the top of the burial mound for a view of the surrounding countryside, although most visitors hurry off to see the Terracotta Warriors Museum after watching a mildly amusing ceremony honoring the emperor who united China. ⊠ *30 km (19 mi) east of Xian in the town of Lintong* 🎫 *Y40* ⊙ *Apr.–Oct., daily 7–7; Nov.–Mar., daily 8–6.*

Xianyang City Museum, formerly a Confucian temple, now houses 3,000 miniature terra-cotta warriors unearthed in 1965. ⊠ *25 km (16 mi) northwest of Xian in the city of Xianyang* 🎫 *Y20* ⊙ *Daily 8–6.*

Tours

Every hotel offers its own guided tours of the area, usually dividing them into eastern area, western area, and city tours. Most tour operators have special English-language tour guides. Lots of tours are available, and prices often vary wildly.

Don't be afraid to bargain, as you might get a much better deal. And check more than one company to make sure you are being charged the going rate. One of the best places to comparison shop is on the 2nd floor of the Bell Tower Hotel, where several tour companies are vying for your business. Try Golden Bridge first, but if you're not satisfied there are other good options. All of them are open until late in the evening.

🔢 Tour-Operator Recommendations **CITS** ⊠ 48 Changan Bei Lu ☎ 029/8539-9999 ⊠ Bell Tower Hotel, 110 Nanda Jie ☎ 029/8760-0227. **Golden Bridge Travel** ⊠ Bell Tower Hotel, 110 Nanda Jie ☎ 029/8760-0219.

EASTERN TOUR By far the most popular option from Xian, tours that head east of the city usually visit the Tomb of the First Qin Emperor, the Terracotta Warriors Museum, and the Huaqing Hot Springs, all located in the town of Lintong. Many tours also stop at the Banpo Matriarchal Clan Village in eastern Xian. The China International Travel Service (CITS) offers this tour for Y350, which includes all admission tickets and an English-speaking guide. The journey takes most of the day; plan on leaving after breakfast and returning in time for dinner.

If you don't want to spend money on a guide, you're better off taking one of the cheap buses that leave constantly from the parking lot between the Xian Train Station and the Jiefang Hotel. The 90-minute journey costs Y10. Make sure the driver knows where you want to be dropped off. To travel between any of the sites in Lintong, a taxi should cost between Y5 and Y10 (although drivers ask foreigners for Y15). To get back to Xian, simply wait along the road for a bus headed to the city.

WESTERN TOUR Less popular than the eastern tour, this excursion varies wildly from operator to operator. Be sure to find out what you're getting for the money. Amateur archaeologists and would-be tomb raiders will hardly be able to tear themselves away from the sites in what's been called China's own Valley of the Kings; others will appreciate some of the relics, but may tire of looking at what appear to be mounds of dirt or holes in the ground.

Of the 18 imperial tombs on the plains west of Xian, a list of the best should include the Qian Tomb, resting place of Tang Dynasty Empress Wu Zetian, China's only female sovereign. A number of her relatives—many sentenced to death by her own decree—are entombed in the surrounding area. The tomb of Prince Yi De contains some beautifully restored frescoes. Other stops on the western tour might include the Xianyang City Museum in Xianyang and the Famen Temple in Famen. CITS offers a customizable Western Tour for between Y400 and Y600 per person. Again, plan on spending the whole day visiting these sites.

Hua Shan. A few hours east of Xian lies one of China's five sacred mountains, a traditional watercolor come to life. The 7,218-foot mountain has lovely scenery, including pines reminiscent of a Dr. Seuss creation and sheer granite walls that rise shockingly out of the surrounding plains. The five peaks of Hua Shan reminded ancient visitors of flower petals, hence the name; translated it means "Flower Mountain." Climbing the mountain is not a trip for the fainthearted: unless you're an Olympic athlete, hiking the main trail to the top will take a good seven to nine hours, some of it along narrow passes on sheer cliffs. Thankfully, there's a cable car ride to North Peak that brings you most of the way up the trail (Y60 one-way, Y110 round-trip). Don't worry about looking like a wimp; there's plenty of climbing left to do from the cable car terminal. From Xian, you can take a train (3 hours, Y12) to Huashan Village, although you'll inconveniently disembark 15km away in the neighboring town of Mengyuan; frequent minibuses (Y5) link the two places. A better choice is one of the tour buses that leave hourly every morning from the parking lot in front of the Jiefang Hotel, across from the train station. Round-trip bus tickets can be had for Y80, although they'd prefer you purchase the inclusive package with all necessary tickets for Y310. ✉ *Y100 entrance; Y60 one-way/Y110 round-trip cable car; Y20 round-trip minibus from Hua Shan Village to the cable car* ☉ *cable car operates daily 7–7.*

Where to Stay & Eat

$–$$$$ ✕ **Tang Dynasty.** Don't confuse the cuisine served in the Tang Dynasty's
Fodor'sChoice popular dinner theater with the specialties available at the separate restaurant. While the former serves mediocre, tourist-friendly fare, the latter specializes in Tang Dynasty–imperial cuisine—a taste you're not likely to find back home at your local Chinese restaurant. Locals praise the abalone and other fresh fish dishes as the finest in Xian. For an unusual evening, book seats at the 7 or 9:30 performances of Tang Dynasty singing and dancing. Time your meal so that you don't miss a minute of the colorful spectacle. ✉ *75 Changan Bei Lu* ☎ *029/8782–2222* ⊟ *AE, MC, V.*

★ $–$$$$ ✕ **Shang Palace Restaurant.** All of Xian's top hotels have elegant eateries, but Shang Palace deserves special mention for dishes that are authentic but approachable. On the menu, classics like honey barbecued

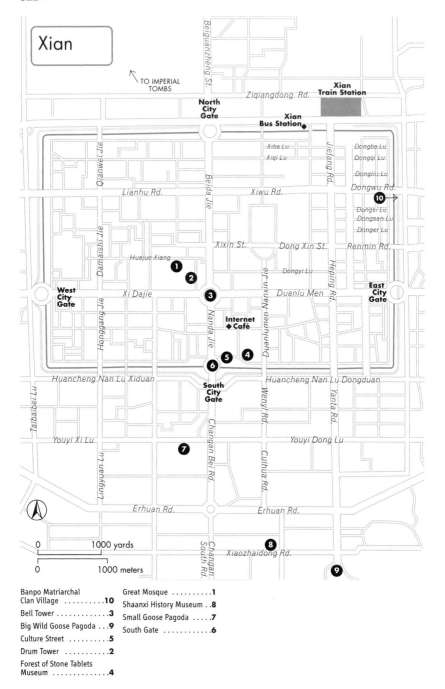

Xian

TO IMPERIAL
TOMBS

Beiguanzheng St.

Xian
Train Station

Ziqiangdong Rd.

North
City
Gate

Xian
Bus Station

Xiba Lu

Qianwei Jie

Jiefang Rd.

Dongba Lu
Dongai Lu

Xiqi Lu

Dongliu Lu

Lianhu Rd.

Xiwu Rd.

Dongwu Rd.

10

Damaishi Jie

Beida Jie

Dongsi Lu
Dongsan Lu
Donger Lu

Xixin St.

Dong Xin St.

Renmin Rd.

Huajue Xiang

1

Dongyi Lu

2

West
City
Gate

Xi Dajie

3

Internet
◆ Café

Duanlu Men

East
City
Gate

Honggang Jie

Nanda Jie

Duanlu-Nanxin Jie

Heping Rd.

5

4

6

Taibaibei Lu

Huancheng Nan Lu Xiduan

South
City
Gate

Huancheng Nan Lu Dongduan

Youyi Xi Lu

7

Wenyi Rd.

Youyi Dong Lu

Lingyuan Lu

Changan Bei Rd.

Cuihua Rd.

Yanta Rd.

Erhuan Rd.

Erhuan Rd.

0   1000 yards

Changan South Rd.

8

0   1000 meters

Xiaozhaidong Rd.

9

Banpo Matriarchal
Clan Village **10**

Great Mosque **1**

Shaanxi History Museum . .**8**

Bell Tower **3**

Small Goose Pagoda **7**

Big Wild Goose Pagoda . . .**9**

South Gate **6**

Culture Street **5**

Drum Tower **2**

Forest of Stone Tablets
Museum **4**

pork and stir-fried chicken with chili sit alongside less familiar dishes like shark's fin soup with chicken and bamboo. As you dine, musicians pluck away in traditional costumes. If you have questions about a dish you've been wanting to try, this is the place to ask; most of the staff here speaks some English. ⊠ *Shangri-La Golden Flower Hotel, 8 Changle Xi Lu* ☎ *029/8325–1000* ▭ *No credit cards.*

¢–$$ ✕ **Lao Sun Jia Restaurant.** This traditional, family-run affair serves some of the best local Islamic specialties in lamb and beef. The decor isn't special, but the food is popular with Xian's large Muslim community. A few famous offerings, such as the roasted leg of lamb or the spicy spareribs of sheep, are a bit pricey, but most dishes are inexpensive. Ask for an English menu. ⊠ *364 Dongda Jie, near the corner of Duanlu Men* ☎ *029/8721–6929* ▭ *No credit cards.*

¢–$$ ✕ **De Fa Chang Restaurant.** If you think dumplings are just occasional snack food, think again. De Fa Chang, one of Xian's most famous restaurants, is known for its dumpling banquet. Don't miss the panfried *guoqie,* stuffed with pork and chives. For the dumpling banquet, head upstairs and choose between the preset menus. Considerably cheaper à la carte dishes can be found downstairs; just grab a plate as a cart passes by your table and be ready to pay on the spot. With red lanterns hanging outside, this four-story behemoth attracts large groups of locals, who sometimes exit singing. ⊠ *Xi Dajie, north side of Bell Tower Sq.* ☎ *029/8721–4060* ▭ *No credit cards.*

¢–$ **Prosperity & Fortune Restaurant** (Tong Sheng Xiang). Don't worry about ordering at this centrally located Muslim restaurant: simply point to a picture on the wall or browse the counter in front of the open kitchen. The most popular dish here is *yangrou paomo,* a delicious lamb soup into which you break small bits of bread. If you feel like having something special, head upstairs for a pricier selection; a whole roasted lamb will set you back Y700. ⊠ *North side of Bell Tower Sq.* ☎ *No phone* ▭ *No credit cards.*

¢–$$ ✕ **Xian Fanzhuang.** This restaurant specializes in local foods with a Muslim flavor as well as "small eats"–street food spruced up for the visitor. Suited business executives and T-shirt-clad college students alike head to the bustling first-floor dining room for the all-you-can-eat buffet (Y22). An adjacent entrance leads to a second-floor restaurant, where more exotic and expensive dishes—algae flavored with orchid, for example—are expertly prepared. An English menu is available. ⊠ *Xian Hotel, 298 Dongda Jie* ☎ *029/8727–3185* ▭ *No credit cards.*

$$$–$$$$ ⊡ **Hyatt Regency.** Bill and Hillary Clinton stayed at this luxury hotel in the heart of the city when they visited in 1998. Near the most popular sights, it is walking distance from the Bell Tower and the East Gate. The beds are extremely comfortable and the large windows provide great views of the city. The guest rooms, however, are smaller than at other comparably priced hotels; chirping birds in the atrium lobby can be annoying when you're trying to fall asleep. ⊠ *158 Dongda Jie, 710001* ☎ *029/8723–1234* 🖶 *029/8721–6799* ⊕ *www.hyatt.com* 🗪 *382 rooms, 22 suites* ♢ *2 restaurants, café, in-room safes, minibars, in-*

9

room broadband, tennis court, gym, bar, nightclub, dry cleaning, laundry service, business services, meeting room, airport shuttle ▭ AE, MC, V.

$$$–$$$$ 🏨 **Shangri-La Golden Flower.** One of the most luxurious hotels in the city,
Fodor's Choice the Shangri-La maintains the chain's usual strict quality. The service here
★ is top-of-the-line in every way, and the English-speaking staff is helpful and friendly. You'll find yourself wondering how they manage to tidy up your room and turn down your bed during the half hour you spent swimming laps in the indoor pool. The hotel is 15 minutes northeast of the city center. *⊠ 8 Changle Xi Lu, 710032 ☎ 029/8323–2981, 800/ 8942–5050 in the U.S. ⌨ 029/8323–5477 ⊕ www.shangri-la.com ➥ 389 rooms, 57 suites ⌂ 2 restaurants, in-room safes, minibars, in-room broadband, indoor pool, gym, 2 bars, nightclub, business services, meeting room ▭ AE, MC, V.*

$$$ 🏨 **Sheraton.** This is a joint venture with high-quality standards and colorfully decorated rooms. Unfortunately, it's 20 minutes west of the city center, making it far from the most popular tourist sites. Still, it's a fine choice if other hotels are booked up. The croissants at breakfast are the best in Xian. *⊠ 262 Fenghao Dong Lu, 710001 ☎ 029/ 8426–1888 ⌨ 029/8426–2188 ⊕ www.starwoodhotels.com ➥ 438 rooms, 17 suites ⌂ 4 restaurants, in-room safes, minibars, in-room broadband, pool, gym, bar, business services, travel services ▭ AE, MC, V.*

★ **$–$$** 🏨 **Bell Tower Hotel.** Relatively inexpensive compared to other hotels in its class, the very popular Bell Tower has spacious, airy rooms with views overlooking downtown Xian. Located directly across from the Bell Tower, this hotel has a great location that puts you within walking distance of many tourist sites. On the 2nd floor, you can compare rates offered by three experienced travel agencies, all competing aggressively for your business. Rooms at the front of the building are more expensive because they have views of the Bell Tower, but some visitors are disturbed by noise from the traffic. *⊠ 110 Nanda Jie, 710001 ☎ 029/ 8760–0000 ⌨ 029/8727–1217 ✐ belltower@ihw.com.cn ➥ 309 rooms, 11 suites ⌂ 2 restaurants, in-room safes, minibars, in-room broadband, bar, babysitting, dry cleaning, laundry service, business services, meeting room, travel services ▭ AE, MC, V.*

$ 🏨 **Howard Johnson Ginwa Plaza.** Don't look for the familiar orange roof here. This is a five-star operation rivaling the best in the city, and is conveniently located just outside the city walls near South Gate. Rooms are outfitted with top-quality European-style furnishings and feature separate workspaces that are much appreciated by travelers. *⊠ 18 Huancheng Nanlu, 710068 ☎ 029/8842–1111 ⌨ 029/8842–9999 ⊕ www.hojochina.com ➥ 324 rooms ⌂ 4 restaurants, in-room safes, minibars, in-room broadband, hair salon, spa, shops, laundry service, business services ▭ AE, MC, V.*

¢ 🏨 **Jiefang.** Catering mostly to Chinese guests, this hotel has relatively clean but rather small rooms. The service is lackadaisical at best. The location, across from the train station, is convenient if you're arriving late at night. ⊠ *181 Jiefang Lu, 710005* ☎ *029/8769–8881* ⊟ *029/ 8769–8666* ⤶ *316 rooms, 3 suites* ⚒ *3 restaurants, hair salon, massage, sauna, laundry service, business services, travel services* ⊟ *No credit cards.*

¢ ⊞ **Liging.** A decent choice if you're looking for something cheap and centrally located, the Liging has rooms that are comfortable, if slightly dingy. Be sure to ask to see a few before you decide. The service is friendly. ⊠ *6 Xida Jie, 710002* ☎ *029/8728–8731 or 029/8721–8895* ⤶ *100 rooms, 3 suites* ⚒ *Restaurant, business services, travel services* ⊟ *No credit cards.*

¢ ⊞ **Wen Yuan Hotel.** Just east of the Drum Tower, this hotel is a good compromise for those who want something inexpensive but not entirely without charm. Rooms here are considerably nicer than what's available elsewhere for the same price. A few of the rooms overlook Xian's Muslim Quarter. ⊠ *45 Xi Dajie, 710001* ☎ *029/8310–3000* ⊟ *029/ 8310–3249* ⤶ *220 rooms, 18 suites* ⚒ *2 restaurants, karaoke, laundry service, dry cleaning, hair salon, business services* ⊟ *AE, MC, V* �|◎| *BP.*

Nightlife & the Arts

One of the busiest parts of town in the evening is the **Muslim Quarter,** where crowds converge to shop, stroll, and eat virtually every night of the week. This is a top spot in town to check out the local color by night. Street-side chefs fire up the stoves and whip up tasty dishes, vendors ply the crowded lanes peddling their wares, and locals and tourists alike jostle in the frenetic pace. If you want to have a great night without spending a lot of money, this is the place.

The impressive song and dance performance at **Tang Dynasty** (⊠ 75 Changan Bei Lu ☎ 029/8782–2222) is the city's most popular evening of entertainment for foreign visitors. Shows begin at 7 and 9:30. The latest European and Japanese techno music draws crowds to **1+1 Club** (⊠ 285 Dongda Jie ☎ 029/8726–3128) even on weekdays. If you're fond of chest-thumping bass, this is the place for you.

Shopping

Predictably, Xian is overloaded with terra-cotta souvenirs. You can get imitation terra-cotta warriors at virtually every tourist site in town. If you want to pick up lots of these replicas for friends back home, try the aggressive vendors outside the Terracotta Warriors Museum; many smaller statues can be had for only Y1.

There is more to buy in Xian, however. On the alley leading to the Great Mosque, the **Hua Jue Xiang Market** (⊠ Hua Jue Xiang) is one of the best places to find interesting souvenirs. Expect the antique you're eyeing to be fake, no matter how vehemently the vendor insists your find is "genuine Ming Dynasty." The shops along **Culture Street** are filled with carved jade, calligraphy, and Shaanxi folk paintings. Even if you don't buy anything, it's a nice place for a stroll.

Continued on page 632

THE
TERRACOTTA
SOLDIERS

DID YOU KNOW?

The thousands of life-size soldiers include charioteers, cavalrymen, archers, and infantrymen. They're all arranged according to rank and duty—exactly as they would have been for a real-life battle. Each one has individual facial features, including different mustaches, beards, and hairstyles.

In 1974, Shaanxi farmers digging a well accidentally unearthed one of the greatest archaeological finds of the 20th century—the Terracotta Soldiers of Qin Shihuang. Armed with real weapons and accompanied by horses and chariots, the more than 8,000 soldiers buried in Qin's tomb were to be his garrison in the afterlife.

Who was Qin Shihuang?

After destroying the last of his rivals in 221 BC, Qin Shihuang became the first emperor to rule over a unified China. He established a centralized government headquartered near modern-day Xianyang in Shaanxi Province. Unlike the feudal governments of the past under which regional officials developed local bases of power, the new centralized government concentrated all power in the hands of a godlike emperor.

Unfortunately for Qin Shihuang's potential heirs, the emperor's inexhaustible hunger for huge engineering projects created high levels of public unrest. These projects, including a precursor to the Great Wall, his own massive tomb, and numerous roads and canals, required the forced labor of millions of Chinese citizens. In 210 BC, Qin died from mercury poisoning during a failed attempt at making himself immortal. Only four years later, his son was overthrown and killed, bringing an ignominious end to China's first dynasty.

A Thankless Job

The construction of Qin Shihuang's gargantuan tomb complex—which includes the Terracotta Soldiers—was completed by more than 700,000 workers over a period of nearly 40 years. The warriors themselves are believed to have been created in an assembly line process in which sets of legs and torsos were fired separately and later combined with individually sculpted heads. Most workers were unskilled laborers; skilled craftsmen completed more delicate work such as the decoration of the tomb and the molding of heads. The soldiers were then painted with colored lacquer to make them both more durable and realistic. It's believed that all of the workers were buried alive inside the tomb (which hasn't yet been excavated) to keep its location and treasures a secret and protect it from grave robbers.

Discovering the Soldiers

Only five years after the death of Qin Shihuang, looting soldiers set fire to the thick wooden beams supporting the vaults. As wood burned and the structure became unsound, beams and earthen walls came crashing down onto the statues, crushing many soldiers and burying all. In many ways, though, the damage to the vaults was a blessing in disguise. The buried Terracotta Soldiers were forgotten to history, but the lack of oxygen and sunlight preserved the figures for centuries.

Since its rediscovery, only a part of the massive complex has been excavated, and the process of unearthing more warriors and relics continues. No one is sure just how many warriors there are or how far the figures extend beyond the already-excavated 700-foot-by-200-foot section. For the time being, most excavation work has stopped while scientists attempt to develop a method of preserving the figures' colored lacquer, which quickly deteriorates when exposed to oxygen.

VISITING THE SOLDIERS

Be sure to walk around to the rear of Vault 1, which contains most of the figures that have already been unearthed. There you can see archaeologists reassembling the smashed soldiers. Vaults 2 and 3 contain unreconstructed warriors and their weapons and give you an idea of how much work went into presenting Vault 1 as we see it today.

Circle Vision Theater

Before heading to the vaults, stop by this 360-degree movie theater and learn how the army was constructed, destroyed, forgotten, and then rediscovered. Although the film is cheesy, it's nonetheless entertaining and informative. It gives a sense of what the area may have been like 2,200 years ago.

Vault 1

Here you'll find about 6,000 warriors, although only 1,000 have been painstakingly pieced together by archaeologists. The warriors stand in their original pits and can only be seen from the walkways erected around the digs. Those in the front ranks are well shaped and fully outfitted except for their weapons, whose wooden handles have decayed over the centuries (the chrome-plated bronze blades were still sharp upon excavation). Walk around to the rear of the vault where you can see terra-cotta soldiers in various states of reconstruction.

(right) Archaeologists have puzzled together almost 1,000 soldiers.

COLORATION

The colored lacquers that were used not only gave the terra-cotta soldiers a realistic appearance, but also sealed and protected the clay. Unfortunately, upon exposure to oxygen, these thin layers of color become extremely brittle and flake off or crumble to dust. Chinese scientists are devising excavation methods that will preserve the coloration of warriors unearthed in the future.

Ready on one knee with bow in hand, these archers are poised to rise and fire a deadly salvo at a moment's notice.

Every cavalry rider is accompanied by a life-size terra-cotta horse.

THE TERRACOTTA SOLDIERS

9

(top) Unreconstructed warriors in Vault 2. (right) The exhibition is a work of art in progress. (opposite page) Visit the museum to see the warrior detail up close.

Vault 2

This vault offers a glimpse of unreconstructed figures as they emerge from the ground. It has remained mostly undisturbed since 1999 when archaeologists found the first tricolor figures—look closely and you can still see pink on the soldiers' faces and patches of dark red on their armor. As with ancient Greek sculptures, the warriors were originally painted in lifelike colors and with red armor. Around the sides of the vault, you can take a close-up look at excellent examples of soldiers and their weaponry in glass cases.

Vault 3

Sixty-eight soldiers and officers in various states of reconstruction stand in what appears to be a military headquarters. Although the condition of the warriors are similar to those in Vault 2, there is one unique figure: a charioteer standing at the ready, though his wooden chariot has been lost to time.

Qinyong Museum

Near Vault 3, an imposing sand-colored pavilion houses two miniature bronze chariots unearthed in the western section of Qin Shihuang's tomb. Found in 1980, these chariots are intricately detailed with ornate gold and silver ornamentation. In the atrium leading to the bronze chariots, look for a massive bronze urn— it's one of the treasures unearthed by archaeologists in their 1999 excavation of an accessory pit near the still-sealed mausoleum. Other artifacts on display include Tang Dynasty tricolor pottery and Qin jade carvings.

GETTING THERE

Practically every hotel and tour company in Xian arranges bus trips to the Terracotta Soldiers as part of an Eastern Tour package. If you aren't interested in having an English-speaking guide for the day, you can save a lot of money by taking one of the cheap buses (Y10 one-way) that leave for the town of Lintong from the parking lot between Xian's train station and the Jiefang Hotel. The ride to the Terracotta Warriors Museum should take between 90 and 120 minutes.

Opening Hours: Mar.–Nov., daily 8:30–5:30; Dec.–Feb., daily 8:30–5.

Admission: Mar.–Nov., Y90 ; Dec.–Feb., Y65. Price includes movie, access to three vaults, and entrance to the Qinyong Museum.

Phone: 029/8139-9001 (main office); 029/8139-9126 (ticket office).

VISITING TIPS

CAMERAS: You can shoot photographs and videos inside the vaults, a change from previous years when guards brusquely confiscated film upon seeing your camera. You still can't use a flash or tripod, however.

SOUVENIRS: You can buy postcards and other souvenirs in the shops outside the vaults and the Circle Vision Theater. Alternatively, you can face the fearsome gauntlet of souvenir hawkers outside the main gates; miniature replica terra-cotta soldiers can be found here for as little as Y1 each. If you're intimidated by the aggressive touts, however, there's nothing available here that you can't get back in Xian. So be strong, don't look them in the eyes, and most important, never stop walking.

TIME: You'll likely end up spending two to three hours touring the vaults and exhibits at the Terracotta Warriors Museum. The time spent here will probably be part of a long day-tour visiting a number of sites—the Hauqing Hot Springs and possibly the Banpo Matriachal Clan Village—clustered around the small city of Lintong, east of Xian.

RAIDERS OF THE LOST TOMB

Qin started construction on his enormous, richly endowed tomb, said to be booby-trapped with automatic crossbows, almost as soon as he took the throne. According to ancient records, this underground palace contained 100 rivers of flowing mercury as well as ceilings inlaid with precious stones and pearls representing the stars and planets. Interestingly enough, mercury levels in the area's soil are much higher than normal, indicating that

there may be truth to those records. Though the site of the tomb was rediscovered to the east of Xian in 1974 (soon after the Terracotta Soldiers were unearthed), the government didn't touch it because it lacked the sophisticated machinery needed to excavate safely. Authorities also executed any locals foolish enough to attempt a treasure-seeking foray.

In 1999, archaeologists finally began excavations

of the area around the tomb and unearthed some fabulous treasures. They've only scratched the surface, however. Most of the tomb still lies buried. In fact, no one is even certain where its main entrance—reportedly sealed with molten copper—is located. Authorities have delayed further excavations until the tomb can be properly preserved rather than risk damaging what may be China's greatest archaeological site.

Side Trips from Xian

A few hours east of Xian lies **Hua Shan,** one of China's five sacred mountains. The 7,218-foot mountain has lovely scenery, including pines reminiscent of a Dr. Seuss creation and sheer granite walls that rise shockingly out of the surrounding plains. The five peaks of Hua Shan (or Flower Mountain) reminded ancient visitors of flower petals. Climbing the mountain is not a trip for the fainthearted, and unless you're an Olympic athlete, hiking the main trail to the top will take a good seven to nine hours, some of it along narrow passes on sheer cliffs. Thankfully, there's a cable car ride to North Peak that brings you most of the way up the trail (Y60 one-way, Y110 round-trip). Don't worry about looking like a wimp; there's plenty of climbing left to do from the cable car terminal. From Xian, you can take a train (3 hours, Y12) to Huashan Village, although you'll inconveniently disembark 15 km away in the neighboring town of Mengyuan; frequent minibuses (Y5) link the two places. A better choice is one of the tour buses that leave hourly every morning from the parking lot in front of the Jiefang Hotel, across from the train station. Round-trip bus tickets can be had for Y80, although they'd prefer you to purchase the inclusive package with all necessary tickets for Y310. ✉ *Y100 entrance; Y60 one-way/Y110 round-trip cable car; Y20 round-trip minibus from Hua Shan Village to the cable car ☉ cable car operates daily 7–7.*

To & from Xian

1½ hrs by plane or 13½ hrs by train southwest of Beijing; 18 hrs by train west of Shanghai.

Xian's main airport is inconveniently located 50 km (30 mi) northwest of the city center in neighboring Xianyang. Those arriving in Xian by train will disembark north of the old city walls. The train station is close to most hotels, so a taxi should cost less than Y10. Most long-distance buses to Xian will drop you off at Jiefangmen, across from the train station.

SHAANXI ESSENTIALS

Transportation

BY AIR

Xian's Xianyang Airport has many daily flights to and from Beijing, Shanghai, Hong Kong, Guangzhou, Chengdu, Kunming, Dunhuang, and Ürümqi. Other domestic destinations are served, but less frequently. International destinations include Japan, Korea, Singapore, and Thailand.

If your hotel doesn't arrange transportation, you have a few options for getting into the city center. Taxis will take you directly to your hotel, but they'll try to squeeze every last yuan out of your wallet; a decent price is around Y120. Hourly buses are a far more economical option, costing Y25. There are six routes to choose from, so you should let the dispatcher know where you're staying.

🛈 Airport Information **Xian Xianyang Airport** ☎ 029/8879-8450.

BY BUS

Just about every bus in Xian passes through the traffic circle around the Bell Tower. Maps on the side of every bus show the route and list destinations. If your Chinese is shaky, it's best to stick to taxis, which are plentiful and cheap.

The long-distance bus station, located on Jiefang Lu across the street and just west of the train station, has buses to Lanzhou, Xining, and other destinations throughout Shaanxi and Henan. Tourist destinations like the Terracotta Warriors Museum are served from the parking lot between the train station and the Jiefang Hotel.

🛈 Bus Information **Xian Bus Station** ✉ Jiefang Lu ☎ No phone.

BY CAR

Because so many of the sights lie outside the city proper, hiring a taxi or a car and driver gives you the freedom to depart when you like instead of waiting for the rest of the tour. Prices start at about Y800 per day, but vary widely based on the type of vehicle and whether you need an English-speaking guide. Every major hotel can arrange car services.

BY TRAIN

The train station, Xian Huochezhan, lies on the same rail line as Lanzhou (10 hours), Dunhuang (23 hours), and Ürümqi (35 hours). Off the Silk Road, other major stops are Beijing (13½ hours), Shanghai (17 hours), Guangzhou (25 hours), Chengdu (16 hours), and Kunming (34 hours). The foreigners' ticket window upstairs above the main ticket office is open daily 8:30 to 11:30 and 2:30 to 5:30. Be aware that it sometimes closes without explanation. First ask for your destination at one of the windows on the far left, then take the receipt to the other side of the room.

🛈 Train Information **Xian Huochezhan** ✉ Huancheng Bei Lu and Jiefang Lu ☎ 029/ 8213-0402.

Contacts & Resources

EMERGENCIES

In case of an emergency, contact your hotel manager for assistance. If you speak Chinese (or are traveling with someone who does), you can also call emergency numbers.

🛈 Emergency Services **Police** ☎ 110. **Fire Department** ☎ 119.

MONEY MATTERS

If you are heading toward Gansu, Qinghai, or Xinjiang, you may want to stock up on cash here in Xian. The use of foreign debit cards is almost impossible as you head farther west, and you'll only be able to cash traveler's checks at Bank of China main branches in major cities. Cash advances on credit cards are possible at most cash machines.

In Xian, Bank of China branches are open weekdays 8 to 7 and weekends 9 to 4.

🏦 **Bank of China** ✉ 396 Dongda Jie ✉ 157 Jiefang Lu.

INTERNET SERVICES

If you have your own laptop, most major hotels in town provide broadband service for about Y30 per day. The massive Lian Long E-Sports Plaza, on the 3rd floor of the Wen Shang Hotel, has more than 900 computers (and a few pool tables). Conveniently located around the corner from the Bell Tower, this Internet café is cheap (Y1to Y3 per hour) and is open around the clock. You can even order food and drinks from your computer terminal.

🏦 **Lian Long E-Sports Plaza** ✉ Wen Shang Hotel, 45 Xi Dajie ☎ No phone.

VISITOR INFORMATION

Besides booking tours, you can also purchase train tickets at the CITS main office. The smaller office in the Bell Tower Hotel is more accustomed to dealing with foreign travelers.

🏦 **Tourist Information** **CITS** ✉ 48 Changan Bei Lu ☎ 029/8539-9999 ✉ Bell Tower Hotel, 110 Nanda Jie ☎ 029/8760-0227.

GANSU

Gansu is the long, narrow province linking central China with the desert regions of the Northwest. For centuries, as goods were transported through the region, Gansu acted as a conduit between China and the Western world. As merchants made their fortunes from silk and other luxuries, the oasis towns strung along the Silk Road became important trade outposts of the Middle Kingdom. But beyond the massive fortress at Jiayuguan lay the end of the Great Wall, the oasis of Dunhuang, and then perdition. Gansu was the edge of China.

Despite its length, the geography of Gansu is not as variable as you might expect. What has long been the poorest province in China is essentially dry, rugged, and barren. The decline of the Silk Road brought terrible suffering and poverty, from which the area has only very recently begun to recover as tourism boosts the local economy.

Lanzhou

Built on the banks of the Yellow River, the capital of Gansu extends along the base of a narrow gorge whose walls rise to 5,000 feet. A city with a long history, Lanzhou has been nearly ruined by rampant industrialization and is now one of the world's most polluted urban areas. Stay here only as long as it takes to arrange transportation to somewhere more pleasant, like Xiahe or Dunhuang.

Exploring Lanzhou

In **Five Spring Mountain Park** (Wuquanshan Gongyuan) you can sip tea among ancient temples and see impressive views of the city below. The five springs that gave the place its name, unfortunately, have dwindled to a trickle. 🎫 Y5 ⊙ Daily 8–7.

After being modernized, the excellent **Gansu Provincial Museum** (Gansu Sheng Bowuguan) is scheduled to reopen sometime in 2007. The most famous item in the museum's collection is the elegant bronze "Flying Horse," considered a masterpiece of ancient Chinese art. Other notable objects include a silver plate indicating contact between China and Rome more than 2,200 years ago, and wooden tablets used to send messages along the Silk Road. ⊠ *3 Xijin Xilu, across from the Friendship Hotel* 🖃 *Y30* ☉ *Tues.–Sun. 9–5.*

The **Mountain of the White Pagoda Park** (Baitashan Gongyuan), laid out in 1958, covers the slopes on the Yellow River's north bank. It's more of a carnival than a place to relax, but it's a great place for people-watching. ⊠ *Entrance at Zhongshan Qiao, the bridge extending over the Yellow River* 🖃 *Y5* ☉ *Daily 7:30–7:30.*

Tours

Gansu Western Travel Service offers a popular day trip to Thousand Buddha Temple and Grottoes that includes all transportation and insurance for around Y340 per person. The company also offers a number of tours to Xiahe, including a five-day trip that also visits the spectacularly beautiful Tibetan temples at Langmusi on the border with Sichuan. A basic two-day tour from Lanzhou costs between Y500 and Y700 per person, including hotel.

🎫 Tour-Operator Recommendations **Gansu Western Travel Service** ⊠ Lanzhou Hotel, 486 Donggang Xilu, Lanzhou ☎ 0931/885-2929 or 138/9331-8956.

Where to Stay & Eat

Many of the best restaurants in Lanzhou are in its upscale hotels; one to try is Zhong Hua Yuan in the Lanzhou Hotel, where an English menu is available. Another place to find a good meal is along Nongmin Xiang Lu, a street that runs behind the Lanzhou Hotel. In the evening, crowds of locals and tourists throng the busy lane lined with lively vendors hawking their cuisine. This is a great place to try the *roujiamo*, a small sandwich filled with onion, chili, and flash-fried lamb or beef.

$–$$$$ ✕ **Xinhai Restaurant** (Xinhai Dajiudian). One of Lanzhou's finest eateries, Xinhai is surprisingly affordable. Lanzhou specialties as well as Cantonese and Sichuanese dishes are pictured on the menu; you can also order from the text-only English menu. Customers claim that the seafood here is the freshest in the city. ⊠ *499 Dongan Xi Lu, next to Legend Hotel* ☎ *0931/886–6078* ▭ *No credit cards.*

¢–$ ✕ **Chuanwei Wang.** You can often tell a good restaurant by the lack of empty tables; at mealtimes, this Sichuanese eatery is always packed. There's no English menu, but pictures of almost every dish make ordering simple. If you're stuck, order *gongbao jiding*, a slightly spicy dish of chicken stir-fried with peanuts. ⊠ *26 Nongmin Xiang Lu, north of Tianshui Lu* ☎ *No phone* ▭ *No credit cards.*

¢ ✕🖵 **Lanzhou Hotel** (Lanzhou Fandian). Built in 1956, this concrete behemoth's Sino-Stalinist exterior hides a modern, extensively refurbished interior. Pleasant service and clean, standard-size rooms make this hotel a good value; the older east and west wings house shabbier but still decent rooms for half the price. At the renowned Chinese restaurant, Zhong Hua Yuan, you can sample the best of local cuisine, from hand-rolled dumplings and roasted lamb shank (served with a side of spices and raw garlic bulbs) to more esoteric entrées like camel's feet soup. ⊠486 *Donggang Xilu, on the corner of Tianshui Lu* ☎ 0931/841–6321 🖷 0931/841–8608 ⇥ 476 rooms, 50 suites ♨ 5 restaurants, minibars, massage, sauna, shops, business services, travel services ⊟ AE, MC, V.

¢–$ 🖵 **JJ Sun Hotel.** From the marble floors in the lobby to the plush furnishings, this is Lanzhou's top luxury hotel. On the west side of the building, the upper floors have sweeping views of the mountains; if you're trying to stay cool, however, be aware that the sun makes these rooms warmer than those on the east side. ⊠ *481 Donggang Xilu* ☎ 0931/ 880–5511 🖷 0931/885–4700 ⊕ *www.jjsunhotel.com* ♨ *Restaurant, in-room safes, minibars, in-room broadband, gym, sauna, dry cleaning, laundry services, business services* ⊟ MC, V.

¢–$ 🖵 **Legend Hotel.** Rooms here are well furnished, although the bathrooms are in need of an update. As it's located right in the heart of downtown, the single-pane windows tend to let in noise from the streets below. ⊠ *529 Tianshui Nanlu, at the corner of Dongang Xilu* ☎ 0931/853– 2888 🖷 0931/852-2333 ⇥ *340 rooms, 21 suites* ♨ *2 restaurants, in-room safes, minibars, in-room broadband, massage, sauna, billiards, table tennis, bar, shop, laundry service* ⊟ AE, MC, V ⲓ◎ⲓ BP.

Nightlife & the Arts

The **Zhengning Lu Night Market,** at the corner of Qingyang Lu and Yongchang Lu, features the usual outdoor assortment of lamb kebabs, hotpot, and noodles.

Side Trips from Lanzhou

Fodor'sChoice ★ One of the only day-trips worth taking from Lanzhou is the **Thousand Buddha Temple and Grottoes** (Bingling Si Shiku). It's filled with Buddhist paintings and statuary, including an impressive 89-foot-tall Buddha carved into a cliff face. Although the art is disappointing compared to the Mogao Grottoes at Dunhuang, the location, in a 200-foot-high canyon dominated by spectacular cliff formations of porous rock, is stunning.

If you travel here on your own, you'll need to catch a bus, a ferry, and a jeep. Don't even try it. It's much easier to book a tour. Gansu Western Travel Service offers a popular day-trip that includes all transportation and insurance for around Y340 per person. 🎟 *Y30 entrance* ☉ *Daily 8–5.*

DID YOU KNOW

The canyon is located along one side of the Yellow River. The journey through a gorge lined by water-sculpted rocks is spectacular. When the canyon is dry you can travel 2½ km (1½ mi) by foot or four-wheel-drive vehicle to see the small community of Tibetan lamas at the Upper Temple of Bingling. The temple (Y10)

DON'T MISS

A daily highlight is the gathering of monks on a lawn for religious debate, when fine points of theology are discussed in the liveliest fashion. The monks charge at each other in groups, hissing good-naturedly, as older monks supervise with a benevolent air. The debate takes place in the afternoon; ask at the ticket office for times. Another interesting daily event is the gathering of hundreds of chanting monks on the steps of the main prayer hall beginning at 11 AM.

itself is nothing special, but the twists and turns of the upper gorge are breathtaking, and the monks are friendly.

Fodor's Choice ★ Located in the remote town of Xiahe, the **Labrang Monastery** (Laboleng Si) is a little piece of Tibet along the Gansu-Qinghai border. A world away from Lanzhou, Xiahe has experienced a dizzying rise in the number of travelers over the past decade. Even Tibetan monks clad in traditional fuchsia robes now surf the Internet, play basketball, and listen to pop music. Yet despite these signs of encroaching modernity, Xiahe is still a wonderful place, attracting large numbers of pilgrims who come to study and to spin the 1,147 prayer wheels of the monastery daily, swathed in their distinctive costume of heavy woolen robes tied with brightly colored sashes.

The Labrang Monastery is the largest Tibetan lamasery outside of Tibet. Founded in 1710, it once had as many as 4,000 monks, a number much depleted due in large part to the Cultural Revolution, when monks were forced to return home and temples were destroyed. Though the monastery reopened in 1980, the government's policy of restricted enrollment has kept the number of monks down to about 1,500.

There are two ways to reach Xiahe: by public bus or by private tour. Buses for Xiahe leave from Lanzhou's South Station (Qiche Nanzhan) every hour or two starting at 7:30 AM and take about 6 hours. Make sure to purchase tickets in advance, as some departures require travel insurance (*baoxian*). Western Travel Service offers a number of tours to Xiahe. ⊠ *2 km (1 mi) west of long-distance bus station* 🖭 *Free; Y25 for guided tour* ⊙ *Sunrise–Sunset.*

To & from Lanzhou
12 hrs by train northwest of Xian; 30 hrs by train southeast of Ürümqi; 5 hrs by train east of Xining.

The city's Zhongchuan Airport is 90 km (59 mi) north of town. Because of this, most people arrive by train. The train station (Lanzhou Huochezhan) is located at the southern end of Tianshui Lu, 1 km (½ mi) south of the city's hotels. Long-distance buses arrive at the East Station (Qiche Dongzhan) on Pingliang Lu, north of the train station. Leaving the city can be a bit more complicated. Buses to major destinations like

The Silk Road: Then & Now

THE HISTORY OF THE SILK ROAD starts in 138 BC, when Emperor Wudi of the Han Dynasty sent a caravan of 100 men to the west, attempting to forge a political alliance with the Yuezhi people living beyond the Taklamakan Desert. The mission was a failure and only two men survived the 13-year return journey, but they brought back with them to Chang'an (present-day Xian) tales of previously unknown kingdoms: Samarkand, Ferghana, Parthia, and even Rome. More important, they told stories about the legendary Ferghana horse, a fast and powerful creature said to be bred in heaven. Believing that this horse would give his armies a military advantage over the Huns, Emperor Wudi sent a number of large convoys to Central Asia in order to establish contact with these newly discovered kingdoms—and to bring back as many horses as possible. These envoys of the Han emperor were the first traders on the Silk Road.

The extension of the Silk Road beyond Central Asia to the Middle East and Europe was due to another ill-advised foreign excursion, this time on the part of the Roman Empire. In 55 BC, Marcus Licinius Crassus led an army to the east against Parthia, in present-day Syria. The battle was one of Rome's greatest military defeats, but some of the survivors were able to obtain Chinese silk from the Parthians. Back in Rome, wearing silk became the fashion, and for the first time in history a trade route was established covering the arduous (5,000-mi) journey between East and West.

It might seem odd today, the two empires knew very little about the origins of their precious cargo. The reason for this common ignorance was the complicated supply chain that transported goods over the Silk Road. No one merchant made the entire journey, but wares were instead brought from kingdom to kingdom, switching hands in the teeming bazaars of wealthy oasis cities along the way.

Over time, the Silk Road became less important due to the opening of sea routes, and was dealt a deathblow by the isolationist tendencies of the Ming Dynasty in the 14th century. Yet today, the Silk Road is being resurrected to transport the modern world's most precious commodity: oil. China's rapid development has created an almost insatiable appetite for energy resources. In the last few years, pipelines have been completed from Kazakhstan and Xinjiang to Shanghai. There's even a long-term plan to create the world's longest pipeline, stretching from Saudi Arabia to China.

All of this oil activity has brought new investment and development to the long-dormant western regions of China. Unfortunately, this modern gold rush is also diluting minority populations and gradually diminishing the exotic remoteness that has long characterized the Silk Road. The best advice: get there as soon as possible.

Xian, Xining, Jiayuguan, and Dunhuang usually leave from East Station, whereas lesser destinations are served by West Station (Qiche Xizhan). Buses to Xiahe depart from South Station (Qiche Nanzhan).

Dunhuang

A small oasis town, Dunhuang was for many centuries the most important Buddhist destination on the Silk Road. Just outside of town, beyond the towering dunes of Singing Sand Mountain, you can see the extraordinary caves of the Mogao Grottoes, considered the richest repository of Buddhist art in the world.

Buddhism entered China via the Silk Road, and as Dunhuang was the point of entry to the Chinese world, it was not long before a temple was established here. By AD 366 the first caves were being carved and painted at the Mogao oasis. Work on the caves continued until the 10th century, after which they were left undisturbed for nearly a thousand years.

Adventurers from Europe, North America, and other parts of Asia began plundering the caves at the end of the 19th century, yet most of the statuary and paintings remain. By far the most astounding find was a "library cave" filled with more than 45,000 forgotten sutras and official documents. The contents were mostly sold to Sir Aurel Stein in 1907, and when translated they revealed the extent to which Dunhuang was an ancient melting pot of cultures and religions.

Today, you'll find a rapidly developing small city that is still, in some ways, a melting pot; tourists from every continent converge upon Dunhuang daily to visit one of the most impressive sites in all of China.

Exploring

❶ The small **Dunhuang Museum** (Dunhuang Bowuguan) displays objects recovered from nearby Silk Road fortifications. If you've visited the Jade Gate or Yangguan Pass, you may enjoy seeing what's been found. Otherwise, the museum will probably only interest Silk Road buffs. ⊠ *8 Yangguan Dong Lu, east of the night market* 🎫 *Y15* ⊗ *Daily 8–6:30.*

❸ South of Dunhuang, the oasis gives way to desert. Here you'll find a gorgeous sweep of sand dunes known as **Singing Sand Mountain** (Ming Sha Shan), named for the light rattling sound that the sand makes when wind blows across the surface At 5,600 feet above sea level, the half-hour climb to the summit is a difficult climb but is worth it for the views, particularly at sunset. Nestled in the sand is **Crescent Moon Lake** (Yueyaquan), a lovely pool that by some freak of the prevailing winds never silts up. Camels, sleds, and various flying contraptions are available at steep prices; try your bargaining skills. ⊠ *Mingshan Lu, 5 km (3 mi) south of town* 🎫 *Y80.*

❷ The magnificent Buddhist **Mogao Grottoes** (Mogao Ku) lie southeast of Dunhuang. At least 40 caves— dating from the Northern Wei in

Fodor'sChoice ★

> **RENT-A-BIKE**
>
> The best way to get around Dunhuang is by bicycle, and you can easily hire one from rental places around town.

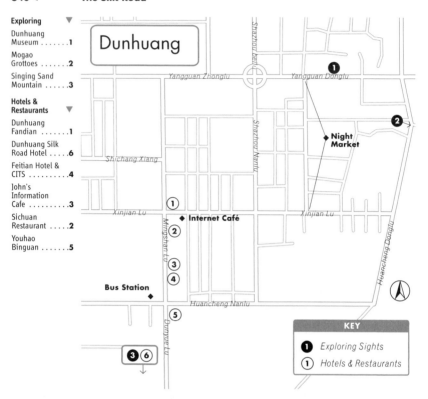

the 4th century AD to the Five Dynasties in the 10th century AD—are open to the public. Which caves are open on a given day depends on the whim of local authorities, but you shouldn't worry too much about missing something. Everything here is stunning. You'll almost certainly visit the giant seated Buddhas in caves 96 and 130, the Tang Dynasty sleeping Buddha in cave 148, and the famous "library" in caves 16 and 17 where 45,000 religious and political documents were uncovered at the turn of the 20th century. A flashlight is a useful item for your visit.

This is one site where you should hire an English-speaking guide. At a cost of only Y20 extra, your understanding of the different imagery used in each cave will increase immeasurably. After the tour, you'll have time to wander around and revisit any unlocked caves. A fine museum contains reproductions of eight caves not usually visited on the public tour. A smaller museum near the library cave details the removal of artifacts by foreign plunderers.

To get here, take a taxi (Y60 to Y100 round-trip) or an hourly tour bus run by CITS (Y20 round-trip). ⊠ *25 km (17 mi) southeast of town* ☎ *No phone* ✉ *Y100 for tour; additional Y20 for English-speaking guide* ⊙ *Daily 8:30–6.*

Tours

If you only have time for one tour, make sure to head to the Mogao Grottoes (Y20). Don't bother with a tour to Singing Sand Mountain, as it's easy enough to reach on your own by taxi. If you're able to spend an extra day in town, take a tour

of sites relating to ancient Dunhuang (Y130). These trips gives you a sense of what it was like to travel on the old Silk Road.

🚩 Tour-Operator Recommendations **Feitian CITS** ✉ 22 Mingshan Lu, in front of the Feitian Hotel ☎ 0937/883-2714.

Where to Stay & Eat

Dunhuang's night market is a 10-minute walk from the most popular hotels. Located between Xinjian Lu and Yangguan Dong Lu, it's worth a visit for cold beer and flavorful lamb kebabs. Small restaurants serving both Western and Chinese fare are clustered together on Mingshan Lu in the center of town.

¢–$ ✗ **John's Information Café.** Cool off after a full day of sightseeing on this trellised patio. Another option is to come before you start your day for a Western-style breakfast and a cup of joe. ✉ *Mingshan Lu, north of the Feitian Hotel* ☎ *No phone* ▭ *No credit cards.*

¢–$ ✗ **Sichuan Restaurant** (Sichuan Canting). Delicious Sichuanese classics like chicken with peanuts, sweet and sour pork, and spicy fried potato strips are available here at very cheap prices. There's even an English menu. ✉ *75 Mingshan Lu, next to the Dunhuang Trade Union Hotel* ☎ *No phone* ▭ *No credit cards.*

★ $–$$ 🏨 **Dunhuang Silk Road Hotel.** This cross between a Chinese fortress and an alpine lodge is the most interesting place to stay in Dunhuang. The large, spacious rooms have historical touches like Ming reproduction furniture and traditional wooden shower buckets. The hotel arranges some great tours, including a sunrise camel ride to the sand dunes of Singing Sand Mountain. The 4th-floor café is the perfect spot to appreciate the dunes from a distance. The hotel's only drawback is its location 3 km (2 mi) south of the town center. ✉ *Mingshan Lu, 736200* ☎ *0937/888–2088* 🖷 *0937/888–2086* ⊕ *www.the-silk-road.com/hotel/dunhuanghotel* ⇆ *292 rooms, 8 suites* ♨ *2 restaurants, gym, sauna, shops, business services, travel services* ▭ *AE, MC, V.*

¢ 🏨 **Dunhuang Fandian.** If you're looking for something mildly luxurious, this lodging in the center of town will fit the bill. Rooms are nicer than at the Feitian Hotel, but without an elevator you'll have to climb the stairs to your room. Foreign currency and traveler's checks can be exchanged in the lobby. ✉ *16 Mingshan Lu, corner of Xinjiang Lu* ☎ *0937/882–2413* ♨ *Business services, travel services* ▭ *No credit cards.*

¢ 🏨 **Feitian Hotel** (Feitian Binguan). Dunhuang's most popular tourist hotel has a variety of clean, comfortable rooms. For a taste of the high life you could even book yourself a deluxe suite. The hotel is home to the CITS travel office and the departure point for popular tour buses. Best of all, it's located in the middle of town. ✉ *22 Mingshan Lu, ½*

9

block north of the bus station ☎ *0937/882–2337* 📠 *0937/882–2337* ♿ *Shop, travel services* 🚫 *No credit cards.*

¢ 🏨 **Youhao Binguan.** Across from the bus station, this is Dunhuang's best budget option. The four-bed dorm rooms on the 4th floor are a great deal at Y30 per person. Hot water flows from 7:30 PM until midnight. Whatever you do, don't use the sub-par laundry service. ✉ *25 Mingshan Lu* ☎ *0937/882–3072* ♿ *Laundry service, travel services* 🚫 *No credit cards.*

Nightlife & the Arts

An evening stroll through the **Dunhuang Night Market**—where you can find cold beer and kebabs—is probably your best bet. To find the night market, walk east on Xinjian Lu from the corner of Mingshan Lu; you can't miss the entrance.

To & from Dunhuang

17 hrs by bus northwest of Lanzhou; 6 hrs by bus west of Jiayuguan.

The easiest and most expensive way to reach Dunhuang is by air, with regular flights from Beijing, Xian, Lanzhou, and Ürümqi. The airport is located near the Mogao Grottoes, with many tour groups arriving in the morning and departing the same evening. The only way to reach town from the airport is by taxi, which should cost around Y20. Buses from Lanzhou and Jiayuguan depart frequently for Dunhuang, dropping you off at the station in the center of town. Most tourists reach the town by rail, the most comfortable but least convenient option: the "Dunhuang" station is actually 120 km (79 mi) north of town. A taxi to Dunhuang should be Y120.

GANSU ESSENTIALS

Transportation

BY AIR

From Lanzhou, there are daily flights to Dunhuang, Beijing, Guangzhou, Shanghai, Chengdu, Ürümqi, and Xian. There are daily flights from Dunhuang to Lanzhou, Beijing, Ürümqi, and Xian.

Lanzhou's airport is 70 km (45 mi) north of the city, making it unpopular with tourists. A public bus costing Y30 per person takes an hour to reach the airport from the China Northwest Airlines office at 512 Donggang Xilu.

Dunhuang's airport is 13 km (8 mi) east of town, on the road to the Mogao Grottoes. A taxi ride from the airport costs Y20 to Y30.

🛫 Airport Information **Dunhuang Airport** ✉ 13 km (8 mi) east of town, near the Mogao Grottoes ☎ 0937/882–5292. **Lanzhou Zhongchuan Airport** ✉ Zhongchuan ☎ 0931/896–8160.

🛫 **China Northwest Airlines** ✉ 512 Donggang Xilu, Lanzhou ☎ 0931/882–1964.

BY BUS

Buses leave Lanzhou's East Bus Station multiple times daily for Xian (14 hours), Dunhuang (24 hours), Ürümqi (32 hours), and Xining (3 hours). Buses for Xiahe (6 hours) leave in the morning from South Station; buy tickets in advance or be sure to bring along your proof of PICC insurance (*see below*).

Dunhuang's long-distance bus station is in the south of town, across from the Youhao Binguan. Buses go to Jiayuguan (7 hours), Lanzhou (24 hours), and Hami (8 hours).

Buses originating in Gansu often require foreigners to show proof of PICC travel insurance before purchasing tickets. It's unclear why this regulation exists, or why there's usually at least one daily bus to each destination that doesn't require the paperwork. You should be able to purchase insurance with your bus ticket, but this is often not the case. You'll probably be better off heading straight to the main PICC office on the north side of Qingyang Lu, just east of Jingning Lu. They'll know why you're there.

🚍 Bus Information **Dunhuang Bus Station** ✉ Dingzi Lu ☎ 0937/882-2174. **Lanzhou East Bus Station** ✉ Ping Yuang Lu ☎ 0931/841-8411. **Lanzhou West Bus Station** ✉ 458 Xijin Dong Lu ☎ 0931/233-3285.

BY TRAIN

Lanzhou's train station is in the southeast section of the city. Trains go to Beijing (24 hours), Shanghai (30 hours), Xian (13 hours), Ürümqi (31 hours), Guangzhou (36 hours), Hohhot (18 hours), Qingdao (37 hours), and Xining (4 hours). Because few trains originate here, buying sleeper tickets in Lanzhou can be difficult; your best bet is to buy tickets early or hope for an upgrade onboard.

The railway station serving Dunhuang is in the small town of Liuyuan, 120 km (74 mi) away. Don't be fooled by the name of the station, which is called "Dunhuang Station" to attract more tourists. Taxis from Liuyuan to Dunhuang cost Y120, or you can ride one of the buses that leave hourly for Y15. Once on the road, the journey takes just over 2 hours.

Western Travel Service can book tickets in advance for trains out of Lanzhou and Liuyuan; otherwise, buy the tickets at the train station.

🚆 Train Information **Lanzhou Train Station** ✉ Houche Zhan Dong Jian, at the southern end of Pingliang Lu and Tianshui Lu ☎ 0931/882-2142. **Liuyuan Train Station** ✉ Liuyuan Huoche Zhan ☎ 0937/557-2995.

Contacts & Resources

MONEY MATTERS

Your best bet is to fill up your money belt before you come to Gansu. If you've run out of traveler's checks or foreign currency to exchange, your only option is to use a credit card to get a cash advance.

🏦 Currency Exchange **Bank of China** ✉ 589 Tianshui Lu, Lanzhou ☎ 0931/888-9942 ✉ Yangguan Zhong Lu, Dunhuang ☎ 0937/263-0510.

9

VISITOR INFORMATION
The only worthwhile tour operator in Lanzhou, Gansu Western Travel Service, has a staff that speaks English.

🚹 Tourist Information **Gansu Western Travel Service** ✉ Lanzhou Hotel, 486 Donggang Xilu, Lanzhou ☎ 0931/885–2929 or 138/9331–8956. **Feitian CITS** ✉ Feitian Hotel, 22 Mingshan Lu, Dunhuang ☎ 0937/883–2714.

QINGHAI

A remote province on the northeastern border of Tibet, Qinghai's sweeping grasslands locked in by icy mountain ranges are relatively unknown to most Chinese people. They tend to think of the province as their nation's Siberia, a center for prisons and work camps. Yet Qinghai shares much of the majestic scenery of Xinjiang combined with the rich culture of Tibet.

Qinghai's relative isolation will soon be a thing of the past, thanks to a recently completed 1,700-km (1,054-mi) rail line to Tibet. For now, the province continues to be sparsely populated, with a little more than 5 million inhabitants. (Yes, that's a tiny number in China.)

Xining

Its name means "Peace in the West," so it's no surprise that Xining started out as a military garrison in the 16th century, guarding the empire's western borders. It was also an important center for trade between China and Tibet. A small city by Chinese standards, with a population slightly more than 1.1 million, Xining is no longer cut off from the rest of China. But the city still feels remote; a far-flung metropolis wedged between dramatic sandstone cliffs, Xining is populated largely by Tibetan and Hui peoples.

For travelers, Xining is a convenient base for visits to the important Kumbum Monastery, which sits just outside the city, and the stunning avian sanctuary of Bird Island, 350 km (217 mi) away on the shores of China's largest saltwater lake.

Exploring Xining

Although most travelers don't come to see Xining, there are a few sights in and around the city. The most important site is the Taoist **North Monastery** (Beichan Si), at the northwest end of town. Construction on this series of mountainside cloisters and pavilions began more than 1,700 years ago during the Northern Wei. Climbing the stairs to the white pagoda at the top gives a view of the entire city sprawled out beneath you. To get here, take a taxi. ✉ *North end of Chanjiang Lu* 🎫 *Free* 🕐 *Dawn–dusk.*

Around Xining

★ The magnificent **Kumbum Monastery** (Ta'Er Si) lies 25 km (15 mi) southwest of Xining. One of the six great monasteries of the Tibetan Buddhist sect known as Yellow Hat—and reputedly the birthplace of the sect's founder, Tsong Khapa—construction began here in 1560. A great reformer who lived in the early 1400s, Tsong Khapa formulated a striking new doctrine that stressed a return to monastic discipline, strict celibacy, and moral and philosophical thought over magic and mysticism. Tsong's followers have controlled Tibetan politics since the 17th century. Still a magnet for Tibetan pilgrims, Kumbum boasts a dozen prayer halls, an exhibition hall, and monks' quarters. Public buses (Y5) to Huangzhong leave frequently from Zifang Jie Bus Station. Get off

at the last stop and walk 2 km uphill or take a put-put (Y2) to the monastery's gates. Taxis from Xining are Y30. ⊠ *Huangzhong* *Y80* ⊙ *Dawn–dusk.*

Tours

You have three choices for arranging tours in Qinghai. Xining's more upscale hotels have travel offices that can help you arrange expensive private tours to Kumbum Monastery or Bird Island with English-speaking guides. For cheaper group tours, head to the Station Hotel or the Post Hotel where the on-site travel agencies specialize in group tours. Be forewarned: you will probably be crammed into a minibus with Chinese tourists. A third option is to hire the services of an enterprising individual like Niu Xiaojun, who's been leading foreigners to off-the-beaten-path destinations for years.

Tour-Operator Recommendations Niu Xiaojun ☎ 1319/579-1105. **Spring & Autumn Travel Service** ⊠ Post Hotel, 138 Huzhu Lu, east of the train station ☎ 0971/817-4957. **Yicai Travel Service** ⊠ Station Hotel, Huochezhan Guanchang ☎ 0971/814-2008.

Where to Stay & Eat

Xining isn't known for its cuisine. Outside of fancy hotels, stick with places that are packed with hungry locals. Whatever you're eating, add a bit of the chili-pepper sauce you'll find on every tabletop; the local variety is only mildly spicy and has a roasted flavor that you won't find anywhere else.

¢–$ ✕ **Jianyin Revolving Restaurant.** Perched atop the 28-story Jianyin Hotel, this slowly revolving restaurant offers mediocre Asian-inspired cuisine. But the food is beside the point. People come here for the spectacular views of the city. There's no minimum, so sipping a cup of tea while enjoying the scenery or playing cards is perfectly acceptable. ⊠ *Jianyin Hotel, 55 Xida Jie, southeast corner of the central square* ☎ *0971/826–1885* ▭ *No credit cards.*

¢ ✕ **Fu Rue Canting.** Popular with people staying next door at the Post Hotel, this Muslim eatery's specialty is *chaomian,* a large plate of noodles fried with mutton and vegetables. It's simple, tasty, and cheap. ⊠ *Huzhu Lu, east of the Post Hotel* ☎ *No phone* ▭ *No credit cards.*

9

¢ ✕ **Xian Yangrou Paomo.** This hole-in-the-wall eatery is known for its huge bowls of hearty mutton soup. Meat, glass noodles, cilantro, and small bits of dense bread are bathed in a mouthwatering broth to make a meal that can satisfy any appetite. Look for a red sign with the easily recognizable characters for Xian. ⊠ *Jianguo Lu, south of the bus station* ☎ *No phone* ▭ *No credit cards.*

$ 🏨 **Yinlong Hotel.** This ultramodern hotel is hands-down the finest lodg-
Fodor'sChoice ing between Xian and Ürümqi. There's an incredible attention to de-
★ tail, from sound-activated lighting in the hallways to bathrooms with a tub and a separate shower. Rooms are exceptionally comfortable and quiet, with views overlooking Xining's central square. ⊠ *38 Huanghe Lu, north side of the central square* ☎ *0971/616–6666* 🖷 *0971/612–7885* ⊕ *www.ylhotel.net* ⇝ *316 rooms* ⌂ *5 restaurants, coffee bar, in-room safe, minibars, massage, sauna, Ping-Pong, billiards, shops, business services, meeting room, dry cleaning, laundry services, travel services* ▭ *AE, MC, V.*

¢ 🏨 **Jianyin Hotel.** A pink-marble foyer entrance greets you at this handsome hotel, the best mid-range option in Xining. It has long been popular with tourists. The rooms are about the same as everywhere else in town, but with an extra layer of glitz. ⊠ *55 Xida Jie* ☎ *0971/826–1887* 🖷 *0971/826–1551* ⇝ *160 rooms, 20 suites* ⌂ *2 restaurants, minibars, hair salon, massage, sauna, bowling, shops, laundry service, business services, meeting room, travel services* ▭ *No credit cards.*

¢ 🏨 **Post Hotel.** If you're looking to meet other backpackers, this popular budget hotel east of the train station is your best bet. For the cheapest dorm-style accommodations you may have to climb six flights of stairs; doubles are mostly on lower floors. The on-site travel agency here is not as popular as the Station Hotel, but offers similar tours. ⊠ *138 Huzhu Lu* ☎ *0971/813–3133* ⌂ *Travel services* ▭ *No credit cards.*

¢ 🏨 **Station Hotel.** Most budget travelers stay here or at the nearby Post Hotel. Rooms at this place on the same square as the train station are cheap but vary in quality considerably; ask to see your room before you decide. Unplug your phone if you don't want it to ring all night with breathless offers of "massage" services. The on-site travel agency offers popular day-trips to Bird Island. ⊠ *Huochezhan Guanchang* ☎ *0971/817–6888* ⌂ *Travel services* ▭ *No credit cards.*

Shopping
Those interested in Tibetan handicrafts will want to stroll through Xining's excellent street markets. The **Jianguo Road Wholesale Market** (⊠ Jianguo Lu, opposite the main bus station) sells everything from traditional Tibetan clothing to the latest CDs.

Side Trip from Xining
★ **Bird Island** (Niao Dao) is the main draw at Qinghai Hu, China's largest inland saltwater lake. The name Bird Island is a misnomer: it was an island until the lake receded, connecting it to the shore. The electric-blue lake is surrounded by rolling hills covered with yellow rapeseed flowers. Tibetan shepherds graze their flocks here as wild yaks roam nearby. Beyond the hills are snowcapped mountains. An estimated 100,000

birds breed at Bird Island, including egrets, speckle-headed geese, and black-neck cranes; sadly, the numbers have been much depleted because of the country's efforts to suppress the spread of avian flu. There are two viewing sites: spend as little time as possible at Egg Island in favor of the much better Common Cormorant Island, where you can see birds flying at eye-level from the top of a cliff. The best months to see birds are May and June. If you're taking a tour to Qinghai Hu, make sure that you're headed here and not the much closer tourist trap known as Qinghai Hu 151. ⊠ *350 km (215 mi) northwest of Xining* ☒ *Y50.*

To & from Xining
4 hrs (225 km [140 mi]) by train or 3 hrs by bus west of Lanzhou; 1,900 km (1,200 mi) northeast of Lhasa.

The airport is 30 km (19 mi) east of the city. Shuttle buses costing Y16 per person can get you to or from the airport in about 40 minutes. If you're traveling with someone else, a taxi (Y40) is a better option. If you arrive by train or bus, you'll be within walking distance of the Post Hotel and the Station Hotel. You can reach the city's more upscale hotels by taking a taxi, a ride that should be less than Y10.

If you're planning on traveling to Tibet, use a well-established travel agent. Bureaucratic formalities mean that you'll still need help obtaining the proper permits.

QINGHAI ESSENTIALS

Transportation

BY AIR
Daily flights link Xining with Beijing, Shanghai, Chengdu, Guangzhou, Xian, and Shenzhen. There is less frequent service to Lhasa, Ürümqi, Qingdao, and Golmud.

Xining Caojiabao Airport, 30 km (19 mi) east of Xining, takes about a half hour to reach by taxi and 40 minutes by shuttle bus. Tickets can be purchased through any travel agent.

🚩Airport Information **Xining Caojiabao Airport** ⊠ 30 km (20 mi) east of Xining ☎ 0971/818-8222.

BY BUS
Tickets for the long, bumpy bus ride to Lhasa can be purchased from any travel agent. These buses may begin running less frequently if the train service to Tibet proves popular. Tickets for the journey to Lanzhou (3 hours) and Xian (15 hours) are available at the long-distance bus station, a few minutes north of the train station. If your next stop is Dunhuang, but you don't want to backpedal to Lanzhou, take the bus to Jiuquan in Gansu and get a connection farther west; the mountain scenery and small Tibetan villages along the way are spectacular.

🚩 Bus Information **Xining Main Bus Station** ⊠ Jianguo Lu, north of the train station ☎ 0971/814-9790.

BY TRAIN

Daily trains link Xining with Lanzhou (4 hours), Xian (15 hours), Beijing (27 hours), and Shanghai (34 hours). Tickets can be purchased at the railway station. Details of the train to Lhasa have not yet been published, but it's likely you'll have to buy tickets through a travel agent.

🚆 Train Information **Xining Railway Station** ⊠ Northern end of Jianguo Lu ☎ 0971/814-9790.

Contacts & Resources

EMERGENCIES

🏥 **Qinghai People's Hospital** ⊠ 143 Gonghe Lu, Xining ☎ 0971/817-7911.

VISITOR INFORMATION

For the moment, the official tourism agencies seem to have given up on Xining. For information, try one of the local tour companies.

XINJIANG

The vast Xinjiang Uyghur Autonomous Region, covering more than 1.6 million square km (640,000 square mi), is China's largest province. Even more expansive than Alaska, it borders Mongolia, Russia, Kazakhstan, Kyrgyzstan, Tajikistan, Afghanistan, and Pakistan. Only 40% of Xinjiang's 19.6 million inhabitants are Han Chinese. About 45% are Uyghur (a people of Turkic origin), and the remainder is mostly Kazakhs, Hui, Kyrgyz, Mongols, and Tajiks. With all of those different faces, it's common for visitors to almost forget at times that this is China.

With an extremely dry climate, Xinjiang gets very little rainfall except in the northern areas near Russia. It gets very cold in winter and very hot in summer, especially in the Turpan Basin where temperatures often sore to 120°F. Visitors usually forgive the extreme weather, however, as they're charmed by the locals and awed by the rugged scenery, ranging from the endless sand dunes of the desert to the pastoral grasslands of the north.

DID YOU KNOW

In the 1980s, archaeologists discovered dozens of tombs in various parts of Xinjiang, with bodies that had been buried for about 3,000 years yet remained remarkably preserved thanks to the arid desert climate. Many of the mummies, believed to be forefathers of the Uyghurs, had northern European features, including fair hair and skin.

Long important as a crossroads for trade with Europe and the Middle East, Xinjiang has nevertheless seldom come completely under Chinese control. For more than 2,000 years, the region has been contested and divided by Turkic and Mongol tribes who—after setting up short-lived empires—soon disappeared beneath the shifting sands of time. In the 20th century, Uyghurs continued to resist Chinese rule, seizing power from a warlord governor in 1933 and claiming the land as a separate republic, which they named East Turkestan. China tightened its grip after the 1949 revolution, however, encouraging Han settlers to emigrate to the province to dilute the Uyghur majority. Today, Uyghurs concede that they have almost no chance of gaining independence, and you'll see lit-

China's Muslims

UYGHUR

The Muslim Turkic people known as Uyghurs (pronounced "WEE-grs") are one of China's largest—and in the eyes of Beijing, most troublesome—minority groups. Uyghurs mostly live in northwest China's Xinjiang, an "autonomous region" that is one of the most tightly controlled parts of the country after Tibet. Uyghurs are descendants of nomadic Turkic Central Asian tribes—they look the least "Chinese" out of all of China's minorities and have a language, food, music, dance, clothing and other customs that have little or no relation to those found elsewhere in China. Yet with a population of nearly 10 million people, most foreigners have never heard of them or their troubled independence movement. Protests and occasional violence in the region during the late 1990s caused Beijing to crack down severely, placing limits on religious education and executing hundreds of suspected Uyghur separatists. The attacks of September 11, 2001 gave the Chinese government further leverage to oppress Uyghurs in the name of fighting terrorism, and Xinjiang has been relatively quiet in recent years.

HUI

Primarily identifiable by their brimless white caps and headscarves, the Hui are ethnically Chinese Muslims. They are descendants of Middle Eastern traders who came to China via the Silk Road, settling down with a Chinese wife after her conversion to Islam. Over a thousand years' time, the Middle Eastern influence on the Hui appearance became diluted to the point where their facial features are now almost impossible to distinguish from those of Han Chinese. Yet because of cultural differences associated with their Islamic faith, Hui tend to associate with other Hui in largely Muslim neighborhoods. Hui reject the eating of several kinds of meat that are popular with Han Chinese, including pork, horse, dog, and several types of birds. In what could be seen as a form of respect by the business-savvy Han Chinese, Hui are also generally considered by the Han to be shrewd businesspeople, perhaps a vestige of their history as the descendants of foreign traders.

9

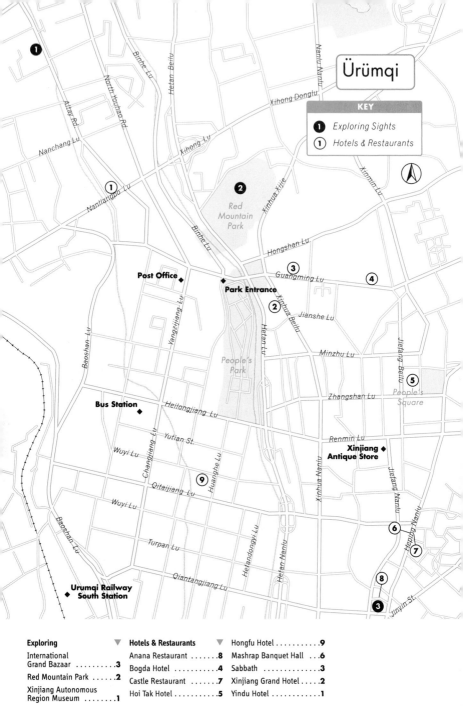

Ürümqi

KEY

1 Exploring Sights

1 Hotels & Restaurants

Red Mountain Park

People's Park

People's Square

Post Office

Park Entrance

Bus Station

Xinjiang Antique Store

Urumqi Railway South Station

Binhe Lu
Hetan Beilu
Nantu Nantu
Xihong Donglu
North Youhao Rd.
Altay Rd.
Nanchang Lu
Xihong Lu
Xinhua Xijie
Kenmin Lu
Nanlianghu Lu
Binhe Lu
Hongshan Lu
Guangming Lu
Xinhua Beilu
Jianshe Lu
Minzhu Lu
Jiefang Beilu
Baoshan Lu
Yangzijiang Lu
Hetan Lu
Zhangshan Lu
Heilongjiang Lu
Yutian St.
Renmin Lu
Wuyi Lu
Changjiang Lu
Qitaijiang Lu
Huanghe Lu
Xinhua Nanlu
Jiefang Nanlu
Wuyi Lu
Turpan Lu
Heiandongyi Lu
Hetan Nanlu
Hepilu Nanlu
Baoshan Lu
Qiantangjiang Lu
Jinyin St.

tle evidence of any remaining aspirations; speaking out against Beijing in public is just too risky.

Ürümqi

Xinjiang's capital and largest city, Ürümqi is at the geographic center of Asia and has the distinction of being the most landlocked city in the world. It's a new city by Chinese standards, little more than barracks for Qing Dynasty troops when it was built in 1763. Once a sleepy trading post, Ürümqi has grown to a sprawling city with just over 2 million inhabitants. Yet despite this modernization, Ürümqi manages to conjure up the past, especially in the Uyghur-populated area near the International Grand Bazaar.

Exploring Ürümqi

3 The streets around the **International Grand Bazaar** were once full of donkey carts and flocks of sheep. Men in embroidered skullcaps and women in heavy brown wool veils remain, and the whole area maintains the bustling atmosphere of a Central Asian street market. You can bargain for Uyghur crafts here, such as decorated knives, colorful silks, and carved jade. Be sure to explore the area, as small shops are tucked into every nook and cranny. ⊠ *Jiefang Lu, 3 km (2 mi) south of the city center.*

Don't miss the exhibition of perfectly preserved mummies at the superb
1 **Xinjiang Autonomous Region Museum** (Xinjiang Zijiqu Bowuguan), 4 km
Fodor's Choice (2½ mi) northwest of the city center. The mummies—including the
★ 4,000 year-old beauty of Loulan—were excavated from tombs in various parts of Xinjiang. In addition, the museum has intriguing fragments of silk brocade, wool rugs, colorful pottery, and hemp-cloth documents discovered with the corpses. The museum shops have a fairly good selection of carpets, jewelry, porcelain, and antiques ready for export. ⊠ *132 Xibei Lu, 1 block west of the Sheraton Hotel* ☎ *0991/453–4453* 🎫 *Y25* ⊙ *Weekdays 9:30–7:30, weekends 10:30–5:30.*

2 Climbing to the top of **Red Mountain Park** (Hong Shan Gongyuan) gives you a picture-perfect view of the snowcapped Heavenly Mountains. An array of incongruously grouped objects—including an eight-story pagoda built by the emperor in 1788 to suppress an evil dragon— are reached via a long set of stairs. If the weather's good, come here in the early evening for the pleasure of seeing the cityscape bathed in the setting sun's golden light. Ignore the cheap carnival rides near the entrance. The park is hard to find, so take a taxi. ⊠ *Off Hongshan Lu* 🎫 *Y10* ⊙ *Daily 6 AM–1 AM.*

WHAT TIME IS IT?

A constant source of confusion for travelers in Xinjiang is figuring out the time. Uyghurs often speak in unofficial Xinjiang time, whereas Han Chinese use standard Beijing time. If in doubt, ask. No matter what time is spoken, you can count on everything in Xinjiang starting two hours later than in Beijing. That is, lunch in Kashgar is usually eaten at 2 PM Beijing Time.

Tours

Ürümqi is a popular place to begin a tour of Xinjiang's vast desert expanses. If your time is limited, a

9

private tour probably makes the most sense. Travel agencies are happy to let you pick and choose from a list of destinations. A four-wheel-drive vehicle will cost around Y1,300 per day; a smaller Volkswagen Santana is Y900 per day.

CYTS, in the parking lot of the Bogda Hotel, offers a wide range of trips lasting from one day to more than three weeks. A tour of sites around Turpan or a trip to the Heavenly Lake can be accomplished in a single day.

Tour-Operator Recommendations CYTS (⊠ 10 Guangming Lu, in the parking lot of the Bogda Hotel ☎ 0991/232–1170). **Grassland Travel Service** (⊠ 2 Renmin Gongyuan Beijie, southwest of the entrance gate to People's Park ☎ 0991/584–1116).

Where to Stay & Eat

Ürümqi is a good place to have your first taste of Uyghur cuisine. Run-of-the-mill Sichuan fare can be found almost everywhere, including at most hotels.

$–$$ ✕ **Sabbath.** At Ürümqi's most out-of-place eatery, you can pretend you're relaxing on a beach in Brazil instead of (1,500 mi) from the nearest ocean. Waiters at this all-you-can-eat *rodizio* (barbecue) fill your plate with flame-roasted steak, shrimp, chicken, and sausage until you're ready to explode. A live Brazilian band plays during dinner. ⊠ 26 *Guangming Lu, west of the Bogeda Hotel* ☎ 0991/886–0601 ➡ No *credit cards.*

¢–$ ✕ **Mashrap Banquet Hall.** If you manage to find this popular restaurant, you'll experience an unforgettable evening of Uyghur culture. Arrive around 8 PM for dinner, and by 9:30 PM you'll be twirling and flapping your arms with locals to the sounds of Uyghur pop music, provided by a live band. The entrance is across the street from Castle Restaurant; Mashrap's neon sign hangs above a slightly shady-looking elevator that will carry you up to the 3rd-floor dining room. ⊠ *Heping Nanlu* ☎ No *phone* ➡ No *credit cards.*

★ ¢–$ ✕ **Castle Restaurant.** The exotic music of Xinjiang plays quietly while the waitstaff—dressed smartly in traditional Muslim garb—tries to keep up with the restaurant's loyal but demanding diners. This is the best place in Ürümqi for sampling Uyghur cuisine. Start with the homemade *suannai* (yogurt), then move on to classic dishes like *laghman* (pulled noodles with lamb and vegetables) and *polo* (rice with lamb and raisins). Those looking to expand their knowledge of the local cuisine should try the *üghüreh* (soup with lamb meatballs and noodles) or the excellent *belkevap* (barbecued lamb chops). ⊠ 132 *Heping Nanlu, north of the International Grand Bazaar* ☎ No *phone* ➡ No *credit cards.*

¢ ✕ **Anana Restaurant.** This popular lunch spot serves classic Uyghur dishes at incredibly cheap prices. You can go with a standard like rice with lamb and raisins, or look at what other people are eating and point. The *rounang* (flat bread baked with lamb inside) is especially good. Wash it all down with a can of Muslim-friendly Zam-Zam Cola, Xinjiang's answer to Coke. To find this place, look for the big red sign. ⊠ *On a small, unmarked street running along the northern wall of the International Grand Bazaar* ☎ No *phone* ➡ No *credit cards.*

$–$$$ 🏨 **Hongfu Hotel** (Hongfu Dajiudian). This upscale hotel offers stylish rooms heavy on frosted glass and dark-wood paneling. There are 11 types of rooms to choose from, so you might want to look at a few before you decide; some have wall-mounted flat-screen TVs. The night market is just steps from the hotel entrance. ✉ *26 Huanghe Lu, corner of Wuyi Lu* ☎ *0991/588–1588* 📠 *0991/582–3188* 🛏 *315 rooms, 18 suites* 🍴 *6 restaurants, in-room safes, minibar, in-room broadband, indoor pool, gym, massage, sauna, laundry, business services, meeting room* ▭ *AE, MC, V.*

$–$$$ 🏨 **Yindu Hotel** (Yindu Jiudian). Xinjiang's finest hotel, the Yindu is testament to the influx of cash that has transformed Ürümqi over the past decade. If you're in town on business, staying here will impress your Chinese contacts. The main drawback is that it's located a couple of kilometers northwest of the city center. You may also be uneasy with the window between the shower and the bed, which the staff explains is "for your wedding night." ✉ *39 Xibei Lu* ☎ *0991/458–0136* 📠 *0991/458–0159* ⊕ *www. yinduhotel.com* 🛏 *312 rooms* 🍴 *6 restaurants, in-room safes, minibars, indoor pool, gym, hair salon, massage, spa, sauna, laundry service, business services, meeting room, travel services* ▭ *AE, MC, V.*

★ ¢–$$$ 🏨 **Hoi Tak Hotel** (Hai De Dajiudian). The most popular tourist hotel in Ürümqi, this gleaming white tower offers first-rate views of the snow-capped Tian Shan Mountains. For the best views, request a room on the east side. Though not huge, the standard rooms are tastefully appointed and have comfortable beds and ample closet space; Internet access is free. ✉ *1 Dongfeng Lu, west side of People's Square* ☎ *0991/ 232–2828* 📠 *0991/232–1818* ⊕ *www.hoitakhotel.com* 🛏 *318 rooms, 38 suites* 🍴 *7 restaurants, in-room safes, minibar, in-room broadband, indoor pool, gym, hair salon, massage, sauna, billiards, bowling, Ping-Pong, nightclub, babysitting, laundry service, business services, meeting room, travel service* ▭ *AE, MC, V.*

¢–$$ 🏨 **Xinjiang Grand Hotel** (Xinjiang Dajiudian). Formerly the Holiday Inn, this hotel offers unremarkable standard rooms in the center of town. However if you're looking for a suite, prices here can be amazingly low—that is, if all the rooms aren't already occupied by long-term guests. Presidential suites can sometimes be had for as little as Y1,200. ✉ *168 Xinhua Bei Lu* ☎ *0991/281–8788* 📠 *0991/281–7422* ⊕ *www.hotelxj.cn* 🛏 *360 rooms, 22 suites* 🍴 *4 restaurants, minibars, in-room broadband, gym, sauna, hair salon, billiards, bar, shops, dry cleaning, laundry service, business services, meeting room, airport shuttle, travel services* ▭ *AE, MC, V.*

¢ 🏨 **Bogda Hotel** (Bogeda Binguan). The city's best budget option, this hotel has rooms that are cleaner and more comfortable than those offered at similarly priced lodgings. Most bathrooms even feature separate shower stalls. For those on a really tight budget, beds in dormitory-style rooms popular with backpackers are only Y20 per night. The CYTS travel agency comes highly recommended. ✉ *10 Guangming Lu* ☎ *0991/886–3910* 📠 *0991/886–5769* 🛏 *248 rooms* 🍴 *3 restaurants, café, gym, hair salon, laundry service, business services, travel services* ▭ *No credit cards.*

Nightlife

As with most Chinese cities, every other block in Ürümqi is blighted by high-price karaoke parlors and blaring discos. Don't worry, there are plenty of places to order a bottle of cold beer. If you're just looking for a cheap bite, the night market on Wuyi Lu—covered by a blanket of tiny white lights—is the place to go.

★ The entertaining song and dance performance at the **International Grand Bazaar Banquet Performance Theater** (⊠ Jiefang Lu, 3 km [2 mi] south of the city center ☎ 0991/855–5491 ⊠ Y168) is preceded by a ho-hum buffet that unsuccessfully tries to capture the delights of Uyghur cuisine. Never mind the food, as this is your best chance to see Uyghur, Uzbek, Kazakh, Tajik, Tartar, and even Irish dancing all in one spectacular evening. Make reservations through your hotel.

Fubar (⊠ Renmin Gongyuan Beijie ☎ 0991/584–4498) is the real thing: a tavern serving cold imported beer and authentic pub grub. The pizza is especially noteworthy. This is the best place in Ürümqi to relax after a day exploring the city. The foreign owners are happy to dispense free travel advice.

Shopping

The **International Grand Bazaar** (⊠ Jiefang Lu, 3 km [2 mi] south of the city center) is the best place to go for Uyghur items like embroidered skullcaps, brightly colored carpets, and hand-carved knives. If it's inexpensive gifts you're after, you will find them here.

Xinjiang Antique Store (⊠ 325 Jiefang Nan Lu, south of Renmin Lu ☎ 0991/282–5161) has a good selection of genuine antique Chinese bric-a-brac, including jade, jewelry, carpets, and porcelain. As all items come with a state-certified export certificate, you won't have to worry about getting your purchase through customs. A smaller branch is located inside the Xinjiang Autonomous Region Museum.

Side Trips from Ürümqi

Fodor'sChoice
★ About a three-hour ride from Ürümqi is the not-to-be-missed **Heavenly Lake** (Tianchi Hu), possibly the prettiest lake in China, surrounded by snow-sprinkled mountains. The water is crystal clear with a sapphire tint. In summer, white flowers dot the hillsides. Unfortunately, tourism has been leaving its ugly footprint. The lake's southern shore is crowded with tour groups posing for snapshots with Mount Bogda in the background. To better appreciate the lake's natural beauty, arrive before the hordes, or stay until after the last bus has departed.

Kazakh families still set up traditional felt tents along the shores of Heavenly Lake from early May to late October, bringing their horses, sheep, and cashmere goats. The Kazakh people have a long history as horse breeders and are known to be skilled riders.

■ TIP→ Most of the yurt dwellers are happy to have you spend the night for about Y20 per person. They can also furnish horses and a guide for a day of riding around the lake. The sleeping quarters are communal, and there's no plumbing. However, you'll have a rewarding glimpse into the way your Kazakh hosts live. It's easy enough to find a place to stay, but you may have difficulty communicating if your Chinese and Kazakh aren't up to snuff.

From Ürümqi, day-tour buses (Y130 round-trip) to Heavenly Lake leave at 9:30 in the morning from a small street beside the north gate of People's Park (Renmin Gongyuan). You'll have from about noon to 6 PM to explore the lake, arriving back in the city at 8 PM. Tickets—usually available up until the bus leaves—can be purchased near the buses. The price includes transportation, admission, and lunch upon arrival.

To & from Ürümqi

2 days (2,250 km [1,400 mi]) by train, 5 hrs by plane northwest of Beijing.

Many people fly to Ürümqi from Beijing or Xian to begin a journey on the Silk Road. The airport is 20 km (12 mi) north of the downtown area and can be reached by taxi (about Y60) in 20 minutes or by Bus 51 (Y1) in less than an hour. Those arriving by train will find themselves about 2 km (1 mi) southwest of the city center. Buses are more complicated: most arrive at Nianzigou, the long-distance bus station on the city's west side, but there are three other stations scattered around town. If you don't arrive at Nianzigou, you'll probably find yourself at Nanjiao Qichezhan (South Station), predictably located a few kilometers south of town.

Turpan

Turpan lies in a desert basin at the southern foot of the Heavenly Mountains. Part of the basin lies 505 feet below sea level, the hottest spot in China and the second-lowest point in the world after the Dead Sea. In summer, temperatures can soar to more than 50°C (120°F), so come prepared with lots of water and sunscreen.

Turpan's claim to fame is its location between the ruins of two spectacular ancient cities, Jiaohe and Gaochang. Most visitors don't linger in Turpan; the best five sites can easily be visited in a single day. But there are other attractions. Surrounded by some of the richest farmland in Xinjiang, Turpan's vineyards are famous for producing several varieties of candy-sweet raisins popular throughout China.

Exploring Turpan

Sugong Mosque (Sugong Ta) and the adjacent **Emin Tower** (Emin Ta) form Turpan's most recognizable image, often featured in tourist brochures. Built in 1777, it commemorates a military commander who suppressed a rebellion by a group of aristocrats. The 141-foot conical tower is elegantly spare, with bricks arranged in 15 patterns. The sunbaked roof of the mosque affords a view of the surrounding lush vineyards. Tours of the area often stop here, but if you've got a couple of hours you can visit on your own. This complex lies 4 km (2½ mi) from the city center at the southeast end of town. ⊠ *Go east on Laocheng Lu, turn right on the last paved road before farmland, known as Qiu Nian Zhong Lu* ☏ *Y20* ☉ *Dawn–dusk.*

The remarkable 2,000-year-old **Karez Irrigation System** (Kanerjing)

> **WORD OF MOUTH**
>
> "Turpan has the ancient ruins of two major cities, a well-sited if rather bare set of cave temples, and other sights. It is the lowest inland place after the Dead Sea."
> —PeterN_H.

9

allowed the desert cities of the Silk Road to flourish despite an unre-lentingly arid environment. In the oasis cities of Turpan and Hami, 1,600 km (990 mi) of underground tunnels brought water—moved only by gravity—from melting snow at the base of the Heavenly Mountains. You can view the tunnels at several sites around the city. Most tour guides take visitors to the largely educational Karez Irrigation Museum. Despite being described as the "underground Great Wall," some visitors are underwhelmed by what are essentially narrow dirt tunnels. ⊠ *888 Xincheng Lu, on the city's western outskirts* 🖼 *Y20* ⊘ *Daily 8–7.*

Around Turpan

★ The ruins of the **City of Gaochang** (Gaochang Gucheng) lie in a valley south of the Flaming Mountains. Legend has it that a group of soldiers stopped here in the 1st century BC on their way to Afghanistan, found that water was plentiful, and decided to stay. By the 7th century the city was the capital of the Kingdom of Gaochang, which ruled over 21 other towns, and by the 9th century the Uighurs had moved into the area from Mongolia, establishing the Kingdom of Kharakojam. In the 14th century Mongols conquered and destroyed the kingdom, leaving only the ruins that can still be seen today. Only the city walls and a partially preserved monastery surrounded by muted, almost unrecognizable shapes remain, an eerie and haunting excursion into the pages of history. Despite repeated plundering of the site, in the early 1900s German archaeologists were able to unearth manuscripts, statues, and frescoes in superb condition. To make the best of your time here, take a donkey cart (time to use your bargaining skills!) to the monastery in the rear right corner; from there, you can walk back toward the entrance through the ruins. ⊠ *30 km (19 mi) east of Turpan* 🖼 *Y20* ⊘ *Dawn–dusk.*

Fodor'sChoice
★
On an island at the confluence of two rivers, the impressive ruins of the **City of Jiaohe** (Jiaohe Gucheng) lie in the Yarnaz Valley west of Turpan. The city, established as a garrison during the Han Dynasty, was built on a high plateau, protected by the natural fortification of cliffs rising 100 feet above the rivers. Jiaohe was governed from the 2nd to the 7th century by the Kingdom of Gaochang and occupied later by Tibetans. Despite destruction in the 14th century by Mongol hordes, large fragments of actual streets and buildings remain, including a Buddhist monastery and Buddhist statues, a row of bleached pagodas, a 29-foot observation tower, and a prison. ⊠ *8 km (5 mi) west of Turpan* 🖼 *Y30* ⊘ *Dawn–dusk.*

★ The **Bezeklik Thousand Buddha Caves** (Bozikelike Qianfo Dong), in a breath-taking valley nestled inside the Flaming Mountains, is an ancient temple complex built between the 5th and 9th century by slaves whose entire lives went into the construction. Many of the fine examples of Buddhist sculpture and wall frescoes were destroyed after Islam came to the region in the 13th century. Other sculptures and frescoes, including several whole murals of Buddhist monks, were removed by 20th-century archaeologists like German Albert von Le Coq, who shipped his finds back to Berlin. Though they remain a feat of early engineering, the caves are in atrocious condition. Go just to see the site itself and the surrounding valley, which is magnificent. Avoid the nearby Buddha Cave con-

Traveling in the Desert

THINGS CAN CHANGE QUICKLY from uncomfortable to painful to dangerous in the intense heat of northwest China's expansive deserts. Temperatures in the summer frequently reach 100°F (40°C), with some areas—the depression around Turpan in particular—soaring to 120°F (50°C). The sun is strong and the air is bone dry. Many of the sites you'll be visiting are remote and lack even the most basic facilities.

In conditions like these, it would be unwise to travel without an abundant supply of water, as well as strong sunscreen, sunglasses, a good hat, toilet paper, and some heat-resistant snacks (dried fruit and nuts are packed with energy and are available everywhere). If you're a fan of cold water, buy frozen plastic bottles in the morning and they'll stay cool until lunchtime, when you should be able to restock.

Water and food are particularly important if you'll be making the long trek across the Taklamakan Desert to the southern Silk Road. The cross-desert highway traverses hundreds of miles of the most inhospitable territory on earth, with just a single gas station located at Tazhong, the halfway point. Should your vehicle become disabled somewhere along that stretch of highway, you may have to wait quite a while before help arrives. The name Taklamakan translates roughly as "he who goes in, never comes out." But by taking a few simple precautions, you can make sure this bit of ancient wisdom doesn't apply to you.

---

structed in 1980 by a local artist; it isn't worth an additional Y20. ✉ *35 km (22 mi) east of Turpan* 🎟 *Y20* 🕐 *Dawn–dusk.*

9

Tours

You could join an organized group tour around Turpan, but you'll likely spend too little time at the best sites and too much time in annoying tourist traps. By taking a slightly more expensive taxi tour you'll be able to choose your own itinerary and spend hours roaming the ruins of Jiaohe and Gaochang. In the off-season you may be able to secure a taxi for the day for as little as Y150, although prices of Y300 are more common during the summer.

📋 Tour-Operator Recommendations **CITS** ✉ Jiaotong Hotel, 230 Laochang Lu ☎ 0995/853-5809.

Where to Stay & Eat

Most hungry visitors stick to the restaurants in and around the Turpan Hotel on Qingnian Lu, a pleasant side street shaded by grape vines. The bazaar across from the bus station is a good place to grab lunch for around Y5. A lively night market with rows of kebab and spicy hotpot stands is on Gaochang Lu, a 10-minute walk north from the Turpan Hotel, just next to the huge public square.

¢–$$ ✕ **Muslim Restaurant.** Like most hotel restaurants in the region, this one is poorly lighted and lacks ambiance, but it does have a hearty variety of standard Uighur dishes: lamb, noodles, and vegetables. ⊠ *Turpan Hotel, 2 Qingnian Nan Lu* ☏ *No phone* ▭ *No credit cards.*

¢–$ ✕ **Chipu Café.** The most popular of the little cafés that cater to foreigners serves a variety of Chinese dishes. The menu is posted on the outdoor blackboard in English. ⊠ *Qingnian Lu, near the Turpan Hotel* ☏ *No phone* ▭ *No credit cards* ☉ *No dinner.*

¢ ✕ **John's Information Café.** The Western food at this popular tourist hangout is far from authentic, but people flock here for the familiar choices and rock-solid travel advice. This is a good place to meet other travelers; they can also rent bikes and wash laundry. ⊠ *Qingnian Lu, opposite the Turpan Hotel* ☏ *0995/852–4237* ▭ *No credit cards.*

¢ ▥ **Turpan Hotel** (Tulufan Binguan). This study in basic geometry, covered in white tile, is the best lodging in town. That isn't saying much, however. Rooms are nothing to write home about, but are relatively clean and large. The Muslim restaurant is quite good, and the gift shop is one exception to Turpan's status as a shopping nonentity. Even if you're not staying here, the indoor swimming pool—open only in the summer—is a good place to cool off after a long day in the desert sun. Admission is Y10 per person. ⊠ *2 Qingnian Nan Lu, south of Laocheng Lu* ☏ *0995/856–8888* ⇗ *219 rooms, 5 suites* ♨ *3 restaurants, indoor pool, gym, shop, laundry service, travel services* ▭ V.

¢ ▥ **Jiaotong Hotel** (Jiaotong Binguan). This budget option isn't a bad place to stay, despite noise from the bus station in the rear and the bazaar across the street. The on-site CITS travel agency makes arranging tours a snap. If you come to Turpan in the off-season, a deluxe suite with a small balcony overlooking the bazaar can be had for as little as Y200. ⊠ *230 Laocheng Lu, next to the bus station* ☏ *0995/853–1320* ⇗ *67 rooms* ♨ *Restaurant, business services, travel services* ▭ *No credit cards.*

Nightlife & the Arts

Much of the nightlife in Turpan consists of drinking beer, crunching sunflower seeds, and kicking back at outdoor tables. Locals head to the night market on Gaochang Lu, at the west end of a large public square.

To & from Turpan

2½–3 hrs (184 km [114 mi]) by bus southeast of Ürümqi, 4 hrs northeast of Korla.

Too close to Ürümqi to have its own airport, Turpan is located inconveniently 60 km (38 mi) south of the nearest train station, in Daheyan. If you arrive by train, take a taxi (Y20) or a public bus (Y8) to reach the city. Most likely, you'll arrive by long-distance bus; the terminal is located in the center of town on the north side of Laocheng Lu. Leaving Turpan is more difficult than arriving: one bus daily departs at noon for Kashgar. For any other destination, you'll have to head back to Ürümqi.

Kashgar

Kashgar, the westernmost city in China, is closer to Baghdad than Beijing. More than 3,400 km (2,100 mi) west of the capital, the city has been a center of trade between China and the outside world for at least 2,000 years. Today, Kashgar is a hub for merchants coming in over the

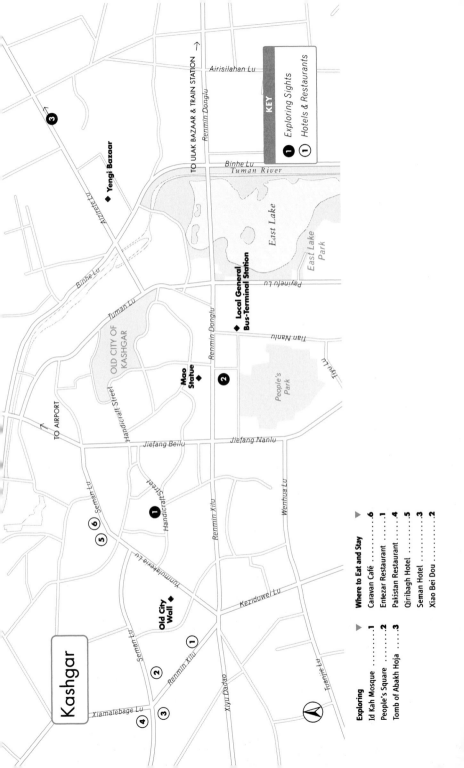

Khunjerab Pass from Pakistan and the Torugart Pass from Kyrgyzstan. When these two treacherous mountain passes are open between May 1 and October 30, Kashgar becomes a particularly colorful city, abuzz not only with curious Western tourists but also with visitors from every corner of Central Asia.

Despite an increasing Han presence in central Kasghar (symbolized by one of the largest Mao statues in the country), the city is still overwhelmingly Uyghur. A great deal of modernization has taken place here since the railway from Ürümqi arrived in 1999, yet parts of Kashgar remain in a time warp. Only a few blocks from newly built karaoke parlors and car dealerships, you can still find blacksmiths, bakers, and cobblers. Much of the city's Uyghur architecture has been demolished, but there are still some traditional houses with ornately painted balconies, as well as large remaining sections of the old city. Most visitors come to Kasghar for the amazing Sunday Market, the largest bazaar in Central Asia and one of the best photo-ops in all of China.

Exploring

❶ Start your tour of the city with a visit to the **Id Kah Mosque** (Ai Tiga'er Qingzhen Si), the center of Muslim life in Kasghar. One of the largest mosques in China, the ornate structure of yellow bricks is the result of many extensions and renovations to the original mosque, built in 1442 as a prayer hall for the ruler of Kashgar. The main hall has a ceiling with fine wooden carvings and precisely 100 carved wooden columns. When services aren't being held, you are free to wander the quiet shaded grounds and even to enter the prayer hall. As this is an active site of worship, women should dress modestly. ⊠ *Ai Tiga'er Guanchang* 🕾 *No phone* 🖃 *Y10* ☉ *Dawn–dusk.*

❸ About 5 km (3 mi) northeast of the city, the **Tomb of Abakh Hoja** (Xiangfei Mu) is one of the most sacred sites in Xinjiang. The sea-green tiled hall that houses the tomb—actually about two dozen tombs—is part of a massive complex of sacred Islamic structures built around 1640. Uyghurs named the tomb and surrounding complex after Abakh Hoja, an Islamic missionary believed to be a descendant of Mohammed who ruled Kashgar and outlying regions in the 17th century. Excavations of the glazed-brick tombs indicate that the first occupant was Abakh Hoja's father, who is buried here along with Abakh Hoja and many of their descendants.

The Han, who prefer to emphasize the site's historical connection to their dynastic empire, call it the Tomb of the Fragrant Concubine. When the

Islam in China

AT LEAST 20 MILLION MUSLIMS live in China, most of them concentrated in areas along the old Silk Road. This is no coincidence, as the teachings of Islam were brought to China by Middle Eastern merchants, some of whom married locals and settled down along the way.

There are two distinct Muslim minority groups in China: the Hui, who are indistinguishable in appearance from the Han Chinese except for the white caps worn by males and the headscarves worn by females, and the Uyghurs (pronounced wee-ghers), a Turkic people with unmistakable Central Asian features. The two groups are almost equal in population—about 10 million each. The Uyghurs live almost exclusively in Xinjiang, whereas the Hui live in large clusters spread throughout the northwest and smaller communities in every major Chinese city.

The greatest difference between Huis and Uyghurs is their orientation toward the country. While the Hui see themselves as a proud Chinese people who long ago converted to Islam, the Uyghurs see themselves as a conquered nation. Throughout the 1990s, Uyghur separatist activities—including several bus bombings in Xinjiang—resulted in a massive crackdown by the central government, leading to accusations of repression, torture, and politically motivated executions. The situation has quieted down over the past few years, but tensions between Uyghurs and Han Chinese are still high.

grandniece of Abakh Hoja was chosen as concubine by the Qing ruler Qianlong in Beijing, Uyghur legend holds that she committed suicide rather than submitting to the emperor. In the Han story, she dutifully went to Beijing and spent 30 years in the emperor's palace, then asked to be buried in her homeland. Either way, her alleged tomb was excavated in the 1980s, and found to be empty. The tomb is a bit difficult to locate, so take a taxi. ⊠ *Off of Aizirete Lu, 2 km (1 mi) east of the Sunday Bazaar* ☎ *No phone* 🎫 *Y15* ☉ *Daily 9–9.*

If you happen to forget which country Kashgar is located in, chances are you aren't standing in **People's Square** (Renmin Guanchang). A statue of Mao Zedong—one of the largest in China—stands with his right arm raised in perpetual salute. The statue is evidence of an unspoken rule in China that directly relates the size of a Mao tribute to its distance from Beijing; the only Mao statue larger than this one is located in Tibet. ⊠ *Renmin Lu between Jiefang Lu and Tian Lu* ☎ *No phone.*

Tours

Kasghar is a tourist-friendly city, so you shouldn't have any trouble arranging tours. Uyghur Tour & Travel Center (also known as Abdul's), in the lobby of the Seman Hotel, offers a "money-back guarantee." It has received high marks from travelers for the past five years. A day-tour of sites within Kashgar will cost about Y400, not including admission tickets. If you're interested in spending a night in the area's only 1,000-star hotel—the Taklamakan Desert—the agency can arrange an all-inclusive overnight camel trek for Y850 per person.

📶 Tour-Operator Recommendations

Uyghur Tour & Travel Center ✉ Seman Hotel, 170 Seman Lu, at Renmin Lu 📞0998/258-5182 ⊕ www.uighurtour.com.

📶 Tour-Operator Recommendations

Uyghur Tour & Travel Center ✉ Seman Hotel, 170 Seman Lu 📞 0998/258-5182 ⊕ www.uighurtour.com.

Where to Stay & Eat

Uyghur food is everywhere in Kashgar. If you get tired of eating lamb, there are some decent restaurants

with Sichuan or even Pakistani food. For something cheap and filling, look for stalls selling everything from juicy melon to almonds to fresh-baked *nang* bread. Hotel reservations are not necessary in Kashgar. Even in the busiest season, there are bound to be plenty of rooms available.

¢–$ ✕ **Caravan Café.** If it's Western food you're craving, head straight to this local institution. Run by a longtime American resident of Kashgar, everything here tastes authentic, if not quite perfect. Customers particularly recommend the quiche, which can be combined with a cold drink and dessert for Y40. If the heat's got you down, go for a fruit smoothie. This is also a good place to pick up travel information. ✉ *120 Seman Lu, next to the Qinibagh Hotel's entrance gate* 📞 0998/298–1864 ⊟ No credit cards.

★ ¢–$ ✕ **Entezar Restaurant** (Yintizaer). Frequented by locals, Entezar is probably your only chance to sample a complete range of Uyghur cuisine. Every word on the menu is translated into English, including helpful descriptions of each dish. For those tired of typical Uyghur fare, Muslim-friendly stir-fry dishes are also available. Forget about a cold beer, though; alcohol is not allowed on the premises. ✉ *30 Renmin Xilu, southeast of the Seman Hotel* 📞 No phone ⊟ No credit cards.

¢–$ ✕ **Xiao Bei Dou.** When you've grown tired of mutton, head here for the best Sichuan-style dishes in Kashgar. Classic selections like sweet-and-sour pork (*tangcu liji*), chicken with peanuts (*gongbao jiding*), and scallion pancakes (*conghuabing*) are all wellprepared. There's plenty of cold beer in the refrigerator, and the 2nd-floor covered terrace is perfect on a warm summer evening. An English menu is available, but the selection is limited. ✉ *285 Seman Lu, east of the Seman Hotel* 📞 No phone ⊟ No credit cards.

¢ ✕ **Pakistan Restaurant.** Foreign restaurants are a rare sight in Kasghar, so this dirt-cheap curry joint is a welcome addition. This is where the city's Pakistani residents wile away their evenings playing cards and sipping tea. To order here, simply state the main ingredient in English: chicken, beef, mutton, or spinach. There are no chopsticks here, as everything is scooped-up using delicious *roti* flat bread. Hot chai tea served with milk is the best way to wash down your meal. This restaurant's sign is covered by a large tree, so look for the tree instead of the sign. ✉ *Seman Lu, opposite the Seman Hotel's rear gate* 📞 No phone ⊟ No credit cards.

¢ ▫ **Qinibagh Hotel** (Qiniwake Binguan). Of Kasghar's two popular hotels, the Qinibagh is in much better shape. Located on the site of the
former British consulate, this hotel has an interesting history. Constructed in 1908, the consulate building—now an attractive Uyghur restaurant—was home to diplomat extraordinaire Sir George McCartney and
his wife for 26 years; their guest list included famous Silk Road travelers like Sven Hedin, Sir Aurel Stein, and Peter Fleming. There are
branches of CITS and John's Information Café, two travel resources,
on the premises. ✉ *93 Seman Lu, northwest of Id Kah Mosque* ☎ *0998/
298–2103* 🖷 *0998/298–2299* ⚒ *4 restaurants, minibars, sauna, bar, laundry service, business services, travel services* ▭ *V.*

¢ ▫ **Seman Hotel** (Seman Binguan). Built in 1890 as the Russian consulate,
this edifice served as a center of political intrigue for many years. The
oldest wing of the hotel is the original consulate, where fans of the "Great
Game" can stay in musty suites decorated with luxurious rugs and old
furniture. The hotel's newer rooms range from comfortable to dilapidated, so be sure to look at a few before you decide. The worst rooms
are adjacent to a large traffic circle; nicer ones surround a pleasant courtyard in the rear. The hotel is very popular with backpackers who come
for the Y15 beds packed into dorm-style rooms. Travel agencies are clustered around the lobby. ✉ *170 Seman Lu, at Renmin Lu* ☎ *0998/258–
2129* 🖷 *0998/258–2150* ⚒ *3 restaurants, shops, laundry service, business services, travel services* ▭ *No credit cards.*

Nightlife & the Arts

In the courtyards of the Seman and Qinibagh hotels, traditional music
and dance are performed frequently in the evening from May through
October. There is usually a cover charge of Y30 per person.

Shopping

Kashgar's famous **Sunday Market** consists of two bazaars with a distance
of almost 10 km (6 mi) between them. The **Yengi Bazaar** on Aizilaiti
Lu, about 1 ½ km (1 mi) northeast of the city center, is open every day,
but on Sunday the surrounding streets overflow with vendors hawking
everything from boiled sheep's heads to trendy sunglasses. In the covered section you can bargain for decorative knives, embroidered fabrics, and all sorts of Uyghur-themed souvenirs. Behind the bazaar, rows
of sleepy donkeys nod off in the bright sunlight, their carts lined up neatly
beside them. For the best photos, however, you'll need to head over to
the **Ulak Bazaar**, a 10-minute taxi ride to the east. Essentially a livestock
market, farmers here tug recalcitrant sheep through the streets, scarf-
shrouded women preside over heaps of red eggs, and old Uyghur men
squat over baskets of chickens, haggling over the virtues and vices of
each hapless hen. In the market for a camel? You can buy one here. On
the outskirts of the market you can get an old-world-style straight-
razor shave from a Uyghur barber or grab a bowl of *laghman* noodles,
knowing that it's flavored with meat that is very, very fresh.

Running alongside the Id Kah Mosque is a narrow lane known as **Hand-
icraft Street.** Walking in either direction you'll find merchants selling everything from bright copper kettles to wedding chests to brass sleigh bells.
At the **Uyghur Musical Instruments Workshop** (✉ 272 Kumdarwaza Rd.

📟 0998/283–5378) you can watch the owner or his apprentice working on Uyghur string instruments—stretching snakeskin or inlaying tiny bits of shell to make a Uyghur guitar called a *ravap*.

Side Trips from Kasghar

6 hrs (200 km [125 mi]) by bus south of Kashgar, near the border with Tajikistan.

The **Karakorum Highway,** a spectacular road winding across some of the most dramatic and inhospitable terrain in the world, traces one of the major ancient silk routes, starting in Kashgar and leading south for 2,100 km (1,300 mi) through three great mountain ranges over the Khunjerab Pass into Pakistan.

DID YOU KNOW

The story behind the highway is as remarkable as the scenery itself. Begun in 1967 by the Chinese government, construction went on for 20 years during which more than 400 lives were lost. Workers blasted through hundreds of miles of solid rock, often hanging by rope over deep gorges to drill holes for dynamite.

Fodor's Choice ★

Six hours south of Kasghar, having followed the Gez River valley deep into the heart of the Pamir Mountains, the highway passes alongside picturesque **Karakul Lake** (Kalakuli Hu). At an elevation of 3,800 meters (12,500 feet), this crystal-blue jewel of a lake is dominated on either side by stunning snowcapped mountains, including the 7,800-meter (25,600-foot) peak of **Muztagata,** the "Father of the Ice Mountains." Arriving at the lake, you'll practically be assaulted by would-be-hosts on camelback, horseback, and motorcycle. Avoid the expensive, touristy yurts along the shore and instead head south of the lake (toward Muztagata) to the charming Kyrgyz village of Subaxcun. The village is farther than it looks, so make use of offers for a free camel or horse ride to your lodging. Accommodations for one night, including dinner and a simple breakfast, should be Y20 to Y40. A two-hour tour of the lake on horseback should be about the same price. Bring warm clothing even in the summer, as the weather can be downright chilly after the sun goes down.

Any travel agent can arrange tours to Lake Karakul, but most people make the breathtaking journey by public bus. Buses headed for Tashkurgan, 2 hours south of the lake, leave Kashgar's long-distance bus station every morning at 10 AM. You'll have to pay the full price of Y44 for your ticket even though you're not traveling the full distance. Bring your passport or you'll be turned back at a border checkpoint in Gezcun. To catch the bus, wait by the side of the highway and flag it down—the bus returning to Kasghar from Tashkurgan passes the lake between 11 AM and 1 PM. A seat should only cost Y40, but enterprising drivers will demand Y50. Either way, the bus is much cheaper than private tours, which will set you back about Y900 per day.

To & from Kashgar

24 hrs (1,175 km [729 mi]) by train southwest of Ürümqi.

Daunted by the long train journey from Ürümqi, many tourists headed for Kasghar travel by air. The airport is 13 km (8 mi) north of the city center; a taxi to or from your hotel shouldn't cost more than Y20. Most people arrive in Kasghar by train; the station is 10 km (6 mi) east of town, not far from the livestock market. Taxis from here will cost about Y15. Kasghar's long-distance bus station is located just east of People's Park in the center of town, although many buses arriving in the city will stop somewhere less convenient to drop you off.

XINJIANG ESSENTIALS

Transportation

BY AIR

Daily flights link Ürümqi with most major Chinese cities, including Beijing, Guangzhou, Shanghai, Xian, Lanzhou, and Chengdu. Destinations within Xinjiang include Kashgar, Hotan, Kuqa, Korla, Altai, and Yining; there are also flights to Dunhuang in Gansu. International destinations include Almaty (Kazakhstan), Bishkek (Kyrgyzstan), Islamabad (Pakistan), Baku (Azerbaijan), as well as Novosobirsk and Moscow in Russia.

🛂 Airport Information **Ürümqi Airport** (Wulumuqi Feijichang) ✉ 16 km (10 mi) northwest of the city in Diwopu ☎ 0991/380-1347. **Kashgar Airport** (Kashi Feijichang) ✉ 10 km (6 mi) north of the city center ☎ 0998/282-3204.

🛂 Carriers **China Southern Airlines** ✉ 26 Guangming Lu, Ürümqi ☎ 0991/882-3300 or 0991/950-333.

BY BUS

Long-distance bus travel is often the only way to travel in Xinjiang if you don't want to wait a day or two for the next available train. Every city in the region is served at least daily by bus from Ürümqi. There's even bus service to Almaty, Kazakhstan.

It's usually a straightforward affair buying tickets from the only station in town, but Ürümqi is more complicated. Unless you're going to Hotan or Altai—which have their own separate bus stations—your best bet is to first look for tickets at Nianzigou Station. If you don't like what's available there, or if your destination is Turpan, head to the South Station (Nanjiao Qichezhan).

Buses (Y130 round-trip) leave for Heavenly Lake (Tianchi Hu) at 9:30 AM from the north gate of Renmin Park. They usually leave the lake at 6 PM and arrive back in Ürümqi at 7:30 PM.

🛂 Bus Information **Kashgar Bus Station** ✉ Tiannan Lu, on the east side of People's Park ☎ 0998/282-9673. **Turpan Bus Station** ✉ 27 Laocheng Lu ☎ 0995/852-2325. **Ürümqi Nianzigou Station** ✉ Western end of Heilongjiang Lu, Ürümqi ☎ 0991/587-8898. **Ürümqi South Station** (Nanjiao Keyunzhan) ✉ Yanerwo Lu, Ürümqi ☎ 0991/286-6635.

BY TRAIN

Daily trains run between Ürümqi and Beijing (48 hours), Shanghai (52 hours), Chengdu (50 hours), Xian (40 hours), and Lanzhou (29 hours). Trains between Ürümqi and Kashgar (24 or 28 hours) depart twice daily; the slow train is half the price of the fast train, but you'll have to do without air-conditioning. Generally, buses are faster and more frequent than trains for travel within Xinjiang.

⁊ Train Information **Ürümqi Train Station** (✉ Qiantangjiang Lu, Ürümqi ☏ 0991/581–4203).

Contacts & Resources

EMERGENCIES

⁊ Police **Ürümqi PSB** ✉ Guangmin Lu, northeast of Renmin Sq ☏ 0991/281-0452. **Kashgar PSB** ✉ 139 Yumulakexiehai Lu, south of the Qinibagh Hotel ☏ 0998/282-2814.

⁊ Hospitals **Chinese Medicine Hospital of Ürümqi** ✉ 60 Youhau Nan Lu, Ürümqi ☏ 0991/242-0963. **Number One People's Hospital** ✉ Jichang Lu, Kashgar ☏ 0998/296-2750.

MONEY MATTERS

In China, there's no place more difficult to run out of money than in Xinjiang. Stock up on cash before you arrive. You can exchange foreign currency and traveler's checks at the main branch of the Bank of China in any major city, but don't even try in small towns and villages. The only thing that can save you if you run out of cash and traveler's checks is a credit card, which you can use to get a cash advance at most ATMs. Debit cards, even those with credit-card logos, don't work.

⁊ Bank of China ✉ 343 Jiefang Nan Lu, at the corner of Minzhu Lu, behind the Hoi Tak Hotel ☏ 0991/283-4222.

INTERNET SERVICES

Major hotels in Ürümqi usually have Internet access. Dragon Netbar, which charges Y1 to Y3 per hour, is open around the clock. This Egyptian-themed Internet café is around the corner from the city's most popular night market.

⁊ Dragon Netbar ✉ 11 Huanghe Lu, near the corner of Wuyi Lu, Ürümqi ☏ No phone.

VISITOR INFORMATION

⁊ Tourist Information **CITS** ✉ Xinjiang Grand Hotel, 168 Xinhua Bei Lu, Ürümqi ☏ 0991/230-5238 ⊕ www.xinjiangtour.com ✉ Jiaotong Hotel, 125 Laocheng Lu, Turpan ☏ 0995/852-1352 ✉ Qinibagh Hotel, 144 Seman Lu, Kashgar ☏ 0998/298-3156.

At a Glance

ENGLISH	PINYIN	CHINESE CHARACTERS
EXPLORING		
SHAANXI	Shǎnxī	陕西
XIAN	Xī'ān	西安
Bank of China	Zhōngguó Yínháng	中国银行
Banpo Matriarchal Clan Village	Bànpō Bówùguǎn	半坡博物馆
Bell Tower	Zhōnglóu	钟楼
Bell Tower Square	Zhōnglóu Guǎngchǎng	钟楼广场
Big Wild Goose Pagoda	Dàyàn Tǎ	大雁塔
Culture Street	Wénhuà Jiē	文化街
Drum Tower	Gǔlóu	鼓楼
Famen Temple	Fǎmén Sì	法门寺
Forest of Stone Tablets Museum	Bēilín Bówùguǎn	碑林博物馆
Great Mosque	Dà Qīngzhēn Sì	大清真寺
Hua Jue Xiang Market	Huà Jué Xiàng Shì Chǎng	化觉巷市场
Huaqing Hot Springs	Huáqīng Chí	华清池
Muslim Quarter	Huímín Xiǎoqū	回民小区
Shaanxi History Museum	Shǎnxī Lìshǐ Bówùguǎn	陕西历史博物馆
Small Goose Pagoda	Xiǎoyàn Tǎ	小雁塔
South Gate	Nánmén	南门
Terracotta Warriors Museum	Bīngmǎyǒng Bówùguǎn	兵马俑博物馆
Tomb of the First Qin Emperor	Qín Shǐhuáng Líng	秦始皇陵
Xian Train Station	Xī'ān Huǒchēzhàn	西安火车站
Xian Xianyang Airport	Xī'ān Xiányáng Fēijīchǎng	西安咸阳飞机场
Xianyang City Museum	Xiányáng Shì Bówùguǎn	咸阳市博物馆
GANSU	Gānsù	甘肃
LANZHOU	Lánzhōu	兰州
EXPLORING		
Five Spring Mountain Park	Wǔquán Gōngyuán	五泉公园
Gansu Provincial Museum	Gānsù Shěng Bówùguǎn	甘肃省博物馆
Labrang Monastery	Lābǔléng Sì	拉卜楞寺
Lanzhou East Bus Station	Lánzhōu Dōng Qìchēzhàn	兰州东汽车站

9

Lanzhou South Bus Station	Lánzhōu Nán Qìchēzhàn	兰州南汽车站
Lanzhou Train Station	Lánzhōu Huǒchēzhàn	兰州火车站
Lanzhou West Bus Station	Lánzhōu Xī Qìchēzhàn	兰州西汽车站
Lanzhou Zhongchuan Airport	Lánzhōu Zhōngchuān Fēijīchǎng	兰州中川飞机场
Mountain of the White Pagoda Park	Báitǎshān Gōngyuán	白塔山公园
Thousand Buddha Temple and Grottoes	Bǐnglíng Sì Shíkū	炳灵寺石窟
Xiahe	Xiàhé	夏河
DUNHUANG	Dūnhuáng	敦煌
EXPLORING		
Dunhuang Airport	Dūnhuáng Fēijīchǎng	敦煌飞机场
Dunhuang Bus Station	Dūnhuáng Qìchēzhàn	敦煌汽车站
Dunhuang Museum	Dūnhuáng Bówùguǎn	敦煌博物馆
Mogao Grottoes	Mògāo Kū	莫高窟
Singing Sand Mountain	Míngshā Shān	鸣沙山
QINGHAI	Qīnghǎi	青海
XINING	Xīníng	西宁
EXPLORING		
Bird Island	Niǎo Dǎo	鸟岛
Green Sea Lake	Qīnghǎi Hú	青海湖
Jianguo Road Wholesale Market	Jiànguó Lù Pīfā Shìchǎng	建国路批发市场
Kumbum Monastery	Tǎ'ěr Sì	塔尔寺
North Monastery	Běichán Sì	北禅寺
Shuijin Xiang Market	Shuǐjǐn Xiàng Shāngchǎng	水井巷商场
Xining Caojiabao Airport	Xīníng Cáojiābǎo Fēijīchǎng	西宁曹家堡飞机场
Xining Bus Station	Xīníng Qìchēzhàn	西宁汽车站
Xining Train Station	Xīníng Huǒchēzhàn	西宁火车站
XINJIANG	Xīnjiāng	新疆
ÜRÜMQI	Wūlǔmùqí	乌鲁木齐
EXPLORING		
International Grand Bazaar	Dà Bāzā	大巴扎
Heavenly Lake	Tiānchí Hú	天池湖

Nianzigou Bus Station	Niǎnzǐgōu Qìchēzhàn	碾子沟汽车站
People's Park	Rénmín Gōngyuán	人民公园
Red Mountain Park	Hóng Shān Gōngyuán	红山公园
Ürümqi Airport	Wūlǔmùqí Fēijīchǎng	乌鲁木齐飞机场
Ürümqi South Bus Station	Wūlǔmùqí Nán Qìchēzhàn	乌鲁木齐南汽车站
Ürümqi Train Station	Wūlǔmùqí Huǒchēzhàn	乌鲁木齐火车站
Xinjiang Autonomous Region Museum	Xīnjiāng Zìzhìqū Bówùguǎn	新疆自治区博物馆
TURPAN	Tǔlǔfān	吐鲁番
EXPLORING		
Bezeklik Thousand Buddha Caves	Bózīkèlǐkè Qiānfódòng	柏孜克里克千佛洞
City of Gaochang	Gāochāng Gùchéng	高昌故城
City of Jiaohe	Jiāohé Gùchéng	交河故城
Karez Irrigation Museum	Kǎnér jǐng Bówùguǎn	坎儿井博物馆
Sugong Mosque & Emin Tower	Émǐn Tǎ	额敏塔
KASGHAR	Kāshí	喀什
EXPLORING		
Id Kah Mosque	Àitígǎ'ěr Qīngzhēn Sì	艾提尕尔清真寺
Karakul Lake	Kālākùlè Hú	喀拉库勒湖
Kasghar Train Station	Kāshí Huǒchēzhàn	喀什火车站
Kashgar Airport	Kāshí Fēijīchǎng	喀什飞机场
People's Square	Rénmín Guǎngchǎng	人民广场
Tomb of Abakh Hoja	Xiāngfēi Mù	香妃墓

9

Tibet

THE ROOFTOP OF THE WORLD

Young Buddhist monk at Sakya Monastery, Tibet

WORD OF MOUTH

"Tibet overland is a trip in itself. The roads were a little muddy—got stuck many times—but it definitely was an adventure and a great trip."

—Boop

WELCOME TO TIBET

TOP REASONS TO GO

★ **Barkhor:** Tibetan Buddhism's holiest pilgrimage circuit, the Barkhor is both the heart of old Lhasa and one of the liveliest people-watching spots in all of China.

★ **Potala Palace:** Towering over Lhasa, this still-impressive palace of the Dalai Lamas was once the world's tallest structure.

★ **Ganden Monastery:** The most remote of the capital's three great monasteries, Ganden offers stunning views of the Lhasa River Valley and surrounding Tibetan farmland from a height of 14,764 feet.

★ **Gyantse Dzong:** The site of fierce fighting between Tibetan and British troops in 1904, this fortress is one of the few remaining symbols of Tibetan military power.

★ **Everest Base Camp:** Stand in awe beneath the world's tallest mountain.

Gyantse Monastery.

XINJIANG UYGUR ZIZHIQU

Wujang

Zhaxigang

**QINGSHAN GAOYUAN
(TIBETIAN PLATEAU)**

**XIZANG ZIZHIQU
(TIBET AUTONOMOUS REGION)**

Dongco

Nyima

Barga

GANGDISE SHAN

Coqen

Siling Co

HIMALAYA

NEPAL

INDIA

Lhaze

Shigatse **3**

**Everest
Base Camp**

Gyantse **2**

Tingri

Guru

0   100 mi

0   100 km

Mt. Everest
(Mt. Qomolangma)

BHU

1 Lhasa: Despite the city's rapid modernization, Lhasa still deserves its reputation as one of China's must-visit destinations. From the crowded back alleys of the Barkhor to the imposing heights of the Potala Palace, a mix of Westerners, local Tibetans, Nepalis, and Han Chinese give this city an atmosphere unlike any other place in the world.

2 Gyantse: Past the sapphire waters of Yamdrok Tso and endless fields of golden highland barley, this small city is the gateway to southern Tibet and the Himalayas. An abandoned fortress high above town is testament to the area's former military importance, while the unique architecture at Pelkor Chode Monastery speaks to the city's history as a melting pot of varied religious denominations.

Camp in the shadow of Mt. Everest.

GETTING ORIENTED

The Tibetan plateau is more than twice the size of France, sandwiched between two Himalayan ridges whose peaks reach an altitude of nearly 9 km (5½ mi). With the recent opening of the rail line and significantly improved roads, Tibet is now more accessible than ever. Lhasa is the best base from which to take day-trips to the fertile Kyi-chu Valley or longer jaunts into the southwestern highlands of Tsang to visit Gyantse, Shigatse, and the Everest region. Every hotel and tour operator can arrange four-wheel-drive jeeps with a driver and/or a guide. Tibet is currently undergoing massive infrastructure improvements, and many roads that were once as bumpy as the steep mountain passes have been flattened into perfect stretches of blacktop. While the improvements are being made, however, you'll still have to use a significant number of dirt roads.

10

3 Shigatse: Tibet's second-largest city, Shigatse, is the traditional capital of the Tsang region and home to the Panchen Lama's seat of power at Tashilhunpo Monastery. The ruined fortress on a hill above town—now being rebuilt as a luxury hotel—is one of the most glaring symbols of the modern world's encroachment on an ancient and sacred land.

4 Everest: You may have trouble breathing when you first sight the majestic peaks of the Himalayas, and not only because of the high altitude. The roof of the world is truly a spectacular place, with roaring snow-melt rivers feeding Tibetan farms and fields of wildflowers below.

TIBET PLANNER

When to go

Like the rest of China, choosing when to visit Tibet is a matter of balancing your tolerance for extreme weather with your tolerance for tourist hordes. The busiest months are July and August, but pleasant weather is common from May through October. If you can come at the beginning or end of the high season you'll have plenty of breathing space to take in the golden roofs of Tibet's monasteries and the icy peaks of the Himalayas. You may want to schedule your trip to coincide with one of Tibet's colorful celebrations including the Birth of Buddha Festival (end of May), the Holy Mountain Festival (end of July), the Yogurt Festival (August), and the Bathing Festival (September). Be aware that if you travel to Tibet in the off-season, many hotels and restaurants may be closed. No matter what time of year you choose to visit, warm clothing, sunglasses, and sunscreen are essential gear for the high-altitude climate.

Lhasa Express

One of history's most audacious engineering projects, the rail line to Lhasa began construction in 2001 after more than 30 years of delays. Chairman Mao first proposed the railroad in the 1960s along with other infrastructure projects just now being realized, like the massive Three Gorges Dam on the Yangtze River. The list of technical challenges confronting the rail line was daunting, as more than 966 km (600 mi) of track needed to be constructed at an altitude of more than 13,000 feet, topping out at Tangula Pass near 17,000 feet. Much of the track rests on semifrozen and constantly shifting permafrost. The line also crosses through six protected environmental reserves, home to endangered species like the Tibetan antelope and snow leopard.

Swiss engineers, experts on frozen terrain, said the project was impossible, but the Chinese government was having none of it. The first passenger train, carrying President Hu Jintao and a host of other dignitaries, rolled into Lhasa's shiny new station on July 1, 2006. The cultural implications of the railroad to ethnic Tibetans—already a minority in their own land—are obvious. The migration of Han Chinese will continue to expand as the traditional Tibetan way of life in many areas rapidly declines in the face of modernization. Politically, the railroad is another firm sign from Beijing that they have no intention of ever letting Tibet break off into a separate political entity; in fact, plans to extend the railway to Tibet's second-largest city, Shigatse, and over the Himalayas to Kathmandu in Nepal are already being developed.

However, the railway isn't completely negative for the locals. A large number of Tibetans make their livelihood from tourism in the region, which has increased dramatically since the opening of the line. The relatively cheap, quick, and comfortable ride by train has also made it possible for Tibetans working and studying in faraway parts of China to return home and visit their families during holidays, something that was nearly impossible when the only practical way to reach Lhasa was an expensive flight.

Getting Around

Outside of Lhasa, Tibet is one of the few places in China where independent travel is almost impossible. Sure, there are cyclists, backpackers, and other rogue types who manage to figure out an unofficial (and usually illegal) way to travel from one remote monastery to the next. But for the rest of us, who prefer to travel comfortably by bus or automobile without fear of imprisonment, the use of an official tour operator is essential.

Private buses for foreign tourists operate during the high season, an economical choice if you're unwilling to spend Y1,000 per day for a private jeep. Four-wheel-drive vehicles (almost always a Toyota Land Cruiser) with drivers are hired out by the many tour outfits based in Lhasa, who will also arrange the necessary permits and tour guides, dependent of course on your travel itinerary.

If you're hoping to explore areas of northern Tibet, like Nagqu and Amdo, be aware that although you can disembark from the train at these stops, you may have difficulty getting back on. People in China have often already purchased every available seat. It's probably best to sit tight until Lhasa and then find another mode of transport to your more off-the-beaten-path destinations.

WHAT IT COSTS In Yuan

RESTAURANTS				
$$$$	**$$$**	**$$**	**$**	**¢**
over 150	100–150	50–99	25–49	under 25
HOTELS				
$$$$	**$$$**	**$$**	**$**	**¢**
over 1,000	500–999	350–499	200–349	under 200

Restaurant prices are for a main course. There is no sales tax in China and tipping is not expected. Hotel prices unless noted are for a standard double room, including taxes.

Cultural Conflict

No matter how remote and underdeveloped Tibet may seem, it's still a tempting destination for the more than one billion people crowded into China's eastern half. As the region's infrastructure is built up and its small towns turn into cities, people looking for job opportunities naturally gravitate here.

Tibetan exile groups accuse the Chinese government of actively encouraging Han migration into the region, but there is no significant evidence to back up this claim. More likely, the continued influx of ethnic Chinese (Han) into Tibet is simply the result of people escaping from fiercely competitive and overcrowded areas in the east.

No matter what's behind the population shift, this much is clear: Han Chinese almost certainly outnumber locals living in the Tibet Autonomous Region (TAR).

One would expect this changing demographic to spell doom for Tibetan culture, but this is not the case. The Barkhor in Lhasa and the area around Tashilhunpo Monastery in Shigatse are certainly Tibetan islands in otherwise increasingly Han cities, but the rest of Tibet remains relatively free from Chinese influence.

The key to understanding migration into the region is that the Han are looking for a better standard of living, not to push Tibetans out of their homeland.

Although Tibet's days as a sheltered mountain kingdom are long gone, you'll find in your travels here that there is still plenty of room for the Chinese and Tibetans to live and prosper together.

10

By Michael D. Manning

Tibet is all you've heard and everything you've imagined: a land of intense sunshine and towering snowcapped peaks, where crystal-clear rivers and sapphire lakes irrigate terraced fields of golden highland barley. The Tibetan people are extremely religious, viewing their daily toil and the harsh environment surrounding them as challenges along the path to life's single goal, the attainment of spiritual enlightenment. The region's multitude of richly decorated monasteries, temples, and palaces is a testament to the dedication of the Tibetan people to their religion. These buildings—including the Potala Palace—were not constructed by forced labor, but by laborers and artisans who donated their entire lives to the accumulation of good karma.

The death, destruction, and cultural denigration of Tibet that accompanied the Chinese invasion in the early 1950s changed this land forever, as did the Cultural Revolution in the late 1960s. Yet the people here remain resilient. Colorfully dressed pilgrims still bring their offerings of yak butter to the temples, and monks work with zeal to repair the damage done to their monasteries. Of course, many young Tibetans, attracted by the wealth and convenience brought by development, have abandoned the traditional ways of their ancestors. Coca-Cola, fast food, and pulsing techno music are popular in Lhasa. Yet it would be a mistake to think that the changes have somehow lessened Tibet's allure as a travel destination. In fact, the presence here of both modern skyscrapers and old stone-block farmhouses only emphasizes the unique and special nature of Tibet, clinging to the past as it takes tentative steps toward the future.

LHASA

The capital of Tibet, Lhasa is a treasure trove of monasteries, palaces, and temples. Geographically the city is divided into a Chinese Quarter to the west and a Tibetan Quarter to the east. The Chinese neighborhood is where you'll find older hotels and Norbulingka Summer Palace. The more colorful Tibetan Quarter is full of small guesthouses, laid-back restaurants, bustling street markets, and Jokhang Temple. There is also a small Muslim Quarter to the southeast of the Barkhor. The old winding lanes in and around the Barkhor are immensely walkable and a great way to rub shoulders with the locals. Don't worry about getting lost: most of the thoroughfares are circular; if you follow the pilgrims, you'll make it back to the circuit.

Exploring

Your main axis of orientation in Lhasa is Beijing Lu, a street that stretches from the Barkhor in the east to as far as Drepung Monastery in the west, passing right in front of the Potala Palace. The easiest way to get from site to site is by taxi, which costs a flat Y10 between most locations in the city. Pedicabs are also available, but agreeing on a price before you hop on is essential; most trips should cost about Y10. Many of the most popular attractions are concentrated in and around the Barkhor area, so walking is always an option.

⑫ Ani Tsangkung Nunnery. This colorful convent has an atmosphere that is livelier than what you'll find at Lhasa's monasteries. Beaming nuns will encourage you to wander through the courtyards, listen to their chanting, and watch them make ornamental butter flowers. There's a simple outdoor restaurant here—popular at lunchtime—where nuns serve up inexpensive bowls of noodles and *momos* (dumplings). The chief pilgrimage site is the meditation hollow where Songtsen Gampo concentrated his spiritual focus on preventing the flood of the Kyi River in the 7th century. ⊠ *Waling Lam, southeast of Jokhang Temple* ☎ *Y30* ☉ *Daily 9–6.*

⑩ Barkhor. Circling the walls of the Jokhang Temple, the Barkhor is not only Tibetan Buddhism's holiest pilgrimage circuit but is also the best spot in Lhasa for people-watching. Look for monks sitting before their alms bowls while the faithful constantly spin their prayer wheels. Unless you want to shock the devout with your blatant disregard for tradition, flow with the crowd in a clockwise direction. This wide pedestrian street is also souvenir central, crammed with stalls where vendors sell prayer shawls, silver jewelry, wall hangings, and just about anything that screams, "I've been to Tibet!" Don't even think about paying what the vendors ask; many of the items can easily be bargained down to less than a quarter of the original price.

② Palha Lupuk Temple. Religious rock paintings dating from as early as the 7th century can be seen at this grotto-style temple. On the 3rd floor you'll find an entrance to a cave with sculptures carved into the granite walls, mostly by Nepalese artists more than a millennium ago. It's a decent temple, but probably only worth the visit if you find yourself in the area with an hour or so to kill. ⊠ *South face of Iron Mountain, on a small street opposite the western end of the Potala Palace* ☎ *Y20* ☉ *Daily 9–8.*

⑪ Jokhang Temple (Da Zhao Si). This temple is the most sacred building in all of Tibet. From the gentle flicker of a butter-lamp light dancing off antique murals, statues, tapestries, and *thangkhas* (scroll paintings), to the air thick with incense and anticipation as thousands of Tibetans pay homage day and night, the temple contains a plethora of sensory delights.

Fodor'sChoice
★

Most likely built in 647 during Songtsen Gampo's reign, the Jokhang stands in the heart of the old town. The site was selected by Queen Wengcheng, a princess from China who became Songtsen Gampo's second wife. His first wife, Princess Bhrikuti from Nepal, financed the building of Jokhang. In her honor, and in recognition of Tibet's strong reliance on Nepal, the Jokhang's main gate faces west, toward Nepal. Among the bits remaining from the 7th century are the four door frames of the inner temple, dedicated to different deities.

10

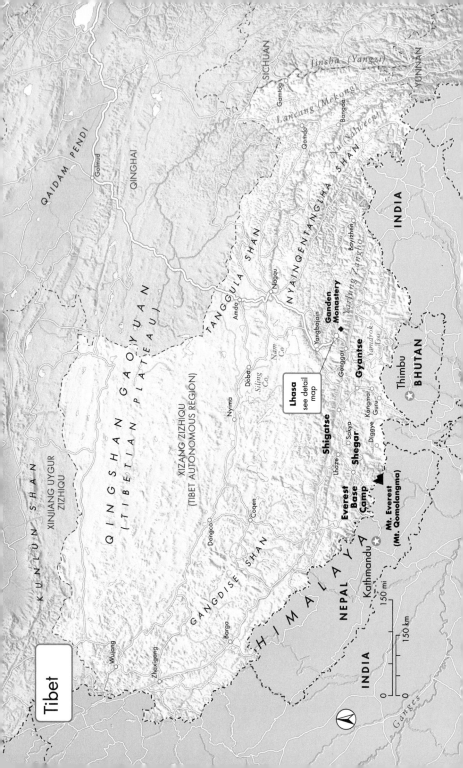

Tibet

Over the centuries, renovations have enlarged the Jokhang to keep it the premier temple of Tibet. Its status was threatened in the 1950s when the Chinese Army shelled it and the Red Guards of the Cultural Revolution ransacked it. During this period, the temple was used for various purposes, including a pigsty. Much of the damage has since been repaired, but a portion of it has been lost forever.

Before entering the Inner Jokhang, you should walk the Nangkhor Inner Circuit in a clockwise direction. It's lined with prayer wheels and murals depicting a series of Buddhist scenes. Continue on to the large Entrance Hall, whose inner chapels have murals depicting the wrathful deities responsible for protecting the temple and the city.

> ## ABOUT THE WEATHER
>
> From November to January, temperatures become frightfully cold (−10°F), but the climate is dry and the skies are blue. Many tourist sights in Lhasa shorten their opening hours in winter months. From June to August highs reach 80°F, although it can feel hotter. Summer sees a bit of rain, and occasionally roads will be closed to popular tourist destinations, including the Everest Base Camp. The best touring conditions occur from mid-April through May as wildflowers bloom and snow begins to melt. September through early November, with its mild weather, is another good option.

Straight ahead is the inner sanctum, the three-story **Kyilkhor Thil,** some of whose many columns probably date from the 7th century, particularly those with short bases and round shafts.

The chapels on the ground floor of the Kyilkhor Thil are the most rewarding. The most revered chapel of the inner hall is **Jowo Sakyamuni Lhakhang,** opposite the entrance. Inside rests a bejeweled 5-foot statue of Jowo Rinpoche—representing the Buddha at age 12—surrounded by adoring disciples. It was brought to Tibet by Queen Wengcheng and somehow has survived, despite a history of being plastered over and buried in sand. On busy days you may have to wait in line to enter this shrine, but it's worth it. On the 2nd floor there are a number of small chapels, although many are closed to visitors. Before you leave, be sure to climb the stairs next to the main entrance up to the Jokhang's ornately decorated golden roof. You'll be rewarded with sweeping views of the Barkhor, the Potala Palace, and the snowcapped mountains beyond Lhasa. ⊠ *Barkhor* 💰 *Y70* 🕙 *Daily 9–6.*

NEED A BREAK?

Located on the eastern leg of the Barkhor Circuit, **Sun Tribe Restaurant** (⊠ 39 Barkhor Dong Jie ☎ 0891/634-1990 ⊟ No credit cards) is a good place to take a break after a visit to the Jokhang Temple. Monks sit around the low tables, chatting and sipping tea. The Tibetan dishes served here—everything from fried yak hooves to mutton with spring onion—are praised by locals as "the real thing."

❸ **Kundeling Monastery** (Gongdelin Si). This monastery is often overlooked by tourists, so it's less crowded than others around Lhasa. If you arrive in the morning, climb to a 2nd-floor chapel to see monks chanting, beating drums, and playing long bronze prayer trumpets. This temple also contains examples of sand painting, in which millions of colorful grains of sand are arranged in a complex pattern over the course of hours or even days. ⊠ *Beijing Zhong Lu and Deji Lu, west of the Potala Palace* 🖃 *Y10* ⊘ *Daily 9–8.*

⓭ **Muslim Quarter.** In perhaps the most Buddhist of cities, the Muslim Quarter—centered around Lhasa's Great Mosque—is a bit of an anomaly. The district was originally intended for immigrants arriving from Kashmir and Ladakh. The Great Mosque (Da Qingzhen Si) was completed in 1716, but very little of the original structure remains. The area is now primarily of interest for its distinct atmosphere and the large concentration of pork-free halal restaurants. ⊠ *Lingkor Nan Lu, west of Lingkor Dong Lu.*

❺ **Norbulingka Palace.** The 7th Dalai Lama (1708–57), a frail man, chose to build a summer palace on this site because of its medicinal spring, and later had his whole government moved here from the Potala Palace. Successive Dalai Lamas expanded the complex, adding additional palaces, a debating courtyard, a pavilion, a library, and a number of landscaped gardens. The most recent addition, built by the current Dalai Lama between 1954 and 1956, is an ornate two-story building containing his private quarters. It turned out to be the place from which, disguised as a soldier, he fled to India on March 17, 1959, three days before the Chinese massacred thousands of Tibetans and fired artillery shells into every building in the complex. Only after searching through the corpses did they realize that the Dalai Lama had escaped.

The work done to repair the damage in the aftermath of the March 1959 uprising is not of high caliber and much of Norbulingka feels run-down. That said, a collection of the Dalai Lama's carriages and automobiles housed in the **Changsam Palace** is worth a look. More fascinating are the personal effects of the current Dalai Lama housed in the **New Summer Palace,** including his radio and phonograph. You can even peek into the Dalai Lama's bathroom. Be sure to look closely at the murals surrounding the current Dalai Lama's throne; on the left behind the throne is perhaps the only portrait of him you'll see anywhere in Tibet. ⊠ *Western end of Luobulingka Lu* 🖃 *Y60* ⊘ *Daily 9–6:30.*

❶ **Potala Palace** (Pudala Gong). Virtually nothing remains of the original 11-story Potala Palace, built in 637 by Songtsen Gampo. What you see today is a 17th-century replacement. The Fifth Dalai Lama, anxious to reestablish the importance of Lhasa as the Tibetan capital, employed 7,000 workers and 1,500 artisans to resurrect the Potala Palace on the 7th-century foundation. The portion called the White Palace was completed in 1653. The Red Palace was not completed until 1694, 12 years after the Dalai Lama's death (which was kept secret by the regent in order to prevent interruption of the construction). The Potala Palace has been enlarged since then, and has been continually renovated. Once the headquarters of Tibet's theocracy, the vast complex is now a museum.

The Potala Palace was the world's tallest building before the advent of modern skyscrapers. Towering above the city from the slopes of Mount

Fodor'sChoice ★

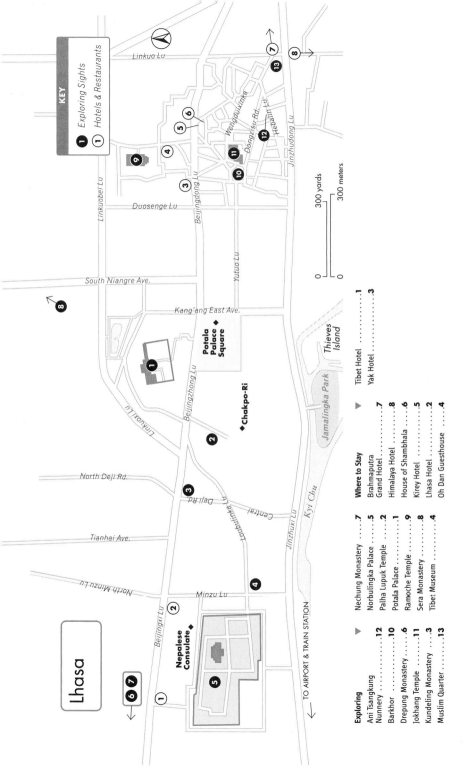

Lhasa

KEY

- ● Exploring Sights
- ① Hotels & Restaurants

◆ Nepalese Consulate

◆ Potala Palace Square

◆ Chakpo-Ri

Jamalingka Park

Thieves Island

Kyi Chu

TO AIRPORT & TRAIN STATION

Streets and landmarks:
Linkuo Lu, Linkuobei Lu, Duosenge Lu, Beijingdong Lu, South Niangre Ave., Kang'ang East Ave., Yutuo Lu, Wengduixinka, Dongzisu Rd., Jinzhudong Lu, Hebalin Lu, North Niangre Lu, North Minzu Lu, Beijingxi Lu, North Deji Rd., Deji Rd., Tianhai Ave., Linkuoxi Lu, Beijingzhong Lu, Minzu Lu, Jinzhuxi Lu, Central Linkuonanlu

0 ____ 300 yards
0 ____ 300 meters

Exploring ▶

Ani Tsangkung Nunnery	**12**
Barkhor	**10**
Drepung Monastery	**6**
Jokhang Temple	**11**
Kundeling Monastery	**3**
Muslim Quarter	**13**
Nechung Monastery	**7**
Norbulingka Palace	**5**
Palha Lupuk Temple	**2**
Potala Palace	**1**
Ramoche Temple	**9**
Sera Monastery	**8**
Tibet Museum	**4**

Where to Stay ▶

Brahmaputra Grand Hotel	**7**
Himalaya Hotel	**8**
House of Shambhala	**6**
Kirey Hotel	**5**
Lhasa Hotel	**2**
Oh Dan Guesthouse	**4**
Tibet Hotel	**1**
Yak Hotel	**3**

Marpori, the structure is 384 feet high; its 1,000 rooms house some 200,000 images. The outer section, the White Palace, was the seat of government and the winter residence of the Dalai Lama until 1951. Inside you can pass through the Dalai Lama's spartan quarters. On either side of the palace are the former offices of the government. The Red Palace, looming above the White Palace, is filled with murals that chronicle Buddhist folklore and ancient Tibetan life. Interspersed among the chapels are eight spectacular tombs covered in nearly five tons of gold. These bejeweled rooms contain the remains of the 5th through 13th Dalai Lamas.

DID YOU KNOW

Underneath the 13-story, 1,000-room fortress are the dungeons, inaccessible to tourists. Justice could be harsh—torture and jail time were the punishments for refusing to pay taxes, displaying anger, or insulting a monk. The worst place to be sent was the Cave of Scorpions, where prisoners were the targets of stinging tails.

The increasing number of visitors makes it difficult to secure tickets for the Potala Palace. Only 500 visitors are allowed in each day. If you're not part of a tour group, here's the drill: arrive at the palace's western gate at 7:30 AM and line up to receive a number; return at 11:30 AM with your passport in order to receive a voucher for the *following day*; return to the palace's front gate the next day at the time indicated on your voucher, when you'll be able to buy a ticket and finally tour the Potala Palace. Don't get discouraged by the difficult process of procuring a ticket; the Potala Palace is worth the trouble. Expect to spend about two hours here. ⊠ *Beijing Dong Lu* ☎ *Y100* ☉ *By appointment.*

⑨ Ramoche Temple (Xiao Zhao Si). This temple was founded by Queen Wengcheng at the same time as the Jokhang Temple. Its three-story structure dates from the 15th century. Despite restorations in the 1980s, it lost much of its former glory after the Chinese used it to house the Communist Labor Training Committee during the Cultural Revolution.

The Ramoche Temple was intended to house the most revered statue of Jowo Rinpoche. A threat of a Chinese invasion in the 7th century induced Queen Wengcheng to hide the statue in the Jokhang Temple. Some 50 years later it was rediscovered and placed within the Jokhang Temple's main chapel. As a substitute, Jokhang reciprocated with a Nepalese statue of Jowo Mikyo Dorje—representing Buddha as an eight-year-old—richly layered in gold and precious stones. It was decapitated during the Cultural Revolution and its torso lost in Beijing. Both head and body were found in 1984, put back together again, and placed in a small chapel at the back of the Ramoche Temple's Inner Sanctum. Be sure to

GETTING AROUND

Taxis are plentiful in Lhasa. A set fare of Y10 will get you almost anywhere within the city limits. Getting to Drepung Monastery will cost about Y40. Minibuses ply a fixed route with fares of about Y2. Bicycle rickshaws are also available for short trips and normally cost Y3, although they're famous for trying to charge foreigners higher prices.

climb to the temple's roof for a spectacular view of the Potala Palace perched high above the rooftops of Lhasa. ⊠ *Xiao Zhao Si Lu, off the north side of Beijing Dong Lu* 🖃 *Y20* ⊙ *Daily 8–4:30.*

❹ **Tibet Museum.** For the Chinese interpretation of Tibetan history, politics, and culture, visit this modern museum. The free personal audio guide provides commentary on important pieces from prehistoric times, Chinese dynasties, and traditional Tibetan life. If you are a scholar of history, you may find

> ### ALTITUDE ALERT
>
> At 12,000 feet, shortness of breath and mild headaches are common during the first few days in Lhasa. These symptoms can be managed by use of a small oxygen canister, herbal remedies, or an aspirin or two. Avoid exertion and drink plenty of water. Severe altitude sickness should be immediately brought to the attention of a physician.

some of the explanations intriguing. ⊠ *Corner of Luobulingka Lu and Minzu Nan Lu, across from the entrance to Norbulingka Palace* 🕾 *0891/ 681–2210* 🖃 *Y30* ⊙ *May–Oct. 9–6:30, Nov.–Apr. 10:30–5.*

Tours

Lhasa is overflowing with travel agencies, any one of which can arrange transportation and an English-speaking guide for sites in and around Lhasa. Most foreign travelers have already purchased tours along with their airline or train tickets, as it is required by Chinese law. Once you're here, you can book other tours if you find there's something else you want to see. A good local agency is Tibet FIT Travel.

🗷 Tour-Operator Recommendations **Tibet FIT Travel** ⊠ 4 Danjielin Lu, Lhasa 🕾 0891/ 634–9239 or 655–2370.

Where to Eat

Take advantage of the competitive market of hybrid restaurants that serve Chinese, Indian, Nepali, Tibetan, and Western fare. Most have sprung up from backpacker haunts serving perennially favorite dishes, from banana pancakes to yak burgers to chicken masala. The most dependable eateries are on hotel or guesthouse premises. However, a more expensive meal does not necessarily mean it's good. A handful of places have a bar area where you can enjoy a predinner tea or cocktail.

★ $$–$$$ ✕ **Shangrila.** Make time in your busy tour schedule for dinner at the Shangrila. As dancers perform traditional routines, your taste buds will be treated to an 18-course Tibetan buffet—a superb opportunity to try indigenous food such as sautéed yak lung, cold yak tongue, and wild sweet potatoes. The colorful scroll paintings that line the walls, the darkwood furniture, and the congenial staffers that happily explain the dishes sets this place apart from other dinner-and-a-show restaurants. Reservations are necessary—sometimes a day in advance—and you should arrive by 7 PM for the best seats. The performance and buffet are a set price of Y80; if you want to skip the buffet, you'll have to fork

10

The Tibetans

Perhaps the most recognizable and well-known minority in China, Tibetans have one of Asia's most unique and colorful cultures. They live primarily on the Tibet-Qinghai Plateau, but they also make their homes in southern Gansu, western and northern Sichuan, and northwestern Yunnan. Their culture is influenced both by Tibet's extreme geography and their unique interpretation of Buddhism, the line between the two often blurred by a "sacred geography," which deifies many of the region's mountains and lakes. Compared with other forms of Buddhism, Tibetan Buddhism (also known as "Lamaism") places far more emphasis on the physical path to enlightenment. This is why the sight of pilgrims prostrating around the base of a sacred mountain or temple for days or weeks on end is a common one in the region.

When Tibet was annexed by China (or "liberated") in 1959, their supreme spiritual leader the Dalai Lama fled in disguise to India where he set up a

Tibetan government-in-exile in Dharamsala, which became known as "little Lhasa." Since then the Dalai Lama has become an international celebrity and has succeeded in making the struggle for Tibetan independence a focus of global attention, drawing strong condemnation—and brutal crackdowns—from Beijing. Few people know that the Dalai Lama has actually for many years no longer insisted on independence, but a more moderate form of autonomy like that enjoyed by Hong Kong and Macau. Yet despite international pressure—and perhaps even because of the attention—there seems little hope that Tibet's status will change in the near future. The Chinese government feels strongly that any weakness shown in regard to Tibet will be used as a pretext for increased separatist activities in Xinjiang and Taiwan.

Meanwhile, Tibet continues to modernize at full-speed, with seemingly every road between Lhasa and Mount Everest being upgraded simultaneously. The rail link between Beijing and Lhasa completed in 2006 is expected to promote "Hanification," or a major increase in the Han Chinese population. With only 2½ million Tibetans living in the Tibet Autonomous Region—and 800 million impoverished Han Chinese nationwide looking for a better way of life—it's only a matter of time before ethnic Tibetans become a small minority in their own homeland.

over a Y50 cover charge. ✉ *12 Beijing Dong Lu, inside the Kirey Hotel* ☎ *0891/636–3800* ▭ *No credit cards.*

$–$$ ✕ **Dunya.** Meaning "The World" in 10 languages, Dunya serves a melting pot of international dishes. The Western food here is slightly disappointing, but the Indian and Nepalese dishes are first rate; both can be complemented by a bottle of Australian wine or a cup of real coffee—both rarities in Tibet. With its exposed-brick interior and a polite English-speaking staff, Dunya feels like a real restaurant, not another hole-in-the-wall eatery. Upstairs is a well-stocked bar with a balcony where you'll often find the Dutch proprietor chatting with customers. ✉ *100 Beijing Dong Lu, next to the Yak Hotel* ☎ *0891/633-3374* ▭ *No credit cards* ⊘ *Closed Nov.–Apr.*

¢–$ ✕ **Makye Ame.** Ask to be seated by the 2nd-floor windows or on the rooftop terrace for some of the best views of the pilgrims on the Barkhor, which passes right by this legendary corner restaurant. Meat eaters will enjoy the fried yak slices, and vegetarians rave about the spinach-tofu ravioli topped with homemade tomato-basil sauce as well as the Indian-style bread stuffed with potato and served with curry and yogurt sauces. Ask the staff to explain the legend of Makye Ame, a mysterious woman immortalized in a poem penned by the Sixth Dalai Lama, who spied her in a bar where the café now stands. To find this place, look for a hand-painted sign reading RESTAURANT. ✉ *Southeast corner of Barkhor* ☎ *0891/632–8608* ▭ *No credit cards.*

¢–$ ✕ **Snowlands.** The well-traveled menu at the Snowlands—covering Chinese, Nepalese, Tibetan, Indian, Italian, and even Mexican cuisine—is **Fodor'sChoice** your guide to the finest meals in Tibet. Join foreign aid workers, local ★ business executives, and the small tour groups who flock in droves to this cozy café near Barkhor. Try the chicken masala with a freshly baked *naan* bread, or feast on grilled yak steak with garlic-butter sauce. This place is hugely popular, and the service can be a little slow, but the food is worth the wait. Fresh cinnamon rolls, apple pie, and croissants are also available. ✉ *4 Danjielin Lu, north of Barkhor* ☎ *0891/633–7323* ▭ *No credit cards.*

¢ ✕ **Tashi.** A popular hangout for foreigners, Tashi is the kind of restaurant where conversations with other diners are inevitable. The most popular dish here is a unique creation called the *bobi,* a kind of tortilla into which sautéed chicken, vegetables, and cream cheese are stuffed. If you're looking to add a bit of heft to your meal, try the delicious cauliflower croquettes, which are deep-fried patties of cauliflower, potato, peas, and carrots. The yak burger is also tasty. ✉ *131 Beijing Dong Lu, at Danjielin Lu* ☎ *0891/633–7305* ▭ *No credit cards.*

Where to Stay

Hotel options in Lhasa have improved significantly in recent years. Ask and you may be shown rooms ranging from a depressing 20-person dormitory to a deluxe suite with private bath, balcony, and minibar. Many of the more expensive hotels even equip their rooms with oxygen machines to ease the effects of altitude sickness. Televisions are now standard, though non-Chinese-language programming is rare. Tibetan guesthouses are a warm and welcoming alternative. Staffed by locals, these lodgings are more personable but some of the shared bathing facilities at the lower-end options can be archaic.

$$$–$$$$
Fodor'sChoice
★
🏨 **Brahmaputra Grand Hotel** (Yaluzangbu Dajiudian). Not only is the Brahmaputra Grand the finest hotel in Lhasa, but it's also one of the most luxurious lodgings in all of China. Opened in 2006, it's billed as the world's only "museum hotel," with every nook and cranny displaying gorgeous Tibetan antiques and artifacts. The only difference here is that everything's for sale. Be careful what you set your heart on, though, as some of the items go for as much as $15,000. The hotel's exterior is a strange mix of Russian and Tibetan architecture, but inside it's all class. From the smartly clad Nepali bellmen to the gently scented hallways with perfect lighting and dark-wood paneling, you'll be impressed every minute of your stay. The hotel's swimming pool and health club are scheduled to open in 2007. The hotel is 2½ km (1½ mi) east of the Barkhor. ⊠ *Gongbutang Lu, Yangcheng Plaza* ☎ *0891/630–9999* 🖨 *0891/630–9888* ⊕ *www.tibethotel.cn* ⊯ *186 rooms* ⅗ *2 restaurants, cable TV, in-room broadband, hair salon, massage, sauna, laundry service, business services, meeting room, travel services* ⊟ *AE, DC, MC, V.*

$$$–$$$$
🏨 **Lhasa Hotel** (Lasa Fandian). If you stay here in July and August, you'll be pleased with the swimming pool—a rare find in Lhasa. The rest of the year you will pay premium rates for an average hotel where the building and the gardens look largely ignored. The hotel is north of the entrance to Norbulingka Palace. ⊠ *1 Minzu Lu* ☎ *0891/683–2221* 🖨 *0891/683–5796* ⊯ *468 rooms, 12 suites* ⅗ *5 restaurants, room service, minibars, cable TV, pool, hair salon, bar, laundry service, business services, currency exchange, meeting rooms* ⊟ *AE, DC, MC, V.*

$$$–$$$$
🏨 **Tibet Hotel** (Xizang Binguan). The rooms in this well-maintained hotel feature a touch of Tibetan style, from the vibrant blue carpeting to the golden silk pillows on the crimson sofas. Couples who want to maximize their time will appreciate the separate tubs and showers in the bathrooms. There are 10 restaurants serving Western and Asian food, but their opening hours are erratic (a problem, as you're quite a way from downtown). Many on the staff speak a little English, but their enthusiasm makes it easy to bridge the communication gap. Rooms in the hotel's rear building are bigger, but slightly older. ⊠ *64 Beijing Xi Lu* ☎ *0891/683–4966* 🖨 *0891/683–6787* ⊯ *333 rooms* ⅗ *10 restaurants, in-room safe, cable TV, in-room broadband, hair salon, laundry service, dry cleaning, business services, travel services* ⊟ *AE, DC, MC, V.*

$$–$$$
🏨 **Himalaya Hotel** (Ximalaya Jiudian). Sliding-glass doors open onto a lavishly appointed foyer defined by four soaring columns, a marble floor, and a central chandelier. The rooms here range from budget rooms to luxurious suites, all featuring Tibetan woodwork and bedding in soothing earth tones. Ask for a room with a view of the Potala Palace. If you want to stay near the Barkhor area, this is your best bet. As a bonus, there are also occasional performances of Tibetan opera. ⊠ *6 Lingkor Dong Lu* ☎ *0891/632–3888* 🖨 *0891/632–1111* ⊯ *133 rooms, 13 suites* ⅗ *Restaurant, cable TV, hair salon, massage, sauna, laundry service, Internet room, business services, meeting room, travel services* ⊟ *AE, MC, V.*

★ **$$–$$$** 🏨 **House of Shambhala.** If you want to stay in a traditional Tibetan dwelling, this quiet boutique hotel may be what you're after. The building, which dates back to the 7th century, was once the home of a high-ranking Tibetan general under the 13th Dalai Lama. Each suite is individually decorated with tangerine-colored walls, hardwood floors,

sheepskin rugs, and exposed roof beams. The king-size beds are covered with hand-beaded duvets, and the bathrooms are tiled in local slate. The staff is friendly and attentive, but few speak much English. On the rooftop terrace you can lounge on a daybed and order from the downstairs restaurant. This hotel is very small, so be sure to reserve far in advance. It is located on a small alley next to the Kirey Hotel. ✉ *7 Jiri Erxiang* ☎ *0891/632–6533* 🖷 *0891/632–6695* 🌐 *www. houseofshambhala.com* 🛏 *10 suites* ⚘ *Restaurant, massage, shop, laundry service* 🖃 *MC, V.*

$$–$$$ 🏨 **Yak Hotel.** Once the first choice for travelers on a tight budget, the Yak now appeals to travelers of all levels. Regardless of what kind of room you choose, it will be immaculate. Even in the most economical of rooms you will find nice touches like Tibetan chests as bedside tables. If you're sensitive to noise, try to get a room toward the back. Dunya restaurant is to the right of the courtyard. ✉ *100 Beijing Dong Lu* ☎ *0891/632–3496* 🛏 *120 rooms* ⚘ *Restaurant, cable TV, bar, laundry service, business center, Internet room* 🖃 *AE, DC, MC, V.*

$ 🏨 **Oh Dan Guesthouse** (Oudan Binguan). An excellent budget choice, this small hotel sits on a busy pedestrian street between the Jokhang and Ramoche temples, only a few minutes north of the Barkhor. Rooms are simple, but comfortable and clean. On the rooftop terrace, you can sip tea and enjoy an awesome view of Lhasa. Avoid the 3rd or 4th floor, as there is no elevator. ✉ *15 Xiao Zhao Si Lu* ☎ *0891/634–4999* 🖷 *0891/ 636–3992* 🛏 *32 rooms* ⚘ *Restaurant, cable TV, shop, laundry service, Internet room, business services, travel services* 🖃 *No credit cards.*

¢–$ 🏨 **Kirey Hotel.** A popular budget hotel, the Kirey is filled with everyone from backpackers to bicyclists to tour groups. Rooms here are spotless, but otherwise unremarkable. Something that is special, however, is that the staff here will wash and dry your laundry free of charge. The location, north of Jokhang Temple, can't be beat. Two excellent restaurants are located in the courtyard. ✉ *105 Beijing Dong Lu* ☎ *0891/632–3462* 🛏 *65 rooms* ⚘ *2 restaurants, cable TV, bicycles, bar, laundry service, Internet room, travel services* 🖃 *No credit cards.*

Nightlife & the Arts

Most visitors to Lhasa are content to take a stroll after dinner before turning in early. If you're looking for a bit of excitement, look no farther than **Neeway Nangma** (✉ 13 Lingkor Bei Lu), the city's most popular disco. An hour spent here watching the dance performances set to both pop and traditional folk songs will clear away any ideas you may have about Tibetan culture being stuck in the past. If you're looking for a quiet spot near the Barkhor to enjoy a drink or a cup of tea after a long day, try **Ganglamedo** (✉ 127 Beijing Dong Lu), across from the Yak Hotel. The bar stocks a wide range of liquors.

Tibetan operas are performed by the **Tibet Shol Opera Troupe** (✉6 Lingkor Dong Lu ☎ 0891/632–1111) in a theater at the Himalaya Hotel.

Shopping

Arts & Crafts

For souvenirs varying from prayer flags to jewel-encrusted horse bridles, stop by one of the hundreds of open-air stalls and small shops that line the roads leading to the Jokhang Temple. Bargain in a tough but friendly manner and the proprietors may throw in extra items for luck. Many of the goods come from around Tibet and Nepal. For quality Tibetan handicrafts, visit **Dropenling** (✉ 11 Chak Tsal Gang Lu ☎ 0891/636–0558), down an alley opposite the Muslim Quarter's main mosque. Unlike other souvenir shops, all the products here are made by Tibetans and all the profits are returned to the local artisan community.

Outdoor Equipment

West of the Potala Palace, **The Third Pole** (✉ 6 Luobulingka Lu ☎ 0891/682–0549) can outfit you with everything you'll need to enjoy the great outdoors, from good hiking shoes to walking sticks to sunglasses. **Wilderness Outside Sports Club** (✉ 182 Beijing Zhong Lu ☎ 0891/682–9365) features a wide selection of outdoor equipment, as well as warm clothing if you're planning a trip to the mountains.

Around Lhasa

Many of Lhasa's best sites are clustered around the city center, but three of the most important are a bit more remote. This trio of monasteries are known as the "three pillars of Tibetan Buddhism," having all been founded by religious patriarch Tsongkhapa at the beginning of the 15th century. All three are worth the effort it takes to reach them, especially Ganden Monastery, located 90 minutes east of Lhasa.

Fodor'sChoice **Ganden Monastery.** If you only have time for one side trip from Lhasa, ★ this rambling monastery with ocher-color walls is your best bet. Established in 1409 by Tsongkhapa, the founder of the Gelugpa sect, its abbot is chosen on merit rather than heredity. Of the six great Gelugpa monasteries, Ganden was the most seriously damaged by Chinese during the Cultural Revolution. Since the early 1980s, Tibetans have put tremendous effort into rebuilding the complex. Some 400 monks are now in residence. Pilgrims come daily from Lhasa to pay homage to the sacred sites and religious relics.

The monastery comprises eight major buildings. The most impressive structure is the **Gold Tomb of Tsongkhapa** (Serdhung Lhakhang) in the heart of the complex, easily recognized by the recently built white *chorten,* or small shrine, standing before the red building. On the 2nd floor is the chapel of **Yangchen Khang,** with the new golden chorten of

Tsongkhapa. The original (1629), made of silver, later gilded, was the most sacred object in the land. In 1959 the Chinese destroyed it, although brave monks saved some of the holy relics of Tsongkhapa, which are now inside the new gold-covered chorten. Be careful walking around this shrine: the buttery wax on the floor is thick and slippery.

If you've got the energy, follow a path that circumambulates the monastery starting from the parking lot. From the path, which leads to the spot where Tsongkhapa was cremated in 1419, you'll be treated to breathtaking views of the Lhasa River Valley. You'll need about an hour to complete the circuit. Buses (Y20 round-trip) to Ganden leave from Barkhor Square in front of Jokhang Temple every morning at 6:30 AM, returning to Lhasa at 3 PM. The beautiful 90-minute ride from Lhasa will give you a glimpse of life in rural Tibet. ⊠ *36 km (22 mi) southeast of Lhasa on main Tibet–Sichuan Hwy.* 🎫 *Y35* 🕐 *Daily 8:30–6.*

★ **Sera Monastery** (Sela Si). This important Gelugpa monastery, founded in 1419, contains numerous temples filled with splendid murals and icons. Originally it was a hermitage for Tsongkhapa and a few of his top students. Within a couple of hundred years it housed more than 5,000 monks.

On the clockwise pilgrimage route, start at the two buildings that will take up most of your visit. **Sera Me Tratsang,** founded in 1419, has a *dukhang* (assembly hall) rebuilt in 1761 with murals depicting Buddha's life. Among the five chapels along the north wall, the one with its exterior adorned with skeletons and skulls is unforgettable. The complex's oldest surviving structure, **Ngagpa Tratsang,** is a three-story college for tantric studies. Here you'll find statues of famous lamas and murals depicting paradise.

Continue to the four-story-high **Sera Je Tratsang,** where Manjashuri, the God of Wisdom, listens to monks engaged in philosophical debate in a courtyard just beyond the temple walls. The extremely animated debates—during which emphatic hand movements signify agreement or disagreement—take place daily starting at 3 PM. Whatever your feelings are about the excitement of debates, this is one you don't want to miss. ⊠ *At the base of Mt. Phurbuchok, 5 km (3 mi) north of Lhasa* 🎫 *Y50* 🕐 *Daily 9–5.*

10

Drepung Monastery. The largest of the Gelugpa monasteries was the residence for lesser lamas. Founded in 1416, it was enlarged in the 16th century by the Second Dalai Lama. By the era of the Fifth Dalai Lama it had become the largest monastic institution in the world, with 10,000 residents. During the Cultural Revolution it suffered only minimally because the army used the building as its headquarters and therefore didn't ransack it as much as other temples. The monastery was reopened in 1980, although the number of resident monks has been severely depleted.

The monastery's most important building is the Tshomchen, whose

> **WORD OF MOUTH**
>
> "Remember just about everything you do in Lhasa requires lots of walking and uphill. Potala Palace is incredibly taxing, even if you are in great shape. So too with the other monasteries. We saw lots of people really struggling with breathing. It is very hard work in the high altitude."   −Don

CLOSE UP

Festivals & Celebrations

TRY TO TIME YOUR VISIT with one of the brilliantly colorful traditional Tibetan festivals. Dancing monks whip up a frenzy to dispel the evil spirits of the previous year at the Year End Festival on the 29th day of the 12th lunar month. The first week of the first lunar month includes Losar (New Year Festival), when Lhasa is filled with Tibetan drama performances, incense offerings, and locals promenading in their finest wardrobe. Grand butter lanterns light up the Barkhor circuit during the Lantern Festival on the 15th of the 1st month. On the seventh day of the fourth month you can join the pilgrims in Lhasa or Ganden to mark the Birth of Sakyamuni (Buddha), or you may want to wait until the 15th for the celebrations of Saga Dawa (Sakyamuni's enlightenment) and join the pilgrims who climb the Drepung Monastery to burn juniper incense. Picnics at the summer palace of Norbulingka are common during the Worship of the Buddha in the second week of the fifth month. During Shötun (Yogurt Festival) in the first week of the seventh month, immerse yourself in the operas, masked dances, and picnics from Drepung (6½ km [4 mi] out of Lhasa) to Norbulingka. During the festival, giant thangkas of the Buddha are unveiled in Drepung Monastery and Tibetan opera troupes perform operas at Norbulingka.

The Tibetan calendar is the same as the lunar calendar, so exact dates as they relate to the Western calendar are only published a year in advance. The approximate dates are as follows: Tibetan New Year (February); the Butter Lantern Festival (late February/ early March); the Birth of Buddha Festival (late May/early June); the Holy Mountain Festival (late July/early August); the one-week Yogurt Festival (August); and the Bathing Festival (September).

vast assembly hall, the **Dukhang,** is noteworthy for its 183 columns, atrium ceiling, and ceremonial banners. Chapels can be found on all three floors, as well as on the roof. In the two-story **Buddhas of Three Ages Chapel** (Düsum Sangye Lhakhang), at the rear of the Dukhang on the ground floor, the Buddhas of past, present, and future are each guarded by two bodhisattvas. To get here, you can hire a taxi from town for between Y40 and Y50. ✉ *Off Beijing Xi Lu, 8 km (5 mi) west of Lhasa* 🎫 *Y50* ⏲ *Daily 9–6.*

Nechung Monastery. Many people skip this 12th-century monastery, but that's a big mistake. With a strong focus on beasts, demons, and the afterlife, Nechung is unlike anything else you'll see in Tibet. Murals on the monastery's walls depict everything from humans being dismembered by dogs and vultures to demons wearing long belts of human skulls engaged in passionate sexual intercourse. Until 1959 this monastery was home to the highly influential Nechung Oracle. Every important decision by a Dalai Lama is made after consulting this oracle, which currently resides in Dharamsala as a member of the government-in-exile. The monastery is 1 km (½ mi) southeast of Drepung Monastery. ✉ *Off Beijing Xi Lu, 8 km (5 mi) west of Lhasa* 🎫 *Y20* ⏲ *Daily 9–5.*

To & from Lhasa

14 hrs by train south of Golmud, 48 hrs by train southwest of Beijing.
2 hrs by plane west of Chengdu, 5 hrs by plane southwest of Beijing.

With the opening of the railroad line in 2006, travelers can now travel easily and cheaply to Tibet from almost anywhere in China. Destinations along the way include Golmud (14 hrs), Xining (26 hrs), Lanzhou (29 hrs), Xi'an (37 hrs), Beijing (48 hrs), Nanjing (40 hrs), Shanghai (53 hrs), and Guangzhou (58 hrs). You'll need a Tibet Travel Permit—which can range from Y200 to Y1,000, depending on who you ask—to buy a train ticket.

The new Lhasa Train Station is located 20 minutes southwest of the city center by taxi (Y50), although a bridge currently under construction should cut both the time and price in half. Flights to Lhasa depart from Beijing (5 hrs), Guangzhou (5 hrs), Xi'an (3½ hrs), Chongqing (3 hrs), and Chengdu (2 hrs). The airport is located 53 km (32 mi) southwest of Lhasa, which takes about 45 minutes by taxi (Y140).

TSANG PROVINCE

The Tibetan province of Tsang includes some of the region's most important historical sites outside of Lhasa, but it's also rich in stunning scenery and dotted with small villages and terraced barley fields filled with brightly decorated yaks. This is your chance to get out of the city and experience rural Tibet, where life seems to have changed little over the past hundred years.

Tours

If you're trying to find the majestic valleys and towering peaks that Tibet conjures up in the imagination, a journey through Tsang should be part of your itinerary. Typically lasting five days, these tours hit all of the hot spots: the brilliant blue waters of Yamdrok Tso Lake, the Dzong Fortress and Pelkor Chode Monastery in Gyantse, the Tashilhunpo Monastery in Shigatse, and the Base Camp below the world's highest peak at Mount Everest.

Every travel agency in Lhasa can arrange this tour for you, but if you want the best deal you should check out the advertisements on the message boards in the courtyards of the Snowlands and Kirey hotels, both located in the Barkhor area. A good price is in the range of Y1,000 per day, which includes all necessary travel permits. Food, lodging, and admission charges to attractions are not included.

10

Gyantse

With small villages of stone houses beside fields of highland barley, Gyantse feels far removed from Lhasa, although the drive is only about six hours. Home to two of Tsang's most impressive sights—the massive tiered Gyantse Kumbum at Pelkor Chode Monastery and the Gyantse Dzong where British soldiers defeated Tibetans in 1904—Gyantse is an essential stop on the journey toward Everest. Tourist dollars have transformed what was once a small village into a small one bustling with hotels, restaurants, and Internet cafés. However, the sites remain impressive and the journey to get here over the Yong-la Pass is unforgettable.

Exploring

Gyantse is easily navigable on foot. Most hotels and restaurants are located along Yingxiong Nan Lu, a few minutes south of the unmistakable Dzong Fortress. The Pelkor Chode Monastery is located 10 minutes' walking northwest of the fortress; both can easily be visited and toured over the course of about three hours.

> ### RUSTIC CUISINE
>
> Outside the capital, the variety of food leaves something to be desired, but in areas commonly visited by tourists you should be able to find a simple meal. You can even order a picnic from your hotel for a countryside trip.

Gyantse Dzong. In the 14th and 15th centuries, Gyantse rose to political power along with the rise of the Sakyapa monastic order. To get an idea of the amount of construction during this period, make the steep climb to the top of this old fortress on the northern edge of town. The building itself isn't in great shape, but you'll be treated to staggering views of the town and the surrounding Nyang Chu Valley. Signs reading JUMP OFF CLIFF aren't making a suggestion, but pointing to the location where Tibetan warriors jumped to their deaths rather than surrendering to British troops in 1904. The best way to see everything here is to wind around the fortress clockwise toward the top, using the long concrete staircase to descend. Be careful, as there's a slippery bit of concrete at the bottom of the stairs. The **Anti-British Imperialist Museum,** located just inside the front gate, is worth a visit for a distorted yet amusing account of the British invasion, sprinkled with obvious bits of propaganda. ⊠ *North end of Yingxiong Lu* ☎ *0892/817–2263* ☏ *Y30* ☉ *Daily 9–6:30.*

★ **Pelkor Chode Monastery.** One of the few multidenominational monastic complexes in Tibet—housing Gelugpa, Sakyapa, and Bupa monks—Pelkor Chode is home to the **Gyantse Kumbum.** Built in AD 1427, this building with its glittering golden dome and four sets of spellbinding eyes rising over uniquely tiered circular architecture is one of the most beautiful in Tibet. Inside there are six floors, each a labyrinth of small chapels adorned with Nepalese-influenced murals and statues. A steep ladder at the rear of the 5th floor provides access to the roof. Impressive in itself, you'll appreciate this complex even more after you've seen it from the heights of Gyantse Dzong. ⊠ *Northwest end of Pelkor Lu* ☎ *0892/ 817–2680* ☏ *Y40* ☉ *Daily 8–7.*

Where to Stay & Eat

¢–$$ ✕ **Fuqi Sichuan.** If you're getting tired of the same old Western–Tibetan hybrid cuisine, there are lots of well-prepared traditional Chinese dishes here from which you can choose. Best of all, there's an English menu, although the prices on it are nearly double what you'd pay ordering in Chinese. ⊠ *10 Yingxiong Nan Lu, near the Gyantse Hotel* ☎ *1351/892– 4212* ▭ *No credit cards.*

¢–$ ✕ **Tashi.** Although it shares the same name and a similar menu with an old favorite in Lhasa, this restaurant is unrelated. Still, the Indian, Tibetan, and Western dishes served in the 2nd-floor dining room are wellliked by

A Once Mighty Empire

THE TIBET AUTONOMOUS REGION (TAR) BEARS ONLY a passing resemblance to what was once a massive empire that encompassed all of Tibet, Qinghai (except for the area around Xining), western Sichuan, and parts of northern Yunnan. Historically, despite their modern-day reputation for being a peaceful people, Tibetans were known as fierce warriors and feared by their neighbors. They even sacked the Chinese capital of Changan, now Xi'an, in the 8th century.

When the Mongols conquered China in the 13th century and founded the

Yuan Dynasty, they also took control of Tibet, adopting Tibetan Buddhism as their official religion. This relationship came back to haunt Tibetans in modern times—it was used by China's successive dynasties and governments to legitimize the nation's claim to Tibet. In 1950, with almost 10 years of experience fighting first the Japanese and then the Nationalist government, the People's Liberation Army entered Tibet and quickly crushed all resistance.

---

visitors, with the yak being highly recommended. ⊠ *North end of Yingxiong Lu, near Pelkor Lu* ☎ *0892/817–2793* ▭ *No credit cards.*

$–$$ ⌂ **Gyantse Hotel** (Jiangzi Fandian). In business since 1986, this government-run hotel is still the top choice in Gyantse. Rooms here are clean and comfortable, if a bit dark and dreary. Amazingly, televisions here have CNN and the BBC available. Make sure to reserve a room in advance, especially during the busy summer months. If no doubles are available, consider sharing a suite with your traveling companions; each contains two bedrooms with king-size beds and separate bathrooms. ⊠ *2 Shanghai Dong Lu, near Yingxiong Lu* ☎ *0892/817–2222* 🖷 *0892/817– 2366* ⏃ *3 restaurants, cable TV, gym, massage, sauna, shops, bar, laundry service, business services* ▭ *No credit cards.*

$ ⌂ **Jian Zang Hotel** (Jiangzi Fandian). Less expensive than the Gyantse Hotel, the Jian Zang is where most backpackers spend the night. The rooms here are clean but otherwise unremarkable, and hot water is always available. ⊠ *14 Yingxiong Nan Lu* ☎ *0892/817–3720* 🖷 *0892/ 817–3910* ⏃ *Cable TV* ▭ *No credit cards.*

To & from Gyantse

6 hrs (180 km/110 mi) by jeep southwest of Lhasa over the Yong-la Pass. 1 ½ hrs (90 km/55 mi) southeast of Shigatse.

Coming from Lhasa, don't let your driver take the longer but faster route through Shigatse to reach Gyantse. Insist on being taken via the dirt road over the Yong-la Pass, where the views are absolutely stunning. Few tourists take this route, and the locals will be genuinely surprised to see you. Once in Gyantse, don't feel the need to rush on to Shigatse the same day; you can spend the night and see the sites in the morning without significantly throwing off your touring schedule.

10

Shigatse

Tibet's second-largest city, Shigatse, is the traditional capital of Tsang and home to the Tashilhunpo Monastery, Tibet's largest functioning monastic institution. The Tsang kings once ruled over the region from the fortress north of town. On its foundations you'll find a newly constructed luxury hotel built to resemble the Potala Palace. Most people only spend a day in Shigatse, visiting the monastery and wandering up and down the city's Walking Street, a tourist-friendly section of Qingdao Lu. Shigatse is quite pleasant, but you haven't traveled all the way to Tibet to see another unremarkable Chinese city.

Exploring

Everything of interest to foreign visitors, including most hotels and restaurants, is located on the stretch of road between the monastery and the fortress, namely Walking Street, which you can recognize by the Chinese-style gates on either end.

Tashilhunpo Monastery. This monastery, one of the six great Gelugpa institutions, is the seat of the Panchen Lama and one of the few religious sites in Tibet not to be destroyed during the Cultural Revolution. Most impressive is the Chapel of Maitreya, housing an 85-foot-high statue of the Future Buddha—the largest in the world—covered in more than 600 pounds of gold. More than a thousand more images are painted on the surrounding walls. You will also be able to visit the Panchen Lama tombs, many of which are lined with photos and sculptures of their later reincarnations. The beautiful stupa of the 10th Panchen Lama, built in 1990 after his death in 1989, is topped with a remarkable likeness of his unmistakable fat, jocular face done in pure gold. As this is the largest functioning monastery in Tibet, the police presence can be a bit heavy at times. Refrain from discussing politics or the Dalai Lama. Don't try to take unauthorized photos, as monks here have been known to manhandle those unwilling to pay for a snapshot. ⊠ *Qingdai Xi Lu* ☎ *0892/882–2114* ⊠ *Y55* ⊗ *Daily 9:30–7.*

Where to Stay & Eat

¢–$$ ✕ **Galgyal Tibet.** Serving both Tibetan and Chinese dishes, this eatery next to the Samdrutse Hotel has a pleasant outdoor seating area. The English menu makes it popular with travelers. A large supply of beer is kept ice cold, the perfect cure for a long day spent under the intense Tibetan sun. ⊠ *8 Qingdao Lu, near Xue Qiang Lu* ☎ *0892/882–6568* ⊟ *No credit cards.*

¢–$ ✕ **Tashi.** Another in a series of unrelated restaurants with the same name, this Nepali-managed eatery specializes in excellent Indian dishes such as chicken butter masala. There's also Western fare. ⊠ *Eastern end of Walking St., near Qingdao Lu* ☎ *0892/883–5969* ⊟ *No credit cards.*

¢–$ ✕ **Yakhead Tibet.** Located in the middle of Walking Street, this restaurant has the most extensive Tibetan menu in town. Only a few words on the menu have been translated into English, but luckily there's also a photograph of every dish. The yak burgers and fried potato momos are especially popular. Look for the sign with a huge carved yak's head above the entrance. ⊠ *14 Walking St.* ☎ *0892/883–7186* ⊟ *No credit cards.*

$-$$ Ⓣ **Manasarovar Hotel.** Until the luxury hotel being built upon the remains of Shigatse's old fortress opens in a year or two, this will remain the best hotel in town. Unfortunately, it's located more than a mile east of the restaurants and shops of Walking Street. Nevertheless, the pleasant rooms have hardwood floors with colorful Tibetan rugs. ⊠ *20 Qing Dao Dong Lu* ☎ *0892/883–9999.*

> ### LODGING OPTIONS
>
> In the major towns outside Lhasa you usually have a choice between bland Chinese hotels and rundown guesthouses, about half of which have hot running water.

¢-$ Ⓣ **Tenzin Hotel.** This is Shigatse's most popular budget hotel, featuring very nice doubles with *en suite* bathrooms and an endless supply of hot water. The hallways and other common areas are decorated with murals depicting various aspects of Tibetan life. There is a half-decent restaurant above the courtyard. ⊠ *8 Bangchelling, across from the Tibetan Market* ☎ *0892/882–2018* 🖷 *0892/883–8080* ♨ *Restaurant, cable TV* ⊟ *No credit cards.*

To & from Shigatse

4½ hrs (280 km/170 mi) west of Lhasa by jeep. 1½ hrs (90 km/55 mi) northwest of Gyantse. 6 hrs (240 km/150 mi) northeast of Shegar.

The perfectly smooth road from Lhasa to Shigatse travels alongside the picturesque Tsangpo River beneath the towering walls of Nimo Gorge. Rather than stopping in Shigatse the first time you pass through, you may want to consider visiting the city on the way back from Everest Base Camp. Driving from Gyantse all the way to Shegar in a single day will maximize the time you have to spend at the mountain by getting a significant chunk of driving out of the way. Shigatse is the only city outside of Lhasa that foreigners can reliably reach by public transportation. Buses leave starting at 7 AM across from the Kirey Hotel in Lhasa.

Shegar

There isn't much of anything to see in Shegar—which also goes by the name New Tingri—a town so small that its two intersecting streets don't even have names. Nevertheless, it's the best place to spend the night before heading down to Rongbuk Monastery for the hike to Everest Base Camp. Supplies in Shegar are more expensive than what you'd pay in Shigatse, but the gouging here is nothing compared to what you'll find closer to Everest. If the accommodations near Everest sound too rough for you, you might even consider making Base Camp a day-trip and spending both nights in the relatively luxurious lodgings in Shegar.

Where to Stay & Eat

¢-$$ ✕ **The Friendly Restaurant** (Youyi Canting). This Sichuanese restaurant is overpriced, but so is almost everything in Shegar. Stick to simple classics like stir-fried egg with tomato or sweet-and-sour pork, which can be ordered from an English menu. ⊠ *Near the intersection* ☎ *0892/ 894–7121* ⊟ *No credit cards.*

¢ ✕ **Restaurant Number One.** Simple but delicious dishes consisting mainly of yak meat, eggs, rice, potatoes, and vegetables are served at this rustic café attached to the Snowland Hotel. These are the only cheap eats in town. ⊠ *Northwest corner of the intersection* ☎ *0892/826–2848* ⊟ *No credit cards.*

$–$$ ✕⌧ **Qomolongma Hotel** (Zhufeng Bingguan). A mediocre government-run hotel, this is nevertheless the best place to stay anywhere near Mount Everest. You'll be comfortable and well rested for your assault on Base Camp the next day, and the walk to your room down what is perhaps the longest hallway on earth will help you get used to the altitude. The restaurant serves both Chinese and Western fare, although we'd recommend sticking with the former. A mountaineering shop can provide you with any last-minute supplies, although water here is three times as expensive as you'll pay at the small shops near the town's gas station. ⊠ *From the intersection, go west over a small bridge and turn left into the entrance* ☎ *0892/826–2775* ⇌ *80 rooms* ⚲ *Restaurant, bar, shop, laundry service, business services, Internet room* ⊟ *No credit cards.*

To & from Shegar

6 hrs (240 km/150 mi) southwest of Shigatse. 3½ hrs (110 km/70 mi) northeast of Rongbuk Monastery and Everest Base Camp.

The long drive from Shigatse to Shegar is necessary if you want to maximize your time at Everest Base Camp. On the way to Mount Everest, you'll encounter a border area checkpoint about 15 minutes outside of town, so don't forget to bring your passport. About 45 minutes later you'll reach Bang-la Pass, with perhaps the world's best view of the Himalayas. On a clear day you can see 4 of the world's 10 highest peaks including Everest, Lhotse, Makalu, and Cho Oyu.

Everest Base Camp

❺ "Because it's there," mountaineer George Mallory quipped in 1922 when asked why he wanted to climb the tallest mountain on the planet. The fabled peak is located in the world's highest national park, Qomolangma Nature Reserve, which is a visual delight that alone is worth the trek from Lhasa. After the monsoon rains in June the hillsides are covered with a variety of blooming flowers and butterflies. Even from April to June the light snow blanketing the rugged ground and along babbling brooks is striking.

You can also visit the world's highest monastery, **Ronguk Monastery,** on your way to Base Camp. There were once 500 monks living here, but now there are only 20 monks and 10 nuns who delight in the company of visitors. It is 8 km (5 mi) along a dirt road from the monastery to Base Camp. The 15-minute drive from the monastery is no longer officially allowed, but plenty of jeeps get through with a little cajoling and perhaps a bit of cash. It's more thrilling, however, to make the three-hour walk, even if it is just to say that you trekked the Everest region. Horse-drawn carts are also available for Y30 per person one-way, making the trip in about an hour. Everest Base Camp is a simple plateau where a number of Tibetan entrepreneurs set up tent hotels where you can have a meal, drink a hot cup of tea, and even spend the night.

Where to Stay & Eat

Sleeping near Mount Everest is a treat, despite the fact that the lodgings available are fairly underwhelming. The Chinese hotel near Rongbuk Monastery is extremely overpriced, and the monastery's own guesthouse is a rundown flophouse popular with backpackers. If you're tough and up for a once-in-a-lifetime experience, stay in one of the tents at Everest Base Camp. It's cold up there, but you can pile on the blankets and keep warm with hot tea. In the morning, you'll be rewarded with the awesome site of the sunrise illuminating the world's highest peak right above your head. There are no true restaurants here, but every tent hotel has a kitchen serving up decent food.

$ ╳▥ **View Station Hotel.** This pink box not far from Rongbuk Monastery is the only hotel-like lodging near Everest Base Camp. Still, for the price you'd expect private bathrooms and consistently hot water, neither of which is available. If you're insistent on staying in a hotel near Mount Everest this place will have to do, but you'd probably be happier heading back to Shegar. ⊠ *North of Rongbuk Monastery* ☎ *No phone* ➫ *40 rooms* ♨ *Restaurant* ▭ *No credit cards.*

¢ ╳▥ **Rongbuk Monastery Guesthouse.** This dingy little guesthouse is the most popular lodging near Mount Everest, mainly because it's the only affordable option with four solid walls. Notable is the guesthouse's prison-style lighting system—lights out at 11 PM—and lack of electrical outlets. Still, the restaurant off of the courtyard is an excellent place to warm up and chat with fellow adventurers after a long day of trekking. ⊠*Across from Rongbuk Monastery* ☎*No phone* ➫*25 rooms* ♨*Restaurant* ▭ *No credit cards.*

To & from Everest Base Camp

14 hrs (670 km/420 mi) southwest of Lhasa by jeep. 3½ hrs (110 km/70 mi) southwest of Shegar (New Tingri).

If you only have eyes for Everest, you can make it here from Lhasa and back in three days. Of course, you'll have to spend about 10 hours driving every day, skip all the sites along the way, and hang out for only an hour or so at Everest Base Camp. Most people make this a five-day trip. Not included in the price of your tour will be the Y65 per person entrance fee, plus Y405 per vehicle, usually split among all the passengers.

TIBET ESSENTIALS

Transportation

BY AIR

Air China, Sichuan Airlines, China Southern Airlines, and China Eastern Airlines all have frequent service to Lhasa. The easiest direct route is from Chengdu, which has as many as 10 daily flights during the summer months for about $200 each way. There are also frequent flights from Beijing, Guangzhou, Xi'an, and Chongqing. If you are coming from Kathmandu, the nonstop flights made three times a week will give you fantastic views of the Himalayas. You must show your permit from the Tibet Tourism Bureau when you check in.

Gongka Airport (LXA) is the only Tibetan airport that can be used by foreigners. A taxi into Lhasa will take about 45 minutes via the new expressway and costs Y150. There is a small café that serves Chinese and Tibetan food adjacent to the departure gates.

Booking a ticket to Lhasa is a complicated process involving a Tibet Tourism Bureau permit. You're much better off letting a travel agent handle this for you rather than attempting to book flights on your own.

🚩 Airport Information **Gongka Airport** (Gonggar Feijichang) ✉ Airport Rd., Gongka County ☎ 0891/618-2220.

BY BUS
Intercity travel by bus is not only long and uncomfortable, it's also illegal for foreigners in almost all of Tibet. In fact, the only bus generally willing to pick up foreigners is the early morning coach from Lhasa to Shigatse that leaves across from the Kirey Hotel.

You can, however, take the pilgrim buses that leave every day at 6:30 AM from Barkhor Square headed to Ganden Monastery.

BY CAR
Travel by car is the only permitted transportation throughout Tibet for foreigners. Travel agencies can arrange a driver and all of the necessary permits for any destination you can imagine, if you're willing to pay the price. If you're headed to Nepal, make sure you arrange a visa in Lhasa before your departure, as you can never be certain whether or not visas will be issued at the border post near Kodari.

BY TRAIN
The train line to Lhasa, which opened in the summer of 2006, has rewritten many of the world's records for extreme engineering. It's the world highest railway, with more than 966 km (600 mi) of track above 13,000 feet, reaching above 16,500 feet in several locations. The line is also home to the world's highest railway station, which at Tangu-la Pass sits at almost 17,000 feet.

The train is comfortable and inexpensive, with free oxygen supplies beneath every seat to ease the uncomfortable symptoms of altitude sickness. Traveling by rail is also the perfect way to see the vast uninhabited expanse of the northern Qinghai-Tibet Plateau, with plenty of yaks and antelopes roaming the hills. With trains now reaching Lhasa from Guangzhou, Shanghai, Nanjing, Beijing, Chengdu, Chongqing, Xi'an, Lanzhou, Xining, and Golmud, there's no reason not to hop aboard for the journey of a lifetime.

🚩 Rail Contact **Tibet Autonomous Region Tourism Office** (Zizhiqu Luyouzhu) ✉ 3 Luobulingka Lu, Lhasa ☻ Daily 8:30-6:30.

Contacts & Resources

CONSULATES

Located between Norbulingka Summer Palace and the Lhasa Hotel, the Nepalese Consulate is open weekdays 10 to 12:30. This is where to get visas if you're continuing on to Nepal.

🛈 **Nepal Nepalese Consulate** ✉ 13 Luobulingka Lu, Lhasa ☎ 0891/683-0609 or 0891/681-5744.

EMERGENCIES

The Tibet Military General Hospital is open 24 hours a day. If you're experiencing mild altitude sickness, pharmacies along Beijing Lu east of the Potala Palace sell oxygen canisters and an effective herbal remedy.

🛈 The **Tibet Military General Hospital** (Xizang Junqu Zongyiyuan) ✉ 3 Zhaji Lu, Lhasa ☎ 0891/632-3364.

HOLIDAYS

Tibet has two sets of holidays: events observed by the People's Republic of China, which shuts down businesses and government offices on these holidays, and Tibetan Buddhist festivals, when pilgrims converge and the streets explode with life and color. The lunar calendar determines the timing of many events, including the Tibetan New Year (February), the Butter Lantern Festival (late February/early March), the Birth of Buddha Festival (late May/early June), the Holy Mountain Festival (late July/early August), the one-week Yogurt Festival (August), and the Bathing Festival (September).

INTERNET SERVICES

In Lhasa, Shigatse, and other decent-size towns throughout Tibet, Internet access is available at almost every hotel and guesthouse for Y5 to Y10 per hour. Internet cafés are also sprinkled almost everywhere, but not to the extent seen in eastern China.

MONEY MATTERS

The larger hotels all offer foreign-exchange service, but cannot process credit-card advances. Only the Bank of China, open weekdays 9 to 1 and 3:30 to 6:30, weekends 10:30 to 3, can facilitate cash advances for Visa and MasterCard. Debit-card withdrawals usually work from the bank's ATM machine. The main Bank of China is west of the Potala Palace, a few minutes' walking north from the yak statues. For most of your needs, however, you may find the branch just east of the Kirey Hotel more convenient.

🛈 **Exchange Services Bank of China** ✉ Lingkor Xi Lu ✉ 20 Beijing Dong Lu.

PASSPORTS & VISAS

ENTERING TIBET A visa valid for the People's Republic of China is required. When you apply for a visa, it's probably best not to share your travel plans with consulate officials. There have been reports of visa applications being denied because of an impending visit to Tibet. You will also need to get a Tibet Tourism Bureau travel permit, which is usually arranged by the travel agent who books your plane or train trip to Lhasa. Travel by train without a permit is possible, but you do so at your own risk.

10

The Chinese government would prefer that you join a guided tour. Groups find it easier to secure a TTB permit as well as permits to visit sites outside of Lhasa. A typical package includes flights to Lhasa and a guide to take you to a hotel. You will then be on your own until your departure when the guide will take you back to the airport. There is no limit, aside from the validity of your Chinese visa, to the length of time you can stay in Tibet.

SAFETY

Don't openly talk politics with Tibetans. If they speak out against the government they may be charged with treason and receive a 20-year jail term. Public Security Bureau personnel are everywhere, sometimes in uniform, sometimes in civilian clothes or even in monks' robes. The PSB monitors civil unrest, visa extensions, crime, and traffic. Beware of the charming Tibetan who may be a secret policeman trying to entrap you into giving him a photograph of the Dalai Lama. You could be detained, deported, and even risk being beaten. PSB offices are in all towns and many of the smaller townships.

TIME

Tibet observes Beijing standard time, which is 7 hours ahead of Greenwich mean time and 12 hours ahead of U.S. eastern standard time.

TOURS

Foreign travelers are required by law to book a tour when securing a Tibet Travel Bureau permit, although enforcement of this regulation is nonexistent. In fact, fewer and fewer foreigners are prebooking tours, preferring the flexibility of arranging travel once they arrive in Lhasa. If you're the independent type, tell your travel agent that you don't want a tour of any kind when you're arranging your flight tickets. Once in Lhasa, visit any tour operator to see what's available. The five-day trip to Everest Base Camp (Y5,000) is the most popular tour, but others include the two-day trip to Nam Tso Lake (Y1,200), the two-day trip to Samye Monastery (Y1,700), and the mammoth 12-day trip to sacred Mount Kailash (Y17,000). One reliable local company is Tibet FIT Travel.

Arranging a tour beforehand will save you time. There are a growing number of tours that can be arranged via the Internet. Agents should be able to advise you on the latest changes to travel restrictions and permit requirements. Typically the cost of an organized tour for a week runs $1,000 to $2,000 per person. When booking a tour, be sure to get confirmation in writing with details about your hotel and meal arrangements.

🛈 Tour-Operator Recommendations **Tibet FIT Travel** ✉ 4 Danjielin Lu, Lhasa ☎ 0891/634-9239 or 655-2370.

VISITOR INFORMATION

🛈 Tourist Information **Tibet Tourism Bureau** ✉ 3 Luobulingka Lu, Lhasa ☎ 0891/683-4315 information, 0891/683-4193 to register a complaint.

At a Glance

ENGLISH	PINYIN	CHINESE CHARACTERS
POINTS OF INTEREST		
TIBET	Xīzàng	西藏
LHASA	Lāsà	拉萨
Ani Tsangkung Nunnery	Āní cāngkōng nígū ān	阿尼仓空尼姑庵
Barkhor	Bākuòjiē	八廓街
Drepung Monastery	Zhébàng Sì	哲蚌寺
Ganden Monastery	Gāndān Sì	甘丹寺
Jokhang Temple	Dà Zhāo Sì	大昭寺
Jowo Sakyamuni Lhakhang	Zhuòmǎ Lākāng	卓玛拉康
Kundeling Monastery	Kūndélín Sì	昆德林寺
Lhasa Gongka Airport	Gònggá Fēijīchǎng	贡嘎飞机场
Lhasa Train Station	Lāsà Huǒchēzhàn	拉萨火车站
Muslim Quarter	Mùsīlín Xiǎo Qū	穆斯林小区
Nechung Monastery	Nǎiqióng Sì	乃穷寺
Norbulingka Palace	Luóbùlínkǎ Gōng	罗布林卡宫
Palha Lupuk Temple	Pàlālǔfǔ Shíkū Miào	帕拉鲁甫石窟庙
Potala Palace	Bùdálā Gōng	布达拉宫
Ramoche Temple	Xiǎo Zhāo Sì	小昭寺
Sera Monastery	Sèlā Sì	色拉寺
Tibet Museum	Xīzàng Bówùguǎn	西藏博物馆
WHERE TO STAY & EAT		
Brahmaputra Grand Hotel	Yǎlǔzàngbù Dàjiǔdiàn	雅鲁藏布大酒店
Dunya	Dūnníyà jiǔbā	敦尼亚酒吧
Himalaya Hotel	Xǐmǎlāyǎ Jiǔdiàn	喜玛拉雅酒店
House of Shambhala	Xiāngbālā dàjiǔdiàn	香巴拉大酒店
Kirey Hotel	Jírì Lǚguǎn	吉日旅馆
Lhasa Hotel	Lāsà Fàndiàn	拉萨饭店
Makye Ame	Mǎjí āmǐ	玛吉阿米
Oh Dan Guesthouse	Ōudān Bīnguǎn	欧丹宾馆
Shangrila	Xiāng Gé Lǐ Lā	香格里拉
Snowlands	Xuě Yù Bīn Guǎn	雪域宾馆
Tashi	Zàxī	扎西

10

Tibet Hotel	Xīzàng Bīnguǎn	西藏宾馆
Yak Hotel	Yà Lǚ Guǎn	亚旅馆
TSANG PROVINCE	Hòu Zàng Dì Qū	后藏地区
GYANTSE	Jiāngzī	江孜
EXPLORING		
Gyantse Dzong	Jiāngzī Zōngshān	江孜宗山
Pelkor Chode Monastery	Bái Jū Sì	白居寺
WHERE TO STAY & EAT		
Fuqi Sichuan	Fūqī Fūqī	夫妻肺片
Gyantse Hotel	Jiāngzī Fàndiàn	江孜饭店
Jian Zang Hotel	Jiànzàng Fàndiàn	建藏饭店
Tashi	Zāxī	扎西
SHIGATSE	Rìkāzé	日喀则
EXPLORING		
Tashilhunpo Monastery	Zāshí Lúbù Sì	扎什伦布寺
WHERE TO STAY & EAT		
Galgyal Tibet	Xī Zàng Zhuǎn Lún	西藏转轮
Manasarovar Hotel	Shénhú Jiǔdiàn	神湖酒店
Tashi	Zāxī	扎西
Tenzin Hotel	Tiānxīn Lǚguǎn	天新旅馆
Yakhead Tibet	Máo Niú Lǚ Guǎn	牦牛旅馆
SHEGAR (NEW TINGRI)	Dìngrì	新定日
EXPLORING		
The Friendly Restaurant	Yǒuyì Fàndiàn	友谊饭店
Qomolongma Hotel	Zhūfēng Bīnguǎn	珠峰宾馆
Restaurant Number One	Dìyī Fàndiàn	第一饭店
MT. EVEREST (QOMOLANGMA)	Zhūmù Lǎngmǎ Fēng	珠穆朗玛峰
EXPLORING		
Rongbuk Monastery	Róngbù Sì	绒布寺
Rongbuk Monastery Guesthouse	Róngbù Sì Zhāodài Suǒ	绒布寺招待所

UNDERSTANDING CHINA

CHINA AT A GLANCE

PRONUNCIATION & VOCABULARY

CHINA AT A GLANCE

Fast Facts

Capital: Beijing
National anthem: *March of the Volunteers*
Type of government: Communist
Administrative divisions: 23 provinces (including Taiwan), 5 autonomous regions, 4 municipalities, 2 special administrative regions (Hong Kong and Macau)
Independence: October 1, 1949
Constitution: December 4, 1982
Legal system: A mix of custom and statute, largely criminal law, with rudimentary civil code
Suffrage: 18 years of age
Legislature: Unicameral National People's Congress; 2,985 members elected by municipal, regional, and provincial people's congresses to serve five-year terms; next elections scheduled for late 2007 or early February 2008
Population: 1.3 billion; the largest in the world
Population density: 138 people per square km (361 people per square mi)

Median age: Female 31.7, male 31.2
Life expectancy: Female 74.3, male 70.3
Infant mortality rate: 25.3 deaths per 1,000 live births
Literacy: 86%
Language: Standard Chinese or Mandarin (official), Yue (Cantonese), Wu (Shanghainese), Minbei (Fuzhou), Minnan (Hokkien-Taiwanese), Xiang, Gan, Hakka dialects
Ethnic groups: Han Chinese 92%; Zhuang, Uygur, Hui, Yi, Tibetan, Miao, Manchu, Mongol, Buyi, Korean, and other nationalities 8%
Religion: Officially atheist but Taoism, Buddhism, Christianity, and Islam are practiced.
Discoveries & Inventions: Decimal system (1400 BC), paper (100 BC), seismograph (AD 100), compass (200), matches (577), gunpowder (700), paper money (800), movable type (1045)

Geography & Environment

Land area: 9.3 million square km (3.6 million square mi), the fourth-largest country in the world, and slightly smaller than the United States
Coastline: 14,500 km (9,010 mi) on the Yellow Sea, the East China Sea, and the South China Sea
Terrain: Mostly mountains, high plateaus, deserts in west; plains, deltas, and hills in east
Islands: Hainan, Taiwan, many smaller islands along the coast
Natural resources: Aluminum, antimony, coal, hydropower, iron ore, lead, magnetite, manganese, mercury, molybdenum, natural gas, petroleum, , tungsten, uranium, vanadium, zinc
ural hazards: Droughts, earthquakes, ls, land subsidence, tsunamis, ons

Environmental issues: Air pollution (greenhouse gases, sulfur dioxide particulates), especially from China's reliance on coal, which is used to generate 70% of the country's electric power. Acid rain is also a consequence of the burning of China's high-sulfur coal, particularly in the north; deforestation; soil erosion and economic development have destroyed one-fifth of agricultural land since 1949; desertification; trade in endangered species; water pollution from untreated wastes; water shortages

China is an attractive piece of meat coveted by all . . . but very tough, and for years no one has been able to bite into it.

— Zhou Enlai,
Chinese Premier, 1973

Economy

Currency: Yuan
Exchange rate: Y8.28 = $1
GDP: $6 trillion
Inflation: −0.4%
Per capita income: Y4,329 ($523)
Unemployment: 9%
Workforce: 744 million; agriculture 50%; industry 22%; services 28%
Debt: $149.4 billion
Major industries: Armaments, automobiles, cement, chemical fertilizers, coal, consumer electronics, food processing, footwear, iron and steel, machine building, petroleum, telecommunications, textiles and apparel, toys

Agricultural products: Barley, cotton, fish, millet, oilseed, peanuts, pork, potatoes, rice, sorghum, tea, wheat
Exports: $325.6 billion
Major export products: Footwear, machinery and equipment, mineral fuels, sporting goods, textiles and clothing, toys
Export partners: U.S. 21.5%; Hong Kong 18%; Japan 14.9%; South Korea 4.8%
Imports: $295.3 billion
Major import products: Chemicals, iron and steel, machinery and equipment, mineral fuels, plastics
Import partners: Japan 18%; Taiwan 11%; South Korea 10%; U.S. 9%; Germany 6%

Political Climate

Since the Chinese Communist Party (CCP) took control of the government in 1949, it has shown little tolerance for outside views. Other major political parties are banned and the government is quick to crack down on movements that it doesn't approve of, most recently the Falun Gong. China's size and diversity complicate national politics, with party control weaker in rural areas, where most of the population lives. Successful politicians have sought support from local and regional leaders and must work to keep influential nonparty members from creating a stir. The decade-long struggle for democracy, which ended in the bloody Tiananmen Square protests of 1989, has fragmented and lost much of its power. The party blamed its rise on foreign agitators and reminds the population that political stability is essential for China's economic growth. The poor handling of the SARS outbreak in early 2003 prompted new calls for government reform.

Did You Know?

• China has nearly 13 million more boys than girls, leading demographers to fear that 40 million Chinese men will remain single in the 21st century.

• The country dropped its Soviet-style centralized economy for a more market-oriented system in 1978. As a result, its GDP had quadrupled by 1998.

• China is the world's largest producer of red meat and rice.

• One out of every three cigarettes in the world is smoked in China.

The nation consumes more than three times the cigarettes puffed away by U.S. smokers.

• Since the revolution, China has had four constitutions in less than 60 years. The first three couldn't keep up with the rapid pace of change, particularly during the Cultural Revolution.

• China executed more than 17,500 people between 1990 and 1999, more than the rest of the world put together.

PRONUNCIATION & VOCABULARY

	Chinese	English Equivalent	Chinese	English Equivalent

Consonants

	Chinese	English Equivalent	Chinese	English Equivalent
b	boat	p	pass
m	mouse	f	flag
d	dock	t	tongue
n	nest	l	life
g	goat	k	keep
h	house	j	and yet
q	chicken	x	short
zh	judge	ch	church
sh	sheep	r*	read
z	seeds	c	dots
s	seed		

Vowels

	Chinese	English Equivalent	Chinese	English Equivalent
ü	you	ia	yard
üe	you + e	ian	yen
a	father	iang	young
ai	kite	ie	yet
ao	now	o	all
e	earn	ou	go
ei	day	u	wood
er	curve	ua	waft
i	yield	uo	wall
i (after z, c, s, zh, ch, sh)	thunder		

Word Order
The basic Chinese sentence structure is the same as in English, following the pattern of subject-verb-object:

He took my pen.	Tā ná le wǒ de bǐ.
s v o	s v o

Nouns
There are no articles in Chinese, although there are many "counters," which are used when a certain number of a given noun is specified. Various attributes of a noun—such as size, shape, or use—determine which

counter is used with that noun. Chinese does not distinguish between singular and plural.

a pen	yìzhī bǐ
a book	yìběn shū

Verbs

Chinese verbs are not conjugated, and they do not have tenses. Instead, a system of word order, word repetition, and the addition of a number of adverbs serves to indicate the tense of a verb, whether the verb is a suggestion or an order, or even whether the verb is part of a question. *Tāzài ná wǒ de bǐ.* (He is taking my pen.) *Tā ná le wǒ de bǐ.* (He took my pen.) *Tā you méi you ná wǒ de bǐ?* (Did he take my pen?) *Tā yào ná wǒ de bǐ.* (He will take my pen.)

Tones

In English, intonation patterns can indicate whether a sentence is a statement (He's hungry.), a question (He's hungry?), or an exclamation (He's hungry!). Entire sentences carry particular "tones," but individual words do not. In Chinese, words have a particular tone value, and these tones are important in determining the meaning of a word. Observe the meanings of the following examples, each said with one of the four tones found in standard Chinese: *mā* (high, steady tone): mother; *má* (rising tone, like a question): fiber; *mǎ* (dipping tone): horse; and *mà* (dropping tone): swear.

Phrases

You don't need to master the entire Chinese language to spend a week in China, but taking charge of a few key phrases in the language can aid you in just getting by. The following supplement will allow you to get a hotel room, get around town, order a drink at the end of the day, and get help in case of an emergency.

Listen to the phrase and repeat what you hear in the space provided.

Common Greetings

Hello/Good morning.	Nǐ hǎo/Zǎoshàng hǎo.
Good evening.	Wǎnshàng hǎo.
Good-bye.	Zàijiàn.
Title for a married woman or an older unmarried woman	Tàitai/Fūrén
Title for a young and unmarried woman	Xiǎojiě
Title for a man	Xiānshēng
How are you?	Nǐ hǎo ma?
Fine, thanks. And you?	Hěn hǎo. Xièxie. Nǐ ne?
What is your name?	Nǐ jiào shénme míngzi?
My name is . . .	Wǒ jiào . . .

Nice to meet you.	Hěn gāoxìng rènshì nǐ.
I'll see you later.	Huítóu jiàn.

Polite Expressions

Please.	Qǐng.
Thank you.	Xièxiè.
Thank you very much.	Fēicháng gǎnxiè.
You're welcome.	Bú yòng xiè.
Yes, thank you.	Shì de, xièxiè.
No, thank you.	Bù, xièxiè.
I beg your pardon.	Qǐng yuánliàng.
I'm sorry.	Hěn baòqiàn.
Pardon me.	Dùibùqǐ.
That's okay.	Méi shénme.
It doesn't matter.	Méi guānxi.
Do you speak English?	Nǐ shuō Yīngyǔ ma?
Yes.	Shì de.
No.	Bù.
Maybe.	Huòxǔ.
I can speak a little.	Wǒ néng shūo yī diǎnr.
I understand a little.	Wǒ dǒng yì diǎnr.
I don't understand.	Wǒ bù dǒng.
I don't speak Chinese very well.	Wǒ Zhōngwén shuō de bù haǒ.
Would you repeat that, please?	Qǐng zài shūo yíbiàn?
I don't know.	Wǒ bù zhīdaò.
No problem.	Méi wèntí.
It's my pleasure.	Lèyì er wéi.

Needs and Question words

I'd like . . .	Wǒ xiǎng . . .
I need . . .	Wǒ xūyào . . .
What would you like?	Nǐ yaò shénme?
Please bring me . . .	Qǐng gěi wǒ . . .
I'm looking for . . .	Wǒ zài zhǎo . . .
I'm hungry.	Wǒ è le.
I'm thirsty.	Wǒ kǒukě.
It's important.	Hěn zhòngyào.
It's urgent.	Hěn jǐnjí.
How?	Zěnmeyàng?

How much?	Duōshǎo?
How many?	Duōshǎo gè?
Which?	Nǎ yí gè?
What?	Shénme?
What kind of?	Shénme yàng de?
Who?	Shuí?
Where?	Nǎli?
When?	Shénme shíhòu?
What does this mean?	Zhè shì shénme yìsi?
What does that mean?	Nà shì shénme yìsi?
How do you say . . . in Chinese?	. . . yòng Zhōngwén zěnme shūo?

At the Airport

Where is . . .	. . . zài nǎr?
customs?	Hǎigūan
passport control?	Hùzhào jiǎnyàn
the information booth?	Wènxùntái
the ticketing counter?	Shòupiàochù
the baggage claim?	Xínglǐchù
the ground transportation?	Dìmìan jiāotōng
Is there a bus service to the city?	Yǒu qù chéng lǐ de gōnggòng qìchē ma?
Where are . . .	. . . zài nǎr?
the international departures?	Guójì hángbān chūfā diǎn
the international arrivals?	Guójì hángbān dàodá diǎn
What is your nationality?	Nǐ shì něi guó rén?
I am an American.	Wǒ shì Měiguó rén.
I am Canadian.	Wǒ shì Jiānádà rén.

At the Hotel, Reserving a Room

I would like a room . . .	Wǒ yào yí ge fángjiān.
for one person	dānrén fáng
for two people	shuāngrén fāng
for tonight	jīntiān wǎnshàng
for two nights	liǎng gè wǎnshàng
for a week	yí ge xīngqī
Do you have a different room?	Nǐ hái yǒu bié de fángjiān ma?
with a bath	dài yùshì de fángjiān
with a shower	dài línyù de fángjiān
with a toilet	dài cèsuǒ de fángjiān
with air-conditioning	yǒu kōngtiáo de fángjiān

How much is it?	Duōshǎo qián?
My bill, please.	Qǐng jiézhàng.

At the Restaurant

Where can we find a good restaurant?	Zài nǎr kěyǐ zhǎodào yìjiā hǎo cānguǎn?
We'd like a(n) . . . restaurant.	Wǒmen xiǎng qù yì gè . . . cānguǎn.
elegant	gāo jí
fast-food	kuàicān
inexpensive	piányì de
seafood	hǎixiān
vegetarian	sùshí
Café	Kāfeī diàn
A table for two	Liǎng wèi
Waiter, a menu please.	Fúwùyuán, qǐng gěi wǒmen càidān.
The wine list, please.	Qǐng gěi wǒmen jiǔdān.
Appetizers	Kāiwèi shíwù
Main course	Zhǔ cài
Dessert	Tiándiǎn
What would you like?	Nǐ yào shénme cài?
What would you like to drink?	Nǐ yào hē shénme yǐnliào?
Can you recommend a good wine?	Nǐ néng tūijiàn yí ge hǎo jiǔ ma?
Wine, please.	Qǐng lǎi diǎn jiǔ.
Beer, please.	Qǐng lǎi diǎn píjiǔ.
I didn't order this.	Wǒ méiyǒu diǎn zhè gè.
That's all, thanks.	Jiù zhèxie, xièxiè.
The check, please.	Qǐng jiézhàng.
Cheers!/Bottoms Up! To your health!	Gānbēi! Zhù nǐ shēntì jiànkāng.

Out on the Town

Where can I find . . .	Nǎr yǒu . . .
an art museum?	yìshù bówùguǎn?
a museum of natural history?	zìránlìshǐ bówùguǎn?
a history museum?	lìshǐ bówuguǎn?
a gallery?	huàláng?
interesting architecture?	yǒuqù de jiànzhùwù?
a church?	jiàotáng?
the zoo?	dòngwùyuán?
I'd like . . .	Wǒ xiǎng . . .
to see a play.	kàn xì.

to see a movie.	kàn diànyǐng.
to see a concert.	qù yīnyuèhuì.
to see the opera.	kàn gējù.
to go sightseeing.	qù guānguāng.
to go on a bike ride.	qí dānchē.

Shopping

Where is the best place to go shopping for . . .	Mǎi . . . zuì hǎo qù nǎr?
clothes?	yīfu
food?	shíwù
souvenirs?	jìniànpǐn
furniture?	jiājù
fabric?	bùliào
antiques?	gǔdǒng
books?	shūjí
sporting goods?	yùndòng wùpǐn
electronics?	diànqì
computers?	diànnǎo

Directions

Excuse me. Where is . . .	Duìbùqǐ . . . zài nǎr?
the bus stop?	Qìchēzhàn
the subway station?	Dìtiězhàn
the rest room?	Xǐshǒujiān
the taxi stand?	Chūzū chēzhàn
the nearest bank?	Zùijìn de yínháng
the hotel?	Lǚguǎn
To the right	Zài yòubiān.
To the left.	Zài zuǒbiān.
Straight ahead.	Wǎng qián zhízǒu.
It's near here.	Jiuzài zhè fùjìn.
Go back.	Wǎng húi zǒu.
Next to . . .	Jǐnkào . . .

Numbers

Cardinal

0	Líng	5	Wǔ
1	Yī	6	Lìu
2	Er	7	Qī
3	Sān	8	Bā
4	Sì	9	Jǐu
10	Shí	30	Sānshí

11	Shíyī	40	Sìshí
12	Shí'èr	50	Wǔshí
13	Shísān	60	Lìushí
14	Shísì	70	Qīshí
15	Shíwǔ	80	Bāshí
16	Shílìu	90	Jǐushí
17	Shíqī	100	Yìbǎi
18	Shíbā	1,000	Yìqiān
19	Shíjǐu	1,100	Yìqiān yìbǎi
20	Ershí	2,000	Liǎngqiān
21	Ershíyī	10,000	Yíwàn
22	Ershí'èr	100,000	Shíwàn
23	Eshísān	1,000,000	Bǎiwàn

Time

What time is it?	Xiànzài shénme shíjiān?
It is noon.	Zhōngwǔ.
It is midnight.	Bànyè.
It is 9:00 A.M.	Shàngwǔ jǐu diǎn.
It is 1:00 P.M.	Xiàwǔ yì diǎn.
It is 3 o'clock.	Sān diǎn (zhōng).
5:15	Wǔ diǎn shíwǔ fēn.
7:30	Qī diǎn sānshí (bàn).
9:45	Jǐu diǎn sìshíwǔ.
Now	Xiànzài
Later	Wǎn yì diǎnr
Immediately	Mǎshàng
Soon	Hěn kuài

Days of the Week

Monday	Xīngqī yī
Tuesday	Xīngqī èr
Wednesday	Xīngqī sān
Thursday	Xīngqī sì
Friday	Xīngqī wǔ
Saturday	Xīngqī lìu
Sunday	Xīngqī rì (tiān)

Modern Connections

Where can I find . . . a telephone?	Zài nǎr kěyǐ shǐ yòng . . . diànhuà?

a fax machine?	chuánzhēnjī?
an Internet connection?	guójì wǎnglù?
How do I call the United States?	Gěi Měiguó dǎ diànhuà zěnme dǎ?
I need . . .	Wǒ xūyào . . .
a fax sent.	fā chuánzhēn.
a hookup to the Internet.	yǔ guójì wǎnglù liánjiē.
a computer.	diànnǎo.
a package sent overnight.	liányè bǎ bāoguǒ jìchū.
some copies made.	fùyìn yìxiē wénjiàn.
a VCR and monitor.	lùyǐngjī he xiǎnshìqì.
an overhead projector and markers.	huàndēngjī he biāoshìqì.

Emergencies and Safety

Help!	Jiumìng a!
Fire!	Jiùhuǒ a!
I need a doctor.	Wǒ yào kàn yīshēng.
Call an ambulance!	Mǎshàng jiào jiùhùchē!
What happened?	Fāshēng le shénme shì?
I am/My wife is/My husband is/ My friend is/Someone is . . .	Wǒ/Wǒ qīzi/Wǒ Zhàngfu/ Wǒ péngyǒu/Yǒu rén . . .
very sick.	bìng de hěn lìhài.
having a heart attack.	xīnzàngbìng fāzuò le.
choking.	yēzhù le.
losing consciousness.	yūndǎo le.
about to vomit.	yào ǒutù le.
having a seizure.	yòu fābìng le.
stuck.	bèi kǎ zhù le.
I can't breathe.	Wǒ bù néng hūxī.
I tripped and fell.	Wǒ bàn dǎo le.
I cut myself.	Wǒ gē shāng le.
I drank too much.	Wǒ jiǔ hē de tài duō le.
I don't know.	Wǒ bù zhīdào.
I've injured my . . .	Wǒ de . . . shòushāng le.
head	tóu
neck	bózi
back	bèi
arm	shǒubèi
leg	tuǐ
foot	jiǎo
eye(s)	yǎnjīng
I've been robbed.	Wǒ bèi qiǎng le.

China Essentials

PLANNING TOOLS, EXPERT INSIGHT,
GREAT CONTACTS

There are planners, and there are those who fly by the seat of their pants. We happily place ourselves among the planners. Our writers and editors try to anticipate all the issues you may face before and during any journey, and then they do their research. This section is the product of their efforts. Use it to get excited about your trip to China, to inform your travel planning, or to guide you on the road should the seat of your pants start to feel threadbare.

GETTING STARTED

We're really proud of our Web site: Fodors. com is a great place to begin any journey. Scan "Travel Wire" for suggested itineraries, travel deals, restaurant and hotel openings, and other up-to-the-minute info. Check out "Booking" to research prices and book plane tickets, hotel rooms, rental cars, and vacation packages. Head to "Talk" for on-the-ground pointers from travelers who frequent our message boards. You can also link to loads of other travel-related resources.

▋ RESOURCES

ONLINE TRAVEL TOOLS

The Web sites listed in this book are in English. If you come across a Chinese-language site you think might be useful, copy the URL into Google, then click the "Translate this page" link. Translations are literal, but generally work for finding out information like opening hours or prices.

All About China
China Digital Times ⊕ http://chinadigital-times.net : an excellent Berkeley-run site tracking China-related news and culture in serious depth. **China National Tourism Office** ⊕ www.cnto.org : a general overview of traveling in China. **China International Travel Service (CITS)** ⊕ www.cits.net/ : the largest comprehensive travel agency in China. **China Travel Services (U.S. site)** CTS ⊕ www. chinatravelservice.com: the state-run travel agency is a helpful starting place when planning trips. **Chinese Government Portal** ⊕ http://english.gov.cn. **China Site** ⊕ www. chinasite.com: a comprehensive portal with links to thousands of China-related Web sites. **Hong Kong Government** ⊕ www.info.gov.hk. **The Oriental List** ⊕ www.datasinica.com: a free Internet mailing list giving extremely reliable information about travel in China.
Business **Business in Hong Kong** ⊕ www. business.gov.hk: a government-run site packed with advice. **China Business Weekly** ⊕ www.chinadaily.com.cn/english/bw/bwtop. html: a weekly magazine from *China Daily*

newspaper. **Chinese Government Business Site** ⊕ http://english.gov.cn/business.htm: provides news, links, and information on business-related legal issues from the Chinese government.
Culture & Entertainment **Chinese Culture** ⊕ www.chinaculture.org: detailed, searchable database with information on Chinese art, literature, film, history and more. The Leisure and Cultural Services Department ⊕ www.lcsd.gov.hk: has access to Web sites for all of Hong Kong's museums and parks through this government portal.
Currency Conversion **Google** ⊕ www. google.com does currency conversion. Just type in the amount you want to convert and an explanation of how you want it converted (e.g., "14 Swiss francs in dollars"), and then voilà. **Oanda.com** ⊕ www.oanda.com also allows you to print out a handy table with the current day's conversion rates. **XE.com** ⊕ www.xe.com is a good currency conversion Web site.
Local Insight **Asia Expat** ⊕ www.asiaxpat. com: gives advice and listings from foreigners living in Beijing, Hong Kong, Guangzhou, and Shanghai. **Asia City Magazines** ⊕ www. asia-city.com: an online version of quirky weekly rags with the lowdown on everything happening in Shanghai and Hong Kong.
Newspapers *China Daily* ⊕ www.chinadaily. com.cn: the leading English-language daily. *People's Daily* ⊕ http://english.peopledaily. com.cn: English edition of China's most popular—and most propagandistic—local daily. *South China Morning Post* ⊕ www.scmp. com: Hong Kong's leading English-language daily.
Safety **Transportation Security Administration** (TSA) ⊕ www.tsa.gov
Time Zones **Timeanddate.com** ⊕ www. timeanddate.com/worldclock can help you figure out the correct time anywhere in the world.
Weather **Accuweather.com** ⊕ www. accuweather.com is an independent weather-forecasting service with especially good coverage of hurricanes. **China Weather**

⊕ http://weather.china.org.cn. **Weather.com** ⊕ www.weather.com is the Web site for the Weather Channel.

Other Resources CIA World Factbook ⊕ www.odci.gov/cia/publications/factbook/index.html has profiles of every country in the world. It's a good source if you need some quick facts and figures.

GREAT CHINESE READS

Big Name Fiction: Gao Xinjiang's *Soul Mountain,* Ha Jin's *Waiting,* and Dai Sijie's *Mr. Muo's Traveling Couch.* **China 101:** *The China Reader: The Reform Era,* edited by Orville Schell and David Shambaugh; *The Search for Modern China,* by Jonathan Spence; and *A History of Hong Kong,* by Frank Welsh. **How about Mao:** Dr Li Zhisui's *The Private Life of Chairman Mao.*

Before your trip, settle in for an evening of Chinese cinema. **Wuxia wonders:** Ang Lee's *Crouching Tiger, Hidden Dragon* and Zhang Yimou's *Hero.* **Arty Drama:** Chen Kaige's *Farewell, My Concubine* and Wong Kar-Wai's *In the Mood for Love.* **Censored in China:** Lou Ye's *Summer Palace.*

VISITOR INFORMATION

For general information before you go, including advice on tours, insurance, and safety, call or visit the Web site of the China National Tourist Office.

The two best-known Chinese travel agencies are the state-run China International Travel Service (CITS) and China Travel Service (CTS), both under the same government ministry. Although they have some tourist information, they are businesses, so don't expect endless resources if you're not buying a tour or flight through them.

In theory, CTS offices cater to sightseeing around their area, and CITS arranges packages and tours from overseas; in reality, their services overlap.

The Hong Kong Tourism Board has stacks of online information about events, sightseeing, shopping, and dining in Hong Kong. They also organize tour packages from the United States, and local sightseeing tours.

China International Travel Service CITS ☎ 626/568-8993 ⊕ www.citsusa.com **China National Tourist Office** New York: ☎ 888/760-8218 ✉ Los Angeles: ☎ 800/670-2228 ⊕ www.cnto.org. **China Travel Service** CTS ☎ 800/899-8618 ⊕ www.chinatravelservice.com. **Hong Kong Tourist Board** (HKTB) ⊕ www.discoverhongkong.com.

∎ THINGS TO CONSIDER

GOVERNMENT ADVISORIES

As different countries have different world views, look at travel advisories from a range of governments to get more of a sense of what's going on out there. And be sure to parse the language carefully. For example, a warning to "avoid all travel" carries more weight than one urging you to "avoid nonessential travel," and both are much stronger than a plea to "exercise caution." A U.S. government travel warning is more permanent (though not necessarily more serious) than a so-called public announcement, which carries an expiration date.

The U.S. Department of State's Web site has more than just travel warnings and advisories. The consular information sheets issued for every country have general safety tips, entry requirements (though be sure to verify these with the country's embassy), and other useful details.

∎ TIP➔ **If you're a U.S. citizen traveling abroad, consider registering online with the State Department (https://travelregistration.state.gov/ibrs/), so the government will know to look for you should a crisis occur in the country you're visiting.**

General Information & Warnings **Australian Department of Foreign Affairs & Trade** ⊕ www.smartraveller.gov.au. **Consular Affairs Bureau of Canada** ⊕ www.voyage.gc.ca. **U.K. Foreign & Commonwealth Office** ⊕ www.fco.gov.uk/travel. **U.S. Department of State** ⊕ www.travel.state.gov.

GEAR

Most Chinese people dress for comfort, so you can plan to do the same. There's little risk of offending people with your dress: Westerners tend to attract attention regardless of their attire. Fashion capitals Hong Kong and Shanghai are the exceptions to the comfort rule: slop around in flip-flops and worn denims and you WILL feel there's a neon "tourist" sign over your head. Opt for your smarter jeans or capri pants for sightseeing there.

Sturdy, comfortable walking shoes are a must: go for closed shoes over Tevas as dust and toe-stomping crowds make them impractical. Northern Chinese summers are dusty and baking hot, so slacks, capris, and sturdy shorts are best. A raincoat, especially a light Goretex one or a fold-up poncho, is useful for an onset of rainy weather, especially in Southern China. During the harsh winters, thermal long johns are a lifesaver—especially in low-star hotel rooms. An overcoat or jacket that reaches below your backside keeps icy winds at bay.

That said, in urban centers you can prepare to be unprepared: big Chinese cities are a clothes shopper's paradise. If a bulky jacket's going to put you over the airline limit, buy one in China and leave it behind when you go. All the other woollies—and silkies, the local insulator of choice—you'll need go for a song, as do brand-name jackets. Scarves, gloves, and hats, all musts, are also easy to find.

Most good hotels have reliable overnight laundry services, though costs can rack up on a long trip. Look outside your hotel for cheaper laundries, and bring some concentrated travel detergent for small or delicate items. Note that it's often cheaper to

> ### WORD OF MOUTH
>
> " . . . unless you'll be attending a formal business or social meeting you will NOT need dressy clothing in China. The Chinese themselves tend to dress quite casually. I would just take one 'smart casual' outfit for eating out, theater performances and the like."   –Neil Oz

buy things than have your own laundered, so if you're even a little interested in shopping, consider bringing an extra, foldable bag to cart purchases home in.

Keep packets of Kleenex and antibacterial hand wipes in your day pack—paper isn't a feature of Chinese restrooms, and you often can't buy it in smaller towns. A small flashlight with extra batteries is also useful. The brands in Chinese pharmacies are limited, so take adequate stocks of your potions 'n' lotions, feminine-hygiene products (tampons are especially hard to find), and birth control. All of these things are easy to get in Hong Kong.

In your carry-on luggage, pack an extra pair of eyeglasses or contact lenses and enough of any medication you take to last a few days longer than the entire trip. You may also ask your doctor to write a spare prescription using the drug's generic name, as brand names may vary from country to country.

> ### WORD OF MOUTH
>
> "One pair of jeans, you can wear the black pants day or night, khakis are nice but no white pants, I like mid-calf pants. I bring a long cotton skirt that can be dressed up or casual. Not sure of the 3/4 coat, silk knit twin sets are very versatile. And stylish yet comfy shoes. Pack light. Since you're a shopper, you can pick up a wrap if it gets cool, and buy a cheap umbrella or a wide brim hat when it rains."
>   –Shanghainese

If you're planning a longer trip or will be using local tour guides, bring a few inexpensive items from your home country as gifts. Popular gifts are candy, T-shirts, and small cosmetic items such as lipstick and nail polish—double-check that none were made in China. Be wary about giving American magazines and books as gifts, as these can be considered propaganda and get your Chinese friends into trouble. Be sure to take enough to keep you entertained, though.

PASSPORTS & VISAS

All U.S. citizens, even infants, need a valid passport with a tourist visa stamped in it to enter China (except for Hong Kong, where you only need a valid passport). It's always best to have at least six months' validity on your passport before traveling to Asia.

PASSPORTS

We're always surprised at how few Americans have passports—only 25% at this writing. This number is expected to grow in coming years, when it becomes impossible to reenter the United States from trips to neighboring Canada or Mexico without one. Remember this: A passport verifies both your identity and nationality—a great reason to have one.

U.S. passports are valid for 10 years. You must apply in person if you're getting a passport for the first time; if your previous passport was lost, stolen, or damaged; or if your previous passport has expired and was issued more than 15 years ago or when you were under 16. All children under 18 must appear in person to apply for or renew a passport. Both parents must accompany any child under 14 (or send a notarized statement with their permission) and provide proof of their relationship to the child.

There are 13 regional passport offices, as well as 7,000 passport-acceptance facilities in post offices, public libraries, and other governmental offices. If you're renewing a passport, you can do so by mail.

Forms are available at passport-acceptance facilities and online.

The cost to apply for a new passport is $97 for adults, $82 for children under 16; renewals are $67. Allow six weeks for processing, both for first-time passports and renewals. For an expediting fee of $60 you can reduce this time to about two weeks. If your trip is less than two weeks away, you can get a passport even more rapidly by going to a passport office with the necessary documentation. Private expediters can get things done in as little as 48 hours, but charge hefty fees for their services.

■ TIP→ Before your trip, make two copies of your passport's data page (one for someone at home and another for you to carry separately). Or scan the page and e-mail it to someone at home and/or yourself.

VISAS

A visa is essentially formal permission to enter a country. Visas allow countries to keep track of you and other visitors—and generate revenue (from application fees). You *always* need a visa to enter a foreign country; however, many countries routinely issue tourist visas on arrival, particularly to U.S. citizens. When your passport is stamped or scanned in the immigration line, you're actually being issued a visa. Sometimes you have to stand in a separate line and pay a small fee to get your stamp before going through immigration, but you can still do this at the airport on arrival. Getting a visa isn't always that easy. Some countries require that you arrange for one in advance of your trip. There's usually—but not always—a fee involved, and said fee may be nominal ($10 or less) or substantial ($100 or more).

If you must apply for a visa in advance, you can usually do it in person or by mail. When you apply by mail, you send your passport to a designated consulate, where your passport will be examined and the visa issued. Expediters—usually the same ones who handle expedited passport applications—can do all the work of obtaining your visa for you; however, there's

PACKING 101

Why do some people travel with a convoy of huge suitcases yet never have a thing to wear? How do others pack a duffle with a week's worth of outfits *and* supplies for every contingency? We realize that packing is a matter of style, but there's a lot to be said for traveling light. These tips help fight the battle of the bulging bag.

MAKE A LIST. In a recent Fodor's survey, 29% of respondents said they make lists (and often pack) a week before a trip. You can use your list to pack and to repack at the end of your trip. It can also serve as record of the contents of your suitcase—in case it disappears in transit.

THINK IT THROUGH. What's the weather like? Is this a business trip? A cruise? Going abroad? In some places dress may be more or less conservative than you're used to. As you create your itinerary, note outfits next to each activity (don't forget accessories).

EDIT YOUR WARDROBE. Plan to wear everything twice (better yet, thrice) and to do laundry along the way. Stick to one basic look—urban chic, sporty casual, etc. Build around one or two neutrals and an accent (e.g., black, white, and olive green). Women can freshen looks by changing scarves or jewelry. For a week's trip, you can look smashing with three bottoms, four or five tops, a sweater, and a jacket.

BE PRACTICAL. Put comfortable shoes atop your list. (Did we need to say this?) Pack lightweight, wrinkle-resistant, compact, washable items. (Or this?) Stack and roll clothes, so they'll wrinkle less. Unless you're on a guided tour or a cruise, select luggage you can readily carry. Porters, like good butlers, are hard to find these days.

CHECK WEIGHT AND SIZE LIMITATIONS. In the United States you may be charged extra for checked bags weighing more than 50 pounds. Abroad, some airlines don't allow you to check bags over 60 to 70 pounds, or they charge outrageous fees for every excess pound—or bag. Carry-on size limitations can be stringent, too.

CHECK CARRY-ON RESTRICTIONS. Research restrictions with the TSA. Rules vary abroad, so check them with your airline if you're traveling overseas on a foreign carrier. Consider packing all but essentials (travel documents, prescription meds, wallet) in checked luggage. This leads to a "pack only what you can afford to lose" approach that might help you streamline.

RETHINK VALUABLES. On U.S. flights, airlines are liable for only about $2,800 per person for bags. On international flights, the liability limit is around $635 per bag. But items like computers, cameras, and jewelry aren't covered, and as gadgetry can go on the list of carry-on no-no's, you can't count on keeping things safe by keeping them close. Although comprehensive travel policies may cover luggage, the liability limit is often a pittance. Your home-owner's policy may cover you sufficiently when you travel—or not.

LOCK IT UP. If you must pack valuables, use TSA-approved locks (about $10) that can be unlocked by all U.S. security personnel.

TAG IT. Always tag your luggage; use your business address if you don't want people to know your home address. Put the same information (and a copy of your itinerary) inside your luggage, too.

REPORT PROBLEMS IMMEDIATELY. If your bags—or things in them—are damaged or go astray, file a written claim with your airline *before leaving the airport*. If the airline is at fault, it may give you money for essentials until your luggage arrives. Most lost bags are found within 48 hours, so alert the airline to your whereabouts for two or three days. If your bag was opened for security reasons in the States and something is missing, file a claim with the TSA.

always an additional cost (often more than $50 per visa).

Most visas limit you to a single trip—basically during the actual dates of your planned vacation. Other visas allow you to visit as many times as you wish for a specific period of time. Remember that requirements change, sometimes at the drop of a hat, and the burden is on you to make sure that you have the appropriate visas. Otherwise, you'll be turned away at the airport or, worse, deported after you arrive in the country. No company or travel insurer gives refunds if your travel plans are disrupted because you didn't have the correct visa.

Getting a tourist visa to China (known as an "L" visa) in the United States is straightforward. Standard visas are for single-entry stays of up to 30 days, and are valid for 90 days from the day of issue (NOT the day of entry), so don't get your visa too far in advance. Costs range from $50 for a tourist visa issued within two to three working days to $80 for a same-day service.

Travel agents in Hong Kong can also issue visas to visit mainland China—the above services cost $25 and $65, respectively. Note: The visa application will ask your occupation. The Chinese don't look favorably upon those who work in publishing or the media. People in these professions routinely state "teacher" under "occupation." Before you go, contact the embassy or consulate of the People's Republic of China to gauge the current mood.
Hong Kong Travel Agents **Japan Travel Agency** ☎ 852/2368-9151 ⊕ www.jta.biz offers the quickest and most efficient visa service. **China Travel Service** CTS ☎ 852/2315-7188 ⊕ www.ctshk.com has 22 branches all over Hong Kong.

Children traveling with only one parent do not need a notarized letter of permission to enter China. However, as these kinds of policies can change, being overprepared isn't a bad idea.

China officially denies visas (and thus entry) to anyone suffering from infectious diseases, including leprosy, AIDS, venereal diseases, and contagious tuberculosis. You must complete information regarding these on applications and on entering the country. However, this information is never checked for tourist visas, though medical tests are required for longer visas.

Under no circumstances should you overstay your visa. To extend your visa, stop by the Entry and Exit Administration Office of the local branch of the Public Security Bureau a week before your visa expires. The office is known as the PSB or the Foreigner's Police; most are open weekdays 9 to 11:30 and 1:30 to 4:30. The process is extremely bureaucratic, but it's usually no problem to get a month's extension on a tourist visa. You need to bring your registration of temporary residency from your hotel and your passport, which you generally need to leave for five to seven days (so do any transactions requiring it beforehand). If you are trying to extend a business visa, you'll need the above items as well as a letter from the business that originally invited you to China saying it would like to extend your stay for work reasons. Rules are always changing, so you will probably need to go to the office at least twice to get all your papers in order.

The Web site ⊕ www.visatoasia.com/china.html provides up-to-date information on visa applications to China.
Chinese Visa Information **Chinese Consulate, New York** ☎ 212/244-9456 ⊕ www.nyconsulate.prchina.org. **Visa Office of Chinese Embassy, Washington** ☎ 202/338-6688 ⊕ www.china-embassy.org. **Visa to Asia** ⊕ www.visatoasia.com/china.html.
U.S. Passport Information **U.S. Department of State** ☎ 877/487-2778 ⊕ http://travel.state.gov/passport.
U.S. Passport & Visa Expediters **A. Briggs Passport & Visa Expediters** ☎ 800/806-0581 or 202/464-3000 ⊕ www.abriggs.com. **American Passport Express** ☎ 800/455-5166 or 603/559-9888 ⊕ www.americanpassport.com. **Passport Express** ☎ 800/362-8196 or 401/272-4612 ⊕ www.passportexpress.com. **Travel Document Sys-**

tems ☎ 800/874-5100 or 202/638-3800 ⊕ www.traveldocs.com. **Travel the World Visas** ☎ 866/886-8472 or 301/495-7700 ⊕ www.world-visa.com.

GENERAL REQUIREMENTS FOR MAINLAND	
PASSPORT	Must be valid for six months after date of arrival.
Visa	Required for U.S. citizens ($25 to $80)
Required Vaccinations	None
Recommended Vaccinations	Hepatitis A and B, typhoid, influenza, booster for tetanus-diphtheria
Driving	Chinese driver's license required
International Departure Tax	Y90 ($11)
Domestic Departure Tax	Y50 ($6)

SHOTS & MEDICATIONS

No immunizations are required for entry into China, but it's a good idea to be immunized against typhoid and Hepatitis A and B before traveling, as well as routine tetanus-diphtheria and measles boosters. In winter, a flu vaccination is also smart, especially if you're infection-prone or are a senior citizen.

■ TIP➔ **In summer months malaria is a risk in tropical and rural areas, especially Hainan and Yunan provinces—consult your doctor four to six weeks before your trip as preventative treatments vary.**

The risk of contracting malaria in cities is small. For more information *see* Health *under* On the Ground in China, *below.*

Health Warnings **National Centers for Disease Control & Prevention** (CDC) ☎ 877/394-8747 international travelers' health line ⊕ www.cdc.gov/travel. **World Health Organization** (WHO) ⊕ www.who.int.

TRIP INSURANCE

What kind of coverage do you honestly need? Do you even need trip insurance at all? Take a deep breath and read on.

We believe that comprehensive trip insurance is especially valuable if you're booking a very expensive or complicated trip (particularly to an isolated region) or if you're booking far in advance. Who knows what could happen six months down the road? But whether or not you get insurance has more to do with how comfortable you are assuming all that risk yourself.

Comprehensive travel policies typically cover trip cancellation and interruption letting you cancel or cut your trip short because of a personal emergency, illness, or, in some cases, acts of terrorism in your destination. Such policies also cover evacuation and medical care. Some also cover you for trip delays because of bad weather or mechanical problems as well as for lost or delayed baggage. Another type of coverage to look for is financial default—that is, when your trip is disrupted because a tour operator, airline, or cruise line goes out of business. Generally you must buy this when you book your trip or shortly thereafter, and it's only available to you if your operator isn't on a list of excluded companies.

If you're going abroad, consider buying medical-only coverage at the very least. Neither Medicare nor some private insurers cover medical expenses anywhere outside of the United States besides Mexico and Canada (including time aboard a cruise ship, even if it leaves from a U.S. port). Medical-only policies typically reimburse you for medical care (excluding that related to preexisting conditions) and hospitalization abroad, and provide for evacuation. You still have to pay the bills and await reimbursement from the insurer, though.

Expect comprehensive travel-insurance policies to cost about 4% to 7% of the total price of your trip (it's more like 12% if you're over age 70). A medical-only

Trip Insurance Resources

INSURANCE COMPARISON SITES		
Insure My Trip.com		www.insuremytrip.com
Square Mouth.com		www.quotetravelinsurance.com
COMPREHENSIVE TRAVEL INSURERS		
Access America	866/807-3982	www.accessamerica.com
CSA Travel Protection	800/873-9855	www.csatravelprotection.com
HTH Worldwide	610/254-8700 or 888/243-2358	www.hthworldwide.com
Travelex Insurance	888/457-4602	www.travelex-insurance.com
Travel Guard International	715/345-0505 or 800/826-4919	www.travelguard.com
Travel Insured International	800/243-3174	www.travelinsured.com
MEDICAL-ONLY INSURERS		
International Medical Group	800/628-4664	www.imglobal.com
International SOS	215/942-8000 or 713/521-7611	www.internationalsos.com
Wallach & Company	800/237-6615 or 504/687-3166	www.wallach.com

policy may or may not be cheaper than a comprehensive policy. Always read the fine print of your policy to make sure that you are covered for the risks that are of most concern to you. Compare several policies to make sure you're getting the best price and range of coverage available.

Even at China's public hospitals foreigners need to pay fees to register, to see a doctor, and then for all tests and medication. Prices are cheap compared to the fancy foreigner clinics that exist in major cities, where you pay $100 to $150 just for a consultation. However, most doctors at public hospitals don't speak English and hygiene standards are low—all the more reason to take out medical insurance.

Hong Kong has excellent public and private health care. Foreigners have to pay for both, so insurance is a good idea. Even for lesser complaints private doctors charge a fortune: head to a public hospital if money is tight. In an emergency you'll always receive treatment first and get the bill afterward—Y570 is the standard ER charge.

BOOKING YOUR TRIP

Unless your cousin is a travel agent, you're probably among the millions of people who make most of their travel arrangements online. But have you ever wondered just what the differences are between an online travel agent (a Web site through which you make reservations instead of going directly to the airline, hotel, or car-rental company), a discounter (a firm that does a high volume of business with a hotel chain or airline and accordingly gets good prices), a wholesaler (one that makes cheap reservations in bulk and then resells them to people like you), and an aggregator (one that compares all the offerings so you don't have to)? Is it truly better to book directly on an airline or hotel Web site? And when does a real live travel agent come in handy?

ONLINE

You really have to shop around. A travel wholesaler such as Hotels.com or Hotel-Club.net can be a source of good rates, as can discounters such as Hotwire or Priceline, particularly if you can bid for your hotel room or airfare. Indeed, such sites sometimes have deals that are unavailable elsewhere. They do, however, tend to work only with hotel chains (which makes them just plain useless for getting hotel reservations outside of major cities) or big airlines (so that often leaves out upstarts like jetBlue and some foreign carriers like Air India). Also, with discounters and wholesalers you must generally pre-pay, and everything is nonrefundable. And before you fork over the dough, be sure to check the terms and conditions, so you know what a given company will do for you if there's a problem and what you'll have to deal with on your own.

■ TIP→ To be absolutely sure everything was processed correctly, confirm reservations made through online travel agents, discounters, and wholesalers directly with your hotel before leaving home.

Booking engines like Expedia, Travelocity, and Orbitz are actually travel agents, albeit high-volume, online ones. And airline travel packagers like American Airlines Vacations and Virgin Vacations—well, they're travel agents, too. But they may still not work with all the world's hotels.

WORD OF MOUTH

" I really enjoyed being in China on my own; I did a lot of reading before I went and I'm glad I did, as nothing can truly prepare you for the reality . . . but it sure does help to have that background!"

An aggregator site will search many sites and pull the best prices for airfares, hotels, and rental cars from them. Most aggregators compare the major travel-booking sites such as Expedia, Travelocity, and Orbitz; some also look at airline Web sites, though rarely the sites of smaller budget airlines. Some aggregators also compare other travel products, including complex packages—a good thing, as you can sometimes get the best overall deal by booking an air-and-hotel package.

The current hotel glut in China means finding accommodation is rarely a problem. Although it's always worth a quick look at online accommodation sites, sometimes dropping an e-mail directly to the hotel itself can get you similar, if not better, rates. To check internal flight prices, eLong is a useful resource—it lists most major domestic airlines at a reasonable rate.

In urban areas, accommodation will probably be the most expensive item on your budget, so it's worth inquiring with travel agents as their rates are often better. That said, many cities, especially Hong Kong, haven't entirely recovered from its post-SARS tourism crisis, and in low season many hotels offer great discounts on their

Web sites. In a nutshell: shop around even more than usual.

WITH A TRAVEL AGENT

If you use an agent—brick-and-mortar or virtual—you'll pay a fee for the service. And know that the service you get from some online agents isn't comprehensive. For example Expedia and Travelocity don't search for prices on budget airlines like JetBlue, Southwest, or small foreign carriers. That said, some agents (online or not) *do* have access to fares that are difficult to find otherwise, and the savings can more than make up for any surcharge.

A knowledgeable brick-and-mortar travel agent can be a godsend if you're booking a cruise, a package trip that's not available to you directly, an air pass, or a complicated itinerary including several overseas flights. What's more, travel agents that specialize in a destination may have exclusive access to certain deals and insider information on things such as charter flights. Agents who specialize in types of travelers (senior citizens, gays and lesbians, naturists) or types of trips (cruises, luxury travel, safaris) can also be invaluable.

A top-notch agent planning your trip to China will make sure you get the correct visa application and complete it on time; the one booking your cruise may get you

a cabin upgrade or arrange to have a bottle of champagne chilling in your cabin when you embark. Complain about the surcharges all you like, but when things don't work out the way you'd hoped, it's nice to have an agent to put things right.

■ TIP→ Remember that Expedia, Travelocity, and Orbitz are travel agents, not just booking engines. To resolve any problems with a reservation made through these companies, contact them first.

Booking hotels and flights for major urban centers is easy to do without a travel agent, though you may get preferable rates (or room upgrades) if you use one. If you're planning to visit farther-flung places, a travel agent can save time and hassle, especially with internal flights, as schedules can change without warning. An agent can track this and adjust your tickets accordingly. Be careful booking with Internet-based Chinese agencies from abroad, as not all are legal travel agencies.

Agent Resources American Society of Travel Agents ASTA ☎ 703/739-2782 ⊕ www. travelsense.org.

China Travel Agents China Highlights China: ☎ 773/283-1999 ✉ U.S.: ☎ 800/268-2918 ⊕ www.chinahighlights.com. **China International Travel Service** CITS Beijing: ☎ 010/6522-2991 ✉ Shanghai: ☎ 021/6289-6925 ✉ U.S.: ☎ 626/568-8993 ⊕ www.citsusa. com ⊕ www.cits.com.cn. **Wings Across Continents Travel Services** Beijing: ☎ 010/5129-6371 ✉ U.S.: ☎ 708/409-1244 ⊕ www. wacts.com.

■ ACCOMMODATIONS

Opening a hotel seems the in-thing to do in China these days. The choice of accommodation (in cities, at least) is wide, and takes in most tastes and budgets. However, that's not to say choosing a hotel is always easy: the Chinese star system is a little unpredictable, and Web sites are often misleading for all but the biggest names. For lesser establishments, try to get recent personal recommendations: the forums on Fodors.com are a great place to start.

WORD OF MOUTH

"We were on our own for a week in Beijing and 5 days in Shanghai, and any difficulties we encountered were minor. Once we realized how easy it was to get around Beijing and do what we wanted to do we were very pleased that we hadn't signed up for a tour.

I recommend buying a good guide book and, as always, doing plenty of pre-trip research, including learning a few common Mandarin words and phrases. This is more for the sake of politeness than in expectation of any serious communication, of course."   –Neil Oz

Location is the first thing you should consider. Chinese cities are usually big, and there's no point schlepping halfway across town for one particular hotel when a similar option is available more conveniently. Consider where you'll be going, then pick your bed.

In major urban centers, many four- or five-star hotels belong to familiar international chains, and are usually a safe—if pricey—bet. You can expect swimming pools, a concierge, and business services here. Locally owned hotels with four stars or less have erratic standards both in and out of big cities, as bribery plays a big part in star acquisition. However, air-conditioning, color TV, and private Western-style bathrooms are the norm for three to four stars, and even lone-star hotels have private bathrooms, albeit with a squatter toilet. Extra-firm beds are a trademark of Chinese hotelerie even in luxury chains.

(⇨ Restaurant & Hotel price charts appear at the beginning of each chapter.)

Most hotels and other lodgings require you to give your credit-card details before they will confirm your reservation. If you don't feel comfortable e-mailing this information, ask if you can fax it (some places even prefer faxes). However you book, get confirmation in writing and have a copy of it handy when you check in.

Be sure you understand the hotel's cancellation policy. Some places allow you to cancel without any kind of penalty—even if you prepaid to secure a discounted rate—if you cancel at least 24 hours in advance. Others require you to cancel a week in advance or penalize you the cost of one night. Small inns and bed-and-breakfasts are most likely to require you to cancel far in advance. Most hotels allow children under a certain age to stay in their parents' room at no extra charge, but others charge for them as extra adults; find out the cutoff age for discounts.

■ TIP➜ Assume that hotels operate on the European Plan (**EP**, no meals) unless we specify that they use the Breakfast Plan (**BP**, with full breakfast), Continental Plan (**CP**, continental breakfast), Full American Plan (**FAP**, all meals), Modified American Plan (**MAP**, breakfast and dinner), or are all-inclusive (**AI**, all meals and most activities).

APARTMENT & HOUSE RENTALS

There's an abundance of furnished rental properties for short- and long-term lets in Beijing, Guangzhou, Hong Kong, Shanghai, and some other cities, too. Prices vary wildly. At the top end are luxury apartments and villas, usually far from the city center and best accessible by (chauffeur-driven) car. Usually described as "serviced apartments" or "villas," these often include gyms and pools, and rents are usually well over $2,000 a month.

There are a lot of well-located mid-range properties in new apartment blocks. They're usually clean, with new furnishings, with rents starting at $500. Finally, for longer, cheaper stays, there are normal local apartments. These are firmly off the tourist circuit and often cost only a third of the price of the mid-range properties. Expect mismatched furniture, erratic amenities, and varying insect populations, although what you get for your money fluctuates, so be prepared to shop around.

Property sites like Move and Stay, Sublet, and Pacific Properties have hundreds of

WORD OF MOUTH

"In retrospect I think that booking [flights] in advance was a very wise decision which saved us considerable aggravation . . . For example, we were told that the flight we wanted at the end of the cruise was cancelled and we would have to take a later one. One of the tour groups on the cruise was unaware of the cancellation and had to wait for a much later flight than ours. Three of the hotels we stayed in were completely full during our stay. If we had just showed up trying to score 'the best' rate we would have been turned away."

–Marija

Online Booking Resources

AGGREGATORS		
Kayak	www.kayak.com	looks at cruises and vacation packages.
Mobissimo	www.mobissimo.com.	
Qixo	www.qixo.com	compares cruises, vacation packages, and even travel insurance.
Sidestep	www.sidestep.com	compares vacation packages and lists travel deals.
Travelgrove	www.travelgrove.com	compares cruises and vacation packages.
BOOKING ENGINES		
Cheap Tickets	www.cheaptickets.com	discounter.
Expedia	www.expedia.com	large online agency that charges a booking fee for airline tickets.
Hotwire	www.hotwire.com	discounter.
lastminute.com	www.lastminute.com	specializes in last-minute travel; the main site is for the U.K., but it has a link to a U.S. site.
Luxury Link	www.luxurylink.com	has auctions (surprisingly good deals) as well as offers on the high-end side of travel.
Onetravel.com	www.onetravel.com	discounter for hotels, car rentals, airfares, and packages.
Orbitz	www.orbitz.com	charges a booking fee for airline tickets, but gives a clear breakdown of fees and taxes before you book.
Priceline.com	www.priceline.com	discounter that also allows bidding.
Travel.com	www.travel.com	allows you to compare its rates with those of other booking engines.
Travelocity	www.travelocity.com	charges a booking fee for airline tickets, but promises good problem resolution.
ONLINE ACCOMMODATIONS		
Asia Hotels	www.asia-hotels.com	good selection of mid- to top-end hotels.
Asia Travel	www.asiatravel.com	popular place to get hotel deals.
CTrip	www.ctrip.com	China-based site, and one of the best places to start looking for hotels.
China Hotel Guide	http://china-hotelguide.com	sometimes has good discounts for better hotels.
China.org.cn	http://hotel.china.org.cn	government-authorized portal with a huge amount of listings.
Hong Kong Hotels Association	www.hkha.org	can often get you great deals, even at the last minute.

Hotelbook.com	www.hotelbook.com	focuses on independent hotels worldwide.
Hotel Club	www.hotelclub.net	good for major cities worldwide.
Hotels.com	www.hotels.com	big Expedia-owned wholesaler that offers rooms in hotels all over the world.
Quikbook	www.quikbook.com	offers "pay when you stay" reservations that allow you to settle your bill when you check out, not when you book.
Sino Hotel	www.sinohotel.com	has a good range of the pricier hotels in big cities.
OTHER RESOURCES		
Bidding For Travel	www.biddingfortravel.com	good place to figure out what you can get and for how much before you start bidding on, say, Priceline.

apartments in major cities. The online classified pages in local English-language magazines or on expat Web sites are good places to start looking for cheaper properties.
Asia Expat ⊕ www.asiaxpat.com. **Pacific Properties** ⊕ www.worthenpacific.com. **Move and Stay** ⊕ www.moveandstay.com. **Sublet.com** ⊕ www.sublet.com.

HOMESTAYS
Single travelers can arrange homestays (often in combination with language courses) through China Homestay Club. Generally these are in upper-middle-class homes that work out at least as expensive as a cheap hotel—prices start from $150 to $180 a week. Nine times out of 10, the family has a small child in need of daily English-conversation classes. China-Homestay.org is a different organization that charges a single placement fee of $300 for a stay of three months or less.
Organizations China Homestay Club ⊕ www.homestay.com.cn. **ChinaHomestay. org** ⊕ www.chinahomestay.org.

HOSTELS
Hostels offer bare-bones lodging at low, low prices—often in shared dorm rooms with shared baths—to people of all ages, though the primary market is young travelers, especially students. Most hostels serve breakfast; dinner and/or shared cook-ing facilities may also be available. In some hostels you aren't allowed to be in your room during the day, and there may be a curfew at night. Nevertheless, hostels provide a sense of community, with public rooms where travelers often gather to share stories. Many hostels are affiliated with Hostelling International (HI), an umbrella group of hostel associations with some 4,500 member properties in more than 70 countries. Other hostels are completely independent and may be nothing more than a really cheap hotel.

Membership in any HI association, open to travelers of all ages, allows you to stay in HI-affiliated hostels at member rates. One-year membership is about $28 for adults; hostels charge about $10 to $30 per night. Members have priority if the hostel is full; they're also eligible for discounts around the world, even on rail and bus travel in some countries.

Budget accommodation options are improving in China. However, the term "hostel" is still used vaguely—the only thing guaranteed is shared dorm rooms aimed at backpackers; other facilities vary. Backpacking hot spots like Yangshuo have lots of options. Beijing, Shanghai, Hong Kong, and Xi'an all have a few decent hostels, but flea-ridden dumps are also common, so always ask to see your room before pay-

10 WAYS TO SAVE

1. Join "frequent guest" programs. You may get preferential treatment in room choice and/or upgrades in your favorite chains.

2. Call direct. You can sometimes get a better price if you call a hotel's local toll-free number (if available) rather than a central reservations number.

3. Check online. Check hotel Web sites, as not all chains are represented on all travel sites.

4. Look for specials. Always inquire about packages and corporate rates.

5. Look for price guarantees. For overseas trips, look for guaranteed rates. With your rate locked in you won't pay more, even if the price goes up in the local currency.

6. Look for weekend deals at business hotels. High-end chains catering to business travelers are often busy only on weekdays; to fill rooms they often drop rates dramatically on weekends.

7. Ask about taxes. Verify whether local hotel taxes are included in quoted rates. In some places taxes can add 20% or more to your bill.

8. Read the fine print. Watch for add-ons, including resort fees, energy surcharges, and "convenience" fees for such things as unlimited local phone service you won't use or a free newspaper in a language you can't read.

9. Know when to go. If your destination's high season is December through April and you're trying to book, say, in late April, you might save money by changing your dates by a week or two. Ask when rates go down, though: if your dates straddle peak and non-peak seasons, a property may still charge peak-season rates for the entire stay.

10. Weigh your options (we can't say this enough). Weigh transportation times and costs against the savings of staying in a hotel that's cheaper because it's out of the way.

ing. New places open all the time, so try to get recommendations from fellow travelers as you go. Note that a private room in a low-end hotel is often just as cheap as so-called hostels; some guesthouses and hotels also have cheaper dorm beds in addition to regular rooms.

China's small but growing Youth Hostelling Association is based in Guangzhou and has a growing list of affiliates. Backpackers.com is a useful resource for booking budget accommodations online. Their prices are higher than the walk-up rate, but it's good to know you have a bed reserved when you arrive.

Backpackers.com ⊕ www.backpackers.com. **Hostelling International–USA** ☎ 301/495–1240 ⊕ www.hiusa.org. **Youth Hostel Association of China** ☎ 020/8734–5080 ⊕ www.yhachina.com.

HOTELS

All hotels listed have private bath unless otherwise noted. Remember that water is a precious resource in China and use accordingly.

When checking in to a hotel, you need to show your passport—the desk clerk records the number before you're given a room. Unmarried couples may occasionally have problems staying together in the same room, but simply wearing a band on your left finger is one way to avoid this complication. Friends or couples of the same sex, especially women, shouldn't have a problem getting a room together. There may, however, be regulations about who is allowed in your room, and it's also normal for hotels to post "visitor hours" inside the room.

▮ AIRLINE TICKETS

Most domestic airline tickets are electronic; international tickets may be either electronic or paper. With an e-ticket the only thing you receive is an e-mailed receipt citing your itinerary and reservation and ticket numbers. The greatest advantage of an e-ticket is that if you lose your receipt, you can simply print out another copy or ask the airline to do it for you at check-in. You usually pay a surcharge (up to $50) to get a paper ticket, if you can get one at all. The sole advantage of a paper ticket is that it may be easier to endorse over to another airline if your flight is canceled and the airline with which you booked can't accommodate you on another flight.

■ TIP➔ Discount air passes that let you travel economically in a country or region must often be purchased before you leave home. In some cases you can only get them through a travel agent.

If you are flying into Asia on a SkyTeam airline (Delta or Continental, for example) you're eligible to purchase their Asia Pass. It covers over 10 Chinese cities (including Beijing, Shanghai, Xi'an, and Hong Kong) as well as destinations in 20 other Asian and Australasian countries. The pass works on a coupon basis; the minimum of three coupons costs $750, whereas six coupons come to $1,410.

Beijing, Xiamen, and Hong Kong are three of the cities included in the One World Alliance Visit Asia Pass. Cities are grouped into zones, and there's a flat rate for each zone. It doesn't include flights from the United States, however. Inquire through American Airlines, Cathay Pacific, or any other One World member. It won't be the cheapest way to get around, but you'll be flying on some of the world's best airlines.

If you're planning to travel to several different Asian destinations, Cathay Pacific's All Asia Pass is an excellent deal. For $1,500 you get a round-trip ticket from New York (JFK), Los Angeles, or San Francisco to Hong Kong, plus 21 days of unlimited travel to 17 other Asian cities. You can pay supplements to add on cities that aren't included and to extend the pass: $350 buys you up to 90 days. If you register for Cathay's online news, there's a $200 discount. If you just want to combine Hong Kong and one other Cathay des-tination, though, go for a regular ticket: the airline generally allows a free Hong Kong stopover.

China Southern Airlines's China Air Pass is excellent value if you're planning to fly to several destinations within the country: the minimum 3-coupon pass comes to $329, and the 10-coupon pass costs $909. The catch? You have to be flying in from abroad on one of their flights. Hong Kong isn't included in the pass, but Shenzhen, just over the border, gets you close enough. Bear in mind that Chinese domestic flight schedules can be very flexible—flights may be changed or canceled at a moment's notice.

Air Pass Info All Asia Pass Cathay Pacific ☎ 800/233-2742 ⊕ www.cathay-usa.com. **Asia Pass** SkyTeam ☎ Continental: 800/523-3273, Delta: 800/221-1212 ⊕ www.skyteam. com. **China Air Pass** China Southern Airlines ☎ 888/338-8988 ⊕ www.cs-air.com. **Visit Asia Pass** OneWorld Alliance ☎ Cathay Pacific: 800/233-2742 ⊕ www.oneworld.com.

■ RENTAL CARS

In a nutshell, self-drive is not a possibility when vacationing in mainland China, as the only valid driver's licenses are Chinese ones. However, this restriction should be cause for relief, as city traffic is terrible, drivers manic, and getting lost practically inevitable for first-timers. Conditions in Hong Kong aren't much better, but you can drive there using a U.S. license.

A far better idea, if you want to get around by car, is to put yourself in the experienced hands of a local driver and sit back and watch them negotiate the tailbacks. All the same, consider your itinerary carefully before doing so—in big cities, taking the subway or walking are often far quicker for central areas. Keep the car for excursions farther afield.

The quickest way to hire a car and driver is to flag down a taxi and hire it for the day—if you're happy with a driver you've used for a trip around town, ask him. After some negotiating, expect to pay between

10 WAYS TO SAVE

1. Nonrefundable is best. If saving money is more important than flexibility, then non-refundable tickets work. Just remember that you'll pay dearly (as much as $100) if you change your plans.

2. Comparison shop. Web sites and travel agents can have different arrangements with the airlines and offer different prices for exactly the same flights.

3. Beware those prices. Many airline Web sites—and most ads—show prices *without* taxes and surcharges. Don't buy until you know the full price.

4. Stay loyal. Stick with one or two frequent-flier programs. You'll rack up free trips faster and you'll accumulate more quickly the perks that make trips easier.

5. Watch those ticketing fees. Surcharges are usually added when you buy your ticket anywhere but on an airline Web site. (That includes by phone—even if you call the airline directly—and paper tickets regardless of how you book).

6. Check early and often. Start looking for cheap fares up to a year in advance. Keep looking until you find a price you like.

7. Don't work alone. Some Web sites have tracking features that will e-mail you immediately when good deals are posted.

8. Jump on the good deals. Waiting even a few minutes might mean paying more.

9. Be flexible. Look for departures on Tuesday, Wednesday, and Thursday, typically the cheapest days to travel. And check on prices for departures at different times and to and from alternative airports.

10. Weigh your options. What you get can be as important as what you save. A cheaper flight might have a long layover, or it might land at a secondary airport, where your ground transportation costs might be higher.

Y350 and Y600, depending on the type of car. Most hotels can make arrangements for you, though they often charge you double that rate—no prizes for guessing whose pocket the difference goes into. As most drivers do not speak English, it's a good idea to have your destination and hotel names written down in Chinese.

Another alternative is American car-rental agency Avis, which includes mandatory chauffeurs as part of all rental packages. A car and driver usually cost Y740 to Y850 ($93 to $110) per day for an economy vehicle such as a locally made Volkswagen Santana. They have offices in Beijing, Hong Kong, Shanghai, Guangzhou, and Shenzhen.

If your heart is set on driving, it is possible for foreigners to get a Chinese license, but you need to have a temporary residence permit. Then it takes a week or two and a whole load of paper-pushing.

▮ VACATION PACKAGES

Packages *are not* guided excursions. Packages combine airfare, accommodations, and perhaps a rental car or other extras (theater tickets, guided excursions, boat trips, reserved entry to popular museums, transit passes), but they let you do your own thing. During busy periods packages may be your only option, as flights and rooms may be sold out otherwise. Packages will definitely save you time. They can also save you money, particularly in peak seasons, but—and this is a really big "but"—you should price each part of the package separately to be sure. And be aware that prices advertised on Web sites and in newspapers rarely include service charges or taxes, which can up your costs by hundreds of dollars.

▮ TIP→ **Some packages and cruises are sold only through travel agents. Don't always assume that you can get the best deal by booking everything yourself.**

Each year consumers are stranded or lose their money when packagers—even large ones with excellent reputations—go out of business. How can you protect yourself? First, always pay with a credit card; if you have a problem, your credit-card company may help you resolve it. Second, buy trip insurance that covers default. Third, choose a company that belongs to the United States Tour Operators Association, whose members must set aside funds to cover defaults. Finally, choose a company that also participates in the Tour Operator Program of the American Society of Travel Agents (ASTA), which will act as mediator in any disputes. You can also check on the tour operator's reputation among travelers by posting an inquiry on one of the Fodors.com forums.

A vacation package to China usually ends up costing much more than booking flights and hotels yourself, though it might be quicker and easier. One of the services the company will provide is arranging your Chinese visa. If you're only staying in big cities, it's just as easy to book your hotel online, though. You don't need a package for other activities in China or Hong Kong—if you want to do organized excursions, it's cheaper to book through a local tour company. You can do this before your trip to be sure of a place on the day you want.

Organizations American Society of Travel Agents (ASTA) ☎ 703/739−2782 or 800/965−2782 ⊕ www.astanet.com. **United States Tour Operators Association** (USTOA) ☎ 212/599−6599 ⊕ www.ustoa.com.

■ TIP➔ Local tourism boards can provide information about lesser-known and small-niche operators that sell packages to only a few destinations.

■ GUIDED TOURS

Guided tours are a good option when you don't want to do it all yourself. You travel along with a group (sometimes large, sometimes small), stay in prebooked hotels, eat with your fellow travelers (the cost of meals sometimes included in the price of your tour, sometimes not), and follow a schedule. But not all guided tours are an

if-it's-Tuesday-this-must-be-Belgium experience. A knowledgeable guide can take you places that you might never discover on your own, and you may be pushed to see more than you would have otherwise. Tours aren't for everyone, but they can be just the thing for trips to places where making travel arrangements is difficult or time-consuming (particularly when you don't speak the language). Whenever you book a guided tour, find out what's included and what isn't. A "land-only" tour includes all your travel (by bus, in most cases) in the destination, but not necessarily your flights to and from or even within it. Also, in most cases prices in tour brochures don't include fees and taxes. And remember that you'll be expected to tip your guide (in cash) at the end of the tour.

Most guided tours to China take in three or four major cities, often combined with a Yangtze River cruise or a visit to far-flung Tibet. You get a day or two in each place, with the same sights featured in most tours. If you want to explore a given city in any kind of depth, you're better doing it by yourself or getting a private guide.

Shopping stops plague China tours, so inquire before booking as to when, where, and how many to expect. Although you're never obliged to buy anything, they can take up big chunks of your valuable travel time, and the products offered are always ridiculously overpriced. Even on the best tours, you can count on having to sit through at least one or two.

Small groups and excellent guides are what Overseas Adventure Travel takes pride in. The Adventure Center has a huge variety of China packages, including trekking, cycling, and family tours. China Focus Travel has 10 different China tours—they squeeze in a lot for your money. Ritz Tours is a mid-range agency specializing in East Asian tours. R. Crusoe & Son is an offbeat company that organizes small group or tailor-made private tours. For something more mainstream, try Pacific Delight; for serious luxury, head to

Artisans of Leisure or Imperial Tours. If you're concerned about responsible tourism, try Wild China, a high-caliber local company with some of the most unusual trips around. For example, one of their cultural trips explores China's little-known Jewish history.

Not all of the companies we list include air travel in their packages. Be sure to check this when you're researching your trip.

Recommended Companies Artisans of Leisure ☎ 800/214-8144 ⊕ www. artisansofleisure.com. **China Focus Travel** ☎ 800/868-7244 ⊕ www.chinafocustravel. com. **Imperial Tours** ☎ 888/296-5306 ⊕ www.imperialtours.net. **Overseas Adventure Travel** ☎ 800/493-6824 ⊕ www. oattravel.com. **Pacific Delight** ☎ 800/221-7179 ⊕ www.pacificdelighttours.com. **R. Crusoe & Son** ☎ 800/585-8555 ⊕ www. rcrusoe.com. **Ritz Tours** ☎ 626/289-7777 ⊕ www.ritztours.com. **The Adventure Center** ☎ 800/228-8747 ⊕ www.adventurecenter. com. **Wild China** ☎ 010/6465-6602 ⊕ www. wildchina.com.

SPECIAL-INTEREST TOURS

ART

Ethnic folk art and the Silk Road are two of the focuses of Wild China's art and architecture tours.
Wild China ☎ 010/6465-6602 ⊕ www. wildchina.com.

BIKING

The Adventure Center has two cycling packages in China, one of which follows the route of the Great Wall. You can hire bikes from them, or take your own. Bike China Adventures organize trips of varying length and difficulty all over China; they encourage you to bring your own bike and give helpful advice on transporting it.

■ TIP→ Most airlines accommodate bikes as luggage, provided they're dismantled and boxed.

Bike China Adventures ☎ 800/818-1778 ⊕ www.bikechina.com. **The Adventure Cen-** ter ☎ 800/228-8747 ⊕ www. adventurecenter.com.

BIRD-WATCHING

Wild China runs an eight-day bird-watching tour in Yunnan, southwest China.
Wild China ☎ 010/6465-6602 ⊕ www. wildchina.com.

CULTURE

Local guides are often creative when it comes to history and culture, so having an expert with you can make a big difference. Learning is the focus of Smithsonian Journeys' small-group tours, which are led by university professors. China experts also lead National Geographic's trips, though all that knowledge doesn't come cheap. Wild China is a local company with some of the most unusual trips around, including visits to ethnic minority groups, Tibet, and little-known Xinjiang province as well as more conventional historical trips and journeys focusing on traditional festivals.
National Geographic Expeditions ☎ 888/966-8687 ⊕ www. nationalgeographicexpeditions.com. **Smithsonian Journeys** ☎ 877/338-8687 ⊕ www. smithsonianjourneys.org. **Wild China** ☎ 010/6465-6602 ⊕ www.wildchina.com.

CULINARY

Artisans of Leisure's culinary tour takes in Shanghai and Beijing from the cities' choicest establishments, with prices to match. Intrepid Travel is an Australian company specializing in budget, independent travel. Their China Gourmet Traveller tour includes market visits, cooking demonstrations, and lots of eating at down-to-earth restaurants. Imperial Tours Culinary Tour combines sightseeing with cooking lectures and demonstrations, and lots of five-star dining.
Artisans of Leisure ☎ 800/214-8144 ⊕ www.artisansofleisure.com. **Imperial Tours** ☎ 888/888-1970 ⊕ www. imperialtours.net. **Intrepid Travel** ☎ 613/9473-2626 ⊕ www.intrepidtravel.com.

ECOTOURS

Wild China's nature-trekking tours include a weeklong hike through a Sichuan nature reserve, home to the Giant Panda. **Wild China** ☎ 010/6465-6602 ⊕ www. wildchina.com.

GOLF

China Highlights organize short golf packages that combine sightseeing with golfing in Beijing, Shanghai, Kunming, Guangzhou, and Guilin. **China Highlights** ☎ 800/268-2918 ⊕ www. chinahighlights.com.

HIKING

The Adventure Center's China hikes include an eight-day walk along the Great Wall, a three-week walk along the route of the Communists' 1934 Long March, and a trip that combines mild hikes with Yangtze cruises and sightseeing. Wild China runs ecologically responsible treks in different parts of China, including Tibet. **The Adventure Center** ☎ 800/228-8747 ⊕ www.adventurecenter.com. **Wild China** ☎ 010/6465-6602 ⊕ www.wildchina.com.

▮ CRUISES

Viking River cruises travel along the Yangtze, ending in Shanghai. The crème de la crème of cruisers, Cunard docks in Hong Kong and Shanghai on its round-the-world trips. Crystal and Princess Cruises both have a variety of packages that call in at Beijing, Shanghai, Hong Kong, and other Asian destinations. Holland America has short China and Japan cruises as well as round-the-world options. Seabourn's Voyage to China spends three days in Shanghai. Star Cruises has trips through southeast Asia that start from, or call at, Hong Kong. Most of the travel agents listed above can arrange Yangtze Three Gorges cruises as part of a package.

Cruise Lines Crystal Cruises ☎ 310/785-9300 or 800/446-6620 ⊕ www.crystalcruises. com. **Cunard** ☎ 800/7CUNARD ⊕ www. cunard.com. **Holland America** ☎ 877/SAIL HAL ⊕ www.hollandamerica.com. **Princess Cruises** ☎ 661/753-0000 or 800/774-6237 ⊕ www.princess.com. **Seabourn Cruise Line** ☎ 305/463-3000 or 800/929-9391 ⊕ www. seabourn.com. **Star Cruises** Hong Kong: ☎ 852/2317-7711 ⊕ www.starcruises.com. **Viking River Cruises** ☎ 877/66VIKING ⊕ www.vikingrivers.com.

TRANSPORTATION

Make no mistake: this is one HUGE country. China's highly efficient train system is an excellent way of getting around if you're not in a hurry, and lets you see how locals travel. The growing network of domestic flights is a quicker travel option.

China's capital, Beijing, is in the northeast. Financial capital Shanghai is halfway down the east coast. The historic city of Nanjing is upriver from Shanghai; head much farther inland and you'll hit the erstwhile capital Xi'an, home to the Terracotta army.

Limestone mountains surround the Guilin area, in southern China. The region's hubs are busy Guangzhou, capital of Guandong province, and Shenzhen, an industrial boomtown on the border with Hong Kong. Though part of China, glitzy Hong Kong is a Special Autonomous Region, and functions as if it were another country.

Smack bang in the middle of China is Sichuan province. Its capital, Chengdu, is an important financial center, and is a transport hub connecting eastern and western China. Kunming is the capital of the southwestern province of Yunnan. Once the gateway to the Silk Road, it's now a gateway for travel to the bordering countries of Myanmar, Laos, and Vietnam.

Despite ongoing international controversy, Tibet, in the far west of the country, remains a Chinese province. Its capital, Lhasa, the historical center of Tibetan Buddhism, is a mind-blowing 3,650 meters (11,975 feet) above sea level on the northern Himalayas.

Vast deserts and grassy plains make up much of northwest China. Here, autonomous Xinjiang province is home to a largely Muslim population. Its capital city, Ürümqi, is the farthest city inland on earth. Nei Mongolia, or Inner Mongolia, is a great swathe of (mostly barren) land that runs across much of the north of China.

Maps with street names in Pinyin are available in most Chinese cities, though they're not always up to date. A few crucial words of Chinese can help decode street names. *Lu* means road, *jie* means street, *dalu* is a main road, and *dajie* is a main street. Those endings are often preceded by a compass point: *bei* (north), *dong* (east), *nan* (south), *xi* (west), and *zhong* (middle). These distinguish different sections of long streets. So, if you're looking for Beijing Xi Lu, it's the western end of Beijing Road.

TRAVEL TIMES FROM BEIJING		
TO	By Air	By Train
Shanghai	2 hours	12 hours
Xi'an	2 hours	11½ hours
Guangzhou	3 hours	22½ hours
Hong Kong	3¾ hours	24 hours
Guilin	3 hours	24 hours
Kunming	3¼ hours	19 hours
Nanjing	1¾ hours	12 hours
Lhasa	6 hours	48 hours
Ürümqi	4 hours	48 hours
Chengdu	4 hours	27 hours

■ TIP→ **Ask the local tourist board about hotel and local transportation packages that include tickets to major museum exhibits or other special events.**

▮ BY AIR

Beijing, Shanghai, and Hong Kong are China's three major international hubs. You can catch nonstop or one-stop flights to China from New York (13¾ to 17 hours), Chicago (13½ to 14½ hours), San Francisco (17 hours), Los Angeles (13 to 16 hours), Sydney (11 to 13 hours), and London (11 to 12 hours). Though most airlines say that reconfirming your return flight is unnecessary, some local airlines cancel your seat if you don't reconfirm.

Play it safe, and check with your airline carefully.

Airlines & Airports **Airline and Airport Links.com** ⊕ www.airlineandairportlinks.com has links to many of the world's airlines and airports.

Airline-Security Issues **Transportation Security Administration** ⊕ www.tsa.gov has answers for almost every question that might come up.

AIRPORTS

Northern China's main hub is the efficient Beijing Capital International Airport (PEK), 27 km (17 mi) northeast of the Beijing city center. Shanghai has two airports: Pudong International Airport (PVG) is newer and flashier than scruffy Hongqiao International Airport (SHA), but Hongqiao is more efficient and closer to downtown. The main hub in southern China is the fabulous Hong Kong International Airport (HKG), also known as Chek Lap Kok. These airports all have good transport connections to the city centers, and both Chinese and Western-style fast-food outlets.

There are also international airports at Guangzhou (CAN), Kunming (KMG), Xiamen (XMN), Shenzhen (SZX), Xi'an (XIY), Chengdu (CTU), and Guilin (KWL), among others.

All Chinese airports have a departure tax of Y90 for international flights (including routes to Hong Kong) and Y50 for domestic. You usually pay before check-in then hand in your coupon at the entrance to the departure hall.

Clearing customs and immigration in China can take a while, especially in the mornings, so make sure you arrive at least two hours before your scheduled flight time.

While wandering Chinese airports, someone may approach you offering to carry your luggage, or even just give you directions. Be aware that this "helpful" stranger will almost certainly expect payment. Many of the X-ray machines used for large luggage items aren't film-safe, so keep films in your carry-on.

Airport Information **Beijing Capital International Airport** ☎ 010/6456-3604 ⊕ www.bcia.com.cn. **Chengdu Shuangliu International Airport** ☎ 028/8570-2649 ⊕ www.cdairport.com. **Guangzhou Baiyun International Airport** ☎ 020/3606-6926 ⊕ www.baiyunairport.com. **Guilin Liangjiang International Airport** ☎ 077/3284-5359. **Hong Kong International Airport** ☎ 852/2181-0000 ⊕ www.hkairport.com. **Kunming Wujiaba Airport** ☎ 0871/312-1220. **Shanghai Hongqiao International Airport** ☎ 021/6268-8918 ⊕ www.shanghaiairport.com. **Shanghai Pudong International Airport** ☎ 021/6908-1388 ⊕ www.shanghaiairport.com. **Shenzhen Bao'an International Airport** ☎ 0755/2777-6216 ⊕ www.szairport.com. **Xi'an Xianyang International Airport** ☎ 029/9978-8450. **Xiamen Gaoqi International Airport** ☎ 0592/570-6017 ⊕ www.xiagc.com.cn.

FLIGHTS

TO & FROM CHINA

Air China is China's flagship carrier. It operates nonstop flights from Beijing and Shanghai to various North American and European cities. Although it once had a slightly sketchy safety record, the situation has improved dramatically, and it is now part of Star Alliance. Don't confuse it with the similarly named China Airlines.

Air Canada has daily flights to Beijing and Shanghai from Vancouver and Montréal. Cathay Pacific flies to Beijing via Hong Kong. China Eastern and China Southern airlines fly from China to the West Coast of the United States. Japan Airlines and All Nippon fly to Beijing via Tokyo. Northwest and United both have service to Beijing from the United States, and United has a nonstop flight to Shanghai from Chicago.

WITHIN CHINA

China Southern is the major carrier for domestic routes, flying to over 80 cities in China. Its main rival is China Eastern.

FLYING 101

Flying may not be as carefree as it once was, but there are some things you can do to make your trip smoother.

MINIMIZE THE TIME SPENT STANDING IN LINE. Buy an e-ticket, check in at an electronic kiosk, or—even better—check in on your airline's Web site before leaving home. Pack light and limit carry-on items to only the essentials.

ARRIVE WHEN YOU NEED TO. Research your airline's policy. It's usually at least an hour before domestic flights and two to three hours before international flights. But airlines at some busy airports have more stringent requirements. Check the TSA Web site for estimated security waiting times at major airports.

GET TO THE GATE. If you aren't at the gate at least 10 minutes before your flight is scheduled to take off (sometimes earlier), you won't be allowed to board.

DOUBLE-CHECK YOUR FLIGHT TIMES. Do this especially if you reserved far in advance. Schedules change, and alerts may not reach you.

DON'T GO HUNGRY. Ask whether your airline offers anything to eat; even when it does, be prepared to pay.

GET THE SEAT YOU WANT. Often, you can pick a seat when you buy your ticket on an airline Web site. But it's not guaranteed; the airline could change the plane after you book, so double-check. You can also select a seat if you check in electronically. Avoid seats on the aisle directly across from the lavatories. Frequent fliers say those are even worse than back-row seats that don't recline.

GOT KIDS? GET INFO. Ask the airline about its children's menus, activities, and fares. Sometimes infants and toddlers fly free if they sit on a parent's lap, and older children fly for half price in their own seats. Also inquire about policies involving car seats; having one may limit seating options. Also ask about seat-belt extenders for car seats. And note that you can't count on a flight attendant to produce an extender; you may have to ask for one when you board.

CHECK YOUR SCHEDULING. Don't buy a ticket if there's less than an hour between connecting flights. Although schedules are padded, if anything goes wrong you might miss your connection. If you're traveling to an important function, depart a day early.

BRING PAPER. Even when using an e-ticket, always carry a hard copy of your receipt; you may need it to get your boarding pass, which most airports require to get past security.

COMPLAIN AT THE AIRPORT. If your baggage goes astray or your flight goes awry, complain before leaving the airport. Most carriers require this.

BEWARE OF OVERBOOKED FLIGHTS. If a flight is oversold, the gate agent will usually ask for volunteers and offer some sort of compensation for taking a different flight. If you're bumped from a flight *involuntarily,* the airline must give you some kind of compensation if an alternate flight can't be found within one hour.

KNOW YOUR RIGHTS. If your flight is delayed because of something within the airline's control (bad weather doesn't count), the airline must get you to your destination on the same day, even if they have to book you on another airline and in an upgraded class. Read the Contract of Carriage, which is usually buried on the airline's Web site.

BE PREPARED. The Boy Scout motto is especially important if you're traveling during a stormy season. To quickly adjust your plans, program a few numbers into your cell: your airline, an airport hotel or two, your destination hotel, your car service, and/or your travel agent.

Smaller Shanghai Airlines has a growing number of national routes, mostly out of Shanghai.

The service on most Chinese airlines is more on par with low-cost American airlines than with big international carriers—be prepared for limited legroom, iffy food, and possibly no personal TV. More important, always arrive at least two hours before departure, as chronic overbooking means latecomers just don't get on.

You can make reservations and buy tickets for flights within China through airline Web sites or with travel agencies. It's worth contacting a Chinese travel agency like China International Travel Service (CITS) (↪ Visitor Information, *above*) to compare prices, as these can vary substantially.

Airline Contacts **Continental Airlines** ☎ 800/523–3273 for U.S. and Mexico reservations, 800/231–0856 for international reservations ⊕ www.continental.com. **Delta Airlines** ☎ 800/221–1212 for U.S. reservations, 800/241–4141 for international reservations ⊕ www.delta.com. **Northwest Airlines** ☎ 800/225–2525 ⊕ www.nwa.com. **United Airlines** ☎ 800/864–8331 for U.S. reservations, 800/538–2929 for international reservations ⊕ www.united.com. **Air Canada** ☎ 888/247–2262, 800/361–8071 TTY ⊕ www.aircanada.com. **Air China** ☎ 800/982–8802 in New York, 800/986–1985 in San Francisco, 800/882–8122 in Los Angeles ⊕ www.airchina.com. **All Nippon** ☎ 800/235–9262 ⊕ www.fly-ana.com. **Cathay Pacific** ☎ 800/233–2742 ⊕ www.cathaypacific.com. **China Eastern** ☎ 800/200–5118, 626/583–1500, or 310/646–1849 in Los Angeles, 415/982–5115 or 650/875–2367 in San Francisco ⊕ www.ce-air.com. **China Southern** ☎ 888/338–8988 ⊕ www.cs-air.com/en. **China Southwest Airlines** ☎ 028/8666-8080 in China ⊕ www.cswa.com/en. **Japan Airlines** ☎ 800/525–3663 ⊕ www.japanair.com. **Shanghai Airlines** ☎ 800/620–8888 ⊕ www.shanghai-air.com.

> ### LUCKY NUMBER
>
> Sichuan Airlines bought the number +86-28-8888-8888 for 2.33 million yuan ($280,723) during an auction of more than 100 telephone numbers in 2003, making it the most expensive telephone number in the world. The number eight (*ba* in Chinese), is considered lucky in China, as it is similar to the Cantonese word for "getting rich."

▮ BY BOAT

Trains and planes are fast replacing China's boat and ferry services. Four- to seven-day cruises along the Yangtze River are the most popular, and thus the most touristy of the domestic boat rides. Both local and international companies run these tours, but shop around as prices vary drastically.

See chapter 8 for specific details on the Yangtze River cruise information.

The Shanghai Ferry Company and the China-Japan International Ferry Company both operate weekly services to Osaka, Japan, from Shanghai. You can purchase tickets for both international and domestic services (in Chinese) at local terminals, or through CITS for a small surcharge.

China-Japan International Ferry Company ✉ 908 Dongdaming Lu, Shanghai ☎ 021/6595-7988. **Shanghai Ferry Company** ☎ 021/6537-5111 ⊕ www.shanghai-ferry.co.jp.

BIKE TRAVEL

Admit it: think of China and you think of bicycles. For millions of Chinese people, they're still the primary form of transport, although the proliferation of cars is making biking less pleasant. Large cities like Beijing, Chengdu, Xi'an, Shanghai, and Guilin have well-defined bike lanes, often separated from other traffic. Travel by bike is extremely popular in the countryside around Guilin, too. Locals don't rate gears much—take your cue from them and just roll along at a leisurely pace.

Note that bikes have to give way to motorized vehicles at intersections. Chinese driving styles might make your first day on wheels a little scary, but take things easy and you'll soon get used to it. If a flat tire or sudden brake failure strikes, seek out the nearest street-side mechanic (they're everywhere), easily identified by their bike parts and pumps.

In major cities, most lower-end hotels and hostels rent bikes. Otherwise inquire at bike shops, CTS, or even corner shops. Few of these places have telephones or Web sites. The going rental rate is Y15 to Y30 a day, plus a refundable deposit, which is often high enough to cover the cost of the bike itself. Check the seat and wheels carefully, or else you'll be stopping to fix flats all day.

Bicycle lights are nonexistent, so cycle with caution at night. Most rental bikes come with a lock or two, but they're usually pretty low quality. Instead, leave your wheels at an attended bike park—peace of mind costs a mere Y0.50. Helmets are just about unheard of in China, though upmarket rental companies catering to foreign tourists usually rent them. They charge much more for their bikes, but they're usually in better condition.

If you're planning a lot of cycling, note that for about Y150 to Y200 you can buy your own basic bike, though expect to pay three or four times that for a mountain bike with all the bells and whistles or for a "Flying Pigeon," the classic heavy-duty model Beijing was once famous for.

The U.S. company Backroads has two different China bike tours; one is suitable for families. Bike China Adventures organizes trips of varying length and difficulty all over China. The Adventure Center runs cycling trips along the Great Wall and in Guilin.

BIKES IN FLIGHT

Most airlines accommodate bikes as luggage, provided they are dismantled and boxed; check with individual airlines about packing requirements. Some airlines sell bike boxes, which are often free at bike shops, for about $20 (bike bags can be considerably more expensive). International travelers often can substitute a bike for a piece of checked luggage at no charge; otherwise, the cost is about $100. Most U.S. and Canadian airlines charge $40 to $80 each way.

Tour Operator Backroads ☎ 800/462-2848 ⊕ www.backroads.com. **Bike China Adventures** ☎ 800/818-1778 ⊕ www.bikechina. com. **The Adventure Center** ☎ 800/228-8747 ⊕ www.adventurecenter.com.

▌ BY BUS

China now has some fabulous luxury long-distance buses with air-conditioning and movies. Most of these services run out of Beijing and Shanghai. However, buying tickets can be complicated if you don't speak Chinese—you may end up on one of the cramped old-style affairs, much like an old-fashioned school bus (or worse). The conditions on sleeper buses are particularly dire. Taking a train or an internal flight is easier and safer, especially in rural areas where bad road conditions make for dangerous rides.

Big cities often have more than one bus terminal, and luxury services sometimes leave from the private depot of the company operating the service. Services are frequent and usually depart and arrive punctually. You can buy tickets for a small surcharge through CITS.

Bus Information CITS offices are located in every city; see specific city listings for contact information. **Hong Kong Tourist Association** (HKTA information hotline) ☎ 852/2807-6177 ⊕ www.hkta.org/login.html.

▌ BY TRAIN

China's enormous rail network is one of the world's busiest. Trains are usually safe and run strictly to schedule. There are certain intricacies to buying tickets, which usually have to be purchased in the city of origin. Train fares are more expensive for foreigners than for the Chinese, and vary drastically depending on where you buy them. You can buy most tickets 10 days in advance; 2 to 3 days ahead is usually enough time, except during the three national holidays—Chinese New Year (two days in mid-January–February), Labor Day (May 1), and National Day (October 1). If you can, avoid traveling then—tickets are sold out weeks in advance and the stations are insanely crowded.

The cheapest place for tickets is the train station itself, where they only accept cash and English is rarely spoken. Most travel agents, including CITS, can book your tickets for a small surcharge (Y20 to Y50), and save you the hassle of going to the station. You can also buy tickets through online retailers like China Train Ticket. They deliver the tickets to your hotel but you often end up paying much more than the station rate.

The train system offers a glimpse of old-fashioned socialist euphemisms. There are four classes, but instead of first class and second class, in China you talk about hard and soft. Hard seats (*yingzuo*) are often rigid benchlike seats guaranteed to numb the buttocks within seconds; soft seats (*ruanzuo*) are more like the seats in long-distance American trains. For overnight journeys, the cheapest option is the hard sleeper (*yingwo*), open bays of six bunks, in two tiers of three. They're cramped, but not uncomfortable; though you take your own bedding and share the toilet with everyone in the wagon. Soft sleepers (*ruanwo*) are more comfortable: their closed compartments have four beds with bedding. Trains between Beijing, Shanghai, Hong Kong, and Xi'an have a deluxe class, with only two berths per compartment and private bathrooms. The non-stop Z-series trains are even more luxurious. Train types are identifiable by the letter preceding the route number: Z is for nonstop, T is for a normal express.

Overpriced dining cars serve meals that are often inedible, so you'd do better to make use of the massive thermoses of boiled water in each compartment and take along your own noodles or instant soup, like locals do. Trains are always crowded, but you are guaranteed your designated seat, though not always the overhead luggage rack. Note that theft on trains is increasing; on overnight trains, sleep with your valuables or else keep them on the inside of the bunk.

You can find out just about everything about Chinese train travel at Seat 61's fabulous Web site. China Highlights has a searchable online timetable for major train routes. The tour operator Travel China Guide has an English-language Web site that can help you figure out train schedules and fares.

China Highlights ⊕ www.chinahighlights.com/china-trains/index.htm. **Seat 61** ⊕ www.seat61.com/China.htm. **Travel China Guide** ⊕ www.travelchinaguide.com/china-trains/index.htm

---

SERIOUS TRAINING

The most dramatic Chinese train experience is the six-day trip between Beijing and Moscow, often referred to as the Trans-Siberian railway, though that's actually the service that runs between Moscow and Vladivostok. Two weekly services cover the 8,047 km (5,000 mi) between Moscow and Beijing. The Trans-Manchurian is a Russian train that goes through northeast China, whereas the Trans-Mongolian is a Chinese train that goes through the Great Wall and crosses the Gobi Desert. Both have first-class compartments with four berths (Y2,500), or luxury two-berth compartments (Y3,000). Trains leave from Beijing Station, which is the cheapest place to buy tickets, though it's easier to get them through CITS. Many Western travel agents specialize in selling Trans-Siberian tickets, but their prices are often much higher.

ON THE GROUND

GREETINGS

Chinese people aren't very touchy-feely with one another, even less so with strangers. Keep bear-hugs and cheek-kissing for your next European trip and stick to handshakes and low-key greetings when you are first meeting local people. Always use people's title and surname until they invite you to do otherwise.

SIGHTSEEING

By and large, the Chinese are a rule-abiding bunch. Follow their lead and avoid doing anything signs advise against. Although you won't be banned from entering any sightseeing spots on grounds of dress, you'd do well to avoid overly skimpy or casual clothes.

China is a crowded country; pushing, nudging, and line-jumping are commonplace. It may be hard to accept, but it's not considered rude, so avoid reacting (even verbally) if you're accidentally shoved.

OUT ON THE TOWN

It's a great honor to be invited to someone's house, so explain at length if you can't go. Arrive punctually with a small gift for the hosts; remove your shoes outside if you see other guests doing so. Eating lots is the biggest compliment you can pay the food (and the cook).

Tea, served free in all Chinese restaurants, is a common drink at mealtimes, though many locals only accompany their food with soup. It's quite normal to order other drinks, though, especially beer.

Smoking is one of China's greatest vices. No-smoking sections in restaurants are nonexistent, and people light up anywhere they think they can get away with it—including on public transport, at times.

Holding hands in public is OK, but keep passionate embraces for the hotel room.

DOING BUSINESS

Time is of the essence when doing business in China. Make appointments well in advance and be extremely punctual, as this shows respect. Chinese people have a keen sense of hierarchy in the office: if you're visiting in a group, the senior member should lead proceedings.

Suits are still the norm in China, regardless of the outside temperature. Women should avoid plunging necklines, heavy makeup, overly short skirts or high heels. Pants are completely acceptable. Women can expect to be treated as equals by local businessmen.

Face is ever-important. Never say anything that will make people look bad, especially in front of superiors. Avoid being pushy or overly buddylike when negotiating: address people as Mr. or Ms. until they invite you to do otherwise, respect silences in conversation and don't hurry things or interrupt. When entertaining, local businesspeople may insist on paying: after a slight protest, accept, as this lets them gain face.

Business cards are a big deal: not having one is like not having a personality. If possible, have yours printed in English on one side and Chinese on the other (your hotel can usually arrange this in a matter of hours). Proffer your card with both hands and receive the other person's in the same way, then read it carefully and make an admiring comment.

Many gifts, like clocks and cutting implements, are considered unlucky in China. Food—especially presented in a showy basket—is always a good gift choice, as are imported spirits. Avoid giving four of anything, as the number is associated with death. Offer gifts with both hands, and don't expect people to open them in your presence.

LANGUAGE

One of the best ways to avoid being an ugly American is to learn a little of the local language. You need not strive for fluency; even just mastering a few basic words and

LOCAL DO'S & TABOOS

CUSTOMS OF THE COUNTRY

"Face" is the all-important issue in China. A cross between pride and social status, it's all about appearances yet its cultural roots run deep. Shame someone publicly, and you may lose their friendship for life; make them look good, and you'll go far. What makes people lose and gain face is complicated, but respect is the key issue. Don't get all upset if things go wrong, especially when reserving tickets and hotel rooms. Instead, be stern but friendly—raising your voice and threatening will get you nowhere. Keep facial expressions and hand gestures to a minimum; when pointing, use your whole hand, not a finger.

Locals often seem less than forthcoming when giving information. Be patient, they're not trying to mislead you, but rather keep you happy by telling you what they think you want to hear. Keep asking questions until you find out what you want.

Residents of big cities like Beijing and Shanghai are used to seeing foreigners, but you may still be stared at, especially if you're not white. In smaller places, the staring may make you feel like a walking museum exhibit. Get used to the cry of *laowai* (a not-very-complimentary word for "foreigner") everywhere you go, too. Simply smile back and treat it all humorously.

Try to keep an open mind about other cultural differences, be it spitting in public, dog meat, or Chinese toilets. The Chinese are a gracious people who will reciprocate kindness.

For guidelines on dining etiquette, *see* Eating Out, *below.*

---

terms is bound to make chatting with the locals more rewarding.

For language fundamentals, *see* Language Notes in the back of the book for an explanation of pronunciation and a vocabulary list. Translations of specific place names are located at the end of every chapter.

Everyone in mainland China speaks Putonghua (*pŭtŹnghuà,* the "common language") another name for Mandarin Chinese. It's written using ideograms, or characters; in 1949 the government also introduced a phonetic writing system that uses the Roman alphabet. Known as Pinyin, it's widely used to label public buildings and station names. Even if you don't speak or read Chinese, you can easily compare Pinyin names with a map.

In Hong Kong the main language spoken is Cantonese, although many people speak English. There are many other local Chinese dialects. Some use the same characters as Putonghua for writing, but the pronunciation is so different as to be unintelligible to a Putonghua speaker. The Chinese government actively discourages mainlanders to use dialects in front of foreigners. There are several non-Chinese languages (such as Mongolia, Uyghur, and Tibetan) spoken by China's ethnic minorities.

Chinese grammar is simple, but a complex tonal system of pronunciation means it usually takes a long time for foreigners to learn Chinese. Making yourself understood can be tricky, however, the Chinese will appreciate your making the effort to speak a few phrases understood almost everywhere. Try "Hello"—*"Ní hǎo"* (nee how); "Thank you"—*"Xiè xiè"* (shee-yeh, shee-yeh); and "Good-bye"—*"Zai jian"* (dzai djan). When pronouncing words written in Pinyin, remember that "q" and "x" are pronounced like "ch" and "sh," respectively; "zh" is pronounced like the "j" in "just"; "c" is pronounced like "ts."

English isn't widely spoken, though the staff in most hotels, travel agencies, and upscale restaurants is the exception. If you're lost and need help, look first to someone

CON OR CONCIERGE?

Good hotel concierges are invaluable—for arranging transportation, getting reservations at the hottest restaurant, and scoring tickets for a sold-out show or entrance to an exclusive nightclub. They're in the know and well connected. That said, sometimes you have to take their advice with a grain of salt.

It's not uncommon for restaurants to ply concierges with free food and drink in exchange for steering diners their way. Indeed, European concierges often receive referral *fees*. Hotel chains usually have guidelines about what their concierges can accept. The best concierges, however, are above reproach. This is particularly true of those who belong to the prestigious international society of Les Clefs d'Or.

What can you expect of a concierge? At a typical tourist-class hotel you can expect him or her to give you the basics: to show you something on a map, make a standard restaurant reservation (particularly if you don't speak the language), or help you book a tour or airport transportation. In Asia concierges perform the vital service of writing out the name or address of your destination for you to give to a cab driver.

Savvy concierges at the finest hotels and resorts can arrange for just about any good or service imaginable—and do so quickly. You should compensate them appropriately. A $10 (Y80) tip is enough to show appreciation for a table at a hot restaurant. But the reward should really be much greater for tickets to that U2 concert that's been sold out for months or for those last-minute sixth-row-center seats for *The Lion King*.

under 30, who may have studied some English in school. In shops, calculators and hand gestures do most of the talking.

A phrase book and language-tape set can help get you started.

Language Resources *Business Companion: Chinese,* by Tim Dobbins and Paul Westbrook, **Living Language/Random House Inc.** ☎ 800/726-0600 ⊕ www.livinglanguage. com. *I Can Read That! A Traveler's Introduction to Chinese Characters,* by Julie Mazel Sussman, **China Books and Periodicals, Inc.** ☎ 415/282-2994 🖷 415/282-0994 ⊕ www. chinabooks.com. *In the Know in China,* by Jennifer Phillips, **Living Language/Random House Inc.** ☎ 800/726-0600 ⊕ www. livinglanguage.com.

▌ BUSINESS SERVICES & FACILITIES

Your hotel (or another nearby mid- to top-end one) is the best place to start looking for business services, including translation. Most are very up-to-speed on businesspeople's needs and can put you in touch with other companies if necessary. Regus and the Executive Centre are international business-services companies with several office locations in Beijing, Shanghai, and Hong Kong. They provide secretarial services, meeting and conference facilities, and office rentals.

The Executive Centre ⊕ www. executivecentre.com. **Regus** ☎ 800/819-0091 ⊕ www.regus.cn.

▌ COMMUNICATIONS

INTERNET

China's major cities are very Internet-friendly for those bearing laptops. Most mid- to high-end hotels have in-room Internet access; if the hotel doesn't have a server but you have a room phone you can usually access a government-provided ISP, which only charges you for the phone call. Wi-Fi is growing exponentially—many hotels and even cafés provide it free.

Many hotels also have a computer with Internet access that you can use. Internet cafés are ubiquitous in big cities, and are rapidly spreading to smaller destinations. It's an unstable business, however, and new ones open and close all the time. Known as *wang ba* in Chinese, they're not usually signposted in English, so ask your hotel to recommend one nearby. Prices (and cleanliness) vary considerably, but start at about Y3 to Y10 per hour.

Remember that there is strict government control of the Internet in China. There's usually no problem with Web-based mail, but you may be unable to access news and even blogging sites.

Cybercafes ⊕ www.cybercafes.com lists over 4,000 Internet cafés worldwide.

PHONES

The good news is that you can now make a direct-dial telephone call from virtually any point on earth. The bad news? You can't always do so cheaply. Calling from a hotel is almost always the most expensive option; hotels usually add huge surcharges to all calls, particularly international ones. In some countries you can phone from call centers or even the post office. Calling cards usually keep costs to a minimum, but only if you purchase them locally. And then there are cell phones (Cell Phones, ⇨ *below*), which are sometimes more prevalent—particularly in the developing world—than landlines; as expensive as cell-phone calls can be, they are still usually a much cheaper option than calling from your hotel.

The country code for China is 86; the city code for Beijing is 10, and the city code for Shanghai is 21. Hong Kong has its own country code: 852. To call China from the United States or Canada, dial the international access code (011), followed by the country code (86), the area or city code without the initial zero, and the eight-digit phone number.

Numbers beginning with 800 within China are toll-free. Note that a call from China to a toll-free number in the United States or Hong Kong is a full-tariff international call.

CALLING WITHIN CHINA

The Chinese phone system is cheap and efficient. You can make local and long-distance calls from your hotel or any public phone on the street. Some pay phones accept coins, but it's easier to buy an integrated circuit (IC) calling card, available at convenience stores and newsstands (*see* Calling Cards, *below*). Local calls are generally free from landlines, though your hotel might charge a nominal rate. Long-distance rates in China are very low. Calling from your hotel room is a viable option, as hotels can only add a 15% service charge.

Chinese phone numbers have eight digits—you only need to dial these when calling somewhere within the city or area you're in. In general, city codes appear written with a 0 in front of them; if not, you need to add this when calling another city within China.

For directory assistance, dial 114. If you want information for other cities, dial the city code followed by 114 (note that this is considered a long-distance call). For example, if you're in Beijing and need directory assistance for a Shanghai number, dial 021–114. The operators do not speak English, so if you don't speak Chinese you're best off asking your hotel for help.

To make long-distance calls from a public phone you need an IC card (⇨ Phone Cards). To place a long-distance call, dial 0, the city code, and the eight-digit phone number.

CALLING OUTSIDE CHINA

To make an international call from within China, dial 00 (the international access code within China) and then the country code, area code, and phone number. The country code for the United States is 1.

IDD (international direct dialing) service is available at all hotels, post offices, major shopping centers, and airports. By international standards prices aren't unreasonable, but it's vastly cheaper to use a long-distance calling card, known as an IP card (*see* ⇨ Calling Cards, *below*). These cards' rates also beat AT&T, MCI, and Sprint hands-down. If you do need to use these services, dial 108 (the local operator) and the local access codes from China: 11 for AT&T, 12 for MCI, and 13 for Sprint. Dialing instructions in English will follow. Access Codes **AT&T Direct** ☎ 800/874-4000, from China: 108-11. **MCI WorldPhone** ☎ 800/444-4444, from China: 108-12. **Sprint International Access** ☎ 800/793-1153, from China: 108-13.

CALLING CARDS
Calling cards are a key part of the Chinese phone system. There are two kinds: the IC card (integrated circuit; *àicei ka*), for local and domestic long-distance calls on pay phones; and the IP card (Internet protocol; *aipi ka*) for international calls from any phone. You can buy both at post offices, convenience stores, and street vendors.

IC cards come in denominations of Y20, Y50, and Y100, and can be used in any pay phone with a card slot—most urban pay phones have them. Local calls using them cost around Y0.30 a minute, and less on weekends and after 6 PM.

To use IP cards, you first dial a local access number. This is often free from hotels, whereas at public phones you need an IC card to do so. You then enter a card number and PIN, and finally the phone number, complete with international dial codes. When calling from a pay phone, both cards' minutes are deducted at the same time—one for local access (IC card) and one for the long-distance call you placed (IP card). There are countless different card brands; China Unicom is one that's usually reliable. IP cards come with face values of Y20, Y30, Y50, and Y100. However, the going rate for them is up to half that, so bargain vendors down.

CELL PHONES
If you have a multiband phone (some countries use different frequencies than what's used in the United States) and your service provider uses the world-standard GSM network (as do T-Mobile, Cingular, and Verizon), you can probably use your phone abroad. Roaming fees can be steep, however: 99¢ a minute is considered reasonable. And overseas you normally pay the toll charges for incoming calls. It's almost always cheaper to send a text message than to make a call, since text messages have a very low set fee (often less than 5¢).

If you just want to make local calls, consider buying a new SIM card (note that your provider may have to unlock your phone for you to use a different SIM card) and a prepaid service plan in the destination. You'll then have a local number and can make local calls at local rates. If your trip is extensive, you could also simply buy a new cell phone in your destination, as the initial cost will be offset over time.

■ TIP➔ **If you travel internationally frequently, save one of your old cell phones or buy a cheap one on the Internet; ask your cell-phone company to unlock it for you, and take it with you as a travel phone, buying a new SIM card with pay-as-you-go service in each destination.**

If you have a tri-band GSM or a CDMA phone, pick up a local SIM card (*sim ka*) from any branch of China Mobile or China Unicom: there are often branches at international Chinese airports. You'll be presented with a list of possible phone numbers, with varying prices—an "unlucky" phone number (one with lots of 4s) could be as cheap as Y50, whereas an auspicious one (full of 8s) could fetch Y300 or more. You then buy prepaid cards to charge minutes onto your SIM—do this straight away as you need credit to receive calls. Local calls to landlines cost Y0.25 a minute, and to cell phones Y0.60. International calls from cell phones are very expensive. Remember to bring an adapter for your phone charger. You can also buy cheap handsets from China Mobile—if you're planning to stay even a couple of days this is probably cheaper than renting a phone.
Cellular Abroad ☎ 800/287-5072 ⊕ www.cellularabroad.com rents and sells GMS

phones and sells SIM cards that work in many countries. **Mobal** ☎ 888/888-9162 ⊕ www.mobalrental.com rents cell phones and sells GSM phones (starting at $49) that will operate in 140 countries. Per-call rates vary throughout the world. **Planet Fone** ☎ 888/988-4777 ⊕ www.planetfone.com rents cell phones, but the per-minute rates are expensive.

▌CUSTOMS & DUTIES

You're always allowed to bring goods of a certain value back home without having to pay any duty or import tax. But there's a limit on the amount of tobacco and liquor you can bring back duty-free, and some countries have separate limits for perfumes; for exact figures, check with your customs department. The values of so-called "duty-free" goods are included in these amounts. When you shop abroad, save all your receipts, as customs inspectors may ask to see them as well as the items you purchased. If the total value of your goods is more than the duty-free limit, you'll have to pay a tax (most often a flat percentage) on the value of everything beyond that limit.

Except for the usual prohibitions against narcotics, explosives, plant and animal material, firearms, and ammunition you can take anything into China that you plan to take away with you. Cameras, video recorders, GPS equipment, laptops, and the like should pose no problems. However, China is very sensitive about printed matter deemed seditious, such as religious, pornographic, and political items, especially articles, books, and pictures on Tibet. All the same, small amounts of English-language reading matter aren't generally a problem. Customs officials are for the most part easygoing, and visitors are rarely searched. It's not necessary to fill in customs declaration forms, but if you carry in a large amount of cash, say several thousand dollars, you should declare it upon arrival.

You're not allowed to remove any antiquities dating to before 1795. Antiques

from between 1795 and 1949 must have an official red seal attached—quality antiques shops know this and arrange it.
U.S. Information **U.S. Customs and Border Protection** ⊕ www.cbp.gov.

▌EATING OUT

In China, meals are really a communal event, so food in a Chinese home or restaurant is always shared—you usually have a small bowl or plate to transfer food from the center platters into. Although cutlery is available in many restaurants, it won't hurt to brush up on your use of chopsticks, the utensil of choice.

The standard eating procedure is to hold the bowl close to your mouth and shovel in the contents without any qualms. Noisily slurping up soup and noodles is also the norm, as is belching when you're done. Covering the tablecloth in crumbs, drips, and even spat-out bones is a sign you've enjoyed your meal. It's considered bad manners to point or play with your chopsticks, or to place them on top of your rice bowl when you're finished eating (place the chopsticks horizontally on the table or plate). Avoid, too, leaving your chopsticks standing up in a bowl of rice—they look like the two incense sticks burned at funerals.

If you're invited to a formal Chinese meal, be prepared for great ceremony, endless toasts and speeches, and a grand variety of elaborate dishes. Your host will be seated at the "head" of the round table, which is the seat that faces the door. Wait to be instructed where to sit. Don't start eating until the host takes the first bite, and then simply help yourself as the food comes around, but don't take the last piece on a platter. Always let the food touch your plate before bringing it up to your mouth; eating directly from the serving dish is bad form.

Chinese food varies considerably from region to region. In the south, rice is the staple carbohydrate; whereas wheat products like bread, dumplings, and noodles are the base of northern cooking. This is often quite oily, with liberal amounts of vinegar; its strong flavors come from garlic, soy sauce, and bean pastes. The food of southern China is known for its use of fresh ingredients and liberal dosing of hot spices.

Meat, poultry, or seafood is present in most Chinese dishes, albeit in small quantities. Vegetables and tofu also play a big role in meals—Chinese vegetarian cookery is excellent, though you often need to go to a dedicated vegetarian restaurant to get it. These restaurants often specialize in tofu cooked so it looks and tastes like different meats. In all Chinese food, dairy products are scarce. Chinese meals usually involve a variety of dishes, which are always ordered communally in restaurants. Eat alone or order dishes just for yourself and you're seriously limiting your food experience.

For information on food-related health issues, *see* Health, *below.*

MEALS & MEALTIMES

Food is a central part of Chinese culture, and so eating should be a major activity on any trip to China. Breakfast is not usually a big deal—congee, or rice porridge (*zhou*) is the standard dish. Most mid- and upper-end hotels do big buffet spreads, whereas blooming café chains provide lattes and croissants in China's major cities.

Snacks are a food group in themselves. There's no shortage of steaming street stalls selling kebabs, grilled meat or chicken, bowls of noodle soup, and the ubiquituous *baozi* (stuffed dumplings).

Many visitors seem to loath eating from stalls—you'd be missing out on some of the best nibbles around, though. Pick a place where lots of locals are eating to be on the safe side.

The food in hotel restaurants is usually acceptable, but vastly overpriced. Restaurants frequented by locals always serve tastier fare at better prices. Don't shy from trying establishments without an English menu—a good phrase book and lots of pointing can usually get you what you want.

If you're craving Western food (or sushi or a curry), rest assured that big cities have plenty of American fast-food chains, and sometimes world-class international restaurants, too. Most higher-end Chinese restaurants have a Western menu, but you're usually safer sticking to the Chinese food.

Meals in China are served early: breakfast until 9 AM, lunch between 11 and 2, and dinner from 5 to 9. Unless otherwise noted, the restaurants listed in this guide are open daily for lunch and dinner. Restaurants and bars catering to foreigners may stay open longer hours.

PAYING

At most restaurants you ask for the bill at the end of the meal, like you do back home. At cheap noodle bars and street stands you often pay up front. Only very upmarket restaurants accept payment by credit card. For guidelines on tipping *see* Tipping, *below.*

Price charts for hotels and restaurants can be found at the beginning of each chapter.

RESERVATIONS & DRESS

Regardless of where you are, it's a good idea to make a reservation if you can. In some places (Hong Kong, for example), it's expected. We only mention them specifically when reservations are essential (there's no other way you'll ever get a table) or when they are not accepted. For popular restaurants, book as far ahead as you can (often 30 days), and reconfirm as soon as you arrive. (Large parties should always call ahead to check the reservations policy.) We mention dress only when men are required to wear a jacket or a jacket and tie.

WINES, BEER & SPIRITS

Forget tea, today the people's drink of choice is beer. Massively popular among Chinese men, it's still a bit of a no-no for Chinese women, however. Tsingtao, China's most popular brew is a 4% lager that comes in liter bottles and is usually cheaper than water. Many regions have their own local breweries, too, and international bands are also available.

When you see "wine" on the menu, it's usually referring to sweet fruit wines or distilled rice wine. The most famous brand of Chinese liquor is Maotai, a distilled liquor ranging in strength from 35% to 53% proof. Like most firewaters, it's an acquired taste.

There are basically no licensing laws in China, so you can drink anywhere, and at any time, provided you can find somewhere open to serve you.

▌ ELECTRICITY

The electrical current in China is 220 volts, 50 cycles alternating current (AC) so most American appliances can't be used without a transformer. A universal adapter is especially useful in China as wall outlets come in a bewildering variety of configurations: two- and three-pronged round plugs, as well as two-pronged flat sockets. Although blackouts are not common in Chinese cities, villages occasionally lose power for short periods of time.

Consider making a small investment in a universal adapter, which has several types of plugs in one lightweight, compact unit. Most laptops and cell-phone chargers are dual voltage (i.e., they operate equally well on 110 and 220 volts), so require only an adapter. These days the same is true of small appliances such as hair dryers. Always check labels and manufacturer in-

structions to be sure. Don't use 110-volt outlets marked FOR SHAVERS ONLY for high-wattage appliances such as hair dryers.
Steve Kropla's Help for World Travelers
⊕ www.kropla.com has information on electrical and telephone plugs around the world.
Walkabout Travel Gear ⊕ www.walkabouttravelgear.com has a good coverage of electricity under "adapters."

▌ EMERGENCIES

If you lose your passport, contact your embassy immediately. Embassy officials can also advise you on how to proceed in case of other emergencies. The staff at your hotel may be able to provide a translator if you need to report an emergency or crime to doctors or the police. Most police officers and hospital staff members don't speak English, though you may find one or two people who do.

Ambulances generally offer just a means of transport, not medical aid; taking a taxi is quicker and means you can choose the hospital you want to go to. Where possible, go to a private clinic catering to expats—prices are sky-high but so are their hygiene and medical standards. Most have reliable 24-hour pharmacies.
U.S. Embassy & Consulate United States Consulate ✉ 1469 Huaihai Zhong Lu, Xuhui District, Shanghai 200031 ☎ 021/6433-6880, 021/6433-3936 for after-hours emergencies ✉ Citizen Services Section, Westgate Mall, 8th fl., 1038 Nanjing Xi Lu, Jingan District

☏ 021/3217-4650 ⊕ http://shanghai. usconsulate.gov. **United States Embassy** ✉ 3 Xiushui Bei Jie, Chaoyang District, Beijing 100600 ☏ 010/6532-3431 Ext. 229 or 010/ 6532-3831 Ext. 264 ⊕ http://beijing. usembassy-china.org.cn. **United States Citizens Services** ✉ 4 Ling Shi Guan Rd., Chengdu 610041 ☏ 028/8558-3992 ⊕ http://chengdu.usembassy-china.org.cn ✉ 1 South Shamian St., Guangzhou 510133 ☏ 020/8518-7605, 020/8121-6077 for after-hours emergencies ⊕ http://guangzhou. usembassy-china.org.cn.

General Emergency Contacts Ambulance ☏ 120. **Fire** ☏ 119. **Police** ☏ 110.

∎ HEALTH

The most common types of illnesses are caused by contaminated food and water. Especially in developing countries, drink only bottled, boiled, or purified water and drinks; don't drink from public fountains or use ice. You should even consider using bottled water to brush your teeth. Make sure food has been thoroughly cooked and is served to you fresh and hot; avoid vegetables and fruits that you haven't washed (in bottled or purified water) or peeled yourself. If you have problems, mild cases of traveler's diarrhea may respond to Imodium (known generically as loperamide) or Pepto-Bismol. Be sure to drink plenty of fluids; if you can't keep fluids down, seek medical help immediately. Tap water in major cities like Beijing and Shanghai is safe for brushing teeth, but buy bottled water to drink and check the bottle is sealed.

∎ TIP➔ If you travel a lot internationally—particularly to developing nations—refer to the CDC's *Health Information for International Travel* (aka Traveler's Health Yellow Book). Info from it is posted on the CDC Web site (⊕ www.cdc.gov/travel/yb), or you can buy a copy from your local bookstore for $24.95.

Infectious diseases can be airborne or passed via mosquitoes and ticks and through direct or indirect physical contact with animals or people. Some, including Norwalk-like viruses that affect your di-

gestive tract, can be passed along through contaminated food. If you are traveling in an area where malaria is prevalent, use a repellant containing DEET and take malaria-prevention medication before, during, and after your trip as directed by your physician. Condoms can help prevent most sexually transmitted diseases, but they aren't absolutely reliable and their quality varies from country to country. Speak with your physician and/or check the CDC or World Health Organization Web sites for health alerts, particularly if you're pregnant, traveling with children, or have a chronic illness.

For information on travel insurance, shots and medications, and medical-assistance companies *see* Shots & Medications *under* Things to Consider *in* Before You Go, *above.*

SPECIFIC ISSUES IN CHINA

There are English-speaking doctors in most major Chinese cities, which generally have an international hospital or clinic, too. Otherwise, the best place to start looking for a suitable doctor is through your hotel concierge, then the local Public Security Bureau. If you become seriously ill or are injured, it is best to fly home, or at least to Hong Kong, as quickly as possible. In Hong Kong, English-speaking doctors are widely available.

Pneumonia and influenza are common among travelers returning from China—talk to your doctor about inoculations before you leave. If you need to buy prescription drugs, try to go to the pharmacies of reputable private hospitals. Do *not* buy them in street-side pharmacies as the quality control is unreliable.

Avian Influenza, commonly known as Bird Flu, is a form of influenza that affects birds (including poultry) but can be passed to humans. It causes initial flu symptoms, followed by respiratory and organ failure. Although rare, it's often lethal. There've been several outbreaks in Hong Kong and China since 2003. The Hong Kong Government now exercises strict control over poultry farms and markets, and there are signs all over town warning against contact with birds. Things aren't so well-controlled in the mainland, however, so ensure any poultry or eggs you consume are well cooked.

Severe Acute Respiratory Syndrome (SARS), also known as atypical pneumonia, is a respiratory illness caused by a strain of coronavirus that was first reported in parts of Asia—notably Hong Kong—in early 2003. Symptoms include a fever greater than 100.4°F (38°C), shortness of breath, and other flulike symptoms. The disease is thought to spread by close person-to-person contact, particularly respiratory droplets and secretions transmitted through the eyes, nose, or mouth. SARS hasn't returned to Hong Kong or China, but many experts believe that it or other contagious, upper-respiratory viruses will continue to be a seasonal health concern.

OVER-THE-COUNTER REMEDIES
Most pharmacies in big Chinese cities carry over-the-counter Western medicines and traditional Chinese medicines. By and large, you need to ask for the generic name of the drug you're looking for, not a brand name. Acetaminophen—or Tylenol—is often known as paracetomol in Hong Kong. Oral contraceptives are also available without prescription, but quality in regular pharmacies varies.

▌HOURS OF OPERATION

Most banks and government offices are open weekdays 9 AM to 5 PM or 6, although close for lunch (sometime between noon and 2). Some bank branches and most CTS tour desks in hotels keep longer hours and are open Saturday (and occasionally Sunday) mornings. Many hotel currency-exchange desks stay open 24 hours. Museums open from roughly 9 AM to 6 PM, six or seven days a week. Everything in China grinds to a halt for the first two or three days of Chinese New Year (sometime in mid-January–February), and opening hours are often reduced for the rest of that season.

Pharmacies are open daily from 8:30 or 9 AM to 6 or 7 PM. Some large pharmacies stay open until 9 PM or even later. Shops and department stores are generally open daily 8 AM to 8 PM; some stores stay open even later in summer, in popular tourist areas, or during peak tourist season.

HOLIDAYS
National holidays in mainland China include New Year's Day (January 1); Spring Festival aka Chinese New Year (late January/early February); Qingming Jie (April 4); International Labor Day (May 1); Dragon Boat Festival (late May/early June); anniversary of the founding of the Communist Party of China (July 1); anniversary of the founding of the Chinese People's Liberation Army (August 1); and National Day—founding of the People's Republic of China in 1949 (October 1); Chongyang Jie or Double Ninth Festival (9th day of 9th lunar month). Hong Kong celebrates most of these festivals, and also has public holidays at Easter and for Christmas and Boxing Day (December 25 and 26). (⇨Festivals & Seasonal Events *in* Chapter 1.)

▌MAIL

Sending international mail from China is extremely reliable. Airmail letters to any place in the world should take 5 to 14 days. Express Mail Service (EMS) is available to many international destinations. Letters within any city arrive the next day, and mail to the rest of China takes a day or two longer. Domestic mail can be subject to search so don't send sensitive materials, such as religious or political literature, as you might cause the recipient trouble.

Service is more reliable if you mail letters from post offices rather than mailboxes. Buy envelopes here, too, as there are standardized sizes in China. You need to glue stamps onto envelopes as they're not self-adhesive. Most post offices are open daily between 8 AM and 7 PM; many keep longer hours. Your hotel can usually send letters for you, too.

You can use the Roman alphabet to write an address. Do not use red ink, which has a negative connotation. You must also include a six-digit zip code for mail within China. Sending airmail postcards costs Y4.50 and letters Y5 to Y7.

Long-term guests can receive mail at their hotels. Otherwise, the best place to receive mail is at the American Express office. Most major Chinese cities have American Express offices with client-mail service. Be sure to bring your American Express card, as the staff will not give you the mail without seeing it

SHIPPING PACKAGES

It's easy to ship packages home from China. Take what you want to send *unpacked* to the post office—everything will be sewn up officially into satisfying linen-bound packages, a service that costs a few yuan. You have to fill in lengthy forms—enclosing a photocopy of receipts for the goods inside isn't a bad idea, as they may be opened by customs along the line. Large antiques stores often offer reliable shipping services that take care of customs in China. Large international couriers operating in China include DHL, Federal Express, and UPS—next-day delivery for a 1-kilogram (2.2-pound) package starts at about Y300. Your hotel can also arrange shipping parcels, but there's usually a hefty markup on postal rates.

Express Services DHL ☎ 800/810-8000 ⊕ www.cn.dhl.com. **FedEx** ☎ 800/988-1888 ⊕ www.fedex.com. **UPS** ☎ 800/820-8388 ⊕ www.ups.com.

▋ MONEY

China is a cheap destination by most North Americans' standards. However, prices vary considerably from place to place—expect your dollar to do more for you in smaller cities than pricey Shanghai or Beijing. The exception to the rule is Hong Kong, where eating and sleeping prices are on a par with the United States.

In mainland China the best places to convert your dollars into yuan are at your hotel's front desk or a branch of a major bank, such as Bank of China, CITIC, or HSBC. All these operate with standardized government rates—anything cheaper is illegal, and thus risky. You need to present your passport to change money.

Although credit cards are gaining ground in China, for day-to-day transactions cash is definitely king. Getting change for big notes can be a problem, so try to stock up on 10s and 20s when you change money. ATMs are widespread, but not always reliable. Hunt around enough, though, and you're sure to find one that accepts your card.

ITEM AVERAGE COST	
Cup of coffee at Starbucks	Y20–Y25
Glass of local beer	Y10–Y30
Cheapest subway ticket	Y3
2-km (1-mi) taxi ride in Beijing or Shanghai	Y10–Y11
Set lunch in a cheap restaurant	Y20
Hourlong foot massage	Y50
Fake Chloé purse	Y200

Prices throughout this guide are given for adults. Substantially reduced fees are almost always available for children, students, and senior citizens.

▋ TIP→ Banks never have every foreign currency on hand, and it may take as long as a week to order. If you're planning to exchange funds before leaving home, don't wait until the last minute.

ATMS & BANKS

Your own bank will probably charge a fee for using ATMs abroad; the foreign bank you use may also charge a fee. Nevertheless, you'll usually get a better rate of exchange at an ATM than you will at a currency-exchange office or even when changing money in a bank. And extracting funds as you need them is a safer option than carrying around a large amount of cash.

■ TIP➜ PIN numbers with more than four digits are not recognized at ATMs in many countries. If yours has five or more, remember to change it before you leave.

ATMs are widespread in major Chinese cities and rates are as good, if not better, than at exchange desks. The most reliable ATMs are HSBC's. They also have the highest withdrawal limit, which offsets transaction charges. Of the Chinese banks, your best bet for ATMs is the Bank of China, which accepts most foreign cards. That said, machines frequently refuse to give cash for mysterious reasons—move on and try another. On-screen instructions appear automatically in English.

ATMs are widely available throughout Hong Kong—most carry the sign ETC instead of ATM. Subway stations are a good place to look if you're having trouble locating one.

CREDIT CARDS

American Express, MasterCard, and Visa are accepted at most hotels and a growing number of upmarket stores and restaurants. Diners Club is less widely accepted.

Throughout this guide, the following abbreviations are used: **AE**, American Express; **DC**, Diners Club; **MC**, MasterCard; and **V**, Visa.

If you plan to use your credit card for cash advances, you'll need to apply for a PIN at least two weeks before your trip. Although it's usually cheaper (and safer) to use a credit card abroad for large purchases (so you can cancel payments or be reimbursed if there's a problem), note that some credit-card companies *and* the banks that issue them add substantial percentages to all foreign transactions, whether they're in a foreign currency or not. Check on these fees before leaving home, so there won't be any surprises when you get the bill.

■ TIP➜ Before you charge something, ask the merchant whether or not he or she plans to do a dynamic currency conversion (DCC). In such a transaction the credit-card *processor* (shop, restaurant, or hotel, not Visa or MasterCard) converts the currency and charges

WORST-CASE SCENARIO

All your money and credit cards have just been stolen. In these days of real-time transactions, this isn't a predicament that should destroy your vacation. First, report the theft of the credit cards. Then get any traveler's checks you were carrying replaced. This can usually be done almost immediately, provided that you kept a record of the serial numbers separate from the checks themselves. If you bank at a large international bank like Citibank or HSBC, go to the closest branch; if you know your account number, chances are you can get a new ATM card and withdraw money right away. **Western Union** (☎ 800/325-6000 ⊕ www.westernunion. com) sends money almost everywhere. Have someone back home order a transfer online, over the phone, or at one of the company's offices, which is the cheapest option. The U.S. State Department's **Overseas Citizens Services** (☎ 202/647-5225) can wire money to any U.S. consulate or embassy abroad for a fee of $30. Just have someone back home wire money or send a money order or cashier's check to the State Department, which will then disburse the funds as soon as the next working day after it receives them.

you in dollars. In most cases you'll pay the merchant a 3% fee for this service in addition to any credit-card company and issuing-bank foreign-transaction surcharges.

Dynamic currency conversion programs are becoming increasingly widespread. Merchants who participate in them are supposed to ask whether you want to be charged in dollars or the local currency, but they don't always do so. And even if they do offer you a choice, they may well avoid mentioning the additional surcharges. The good news is that you *do* have a choice. And if this practice really gets your goat, you can avoid it entirely thanks to American Express; with its cards, DCC simply isn't an option.

Reporting Lost Cards American Express
☎ 800/992-3404 in the U.S. or 336/393-1111

collect from abroad ⊕ www.americanexpress. com. **Diners Club** ☎ 800/234-6377 in the U.S. or 303/799-1504 collect from abroad ⊕ www.dinersclub.com. **MasterCard** ☎ 800/622-7747 in the U.S. or 636/722-7111 collect from abroad, 800/110-7309 in China ⊕ www.mastercard.com. **Visa** ☎ 800/847-2911 in the U.S. or 410/581-9994 collect from abroad, 800/711-2911 in China. ⊕ www.visa.com.

CURRENCY & EXCHANGE

The Chinese currency is officially called the yuan (Y), and is also known as *renminbi* (RMB), or "People's Money." You may also hear it called *kuai*, an informal expression like "buck." It's pegged to the U.S. dollar at around Y8.

Both old and new styles of bills circulate simultaneously in China, and many denominations have both coins and bills. The Bank of China issues bills in denominations of 1 (burgundy), 2 (green), 5 (brown or purple), 10 (turquoise), 20 (brown), 50 (blue or occasionally yellow), and 100 (red). There are 1 yuan coins, too. The yuan subdivides into 10-cent units called *jiao* or *mao*; these come in bills and coins of 1, 2, and 5. The smallest denomination is the *fen*, which comes in coins (and occasionally tiny notes) of 1, 2, and 5. Counterfeiting is rife in China, and even small stores inspect notes with ultraviolet lamps. Change can be a problem—don't expect much success paying for a Y13 purchase with a Y100 note, for example.

Exchange rates in China are fixed by the government daily, so it's equally good at branches of the Bank of China, at big department stores, or at your hotel's exchange desk, which have the added advantage of often being open 24 hours a day. Any lower rates are illegal, so you're exposing yourself to scams. A passport is required. Hold on to your exchange receipt, which you need to convert your extra yuan back into dollars.

In Hong Kong, the only currency used is the Hong Kong dollar, divided into 100 cents. Three local banks (HSBC, Standard Chartered, and the Bank of China) all issue bills and each has their own designs. At this writing, the Hong Kong dollar was pegged to the U.S. dollar at approximately 7.8 Hong Kong dollars to 1 U.S. dollar. There are no currency restrictions in Hong Kong. You can exchange currency at the airport, in hotels, in banks, and through private money changers scattered through the tourist areas. Banks usually have the best rates, but as they charge a flat HK$50 fee for non-account holders, it's better to change large sums infrequently. Currency-exchange offices have no fees, but they offset that with poor rates. Stick to ATMs whenever you can.

■ TIP→ Even if a currency-exchange booth has a sign promising no commission, rest assured that there's some kind of huge, hidden fee. (Oh . . . that's right. The sign didn't say no *fee*.) And as for rates, you're almost always better off getting foreign currency at an ATM or exchanging money at a bank.

TRAVELER'S CHECKS & CARDS

Some consider this the currency of the cave man, and it's true that fewer establishments accept traveler's checks these days. Nevertheless, they're a cheap and secure way to carry extra money, particularly on trips to urban areas. Both Citibank (under the Visa brand) and American Express issue traveler's checks in the United States, but AmEx is better known and more widely accepted; you can also avoid hefty surcharges by cashing AmEx checks at AmEx offices. Whatever you do, keep track of all the serial numbers in case the checks are lost or stolen.

Most hotels don't accept traveler's checks as payment, and only some branches of the Bank of China exchange them, usually at a worse rate than cash. Consider bringing some purely as backup, in case of credit-card theft.

American Express now offers a stored-value card called a Travelers Cheque Card, which you can use wherever American Express credit cards are accepted, including ATMs. The card can carry a minimum of $300 and a maximum of $2,700, and it's a very safe way to carry your funds. Although you can get replacement funds in 24 hours if your card is lost or stolen, it doesn't really strike us as a very good deal. In addition to a high initial cost ($14.95 to set up the card, plus $5 each time you "reload"), you still have to pay a 2% fee for each purchase in a foreign currency (similar to that of any credit card). Further, each time you use the card in an ATM you pay a transaction fee of $2.50 on top of the 2% transaction fee for the conversion—add it all up and it can be considerably more than you would pay when simply using your own ATM card. Regular traveler's checks are just as secure and cost less.

American Express ☎ 888/412-6945 in the U.S., 801/945-9450 collect outside of the U.S. to add value or speak to customer service ⊕ www.americanexpress.com.

▌RESTROOMS

Public restrooms abound in mainland China—the street, parks, restaurants, department stores, and major tourist attractions are all likely locations. Most charge a small fee (usually less than Y1), but seldom provide Western-style facilities or private booths. Instead, expect squat toilets, open troughs, and rusty spigots; WC signs at intersections point the way to these facilities. Toilet paper is a rarity, so carry tissues and antibacterial hand wipes in your day pack. The restrooms in the newest shopping plazas, fast-food outlets, and deluxe restaurants catering to foreigners are generally on a par with American restrooms. In post-SARS Hong Kong, public restrooms are well maintained. Alternatively, dip into malls or the lobby of big international hotels to use their loos.

Find a Loo The Bathroom Diaries ⊕ www.thebathroomdiaries.com is flush with unsanitized info on restrooms the world over—each one located, reviewed, and rated.

> ### WORD OF MOUTH
>
> "Feel free to wear your usual jewelry in China, I think it's the safest place I have lived in, although one must still exercise reasonable caution. People say there is some bag snatching, but I haven't seen or experienced same myself. It could be carried out by out-of-towners who are not able to get work in the big city."
>
> –Fenno

▌SAFETY

There is little violent crime against tourists in China, partly because the penalties are severe for those who are caught—China's yearly death-sentence tolls run into the thousands. Single women can move about without too much hassle. Handbag-snatching and pickpocketing do happen in markets and on crowded buses or trains—keep an eye open and your money safe and you should have no problems. Use the lockbox in your hotel room to store any valuables, but always carry your passport with you for identification purposes.

China is full of people looking to make a quick buck. The most common scam involves people persuading you to go with them for a tea ceremony, which is often so pleasant that you don't smell a rat until several hundred dollars appear on your credit-card bill. "Art students" who pressure you into buying work is another common scam. The same rules that apply to hostess bars worldwide are also true in China. Avoiding such scams is as easy as refusing *all* unsolicited services—be it from taxi or pedicab drivers, tour guides, or potential "friends."

Chinese traffic is as manic as it looks, and survival of the fittest (or the biggest) is the main rule. Crossing streets can be an extreme sport. Drivers rarely give pedestrians the right-of-way and don't even look for pedestrians when making a right turn on a red light. Cyclists have less power but are just as aggressive.

The severely polluted air of China's big cities can bring on, or aggravate, respiratory problems. If you're a sufferer, take the cue from locals, who wear surgical masks, or a scarf or bandana as protection.

■ TIP→ Distribute your cash, credit cards, I.D.s, and other valuables between a deep front pocket, an inside jacket or vest pocket, and a hidden money pouch. Don't reach for the money pouch once you're in public.

▮ TAXES

There is no sales tax in China or Hong Kong. Mainland hotels charge a 5% tax; bigger, joint-venture hotels also add a 10% to 15% service fee. Some restaurants charge a 10% service fee.

A departure tax of Y50 (about $6) for domestic flights and Y90 (about $11) for international flights (including flights to Hong Kong and Macau) must be paid in cash in dollars or yuan at the airport. People holding diplomatic passports, passengers in transit who stop over for less than 24 hours, and children under 12 are exempt from the departure tax.

▮ TIME

The whole of China is 8 hours ahead of London, 13 hours ahead of New York, 14 hours ahead of Chicago, and 16 hours ahead of Los Angeles. There's no daylight saving time, so subtract an hour in summer.

▮ TIPPING

Tipping is a tricky issue in China. It's officially forbidden by the government, and locals simply don't do it. In general, follow their lead without qualms. Nevertheless, the practice is beginning to catch on, especially among tour guides, who often expect Y10 a day. Official CTS representatives aren't allowed to accept tips, but you can give them candy, T-shirts, and other small gifts. You don't need to tip in restaurants or in taxis—many drivers insist on handing over your change, however small.

In Hong Kong, hotels and major restaurants usually add a 10% service charge; however, in almost all cases, this money does not go to the waiters and waitresses. Add on up to 10% more for good service. Tipping restroom attendants is common, but it is generally not the custom to leave an additional tip in taxis and hair salons, and unheard of in theaters and cinemas.

EFFECTIVE COMPLAINING

Things don't always go right when you're traveling, and when you encounter a problem or service that isn't up to snuff, you should complain. But there are good and bad ways to do so.

TAKE A DEEP BREATH. This is always a good strategy, especially when you are aggravated about something. Just inhale, and exhale, and remember that you're on vacation. We know it's hard for Type A people to leave it all behind, but for your own peace of mind, it's worth a try.

COMPLAIN IN PERSON WHEN IT'S SERIOUS. In a hotel, serious problems are usually better dealt with in person, at the front desk; if it's something quick, you can phone.

COMPLAIN EARLY RATHER THAN LATE. Whenever you don't get what you paid for (the type of hotel room you booked or the airline seat you prereserved) or when it's something timely (the people next door are making too much noise), try to resolve the problem sooner rather than later. It's always going to be harder to deal with a problem or get something taken off your bill after the fact.

BE WILLING TO ESCALATE, BUT DON'T BE HASTY. Try to deal with the person at the front desk of your hotel or with your waiter in a restaurant before asking to speak to a supervisor or manager. Not only is this polite, but when the person directly serving you can fix the problem, you'll more likely get what you want quicker.

SAY WHAT YOU WANT, AND BE REASONABLE. When things fall apart, be clear about what kind of compensation you expect. Don't leave it to the hotel or restaurant or airline to suggest what they're willing to do for you. That said, the compensation you request must be in line with the problem. You're unlikely to get a free meal because your steak was undercooked or a free hotel stay if your bathroom was dirty.

CHOOSE YOUR BATTLES. You're more likely to get what you want if you limit your complaints to one or two specific things that really matter rather than a litany of wrongs.

DON'T BE OBNOXIOUS. There's nothing that will stop your progress dead in its tracks as readily as an insistent "Don't you know who I am?" or "So what are you going to do about it?" Raising your voice will rarely get a better result.

NICE COUNTS. This doesn't mean you shouldn't be clear that you are displeased. Passive isn't good, either. When it comes right down to it, though, you'll attract more flies with sugar than with vinegar.

DO IT IN WRITING. If you discover a billing error or some other problem after the fact, write a concise letter to the appropriate customer-service representative. Keep it to one page, and as with any complaint, state clearly and reasonably what you want them to do about the problem. Don't give a detailed trip report or list a litany of problems.

INDEX

PHOTO CREDITS

Cover Photo (Farmer walking on a terraced rice field, Longsheng, Guangxi region): *Daryl Benson/ Masterfile.* 5, *Dennis Cox/age fotostock.* 8, *JLImages/Alamy.* 9, *John W. Warden/age fotostock.* 10 (top), *Martyn Vickery/Alamy.* 10 (bottom), *Keren Su/China Span/Alamy.* 11, *Sylvain Grandadam/age fotostock.* 12, *Dennis Cox/Alamy.* 13 (left), *Lon Linwei/Alamy.* 13 (right), *China National Tourist Office.* 14, *Luis Castañeda/age fotostock.* 15 (left), *Dbimages/Alamy.* 15 (right), *San Rostro/age fotostock.* 23, *SuperStock/ age fotostock.* 24 (top right), *José Fuste Raga/age fotostock.* 24 (bottom right), *Mary Evans Picture Library/Alamy.* 25 (top left), *China National Tourist Office.* 25 (bottom left), *Visual Arts Library (London)/Alamy.* 25 (right), *Panorama Media (Beijing) Ltd./Alamy.* 26 (left), *Popperfoto/Alamy.* 26 (top right), *Eddie Gerald/Alamy.* 26 (bottom right), *North Wind Picture Archives/Alamy.* 27 (left), *Beaconstox/Alamy.* 27 (top right), *Bruno Perousse/age fotostock.* 28 (left), *Kevin O'Hara/age fotostock.* 28 (bottom right), *A.H.C./age fotostock.* 29 (top left), *Tramonto/age fotostock.* 29 (bottom left), *ImagineChina.* 29 (right), *Iain Masterton/Alamy.* **Chapter 1: Beijing:** 31, *Superstock/age fotostock.* 34, *Tim Graham/Alamy.* 40-41, *ImagineChina.* 41 (bottom), *Juan Carlos Muñoz/age fotostock.* 42, *Luis Castañeda/age fotostock.* 43 (top), *Dennis Cox/age fotostock.* 43 (top center), *Richard T. Nowitz/age fotostock.* 43 (bottom center), *Imag-*

ABOUT OUR WRITERS

Joshua Samuel Brown's work has appeared in a strange and eclectic variety of publications across the globe. His writing and photography can be seen at www.josambro.com, and his first book, *Vignettes of Taiwan,* is available through Amazon. Joshua updated the Pearl River Delta chapter, the Guangxi and Guizhou sections of the Southwest chapter, the Xiamen section of East Coast chapter, and wrote the Spirituality in China, A Culinary Tour of China, the Age of Empire articles. He also wrote Quintessential China and the If You Like articles in the front of the book.

Chris Horton first came to China in 1998 to study Chinese in Beijing. Since then he has worked in Dali as a cafe manager, Shanghai as a magazine and book editor and Kunming as a business consultant. Work aside, he travels around Yunnan whenever he has free time, preferably by bike. Chris updated the Yunnan section of the Southwest chapter, wrote China in the 21st Century, and the ethnic minorities articles that are scattered throughout the book.

Helena Iveson has called China home for nearly 5 years. She packed her bags and moved there after finishing a Masters in International Journalism in London. She is a freelancer for the BBC, the *South China Morning Post,* and newspapers in Britain and Australia, as well as a presenter on China's international English language television station, CCTV9. Helena wrote the Hebei and Shandong sections of the Beijing to Shanghai chapter.

Michael D. Manning has lived in Xinjiang since 2005, setting up China's largest sun-dried tomato operation and maintaining a popular website focused on the country's remote western regions (china.notspecial.org). He has worked for news outlets as diverse as NBC News and *High Times,* with a bit of English teaching thrown in for good measure. Michael is the author of the Tibet and Silk Road chapters, and Great Itineraries in the front of the book.

Sascha Matuszak, is a freelance writer based in Chengdu, Sichuan Province and a regular contributor to newspapers and magazines around the Pacific Rim and in the American Midwest. In addition to fine cuisine, Sascha enjoys playing chess and sipping wine. Sascha updated the Chongqing and Sichuan chapters.

Victoria Patience grew up in Hong Kong, and she's never stopped calling Asia home. Her first solo trip was through China, aged 16, and she's been fascinated with the country ever since. A train ride from Hong Kong took her all the way to London, where she studied Spanish and Latin American literature. She now lives in Buenos Aires, but returns to Asia regularly. Victoria penned the "All the Tea in China" article and contributed greatly to both Hong Kong Shopping and Exploring. She also put her research and writing skills to work on Essentials at the end of the Beijing, Shanghai, and Hong Kong chapters and at the back of the book.

Will Thomson is a writer, radio producer, member of the American Anthropological Association, and is now researching an anthropological cookbook on Chinese rural food traditions. His work has appeared on National Public Radio, the *Boston Globe,* and PBS Online NewsHour. Currently a doctoral candidate at New York University, his focus is the rapid urbanization of 21st century China and the growing friction between new cities and old institutions. Will updated the Jiangsu and Anhui sections of the Beijing to Shanghai chapter, and the Zhejiang section of Eastern China.

BEIJING CONTRIBUTORS

Dinah Gardner has written more than a dozen guidebooks on Asia and still refuses to wear a conical bamboo hat. She updated the Historical Sights and Arts Nightlife sections. A native New Yorker and long time Beijing resident, **Alex Miller**

wrote about Beijing's neighborhoods and side trips for this edition. **Katharine Mitchell** writes for various publications in China and abroad. She holds a MA in Literature from the University of Mississippi and a MFA in Fiction Writing from the University of Montana. She updated the Shopping section.

Eileen Wen Mooney has lived in Taiwan, Hong Kong, and China for more than 20 years—the last 12 have been in Beijing. She lent her incredible know-how and insider secrets to the Where to Eat and Where to Stay chapters for the Beijing chapter. **Paul Mooney,** a New York native, is a freelance writer who has studied and worked in Asia for more than 25 years. He is the author of several travel books and updated the Experience and Neighborhoods section for this book. When **Alex Pasternack** is not teaching or exploring the hutong by bicycle, he writes about the environment, art, and architecture for *That's Beijing.* For this edition, he wrote about the Great Wall.

HONG KONG CONTRIBUTORS

Hiram Chu, who lives in China and writes for several English-language publications, covered Macau. **Eva Chui Loiterton,** who contributed to the nightlife and exploring sections of Hong Kong, currently she divides her time between writing and working in Hong Kong's TV and film industries. **Robin Goldstein,** a U.S.-based food critic and veteran Fodor's writer, was happy to travel to Hong Kong to investigate its restaurants and hotels. **Sofia A. Suárez,** who writes weekly style and art columns for the *South China Morning Post,* put her fashion savvy to work on the "It Suits You" article and all the specialty store reviews in Hong Kong's shopping section.

SHANGHAI CONTRIBUTORS

David Taylor has spent the last three working as a writer and editor, and updated the dining chapter of Shanghai. **Lisa Movius** has written extensively about China's contemporary art, culture, society and economy. She updated the Arts & Nightlife chapter. Back in the U.S. after serving as a foriegn newspaper correspondent in Shanghai, **Rachel Berlin** wrote the lodging chapter for the Shanghai chapter. **Elyse Singleton** has been living in Shanghai since 2001. She has traveled extensively through China as a writer and photographer and wrote the Experience and Neighborhoods section, as well as the Markets piece.